Twentieth-Century
Literary Criticism

Guide to Gale Literary Criticism Series

For criticism on	Consult these Gale series
Authors now living or who died after December 31, 1959	*CONTEMPORARY LITERARY CRITICISM (CLC)*
Authors who died between 1900 and 1959	*TWENTIETH-CENTURY LITERARY CRITICISM (TCLC)*
Authors who died between 1800 and 1899	*NINETEENTH-CENTURY LITERATURE CRITICISM (NCLC)*
Authors who died between 1400 and 1799	*LITERATURE CRITICISM FROM 1400 TO 1800 (LC)* *SHAKESPEAREAN CRITICISM (SC)*
Authors who died before 1400	*CLASSICAL AND MEDIEVAL LITERATURE CRITICISM (CMLC)*
Authors of books for children and young adults	*CHILDREN'S LITERATURE REVIEW (CLR)*
Black writers of the past two hundred years	*BLACK LITERATURE CRITICISM (BLC)*
Short story writers	*SHORT STORY CRITICISM (SSC)*
Poets	*POETRY CRITICISM (PC)*
Dramatists	*DRAMA CRITICISM (DC)*
Major authors from the Renaissance to the present	*WORLD LITERATURE CRITICISM, 1500 TO THE PRESENT (WLC)*

For criticism on visual artists since 1850, see
MODERN ARTS CRITICISM (MAC)

ISSN 0276-8178

Volume 52

Twentieth-Century Literary Criticism

**Excerpts from Criticism of the
Works of Novelists, Poets, Playwrights,
Short Story Writers, and Other Creative Writers
Who Lived between 1900 and 1960,
from the First Published Critical
Appraisals to Current Evaluations**

Laurie Di Mauro
Editor

Jennifer Brostrom
Jeffery Chapman
Jennifer Gariepy
Margaret A. Haerens
Drew Kalasky
Marie Lazzari
Thomas Ligotti
Sean René Pollock
David Segal
Janet Witalec
Associate Editors

 Gale Research Inc. • *DETROIT* • *WASHINGTON, D.C.* • *LONDON*

STAFF

Laurie Di Mauro, *Editor*

Jennifer Brostrom, Jeffery Chapman, Jennifer Gariepy, Margaret A. Haerens, Drew Kalasky, Marie Lazzari, Thomas Ligotti, Sean René Pollock, David Segal, Janet Witalec, *Associate Editors*

Pamela Willwerth Aue, Christine M. Bichler, Patrick L. Bruch, Nancy Dziedzic, Matthew McDonough, Lynn M. Spampinato, *Assistant Editors*

Jeanne A. Gough, *Permissions & Production Manager*
Linda M. Pugliese, *Production Supervisor*
Donna Craft, Paul Lewon, Maureen A. Puhl, Camille P. Robinson, Sheila Walencewicz, *Editorial Associates*
Jill H. Johnson, *Editorial Assistant*

Sandra C. Davis, *Permissions Supervisor (Text)*
Maria L. Franklin, Josephine M. Keene, Michele Lonoconus, Shalice Shah, Kimberly F. Smilay, *Permissions Associates*
Jennifer A. Arnold, Paula M. Labbe, Brandy C. Merritt, *Permissions Assistants*

Margaret A. Chamberlain, *Permissions Supervisor (Pictures)*
Pamela A. Hayes, Keith Reed, *Permissions Associates*
Susan Brohman, Arlene Johnson, Barbara A. Wallace, *Permissions Assistants*

Victoria B. Cariappa, *Research Manager*
Maureen Richards, *Research Supervisor*
Robert S. Lazich, Mary Beth McElmeel, Donna Melnychenko, Tamara C. Nott, Jaema Paradowski, *Editorial Associates*
Karen Farrelly, Julie Leonard, Stefanie Scarlett, *Editorial Assistants*

Mary Beth Trimper, *Production Director*
Catherine Kemp, *Production Assistant*

Cynthia Baldwin, *Art Director*
Barbara J. Yarrow, *Graphic Services Supervisor*
C. J. Jonik, *Desktop Publisher*
Willie F. Mathis, *Camera Operator*

Library of Congress Catalog Card Number 76-46132
ISBN 0-8103-2430-X
ISSN 276-8178

Printed in the United States of America
Published simultaneously in the United Kingdom
by Gale Research International Limited
(An affiliated company of Gale Research Inc.)
10 9 8 7 6 5 4 3 2 1

I(T)P

The trademark **ITP** is used under license.

Contents

Preface vii

Acknowledgments xi

v

Preface

Since its inception more than ten years ago, *Twentieth-Century Literary Criticism* has been purchased and used by nearly 10,000 school, public, and college or university libraries. *TCLC* has covered more than 500 authors, representing 58 nationalities, and over 25,000 titles. No other reference source has surveyed the critical response to twentieth-century authors and literature as thoroughly as *TCLC*. In the words of one reviewer, "there is nothing comparable available." *TCLC* "is a gold mine of information—dates, pseudonyms, biographical information, and criticism from books and periodicals—which many libraries would have difficulty assembling on their own."

Scope of the Series

TCLC is designed to serve as an introduction to authors who died between 1900 and 1960 and to the most significant interpretations of these author's works. The great poets, novelists, short story writers, playwrights, and philosophers of this period are frequently studied in high school and college literature courses. In organizing and excerpting the vast amount of critical material written on these authors, *TCLC* helps students develop valuable insight into literary history, promotes a better understanding of the texts, and sparks ideas for papers and assignments. Each entry in *TCLC* presents a comprehensive survey of an author's career or an individual work of literature and provides the user with a multiplicity of interpretations and assessments. Such variety allows students to pursue their own interests; furthermore, it fosters an awareness that literature is dynamic and responsive to many different opinions.

Every fourth volume of *TCLC* is devoted to literary topics that cannot be covered under the author approach used in the rest of the series. Such topics include literary movements, prominent themes in twentieth-century literature, literary reaction to political and historical events, significant eras in literary history, prominent literary anniversaries, and the literatures of cultures that are often overlooked by English-speaking readers.

TCLC is designed as a companion series to Gale's *Contemporary Literary Criticism,* which reprints commentary on authors now living or who have died since 1960. Because of the different periods under consideration, there is no duplication of material between *CLC* and *TCLC*. For additional information about *CLC* and Gale's other criticism titles, users should consult the Guide to Gale Literary Criticism Series preceding the title page in this volume.

Coverage

Each volume of *TCLC* is carefully compiled to present:

- criticism of authors, or literary topics, representing a variety of genres and nationalities

- both major and lesser-known writers and literary works of the period

- 10-15 authors or 4-6 topics per volume

- individual entries that survey critical response to each author's work or each topic in literary history, including early criticism to reflect initial reactions; later criticism to represent any rise or decline in reputation; and current retrospective analyses.

Organization of This Book

An author entry consists of the following elements: author heading, biographical and critical introduction, list of principal works, excerpts of criticism (each preceded by an annotation and followed by a bibliographic citation), and a bibliography of further reading.

- The **Author Heading** consists of the name under which the author most commonly wrote, followed by birth and death dates. If an author wrote consistently under a pseudonym, the pseudonym will be listed in the author heading and the real name given in parentheses on the first line of the biographical and critical introduction. Also located at the beginning of the introduction to the author entry are any name variations under which an author wrote, including transliterated forms for authors whose languages use nonroman alphabets.

- The **Biographical and Critical Introduction** outlines the author's life and career, as well as the critical issues surrounding his or her work. References to past volumes of *TCLC* are provided at the beginning of the introduction. Additional sources of information in other biographical and critical reference series published by Gale, including *Short Story Criticism, Children's Literature Review, Contemporary Authors, Dictionary of Literary Biography,* and *Something about the Author,* are listed in a box at the end of the entry.

- Most *TCLC* entries include **Portraits** of the author. Many entries also contain reproductions of materials pertinent to an author's career, including manuscript pages, title pages, dust jackets, letters, and drawings, as well as photographs of important people, places, and events in an author's life.

- The **List of Principal Works** is chronological by date of first book publication and identifies the genre of each work. In the case of foreign authors with both foreign-language publications and English translations, the title and date of the first English-language edition are given in brackets. Unless otherwise indicated, dramas are dated by first performance, not first publication.

- Critical excerpts are prefaced by **Annotations** providing the reader with information about both the critic and the criticism that follows. Included are the critic's reputation, individual approach to literary criticism, and particular expertise in an author's works. Also noted are the relative importance of a work of criticism, the scope of the excerpt, and the growth of critical controversy or changes in critical trends regarding an author. In some cases, these annotations cross-reference excerpts by critics who discuss each other's commentary.

- **Criticism** is arranged chronologically in each author entry to provide a perspective on changes in critical evaluation over the years. All titles of works by the author featured in the entry are printed in boldface type to enable the user to easily locate discussion of particular works. Also for purposes of easier identification, the critic's name and the publication date of the essay are given at the beginning of each piece of criticism. Unsigned criticism is preceded by the title of the journal in which it appeared. Some of the excerpts in *TCLC* also contain translated material. Unless otherwise noted, translations in brackets are by the editors; translations in parentheses or continuous with the text are by the critic. Publication information (such as footnotes or page and line references to specific editions of works) have been deleted at the editor's discretion to provide smoother reading of the text.

- A complete **Bibliographic Citation** designed to facilitate location of the original essay or book follows each piece of criticism.

- An annotated list of **Further Reading** appearing at the end of each author entry suggests secondary sources on the author. In some cases it includes essays for which the editors could not obtain reprint rights.

Cumulative Indexes

- Each volume of *TCLC* contains a cumulative **Author Index** listing all authors who have appeared in Gale's Literary Criticism Series, along with cross references to such biographical series as *Contemporary Authors* and *Dictionary of Literary Biography*. For readers' convenience, a complete list of Gale titles included appears on the first page of the author index. Useful for locating authors within the various series, this index is particularly valuable for those authors who are identified by a certain period but who, because of their death dates, are placed in another, or for those authors whose careers span two periods. For example, F. Scott Fitzgerald is found in *TCLC*, yet a writer often associated with him, Ernest Hemingway, is found in *CLC*.

- Each *TCLC* volume includes a cumulative **Nationality Index** which lists all authors who have appeared in *TCLC* volumes, arranged alphabetically under their respective nationalities, as well as Topics volume entries devoted to particular national literatures.

- Each new volume in Gale's Literary Criticism Series includes a cumulative **Topic Index,** which lists all literary topics treated in *NCLC, TCLC, LC 1400-1800,* and the *CLC* yearbook.

- Each new volume of *TCLC,* with the exception of the Topics volumes, includes a **Title Index** listing the titles of all literary works discussed in the volume. In response to numerous suggestions from librarians, Gale has also produced a **Special Paperbound Edition** of the *TCLC* title index. This annual cumulation lists all titles discussed in the series since its inception and is issued with the first volume of *TCLC* published each year. Additional copies of the index are available on request. Librarians and patrons will welcome this separate index; it saves shelf space, is easy to use, and is recyclable upon receipt of the following year's cumulation. Titles discussed in the Topics volume entries are not included *TCLC* cumulative index.

Citing *Twentieth-Century Literary Criticism*

When writing papers, students who quote directly from any volume in Gale's literary Criticism Series may use the following general forms to footnote reprinted criticism. The first example pertains to materials drawn from periodicals, the second to material reprinted from books.

[1]T. S. Eliot, "John Donne," *The Nation and the Athenaeum,* 33 (9 June 1923), 321-32; excerpted and reprinted in *Literature Criticism from 1400 to 1800,* Vol. 10, ed. James E. Person, Jr. (Detroit: Gale Research, 1989), pp. 28-9.

[2]Clara G. Stillman, *Samuel Butler: A Mid-Victorian Modern* (Viking Press, 1932); excerpted and reprinted in *Twentieth-Century Literary Criticism,* Vol. 33, ed. Paula Kepos (Detroit: Gale Research, 1989), pp. 43-5.

Suggestions Are Welcome

In response to suggestions, several features have been added to *TCLC* since the series began, including annotations to excerpted criticism, a cumulative index to authors in all Gale literary criticism series, entries devoted to criticism on a single work by a major author, more extensive illustrations, and a title index listing all literary works discussed in the series since its inception.

Readers who wish to suggest authors or topics to appear in future volumes, or who have other suggestions, are cordially invited to write the editors.

Acknowledgments

The editors wish to thank the copyright holders of the excerpted criticism included in this volume, the permissions managers of many book and magazine publishing companies for assisting us in securing reprint rights, and Anthony Bogucki for assistance with copyright research. We are also grateful to the staffs of the Detroit Public Library, the Library of Congress, the University of Detroit Library, Wayne State University Purdy/Kresge Library Complex, and the University of Michigan Libraries for making their resources available to us. Following is a list of the copyright holders who have granted us permission to reprint material in this volume of *TCLC*. Every effort has been made to trace copyright, but if omissions have been made, please let us know.

COPYRIGHTED EXCERPTS IN *TCLC*, VOLUME 52, WERE REPRINTED FROM THE FOLLOWING PERIODICALS:

The Armchair Detective, v. 22, Winter, 1989. Copyright © 1989 by *The Armchair Detective*. Reprinted by permission of the publisher.—*Biography,* v. 6, Spring, 1983. © 1983 by the Biographical Research Center. All rights reserved. Reprinted by permission of the publisher.—*The Centennial Review,* v. XV, Fall, 1971 for "Henry Adams' Satire on Human Intelligence: Its Method and Purpose" by Henry B. Rule. © 1971 by *The Centennial Review*. Reprinted by permission of the publisher and the author.—*The CEA Critic,* v. XLI, January, 1979. Copyright © 1979 by the College English Association, Inc. Reprinted by permission of the publisher.—*Children's Literature Association Quarterly,* v. 8, Fall, 1983. © 1983 Children's Literature Association. Reprinted by permission of the publisher.—*Comparative Drama,* v. 20, Summer, 1986. © copyright 1986, by the Editors of *Comparative Drama*. Reprinted by permission of the publisher.—*Fitzgerald/Hemingway Annual: 1976,* 1978 for "Save Me the Waltz' as a Novel" by Meredith Cary. Copyright © 1978 by Gale Research Inc. Reprinted by permission of the author.—*Fitzgerald/Hemingway Annual: 1977,* 1978 for "Rivalry and Partnership: The Short Fiction of Zelda Sayre Fitzgerald" by W. R. Anderson. Copyright © 1977 by Gale Research Inc. Reprinted by permission of the author.—*Foundation,* n. 38, Winter, 1986-87 for "Verne's Amazing Journeys" by M. Hammerton. Copyright © 1986 by the Science Fiction Foundation. Reprinted by permission of the author.—*Forum,* v. 12, 1975. Copyright, 1975, by Events Publishing Company, Inc. Reprinted by permission of Current History, Inc.— *Journal of Popular Culture,* v. XI, Winter, 1977. Copyright © 1978 by Ray B. Browne. Reprinted by permission of the publisher.—*The Journal of Narrative Technique,* v. 12, Fall, 1982. Copyright © 1982 by *The Journal of Narrative Technique*. Reprinted by permission of the publisher.—*The New York Herald Tribune Books,* October 30, 1932. Copyright 1932, renewed 1960, New York Herald Tribune Inc. All rights reserved. Reprinted by permission.—*The New York Times Book Review,* July 3, 1932; October 16, 1932. Copyright 1932, renewed by The New York Times Company. Both reprinted by permission of the publisher.—*The New Yorker,* v. XXXVIII, November 1, 1952 for "Turns for the Worse" by Anthony West. Copyright 1952, renewed 1980 by The New Yorker Magazine, Inc. Reprinted by permission of the author./ v. XXII, November 30, 1946. Copyright 1946, renewed 1973 by The New Yorker Magazine, Inc. Reprinted by permission of the publisher.—*Russian Literature Triquarterly,* n. 8, 1974. © 1974 by Ardis Publishers. Reprinted by permission of the publisher.—*The Russian Review,* v. 42, October, 1983 for "Zabolotsky's 'The Triumph of Agriculture' : Satire or Utopia?" by Irene Masing-Delic. Copyright 1983 by The Russian Review, Inc. Reprinted by permission of the author.—*Scando-Slavica,* v. XX, 1974 for "Some Themes and Motifs in N. Zabolockij's 'Stolbcy'" by I. Masing-Delic. Copyright © by the Associaton of Scandinavian Slavists and Baltologists. Reprinted by permission of the author.—*The Sewanee Review,* v. LXXXVIII, Spring, 1980. © 1980 by The University of the South. Reprinted with the permission of the editor of *The Sewanee Review*.—*Slavic and East-European Journal,* n.s. v. X, Summer, 1966. © 1966 by AATSEEL of the U.S., Inc. Reprinted by permission of the publisher.—*The Southern Humanities Review,* v. XVIII, Winter, 1984 for "Henry Adams and the Education of His Readers" by Linda A. Westervelt. Copyright 1984 by Auburn University. Reprinted by permission of the author.—*Tulane Studies in English,* v. 2, 1977. Copyright © 1977 by Tulane University. Reprinted by permission of the publisher.

of the author.—McHugh, Roland. From *The "Finnegans Wake" Experience.* University of California Press, 1981. © 1981 by The Regents of the University of California. Reprinted by permission of the publisher.—Meyer, Hans Georg. From *Henrik Ibsen.* Translated by Helen Sebba. Frederick Ungar Publishing Co., 1972. Copyright © 1972 by The Ungar Publishing Company. Reprinted by permission of the publisher.—Moi, Toril. From "Representation of Patriarchy: Sexuality and Epistemology in Freud's Dora," in *In Dora's Case: Freud—Hysteria—Feminism.* Exited by Charles Bernheimer and Claire Kahane. Columbia University Press, 1985. Copyright © 1985 Columbia University Press. All rights reserved. Used by permission of the publisher.—Pierce, John J. From *Foundations of Science Fiction: A Study in Imagination and Evolution.* Greenwood Press, 1987. Copyright © 1987 by John J. Pierce. All rights reserved. Reprinted by permission of permission of Greenwood Publishing Group, Inc., Westport, CT.—Piper, Henry Dan. From *F. Scott Fitzgerald: A Critical Portrait.* Holt, Rinehart and Winston, 1965. Copyright © 1965 by Henry Dan Piper. All rights reserved. Reprinted by permission of Henry Holt and Company, Inc.—Rose, Mark. From "Jules Verne: Journey to the Center of Science Fiction," in *Alien Encounters: Anatomy of Science Fiction.* Cambridge, Mass.: Harvard University Press, 1981. Copyright © 1981 by the President and Fellows of Harvard College. All rights reserved. Excerpted by permission of the publisher and the author.—Savater, Fernando. From *Childhood Regained: The Art of the Storyteller.* Translated by Frances M. López-Morillas. Columbia University Press, 1982. Copyright © 1982 Columbia University Press. All rights reserved. Used by permission of the publisher.—Symons, Julian. From *Mortal Consequences: A History—From the Detective Story to the Crime Novel.* Harper & Row, Publishers, 1972. Copyright © 1972 by Julian Symons. All rights reserved. Reprinted by permission of Curtis Brown Ltd., London on behalf of Julian Symons.—Trilling, Lionel. From *The Liberal Imagination: Essays on Literature and Society.* The Viking Press, 1950. Copyright 1950 by Lionel Trilling. Copyright renewed © 1978 by Diana Trilling and James Trilling. Reprinted by permission of the Estate of Lionel Trilling.—Weigand, Hermann J. From *The Modern Ibsen: A Reconsideration.* Holt, 1925. Copyright, 1925, by Henry Holt and Company, Inc. Copyright, 1953 by Hermann Weigand. All rights reserved. Reprinted by permission of Henry Holt and Company, Inc.—Wright, Elizabeth. From *Psychoanalytic Criticism: Theory in Practice.* Methuen, 1984. © 1984 Elizabeth Wright. All rights reserved. Reprinted by permission of the publisher.—Zweig, Stefan. From *Mental Healers: Franz Anton Mesmer, Mary Baker Eddy, Sigmund Freud.* Translated by Eden Paul and Cedar Paul. The Viking Press, 1932. Copyright 1932, renewed 1959 by Viking Press, a division of Penguin Books USA Inc. Reprinted by permission of the publisher.

PHOTOGRAPHS AND ILLUSTRATIONS APPEARING IN *TCLC*, VOLUME 52, WERE RECEIVED FROM THE FOLLOWING SOURCES:

Reproduced by the permission of Harold Ober Associates Incorporated: **p. 53;** Jacket of *Save Me the Waltz,* by Zelda Fitzgerald. Charles Scribner's Sons, 1932. Reprinted by permission of Charles Scribner's Sons, an imprint of Macmillan Publishing Company: **p.63;** Collection of Arlyn Bruccoli: **p. 73;** Sigmund Freud Copyrights: **p. 79;** Courtesy of E.L. Freud: **pp. 83, 95;** Theatre Collection, The New York Public Library at Lincoln Center, Astor, Lenox, and Tilden Foundations: **p. 167;** The Anderson Galleries, sale 1794, 14-16 January 1924: **p. 196;** Excerpt from *Finnegan's Wake,* by James Joyce. Copyright 1939 by James Joyce, copyright renewed ©1967 by Giorgio Joyce and Lucia Joyce. Reprinted in the United States and Canada by permission of Viking Penguin, a division of Penguin Books USA Inc. Reprinted in the British Commonwealth by permission of Faber & Faber Ltd.: **p. 211;** Reprinted by permission of the Estate of Lucia Joyce: **p. 221;** The Granger Collection, New York: **pp. 231, 306;** British Museum: **p. 241;** Courtesy of Family of Mary Roberts Rinehart: **p. 289.**

The Education of Henry Adams

Henry Adams

The following entry presents criticism of Adams's autobiography *The Education of Henry Adams: A Study in Twentieth-Century Multiplicity* (1907). For discussion of Adams's complete career, see *TCLC*, Volume 4.

INTRODUCTION

Although disparaged by Adams himself as a "failure," *The Education of Henry Adams* is today considered one of the most important literary documents of American life and philosophy. Presenting a selective and deliberately incomplete view of its author's life, the book combines autobiography, memoir, and historical treatise in demonstrating how Adams arrived at his view of history as marked by disharmony and dispersion.

Adams was born into a prominent New England family that included his great-grandfather John Adams, who served as the second president of the United States, and his grandfather John Quincy Adams, the nation's sixth president. Adams initially prepared for a career in politics, expecting to share in his family heritage of power and influence, but restlessness and pessimism over the corruption and short-sightedness of American political life eventually compelled him to pursue a literary career. He attended Harvard and later traveled to England, where he served as private secretary to his father, then Minister to Great Britain. Upon returning to the United States, Adams moved to Washington, D.C., and published articles on politics and political philosophy prior to accepting a teaching position at Harvard that carried with it the editorship of the *North American Review*. Because his family's wealth freed him from the need to earn an income, Adams eventually resigned these positions and devoted himself exclusively to writing. He died in 1918.

The Education of Henry Adams was originally published privately in 1907 in a special limited edition. Although it sold to only about one hundred readers prior to Adams's death, the book achieved widespread popularity following its republication that same year among the "generation of futilitarians," in Louis Kronenberg's phrase, who had experienced the chaos and hopelessness of World War I. Subtitled simply "An Autobiography" in 1918, *The Education* was carefully revised and the current subtitle restored in a 1973 edition edited by Adams's principal biographer, Ernest Samuels. Although Adams acknowledged his debt to previous autobiographers in *The Education,* including European philosophers Jean-Jacques Rousseau and Saint Augustine as well as American autobiographers Benjamin Franklin and Henry James, critics generally agree that the book is less a work of self-revelation than an attempt at historical synthesis. The central theme is posited in Adams's subtitle, "A Study in Twentieth-Century Multiplicity," and is a continuation of his earlier philosophical history of the Middle Ages, *Mont Saint Michel and Chartres: A Study in Thirteenth-Century Unity.* The clash between the opposing concepts of unity and multiplicity forms the basis of the two books. In *Mont Saint Michel* Adams posed the Virgin as the symbol of the social, spiritual, and aesthetic harmony that he believed existed in the Middle Ages. Applying an entropic theory of history—the belief that systems and societies steadily break down and collapse over time—Adams presented in *The Education* the image of the dynamo as the symbol of the modern world's fall from a state of unity to one of conflict-ridden multiplicity.

In *The Education,* Adams attempted to examine his life objectively, referring to himself in the third-person voice and employing the literary convention of the manikin, as used by Thomas Carlyle in his *Sartor Resartus* and Jean-Jacques Rousseau in his *Confessions.* In his preface to the 1907 edition of *The Education,* Adams concurred with Rousseau's description of the *Confessions* as "a warning against the Ego." According to Adams, the ego has "become a manikin on which the toilet of education is to be draped in order to show the fit or misfit of the clothes. The object of study is the garment, not the figure." Rather than focusing on himself—a subject—Adams focused on his education—an object—using this distanced self-study to demonstrate to students how the education "fitted on" Adams and his contemporaries had failed to prepare them for the chaos and multiplicity of the modern world.

Critical discussion of *The Education* focuses mainly on the manikin trope and on the book's fragmentary nature, with many commentators noting that both serve to show that Adams revealed more by what he did not include than by what he did. Carolyn Porter has written that although the manikin was meant to serve as a "detached observer," the book inadvertently exposes "what Adams has tried to repress—that the figure was a participant in, as well as an observer of, the events whose progress he is designed to measure." In trying to remain detached, Adams also left out much personal information, including any mention of his marriage or the suicide of his wife, Marian Hooper Adams. Hayden White commented that the gap in the text "reinforces the thesis of the emptiness of life that Adams adumbrates in the figure of the 'manikin' throughout the book. Adams cannot account for this emptiness, ontological in nature as he envisions it, either by historical-empirical-narrative methods . . . or by aprioristic, deductive, and speculative methods." Perhaps more important for Adams's questioning of theoretical and philosophical assumptions than for its literary value or actual conclusions, *The Education of Henry Adams* best demonstrates Adams's conscientious approach to addressing perennial and modern issues in history, literature, and philosophy.

CRITICISM

The New Republic   (essay date 1918)

[*In the following review, the anonymous critic provides a positive assessment of* The Education of Henry Adams.]

Henry Adams was born with his name on the waiting list of Olympus, and he lived up to it. He lived up to it part of the time in London, as secretary to his father at the Embassy; part of the time at Harvard, teaching history; most of the time in Washington, in La Fayette Square. Shortly before he was born the stepping stone to Olympus in the United States was Boston. Sometimes Boston and Olympus were confused. But not so long after 1838 the railroads came, and while Boston did its best to control the country through the railroads there was an inevitable shift in political gravity, and the centre of power became Ohio. It was Henry Adams's fate to knock at the door of fame when Ohio was in power; and Ohio did not comprehend Adams's credentials. Those credentials, accordingly, were the subject of some wry scrutiny by their possessor. They were valid, at any rate, at the door of history and Henry Adams gave a dozen years to Jefferson and Madison. It was his humor afterwards to say he had but three serious readers—Abram Hewitt, Wayne McVeagh and John Hay. His composure in the face of this coolness was, however, a strange blending of serenities derived equally from the cosmos and from La Fayette Square. He was not above the anodyne of exclusiveness. Even his autobiography, a true title to Olympus, was issued to a bare hundred readers before his death, and was then deemed too incomplete to be made public. It is made public now nominally for "students" but really for the world that didn't know an Adams when it saw one.

For mere stuff the book is incomparable. Henry Adams had the advantage of full years and happy faculty, and his book is the rich harvest of both. He had none of that anecdotal inconsequentiality which is a bad tradition in English recollections. He saved himself from mere recollections by taking the world as an educator and himself as an experiment in education. His two big books were contrasted as *Mont-Saint-Michel and Chartres: A Study of Thirteenth-Century Unity,* and *The Education of Henry Adams: A Study of Twentieth-Century Multiplicity.* The stress on multiplicity was all the more important because he considered himself eighteenth century to start with, and had in fact the unity of simple Americanism at the beginning.

Simple Americanism goes to pieces like the pot of basil in this always expanding tale of a development. There are points about the development, about its acceptance of a "supersensual multiverse," which only a Karl Pearson or an Ernst Mach or a Balfour could satisfactorily discuss or criticize. A reader like myself gazes through the glass bottom of Adams's style into unplumbed depths of speculation. Those depths are clear and crisp. They deserve to be investigated. But a "dynamic theory of history" is no proper inhabitant of autobiography, and "the larger synthesis" is not yet so domesticated as the plebeian idea of God. That Adams should conduct his study to these ends is, in one sense, a magnificent culmination. A theory of life is the fit answer to the supersensual riddle of living. But when the theory must be technical and even professional, an autobiography has no climax in a theory. It is better to revert, as Adams does, to the classic features of human drama: "Even in America, the Indian Summer of life should be a little sunny and a little sad, like the season, and infinite in wealth and depth of tone—but never hustled." It is enough to have the knowledge that along certain lines the prime conceptions were shattered and the new conceptions pushed forward, the tree of Adams rooting itself firmly in the twentieth century, coiled round the dynamos and the law of acceleration.

Whatever the value of his theory, Henry Adams embraced the modernity that gradually dawned on him and gave him his new view of life. Take his enthusiasm for world's fairs as a solitary example. One might expect him to be bored by them, but Hunt and Richardson and Stanford White and Burnham emerge heroically as the dramatizers of America, and Henry Adams soared over vulgarity to a perception of their "acutely interesting" exhibits. He was after—something. If the Virgin Mary could give it to him in Normandy, or St. Louis could give it to him among the Jugo-Slavs and the Ruthenians on the Mississippi, well done. No prejudices held him back. He who could interpret the fight for free silver without a sniff of impatience, who could study Grant without the least filming of patriotism, was not likely to turn up his nose at unfashionable faiths or to espouse fashionable heresies. He was after education and any century back or forward was grist to his mill. And his faith, even, was sure to be a sieve with holes in it. "All one's life," as he confesses grimly, "one had struggled for unity, and unity had always won," yet "the multiplicity of unity had steadily increased, was increasing, and threatened to increase beyond reason." Beyond reason, then, it was reasonable to proceed, and the son of Ambassador Adams moved from the sanctity of Union with his feet feeling what way they must, and his eye on the star of truth.

So steady is that gaze, one almost forgets how keen it is. But there is no single dullness, as I remember, in 505 large pages, and there are portraits like those of Lodge or La Farge or St. Gaudens or the Adamses, which have the delicacy and fidelity of Holbein. A colorist Adams is not, nor is he a dramatist. But he has few equals in the succinct expressiveness that his historical sense demands, and he can load a sentence with a world of meaning. Take, for instance, the phrase in which he denies unity to London society. "One wandered about in it like a maggot in cheese; it was not a hansom cab, to be got into, or out of, at dinnertime." He says of St. Gaudens that "he never laid down the law, or affected the despot, or became brutalized like Whistler by the brutalities of his world." In a masterly chapter on woman he summed up,

> The woman's force had counted as inertia of rotation, and her axis of rotation had been the cradle and the family. The idea that she was weak

revolted all history; it was a palaeontological falsehood that even an Eocene female monkey would have laughed at; but it was surely true that, if force were to be diverted from its axis, it must find a new field, and the family must pay for it . . . She must, like the man, marry machinery.

In Cambridge

> the liveliest and most agreeable of men—James Russell Lowell, Francis J. Child, Louis Agassiz, his son Alexander, Gurney, John Fiske, William James and a dozen others, who would have made the joy of London or Paris—tried their best to break out and be like other men in Cambridge and Boston, but society called them professors, and professors they had to be. While all these brilliant men were greedy for companionship, all were famished for want of it. Society was a faculty-meeting without business. The elements were there; but society cannot be made up of elements—people who are expected to be silent unless they have observations to make—and all the elements are bound to remain apart if required to make observations.

Keen as this is, it does not alter one great fact, that Henry Adams himself felt the necessity of making observations. He approached autobiography buttoned to the neck. Like many bottled-up human beings he had a real impulse to release himself, and to release himself in an autobiography if nowhere else, but spontaneous as was the impulse, he could no more unveil the whole of an Adams to the eye of day than he could dance like Nijinski. In so far as the Adamses were institutional he could talk of them openly, and he could talk of John Hay and Clarence King and Henry Cabot Lodge and John La Farge and St. Gaudens as any liberated host might reveal himself in the warm hour after dinner. But this is not the Dionysiac tone of autobiography and Henry Adams was not Dionysiac. He was not limitedly Bostonian. He was sensitive, he was receptive, he was tender, he was more scrod than cod. But the mere mention of Jean Jacques Rousseau in the preface of this autobiography raises doubts as to Henry Adams's evasive principle, "the object of study is the garment, not the figure." The figure, Henry Adams's, had nagging interest for Henry Adams, but something racial required him to veil it. He could not, like a Rousseau or "like a whore, unpack his heart with words."

The subterfuge, in this case, was to lay stress on the word "education." Although he was nearly seventy when he laid the book aside and although education means nothing if it means everything, the whole seventy years were deliberately taken as devotion to a process, that process being visualized much more as the interminable repetition of the educational escalator itself than as the progress of the person who moves forward with it. Moves forward to where? It was the triumph of Henry Adams's detachment that no escalator could move him forward anywhere because he was not bound anywhere in particular. Such a man, of course, could speak of his life as perpetually educational. There was no wolf to devour him if his education in dodging wolves proved incomplete. Faculty qua faculty could remain a permanent quandary to him, so long as he were not forced to be vocational, so long as he could speculate on "a world that sensitive and timid natures could regard without a shudder."

The unemployed faculty of Henry Adams, however, is one of the principal fascinations of this altogether fascinating book. What was it that kept Henry Adams on a footstool before John Hay? What was it that sent him from Boston to Mont-Saint-Michel and Chartres? The man was a capable and ambitious man, if ever there was one. He was not merely erudite and reflective and emancipatingly sceptical, he was also a man of the largest inquiry and the most scrupulous inclusiveness, a man of the nicest temper and the sanest style. How could such justesse go begging, even in the United States? Little bitter as the book is, one feels Henry Adams did go begging. Behind his modest screen he sat waiting for a clientage that never came, while through a hole he could see a steady crowd go pouring into the gilded doors across the way. The modest screen was himself. He could not detach it. But the United States did not see beyond the screen. A light behind a large globule of colored water could at any moment distract it. And in England, for that matter, only the Monckton Milneses kept the Delanes from brushing Adams away, like a fly.

The question is, on what terms did Adams want life? It is characteristic of him that he does not specify. But one gathers from his very reticence that he had least use of all for an existence which required moral multiplicity. Where he seems gravest and least self-superintending is in those criticisms of his friends that indicate the sacrifice of integrity. He was no prig. Not one bleat of priggishness is heard in all his intricate censure of the eminent British statesmen who sapped the Union. But there is a fund of significance in his criticism of Senator Lodge's career, pages 418 and on, in which "the larger study was lost in the division of interests and the ambitions of fifth-rate men." It is in a less concerned tone that the New Yorker Roosevelt is discussed. "Power when wielded by abnormal energy is the most serious of facts, and all Roosevelt's friends know that his restless and combative energy was more than abnormal. Roosevelt, more than any other man living within the range of notoriety, showed the singular primitive quality that belongs to ultimate matter—the quality that mediaeval theology assigned to God—he was pure act." Pure act Henry Adams was not. If Roosevelt exhibited "the effect of unlimited power on limited mind," he himself exhibited the contrary effect of limited power on unlimited mind. Why his power remained so limited was the mystery. Was he a watched kettle that could not boil? Or had he no fire in his belly? Or did the fire fail to meet the kettle? Almost any problem of inhibition would be simpler, but one could scarcely help ascribing something to that refrigeration of enthusiasm which is the Bostonian's revenge on wanton life force. Except for his opaline ethics, never glaring yet never dulled, he is manifestly toned down to suit the most neurasthenic exaction. Or, to put it more crudely, he is emotion Fletcherized to the point of inanition.

Pallid and tepid as the result was, in politics, the autobiography is a refutation of anaemia. There was, indeed, something meagre about Henry Adams's soul, as there is something meagre about a Japanese color-print or a butterfly.

But the lack of sanguine or exuberant feeling, the lack of buoyancy and enthusiasm, is merely a hint that one must classify, not a command that one condemn. For all this book's parsimony, for all its psychological silences and timidities, it is an original contribution, transcending caste and class, combining true mind and matter. Compare its comment on education to the comment of Joan and Peter—Henry Adams is to H. G. Wells as triangulation to tape-measuring. That profundity of relations which goes by the name of understanding was part of his very nature. Unlike H. G. Wells, he was incapable of cant. He had no demagoguery, no mob-oratory, no rhetoric. This enclosed him in himself to a dangerous degree, bordered him on priggishness and on egoism. But he had too much quality to succumb to these diseases of the sedentary soul. He survives, and with greatness. (pp. 169-71)

F. H., "Henry Adams," in The New Republic, Vol. XVII, No. 214, December 7, 1918, pp. 169-71.

Kenneth MacLean   (essay date 1959)

[*In the essay below, MacLean discusses the window as a metaphor for the imaginative faculties and the cross as a symbol of the union of bipolar ideas in* The Education of Henry Adams.]

A distinguishing paradox of Western literature of recent time is the frequent combining, in even measures of poetry and prose, of the matters of society and history with those of personality and the individual. The *Education of Henry Adams* so combines. Its formal interest as social history cannot be overstated. In its earlier sections it moves through the mind of nineteenth-century New England—the lingering of the Enlightenment, the calm of Harvard, the shattering dilemmas of the Civil War. During this war Adams acted as private secretary for his father who was the United States Minister in London, and the second large movement of this volume presents a great deal of nineteenth-century England as this society moved further into its industrial phase—London growing smaller as it doubled in size. We see the scene, and we are introduced to the greater tones of government, literature, and country-house life. Further on, into the 70's and after, the *Education* brings us back to this continent where a Pennsylvania mind, devoted to "work, whiskey, and cards," was creating the new America of railways, oil, dynamos, hoping to find Fortune asleep in an elevator. The last chapters, less social than philosophical, deal sceptically with dominant turn-of-the-century theories and syntheses, while developing Adams' own questionable laws of inertia and acceleration. In the later pages, too, the reader is carried into the sleepy trades, into the religion of the Far East, and finally into the mediaeval religion of the nearer West. Within this impressive socio-philosophical story (of greatest value in itself, and clearly the work of the admirable historian of *Jefferson and Madison*) there moves, even as valuably, a private spirit, a private secretary, in full literary and imaginative intimacy.

At moments the *Education* seems to breathe among those pleasant intimacies of French life which were given a final

expression in the Impressionists—the walk, the book, the meal, the solitary observation, as single as one's glass of absinthe before dinner in the Palais Royal. It includes older, sharper English intimacies as well. It incorporates some of that enormous solitude of Gibbon. It suggests, too, the close domesticity of Sterne, the confining atmosphere of Cowper. Rooms and shadowy shades lead into personal corners and enclosures that are suffocating, claustrophobic, even shameful. The maggot is lost in the cheese; the earthworm is feeling for a light at the end of the corridor. The valley of life grows thin and narrow—narrow often with the resolved meanings of the imagination. The long gloom of Norwegian fiords, the sleeping distances of Russian inertia, startle this small inside life.

The intimacy of the *Education* is finally of the kind which moves among those sensitive images of thought, beyond which education does not go. Its intimacy is imaginative. It touches the skin. For comparable imaginative attentions, the *Prelude* and *Tristram Shandy* offer parallels. Adams indeed begins as Wordsworth's child and as poor Tristram, and something of the delicacy of both these spirits pursues the whole of *Education.* His name is Groombridge. Henry Adams is of course often, less attractively, Mr. Shandy the philosopher and idea-ist.

In approaching and preserving the sensitive imaginative moment, Adams perhaps drew obliquely upon his *Mont-Saint-Michel and Chartres* of 1904, written just before the *Education.* Adams' late and decisive interest in Gothic architecture was stimulated by his old friend and travelling companion John La Farge, who was interested professionally in mediaeval glass.

> The hunt for the Virgin's glass opened rich preserves. Especially the sixteenth century ran riot in sensuous worship. Then the ocean of religion, which had flooded France, broke into Shelley's light dissolved in star-showers thrown, which had left every remote village strewn with fragments that flashed like jewels, and were tossed into hidden clefts of peace and forgetfulness.

"Chartres is all windows," Adams said. And so is the *Education.* It is proper to regard its sharply bright imaginative moments (there are perhaps a hundred or more) as psychological windows enclosing the soul, shining across a pearl-grey mental grisaille. The prose, Norman and New England—often salty and cold—is the stonework in this fenestration. The *Prelude* suggests similar windows of personal design, many of them close to glassy lake and blue water, and hence rather literally Gothic. However various, for both Wordsworth and Adams the Gothic light was greatly of French origin.

In many imaginative moments in the *Education* Adams has actually included the literal frame of a window. As a young messenger to Sicily in 1860, Adams interviewed Garibaldi while the soldier banqueted at sunset with his "pirates" in the Senate House at Palermo. Dressed in the red shirt, Garibaldi left the table and sat in a window to talk with Adams. At a window in La Fayette Square in Washington, Hay and Adams stood in 1892 looking quizzically at old Civil War soldiers tottering along to their clubs and their cocktails and cards. Three times he refers to the window here. From a club window in New York in 1904, Adams observed the imaginative collisions on Fifth Avenue.

> A traveller in the highways of history looked out of the club window on the turmoil of Fifth Avenue, and felt himself in Rome, under Diocletian, witnessing the anarchy, conscious of the compulsion, eager for the solution, but unable to conceive whence the next impulse was to come or how it was to act. The two-thousand-years failure of Christianity roared upward from Broadway, and no Constantine the Great was in sight.

In these late years Adams was crossing Poland and Russia by train, seeing other surfaces of conflict and chaos.

> . . . From the first glimpse one caught from the sleeping-car window, in the early morning, of the Polish Jew at the accidental railway station, in all his weird horror, to the last vision of the Russian peasant, lighting his candle and kissing his ikon before the railway Virgin in the station at St. Petersburg, all was logical, conservative, Christian and anarchic.
>
> Studied in the dry light of conservative Christian anarchy, Russia became luminous like the salt of radium; but with a negative luminosity as though she were a substance whose energies had been sucked out—an inert residuum—with movement of pure inertia. From the car window one seemed to float past undulations of nomad life—herders deserted by their leaders and herds—wandering waves stopped in their wanderings—waiting for their winds or warriors to return and lead them westward; tribes that had camped, like Khirgis, for the season, and had lost the means of motion without acquiring the habit of permanence.

Here, finally in illustration, is a very late "window"—chaotic, too.

> One late afternoon, at midsummer, the Virgin's pilgrim was wandering through the streets of Troyes in close and intimate conversation with Thibaut of Champagne and his highly intelligent seneschal, the Sieur de Joinville, when he noticed one or two men looking at a bit of paper stuck in a window. Approaching, he read that M. de Plehve had been assassinated at St. Petersburg. The mad mixture of Russia and the Crusades, of the Hippodrome and the Renaissance, drove him for refuge into the fascinating Church of St. Pantaleon near by. Martyrs, murderers, Caesars, saints and assassins—half in glass and half in telegram; chaos of time, place, morals, forces and motive—gave him vertigo.

The imaginative moment is often very literally a window moment. Less literally, all imaginative moments in the *Education* are the windows of this personal church in which Adams stands, often painfully, at centre. The yellow kitchen floor at Mount Vernon Street, the rush of Swinburne's talk in the smoky bedroom at Fryston, war papers on the turf at Wenlock Abbey, his sister's sickroom glowing in the sensuous Tuscan light—all these images are part of the personal glass. The meaningless French novel, in turn, is thrown out the train window. The questionable little red-chalk Rafael is held up to the window. At an afternoon function at Miss Burdett Coutts's home in Stratton Place, the uncomfortable young private secretary tried to hide in the embrasure of a window.

As the "rosy sanctuary" rises in the far regions of this mind, the outward becomes the inward in that conversion of form which is romanticism. The psychological architecture of the *Education* is a striking monument of this romantic inward style. Its inner manners are deeply supported by an appropriately probing analysis. The "burning-glass" of Henry James often explores in human character unrecognized ranges of simplicity, paradox, sexuality, moral confusion, torpor. The analytical manner of the *Education* is the proper aesthetic friend of its inward imaginative style.

The imaginative moments preserved in the *Education* are those which time has selected for meaning and symbol. Time effects imaginative consolidations, operating even as distance in the far voyage of the Ancient Mariner. The *Education* is the story of objects rising into symbols through the perspective of years.

The imaginative moments preserved in the *Education* are those which time has selected for meaning and symbol. Time effects imaginative consolidations, operating even as distance in the far voyage of the Ancient Mariner. The *Education* is the story of objects rising into symbols through the perspective of years.

The imaginative process is slow, hesitant, irregular. The natural world, in contrast, generally shows a more steady motion—"a single, continuous, unbroken act." The seventeenth century was probably very much the age of motion, and the thought of this century in all regards acts as a sharp filter for Adams. The seventeenth-century "Coy Mistress" of Andrew Marvell is a poem of motion, which we may guess (or wish) Adams knew. Against the steady and inexorable way of real time Marvell has set imaginative time, with its slow and exotic accumulations. Two ways of time are observed in the *Education.* "This was the journey he remembered. The actual journey may have been quite different, but the actual journey has no interest for education." Wind and waves, drift and surf—motions of the sea—are a part of its natural time. Real time is carried along, too, by the locomotions of the nineteenth century—the railway which took the boy of twelve, in 1850, to Washington; the new Cunarders whose smoke could be seen from the Quincy hills. When he was past fifty, Henry Adams learned to ride the new bicycle. In 1904, he bought the new automobile to use in his study of the cathedrals of northern France. The tourists encountered in the *Education* seem to be travelling by real time.

Imaginative time is different. Adams includes in the *Education* many images to suggest imagination's languid procedure. He employs those deliberate images of *walking* and *staircase* which belong to the time world of Sterne. He stands often in the stairway of thought. He walks with his thoughts in a room over his father's head during one of those congested Civil War nights which he spent as a young man in London. An image of similar effect is the *step.* It was very much a part of his imagination that the young Gibbon sat, in the evening of the day of history, on the *steps* of Santa Maria di Ara Coeli—imagination resting in and above time. Adams' *steps* are very close to the education theme. The still moment is sometimes one of a meaningful illness. The *Education* begins with the child's scarlet fever—a first memory being that of a gentle aunt "entering the sick-room bearing in her hand a saucer with a baked apple." In later years Adams lay ill in London, in Wordsworth's Waste Land city—the wounded knight of Western myth perhaps, needing to read a sign but only remembering.

> The time was the month of January, 1892; he was alone, in hospital, in the gloom of midwinter. He was close on his fifty-fourth birthday, and Pall Mall had forgotten him as completely as it had forgotten his elders. He had not seen London for a dozen years, and was rather amused to have only a bed for a world and a familiar black fog for horizon. The coal-fire smelt homelike; the fog had a fruity taste of youth; anything was better than being turned out into the wastes of Wigmore Street. He could always amuse himself by living over his youth, and driving once more down Oxford Street in 1858, with life before him to imagine far less amusing than it had turned out to be.

Earlier in England, in the summer of 1870 which was painfully marked by his sister's death and also by the war, Adams went to stay at Wenlock Abbey with his friends the Milnes Gaskells, who had restored a part of the abbey, the Prior's house, to use as a country home. "Lying on the turf, the ground littered with newspapers, the monks studied the war correspondence." The *green turf* (and *grass*) may be felt here to have that same blunting way against time which, as an image, it effects in Wordsworth's poetry. *Summer* is sometimes for Adams, as so frequently and pleasantly for the late nineteenth-century painter, the serene point.

> . . . The happiest hours of the boy's education were passed in summer lying on a musty heap of Congressional Documents in the old farmhouse at Quincy, reading *Quentin Durward, Ivanhoe,* and *The Talisman,* and raiding the garden at intervals for peaches and pears.

Summer afternoons at Wenlock could be as timeless.

> One's instinct abhors time. As one lay on the slope of the Edge, looking sleepily through the summer haze towards Shrewsbury or Cader Idris or Caer Caradoc or Uriconium, nothing suggested sequence. The Roman road was twin to the railroad; Uriconium was well worth Shrewsbury; Wenlock and Buildwas were far superior to Bridgnorth. The shepherds of Caractacus or Offa, or the monks of Buildwas, had they approached where he lay in the grass, would have taken him only for another and tamer variety of Welsh thief. They would have seen little to surprise them in the modern landscape unless it were the steam of a distant railway. One might mix up the terms of time as one liked, or stuff the present anywhere into the past, measuring time

> by Falstaff's Shrewsbury clock, without violent sense of wrong, as one could do it on the Pacific Ocean; . . .

It was in the summers, at the turn of the century, that Adams' studies of French glass were made.

> In the long summer days one found a sort of saturated green pleasure in the forests, and gray infinity of rest in the little twelfth-century churches that lined them, as unassuming as their own mosses, and as sure of their purpose as their round arches; . . .

The imaginative process is slow, irregular. It is also catastrophic in its procedure, its knowledge coming with sudden shock. In suggesting such process, Adams uses a particular type of image: *shock, chasm, stride, kick, convulsion, explosion, rupture, breach, upheaval, overthrust, sudden warping, falling ceiling, falling wall.* A wall fell in the mind as he first felt Beethoven's imagination. As a nineteenth-century writer, Adams was most attentive to geologic and so-called evolutionary themes. He could sit on the Wenlock edge of time, feeling the presence below him of his fish ancestry. He could look into Quincy Bay and sense quite un-Mayflower cousinship with its watery inhabitants, including the shark. His idioms of evolution and geology are directly effective (indeed, perhaps new in the vocabulary of imagination) for suggesting the catastrophic way of the imagination—its jumps, its slow violence. Imagination is indeed that Friar Bacon's head which announced "Time had passed!"

And so the images "fade behind the present." After late grasshopper summer, life grows frail, grows thin as the elm trees. But a saintly and severe spareness of scene takes over, like that in which the aged leech-gatherer sat, of rocks and pools which have become simple and clear with symbolic meaning. Life grows young with meaning, as it did for Wordsworth. Adams, too, sailed, if rather roughly, to Byzantium. The drift finds the seeker. By the time education has taken place, imaginative resolutions have been achieved to the point of a sharp, an almost Eastern symbolism: "only on the edge of the grave can man conclude anything." There is little imagery in the *Education* that is literal—"cheap imagination"; there is much that is symbolic. *Line* and *street, black* and *white, smoke, mountain* and *attic, triangle* and *thread, Rome* and *Paris* and *Mt. Vernon*—all are symbols. In this resolution the prose abounds in interrelations. Diction re-echoes. The essential phrase sticks. Emerson had said that for those who trust themselves, all objects will acquire meaning. The *Education* is the fulfilment of such personal trust. Those intimate ceremonies, which are the flower of the personal life, have here produced meanings, and, in a further degree, certain enchantments.

In the *Education* the imagery has been resolved into male and female patterns. Woman, wherever she appears, is the principle of vitality. She is the lyric impulse in this text: "the first fresh breath of leafless spring"; the snow singing under the runners. Shelley is clearly helpful here. The feminine excites the scene of nature, particularly that moving Southern landscape which the twelve-year-old boy saw on spring days in Maryland. Perhaps it is the Negro mother of the South who softly shadows these Adams landscapes, even as in a Whitman poem.

> The Potomac and its tributaries squandered beauty. Rock Creek was as wild as the Rocky Mountains. Here and there a negro cabin alone disturbed the dogwood and the judas-tree, the azalea and the laurel. The tulip and the chestnut gave no sense of struggle against a stingy nature. The soft, full outlines of the landscape carried no hidden horror of glaciers in its bosom. The brooding heat of the profligate vegetation; the cool charm of the running water; the terrific splendor of the June thunder-gust in the deep and solitary woods, were all sensual, animal, elemental. No European spring had shown him the same intermixture of delicate grace and passionate depravity that marked the Maryland May.

Other ladies belong to this landscape.

> The broad Potomac and the coons in the trees, the bandanas and the boxhedges, the bedrooms upstairs and the porch outside, even Martha Washington herself in memory, were as natural as the tides and the May sunshine; . . .

Here again is spring in Washington, gentle as in Rome, with a classical feminine presence.

> When spring came, he took to the woods, which were best of all, for after the first of April, what Maurice de Guérin called "the vast maternity" of nature showed charms more voluptuous than the vast paternity of the United States Senate. Senators were less ornamental than the dogwood or even the judas-tree. They were, as a rule, less good company. Adams astonished himself by remarking what a purified charm was lent to the Capitol by the greatest possible distance, as one caught glimpses of the dome over miles of forest foliage. At such moments he pondered on the distant beauty of St. Peter's and the steps of Ara Coeli.

The boy made his first trip to Washington with his father to see his grandmother who was ill. "The softness of his gentle old grandmother as she lay in bed and chatted with him, did not come from Boston." Even in age and illness the grandmother can be associated with that vitality which is natural and Southern. This grandmother, Louisa, Adams made the first extensive feminine portrait in the *Education.* Educated in Nantes, she brought, to the White House and later to Quincy, her Sèvres, her Queen Anne, and the spirit itself of the silver age. She was indeed a Romney portrait in silver grey. The characteristic woman of the *Education* is an eighteenth-century spirit, whose vitality is that of intelligence and gaiety. Central woman in the *Education* is the sister, Mrs. Charles Kuhn, who died at Bagni di Lucca of lockjaw which developed from a foot injury received in a cab accident. "She faced death, as women mostly do, bravely and even gaily. . . ." In this striking and central moment of the *Education,* the vitality of a woman is allowed to be seen as participating and sharing in the vitality of the death which destroys her. Mrs. Henry Adams (Clover), whose death too was tragic, clearly belonged with the Millamants, among the bright mysteries of the eighteenth century—"a lightly-sparred

yacht." Woman in nature and woman in society form something of a progress in the *Education* moving in the direction of the Virgin who is the sum of energies. The vital language of woman in the *Education* is somewhat modified by sharp observations on Pocahontas, Queen Victoria, and generally on the New York woman. Adams, too, could allow himself to imagine a wrinkled Venus.

Girls in summer dresses, and young men in black orators' gowns, "singularly wanting in enthusiasm"—the contrasting male imagery of the *Education* develops into patterns of ineptitude. A certain Shandyism controls Adams' masculine representation. From his boyhood he remembers his grandfather, the old President, making fruitless experiments in his dressing-closet with caterpillars under glass tumblers. His caterpillars never became moths and butterflies.

> The Madam bore with fortitude the loss of the tumblers which her husband purloined for these hatcheries; but she made protest when he carried off her best cut-glass bowls to plant with acorns or peachstones that he might see the roots grow, but which, she said, he commonly forgot like the caterpillars.

In his last illness the old President sat paralysed in a tall-backed, invalid armchair, on one side of the spare bedroom fireplace—old friends dozing beside him. He died in wintry February, and funeral services were held in the Quincy church, with which the boy associated grey and bald heads. In Washington sober Shandean eyes saw the uncompleted square marble shaft which was to honour the first President, standing in a shabby city whose few completed buildings looked "like white Greek temples in the abandoned gravel-pits of a deserted Syrian city." From the Lincoln Inaugural Ball of March 1861 Adams preserved this rustic literary festoon.

> He saw Mr. Lincoln but once; at the melancholy function called an Inaugural Ball. Of course he looked anxiously for a sign of character. He saw a long, awkward figure; a plain, ploughed face; a mind, absent in part, and in part evidently worried by white kid gloves; features that expressed neither self-satisfaction nor any other familiar Americanism, but rather the same painful sense of becoming educated and of needing education that tormented a private secretary, above all a lack of apparent force.

While Adams seems to assign a sterile symbolism to all masculine figures, his Bohemianism allowed him to indicate severely the particular degree of impotence in the English scene. To a masculine portrait, with arm in sling and hair parted in the middle, he often added either dullness or a restless nervous colouring—some of both these tones perhaps derived from seventeenth- and eighteenth-century English satiric portraiture. The *Chartres* carried its complement of unsatisfactory male figures. The heavily negatived *Education* is itself written in terms of this masculine psychology. Adams is "the masculine philosopher."

". . . No woman had ever driven him wrong; no man had ever driven him right." Woman is made the centre of values in the *Education*—nature, society, religion. Many old values are attached to her. Like Rome itself, the *Education* is "full of soft forms felt by lost senses." With woman Adams joins the agrarian eighteenth century and an isolated Mt. Vernon, "with no practicable road to reach it." The old society of "agriculture, handwork, and learning" was hers. The age of humanism, when books were still "the source of life," seems to be a part, too, of this broadly associated province of woman. A striking passage with a humanistic theme is that oddly Wordsworthian "boyhood-games" description of the defeat of the Boston Latin School in a snowball fight with town boys. Stones reinforced the soft snow and high foreheads bled as the humanities retreated before the newer social energies. Adams often rivals Gibbon in his power of giving poetic value to the humanities, which, clerical and mediaeval, can be placed in woman's and the Virgin's province.

To the masculine image he attaches the new energies of the scientific nineteenth century. Perhaps something of Hawthorne's mind directed Adams in this association, for Hawthorne linked (unhappily) maleness and science. The state as a power attempting to direct the energy of science is also given masculine association in the *Education.* The frustration symbols indicate Adams' spoken persuasion that scientific energy, being non-human (unlike the feminine retainers) is not controllable. "Excess of power . . . held by inadequate hands." Adams saw the scientific energies as accelerating towards chaos and death—moving into a disappearing path. Guns flashed their barrels in the snow halting Adams' sister at the Stelvio Pass, "where the glacier of the Ortler Spitze tumbled its huge mass down upon the road"—science and state presenting barriers to the true energies of life. Adams can strongly represent the sensation of the rising physical powers of the nineteenth century. He sketches the "frantic outline" of New York. In one personal spot of imagination he painfully seized the strength of the Northern armies emergent in the spring of 1863. The foundations of his opposition to scientific power are perhaps most deeply placed in an essential pacifism, inheritable from Gibbon and Shelley alike. The effect on the human being of relation to scientific power is, paradoxically, the inflation of the helpless ego. Adams' Senate Chamber is a scene of "irritated egotism." With pathos he presents in the later pages of the *Education* the breakdown of his great friends John Hay and Clarence King—both members of the little "Five of Hearts"—the statesman and the scientist. "A friend in power is a friend lost," in multiple ways. Adams is a great writer of masculine epitaphs, both English and American.

In the cathedral of Chartres, Blanche of Castile glares across the transept at Pierre de Dreux. The *Education* presents just such a divided imagination. Matthew Arnold saw his time as wanting a singleness of imagination. Adams, too, speaks as a scholar-gipsy, thinking "Arnold the best form of expression in his time." In Arnold the heathen armies fight at night. The conflict is made more open, more glaring, and rather less Victorian in the *Education.*

"Life was a double thing." Adams' harshest indictment (especially appropriate to Southerners, Senators, and railway superintendents) was that of being simple, of being in-

capable of "admitting two." His own father saw the ironies and let them stand. He did not know cant. He was not a schoolmaster, "a man employed to tell lies to little boys." The Jewish mind Adams can call "complex." He liked La Farge's mind, "opaline with infinite shades and refractions of light, and with color toned down to the finest gradations." One can hardly draw out the doubleness, the manifold crosslight that belongs to Adams' text. Winter and summer, the binary star, the lobes of the brain—there is a natural principle of doubleness. Moreover, ideas reflect and call up opposites, as shade belongs to light, the lender to the borrower. There is an added temporal doubleness, when what is past is seen in conflict with what is present. England especially seemed the centre of "the fantastic mystery of coincidences." It is evident that Adams is everywhere pursuing the imagination as an associationist. His chief associational emphasis is one which explores the language of opposites—of anarchy and complexity. His guides in the field of opposites are Locke and Sterne, Wordsworth and Keats, and perhaps particularly Hazlitt, a spirit evenly irritated and embittered. Hegel is a German guide, along with Kant and Schopenhauer. The conflict in the human imagination is disturbingly set off by a kind of agreeable biological and physical "associationism," whereby fish blends into man, and mass becomes motion in an easy purposeless "interconversion of forms."

The image of the cross lies in the centre of the Adams text, relating, as it were, the windows. It is a hidden image—the psychological point where the two dreams cross, of pleasure and pain. The cross exercises a similar psychological place in the middle, troubled passages of the *Prelude.* Adams touched openly the cross image as he passed from Blake's black London over to Holland, to enter the ripe beauty of still-sixteenth-century Antwerp. As their ship, the Baron Osy, steamed up the Scheldt in the morning mists, a travelling band began playing, and peasants dropped their tools to dance in the field. The cross is constant in Adams' questioning text, playing into every irony, every paradox, every wish and defeat. Adams had noted the omission of the crucifixion on Chartres' central portal. "Everything is there except misery." The architectural cross-thrust in a Chartres results in equilibrium, not conflict.

The cross image stands at the centre of what is probably a large pattern of religious images in the *Education.* There is a harsh religious story, of Cain and Abel, of vice, of the worldly wise, of exile, of the broken pitcher. As a child of twelve Adams was presented in the temple of the blue-coated American Senators. Lyrical notes, too, obtain—of Eden and the smell of trees, of the rainbow that protects. Vaguely lost in the starry evening in Estes Park in Colorado after a day of fishing, Adams allowed his mule to carry him along to that cabin where he meets for the first time Clarence King. The religious symbols of Adams' New England text, themselves in conflict, surround a central psychological cross. "For he knew no longer the good from the bad." "For he knew not where to turn."

Something further is produced, and the conflict of opposites presents, through the cross, something further in the way of form. It is this further thing which is the advanced style of the *Education.* The conflict of knowns becomes the unknown, the "obstacle in the dark." Now one enters the region of a truly tuneless, questioning prose. Now one meets the tree which is not the happy tree of imagination. Instead, there is "a personal grief in every tree." Now we see the bird, not of Marvell's and Keats's enchanted bough, but another bird of imagination—the vulture, the screaming macaw, the dove that has lost its taste for olives. Now we hear the ironic echo of Wordsworth's much happier language. The *Prelude*'s water language is perverted into seawrecks. We hear echoes, too, of the language of an unfit eighteenth-century optimism. Whitman's purple scene becomes an irony. Here is a new jungle world, of lightweights and heavyweights. Proceeding with the cross, Adams has developed those perplexed styles of imagination suitable to his society of February faces. Here is modern imagination, "nervous as wild beasts." Here is the "garden of innate disorder," spotty, scrappy, restless, accidental, strange. This is the sublime—unlike the beautiful *Chartres.* This is experience—unlike the innocent *Chartres.* "Life could not go on so beautiful and so sad." "Life is so gay and horrid!" In the parish church in Champagne or Touraine, Adams always stopped to look at the window of fragments,

> where one's glass discovered the Christ-child in his manager, nursed by the head of a fragmentary donkey, with a Cupid playing into its long ears from the balustrade of a Venetian palace, guarded by a legless Flemish *leibwache*, standing on his head with a broken halbert; all invoked in prayer by remnants of the donors and their children that might have been drawn by Pouquet or Pinturicchio, . . .

Paradoxically, though, it was Rome which best suggested the disordered modern style.

The divided imagination receives tone from the very element of glass in these personal windows. There is special consideration given in the *Education* to glass and related images (mosaic, marble, porcelain, crystal, antimony, pearl, diamond, mirror). Glass is sometimes the cutting surface which education works upon. It is the mental substance, the "glassy essence." In the *Chartres* Adams uses the phrase "delirium of colored light," suggesting perhaps those associations with glass which obtain faintly in eighteenth-century writing (Pope and Watts, for instance) and in romantic writing (Coleridge and Poe, for instance). The hint is rather strong in the passage on Adams' German schooling.

> The future Kaiser Wilhelm I, regent for his insane brother King Friedrich Wilhelm IV, seemed to pass his time looking at the passers-by from the window of his modest palace on the Linden.

Colour plays a striking part in the *Education,* and it is proper to stress Adams' love of colour, so evident in the *Chartres.* The rose window in Chartres is "our Lady's promise of Paradise." Chartres was a bird lighting on the ground. The yellow-legs of New England shores are noted. Miss Stevenson has said that Adams "won back in color something remembered from his childhood." The boy had even tasted the colour of the letters in his speller. Perhaps

in the *Education* colour turns from *yellow* to *black,* on to *blue* and *green.* This is colouring somewhat like that of the *Prelude.* No one so attached to colour, and who knew as well the philosophy of illusion, would be unaware of that particular language of illusion which, from the seventeenth century on, was associated with colour. Adams knew what it was to have the stage-scenery of the senses collapse, as in the summer of his sister's death. Snow and the glacial periods (or "intermittent chills") operate in the *Education* like the white of Moby Dick, as a reality below the illusion of colour. "Glow, like iron at dull heat"— Adams could use colour glaringly. The light from the thousand candles shining on spring nights over the empty St. Louis Exposition was phantom-like: "by night Arabia's crimson sands had never returned a glow half so astonishing." This historian can stand "green with horror." "The clouds that gather round the setting sun do not always take a sober coloring from eyes that have kept watch on mortality." Indirectly, Adams employs throughout the *Education* the colour that belongs to the agony of the Cross.

Colour and glass in their essences add direct tone to the troubled imagination of the *Education.* (pp. 332-44)

Kenneth MacLean, "Window and Cross in Henry Adams' 'Education'," in University of Toronto Quarterly, *Vol. XXVIII, No. 4, July, 1959, pp. 332-44.*

Herbert F. Hahn   (essay date 1963)

[*In the following essay, Hahn disputes the notion that Adams meant only to convey his personal sense of failure in* The Education, *arguing instead that he used his failure as a literary device to show the dramatic irony inherent in pursuing education during rapidly changing times.*]

Anyone beginning to read Henry Adams' *Education* for the first time gets the impression from the very first chapters that Adams thought his life had been a failure, and that he considered it a failure because his education had not fitted him to play a useful part in the new and different world that was coming into being in the nineteenth century. The book can therefore be taken—so it seems—as a protest, based on one man's experience, against the effect of technology and industrialism on the personal values of the social system which they displaced.

Throughout the book Henry Adams gives the impression of a man who wished to participate actively in affairs but always missed the chance to function effectively. There is a certain poignancy in his desire to understand why a man like himself, who started with every apparent advantage and set out with such faith and eagerness, should have ended with so little accomplished. His antecedents and his personal attainments had indicated a career in the Adams tradition; yet he never found an opportunity to make a contribution to his time comparable with what his forebears had accomplished.

This presentation of himself as a failure has usually been accepted by Adams' readers at face value. In the 1920's a whole "generation of futilitarians" (Louis Kronenberger's phrase) found that Adams' theme of maladjustment between a cultivated personality and an increasingly mechanized civilization presented exactly the predicament which they were experiencing. His book became the Bible of the younger generation struggling with the frustrations of a world they neither made nor understood.

Could it be, on the other hand, that the dominant theme of Henry Adams' book was a literary device of the author's rather than a reflection of the facts? One recent critic has advanced the theory that Henry Adams fancied himself as the "heroic failure" of a modern epic. From this point of view, the dramatic irony inherent in the repeated assertions that Adams never felt at home in the world and despaired of ever playing a significant part in it was a consciously cultivated irony. If true, this view of Adams' intention helps to explain some things about the book which otherwise strike the reader as puzzling. There is, for example, in the chapters devoted to Adams' travel-years after graduation a certain tone of insouciance—a pose of naiveté—which leaves the reader with a very inadequate sense of how Adams reacted to the things he saw in Europe. He seems to be trying to emphasize the *lack* of "education" to be gained from the experiences available to a young man of his background in his day. And yet we know from the famous letters Adams wrote on subsequent travels that he was capable of responding richly to experience. In the *Education,* however, he gives the impression of making the grand tour without zest and of finding most things rather empty of meaning for him. This impression does not accord with what is otherwise known of his temperament. His attitude becomes understandable, however, if it can be regarded as a consciously planned device for emphasizing his "failure" to find an acceptable place in a civilization with which he felt himself out of tune.

Actually, the burden of Henry Adams' complaint was not his own "failure" to adjust to the world but the realization that the world in which he lived as an adult had changed so much from the world in which he grew up as a child that the traditional values of his upbringing had become meaningless and inapplicable. A relatively uncomplicated agrarian America, operating on the basis of stern but comprehensible Puritan principles, was rapidly being transformed into a highly complex industrialized state, with a bewildering shift in the principles on which it operated and an apparent exclusion of morality from the political means for achieving its goals. The disappearance of the sort of world in which an Adams could have functioned and its displacement by a new world which required a type of "education" such as no previous Adams had ever had—that is the real theme of Henry Adams' long book. He took pleasure, it is true, in presenting himself as an anachronism from a former age and indulged his tragic feeling of having been born too late. But behind the mask of "the tragic failure" was another Henry Adams who was not lamenting his fate so much as making a genuine effort to understand the times that were out of joint.

Henry Adams knew that a man must thoroughly understand the world in which he finds himself in order to be able to grapple with it. He sensed that his "education" in the ways of the new world would require him, first of all, to unlearn everything that he had been taught. However, he *believed* in the values of his grandfather's world; it was the rejection of those values by the new world, rather than his own failure to accommodate himself to it, that represented for him the real tragedy he was writing about. Nevertheless, he felt it was important to get beyond the perspectives of his traditional background and to make the attempt to understand the contemporary world. Lacking the opportunity to participate in affairs, he became an observer and commentator, writing detailed accounts of the political events he was living through, frequently with penetrating remarks on the personalities of the chief participants. His political chapters served the purpose of underlining the corruption, vulgarity, and cynicism of the modern world from which he felt himself alienated. Until Lincoln Steffens painted the same picture in more vivid colors and with much greater detail, Adams' account of the unprincipled dealings in American public life was the classic portrayal of a burgeoning business civilization creating a chaos in which self-interest was the sole guiding principle.

But political events and economic developments were only the surface features, after all. Henry Adams' education in the nature of the modern world would not be complete—at least, he would never be satisfied—until he had fathomed the driving forces and motivations that accounted for the surface phenomena. He understood in a general way that modern science with its practical achievements was responsible for the transformations which had changed the easy-going world of his forebears into a totally different, enigmatic world, that nevertheless seemed amazingly alive. But he doubted the correctness of the common point of view which regarded progress as inevitable and the American brand of material achievement as the climax of all progress. What Henry Adams really sought from his "education" was a standard or principle of interpretation by which he could estimate the truth of the world-view which made a virtue of chaos as long as it seemed to further "progress." As one who had been brought up in a tradition that gave great satisfaction through the unity and consistency of meaning it assigned to life, he was genuinely concerned to discover how it was possible to find a comparable satisfaction in a world that had become so complex and contradictory as to lose all unity and consistency of meaning.

Adams failed to solve the problem, at first, because he assumed from the start that satisfaction in life would be found only by those who learned to *control* the complicated, multiple forces dominant in the world in their time. When he saw politicians and business men who were not "educated," in his sense, doing *just that* with phenomenal success, and when he saw men like his friend Clarence King failing miserably even though trained (educated) for exercising such control, he became pessimistic about the value of "education" as a means of finding satisfaction in life. For him, satisfaction meant understanding as well as controlling. He observed, however, that the successful men of his day controlled the forces operating in the world without understanding them, or even being conscious of a need to understand them. Adams, therefore, despaired of the possibility of finding any principle of action in modern life that gave unity of meaning to the diverse activities it engendered.

Adams, however, was not prepared to accept "multiplicity" as any more than a descriptive term for the modern situation: it could not be made, his whole temperament told him, into a philosophical justification for the situation. And so, he continued to study, to observe, and to weigh, in a constant search for the meaning of his contemporary environment. He gave up, for the time being, the attempt to identify a unifying principle in the world as he knew it; and turning to the world of the Middle Ages, where unity and significance had permeated all of life, he proceeded to study it thoroughly in order to find out its secret. It has been customary to regard Henry Adams' love affair with the Middle Ages as a nostalgic search for the very things he missed in modern civilization. The contrast between the two ages is striking enough: on the one hand, chaos without meaning; on the other, a unifying principle that gave significance to all the parts. But when Henry Adams immersed himself in the medieval outlook on life, it was not to "go home" to a world for which he felt an instinctive sympathy—actually he had been unaware of such a world before his tour of Normandy with the Henry Cabot Lodges. It was rather to gain perspective on his *own* world that he sought to understand medieval "unity" in contrast to nineteenth-century "multiplicity."

So satisfying did Henry Adams find the assurance and confidence reflected in the medieval point of view that he almost surrendered to it, and bowing himself before the Virgin of Chartres he asked for the peace that would come from understanding himself and his world as clearly as the Virgin's followers understood theirs. Significantly, he did not ask for "the peace which *passeth* understanding"; he insisted on *having* understanding; as a child of the scientific age, he *had to know*. So, wistfully, he started "once more" his search for "education" (enlightenment).

The real significance of Henry Adams' *Education* is not the story of maladjustment that it tells, nor yet the contrast between two civilizations that it makes, but the explanation which the author eventually worked out for the trend of civilization from medieval unity to modern multiplicity. In a series of brilliant though still ironic chapters (31-34), Adams summed up what he had learned from his lifelong search for understanding of the world in which he lived. These philosophical chapters have seldom been taken quite seriously; they have sometimes been brushed aside as derivative: the chief idea in them came from the author's brother, Brooks Adams. But there is a philosophy of history in them, seemingly artificial because applied too mechanically, yet containing an explanation of modern "chaos" and the "multiplicity" of modern civilization which has proved to be so appropriate and so illuminating that it deserves reconsideration.

Henry Adams had learned, first of all, that modern science (itself an attempt to discover the immutable "laws of nature") had ended by discovering, in modern physical theory, that there were no simple, immutable laws of nature which gave unity, consistency, and order to the universe; that, rather, the laws of the physical world seemed to be

infinitely complex, not always consistently predictable in their application, and hence undependable as a basis for finding order in the universe. In a word, Henry Adams came to the realization that such a system of order and unity as the medieval synthesis was the creation of the mind of man imposing its desire for simplicity and significance on the phenomena of the world at large. As he said himself, "Chaos was the law of nature; Order was the dream of man."

Henry Adams had learned, in the second place, that the discoveries of modern science, destructive as they were to philosophical conceptions of the universe, were nevertheless making constructive contributions to the material comfort of mankind in the universe, by increasing man's knowledge of the number and kinds of physical energies available for application to his needs. As man's knowledge of the physical forces of nature became more complex (less unified even in theory), man's opportunities for bending them to his purposes increased proportionately. The "multiplicity" or complexity of modern industrialized life, in other words, corresponded to the actual "chaos" of forces existing in the physical universe.

In the light of these insights, it had been pointless as well as fruitless for Henry Adams to look for a unifying principle to explain the modern world. Multiplicity of conflicting forces was its chief characteristic, and inevitably so. Man might try to impose his control over the physical forces of nature and upon the human energies of society, but the resulting "order" was not inherent in either nature or society, and it lasted only as long as the mind of man thought the one and willed the other. Philosophically speaking, there was no "God" to give significance to the universe of forces and the world of energies. Logically, therefore, there was nothing wrong with the modern tendency to establish control of these forces and energies without understanding them. In relation to the universe and the world, men had become "as gods"—without the divine capacity, of course, to give real significance to what they were doing with their new powers. The significant fact, for Henry Adams, was that the tendency was irreversible. He had come to realize that there was no going back, that a world of meaningful unity had never really existed (outside the human mind), that a world of chaotic, conflicting forces corresponded more nearly to the reality than all the orderly worlds created by man's imagination and reason.

The most famous part of Henry Adams' philosophy of history was what he called "the law of acceleration" (unconsciously demonstrating within himself his view that, though there be no actual laws, even in history, the mind will impose law as a device to help itself understand what it is talking about). He thought he saw in history a consistent trend toward *increasing* control over the forces of nature. Starting in a small way with the discovery and exploitation of the power of a water wheel and the power in a windmill, man had then, with smaller and smaller gaps of time between discoveries, but larger and larger amounts of power at his disposal, proceeded to find and use steam power electric power, and so on. Henry Adams was convinced that this "acceleration" in man's control of nature's forces would continue in geometric proportion, until (he predicted) man would have discovered within fifty years of Adams' time the ultimate source of power locked in the atom.

In his own generation, the symbol of modern man's control of force was the dynamo, which Henry Adams found to be the most fascinating embodiment of ultimate power under complete control yet devised. Fascinating he found it to watch in operation—but appalling to think about in its implications. As a symbol of force under control, it helped to explain to him the nature of the civilization in which he lived. As a prophecy of the trend of civilization, it suggested increasing efficiency in man's control of ultimate force until the human race reached the point where it could even destroy itself with atomic energy. This eventuality Henry Adams could not regard with complacency. He could not accept the view of his contemporaries that the history of mankind in modern times was a story of inevitable progress upwards. "Complexity, Multiplicity, even a step towards Anarchy, it might suggest, but what step towards perfection?"

It was not the ultimate denouement, however, that troubled Henry Adams in his innermost depths. That denouement, after all, remained only a logical possibility; it was not inevitably a foregone conclusion. He saw another already taking place which appalled him more specifically. As man's control of the forces of nature increased in efficiency, his will to dominate the social energies of mankind also increased, with a resulting tendency to *concentrate* the power inherent in the forces of society, again for the sake of efficiency. In other words, the technological advance of mankind was inexorably accompanied by a trend to regimentation and the collectivization of man's social relationships. It was the progressive destruction of human values in the accelerating trend towards a power civilization that appalled Henry Adams the most.

Here was the real tragedy of living in modern times. Critics are mistaken to emphasize the tragedy implicit in the *Education* as a personal one for Henry Adams. Adams would have insisted that he was describing a situation that constituted a tragedy for all thoughtful and sensitive souls. With the increase in the means of control over energy and power, all that was distinctively human in human life was gradually being supplanted by all that was mechanical and impersonal. Adams' book was not simply a protest against an intolerable situation by one who had been most uncomfortable in it; it was an attempt to instruct a whole new generation in the conditions under which life in modern times was being lived, and to emphasize that no other conditions were possible under the circumstances.

Henry Adams made all this sound very pessimistic. But behind the pessimistic tone of his discussion it is possible to discern a positive note of emphasis on continuing human values, particularly the human capacity for thought. It is true that, in its context, his quotation from Karl Pearson: "Order and reason, beauty and benevolence, are characteristics and conceptions which we find solely associated with the mind of man," sounds like a pessimistic acknowledgement of the fact that the universe does *not* contain order and reason but is essentially meaningless. On the other hand, like several ironic passages in Adams' last chapters, the quotation conceals his faith that, though the universe be meaningless, the very attempt of the human mind to create meaning from its diverse phenomena is the source of all truth and beauty and value in the *human* world. The meaningless chaos of the universe, though eternal, was as nothing compared with the ephemeral, but significant, flash of a human mind in the cosmic darkness.

Again, Henry Adams' parable of the young oyster, in which he compared the human mind to that little animal

---

An excerpt from *The Education of Henry Adams*

Psychology was to him a new study, and a dark corner of education. As he lay on Wenlock Edge, with the sheep nibbling the grass close about him as they or their betters had nibbled the grass—or whatever there was to nibble—in the Silurian kingdom of Pteraspis, he seemed to have fallen on an evolution far more wonderful than that of fishes. He did not like it; he could not account for it; and he determined to stop it. Never since the days of his *Limulus* ancestry had any of his ascendants thought thus. Their modes of thought might be many, but their thought was one. Out of his millions of millions of ancestors, back to the Cambrian mollusks, every one had probably lived and died in the illusion of Truths which did not amuse him, and which had never changed. Henry Adams was the first in an infinite series to discover and admit to himself that he really did not care whether truth was, or was not, true. He did not even care that it should be proved true, unless the process were new and amusing. He was a Darwinian for fun.

From the beginning of history, this attitude had been branded as criminal—worse than crime—sacrilege! Society punished it ferociously and justly, in self-defence. Mr. Adams, the father, looked on it as moral weakness; it annoyed him; but it did not annoy him nearly so much as it annoyed his son, who had no need to learn from Hamlet the fatal effect of the pale cast of thought on enterprises great or small. He had no notion of letting the currents of his action be turned awry by this form of conscience. To him, the current of his time was to be his current, lead where it might. He put psychology under lock and key; he insisted on maintaining his absolute standards; on aiming at ultimate Unity. The mania for handling all the sides of every question, looking into every window, and opening every door, was, as Bluebeard judiciously pointed out to his wives, fatal to their practical usefulness in society. One could not stop to chase doubts as though they were rabbits. One had no time to paint and putty the surface of Law, even though it were cracked and rotten. For the young men whose lives were cast in the generation between 1867 and 1900, Law should be Evolution from lower to higher, aggregation of the atom in the mass, concentration of multiplicity in unity, compulsion of anarchy in order; and he would force himself to follow wherever it led, though he should sacrifice five thousand millions more in money, and a million more in lives.

Henry Adams, in his The Education of Henry Adams, *Riverside Press, 1918.*

"secreting its universe to suit its conditions until it had built up a shell of nacre that embodied all its notions of the perfect," but "perishing in the face of the cyclonic hurricane or the volcanic upheaval of its bed," sounds like a realistic recognition of the fact that the universe has no interest in the existence of man and offers him only complete annihilation (death) as his ultimate fate. Few writers have described more pitilessly how completely indifferent the universe seems to be to the aspirations and strivings of the human race. Yet, behind the irony of the parable was the implication that it was precisely the aspiration and the striving that gave meaning, if only temporarily, to all that was human in an otherwise impersonal universe.

What Henry Adams accomplished in his *Education* was not only to describe remorselessly what kind of a world the modern world had become—philosophically, as well as politically and economically; he also provided a point of view with which to face that world without despair. (pp. 444-49)

> *Herbert F. Hahn, " 'The Education of Henry Adams' Reconsidered," in* College English, *Vol. 24, No. 6, March, 1963, pp. 444-49.*

Vern Wagner (essay date 1969)

[*In the following excerpt from his book* The Suspension of Henry Adams: A Study of Manner and Matter, *Wagner examines the style, structure, and the theme of failure in* The Education.]

Adams wrote to William James in 1908 about his *Education* which he had published privately the previous year:

> As for the volume [*Education*], it interests me chiefly as a literary experiment, hitherto, as far as I know, never tried or never successful. Your brother Harry tries such experiments in literary art daily, and would know instantly what I mean; but I doubt whether a dozen people in America—except architects or decorators— would know or care.

> I care little myself, and have put too many such *tours-de-force* into the fire, to bother about explanation. This will probably follow the others, for I have got it so far into shape that I can see the impossibility of success. It is the old story of an American drama. You can't get your contrasts and backgrounds.

The noteworthy referent is to "architects and decorators," and the noteworthy description is "literary experiment." Did Adams succeed in it or did he not? In the "Editor's Preface" (dated September 1918 and signed by Henry Cabot Lodge) he wrote of the volume, "The point on which the author failed to please himself, and could get no light from readers or friends, was the usual one of literary form. . . . The scheme became unmanageable as he approached his end. . . . and he could not satisfy himself with his workmanship." He said the book was "avowedly incomplete." What dissatisfied him? The book is clearly what he intended it to be, a sequel to *Chartres:* a study of twentieth-century multiplicity as opposed to the former's being a **"Study of Thirteenth-Century Unity."** The last three chapters, like the last three of *Chartres,* are the climax of all that preceded. He wrote Barrett Wendell in

1909 that he thought these six chapters comprised a single essay. They do come to seem that—but one must read carefully everything else in the two volumes to see it.

It seems to me, therefore, that the whole matter of the *Education* must be dealt with in detail to see what its manner is—its architecture and its decoration. Adams said . . . "The pen works for itself, and acts like a hand, modelling the plastic material over and over again to the form that suits it best." Like the painter, sculptor, architect, composer, photographer or choreographer, the writer as artist knows a satisfactory result comes only from finding a proper form for the matter of his thought. Each knows an idea in the depths and recesses of his mind communicates successfully only through proper form, and the final form is likely to be only an approximation of his fullest thought. All would-be artists are mutes until they learn speech, and none ever learns enough of that. Colors, lines, sounds, shapes and steps as well as words, unless they are ordered into intelligible *form,* remain gibberish, and the form that results, the "artistic product," must always seem to the artist insufficient. That Henry Adams was aware of this explains why he declared his *Education* "avowedly incomplete," why his workmanship dissatisfied him, why he failed to please himself. He did not realize his ideal. But to judge how far he did succeed in giving appreciable form to his material his readers must examine both, concentrating on the point where they meet, at the juncture.

A survey of the general impact of the *Education* shows that it provides surging waves of intricacies, of no certainties in the labyrinthine world. There is gnarliness, if waves could gnarl. Overall the book seems to be late Gothic architecturally speaking—or architectonically—in contrast to the Norman Romanesque of the *History,* a book that matches Mont-Saint-Michel with its presumed faith in flatly declared facts, in simplicity, in clarity, in weight and mass. In the *Education* a great wealth of facts clash against one another, startling facts, obscure facts, perhaps wrong ones. One reason they may even be excused when they are wrong is that, as Adams said in Chapter III, "Washington," describing a boyhood trip there in 1850, "the actual journey has no interest for education. The memory was all that mattered." The actual history Adams reported in his study of education in the last two-thirds of the nineteenth century, meaning exactness in dates and other accuracies, is not significant to anyone but the student of fact. Facts are symbols in the *Education* as they are in *Chartres;* facts became images. When on that 1850 trip to Washington Henry visited the White House with his father, he wrote later he "half thought he owned it, and took for granted that he should some day live in it." It is unimaginative to suppose that he meant to be literal. For the late Henry Adams facts helped little for, as he wrote in the *Education,* "all opinion founded on fact must be error, because the facts can never be complete, and their relations must be always infinite."

Contortions of both sentences and matter produced peculiar distortions in the *Education.* Chapters end with downbeats that shatter the shore of a reader's perceptions. The entire tone is excessively lugubrious for a book about a presumably ebullient nineteenth century and not its *fin de siècle* decade alone. The sentences are so intricately and heavily weighted at the ends that they spoil any impression of flat statement. Their unbalance spoils that sense of rhythmic flux balanced sentences succeeded in conveying, I think, in the *History.* The clearcut order of the paragraphs themselves always counteract as sure as reefs the turgid flow of the sentences they contain. Jokes of all kinds curl atop powerful waves—sad, malicious, sharp, lightsome. They float above the somber tone, accentuating it. Sudden solemn aphorisms appear like islands or lifebuoys anchored in the ebb and flow of observations recording a movement called an education that beat about for nearly seventy years to end in the peculiar calm of "failure" at last, a word heavily charged with negation, loss, sorrow and hopelessness, the end to the storm of life. "Failure" is a cry from one drowning in a sub-aqueous world; it knells constant warnings about the uselessness of the human effort to learn about and finally to understand the content of the reefs, rocks and earthquakes, the whirlpools, cyclones, hurricanes and catastrophes that endanger all floating vessels seeking anchorage in peace and conclusion.

Most readers of Henry Adams agree with his brother Brooks who wrote of Henry in 1919, "he poses, more or less throughout his book, as having been a failure and a disappointed man." This is true enough, for one interpretation of the *Education* is that it is a treatise on failure. But Brooks added,

> He was neither the one nor the other, as he knew well. He was not a failure, for he succeeded, and succeeded brilliantly, in whatever he undertook, where success was possible; and he was not disappointed, for the world gave him everything he would take.

Examined in the light Brooks used here the declaration is sound enough: the honorary degree Harvard offered Adams in 1892 proves his success as a professor of history there from 1871-1877. No one has found he failed as editor of the *North American Review* for the same period. And the current status his historical work enjoys demonstrates his triumph as an historian. Why then did Adams pose as a failure? The answer is that he sought success in places where, as his brother hinted, it was not possible. He arrived at manhood to find a society blasted and coarsened by a Gilded Age he found he could not understand. He studied a science that not only wrecked the foundations of accepted religion but could not explain itself—a science that uncovered the *Pteraspis* and the *Terebratula,* puzzling creations that jeered at pure evolutionary theory. This science in 1901 finally produced radium which threw into question all scientific law to that date. In general he failed constantly to be prepared or equipped for events and happen-chance that occurred, nearly always experiences that surprised him.

But he meant failure in a worldly sense too, despite the surface evidence. He used a stronger light than his brother did. As a teacher, he said he did not know what to teach or for what purpose: "History is a tangled skein that one may take up at any point, and break when one has unravelled enough; but complexity precedes evolution." The

Pteraspis, the first known vertebrate before whom there is no recognizable ancestor, "grins horribly from the closed entrance." As an editor he chalked up another failure: he could only become "an authority on advertising." And as an historian "He had no notion whether . . . [his histories] served a useful purpose." He implied finally that they did not, and in the second of his last and most provocative studies, *A Letter to American Teachers of History* (1910) he showed that he saw the second law of thermodynamics to be the probable governing law of the progressive universe with Entropy—which is indeed silence—the likely goal. Thus he justified his claim of failure on broader grounds than his brother Brooks would admit to. One cannot therefore accept Brooks's assertion that it was merely a pose.

To Adams education fully thought of should contain training for aspects of life no school or educator had ever provided save Jean Jacques Rousseau, perhaps, whom he had praised in the first preface to the *Education,* but whose greatness as an educator was "in the manner of the eighteenth century." Beginning the chapter "Twenty Years After (1892)" he said, "education should try to lessen the obstacles, diminish the friction, invigorate the energy, and should train minds to react, not at haphazard, but by choice, on the lines of force that attract their world." When, however, he discovered the lines of force were beyond knowing until too late, and that choice or no choice made no difference, then in training minds to act by choice education "may be shown to consist in following the intuitions of instinct" while the conscious mind remained observant but silent—the most economical behavior. It is the position of the Rajah in the 1891 poem **"Buddha and Brahma."**

The great lesson Adams teaches in the **Education** is the old one of **"Buddha and Brahma"** with good temper added; he presented it concisely in the second preface to the book: "in the immediate future, silence next to good-temper was the mark of sense." The same statement occurs in the final chapter. In his letters he persistently said the same with slight variation, and with "good temper" implied in his wording. To Cecil Spring Rice, for example, he wrote in 1897, "All that remains is to hold one's tongue, and vomit gracefully, until the time comes when no man needs to be sea-sick more." In 1905 he wrote Margaret Chanler even more succinctly, "Silence alone is respectable and respected. I believe God to be Silence." He did not arrive at this thought easily. It resulted from what he found was his incapacity to shape his own destiny, to influence the course of human affairs in society itself and, more important, to understand the meaning of human affairs and destiny itself. He wrestled perpetually, only to have this idea confirmed so often, thoroughly and finally that it is a considerable result.

The **Education** begins with a sophomoric question: "Where was he?—where was he going?" The splendid irony is that wherever it has been asked the question is one unanswered by all philosophy and human thought.

Bernard DeVoto declared that after reading the book more than a dozen times he got an intense pleasure from perceiving how much of what Adams passes a magisterial judgment on he was altogether ignorant of how superhumanly absurd much of his reasoning is, on the basis of what gigantic misconceptions he announced certainties where almighty God would have proceeded tentatively.

The comment typifies the resentful criticism Adams has received from many critics whose lack of perception I excuse because Adams did not succeed for them as an artist. Many take Adams' use of the word "ignorance" in too small a sense when he meant it to represent an ironic image of great inconclusion. Many so mistake Adams' pompous phraseology of exaggerated statements as "magisterial judgment" that they do not see the addition of circumlocutions, hesitations and elaborate protective phrases accentuate the ignorance he claimed by cancelling his boldest remarks. Many more than Mr. DeVoto see Adams' hyperbolic declarations as such "gigantic misconceptions" they are unable to see what appear to be "certainties" are only mock answers stated definitively to point up the fundamental fact of uncertainty, in nearly every case protected by some sort of "maybe."

Adams had said in *Chartres:*

> An artist, if good for anything, foresees what his public will see; and what his public will see is what he ought to have intended—the measure of his genius. If the public sees more than he himself did, this is his credit; if less, this is his fault.

Henry Adams' major failure has been, to date, as an artist. It is a failure I seek to correct. His "superhumanly absurd" reasoning was, I think, humor. . . . So are his judgments—pretended—and his certainties—overly pronounced. His claim of ignorance was serious but not simple. The declaration, "He knew enough to be ignorant," is plain to the point of being annoyingly flat; and magisterial by itself it is even insulting if the reader emphasizes the "He." But its content as thought is hardly absurd if one reads on:

> His course had led him through oceans of ignorance; he had tumbled from one ocean into another till he had learned to swim; but even to him education was a serious thing.

Then follows a famous passage:

> A parent gives life, but as parent, gives no more. A murderer takes life, but his deed stops there. A teacher affects eternity; he can never tell where his influence stops.

Teacher-recruitment posters bear this quotation, a weighty inducement to the idealistic young to take up the task of affecting eternity through teaching. One hardly sees the caution implied in the final clause, but to consider the effect of ignorant tutoring sobers the view. The rest of the paragraph is just as decided, but it unmistakably corrects anyone whose ambition to shape eternity is overweening:

> A teacher is expected to teach truth, and may perhaps flatter himself that he does so, if he stops with the alphabet or the multiplication table, as

a mother teaches truth by making her child eat with a spoon; but morals are quite another truth and philosophy is more complex still. A teacher must either treat history as a catalogue, a record, a romance, or as an evolution; and whether he affirms or denies evolution, he falls into all the burning faggots of the pit. He makes of his scholars either priests or atheists, plutocrats or socialists, judges or anarchists, almost in spite of himself. In essence incoherent and immoral, history had either to be taught as such—or falsified.

I think the *Education* adds up to humor in the largest sense: it is a treatise on inconclusion. The manner of its writing meets the chaos of its matter in a juncture that images suspension. "Gnarliness" is the word to characterize the complex description of movements in the lifetime of a man who ended nowhere, in the maze where he had begun, at no fixed point. Adams learned a powerful lesson. Not being positive but severely restrictive if not negative, it appears to many readers worth little. Simply stated it is this: failure described any education for the twentieth century that concludes understanding means something else than ignorance. Or: failure necessarily results from any education aiming at unified, orderly, patterned learning. Or: education properly considered results in silence.

But this was only part of Adams' education. Were it all, the *Education* should be consistently heavy and somber and gloomy. It is not. "Funniness" decorates the basic pattern, funniness of expression, of episodes, of thought; the whole elaborated hyperbole of the style encourages that essential beyond silence, "good temper," the only safe tower beyond tragedy. The *story* of the *Education,* as the writer himself defined it, deals with the adventures of Henry Adams "in search of an education, which, if not taken too seriously, tended to humor."

One device that accentuates the humor is Adams' treatment of himself throughout the book as a littler man than he was in fact though that was little—five feet three inches high. He was a Lilliputian. He was a tiny manikin, a "homunculus" who crawled down gangplanks. He sat and stared helplessly into the future. He hid in rooms. He shook his "white beard in silent horror." He flung up his little arms in helplessness, or he flung them around another figure, or he fell, nearly faint, into other arms outstretched. But the "figure" that Henry Adams depicted finally emerges from his book as a reflection of one man's mental mirror, one finally very like that of Edward Gibbon, that "fat little historian" who when gazing at Gothic cathedrals "darted a contemptuous look on the stately monuments of superstition," but who must have felt respect for them as for any objects worthy of his "vast study and active mind." Eighteenth-century Gibbon scorned the structures Adams succeeded in feeling in *Mont-Saint-Michel and Chartres,* but he would not have dismissed them. The picture of Gibbon Adams presents is only amusing until one realizes Adams gave strong respectability to the airs of this stout-minded little man. So Don Quixote also inspires respect if we think of him occasionally as Cervantes' ironic protest against woman-inspired "courtesy." A like air of respectability arises about short Henry Adams too whose cry of "Failure" sounds so specious. Like Gibbon, like the Noble Spanish Knight, Henry Adams stands up from his book so pitifully little and yet so greatly stout a man that the impression is miniature grotesque. He invites our laughter while he attracts our sympathy. By creating such a *persona* Adams went far in creating one of the effective paradoxes of his work.

The major result of my analysis of the *Education* shows it to be a careful work of art. Adams imposed artistic order on disorderly material, patterns on confusion; he gave a form to plasticity. Paradoxically, he fixed shapelessness on matter. He created art through successful technique. But he is far beyond artisanship. His technique is a success of mind, the final essential, I think, in the greatest art. All the factors are linked . . . to the point we must consider: at the juncture. In this case the principal factor of humor becomes by means of the writing the final matter of the work. Adams' pen finally traced out the main sequence of his thought. Realizing the necessity for striking out, what he left was purposeful. What may seem side-paths ultimately appear for what they are: necessary stops along the main lines of force. To avoid shapelessness he did employ his pen to model the plastic material of his education "over and over again to the form that suits it best." The result was a very clear fundamental structure.

Chronology is the basic arrangement of the *Education* and each of the thirty-five chapters advanced Adams' story of education one or more years from 1838 to 1905. (Often Adams stepped into the future to look back on the experiences he related for a particular year, but when moving so he always showed he had not come to know later what he did not know at the time.) This arrangement provides the reader of the *Education* the common excitement of any narrative in ordinary time sequence; but it is somewhat deceptive since the material was always selected only from the experiences Adams claimed contributed to his education. In Chapter II, "Boston," he explained this in describing his education "at the moment when character is plastic" from the years 1848 to 1854 when he was between the ages of ten and sixteen. He presented here a caution the reader should note carefully in reading all of the book:

> This is the story of an education, and the person or persons who figure in it are supposed to have values only as educators or educated. The surroundings concern it only as far as they affect education.

Adams wanted his readers to consider him as an *image* of nineteenth-century education, an image that serves as a symbol; in this way he could focus on the abstraction "education."

In a letter to John Hay in 1883 Adams wrote:

> Trollope has amused me for two evenings. I am clear that you should write autobiography. I mean to do mine. After seeing how coolly and neatly a man like Trollope can destroy the last vestige of heroism in his own life, I object to allowing mine to be murdered by any one except myself.

But to think of the *Education* as being what Adams meant by his autobiography so weakens its point that one can see

then only a misleading account of a particular life that is unique and therefore limited. In the "Preface" dated 1907, Adams wrote at greater length on this issue:

> As educator, Jean Jacques was, in one respect, easily first: he erected a monument of warning against the Ego. Since his time, and largely thanks to him, the Ego has steadily tended to efface itself, and, for purposes of model, to become a manikin on which the toilet of education is to be draped in order to show the fit or misfit of the clothes. The object of study is the garment, not the figure. The tailor adapts the manikin as well as the clothes to his patron's wants. The tailor's object, in this volume, is to fit young men, in universities or elsewhere, to be men of the world, equipped for any emergency; and the garment offered to them is meant to show the faults of the patchwork fitted on their fathers.

If it is an autobiography, several sharp criticisms of the book are quite justified. One is that the use of the third person throughout would be a specious pretense of objectivity: Adams meant all along to insinuate himself into the reader's consciousness. Thus, goes this interpretation, Adams did in effect cheat. And Rousseau was more "honest" and so are all other autobiographers. Worse: if the book is autobiography, the gaps in Adams' account, explanations not given, sly hints not explained, references not followed out, all are further deception. The most spectacular omission is the story of the twenty years from 1871 to 1892. Only too briefly did he discuss his work as teacher, editor and historian then, in Chapter XX and XXI. An account of his marriage and his wife's suicide is missing entirely. Matched against the thoroughness with which he seemingly dealt with his life until 1871, the omission seems a fraud. But Adams included his own oblique defense, one not sufficiently noted. He began Chapter XXI, "Twenty Years After (1892)"

> Once more! this is a story of education, not of adventure! It is meant to help young men—or such as have intelligence enough to seek help—but it is not meant to amuse them. What one did—or did not do—with one's education, after getting it, need trouble the inquirer in no way; it is a personal matter only which would confuse him.

He was fully aware his book would call attention to himself, that the figure is of emphatic interest. He wrote in the last paragraph of his 1907 Preface:

> The mankind, therefore, has the same value as any other geometrical figure of three or more dimensions, which is used for the study of relation. For that purpose it cannot be spared; it is the only measure of motion, of proportion, of human condition; it must have the air of reality; must be taken for real; must be treated as though it had life. Who knows? Possibly it had!

Thus the remark that what the manikin did with his education after getting it would only confuse the reader is true enough because personal matters would deflect the reader from the main sequence of his thought.

Such an interpretation explains more than the treatment of the prime manikin, Henry Adams. It explains the curious treatment of most of the other figures who appear in the book. The first one of importance is his father Charles Francis Adams, especially dominant because "His father's character was therefore the larger part of his education, as far as any single person affected it." "Character" differs in direction of meaning from "man," the former being less whole than the latter; character is not necessarily the man. Adams presented a sensitive and subtle analysis of Charles Francis Adams but not a full portrait. He was, says his third son, the man of perfect poise who "stood alone" in his age in Boston and "set up a party of his own . . . [that] became a chief influence in the education of the boy Henry . . . and violently affected his character." The *character* of Mr. Adams that emerges from Henry Adams' presentation (some six to eight pages) is curiously cold and unloved. He did not, like the Presidents who were his father and grandfather (nor like at least two of his sons, Henry and Brooks) reveal restlessness. To his son Henry he "possessed the only perfectly balanced mind that ever existed in the name." But his son rejected him finally as a useful educator because his balance was so fixed and settled, so fully an inheritance from Puritan ancestry. He was—I think the word must be—a grotesque. His "business in life was to get past the dangers of the slave-power, or to fix its bounds at least."

> The task done, he might be content to let his sons pay for the pilotage; and it mattered little to his success whether they paid for it with their lives wasted on battle-fields or in misdirected energies and lost opportunity.

This may be a very personal complaint, but I think Adams meant not only his father's sons but all the following generation were forfeit to his father's fixed balance of mind. By strong implication though not by direct revelation Henry Adams exhibits strong objection to his father's character in the role of educator, though not to his father "personally" considered.

Yet if his perfection meant positively that his father was no snob, flatterer, or vilifier, nor envious, jealous, vain, conceited, arrogant or full of pride, why did Henry not profit from the education such character provided? Henry Adams was after all in "search of a father." It is because Charles Francis Adams was a negative educational force. Henry Adams declared flatly:

> The generation that lived from 1840 to 1870 could do very well with the old forms of education; that which had its work to do between 1870 and 1900 needed something quite new.

"Charles Francis Adams was singular for mental poise," yet his memory was hardly above the average; his mind was not bold like his grandfather's or restless like his father's, or imaginative or oratorical—still less mathematical; but it worked with singular perfection, admirable self-restraint, and instinctive mastery of form. Within its range it was a model.

The trouble was its narrowness of range, and in his son's analysis he appears to be what his critics found also, for "They called him cold."

In contrast his father's intimates during the years 1848-

1854 to whose talk young Henry listened constantly, John G. Palfrey, Richard H. Dana and Charles Sumner, seem warm and human. All of them together, however, provided no more education "fitting him for his own time" than anything else because they "were all types of the past" convinced that their sort of world that "had always existed in Boston and Massachusetts Bay, was the world which he was to fit." They were part of the "same upper-class *bourgeoisie*" that comfortably felt the same way in France and in England and wanted to in Italy and Germany. In Boston it meant that "nothing exacted solution" because—the most succinct summation Adams provided in the chapter—"Boston had solved the universe."

The education of Henry Adams in these years from all sources came to this:

> All experience since the creation of man, all divine revelation or human science, conspired to deceive and betray a twelve-year-old boy who took for granted that his ideas, which were alone respectable, would be alone respected.

The list of specific items that began to make up his education is considerable, and all added up to nothing. His father belonged to the past. The church represented only the disappearance of religion. Emerson, who did protest in part, was *naïf* if we consider him an element in education needed for the period 1870-1900. The reading he began caused him "In the want of positive instincts" to drift into "the mental indolence of history." The family "was rather an atmosphere than an influence." Outside influences were negative. "He always reckoned his school days, from ten to sixteen years old, as time thrown away," because they failed to provide him with the four necessary tools he later needed—mathematics, French, German and Spanish. The amusements about him—skating, sleighing, billiards—taught him nothing "likely to be of use to him in the world." He was, all told, educated as a standardized Boston type, and no one knew whether such a type was fitted to deal with life in the late nineteenth century. As it turned out it was not.

Amid this list of educational failures in his youth, one thing of value he did learn: "Only in one way his father rendered him a great service by trying to teach him French and giving him some idea of a French accent." Everything else of value is described grudgingly. "His father made no effort to force his mind, but left him free play, and this was perhaps best." He had learned to read, and books remained the source of life, but "as in the eighteenth century," in the sense of the past. His happiest hours were devoted to Sir Walter Scott and raiding the garden for peaches and pears, he says finally. "On the whole he learned most then." What *Ivanhoe* and peaches taught he does not say. Nor does he say they contributed to weaving any garment of education. At the age of sixteen Adams appeared to lack all but a thread of any patchwork of education and was about as naked of it as the day he was born. He had acquired only the stamp of education sealed in 1848 on the older Puritan generation, an inheritance he and other men whose lives were to "fall" in the generation between 1865 and 1900 had to get rid of if they were to "take the stamp that belonged to their time. This was their education."

Despite the roughly chronological order of the material, then, the special selection and treatment of details all deal with education alone. This shows how far removed from usual autobiography the book is. Each chapter builds on the preceding one in a steady progression in simple narrative time but, more important, they all build into complexity. Adams never left his single, central subject, education, the clear, unifying element of the whole. He wrote of his friend Henry James that he "taught the world to read a volume for the pleasure of seeing the lights of his burning-glass turned on alternate sides of the same figure." Adams did the same thing in reverse: He turned lights on the educative sides of various figures as they affected the same object, the garment of education.

In structure one sees the book in two parts. The first, Chapters I-XX, describes the material of a mid-nineteenth-century education (to 1870) to be used by the later nineteenth-century active man of the world. Passing by the twenty years of active life when Adams applied his first education, because that matter was personal as I have noted, the final half of the book rises above the specific details so fully mentioned in the first to a lofty plateau of observation and speculation. In it Adams largely disengaged himself from daily facts to deal with great ideas, using his chronology as a bare frame on which to build his thinking, a frame that gives movement to the whole. The chapter titles themselves show how he advanced in the treatment of his material. The first six chapters have simple place names. As the book progresses the chapter titles become increasingly more abstract until at the last (especially the very last one) they become obscure in meaning.

The simple chronology Adams employs disguises another arrangement of the material: The chapters fall into groups, and each revolves about a single object. There are six of these sections in all, each a fairly complete essay. The divisions are not notable as one reads the book since the author did not mark them off. But marked breaks occur in the subject matter. As I count the sections, they are as follows:

Section I	—I-VI	: Education in Childhood and Youth
" II	—VII-XV	: Education by Englishmen
" III	—XVI-XX	: Education to Failure
" IV	—XXI-XXIV	: Education in Indian Summer
" V	—XXV—XXXII	: Education in Force
" VI	—XXXIII-XXXV	: Education as Inconclusion

A remarkable stylistic device Adams employed has to do with his paragraph structure. A glance shows the paragraphs run to a surprisingly uniform length, usually two to a page with few exceptions either very long or very short. And the chapters are uniform also in that they are roughly equal in the number of pages they contain, but more surprisingly in the number of paragraphs. One has forty-four, one but twelve, and the rest range from eighteen to thirty-three, the most common number being twenty-eight. Six chapters have that many. Only two contain more than thirty paragraphs, and five less than twenty. In blueprint form the book is steady and even, progressing, outwardly at least, step by even step, matching the steady progression of the chronology. Yet this even flow

of paragraphs and years is not monotonous for it serves to create a counterpoise, counteracting the extravagant content *of* the paragraphs.

As I examined the paragraphs themselves one at a time I noted a general pattern of structure that has, again, a remarkable and almost monotonous consistency. Adams seldom varied the pattern. For the most part they are formal, textbook paragraphs similar to those of the *History,* each one a "free unit." More often than not the first sentence is the topic sentence, a declaration clamped by the final one that is a restatement of it and a half step beyond it, usually a step into generalization. In addition, a great many of the paragraphs are so constructed that the first sentence can be read with the last to make considerable sense. One gets the firm impression that Adams set up his paragraphs with his final sentence well in mind as he proceeded to develop his initial topic sentence. A few paragraphs chosen at random will demonstrate this framework:

> 1. Pp. 44-45: (First sentence:) "The boy could not have told her [his aunt]; he was nowhere near an understanding of himself." (Last sentence:) "Even at twelve years old he could see his own nature no more clearly than he would at twelve hundred, if by accident he should happen to live so long." Paragraph content: The confused impression of Washington on the Boston boy of twelve, who had a taint of Maryland blood.

> 2. P. 201: (First sentence:) "Least of all did Motley mean that the taste or the manners were perfect." (Last sentence:) "He meant something scholarly, worldly, and modern; he was thinking of his own tastes." Paragraph content: The extreme contrast between the badness and the best qualities of English society.

> 3. Pp. 264-265: (First sentence:) "Badeau took Adams to the White House one evening and introduced him to the President and Mrs. Grant." (Last sentence:) "Adam, according to legend, was such a man." Paragraph content: To compare Grant to Garibaldi to show that each was archaic.

> 4. P. 429: (First sentence:) "Rid of man and his mind, the universe of Thomas Aquinas seemed rather more scientific than that of Haeckel or Ernst Mach." (Last sentence:) "Mind and Unity flourished or perished together." Paragraph content: The ironic fact that Aquinas really demonstrated more unity by far than modern science, though unscientific.

But what lies between these sturdy first and last sentences of such conventional paragraphs is an elaboration of details and arguments into sentences that particularly distinguish Adams' style. In a sense he drove these two sentences apart with those that lay between, those remarkable, rich sentences so very full of lively thought, so involved and so various. These sentences forming the contents of the paragraphs are, in fact, so convoluted, containing so rich a vocabulary and wealth of allusions, the underlying structure is hardly evident at all since the sentences within them compel such attention from the reader the signs of their framework are almost entirely obscured. Furthermore, the paragraphs are not free units at all in the sense that they can usually be extracted from the larger whole for their fullest meaning. Time and again the reader cannot discover this until well into a following paragraph, sometimes well beyond the next two or three. So, stylistically, Adams created a paradox. The ordered unity of the paragraphs is countered by the gnarly content within them to result in a series of struggling sentences that dispel the very artistic order the paragraph form appears to give them.

One other fact is evident as one studies the structure of the book. It clearly shows Adams' conscious artistry. Key words such as chaos, multiplicity, failure and force are all used sparingly at first. Their use gradually and unobtrusively picks up until the frequency of their appearance is, though not overbearing, particularly heavy and noticeable. So, for example, the word "force" appears in Chapter I nine times. But in Chapter XXV it occurs forty-two times. And in Chapter XXXIII, seventy-four times, nine times in the first two paragraphs alone. (pp. 85-101)

> *Vern Wagner, in his* The Suspension of Henry Adams: A Study of Manner and Matter, *Wayne State University Press, 1969, 268 p.*

Henry B. Rule   (essay date 1971)

[*In the following essay, Rule argues that Adams creates two oppositional fictional characters in* The Education—*the Private Secretary and the Blighted Bostonian—in order to satirize his own historical experience in the wake of disruptive social and scientific changes.*]

In *The Education of Henry Adams,* Adams satirized himself for very much the same reason that he had taunted Thomas Jefferson in his nine-volume *History of the United States.* Both men became figures of irony because they failed to adapt themselves to the conditions of their times. Just as Jefferson attempted to legislate in a war-torn world as though eternal peace were at hand, so Adams preached the efficacy of Divine Education and the Moral Law in the age of Grant as though the millennium were about to dawn.

The *History* and the *Education,* however, express large philosophical differences concerning man's relation to the cosmos. The lesson of the *History* is that man must understand the facts of his environment if he is to be effective as a moral agent. But the *Education* emphasizes the almost insurmountable difficulties that confront man in his effort to understand his surroundings. The shock of tragedy and the sense of being left behind by a runaway world forced Adams to re-examine the rather simple moral formulas of the *History.* The more Adams studied his world, the more bewildering became the problem of epistemology. Religion offered no help. The gentle rationalism of the Unitarian Church had destroyed the religious sense early in Adams' boyhood. Besides, what place had the childlike mysteries of Jesus Christ and the Virgin Mary in the world of railroads, Grant politics, dynamos, and x-rays? Nor could he any longer rely on history as a means of understanding his milieu. He had written a dozen volumes of American History in an effort to establish "a necessary sequence of human movement," but he could no longer be satisfied with the results, for there was no common agreement among men as to what the facts of history were, nor could he find an exact method of measuring them. So Adams turned to science, the modern religion, in his efforts to find meaning in the universe. After years of scientific study, he found himself more confused than ever concerning the nature of the forces around him:

> He knew no more than a firefly about rays—or about race—or sex—or ennui—or a bar of music—or a pang of love—or a grain of musk—or of phosphorus—or conscience—or duty—or the force of Euclidian geometry—or non-Euclidian—or heat—or light—or osmosis—or electrolysis—or the magnet—or ether—or *vis inertiae*—or gravitation—or cohesion—or elasticity—or surface tension—or capillary attraction—or Brownian motion—or some scores, or thousands, or millions of chemical attractions, repulsions or indifferences which were busy within and without him. . . .

Out of Adams' lifelong frustrated effort to gain knowledge stems the theme and satiric tone of the *Education.* The theme of the *Education* is the feebleness of the human intellect—man's blind devotion to *a priori* ideas which have no relation to the chaos outside of him, his inability to achieve his goals in an uncaring universe, his futile attempts to understand the complexities around him. As Adams himself said, the *Education* is an illustration of his aphorism "that it is impossible to underrate human intelligence—beginning with one's own."

The satiric tone of the *Education* links it to such masterpieces of irony and satire as *Don Quixote, Candide,* and *Gulliver's Travels.* Don Quixote, Candide, Lemuel Gulliver, and Henry Adams are literary brothers: each stands for the little idealist who is pushed, smashed, and *educated* by the world. Each in his suffering and isolation serves as a "center of indifference"; through the eyes of each the reader can appraise the comic and tragic ironies of the human situation. The *Education,* then, contrary to common critical opinion, is primarily neither biography nor history nor philosophy, but it is one of the nineteenth century's greatest works of satire and irony.

The process by which Adams achieved this tone is closely related to the Double Technique long familiar to the audiences of comedies from the *Amphitryon* of Plautus to the *Comedy of Errors* of Shakespeare. By using the third person point of view, rather than the traditional first person of autobiographies, Adams was able to project dramatically certain facets or "doubles" of his personality so that he could smile satirically at them as if they were comic characters in a play or novel who resembled Henry Adams superficially but were far different from the complex real man. The Double Technique was the means by which Adams simplified and isolated the issues that he wished to attack. By turning aspects of his life and personality into "characters," he was able to gain the objectivity, the aesthetic distance, that satire and irony require. The sense of containing within themselves a number of personalities is not unusual among extremely sensitive and complex men. Adams might have been thinking of himself when he remarked of William Gladstone: "Of course in him, as in most people, there were two or three or a dozen men; in these emotional, abnormal natures, there are never less than three."

Adams' own highly self-conscious feelings of schizophrenia can be traced in some degree in the collections of his letters. The sense of doubleness that one has in periods of disappointment and frustration, the sense that one is two persons—the person who fails and the person who ironically analyzes his own failure—was expressed by Adams in a letter as early as 1862:

> You find fault with my desponding tone of mind. So do I. But the evil is one that probably lies where I can't get at it. I've disappointed myself, and experience the curious sensation of discovering myself to be a humbug. How is this possible? Do you understand how, without a double personality, *I* can feel that *I* am a failure? One would think that the *I* which could feel that, must be a different *ego* from the *I* of which it is felt.

In 1882, Adams' troubled conscience produced a passage which augured with remarkable accuracy the Double Technique in the *Education:* "My ideal of authorship," Adams wrote, "would be to have a famous *double* with another name, to wear what honors I could win. How I should enjoy upsetting him at last by publishing a low and shameless essay with woodcuts in his name!"

After the suicide of his wife, Adams' sense of possessing a double consciousness increased. The violence of the emotional explosion that occurred in 1885 produced in Adams the feeling that he had lived two separate lives—one before his personal tragedy and one after: ". . . I feel that the history is not what I care now to write, or want to say, if I say anything," he wrote in 1891. "It belongs to the *me* of 1870; a strangely different being from the *me* of 1890." Not only did he feel that the Adams of the past was a stranger to the Adams of the present, but he also felt that there were mutually exclusive Adamses of the present: "I have gone on talking, all that time," he once declared, "but it has been to myself—and to her. The world has no part in it. One learns to lead two lives, without education." These multiple personalities—before and after tragedy, public and private—produced the tensions that resulted in the self-irony of the *Education:* "If anyone in particular exists whom I long to contradict before he opens his mouth, it is I," Adams once said.

Adams' habit of viewing consciousness as multiple became so confirmed that he began to make jokes on the subject: "I am in Florida until further notice," he wrote in 1896. "Only my Mahatma, or *double,* remains in Washington, and Mahatmas don't count." But more important, he began to think of his doubles as works of art, his own creations with which he could do as he pleased. For instance, the origin of the satirical tone of the *Education* is described in a letter written in 1903.

> Remember that, after all, I am, or have been, human, and that nothing human has any longer the slightest interest to me, if it resembles my-

self. That particular form of boredom, in all of its varieties, can only be saved by putting into it what never was there—a sense of the ridiculous.

The later correspondence is filled with delightful passages in which Adams described his antics as if he were a playwright creating comic character parts. To take one example:

> I run about among my friends holding everybody's hand with unctuosity, calling everybody by the wrong names, and asking about all the children who never existed. Then I go into fits of laughter at their meek embarrassment, and ask what their names are, anyway, and how the devil they come to know mine. There is really something very droll about one's dotage. The role is so confoundedly familiar, as played by the past actors, that one feels horribly tempted to make fun of young Hamlet and Laertes and Ophelia, and ask straight out before the audience what sort of idiots they take themselves to be, that they should think they could teach something to Uncle Polonius.

In the *Education,* Adams created two major roles for his doubles to play. The role of the Private Secretary satirizes directly Adams' own impotence and ignorance, while at the same time it uncovers the futility and failure of the world's greatest leaders. The second role—that of the Blighted Bostonian—satirizes the failure of an eighteenth century mind to adapt itself to the conditions of the nineteenth century. The failure of mind that both roles illustrate is designed to dramatize the major moral of the book—the urgent need for greater mind power to understand and control the technical, political and economic forms of power that dominate the modern world.

Adams created the role of the Private Secretary, who is the main actor in about a fourth of the *Education,* in order to make some of his most acid attacks on the foibles of the human intellect. His method of attack was Socratic. By emphasizing the ignorance and insignificance of the Private Secretary, Adams made the ironic revelation that this servant of "a rather low order" was no less blind and impotent than those whom the world regarded as wise and powerful. Unflaggingly, he attached the lowliest epithets to the Private Secretary. He was a "herring-fry in a shoal of moving fish," a "young mosquito" buzzing admiration into the ears of his friends, unaware that sooner or later he would be slapped; he wandered around in society "like a maggot in cheese," and he followed his betters about with the unthinking obedience of "a little dog." At times, Adams dramatized the triviality of the Private Secretary in little comic scenes:

> . . . he gave his name as usual at the foot of the staircase, and was rather disturbed to hear it shouted up as "Mr. Handrew Hadams!" He tried to correct it, and the footman shouted more loudly: "Mr. Hanthony Hadams!" With some temper, he repeated the correction, and was finally announced as "Mr. Halexander Hadams," and under this name made his bow for the last time to Lord Palmerston, who certainly knew no better.

These epithets and scenes, however, are merely a part of Adams' satiric scheme for attacking the ignorance and helplessness of the great men of the world. When the incomprehension and impotence of the lowly Private Secretary are used as water marks for measuring the level of knowledge and strength in others, the reader learns that the great and wise of the earth were as ignorant and helpless as the "infantile" Private Secretary. Adams described the Private Secretary in Washington in 1860 as "surely among the most ignorant and helpless" of all the crowd that swarmed about him. But the reader soon learns that the nation's greatest statesmen could no more understand and control the forces around them than could the Private Secretary. The Southern politician, held up by all the world as the standard of statesmanship, was mad, the victim of hallucinations. Even the new President, Abraham Lincoln, seemed to have the same painful need for education "that tormented a private secretary." Observing at close range the greatest American statesmen of the day—Lincoln, Seward, Sumner—the Private Secretary could only learn that "they knew less than he."

The same pattern of irony emerges from the Private Secretary's London adventures. Once again Adams compared the knowledge of his double to that of the world's greatest statesmen and arrived at the conclusion that the lowly Private Secretary was "as ignorant as the best informed statesman." In the London of 1861, he had "the most costly tutors in the world." Among them were Prime Minister Lord Palmerston, Foreign Secretary Lord Russell, and Chancellor of the Exchequer Mr. Gladstone. Yet the only profit that he gained from this "immense staff of teachers" was that their most confidential associates understood them no better than he. Indeed, "all the world had been at cross-purposes, had misunderstood themselves and the situation, had followed wrong paths, drawn wrong conclusions, had known none of the paths." In a magnificent understatement, Adams concluded that "ignorance was not confined to the young and insignificant, nor were they the only victims of blindness." This rule, moreover, did not apply to statesmen alone. In the chapters entitled "Dilettantism" and "Darwinism," the innocent Private Secretary uncovered in the same Socratic manner intellectual confusions among leaders in art and science. Thus the role of the Private Secretary was designed to reveal failure of intellect, whether American or British, among statesmen, art experts, or scientists—each, learned and simple, like the Private Secretary, was "lost in the darkness of his own gropings." Unlike the Private Secretary, however, the mass of men who crushed about him seemed "ignorant that there is a thing called ignorance."

The chief cause of this mental bankruptcy was what Adams called "*vis inertiae*"—the continuation of the mind along lines of force that may have been useful once, but which now are at variance with a dynamic world. Lord Palmerstone's laugh was a sardonic reminder to the Private Secretary of a mind burdened by concepts of the past inapplicable to present reality, yet so protected by a thick crust of egotism that it was unable to recognize its own failure:

> The laugh was singular, mechanical, wooden, and did not seem to disturb his features.

"Ha! . . . Ha! . . . Ha!" Each was a slow, deliberate ejaculation, and all were in the same tone, as though he meant to say: "Yes! . . . Yes! . . . Yes!" by way of assurance. It was a laugh of 1810 and the Congress of Vienna.

Except for men like Grant, who have no mind at all, each of the main characters in the *Education,* from Senator Sumner to Lord Palmerston, fail because of the anachronistic qualities of their thought. But the most vivid example of *vis inertiae,* illustrative of all the others, is Adams' second double, whom for descriptive purposes I have labeled the Blighted Bostonian.

The Blighted Bostonian was a close cousin to Don Quixote, a character who was never far from Adams' mind. Both Don Quixote and the Blighted Bostonian were types; that is, they had exaggerated and sharply defined qualities representative of their environments. According to Henri Bergson, one of Adams' favorite philosophers, a type is always comic:

> Every comic character is a *type.* Inversely, every resemblance to a type has something comic in it. . . . It is comic to fall into a ready-made category oneself into which others will fall, as into a ready-made frame; it is to crystallize into a stock character.

In the first several chapters of the *Education,* Adams described the stock of ideas that made the Blighted Bostonian a strongly delineated type of New England idealism, "*type* bourgeois-bostonian," as Adams once put it. The New Englander, according to Adams, viewed the world with "the instinct of resistance," as a thing of evil to be reformed; it was the duty of the New Englander not only to reform the evil of the world, but also to hate it. He could fight evil forces without doubts or hesitations, for right and wrong were clearly recognizable, dogmatic, a priori. His program for solving the problem of evil in human affairs was simple and certain:

> Politics offered no difficulties, for there the moral law was a sure guide. Social perfection was also sure, because human nature worked for Good, and three instruments were all she asked—Suffrage, Common Schools, and the Press. On these points doubt was forbidden. Education was divine, and man needed only a correct knowledge of facts to reach perfection.

As a member of the Adams clan, the high priests of New England politics, the Blighted Bostonian was inspired by these components of New England idealism with irresistible force and solemnity. He was never allowed to forget the ponderous significance of being an Adams. Every Sunday during his childhood he sat in the country church of Quincy behind the bald head of his president grandfather, John Quincy Adams, and below a memorial tablet dedicated to the honor of his president great-grandfather, John Adams. The impressive pomp of the funeral service for John Quincy Adams in 1848, with its expressions of "national respect and family pride," followed by a eulogy delivered in Faneuil Hall by the boy's uncle, Edward Everett, the foremost orator of his day, could not but impress on the boy the grandeur of the Adams tradition. But

Adams the observer could foresee the ironic incongruity between his double's illusions and the facts of the future:

> All experience since the creation of man, all divine revelation or human science, conspired to deceive and betray a twelve-year-old boy who took for granted that his ideas, which were alone respectable, would be alone respected.

"Inertia is the law of mind as well as of matter," wrote Adams as he observed the constant impact of reality on the illusions of the Blighted Bostonian. When the inertia of mind is strong enough—that is, when fixed ideas are sufficiently cemented within the mind—the collision of ideas and reality is likely to be completely shattering. Then a kind of mental paralysis results, when relatively simple problems seem enormously complex and action seems hopeless.

One of his first collisions with reality occurred at the age of twelve while he was on the road from Washington to Mount Vernon:

> Bad roads meant bad morals. The moral of this Virginia road was clear, and the boy fully learned it. Slavery was wicked, and slavery was the cause of this road's badness which amounted to social crime—and yet, at the end of the road and product of the crime stood Mount Vernon and George Washington.

This paradox apparently puzzled the Blighted Bostonian all the rest of his life. How could one deal with a moral problem that deduced George Washington "from the sum of all wickedness?" Adams the scientific historian could have easily resolved this paradox, for it is obvious that many forces other than slavery produced George Washington. But Adams, the Blighted Bostonian, once his ideals were confounded by reality, could think only in irreconcilable opposites, paradoxes without solutions. The categories of good and bad, George Washington and slavery, were so firmly fixed in his mind that once he saw that they did not conform to reality, he was overwhelmed by the complexities of the world. The resulting mental paralysis, at once comic and tragic, made him a creature of irony.

The Blighted Bostonian's visit to Rome in 1860 produced a similar state of mental paralysis. In his youth he had had firmly implanted in his mind the faith that man was eternally evolving toward perfection. But "Rome could not be fitted into an orderly, middle class, Bostonian systematic scheme of evolution." All that he could learn from Rome was chaos, catastrophe, "the just judgments of an outraged God against all the doings of man." The shock of this violent contradiction to his ideals was even greater than when he had tried to deduce George Washington "from the sum of all wickedness." In his stunned bewilderment, he could only repeat to himself, "Why! Why!! Why!!!"

Thus the Blighted Bostonian, setting forth like Don Quixote to bring about a Golden Age, was constantly shattered by the impact of realities on his illusions. Always the reaction was in some form of paralysis. Sometimes the response was one of shocking disillusionment, fixed in the mind forever, as when Charles Sumner, who in the boy's hero-worshipping eyes represented the quintessence of New England idealism and greatness, suddenly broke relations with the Adams family in the winter of 1860-1861. Sometimes it was one of intense self-abasement, as when he met Algernon Swinburne in 1862, whose wild genius was everything Boston conservatism was not. The reaction was one of helpless defeat when the announcement of Grant's cabinet in 1869 proved to the young man that party politics were to rule the nation. When he learned from his experience as a Harvard professor that even "divine" education was a fraud and failure, the disillusionment of Adams' idealistic double was so great that quietism and retreat from the world were his only resource.

One of the ironies that resulted from this constant state of mental shock was the Blighted Bostonian's steady drift toward destinations he did not seek. This dreamlike passivity to the forces around him was foreshadowed in one of the earliest episodes of his life. One day, when a child, he passionately rebelled against going to school. He was about to win his battle when the door to his president grandfather's library opened, and the old man came slowly down the stairs like the embodiment of Fate. Putting his hat on his head, he "took the boy's hand without a word, and walked with him, filled with awe, up the road to the town." The old man was close to eighty; surely, the boy thought, he would not walk nearly a mile "on a hot summer morning over a shadeless road to take a boy to school." The boy could have easily broken away, but he "saw all of his strategic points turned, one after another, until he found himself seated inside the school, and obviously the centre of curious if not malevolent criticism." Then the grandfather released his hand and departed. This episode may be viewed as an allegory of the Blighted Bostonian's life. He hated the tendencies of his age, and yet Fate led him by the hand to the schoolhouse of experience despite his hatred. He watched all of his strategic points of escape from failure pass by—politics, diplomacy, science—but he was paralyzed to act.

Adams' metaphorical language emphasized the ironic contrast between the Blighted Bostonian's feeble will and the forces that dominated him. From the beginning, he had been "dragged hither and thither, like a French poodle on a string, following always the strongest pull, between one form of unity or centralization and another." After returning from his abortive attempt to find an education in Germany, he "dropped back on Quincy like a lump of lead; he rebounded like a football, tossed into space by an unknown energy." In English society, he found himself in "dead-water, and the parti-colored, fantastic cranks swam about his boat, as though he were the ancient mariner, and they the saurians of the prime." The wake of the Civil War left him "a flotsam or jetsam of wreckage." And in his old age, he passively watched "the apparent movement of the stars in order to guess [his] declination."

Thus through drama and metaphor, Adams presented the story of the Blighted Bostonian, the tragicomic history of a man born between two worlds—the eighteenth century world of Ciceronian politics and simple handicraft and the nineteenth century world of Grantism and the technical knowledge that revolutionized the political and social habits of the nation. Because of the *vis inertiae* of mind, he was no more able to understand or control this environment than the Indian or the buffalo.

The value and significance of Adams' satire on mind in the *Education* have been frequently misunderstood by its critics. One mistake that critics have made is to confound the Henry Adams in the *Education* with Henry Adams the man—a confusion which should be erased by an understanding of the Double Technique that this study has attempted to explain. The naive, infantile Private Secretary was not the vigorous and ambitious young man who supported his father's diplomacy by writing sophisticated propaganda in American newspapers or the energetic young scholar who made his literary debut in the *North American Review* with a series of brilliant articles on historical, economic, and scientific subjects. Nor was the tired, defeated Blighted Bostonian, whom I have described above, the Henry Adams who was one of Harvard's greatest teachers and who wrote a dozen volumes of historical masterpieces. The Henry Adams in the *Education* was a literary creation, made up of certain elements of the personality and experience of Henry Adams the man, but transformed and shaped by the artistic imagination so as to produce a moral.

A strange failure to recognize this moral is the second mistake of those critics who describe the satire and irony in the *Education* as perverse, without intellectual content. A passage in one of Adams' letters states simply and clearly the moral problem that the *Education* poses:

> What is the end of doubling up our steam and electric power every five years to infinity if we don't increase thought power? As I see it, the society of today shows no more thought power than in our youth, though it showed precious little then. To me, the whole lesson lies in this experiment. Can our society double up its mind-capacity? It must do it or die; and I can see no reason why it may not widen its consciousness of complex conditions far enough to escape wreck; but it must hurry.

The need for new and increased mental energies to control the explosive new forces released by science is exactly the moral point dramatized by the roles of the Private Secretary and the Blighted Bostonian. It is the lesson emphasized by all of the various forms of intellectual blindness, vapidity, and inertia illustrated throughout the *Education.* It is also the point stressed in the series of chapters in the last third of the book expounding the "Dynamic Theory of History." It is the lesson that unifies both the dramatic and expository sections of the *Education.*

Adams was not a cynical nihilist as some critics have described him. His concern for civilization was deeply felt. Almost alone in a world that had become drunk with scientific power he saw that the scientific attitudes that he had once served faithfully had banished Divinity from the universe and were poised to destroy civilization on earth. His "Preface" to the *Education* and a number of his letters show that while writing the book he thought of himself as

a modern St. Augustine. The City of Rome, its wickedness and its probable doom, was a subject of both Henry Adams and St. Augustine. Both prophets saw man's predicament in a quite similar light, although their solutions to that predicament differed. St. Augustine's "God's commands" and Adams' naturalistic forces both result in man's becoming dependent on powers greater than his own. For St. Augustine, man's salvation lay in fleeing from the City of Rome and finding sanctuary in the City of God. For Adams, there was no City of God; man's only hope is to develop his mind to the extent that he can govern the City of Rome and guide it from catastrophe. To dramatize the mental infirmities that prevent the consummation of that hope is the whole purpose of that form of self-satire which I have called the Double Technique. (pp. 430-44)

> *Henry B. Rule, "Henry Adams' Satire on Human Intelligence: Its Method and Purpose," in* The Centennial Review, *Vol. XV, No. 4, Fall, 1971, pp. 430-44.*

Earl N. Harbert   (essay date 1977)

[*An American writer and educator, Harbert is the author of* The Force So Much Closer Home: Henry Adams and the Adams Family *(1977),* Henry Adams: A Reference Guide *(1977), and* Critical Essays on Henry Adams *(1981). In the following essay he discusses the relation of* The Education of Henry Adams *to the tradition of autobiography exemplified by the* Confessions *of Jean-Jacques Rousseau and the Roman philosopher Augustine.*]

For readers who have been fascinated by *The Education of Henry Adams,* the most significant event of recent years was the appearance in 1973 of a carefully revised edition, corrected according to the author's final intentions and edited by Adams's chief biographer, Ernest Samuels. At long last, and for the first time since the book was put on sale in 1918, the title page of the *Education* appears without the infamous and misleading subtitle, "An Autobiography." Those two words, added to the 1918 version without authorization from Adams himself, who died before that printing appeared, have been largely responsible for a general confusion about the author's intentions, and, in turn, for a profusion of conflicting opinions, comments, and judgments concerning the final success or failure of Adams's achievement. Yet, all together this almost uncollectable critical response to the book forms at best a partial truth; for by any conventional definition, at least, the *Education* must be seen to offer us something much larger than the usual understanding of "autobiography" allows. How the shade of Henry Adams, at his sardonic best, must relish the last of his many jokes—this one played unintentionally on the three generations of readers who have helped to keep the *Education* alive.

All this is not to say that the book is free of autobiographical influences. Quite the contrary: many scholars have noted the author's debts to Rousseau and Augustine, to the private literature of the Adams family, especially the diaries of John and John Quincy Adams; and to that peculiarly American strain of personal narrative which can be traced, with some variations, from the Puritans, through Jonathan Edwards and Benjamin Franklin, to Henry James and Henry Adams. And convincing evidence of indebtedness to an autobiographical tradition is provided by Adams himself in his "Preface" to the *Education,* where he acknowledges a familiarity with a variety of personal narratives in the various forms of confessions, autobiographies, and memoirs, mentioning their authors by name. From the perspective of our usual interest in admitted and implied influences, then, Adams's reliance on a great autobiographical tradition is well established. So a sound case can be made—for treating his book as an impressive extension of that older tradition into the twentieth century. But, in fact, the *Education* should also be thought of, at least in part, as the first modern American autobiography, a seminal volume, as important in its way as was T. S. Eliot's announcements of modernity in his best poetry of the same period. To realize just how modern the *Education* really is, a reader need only compare it with the *Autobiography* of Henry's older brother, Charles Francis Adams II, published in 1916. Charles's book shows what the mere conjunction of the well-established family writing habit, with a prosaic tradition of memoir-writing, and a pedestrian historical outlook could be expected to produce in the work of an almost exact contemporary. Nowhere in Charles's *Autobiography* does one find the play of artistic imagination that stamps Henry's *Education* as a unique work of genius, an account that is at once both traditional and highly experimental. For the *Education* is an American classic, and readers must take it on its own terms or fail to comprehend its full meaning.

Nor was this uniqueness lost to T. S. Eliot himself. In one of the earliest reviews of Adams's book, titled "A Sceptical Patrician" and printed in the *Athenaeum* in 1919, the poet warned: "It is doubtful whether the book ought to be called an autobiography, for there is too little of the author in it." Unfortunately, while most readers of the very popular *Education* have recognized its autobiographical possibilities, few have taken Eliot's warning seriously enough.

Aside from Eliot's cautionary advice, which Adams had no opportunity to read, any more than he had a chance to strike the misleading subtitle from later reprintings, there is abundant external evidence that the author did not plan his work as simply yet another contribution to the tradition of American autobiography. Here, Adams's personal correspondence is extremely useful in putting us on the track of his thoughts concerning the autobiographical form in literature, even before he began the *Education.* Writing to Henry James in 1903 about the latter's biography of William Wetmore Story, Adams said:

> The painful truth is that all of my New England generation, counting the half-century, 1820–1879, were in actual fact only one mind and nature; the individual was a facet of Boston . . . Type Bourgeois bostonian [sic]! A type quite as good as another but more uniform. . . . God knows that we knew our want of knowledge! the [sic] self-distrust became introspection—nervous self-consciousness—irritable dislike of America, and antipathy to Boston.

> So you have written not Story's life, but your own and mine—pure autobiography. . . .

Later, after he had completed the *Education,* Adams sent a copy of the private printing to James in 1908, together with a letter that explained: "The volume is a mere shield of protection in the grave. I advise you to take your own life in the same way, in order to prevent biographers from taking it in theirs." The truth found by biographers and autobiographers could prove to be "painful truth" indeed. As a biographer himself, Henry Adams knew this firsthand, having written the lives of Albert Gallatin, John Randolph, and Aaron Burr before he began the *Education.* Certainly the possibilities for using some version of autobiography as a "shield of protection" had occurred to Adams as early as 1891, when he wrote to his English friend, Charles Milnes Gaskell: "The moral seems to be that every man should write his life, to prevent some other fellow from taking it." So Adams determined to take his own life in literature but in a unique way, as he turned a chronological narrative of personal experience into an autobiographical literary experiment.

In the *Education* itself, perhaps the most obvious signal of the author's extraordinary intentions may be found on the "Contents" page. Surely a superb historian like Adams could do better than to leave such a hiatus as that between Chapter XX, entitled "Failure (1871)" and Chapter XXI, entitled "Twenty Years After (1892)." For "protection," of course, he had seen fit to leave this period in his life blank—a gap that excluded every detail of his relationship with Marion Hooper Adams, the wife who is never mentioned in the *Education.* Gone too, along with the personal version of his marriage, is all pretense to confessional sincerity or historical accuracy and completeness. Instead, as Adams makes clear, the reading game must be played by the author's own rules.

Nowhere is this made so clear as in the "Preface" to the *Education.* From that point onward in the book, the introduction of a "manikin" figure called "Henry Adams" serves to protect the real author from excessive self-revelation, by offering the disguise of personal experience as a covering for didactic art. From almost the first word, the reader is warned that he should not expect another confessional in the tradition of Rousseau or of the American Puritans. For Adams, the *Confessions,* although written like the *Education* "in the manner of the eighteenth century," can be instructive in the twentieth century only when correctly viewed or read. Timely interpretation emphasizes personal limitations rather than accomplishments, and makes the *Confessions* useful as a warning and not as a model.

> As educator, Jean Jacques was in one respect, easily first; he erected a monument of warning against the Ego. Since his time, and largely thanks to him, the Ego has steadily tended to efface itself, and, for purposes of model, to become a manikin on which the toilet of education is to be draped in order to show the fit or misfit of the clothes. The object of study is the garment, not the figure. The tailor adapts the manikin as well as the clothes to his patron's wants. The tailor's object, in this volume, is to fit young men, in uni-

versities or elsewhere, to be men of the world, equipped for any emergency; and the garment offered to them is meant to show the faults of the patchwork fitted on their fathers. . . .

The manikin, therefore, has the same value as any other geometrical figure of three or more dimensions, which is used for the study of relation. For that purpose it cannot be spared; it is the only measure of motion, of proportion, of human condition; it must have the air of reality; must be taken for real; must be treated as though it had life. Who knows? Possibly it had!

Enter the manikin "Henry Adams" and exit all pretense of conscious self-revelation. As the author tells us 432 pages later,

Of all studies, the one he would rather have avoided was that of his own mind. He knew no tragedy so heart-rending as introspection, and the more, because—as Mephistopheles said of Marguerite—he was not the first. Nearly all the highest intelligence known to history had drowned itself in the reflection of its own thought, and the bovine survivors had rudely told the truth about it, without affecting the intelligent.

Here, the "painful truth" Adams first had described to James emerged more painful still. The source was not simply personal revelation of the usual kind—the embarrassing details of an outward life—but rather the traditional autobiographical practice of looking inward, and of telling truthfully what one has found. Far better to spare the pain and turn away from self, to teach, instead, in the words of the "Preface," ". . . young men, in universities or elsewhere, to be men of the world equipped for any emergency." And teach, Adams did in the pages of his book.

This is not the place to trace in detail the many lessons in politics, religion, philosophy, science, and art—which measure the author's didactic intention in the *Education.* These main lines of educative force also provide themes for the narrative; while the manikin's example demonstrates over and over the repeated "failure" of the subject ever to learn enough. Gradually, by accretion, this "failure" grows to seem conclusive—just as certain as the failure, in Adams's mind, of Rousseau in his *Confessions* to provide any effective guidance for modern man. Yet the larger, more general lesson here is one of change and not of failure alone; and to give it force, the author concentrates his attention on a central human figure, the persona Henry Adams, who grows from child to man as he tries out, for the reader's benefit, a variety of possibly educational experiences.

But finally the life of "Henry Adams" by itself does not teach enough to satisfy the author, who tells us why:

Truly the animal that is to be trained to unity must be caught young. Unity is vision; it must have been part of the process of learning to see. The older the mind, the older its complexities, and the further it looks, the more it sees, until even the stars resolve themselves into multiples; yet the child will always see but one.

Experience has led the manikin away from unity and instinct, and time has played him false, even while it pretended to educate.

In the face of such change, man must seek to recapture a sense of instinctive unity in art, as Adams hoped to do in his *Education.* For him, art was the only possible alternative to chaos, although for others who may be better educated than he, the author holds out another possibility of scientific unity, especially in the final chapters of his book and in his later essays. But the *Education* tells Henry Adams's story, beginning with his origins in "Quincy" (Chapter I) and "Boston" (Chapter II), and ending with the futuristic speculations that radiated from his mature mind. Put together in his way, the whole story is an experiment in didactic art—taking up in the twentieth century where Rousseau and Franklin left off. For, much as when he was a classroom instructor at Harvard College, the author of the *Education* still kept his faith in the timeless value of the teacher, who could shape human thought into worldly force, and effectively link the past and present with an uncertain future. As Adams wrote in the *Education,* "A teacher affects eternity; he can never tell where his influence stops." By reaching out to the "one [mind] in ten" that "sensibly reacts" to such teaching, the writer hoped to have his autobiographical lessons accepted by his readers in the same way that, in the "Preface," he claimed to use Rousseau's *Confessions,* as "a monument of warning against the Ego."

Finally, only the vigorously reacting mind, Adams believed, could benefit fully from lessons which otherwise became surface polish for the merely passive manikin:

The object of education for that mind should be the teaching itself how to react with vigor and economy. No doubt the world at large will always lag so far behind the active mind as to make a soft cushion of inertia to drop upon, as it did for Henry Adams; but education should try to lessen the obstacles, diminish the friction, invigorate the energy, and should train minds to react, not at haphazard, but by choice, on the lines of force that attract their world. What one knows is, in youth, of little moment; they know enough who know how to learn.

That rare tenth mind alone knows how to learn: it follows out Adams's lines of force and interest only to react against the egoistic example of the manikin. For that mind only, Adams holds out the hope of being prepared "by choice" to "jump" and stay ahead of the other expanding forces in the universe. Just such a mind might well succeed where the author knew himself to have failed; it might complete a patterning of life and experience with a mastery that would turn chaos into orderly design. Yet, so far as Adams could see in the *Education,* all education based on example—at least human example—was already obsolete. Traditional autobiography, like other forms of human experience, seemed to have reached the end of its usefulness, as education and as art.

What was left to Adams and to modern literature was experiment. So he attempted to turn his narrative of personal experience into something both artistic and useful. Alongside the warnings provided by the chronological gap in the narrative and by the manikin subject, the author developed a vocabulary of symbols, used to tie past experience to future possibility by drawing on instinct rather than reason. The most famous example, of course, is Chapter XXV, "The Dynamo and the Virgin," perhaps the best evidence that the *Education* can be read as modern art, as many anthologies testify.

I do not pretend in this brief survey to judge the *Education* either a failure or a success as art. Still it should be useful to point out that the overall effect of Adams's symbolic treatment—like the picture of the titular character in the book who is both manikin and tailor, and the impression created by the before-and-after organization—is once again to underscore division or contradiction in human experience, and to deny the possibility of unity in the "vision" of the aging author. Perhaps the "child will always see but one"; yet the reader of the *Education,* on the other hand, is left to yearn for such childish unity—in subject matter, organization, and conclusion. The book lacks even an imposed authorial unity, in the form of a single symbolic pattern; and the reader cannot order the various lines of force and thought by reference to some convenient symbol, like the pond in *Walden*.

For Adams, "Chaos was the law of nature; Order was the dream of man." By telling us only what he wanted to about his own life, Henry Adams played the part of a natural man who yet remained always something of a dreamer. While he was a teacher, he was also an artist, who sought to make his own story into didactic art of a high order, still leaving all judgments about his ultimate success to his readers. Meanwhile, the lessons of his life became theirs to use as they saw fit. Properly, the final words about the didactic value of an autobiography might be expected to belong to the author, who could best summarize the meaning of his own life. But in Adams's case, the authorial strategy was different. At the time that he was writing his life story, the author of the *Education* showed that he was too nimble or too evasive to be caught without "protection" and a "shield" for the future. In a letter to E. D. Shaw, the artist managed to shift the burden of interpretation from intention to response, as he showed how he had made the substance of his own experience into a heuristic experiment, designed to test his audience rather than to reveal himself:

> All considerable artists make a point of compelling the public to think for itself, and their rule is to require each observer to see what he can, and this will be what the artist meant. To the artist the meaning is indifferent. Every man is his own artist before a work of art.

Taken as autobiography, then, the *Education* is most of all "a work of art." The genius of Adams's experiment in modernity lies in his dramatic conversion of the narrative and didactic conventions he had inherited—the stuff of traditional autobiography—to his own unique purposes. For, while he kept the surface appearance of the narrative of personal experience, perhaps to convince the public that they knew exactly what he was doing, Adams also offered

his readers full artistic license to make every one of them his own autobiographer. (pp. 133-41)

Earl N. Harbert, "Henry Adams's 'Education' and Autobiographical Tradition," in Tulane Studies in English, *Vol. 22, 1977, pp. 133-41.*

B. L. Reid   (essay date 1980)

[*Reid was an American writer and educator whose works include* The Long Boy and Others: Eighteenth Century Studies *(1969) and* Necessary Lives: Biographical Reflections *(1990), from which the essay below is taken. Originally published in* The Sewanee Review *in 1980, the essay provides an overview of* The Education of Henry Adams.]

The Education of Henry Adams is a work of such subtlety and sophistication that it is hard to believe it was written by an American—written, at that, a good forty years before we all got so complicated and clever. For beauty of thought and style, for authentic difficulty, earned density of matter and manner, I can think of nothing to compare with it but the greatest novels of Henry James, and even they are finally less resistant and elusive. "Words are slippery and thought is viscous," Adams remarks on page 451, when we are long past the need to be told. It is important to remember that James and Adams were friends, that they were doing their finest and most complex work at exactly the same time, in the first years of the new century; and it is some comfort to see that William James, brother to one and friend to both, found reading them hard to the point of exasperation.

In talking of his book, as in talking of his life in his book, Adams adopted the pose of failure. When he completed his manuscript early in 1907 he had forty copies printed privately, then another sixty copies, to be sent about to friends for judgment and revision. He invited his friends, especially those mentioned in the book, to cut and slash and emend at will. He kept saying that the book had fallen so far short of his hopes that he was more than half inclined to suppress it altogether; and indeed he never brought it out himself, though he did authorize a posthumous edition in the copyright of the Massachusetts Historical Society, and that was published by Houghton Mifflin in 1918. In letters accompanying the privately circulated copies Adams applied a humorous rhetoric of hyperbolical deprecation. "The *Education* . . . is a picture of my aphorism that it is impossible to underrate human intelligence—beginning with one's own," he wrote to Margaret Chanler. "I am ashamed of it, and send it out into the world only to be whipped." To William James he described himself as "the champion failer of all" and lamented that he had been able to carry his design only far enough to "see the impossibility of success." Both Jameses were too intelligent not to admire Adams's *Education.* Neither the life nor the book is a failure. One can see the sense in which, by Adams's supernal standards, neither is a success; but surely by any reasonable moral or aesthetic measure both are intricate and beautiful. I judge the *Education* to be the single book of highest distinction ever produced by an American.

Ordinarily in dealing with a work of literature the first problem is to find a handle to turn the work about so as to measure its achievement against its ambition. In dealing with the *Education* the most obvious handle, and one we dare not let go, is the phenomenon of one's bafflement, the book's unique combination of slipperiness of language— its quicksilver style—and viscosity or profundity of thought: its density of ideas and its immense range of learning, within which the voice of Adams moves with an elegant elliptical allusiveness, a kind of tough dandyism of mind, at once lofty, fastidious, and robust. In fact Adams is far more seeming-candid than most writers in offering himself for manipulation: handles stick out all round his work, as in that crazy sentence-making machine that Gulliver finds in the Academy of Lagado. All of his statements of design are helpful in some degree, even when they border on disingenuousness.

To William James he described the book as a piece of intellectual therapy, written like his *Mont-Saint-Michel and Chartres* "to clean off a bit of the surface of my mind . . . always to clean my own mind." In writing to his dear friend Charles Milnes Gaskell of Wenlock Abbey in Shropshire, Adams first described his *Education* offhandedly as "my last Will and Testament," but he went on to speak of something more fundamental, his outright elegiac motive: "The volume is wholly due to piety on account of my father and John Hay." In a second letter to Gaskell a few days later he remarked that if he published his book, "I shall have survived, buried, and praised my friends, and shall go to sleep myself. *It is time.*" He was in his sixty-ninth year, but he had been feeling, or at any rate talking, like an old man for a good many years. The elegiac is a dominant note in the *Education,* one of its most resonant and affecting.

Equally affecting is Adams's wish to write a helpful book, of service particularly to young persons seeking a way to an education that will help them to plan and conduct a life in the terrifying "multiplicity" of the new century. His own "failures" were to be exemplary and monitory, to help, as he put it in his 1907 preface, "to fit young men, in universities or elsewhere, to be men of the world, equipped for any emergency." An extravagant hope for any education, surely, but always pragmatical in impulse. To Gaskell he presented his volume more simply and touchingly as a kind of emeritus performance of a failed Harvard professor of history and failed historian of contemporary affairs: "my closing lectures to undergraduates in the instruction abandoned and broken off in 1877." Deadly serious in his aim to contribute to a reform in education, particularly in the teaching and learning of history, he intended to circulate his book, accompanied by his long supplementary essay, **"The Rule of Phase Applied to History,"** at large among American teachers of history. This scheme was later abandoned.

Adams's address to an intended audience of students may remind one of Thoreau's remark in the second paragraph of *Walden:* "Perhaps these pages are more particularly addressed to poor students." Benjamin Franklin had undertaken his *Autobiography* in 1771 in the form of a letter to his son, to tell a story of a successful and happy life, possibly "fit to be imitated"; and he picked it up again in 1784, he says, on the urging of friends such as Benjamin Vaughan who admired what they had seen of his account of "the manners and situation of a rising people" and of a personal life that might "induce more men to spend lives fit to be written." Adams himself cites Franklin as his American predecessor in presenting a memoir as a "model . . . of self-teaching." Franklin's book is a small classic, nourishing and charming, but it reads like a primer alongside *The Education of Henry Adams.*

The models Adams mentions repeatedly are the confessions of St. Augustine and Jean-Jacques Rousseau, though he considers both of them ultimately failures, going awash in metaphysics and egotism respectively. If Adams wishes his *Education* to be exemplary and monitory, the self is his necessary subject, but he seeks at all costs to avoid the traps of the ego. He resorts to all sorts of self-distancing and self-diminishing devices, such as the clothes metaphor he borrows from *Sartor Resartus,* by which he becomes the Teufelsdröckh of his own tale, a "lay-figure" or "manikin" who (or which) is to be "taken for real" and "treated as though it had life" ("Who knows?" says Adams; "Possibly it had!"), as it rickets about in the "garment" of its education to show forth to students "the faults of the patchwork fitted on their fathers." This resolve to avoid self-celebration comes near to taking command of the book, both matter and manner, dictating basic decisions in regard to point of view, selection, emphasis, tone, language itself.

We must see that Adams judges the failures of Augustine and Jean-Jacques to be failures of art, for his own ambition was consciously literary: he wished to work not primarily as historian or as biographer but as artist. Augustine alone among memoirists, he thought, had possessed a genuine "idea of literary form,—a notion of writing a story with an end and object, not for the sake of the object, but for the form, like a romance," and he failed because he could not sustain his conceived artistic shape, his drama. Adams's own purpose and his own failure had been of the same order, he felt when he had finished, or abandoned, his manuscript. He had written his *Mont-Saint-Michel and Chartres* and his *Education,* he told Edith Morton Eustis, not in order "to teach others, but to educate myself in the possibilities of literary form." He went on: "Between artists, or people trying to be artists the sole interest is that of form. . . . The arrangement, the construction, the composition, the art of climax are our only serious study." We note the personal possessive pronoun. He wrote William James that the *Education* "interests me chiefly as a literary experiment, hitherto, as far as I know, never tried or never successful," and he went on to specify the kinship of art he felt with Henry James: "Your brother Harry tries such experiments in literary art daily, and would know instantly what I mean." When he wrote Henry James on May 6, 1908, he addressed him with jocular geniality as *frater.*

In his only reference in the *Education* to James's novels, Adams remarks that "Henry James had not yet [in 1862] taught the world to read a volume for the pleasure of seeing the lights of his burning-glass turned on alternate sides of the same figure." In 1908 he saw himself as having joined James in such experiments and failed at the enterprise. In a letter to his dear friend Elizabeth Cameron he made another crucial use of his metaphor of light and angle of view. He was being tempted to publish his *Education,* he said, chiefly as a way to avoid the pressure of demands that he do an outright memoir of John Hay: "All memoirs lower the man in estimation." He wished instead to give Hay a just elevation, and the best device for that was some such elliptical view as the *Education* employed: "Such a side light is alone artistic." Adams's light would not be a burning-glass but something more shifting, shaded, and oblique.

Perhaps Adams's most helpful comments in the letters surrounding the *Education* have to do with its structure, "the arrangement, the construction, the composition"— what James would have called *ordonnance.* In writing to Barrett Wendell, for example, Adams links himself cheerfully with Augustine and Rousseau as failers in an enterprise of impossible difficulty: "We have all three undertaken to do what cannot be successfully done—mix narrative and didactic purpose and style." I take the grammar of the latter clause to imply not two counters but three: story, argument, style. He, Augustine, and Rousseau had all attempted the "*tour-de-force* of writing drama with what is essentially undramatic."

Yet Adams feels that his task was the hardest of the three, and his failure perhaps the least shaming, owing to the greater perplexity for an American in trying to find and fix a satisfactory "atmosphere." To Elizabeth Cameron he also described his struggle "to keep an atmosphere." The idea is complex and none too clear as Adams applies it. By the term itself he probably meant what we more commonly call context or background, and he used the latter term to William James: "It is the old story of an American drama. You can't get your contrasts and backgrounds." With more than a dozen volumes of American history, biography, and fiction behind him, Adams presumably knew what he was talking about. But why was an American atmosphere or background so hard to fix? He leaves us to sort the matter out for ourselves. My assumption is that he had in mind the relative thinness, the lack of density and definition, the something anarchic and formless in our culture, its reluctance to take shapes and hold them, our heterogeneousness and our lingering infantilism, our way of growing bigger and older without growing up, the shifting baby-fat that keeps moving under the national skin.

To describe the structure of his book in the usual sense of order, proportion, scope, Adams offered a typically amusing and intricate figure in a letter to James Ford Rhodes:

> If you can imagine a centipede moving along in twenty little sections (each with a mathematical formula carefully concealed in his stomach) to the bottom of a hill; and then laboriously climbing in fifteen sections more (each with a new mathematical formula carefully concealed in its stomach) till it can get up on a hill an inch or two high, so as to see ahead a half inch or so, you will understand in advance all that the **"Education"** has to say.

This is Adams's way of saying that his book moves in a system of twenty chapters, about three hundred pages, carrying his story from "Quincy" in 1838 to "Failure" in 1871 (the bottom of the hill); then, after a startling hiatus in the narrative, a further fifteen chapters, about two hundred pages, moving from "Twenty Years After" in 1892 to "Nunc Age" in 1905.

In reading one comes slowly and perhaps sullenly to recognize that Adams is a good deal less interested in "narrative" than in "didactic purpose." Particularly after he breaks off his story abruptly in 1871, there is less and less narrative, more and more abstraction, speculation, philosophical postulating. A book that willfully leaps over twenty years in the life of its "subject" can hardly call itself a Life: Adams's own proposed subtitle was "A Study of Twentieth-Century Multiplicity." He meant what he said when he called the central persona a manikin and a lay-figure. In the later chapters especially the light strikes more and more from the side; the lay-figure scarcely moves in body. What moves, ever more boldly and subtly, is the mind inside.

One may feel the emphases of the book as divided, elusive, even evasive; still Adams plays basically fair in the matter of the superior weight he will assign to argument. Writing to William James he pretended to have practiced a sleight of hand: trusting, he says, to the smallness and inattentiveness of his audience, he had "hid" in the last hundred pages of *Mont-Saint-Michel and Chartres* "a sort of anchor in history"; then in the *Education,* conceived as "a companion study of the twentieth century," he had proceeded to "hide" a supplementary hundred pages of historical theory in the midst of "a stack of rubbish meant only to feed the foolish." This is to scoff at his reader and at four-fifths of his own book: his hyperboles can be merely exasperating. To Henry James he put the case more plainly: the *Education* was conceived as "a completion and mathematical conclusion from the previous volume about the Thirteenth Century,—the three concluding chapters of this being only a working out to Q.E.D. of the three concluding chapters of that." Not only in letters but in his prefaces and in his main text, Adams kept trying to make clear that his subject was not The Life of Henry Adams but the failure of a figure called Henry Adams to accumulate an education requisite for living in the real world, the world that the historian must understand or at least chronicle honestly. The manikin is used, he says in his 1907 preface, because he is indispensable "for the study of relation."

Yet "the object of study," he insists, "is the garment, not the figure." In the ventriloquizing "Editor's Preface" which he wrote in 1916 to appear over the signature of Henry Cabot Lodge in the 1918 public edition, Adams called the *Education* a "sequel" to *Mont-Saint-Michel and Chartres,* always designed as such, and went on to quote the paragraph concluding chapter 29 that specifies such a relationship. The poor thing had failed, he lamented, because the author had not been able to master his literary form, especially at the end: "Probably he was . . . trying only to work into it his favorite theory of history."

But it is high time to try to observe Adams's mingled purposes of story, argument, style going about their business of forming the work of art at which he professed to have failed. If this is failure, one must finally ask of the art as of the life, then what on earth is success?

The dominance of the didactic accumulates slowly, intensifying and spreading until at the end it almost entirely displaces other motives. Yet the didactic is not what first catches the eye, though it is quietly at work from the beginning. It seems absurd to say of a work that is in some sense autobiographical that it is self-conscious; but the self-consciousness of the *Education* is a special genus, born of didactic intention. This is not the ordinary self of autobiography, free like Whitman's self to lean and loaf at its ease, casually free to report its own doing, in whatever order of feeling, thought, and action. Adams's self is constrained by its function as exemplar, a datum, a proof in an argument, a figure in a demonstration.

This motive, not modesty actual or posed, directs the crucial decision to speak of the self always in the third person, to say not "I" but "he" or "Adams." The effects of such a simple device are complex and startling. Logically the third person, by distancing, ought to objectify; and Adams would justify it on those grounds, or pretend to do so. But it does not work that way in the *Education:* it abstracts, but it does not objectify. The self is not so much set off in a middle distance as set slightly to one side, while the writer's observing eye looks on with an obliqueness merely assumed or fictional. The abstracting effect of the third-person eye and voice works curiously to intensify rather than to diminish self-consciousness: we are always aware of the self self-consciously avoiding self-consciousness in order to posit a self that is merely phenomenal. The conception is fiendishly artful, so superbly managed that one is not only caught but deeply moved—by the motive as well as by the art.

Furthermore the third-person angle of narration contributes profoundly to the elegiac effect that richly pervades the whole book. We are always aware that it is old man Adams who has chosen to make a manikin of the self and set it to mime its way through a disenchanting, even humiliating demonstration, and who looks back over the pathetic phases of its failure across a span of seventy years with a reminiscent irony, an eye that is disappointed and resigned but also indulgent, amused, grateful.

The discovery of how good Adams is at the novelist's craft of narrative, character, atmosphere makes one lament his decision to throw his main force on the side of historical argument, and it may make one feel the more surly about struggling with the intricacies of the argument itself. The discovery occurs early, for in his first chapters, particularly in his first pages, Adams does some of the best pure writing ever produced in this country.

The long first chapter, "Quincy (1838-1848)," is brilliant in local vividness and suggested range, and it contains the whole book in miniature. It sets moving the master metaphor fundamental to the book's habit of artifice: the figure of life as a "game" which Adams never quite joined as a player because he "lost himself in the study of it"—characteristically a study mainly of the "errors" of the

players. Failure is foreknown; the autumnal melancholy of the tale to come is forefelt. The "detached" third-person point of view is assumed from the beginning: a male child is born in February 1838 in the shadow of Boston State House. But Adams does not pretend that this "he," this "ten pounds of unconscious babyhood," is an Everybaby. This is not just any manikin but one with a name that entails a destiny. "It's a complex fate, being an American," wrote Henry James, who also described himself as "a citizen of the James family." Adams was an American, a New Englander, an Adams—all being forms of fate, as he is superbly aware. He is born into "a nest of association so colonial—so troglodytic"; in church on Sunday the boy reads, over the bald head of his grandfather President John Quincy Adams, the plaque in memory of his greatgrandfather President John Adams. "You'll be thinkin' you'll be President too," the Irish gardener says to him sardonically. (Not everyone has an Irish gardener.) The boy is surprised at the doubt implied in the statement.

The early omens are dubious. He belongs to the third generation after President John, he is the youngest of three brothers, and a severe attack of scarlet fever in his fourth year turns him into the runt of the litter: he "fell behind his brothers two or three inches in height, and proportionally in bone and weight." The effect upon his "character and processes of mind," Adams suggests tentatively, may have been a certain "fining-down process of scale," and an intensification of his natural inclination to the New Englander's critical cast of mind: "The habit of doubt; of distrusting his own judgment and of totally rejecting the judgment of the world; the tendency to regard every question as open; the hesitation to act except as a choice of evils; the shirking of responsibility; the love of line, form, quality; the horror of ennui; the passion for companionship and the antipathy to society." But Adams has no intention of presenting himself as neurasthenic. He remarks once that as a boy his nerves were "delicate" and that when he was older he "exaggerated" that weakness. He treats the matter frankly and drops it, and we hear hardly another word of nerves or health of any kind. He thinks of himself as "normal" and believes that others so regard him.

No, he insists, what is to be "peculiar" in his nature will be a function of "education," not "character"; and he gives us thus early a view of the complex things he will mean by his key term, a definition inclusive enough to carry us to the end of the long book: "From cradle to grave this problem of running order through chaos, direction through space, discipline through freedom, unity through multiplicity, has always been, and must always be, the task of education, as it is the moral of religion, philosophy, science, art, politics, and economy." What he has described is his whole permanent field of attention. In these early pages Adams gives us as well the decisive first datum in the education, his grounding, blood and bones, in the blunt and beautiful rhythm of New England seasons, which he sets in a classical rhetorical frame of comparison and contrast: the long cold white winter in which the earth seems to die and men and animals stumble about like somnambular spirits, followed by the shockingly sudden and complete resurrection of the miraculous green world in the "drunken" summer. Adams uses the seasonal cycle brilliantly, as fact and trope: "The double exterior nature gave life its relative values. Winter and summer, cold and heat, town and country, force and freedom, marked two modes of life and thought, balanced like lobes of the brain." A sensitive boy who grows up in New England weather takes the lesson of bifurcation into his tissues: "life was double."

Already we begin to sense the basic strategy of the book, as much a matter of temperament as of design, adopted more or less helplessly because it is its author's cast of mind. The discipline of dividedness, of ambiguity, the sense of duality as the habit of fact as of perception pervades this first chapter, and it will grow ever more beautiful and baffling. As summer and country are set against winter and town, so freedom is set against constraint, youth against age, moral and political Adamses against banking Brookses: Grandfather John Quincy Adams gives Bibles; Grandfather Peter Chardon Brooks gives silver mugs. Grandmother Louisa Catherine Johnson Adams, "the Madam," embodies dividedness: half English and half American, dragged about the capitals of the world by chances of war and politics, settled at last in a colonial house with Queen Anne paneling and Louis Seize furniture, in old age in the middle of the American nineteenth century she still seems lost. It is no wonder that Henry Adams should trace to her a strain of ambivalence in his genetic equipment: "those doubts and self-questionings, those hesitations."

For Adams the crucial dividedness is temporal. By heritage, by temperament, by moral, political, and aesthetic inclination, he feels himself to be a throwback to an age already dead, "a child of the eighteenth century." Yet before he is six he has seen the twentieth century foretold by the railroad, the steamship, the telegraph, and it is a citizen of the twentieth century who tells the whole story of the *Education.* By the end he has worked his way through to a humorous and reluctant peace: old Henry Adams has just discovered that the best way to follow the track of the Virgin in French medieval stained glass is by motor car. It was the nineteenth century, the real arena of his living, with which Adams could never make peace. "He never could compel himself to care for nineteenth-century style," he remarks laconically in his first chapter. The temper that set him against the temper of his time, so that he never willingly inhabited his life, freed him to play the revenant, the alien and skeptical sojourner.

At one early point Adams appears flatly to deny any such alienation. He says roundly: "To his life as a whole he was a consenting, contracting party and partner from the moment he was born to the moment he died." But the whole weight and coloring of the story as it accumulates show the disingenuousness of the statement. He is trying to protect the fiction of the representativeness of his Henry Adams manikin, whose exemplary function works only if he is accepted as a "consciously assenting member" of his age. The more illuminating metaphor is his conventional life-game figure. Adams had been, originally, willing to play the game of his age, to contend for plums and power within its cynical rules, and he knew the cards he held

were the strongest; but instead of playing he "lost himself in study" of the game, as he says. It was "failure" that turned him into a suave Thersites: spectator, learned student, critic, and ironical chronicler of a bitter comedy. Hence that persistent light from the side.

Adams's obsessive theme of personal failure is hyperbolical and to an irritating degree perverse—at once self-indulgent and self-flagellant, almost masturbatory—but it is more than a mere trope. By the measure of his own very large ambitions for worldly power (to be exercised, of course, with Adams and eighteenth-century highmindedness) he was indeed established early as a failure. But the age fails with him, far more consequentially, and it is in his function as critic that Adams is a "consenting member" of the public process. Consent need not imply applause. Yet along the way to failure Adams does find much to praise in the way of human performance: hence the profound and touching effect of elegy and eulogy in the *Education.*

His early perception of life as double is the primitive movement in the definition of education as a struggle to "run" order through chaos, unity through multiplicity. The definition, formed in study and experience, is both cause and effect of Adams's Hegelian habit of mind which finds antithesis everywhere set against thesis; but it is moral and intellectual energy that impels the mind to drive toward ever higher synthesis. The highest synthesis, the highest knowable truth, presumably must be an affair of tone, the shade into which all the warring opposites finally coalesce. The very first sensuous experience Adams can remember is a kind of absolute, unshaded: a child of three sitting on a yellow-painted kitchen floor in a patch of hard sunlight. The characteristic quality of New England light was "glare": "The boy was a full man before he ever knew what was meant by atmosphere. . . . After a January blizzard, the boy who could look with pleasure into the violent snow-glare of the cold white sunshine, with its intense light and shade, scarcely knew what was meant by tone." Knowledge of tone was to be reached "only by education." *The Education of Henry Adams* is ultimately a triumph of the achievement of tone, in the most ramified sense: tone as knowledge, tone as commensurate style.

"Failure" is the twentieth section of his down-slanted "centipede" of structure, and it closes the long first movement of the book. Adams extends the chapter through an account of the summer following his first year of teaching, chiefly to include his first meeting with Clarence King, presented as a benign crisis in his own history, a rounding and closing of a long phase of education and a beginning of "life." Adams had traveled west as a "friend of geologists" to take a spectator's part with one of the field parties of the Fortieth Parallel Survey which was mapping the geology of a hundred-mile-wide belt along the line of the newly completed Union Pacific Railroad. Such a gesture of the still disheveled young republic seeking definition of itself was bound to appeal to Adams for its transcendental quality, and bound to strike him as symbolically right to produce, at its western terminus, Henry Adams on a solitary mule, belated and lost, stumbling through the dark in a canyon of Estes Park to discover Clarence King in a lamplit Rocky Mountain cabin. It won't do to smile at this kind of thing: fate is fate, and we must grant a sufficiently poetical mind its right to play. A Dantesque density surrounds the meeting of Adams and the gay, paradoxical, star-crossed young man of such preternatural charm and high capacity; and though beyond this point King is only flickeringly visible in the book, like Charles Francis Adams and John Hay and the literally invisible Marian Hooper Adams he is a resident ghost, a shade enriching its mysterious and beautiful texture.

The most astonishing of Adams's elaborate strategies of structure is a negative act: the decision to leave a gap of a full twenty years in his narrative. The hiatus occurs not in the act of writing but in the stuff of the book, the material of the narrative. Adams does not set his task aside for many years and then pick it up again where he left off, as Franklin did; his writing was quite swift and continuous, most of it done in 1904-1905, and within that process he decided to leave the hiatus—as a structural member of the work, a design of ellipsis. It was a bold decision and at first glance a perverse one, the coarsest of Adams's perversities. What staggers the reader is that what he chooses to pass over are his twenty years of "success," the years when he was "doing his work," when he was most fully "living" by an ordinary measure of biographical matter. It is not easy to think of any other autobiographer who so resolutely turns his back when he might have been puffing out his chest.

The case is less absolute than I am making it sound. Adams has already shown us a summary sketch of his career as teacher and editor, and that carries us to 1877. And in "Twenty Years After," in a still more sketchy and elliptical treatment, he does tell us what he had "done" in the interval down to 1892: with Grant off the scene and W. M. Evarts and Hay in the State Department, Adams had gone back to Washington to be a "stable-companion to statesmen, whether they liked it or not," and to "write history"; in fifteen years or so he had produced an "altogether ridiculous" number of printed volumes. But such vague laconicisms encompass an enormous willed reticence. The "altogether ridiculous" formula, for example, covers the most varied and distinguished canon of his generation—not only the monumental nine-volume *History of the United States during the Administrations of Jefferson and Madison,* but also two volumes of biography, a collection of historical essays, and two stylish and original novels to which Adams never even put his name. He pretends to no impact on the culture of the day; like Henry James's Dencombe in "The Middle Years," he says he had "worked in the dark," and Adams reckons only three "serious readers": Abram Hewitt, Wayne McVeagh, and John Hay.

The largest and most moving of these withholdings is Adams's refusal to speak at all of his marriage—thirteen happy years from 1872 to 1885 with Marian Hooper Adams in Cambridge, Washington, and Europe, terminated by her suicide in a period of deep depression following the death of her father. The closest Adams comes to any reference to his wife or his marriage is the enigmatic paragraph at the end of "Twenty Years After," as hooded and haunting as Saint-Gaudens's memorial figure itself, his brooding communion with which in the spring of 1892 recalls another Henry James situation—Marcher at the end of "The Beast in the Jungle." Adams is expressing, by his withholding, what Ernest Samuels calls his "somber pose" that he had died when his wife died: her death "broke his life in halves," as he wrote elsewhere; and the second half of his life, as of his book, is "posthumous" in feeling, a ghost's drifting reverie. But indeed her unmentioned death colors the whole book, and is the profoundest source of its elegiac feeling. Surely we need look little farther for the psychology of the twenty-year hiatus. Adams could not talk in detail of the period without talking of his marriage, and he could not bear to talk of it.

Odd as it may seem to go on at such length about something that is not present in the work being examined, in dealing with the *Education* one needs to work in the spirit of Stevens's Snow Man, who wished to attend not only to "nothing that is not there" but also to "the nothing that is." When an autobiographer chooses to pass over the twenty most productive years of his life, he creates a negation that is a phenomenon in itself, a nothing that is. The missing marriage is a negation within the negation, and if its beauty and grievousness largely explain the emotional logic of omission, the logic of literary tactics needs to be sought elsewhere. The primary fact, as he himself insists, is that Adams is not really writing autobiography in the ordinary sense. His renewed insistence, in exclamatory form, in the opening sentence of chapter 21, "Twenty Years After," carries something of the force of the reinvocation of the Muse as Spenser or Milton or Pope draws a deep breath for the last movement of epical action: "Once more! this is a story of education, not of adventure!" He now carefully restates his purpose: "It is meant to help young men—or such as have intelligence enough to seek help—but it is not meant to amuse them." The *Education* is more a pragmatic philosophical treatise than it is an autobiography, and Adams now ceremonially redefines "education" for the "barely one man in a hundred" who "owns a mind capable of reacting to any purpose on the forces that surround him": "The object of education for that mind should be the teaching itself how to react with vigor and economy. . . . Education should try to lessen the obstacles, diminish the friction, invigorate the energy, and should train minds to react, not at haphazard, but by choice, on the lines of force that attract their world."

If I understand his grammar, by "reacting to any purpose on" he means "to influence, to work usefully upon." Hence an account of the uses to which he put his education would seem to be very much in point. But Adams is already committed to presenting his education as failure, and so he has had to ignore twenty years of productive "life" in order to avoid the skewing effect of success. This tactic, in combination with his definition above, involves him in another paradox. What matters is action, yet what Adams "did" with his education is not the "inquirer's" proper concern: "It is a personal matter which would only confuse him." The inquirer who would have enjoyed an opportunity to be confused by all that personal matter must make the best of his deprivation. It would have been one thing, sufficiently cynical, if Adams had chosen directly to apply the label of failure to his twenty years of marriage, publication, and stable-companionship with statesmen. Perhaps the case is that he could have validated such a view only by treating his wife's suicide as decisive; and though that may indeed have been his deepest feeling, the event itself is for him literally unspeakable.

Adams picks up his narrative, in the increasingly vague sense in which he is writing narrative, at a point of low vitality: "Education had ended in 1871 [when he 'began to apply it for practical uses like his neighbors']; life was complete in 1890; the rest mattered so little!" After twenty years of concentrated work, he had "thought his own duties sufficiently performed and his account with society settled." He has "enjoyed his life amazingly," but it seems to him essentially finished, and in any case he is tired and low in nervous energy, so he has simply broken things off. Now, nearing fifty-four years of age in January 1892, he lies glooming in a London hospital after a minor operation. He had just "come up from the South Seas with John La Farge"—a phrase that covers more than a year of travel with his painter friend. It is a bit dashing to be told, with twenty-five years, fifteen chapters, two hundred pages still to go, that life is over and what remains matters little; but one has learned by now to play these games with Adams, to fall into sympathy with his mood and manner, and to await rewards with confidence.

One has now come face to face, I think, with the crux of Adams's artistic problem at which he thought he had failed: how to make "dramatic," or shapely and interesting, material that is essentially undramatic—as he has resolved to limit it. After this point narrative virtually disappears. In effect Adams almost ceases to act visibly; he moves, driftingly, from place to place, but his basic action goes on in the mind, as thought—observation, speculation, formulation. As the narrative energy diminishes, the philosophical energy intensifies, the texture of thought and speech grows ever more dense, the whole enterprise more complex, more interesting or less interesting according to taste. Even in the "posthumous" phase of his life, Adams has not ceased to live a rich personal life, though it is blighted by his widowerhood and then by his hopeless attachment to Elizabeth Cameron, wife of his friend in the Senate. Hence, though he has now chosen to act by thinking, he also acts by feeling. His way of expressing feeling is classical in kind—reticent, elliptical, underspecified, suggestive; but the feeling itself is so rich, so strong, so intelligent that it takes subterranean control of the book and of one's responses to it.

Adams's education did not cease in 1871, any more than his life ended in 1890. Both continue for the whole span of the book, to 1905—and beyond. But direction and emphasis, the rhythm of energy, change in the education as in the life. When the life has moved into the mind, it is too late to train oneself for effective action or reaction upon "the lines of force that attract [one's] world." Education also moves into the mind, to become a sifting and sorting and formulating, an effort to set things straight in their patterns. It is, personally, an appeasement of the mind's hunger for order, and, less personally, a powerful continu-

ing tutorial urge, a desire to transmit a body of insight that will free younger men to act with more intelligence and less waste.

Henry Adams was blessed with one of the richest of human gifts, a genius for friendship, and surely no man of his day possessed a larger, warmer, or more brilliant circle of friends of both sexes. Persons of high gifts themselves, of his own age and also younger, enjoyed his company and treasured his affection and approval. As a houseguest or traveling companion he was welcomed for weeks or months at a stretch by men like King, La Farge, Saint-Gaudens and by families such as the Camerons, the Lodges, the Hays, the Roosevelts. His own talk was copious, witty, full of meat, as were his letters. The *Education* itself makes none of these claims; it simply cites occasions whose mere recurrence proves the case.

Adams and John Hay had had the exquisite satisfaction of building adjoining houses in Lafayette Square in Washington in 1884-1885, designed by Adams's good friend Henry Hobson Richardson, probably the finest of American Victorian architects; but Marian Adams had hardly lived to occupy her house, and after her death Henry Adams spent as much time in travel or residence abroad, especially in Paris, as he spent in Washington. His journeys were so numerous and so adventitious, and his account of them so systematically sidelong and impressionistic, that it is pointless to try to follow them. The journeys were social and intellectual in function, like the whole action of Adams's life now, and it is really the intricate movement of his mind that one must try to follow—dazzled, confused, and profoundly impressed by the almost arrogant masterliness of flight as a mind launches, soars, dives, hovers, perches, launches again. The whole of that flight is far too wide and complex to review; every reader must give himself the pleasure and the exasperation of following it for himself. A mere outline is task enough.

The hazy autumnal atmosphere of this long final movement is suggested by characteristic chapter headings: "Silence," "Indian Summer," "Twilight," "Vis Inertiae," "Nunc Age." Autumn, Adams writes of the season itself, should be "a little sunny and a little sad." His own autumn is more sad than sunny, and we can feel the soreness of his heart within the tone of his beautifully stylized gaiety. The passing of time, and of friends, is a part of it, naturally, and Adams names his own age almost every year as he moves from his middle forties to his late sixties. A newly authentic sense of failure colors the mood as well. Adams's life now does really feel in a sense "posthumous." The persons he has loved most are dead, or otherwise unreachable, or failing along with him. He has put his work behind him: it is well enough in its way, but sadly limited in outreach for a boy who had dreamed of "controlling power in some form." He confesses in his understated way his sense of the irony of the fact that no public office has ever been offered to him, but he has put away the ambition to be a public man and the deprivation hardly seems to matter any more. What is left is ennui, restlessness, fear, and above all the passion of the mind to know before it dies—education in that desperate and beautiful sense. It is for that reason that the spectacle of life still matters, that the aging mind still drives itself to go over and over all it knows, and to keep on adding to its store.

Adams has not altogether given up his interest in politics and current affairs, but he watches such things now in a much more detached and musing spirit, as one datum among many in the huge design he is trying to puzzle out. He is on the track of the track of force, trying to understand the shape of the movement of power in time; he is more interested in the past and the future than in the present, though of course the present matters acutely as the most visible cusp in the graph of movement. The "honest historian," Adams remarks, must not take a partisan view of his data: "To him even the extinction of the human race should be merely a fact to be grouped with other vital statistics." He seemed now to care little what way national or international affairs drifted, except in the very personal sense that the reputation and even the health of John Hay as secretary of state were bound up with the drift. Adams describes himself, Hay, and Clarence King as "inseparable" after 1879, but King spends so much of his life "underground"—in the doubly punning sense of his mining operations and his secret common-law marriage to a black woman in New York—that he remains a shadow in the narrative, and it is Hay who matters most to Adams as a friend of the bosom, and hence to the reader. Adams views Hay's tenure as a triumph at the cost of life.

But the larger triumph of the quarter-century is the vast increase and "concentration" of mechanical power, and of the money-power that will manage and exploit it, the "banker's Olympus" of capitalism. As an honest historian Adams must be the fascinated recorder of that process; but he can take no pleasure in it, for it means the death of his class and of the eighteenth-century principles he has fought for all his life: "strict construction, limited powers, George Washington, John Adams, and the rest." This social and political death leaves Adams feeling "posthumous" in yet another sense, and farther and more scornfully distanced from the tide of affairs.

In his famous chapter 25, "The Dynamo and the Virgin," Henry Adams describes the habits of his guild: "Historians undertake to arrange sequences,—called stories, or histories—assuming in silence a relation of cause and effect. These assumptions, hidden in the depths of dusty libraries, have been astounding, but commonly unconscious and childlike." In the same rueful paragraph he sketches his own historian's history:

> Adams, for one, had toiled in vain to find out what he meant. He had even published a dozen volumes of American history for no other purpose than to satisfy himself whether, by the severest process of stating, with the least possible comment, such facts as seemed sure, in such order as seemed rigorously consequent, he could fix for a familiar moment a necessary sequence of human movement. The result had satisfied him as little as at Harvard College. Where he saw sequence, other men saw something quite different, and no one saw the same unit of measure.

The one thing he "insisted" on was "a relation of sequence," refusing to accept the anarchy of randomness:

one thing must follow another not by chance but according to some motive, logic, shape, an order at least of energy if not of conscious design. To this hypothesized sequential energy of history he assigns the name *attraction*. He is willing to find it anywhere, but he insists on finding it somewhere: "The matter of direction seemed vital."

In the autumnal mood of his late years, "holding open the door into the next world," a "Teufelsdröckh," a "stranded Tannhäuser," a "dove of sixty years old, alone and uneducated, who has lost his taste even for olives," but still "passionately seeking education," Adams continues to study "his ignorance in silence." His historian's object is "to triangulate from the widest possible base to the furthest point he thinks he can see, which is always far beyond the curvature of the horizon." Seeking to widen his base, and to understand it newly, he spends months and years conning again his old knowledge and adding new. His aim is "to follow the track of the energy," or, reversing his figure, "to keep in front of the movement, and, if necessary, lead it to chaos, but never fall behind. Only the young have time to linger in the rear." Such an objective, he considered, was "not extravagant or eccentric. One sought no absolute truth. One sought only a spool on which to wind the thread of history without breaking it." Adams's thinking, phenomenally rangy and ingestive, comes to concentrate gradually on two main lines, finally a single line, a concept of force or power as religious as it is scientific.

The Dynamo and the Virgin, both so quiet, so chaste, so powerful, so mysterious, merge at last in the mind. Adams finds himself describing the Virgin as the "animated dynamo," implying reproduction and hence a principle of infinity. In the great gallery of machines at the Paris exposition of 1900, he "found himself lying . . . with his historical neck broken by the sudden irruption of forces totally new":

> He began to feel the forty-foot dynamos as a moral force, much as the early Christians felt the Cross. The planet itself seemed less impressive, in its old-fashioned, deliberate, annual or daily revolution, than this huge wheel, revolving within arm's-length at some vertiginous speed, and barely murmuring—scarcely humming an audible warning to stand a hair's-breadth further for respect of power—while it would not wake the baby lying close against its frame.

"Before the end," he continues, "one began to pray to it; inherited instinct taught the natural expression of man before silent and infinite force." One approaches the Dynamo, like the Virgin, with fear or love but certainly with respect: each is an "occult mechanism." I suppose one must conclude that Henry Adams ended up seeking God— though, looking down from his historian's Olympus, he will not thank one for saying so.

With his poetical rationalism, his superbly mortal intelligence, Adams had been in flight from religion all his life; but it did him no more good than it did Jonah, in Melville's phrase, "to flee world-wide from God." An implicit reverentness, sometimes nearly, reluctantly explicit, thickens and irradiates the long last movement of the *Education.* When the old student Henry Adams "imagines" himself three hundred years old in a sixteenth-century French church, "kneeling before the Virgin's window in the silent solitude of an empty faith, crying his culp, beating his breast, confessing his historical sins, weighed down by the rubbish of sixty-six years' education, and still desperately hoping to understand," he means to project a hyperbolical persona, bitterly humorous; but it is hard to mistake the rich sympathy for the image in the breast of the man who made it. The self scrutinizes itself rationally but with affectionate pity: the image is formed out of feeling too deep to accept burlesque.

The only religion Adams "professes"—after the great expositions of Chicago in 1893, Paris in 1900, and St. Louis in 1904—is "the religion of World's Fairs," by which he means his terrified attempt to understand and to "triangulate" the mighty new mechanical energies, the burly children of science at work on natural force. Chicago had seemed to Adams "the first expression of American thought as a unity," yet a thought that frightens and disgusts him, hardly thought at all but the more or less mindless elevation of mechanical power, with its necessary and equally offensive concomitants in politics and finance. In Paris his historical neck had been broken not only by the dynamos but by Röntgen rays, radium, and the internal combustion engine—occult mechanisms that seemed to imply anarchy, inscrutability in fundamental physical processes. By 1904 in St. Louis, the new American seemed to be confirmed as "the servant of the powerhouse, as the European of the twelfth century was the servant of the Church": he was "the child of steam and the brother of the dynamo."

Adams's concentration upon twin lines of force, spiritual/theological and mechanical/scientific, symbolized by the Virgin and the Dynamo, represented the culmination of a profoundly impressive discipline of scrutiny and rejection, too long—lifelong really but intensified in these final fifteen years—and too intricate to review here. His range and subtlety carried him not only deeply but repeatedly into history, of course, but also into politics, sociology, economics, psychology, literature, art, philosophy, and above all into theology and science, upon which bifurcation he may be said to have settled at last, more or less despairingly and by an act of will: "Satisfied that the sequence of men led to nothing and that the sequence of their society could lead no further, while the mere sequence of time was artificial, and the sequence of thought was chaos, he turned at last to the sequence of force." Seeking unity he had traveled continents and ransacked libraries and his own mind, and everywhere he had found only multiplicity. Even the line of natural force, which had hitherto seemed the one sure unity, was turning out under the new chemistry and physics to be as anarchic as the line of thought. What did appear certain was the vertiginous increase of power which, for its control and exploitation, was forcing society into modes of concentration at which Adams stared with pessimism and fastidious distaste.

His sense of reeling multiplicity everywhere about him drove Adams to join his young friend Bay Lodge in the "party" they called, only half humorously, the Conservative Christian Anarchists. With Hegel and Schopenhauer

as patron saints, the little node of beleaguered intellectual aristocrats, acting on the great principle of contradiction, followed ideas from statement to dispersal to negation to reformulation, ad infinitum. Adams argued that "in the last synthesis, order and anarchy were one, but that the unity was chaos"; but then he reflected that he would be "equally obliged to deny the chaos." In a half-dozen of the most brilliant paragraphs in American writing he follows the tortuous track toward the higher synthesis and the "universal which thinks itself, contradiction and all." The moral of this desperate intellectual comedy is that the wholly serious mind can never satisfy itself, never rest; yet, if it is not to be merely paralyzed by ambivalence, it must force itself to pause and perch long enough to mine some limited area as deeply as it can penetrate. And so Adams's brain seizes the Virgin and the Dynamo and tosses them from lobe to lobe. He imagines himself as crawling like Sir Lancelot in the twelfth century along a knife-edge dividing "two kingdoms of force which had nothing in common but attraction"—their drive, energy, impact upon his own mind. The inscrutable "rays" that stood to him for the new science seemed "a revelation of mysterious energy like that of the Cross." Adams "made up his mind to venture it; he would risk translating rays into faith." In a sense, I suppose, he risks translating faith into rays, or science. His awe and love to go to the Virgin, his awe and fear to the Dynamo; his intellectual energy goes to both energies.

In the summer of 1895, when he visits twelfth- and thirteenth-century churches in Normandy, Caen, Coutances, Mont-Saint-Michel, in company with Mrs. Lodge and her two sons, the Virgin and the mysteries of faith begin to be resurrected for Adams's mind as powerful counters in the history of thought. Helped by these fresher minds to throw off the obscuring "German" bias lingering from his youth, he is awakened to a disturbing and seductive "new sense of history," an intuition of a strange and beautiful line of force that demands a new mode of understanding. But in the summer of 1899, alone in Paris and "hunted by ennui," he "entered the practice of his final profession" by undertaking a systematic survey, or "triangulation," of the twelfth century. In the late autumn John La Farge arrived on the scene, bringing his artist's and student's expertise in the stained glass in which the medieval men limned the images of their faith, as well as his bracing jibe "Adams, you reason too much!" Now Adams's study of the Virgin, particularly at Chartres, began to move in a more intuitive rhythm toward a point. To evoke the presence of La Farge the artist, Adams applies the glass-palette as fact and figure: "In conversation La Farge's mind was opaline with infinite shades and refractions of light, and with color toned down to the finest gradations. In glass it was insubordinate; it was renaissance; it asserted his personal force with depth and vehemence of tone never before seen."

Adams's "idol" Gibbon, in a phrase he quotes with hilarity, had "darted a contemptuous look on the stately monuments of superstition," the Gothic cathedrals. Adams's own look is baffled, awed, adoring, for the Virgin blends in his mind not only with Christ who is Love but with Venus who is Love again. She becomes Woman, sex, reproduction, the mysterious inspirer and continuator not only of faith but of the basic racial energy. After 1895, culminating a lifetime's admiration of Woman, Adams begins "to feel the Virgin or Venus as force"; she was "the highest energy ever known to man, the creator of four-fifths of his noblest art," and "all the steam in the world could not, like the Virgin, build Chartres." That seemed a kind of given, a historical fiat. But Adams is too honest to abandon either stream of force, faith or science, Virgin or Dynamo; and he must continue to live torn, like Adam in the garden, "between God who was unity, and Satan who was complexity."

The new physics had casually transformed "the scientific synthesis commonly called Unity" into "the scientific analysis commonly called Multiplicity. The two things were the same, all forms being shifting phases of motion." So rebuffed, the elderly seeker of Unity yearned simply to drop "the sounder into the abyss—let it go," hence to give up the chase entirely. Adams "saw his education complete, and was sorry he ever began it." It is the sense of the moral and political cynicism thickening around him that will not let him rest: "He repudiated all share in the world as it was to be, and yet he could not detect the point where his responsibility began or ended." Despairingly and bravely, he resolves simply to will a double concentration: he will face and study Multiplicity as a fact, and at the same time study the nearest thing to Unity he can see.

"Any schoolboy could see," as Adams puts it in one of his exasperating ritual phrases, that man "as a force" had to be measured "by motion, from a fixed point." For his fixed point he settled upon the century from 1150 to 1250, as expressed in the French cathedrals and the thought of Aquinas, as the period when men had felt most powerfully at least the illusion of Unity: "The point of history when man held the highest idea of himself as a unit in a unified universe." Beginning there, and working in philosophy and mechanics, he would attempt to "measure motion down to his own time without assuming anything as true or untrue, except relation," so to produce a volume to be called *Mont-Saint-Michel and Chartres: A Study of Thirteenth-Century Unity.* Thereafter, having fixed "a position for himself," he would confront twentieth-century Multiplicity in *The Education of Henry Adams.* With these two "points of relation" established, he could triangulate: "He hoped to project his lines forward and backward indefinitely, subject to correction from anyone who should know better." A bold program, surely, for a man of sixty-five. At past fifty Adams had "solemnly and painfully" learned to ride a bicycle. Now the double motives of his quest came together amusingly when the "elderly and timid single gentleman" bought an automobile, one of the new "nightmares" capable of a hundred kilometers an hour, and in such a juggernaut followed the track of the Virgin about France:

> For him, the Virgin was an adorable mistress, who led the automobile and its owner where she would, to her wonderful palaces and chateaux, from Chartres to Rouen, and thence to Amiens and Laon, and a score of others, kindly receiving, amusing, charming and dazzling her lover, as though she were Aphrodite herself, worth all

else that man ever dreamed. He never doubted her force, since he felt it to the last fibre of his being, and could no more dispute its mastery than he could dispute the force of gravitation of which he knew nothing but the formula. He was only too glad to yield himself entirely, not to her charm or to any sentimentality of religion, but to her mental and physical energy of creation which had built up these World's Fairs of thirteenth-century force that turned Chicago and St. Louis pale.

Old Man Adams is wide awake to such conjunctions as comedy; yet the energy behind the enterprise was a despair so wide that it had to be defied if life was to continue. If in the most general sense Adams was seeking God (and finding mostly Satan), the thing he was fleeing was Self. Beyond all things he dreaded the final solipsism of being driven to the mind, his own mind, to find a locus of order or value—Unity. "Of all studies," he wrote, "the one he would rather have avoided was that of his own mind. He knew no tragedy so heartrending as introspection." Psychology had always seemed to him the least wholesome of his numerous sciences, and it is with pity and revulsion that he presents the figure of enlightened modern psychological man, the man who "knew" that "his normal condition was idiocy, or want of balance, and that his sanity was unstable artifice. His normal thought was dispersion, sleep, dream, inconsequence; the simultaneous action of different thought-centres without central control. His artificial balance was acquired habit. He was an acrobat, with a dwarf on his back, crossing a chasm on a slack-rope, and commonly breaking his neck." If the universe is to be "known only as motion of mind," and the property of mind is to "dissolve," then the condition of the serious seeker is heartrending indeed. It is at least in part with revulsion and defiance that Adams turns to the Virgin and the Dynamo: they are the creatures least like himself.

The turn is the act of a despairing yet indomitable intelligence, and there is great sadness in its resignation, as there is grandeur in its resoluteness. The man who had set out to know everything ends up wondering if anything is to be known. The direction of the turn has a great deal to do with both the form and the tone of the *Education.* The wish to move outside the self, to use it but not to depend upon it, not to live exclusively there, dictates the turn away from straight autobiography; the adoption of the view from the side in third-person narration turns the self into datum, a documentary or exemplary rather than a dramatic or even a subjective persona. The pessimism or resignation, the slow falling back from the dream, gives emotional and philosophical density to the elegiac mood of the whole book—which was written, after all, after these matters had been settled, for the most part sadly, in Adams's mind.

The long complex lines of thought, traced here so sketchily, fill perhaps two-thirds of the space in the final fifteen segments of Adams's centipede of structure. The rest of the space is occupied mainly by political affairs, noticed in large general international terms centering on the career of John Hay in the State Department, which Adams treats as a personal triumph that is ultimately suicidal.

Adams's handling of the decline and death of Hay and King, so brief and so feeling as it is, sharpens the general autumnal air to a point of wintry chill. King, "the best and brightest man of his generation," goes first, late in 1901. For Adams there is comfort in the fact that he dies off-stage, but a grinding wretchedness in contemplating the loneliness of his end in a California inn. Hay, who in Adams's view was killing himself in the country's service, lasts till 1905; and his death at Nauheim where Adams had just left him for rest and treatment is used by Adams to close his book, an event of implicit suicide beyond which he does not wish to speak: the rest is silence.

"Nunc Age"—Now Go—is his title for his last short chapter. "One walks with one's friends squarely up to the portal of life, and bids goodbye with a smile. One has done it so often!" Earlier Adams had remarked that "the affectation of readiness for death is a stage role, and stoicism is a stupid resource." But it was the only resource and Adams was reduced to it now. In its reticently eloquent way, the *Education* has been a paean to friendship all the way. Adams's rich quiet affectionateness is one of the book's primary sources of strength, as impressive as its cranky intellectual brilliance—though I wonder if it is any more moving. The book's triumph is compound and complex, a property of mind, of feeling, and of style. (pp. 65-88)

> B. L. Reid, "The View from the Side," in his Necessary Lives: Biographical Reflections, *University of Missouri Press, 1990, pp. 65-88.*

James Goodwin   (essay date 1983)

[*In the following essay, Goodwin examines Adams's use of a self-effacing narrative style in* The Education, *his ambivalence toward his family and national heritage, and his leanings toward anti-Semitism during his later years.*]

In many respects *The Education of Henry Adams* is a literary counterpart to the nameless grave site where Henry Adams and his wife Marian are buried. The site is dominated by a dramatic and now well-known bronze statue commissioned by Adams in memory of Marian and created by the sculptor Augustus Saint-Gaudens. Following Adams' stipulations, the graves are prominent but they do not disclose the identities of their occupants. In equivalent fashion, *The Education* gives prominence to the name Henry Adams but effaces and withholds much personal and identifying material of the life it commemorates. The process of self-effacement conducted in the book is perhaps most apparent in Adams' exclusive use of third-person forms of address to narrate his life and times. Though we are inclined to think of autobiography as a testament to subjectivity, Adams' book seems more like a memorial to impersonality.

The family name Adams is a national monument in its own right, as the autobiographer self-consciously reiterates from the opening pages of *The Education* to the conclusion. The surname and its wealth of historical connotations are judged, in early chapters, to be an impediment to success in any twentieth-century endeavor. In closing

chapters, the surname stands as ironic commentary on the inadequacies of America's colonial heritage in the modern era. Henry Adams' movements over a lifetime between Quincy, Boston, Cambridge and Washington marked the increasing degree of his deviation from the family record of political service. During his undergraduate years, the portraits of Presidents John Adams and John Quincy Adams hanging in Harvard Hall were a reminder of that unmatched record. He returned to Harvard College twelve years later to teach history, having abandoned thoughts of a government position in Washington. The chapter that recounts the return to his alma mater summarizes in its title Adams' estimate of his progress in the world to that point: "Failure (1871)."

In proceeding to an analysis of Adams' own sense of nullity, a clarification of terms is necessary. The most common understanding of the term *non-person* is a political one. In modern context, it refers to individuals liquidated under totalitarian regimes. Whenever possible, the totalitarian state erases from public life and official history all vestiges of its victims' existence. Some of the term's political implications will be applied to *The Education of Henry Adams* later in the present essay. The term refers initially, however, to a grammatical distinction explained in the work of the French linguist Emile Benveniste. The distinction clarifies the nature of Adams' self-references in *The Education,* whose narrative sets forth a representation of the modern self, a critique of the age, and a theory of history. In accordance with Benveniste's discussion of subjectivity in language, we can say that Henry Adams is a non-person in his own autobiography. Furthermore, that sense of self is consistent with Adams' opinions on modern society and his predictions about the course of history.

In analyzing the functions of personal pronouns, which are fundamental to the expression of selfhood in autobiography, Benveniste concludes that of the three singular forms—*I, you, he/she*—only *I* and *you* truly signify one's person as it is situated within language. According to his analysis, *I* is defined as "the individual who utters the present instance of discourse containing the linguistic instance *I.*" The definition appears to be tautological because it concerns an "empty" and self-referential sign that is given meaning only when it is enacted in speech or writing. From this perspective, *I* is an intersubjective grammatical category that assumes a *you* to whom discourse in the first-person is directed. Under Benveniste's revised schema of pronouns, the so-called third-person plainly does not fulfill the linguistic conditions of *person-hood.* A sentence containing *he* as its grammatical subject does not necessarily refer to the instance of discourse that contains *he* or to its speaker. Unlike an intrinsically personal pronoun and its functional subjectivity, a non-personal pronoun has as its referent someone or something outside the discourse itself. Furthermore, in a narrative where the narrator does not intervene in his own person (as *I,* in other words), the third-person can be said to signify the absence of person. This effect of the third-person in *The Education,* on which its other rhetorical strategies are based, promoted the following reaction from T. S. Eliot: "It is doubtful whether the book ought to be called an autobiography, for there is too little of the author in it."

The linguistic distinction between person and non-person is readily borne out by comparison of *The Education* to Rousseau's *Confessions.* Indeed, Adams invites the comparison in *The Education*'s preface, where he quotes famous lines from that book's overture as, in his words, a "warning against the Ego." Nominally addressed to God, Rousseau's opening words are truly a celebration of subjectivity and a direct challenge to the reader (the genuine addressee) to equal the book's candor. Though the overture starts as an entreaty, it rapidly shifts to a hortatory, even imperious, mood:

> Let the last trumpet sound when it will, I shall come forward with this work in my hand, to present myself before my Sovereign Judge, and proclaim aloud: "Here is what I have done, and if by chance I have used some immaterial embellishment it has been only to fill a void due to a defect of memory. I may have taken for fact what was no more than probability, but I have never put down as true what I knew to be false. I have displayed myself as I was, as vile and despicable when my behaviour was such, as good, generous, and noble when I was so. I have bared my secret soul as Thou thyself hast seen it, Eternal Being! So let the numberless legion of my fellow men gather round me, and hear my confessions. Let them groan at my depravities, and blush for my misdeeds. But let each one of them reveal his heart at the foot of Thy throne with equal sincerity, and may any man who dares, say 'I was a better man than he.' "

Here, as elsewhere in the *Confessions,* first-person discourse is performatory. By uttering a pledge of sincerity, Rousseau makes that pledge; utterance and authorial action converge. Rousseau's sole anxiety as narrator is that he will fail to fulfill the compulsion to confess. He writes, "I have only one thing to fear in this enterprise; not that I may say too much or tell untruths, but that I may not tell everything and may conceal the truth." In general, through the first-person the *Confessions* asserts an unmediated correspondence between narrative, discourse and author.

Adams' opening rhetorical stance, in contrast to Rousseau's, offers a case study in indirection and self-effacement. To say the least, he puts himself at several removes from the life narrated. Like Rousseau, Adams stipulated that his autobiography be published posthumously. But, where the *Confessions* opens with a good-humored evocation of the Last Judgment that universalizes death, *The Education* opens with stark references to the author's failing health and to the public silence into which he had lapsed after a paralyzing stroke in 1912. As biographer Ernest Samuels has documented, the so-called Editor's Preface signed by Henry Cabot Lodge, and dated months after the author's death in 1918, was in fact written by Adams in early 1916. Through this editorial death mask Adams refers to the unmanageable difficulties encountered "as he approached his end"—that is, the end of *The Education* and of life itself. Thus, fully two years before his death, Adams triangulates the time frame of his narrative to a point beyond the grave. Requests made at the end of 1915 that *The Education* be published in his lifetime momentar-

ily attracted Adams' interest. But he soon reasserted his initial resolution to leave the matter to executors. As the new year 1916 approached, he declined all entreaties for immediate publication with the explanation: "Unfortunately, I am really dead,—stone coffin cold,—and I cannot go on with the old life. . . . The book is, as I have said, not in a condition to appear as a work of mine."

The author's Preface to *The Education* offers explication of the book's distancing effect, but it scarcely brings Adams any closer to the narrative surface. Claiming self-effacement to be the trend of history since the era of Romantic egoism, Adams holds that for the purposes of education the ego serves only as a "manikin" and that only the fit for others, not the original figure, is of lasting consequence. Though the analogy to tailoring has its origin in Carlyle, in *The Education* manikin is much more a sarcastic diminutive for *man* than it is an allusion to Teufelsdröckh's clothes philosophy. Devised as a sign of modern man's powerlessness, the image subordinates the dread of being a nonentity to the spirit of historical inquiry. As the Preface explains, Adams' own person is to serve as the fundamental unit of measure in *The Education*'s "study of relation" in the "human condition." Not the immediate agent of discourse and history Rousseau depicts, the self for Adams is instead their object and accessory. And, rather than the coincidence of utterance and authorial action proposed in the *Confessions,* their dissociation is the ambition of Adams' narrative. Adams insists that it is only for the purposes of demonstration that the manikin persona "must have the air of reality; must be taken for real; must be treated as though it had life." Such a point of view requires a new term for our lexicon of the rhetoric of narrative; I suggest *necrospective.* As the narrative approaches its end, Adams describes himself as "a man who, holding open the door into the next world, regarded himself as merely looking round to take a last glance of this."

The scarcity of explicit personal revelations in *The Education,* which for T. S. Eliot calls into question its status as autobiography, is in truth one aspect of Adams' innovations in the autobiographical mode. What is remarkable about the narrative is not that there is really so little of the author in it but that the narrative depicts the author on such a diminished scale. The explanation for this trait is to be found, at least in part, in new theories of psychology, which Adams contemplated with grave apprehension. At the conclusion of the chapter "The Abyss of Ignorance" Adams numbers subconscious impulses among the supersensuous forces that, like X-rays, put the lie to society's body of acquired knowledge and open the mind directly onto chaos. The psyche is for Adams a balancing act in which stability is maintained through ingrained habit and external devices. Only through vigilant artifice, or the escape route of death, can the certain prospect of a "dissolving mind" be forestalled. The artifice and the escape are attained in *The Education* through the act of writing, which preserves Adams' identity as, at best, a failure and, at worst, a nullity. Outside the metaphor of education, it is chiefly as a failed writer that Adams identifies himself in the first thirty-three years, and twenty chapters, of *The Education.* The chapter "Failure," which marks the close of that period, contends that editorship of the *North Amer-*

ican Review effectively put an end to his writing career for seven years and meant that, as an author, "he was totally forgotten."

Though Adams recalls early events in his writing life with vivid detail, the narrative tone in which these events are presented insists that they are scarcely memorable. The facts of the matter are, to be sure, more flattering, but here we will follow the account *The Education* provides. As with so many later choices of direction in life, Adams first decided on a literary career because all else seemed to have failed him. He inaugurated the career as a student at Harvard, where he learned to anticipate failure in the pursuits for which a Harvard education prepared most of its undergraduates. Given the intellectual and social environment that prevailed at Harvard, Adams' ambition to be a writer was an unlikely one. He describes the choice as typical of his behavior in its uncommon and antiquated character. With a self-deprecating tone he considers typical of the Harvard man, however, Adams maintains that his talents as a collegian were far from uncommon. Even at the time, Adams states, his writing "seemed to him thin, commonplace, feeble." Throughout the account of early years readers are aware, of course, that the narrative point of view is controlled by an eminently accomplished writer in his sixties, one who has made a name for himself among the intelligentsia of the United States and England many times over as essayist, biographer, editor, historian and—by word of mouth—as novelist.

The first honor of his literary career, election as Class Day Orator at Harvard, Adams considered to be wrongly awarded since he thought himself largely unrepresentative of the graduating class. Yet, in his opinion it is precisely such negative self-evaluation that to a great extent typified the Harvard graduate, whose strongest traits were "self-criticism and self-consciousness." Thus, only in his commonplaceness did Adams feel akin to his classmates and, in that, they served as "so many mirrors of himself, an infinite reflection of his own shortcomings." Measured against others of his generation, Adams finds himself no better and little worse. In *The Education* this act of self-assessment through external standards is a method of self-portraiture based on foreshortened perspectives. Adams' self-irony in *The Education* is fitted for a manikin. One might expect the college youth to be diminutive in stature in the estimation of the distinguished writer, but even in an autobiographical statement Adams prepared for the senior yearbook his ambitions are expressed in a negative and devaluing manner: "My wishes are for a quiet and a literary life, as I believe that to be the happiest and in this country not the least useful."

Adams habit of belittling himself as a writer—captured most succinctly in "HOMUNCULUS SCRIPTOR," the mock epitaph he composed—may well have developed in reaction against the unassailable distinction of the Adams' family name. The ring to that name for Americans is above all political, but to the young Henry Adams it was equally literary, for there was a long and distinguished family tradition in public letters. In fact, down through his own generation the Adams' sons served as editors of their forefathers' political papers and as their official biogra-

phers. Father Charles Francis Adams found time in his prominent career as state legislator, newspaperman, foreign minister, and U.S. Congressman to write lives of his grandfather and grandmother, John and Abigail Adams, and to edit their papers and letters in addition to those of his father, John Quincy Adams. At about age ten, Henry Adams helped proofread the ten-volume *Works of John Adams* his father was then preparing. Picture for a moment grandson and great-grandson laboring over the literary remains of their ancestor, an American founding father. The Adams descendants were, as we see, the literary executors of their forefathers. Henry Adams was also, in some sense, their literary executioner.

Traditionally, writing for the Adams men was an adjunct to law and government, which was the genuine business of their lives. Like Hawthorne, Adams found no clear precedent within family history for writing as a career entirely in itself. Through two attempts to study law in preparation for the bar examinations, Henry Adams made first steps toward a career in keeping with family tradition. His progress was quickly halted, however—first by the lure of foreign travel, then by opportunities to accompany his father to Washington and London as personal secretary. Privy to the inner councils of Congress for a year and of the United States legation in England for seven, Henry Adams concluded that he was ill-fitted for politics or diplomacy. Education in these professions was, he wrote, "a long mistake." During this period, according to his autobiography, the only instruction of lasting value was in the form of writing lessons. They constituted a major part of his literary apprenticeship. From Washington Adams published a number of political items in Boston papers and from London he contributed frequently to the *New York Times,* but in *The Education* he characterizes his writing activities for the eight years as principally those of a functionary and copyist. Adams' anonymity as a correspondent was breached the first year of residence in London (1861) and he shortly thereafter put a stop to what was becoming a career in journalism. The shadows of Boston State House had loomed over the circumstances of his birth; his career as a mature essayist and historian began under the shadow of Minister Charles Francis Adams' diplomatic achievements. In the capacity of private secretary to the Minister, Henry Adams did all writing literally in the name of his father and, at that, he was not writing for publication but for the government's confidential records.

Since this was unquestionably a formative phase in his literary life, it is important to consider the scene from *The Education* in which Adams characterizes his duties and capabilities in the year 1863, at age twenty-five. After the outbreak of civil war in the United States, his father was engaged in a political struggle to halt British manufacture of warships destined for the Confederate navy. With his older brother Charles in the thick of military action at home, Henry Adams thought of his position abroad as that of a dutiful, unimaginative "volunteer" for the Minister. To Adams' mind, his role in the diplomatic skirmishes between the Union and the British government amounted to nothing since he was only a noncombatant, "sent to the rear" for safety. The issue of the warships was resolved successfully for the Union side immediately after the Minister sent to the British Foreign Secretary a declaration whose phrasing became famous. The dispatch closed with the sentence: "It would be superfluous in me to point out to your lordship that this is war!" To display his abilities as an apprentice writer and historian, Adams supposes that his father had asked him at the time to draft an explanatory paragraph on this sentence. In the character of private secretary, Adams develops what he takes to be the three-fold implication of the Minister's opening phrase. The point of the exercise in explication is to show that the rhetorical sway of "It would be superfluous in me" is for the most part unsensed by Adams' own "copying eye." As a *trope,* the phrase is a perfect example of *litotes,* or understatement; as a diplomatic strategy, it superbly balances caution with threat. Within *The Education*'s narrative, the implications of Minister Adams' declaration are made clear *before* the commentary is inserted, even for a reader previously unaware of the incident's details. What is superfluous to the declaration, as the autobiography facetiously demonstrates, is precisely the wordy commentary the clerk Henry Adams would have provided.

As with Charles Francis Adams' style of expression, so with his character, in the son's view: "The Minister's mind like his writings showed a correctness of form and line that his son would have been well pleased had he inherited." These seemingly enviable qualities of mind are expanded upon in an earlier chapter:

> Charles Francis Adams was singular for mental poise—absence of self-assertion or self-consciousness—the faculty of standing apart without seeming aware that he was alone—a balance of mind and temper that neither challenged nor avoided notice, nor admitted question of superiority or inferiority, of jealousy, of personal motives, from any source, even under great pressure. This unusual poise of judgment and temper, ripened by age, became the more striking to his son Henry as he learned to measure the mental faculties themselves, which were in no way exceptional either for depth or range. Charles Francis Adams's memory was hardly above average; his mind was not bold like his grandfather's or restless like his father's, or imaginative or oratorical—still less mathematical; but it worked with singular perfection, admirable self-restraint, and instinctive mastery of form. Within its range it was a model.

What the son finds distinctive about the father is thus not intellectual daring but restraint, not inventiveness but modest mastery, not flourish but balance. By aligning the quotations above, the reader detects relief on Henry Adams' part in the tacit admission that he is not truly his father's son with respect to the elder's "correctness of form and line." These are necessary attributes for the responsible and successful statesman but they are too narrow to suit the ultimate purposes of the creative writer and speculative thinker. When the son distinguishes the father from his forefathers by earmarking the qualities they possessed and he lacks, the reader has good reason to put the name Henry Adams beside the unclaimed "imaginative or oratorical" ability. Only it will enable the son to gain that

"depth and range" unreached by the father. *The Education* is infused with the conviction that the twentieth century denies the serious writer the mastery of form, the unity, enjoyed by the father in diplomacy and by Saint Augustine in autobiography. The agitated, assertive and adventurous mind, not the poised and restrained one, will provide the speculative history required to understand the era of dynamos. And, of course, Adams believed that the historian must develop "mathematical" abilities in order to account for recent historical change.

In fitting young men for the modern era, *The Education*'s preface advises, the manikin-author is committed to find fault with "the patchwork fitted on their fathers." Where the manikin-author is personally concerned, it means breaking the mold of paternal tradition, which is described as follows: "C. F. Adams was sure to do what his father had done, as his father had followed the steps of John Adams, and no doubt thereby earned his epithets." That the political world expected no less of young Henry Adams he knew full well. In the public announcement of his identity that prompted Adams to quit the newspapers at the end of 1861, for instance, the editor of the Boston *Courier* advised readers that the London correspondent

> has by no means degenerated from the hereditary ability of his family,—which now for four generations has either fulfilled high expectations, or, as in the present case, has given promise of future distinguished usefulness to the country.

Though *The Education* relentlessly minimizes Adams' usefulness, it also reveals that he meant to be of service to the country, but in ways self-consciously separate from those of his ancestors. We have seen that Henry Adams repudiates much of the family heritage of mind and character as ill-suited for modern times. Furthermore, the childless autobiographer wrote *The Education* in the awareness that he left behind no body of writing connected with public life to be edited by descendants, as the Adams men traditionally had done. Though one fourth-generation direct descendant, Charles Francis Adams, Jr., acted consistent to family usage by writing a biography of their father, his brothers Henry and Brooks arranged in 1905 to bar the public from the Adams archives for at least fifty years. Brooks abandoned his biography of John Quincy Adams after Henry annotated the manuscript copiously and criticized it severely. In explanation, Henry expressed contempt for the sixth President and loathing for that era. But he found himself and his own times no better: "The picture of our wonderful grandpa is a psychologic nightmare to his degenerate and decadent grandson."

Adams' suppression of egoism and his self-devaluation in *The Education* can be understood as a psychological defense that compensates for rebellion against paternal tradition. In accepting the phenomenon of multiple personality as described in the new psychology, Adams seems aware that the self-image *The Education* projects is a species of reaction-formation that reverses significant traits in the book's portrait of his father. The self-consciousness Adams says his father lacks entirely he possesses in excess. Where this trait would otherwise promote Romantic egoism, Adams confines its influence to the private sphere. In turn, the privacy of person so jealously guarded in *The Education* strikes the reader as a reaction against prominence of the family name in the public arena. Adams' most ambitious assertions of imagination he offered to the public anonymously (the novel *Democracy*), pseudonymously (the novel *Esther*), and posthumously (*The Education*). The large reprinting of *Mont-Saint-Michel and Chartes* for public sale in 1913 represents something of an exception to this practice, but when the work was originally printed in 1904 in a private and limited edition his name did not appear on the title page. Adams' most serious bid for public usefulness as a writer is his nine-volume history of the United States under the administrations of Jefferson and Madison. *The Education* disparages this work, to which he devoted more than ten years, calling it a merely local history whose audience numbered scarcely more than three readers.

While *The Education* singles out the father for his mental poise, it burlesques the son's precarious balance of mind. With an image that Samuel Beckett later uses to similar effect, Adams compares the modern psyche to a bicycle rider "mechanically balancing himself by inhibiting all his inferior personalities, and sure to fall into the subconscious chaos below, if one of his inferior personalities got on top." In this analogy, the only steady truth is the "sub-conscious chaos below." As surely as the supersensuous force of radium is "parricidal," so is the force of the subconscious. Both determine Adams' identity as "an American in search of a father," his self-characterization in a period when his father was still alive. After the latter's death, Henry expressed these sentiments about writing a life of his father:

> These biographies are murder, and in this case, to me, would be both patricide and suicide. They belittle the victim and the assassin equally. . . . I have sinned myself and deeply, and am no more worthy to be called anything, but, thank my diseased and dyspeptic nervous wreck, I did not assassinate my father.

Yet, as the above textual analysis strives to demonstrate, for Adams autobiography becomes no less an act of patricide than such a biography would be. In a compounded sense autobiography is for the son an exercise in belittling himself and, finally, in killing himself. In preparing *The Education,* Adams thought of himself as his own literary executor and executioner. The cover letter accompanying the copy sent to Henry James makes clear this intention: "The volume is a mere shield of protection in the grave. I advise you to take your own life in the same way, in order to prevent biographers from taking it in theirs." To narrate a life history with such motives is an act of necrospection.

The very ambition of Adams to treat history as a science makes *The Education* the instrument of his own symbolic destruction. Described by Adams as the intellectual effort "to fix a position for himself," the book posits him as a known quantity in order to proceed with the historical study of relations. We have seen that such effort is based on extrapolation—or triangulation—beyond Adams' life; indeed, it assumes his death so that individual existence

can be treated as a fixed position in the modern era, whose changes are unprecedented. Within the book's own terms, to treat an unknowable like the multiplicity of the modern individual's life and mind as known is to substitute matter for force, the inert for flux. *The Education* is an avowed attempt at historical synthesis. Unlike the scientific syntheses it refers to, however, the self-history alleges that "a point must always be soon reached where larger synthesis is suicide." The instance in world history where that point had been reached, according to *The Education,* was the turn of the nineteenth century into the twentieth, when political terrorism surged in Russia and the West, particularly in the form of suicidal assassination plots. To the "conservative Christian anarchist" (Adams' epithet for himself in this period), these plots brought an explosive end to society's complacent ideas of progress. Though Adams welcomed their consequences, the plots also caused him to wonder "which was he—the murderer or the murdered?"

Adams' education is as an historian, and as a writer of history the third- or non-person form of address comes naturally to him; it gives primacy to the event and not to the person. First-person address, on the other hand, is adapted to the speaker or the writer and centers expression on that individual as the point of origin. In linguistic terms, as Benveniste has argued, the differences between non-person and first-person forms of address correspond to differences between two types of expression—*history* and *discourse.* History entails the narration of past events, with the three components narration, past and events standing in equal importance. It imposes special limitations upon verbal categories of person and tense. Conventional autobiographical references to the historian as narrator (as *I*) and to the time frame of composition (the historian's *now*) are excluded. The present tense is avoided, with the exception of an atemporal mode such as the present of definition. For the simple future tense there is a substitute prospective tense. Benveniste observes that the fundamental tense in historical narration is "the tense of the event outside the person of a narrator." The extent to which *The Education of Henry Adams* employs these limitations on person and tense is evident on every page.

Discourse organizes expression in the category of linguistic person and in tenses related to the time frame of composition. The correlations of person and tense in discourse are signs of subjectivity (in the grammatical sense). Discourse situates person within the moment of expression. History situates the narrator outside the narrative. This is not to say, however, that historical writing is always devoid of discourse. Language, by its nature, permits immediate transfer from one form of expression to the other. Historical narration can be interrupted by discourse in order to permit the historian to comment on events and evidence. Gibbon and Michelet shape their histories around a point of discourse with which they identify themselves. For Gibbon that point is the ruins of the Roman Capitol and the ruin of an empire; for Michelet it is the French Revolution. In *The Education* the point of discourse for Adams is not a past or present event, but a future one: the moment of his own extinction. To follow definitions Roland Barthes formulates in his study of Balzac, Adams is present in *The Education* as a *figure* but not as a *person*. Not indicative of a psychological or philosophical entity, which would involve moral freedom and individual motives, the figure named Henry Adams functions in *The Education* as a textual site, as "an impersonal network of symbols combined under the proper name," in Barthes' words.

Fundamental to the book's attempt at historical synthesis is its exclusive use of third-person narration. In addition to the name Adams and the various epithets (of which "student" and "historian" are probably the most frequent), impersonal (*it*) and indefinite (*one*) pronouns also appear regularly as sentence subjects. In an essay on the style of autobiography, Jean Starobinski writes that such use of the third-person as a mode of self-reference suggests "solidification by objectivity." Starobinski finds as well that the "effacing of the narrator (who thereby assumes the impersonal role of historian) . . . works to the benefit of the event, and only secondarily reflects back upon the personality of the protagonist the glitter of actions in which he has been involved." In Adams' case, the "event" thus foregrounded is no less than the extinction of individuality.

The synthesizing consciousness of Henry Adams, which is the manifest rationale for *The Education*'s third-person form of address, quantifies individual life and reduces mind into the objects, not the movers, of modern history. The autobiography's narrative sets forth a theory of history in the closing chapters. The logic of history outlined there makes it appear that the individual is a nonentity at the mercy of historical and supersensual forces whose effects increase at an accelerating pace. By casting himself as a non-person, Adams demonstrates a historiography that sets "the feeble atom or molecule called man" adrift in a chaotic multiverse. What order and meaning the historian can provide are in calculations of energy and of massive phases abstracted completely from human factors. Within three years of completing *The Education*, Adams elaborated the theory in two essays, **"The Rule of Phase Applied to History"** and *A Letter to American Teachers of History*. The analogy between history and physical science reaches its terminus in the *Letter*. Human life considered as energy is a form of physical energy and is thus governed by the laws of physics. For Adams the most general and inevitable of these laws is the second law of thermodynamics, which states that the universe's energy is being constantly dissipated and is recoverable only at the cost of still greater energy. The tendency of history is thus the tendency toward entropy and the historian must "define his profession as the science of human degradation."

Adams terms the dynamic theory of history proposed in *The Education* "a vicious circle" whose "mathematical completeness approached perfection." R. P. Blackmur, in his unfinished study recently published, considers Adams' determinism to be a "circular argument in which the circle narrows to nothing." Blackmur's singularly sympathetic response to the play of thought in Adams' work balks at the final two historical essays, which he thinks represents "the breakdown, rather than the completion, of the ma-

ture mind." Considering the rhetoric of self-reference and the view of history in *The Education,* however, **"The Rule of Phase"** and the *Letter* can be seen to embody the necessary extension into pure theory of Adams' mature beliefs. The political sense of the term *non-person* is relevant here. The totalitarian state institutes the elimination of individuals and of entire classes or races of people in the name of historical necessity and scientific progress. While no sensible person could accuse Henry Adams of having publicly encouraged such practices, personal principles that can be accurately defined as totalitarian in nature are evident in many of his judgments against society and the modern period, including the one he makes in a letter to an English friend in 1893:

> I am myself more than ever at odds with my time, I detest it, and everything that belongs to it, and live only in the wish to see the end of it, with all its infernal Jewry.

Adams' anti-Semitism, like Ezra Pound's, functions in part as a personification of his historical pessimism. But it is by no means only that, and one commits a serious error in passing over such expressions of hatred as merely transient or secondary in the work of either writer. J. C. Levenson commits this error when he concludes that the anti-Semitism in Adams' writing should be viewed as "a datum of personal psychology like insomnia or addiction to privacy." Levenson finds that virulent reference to Jews "disfigures" Adams' late works, but he contends that it does so "inessentially." The Jew is essential, however, to the imagery in *The Education,* which opens with a comparison to the imagined circumstances at birth of an archetypal "Israel Cohen." Elsewhere, Adams adopts the racist caricature of "the Jew banker" to deplore corruption within the contemporary leisure class. In the chapter on his year of study in Berlin, he expresses revulsion toward the "derisive Jew laughter of Heine" that he fancies echoed among German intellectuals during the 1850's. In another chapter he conveys his sense of estrangement from American society in depicting its ready assimilation of the immigrant Jew "still reeking of the Ghetto, snarling a weird Yiddish." Ernest Samuels considers the vein of anti-Semitism in Adams "unfortunate" and attributes it to the Dreyfus affair and the French propaganda campaigns of the 1890's, which "lent a new vocabulary to the social satirist." Yet, Adams' anti-Semitism is already distinct in 1888, when in a letter to Elizabeth Cameron he protests the circumstance that "the German Jew should be the aim and end of our greatest triumphs in science and civilisation."

The social and economic evolution that led to the elevation of Jews to positions of power and privilege—in actual proportions far below the one Adams hysterically conjectured—is for him a symptom of the degeneration of Western Culture. Adams' pessimism and nihilism rationalize anti-Semitism within a sweeping interpretation of history. In the context of American history, Adams identifies the emergence of a powerful immigrant social class as an immediate threat to the survival of the country's traditional ruling class. The rising class is personified in the figure of "a Polish Jew fresh from Warsaw or Cracow—. . . a furtive Yacoob or Ysaac." *The Education* indulges in racial antagonism that stems from the irony, tinged with resentment, that he, an Adams, "American of Americans, with Heaven knew how many Puritans and Patriots behind him" is eclipsed from power by a recently settled population. Unexpectedly, he identifies himself with the country's original victims of European settlement: "he was no worse off than the Indians or the buffalo who had been ejected from their heritage by his own people." Adams' one consolation is that "the defeat was not due to him, nor yet to any superiority of his rivals." The "defeat" is Adams' symbol for the loss by America's old elite of their customary powers. The "defeat" is fictional rather than historical. At the time Adams wrote, the composition of the ruling class was, more accurately, being expanded and diversified with the internationalization of capital.

As we see, Adams relates his sense of personal nullity to the rise of an immigrant population and the accompanying decline of the nation's first families. In this matter, his social analysis is formulated in terms of racial threat. The crowning irony is that Adams, supposing himself a member of an endangered elite, summons an analogy to the victims of that elite's genocidal policies. Adams seems to relish the role of victim, which is a purely imaginary one in his case. This sense of victimization is consistent with his determinist views on history. To Adams' mind, history's progressive concentration of material forces has made the modern self—whether it be that of poet or politician—a nonentity. Through an ironic inversion typical of Adams' imagination, defeat of the modern self is transposed into a victory for the objective, scientific method of historical analysis.

For the critic Philippe Lejeune, autobiography in the third person is a means of internal distancing and self-confrontation. Related psychological effects are involved in *The Education*'s form of address, but on an idiomatic level Adams' use of the non-person as self-reference has one major additional effect. *He* can serve as a form of address referring to someone present when one wishes to remove him from the personal sphere. In this form *he* can be employed in two expressions with opposite values. On the one hand, it can stand as a sign of respect, as in the polite phrase "His Majesty." On the other, it can convey scorn by indicating that the individual addressed is unworthy of personal acknowledgment. Adams intensifies the affect of self-annihilation in his autobiography through uses of the latter non-personal form. As reflected in *The Education*'s rhetorical tactic of casting him as a nonperson, Adams is an historian who posits depersonalization as a cardinal premise. In the *Letter* he proposes to "treat primitive humanity as a volume of human molecules of unequal intensities, tending to dissipate energy, and to correct the loss by concentrating mankind into a single, dense mass." The *Letter* legitimizes the premise of depersonalization as the dictate of modern history and contemporary science.

The link of Adams' anti-Semitism and his theory of history with totalitarian thought becomes clearer when we consider them in the context of Hannah Arendt's study *The Origins of Totalitarianism*. Reflecting on the extent of "organized oblivion" of individualism under totalitarian rule,

Arendt concludes that in such circumstances a victim's death is deprived of "its meaning as the end of a fulfilled life." The death of one the state has already made into a non-person through arrest or exile simply sets "a seal on the fact that he had never really existed." Adams expresses a comparable estimation of the individual matter of life and death when he advises readers of *The Education* that the manikin-author "must be treated as though it had life. Who Knows? Possibly it had!" Though the tone here is jocular, Adams is no less thorough than totalitarian policy in making individual existence seem superfluous. The images of degradation, failure and anomie in Adams' late work delineate a consciousness that, following Arendt's analysis, is in accord with totalitarian ideology in significant respects.

Arendt observes that total power is maintained only as long as the state keeps the masses in a constant pitch of mobilization and movement. This policy of impermanence and the propaganda against democratic political order produce conditions whereby "neither nature nor history is any longer the stabilizing source of authority for the actions of mortal men" and state terror can prevail. For Adams, as for Oswald Spengler (whose *Decline of the West* was published the year of Adams' death), the historical direction Western society has taken is irretrievably one toward corruption and ultimate dissolution. In his *Letter to American Teachers of History*, Adams describes the historical motion of his times as an entropic trajectory that is unalterable. As final proof of this dire forecast, Adams offers testimony from contemporary speculations in the fields of medicine and psychology about world-wide "enfeeblement of the Will" and the degeneration of national populations into the "crowd." While Adams never actively associated with any extremist political movements, he drew the worst possible conclusions about the modern era and on these conclusions based his historiography.

While in France during the Dreyfus affair, Adams read with enthusiasm the outpouring of reactionary propaganda, particularly the journalism of Edouard Drumont. In July 1896, he writes: "Here I pass the day reading Drumont's anti-semitic ravings, . . . buying every newspaper I can lay my hands on, to see if I can find the limits of the chaos of Europe." A month later he informs a correspondent: "I read with interest actually the extravagance of Drumont—*France Juive, Libre Parole*, and all. Suppose you try his '*Dernière Bataille*,' or '*La Fin d'un Monde*.' . . . But of course, all this is anarchy pure and simple." A taste for political apocalypse and a delight in social chaos are components of Adams' nihilism. The escalating turmoil over Dreyfus confirmed the pessimism that underlies his later theory of history. The historiography proves compatible with the inhuman outlook of totalitarianism.

The form of narration and the rhetoric of self-reference in *The Education* conform to the ideology reflected in Adams' dynamic theory of history and rule of phase. Shaped as history and as a demonstration of the theory and rule, the autobiography organizes its materials in a strict chronology. Chapter titles are accompanied by dates, which are arranged in the absolute sequence of an annal. In the original, private edition of 1907, the dates alone stood as chapter titles. The one exception to the book's temporal continuity is the unnarrated twenty year period that separates chapters twenty and twenty-one. This lacuna in the narrative is an autobiographical example of the historical discontinuity Adams argues in the concluding chapters. The last chapter, dated 1905, covers the period in which Adams was completing *The Education,* but the form of address remains in the tense and person of historical narration.

The first five years of the new century, years contemporary to the conception and completion of the book, are functionally an excluded present in the narrative. Adams viewed the century's inaugural decade as the breaking point in the continuity of Western history:

> The movement from unity into multiplicity, between 1200 and 1900, was unbroken in sequence, and rapid in acceleration. Prolonged one generation longer, it would require a new social mind. As though thought were common salt in indefinite solution it must enter a new phase subject to new laws. Thus far, since five or ten thousand years, the mind had successfully reacted, and nothing yet proved that it would fail to react—but it would need to jump.

On the plane of autobiographical chronology, Adams' lifetime thus falls within the terminal phase of the old historical order.

In consigning personal experience to history, Adams casts his current reflections, opinions and comparisons (materials that conventionally belong to discourse) in forms of the past tense. Historical narration—in which no person speaks and the events seem to narrate themselves—is thus sustained. The authority behind *The Education*'s speculations on modern society and politics is not acknowledged to be personal. Instead, history itself is made to speak, as in the following reification and personification: "History saw few lessons in the past that would be useful in the future." Through such formulations, the non-person form of address in *The Education* reflects an abdication of individual power, of political agency and of historical responsibility. The lesson taught through *The Education*'s rhetoric, form of narration and theory of history is one of submission and "passive obscurity" in the face of historical destiny (pp. 117-34).

> *James Goodwin, "The Education of Henry Adams: A Non-Person in History," in* Biography, *Vol. 6, No. 2, Spring, 1983, pp. 117-35.*

Linda A. Westervelt (essay date 1984)

[*In the following excerpt, Westervelt argues that, despite his apparent aversion to categorical systems of order, Adams uses doubleness in* The Education of Henry Adams *as a contradictory means of imposing order and education on his readers.*]

Since education for Henry Adams is the process of inventing a method with which to assimilate experience, without the possibility of a final ordering system, it seems important to examine the apparent contradiction between the numerous instances of doubleness, a central ordering principle of theme and style in *The Education,* and Adams' claim that any attempt at ordering must falsify experience. Not original to *The Education,* doubleness is inherent in autobiography: the self-conscious teller and the observed self, the time of the telling and the time of the action, fiction and fact. Even beyond these generic qualities, Adams incorporates and calls attention to other thematic and stylistic dualities. From the outset Adams makes a special claim to doubleness as central and even peculiar to his experience: "From the earliest childhood the boy was accustomed to feel that, for him, life was double." His experience entices Adams with the possibility of an ordering principle, but one which he repeatedly rejects. Doubleness, both invented and discovered, becomes a test, a way of setting up a problem for examination, a method whose vulnerability to revision is its main feature and its flaw. Because it is never final, this revision, which offers the chance to gain insights by changing one's view and thus to transcend formally the earlier, more limited self, consoles Adams for the passage of time. Then, engaging the reader in evaluating the doubles that the text sets up, Adams creates a bond with the reader, a potential source of greater consolation. Looking at doubleness in the theme, sentence structure, and "manikin" will help in understanding Adams' attention to educating the reader.

Adams represents doubleness as a way of shaping and informing nearly all his experience: Adams/Brooks, Quincy/Boston, type/variation, success/failure, the Virgin/the Dynamo, multiplicity/unity. Among these, the first two sets seem provided, while others (including the chapter titles) seem imposed by the author. Adams juxtaposes these poles, not to synthesize them, but to hold them at the same time, in order to see how each constitutes the other. For example, explaining Quincy as "summer and country," the "multiplicity of nature," and Boston as winter, town, and "compulsory learning" characterizes each more fully by describing its opposite. Although Adams grants Quincy and Boston separate chapters, Boston is introduced early in the Quincy chapter and Quincy is mentioned throughout the Boston chapter. The forces are "hostile" and "separated" or distinct, yet they are attractive and inseparable, with each pole existing fully only in light of the other. Together they are a unit, but not a unity or a synthesis. The closest one can come to truth is to hold both in mind at once, but to prevent their losing their particularity or their identity by merging them in thought.

From the outset Adams carefully avoids setting up any poles as a comfortable "either / or." For example, his "Washington education" consists of his perceiving George Washington and Mount Vernon as a contradiction of the South:

> To the New England mind, roads, schools, clothes, and a clean face were connected as part of the law of order or divine system. The moral of this Virginia road was clear, and the boy fully learned it. Slavery was wicked, and slavery was the cause of this road's badness which amounted to social crime—and yet, at the end of the road and product of the crime stood Mount Vernon and George Washington.

Washington is "an ultimate relation, like the Pole Star," which stays constant and is a source of direction amidst the chaos. Mount Vernon is not a synthesis of New England and the South, nor is it a new pole against which to form another opposition. It is a kind of center, yet it exists outside the opposition. Washington is an accident. His existence at Mount Vernon prevents any easy pigeonholing and denies the absolute designation of New England and the South as contraries. This early lesson teaches Adams both the desire for unity and the need to resist such oversimplification. If Adams sees either pole, such as Quincy or Boston, the North or the South, order or chaos, as able to supplant or to incorporate the other or if he sees the two poles as reconcilable, he falsifies experience. The opposition between North and South remains valid, but, because of Washington, the two categories are not exclusive, nor is the division entirely reliable as a principle upon which to base value judgments. One can come closest to understanding the poles by viewing them from an interface or "knife-edge" between them and seeing both, not as constituting a spectrum, but as commenting on one another. The two poles must be held in suspension, with perception moving rapidly between the two.

Before turning to the reflection of this way of seeing in Adams' style, two further examples of dualism in the theme of *The Education* must be considered, examples which emphasize the tension of the dualism and also incorporate the idea of process. Autobiography, more than any other kind of book, is a revenge against time in that it is the author's attempt to make himself permanent by means of the book. He gets not the chance to live again, as Benjamin Franklin humorously wished, but the chance to see again and to make past acts permanent via writing, which will be re-experienced by readers in the future. If he does not "re-live," he can "re-view" and "revise" to the extent that he selects and gives form to the events of his life. Autobiography also exists outside linear time in the sense that the author creates mythic time by bringing the past into the present and forcing them to co-exist in an eternal present. The time of the narrative transcends linear time since the entire life is present at once with each of its aspects reflecting on every other as the result of their being informed by the author's way of perceiving them and of their existing continuously in the book. Yet within this mythic time that his autobiography creates, Adams demythologizes the ideas of education and unity, the self, heritage, and America: education was a failure and "Unity was the dream of man." Nor does he allow the reader any illusion of escape from linear time, especially with his description of his sister's death, his comparison of America with Rome, and his discussion of entropy, the theory that the universe is running down and gradually moving towards stasis. Throughout *The Education,* rather than downplaying the opposition between the poles, here mythic time and linear time, Adams actually heightens the conflict by refusing to ignore either one or to make them harmonious and thus creates tension in the book. The pain of Louisa's death is brought into the present of the book with the possibility, inherent in the genre, that this special space of the text might offer consolation by giving meaning to the loss. Adams chooses to write in a genre which, by definition, allows the opportunity for mythologizing or transforming the life and thus might offer solace, but which, in theme and style, he forces to undercut this sort of renewal.

A second example, the Dynamic Theory of History, contains a similar tension, but it also emphasizes the idea of process and thus adds another dimension to doubleness. Here the tension exists between Adams' desire for a metatheory, a formula against which to evaluate experience and to make value judgments, and his knowledge that the concept is not possible and that any such theory is inadequate. His theory, or his way of "account[ing] to himself for himself somehow," is as inclusive and as close to some abstract notion of "truth" as possible, at the same time that it is personal, tentative, and temporary. The theory, like *The Education* for which it is a climax, attempts to include in a sort of quivering balance an end or synthesis that is still in process (by being continuously verified), particular instances within a holistic overview, chaos and unity. Denying rest and refusing to limit the plenitude of experience arbitrarily, Adams affirms multiplicity. However, Adams' chief certainty—that until he dies his understanding will be revised continuously—undermines the idea that writing an autobiography gains its author revenge against time and allows him to live on. Continued existence is problematic, not only because Adams' opinions may change, but also because his readers, if any, will have changed. He discusses this problem of audience in Chapter XXXIV:

> He could see that the new American—the child of incalculable coal-power, chemical power, electric power, and radiating energy, as well as of new forces yet undetermined—must be a sort of God compared with any former creation of nature. . . . Every American who lived into the year 2000 would know how to control unlimited power. He would think in complexities unimaginable to an earlier mind. . . . To him the nineteenth century would stand on the same plane with the fourth—equally childlike—and he would only wonder how both of them, knowing so little, and so weak in force, should have done so much.

The last sentence, especially, sounds plaintive—a plea that the twentieth-century man respect his ancestor, who, however "weak" and ignorant, has made the new man possible. Although Adams hints in *The Education* that "barely one in ten" minds can profitably respond to such teaching as his book offers and in a letter claims that he prefers this elite audience, his mentioning readers reveals his facing the problem of audience.

The doubles proliferate. The certainty of unpredictable revision, the same certainty that makes Adams' theory dynamic while it qualifies his revenge against time, also denies the contradictory idea that in producing the book the author reifies, or in a sense kills, himself. This second pole, reification, surfaces in *The Education* as well as in the circumstances of its publication. Writing about the proposed *Education* to Henry James, Adams puns on writing one's autobiography as "tak[ing one's] own life": "I advise you to take your own life in the same way, in order to prevent biographers from taking it in theirs." The depersonalized "manikin," literally a form, is constructed. As artifact it serves not as an ideal or a representative, but as a convenience. The sacrifice of the ego, Adams implies in the Preface, is necessary if "the study of relation" is to be accurate. However, his restricting *The Education* to one hundred privately printed copies for eleven years, a provisional version open to revision by others as well as by himself, his threat to destroy the manuscript, and his refusal to allow publication or completion of the manuscript, to cause its continued existence as an object, until after his death offer evidence of Adams' resistance to reification. Insisting on a "dynamic" theory, Adams causes the text itself to include activity and thus resist stasis. Adams draws attention to the feared pole—here self-destruction and elsewhere failure, diachronic or linear time, and chaos—and refuses the reader comfortable illusions. At the same time, though, the relationship between the poles, the necessity of one's constituting the other, assures the reader that the feared pole will not supplant the other: process, success, synchronic or mythic time, and unity exist as surely as their counterparts. Both are equally valid. The duality does not disappear into a hierarchy. By insisting that both poles, process and reification, exist at once, Adams compels the reader to consider that the lesson is not in either pole but hovers in the changing, dynamic relationship between them. Thus, while the tension that results from refusing to deny either pole in a duality destroys illusions, the tension is also creative since it incorporates process into the book and so works against the objectification of self which writing a book entails. Both living on and reification are true and not true at the same time: *The Education* exists as a book, a thing, and yet the education it describes denies the possibility of education as an entity. This balancing on the "knife-edge," the means by which Adams' education has proceeded, finds its fullest expression in the Dynamic Theory of History, but the paradigm appears in the sentence structure as well.

At crucial points in *The Education,* Adams uses a sentence pattern—SV; but SV—which holds time in suspension while it forces the reader to hover between the two poles. Two of these sentences seem particularly noteworthy, the first because it sets forth at the outset the paradox of Adams' position, and the second because it comments on order. On the first page of the text of *The Education,* Adams writes:

> Had he been born in Jerusalem under the shadow of the Temple and circumcised in the Synagogue by his uncle the high priest, under the name of Israel Cohen, he would scarcely have been more distinctly branded, and not much more heavily handicapped in the races of the coming century, in running for such stakes as the century was to offer; but, on the other hand, the ordinary traveller, who does not enter the field of racing, finds advantage in being, so to speak, ticketed through life, with the safeguards of an old, established traffic.

Adams uses Judaism metaphorically to imply his specialness. It would not have mattered if he had been branded as an outsider; such marking could hardly have hindered him in a political career more than the name Adams. If he enters "the races," the name, which ought to entitle

him to privilege, is a hindrance. Paradoxically, Adams can enjoy advantage from his ancestry only if he gives up the career that the heritage seems to make appropriate for him. He is one of the "chosen," but the mark has mysteriously become a "handicap." The paradox is heightened by the structure of the compound-complex sentence, a structure which can hold the opposites in balance. The first part of the sentence is complex and defines the heritage or "brand" as a limitation. A semicolon and "but" divide the independent clauses. The re-definition which follows provides the contradiction: the one who does not enter the race "finds advantage" in being ticketed. With the choice not to run, the "brand" becomes a "ticket," a "safeguard." Using the conjunction "but," Adams contrasts two similar grammatical elements which are joined in one sentence. "But" signals a change of direction to the reader, at the same time that it does not suggest mutually exclusive alternatives (or), additions (and), explanations (for), or denials (nor). Rather, "but" heightens the double change of expectation. In the first part, the reader might suppose heritage to be an advantage, but it is a limitation. Then, what follows "but" denies the very expectation fostered in the first part of the sentence: it turns out that heritage can be advantageous, after all, albeit in a curtailed way. The second part of the sentence expands and revises the first part, but the second part does not supplant or destroy the first. "But" links the two parts and implies their similarity and their difference at the same time.

This recurring sentence structure—the compound sentence whose elements are joined and contrasted by "but"—reflects not only the doubleness of life that intrigues Adams, but also the particular relation which the poles have to one another. Adams oscillates between two contradictory opinions, each of which is held in succession. Because they are written, they exist as two fixed points in the text. However, when they are perceived by a reader, who reads the words in linear sequence, the second pole supplants the first. On reflecting further, however, the reader understands that since the poles or contraries constitute each other, neither destroys the other. Both parts of the sentence exist in a dynamic relationship. Just as Adams avoids oversimplifying the opposition between Quincy and Boston, he also resists closure with his sentence structure. Its openness invites the reader to return to the beginning of the sentence and then move back and forth between the two parts. Of course, the reader may not respond to the openness—either by not perceiving it or by attempting synthesis to resolve the confusion—but Adams' calling attention to the sentence pattern by repetition indicates his attempt to educate the reader to a new way of seeing. (pp. 23-8)

Besides creating expectations by means of his style, Adams shows more direct concern for his reader's response, a feature appropriate to a work that claims to be didactic. Whether the autobiographer wants to justify his life, to receive the affirmation of his community, to teach, or simply to shape his life into an artistic form, he, more than other narrative artists, overtly reveals his consciousness that his text must be realized by the reader if he is to succeed. The relationship between author and reader, with the open-ended text as a meeting ground, offers one more opportunity to study doubleness in *The Education.* That relationship becomes more apparent, however, when the manikin, Adams' lens, is more clearly understood.

Adams' writing an autobiography, a genre whose generating impulse is self-revelation, contrasts with his referring to himself in the third person and his omitting and changing the facts of his life, both of which obscure rather than reveal him. On the one hand, despite the use of third person, the distance between the author and the manikin is often small. *The Education* is not impersonal; the reader can easily substitute "I" for "he" without making other significant changes. Adams never wonders what "he" thought. He does not cast doubt on his knowledge of the manikin's thoughts, as otherwise omniscient narrators sometimes do in novels. When the manikin is in doubt about the effect of scarlet fever, for example, the narrator does not question or go beyond the manikin's assessment: "Henry Adams never could make up his mind. . . ." In other words, the narrator and the manikin appear to hold the same view. Nevertheless, even though the potential for identification exists, with his use of the third person pronoun Adams never allows the narrator of *The Education* to be viewed as identical with the subject, however close they may seem. Subject and object tend to merge in autobiography with the use of "I." Adams' use of the third person pronoun prevents this fusion of subject and object by treating them as poles, and thus he forces the reader to remain aware that they are separate, even at the end when the older manikin increasingly resembles the narrator. Indeed, by dramatizing the generic division between self-conscious teller and observed self, Adams makes explicit that he both creates himself and gives value to his creation by writing it down, even at the sacrifice of the illusion that the actual author can live on via a text.

Often in *The Education,* Adams makes the point that particular theories do not concern him except as they reveal a deeper structure:

> No one means all he says, and yet very few say all they mean, for words are slippery and thought is viscous; but since Bacon and Newton, English thought had gone on impatiently protesting that no one must try to know the unknowable at the same time that everyone went on thinking about it. The result was as chaotic as kinetic gas; but with the thought a historian had nothing to do. He sought only its direction.

Adams makes similar statements about other theories elsewhere in *The Education* and about Catholic theology in *Mont-Saint-Michel and Chartres.* This way of presenting the goal of his quest offers a clue to the status of the manikin. Adams is anxious to focus the readers's attention not on particulars but on generalizations—movement and structure. With Rousseau's *Confessions* as a warning against egotism, Adams chooses to examine the education, not the self. As reflector, the manikin, in an ironic reversal of the metaphor of the form on which clothing is draped, divests himself or "get[s] rid of his own beliefs because they color what he sees." Thus, he empties himself or offers himself as a fixed "point of relation" representative of the multiplicity of the twentieth century. Using himself plus Amiens Cathedral and Thomas Aquinas as fixed

points in the thirteenth century, Adams can triangulate and project into the future. "As teacher, he needed to speak for others than himself." Using the manikin to represent objectivity, the emptying of the self necessary to the search for essence, Adams teaches the reader to look beyond the particulars to uncover the form.

On the other hand, it is primarily "by action on man [that] all known forces may be measured." To measure change requires a perceiver:

> Clearly if he was bound to reduce all these forces to a common value, this common value could have no measure but that of their attraction on his own mind. He must treat them as they had been felt; as convertible, reversible, interchangeable attractions on thought. He made up his mind to venture it; he would risk translating rays into faith.

If one can "know nothing but the motions which impinge on his senses," then Adams, who lived figuratively in the eighteenth and literally in the nineteenth and twentieth centuries and who is both curious and receptive to change, is a particularly valuable vehicle. Because of his heritage and early education, he claims to have special understanding of the transition from the eighteenth to the nineteenth century. Because of his later self-imposed search for education, he registers the moment of transition from the nineteenth to the twentieth century. Early in *The Education,* Adams characterizes himself as a "variation" of the type of the Adams and Brooks families. His being a variation, a spectator rather than an actor, the only male Adams in four generations not to hold public office or to be a lawyer, fits him for his search, since he has been able to devote his energy to "reacting" rather than to doing. For example, he and Hay can discuss international relations, but Adams is the freer because, while he has similar knowledge, he remains independent of public opinion and does not have to expend energy implementing the policies he creates. In another context, that of Darwin's theory, "variation" permits evolution. As a "variation," Adams is a deviation, the beginning of a new line.

Yet Adams writes of "risk" and "venture," calls this new education "hazardous," and compares himself with "Sir Lancelot." He describes being carried away by his hobby, writes of having offered himself to the task but of wanting to "escape" what he has to see. When Adams decides to continue his quest, the words imply that in risking the vision of chaos he may be annihilated:

> Beyond the lines of force felt by the senses, the universe may be—as it has always been—either a supersensuous chaos or a divine unity, which irresistibly attracts, and *is either life or death to penetrate* (my emphasis).

From both directions, then, becoming a manikin and accepting the role of perceiving knight, Adams risks death. But, as with the Dynamic Theory of History, he refuses the illusions that would follow if he were to ignore or favor one perspective over the other. Besides exposing himself to terrible knowledge, Adams, with even more ambivalence, lays himself open to prying eyes and offers himself as the one who marks and celebrates the moment of discontinuity, although he limits the exposure in this last sense. The special attributes that make Adams the appropriate filter—his heritage, his education, his responsiveness, and the time he has been given—also, as one "brought up among Puritans," make him liable to render an account "for himself" and so make his continuing his education a "duty."

As a balancing mechanism, a "convenience" for measuring force that must first have been "felt" by a particular person, the manikin is precarious, for Adams still faces self-destruction from without and within: misunderstanding by his readers, exposure to chaos, reification, error from subjectivity and narrow vision, becoming outmoded, embarrassment. But Adams' writing *The Education* anyway affirms the value of the self as the basis for value judgments and the acceptance of this responsibility. The lesson is as much in the last part of *"Vis Nova,"* the preface to **"A Dynamic Theory of History,"** as in the theory itself, for in *"Vis Nova"* Adams concludes that, while the temptation is to avoid responsibility, one must "account *to himself* for himself" if he has any "self-respect" (my emphasis). Having wondered in *The Education* if he is "worth educating," he writes later in a letter that the book has "served its only purpose by educating *me.*" His attempt at interpretation, *The Education,* constitutes his act of faith in himself as worthy of education. Nevertheless, despite the resistance to the reader which Adams shows with his claim that the book benefits only him, with his remarks that very few can respond to education, with his ambivalence toward publication, and with his protective invention, the manikin, once he decides to publish, even posthumously, Adams allows the text to be realized by its readers. Thus, he recognizes others as worthy of being educated as well. In a letter to Elizabeth Cameron, 13 May 1905, Adams displays less indignation than usual in his later letters:

> Among the two or three hundreds of millions of people about us in Europe and America, our public could hardly be five hundred. . . . For my own practical life, the number has certainly never exceeded a score. Anything which has helped to bring that score into closer understanding and sympathy, has been worth doing. Any expression which makes on me the illusion of having done anything towards sympathy,— apart from the effect of making me hopeless,—is as near positive satisfaction as St. Francis or Pascal or I could reach. We never despised the world or its opinions; we only failed to find out its existence.

It is here, nevertheless—between the poles of author and reader—that the most serious tension of the book exists. That the incompleteness of the text is protective, making it difficult, even private, has been shown, but the incompleteness is also openness and so, paradoxically, affirms the reader's activity by requiring him to participate.

The last chapter of *Mont-Saint-Michel and Chartres,* "St. Thomas Aquinas," which Adams says is crucial to understanding the end of *The Education,* clarifies his concept of audience. Adams resembles Aquinas in terms of both the range of thought he attempts and the freedom that he ac-

cords man. In *Chartres,* Adams makes an extended analogy between the theology of St. Thomas and the architecture of the Cathedral at Beauvais, both of which were begun at the high point of medieval thought, but neither of which was completed. Adams fears that just as the thought that inspired the cathedral of Thomas is outmoded at the time of its building, so too the written text will no longer have a wide audience, only a "band of survivors." He worries that he will seem naive to the twentieth-century man, superior in his ability to "deal in contradictions," control "unlimited power," and think with a "new social mind."

The central problem for medieval architect and theologian, both artists according to Adams, is one of audience. Cathedral and philosophy are each constructed as a meeting place between man and God, but "the process of getting God and man under the same roof—of bringing two independent energies under the same control—required a painful effort." Once Adams authorizes publication of *The Education,* the text becomes as public as the theology of Thomas or the cathedrals of the Middle Ages. As an encyclopedic work of art that uses the past to survey the future, Adams' text is also a meeting place, a symbolic space where reader and author can consider ultimate matters. Writing with a didactic purpose, Adams works for man, even "drags" him into the edifice which is "cold," barren, and "failed" in its purpose without an audience. Again, Adams takes his clue from Thomas' apparently contradictory solution: allowing that man has free will. Instead of despairing that the reader has power, even ultimate power, in completing or rejecting the text, Adams exploits this potential by proposing to be his descendant's "pupil":

> For this new creature, born since 1900, a historian asked no longer to be teacher or even friend; he asked only to be a pupil, and promised to be docile, for once, even though trodden under foot. . . .

This role is not literally possible except perhaps in Adams' having imagined and anticipated the twentieth-century man and written *The Education* in part responding to what that vision has taught him. Adams' role as pupil implies a dialogue with the reader, the twentieth-century man, a phenomenological view of the text whereby the reader, in realizing the text, recreates the manikin whom it presents, "treating it as though it has life" and in that way giving it life.

But, in asking the twentieth-century man to teach him, Adams toys with anarchy in the form of the dissolution of his text into multiple interpretations by his audience and so follows the example of the Virgin, whose force is fecundity. His generosity is a compliment to the reader. Although Adams must have power in order to share it, he calls attention in this passage to his willingness to do so, somewhat as the Virgin dispenses grace. The submissiveness of his posture is notable: "asked only," "promised to be docile," "trodden under foot." Adams more commonly refers to himself in *The Education* as a "student," but here he uses "pupil," a more modest word which originally meant a minor or a ward and only later came to mean one, especially a young person, who is taught. In diminishing the importance of his priority to the reader, Adams limits the customary assumption that a text creates its reader and so destroys the hierarchy between reader and author. In minimizing his priority, Adams constitutes the text as a space where reader and author are both active and creative. Paradoxically, in acknowledging his role as pupil, he becomes a teacher in the fullest sense.

With theme, sentence structure, manikin, and now his relationship with the reader, Adams denies hierarchy, even at the expense of "form," because such systematizing is inconsistent with his epistemology as well as because it leaves out experience which he feels to be true. Hierarchy is a reductive and arbitrary ordering principle which heeds neither chaos nor the reason for man's compulsive search for order. As Adams sees the matter, humans search for order so consistently because of the intuition that chaos underlies reality and because of the fear which accompanies this hunch. Always looking beyond, Adams here is looking for the motive behind the insistent urge. Therefore, he incorporates chaos into the book via gaps and puzzles, tension, process, irony, and disillusionment in order to compel the reader to feel the confusion and to enact the failure of the search, the toppling of certainties each time. Adams does not prove that the process is futile. Rather, his purpose is just the opposite: he demonstrates that the urge is insistent, and he persuades the reader to value it. The one "correct" insight that man has always had is to value the search, however he has symbolized the forces he sought. Since all man can know is what he feels, unity, as a motivating principle, has a truth value, even if the particular theories invented to support it are not true. Further, the value of the principle originates with man and may not exist as an outside standard. The pursuit does not matter, except to the self. Adams affirms that, although man may make "blunders" in conceiving particular theories, "he never made a mistake in the value he set on the whole." Just as Thomas Aquinas argues *"ab defectu"* to prove "the perfection of a machine by the number of its imperfections," Adams declares that the value of the search is demonstrated by the failure of the results, for the fact that man keeps searching is testimony to his vigor. Leaving the text open and envisioning his reader as having such freedom, Adams risks anarchy—the absence of the restraint and order that a text imposes on the reader, a fluidity that would deny the text as an entity. If Adams has taught his reader "how to react," then *The Education,* his act of faith in himself, becomes his act of faith in the twentieth-century man. (pp. 30-6)

> *Linda A. Westervelt, "Henry Adams and the Education of His Readers," in* The Southern Humanities Review, *Vol. XVIII, No. 1, Winter, 1984, pp. 23-37.*

FURTHER READING

Conder, John J. "*The Education of Henry Adams:* The Cre-

ation of a World of Force." In his *A Formula of His Own: Henry Adams's Literary Experiment,* pp. 85-151. Chicago: University of Chicago Press, 1970.

Examines the diverse themes of individual chapters in *The Education.*

Cooley, Thomas. "The Dissolving Man: Henry Adams." In his *Educated Lives: The Rise of Modern Autobiography in America,* pp. 27-49. Columbus: Ohio State University Press, 1976.

Contends that Adams unconsciously communicated a sense of his own psychological determinism in *The Education* in his seemingly objective emphasis on mechanistic historical and cultural forces.

Leslie, Shane. Review of *The Education of Henry Adams,* by Henry Adams. *The Dublin Review* 164, No. 329 (April-June 1919): 218-32.

Favorable overview of *The Education.*

Lesser, Wayne. "Criticism, Literary History, and the Paradigm: *The Education of Henry Adams.*" *PMLA* 97 (May 1982): 378-94.

Seeks to explain *The Education* "as a disciplinary inquiry and to demonstrate the necessity of understanding the book's achievement in terms of its disciplinary aims and reflective procedures."

Levenson, J. C. "Modern Man in a Multiverse." In his *The Mind and Art of Henry Adams,* pp. 289-350. Cambridge, Mass.: Riverside Press, 1957.

Discusses the influence of Adams's social and political beliefs on *The Education.*

Mitchell, Lee Clark. "'But This Was History': Henry Adams' 'Education' in London Diplomacy." *The New England Quarterly* LII, No. 3 (September 1979): 358-76.

Traces Adams's account in *The Education* and in his personal letters of his years in London, contending that "to dramatize his twin themes of chaos in the world and the failure of education, Adams knowingly falsified motives and deliberately misinterpreted events to a degree previously unsuspected."

Monteiro, George. "Henry Adams' Jamesian Education." *The Massachusetts Review* XXIX, No. 2 (Summer 1988): 371-84.

Examines the social and literary connections between Adams and Henry James.

Smith, Thomas R. "The Objectivity of *The Education of Henry Adams.*" In *Studies in Autobiography,* edited by James Olney, pp. 151-62. New York: Oxford University Press, 1988.

Asserts that while Adams created a facade of objectivity through his use of the "manikin" and third-person narrative, the book nonetheless discloses both the "authority of the narrating voice" and the story of its protagonist.

White, Hayden. "Method and Ideology in Intellectual History: The Case of Henry Adams." In *Modern European Intellectual History: Reappraisals and New Perspectives,* edited by Dominick LaCapra and Steven L. Kaplan, pp. 280-310. Ithaca, NY: Cornell University Press, 1982.

Cites *The Education* in a discussion of the applicability of various critical theories to the study of intellectual history.

Williams, H. H. Review of *The Education of Henry Adams,*

by Henry Adams. *The Monist* XXXI, No. 1 (January 1921): 149-59.

Surveys Adams's philosophy as reflected in *The Education*.

Additional coverage of Adams's life and career is contained in the following sources published by Gale Research: *Contemporary Authors,* Vols. 104, 133; *DISCovering Authors; Dictionary of Literary Biography,* Vols. 12, 47; and *Twentieth-Century Literary Criticism,* Vol. 4.

Zelda Sayre Fitzgerald

1900-1948

American novelist, short story writer, essayist, and nonfiction writer.

INTRODUCTION

Best known as the wife of American author F. Scott Fitzgerald, Fitzgerald is the author of short stories, essays, and the semiautobiographical novel *Save Me the Waltz*. While this work has been assessed as simplistically plotted and confusingly written, Fitzgerald has been commended for her portrayal of a woman seeking personal fulfillment through artistic expression.

Born in Montgomery, Alabama, Fitzgerald was the youngest daughter of a conservative Southern family. She met Scott Fitzgerald shortly after her graduation from high school and married him two years later. The couple's glamorous, fast-paced life in New York City and later in Paris epitomized the excesses of the Jazz Age. Their marriage, however, was strained by several factors, including Fitzgerald's desire to achieve on her own the same renown that her husband attained with the novels *This Side of Paradise,* published in 1920, and *The Beautiful and Damned,* published in 1922. Fitzgerald studied painting and other arts and crafts, and at the age of twenty-seven began several years of training in ballet, at which she proved unsuccessful. In 1930 she suffered an emotional breakdown and was institutionalized for the first of many times. She died in a fire in 1948 while she was a patient at a sanitarium in Asheville, North Carolina.

Fitzgerald began writing short stories and essays during the early years of her marriage, taking as her themes the Jazz Age and a youth culture characterized by unprecedented social freedom. Scott Fitzgerald revised and edited much of her work during this period, and these pieces were often published under his name or under a joint byline to capitalize on his greater fame. Between April 1929 and March 1930, while living in Paris, Fitzgerald composed the stories that became known as the "girls series." Critics agree that this story sequence—which includes "The Southern Girl," "The Girl with Talent," "A Millionaire's Girl," and "Poor Working Girl"—demonstrates the growth of her talent, as the stories evolve from undeveloped character sketches to concretely detailed accounts written from a sympathetic but objective narrative perspective. W. R. Anderson contended that these writings "are a record of Zelda Fitzgerald's struggle toward seriousness of expression, of her growth toward competence in literary technique, and of her husband's continuing but increasingly sparing and wary guidance." The story "Miss Ella," published in the December 1931 issue of *Scribner's,* is thought to be Fitzgerald's first work written without her husband's guidance; critics consider it superior in plotting and characterization to the pieces in the "girls" series. "A Couple of Nuts," published in *Scribner's* in August 1932, is widely regarded as her most accomplished work of short fiction. This story follows a young couple's degeneration from innocent romantic adventurers amid the decadent circles of European cafe society to victims of emotional and moral disintegration.

While under treatment for a psychological collapse in 1932, Fitzgerald was encouraged by her doctor to write as a means of therapy, and during a few weeks in a mental institution she completed the first draft of *Save Me the Waltz.* Set in the 1920s, the novel details the life of Alabama Beggs, a rebellious young Southern woman who marries successful artist David Knight. Together they join the flamboyant social elite of New York, Paris, and the Riviera. Seeking self-sufficiency and an identity separate from that of her husband, Alabama leaves him to embark on a career in ballet. On the verge of spectacular success, she contracts an illness that ends her dancing career. Ultimately, she returns to the South to make peace with her dying father, and the novel concludes with the Knights reunited. Many commentators have noted that this fictionalized and wildly romanticized treatment of the Fitzgeralds' own lives covers virtually the same ground as Scott Fitzgerald's *Tender Is the Night,* on which he had been working for nearly a decade at the time that Zelda Fitzgerald wrote her novel. Most reviewers criticized the book's excessively elaborate, obscure prose and its numerous grammatical errors, but acknowledged that Fitzgerald evoked the mood of the era. Modern commentators are divided in their assessments. Some value the novel for providing a woman's perspective on characters and events covered in a more famous novel by a male author, while others disparage Fitzgerald's arrogation of what Scott Fitzgerald considered "his material." Some critics maintain that although *Save Me the Waltz* is technically flawed, it remains a poignant, sensitive account of a woman's search for personal identity.

PRINCIPAL WORKS

Eulogy on the Flapper (essay) 1922; published in journal *Metropolitan Magazine*

Save Me the Waltz (novel) 1932

Bits of Paradise: 21 Uncollected Stories by F. Scott and Zelda Fitzgerald [with F. Scott Fitzgerald] (short stories) 1973

Zelda Fitzgerald: The Collected Writings (short stories and novel) 1991

CRITICISM

The New York Times Book Review   (essay date 1932)

[*In the following review of* Save Me the Waltz, *the critic faults Fitzgerald's writing style as clumsy and inflated but acknowledges her ability to create realistic characters and an intriguing plot.*]

Mrs. Fitzgerald's book [**Save Me the Waltz**] is a curious muddle of good psychology and atrocious style. The slow rift between a formerly devoted young husband and wife, as success both worldly and artistic comes to the husband and leaves the wife behind; the frantically hard work of the wife to make herself a career quite separate from his, and her tragic failure to do so, make up a story which has possibilities, although it is not new, and which gains steadily in vitality as it moves along. And although the background of post-war New York and the Paris of boites-de-nuit and the Ritz bar has been overworked, yet it would still serve quite well for a little while longer. Mrs. Fitzgerald, however, has almost crushed the life out of it with a weight of unwieldy metaphor; and in searching for the startling phrase has often descended to the ludicrous, as in "she lay staring about, conscious of the absence of expression smothering her face like a wet bath-mat." It is a pity, too, that the publishers could not have had more accurate proofreading; for it is inconceivable that the author should have undertaken to use as much of the French language as appears in this book, if she knew so little of it as this book indicates—almost every single French word (and there are many), as well as many foreign names and a good many plain English words, are misspelled. This may sound like a small thing, but to meet such mistakes on practically every page is so annoying that it becomes almost impossible to read the book at all.

"Of the Jazz Age," in The New York Times Book Review, *October 16, 1932, p. 7.*

New York Herald Tribune Books   (essay date 1932)

[*The following is a favorable assessment of* Save Me the Waltz.]

Save Me the Waltz is the last will and testament, so to speak, of a departed era that began as a barroom ballad and ended as a funeral oration. Until Mrs. Fitzgerald reminded us, we had almost forgot the gay procession of Americans who sought their salvation in the basements of Montmartre, along the sunny Riviera, at Nice, Juan les Pins, Mentone. Except for the few who escaped to Majorca, the disillusioned rest drank a farewell sherry-flip and returned to the land of comic-strips and skyscrapers.

This is approximately the fate of Alabama Beggs, the heroine who somersaults through the pages of this novel. We are informed very early that she had something of the incorrigible rebel in her, and wasn't to be browbeaten or cajoled by papa and mama Beggs, as her sisters were, into a commonplace marriage. Flirting with the town sheik was fun enough, but Alabama never let that interfere with her plans for the future. When one of her first suitors asked her if she could live on five thousand a year she replied:

"I could, but I don't want to."
"Then why did you kiss me?"
"I had never kissed a man with a mustache before."

While she liked to think she was a hardboiled experimentalist—a new female type which the war fertilized—she was in her heart an uncompromising sentimentalist not unlike the kind she read about in the frayed family copy of Boccaccio; she wanted to live in a big city, preferably New York. David Knight, a young fresco painter, offered her both. The marriage knot officially tied, they set out for the vertical city, where, like true children of the metropolis, they soon learned to get plastered on bathtub gin and waddle in gayety.

We see them next in Normandy eating lobsters, mixing drinks with anonymous celebrities, and looking appropriately bored. Here the call of the flesh came hazardously near compromising Alabama and breaking up the Knight household. In Paris Alabama did penance by punishing the flesh in a ballerina school. She was forced, however, through illness to abandon a career she never really wanted. The Knights (there are three now, a daughter having been added in the interim) are called home to bury old Judge Beggs, and they get unexplainably maudlin over sentiments they never valued too highly.

What, you may naturally ask, is the purpose of all this apparently aimless gyration? Mrs. Fitzgerald's answer would probably be: none whatsoever. The Knights were just like any other average American pre-depression adventurers. They thought that happiness, like prosperity, was just around the corner. If they learned anything for all their trouble, it was this: that to take life too seriously is almost as fatal as not taking it seriously enough.

That may explain, to some extent, why Mrs. Fitzgerald refuses to recognize the validity of pure tragedy, and why she converts every tragic situation into a harlequinade. At first the reader is amused by this; later he begins to suspect the author of completely depriving her characters of their will. At times the story comes dangerously near losing all emotional credibility.

There is a constant recurrence of exaggerated images such as: "Sylvia flopped across the room like an opaque protoplasm propelling itself across a sand bank"; or, "Her body was so full of static from the constant whip of her work that she could get no clear communication with herself."

We may attribute this, and other disturbing elements, to the fact that this is Mrs. Fitzgerald's first attempt to master the novel form (although she has done admirably with the short-story). **Save Me The Waltz** can, however, be read with considerable pleasure. The writing has a masculinity that is unusual; it is always vibrant and always sensitive. (pp. 10-11)

A review of "Save Me the Waltz," in New

York Herald Tribune Books, *October 30, 1932, pp. 10-11.*

Henry Dan Piper   (essay date 1965)

[*An American educator and critic, Piper served as editor of a 1971 edition of F. Scott Fitzgerald's* The Great Gatsby *(1925). In the following excerpt from his* F. Scott Fitzgerald: A Critical Portrait, *he analyzes* Save Me the Waltz *in terms of its autobiographical content and assesses its merit as a novel.*]

Quite apart from its connection with *Tender Is the Night,* Zelda Fitzgerald's novel, *Save Me the Waltz,* deserves attention for several other reasons. It was one of the first and still is one of the best stories that has been written by an American about the career of a ballerina. It is also one of the authentic literary documents of the post-World War I decade. Who, after all, was better qualified to write the history of the American girl during that era than Zelda? A child of the century, born in 1900, she had sat for her portrait as Rosalind, first of the flappers, in *This Side of Paradise* and had married its author before she was twenty years old.

During the decade that followed, no one accepted the new philosophy of the flapper more completely nor defended it more outspokenly than did Zelda. "All neurotic women of thirty and all divorce cases, according to the papers, . . . [can] be traced to the flapper," she had written in 1922 in a popular magazine article vindicating her way of life. "As a matter of fact she hasn't yet been given a chance. I know of no divorcées and no neurotic women of thirty who were flappers." But before she herself was thirty, her own marriage had fallen apart and she was confined to a mental institution. Exactly a decade elapsed between her marriage in April, 1920, and her collapse into schizophrenia in Paris in April, 1930.

During the decade preceding World War I, the American girl had won her freedom, so to speak, at the barricades—striking for better working conditions, going to jail for the right to vote, and otherwise assuming the traditional male prerogatives. As a result, her younger sister, the post-war flapper, was given her freedom before she had actually earned it. For the girl whose twentieth birthday fell during the year 1920, as Zelda's did, it seemed for one historic moment as though there were nothing she could not do or be, if she tried hard enough. But only at a price. Few documents surviving from the 1920's record more movingly than Zelda's novel the price the women of her generation paid for their boundless sense of freedom. *Save Me the Waltz* deserves to be read by everyone who ever shared Zelda's belief that happiness consists in doing just what one wants, or who ever envied her because she had the opportunity to live by that principle.

But a word of caution. The reader who opens *Save Me the Waltz* for the first time without advance warning is bound to be puzzled and exasperated by Zelda's baffling literary style. What, for example, is he to make of a passage such as this, right at the beginning of the story?

> Incubated in the mystic pungence of Negro

mammies, the family hatched into girls. From the personification of an extra penny, a street-car ride to whitewashed picnic grounds, a pocketful of peppermints, the Judge became, with their matured perceptions, a retributory organ, an inexorable fate, the force of law, order, and established discipline. Youth and age: a hydraulic funicular, and age, having less of the waters of conviction in its carriage, insistent on equalizing the ballast of youth. The girls, then, grew into the attributes of femininity, seeking respite in their mother from the exposition of their young-lady years as they would have haunted a shady grove to escape a blinding glare.

Fortunately this turgid prose clears up about a third of the way through *Save Me the Waltz,* and Zelda's writing begins to take on professional luster and sparkle. By then, the reader has discovered that he is participating in a remarkable experience. Before the reader's eyes, as it were, Zelda has succeeded in imposing imaginative order on the raw material of her shattered past, and in giving it objective structure and meaning. What began as a haunted nightmare has been transformed into a lucid and moving story. Understandably, the reader accustomed to a Faulkner's or a Dostoevski's more artful rendering of a diseased state of mind flinches at first before Zelda's much cruder transcriptions of reality. But, before long, he is watching fascinated as her imagination detaches itself from the crazy burden of personal history and creates a story capable of commanding his attention and sympathy. The result is a novel of cumulative power that continues to reverberate in the memory long after it has been laid aside.

The facts of Zelda Fitzgerald's life differed little from those of her heroine, "Alabama Beggs." (pp. 193-95)

Quite likely many of the stories about her drinking and petting and swimming in the nude were exaggerated. If they were, no one cared less than Zelda. Certainly, they did nothing to diminish her popularity with the college boys at Alabama State and Georgia Tech, where she was in constant demand for dances and house parties, or with the young officers stationed at nearby Camp Sheridan. Like her heroine, Alabama Beggs, she was eager to marry and escape "from the sense of suffocation that seemed to her to be eclipsing her family, her sisters and mother." But as she frankly admitted to Fitzgerald, she did not intend to do so until she had found someone with enough money to gratify her desire for expensive adventures.

> She, she told herself, would move brightly along high places and stop to trespass and admire, and if the fine was a heavy one—well, there was no good in saving up beforehand to pay it. Full of these presumptuous resolves, she promised herself that if, in the future, her soul should come starving and crying for bread it should eat the stone she might have to offer without complaint or remorse. Relentlessly she convinced herself that the only thing of significance was to take what she wanted when she could.

Like Alabama, too, Zelda "want[ed] life to be easy and full of pleasant reminiscences. . . . Obligations were to Alabama a plan and a trap laid by civilization to ensnare and cripple her happiness and hobble the feet of time." Marriage, instead of an assumption of new responsibilities, was an escape from old ones. "I believe it has always been understood between us," Alabama reminds David Knight, her artist husband, after their marriage, "that we would not interfere with each other." To this principle Zelda herself clung determinedly during the next ten years. When, successively, New York, St. Paul, Long Island, and Wilmington bored her, there was always her beloved Paris, where the parties never ceased. "Nobody knew whose party it was," she wrote in *Save Me the Waltz.* "It had been going on for weeks. When you felt you couldn't survive another night you went home and slept, and when you got back a new set of people had consecrated themselves to keeping it alive." Later, in a Paris night club, when the waiter brings the check, Alabama insists on paying for everything herself. "This is my party," she tipsily insists, ". . . I've been giving it for years."

But finally even the Paris parties lose their savor. "I can't stand this any longer," she cries pathetically to her husband after one especially hectic evening. "I don't want to sleep with the men or imitate the women, and I can't stand it! . . . Oh, David . . . I'm much too proud to care—pride keeps me from feeling half the things I ought to feel." But David, who by now is tired of her drinking and carousing, and who has his own career as a successful painter to occupy him, can only answer impatiently, "Care about what? Haven't you had a good time?"

Then one evening Alabama's life suddenly assumes fresh

Zelda Fitzgerald's self-portrait, believed to be done in the early 1940s.

purpose and meaning. Like all the other evenings, this particular one has begun in the usual way with a crowd of drunken expatriates in the American bar of a fashionable Paris hotel. Besides Alabama and David, there are Dickie Axton ("She shot her husband in the Gare de l'Est"), Dickie's friend, a certain Miss Douglas ("She was English. You couldn't tell whom she had slept with"), and Miss Douglas' companion, an American musician named Hastings ("an intangible reprobate, discouraging people and living like a moral pirate"). From the American bar, these charming people move on restlessly to one entertainment after another, including a program of Russian ballet at the Théâtre du Châtelet. Here, watching the dancing, Alabama is struck by the contrast between its disciplined grace and beauty and the ugly confusion of her own existence. Afterwards, in a crowded, smoke-filled night club, she is introduced to a Russian princess who has once been a star with the Imperial ballet corps, and who now trains dancers in her own studio for Diaghilev. Impressed once more by the contrast between the noisy disorder of their surroundings and this woman's poised serenity, Alabama impetuously persuades the princess to let her attend one of her ballet classes.

Once Alabama's dance lessons begin, the muddy language of *Save Me the Waltz* immediately starts to clear up. Instead of image-encrusted expository prose, we get dramatic scenes of great power. Leaving the chaos of her youth behind, Zelda has now reached the most satisfying period of her life: those afternoons in 1928 and 1929 that she spent dancing in the Paris studio of Lubov Egorova, the Princess Troubetsky. Following her retirement from the Russian Imperial ballet, where she had been a famous prima ballerina, Egorova had opened a school in Paris in 1923 at the instigation of Diaghilev. Zelda met her two years later through the Gerald Murphys, whose small daughter attended one of her ballet classes.

Alabama's husband, the successful David Knight, has nothing but scorn for his wife's dream of becoming a professional dancer. She is much too old to begin; and her grueling afternoons, sweating in front of a mirror at the ballet bar, exasperate him. "Are you under the illusion that you'll ever be any good at that stuff?" he inquires patronizingly. "There's no use killing yourself. I hope that you realize that the biggest difference in the world is that between the amateur and the professional in the arts." When she tries to tell him about the pleasure she finds in her lessons, he laughs and calls her a mystic. "You're not the first person who's ever tried to dance. . . . You don't need to be so sanctimonious about it."

Finally, after long weeks of practice, Alabama is given the chance to make her professional debut in a theater in Naples. On Madame's recommendation, she has been invited to dance with the ballet corps of an Italian opera company. The scenes describing her adventures living in a seedy boardinghouse, and performing with a broken-down troupe of Neapolitan singers and dancers, are among the funniest in the novel. Equally comic, but more poignant, are Zelda's descriptions of Alabama's husband and their small daughter impatiently waiting in a dull Swiss summer hotel for news of her opening night triumph. It is hard to believe that the dazed mind which began this story has been able to attain such mastery over her material. But now Zelda is completely detached from her past, and can shape it with cool, controlled prose.

She has finally left her personal tragedy behind and soared off on the wings of her imagination. Actually, the invitation to dance professionally that Zelda had longed for with such impatience never came. Nor was she ever able to convince Fitzgerald that she too had creative talent. Instead she wore herself out in Egorova's studio until she broke down and was forced to give up her dreams of becoming a professional *danseuse.*

Once Alabama has achieved her triumphant debut as a ballerina, *Save Me the Waltz* plunges back again into nightmarish fantasy. Alabama's foot becomes infected, and she eventually collapses into raving delirium. When she awakens in a hospital, she learns that, in order to save her foot, the surgeon has had to cut the tendons; she will never be able to dance again. Her husband, who has hurried from Switzerland, does his best to comfort her. But because he has never realized what her dancing meant to her, his words are of little help. "We have each other," he says. "Yes—what's left," is her bitter reply. "She had always meant to take what she wanted from life. Well—she hadn't wanted this."

Soon afterward she gets word that her father is seriously ill, and with David and their daughter, Bonnie, she hastens home. Faced for the first time with the realization that her father is going to die, Alabama wonders how she will survive her loss.

> She thought of the time when she was little and had been near her father—by his aloof distance he had presented himself as an infallible source of wisdom, a bed of sureness. She could trust her father. She half-hated the unrest of David, hating that of herself that she found in him. Their mutual experiences had formed them mutually into an unhappy compromise. That was the trouble; they hadn't thought that they would have to make any adjustments as their comprehensions broadened their horizons, so they accepted those necessary reluctantly, as compromise instead of change. They had thought they were perfect. . . .

Without her father, Alabama thinks, she will have lost her last resource. Or will she? "It will be me who is the last resource," she tells herself, "when my father is dead."

After his funeral Alabama withdraws more and more into her own secret world. At the end of the novel, when David finds her brooding alone in a dark corner and asks what she is thinking about, she can only tell him, "Forms, shapes of things." These words remind us of the incident several chapters earlier in which Alabama had come into Madame's studio one day and discovered the old princess serenely sitting all alone studying the vacant distance. "What do you find in the air that way?" Alabama had inquired. "Forms, child, shapes of things." "Is it beautiful?" she asked. "Yes." "I will dance it," Alabama had promised. Now she can only weave and reweave the shattered fragments of her dreams into a private ballet of her own.

"Why have we practically wasted the best years of our lives?" David asks impatiently in the novel's concluding pages. "So that there will be no time left on our hands at the end," is Alabama's answer. ". . . [T]he object of the game is to fit things together so that when Bonnie [their small daughter] is as old as we and investigates our lives, she will find a beautiful harmonious mosaic." To the making of this secret mosaic Zelda was to devote the rest of her life, until she died in a disastrous fire (along with eight other women patients) at Highland Hospital for Nervous Diseases near Asheville, North Carolina, on March 11, 1948.

Thus, *Save Me the Waltz* is a great deal more than a clinical document of schizophrenia. "It's very difficult to be two simple people at once—one who wants to have a law to itself and the other who wants to keep all the nice old things and be loved and safe and protected," she says of her heroine in a passage that combines Zelda's own lawless grammar with her pathetic need for order and security. With one side of her nature she continued to cling to the moral certainties represented by her father, while at the same time she let herself be swept up in the hectic quest for new experiences. "We grew up founding our dreams on the infinite promises of American advertising," Alabama admits ruefully at one point toward the end of the novel. "I *still* believe that one can learn to play the piano by mail and that mud will give you a perfect complexion.

What makes Zelda's novel such a remarkable experience is that we are able to participate to such a degree in her effort to impose imaginative unity on her divided and shattered past. She begins by trying to write conventional, straightforward narrative history. But because she has no stable point of view from which to judge her experience, the result is chaos. She cannot reduce her past to an orderly chronological arrangement of facts, nor can she establish fruitful cause-and-effect relationships, nor make meaningful generalizations. Take, for example, the passage quoted at the beginning of this chapter, in which she confronts for the first time the problem of writing about her father. Unable to sort out or to control her feelings about Judge Sayre, she can only pile on top of one another the welter of images that are associated in her memory with him.

However, once Zelda reaches the point where her life takes on purpose and meaning—in the dancing studio of Egorova—the chaos in her writing (and her mind) disappears. No wonder she clung to those dancing lessons as persistently as she did, despite Fitzgerald's objections and lack of sympathy. They gave her the first security she had known since leaving Montgomery. Her dancing became for her a total—a religious—commitment. When, in *Save Me the Waltz,* she later tried to express what dancing meant to her, she inevitably fell back on religious metaphor and imagery. "My friend tells me you want to dance. Why?" Madame asks Alabama curiously at the first lesson. "You have friends and money already." "[Because] . . . it seemed to me—Oh, I don't know. As if it held all the things I've always tried to find in everything else," Alabama replies intensely.

This first glimpse of the dance as an art opened up a world. "Sacrilege," she felt like crying out to the posturing abandon of the past. . . . It seemed to Alabama that, reaching her goal, she would drive the devils that had driven her—that, in proving herself, she would achieve that peace which she imagined went only in surety of one's self—that she would be able, through the medium of the dance, to command her emotions, to summon love or pity or happiness at will, having provided a channel through which they might flow. . . . David's success was his own—he had earned his right to be critical—Alabama felt that she had nothing to give the world and no way to dispose of what she took away.

The hope of entering Diaghilev's ballet loomed before her like a protecting cathedral.

Afterwards, when a friend asks Alabama why she insists on wearing herself out at her lessons day after day, Zelda says in her defense:

[She] had never felt so close to a purpose as she did at that moment. . . . She felt that she would know [the answer] when she could listen with her arms and see with her feet. It was incomprehensible that her friends should feel only the necessity to hear with their ears. That was "Why."

This longing for total communication—to speak, as it were, with the voice of God—was for Zelda a passionate compulsion. In her writing, as in her dancing and her painting, she was continually trying to transcend the limits of physical reality, to "listen with her arms and see with her feet." It was mad, of course, but it was the madness of the artist. It shows up also in the painting to which she turned with considerable success after she was no longer able to dance. In 1934, a showing of her work was held in a Manhattan gallery. One painting of which she was especially fond, now in the municipal art gallery in Montgomery, represented two dancers in motion, their legs and arms oddly distorted. "I painted them that way to express the pure quality of what it was they were dancing," she told me when she showed it to me in 1947. "It wasn't the dancers but the step itself that I wanted to paint."

The need to go beyond the borders of the senses, to express the inexpressible, was also responsible for her weird, synesthetic prose. In writing of this type, the senses become confused. Trumpets blare scarlet colors, the blue sky feels cool, the deserts burn with a yellow intensity, and smells, odors, tastes, visual images, and tactile sensations pile up on another. It is a kind of writing frequently exhibited by schizoid personalities, often with fresh and striking results. Although it is disturbing when first encountered at the beginning of *Save Me the Waltz,* where it often rages uncontrolled, it sometimes endows Zelda's prose with an elegant intensity.

High parabolas of Schumann fell through the narrow brick court and splashed against the red walls in jangling crescendo . . . Asthmatic Christmas bells tolled over Naples: flat metallic sheets of sound like rustled sheafs of roofing. . . . The afternoon . . . scratched itself on the yellow flowers. . . .

Yellow roses she bought with her money like Empire satin brocade, and white lilacs and pink tulips like moulded confectioner's frosting, and deep-red roses like a Villon poem, black and velvety as an insect wing, cold blue hydrangeas clean as a newly calcimined wall, the crystalline drops of lily-of-the-valley, a bowl of nasturtiums like beaten brass, anemones pieced out of wash material, and malignant parrot tulips scratching the air with their jagged barbs, and the voluptuous scrambled convolutions of Parma violets. She bought lemon-yellow carnations perfumed with the taste of hard candy, and garden roses purple as raspberry puddings, and every kind of white flower the florist knew how to grow. She gave Madame gardenias like white kid gloves, and forget-me-nots from the Madeleine stalls, threatening sprays of gladioli and the soft, even purr of black tulips. She bought flowers like salads and flowers like fruits, jonquils and narcissus, poppies and ragged robins, and flowers with the brilliant carnivorous qualities of Van Gogh. She chose from windows filled with metal balls and cactus gardens of the florists near the rue de la Paix, and from the florists uptown who sold mostly plants and purple iris, and from florists on the left bank whose shops were lumbered up with wire frames of designs, and from outdoor markets where the peasants dyed their roses to a bright apricot, and stuck wires through the heads of the dyed peonies.

Such jagged imagery is especially suited to the nightmare agonies that Alabama undergoes while she is in the hospital in Naples. Here Zelda was remembering her own delirium in the Swiss mental sanatorium in 1930:

The walls of the room slid quietly past, dropping one over the other like the leaves of a heavy album. They were all shades of grey and rose and mauve. There was no sound when they fell.

Two doctors came and talked together. What did Salonika have to do with her back?

"I've got to have a pillow," she said feebly. "Something broke my neck!"

The doctors stood impersonally at the end of the bed. . . . "This afternoon, then, at three," said one of the men, and left. The other went on talking to himself.

"I can't operate," she thought he said, "because I've got to stand here and count the white butterflies today."

"And so the girl was raped by a calla-lilly," he said, "—or, no, I believe it was the spray of a shower bath that did the trick!" he said triumphantly.

He laughed fiendishly. How could he laugh so much of "Pucinello." And he as thin as a matchstick and tall as the Eiffel Tower! . . .

. . . The walls began again. She decided to lie there and frustrate the walls if they thought they could press her between their pages like a bud from a wedding bouquet. For weeks Alabama lay there. The smell of the stuff in the bowl took the skin off her throat and she spat red mucous. . . .

. . . Sometimes her foot hurt her so terribly that she closed her eyes and floated off on the waves of the afternoon. Invariably she went to the same delirious place. There was a lake there so clear that she could not tell the bottom from the top; a pointed island lay heavy on the waters like an abandoned thunderbolt. Phallic poplars and bursts of pink geranium and a forest of white-trunked trees whose foliage flowed out of the sky covered the land. Nebulous weeds swung on the current: purple stems with fat animal leaves, long tentacular stems with no leaves at all, swishing balls of iodine and curious chemical growths of stagnant waters. Crows cawed from one deep mist to another.

Save Me the Waltz ultimately fails as a novel. Except for a few comic scenes in the second half, it rarely arouses any emotion except pity. Its humanity lies less in its art than in its documentary proof of the remarkable survival powers of the imagination. Although Zelda, when she wrote it, was unable to cope rationally with either her literal past or the immediate everyday world, she was still capable of inventing an imaginary world of striking beauty and order. The world in which Alabama dances and fulfills herself is a true one—a finer and more convincing one than the ruins from which it had been created by Zelda's imagination. It is a world that she was able to view with humor and detachment, and she succeeded in conveying her feelings about it with insight and passion.

Certainly, *Save Me the Waltz* offers a more sensitive account of the deranged wife's view of her marriage than we find in her husband's version, *Tender Is the Night.* The disturbing thing about both novels is their authors' mutual failure to comprehend the other's point of view. Dick Diver and Alabama Beggs, the two centers of interest, are proof that the more unsympathetic portraits of their respective spouses, Nicole Diver and David Knight, must be heavily discounted. No wonder the Fitzgerald marriage failed. Nor is it surprising that, after spending the spring and summer of 1932 correcting both the manuscript and the galley proofs of *Save Me the Waltz,* Fitzgerald, on returning to his novel, should have extensively overhauled and expanded his plans. How elaborate that overhauling was we do not know precisely. But in the process, *Tender Is the Night* clearly became a defense of his role in their marriage. (pp. 196-204)

> *Henry Dan Piper, in his* F. Scott Fitzgerald: A Critical Portrait, *Holt, Rinehart and Winston, 1965, 334 p.*

W. R. Anderson   (essay date 1978)

[*In the following essay, Anderson traces Fitzgerald's development as a writer from her first short stories to* Save Me the Waltz, *and examines "the interrelationship between her writing and the literary career of her husband."*]

The recent publication of *Bits of Paradise: 21 Uncollected Stories By F. Scott and Zelda Fitzgerald* was, in part, a

---

> **Zelda Fitzgerald discusses her perception of the world while hospitalized in Paris:**
>
> Every day it seems to me that things are more barren and sterile and hopeless—In Paris, before I realized that I was sick, there was a new signifigance to everything: stations and streets and façades of buildings—colors were infinite, part of the air, and not restricted by the lines that encompassed them and lines were free of the masses they held. There was music that beat behind my forehead and other music that fell into my stomach from a high parabola and there was some of Schumann that was still and tender and the sadness of Chopin Mazurkas—Some of them sound as if he thought that he couldn't compose them—and there was the madness of turning, turning, turning through the deciciveness of Litz. Then the world became embryonic in Africa—and there was no need for communication. The Arabs fermenting in the vastness; the curious quality of their eyes and the smell of ants; a detachment as if I was on the other side of a black gauze—a fearless small feeling, and then the end at Easter—But even that was better than the childish, vacillating shell that I am now. I am so afraid that when you come and find there is nothing left but disorder and vacuum that you will be horror-struck. I don't seem to know anything appropriate for a person of thirty: I suppose it's because of draining myself so thoroughly, straining so completely every fibre in that futile attempt to achieve with every factor against me—Do you mind my writing this way? Don't be afraid that I am a meglo-maniac again—I'm just searching and it's easier with you—
>
> You'll have to re-educate me—But you used to like giving me books and telling me things. I never realized before how hideously dependent on you I was—Dr. Forel says I won't be after. If I can have a clear intelligence I'm sure we can use it—I hope I will be different [.I?] must have been an awful bore for you.
>
> Why do you never write me what you are doing and what you think and how it feels to be alone—
>
> *Zelda Fitzgerald, in an undated letter to F. Scott Fitzgerald, excerpted in* Zelda: A Biography, *by Nancy Milford, 1970.*

---

witness to the growth of interest in the fiction of Zelda Sayre Fitzgerald. *Bits of Paradise* reprints ten pieces which she wrote, alone or in conjunction with her husband. All of them had been published in periodicals during her lifetime, but they were, at last, being accorded the more permanent stature of book publication, in company with eleven of Scott Fitzgerald's previously-uncollected stories. If one eliminates the very brief sketch **"The Continental Angle"**—arguably a nonfiction essay in gustatory nostalgia, on the order of Mrs. Fitzgerald's lengthier pieces **" 'Show Mr. and Mrs. F. to Number—' "** and **"Auction—Model 1934"**—a survey of the stories in *Bits of Paradise* provides a consistent index to the awakening and growth of Zelda Fitzgerald's interest in fiction as a creative art form. This paper makes such a survey.

The objective of the survey is twofold: first, to trace Zelda Fitzgerald's progress as she moved from her first tentative efforts in fiction through a series of increasingly more ambitious undertakings toward her novel *Save Me the Waltz;* second, to explore the interrelationship between her writing and the literary career of her husband. Zelda Fitzgerald also wrote a small body of nonfiction—reviews, essays, articles for women's magazines. These pieces are considered only peripherally in their relationship to the published fiction, as are the references to unpublished and presumably lost stories, references which occasionally surface in the Fitzgeralds' correspondence.

Zelda Fitzgerald has typically been understood as blessed with a flare for brilliant but unsustained creative expression, as a woman possessed with an unstable talent and little esthetic or educational background with which to discipline that talent. Nancy Milford's biography *Zelda* has, of course, largely corrected this glib assessment. Examination of the development of Mrs. Fitzgerald's short stories substantiates Milford's findings that, despite the emotional chaos in which her marriage and her life foundered, Zelda Fitzgerald's groping efforts to find self-definition in artistic achievement resulted in fundamentally consistent growth toward control and purpose in her writing.

That progress was, to be sure, extremely complicated by the intricacies of her relationship, personally and artistically, with her husband. As Milford has shown, theirs was a union marked by extremes—exuberant happiness turning to mutually-destructive rivalry, conflict, and jealousy. Yet, as she also demonstrates with discernment, the Fitzgeralds were, even in their most agonized alienation, dependent on each other, emotionally and otherwise.

One facet of that interdependence surfaced in their writing. Certainly Scott Fitzgerald *needed, used* Zelda Fitzgerald. He seized upon her freshness, her ready acceptance of life, both to reinforce his own romantic worldview, and to provide—from her letters, diaries, and from his observations of her actions—subject matter for his fiction. In her writing, Zelda Fitzgerald was similarly dependent on him. She turned to his work for guidance, discipline, examples, and patterns. She relied on him for suggestions and corrections. Most importantly, as he used their life together as an inexhaustible repository of experiential subject matter, so she increasingly came to draw upon the joys, conflicts, and disappointments of their marriage. Most writers, of course, call on their own experiences as bases for creation. The Fitzgeralds, however, shared a sensibility which depended much more heavily than usual on that artistic wellspring. Zelda Fitzgerald, like her husband, saw life in those intensely romantic, intensely subjective terms which naturally emphasized personal experience, and emotional response to the experience, almost exclusively as the fundamental subject matters of fiction.

With such a sensibility, writing is, in part, a method of self-definition. Two writers striving to find meaning, value, and achievement from a common experience are almost assuredly headed for conflict; such was certainly the case with the Fitzgeralds. Writing fiction became, for Zelda Fitzgerald, part of her intensive struggle for spiritual independence. Like her dancing and painting, her writing took on, in her eyes and in those of her husband, an ominous tinge of rivalry. Thus, as she came closer to writing *good,* serious fiction, the interrelationship, as it is demonstrated in this survey, became more and more complex. Fitzgerald continued throughout his life to assist and encourage his wife's literary efforts; yet, as she became increasingly proficient, he demonstrated increased resentment and annoyance that she was attempting to establish herself in his field, using his expertise, and (most disturbingly) drawing on "his" material—their experiences.

At the beginning, however, Fitzgerald seems to have enjoyed Zelda Fitzgerald's forays into writing. In the early years of their marriage, as they became figures of public interest, she was given the opportunity to contribute brief articles to several periodicals—interviews, a review of *The Beautiful and Damned,* "authoritative" articles on the flapper. These pieces, of course, played on their mutual popularity, and their supposed "Jazz Age" lifestyle together. The process by which these fledgling efforts led to a desire to write fiction is unclear; however, by 1923 Zelda Fitzgerald was engaged in composition of her first short story, which would ultimately find publication as **"Our Own Movie Queen,"** under her husband's name.

The Fitzgeralds were living in Great Neck at that time. Scott Fitzgerald was occupied with the production of his play *The Vegetable,* and with planning his third novel. Nevertheless, he found time to assist Zelda Fitzgerald with the story, which was completed in November. The degree to which Fitzgerald was involved is uncertain. The notations he made in his *Ledger,* his personal account book of his life and literary career, exemplify that uncertainty. He includes it in his "Record of Published Fiction," but notes that it is "Two thirds written by Zelda. Only my climax and revision."—yet credits its entire earnings to himself. In the section entitled "Money Earned by Writing since Leaving Army," however, he notes it as "(half Zelda)," yet credits the entire $900.00 income (after a ten per cent agent's fee) to his own earnings. In the section devoted to "Zelda's Earnings" he also claims half-authorship and divides the income equally, crediting his wife with having earned $450.00 from the story.

At the same time, Zelda Fitzgerald was telling an interviewer about her efforts to write fiction:

> "I like to write. Do you know, I thought my husband should write a perfectly good ending to one of the tales, and he wouldn't! He called them 'lop-sided,' too! Said that they began at the end."

She told an interviewer that she had written three stories, although only **"Our Own Movie Queen"** survives from that time. The interview also sounded two portentous notes. First, it expressed Mrs. Fitzgerald's interest in finding a creative outlet of her own. She was beginning, albeit with self-conscious amateurism, ventures into a field she would subsequently come to term her "work." The second implication of importance is that Fitzgerald apparently was willing to offer her passing guidance and correction, but did not take her "work" seriously enough to become deeply involved in it.

Taken in conjunction with the *Ledger* entries, then, the interview indicates that Fitzgerald's contributions to **"Our Own Movie Queen"** were probably not major. What interested him about it was its potential marketability: he first attempted to sell it to the Hearst publishing corporation, as partial fulfillment of a contract with Hearst's *Cosmopolitan* for options on all his stories during 1923, which would explain his sole by-line. The story was finally placed with the *Chicago Sunday Tribune,* where it appeared in 7 June 1925. Undoubtedly, the fact that the *Tribune* thought it was buying a Scott Fitzgerald piece accounted for the high price of a thousand dollars.

A typescript of **"Our Own Movie Queen"** exists in the F. Scott Fitzgerald papers at the Princeton University Library. It evidences extensive editorial revision in Fitzgerald's hand, almost completely in the form of deletions of words, phrases or passages. The effect is an overall tightening of the story; however, there is no evidence, at this stage, of any substantial addition of passages or of ideas by Fitzgerald. Unless his contributions came at earlier stages, **"Our Own Movie Queen"** would seem to have been principally Zelda Fitzgerald's creation. Certainly the finished story is not one which would add particular luster to his reputation. It is a brittle, "slick," satiric piece. Its tone and mood are, perhaps, akin to those of Scott Fitzgerald's less-serious magazine stories of the period—"Jemina"—as well as to the glib facetiousness of Zelda Fitzgerald's nonfiction pieces such as the review of *The Beautiful and Damned* which she wrote for the *New York Tribune* of 2 April 1922—the review which contains this sample of Mrs. Fitzgerald's humor:

> It seems to me that on one page I recognized a portion of an old diary of mine which mysteriously disappeared shortly after my marriage, and also scraps of letters which, though considerably edited, sound to me vaguely familiar. In fact, Mr. Fitzgerald—I believe that is how he spells his name—seems to believe that plagiarism begins at home.

As part of its tone of sophisticated wit, **"Our Own Movie Queen"** adopts a consistently superior attitude, verging on condescension, toward its humorously-named heroine, Gracie Axelrod. She is a poor girl, who wreaks a plebian's revenge on the snobbish Blue Ribbon family. Yet, the reader is invited to see her, within limits, as a woman capable of taking care of herself in the world, by manipulation of her physical attractiveness, and through a certain self-protective predatoriness. To this extent, she is Zelda Fitzgerald's version of the tough, selfish, but attractive young women who populate so much of her husband's fiction. Gracie is not aristocratic or wealthy—few of Mrs. Fitzgerald's heroines are—but she shares qualities of self-absorption, self-sufficiency, and attractiveness with women such as Judy Jones of "Winter Dreams."

Like much of Fitzgerald's fiction, **"Our Own Movie Queen"** also turns to personal experience for some of its setting—a midwestern locale, patterned, apparently, on the twin cities of Minneapolis / St. Paul. The Fitzgeralds had lived in St. Paul in 1921-1922; Zelda Fitzgerald could draw on her outsider's impressions of her husband's city, as he had drawn on his impressions of her home town for stories such as "The Jelly Bean" and parts of "The Ice Palace."

Whatever the degree of his participation in its composition, **"Our Own Movie Queen"** certainly shows the mark of Scott Fitzgerald's influence. Despite its rudimentary characterization, trick ending, and overall slickness, he was not ashamed to claim it as his own creation, at least for the sake of selling it. As a beginning venture into writing it must have given Zelda Fitzgerald a sense of accomplishment: it had been accepted professionally, by her literary mentor, and by a paying publisher.

Zelda Fitzgerald was, however, by no means ready to embark on a literary career. For the next five and a half years she contented herself with a continuation of the role of the amateur dabbler, writing occasional magazine pieces, such as **"Does a Moment of Revolt Come Sometime to Every Married Man?"** and **"What Became of Our Flappers and Sheiks?,"** both of which were published in *McCall's* magazine (March 1924 and October 1925, respectively), or **"The Changing Beauty of Park Avenue,"** which appeared in *Harper's Bazaar* in January 1928. The typescript of the latter, like the typescript of **"Our Own Movie Queen,"** in the Zelda Sayre Fitzgerald papers at Princeton, bears corrections and editing in Scott Fitzgerald's hand, evidence that he continued to take an interest in his wife's writing, as a proud parent would encourage the inventiveness of a precocious child. A measure of the kind of writing she was producing may be derived from the fact that, by 1928, her market was the youth-cult-oriented *College Humor,* a magazine for which Fitzgerald had little respect, considering it only a market for hastily-written or second-rate material. Apparently, however, he had no objection to selling *College Humor* two of Zelda Fitzgerald's humorous sketches, which were published as though written by both Fitzgeralds. **"Looking Back Eight Years"** appeared in June 1928, and **"Who Can Fall in Love After Thirty?"** the following October. The *Ledger,* which attributes them entirely to Mrs. Fitzgerald, discloses that the first one was apparently sold directly to the magazine, for $300.00, while the second one brought $200.00, less ten per cent commission—indicating that Fitzgerald's agent, Harold Ober, handled its negotiations.

By Scott Fitzgerald's standards, such prices scarcely warranted his signature—he earned $25,732.96 that year, by his own count—but *College Humor* was apparently sufficiently pleased to commission a series of six articles, of approximately five thousand words each, treating different types of girls. The series is first described in an office memorandum of 14 February 1929, by Fitzgerald's literary agent, Harold Ober.

> Scott Fitzgerald said that Zelda would do six articles for *College Humor,* that he would go over them and fix them up and that the articles would be signed with both their names. . . . He said we had better leave the price until they did the first article.
>
> They are to be articles about different types of girls. I should think they ought to pay $500 for them, if they are four or five thousand words in length.

The inference from the memorandum is that Fitzgerald had made the preliminary arrangements himself with

H. N. Swanson, editor of *College Humor.* What is not clear is whether Swanson realized he would be paying for pieces basically written by Mrs. Fitzgerald; he may not have cared, so long as both names were signed. On the following day, Swanson and Ober met. Swanson suggested a list of types of girls to be evoked—city debutante, young married, modern, Southern, country club, western, and New York society woman. He also requested that the pieces be "story articles," rather than "philosophical discussions," and suggested techniques to be utilized. Ober wrote Fitzgerald of the agreement with Swanson:

> He thought each girl could be given a name and she could be described as a certain kind of girl because at such and such a party, she did so and so. In other words, she could be described by instances in her life, things that she did, rather than things that were said about her, etc.

Swanson obviously wanted short stories, not satiric humor. If he expected Fitzgerald himself to be deeply involved in their composition, however, he was truly bargain-hunting, for Fitzgerald's stories at that time, which were going exclusively to *The Saturday Evening Post,* sold for $3500.00 each.

If, on the other hand, Zelda Fitzgerald could write them, with some guidance and polishing from her husband, they would provide some easy revenue. More important, assuredly, they would provide diversion for her. By early 1929, the growing friction and tension in the Fitzgeralds' marriage had become serious. Fitzgerald was drinking heavily and worrying about his inability to make progress with his fourth novel, the final version of which would be *Tender Is the Night.* Zelda Fitzgerald, frustrated and disappointed in her inability to derive fulfillment from her role as decorative wife of a famous author, was increasingly struggling to find serious creative achievement in her own right. Her effort to become a ballet dancer occupied much of that struggle, but, as Nancy Milford has pointed out, the articles she had written during 1927 and 1928 were also manifestations of her groping search for meaning in her life. Her need for artistic achievement would, in the next few years, become, obsessively, the central concern of her life, what she would later come to term in communications with her husband and her psychiatrists, her *work.* There is considerable significance in that terminology: "work" connotes professional achievement, not amateur expression.

Zelda Fitzgerald's increasingly intense interest in her work, then, coincided with Swanson's requirements, to lead her back to the effort to write fiction. She had finished the first of the "girl" sketches by the beginning of March, while the Fitzgeralds were still living at "Ellerslie," near Wilmington, Delaware. Entitled **"The Original Follies Girl,"** it was brief (around 2000 words) and sketchy in plot and characterization. Nevertheless, Ober sold it to Swanson for $400.00, and was confident he could get $500.00 apiece for the rest of the series.

Almost immediately, the Fitzgeralds sailed to France. For the next year, while they divided their time between Paris and the Riviera, Zelda Fitzgerald evidently threw herself into her writing with increasing intensity—the obsessive

intensity with which she pursued ballet studies. By mid-April, she had finished **"Poor Working Girl"** and had sent it to Ober; **"The Southern Girl"** followed in June; **"The Girl the Prince Liked"** in August; **"The Girl with Talent"** in October; and **"A Millionaire's Girl"** in March 1930. As a group, they are a record of Zelda Fitzgerald's struggle toward seriousness of expression, of her growth toward competence in literary technique, and of her husband's continuing but increasingly sparing and wary guidance.

Fitzgerald's correspondence and the typescripts of the "Girl" series included in the F. Scott Fitzgerald papers at Princeton—there are typescripts for all the stories except **"The Southern Girl"** with holograph corrections by both Scott and Zelda Fitzgerald—indicate that, while Fitzgerald continued to play some part in the conception and planning of the stories, Zelda Fitzgerald took an increasingly craftsmanlike interest in composition and revision of what was steadily becoming *her* work.

The extent to which Fitzgerald was involved in originating the "Girl" pieces is difficult to assess. He was certainly involved, from time to time, in at least some stages of writing of some, if not all, of the stories. Harold Ober, in fact, became alarmed that Fitzgerald might be engaging himself too deeply in the composition of what were, to him as to Fitzgerald, minor "sketches." On 8 October 1929, he wrote Fitzgerald:

> I agree with you that it is a mistake for you to use up material on these articles that you could use in stories. Of course as this one . . . ["**The Girl with Talent**"] stands, it is more a sketch than a story, although it is a beautifully done sketch. . . . if you have any more ideas that will make stories, don't put them into this form.

Fitzgerald probably agreed with and for the most part accepted Ober's advice; he was, at that time, struggling with the material which would eventually become *Tender Is the Night,* as well as attempting to write short stories, and he surely could not have had much time to devote to his wife's work. Nevertheless, he must have remained involved on at least a sporadic basis right through the last of the series to be written, **"A Millionaire's Girl."** Several years after its composition, he would write to Zelda Fitzgerald acknowledging that, as with other of their joint efforts, his contributions to that story had consisted principally in suggesting a theme and revising the completed manuscript.

While that letter suggests that Fitzgerald was continuing to assist and guide his wife's writing, the evidence of the typescripts at Princeton indicates that she was becoming increasingly self-sufficient, playing a more important part in the revisions of her work. Fitzgerald may have been suggesting editorial changes, but if so, they came in early stages of composition. The extensive editorial revision on the five typescripts at Princeton is almost entirely in Zelda Fitzgerald's hand, a marked contrast with the revision in her husband's holograph on the typescripts of earlier work such as **"Our Own Movie Queen"** and **"The Changing Beauty of Park Avenue."** The titles and by-lines of all five pieces are written in Fitzgerald's hand, in some cases changing titles which Zelda Fitzgerald had supplied. For instance, **"The Girl the Prince Liked"** originally was entitled, in Zelda Fitzgerald's holograph, "The Story Book Girl." There are occasional revisions in the typescripts in Fitzgerald's hand—word changes, an added phrase, and in one instance, several words lined through in the black ink in which corrections identifiable as his are elsewhere made. However, these revisions are sparingly made. In fact, two of the typescripts, **"The Original Follies Girl"** and **"Poor Working Girl,"** apparently bear no revisions at all by him, other than the added titles.

On the other hand, all five typescripts were thoroughly revised in Zelda Fitzgerald's holograph. In most instances, her corrections are minor—reorganizing and tightening wordy phrases; sharpening images; substituting more effective adjectives or verbs. Three of the stories, however, bear evidence of her enhanced interest in the details of craftsmanship, of careful revision. The final paragraph of **"The Original Follies Girl,"** for instance, was added in revising the typescript, adding to the story's tone of elegaic wistfulness:

> Gay was too good a companion and too pretty to go dying like that for a romanticism that she was always half afraid would slip away from her.

She similarly revised **"The Girl the Prince Liked,"** giving it a completely new ending, and apparently discarding the earlier conclusion. Again, the mood of sustained, isolated loss—a mood which may have been suggested by the "dying fall" endings of a number of her husband's stories—is strengthened. The accompanying photograph shows the revised ending.

However, the last of the series, **"A Millionaire's Girl,"** received the most extensive rewriting. Nine of its twenty-seven pages of triple-spaced typescript were heavily revised; four of these include paragraph-length additions aimed at exploring in greater depth the emotional reactions of characters, or heightening descriptive imagery to influence mood. One example may serve to illustrate the kind of craftsmanship Mrs. Fitzgerald was learning to apply. The principal characters are Caroline—a talented and beautiful social climber—and Barry—a wealthy and aristocratic man with whom she has fallen in love. His family, of course, has objected, and has attempted to bribe her to break off their engagement. There is an argument in Ciro's Club, after which Caroline and Barry part ways. The typescript did not explore the nature of the disagreement, leaving the impression that Caroline petulantly attacked Barry for having the sort of family who would insult her. The sense of the typescript version may be derived if one reads the story as printed in *Bits of Paradise,* skipping the middle paragraph on page 257. That paragraph, as may be seen in the accompanying photograph, was added, in Zelda Fitzgerald's hand, to the typescript. It reads:

> Everyone was delighted with so public and melodramatic a *crise* in a romance that had inspired so much envy. Before they left even the waiters in the place had gleaned the story of Caroline's foolish acceptance of a nice big check and an automobile from Barry's father. She claimed to Barry that she had not understood it was to

have been the reward for letting him go and he claimed in no uncertain terms that she was fundamentally, hopelessly and irreclaimably dishonest. It seems too bad that they couldn't have done their claiming at home because then they might have patched up the mess. But too many people had witnessed the scene for either of them to give in an inch.

The addition makes specific the causes of the dissolution of the romance, while it adds depth to the characterization of both principals. Caroline becomes more naively opportunistic, while Barry is made to display more clearly the pompous rigidity of his breeding. Both are exposed as proud, mettlesome personalities.

To be sure, these revisions may have, in whole or in part, been suggested by Fitzgerald as he read the typescripts; however, the fact that there are some minor additions in his holograph to several of the typescripts makes the likelihood strong that the additions in Zelda Fitzgerald's hand reflect her own thinking. This evidence of substantially increased attention to the details of literary craftsmanship, as she began more and more to consider herself a writer in her own right, is matched by the steadily improving skills she was developing, from story to story, as she moved through the series. **"The Original Follies Girl"** and **"Poor Working Girl,"** the first two pieces she wrote, were scarcely more than sketches. The first one, which was published in the July 1929 *College Humor,* followed, sympathetically, the fortunes of a beautiful performer, Gay, who surrounded her life with objects and fine clothing, to create a sense of position and accomplishment through possessions and the flair for displaying them with panache. Little characterization slipped in, although there were occasional glimpses of Gay's feelings and thoughts.

The second, **"Poor Working Girl,"** was much more flippant, going back to some of the tone of **"Our Own Movie Queen."** There was no effort to create reader sympathy for Eloise Everette Elkins, a vacuous, poorly-educated girl from a small-town middle class background. The reader merely follows her as she fails miserably as a governess, abandons her vague plans for a stage career, and settles down to a dreary career as the pretty girl in the electric company's offices. A note of pathos was added at the end, as we are informed that Eloise is the end-product of "worn-out stock." Apparently not even Swanson was very happy with this story, since he postponed publication until January 1931, at the end of the series.

Harriet, the "Southern Girl" of the third sketch, which appeared in the February 1930 *College Humor,* received more sympathy and attention from her creator. While her story retains some of the air of the mood piece, designed to create sympathy for the disciplined, self-sufficient belle, making the best of the straitened circumstances into which her family has fallen, a basic plot was added. In tracing the complications of separate romances between Harriet and a pair of young men from Ohio, Zelda Fitzgerald reconsidered the theme of incompatibility between Southerner and Northerner her husband had studied in "The Ice Palace." A saccharin resolution mars the story, but it was a decided advance over the first two.

"The Girl the Prince Liked" and **"The Girl with Talent"** were more ambitious efforts. Each was over 3000 words in length, and followed its heroine through a more sustained and complicated plot, as the two women—"girl" was no longer an applicable term—fought to find excitement and happiness outside the confines of conventional, if affluent, marriages. Both move restlessly to Europe, abandoning husband and children in search of adventure and fulfillment, respectively, as the mistress of the Prince of Wales, and as a cabaret performer. **"The Girl the Prince Liked,"** which appeared in the February 1930 *College Humor,* is perhaps the stronger story, in that it closes on a note of ironic self-recognition as Helena is left with her memories, both of her conquest, and of what she sacrificed for it—a self-possessed but toughened international femme fatale. Lou, in **"The Girl with Talent,"** is permitted a more conventional happy ending, as she suddenly, but ironically, finds another husband and has another child, settling down in China to the same kind of bourgois contentment she fled in New York. The "happy" ending was more appropriate for *College Humor,* in the April 1930 issue in which the story appeared, than had been the starker closing of the earlier story; only the endings varied, however. The stories shared otherwise a quality of increased narrative achievement which was the result of Zelda Fitzgerald's increased attention to a number of facets of fictional technique.

The most striking and effective of these technical devices was the development of a narrative perspective which permitted her to create both a sense of involved immediacy with her characters, and a level of detached judgment. At first, as it began to emerge in the "Girl" series, it was little more than an unidentified narrative voice, a first-person author-observer, undefined by sex or character, who described the appearances and actions of Gay, the "Follies Girl," and Eloise, the "Working Girl," as if it were present as an element of their environment, observing, offering ironic closing assessments, but rarely privy to their thoughts, other than in an occasional limited-omniscient glimpse. In **"Southern Girl,"** however, the voice became at times plural—a narrative "we," more closely identified with the specific social fabric of the small Southern community, analogous to the perspective later used, for instance, by William Faulkner in "Smoke" and *The Town.* Yet the narrator could become an individual separating from the community to drift away, as did the protagonist:

> I left Jeffersonville about then, but I can imagine how the winter came and the groups about the parlor at Harriet's grew bigger and perhaps younger.

The process of individualization of the narrator permitted flexibility of scene; "I" left Jeffersonville, in part, so that when Harriet visited New York there would be an observer. A sense of distance was also achieved, but at the same time, the observer-narrator also began to participate more immediately, more actively, in the destiny of the protagonist. In **"The Girl the Prince Liked"** and **"The Girl with Talent,"** the narrator became a party—sometimes conspiratorially, frequently disapprovingly—to the increasingly self-destructive life-styles of the protagonists, even attempting to become involved at one point in a subtle marital conflict between Lou and her first husband.

Zelda Fitzgerald may not have consciously patterned her narrator after the observer-participants her husband had employed so effectively in *The Great Gatsby* or "The Rich Boy." Nevertheless, by the time she had come to composition of **"A Millionaire's Girl,"** she had honed a tool which, like Nick Carraway, simultaneously permitted access to events, judgmental detachment, and, to the extent that the narrator is sensitive to the ominous self-destructive nature of a quality of life shared with the protagonist, a sense of involvement in their struggles.

That element of involvement is even stronger in Zelda Fitzgerald's stories. Carraway came to know himself and his society through Gatsby's tragedy, but it was not essentially *his* tragedy; there is, by the end of the "Girl" series, almost a sense of fusion between narrator and protagonist, as though the narrative identity were a self-questioning element of the protagonist's psyche. That identity is confusingly complicated in **"A Millionaire's Girl"** by the fact that the narrator is identified at one point as one of the Fitzgeralds, as Caroline and Barry become engaged during a visit to a suburban home jokingly referred to as "Fitzgerald's Roadhouse." Later, the narrator is found on the same transcontinental train as Caroline, and becomes her confidant and adviser in Hollywood, sharing to a degree her romantic confidence in success, but privately doubting that her marriage to Barry will survive the tempests of conflicting values and ambitions.

As her narrator became more and more important as a focus of evaluation and interpretation, Zelda Fitzgerald was also learning the value of descriptive setting in suggesting mood. The opening passages of **"The Southern Girl"** and **"A Millionaire's Girl"** for instance, do far more than simply describe Jeffersonville or New York: they prepare the reader for the kind of personality on which the story will focus, and at the same time economically establish, by accretion of detail, an air of dreamy verisimilitude.

Both the narrator-protagonist fusion and the use of concrete, if romanticised, detail were elements of an increasing proficiency in manipulation of personal experience. It was the growth of a communicated sense of deeply-felt personal struggle which, as much as any quality, lifted the last of the "Girl" series beyond the realm of amateur mood-sketch. In her protagonists, Zelda Fitzgerald was more and more acutely objectifying her own inner struggles for a sense of identity and achievement; simultaneously, through her narrative commentator, she was weighing the consequences of talent subordinated to marriage, or the equally foreboding consequences of a life in which love and romance are subordinated to the search for individual freedom. To be sure, the increased technical sophistication and seriousness of theme could not find full expression in too-brief stories hampered by glib endings—"happy" reversals or sophisticated cynicism. Nevertheless, by the end of the series, Zelda Fitzgerald was writing stories which both her husband and his literary agent recognized as being too good to waste on *College Humor.*

Even as the series progressed, Harold Ober had been able

to persuade Swanson to raise the price of the stories, first to $500.00, then to $800.00. However, as Mrs. Fitzgerald came to an increasingly proficient level, calling more and more deeply on a common store of experience which her husband considered "his" material, Fitzgerald wrote to Ober that he felt the price for **"The Girl with Talent"** should be raised to at least $1000.00. His concern was primarily financial (he suggested, for instance, that, if Swanson would not meet the increase, his name be dropped from the articles); but he was perhaps also increasingly aware of the degree to which Mrs. Fitzgerald's writing was drawing on his professional resources. He was not jealous, but he felt the improved quality demanded more appreciation, and was willing to attempt genteel extortion to obtain it.

This background partially explains the fact that **"A Millionaire's Girl"** was sold, not to *College Humor,* but to *The Saturday Evening Post,* for a substantially enhanced price ($4000.00), as the product of Scott Fitzgerald's pen alone. Upon receipt of the typescript, with its title corrected in Fitzgerald's hand, Ober apparently thought it was his story alone, and judged it worthy of the *Post.* Ober subsequently offered profuse apologies to Zelda Fitzgerald, but both he and Fitzgerald presumably realized that to acknowledge publicly that the story had been substantially hers would be to risk trouble with both *College Humor* and *The Saturday Evening Post.* In his *Ledger,* however, Fitzgerald took care to ascribe its authorship entirely to Mrs. Fitzgerald. If she was not permitted the pleasure of acknowledged success, she could at least take comfort in self-satisfaction that her story had been accepted as worthy of her husband, and that it had earned more than all her previous writing together.

Unfortunately, by the time the story appeared in the 17 May 1930 *Saturday Evening Post,* Zelda Fitzgerald had undergone her first major psychological collapse. As she began to recuperate, first at Valmont, then at Prangins, Switzerland, she apparently concentrated on writing as a kind of self-protective therapy. Unable to dance, she increasingly turned to writing as her "work." Fitzgerald also evidently seized upon her writing as a therapeutic exercise, taking great pains, through both the Ober office and Maxwell Perkins, his editor at Scribners, to find publication outlets for her stories and sketches. As early as 8 June 1930, she had completed a story, which he was anxious to send off to New York. By mid-July, he had sent three stories or sketches, probably including one, to Ober, to be shown, among other possible buyers, to Perkins for *Scribner's Magazine.* These stories, which were never sold, have not been found among the Fitzgerald papers. Their titles—"A Workman," "The Drought and the Flood," and "The House"—take on almost symbolic qualities emphasizing productive labor, structure, and disaster, when one realizes the conditions under which they were written.

Although Maxwell Perkins, speaking for the editor of *Scribner's Magazine,* expressed admiration for the imagistic power of the stories, he wrote Fitzgerald on 5 August 1930 rejecting them. These are presumably the same sketches which, in November, Fitzgerald was urging Ober to submit to *Century Magazine* or *The New Republic,*

under the blanket title "Stories from a Swiss Clinique." On 6 January 1931, Ober wrote Fitzgerald that Edmund Wilson, at *The New Republic,* had agreed to keep the sketches for possible use, although he had not been encouraging, since that magazine rarely published fiction. Wilson may have simply been acting from friendship for the Fitzgeralds, of course; but at least Ober's letter confirms that Zelda Fitzgerald's fiction continued to have potential for consideration. No further record of these stories, however, has surfaced.

As she became somewhat better adjusted to life at the Forel clinic at Prangins, Zelda Fitzgerald was able to write a story which found better fortune. Fitzgerald sent "Miss Bessie" to Ober sometime in the fall of 1930. By mid-November, Ober had submitted it to *Scribner's Magazine,* which accepted, for the price of $150.00, provided that Mrs. Fitzgerald would revise what Maxwell Perkins termed, in a letter of 12 November to Fitzgerald, her more "remote" and "too numerous" similes and metaphors. Unpublished correspondence of early 1931 between Perkins and Fitzgerald, which may be seen in the Charles Scribner's Sons Archive at Princeton University Library, contains frequent passing reference to the revision, in proof, of "Miss Bessie." Whether from a genuine belief in the merit of the story, or a desire to find some encouraging stimulus for his wife—or a combination of both reasons, Fitzgerald devoted considerable attention to the story, which ultimately appeared under the revised title **"Miss Ella"** in the December 1931 issue of *Scribner's Magazine.*

A heavily-corrected set of galley proofs of the story exists in the Zelda Sayre Fitzgerald papers at Princeton. The revisions, in a hand which appears to be Zelda Fitzgerald's, are directed primarily at complying with Perkins' requests that some of the more abstract metaphorical passages be made more coherent. In addition to substitutions of words for greater clarity of diction, wordy or vague passages are pared down or rewritten. There is, however, no major reorientation of plot or characterization. Although Scott Fitzgerald may have participated in the revision process, it appears more likely, from the correspondence concerning the story and from the fact that revisions were made in proof stages, that the basic composition is wholly Zelda Fitzgerald's. While her husband may have lent his incisive instinct for diction and phrasing in the revision stage, **"Miss Ella"** was, more than any of her earlier work, essentially her creation.

The story evidences a creative continuity with the "Girl" series. Point of view is again focussed through a peripheral observer-participant, a young person who seems to be a relative, or intimate, of the family of the protagonist, the spinster of the title. The age and sex of the narrator are never specified, although the nature of the observations offered—details of dress materials, the description of Miss Ella's triangular love story from an essentially feminine perspective—suggests a young girl, receptive to and appreciative of the complexities of Miss Ella's unhappiness.

When he first read the story, Maxwell Perkins was much taken with treatment of both protagonist and narrator. He wrote Fitzgerald:

. . . it did give a very complete strong sense of a character in this Southern old maid. It was moving in that way, but it had another quality that was still more moving.—In some way it made the reader share the feelings of the young girl through whose eyes Miss Bessie was seen, so that she was not only real, and in some degree was not real, but was as the young girl saw her.

Miss Ella's character is strong because she has continued to function, despite some mysterious personal tragedy which has made her a spinster. But it is the sense of *identity,* of sympathy, between the narrator and Miss Ella which makes the story work. As the mystery—an effective element of suspense is created as we wait for the explanation of Miss Ella's spinsterhood—is unfolded by the narrative voice, the reader is swept into the events. Narrator and reader seem not merely present but also involved as a rejected suitor commits suicide on the day of Miss Ella's wedding to his rival, sealing her self-denying rejection of marriage and happiness. In effect, the narrator, who had not been born when the events occurred, and who never reveals how she knows of them, *becomes* Miss Ella, leading the reader into a mind and soul rigidly bound in guilty self-denial. The effect is to suffuse the story with a Faulknerian air of psychological tension; repressed, self-punishing fury; effectively, if unrealistically, symbolized by the suicide weapon, deliberately left as a *memento mori* in the summer house.

Zelda Fitzgerald was continuing to explore the complexities of the feminine psyche struggling unsuccessfully for mature fulfillment. **"Miss Ella,"** however, achieved deeper resonance and integrity through its more consistent sounding of the note of ruin and waste which had occasionally surfaced in the "Girl" stories. It was grounded in her own unhappiness, and it attempted to marshal that unhappiness seriously, without cynicism or artificiality. Miss Ella had courage and dignity, and a certain romantic glamor, but they were founded on repressed sensuality and agonized guilt. Without being at all autobiographical, the story drew its strength from the sense of lost opportunities and unattained ecstasy which had come to characterize the lives of both Fitzgeralds.

The effort to make art of her internal conflicts may have aided Zelda Fitzgerald in her recuperation. At any rate, by September 1931, she had been permitted to leave Prangins, to return to the United States to settle in Montgomery, Alabama, the home town which had provided the ambience of **"Miss Ella."** While her husband went to Hollywood on a screenwriting job, she threw herself feverishly into her own work. She was also, according to Nancy Milford, beginning systematically to reread her husband's short fiction, both as a means of re-establishing rapport with him and with former happiness, and as a disciplined effort to study and benefit from his fictional techniques.

Milford credits Zelda Fitzgerald with writing, during the next six months, seven short stories, in addition to the first draft of her novel, *Save Me the Waltz.* Of these, apparently only **"A Couple of Nuts,"** her last published short story, has survived. The story may have actually been written at Prangins; if not, it must have been one of the first of this new group of stories, since it was in Maxwell Perkins'

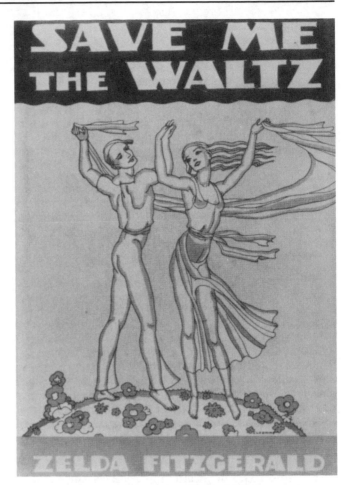

Dust jacket for Save Me the Waltz.

hands by mid-October, only a month after Zelda Fitzgerald's release from Prangins. On 21 October, Perkins wrote to Fitzgerald:

> I think there is no doubt that Zelda has a great deal of talent, and of a very colorful, almost poetic kind. In the case of the particular story, **"The Two Nuts"** I think perhaps the color and all that, rather overwhelmed the story.

Perkins went on to praise the story's metaphorical freshness, although he felt that that quality interfered with its continuity. Nevertheless, he returned it for revision, with the possibility that *Scribner's Magazine* might accept it. Whether Fitzgerald, who was about to depart for Hollywood, was himself involved in the revision is unclear; no manuscript or other pre-publication version is known to exist. In the absence of other evidence, it is quite likely that Zelda Fitzgerald completed her own revisions of this story. The revised story was acceptable to *Scribner's Magazine,* which published **"A Couple of Nuts"** in its August 1932 issue.

The story is usually assessed as her most accomplished short fiction. Matthew J. Bruccoli terms it " . . . Zelda Fitzgerald's best effort— . . . closer to a real story than any of the others." ["Preface," **Bits of Paradise**] Nancy Milford finds that in it, " . . . Zelda was in control of her talent." There are no major new departures in technique in the story: point of view is channelled, once again, through an unnamed narrator-participant, who moves in the same decadent world of European cafe society as the protagonists, a young couple named Larry and Lola. To be sure, the narrator's plane of existence differs: she (or possibly even "he") is an established habitue of the salons, clubs, and villas of the Parris-Cannes axis, while the protagonists are adventuresome night-club entertainers, attempting to parlay their talent, youth, and physical charm into success and acceptance.

The narrator follows them through a metamorphosis from a kind of cynical innocence which accepted life—including marriage—as a grand romantic adventure to dissipation and dissolution: they cease to have *adventures* and become mere adventurers.

That process is precipitated by a new character in Zelda Fitzgerald's cast of standards, a charming, wealthy, but thoroughly amoral socialite, Jeff Daugherty, who toys with the transparent ambitions of the couple as idly as he carries out a passing liasion with Lola. Daugherty is a master of social ease and coordination, but about him clings a perceptible aura of what Milford has termed "ruin," a major thematic component of the story. He is an almost allegorical personification of illusory superficial glamor masking meaningless and psychically destructive unproductiveness. Even flight to the United States cannot preserve the romantic and artistic integrity of Lola and Larry's marriage. A former wife of Daugherty, as decadently predatory as her ex-husband, completes the destruction. Her seduction of Larry leads to scandal, threatened divorce, and his death, appropriately the result of storm at sea.

The narrator (thus vicariously, the reader) has refrained from actively intervening out of lassitude and, perhaps, class loyalty. Consequently, the narrator becomes implicated in the decay and moral irresponsibility represented in the characterization, plot, and setting. Zelda Fitzgerald called on all her practice to suffuse the story with a sustained tone, ominous and sinister, of loss and destruction. Her physical descriptions reinforce the moral qualities of the story. For instance, as Larry bends all his efforts toward retaining a pretence of nonchalant ignorance of a summer affair between Lola and Daugherty, the couple (along with the narrator, of course) remain too long on the Riviera:

> Jeff left with his fatuous coterie. We three shivered alone in the prickly sunshine of the beach. The ocean turned muddy and our bathing clothes didn't dry from one brisk swim to another; we grew irritable with the unspent tang of the sea.

The beach's sudden loss of charm, coincident with the departure of Daugherty, reinforces the illusory nature of his social magic, and prefigures the death of romance and happiness.

"A Couple of Nuts" also displayed Mrs. Fitzgerald's mastery of irony as a device for control. The narrator, with self-deprecating wit, analyzes her unwillingness to act to save the youngsters. More ironically, Lola ends the story by describing Daugherty and his ex-wife as "a couple of nuts," the same phrase Daugherty had used to dismiss Larry and Lola from his consideration. Lola's phrase betrays her almost-total lack of appreciation of the enormity of the evil which had crushed her fragile dreams.

Without writing veiled autobiography, Zelda Fitzgerald had learned to turn her own experience, including internal torment and struggle, to account in creating moving and affecting fiction. She still needed the guidance and correction of others, but she was surely pleased with the maturity and depth of "Miss Ella" and "A Couple of Nuts." She had begun to consider herself a fledging professional. One indication of her increased self-confidence is that she began to send manuscripts directly to Ober, without waiting to submit them for her husband's suggestions and revisions. A more substantial indication was the novel she had begun to write in early 1932. Her progress, from "Our Own Movie Queen" through the "Girl" series had enhanced her narrative and technical capacities to a point at which she evidently felt herself worthy and capable of artistic independence from her husband.

That desire for independence had undoubtedly been spurred by an increasingly ambivalent attitude on Scott Fitzgerald's part. He had always been patient with his wife's attempts to write, particularly as he felt they amused her, or offered therapeutic occupation. But he had from time to time exhibited a sense of possessive superiority, particularly when she attempted more "serious" writing, with its inevitable infringement on a reservoir of deeply-felt personal experience he insisted was "his" material. In 1930, he had written to one of his wife's doctors that, if he had to choose between her health and his profession, the choice would be in favor of his ambitions to be part of English literature. As he struggled more and more desperately to compose a novel based in themes of loss and the decay of dreams, and set in the France of Parisian night clubs and Riviera villas, he may well have begun to consider his wife's work amateurish pilferings from his own writing. He certainly would have that reaction to her novel, when he finally saw its manuscript, leading up to a tense confrontation, in 1933, in which he described her as a third-rate writer whose efforts were robbing him of his material. Thus, the knowledge, in 1932, that he harbored such resentments assuredly played a part in Zelda Fitzgerald's increased efforts toward independence. In explaining to Fitzgerald why she had submitted the manuscript of *Save Me the Waltz* to Scribners without first showing it to him, she wrote:

> Also, feeling it to be a dubious production due to my own instability I did not want a scathing criticism such as you have mercilessly—if for my own good given my last stories, poor things.

The aura of rationalized self-justification is there, of course. Nevertheless, there is also the ring of unpleasant truth in emotion-laden words like "scathing" and "mercilessly." By 1932, the quality of Zelda Fitzgerald's writing had truly improved to a point at which she must have seemed to her husband a kind of ungrateful rival. It is surely not necessary to see her as his artistic equal to recognize that, through the example, opportunities, guidance Fitzgerald had given her, she had been able to nurture her creative flair into literary talent of sufficient merit to threaten his uniqueness in a way that would have serious repercussions as she turned to the novel for which her stories had been preludes.

The body of Zelda Fitzgerald's fiction is too small, and for the most part insufficiently distinguished, to judge whether, with better fortune, she might have truly achieved her goal of professional mastery. Nevertheless, stories such as **"Miss Ella,"** and **"A Couple of Nuts"** demonstrate that her sporadic apprenticeship to her husband had had very valuable results. By the time she had published her last short story, she was well on her way to a literary self-sufficiency rooted in tempestuous partnership with Scott Fitzgerald. Whether she would ever have achieved a truly independent professional stature is a moot question. That she had the ability to write moving and true fiction is amply witnessed in her last short stories. (pp. 19-40)

> *W. R. Anderson, "Rivalry and Partnership: The Short Fiction of Zelda Sayre Fitzgerald," in* Fitzgerald/Hemingway Annual: 1977, 1978, pp. 19-42.

Meredith Cary   (essay date 1978)

[*In the following essay, Cary examines the structure of* Save Me the Waltz.]

It has proved all too easy to read Zelda Fitzgerald's novel, *Save Me the Waltz,* in terms of illness, seeing in the metaphoric style primarily the reflection of a diseased imagination and discounting the content as being so neurotically antagonistic to men and so contentiously autobiographical as to be of no value except to biographers. Such a view is understandable if the novel is considered to be on the losing side of a kind of novelistic duel between Zelda Fitzgerald's *Save Me the Waltz* and F. Scott Fitzgerald's *Tender Is the Night*—an approach which is tempting because of the flamboyance of the personalities, the commonality of the artistic material drawn upon, and the conjunction of the actual writing of the two novels. However, it is necessary to observe that whereas it is Zelda Fitzgerald's novel which is usually condemned as excessively autobiographical, it is Scott Fitzgerald's novel which in fact details the lives of an alcoholic and a mental patient. Since an easy recognition of the personalities and problems has not caused *Tender Is the Night* to be simplistically assigned to a sub-literary category, it should be possible to approach *Save Me the Waltz* as something other than an associational curiosity. The reward for doing so is the discovery of a work exhibiting impressive artistic control of both form and content—the patterns of metaphor, the narrative structure and the character delineations reveal *Save Me the Waltz* to be a thoughtful and carefully balanced study of a search for individuality, social relevance, and order.

The structure of the novel is, appropriately, orderly. Divided into four sections, it treats in two phases—first the training for the experience and then the experience itself—each of the two central concerns of the main character—

Alabama Beggs. There is the childhood which is the only training offered the young girl for the marriage which represents her life. And when she becomes disillusioned with the marriage and retreats from "life" to "art," there is her training in the dance and finally her career as a ballerina. The events which flesh out these four sections depict the will to succeed and the recognition of failure of a talented woman driven to excel in both areas.

Alabama's childhood is influenced primarily by the personalities of her father and her mother, and by the expectations of the society in which she grows up. Opening the novel with a description of the character of Judge Beggs in the metaphor of a castle, Zelda Fitzgerald suggests the crucial importance of both the negative and positive implications of his personality as a father. "Impregnable" because of his intellect, his integrity and his unapproachability, he is a "living fortress" for his children, who, as long as they belong to him rather than to themselves, are convinced they can "do anything and get away with it."

While he protected his children from society, he also protected himself from them, however, declaring "without humor, 'I will build me some ramparts surrounded by wild beasts and barbed-wire on the top of a crag and escape this hoodlum.' " This extension of the castle metaphor for his private use within the family enclosure suggests the inevitability of his children's reactions to him as to fragments of a personality beyond their reach. When they were small, he seemed to be "the personification of an extra penny, a street-car ride to whitewashed picnic grounds, a pocketful of peppermints." As teenagers, they perceived him as "a retributory organ, an inexorable fate, the force of law, order, and established discipline." In both stages, they grasp only the function, having no means of approaching close enough to perceive the man. They therefore learn only his rules, not his values, and so they are hampered by his remoteness from them just as they are "crippled" by the family remoteness from society.

Inevitably, the girls "seek respite in their mother" from so unyielding a presence. Their mother, Millie, is an "emotional anarchist" of "wide and lawless generosity." In contrast to the paternal view of them as "hoodlum," Millie announces that "If my children are bad . . . I have never seen it." Unjudging either of her husband or her children, she urges the girls to avoid confrontations with their father, not through obedience but through "making their arrangements outside."

For Alabama, this model of femininity as accommodating rather than judging is reinforced by the observation of her older sister's behavior on dates. Her sister changes into a

> more fluctuating, more ingratiating person, as she confided herself to the man. She wished it were herself. There would be her father at the supper table. It was nearly the same; the necessity of being something that you really weren't was the same. Her father didn't know what she really was like.

Unlike Millie, whose personality really did disappear into her wifehood even to the abandonment of her own family in favor of her service to her husband's people, Alabama learns to conceal, not to cancel, what she is "really like." In a phrase the repetition of which measures the development of Alabama's growing perception of the discrepancy between the ideal and the possible, she convinces herself that "the only thing of any significance was to take what she wanted when she could." But even from the beginning, the ruthlessness of such a plan is modified by her counter-drive toward "paying for things I do—it makes me feel square with the world." Thus, by the time her introductory portrait is complete, what she "really" is emerges as a chaotic mixture of the will and self-righteous integrity of her father and the yieldingness and non-judging sympathy of her mother. If her mother perceives Alabama's characteristic drive to be "more conquering" than her sister, still, Alabama's childhood concept of what makes people interesting is that "things happen" to them. Such a blend of dominance and passivity, embodied in the extremes of her parents, becomes the framework on which the individual Alabama matures.

Her maturation is, inevitably in such an environment, marked in sexual rather than vocational terms. Her inspection of her mother and sisters leads the teenaged Alabama to conclude that there is "nothing to do but drink and make love." However, such a conclusion is only partially appropriate. At first Alabama submits herself to David, imagining herself being "pulled finer and smaller like those streams of spun glass that pull and stretch till there remains but a glimmering illusion." So totally is she subsumed by her lover's personality that she seems to herself to have "crawled into the friendly cave of his ear" where she becomes lost among "the deep trenches of the cerebellum," the desolate "mystic maze" of "vast tortuous indentations" which lead her round and round until she becomes hysterical. The metaphor suggests both the concept of femininity which her childhood has given her and her inability to fit its pattern: it is not really within her character to disappear into David as Millie disappeared into the Judge.

In the footsteps of her mother, however, she masks her reaction well enough that David and her father dispose of her as if she were uncomplicatedly her mother's child. David's view of the relationship is the conventional one, and so he asks her father, not Alabama herself, about the marriage. To Alabama, he observes merely that "you are my princess and I'd like to keep you shut forever in an ivory tower for my private delectation." Her submissiveness is quite casually assumed by the egotistical young artist, who has linked the name of "Miss Alabama Nobody" with that of "David David Knight Knight Knight." But Alabama, who has just escaped her father's "fortress," is not charmed by the image. The "real" Alabama, whom neither her father nor her young lover perceives, asks David not to mention the ivory tower again. And on her honeymoon, she tells herself that "no power on earth could make her do anything . . . any more, except herself."

The conflict between their views of their relationship is not immediately disastrous, partly because both seem to assume the establishment of a new home something on the order of the Beggs'. The differences, however, are significant. The judge has so fixed a sense of place that he does not even momentarily consider moving from his home when it becomes too large on the departure of his children. In contrast, David and Alabama drift among hotels and rented houses, changing not only addresses, but cities and even countries. That they are working not on a fortress but on an encampment that cannot be defended is suggested by their inability to repel invasion even temporarily. For example, Alabama brings her parents to her home only to discover "drunks in the hammock" who invade the diningroom during dinner and who, even when paid to leave, can not be prevented from reeling back into the kitchen during the night.

Similarly, Provence, where they settle for a time, seems to Alabama to be a place where keeps and battlements crumble and moats fill harmlessly with honeysuckle. The metaphor recalls most immediately the image of the Judge—appropriately, since it is at this stage in her life that Alabama faces the extent to which her father's pattern of marriage is inappropriate to her character. Further, Provence is in Europe's "south," a concept of locale which David sees as appropriate to Alabama but not to himself. The notion that it is congenial to one but not to the other emblemizes the crumbling of their relationship, for it was with their acute sense of closeness that they expected to replace the geographical sense of home which was a major portion of the Judge's strength.

In the beginning, they are agreed that their joint personality should be David's. David's fame emphasizes Alabama's observation that it is "a man's world," and she makes an effort to be "feminine" in her mother's way, expressing a longing to live "without premeditation," insisting that she will be content to "luxuriate in this voluptuous air and grow fat on bananas and Chablis while David Knight grows clever." But even her declarations of dependency embody an ominous ambivalence. She remarks to her daughter that "I am so outrageously clever that I believe I could be a whole world to myself if I didn't like living in Daddy's better." David is to *grow* clever while Alabama *is* clever: it is a strikingly poor basis on which to submerge Alabama's personality. Further, it suggests that another of the difficulties facing the marriage is the extent to which David's character differs from that of the Judge.

David does not tower over Alabama in maturity any more than in cleverness. For example, he indulges in tantrums over minor irritations such as his ranting that it "ruined his talent to have his buttons torn off in the laundry." But the problem is not altogether David's. Her recognition of David's limitations does not prevent Alabama from casting him as a kind of father substitute when she finds it convenient. She assumes that he will organize their life and then blames him for her boredom, as she blamed her father during her childhood. To be sure, the charge is not wholly irresponsible since David's view of a woman's role is a devastatingly limiting one. He assumes that Alabama will find some painless way of going into cold storage while he works and emerge as a compliant feature of his social life when he wishes to be amused. And when she complains of boredom to him, his notion of a solution is to suggest a party.

As was prefigured by the metaphors of their courtship, Alabama makes an attempt at the sort of life David imagines, with endless reading and abortive attempts to sew. But the "female role" is simply inappropriate to her. She cannot keep the servants from stealing, she cannot dominate the cook sufficiently to get any variety into the family meals, she cannot keep the house free of insects. The passage in which she discovers her pregnancy embodies the various elements of her problem. In an "incompetent" discussion of the problem, David suggests that Alabama ask her mother for advice. But Alabama objects: "Oh, David—don't! She'd think I wouldn't know how." In fact, of course, no matter what may be her family's view of the normal and basic function of womanhood, she doesn't "know how."

Her lack of an instinctive understanding of the conventional role is further illustrated in the flirtation which overtly triggers the breakdown of the marriage. She has been accustomed to attention for her wit in her own language. But at the party which was to relieve her boredom, she discovers that she does not understand French well enough to be clever. And noticing that it is David alone, rather than the pair of them, who receives the attention, she turns to the international form of communication—falling into a love affair out of boredom and a demolished sense of worth.

However, love affairs between people who cannot talk to each other are predictably useless. Alabama buys a French dictionary and her lover buys an English dictionary, but she does not really want to sneak to his apartment to consummate the flirtation, and his final letter is in interminable French which Alabama can only destroy unread. It was an affair of appearances only—they are both blond and brown and beautiful—and so it is the photograph which accompanied the letter which has meaning for Alabama: "Though it broke her heart, she tore the picture too. It was the most beautiful thing she'd ever owned in her life, that photograph. What was the use of keeping it?"

The implications are complex. She has no instinct to clutch the past. She has discovered something—in the realm of appearances, at least—more beautiful than David and his painting. That the relationship has been a matter of surfaces only is not in itself a basis on which to turn away from it, for the affair constitutes an admission that her life with David does not make room for the "real" Alabama either. She concludes that "Jacques had passed over that much of their lives like a vacuum cleaner" not entirely because David is repellently outraged—yelling about "foreigners," "wops" and "kikes"—but because, for her as well, the experience has "vacuumed up" the idle happiness of her marriage to David, just as her marriage had cancelled the security derived from her father. Recognizing a turning point, she re-edits her earlier understanding of life's process: "You took what you wanted from life, if you could get it, and you did without the rest."

It is in response to this new insight into the necessity of sometimes doing without that her solution emerges from the tangle of emotions embodied in the episode which closes the marriage section of her story. Having retreated to Paris to escape the "south" which has become symboli-cally obnoxious to David, they attend a party where David flirts with the guest of honor. The hostess describes Gabrielle Gibbs to Alabama as a "half-wit" who has a body like marble. David supplies the speculation that her marble is arrestingly covered throughout with blue veins. To Alabama, who is introduced to her as she is being sick in the bathroom, Gabrielle is simply a blonde drunk on the bathroom floor, so disorderly that "a platinum wisp floated in the bowl of the toilet." But to the rest of the party, Gabrielle is "the center of something" and Alabama feels painfully inferior. Although it is Gabrielle who is wallowing around the bathroom floor, it is Alabama whom the hostess ushers out of the room "like a maid gathering dust off the parlor floor." While David tries to impress the dancer by speculating that she wears something "boyish underneath your clothes," it was Alabama who gave him the idea by actually wearing silk BVDs. To add to her sense of outrage at David's use of her, Alabama is advised by others in the party as to her wifely role. She is told of her "need to be bossed," and when she objects that she wants to direct her own life, if she could only find its direction, she is reminded: "You've a child, haven't you?"

The conventional role has its appeals for her, and so she whimpers to David that she wishes she could "live in your pocket," but David sensibly objects that she would slip through a hole she had forgotten to darn. The normal is simply not her role, a difficulty echoed in the hostess' remark that dancing "would be the very thing for Alabama. I've always heard she was a little peculiar—I don't mean actually batty—but a little difficult. An art would explain." It is a view which finally makes sense to Alabama. She has come to realize that she cannot rest as a function of her husband and her daughter. And yet she is sufficiently convinced by her mother's type of femininity to agree that her failure to adapt to the image requires an "explanation." She therefore vows to become "as famous a dancer as there are blue veins over the white marble of Miss Gibbs." Her intention is to justify her character, lend direction to her life, and compete with "the center of something."

Alabama plunges into her training for the dance as deliberately and as wholeheartedly as she had pursued the other phases of her life. Although the original decision was made somewhat on the spur of the moment and resulted at least superficially from her taking seriously the idle flippancy of a social wit, Alabama works out a careful rationale for her new pursuit. "She tried to weave the strength of her father and the young beauty of her first love with David, the happy oblivion of her teens and her warm protected childhood into a magic cloak." She was determined, having despaired of "careless" happiness, to "command her emotions, to summon love or pity or happiness at will," to "drive the devils that had driven her." Because the dance demands self-discipline and represents ordered beauty, she pursues it as a means of forcing those missing qualities onto her unsatisfactory life.

Since the qualities at issue are those which have triggered David's irritation with their marriage, Alabama's studies at first seem to promise rescue for the foundering marriage as well as release for the "real" Alabama. But David very soon stops being pleased at the increased free time Alabama's absorption gives him and turns instead to complaints about the loss of home life. The inevitable recriminations quickly billow into brutal competition. Each feels the other is incapable of understanding the rival art. And instead of shifting their ground to the larger idea of a general concept of art which would include both painting and the dance, David develops a pattern of undercutting Alabama's efforts as those of the permanent amateur in contrast to the professionalism he has the income to document. Although he says he will help her become a dancer, he "did not believe that she could become one," and he continues to treat her like one of his possessions, exhibiting her to his friends "as if she were one of his pictures" and inviting them to feel her muscle.

When, despite his interference and complaints, Alabama does receive an offer to dance professionally, David is convinced there is "something accidental" about the offer and refuses to allow her to consider taking it. Further, since the offer is from a company in Naples—the "south"—David will not consider moving the household even though Alabama's work is geographically tied while his is not: he could paint anywhere, if he would.

The passage with which the third section of the novel concludes sums up this tangle of conflicting influences on Alabama and on the marriage. As long as Alabama was merely training for the dance, she could avoid a confrontation over the deterioration of her marriage by spending more and more time at the studio. But the job offer precipitates a decision. Since it negates David's most vocal claim to dominion over Alabama—that she is ineradicably an amateur and therefore beneath his professionalism—it triggers a greater insistence on his part for some symbolic submission from her in other ways. Always to some extent her mother's daughter, Alabama at no time seems to question David's right to make the rules applicable to the marriage. Therefore she does not challenge his notion that her becoming a professional dancer will require their separation. Nor does she contradict his decision that Bonnie must stay in Paris rather than accompany her mother to a region where there will be no French schools.

The marriage has for a long time seemed so bankrupt to her that she may be responding principally to their mutual sense of "unconscious relief" at the separation. However, her obedience in the disposition of Bonnie is not so willing. She has tried to involve Bonnie in the dance with her in order to overcome the child's objection that "it is too 'sérieuse' to be the way Mummy is." But Bonnie continues to feel that her mother was nicer before she began to dance, and Alabama recognizes in her child the longings which she herself felt so overwhelmingly for something "pretty and stylized in her life." When she finds in Bonnie's drawing book a picture in which "two figures held hands gingerly," and which Bonnie has labeled "c'est trés chic, mes parents ensemble," Alabama is defeated. She cannot turn away from her daughter's family view. Bonnie wants her parents together no matter how "gingerly" the alliance. It is appropriate that the recognition should make Alabama feel "sick and middle-aged" since her choice involves setting aside her own drive for beauty and order in favor of the same drive in the coming generation.

If the matter had rested there, the dancer's defeat would have been uncomplicated. However, family life is organized by David's opinions and not by Bonnie's. And David's response to her giving up makes clear that he is not thinking of them as "parents together" but as a man with his subsidiaries. He consoles Alabama by promising to "try to arrange something" in America. The patronizing reminder that he expects to organize her opportunities as well as set up her limitations makes clear that he sees the decision as a contest which he has won. Before the job offer, Alabama had no real choice but to submit to David's demands for obedience and subservience, for even if David had been able to accept a relationship of equals, Alabama's own view of marriage was too like that of her parents to allow her to demand or even visualize such an arrangement. Therefore, when David's arrogance rouses her from the temporary delusion of Bonnie's view of them together, she recoils into the dance. For the first time, she has a choice.

The result of the choice is far from clear cut, however. She is an undoubted success, professionally. And although she misses Bonnie, she is not really a competent parent, as is symbolized by the disastrous party she gives Bonnie during the child's visit to Naples. Nor does she feel much kinship to her daughter, who has stopped her dancing lessons as soon as Alabama is no longer there to require them of her, and whose increasing snobbishness brings forth complaints that Italian trains de luxe are not sufficiently luxurious. David is really no better a parent than is Alabama, as is indicated by the parallel inept party he arranges for Bonnie upon her return to France, but her snobbishness motivates the child's preference for living in her father's wealthier, more social world in Paris.

In contrast to the society which collects around David, Alabama is "always alone." Even her fellow dancers cannot understand her reasons for dancing when she has a husband and child. The complete isolation which her choice has brought upon her is emphasized in the hospital sequence with which her independence ends. Though she is alone—remote from society and family, as her father was—she is not impregnable as he was. Her career stops when the tendons in her foot are cut as a result of the blood poisoning she develops from the effects of the glue of her dancing slipper which invades a neglected blister on her toe.

The disaster is not simply bad luck. Having started too late to train for the dance—partly because of her own waywardness and partly through her parents' lack of ambition for a daughter—she must work too hard to recover the time. Self-controlled only through decision and not through basic personality, she is undisciplined in areas her attention does not touch, and therefore she neglects the blisters she sees as simply one element of the central masochism of any discipline. Unsure of the exclusive value of building a "whole world to herself" as opposed to living in David's world, she is insufficiently egotistical—in contrast to Gabrielle Gibbs, or Arienne, a less talented but more dedicated fellow student at ballet school—to secure her future through attention to inartistic detail. She has pursued the dance because it is beautiful and because it represents order—in other words, because it is not life for her. Her father's impregnability came from "paring your perceptions to fit into the visible portion of life's mosaic," whereas Alabama, believing in the "infinite promise of American advertising," remains vulnerable to reality.

In contrast to her childhood intention to "bring forth sweet-smelling blossoms from the hardest of rocks, and night-blooming vines from barren wastes," she confronts in the hospital a different kind of unnatural growth: "Nebulous weeds swung on the current: purple stems with fat animal leaves, long tentacular stems with no leaves at all, swishing balls of iodine and the curious chemical growths of stagnant waters." Where she had intended extraordinary beauty, she concludes in her delirium that her struggle toward differentness has produced only grotesque and repellent abnormality. The distressed imagery merges into David's reassurance that "it has brought us together again." The meaning of that palliative to the demoralized Alabama is the silent revision of her life's rule: "she had always meant to take what she wanted from life. Well—she hadn't wanted this."

When Alabama rises from the hospital bed which signals the end of her dreams of the dance in order to attend her father's deathbed, the novel returns to the imagery of its opening scenes. Alabama considers that she is returning to the "peaceful" place where she "was little," but the differences in her perceptions indicate the extent of her change. The final series of images involving parents and home is pervaded by her "shocked" realization: "without her father the world would be without its last resource. But . . . it will be me who is the last resource when my father is dead." The man who had, in the beginning, been a "living fortress" now lies "withering on the bed." Alabama at last remembers how she used to "gloat when something went wrong" as a symbolic breaching of her father's invulnerability. Though still sensitive to the "noble completeness" of her father's life, she now understands the mechanism of that completeness. Her father's house is small—smaller than those the grown up children live in. Its size is an equivalent of the less tangible curtailment which is his life method.

Money is the image which most clearly represents his limitations. He has saved the first coins he ever earned. His response to the early death of his only son is to ask in a "heartbreaking" cry how he can be expected to pay for the funeral. His parallel response to his own death is to hand Millie a check to cover his funeral expenses, stipulating that he wants it back if he doesn't die. "We can't afford this sickness," he says, "over and over," as he languishes toward death, and his last words are, "this thing is costing money." The accumulating references build an image of a man who limits his perceptions of life to tangible elements.

It is to such an individual that Alabama turns, seeking "some kind of shelter" from her prolonged struggle with life's less tangible results. Failing to allow for the discrepancy of their life methods, she formalizes her own experience into a final question for the "infallible" man who symbolizes justice, both publicly, as a judge, and personally, as her father. She asks if "our bodies are given to us as counterirritants to the soul," and why, in that case, bodies "fail" when they should bring surcease from "tortured minds," just as souls "desert us as a refuge" when "we are tormented in our bodies." Why has the dance failed to relieve her of the disappointments of marriage; why has her body failed her in the dance? "Ask me something easy," answers the dying man.

The ritual of transmission is complete. Alabama recalls her childhood rage at discovering that Santa Claus could exist as a myth that was not true. Yet she "feeds" on memories of her father "like converts imbibing a cult," even while she recognizes his small house, his failure to leave a final message, his limitation to the realm of "easy" questions. This resignation where once she would have been enraged marks the beginning of a new attempt to bring order and meaning to her life. She explains to David that "the object of the game" is to create "a beautiful harmonious mosaic of two gods of the hearthstone" so that when Bonnie is adult she will feel "less cheated" and will "believe that her restlessness will pass." She will attempt to set aside her own despair by deliberately creating an illusion for Bonnie. She will cherish the "cult" of parenthood—as distinct from the father who bequeathed her "many doubts"—by turning her attention to Bonnie's impression of their world.

Her vision is an attempt at compromise. Alabama recalls that "when she had wanted her own way about things," her father had told her that "if you want to choose, you must be a goddess." Her invocation of "two gods" echoes the language of the Judge's remark at the same time that her calling for "gods of the hearthstone" shows her effort to "choose" limitation in the form of the "conventional" role she recognizes as suitable for her mother and sister.

Domesticity does seem to be the only role left open to Alabama, and yet her ability to "choose" it appears to be limited by more than the difficulty implied by her father's attitude toward choice. David objects to what he considers "middle-aged moralizing." Bonnie misunderstands Alabama's concern with good manners. And the family "hearthstone" is a rented house through which the twilight flows like the "clear cold current of a trout stream." This final image, which incorporates a state of flux into the basic conditions of life, emphasizes the contrast between the perpetually moving household Alabama offers Bonnie and the "fortress" her father had seemed to create for her.

The possibility for success of Alabama's new "choice" is spelled out in the exchange which ends a party she and David have given on the basis of their re-established marriage:

> "I'm going to air the room a little," said Alabama. "I wish people wouldn't set wet glasses down on rented furniture."
>
> "Alabama," said David, "if you would stop dumping ash trays before the company has got well out of the house we would be happier."
>
> "It's very expressive of myself. I just lump everything in a great heap which I have labelled 'the

past,' and, having thus emptied this deep reservoir that was once myself, I am ready to continue."

She has remained a person "to whom things happen," but because of her own character and because of the society in which she lives, the happenings have served to cancel, to vacuum up, to empty the reservoir which she had hoped would prove a collecting pool. Compelled by energy and a dream of order, she applies herself to the role her family and society offer her. Searching for a life method whereby housework will prove "expressive of herself," she imagines she will order the past by dumping ashes. But David's complaint is justified regarding both housework and marriage. It is true that they would both be "happier" if she could resign herself to simply cleaning up instead of symbolizing order, if she could stop noticing that David is being courted for his remarkable artist's insight into the ballet—an insight which is derived from her own defeated efforts.

However, the "devils" which drive Alabama make such capitulation impossible to her. Torn between her father's inflexible will and her mother's conventional role, her own creativity and her society's norm, she is bound for defeat in every realm of life, from dancing to cleaning ashtrays. Her realism forces her to a recognition of the discontinuity between her present desire for resignation and the quality of her past integrity which produced the struggle that "was once myself." It is only her gallantry which allows her, though "empty," to continue.

From the beginning, Alabama's assumption of her own competence is clear. Her childhood contribution to her family's conversation on the awkwardness of crabs is to say "I believe I could make one . . . if I had the material." Such a God-complex might have been offensive in a more self-serving individual. But this drive is modified in Alabama by a remarkable honesty in analyzing the creature she did help to create: herself. In giving Alabama a part to play in her own making, Zelda Fitzgerald avoided the bathos which is a danger in the representation of defeat. Alabama's own personality, character and biology contribute centrally to her downfall. Her flamboyancy prevents her from succeeding at wifely things. Her lack of self-discipline defeats her talent. Her motherhood, her age and vulnerability to disease focus her other difficulties into a pattern of despair. Her biology is important also in that it informs her relations with her family and her society. The people with whom Alabama deals—her father, mother, husband, daughter, friends and colleagues—present a united view of the female role. And Alabama shares their view of normal womanhood. An additional part of her difficulty, then, is her conception of her own helpless abnormality.

In structuring Alabama's problem in this way, Zelda Fitzgerald avoided the polemic common in representations of the female version of defeat. The function of the novel is to trace the causes of Alabama's downfall, but the pattern of causation is so intricate and diversified and the responsibility so inadvertent that no villain is produced. Rather than assigning blame, Zelda Fitzgerald fleshes forth a situation and its results. This avoidance of oversimplification is the key to the novel's power. Dispassionately evoking the intricacy of the counterbalancing and contradicting elements of character and environment, Zelda Fitzgerald creates a convincing pattern out of apparent chaos and happenstance. In this lies the literary value of the work. (pp. 65-78)

Meredith Cary, " 'Save Me the Waltz' as a Novel," in Fitzgerald/Hemingway Annual: 1976, *1978, pp. 65-78.*

F. Scott Fitzgerald on *Save Me the Waltz*:

Turning up in a novel signed by my wife as a somewhat anemic portrait painter with a few ideas lifted from Clive Bell, Leger, etc. puts me in an absurd & Zelda in a ridiculous position. The mixture of fact & fiction is calculated to ruin us both, or what is left of us, and I can't let it stand. Using the name of a character I invented to put intimate facts in the hands of the friends and enemies we have accumulated *en route*—my God, my books made her a legend and her single intention in this somewhat thin portrait is to make me a non-entity.

F. Scott Fitzgerald, in a letter quoted in Scott Fitzgerald, *Scribner's, 1962.*

Victoria Sullivan   (essay date 1979)

[*Sullivan is an American educator, playwright, and critic. In the following essay, she maintains that apart from autobiographical considerations,* Save Me the Waltz *is worthy of critical attention for its poetic style, evocation of scene and personality, and subject matter.*]

Since Zelda Sayre Fitzgerald wrote a brilliant novel, **Save Me the Waltz**, published in the fall of 1932, one might well wonder why critics consistently fail to note her work, even when focusing on modern women writers. Large-scale ignorance of her worth as a writer is not the result of her having produced only one novel; after all, Kate Chopin wrote only *The Awakening*. No, clearly this critical disregard may be attributed to the fact that Zelda was married to F. Scott Fitzgerald, and that as his wife she became a legendary social figure. Her mythic image as the schizophrenic party-girl, riding on the tops of taxis and diving into fountains, has continued to flourish into the 1970's, while her writing has been relegated to the category of quaint footnote to Scott's literary career. However, to read **Save Me the Waltz** with an open mind is to be disabused of the notion that it is only the case history of a deranged wife. In fact it is as much a product of the creative imagination as any novel.

Nevertheless Zelda's creativity has regularly been viewed as a symptom of jealousy, a misguided effort to compete with or undercut her husband. Hemingway's biased but still classic assessment of Zelda in *A Moveable Feast* (New York: Bantam Books, 1965) is often cited as hard evidence:

Zelda was jealous of Scott's work and as we got

to know them, this fell into a regular pattern. . . . He would start to work and as soon as he was working well Zelda would begin complaining about how bored she was and get him off on another drunken party. . . . when he was drunk he would usually come to find me and, drunk, he took almost as much pleasure interfering with my work as Zelda did interfering with his.

Of course Hemingway is hardly the most objective person to pass judgement on the marriage, since there was strong hostility between himself and Zelda. She at one time described him as "bogus," and another time as "a pansy with hair on his chest." Still, his claim that Zelda was jealous tends to be accepted totally uncritically, even in the Afterword to the Signet paper edition of *Save Me the Waltz* (New York, 1968), where Matthew J. Bruccoli asserts: "That she competed with her husband for attention and even tried to rival him through her painting, writing, and dancing is clear." True, such an assessment does not comment on the quality of her work, but Bruccoli's position is disturbing in that it presents an interpretation—that she was almost solely motivated by rivalry in all she did—as a fact.

With such a patronizing attitude towards Zelda's artistic drive, *Save Me the Waltz* continues to be considered what Harry T. Moore has labeled "a literary curio" (Preface, *Save Me the Waltz,* 1967). Because of its autobiographical content, there is an interesting double standard revealed in critics' attitudes towards such a novel: if the critic admires the work, he finds that the autobiographical material has been cunningly transformed into art; if he is unsympathetic, he condemns it as "rather literally autobiographical," as Moore remarks of *Save Me the Waltz.* Then, too, the critic may damn the work by treating it as some sort of revealing secondary source; for instance Bruccoli claims that this novel is "worth reading partly because anything that illuminates the career of F. Scott Fitzgerald is worth reading." What is ignored here is that fiction is often spun from the thread of autobiographical perception; one would hardly call to ask Dickens, Joyce, D. H. Lawrence, Hemingway, or Scott Fitzgerald for such a practice.

Obviously Zelda used life's raw material, but as with any novelist it is the skill with which she shaped her material that ought to concern us. By not considering her work a fully realized novel, certain critics have relieved themselves of the need to discuss Zelda's artistry—her ironic technique, her thematic concerns, her use of recurring metaphors—because they have never admitted its existence. However, judged on the merits of its unique vision, style, and insight, *Save Me the Waltz* can stand on its own as a work of fiction.

Actually Zelda had been writing with skill and style since her adolescence, a talent recognized immediately by Scott, who regularly made use of her diaries and letters in creating his outrageous, glamorous heroines, such as the charming debutante Rosalind in *This Side of Paradise.* During the late 1920's and early 1930's Zelda co-authored a number of stories with Scott, and in a few instances her stories even went out under his name because they drew higher payments that way: $500 for a Zelda Fitzgerald story, and $4000 for one signed by Scott alone. Surely such a practice discouraged any sense of herself as a serious writer. Yet early in 1932, shortly after her father died, and on the verge of a second mental breakdown, she nonetheless started a novel.

Scott was busy with *Tender Is the Night,* a work which went through numerous revisions over nine discouraging years. Drinking heavily at the time, he was extremely antagonized by what he considered to be Zelda's stealing of "his" material. The material was their married life. Because they married in 1920, when Zelda was not quite twenty years old and Scott twenty-four, in effect Zelda's whole adult life was included in this raw material Scott claimed as his alone. Undeterred by her husband's territorial imperative, Zelda in several months of intense work completed the first draft of her novel.

The story traces the life of Alabama Beggs from childhood through romantic marriage to rising young painter David Knight, into motherhood, and finally to a chilling climax in her aborted career as a ballet dancer. A lively, bold, self-conscious southern belle, Alabama Beggs grows up with both a thirst for life and a need to be noticed. She is the golden girl—talented, picture pretty, and witty—with a loving mother, stern father, and a multitude of adoring beaus. She appears to be the American dream incarnate, but like all such fantasy creatures in serious works of art, life will exact a heavy price for her rites of passage into the cold world of reality. The dream must be destroyed.

There are three major areas in which Zelda's novel is unique and worthy of critical attention: its poetic style; its ironic evocation of scene and personality; and its subject matter, both the detailed description of the creation of a ballet dancer and the brutal, lyrical portrait of a woman destroyed in her efforts to achieve autonomy.

Stylistically the novel is not a smooth whole. In fact the first forty pages, where Zelda is still finding her narrative voice, are marred by excessive overlapping of images and eccentric word choices. Perhaps she was struggling to impress, although this style only slows the reader, and no doubt has turned away a number of the curious. But as the story progresses, the writing changes. One of Zelda's strengths is an eye for telling detail; she merely had to learn to control her technique. A skilled editor would have helped. When Scribners did publish it, the novel appeared with almost no publicity and printed on unusually cheap paper, a rather extraordinary practice for that prestigious publishing house. It was one more indication of the power of Scott's disapproval, since Scribners was also his publisher.

Zelda's style is characterized by a fusion of the visual and the psychological perception. She regularly infuses animation and spirit into the inanimate object or place; this is particularly the case in her descriptions of various domestic environments. Always Zelda senses the disjunction of the worlds in which she moves. Early in the novel she projects this emotional disjunction in a description of Alabama's childhood home, a place where the oppressively idealized father leaves his strange mark on everything:

> Dusk leaves no shadows or distortions in his rooms but transfers them to vaguer, grayer worlds, intact. Winter and spring, the house is like some lovely shining place painted on a mirror. When the chairs fall to pieces and the carpets grow full of holes, it does not matter in the brightness of that presentation. The house is a vacuum for the culture of Austin Beggs' integrity. Like a shining sword it sleeps at night in the sheath of his tired nobility.

Here she captures the sense of unreality (the house like a painting on a mirror, a picture within a picture), suffocation, decay, and alienation, but overloads the perception with the awkward and excessive alliteration of the shining sword which sleeps in the sheath of the father's tired nobility.

Later in the novel she attempts the same sort of subjective/objective fusion, but with greater control and power, as in a description of the expatriate party life:

> Nobody knew whose party it was. It had been going on for weeks. When you felt you couldn't survive another night, you went home and slept and when you got back, a new set of people had consecrated themselves to keeping it alive. It must have started with the first boatloads of unrest that emptied themselves into France in nineteen twenty-seven. Alabama and David joined in May, after a terrible winter in a Paris flat that smelled of a church chancery because it was impossible to ventilate. That apartment, where they had fastened themselves up from the winter rain, was a perfect breeding place for the germs of bitterness they brought with them from the Riviera.

In this paragraph Zelda reveals both the anonymity and the frantic hunger of the post World War I hedonism and despair. The mood is again one of dissociation, but curiously colored by the domestic detail of the Paris flat that is impossible to ventilate. The perverse unhealthiness of their situation is emphasized by "the germs of bitterness" they carry with them.

Not all her images are so bleak. Consider the special, almost divine qualities of the artist husband, David, conveyed in an early description:

> There seemed to be some heavenly support beneath his shoulder blades that lifted his feet from the ground in ecstatic suspension, as if he secretly enjoyed the ability to fly but was walking as a compromise to convention.

Here she combines an image of the supernatural and unreal, David as angel, with the simultaneous recognition that convention demands that one compromise—so David cannot be allowed to fly. Of course throughout the novel flight is a potent symbol. It is the ballet dancer's ultimate goal, or at least the illusion of flight. Flying also represents transcedence and it is significant that Alabama's unconsummated but dramatic affair is with a young French aviator. After the liaison is discovered and destroyed by David, she receives the false information that the flyer has crashed, the negative corollary of flight. In fact he flies off to the exotic land of China with a broken heart. Flight

and, for Alabama, dance may be emblematic of escape—a supernatural means of leaving this ordinary world of unventilated apartments and tired paternal nobility.

Of Alabama's growing absorption in and dedication to ballet, Zelda notes: "Her life outside was like trying to remember in the morning a dream from the night before." Dance has become the only significant reality with life itself becoming the dream. Yet the activity of dancing may produce imagery of a distorted and perverse morbidity as well. In a paragraph that develops by unusual analogy, Zelda moves from a macabre image of war, soldiers dancing with corpses, to Alabama's own grotesque domestic musings:

> The macabre who lived through the war have a story they love to tell about the soldiers of the Foreign Legion giving a ball in the expanses around Verdun and dancing with the corpses. Alabama's continued brewing of the poisoned filter for a semiconscious banquet table, her insistence on the magic and glamor of life when she was already feeling its pulse like the throbbing of an amputated leg, had something of the same sinister quality.

Not until the end of the long second sentence does the metaphor close on the shared sinister quality. What strikes one is the dancer's fascination with the most macabre of balls linked to the bizarre psychological brewing of a poisonous filter for some narcotic banquet. There are intimations of a perverse fairy tale here, in her insistence on the magic and glamor of life mixed with the rotting victims of World War I—all this served up on a platter that throbs like an amputated leg. It is the Brothers Grimm done one better (similar in its disturbing overtones to Anne Sexton's marvelously destructive poetic renditions of folk and fairy tales).

Zelda describes the pain of the process of becoming a dancer with precision:

> Alabama rubbed her legs with Elizabeth Arden muscle oil night after night. There were blue bruises inside above the knees where the muscles were torn. . . . In her bathing suit she tried to stretch on the high back of a Louis Quatorze sofa. She was always stiff, and she clutched the gilt flowers in pain. She fastened her feet through the bars of the iron bed and slept with her toes glued outward for weeks. Her lessons were agony.

Surely the pain is heroic, but also suggestive of the dance of death in its almost religious fanaticism. This tough, brutal process of personally inflicted torture is only ironically highlighted by the appurtenances of luxury, such as the Elizabeth Arden muscle oil and the gilded Louis Quatorze sofa. Still blue bruises heal. However, just at the moment it starts to take off, Alabama's career is destroyed by a small injury, which becomes seriously infected and leads to the disastrous surgery.

During the many weeks that she is confined to the hospital, Alabama occasionally hallucinates from the pain, and even when rational her vision has a touch of the schizophrenic:

"I must be very thin," she thought. The bedpan cut her spine, and her hands looked like bird claws. They clung to the air like claws to a perch, hooking the firmament as her right to a foot rest. Her hands were long and frail and blue over the knuckles like an unfeathered bird.

Typically she is once again torn between her need to escape earth's limitations, hooking the firmament, and the demands of the grotesquely mundane bedpan. The "unfeathered bird" is a particularly appropriate image for the hospitalized Alabama, since she had hoped so desperately that dance would free her, unburden her, let her fly like a winged creature. Earlier, "Her pas de bourrée progressed like a flying bird," and once when one of her fellow students asked her why she wished to be a dancer since she already possessed a husband, Alabama had explained: "Can't you understand that I am not trying to get anything—at least I don't think I am—but to get rid of some of myself?" She had been dreaming of soaring off the ground into the sky, and it was her tragedy that she was brought back to earth with a vengeance.

Zelda's most effective stylistic device is the use of recurring images and metaphors that build a sustained mood in the novel. Rich in illogic, these images nonetheless cohere and develop certain specific thematic concerns: one, the domestic environment as a negative, alienating, and sometimes dangerous milieu; two, the need to escape through transcendence, flight, dance, and unreality; and three, a recognition that pain and dissociation may be the price that one pays for pursuing a dream.

Zelda Fitzgerald has captured her schizophrenic vision in the language of metaphor, following her heroine from promising girlhood to adult disillusionment. She leaves David and Alabama both alive and wounded. In the final image of the novel:

> They sat in the pleasant gloom of late afternoon, staring at each other through the remains of the party; the silver glasses, the silver tray, the traces of many perfumes; they sat together watching the twilight flow through the calm living room that they were leaving like the clear cold current of a trout stream.

This very calmness is the antithesis of the flight Alabama has been seeking. It is the end of the day and the decade, but they have survived.

Save Me the Waltz is a chronicle of survival at great cost. Far less indulgent and romantic in its vision than either *Tender Is the Night* or *The Last Tycoon*, *Save Me the Waltz* is one of the more moving novels of female consciousness produced in the 1930's. Certainly Zelda Sayre Fitzgerald has been too long ignored among twentieth-century women writers. She deserves to be read and appreciated. (pp. 33-5, 37-9)

Victoria Sullivan, "An American Dream Destroyed: Zelda Fitzgerald," in The CEA Critic, *Vol. XLI, No. 2, January, 1979, pp. 33-5, 37-9.*

Linda W. Wagner   (essay date 1982)

[*Wagner is an American educator, critic, and poet. In the following essay, she analyzes the structure, themes, and style of* Save Me the Waltz.]

Ornamental, rococo, Zelda Fitzgerald's style in the beginning of her only novel, *Save Me the Waltz,* mimicks the adolescent flightiness of her protagonist, Alabama Beggs. Later in the book, as Alabama's father dies and she herself is ill, however, Fitzgerald's style is somber, spare, direct. Few writers have adapted their language and prose rhythms so capably to the emotional tone of the scene being described. *Save Me the Waltz* is both tone poem and highly evocative picture of what it means to a female child to grow up, to grow into the bleak recognition that being female in America is—or was at the turn of the century—synonymous with being inferior.

When Fitzgerald piles adjective upon adjective, building the incremental and breathless style that conveys Alabama's wistful charm, she runs the risk of losing her readers' sympathies. The prose suggests that there is no tragedy here, in Alabama's search for self and place. There is only an all-too-common theme of fearfulness and displacement.

> The swing creaks on Austin's porch, a luminous beetle swings ferociously over the clematis, insects swarm to the golden holocaust of the hall light. Shadows brush the Southern night like heavy, impregnated mops soaking in oblivion to

Zelda Fitzgerald's untitled painting of dancers.

the black heat from whence it evolved. Melancholic moonvines trail dark, absorbent pads over the string trellises.

"Tell me about myself when I was little," the youngest girl insists. She presses against her mother in an effort to realize some proper relationship.

"You were a good baby."

Consistent with this introductory scene, *Save Me the Waltz* shows Alabama's being pigeon-holed from the beginning of her life into the proper female roles: good girls don't cry, tease, whine. They do, however, defer to fathers, marry for money, and keep the family name respected. Her two older sisters, Dixie and Joan, set examples in all respects. When Dixie's former boyfriend commits suicide and she has a nervous breakdown, angry that her father had broken up the affair, her father's only comment is that he will not tolerate such "emotional nonsense." When his only son dies, he throws the bill for the funeral into his wife's lap and demands that she explain how he can pay such a bill. As Fitzgerald deftly shows, Judge Beggs is a tyrant. Viewed positively, he is "a living fortress," capable of carrying all the women of his family on his shoulders. But she also shows the ways his meek wife Millie has learned to get past his rigidity, calling her an "emotional anarchist" who permits whatever will work to keep peace and sanity. Millie's children are her primary concern. She does battle daily with her husband—although he does not realize the battle—over them. But the price for her success is complete personal and moral compromise.

Alabama's search for identity underscores her mother's relinquishment of her own being. Although she could manage only "a strong sense of her own insignificance" just as she is ready to marry, Alabama as a child knows that "she is like nothing at all and will fill out her skeleton with what she gives off . . . what effort she makes will become herself." As a teenager she claims that she must quit school, because she already knows "everything." And in some ways, Fitzgerald proves, Alabama does. As she watches her sister Joan meld into her boyfriend's personality, she thinks:

> There would be her father at the supper table. It was nearly the same; the necessity of being something that you really weren't was the same. Her father didn't know what she really was like, she thought.

Alabama also knows that marriage is not the blending of two personalities into one perfect whole, as the romanticists would have it, but rather that marriage is a selfish state, "that one person never seeks to share the future with another, so greedy are secret human expectations." "Being in love is simply a presentation of our pasts to another individual, mostly packages so unwieldy that we can no longer manage the loosened strings alone." Superior to her mother in that she insists on paying for the things she does, on recognizing them for what they really are—infidelities, lies, superficialities, Alabama seems to have a clear idea of what her various courtships with the military suitors finally mean. Yet when she meets David Knight, blond Adonis and would-be-painter, she falls into all the cultural expectations.

One key scene is David's carving on the country club doorpost: " 'David,' the legend read, 'David, David, Knight, Knight, Knight, and Miss Alabama Nobody.' 'Egotist,' she protested." The memory of the legend comes to haunt her, however, as she submits to giving up her name in the marriage ceremony and hearing repeatedly how famous David will become. Ironically, Alabama Beggs—whose street is also named for her family—has a much more prestigious name than does David. The pattern of female subservience, and Alabama's suppressed anger because of it, begins here. Fitzgerald follows this scene with an intimate lovers' conversation before the fire. Alabama imagines crawling into David's mind, becoming lost in the uniform "sleek grey matter" and hysterically beginning to run. Her commitment to him occurs because "So much she loved the man, so close and closer she felt herself that he became distorted in her vision, like pressing her nose upon a mirror and gazing into her own eyes. . . . She felt the essence of herself pulled finer and smaller like those streams of spun glass that pull and stretch till there remains but a glimmering illusion. She felt herself very small and ecstatic." The image becomes complete when David writes her repeatedly that she is his princess in the tower, and that he will keep her there forever. "Alabama asked him not to mention the tower again."

Even before the close of Part One of the novel, however, David confesses infidelity and the projection of trouble is clear. When a woman's identity is encompassed in the role of wife, when her worth is based almost entirely on her physical self—her "beauty," then physical betrayal is the ultimate rejection. Part Two opens with an abrupt description of the Knight's enormous and expensive bed. They have been married three years; they are famous, and wicked. They are also pregnant, even though David keeps ignoring that element in their lives, just as he will largely ignore the daughter Bonnie when she has been born.

The skill with which Fitzgerald conveys this common theme and event pattern has been generally ignored. Even the opening pages of *Save Me the Waltz* have dual purposes. They describe the personalities of Alabama's father and mother, showing her firm entrenchment in the myth of father as protector and mother as his helpmeet; but they also show the rigid role division within the Beggs family. For all the seeming unconventionality of the Knights' culture, David's expectations are just as traditional as Alabama's father's, and—most unfortunate of all—Alabama's expectations are equally traditional. She has been reared in a home where the aura of permanence and protection surrounds her: "the house is like some lovely shining place painted on a mirror." Evanescent as that aura was whenever it came in conflict with people's emotional needs, Alabama still believed in it. She saw that that mood resulted from her mother's work, and assumed the role of making David's world lovely and shining. Part Two of the novel shows his unfaithfulness with a woman who makes no pretense of being comforting or devoted, and his act shatters all Alabama's expectations.

Her anger leads to her own infidelity but more important,

to a search for some way to give meaning to her life. Being David's wife has become hollow, and she does not yet see the value in being only Bonnie's mother. Alabama's turn to the study of ballet, and her comparative success in that study, is the subject of the two concluding segments of the novel.

Perhaps because of its structure rather than its themes or language, *Save Me the Waltz* deserves to be known as a modernist novel. Readers might presume to know the "story" the book tells—the beautiful Southern Zelda Sayre, her father's darling, carried off by the Northern lieutenant-writer to a life of exotic companionship, drinking, and behavior calculated to gain media coverage as well as friends' approval. Later, but not much later, after the birth of Scottie, Zelda attempts to become a writer and a dancer (the literary world frowns at her "competitiveness"). And from 1930 on, she lives in one mental institution after another. Even though *Save Me the Waltz* is autobiographical and chronological, it is also interestingly fragmented. Events do not follow events in an expected order; scenes juxtapose with other scenes, and Fitzgerald uses very little formal transition. By presenting the story from Zelda/Alabama's perspective, the novel focuses on the emotionally crucial happenings. We see David's infidelity but we know almost nothing about the Knights' first three years of marriage. That he plans an affair because, in his words, "my work's getting stale. I need new emotional stimulus," makes Alabama doubly furious. She not only loses her husband; she is reminded again that her life is of little worth compared to that of the artist, that she has nothing of importance to do or to think about.

Alabama's own unfaithfulness is retaliation both conscious and unconscious. She will pay Knight back in his own coin. She will also become an artist. And in the process of learning to dance, she replaces the former idols in her life—her father and David—with the Russian ballerina who is her teacher. Fitzgerald's description of Madame is one of the best portrayals in American literature of the older woman who is dedicated to, and impassioned by, her work. In the structure of Parts Three and Four, the tacit recognition that Alabama has formerly misplaced her allegiances becomes clear. Women can help other women find their strengths. The adversarial role Alabama used with other women disappears, and she is able to know her limitations, and theirs, without disappointment.

Given the elliptical structure of *Save Me the Waltz,* Fitzgerald yet manages to develop suspense and classic rising action. The four sections of the novel underscore the importance of having the book tell Zelda/Alabama's story, rather than the story of the Knights as a pair. David's ostensible success would have alleviated the sense of tragedy implicit in the story line of his wife. Section One gives Zelda/Alabama's background and her change of venue, from her father's house to the proprietorship of David Knight. Section Two shows her vacillating loyalty, as she sees the flaws in her husband's character (which at times mirror her own) and tries to find ways around conflict with him. For her, the best recourse is to work at an art of her own. Part Three describes the pain and effort as Alabama becomes a proficient ballerina, while the conflicts

at home are muted (at least in this published version of the novel; Scott Fitzgerald and Scribners made many changes in the manuscript Zelda originally submitted).

Part Four begins the fantasy of the novel, as Alabama leaves David and their daughter Bonnie to take a role in a professional ballet company in Rome. (In real life, Zelda refused that offer and instead went to Africa with Scott.) In the fiction, Alabama falls seriously ill at the same time her father does. She lives but surgery on her foot cripples her and she will never dance again. Her acceptance of that fact, her acquiescence when David reappears to care for her, and her confusion when they return to America to see her dying father bring the novel to a realistic, unflinching end. There is no sense of a fairy-tale in this account of a princess who marries a prince (or knight).

Save Me the Waltz ends with a pall of sadness over Alabama's lost career and the Knights' fading marriage. Yet Alabama continues largely for Bonnie's sake, her anger modulated into a lament for the impermanence of her life with David, the futility of her attempts to create a "home." The novel closes with a passage as evocative as the last page of the much more famous Fitzgerald novel, *The Great Gatsby,* as Alabama tries to substitute defiance for sorrow:

> "I'm going to air the room a little," said Alabama. "I wish people wouldn't set wet glasses down on rented furniture."
>
> "Alabama," said David, "if you would stop dumping ash-trays before the company has got well out of the house we would be happier."
>
> "It's very expressive of myself. I just lump everything in a great heap which I have labelled 'the past,' and, having thus emptied this deep reservoir that was once myself, I am ready to continue."
>
> They sat in the pleasant gloom of late afternoon, staring at each other through the remains of the party: the silver glasses, the silvery tray, the traces of many perfumes; they sat together watching the twilight flow through the calm living-room that they were leaving like the clear cold current of a trout stream.

Moving past permanence, equating vitality with changes in place, the Knights existed only as shadows of real people. Fitzgerald's assertion is that neither David, for all his success, nor Alabama, for all her beauty, reached any kind of promise; and that Alabama's futility was the more damaging because she had once found purpose through the dance. To lose what one has known as joy—David, the dance, security in her father's house—is worse than not having known it. Fitzgerald's choice of title brings the several plot lines together effectively.

Although one usually thinks of the gentleman asking for a waltz to be saved, Fitzgerald shows Alabama thinking of David on the dance floor. She is the person who loves dancing; David can only admit "I never could waltz anyway." That Alabama later finds her identity in and through the dance is further elaboration on the image. Her art, however, is private; it is not something one could perform in drawing rooms. It has no ornamental value and, rather than enhancing David's life, it disrupts it.

Even Alabama's father is linked to the dance image. One of the last memories of him is meeting his future wife at a New Years ball. Alabama is surprised at this recollection; she "had never pictured her father dancing." Neither could she accept the frailty and self-absorption of the dying man. She assumes that he will have some kind of final message for her, that she is still the center of his life, and she searches long after his death for that precious word. What she feels as abandonment only reinforces her sense of loss and crumbling self-esteem.

The title *Save Me the Waltz* gains its force from the juxtaposition of the first two words—*save me*—with the last. The flightiness and superficiality of the Southern culture, of romance, of a woman's world of parties and gossip suggested by the waltz image are at cruel variance with Alabama's real needs. Her turn to ballet was a religious passage, a means of finding value through extreme dedication, pain, effort. Defeated (in the fiction) by the very body that was to be her means into the world of art, she spoke about her loss seldom: we would never expect to hear the title phrase from Alabama's lips. The physical and spiritual terror of her existence, portrayed so well in this novel, was that her life did continue, a fabric of arguments of proper social codes, balanced check books, and David's important work as painter. *Save Me the Waltz* is an ironic fiction which paints the disspirited modern woman as vividly as Eliot's *The Waste Land* did the modern temper.

For those readers who knew the story of the destructive Fitzgerald marriage, *Save Me the Waltz* made an almost unthinkably direct and remorseless statement. Fitzgerald's anger when he learned that Zelda had written the book in two months of her stay at the Phipps Clinic, with the support of psychiatrist Mildred Squires, to whom the book is dedicated, tells volumes about the competitiveness between the two. As more and more is learned about madness and about cultural pressures, readers may be able to reconcile the differences among Fitzgerald biographers, and come closer to the truth about "support" which might be termed "overprotectiveness," "love" which might be called "possession," and even "madness" which might be described as socially-approved escape.

Reviewers contemporary with the novel in 1932, however, were interested in the book largely because it was written by F. Scott Fitzgerald's wife. Published in October of 1932 to very little fanfare by Scribners, *Save Me the Waltz* sold fewer than 1400 copies and brought Zelda only $120 in royalties. Reviews were circumspect, mixed, and brief.

Arthur D. Pierce saw that the novel was "a cry from the heart of the woman . . . resolved to pay gladly for the freedom she deliberately determined to have" but several other reviewers found the novel "shallow." As Jane Morrison wrote, "The novel is a wordy and voluminous portrayal of twentieth century life as it is imagined, rather than as it really is." One thinks of Charlotte Perkins Gilman's *The Yellow Wallpaper,* published so many years before in 1899, and wonders how often women's stories will be written off as fantasy. Readers seemed bent on refusing

to recognize the reality of the book, in fact; W.E.H. complained in *The Boston Transcript* that "The power of such a novel would be stronger if the reader could discern the author's own feeling in regard to her characters." When readers mentioned the life of the Fitzgeralds and the other Paris expatriates, they were likely to carp at Zelda for reusing the materials of *The Beautiful and Damned.*

One of the difficulties with *Save Me the Waltz*—the structure which depended for coherence on juxtaposition and a free-floating sequence of events—was also its strength narratively, in that structure also showed character. Charlotte Becker compared Fitzgerald's methods to those of the Follies, but found them effective; she admired Zelda for writing "in a style of her own" and with "sensitive talent." C.F.R. in the *Philadelphia Public Ledger* found the book "constructive in thought, clever in execution, fascinating and brisk," revealing "a distinct, forceful personality." *Save Me the Waltz* is "sincere and distinctive." "With deft turns here and there she creates a complete impression without indulging in long discursive passages. Her style is succinct and refreshing, clear and under perfect control." Dorothea Brande, too, in the *Bookman,* complains about Fitzgerald's vocabulary but concludes that "There is a warm, intelligent, undisciplined mind behind *Save Me the Waltz.*" Even the *New York Times,* mentioning her "atrocious style," praises the novel and notes that it gains "vitality" as it moves along.

Most readers know that Zelda helped Scott with his writing. Rather than relegate her aid to spelling corrections, perhaps we should note her own published stories and essays, and the fact that in the early 1930s Scott published several stories that were entirely Zelda's work under his own name, so magazines would pay high rates. *Save Me the Waltz* was, then, not a usual "first novel" but the culmination of many years of Zelda's working with words and considering herself a writer. As she wrote in March, 1932, to Scott about the book:

> I am proud of my novel, but I can hardly restrain myself enough to get it written. You will like it—It is distinctly Ecole Fitzgerald, though more ecstatic than yours—Perhaps too much so.

Zelda's recognition that her style was "ecstatic" suggests that her lush vocabulary and impressionistic structure was intentional. She knew how to write the way her husband did but she purposely chose to write the way *she* did. One of the closing scenes of the novel, that in which David is allowed to visit Alabama after her long stay in the hospital, illustrates her spare description, albeit highly figurative, and her rapid progression from idea to idea, scene to scene:

> Twice a day he came to the hospital and listened to the doctors telling about blood poison.
>
> Finally they let him see her. He buried his head in the bedclothes and ran his arms underneath her broken body and cried like a baby. Her legs were up in sliding pulleys like a dentist's paraphernalia. The weights ached and strained her neck and back like a medieval rack.
>
> Sobbing and sobbing, David held her close. He

felt of a different world to Alabama; his tempo was different from the sterile, attenuated rhythms of the hospital. He felt lush and callous, somehow, like a hot labourer. She felt she hardly knew him.

He kept his eyes glued persistently to her face. He hardly dared look at the bottom of the bed.

"Dear, it's nothing," he said, with affected blandness. "You will be well in no time." Somehow she was not reassured. He seemed to be avoiding some issue. Her mother's letters did not mention her foot and Bonnie was not brought to the hospital.

"I must be very thin," she thought. The bedpan cut her spine, and her hands looked like bird claws. They clung to the air like claws to a perch. . . . Her hands were long and frail and blue over the knuckles like an unfeathered bird.

What Fitzgerald achieves in this brief segment is a tribute to the restrained, highly-imaged style she has carved. David's evasiveness, his frantic need to protect (even at the cost of honesty), his rhetoric create a person so different from Alabama's weary sense of truth that he might as well be a "hot labourer," someone far outside the realm of Alabama and David's social milieu. Once Fitzgerald gives us his description through the tough image, she continues to describe him as a pretender. Then, after five paragraphs about David and David's fantasies, she switches abruptly (but reasonably—our attention has indirectly been on Alabama throughout because she is the one who is sick) to the monologue of the protagonist. The five opening words, "I must be very thin," coalesce impressions made throughout the preceding pages, and Fitzgerald pounds home the impression with the image of the bedpan, followed by the more moving picture of the hands as bird claws, a picture that takes shape through subsequent color and detail.

Again and again through *Save Me the Waltz*, Fitzgerald manages to create and evoke simultaneously. The reader receives an apt and accurate picture, but enough tension occurs in the image to set loose reverberations that echo and swirl, coloring later references, blending the separate scenes into one narrative, a narrative which was, and is, not only "a cry from the heart of a woman" but also a haunting novel. (pp. 201-08)

> *Linda W. Wagner, " 'Save Me the Waltz': An Assessment in Craft," in* The Journal of Narrative Technique, *Vol. 12, No. 3, Fall, 1982, pp. 201-09.*

FURTHER READING

Bibliography

Bruccoli, Matthew J. "Zelda Fitzgerald's Publications." In his *F. Scott Fitzgerald: A Descriptive Bibliography*, pp. 299-309. Pittsburgh: University of Pittsburgh Press, 1972.
Chronological listing including periodical publication information.

Biography

Mayfield, Sara. *Exiles from Paradise: Zelda and Scott Fitzgerald.* New York: Delacorte Press, 1971, 309 p.
Partisan account of the Fitzgeralds' lives. Mayfield treats passages from Zelda Fitzgerald's published fiction as biographical fact and assesses Zelda as an enormously talented writer who was systematically repressed by her husband and his associates.

Mellow, James R. *Invented Lives: F. Scott and Zelda Fitzgerald.* Boston: Houghton Mifflin Company, 1984, 569 p.
A detailed biographical account of the Fitzgeralds' marriage that Mellow asserts is "about the personal cost of American success and American failure."

Milford, Nancy. *Zelda: A Biography.* New York: Harper & Row Publishers, 1970, 424 p.
Close examination of Fitzgerald's life, career, and marriage.

Smith, Scottie Fitzgerald. Foreword to *Bits of Paradise: 21 Uncollected Stories by F. Scott and Zelda Fitzgerald*, pp. 1-7. London: Bodley Head, 1973.
Reminiscence by the Fitzgeralds' daughter.

Criticism

Bruccoli, Matthew J. "A Note on the Text." In *Save Me the Waltz*, by Zelda Fitzgerald, pp. 239-55. Carbondale: Southern Illinois University Press, 1967.
Account of the novel's composition, various drafts and revisions, and publication history.

———. Preface to *Bits of Paradise: 21 Uncollected Stories by F. Scott and Zelda Fitzgerald*, pp. 8-13. London: Bodley Head, 1973.
Provides periodical publication information and offers some critical assessment.

Fryer, Sarah Beebe. "Nicole Warren Diver and Alabama Beggs Knight: Women on the Threshold of Freedom." *Modern Fiction Studies* 31, No. 2 (Summer 1985): 318-26.
Compares the treatment of similar subject matter in F. Scott Fitzgerald's *Tender Is the Night* and Zelda Fitzgerald's *Save Me the Waltz*, maintaining that the latter work possesses the "uncommon distinction of viewing from a woman's perspective events and characters made famous by a male author."

Going, William T. "Two Alabama Writers: Zelda Sayre Fitzgerald and Sara Haardt Mencken." *The Alabama Review* XXIII, No. 1 (January 1970): 3-29.
Examines the similarities in the lives of Fitzgerald and Mencken, the parallel themes found in their works, and their disparate personalities.

Hellman, Geoffrey. "Beautiful and Damned." *The Saturday Review of Literature* (New York) IX, No. 14 (22 October 1932): 190.
Commends isolated sections of *Save Me the Waltz* but considers the book flawed by Fitzgerald's reliance on intricate metaphor.

Moore, Harry T. Preface to *Save Me the Waltz*, by Zelda

Fitzgerald, pp. vii-xi. Carbondale: Southern Illinois University Press, 1967.

> Critical assessment focusing on the novel's publication history and shared themes with *Tender Is the Night.*

Tavernier-Courbin, Jacqueline. "Art as Woman's Response and Search: Zelda Fitzgerald's *Save Me the Waltz.*" *The Southern Literary Journal* XI, No. 2 (Spring 1979): 22-42.

> Favorable assessment of *Save Me the Waltz,* discussing the novel in relation to Fitzgerald's life.

Additional coverage of Fitzgerald's life and career is contained in the following sources published by Gale Research: *Contemporary Authors,* Vols. 117, 126; and *Dictionary of Literary Biography Yearbook, 1984.*

Sigmund Freud

1856-1939

Austrian psychologist, neurologist, nonfiction writer, essayist, biographer, and autobiographer.

INTRODUCTION

Freud is considered one of the most influential and controversial thinkers of the twentieth century for his development of the theories and methodologies of psychoanalysis. Central to his theory is the concept of the unconscious, which he described as a primitive region of the psyche containing emotions, memories, and drives that are hidden from and repressed by the conscious mind. Freud's formulation of a method for retrieving and analyzing repressed psychic material established psychoanalysis as an indispensable form of therapy in treating neurotic disorders, many of which were first identified by Freud and his followers. Freud has also exerted a profound influence on the broader culture of the twentieth century, inspiring artists, writers, critics, and filmmakers. Many of the psychoanalytic terms that Freud coined—"narcissism," "repression," "transference,"—have entered the vernacular of several languages. Despite the widespread application of the principles of psychoanalysis in the field of psychology, Freud's writings continue to ignite controversy in such diverse disciplines as feminist literary theory, linguistics, and hermeneutics.

Freud was born in Freiberg, Moravia. At the age of four he moved with his family to Vienna, Austria, where he spent the remainder of his life, with the exception of a brief period of exile in London shortly before his death. After graduating summa cum laude from the Sperl Gymnasium, Freud enrolled at the University of Vienna as a medical student. In 1876 he entered Ernst Brücke's Institute of Physiology as a research scholar and concentrated on the histology of nerve cells. He graduated from the institute in 1881 and a year later began practicing at the Vienna General Hospital, moving between several departments, including Internal Medicine, the Psychiatric Clinic, and the Department of Nervous Diseases. After he obtained a license in neuropathology, Freud left the hospital permanently. He obtained a travel grant to study in Paris under neurologist Jean-Martin Charcot, who used hypnosis to analyze and treat hysteria, a psychological condition encompassing a broad range of emotional, sensory, visceral, and vasomotor disorders. In 1886 Freud started his private practice in neuropathology and a year later began using hypnosis as an analytic and therapeutic method. Freud soon abandoned hypnosis, however, believing that it placed the therapist in an intrusive and manipulative role and that it was an ineffective means of gaining access to his patients' unconscious emotions. By 1895 Freud began formulating his theory of free association, a method

which allowed his patients to freely summon submerged impressions and memories. Freud eventually reached the conclusion that all neuroses are sexually based, and that his patients' symptoms were products of repressive forces that mask conflicting drives within the dynamic regions of the psyche. He termed these regions the id, ego, and superego. According to Freud, the id is the source of instinctual needs and drives; the ego the site of reason and conscious awareness; and the superego the source of conscience and morality. During this same period, Freud arrived at his famous dictum that every dream is the fulfillment of an unconscious wish. In addition to operating his private practice, delivering lectures, and writing such works as *Die Traumdeutung* (*The Interpretation of Dreams*) and *Zur Psychopathologie des Alltagslebens* (*Psychopathology of Everyday Life*), Freud founded the Vienna Psychoanalytical Society in 1908, and two years later, the International Psychoanalytical Association (IPA).

After 1910 the psychoanalytic movement gained steady impetus, while simultaneously generating vehement opponents, some of whom were former colleagues of Freud, including Alfred Adler and Carl Jung. Adler disagreed with the psychosexual basis of Freud's psychology and formed a discipline known as individual psychology, which postulated that inferiority complexes were the basis for neurotic disorders. Jung emphasized the positive potential of religious impulses for integrating and resolving personality conflicts and theorized that the unconscious is a collective entity which transmits archetypal cultural values and symbols. In the United States the psychoanalytic movement generally encountered less resistance, though Freud disparaged its acceptance as the result of popular accounts of his theories and irresponsible translations of his books. In his later works, including *Die Zukunft einer Illusion* (*The Future of an Illusion*), *Das Unbehagen in der Kultur* (*Civilization and Its Discontents*), and *Der Mann Moses und die monotheistische Religion* (*Moses and Monotheism*), Freud focused on religion as a cause of neurotic illness that afflicts both individuals and society as a whole. During the 1930s, Freud was denigrated by the Nazis as a "degenerate" Jewish thinker, and his books were burned at public rallies. Despite the perilous political situation in Austria after the 1938 German invasion, Freud remained in Vienna for several months before fleeing to England, where he spent the final year of his life. Freud died of cancer in 1939.

Freud's ideas continue to generate controversy, particularly in the fields of psychotherapy, literary criticism, religious studies, and anthropology. One of the most pervasive objections to psychoanalysis is that it is a reductionist attempt to attribute all human behavior to sexual impulses. Marxist and feminist critics argue that since Freud drew upon his own personal neuroses as a model for the human psyche in general, his psychology has strong bourgeois and phallocentric biases. Clinical psychiatrists are frequently indifferent or hostile towards psychoanalysis, emphasizing that the majority of mental illnesses, including most psychoses, can be understood and treated as neurochemical abnormalities. Nevertheless, most scholars readily acknowledge that Freud was one of the major thinkers of the modern era for his formulation of a comprehensive theory of the human mind, his revolutionary approach to therapy, the originality of his work, and the remarkable diffusion of his ideas in twentieth-century culture.

PRINCIPAL WORKS

Studien über Hysterie [with Josef Breuer]   (case studies) 1895
   [*Studies in Hysteria*, 1909]
Die Traumdeutung   (nonfiction)   1900
   [*The Interpretation of Dreams*, 1913]
Über den Traum   (nonfiction)   1901
   [*On Dreams*, 1914]
Zur Psychopathologie des Alltagslebens   (nonfiction) 1901
   [*Psychopathology of Everyday Life*, 1914]
Bruchstück einer Hysterie-Analyse   (case study)   1905

["Fragment of an Analysis of a Case History," published in *Collected Papers*, Vol. 3, 1925]
Drei Abhandlungen zur Sexualtheorie   (essays)   1905
   [*Three Contributions to the Sexual Theory*, 1910; also published as *Three Essays on the Theory of Sexuality*, 1949]
Der Witz und seine Beziehung zum Unbewussten   (nonfiction)   1905
   [*Wit and Its Relation to the Unconscious*, 1916]
Beiträge zur Psychologie des Liebeslebens   (nonfiction) 1910
   [*Contributions to the Psychology of Love*, 1925]
Eine Kindheitserinnerung des Leonardo da Vinci   (biography)   1910
   [*Leonardo da Vinci: A Psychosexual Study of Infantile Reminiscence*, 1916]
Über Psychoanalyse: Fünf Vorlesungen   (lectures)   1910
   [*The Origin and Development of Psychoanalysis*, 1910; also published as *Five Lectures on Psychoanalysis*, 1911]
Totem und Tabu: Über einige Übereinstimmungen im Seelenleben der Wilden und der Neurotiker   (nonfiction)   1912
   [*Totem and Taboo: Resemblances between the Psychic Lives of Savages and Neurotics*, 1918]
Zur Geschichte der psychoanalytischen Bewegung   (nonfiction)   1914
   [*The History of the Psychoanalytic Movement*, 1916]
Vorlesungen zur Einführung in die Psychoanalyse. 3 vols.   (nonfiction)   1917
   [*A General Introduction to Psychoanalysis*, 1920; also published as *Introductory Lectures on Psychoanalysis*, 1922]
Jenseits des Lustprinzips   (nonfiction)   1920
   [*Beyond the Pleasure Principle*, 1922]
Massenpsychologie und Ich-Analyse   (nonfiction)   1921
   [*Group Psychology and the Analysis of the Ego*, 1922]
Das Ich und das Es   (nonfiction)   1923
   [*The Ego and the Id*, 1927]
Selbstdarstellung   (autobiography)   1925
   [*An Autobiographical Study*, 1935]
Die Frage der Laienanalyse: Unterredungen mit einem Unparteiischen   (nonfiction)   1926
   [*The Problem of Lay-Analyses*, 1927; also published as *The Question of Lay-Analysis: An Introduction to Psychoanalysis*, 1947]
Hemmung, Symptom und Angst   (nonfiction)   1926
   [*Inhibition, Symptom and Anxiety*, 1927]
Die Zukunft einer Illusion   (nonfiction)   1927
   [*The Future of an Illusion*, 1928]
Das Unbehagen in der Kultur   (nonfiction)   1930
   [*Civilization and Its Discontents*, 1930]
Neue Folge der Vorlesungen zur Einführung in die Psychoanalyse   (lectures)   1933
   [*New Introductory Lectures on Psychoanalysis*, 1933]
Die endliche und unendliche Analyse   (nonfiction)   1937
   [*Analysis Terminable and Interminable*, 1937]
Der Mann Moses und die monotheistische Religion   (nonfiction)   1939
   [*Moses and Monotheism*, 1939]
Abriss der Psychoanalyse   (nonfiction)   1940
   [*An Outline of Psychoanalysis*, 1940]

CRITICISM

The Nation　(essay date 1913)

[*In the following negative review of* The Interpretation of Dreams, *the critic provides an overview of Freud's dream theories. While praising certain of Freud's earlier contributions to psychiatry, the reviewer faults this work for its lack of scientific rigor and validity.*]

Professor Freud's work in psychotherapeutics, and the effective results gained in connection with his "psychoanalytic method," have attracted wide attention among psychiatrists and the medical fraternity. This method consists in inducing a patient to avoid all attempt at guiding his thoughts, and to report the images and ideas which spontaneously appear to him under these conditions. Many of the images, etc., which thus arise in the patient's mind evidently relate to experiences long since forgotten, which the practitioner is able to recall to the patient by skilful questioning. Our author and his followers hold that we are able by this method to discover the basis of certain obsessions and phobias, the evil effects of which may be removed by what may be called a cathartic treatment. In the course of his many psycho-analyses Freud has been much impressed by the important fact that the forgotten experiences resuscitated by this means bear a striking resemblance to the content of dream life, and this has led him to adopt the theory of dreams presented in [*The Interpretation of Dreams*]. The drift of the author's argument is far from clear, being obscured by great diffuseness and occasional elusiveness of statement. Readers are therefore in danger of being led by his abounding self-confidence and enthusiasm to accept without question his clever interpretations which are given with great wealth of detail, and to accept without due criticism the dream theory which these interpretations are supposed to substantiate.

Stripped of all illustrative material, the theory may be stated as follows: Our author's main interest is centred upon the thesis that every dream is the fulfilment of an unconscious wish. He conceives of this wish as an active entity which strives to rise into full consciousness and to effect its realization, this being thwarted by the action of another entity which he designates as the "censor." "The psychic activity in dream formation resolves itself into two functions—the provision of the dream thoughts" which are unconscious, "and the transformation of these into the dream content." This latter activity is "peculiar to dream life and characteristic of it, . . . something qualitatively altogether different from waking thought, and therefore not in any way comparable to it. It does not, in general, think, calculate, or judge at all, but limits itself to transforming. . . . This product, the dream, must at any cost be withdrawn from the censor"; this being accomplished by a variety of devices. The dream under his view would not occur unless it had a special function, which is thus described: "The dream has taken it upon itself to bring the liberated excitement of the unconscious back under the domination of the fore-conscious; it thus affords relief for the excitement of the unconscious, and acts as a safety valve for the latter."

Before examining this theory in detail we may well call attention to two contributions to psychology made by Professor Freud in other works, and brought into prominence in the book before us. It is, of course, no discovery of his that there exists an elusive psychic field, commonly spoken of among us as "subconsciousness," which is quite beyond the limits of awareness, and which has its influence upon the psychic field of which we are aware (our author's "fore-consciousness"); but this fact has only of late years gained adequate attention from psychologists, who, in the face of the phenomena brought to view by Freud's investigations, can no longer ignore its significance. His results also force upon our notice the fact, of which again, however, he is not the discoverer, that consciousness is a complex system of psychic systems, even as the nervous system whose activities correspond with consciousness is a complex system of minor nerve systems. Here again psychologists must acknowledge that the emphasis laid upon the "unity of consciousness" has led them to overlook facts which our author's studies compel them to take account of.

This latter point leads us at once to the consideration of the doctrine of the "censor" to which our author gives so great prominence. This "censor" is spoken of as a psychic system or clever psychic entity which resists the "penetration to consciousness of the dream thoughts," and which our author likens "to the Russian newspaper censor on the frontier, who allows to fall into the hands of his protected readers only those foreign journals that have passed under the black pencil." When the censor fears that the dream thought will escape his vigilance he resorts to all sorts of artifices to forestall its persistency. He changes the dream so that it becomes repugnant rather than attractive. He moulds the dream by distortion; by displacement and condensation; by substitutions; by the suppression and inversion of pleasure-pain and emotional reactions; by making it appear foolish and disconnected; by forcing us to forget it upon awakening. Never, indeed, should we have a dream but for the fact that "the sleeping state makes dream formation possible by diminishing the endopsychic factor."

The layman certainly must see in this conception much that will appear to him fantastic, if not absurd. The psychologist must see in it the building of a huge structure upon a very slim and unstable foundation. It is to be agreed, of course, that the psychic system of which we are aware in waking life, moulded as it has been, and is, by the social influences that surround us, prevents the fruition of desires and frustrates the development of thought trains which are inimical to our welfare as social beings. But this acknowledgment does not warrant us in holding that this wide-awake consciousness is an entity so separate and diverse from the other psychic systems within us as our author would have us believe. All the evidence before us leads to the view that consciousness is fundamentally of the same nature through and through: that differences of systemic form occur within it; but that these are always in some measure correlated and are constantly more or less influential in determining the nature of that field of consciousness of which we are aware: this being quite compatible with the fact that when we feel consciousness to be less than fully alert prominence is gained by other psychic systems than that which is evidenced in moments of full alertness.

Passing over the final labored and obscure elaboration of this censorship, which points to another censor governing "the transition from the fore-conscious to the occupation of consciousness," we may turn to the main thesis, viz., that "the content of the dream is the fulfilment of a wish; its motive is a wish." This thesis is based on the author's analysis of dream contents which, if allowed to develop, very frequently, if not usually, bring into prominence some wish which in the dream is felt to be realized. This fact none will deny, but question at once arises whether this is a special characteristic of dream consciousness. It surely is true that the development of the thoughts which arise in everyday wide-awake life also constantly yields wishes that are immediately followed by pictures of the consequences of their imagined fulfilment. In this characteristic of dream life we therefore find no unique psychic functioning.

But in dream life, as in wide-awake life, there are many cases where wishes are not observable. This fact, however, does not balk our theorist, who warns us that his "doctrine does not rest upon the acceptance of the manifest dream content, but has reference to the thought content which is found to lie behind the dream by the process of interpretation." And here he displays extraordinary ingenuity in ferreting out dream wishes where none at first appears, by methods which, by the way, would yield very similar results if applied to normal waking consciousness. In his other writings our author has given evidence of a morbid tendency to over-emphasize the potency of erotic influences in all of experience, and in the field here considered the results of this preconception are conspicuous, leading him to improbable and revolting explanations. It may be true that these influences are very powerful in our adult lives; true also that they have been powerful in infantile life, and by their early activity have resultants which are felt as we come to mature. It is to be noted, however, that the traces thus left are likely to appear in wide-awake life when we allow our thoughts to flow without restriction, as well as in dream life, which latter is so closely allied with our uncontrolled waking states that we are led to speak of the latter as "day dreaming." All this may be granted, however, without forcing us to follow our author in his insistence that virtually all such dream wishes must have this origin. The illegitimacy of his method is evidenced in many directions; notably, for instance, in the interpretation of dreams of "dental irritation." It may be illustrated by reference to his explanation of dreams which picture the death of beloved parents. He is unable to "use the dream as a proof that" the dreamer "wishes them dead *now*. The theory of dreams . . . is satisfied with concluding that the dreamer has wished them dead—at some one time in childhood." The antagonism of children to parents who punish them is thus made to explain certain of these death dreams; but the largest proportion of them he would account for as due to infantile erotic influences. The man dreams of the death of his beloved father because in childhood he had felt sexual attraction towards his mother, and had wished for the death of his father who was his effective rival. Apart from the forced and repulsive nature of this explanation it can evidently apply only to dreams where the dead parent is of the same sex as the dreamer, and is negatived by the fact that these death dreams frequently refer to parents of the opposite sex. He agrees that this sometimes happens, but contends that it is exceptional, without attempting in any way to substantiate this claim.

Finally, when we turn to our author's thesis that the dream has a special function, we find ourselves naturally led to assume a skeptical attitude by the fact that throughout the whole of his studies evidence constantly appears which leads us to note the closest of relations between our wide-awake and our dream consciousness. This our author accepts or denies as occasion requires. He agrees "that all the material composing the content of the dream in some way originates in experience"; that "the experiences of the previous day furnish the immediate material for its content"; that the dream thoughts "are usually found to be a complex of thoughts and memories of the most intricate possible construction, and to possess all the properties of the thought processes which are known to us from waking life"; and even goes so far as to say that Aristotle was correct in holding that "the dream is a continuation of thinking in sleep." Yet, as we have seen above, he bases his theory upon the assumption that there is an activity in the transformation of dream thoughts into dream content which is "something qualitatively altogether different from waking thought, and therefore not in any way comparable to it," and he finally asks us to believe that "it is quite impossible to explain the dream as a psychic process."

One cannot close this book without a sense of depression. The author is a man of great ability, who has won distinction in connection with his use of the psycho-analytic method, and who is believed to have done great service in his special field by a large group of his professional brethren, not all of whom, however, agree that his theoretical positions are valid. But his mode of thought as displayed in this book is indicative of a total lack of the characteristics which lead to scientific advance. In it he portrays himself as one whose scientific judgment cannot be trusted, and this must lead even his most enthusiastic followers to question whether they are not overestimating the value of his work in other directions. He presents an example of the dangers connected with the extreme specialization characteristic of the educational systems of our day, which fails to strengthen the sense of logical values so important to the development of a true science. Their appreciation would have led our author to use caution in the adoption of doubtful hypotheses, and to hesitate to take the attitude of a special pleader who emphasizes all evidence favorable to the hypothesis adopted, and minimizes, if he does not overlook entirely, all evidence that is unfavorable. The value of his practical work in relation to hysteria and kindred problems will be remembered long after his theory of dreams has been forgotten. (pp. 503-05)

A review of "The Interpretation of Dreams," in
The Nation, *Vol. 96, No. 2498, May 15, 1913,
pp. 503-05.*

The New Republic   (essay date 1918)

[*In the following review of* Totem and Taboo, *the critic
praises Freud's investigation into the origins of human
behavior.*]

Professor Freud's volume [***Totem and Taboo***] is an attempt to enlist psychoanalytic study for the elucidation of these two ethnological problems. The book sees in the taboo a somewhat familiar phenomenon. The original meaning of totemism is more baffling. This it seeks "through its infantile traces, that is, through the indications in which it reappears in the development of our own children." These hypotheses are intended for "students of ethnology, philology, folklore and of the allied sciences," as well as psychoanalysts, but the author does not propose to do much more than stimulate his readers. His chapters, he says, "will furnish the former [the ethnologists] with sufficient insight into the new psychological technique, nor will the psychoanalysts acquire through them an adequate command over the material to be elaborated." But the suggestion is clear, the large and luminous hypothesis, and it is for some one else to amplify.

Those who are outside both ethnology and psychoanalysis may not expect to find much in these four essays, but perhaps one outsider may say that the book is extraordinarily provocative. It is not easy for the outsider to read it. While reading it his undisciplined mind takes some impressions much better than others, as if the ink of attention were not evenly or cleanly distributed. The result is muggy and blurred. But with all the disadvantages of imperfect apprehension and distressing inconclusion when the book is finished (I speak for myself) there is a thrilling sense of having had contact with a mind at work on the root-problems of human behavior. Much that is shoved out of sight is indispensable to the understanding of society, and it is the merit of Freud's excursion into the psychic life of savages that he finds exciting and illuminating clues to the aberrations of men and women and their intractability in the harness of civilization today. By groping among the brutal and bloody origins of society in the interest of psychology something emerges beside the usual dry memoranda on the Barongos and the Wakambas. A living connection is established between the Barongos and the people we know best. Freud is aware, of course, of the peculiar dangers of his own specialism. "An intellectual function in us demands the unification, coherence and comprehensibility of everything perceived and thought of, and does not hesitate to construct a false connection if, as a result of special circumstances, it cannot grasp the right one." How far Freud has avoided these temptations the expert must decide. He himself admits "improbability" in his own amazing conclusion that "the beginnings of religion, ethics, society, and art meet in the Oedipus complex." But in stating this "remarkable convergence" it is only fair to Freud to show the temper of his own comment on his conclusion. "This is in entire accord," he believes, "with the findings of psychoanalysis, namely, that the nucleus of all neuroses, as

far as our present knowledge goes, is the Oedipus complex. It comes as a great surprise to me that these problems of racial psychology can also be solved through a single concrete instance, such as the relation to the father. Perhaps another psychological problem must be included here. We have so frequently had occasion to show the ambivalence of emotions in its real sense, that is to say the coincidence of love and hate towards the same object, at the root of important cultural formations. We know nothing about the origin of this ambivalence. It may be assumed to be a fundamental phenomenon of our emotional life. But the other possibility seems to me also worthy of consideration: that ambivalence, originally foreign to our emotional life, was acquired by mankind from the father complex (that is to say, the parent complex), where psychoanalytic investigation of the individual today still reveals the strongest expression of it."

The important point here is Freud's recognition of ambivalence. Just as no physical twinge is without its significance in physiology, so no psychic twinge is without its significance in psychology, and Freud's magnificent service is to recognize and account for those awkward and disregarded emotions—such as mingled love and hate—of which life is full. There may be fancifulness in his adaptation of the Darwinian anecdote, his account of the tyran-

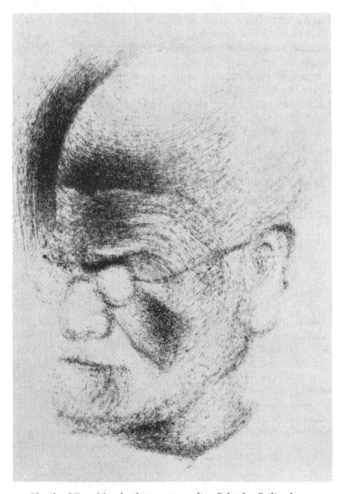

Sketch of Freud by the famous surrealist, Salvador Dali, who accompanied Stefan Zweig on a visit to Freud in July 1938.

nous father slain by the oppressed sons who thereafter preclude sex-rivalry and incest and thereby give rise to the totem. But there is absolutely no fancifulness in the facts he faces. In the end the knowledge of man's psyche may no more resemble Freud's than our present knowledge of the circulation of the blood resembles the Greeks'. But the adventure opened out by Freud is beyond doubt a supreme adventure, and his version of totem and taboo shows the same livingness of conception as his portrayal of Leonardo and his establishment of the meaning of dreams.

What significance has it for the layman? A group with the totem of the bull-moose is no longer forced to look for mates among the elephants and the donkeys. A bull-moose may marry a cow-moose, if he wants to. Similarly, one may be an elk or a wolf's head or an eagle or a Bones without exhibiting any of the other traces of infantility. The humiliating initiation into secret societies undoubtedly exhibits the same ambivalence that accompanies the selection of a king among savages. There is something arcane about the mere fact of a secret society. But what of it? How does it bear on conduct today? To read *Totem and Taboo* is to find many answers. It is to see in a new light our hero-worships and hero-slayings, our anxiety to believe that Hindenburg has once more died of apoplexy, our willingness to burn people in effigy and to make psychological short-cuts under the urgency of passion. Our little brown brothers are still inside us. We are bone and tissue with them. If we partake of communion instead of cannibalism, we are still fraternal with cannibalism. Freud's establishment of the Oedipus complex as central is probably correct. Even if not correct, the investigation is at the kernel of psychological science. There is a man in us that is still a cave-dweller, and our own brain and heart is the cave. Into that cave Freud has thrown a ray of research, and the darkest outsider is given to see. (pp. 347-48)

> *Francis Hackett?, in a review of "Totem and Taboo," in* The New Republic, *Vol. XV, No. 194, July 20, 1918, pp. 347-48.*

H. W. Frink   (essay date 1921)

[*In the following review, Frink states his opinion that Freud's* A General Introduction to Psychoanalysis *is superior to all prior expositions on psychoanalysis.*]

The struggle of the science of psychoanalysis for recognition has been attended by unusual circumstances. There has been extraordinary prejudiced resistance on the one hand, and much foolish enthusiasm on the other. For the material that comes under survey [in Freud's *A General Introduction to Psychoanalysis*] is in great measure the common property of every man. And because he finds himself involved in some of its disclosures, he feels qualified to pass upon its merits. Throughout, Freud's doctrines have thus had to contend with judgments growing almost entirely out of subjective factors; truly scientific opposition, criticism, or, indeed, indorsement, has been rather rare.

The period in which almost universal opposition to psychoanalysis was the rule is now merging into one of equally unfortunate popularity, which has resulted in uncontrolled distortion of its data, and abuse of the purposes for which it was originally conceived. Happily, the abuse and misconception to which Freud's doctrines are now subject can hardly be laid to the blame either of those who originated the method or of those who have taken it seriously. Rather is it due to the large amount of pseudo-scientific literature that has grown up about the subject, and more especially to the freedom with which the journalist and the dilettante have appropriated its material. The number of popular expositions of analysis has of recent years become very large indeed. Few of these books have any merit. Most of them are written by individuals who have had no opportunity for personal experience with the method and possess none of the training essential to its mastery. This literature has, moreover, given a controversial aspect to the matter, which has no bearing on actual practice, and has served only to confuse the public and to spread the many misconceptions that prevail.

It is, therefore, a great relief to have at last a systematic presentation of psychoanalysis from Freud himself, with whose authority no man can compete while he is alive. The new book is a translation of a series of twenty-eight lectures, covering in an introductory way the main essentials of psychoanalytic theory. Undoubtedly it is the finest exposition of the subject yet written, while in addition it gives us a personal touch with the author which none of his earlier works afford. Those who have followed Freud's later writings closely will find little that is new in this book, for it contains almost nothing that he has not discussed more fully elsewhere. On the other hand, those who have read only such of Freud's works as have been translated into English, or have relied upon expositions by other writers to give them an acquaintance with his teachings, will find much that is new to them, and much, perhaps, that to a certain class will be distasteful and disappointing. For the very ease and simplicity of this presentation make even more apparent than do the author's most technical writings the intricacy, the difficulty, and the seriousness of his subject, and make apparent to what a wide extent the superficial notions current about it depart from what Freud has actually attempted to teach. Those, therefore, who have looked upon psychoanalysis as a plaything, as a philosophy for the parlor radical, or as a means of imparting thrills and color to studio life, will find this book greatly disappointing and little to their taste.

The book is divided into three parts, the first of which deals with the Psychology of Errors, the second with the Dream, and the last with the General Theory of the Neuroses.

The first part is devoted to the proof of the hypothesis that the slip of the tongue, the seemingly "chance" act and error are psychologically determined by motives which cannot enjoy free conscious exercise. These phenomena ordinarily are symptoms of the mutual interference of two opposing intentions, one of which usually has undergone repression. Part Two discusses the dream as a psychic phenomenon. It is in the study of the dream that Freud gives his theory of wish fulfilment and acquaints the reader with the phenomena of resistance and censorship, and with some of the specific mechanisms to which the dream is subject that make it apparently unintelligible to the waking mind. The dream is a type of thinking, governed by certain dynamic forces, the source and function of which are more fully discussed in the latter portion of the book. The dream is moreover amenable to interpretation in the light of the individual's experiences, aims, and conflicts: it is a manifestation of desire, and affords an outlet to the impulses which have been rigidly repressed in conscious thinking. In this latter regard it resembles the neurosis, and hence it is that the dream is one of the central points of interest in psychoanalysis.

From these considerations drawn from phenomena common to normal and neurotic alike, Freud takes us to the study of the neuroses. He selects sufficient material to convey a fairly complete exposition of his Libido Theory, its development and relation to symptoms. He also discusses very frankly both the scope and the limitations of his method.

It must be pointed out here that most of the opposition that psychoanalysis has encountered was not directed toward the method itself, but to some of the explanations concerning the source of neurotic conflict. And those who are accustomed to regard the freedom with which an author discusses the sexual life of man as a sign of his depravity will find much they can find fault with in this book. These individuals do not for the most part understand their own prejudices, and forget that psychoanalytic theory was deductively evolved. Psychoanalysis was a bold departure in method, but the results of its application have demonstrated the insufficiency of the premises and methods current in introspective psychology. It alone furnished an approach to the forces that maintain the continuity of personality and govern its economy in normal and diseased alike. It, for the first time, clearly revealed a vast aspect of psychic life hitherto unexplored, the Unconscious, and supplied psychology with the much needed dynamic unit, the urge for gratification, the "unconscious wish."

The average person who readily acknowledges the existence of physical phenomena beyond his immediate perception is not conscious of the entire series of sense and apperceptive integrations which began to form on the day of his birth, and which furnish him with the conditions in which all phenomena in the physical world are placed. Yet consciousness or awareness is the only criterion he has for the existence of occurrences in his psyche; he is at no time aware of the great mass of former experiences, feelings, and efforts which make him a distinct personality, and which are now part of the thinking mass, though it has no direct access to consciousness.

This simple fact, that unconscious memories and motives exist, is the vital premise of psychoanalysis. And it is not a premise valid only for the neurotic. It is the product of man's adaptation to social life, as a result of which his every impulse and wish cannot be gratified without censorship from educational and moral influences. If an impulse is subservient to an elemental need of the individual, its energy is indestructible and seeks some manner of gratification. But in the course of life, memories, impulses, and motives become subject to a selective principle, namely quality, in relation to the elemental needs and desires of

the personality and their possibility of gratification. The material on which repressing forces operate is more or less uniform; the most elemental needs of life are hunger and love. In man's present state of organization, the needs of hunger do not entail great struggle for the individual until maturity. His love needs, however, appearing far earlier than was once supposed, are gratified at first quite independently of environment. The first activities of feeding and alimentation make the organs which serve these ends the first receptors of pleasurable stimuli, and activities connected with them are, independent of their usefulness, indulged in for the pleasure they yield. These activities are abruptly checked by the earliest education instituted, and the individual must learn to associate qualities with them other than those previously entertained. Hereafter, in the gratification of his erotic needs the individual encounters the greatest struggle. The long latent period between the time he appreciates erotic pleasure and the time when opportunity is given for permissible gratification is thus filled with many possibilities. The interaction of individual desire and environmental conditions is the seat of constant strife, and the type of adaptation is determined by factors in constitution and character which are as yet not clearly understood. The neurosis is one form of adaptation, and despite its glaring departures, its devious and costly procedure, it is purposeful, and true to the principle that directs all effort, and consistent with the laws that govern all thought. (pp. 236-37)

H. W. Frink, in a review of "A General Introduction to Psychoanalysis," in The Nation, *New York, Vol. CXII, No. 2901, February 9, 1921, pp. 236-37.*

Henry Hazlitt   (essay date 1930)

[*An American writer and editor, Hazlitt is the author of over fifteen books, including* Economics in One Lesson *(1946),* What You Should Know about Inflation *(1960),* The Foundations of Morality *(1964), and* Man vs. the Welfare State *(1969). In the following mixed review of* Civilization and Its Discontents, *Hazlitt praises the scope and originality of the work, but reproaches Freud for what he sees as faulty reasoning and untenable conclusions.*]

A new volume by the most influential thinker of our time (next to Einstein) is certain to be an event; and its broad subject makes the present essay particularly noteworthy. [Freud's ***Civilization and Its Discontents***] is written for the most part with remarkable lucidity, and we are indebted to the translator for carrying the original over into an English prose highly attractive on its own account.

Suggestive and shrewd as it is in its detailed discussions, however, the essay lacks a certain structural clarity. It frequently misleads the reader regarding the direction of its argument, and it would be difficult to summarize its winding course and numerous subordinate discussions. Freud begins with the assertion that life as we find it is too hard for us, and that we are driven to various palliative remedies, principally three: (1) powerful diversions of interest, such as science and "cultivating our gardens," which lead us to care little about our misery; (2) substitutive gratifications, which lessen it, such as art offers, "illusions in contrast to reality"; and (3) intoxicating substances, which make us insensitive to it. After indicating the limitations of these and other methods for achieving happiness, Freud concludes that its attainment is a sheer impossibility; the whole constitution of things runs counter to it:

> Suffering comes from three quarters: from our own body, which is destined to decay and dissolution, and cannot even dispense with anxiety and pain as danger signals; from the outer world, which can rage against us with the most powerful and pitiless forces of destruction; and finally from our relations with other men. The unhappiness which has this last origin we find perhaps more painful than any other.

Yet though our goal of happiness remains unattainable, we cannot give up the effort to come nearer to realization of it. This struggle we must make both as individuals and collectively. The collective struggle results in the growth of civilization and culture. Rejecting such vague teleological concepts as "progress," Freud proceeds to analyze the elements of which civilization is composed. The most important consist of all the activities and possessions which men use to make the earth serviceable to them, to protect them against the tyranny of natural forces, and so on. In the last generations man has established his dominion over nature in a way never before imagined. But men are beginning to perceive that all this newly won power has not made them feel any happier. This, according to Freud, is no ground for inferring that technical progress is worthless from the standpoint of happiness; the valid conclusion is merely that power over nature is not the only condition of human happiness, just as it is not the only goal of civilization's efforts.

Considering in turn the place in culture of beauty, cleanliness, order, and the value set upon the higher mental activities, Freud arrives finally at a consideration of the ways in which social relations are regulated. This involves the setting up of law, or "right," against "brute force," or, in other words, the use of the strength of the mass to curb the strength of any single individual. From a wider viewpoint, civilization is built upon the renunciation by individuals of instinctive gratifications, and the privations this involves are the cause of the antagonism against which all civilization has to fight. As one might expect, Freud attaches high importance to the sexual privations, but in this volume his chief emphasis is on the all but universal instincts of aggression and destruction. In addition to the instinct of self-preservation, he concludes that there must exist an opposing "death instinct," from which the instinct of aggression is derived. It is this instinct of aggression that constitutes the most powerful obstacle to culture, and even threatens its destruction:

> Men have brought their powers of subduing the forces of nature to such a pitch that by using them they could now very easily exterminate one another to the last man. They know this—hence arises a great part of their current unrest, their dejection, their mood of apprehension.

In this situation Freud does not pretend to have any facile solution or consolation to offer; indeed, he thinks we may yet have to accustom ourselves to the idea that "there are certain difficulties inherent in the very nature of culture which will not yield to any efforts at reform."

He concludes with an elaborate analysis of the moral conscience. In the child, conscience can best be designated the dread of losing love—usually of the father and mother. In the adult this process is more complicated: conscience becomes a part of the ego that distinguishes itself from the rest as a "super-ego," and "exercises the same propensity to harsh aggressiveness against the ego that the ego would have liked to enjoy against others. The tension between the strict super-ego and the subordinate ego we call the sense of guilt." Freud dilates upon this because he wishes "to represent the sense of guilt as the most important problem in the evolution of culture, and to convey that the price of progress in civilization is paid in forfeiting happiness through the heightening of the sense of guilt."

I do not find this part of his essay very convincing. I see no evidence, for example, that the sense of guilt has increased as civilization has progressed; there is even reason for believing the contrary. Has the sense of guilt increased since the Victorian age? Since the days of the medieval saints? Is it established that primitive man, when he violated a tribal taboo, felt less guilt than modern man when he violates one of our own taboos? The representation of the conscience as a super-ego tyrannizing over the ego strikes me as equally dubious. It is all very well to speak this way if one is frankly using a metaphor; indeed, I suspect that it is his ingratiating use of just such metaphors that accounts for Freud's deep appeal to many minds. He makes the life of the soul seem vivid to them; he dramatizes it memorably. But metaphors are not science, and satisfaction with them may delay real investigation. I do not see why the whole personality need be split in two in order to explain "conscience," or why we must invent an entity ("an agency or institution in the mind," as Freud calls the "super-ego") to describe a process. Nor does it seem necessary, again, to create a special "death instinct" to account for the facts Mr. Freud presents. This weakness for solution by gratuitous assumption, for inventing names and calling them explanations, is certainly not unfamiliar to Mr. Freud's readers; and he is capable here, as in previous volumes, of some appallingly fantastic reasoning. Yet if Mr. Freud's is not a thoroughly trustworthy mind, it is none the less, one need hardly add, an immensely interesting one, and surely one of the most seminal of our era. *Civilization and Its Discontents,* in spite of its few vagaries, must be set down an impressive and absorbing contribution to the great problem of happiness under our civilization. (pp. 299-300)

Henry Hazlitt, "The Neurosis of Civilization," in The Nation, *New York, Vol. CXXXI, No. 3402, September 17, 1930, pp. 299-300.*

Stefan Zweig   (essay date 1931)

[*Zweig was an Austrian biographer, short story writer, novelist, dramatist, autobiographer, poet, essayist, critic, librettist, and translator. His works are humanistic in nature and address the possibilities of transcending lin-*

guistic and cultural barriers between different nationalities. A Jewish pacifist who strove to insulate his work from politics, Zweig became severely depressed by the news of Hitler's military conquests and committed suicide in 1942. In the following excerpt from his Mental Healers: Franz Anton Mesmer, Mary Baker Eddy, Sigmund Freud, *which was originally published in German, Zweig discusses Freud's profound influence on twentieth-century psychology, stating that psychoanalysis "altered all the standards of our mental dynamics."]*

A very definite effort is needed to forget anything that has long been familiar, to return deliberately from a higher stage of perception or understanding to a more simple one. Thus it is difficult today to recall clearly the attitude of the scientific world of 1900 to the notion of the unconscious. The psychology of those earlier days, the pre-Freudian psychology, recognized clearly enough that the conscious activity of our reason did not comprise the whole of our mental operations, and that behind or below the working of the intelligence there were operative, in the shadows, other mental forces which were no less a part of our being. But these earlier psychologists could not make effective use of this notion of the unconscious, for they had never seriously tried to subject it to scientific investigation. The philosophy of the closing years of the nineteenth century was concerned to study psychical manifestations only insofar as they occurred within the brightly illuminated circle of consciousness. It was regarded as absurd, as a contradiction in terms, to consider anything unconscious as a possible content of the mind, which was looked upon as conscious by definition. A feeling did not become a feeling until it could be plainly felt; the will was not the will until it willed in full awareness of doing so. So long as mental phenomena failed to rise into the level of the conscious life, psychology excluded them from the domain of science as intangible and imponderable.

Adopting the technical term "unconscious" for use in psychoanalysis, Freud gave it a new meaning. Far from accepting the view that only the conscious operations of the mind are mental, and that therefore the unconscious must belong to an entirely different or completely subordinate category, he insisted that all the workings of the mind are primarily unconscious happenings; that those which become conscious are not of an utterly different or of a superior order to those which remain unconscious, inasmuch as their entry into consciousness is, so to say, a quality imposed upon them from without, like light falling upon an object. A table is equally a table whether it remains invisible in a pitch-dark room or is made visible to the observer by switching on the electric light. All that has happened in the latter case is that the light has made its presence evident to the senses of the observer, but the table was there before, and has not been created by the light. Doubtless when illuminated it has become more plainly perceptible and can be more effectively and accurately measured than it could be before the light was switched on; although even in the darkness its dimensions could have been roughly ascertained by another sense than that of vision, namely by the sense of touch. Logically, then, the table that is invisible in the darkness belongs to the material world no less than does the visible table; and in psychology, likewise, the

unconscious is part of the mind no less than the conscious. Consequently, when Freud used the term "unconscious" it was no longer in the sense of "unknowable," and as he used the word it entered for the first time into the domain of science. In this way psychology, given a new criterion of attention, equipped with a diving-bell enabling it to explore the depths of the mind and no longer as of old restricted to an examination of the surface, became at length (and once more!) a true science of the mind, a practically applicable and most salutary science of life.

This discovery of a new field of research, this fundamental transformation and vast expansion of the area in which our mental energies are known to operate, has been Freud's supreme act of genius. Almost at one step, the cognizable sphere of the mind has been made many times larger than before. It has been given a third dimension, that of depth, in addition to the superficial dimensions of length and breadth. After the event, epoch-making ideas are apt to seem simple and self-evident; and to some, therefore, the change thus effected may appear a trifling matter. The fact is, however, that it has altered all the standards of our mental dynamics. Probably in days to come this creative moment in the history of psychology will rank in importance in the story of human knowledge with those when, in their several days, Copernicus and Kant altered their respective contemporaries' whole outlook on the universe. Already after no more than thirty years, the academic picture of the mind at the turn of the century seems as dull-witted, fallacious, and narrow as a Ptolemaic map wherein a small fraction of our world, all that was known to the ancient geographers, is depicted as the entire cosmos. Like those naïve cartographers, the pre-Freudian psychologists were content to describe the unexplored continents of the mind as "terra incognita"; and when they alluded to the vast region of the unconscious, all that they meant was a region beyond the scope of the knowable. They opined, indeed, that somewhere within the mind there must be a dark reservoir into which our unused memories must flow, to be stored away there in oblivion; a warehouse, or rather a lumber-room, wherein the forgotten and unutilized must lie in chaotic and purposeless disorder; perhaps even an arsenal of out-of-date weapons and implements to which memory might turn now and again in order to bring back into consciousness some article for which a use could temporarily be found. But the essential outlook of pre-Freudian science was that this unconscious realm was wholly passive, completely inert; a domain of life that was over and done with, of a past that had had its day and had ceased to be—a magazine of spent forces which could have no influence on the present activities of the mind.

Freud's conception was frankly opposed to this. In his view the unconscious, far from being a mortuary for decayed remnants of the mental life, was the primal substance out of which that life was made, whereas it was but a small fragment of the mind which entered the illuminated region of consciousness. The major, the unilluminated part of the mind, the so-called unconscious, was anything but decayed and undynamic. It is, says Freud, no less actively at work than the conscious mind in moulding our

Thomas Mann on Freud:

We know that Sigmund Freud, . . . founder of psychoanalysis as a general method of research and as a therapeutic technique, trod the steep path alone and independently, as physician and natural scientist, without knowing that reinforcement and encouragement lay to his hand in literature. He did not know Nietzsche, scattered throughout whose pages one finds premonitory flashes of truly Freudian insight; he did not know Novalis, whose romantic-biologic fantasies so often approach astonishingly close to analytic conceptions; he did not know Kirchgaard, whom he must have found profoundly sympathetic and encouraging for the Christian zeal which urged him on to psychological extremes; and, finally, he did not know Schopenhauer, the melancholy symphonist of a philosophy of the instinct, groping for change and redemption. Probably it must be so. By his unaided effort, without knowledge of any previous intuitive achievement, he had methodically to follow out the line of his own researches; the driving force of his activity was probably increased by this very freedom from special advantage. And we think of him as solitary—the attitude is inseparable from our earliest picture of the man. Solitary in the sense of the word used by Nietzsche in that ravishing essay "What is the Meaning of Ascetic Ideals?" when he characterizes Schopenhauer as "a genuine philosopher, a self-poised mind, a man and gallant knight, stern-eyed, with the courage of his own strength, who knows how to stand alone and not wait on the beck and nod of superior officers." In this guise of man and gallant knight, a knight between Death and the Devil, I have been used to picture to myself our psychologist of the unconscious, ever since his figure first swam into my mental ken.

Thomas Mann, in his Freud, Goethe, Wagner, *1937.*

thoughts and feelings, being indeed, presumably, the more active and influential moiety of our mental existence. He who fails to make due allowance for the unconscious element in all our decisions is making a great mistake, for he is ignoring the chief factor of our internal tensions. He is like one who should estimate the size and the destructive possibilities of an iceberg only upon the ground of what is visible above the surface of the water, whereas nine-tenths of the colossus lie beneath the waves. That man deceives himself grossly who believes that our conscious thoughts, the energies of which we are fully aware, exclusively determine our feelings and doings. Our life does not move freely in the domain of the rational, but is continually exposed to the working of unconscious forces. From moment to moment, influences from an apparently forgotten past stream fatefully into our living present.

Thus man is far less splendidly master of himself than he used to suppose. Far less than was formerly imagined does the upper world of consciousness really belong to the alert will and the positive intelligence, for the lightning-flashes which are our real decisions emerge from the dark cloud of the unconscious, and from the depths of the impulsive life come the earthquake thrusts that determine our destiny. In that obscure realm, huddled together pell-mell, lies all that, in the sphere of the conscious, seems delimited in orderly fashion by the transparent walls of the categories of space and time. The buried desires of a long-forgotten childhood still live greedy lives in the unconscious, accounting for the otherwise unaccountable lusts that drive us like chaff before the wind. Terrors and anxieties which have no meaning for the conscious mind, rise from the depths and suddenly take control of our nerves. Nay more, cravings that belong, not to our own individual past, but to that of mouldered generations and savage primitives from whose loins we have sprung, are still rooted in our being and decide our latter-day activities. From the depths come the most genuinely personal of our deeds; from a region we cannot fathom with our waking intelligence emerge the shafts of inexplicable illumination and the forces which are mightier than all that in the conscious we term "ourselves." Unknown to the conscious self, there abides in the twilight that ancient ego which the civilized ego has forgotten or refuses to acknowledge; that primal ego which, being ignored by the conscious self, takes vengeance from time to time by throwing off the veneer of civilization. The untamable instincts of this primal being are still the hot blood circulating within us; and ever and again the will of the unconscious becomes active, bestirs itself, emerges into the full light of day, becomes conscious, and discharges its energy in action. "I also am," saith he; "I also will do."

With every word that we speak, and in every action that we perform, we are simultaneously engaged in repressing unconscious impulses. Unceasingly our moral sense, our civilized sentiment, must be on the defensive against the savage promptings of instinct. Thus it comes to pass that our whole mental life is an incessant, an arduous, an unending struggle between conscious and unconscious volitions, between responsible behaviour and the irresponsibility of our impulses. Yet even the ostensibly unconscious has a definite significance in its manifestations, however incomprehensible they may seem to us; and for Freud the task of the new psychology was to make the significance of these unconscious stirrings within himself plain to every individual. Not until we have thrown light into the subterranean regions of an individual's mind shall we really know the world of the feelings; not until we have explored the abysses of the unconscious shall we know the real cause of troubles and disorders of the conscious. No one needs a psychologist or a psychopath to teach him what he consciously knows. It is where conscious knowledge fails, it is where the workings of the unconscious are concerned, that the psychoanalyst can give help and bring healing.

But how are we to get down into this twilit realm? The psychologist of the schools gives us no assistance here. Traditional science flatly denies the possibility of studying the phenomena of the unconscious, since they elude measurement with instruments of precision. The old psychology could work only in the daylight, could deal only with the clear-cut realm of consciousness. Wordless things, and those which spoke only the language of dreams, were ignored. Now that Freud has lived and written, these ancient outlooks have crumbled, and are fit only for the scrap-heap. According to him, the unconscious is by no means dumb. It has plenty to say, though it uses other signs and symbols, talks a different language from the conscious. Obviously, therefore, one who wishes to travel into his own depths and learn what goes on there must master the language of this new world. Like the Egyptologists with the Rosetta stone, Freud began by interpreting one sign after another, building up by degrees a vocabulary and a grammar of this tongue of the unconscious until he had become able to understand and to make comprehensible to others the voices that exhort us or allure us behind our waking words and our waking consciousness and to whose bidding we generally pay more heed than to that of our recognized will. One who has learned a new language has acquired new senses, has got possession of the key to a new world. Thus it was that Freud's "depth-psychology," his psychology of the unconscious, revealed a mental world that had been hitherto unknown, with the result that psychology, which to nineteenth-century scientists had been no more than an epistemological observation of the processes of consciousness, became once more what it should never ceased being, "Seelenkunde," a true science of the mind. No longer does one of the hemispheres of the mind, one hemisphere of the internal cosmos, lie unregarded in the moonlight of science. As the years pass, the outlines of our knowledge of the unconscious are being filled in, so that it grows ever plainer that we are winning an entirely new insight into the wonderfully significant structure of our mental world. (pp. 289-95)

> *Stefan Zweig, "The Realm of the Unconscious," in his* Mental Healers: Franz Anton Mesmer, Mary Baker Eddy, Sigmund Freud, *translated by Eden Paul and Cedar Paul, The Viking Press, 1932, pp. 289-95.*

Carl Gustav Jung　(essay date 1933)

[*Jung was a Swiss psychologist and creator of "analytical psychology," the theoretical basis of which grew out of his early study of psychoanalysis under Freud. Disagreeing with Freud's theory of the unconscious sexual origin of neurosis, Jung developed a school of psychology based on the hypothesis that the source of human psychic life resides both in the individual's personal history, the "individual unconscious," and in the collective history of humanity, the "collective unconscious." In Jung's psychology, archetypal patterns from mythology and folklore replace the unconscious sexual conflicts of Freud's system as a source of illumination for common patterns in human behavior. Jung also discerned archetypal patterns in modern literature, a practice that has led to a modern school of literary criticism. In the following excerpt from his* Modern Man in Search of a Soul, *Jung differentiates himself and his psychology from Freud, censuring Freud's reductionist tendencies and his misunderstanding of the religious impulse.*]

The difference between Freud's views and my own ought really to be dealt with by someone who stands outside the circles of influence of those ideas which go under our respective names. Can I be credited with sufficient impartiality to rise above my own ideas? Can any man do this? I doubt it. If I were told that someone had rivalled Baron Münchausen by accomplishing such a feat, I should feel sure that his ideas were borrowed ones.

It is true that widely accepted ideas are never the personal property of their so-called author; on the contrary, he is the bond-servant of his ideas. Impressive ideas which are hailed as truths have something peculiar to themselves. Although they come into being at a definite time, they are and have always been timeless; they arise from that realm of procreative, psychic life out of which the ephemeral mind of the single human being grows like a plant that blossoms, bears fruit and seed, and then withers and dies. Ideas spring from a source that is not contained within one man's personal life. We do not create them; they create us. To be sure, when we deal in ideas we inevitably make a confession, for they bring to the light of day not only the best that in us lies, but our worst insufficiencies and personal shortcomings as well. This is especially the case with ideas about psychology. Whence should they come except from the most subjective side of life? Can experience with the objective world save us from subjective prejudgements? Is not every experience, even in the best of circumstances, to a large extent subjective interpretation? On the other hand, the subject also is an objective fact, a piece of the world. What issues from it comes, after all, from the universal soil, just as the rarest and strangest organism is none the less supported and nourished by the earth which we all share in common. It is precisely the most subjective ideas which, being closest to nature and to the living being, deserve to be called the truest. But what is truth?

For the purposes of psychology, I think it best to abandon the notion that we are today in anything like a position to make statements about the nature of the psyche that are "true" or "correct." The best that we can achieve is true expression. By true expression I mean an open avowal and a detailed presentation of everything that is subjectively noted. One person will stress the forms into which this material can be worked, and will therefore believe that he has created what he finds within himself. Another will lay most weight upon the fact that he plays the part of an observer; he will be conscious of his receptive attitude, and insist that his subjective material presents itself to him. The truth lies between the two. True expression consists in giving form to what is observed.

The modern psychologist, however unbounded his hopes, can hardly claim to have achieved more than the right sort of receptivity and a reasonable adequacy of expression. The psychology we at present possess is the testimony of a few individuals here and there regarding what they have found within themselves. The form in which they have cast it is sometimes adequate and sometimes not. Since each individual conforms more or less to a type, his testimony can be accepted as a fairly valid description of a large number of people. And since those who conform to other types belong none the less to the human species, we may conclude that the description applies, though less fully, to them too. What Freud has to say about sexuality, infantile pleasure, and their conflict with the "principle of reality," as well as what he says about incest and the like, can be taken as the truest expression of his own psychic make-up. He has given adequate form to what he has noted in himself. I am no opponent of Freud's; I am merely presented in that light by his own short-sightedness and that of his pupils. No experienced psychotherapist can deny having met with dozens of cases at least which answer in all essentials to Freud's descriptions. By his avowal of what he has found in himself, Freud has assisted at the birth of a great truth about man. He has devoted his life and his strength to the construction of a psychology which is a formulation of his own being.

Our way of looking at things is conditioned by what we are. And since other people are differently constituted, they see things differently and express themselves differently. Adler, one of Freud's earliest pupils, is a case in point. Working with the same empirical material as Freud, he approached it from a totally different standpoint. His way of looking at things is at least as convincing as Freud's, because he also represents a well-known type. I know that the followers of both schools flatly assert that I am in the wrong, but I may hope that history and all fairminded persons will bear me out. Both schools, to my way of thinking, deserve reproach for over-emphasizing the pathological aspect of life and for interpreting man too exclusively in the light of his defects. A convincing example of this in Freud's case is his inability to understand religious experience, as is clearly shown in his book: *The Future of an Illusion.* For my part, I prefer to look at man in the light of what in him is healthy and sound, and to free the sick man from that point of view which colours every page Freud has written. Freud's teaching is definitely one-sided in that it generalizes from facts that are relevant only to neurotic states of mind; its validity is really confined to those states. Within these limits Freud's teaching is true and valid even when it is in error, for error also belongs to the picture, and carries the truth of a true avowal. In any case, Freud's is not a psychology of the healthy mind.

The morbid symptom in Freud's psychology is this: it is based upon a view of the world that is uncriticized, or even unconscious, and this is apt to narrow the field of human experience and understanding to a considerable extent. It was a great mistake on Freud's part to turn his back on philosophy. Not once does he criticize his premises or even the assumptions that underlie his personal outlook. Yet to do so was necessary, as may be inferred from what I have said above; for had he critically examined his assumptions, he would never have put his peculiar mental disposition naïvely on view, as he has done in *The Interpretation of Dreams.* At all events, he would have had a taste of the difficulties which I have met with. I have never refused the bitter-sweet drink of philosophical criticism, but have taken it with caution, a little at a time. All too little, my opponents will say; almost too much, my own feeling tells me. All too easily does self-criticism poison one's naïveté, that priceless possession, or rather gift which no creative man can be without. At any rate, philosophical criticism has helped me to see that every psychology—my own included—has the character of a subjective confession. And yet I must prevent my critical powers from destroying my creativeness. I know well enough that every word I utter carries with it something of myself—of my special and unique self with its particular history and its own particular world. Even when I deal with empirical data, I am necessarily speaking about myself. But it is only by accepting this as inevitable that I can serve the cause

of man's knowledge of man—the cause which Freud also wished to serve, and which, in spite of everything, he has served. Knowledge rests not upon truth alone, but upon error also.

It is perhaps here, where the question arises of accepting the fact that every psychological teaching which is the work of one man is subjectively coloured, that the line between Freud and myself is most sharply drawn.

A further difference seems to me to consist in this, that I try to free myself from all unconscious and therefore uncriticized assumptions as to the world in general. I say "I try," for who can be sure that he has freed himself from all his unconscious assumptions? I try to save myself at least from the crassest prejudices, and am therefore inclined to recognize all manner of gods provided only that they are active in the human psyche. I do not doubt that the natural instincts or drives are forces of propulsion in human life, whether we call them sexuality or the will to power; but I also do not doubt that these instincts come into collision with the spirit, for they are continually colliding with something, and why should not this something be called spirit? I am far from knowing what spirit is in itself, and equally far from knowing what instincts are. The one is as mysterious to me as the other, yet I am unable to dismiss the one by explaining it in terms of the other. That would be to treat it as a mere misunderstanding. The fact that the earth has only one moon is not a misunderstanding. There are no misunderstandings in nature; they are only to be found in the realms that man calls "understanding." Certainly instinct and spirit are beyond my understanding. They are terms that we allow to stand for powerful forces whose nature we do not know.

As may be seen, I attribute a positive value to all religions. In their symbolism I recognize those figures which I have met with in the dreams and fantasies of my patients. In their moral teachings I see efforts that are the same as or similar to those made by my patients, when, guided by their own insight or inspiration, they seek the right way of dealing with the forces of the inner life. Ceremonial, ritual, initiation rites and ascetic practices, in all their forms and variations, interest me profoundly as so many techniques for bringing about a proper relation to these forces. I likewise attribute a positive value to biology, and to the empiricism of natural science in general, in which I see a herculean attempt to understand the human psyche by approaching it from the outer world. I regard the gnostic religions as an equally prodigious undertaking in the opposite direction: as an attempt to draw knowledge of the cosmos from within. In my picture of the world there is a vast outer realm and an equally vast inner realm; between these two stands man, facing now one and now the other, and, according to his mood or disposition, taking the one for the absolute truth by denying or sacrificing the other.

This picture is hypothetical, of course, but it offers a hypothesis which is so valuable that I will not give it up. I consider it heuristically and empirically verified; and what is more, it is supported by the *consensus gentium.* This hypothesis certainly came to me from an inner source, though I might imagine that empirical findings had led to its discovery. Out of it has come my theory of types, and also my reconciliation with views as different from my own as those of Freud.

I see in all happening the play of opposites, and derive from this conception my idea of psychic energy. I hold that psychic energy involves the play of opposites in much the same way as physical energy involves a difference of potential, which is to say, the existence of such opposites as warm and cold, high and low. Freud began by taking sexuality as the only psychic driving power, and only after my break with him did he grant an equal status to other psychic activities as well. For my part, I have subsumed the various psychic drives or forces under the concept of energy in order to avoid the arbitrariness of a psychology that deals with drives or impulses alone. I therefore speak, not of separate drives or forces, but of "value intensities." By what has just been said I do not mean to deny the importance of sexuality in psychic life, though Freud stubbornly maintains that I do deny it. What I seek is to set bounds to the rampant terminology of sex which threatens to vitiate all discussion of the human psyche; I wish to put sexuality itself in its proper place. Common-sense will always return to the fact that sexuality is only one of the life-instincts—only one of the psycho-physiological functions—though one that is without doubt very far-reaching and important.

Beyond all question, there is a marked disturbance today in the realms of sexual life. It is well known that when we have a bad toothache, we can think of nothing else. The sexuality which Freud describes is unmistakably that sexual obsession which shows itself whenever a patient has reached the point where he needs to be forced or tempted out of a wrong attitude or situation. It is an over-emphasized sexuality piled up behind a dam; and it shrinks at once to normal proportions as soon as the way to development is opened. It is being caught in the old resentments against parents and relations and in the boring emotional tangles of the family situation which most often brings about the damming-up of the energies of life. And it is this stoppage which shows itself unfailingly in that kind of sexuality which is called "infantile." It is really not sexuality proper, but an unnatural discharge of tensions that belong to quite another province of life. This being so, what is the use of paddling about in this flooded country? Surely, straight thinking will grant that it is more important to open up drainage canals. We should try to find, in a change of attitude or in new ways of life, that difference of potential which the pent-up energy requires. If this is not achieved a vicious circle is set up, and this is in fact the menace which Freudian psychology appears to offer. It points no way that leads beyond the inexorable cycle of biological events. This hopelessness would drive one to exclaim with Paul: "Wretched man that I am, who will deliver me from the body of this death?" And our man of intellect comes forward, shaking his head, and says in Faust's words: "Thou art conscious only of the single urge," namely of the fleshly bond leading back to father and mother or forward to the children that have sprung from our flesh—"incest" with the past and "incest" with the future, the original sin of the perpetuation of the family situation. There is nothing that can free us from this bond except that opposite urge of life, the spirit. It is not the children of the flesh, but the "children of God" who know freedom. In Ernst Barlach's tragic novel of family life, *Der Tote Tag,* the mother-dæmon says at the end: "The strange thing is that man will not learn that God is his father." That is what Freud would never learn, and what all those who share his outlook forbid themselves to learn. At least, they never find the key to this knowledge. Theology does not help those who are looking for the key, because theology demands faith, and faith cannot be made: it is in the truest sense a gift of grace. We moderns are faced with the necessity of rediscovering the life of the spirit; we must experience it anew for ourselves. It is the only way in which we can break the spell that binds us to the cycle of biological events.

My position on this question is the third point of difference between Freud's views and my own. Because of it I am accused of mysticism. I do not, however, hold myself responsible for the fact that man has, everywhere and always, spontaneously developed religious forms of expression, and that the human psyche from time immemorial has been shot through with religious feelings and ideas. Whoever cannot see this aspect of the human psyche is blind, and whoever chooses to explain it away, or to "enlighten" it away, has no sense of reality. Or should we see in the father-complex which shows itself in all the members of the Freudian school, and in its founder as well, convincing evidence of any release worth mentioning from the inexorable family situation? This father-complex, fanatically defended with such stubbornness and over-sensitivity, is a cloak for religiosity misunderstood; it is a mysticism expressed in terms of biology and the family relation. As for Freud's idea of the "super-ego," it is a furtive attempt to smuggle in his time-honoured image of Jehovah in the dress of psychological theory. When one does things like that, it is better to say so openly. For my part, I prefer to call things by the names under which they have always been known. The wheel of history must not be turned back, and man's advance towards a spiritual life, which began with the primitive rites of initiation, must not be denied. It is permissible for science to divide its field of enquiry and to set up limited hypotheses, for science must work in that way; but the human psyche may not be parcelled out. It is a whole which embraces consciousness, and is the mother of consciousness. Scientific thought, being only one of its functions, can never exhaust all the possibilities of life. The psychotherapist must not allow his vision to be coloured by the glasses of pathology; he must never allow himself to forget that the ailing mind is a human mind, and that, for all its ailments, it shares in the whole of the psychic life of man. The psychotherapist must even be able to admit that the ego is ill for the very reason that it is cut off from the whole, and has lost its connection with mankind as well as with the spirit. The ego is indeed the "place of fears," as Freud says in *The Ego and the Id,* but only so long as it has not returned to the "father" and "mother." Freud shipwrecks on the question of Nicodemus: "Can a man enter his mother's womb a second time and be born again?" To compare small things with great, we might say that history repeats itself here, for the question once more comes to the front today in a domestic quarrel of modern psychology.

For thousands of years, rites of initiation have been teaching spiritual rebirth: yet, strangely enough, man forgets again and again the meaning of divine procreation. This is surely no evidence of a strong life of the spirit; and yet the penalty of misunderstanding is heavy, for it is nothing less than neurotic decay, embitterment, atrophy and sterility. It is easy enough to drive the spirit out of the door, but when we have done so the salt of life grows flat—it loses its savour. Fortunately, we have proof that the spirit always renews its strength in the fact that the central teaching of the ancient initiations is handed on from generation to generation. Ever and again human beings arise who understand what is meant by the fact that God is our father. The equal balance of the flesh and the spirit is not lost to the world.

The contrast between Freud and myself goes back to essential differences in our basic assumptions. Assumptions are unavoidable, and this being so, it is wrong to pretend that we have made no assumptions. That is why I have dealt with fundamental questions; with these as a starting-point, the manifold and detailed differences between Freud's views and my own can best be understood. (pp. 115-24)

> *C. G. Jung, "Freud and Jung—Contrasts," in his* Modern Man in Search of a Soul, *translated by W. S. Dell and Cary F. Baynes, 1933. Reprint by Harcourt, Brace & World, Inc., n.d., pp. 115-24.*

Karl Menninger   (essay date 1939)

[*An American psychiatrist, educator, and writer, Menninger is the author of such books as* Man Against Himself *(1938),* The Crime of Punishment *(1968),* Whatever Became of Sin? *(1973), and* The Human Mind Revisited *(1978). In the following review, Menninger provides an overview of* Moses and Monotheism, *underscoring the importance of Freud's analysis of religious orthodoxy and the historical continuity of world religions.*]

If, in some magical way, Plato or Galileo were to reappear on this earth, and to remain silent for six years, the announcement of a book expressing his most recent ideas would justly be an event of surpassing importance. Every newspaper and magazine in the civilized world would be endeavoring to obtain the privilege of reprinting, and columns would be filled with interviews, comments, analyses, discussions, perhaps even refutations. And yet in June, 1939, there appears the first book, [*Moses and Monotheism*], in six years from the pen of a man whose intrepidity and originality of thought, whose intuitive brilliance, whose fruitful adventures into the unknown have already given him a place in history comparable to that of such notable predecessors as those mentioned. And if there have been no headlines (which is not entirely the case) and as yet no reprinting, no interviews, no frontpaging, it must be ascribed in part to the blind spots which always afflict us with respect to a contemporary genius, in part to the modest and retiring nature of this particular genius, and in part to the curious fear and taboos attaching to every revolution in the established conceptions of organized society.

For fifty years Sigmund Freud has devoted himself to the study of human life. But he has directed his attentions not to those aspects of life which were the most obvious, not to the external manifestations but to the internal operations, the machinery of the soul. In the modern concept of the word, Freud discovered psychology. More accurately, he discovered the technique for studying subsurface psychology, and he has used this instrument with indefatigable patience and incredible courage. He made no secret of his method or of his findings, and he built his theories and modified them from time to time, on the basis of what he and his followers learned from clinical experience.

Some twenty years ago, in the ripeness of middle life, he gave still further evidence of his temerity by going beyond his facts in the construction of theories to explain the data which he had accumulated and to anticipate the discovery of new facts and the correction of old prejudices. In a sense, these theories were but the extension of conclusions about human psychology drawn from his empirical observations, conclusions which can no longer be called hypotheses because they have been so amply supported and verified by the observations of many other scientists. Each new pronouncement of this great genius has been met by storms of objection, refutation, ridicule and skepticism. And time after time, following the initial storm, the reaction against his quiet proposals has died down and their authority become established. I would not give the impression that every postulation of Freud's has been substantiated, because this is far from being the case. Freud has altered and revised many of his original propositions and conclusions, some of them several times. Although he still retains his originality of thought and his courage to venture into unknown territories armed only with the knowledge that he has acquired in the investigation of the human mind, he still records his ideas with a diffidence and tenuousness which are in sharp contrast to the arrogant positivism of some of his skeptics.

Moses and Monotheism has already been reviewed so frequently that its essential content is probably well known to most readers of this journal. In substance Freud turns his attention to the psychological implications of the religious concepts which dominate the occidental world. He does not explicitly say so, but he is obviously intrigued with the contemporary illustrations of the ancient quip that half the world worships the Jew and the other half hates him. Of course, the bitter truth is that, to a considerable extent, the half which worships the Jew is the same half that hates him. But Freud's book is not primarily a study of anti-Semitism, having only an indirect bearing on that problem, although he does come to the conclusion that "hatred for Judaism is at bottom hatred for Christianity."

Freud's thesis is that there is support in psychology, anthropology, biblical exegesis and history that Moses was born an Egyptian, that he "chose" a group of Semitic captives to be his special wards and, inspired by the ideas of Amenhotep IV, instructed these Semites with regard to monotheistic conceptions and what was later called the Elohim religion; that he likewise taught them the Egyptian custom of circumcision, and that he led them toward Palestine. The theory continues, to the effect that these semi-civilized nomads reacted first positively and then negatively toward the idealistic "Moses religion," fluctuating constantly between it and a return to a polytheistic worship, absorbed Jahve (Jove) elements into their Midianite Elohim concepts, and thus became sufficiently bellicose to kill their idealistic leader and to conquer and displace the Canaanite tribes. Thereafter, Freud assumes, a second and false Moses was set up as their leader. But the blood guilt for the murder of their emancipator continued to obsess them so that their religion became dominated by ceremonials of atonement, sacrifice and purification. In spite of these, or perhaps because of them, the Jews continued to oscillate between monotheism and polytheism, fleeing centrifugally from the Moses concept to the polytheistic faiths and practices of surrounding tribes and then centripetally back again to rigorous monotheism and nationalism. Anyone familiar with the historical books of the Old Testament must recall the monotonous repetitiousness of the good kings and bad kings, of the idolators and the prophets.

A. A. Brill on Freud:

In a number of his works Freud exposes his innermost feelings, so that he who reads will find there his real autobiography, and in some, notably, *The Interpretation of Dreams,* he touches on the Jewish problem. But his first encounter of this problem is described in his autobiography, where he states that he came face to face with it when he entered the university in 1873. It struck him as unreasonable that he was supposed to feel inferior and extra-national because he was a Jew. "I rejected the first," he states, "with all resoluteness. I could never grasp why I should be ashamed of my origin, or, as they began to say, of my 'race.' As to the nationality which was denied me, I gave this up without much regret." He felt that there would surely always be a bit of room for a zealous fellow worker within the sphere of mankind without the necessity of any enrollment. "But these first university impressions produced one very important result for the future. I became familiar early with my destiny—to belong to the opposition and to be proscribed from the 'compact majority.' A certain independence of judgment was in this way developed."

A. A. Brill, in his introduction to The Basic Writings of Sigmund Freud, *1938.*

Freud agrees with Christian theology that although Jesus was killed, he let himself be killed as a voluntary sacrifice—innocent himself, but representing those who had "sinned." By thus taking upon himself the guilt of the others—the guilt for the "original sin," which was the murder of the primeval father (Moses)—he set free those "sons" who could identify themselves with him. These theological principles were worked out and generalized by the brilliant Jewish theologian, Paul of Tarsus, so that Christianity became the successor to Judaism, the latter becoming a "fossil" religion. The Christians, then, were those Jews who could say, "Yes, you and we killed our God, but we

have admitted it and atoned for it and are cleansed from the guilt of it, but you (other Jews) will not admit it. You will not allow yourselves to be represented by the sacrifice of Jesus as we have, and so you must go on suffering and feeling guilty." But in elaborating this extension of Judaism, primitive Christianity receded from the austere heights of the Moses religion, Freud says, and became patently polytheistic, absorbing elements from Greek and Roman ideologies.

This is the thesis of *Moses.* The questionable validity of the exigetical and historical proof Freud frankly concedes, but its psychological soundness he defends, and he is fully justified in doing so. It might be in order to indicate what is meant by psychological validity in contrast to historical validity. For example, the proposition that Moses had been killed by the children of Israel in the desert has been advanced and believed by others, but many historians will probably continue to declare that the evidence for it is entirely unsubstantial, that it has, therefore, no historical validity. Freud admits this possibility, but maintains correctly that it does have psychological validity. The consequences, the succeeding events, were precisely what one could have predicted had the murder occurred. As a matter of fact, it need not have actually occurred, provided it were generally desired, for in the depths of the human mind the intention or wish to perform an act is, as every psychiatrist and psychoanalyst knows, burdened with a sense of guilt scarcely less intense than that caused by the actual act itself. That the Jews rebelled against Moses, fought his leadership, disobeyed his regulations, "murmured against" him, is abundantly attested in the Bible, and there can be little doubt but that they *wanted* to kill him.

Therefore, Freud does not have to prove that the Jews killed Moses; he needs only to prove that they wanted to, and felt as if they had done so. He points out that the Jews are a people burdened with a tremendous sense of guilt which drives them constantly on the one hand to make atonements and propitiations to God and to their consciences, and on the other hand (a point which Freud does not mention specifically) to indulge in provocative behavior, behavior that is sometimes described as masochistic.

Psychological validity is further to be found in the illustration of the cyclic pattern of disadvantageous behavior, which in an earlier essay Freud described as due to the "repetition compulsion." The Jews did kill Jesus and, so far as we know, Jesus, like Moses, had committed no worse crime than that of having exhorted his people to worship a single, living God and to give decent treatment to one another. It is to Freud's frank admission that the Jews killed Jesus that some Jewish critics of the book object. In the first place, they say, it is not true; it was the Roman soldiers who killed Jesus, not the Jews. In the second place, even if it were true, one should not mention it just now.

Such objections on the part of the Jews are eloquent testimony to the soundness of Freud's main thesis. To evade the issue on a technical basis, to say, "Yes, of course, the Jews wanted to get rid of Jesus and had him tried in a Roman court, but it was not actually they who stuck the cross in the ground," is a kind of legalistic sophistry which only places those who use it in a bad light. It is as if they would say that the Jews wanted to kill Jesus, but sought a way to accomplish it without assuming the responsibility. Freud does not evade the responsibility or the accusation; he interprets it. One such honest scientific effort to get at the truth, as Freud makes in this book, does more to combat anti-Semitic prejudice than do a dozen eulogies of Jewish accomplishment or a hundred denials of Jewish wickedness or a thousand schemes for attempting to suppress (for supposedly strategic reasons) the abilities or opinions of brilliant men who happen to be Jews.

In pursuance of our thesis as to the psychological validity of the theory, it may be pointed out that whether the Jews were unanimous in their condemnation of Jesus (which they were not) or whether Jesus was killed through the machinations of a few leaders who felt imperiled by his doctrines, is not important. The important fact is that the Jewish conscience acts repeatedly in denial of the accusation of murder. This is intertwined with the tendency of the Christians, or I should say some Christians, to unload their own sense of guilt onto the Jews instead of onto Jesus. Who was actually responsible for the death of Jesus is a moral question and one in which psychology is not interested. What is psychologically important is that Christians and Jews react to guilt feelings, and react to them in ways which are superficially different but actually, in the last analysis, the same—by denial, by atonement, by ritualistic sacrifice.

It would be a narrow interpretation to regard *Moses and Monotheism* only as an analytic interpretation of the Jewish people and their peculiar history. The real importance of the theories elaborated in this book depends upon their universality. For what the Jews did and what the Jews do are what all people do. Someone has said that the Jews are like everyone else, only more so, and Freud has taken advantage of this acute observation to show that certain ideals of self-importance and separation inculcated in the early demarcation of this group enable us to study the application of the psychology of the individual to the psychology of a larger group. And just as Freud is able to interpret the history of the Jews in the light of his knowledge of the psychological history of the individual, so in this Jewish group pattern one can see certain world patterns. Yet, it would be carrying the implications too far to say that the American people still punish themselves for their burden of guilt in connection with the despoliation, robbery and murder of the Indians and the enslavement of the Africans, or that the British people must still atone for the rape of India and South Africa, and so on with France and Spain. It would be a false extension of Freud's theory to think in these terms, because the crimes of these countries were not the crimes of the whole people, as in the case of Freud's illustration. Society has emerged from the tribal group to larger and more complicated units, the mass psychology of which we do not fully understand. But toward an ultimate understanding of them this masterful contribution of Freud's to the psychology of one clear-cut group of people, whose detailed history is a part of our intellectual and social heritage, must be regarded as fundamental.

It is a pity that Freud did not continue the application of his theory of the oscillations of religious interest between monotheism and polytheism, between Elohim and Jahve-Baal, one step farther. His failure to do so stems in part from a curious Viennese provincialism with which he has always been afflicted. For, just as the early church theology and its subsequent Roman development represented another swing away from monotheism into a more or less militant polytheism, so the Protestant Reformation represented a swing back to the monotheistic Elohim religion of Moses. In essence Protestant Christianity, the Moses religion of Elohim and the Ikhnaton worship of Aton are analogous and in a sense continuous. Hence, it is no mere accident of geography that the Protestant Christians of England and the United States should have been the defenders and friends of the persecuted Jews of Germany and Austria, or that the Catholics, on the other hand, in spite of the possibility that they may meet the same fate as the Jews, should have stubbornly defended the fascist regimes of Franco and Mussolini and, indirectly, of Hitler. It is true that most of the Nazis of Austria and Germany are, or were, nominally Protestants, but it is also significant that under the Nazi regime they are being compelled to relinquish this Judaic faith. If one finds no Catholic figure in Europe corresponding to the Protestant Niemoeller, it is not because Catholics are not brave and willing to suffer and die for their faith. It is because Hitler is exactly right when he says that Christianity, meaning Protestant Christianity, is Jewish, that is to say, a monotheistic Moses religion; Catholicism, on the other hand, as Freud says, is polytheistic and in this sense non-Jewish. Freud neglects to make this exceedingly important distinction, but throughout his book refers to Christianity as if it were synonymous with Catholicism.

Similarly, Freud neglects the fact that reformed Judaism is also a return to the spirit of the Elohim religion, with far less emphasis upon rituals of atonement and propitiation and far more upon the improvement of the interpersonal relationships between human beings. It no longer struggles with the temptation to return to the many gods, subtly implied in that clarion cry of orthodox Judaism, *"Schma, Israel, adonoi elohainu, adonoi echad!"* "Hear, O Israel, the Lord is our *Gods* [sic] the Lord is one!" On a psychological basis Protestant Christianity and reformed Judaism should long since have become amalgamated, since both in theory and in practice they represent one great religious ideology as opposed to the utterly different ideology of Catholicism. It is not our function to evaluate these any more than does the author of *Moses and Monotheism,* and it may be that the Jahve system can better serve the needs of some human beings than the monotheistic system. There is much to indicate that it better serves the uses of autocracy and tyranny. But there should be no shutting of one's eyes to the facts that this is the real distinction between these world religions, and not the many trivia which are advanced to maintain secular separatism.

This is the great social message of Freud's book. Superstitious religion stems from the neurosis of the individuals that compose society and serves regularly to cloak the actions of hate in a pious disguise. Such religion is based on the theory that men were made by "the gods" in their image. Religious concepts which recognize that man created God, that he is an ideal constructed from unconscious memories of a benign father with the highest aspirations of human thought, that he represents not some shibboleth for the entrance into a future life, but the index of an increased regard for the dignity of present-day human life—this is the spirit of a civilized, intelligent religion. But like the Aton religion, the Moses religion, the Elohim religion, the Jesus religion, it is not one which lends itself to vigorous exploitation. In this sense it suffers the weakness of democracy as compared to the strength of autocracy. Its strength is internal rather than external. The ultimate victory of this kind of religion would be marked by its official disappearance; man will have achieved the social wisdom that would make religious idealism no longer necessary. (pp. 23-5)

> Karl Menninger, "Death of a Prophet," in The New Republic, *Vol. LXXXXX, No. 1288, August 9, 1939, pp. 23-5.*

Lionel Trilling   (essay date 1950)

[*A widely respected American critic and literary historian, Trilling was also an essayist, editor, novelist, and short story writer. His exploration of liberal arts theory and its ethical dimensions led Trilling to write not only as a literary critic, but as a social commentator as well. A liberal and a humanist, Trilling judged the value of a text by its contribution to culture and, in turn, regarded culture as indispensable for human survival. Trilling focused in particular on the conflict between the individual and culture, maintaining that art had the power to "liberate the individual from the tyranny of his culture in the environmental sense and to permit him to stand beyond it in an autonomy of perception and judgement." In the following essay, Trilling considers Freud's theories about art and the influence of psychoanalysis on twentieth-century criticism and literature.*]

The Freudian psychology is the only systematic account of the human mind which, in point of subtlety and complexity, of interest and tragic power, deserves to stand beside the chaotic mass of psychological insights which literature has accumulated through the centuries. To pass from the reading of a great literary work to a treatise of academic psychology is to pass from one order of perception to another, but the human nature of the Freudian psychology is exactly the stuff upon which the poet has always exercised his art. It is therefore not surprising that the psychoanalytical theory has had a great effect upon literature. Yet the relationship is reciprocal, and the effect of Freud upon literature has been no greater than the effect of literature upon Freud. When, on the occasion of the celebration of his seventieth birthday, Freud was greeted as the "discoverer of the unconscious," he corrected the speaker and disclaimed the title. "The poets and philosophers before me discovered the unconscious," he said. "What I discovered was the scientific method by which the unconscious can be studied."

A lack of specific evidence prevents us from considering the particular literary "influences" upon the founder of

Freud examining the manuscript of his final work, Moses and Monotheism.

psychoanalysis; and, besides, when we think of the men who so clearly anticipated many of Freud's own ideas— Schopenhauer and Nietzsche, for example—and then learn that he did not read their works until after he had formulated his own theories, we must see that particular influences cannot be in question here but that what we must deal with is nothing less than a whole *Zeitgeist,* a direction of thought. For psychoanalysis is one of the culminations of the Romanticist literature of the nineteenth century. If there is perhaps a contradiction in the idea of a science standing upon the shoulders of a literature which avows itself inimical to science in so many ways, the contradiction will be resolved if we remember that this literature, despite its avowals, was itself scientific in at least the sense of being passionately devoted to a research into the self.

In showing the connection between Freud and this Romanticist tradition, it is difficult to know where to begin, but there might be a certain aptness in starting even back of the tradition, as far back as 1762 with Diderot's *Rameau's Nephew.* At any rate, certain men at the heart of nineteenth-century thought were agreed in finding a peculiar importance in this brilliant little work: Goethe translated it, Marx admired it, Hegel—as Marx reminded Engels in the letter which announced that he was sending the book as a gift—praised and expounded it at length, Shaw was impressed by it, and Freud himself, as we know from a quotation in his ***Introductory Lectures,*** read it with the pleasure of agreement.

The dialogue takes place between Diderot himself and a nephew of the famous composer. The protagonist, the younger Rameau, is a despised, outcast, shameless fellow; Hegel calls him the "disintegrated consciousness" and credits him with great wit, for it is he who breaks down all the normal social values and makes new combinations with the pieces. As for Diderot, the deuteragonist, he is what Hegel calls the "honest consciousness," and Hegel considers him reasonable, decent, and dull. It is quite clear that the author does not despise his Rameau and does not mean us to. Rameau is lustful and greedy, arrogant yet self-abasing, perceptive yet "wrong," like a child. Still, Diderot seems actually to be giving the fellow a kind of superiority over himself, as though Rameau represents the elements which, dangerous but wholly necessary, lie beneath the reasonable decorum of social life. It would perhaps be pressing too far to find in Rameau Freud's id and in Diderot Freud's ego; yet the connection does suggest itself; and at least we have here the perception which is to be the common characteristic of both Freud and Romanticism, the perception of the hidden element of human nature and of the opposition between the hidden and the visible. We have too the bold perception of just what lies hidden: "If the little savage [i.e., the child] were left to himself, if he preserved all his foolishness and combined the violent passions of a man of thirty with the lack of reason of a child in the cradle, he'd wring his father's neck and go to bed with his mother."

From the self-exposure of Rameau to Rousseau's account of his own childhood is no great step; society might ignore or reject the idea of the "immorality" which lies concealed in the beginning of the career of the "good" man, just as it might turn away from Blake struggling to expound a psychology which would include the forces beneath the propriety of social man in general, but the idea of the hidden thing went forward to become one of the dominant notions of the age. The hidden element takes many forms and it is not necessarily "dark" and "bad"; for Blake the "bad" was the good, while for Wordsworth and Burke what was hidden and unconscious was wisdom and power, which work in despite of the conscious intellect.

The mind has become far less simple; the devotion to the various forms of autobiography—itself an important fact in the tradition—provides abundant examples of the change that has taken place. Poets, making poetry by what seems to them almost a freshly discovered faculty, find that this new power may be conspired against by other agencies of the mind and even deprived of its freedom; the names of Wordsworth, Coleridge, and Arnold at once occur to us again, and Freud quotes Schiller on the danger to the poet that lies in the merely analytical reason. And it is not only the poets who are threatened; educated and sensitive people throughout Europe become aware of the depredations that reason might make upon the affective life, as in the classic instance of John Stuart Mill.

We must also take into account the preoccupation—it began in the eighteenth century, or even in the seventeenth—with children, women, peasants, and savages, whose mental life, it is felt, is less overlaid than that of the educated adult male by the proprieties of social habit. With this preoccupation goes a concern with education and personal development, so consonant with the historical and evolutionary bias of the time. And we must certainly note the revolution in morals which took place at the instance (we might almost say) of the *Bildungsroman*,

for in the novels fathered by *Wilhelm Meister* we get the almost complete identification of author and hero and of the reader with both, and this identification almost inevitably suggests a leniency of moral judgment. The autobiographical novel has a further influence upon the moral sensibility by its exploitation of all the modulations of motive and by its hinting that we may not judge a man by any single moment in his life without taking into account the determining past and the expiating and fulfilling future.

It is difficult to know how to go on, for the further we look the more literary affinities to Freud we find, and even if we limit ourselves to bibliography we can at best be incomplete. Yet we must mention the sexual revolution that was being demanded—by Shelley, for example, by the Schlegel of *Lucinde,* by George Sand, and later and more critically by Ibsen; the belief in the sexual origin of art, baldly stated by Tieck, more subtly by Schopenhauer; the investigation of sexual maladjustment by Stendhal, whose observations on erotic feeling seem to us distinctly Freudian. Again and again we see the effective, utilitarian ego being relegated to an inferior position and a plea being made on behalf of the anarchic and self-indulgent id. We find the energetic exploitation of the idea of the mind as a divisible thing, one part of which can contemplate and mock the other. It is not a far remove from this to Dostoevski's brilliant instances of ambivalent feeling. Novalis brings in the preoccupation with the death wish, and this is linked on the one hand with sleep and on the other hand with the perception of the perverse, self-destroying impulses, which in turn leads us to that fascination by the horrible which we find in Shelley, Poe, and Baudelaire. And always there is the profound interest in the dream—"Our dreams," said Gerard de Nerval, "are a second life"—and in the nature of metaphor, which reaches its climax in Rimbaud and the later Symbolists, metaphor becoming less and less communicative as it approaches the relative autonomy of the dream life.

But perhaps we must stop to ask, since these are the components of the *Zeitgeist* from which Freud himself developed, whether it can be said that Freud did indeed produce a wide literary effect. What is it that Freud added that the tendency of literature itself would not have developed without him? If we were looking for a writer who showed the Freudian influence, Proust would perhaps come to mind as readily as anyone else; the very title of his novel, in French more than in English, suggests an enterprise of psychoanalysis and scarcely less so does his method—the investigation of sleep, of sexual deviation, of the way of association, the almost obsessive interest in metaphor; at these and at many other points the "influence" might be shown. Yet I believe it is true that Proust did not read Freud. Or again, exegesis of *The Waste Land* often reads remarkably like the psychoanalytic interpretation of a dream, yet we know that Eliot's methods were prepared for him not by Freud but by other poets.

Nevertheless, it is of course true that Freud's influence on literature has been very great. Much of it is so pervasive that its extent is scarcely to be determined; in one form or another, frequently in perversions or absurd simplifications, it had been infused into our life and become a component of our culture of which it is now hard to be specifically aware. In biography its first effect was sensational but not fortunate. The early Freudian biographers were for the most part Guildensterns who seemed to know the pipes but could not pluck out the heart of the mystery, and the same condemnation applies to the early Freudian critics. But in recent years, with the acclimatization of psychoanalysis and the increased sense of its refinements and complexity, criticism has derived from the Freudian system much that is of great value, most notably the license and the injunction to read the work of literature with a lively sense of its latent and ambiguous meanings, as if it were, as indeed it is, a being no less alive and contradictory than the man who created it. And this new response to the literary work has had a corrective effect upon our conception of literary biography. The literary critic or biographer who makes use of the Freudian theory is no less threatened by the dangers of theoretical systematization than he was in the early days, but he is likely to be more aware of these dangers; and I think it is true to say that now the motive of his interpretation is not that of exposing the secret shame of the writer and limiting the meaning of his work, but, on the contrary, that of finding grounds for sympathy with the writer and for increasing the possible significances of the work.

The names of the creative writers who have been more or less Freudian in tone or assumption would of course be legion. Only a relatively small number, however, have made serious use of the Freudian ideas. Freud himself seems to have thought this was as it should be: he is said to have expected very little of the works that were sent to him by writers with inscriptions of gratitude for all they had learned from him. The Surrealists have, with a certain inconsistency, depended upon Freud for the "scientific" sanction of their program. Kafka, with an apparent awareness of what he was doing, has explored the Freudian conceptions of guilt and punishment, of the dream, and of the fear of the father. Thomas Mann, whose tendency, as he himself says, was always in the direction of Freud's interests, has been most susceptible to the Freudian anthropology, finding a special charm in the theories of myths and magical practices. James Joyce, with his interest in the numerous states of receding consciousness, with his use of words as things and of words which point to more than one thing, with his pervading sense of the interrelation and interpenetration of all things, and, not least important, his treatment of familial themes, has perhaps most thoroughly and consciously exploited Freud's ideas.

It will be clear enough how much of Freud's thought has significant affinity with the anti-rationalist element of the Romanticist tradition. But we must see with no less distinctness how much of his system is militantly rationalistic. Thomas Mann is at fault when, in his first essay on Freud, he makes it seem that the "Apollonian," the rationalistic, side of psychoanalysis is, while certainly important and wholly admirable, somehow secondary and even accidental. He gives us a Freud who is committed to the "night side" of life. Not at all: the rationalistic element of Freud is foremost; before everything else he is positivistic. If the interpreter of dreams came to medical science through Goethe, as he tells us he did, he entered not by

way of the *Walpurgisnacht* but by the essay which played so important a part in the lives of so many scientists of the nineteenth century, the famous disquisition on Nature.

This correction is needed not only for accuracy but also for any understanding of Freud's attitude to art. And for that understanding we must see how intense is the passion with which Freud believes that positivistic rationalism, in its golden-age pre-Revolutionary purity, is the very form and pattern of intellectual virtue. The aim of psychoanalysis, he says, is the control of the night side of life. It is "to strengthen the ego, to make it more independent of the super-ego, to widen its field of vision, and so to extend the organization of the id." "Where id was,"—that is, where all the irrational, non-logical, pleasure-seeking dark forces were—"there shall ego be,"—that is, intelligence and control. "It is," he concludes, with a reminiscence of Faust, "reclamation work, like the draining of the Zuyder Zee." This passage is quoted by Mann when, in taking up the subject of Freud a second time, he does indeed speak of Freud's positivistic program; but even here the bias induced by Mann's artistic interest in the "night side" prevents him from giving the other aspect of Freud its due emphasis. Freud would never have accepted the role which Mann seems to give him as the legitimizer of the myth and the dark irrational ways of the mind. If Freud discovered the darkness for science he never endorsed it. On the contrary, his rationalism supports all the ideas of the Enlightenment that deny validity to myth or religion; he holds to a simple materialism, to a simple determinism, to a rather limited sort of epistemology. No great scientist of our day has thundered so articulately and so fiercely against all those who would sophisticate with metaphysics the scientific principles that were good enough for the nineteenth century. Conceptualism or pragmatism is anathema to him through the greater part of his intellectual career, and this, when we consider the nature of his own brilliant scientific methods, has surely an element of paradox in it.

From his rationalistic positivism comes much of Freud's strength and what weakness he has. The strength is the fine, clear tenacity of his positive aims, the goal of therapy, the desire to bring to men a decent measure of earthly happiness. But upon the rationalism must also be placed the blame for the often naïve scientific principles which characterize his early thought—they are later much modified—and which consist largely of claiming for his theories a perfect correspondence with an external reality, a position which, for those who admire Freud and especially for those who take seriously his views on art, is troublesome in the extreme.

Now Freud has, I believe, much to tell us about art, but whatever is suggestive in him is not likely to be found in those of his works in which he deals expressly with art itself. Freud is not insensitive to art—on the contrary—nor does he ever intend to speak of it with contempt. Indeed, he speaks of it with a real tenderness and counts it one of the true charms of the good life. Of artists, especially of writers, he speaks with admiration and even a kind of awe, though perhaps what he most appreciates in literature are specific emotional insights and observations; as we have noted, he speaks of literary men, because they have understood the part played in life by the hidden motives, as the precursors and coadjutors of his own science.

And yet eventually Freud speaks of art with what we must indeed call contempt. Art, he tells us, is a "substitute gratification," and as such is "an illusion in contrast to reality." Unlike most illusions, however, art is "almost always harmless and beneficent" for the reason that "it does not seek to be anything but an illusion. Save in the case of a few people who are, one might say, obsessed by Art, it never dares make any attack on the realm of reality." One of its chief functions is to serve as a "narcotic." It shares the characteristics of the dream, whose element of distortion Freud calls a "sort of inner dishonesty." As for the artist, he is virtually in the same category with the neurotic. "By such separation of imagination and intellectual capacity," Freud says of the hero of a novel, "he is destined to be a poet or a neurotic, and he belongs to that race of beings whose realm is not of this world."

Now there is nothing in the logic of psychoanalytical thought which requires Freud to have these opinions. But there is a great deal in the practice of the psychoanalytical therapy which makes it understandable that Freud, unprotected by an adequate philosophy, should be tempted to take the line he does. The analytical therapy deals with illusion. The patient comes to the physician to be cured, let us say, of a fear of walking in the street. The fear is real enough, there is no illusion on that score, and it produces all the physical symptoms of a more rational fear, the sweating palms, pounding heart, and shortened breath. But the patient knows that there is no cause for the fear, or rather that there is, as he says, no "real cause": there are no machine guns, man traps, or tigers in the street. The physician knows, however, that there is indeed a "real" cause for the fear, though it has nothing at all to do with what is or is not in the street; the cause is within the patient, and the process of the therapy will be to discover, by gradual steps, what this real cause is and so free the patient from its effects.

Now the patient in coming to the physician, and the physician in accepting the patient, make a tacit compact about reality; for their purpose they agree to the limited reality by which we get our living, win our loves, catch our trains and our colds. The therapy will undertake to train the patient in proper ways of coping with this reality. The patient, of course, has been dealing with this reality all along, but in the wrong way. For Freud there are two ways of dealing with external reality. One is practical, effective, positive; this is the way of the conscious self, of the ego which must be made independent of the super-ego and extend its organization over the id, and it is the right way. The antithetical way may be called, for our purpose now, the "fictional" way. Instead of doing something about, or to, external reality, the individual who uses this way does something to, or about, his affective states. The most common and "normal" example of this is daydreaming, in which we give ourselves a certain pleasure by imagining our difficulties solved or our desires gratified. Then, too, as Freud discovered, sleeping dreams are, in much more complicated ways, and even though quite unpleasant, at the service of this same "fictional" activity. And in ways yet more complicated and yet more unpleasant, the actual neurosis from which our patient suffers deals with an external reality which the mind considers still more unpleasant than the painful neurosis itself.

For Freud as psychoanalytic practitioner there are, we may say, the polar extremes of reality and illusion. Reality is an honorific word, and it means what is *there;* illusion is a pejorative word, and it means a response to what is *not there.* The didactic nature of a course of psychoanalysis no doubt requires a certain firm crudeness in making the distinction; it is after all aimed not at theoretical refinement but at practical effectiveness. The polar extremes are practical reality and neurotic illusion, the latter judged by the former. This, no doubt, is as it should be; the patient is not being trained in metaphysics and epistemology.

This practical assumption is not Freud's only view of the mind in its relation to reality. Indeed what may be called the essentially Freudian view assumes that the mind, for good as well as bad, helps create its reality by selection and evaluation. In this view, reality is malleable and subject to creation; it is not static but is rather a series of situations which are dealt with in their own terms. But beside this conception of the mind stands the conception which arises from Freud's therapeutic-practical assumptions; in this view, the mind deals with a reality which is quite fixed and static, a reality that is wholly "given" and not (to use a phrase of Dewey's) "taken." In his epistemological utterances, Freud insists on this second view, although it is not easy to see why he should do so. For the reality to which he wishes to reconcile the neurotic patient is, after all, a "taken" and not a "given" reality. It is the reality of social life and of value, conceived and maintained by the human mind and will. Love, morality, honor, esteem—these are the components of a created reality. If we are to call art an illusion then we must call most of the activities and satisfactions of the ego illusions; Freud, of course, has no desire to call them that.

What, then, is the difference between, on the one hand, the dream and the neurosis, and, on the other hand, art? That they have certain common elements is of course clear; that unconscious processes are at work in both would be denied by no poet or critic; they share too, though in different degrees, the element of fantasy. But there is a vital difference between them which Charles Lamb saw so clearly in his defense of the sanity of true genius: "The . . . poet dreams being awake. He is not possessed by his subject but he has dominion over it."

That is the whole difference: the poet is in command of his fantasy, while it is exactly the mark of the neurotic that he is possessed by his fantasy. And there is a further difference which Lamb states; speaking of the poet's relation to reality (he calls it Nature), he says, "He is beautifully loyal to that sovereign directress, even when he appears most to betray her"; the illusions of art are made to serve the purpose of a closer and truer relation with reality. Jacques Barzun, in an acute and sympathetic discussion of Freud, puts the matter well: "A good analogy between art and *dreaming* has led him to a false one between art and *sleeping.* But the difference between a work of art and a dream is precisely this, that the work of art *leads us back to the outer reality by taking account of it.*" Freud's assumption of the almost exclusively hedonistic nature and purpose of art bar him from the perception of this.

Of the distinction that must be made between the artist and the neurotic Freud is of course aware; he tells us that the artist is not like the neurotic in that he knows how to find a way back from the world of imagination and "once more get a firm foothold in reality." This however seems to mean no more than that reality is to be dealt with when the artist suspends the practice of his art; and at least once when Freud speaks of art dealing with reality he actually means the rewards that a successful artist can win. He does not deny to art its function and its usefulness; it has a therapeutic effect in releasing mental tension; it serves the cultural purpose of acting as a "substitute gratification" to reconcile men to the sacrifices they have made for culture's sake; it promotes the social sharing of highly valued emotional experiences; and it recalls men to their cultural ideals. This is not everything that some of us would find that art does, yet even this is a good deal for a "narcotic" to do.

I started by saying that Freud's ideas could tell us something about art, but so far I have done little more than try to show that Freud's very conception of art is inadequate. Perhaps, then, the suggestiveness lies in the application of the analytic method to specific works of art or to the artist himself? I do not think so, and it is only fair to say that Freud himself was aware both of the limits and the limitations of psychoanalysis in art, even though he does not always in practice submit to the former or admit the latter.

Freud has, for example, no desire to encroach upon the artist's autonomy; he does not wish us to read his monograph on Leonardo and then say of the "Madonna of the Rocks" that it is a fine example of homosexual, autoerotic painting. If he asserts that in investigation the "psychiatrist cannot yield to the author," he immediately insists that the "author cannot yield to the psychiatrist," and he warns the latter not to "coarsen everything" by using for all human manifestations the "substantially useless and awkward terms" of clinical procedure. He admits, even while asserting that the sense of beauty probably derives from sexual feeling, that psychoanalysis "has less to say about beauty than about most other things." He confesses to a theoretical indifference to the form of art and restricts himself to its content. Tone, feeling, style, and the modification that part makes upon part he does not consider. "The layman," he says, "may expect perhaps too much from analysis . . . for it must be admitted that it throws no light upon the two problems which probably interest him the most. It can do nothing toward elucidating the nature of the artistic gift, nor can it explain the means by which the artist works—artistic technique."

What, then, does Freud believe that the analytical method can do? Two things: explain the "inner meanings" of the work of art and explain the temperament of the artist as man.

A famous example of the method is the attempt to solve the "problem" of *Hamlet* as suggested by Freud and as carried out by Dr. Ernest Jones, his early and distinguished follower. Dr. Jones's monograph is a work of painstaking scholarship and of really masterly ingenuity. The research undertakes not only the clearing up of the mystery of Hamlet's character, but also the discovery of "the clue to much of the deeper workings of Shakespeare's mind." Part of the mystery in question is of course why Hamlet, after he had so definitely resolved to do so, did not avenge upon his hated uncle his father's death. But there is another mystery to the play—what Freud calls "the mystery of its effect," its magical appeal that draws so much interest toward it. Recalling the many failures to solve the riddle of the play's charm, he wonders if we are to be driven to the conclusion "that its magical appeal rests solely upon the impressive thoughts in it and the splendor of its language." Freud believes that we can find a source of power beyond this.

We remember that Freud has told us that the meaning of a dream is its intention, and we may assume that the meaning of a drama is its intention, too. The Jones research undertakes to discover what it was that Shakespeare intended to say about Hamlet. It finds that the intention was wrapped by the author in a dreamlike obscurity because it touched so deeply both his personal life and the moral life of the world; what Shakespeare intended to say is that Hamlet cannot act because he is incapacitated by the guilt he feels at his unconscious attachment to his mother. There is, I think, nothing to be quarreled with in the statement that there is an Oedipus situation in *Hamlet;* and if psychoanalysis has indeed added a new point of interest to the play, that is to its credit. And, just so, there is no reason to quarrel with Freud's conclusion when he undertakes to give us the meaning of *King Lear* by a tortuous tracing of the mythological implications of the theme of the three caskets, of the relation of the caskets to the Norns, the Fates, and the Graces, of the connection of these triadic females with Lear's daughters, of the transmogrification of the death goddess into the love goddess and the identification of Cordelia with both, all to the conclusion that the meaning of *King Lear* is to be found in the tragic refusal of an old man to "renounce love, choose death, and make friends with the necessity of dying." There is something both beautiful and suggestive in this, but it is not *the* meaning of *King Lear* any more than the Oedipus motive is *the* meaning of *Hamlet.*

It is not here a question of the validity of the evidence, though that is of course important. We must rather object to the conclusions of Freud and Dr. Jones on the ground that their proponents do not have an adequate conception of what an artistic meaning is. There is no single meaning to any work of art; this is true not merely because it is better that it should be true, that is, because it makes art a richer thing, but because historical and personal experience show it to be true. Changes in historical context and in personal mood change the meaning of a work and indicate to us that artistic understanding is not a question of fact but of value. Even if the author's intention were, as it cannot be, precisely determinable, the meaning of a work cannot lie in the author's intention alone. It must also lie in its effect. We can say of a volcanic eruption on an inhabited island that it "means terrible suffering," but if the island is uninhabited or easily evacuated it means something else. In short, the audience partly determines the meaning of the work. But although Freud sees something of this when he says that in addition to the author's intention we must take into account the mystery of *Hamlet's* effect, he nevertheless goes on to speak as if, historically, *Hamlet's* effect had been single and brought about solely by the "magical" power of the Oedipus motive to which, unconsciously, we so violently respond. Yet there was, we know, a period when *Hamlet* was relatively in eclipse, and it has always been scandalously true of the French, a people not without filial feeling, that they have been somewhat indifferent to the "magical appeal" of *Hamlet.*

I do not think that anything I have said about the inadequacies of the Freudian method of interpretation limits the number of ways we can deal with a work of art. Bacon remarked that experiment may twist nature on the rack to wring out its secrets, and criticism may use any instruments upon a work of art to find its meanings. The elements of art are not limited to the world of art. They reach into life, and whatever extraneous knowledge of them we gain—for example, by research into the historical context of the work—may quicken our feelings for the work itself and even enter legitimately into those feelings. Then, too, anything we may learn about the artist himself may be enriching and legitimate. But one research into the mind of the artist is simply not practicable, however legitimate it may theoretically be. That is, the investigation of his unconscious intention as it exists apart from the work itself. Criticism understands that the artist's statement of his conscious intention, though it is sometimes useful, cannot finally determine meaning. How much less can we know from his unconscious intention considered as something apart from the whole work? Surely very little that can be called conclusive or scientific. For, as Freud himself points out, we are not in a position to question the artist; we must apply the technique of dream analysis to his symbols, but, as Freud says with some heat, those people do not understand his theory who think that a dream may be interpreted without the dreamer's free association with the multitudinous details of his dream.

We have so far ignored the aspect of the method which finds the solution to the "mystery" of such a play as *Hamlet* in the temperament of Shakespeare himself and then illuminates the mystery of Shakespeare's temperament by means of the solved mystery of the play. Here it will be amusing to remember that by 1935 Freud had become converted to the theory that it was not Shakespeare of Stratford but the Earl of Oxford who wrote the plays, thus invalidating the important bit of evidence that Shakespeare's father died shortly before the composition of *Hamlet.* This is destructive enough to Dr. Jones's argument, but the evidence from which Dr. Jones draws conclusions about literature fails on grounds more relevant to literature itself. For when Dr. Jones, by means of his analysis of *Hamlet,* takes us into "the deeper workings of Shakespeare's mind," he does so with a perfect confidence that he knows what *Hamlet* is and what its relation to Shakespeare is. It is, he tells us, Shakespeare's "chief masterpiece," so far superior to all his other works that it may

be placed on "an entirely separate level." And then, having established his ground on an entirely subjective literary judgment, Dr. Jones goes on to tell us that *Hamlet* "probably expresses the core of Shakespeare's philosophy and outlook as no other work of his does." That is, all the contradictory or complicating or modifying testimony of the other plays is dismissed on the basis of Dr. Jones's acceptance of the peculiar position which, he believes, *Hamlet* occupies in the Shakespeare canon. And it is upon this quite inadmissible judgment that Dr. Jones bases his argument: "It may be expected *therefore* that anything which will give us the key to the inner meaning of the play will *necessarily* give us the clue to much of the deeper workings of Shakespeare's mind." (The italics are mine.)

I should be sorry if it appeared that I am trying to say that psychoanalysis can have nothing to do with literature. I am sure that the opposite is so. For example, the whole notion of rich ambiguity in literature, of the interplay between the apparent meaning and the latent—not "hidden"—meaning, has been reinforced by the Freudian concepts, perhaps even received its first impetus from them. Of late years, the more perceptive psychoanalysts have surrendered the early pretensions of their teachers to deal "scientifically" with literature. That is all to the good, and when a study as modest and precise as Dr. Franz Alexander's essay on *Henry IV* comes along, an essay which pretends not to "solve" but only to illuminate the subject, we have something worth having. Dr. Alexander undertakes nothing more than to say that in the development of Prince Hal we see the classic struggle of the ego to come to normal adjustment, beginning with the rebellion against the father, going on to the conquest of the super-ego (Hotspur, with his rigid notions of honor and glory), then to the conquests of the *id* (Falstaff, with his anarchic self-indulgence), then to the identification with the father (the crown scene) and the assumption of mature responsibility. An analysis of this sort is not momentous and not exclusive of other meanings; perhaps it does no more than point up and formulate what we all have already seen. It has the tact to *accept* the play and does not, like Dr. Jones's study of *Hamlet,* search for a "hidden motive" and a "deeper working," which implies that there is a reality to which the play stands in the relation that a dream stands to the wish that generates it and from which it is separable; it is this reality, this "deeper working," which, according to Dr. Jones, produced the play. But *Hamlet* is not merely the product of Shakespeare's thought, it is the very instrument of his thought, and if meaning is intention, Shakespeare did not intend the Oedipus motive or anything less than *Hamlet;* if meaning is effect then it is *Hamlet* which affects us, not the Oedipus motive. *Coriolanus* also deals, and very terribly, with the Oedipus motive, but the effect of the one drama is very different from the effect of the other.

If, then, we can accept neither Freud's conception of the place of art in life nor his application of the analytical method, what is it that he contributes to our understanding of art or to its practice? In my opinion, what he contributes outweighs his errors; it is of the greatest importance, and it lies in no specific statement that he makes about art but is, rather, implicit in his whole conception of the mind.

For, of all mental systems, the Freudian psychology is the one which makes poetry indigenous to the very constitution of the mind. Indeed, the mind, as Freud sees it, is in the greater part of its tendency exactly a poetry-making organ. This puts the case too strongly, no doubt, for it seems to make the working of the unconscious mind equivalent to poetry itself, forgetting that between the unconscious mind and the finished poem there supervene the social intention and the formal control of the conscious mind. Yet the statement has at least the virtue of counterbalancing the belief, so commonly expressed or implied, that the very opposite is true, and that poetry is a kind of beneficent aberration of the mind's right course.

Freud has not merely naturalized poetry; he has discovered its status as a pioneer settler, and he sees it as a method of thought. Often enough he tries to show how, as a method of thought, it is unreliable and ineffective for conquering reality; yet he himself is forced to use it in the very shaping of his own science, as when he speaks of the topography of the mind and tells us what a kind of defiant apology that the metaphors of space relationship which he is using are really most inexact since the mind is not a thing of space at all, but that there is no other way of conceiving the difficult idea except by metaphor. In the eighteenth century Vico spoke of the metaphorical, imagistic language of the early stages of culture; it was left to Freud to discover how, in a scientific age, we still feel and think in figurative formations, and to create, what psychoanalysis is, a science of tropes, of metaphor and its variants, synecdoche and metonymy.

Freud showed, too, how the mind, in one of its parts, could work without logic, yet not without that directing purpose, that control of intent from which, perhaps it might be said, logic springs. For the unconscious mind works without the syntactical conjunctions which are logic's essence. It recognizes no *because,* no *therefore,* no *but;* such ideas as similarity, agreement, and community are expressed in dreams imagistically by compressing the elements into a unity. The unconscious mind in its struggle with the conscious always turns from the general to the concrete and finds the tangible trifle more congenial than the large abstraction. Freud discovered in the very organization of the mind those mechanisms by which art makes its effects, such devices as the condensations of meanings and the displacement of accent.

All this is perhaps obvious enough and, though I should like to develop it in proportion both to its importance and to the space I have given to disagreement with Freud, I will not press it further. For there are two other elements in Freud's thought which, in conclusion, I should like to introduce as of great weight in their bearing on art.

Of these, one is a specific idea which, in the middle of his career (1920), Freud put forward in his essay *Beyond the Pleasure Principle.* The essay itself is a speculative attempt to solve a perplexing problem in clinical analysis, but its relevance to literature is inescapable, as Freud sees well enough, even though his perception of its critical im-

portance is not sufficiently strong to make him revise his earlier views of the nature and function of art. The idea is one which stands besides Aristotle's notion of the catharsis, in part to supplement, in part to modify it.

Freud has come upon certain facts which are not to be reconciled with his earlier theory of the dream. According to this theory, all dreams, even the unpleasant ones, could be understood upon analysis to have the intention of fulfilling the dreamer's wishes. They are in the service of what Freud calls the pleasure principle, which is opposed to the reality principle. It is, of course, this explanation of the dream which had so largely conditioned Freud's theory of art. But now there is thrust upon him the necessity for reconsidering the theory of the dream, for it was found that in cases of war neurosis—what we once called shell-shock—the patient, with the utmost anguish, recurred in his dreams to the very situation, distressing as it was, which had precipitated his neurosis. It seemed impossible to interpret these dreams by any assumption of a hedonistic intent. Nor did there seem to be the usual amount of distortion in them: the patient recurred to the terrible initiatory situation with great literalness. And the same pattern of psychic behavior could be observed in the play of children; there were some games which, far from fulfilling wishes, seemed to concentrate upon the representation of those aspects of the child's life which were most unpleasant and threatening to his happiness.

To explain such mental activities Freud evolved a theory for which he at first refused to claim much but to which, with the years, he attached an increasing importance. He first makes the assumption that there is indeed in the psychic life a repetition-compulsion which goes beyond the pleasure principle. Such a compulsion cannot be meaningless, it must have an intent. And that intent, Freud comes to believe, is exactly and literally the developing of fear. "These dreams," he says, "are attempts at restoring control of the stimuli by developing apprehension, the pretermission of which caused the traumatic neurosis." The dream, that is, is the effort to reconstruct the bad situation in order that the failure to meet it may be recouped; in these dreams there is no obscured intent to evade but only an attempt to meet the situation, to make a new effort of control. And in the play of children it seems to be that "the child repeats even the unpleasant experiences because through his own activity he gains a far more thorough mastery of the strong impression than was possible by mere passive experience."

Freud, at this point, can scarcely help being put in mind of tragic drama; nevertheless, he does not wish to believe that this effort to come to mental grips with a situation is involved in the attraction of tragedy. He is, we might say, under the influence of the Aristotelian tragic theory which emphasizes a qualified hedonism through suffering. But the pleasure involved in tragedy is perhaps an ambiguous one; and sometimes we must feel that the famous sense of cathartic resolution is perhaps the result of glossing over terror with beautiful language rather than an evacuation of it. And sometimes the terror even bursts through the language to stand stark and isolated from the play, as does Oedipus's sightless and bleeding face. At any rate, the Aristotelian theory does not deny another function for trage-dy (and for comedy, too) which is suggested by Freud's theory of the traumatic neurosis—what might be called the mithridatic function, by which tragedy is used as the homeopathic administration of pain to inure ourselves to the greater pain which life will force upon us. There is in the cathartic theory of tragedy, as it is usually understood, a conception of tragedy's function which is too negative and which inadequately suggests the sense of active mas-tery which tragedy can give.

In the same essay in which he sets forth the conception of the mind embracing its own pain for some vital purpose, Freud also expresses a provisional assent to the idea (earli-er stated, as he reminds us, by Schopenhauer) that there is perhaps a human drive which makes of death the final and desired goal. The death instinct is a conception that is rejected by many of even the most thoroughgoing Freudian theorists (as, in his last book, Freud mildly noted); the late Otto Fenichel in his authoritative work on the neurosis argues cogently against it. Yet even if we re-ject the theory as not fitting the facts in any operatively useful way, we still cannot miss its grandeur, its ultimate tragic courage in acquiescence to fate. The idea of the real-ity principle and the idea of the death instinct form the crown of Freud's broader speculation on the life of man. Their quality of grim poetry is characteristic of Freud's system and the ideas it generates for him.

And as much as anything else that Freud gives to litera-ture, this quality of his thought is important. Although the artist is never finally determined in his work by the intel-lectual systems about him, he cannot avoid their influence; and it can be said of various competing systems that some hold more promise for the artist than others. When, for example, we think of the simple humanitarian optimism which, for two decades, has been so pervasive, we must see that not only has it been politically and philosophically in-adequate, but also that it implies, by the smallness of its view of the varieties of human possibility, a kind of check on the creative faculties. In Freud's view of life no such limitation is implied. To be sure, certain elements of his system seem hostile to the usual notions of man's dignity. Like every great critic of human nature—and Freud is that—he finds in human pride the ultimate cause of human wretchedness, and he takes pleasure in knowing that his ideas stand with those of Copernicus and Darwin in making pride more difficult to maintain. Yet the Freud-ian man is, I venture to think, a creature of far more digni-ty and far more interest than the man which any other modern system has been able to conceive. Despite popular belief to the contrary, man, as Freud conceives him, is not to be understood by any simple formula (such as sex) but is rather an inextricable tangle of culture and biology. And not being simple, he is not simply good; he has, as Freud says somewhere, a kind of hell within him from which rise everlastingly the impulses which threaten his civilization. He has the faculty of imagining for himself more in the way of pleasure and satisfaction than he can possibly achieve. Everything that he gains he pays for in more than equal coin; compromise and the compounding with defeat constitute his best way of getting through the world. His best qualities are the result of a struggle whose outcome

is tragic. Yet he is a creature of love; it is Freud's sharpest criticism of the Adlerian psychology that to aggression it gives everything and to love nothing at all.

One is always aware in reading Freud how little cynicism there is in his thought. His desire for man is only that he should be human, and to this end his science is devoted. No view of life to which the artist responds can insure the quality of his work, but the poetic qualities of Freud's own principles, which are so clearly in the line of the classic tragic realism, suggest that this is a view which does not narrow and simplify the human world for the artist but on the contrary opens and complicates it. (pp. 32-54)

> *Lionel Trilling, "Freud and Literature," in his* The Liberal Imagination: Essays on Litera-ture and Society, *1950. Reprint by Harcourt Brace Jovanovich, 1979, pp. 32-54.*

Erich Fromm   (essay date 1979)

[*Fromm was a German-born American philosopher, psy-choanalyst, writer, and educator whose work was strong-ly influenced by Freud and Karl Marx. Throughout his career, Fromm strove toward an understanding of human existence based upon the breaking down of bar-riers—between individuals as well as between schools of thought. Fromm's central concern was the application of psychoanalysis, sociology, philosophy and religion to the peculiar problems of humanity in modern industri-alized society, and he labeled his basic position a form of "social humanism." In his most famous book,* Escape from Freedom *(1941), Fromm characterized the mod-ern individual as a creature who is bound to an illusory freedom which, while granting him "independence and rationality, has made him isolated and, thereby, anxious and powerless." Although Fromm acknowledged the power of psychoanalysis as a tool for illuminating neuro-ses, he felt that Marx was superior to Freud because he believed in the possibility that humanity could be per-fected. As Fromm stated in an interview, "If Freud could have imagined a classless and free society he would have dispensed with the ego and id as universal categories of the human mind." The following excerpt from his* Greatness and Limitations of Freud's Thought, *which was orginally published in German, Fromm assesses the strengths and weaknesses of Freud's theories on the unconscious and the Oedipus complex.*]

To be sure, Freud was not the first to discover the phe-nomenon that we harbor thoughts and strivings which we are not aware of—that is to say, which are unconscious—and live a hidden life in our psyche. But Freud was the first to have made this discovery the center of his psycho-logical system and he investigated unconscious phenome-na in the greatest detail, with astonishing results. Basically Freud dealt with a discrepancy between thinking and being. We think one thing, for instance that our behavior is motivated by love, devotion, sense of duty, et cetera, and we are not aware that instead it is motivated by the wish for power, masochism, dependency. Freud's discovery was that what we think is not necessarily identical with what we are; that what a person thinks of himself may be, and usually is, quite different or even completely in contradiction to what he really is, that most of us live in a world of self-deception in which we take our thoughts as representing reality. . . . (pp. 21-2)

Freud's great discovery, with its fundamental philosophical and cultural consequences, was that of the conflict between thinking and being. But he restricted the importance of his discovery by assuming that essentially what is repressed is awareness of infantile sexual strivings and that the conflict between thinking and being is essentially that between thinking and infantile sexuality. This restriction is not surprising. As I said before, being under the influence of the materialism of his time, Freud sought the contents of that which was repressed in those strivings which not only were psychical and physiological at the same time, but also, which was obvious, were repressed in the society in which Freud lived—more specifically, in the middle class, with its Victorian morality, from which Freud and most of his patients came. He found proof that pathological phenomena—hysteria for instance—sometimes were expressions of repressed sexual strivings. What he did was to identify the social structure of his class and its problems with the problems inherent in human existence. This was indeed one of Freud's blind spots. For

him, bourgeois society was identical with civilized society, and while he recognized the existence of peculiar cultures that were different from bourgeois society, they remained for him primitive, undeveloped.

Materialistic philosophy and the widespread repression of the awareness of sexual desires were the basis from which Freud constructed the contents of the unconscious. In addition he ignored the fact that very often sexual impulses do not owe their presence or intensity to the physiological substratum of sexuality, that on the contrary they are often the product of entirely different impulses which in themselves are not sexual. Thus a source of sexual desire can be one's narcissism, one's sadism, one's tendency to submit, plain boredom; and it is well known that power and wealth are important elements in arousing sexual desires.

Today, only two or three generations after Freud, it has become obvious that in the culture of the cities, sexuality is not the main object of repression. Since mass man is dedicated to becoming a *Homo consumens,* sex has become one of the main articles of consumption (and in fact one of the cheapest) creating the illusion of happiness and satisfaction. The conflicts to be observed in man, between conscious and unconscious strivings, are diverse. Here is a list of some of the more frequent of these conflicts:

> consciousness of freedom—unconscious unfreedom
>
> conscious good conscience—unconscious guilt feeling
>
> conscious feeling of happiness—unconscious depression
>
> conscious honesty—unconscious fraudulence
>
> consciousness of individualism—unconscious suggestibility
>
> consciousness of power—unconscious sense of powerlessness
>
> consciousness of faith—unconscious cynicism and complete lack of faith
>
> consciousness of loving—unconscious indifference or hate
>
> consciousness of being active—unconscious psychic passivity and laziness
>
> consciousness of being realistic—unconscious lack of realism

These are the true contradictions of today which are repressed and rationalized. They existed already during Freud's time but some of them not as drastically as they do now. But Freud paid no attention to them because he was fascinated by sex and its repression. In the development of orthodox Freudian psychoanalysis infantile sexuality still remains the cornerstone of the system. Analysis thus has served as a resistance against touching the real and most decisive conflicts within man and between men.

Another of the great discoveries of Freud is what is called the Oedipus complex, and he postulated that the unsolved Oedipus complex is at the bottom of every neurosis.

What Freud meant by the Oedipus complex is easily understood: The little boy, because of the awakening of his sexual strivings at an early age, say four or five years, develops an intense sexual attachment to and desire for his mother. He wants her, and the father becomes his rival.

Max Eastman on Freud:

Science . . . is no supernal enterprise; it is nothing but the skilled, persistent, and appropriate use of the mind, and the stores of human knowledge, about any problem. It does, however, require at least three qualifications in the scientist: the discipline of suspended judgment, a mastery of the knowledge relevant to his problem, a sustained passion for verification. Freud had none of these qualifications. He jumped to conclusions with the agility of a trained athlete. He was (to quote Dr. [Ernest] Jones) "ill-informed in the field of contemporary psychology and seems to have derived only from hearsay any knowledge he may have had of it"— he did not even sense, for instance, the elementary distinction between idea and perception. He had a temperamental distaste for experiment, and no impulse at all toward verification. The idea of submitting his "insights," his "intuitions," his "explorations of the unconscious," to confirmation *by someone else* seems to have been particularly alien to his intensely emotional and recklessly inventive mind. His attitude toward other people's findings may be inferred from the ferocious demand he made of his sweetheart that she join him in hating her brother. He would break off his engagement, he threatened, if this happy consensus of opinion was not attained.

To me he was less like Newton, or Darwin, or any of the great men of science, than like Paracelsus—a man who made significant contributions to science, but was by nature given to infatuation with magical ideas and causes. Freud's contributions were, to be sure, immeasurably greater than those of Paracelsus, but there is a similar admixture of midnight fabrication in them.

> *Max Eastman, in his* Great Companions: Critical Memoirs of Some Famous Friends, *1942.*

He develops hostility toward the father and wants to replace him and, in the last analysis, to do away with him. Feeling his father to be his rival the little boy is afraid of being castrated by the father-rival. Freud called this constellation the Oedipus complex because in the Greek myth it is Oedipus who falls in love with his mother without awareness that the beloved woman is his mother. When the incest is discovered he blinds himself, a symbol for castrating himself, and leaves his home and kin, accompanied only by his daughter Antigone.

Freud's great discovery here is the intensity of the attachment of the little boy to his mother or a mother figure. The degree of this attachment—of the wish to be loved and cared for by mother, not to lose her protection and, in many men, not to give up mother but rather to see her in women who, although the man's age, signify a mother for him—cannot be overestimated. This attachment exists in girls too but it seems to have a somewhat different outcome which has not been made clear by Freud, and which is indeed very difficult to understand.

The attachment of a man to his mother, however, is not difficult to understand. Even in intrauterine life she is his world. He is completely part of her, nourished by her, enveloped by her, protected by her and even after birth this situation does not change fundamentally. Without her help he would die, without her tenderness he would become mentally sick. She is the one who gives life and on whom his life depends. She can also take life away by refusing to fulfill her motherly functions. (The symbol of the mother's contradictory functions is the Indian goddess Kali, the creator of life and its destroyer.) The father's role in the first years of life is almost as negligible as his incidental function of procreating a child. While it is a scientific truth that the male sperm must unite with the female egg, it is an experiential truth that the man has practically no role whatsoever in the procreation of a child and the care for its life. Psychologically speaking, his presence is quite unnecessary and can be fulfilled equally well by artificial insemination. He may play a role again when the child reaches the age of four or five, as the one who teaches the child, who serves as an example, who is responsible for his intellectual and moral upbringing. Unfortunately he is often an example of exploitativeness, irrationality and immorality. He usually wants to mold his son in his own image so that he becomes useful to him in his work and becomes the heir to his possessions, and also to compensate him for his own failures by achieving what the father did not achieve.

The attachment to and dependence on the mother figure is more than an attachment to a person. It is a longing for a situation in which the child is protected and loved and has not yet any responsibility to bear. But it is not only the child who has that longing. If we say the child is helpless and hence needs the mother we must not forget that every human being is helpless in relation to the world as a whole. To be sure, he can defend himself and take care of himself up to a point, but considering the dangers, uncertainties, risks with which he is confronted, and on the other hand how little power he has to cope with physical illness, poverty, injustice, it seems open to question whether the adult is less helpless than the child. But the child has a mother who by her love wards off all dangers. The adult has—nobody. Indeed he may have friends, a wife, a certain amount of social security, yet even so the possibility of defending himself and of acquiring what he needs is very fragile. Is it surprising that he carries with him the dream of finding a mother again or of finding a world in which he can be a child again? The contradiction between the loving of the paradisiacal child existence and the necessities that follow from his adult existence can be rightly considered the nucleus of all neurotic developments.

Where Freud erred, and had to err because of his premises, was that he understood the attachment to mother as essentially one of a sexual nature. Employing his theory of infantile sexuality it was logical for him to assume that what binds a little boy to his mother is that she is the first woman in his life, close to him, and gives his sexual desires a natural object for which he has longed. This too is to a large extent true. There is ample evidence that the mother is for the little boy not only an object of affection but an object of sexual desire. But—and here is Freud's great error—it is not the sexual desire which makes the relationship to mother so intense and vital and the figure of the mother so important, not only in childhood but maybe for a person's entire life. Rather, this intensity is based on the need for the paradisiacal state I just spoke about.

Freud overlooked the well-known fact that sexual desires per se are not characterized by great stability. Even the most intense sexual relationship, if it is without affection and strong emotional ties, the most important being love, is rather short-lived and if one gives it six months one is probably being liberal. Sexuality as such is fickle and even more so perhaps in men, who are roving adventurers, than in women in whom the responsibility for a child gives sex a more serious meaning. To assume that men should be bound to their mothers because of the intensity of a sexual bond that had its origin twenty or thirty or fifty years earlier is nothing short of absurd considering that many are not bound to their wives after even three years of a sexually satisfactory marriage. Indeed, for little boys the mother may be an object of desire because she is one of the first women close to him, but it is also true, as Freud reports in his own case histories, that they are just as willing to fall in love with a little girl of their own age and have passionate love affairs with them, with mother relatively forgotten.

One does not understand the love life of a man if one does not see how it wavers between the wish to find the mother again in another woman, and the wish to get away from mother and to find a woman who is as different from the mother figure as any woman possibly could be. This conflict is one of the basic causes of divorce. It easily happens that the woman is not a mother figure when the marriage begins, but in married life, in which she takes care of the household, she often becomes a kind of disciplinarian who holds the man back from his childhood wish for new adventures; by this very fact, she assumes the function of the mother and as such is wanted by the man, and at the same time he is afraid of and repelled by her. Often an older man falls in love with a young girl, among other reasons because she is free from all motherly features and as long as she is infatuated with him the man has the illusion of having escaped his dependence on the mother figure. Freud in his discovery of the Oedipal tie to the mother uncovered one of the most significant phenomena, namely man's attachment to mother and his fear of losing her; he distorted this by explaining it as a sexual phenomenon and thus obscured the importance of his discovery that the longing for mother is one of the deepest emotional desires rooted in the very existence of man.

The other part of the Oedipus complex, the hostile rivalry with the father, culminating in the wish to kill him, is an equally valid observation which, however, has not necessarily anything to do with the attachment to mother. Freud gives a universal meaning to a feature that is characteristic only of patriarchal society. In a patriarchal society the son is subject to the father's will; he is owned by the father and his fate is determined by the father. In order to be the heir of the father—that is, broadly speaking, to be successful—he must not only please the father, he must submit to him, obey him and replace his own will with that of the father. As always, oppression leads to hate, to a wish to liberate oneself from the oppressor, and in the last analysis, to eliminate him. We see this situation clearly in examples such as the old peasant who rules like a dictator over his son, his wife, until the day he dies. If that day is far off, if the son reaches the age of thirty or forty or fifty and still has to accept the domination of his father, then indeed in many cases he will hate him as an oppressor. In the modern business world all this is greatly mitigated: the father does not usually own property to which the son would be heir, since the advancement of younger people is based to a large extent on their own capacities, and only rarely, as in personally owned enterprises, does the longevity of the father keep the son in an inferior position. Nevertheless, these are very recent developments and it is fair to say that through several thousand years of patriarchal society there was a built-in conflict between father and son based on the father's control over the son and the son's wish to rebel against it. Freud saw this conflict but did not recognize it for what it is, namely a feature of patriarchal society; instead he interpreted it as essentially the sexual rivalry between father and son.

Both observations, the nonsexual desire for protection and safety, the paradisiacal bliss, and the conflict between father and son as a necessary by-product of patriarchal society, were combined by Freud into a unit in which the attachment to mother was sexual and hence the father became a rival, a name to be feared and hated. The hatred toward the father because of sexual rivalry for mother has often been demonstrated by certain sayings of little boys, which are not infrequent: "When father dies I will marry you, Mommy." Such sayings are used as proof of the murderous impulses of the little boy and the extent of his rivalry with his father.

I do not believe they prove anything of the kind. Naturally the little boy has impulses during which he wants to be big like the father and to replace the father as a favorite of his mother. It is natural that in the between state in which all children over four live, of neither really being infants any-

more nor being treated as adults, they have the wish to be big like adults; but the sentence *When father dies I shall marry you* is given undue weight by so many to mean that this little boy really wants his father to be dead. The little boy has no idea of what death is, and all he is really saying is "I wish father was away, so that I can get all her attention." To conclude that the son deeply hates the father, a hatred which includes this death wish, is to pay little attention to the world of imagination of the child and to the difference between him and the adult.

Let us have a look at the Oedipus myth in which Freud saw confirmed his construction of the tragic nature of the incestuous wishes of the little boy and the rivalry with the father. Freud dealt only with the first of Sophocles' trilogy, *Oedipus Rex,* and this tragedy tells us that an oracle has told Laius, the King of Thebes, and his wife, Jocasta, that if they have a son this son will kill his father and marry his own mother. When a son, Oedipus, is born to them, Jocasta decides to escape the fate predicted by the oracle by having the infant killed. She give Oedipus to a shepherd, who is to abandon the child in the woods with his feet bound so that he will die. But the shepherd, taking pity on the child, gives the infant to a man in the service of the King of Corinth, who in turn brings him to his master. The king adopts the boy, and the young prince grows up in Corinth not knowing that he is not the true son of the King of Corinth. He is told by the oracle in Delphi that it is his fate to kill his father and to marry his mother. He decides to avoid this fate by never going back to his parents. Leaving Delphi he engages in a violent argument with an old man riding in a carriage, loses his temper and slays the man and his servant without knowing that he has slain his father, the King of Thebes.

His wanderings lead him to Thebes. There the Sphinx is devouring the young men and women of the city, and she will cease doing so only if someone can find the right answer to a riddle she asks. The riddle is this: "What is it which first goes on four, then on two, and eventually on three?" The city of Thebes has promised that anyone who can solve the riddle and thus free the city from the Sphinx will be made king and will be given the king's widow for a wife. Oedipus undertakes the venture. He finds the answer—which is *man,* who as a child walks on four, as an adult on two, and in his old age on three (with a cane). The Sphinx throws herself into the ocean, the city is saved from calamity and Oedipus becomes king and marries Jocasta, his mother.

After Oedipus has reigned happily for some time, the city is ravaged by a plague which kills many of its citizens. The seer, Teiresias, reveals that the plague is the punishment for the twofold crime which Oedipus has committed, patricide and incest. Oedipus, after having tried desperately not to recognize this truth, blinds himself when he is compelled to see it, and Jocasta commits suicide. The tragedy ends at the point where Oedipus has suffered punishment for a crime which he committed unknowingly and in spite of his conscious effort to avoid committing it.

Was Freud justified in concluding that this myth confirms his view that unconscious incestuous drives and the resulting hate against the father-rival are to be found in every male child? Indeed, it does seem as if the myth confirms Freud's theory, and that the Oedipus complex justifiably bears its name.

If we examine the myth more closely, however, questions arise which cast some doubts on the correctness of this view. The most pertinent question is this: if Freud's interpretation is right, we should expect to be told that Oedipus meets Jocasta without knowing that she is his mother, falls in love with her and then kills his father, again unknowingly. But there is no indication whatsoever that Oedipus is attracted by or falls in love with Jocasta. The only reason we are given for Oedipus' marriage to Jocasta is that she, as it were, goes with the throne. Should we believe that a story, the central theme of which constitutes an incestuous relationship between mother and son, would entirely omit the element of attraction between the two? This question is all the more weighty in view of the fact that, in the older versions, only once does the oracle predict marriage to the mother, in the version by Nikolaus of Damascus, which according to Carl Robert is based on a relatively recent source.

Considering this question we might formulate a hypothesis, namely that the myth can be understood as a symbol not of the incestuous love between mother and son but of the rebellion of the son against the authority of the father in the patriarchal family; that the marriage of Oedipus and Jocasta is only a secondary element, only one of the symbols of the victory of the son, who takes his father's place and with it all his privileges.

If we are thinking only of *Oedipus Rex* this hypothesis remains at best a hypothesis, but its validity can be decided by examining the whole Oedipus myth, particularly in the form presented by Sophocles in the two other parts of the trilogy, *Oedipus at Colonus* and *Antigone.* This examination leads to a very different and new understanding in the form presented by Sophocles in the two other parts between patriarchal and matriarchal cultures.

In *Oedipus at Colonus* we find Oedipus exiled by Creon and accompanied by his daughters Antigone and Ismene, while his sons Eteocles and Polyneices refuse to help their blind father, whose throne they fight for. Eteocles wins but Polyneices, refusing to yield, seeks to conquer the city with outside help and to wrest power from his brother.

Thus far we have seen that one topic of the trilogy is the hate between father and son in a patriarchal society, but if we look at the trilogy as a whole we discover that Sophocles is speaking of the conflict between the patriarchal and the earlier matriarchal world. In the patriarchal world sons are fighting their fathers and fighting each other; the victor is Creon, the prototype of a Fascist ruler. Oedipus, however, is not accompanied by his sons but by his daughters. It is they on whom he relies while his relation to his sons is one of mutual hate. Historically, the original Oedipus myth, in the versions which existed in Greece and upon which Sophocles built his tragedy, gives an important clue. In these formulations, the figure of Oedipus is always connected with the cult of the earth goddesses, the representatives of matriarchal religion. In almost all versions of the myth, from parts which deal with the exposure

of Oedipus as an infant to those which are centered around his death, traces of this connection can be found. Thus, for instance, Eteonos, the only Boeotian city which had a cult shrine of Oedipus and where the whole myth probably originated, also had the shrine of the earth goddess Demeter. At Colonus (near Athens), where Oedipus finds his last resting place, was an old shrine of Demeter and the Erinyes which had probably existed prior to the Oedipus myth. As we shall see, Sophocles has emphasized this connection between Oedipus and the chthonic goddesses in *Oedipus at Colonus.*

Oedipus' return to the grove of the goddesses, though the most important clue, is not the only one to the understanding of his position as representative of the matriarchal order. Sophocles makes another and very plain allusion to matriarchy by having Oedipus refer to Egyptian matriarchy when he tells about his daughters. This is the way he praises them: "O true image of the *ways of Egypt that they show in their spirit and their life! For there the men sit weaving in the house, but the wives go forth to win the daily bread.* And in your case, my daughters, those to whom these toils belonged keep the house at home like girls, while ye, in their stead, bear your hapless father's burden."

The same trend of thought is continued by Oedipus when he compares his daughters to his sons. Of Antigone and Ismene he says: "Now, these girls preserve me, these my nurses, *these who are men not women,* in true service: but ye are aliens, and no sons of mine."

In *Antigone* the conflict between the patriarchal and matriarchal principles finds its most radical expression. Creon, the ruthless authoritarian, has become the tyrant of Thebes, Oedipus' two sons have been killed, one while attacking the city to gain power, the other while defending it. Creon has ordered that the legitimate king should be buried and that the challenger's body should be left unburied, the greatest humiliation and dishonor to be done to a man, according to Greek custom. The principle that Creon represents is that of the supremacy of the law of the state over ties of blood, of obedience to authority over allegiance to the natural law of humanity. Antigone refuses to violate the laws of blood and of the solidarity of all human beings for the sake of an authoritarian, hierarchial principle. She stands for the freedom and happiness of the human being as against the arbitrariness of male rule. Therefore the Chorus can say, "Wonders are many, and none is more wonderful than man." In contrast to her sister Ismene who feels that women have to capitulate to the power of men, Antigone defies the principle of patriarchy. She follows the law of nature and equality and all-embracing motherly love and says, "It is not my nature to join in hating but in loving." Creon, his masculine superiority challenged, says, "Now verily I am no man, she is the man if this victory shall rest with her and bring no penalty," and turning to his son who has fallen in love with Antigone, he says, "Yea, this my son should be thy heart's fixed law—in all things to obey thy father's will." He continues, "*But disobedience is the worst of evils.* This it is that ruins cities; this makes home desolate; by this, the ranks of allies are broken into headlong rout; but, of the lives whose course is fair, the greater part owes safety to obedience. *Therefore we must support the cause of order, and in no wise suffer a woman to worst us. Better to fall from power, if we must, by a man's hand; than we should be called weaker than a woman."*

The conflict between Creon the patriarch and Haemon the rebel against patriarchy and the defender of women's equality, comes to climax when Haemon's answer to his father's question "Am I to rule the land by other judgment than my own?" is "That is no city which belongs to one man . . . Thou wouldst make a good monarch of a desert." Upon which Creon answers, "This boy, it seems, is the *woman's* champion." And Haemon points to the power of the matriarchal goddesses: "And for thee, and for me, and for the *gods below.*" (The gods below are the mother goddesses.) The conflict comes to its end. Creon has Antigone buried alive in a cave—again a symbolic expression of her connection with the goddesses of the earth. Stricken by panic, Creon tries to save Antigone but in vain. Haemon attempts to kill his father and when he fails, he takes his own life. Creon's wife, Eurydice, upon hearing the fate of her son, kills herself, cursing her husband as the murderer of her children. Creon has won physically. He has killed his son, the woman his son loved, and his wife, but morally he is indeed in bankruptcy, and admits it: "Ah me, this guilt can never be fixed on any other mortal kind, for my acquittal! I, even I, was thy slayer, wretched that I am—I own the truth. Lead me away, O my servants, lead me hence with all speed, whose life is but as death! . . . Lead me away, I pray you; a rash, foolish man; who have slain thee, ah, my son, unwittingly, and thee, too, my wife—unhappy that I am! I know not which way I should bend my gaze, or where I should seek support; for all is amiss with that which is in my hands;—and yonder again, a crushing fate hath leapt upon my head."

If we look now at the whole trilogy we must come to the conclusion that incest is not the main idea or even essential to the vision Sophocles expressed there. It may appear so if we read only *Oedipus Rex* (and how many people who speak glibly of the Oedipus complex have read the trilogy?), but considering the entire trilogy, Sophocles deals with the conflict between the matriarchal principle of equality and democracy represented by Oedipus, and the principle of patriarchal dictatorship of "law and order" represented by Creon. While patriarchy remains the victor in terms of power, its principles are morally defeated in the debacle of Creon who recognizes that he has achieved nothing but death. (pp. 23-36)

> *Erich Fromm, in his* Greatness and Limitations of Freud's Thought, *New American Library, 1980, 148 p.*

Sarah Kofman   (essay date 1980)

[*A French educator and critic, Kofman is the author of* Nietzsche et la métaphor, L'Enfance de l'art, *and* Nietzsche et la scène philosophique. *In the following excerpt from her* The Enigma of Woman: Woman in Freud's Writings *(1985), which was originally published in French in 1980, Kofman offers a feminist and poststructuralist psychoanalysis of Freud's duplicitous and misogynistic stance towards women.*]

Didn't Freud himself predict it? Feminists would take to the warpath against his texts, which, on the subject of women, would be seen as rife with masculine prejudice. The woman question has indeed provoked opposition not only from without but from within the very heart of psychoanalysis, has unleashed a veritable internecine war: women analysts are turning psychoanalysis against its founder, accusing him of taking sides, of siding with his sex, because of his sex. In brief, they say, on the question of woman, a man, even a Freud, cannot produce objective, neutral, scientific discourse: he can only *speculate,* that is, philosophize, construct a system destined to justify an idée fixe, a tendentious view based not on observation but on self-perception. So he cannot help verging on madness, paranoia.

In his lecture **"Femininity" ("Die Weiblichkeit")**, a text recently denigrated—to put it mildly—by a woman psychoanalyst, speaking to men and women ("Ladies and Gentlemen," he says at the beginning of his talk, repeating an apparently banal formula in order to bring out all its enigmatic strangeness later on), Freud emphasizes—not without irony—that every time any point is made against women, female psychoanalysts suspect men of deeply rooted masculine prejudices that prevent them from being impartial.

Freud avails himself of various arguments in an effort to dispel such suspicions. He maintains that the use of psychoanalysis as a weapon in the controversy is not enough to decide the issue, does not make it possible to choose between himself and the women analysts. Psychoanalysis is a *two-edged* sword that may well be used against women's discourse, he argues, for it allows us to understand that the female sex cannot accept, or wish to accept, anything that runs counter to its strongest desires, anything that contradicts, for example, the equality with men that women so ardently seek. Psychoanalysis thus allows us to understand why "feminists" adamantly reject the Freudian concept of the feminine superego, for according to them this concept originates merely in man's "masculinity complex" and serves as a theoretical justification for men's innate tendency to belittle and repress women.

Almost always, in fact, it is the concept of the *feminine superego* and its corollary, women's intellectual and cultural inferiority, that give rise to controversy. It takes real heroism for Freud to make his explosive conclusions public:

> I cannot evade the notion (though I hesitate to give it expression) that for women the level of what is ethically normal is different from what it is in men. Their super-ego is never so inexorable, so impersonal, so independent of its emotional origins as we require it to be in men. Character-traits which critics of every epoch have brought up against women . . . would [all] be amply accounted for by the modification in the formation of their super-ego. . . . We must not allow ourselves to be deflected from such conclusions by the denials of the feminists, who are anxious to force us to regard the two sexes as completely equal in position and worth.

And with regard to the different outcomes of the Oedipus complex in girls and boys, outcomes responsible for the differences in their respective superegos, "here the feminist demand for equal rights for the sexes does not take us far."

I, Freud, Truth, I speak, and Truth will soon be able to resist all pressures, all more or less hysterical "feminist" demands; for, O women, if you seek to use psychoanalysis against me, I shall be much better prepared to turn it back against you, even while I pretend to be granting you some concessions, agreeing to some compromises in order to put an end to the battle of the sexes between us, and to reestablish among male and female psychoanalysts a "polite agreement": in my lordly fashion I freely grant you that "pure femininity" and "pure masculinity" are purely theoretical constructions and that the content of such speculative constructions remains quite uncertain. I am prepared to grant, too, that most men fall far short of the masculine ideal, for "all human individuals, as a result of their bisexual disposition and of cross-inheritance, combine in themselves both masculine and feminine characteristics."

In this internecine war, the thesis of bisexuality is a weapon that is supposed to put an end to the accusations made by women psychoanalysts: Freud's injurious discourse on women no longer concerns *them,* for they are exceptions to the rule, more masculine than feminine.

> The discussion of [femininity] has gained special attractiveness from the distinction between the sexes. For the ladies, whenever some comparison seemed to turn out unfavourable to their sex,

were able to utter a suspicion that we, the male analysts, had been unable to overcome certain deeply-rooted prejudices against what was feminine, and that this was being paid for in the partiality of our researches. We, on the other hand, standing on the ground of bisexuality, had no difficulty in avoiding impoliteness. We had only to say: "This doesn't apply to *you.* You're the exception; on this point you're more masculine than feminine."

More masculine than feminine, if not homosexual. **"The Psychogenesis of a Case of Homosexuality in a Woman"** emphasizes that the patient "was in fact a feminist; she felt it to be unjust that girls should not enjoy the same freedom as boys, and rebelled against the lot of women in general."

The thesis of bisexuality not only is the thesis that Freud is defending, it also serves as his defense against accusations of anti-feminism; and it, too, is double-edged. It allows Freud to repeat the most tenacious, the most traditional, the most metaphysical phallocratic discourse: if you women are as intelligent as men, it is because you are really more masculine than feminine. Thus it allows him to shut women up, to put an end to their demands and accusations. But this thesis also makes it possible to displace the metaphysical categories that it renders problematic, since it proclaims the purely speculative character of the masculine/feminine opposition. The thesis of bisexuality thus implies that Sigmund Freud himself could not have been *purely and simply* a man (*vir*), that he could not have had (*purely*) masculine prejudices. That charge only reveals the metaphysical prejudices of those who press it.

Freud's consulting-room in London, rearranged by his son Ernst after the move from Vienna.

Freud never appeals to this argument in his own defense, however, never exhibits his femininity as he indulges in exposing the masculinity of his female colleagues. The thesis of bisexuality, declared valid in principle for all humans, is in the last analysis used only as a strategic weapon in connection with women; we shall have the opportunity to verify this. And it is as though Freud were loudly proclaiming the universality of bisexuality in order better to disguise his silent disavowal of his own femininity, his paranoia. (pp. 11-15)

It is indeed against the potential suspicion of paranoia that Freud seeks in particular to defend himself whenever he distinguishes, like a typical positivist, between (philosophical) speculation and (scientific) observation, or whenever he denies having any sort of gift for philosophy. It is always his opponents—Jung, for example—who are speculative. Thus what is fundamentally at stake in **"On Narcissism: An Introduction"** is the demonstration that narcissism, particularly with regard to paranoia, lends itself to sterile and insane speculations. This text is a polemical denunciation of Jung's philosophical monism—Jung, who thinks he can dispense with the libido's sexual specificity, with the distinction between the energy of the ego's drives and its libido, between the ego's libido and that of the object, between sexual libido and nonsexual energy. This speculative economizing can be achieved only at the expense of observation and to the benefit of "barren theoretical controversy." By way of contrast, Freud's distinctions, his persistent dualism, result from his elaborations based on close observation of neurotic and psychotic processes and from his pursuit of a hypothesis "to its logical conclusion, until it either breaks down or is confirmed." To barren speculation Freud opposes the productive model of physics:

> That is just the difference between a speculative theory and a science erected on empirical interpretation. The latter will not envy speculation its privilege of having a smooth, logically unassailable foundation, but will gladly content itself with nebulous, scarcely imaginable basic concepts, which it hopes to apprehend more clearly in the course of its development, or which it is even prepared to replace by others. For these ideas are not the foundation of science upon which everything rests: that foundation is observation alone. They are not the bottom but the top of the whole structure, and they can be replaced and discarded without damaging it. The same thing is happening in our day in the science of physics, the basic notions of which as regards matter, centres of force, attraction, etc., are scarcely less debatable than the corresponding ideas in psycho-analysis.

"I am not Jung, I am not paranoid," Freud reiterates endlessly.

What Freud seems to need to prove in the **"Femininity"** lecture is that he, Freud—he insists on this at the end of his talk (a classic denegation!)—is not the victim of an idée fixe, even though he never ceases to stress the importance of the role the lack of a penis plays in the formation of femininity. It is no accident that the lecture begins, here again, by contrasting observation with speculation: you cannot

evaluate the sexual position of my discourse, for it is not the pathological subject Sigmund Freud that is speaking or speculating, it is the transcendental subject of science, whose affirmations are based entirely on observed facts: "To-day's lecture . . . brings forward nothing but observed facts, almost without any speculative additions." With respect to those facts "I" play no role, do not take sides.

If we recall that in *Beyond the Pleasure Principle* Freud does not hesitate to present the hypothesis of the death wish as purely speculative, as possibly having only mythic roots, the strenuous hostility to speculation he displays here may seem suspect: the whole campaign he is waging against the speculative no doubt in some way works to his advantage; perhaps it is to enhance one's own stature that one claims not to be playing a role or taking sides. In any event, the appeal to observation has the immediate object of cleansing Freud of any taint of partiality by making *women psychoanalysts his accomplices.* He repeats this endlessly: the observations of these "excellent female colleagues" furnished his most important material, first enlightened him on female sexuality. He has only added some clarifications, has better isolated certain points that they have already brought to light. His work is only one contribution among others and he has limited himself to bringing out the most important points of agreement or disagreement. Whereas elsewhere Freud insists on the priority of his own discoveries even while recognizing that they have often been foreshadowed by some brilliant poets, here for strategic reasons he has to deny the paternity of his ideas and openly to display his debt to the female analysts.

> Since [my] subject is woman, I will venture on this occasion to mention by name a few of the women who have made valuable contributions to this investigation. Dr. Ruth Mack Brunswick [1928] was the first to describe a case of neurosis which went back to a fixation in the pre-Oedipus stage and had never reached the Oedipus situation at all. . . . Dr. Jeanne Lampl-de Groot [1927] has established the incredible phallic activity of girls towards their mother by some *assured observations,* and Dr. Helene Deutsch [1932] has shown that the erotic actions of homosexual women reproduce the relations between mother and baby.

The appeal to observation has a fundamental strategic value here, and Freud does not seem to consider that it may be incompatible with the haste he is demonstrating elsewhere by publishing, against all scientific caution, results that by his own admission have not been completely verified, on the grounds that little time remains to him, though earlier he managed to hold back the Dora case for four or five years before divulging the *secret* of his patient out of pure duty to science . . . ; on the grounds, too, that the women psychoanalysts will in any case be able to exploit and complete his work: "I feel justified in publishing something which stands in urgent need of confirmation before its value or lack of value can be decided," he writes at the beginning of **"Some Psychical Consequences of the Anatomical Distinction between the Sexes."** (pp. 16-19)

In haste to write about women in order to outdistance women once again, in haste to write for fear that death may outdistance him: it is as if up to the very last moment Freud had been shrinking from the impossible task of writing about women; the texts on female sexuality, stressing the new importance of the preoedipal relation of daughter to mother and casting doubt on the status of the Oedipus complex as the core of neuroses, are all late texts, "a product of the very last few years." A retreat in the face of the task at hand which is perhaps a retreat in the face of female sexuality itself, because of the horror/pleasure it provokes, because of the death threat that it is thought to bear. For neither death nor woman's sex can be faced directly. To write about female sexuality is to disclose a dangerous secret, is in one way or another to display openly, to dis-cover, woman's fearsome sex. A sex that is all the more fearsome and threatening for man in that he feels vulnerable—and guilty.

Here we cannot help thinking of Spinoza, whose death left his *Tractatus theologico-politicus* unfinished just as he was about to confront the question of women in the political sphere and just when he had deprived women, along with servants, of all political rights, even under the ideal democratic regime.

Wanting to have the last word on women—doesn't that always mean running the risk that goes with last words? Doesn't the desire to get to the heart of the matter, to bring the riddle to an end, entail the risk of reaching *the end*? This accounts for Freud's extreme restraint on the subject of women over a long period of time, the period during which he set up a simple parallelism and a simple symmetry, for example, between the girl's Oedipus complex and the boy's; only later, with the preoedipal phase, came the discovery of the woman as *totally other,* and then there was the ultimate haste to publish, the anxiety in the face of death.

It was not the first time in Freud's career that anxiety over death underlay his decision to publish a text that he had held back a long time (five years). He had done the same thing with *The Interpretation of Dreams,* at a time when Freud's age alone could not justify an objective fear of death.

This becomes clear in the famous dream in which Brücke proposes that Freud dissect his own pelvis. The crucial feature of this dream—showing that, its manifest content notwithstanding, it is indeed a dream of wish fulfillment—is that the dreamer does not experience the *feeling of horror (Grauen)* that ought objectively to be connected with the dissection, with such a "strange task." Freud interprets the dream as follows:

> The dissection meant the self-analysis which I was carrying out, as it were, in the publication of this present book about dreams—a process which had been so distressing to me in reality that I had postponed the printing of the finished manuscript for more than a year. A wish then arose that I might get over this feeling of distaste; hence it was that I had no gruesome feeling ['*Grauen*'] in the dream. But I should also have been very glad to miss growing grey—'*Grauen*'

in the other sense of the word. I was already growing quite grey, and the grey of my hair was another reminder that I must not delay any longer.

This fragment of interpretation with the crucial wordplay on *Grauen* is not part of the central analysis of the dream, but is tacked on through association of ideas to the analysis of the dream of the journeyman tailor who became a famous poet. This latter dream seems to contradict the general law of dreams as wish fulfillment: it appears, indeed, to be a dream of punishment, but analysis reveals that the unconscious desire underlying the dream is the desire to remain young—a painful desire in the aging man, and one that is never appeased. With the dream of the journeyman tailor Freud associates, in addition to the Brücke dream, another of his own in which he finds himself back in the "gloomiest and most unsuccessful year" of his medical career, when he did not yet have a job and did not know how he would manage to earn his living. Even so, this return to an unhappy time of life is indeed wish fulfillment, since it is a return to the period of his youth: "I was once more young, and, more than everything, *she* was once more young—the woman who had shared all these difficult years with me. . . . I had a choice open to me between several women whom I might marry!" Nostalgia for youth, as this last association proves, is always nostalgia for sexual potency, just as ideas of death and old age are always connected with the idea of impotence: this is confirmed by the interpretation of the dream of "an elderly gentleman [who] was awakened one night by his wife, who had become alarmed because he was laughing so loudly and unrestrainedly in his sleep. . . . The dream-work succeeded in transforming the gloomy idea of impotence and death into a comic scene, and his sobs into laughter."

In other words, the death anxiety that assails Freud and leads him to publish *The Interpretation of Dreams* is not "pure" death anxiety; it is inseparable from anxiety related to the limitation of sexual potency. And to publish *The Interpretation of Dreams* is not only to outdistance the death that is to come, it is in every sense to recapture youth, potency, even omnipotence: this publication, in fact, should confer *immortality* on its author, the immortality of the heroes and great men who could set out for an "unknown land which scarce an alien foot has pressed" from time immemorial, could reveal "strange things," defy all taboos, including that of incest. By its unheard-of revelations, the publication of *The Interpretation of Dreams* is to transform Freud into a superman, make him a rival of that Oedipus who "resolved the dark enigma, noblest champion and most wise." A superman, indeed a demigod: the dream in which Freud identifies with Hercules cleaning out the Augean stables (with a "long stream of urine" he would cleanse the science of neuroses of all its errors and prejudices) ends with the megalomanic affirmation: "in short, . . . I was a very great man."

Through the publication of this work, Freud was to achieve not only his infantile desire of immortality but also what his father, the Jew Jakob, had been unable to accomplish, so that his son had to accomplish it in his stead. To the son's great disappointment, Freud's father—as we know from the famous anecdote of the cap knocked to the ground by a Christian—was not a hero, although later, in his dreams, the son gives shape to his nostalgia for a heroic father modeled on Hannibal's: " 'To stand before one's children's eyes, after one's death, great and unsullied'—who would not desire this?" After telling the story of the cap, Freud writes:

> This struck me as *unheroic* conduct on the part of the big, strong man who was holding the little boy by the hand. I contrasted this situation with another which fitted my feelings better: the scene in which Hannibal's father, Hamilcar Barca, made his boy swear before the household altar to take vengeance on the Romans. Ever since that time, Hannibal had had a place in my phantasies. . . . To my youthful mind Hannibal and Rome symbolized the conflict between the tenacity of Jewry and the organization of the Catholic church.

Against this background we can understand the complex factors that may have led Freud to put off publishing *The Interpretation of Dreams* even though the work was destined to confer immortality on its author (in one passage Freud alludes to a request made by Louise N. the previous evening to borrow one of his books, whereupon he proposed instead a book by Rider Haggard, for his "own immortal works" had not yet been written), and even though another dream confirms his desire to be done with *The Interpretation of Dreams* in order to become independent at last and fulfill all his desires (this is the botanical dream in which the initial situation is the same as in the Brücke dream: in the one case Freud sees *before him* his own pelvis, in the other he sees *before him* the monograph he has written on the genus *Cyclamen*: "I saw the monograph which I had written *lying before me*. . . . I had had a letter from my friend [Fliess] in Berlin the day before in which he had shown his power of visualization: 'I am very much occupied with your dream-book. *I see it lying finished before me and I see myself turning over its pages.*' How much I envied him his gift as a seer! If only *I* could have seen it lying finished before me!" "The dream . . . [was] a passionately agitated plea on behalf of my liberty to act as I chose to act and to govern my life as seemed right to me and me alone." We can now understand why Freud, despite his strong desire for publication, nevertheless postponed it, why the idea of publication was so painful to him, stirred up in him a feeling of horror (*Grauen*), gave him gray hair (*grauen*) . . . ; we can understand why the dream about Brücke, in which he seems finally to satisfy his desire, is at the same time a dream of anguish in which, far from attaining the immortality he desires, he sees himself in a wooden house identified by association with a grave (although the grave is Etruscan, this being a dream ruse to make him accept the unacceptable, to transform "the gloomiest of expectations into one that was highly desirable," just as the heroine, the woman guide, of *She*, the book lent the evening before to Louise N., instead of retrieving immortality for herself and others meets death in a mysterious subterranean fire). The only consolation the dream affords is that perhaps the children will obtain what was denied the father, those children who are their parents' sole access to immortality, those chil-

dren who are one with their parents, in a way, as that "strange book" also indicates, that novel in which a character's identity is maintained through successive generations over a period of two thousand years.

By conferring immortality upon myself through my publication, I make a gift of it also to my father, with whom I identify, as my own children will one day confer it upon me by living after me: such may be the meaning of this dream. But it may also be interpreted differently: I deny myself immortality and bequeath it only to my children out of guilt toward my father, who was unable to attain it himself for lack of heroism.

Guilt at having succeeded where the father failed thus explains his delay in publishing (he waited five years)—as Hannibal delayed before entering Rome, as Moses waited to enter the Promised Land. Generally speaking, guilt explains why Freud always postponed fulfillment of his desires or his ambitions, why he put off his marriage for five years, why he waited five years to take his medical examinations. The delays can thus be attributed to inhibition, but also to the fact that Freud always had the *strength* to postpone the immediate satisfaction of his desires in order to satisfy them more fully later on. As if five years of life did not count for him, as if he had all the time in the world ahead of him, as if he knew that in spite of his delays he would nevertheless achieve his aims. Symptomatically, he sets five years as the length of treatment of the patients to whom he is closest: what are five years of life in comparison with all the benefits that analysis offers? Freud knows that in spite of having a poor Jew for a father (whom he replaces in a dream by the professor Meynert, thanks to whom Freud, had he been the professor's son, would have advanced more rapidly), indeed thanks to his own—Jewish—tenacity, he will succeed in the end. " 'And just as I succeeded in the end in *that,* though you would not believe it, so I shall achieve *this,* too,' " he notes in interpreting the "absurd" dream in which his father declares that he was married in *1851* after getting drunk and being locked up. This marriage resulted in the immediate birth of his son Sigmund—in *1856.*

This dream proves that father Jakob did not have the strength to postpone the satisfaction of his own desires, that he was unable to accomplish the psychic exploit that matters most to a man, that of rising above his own nature (cf. the conclusion of "The Moses of Michelangelo"). He got drunk (which in the symbolic language of dreams means that he made love), got his future wife pregnant, had to get married in a hurry, had to falsify his son's birth-date by two months in order to conceal his guilt (two months transformed in Freud's dream into five years the better to cleanse the father's stain), as Freud declares that the paternal figure in this dream, an exception to the rule, plays the role of straw man, that this figure merely represents Professor Meynert, who had said of himself: " 'You know, I was always one of the clearest cases of male hysteria.' " Thus Freud conceals the paternal hysteria and takes it upon himself to accomplish the feat that his father was unable to perform: the "heroic" postponement of the satisfaction of his desires, giving the lie to the proverb "like father, like son," while contriving to do just the opposite in his dreams so as to create a father in his own image.

So Freud always postpones the satisfaction of his desires, killing two birds with one stone: he shows his own superiority to his father, and he punishes himself for succeeding where his father failed.

That is why, in the Brücke dream, in order to publish his book, to make himself independent and immortal, he needs paternal authorization, even an order emanating from that substitute father, old Brücke. For why did he choose old Brücke if not because "even in the first years of my scientific work it happened that I allowed a discovery of mine to lie fallow until an energetic remonstrance on his part drove me into publishing it," and because the evening before, when he went to see Louise N., he felt that she was pressing him to publish, transmitting someone else's orders: " 'Well, when are we to expect these so-called ultimate explanations of yours which you've promised even *we* shall find readable?' she asked, with a touch of sarcasm. At that point I saw that someone else was admonishing me through her mouth . . . "?

All this, however, cannot in itself explain the delay in publishing *The Interpretation of Dreams,* the shame that Freud says he felt in making public a work that would betray such a large part of his most private character:

> After all, the best of what you know
> May not be told to boys,

a work that would reveal "such strange things," things that horrify him and that threaten to horrify others: how is it that taking the father's place "heroically" could be so shameful and terrible? Unless this "heroism," like that of Oedipus, consists not only in "killing" the father (Oedipus' father, according to Plato, also begat his son while he was drunk) but also in sleeping with the mother. Unless the son's heroism can be achieved only *by virtue of the mother's complicity and preferential love.*

In the Brücke dream, it is a maternal figure, Louise N., who *presses* him to publish, to become a hero (even though the interpretation casts her in the role of simple intermediary). Similarly, the dream of the three Fates casts the mother in the role of an educator who teaches her son to defer his desires by making him wait before appeasing his hunger: it is she who teaches him "heroism." In a note to *The Interpretation of Dreams* concerning the oedipal dreams of some classical heroes (Julius Caesar's dream of relations with his mother, Herodotus' dream of Hippias), dreams already interpreted in the classical period as favorable signs, signs of possession of (Mother) Earth, or of a reconquest of lost authority (like the Tarquinian oracle affirming that the first man to kiss his mother would be master of Rome), Freud remarks that "people who know that they are preferred or favoured by their mother give evidence in their lives of a peculiar self-reliance and an unshakeable optimism which often seem like heroic attributes and bring actual success to their possessors." Finally, in Supplement B of **"Group Psychology and the Analysis of the Ego,"** at the point where Freud is showing how the first epic poet invented the myth of the hero—"A hero was a man who by himself had slain the father"—he adds:

"The transition to the hero was probably afforded by the youngest son, the *mother's favourite,* whom she had protected from paternal jealousy, and who, in the era of the primal horde, had been the father's successor."

Now Freud, although the eldest son, indeed thought he was his mother's favorite. With respect to the dream in which he aspires to the title of *professor extraordinarius,* he wonders:

> What, then, could have been the origin of the ambitiousness which produced the dream in me? At that point I recalled an anecdote I had often heard repeated in my childhood. At the time of my birth an old peasant-woman had prophesied to my proud mother that with her first-born child she had brought a great man into the world. Prophecies of this kind must be very common: there are so many mothers filled with happy expectations and so many old peasant-women and others of the kind who make up for the loss of their power to control things in the present world by concentrating it on the future.

If Freud hesitates to publish *The Interpretation of Dreams* and experiences death anxiety on his own account and his mother's, it is because this publication entails the formidable risk of exposing to everyone his double crime and revealing his mother's complicity. The dream of the dead mother that Freud had when he was seven or eight years old (the age at which the incident between his father and the Christian over the cap is supposed to have occurred) confirms that the death anxiety on his mother's behalf refers to the son's incestuous desires: in this dream he sees his

> *beloved mother, with a peculiarly peaceful, sleeping expression on her features, being carried into the room by two (or three) people with birds' beaks and laid upon the bed.* . . . I was not anxious because I had dreamt that my mother was dying; but I interpreted the dream in that sense in my preconscious revision of it because I was already under the influence of the anxiety. The anxiety can be traced back, when repression is taken into account, to an obscure and evidently sexual craving that had found appropriate expression in the visual content of the dream.

To publish one's dreams is to make known to everyone one's own (fantasmatic) incestuous relations. Freud is himself another Oedipus, not only because he too has been able to solve famous riddles, to head for unknown regions where no one has ever before set foot, but also—for the one is always a corollary of the other—because he has (although only in dreams, and that is what distinguishes him from Oedipus) "killed" his father and slept with his mother. He who seeks to know the deep mysteries of nature must not be afraid to violate natural laws, to appear to everyone as a monster, *horrible visu:* such is the lesson of the Oedipus myth, as Nietzsche had already exposed it in *The Birth of Tragedy.* Supreme wisdom requires supreme monstrosity. To be a hero is always also to be a monster who runs the risk of arousing a feeling of horror (*Grauen*) and of being cast out of society like a *pharmacos* instead of acquiring the immortality one has been seeking.

Moreover, if we recall that Freud uses the same term, *Grauen,* to designate the feeling experienced by most men when confronted by a woman's (the Mother's) genitals (represented symbolically by the Medusa's head)—a feeling of horror that may well make one's hair turn gray (*grauen*) overnight—we may wonder whether "these strange, unknown things" that Freud reveals in *The Interpretation of Dreams* are not more specifically concerned with woman's sex, the Mother's, upon which the dreamer has dared to cast his glance, at the risk of being blinded, of being castrated, and of seeing his mother, like Jocasta, hang herself.

Throughout his work Freud notes the horror and terror that women's genitals inspire, and the disastrous influence that woman is thought to have on man. By virtue of her sex, woman cannot fail to bring about man's ruin. The *Autodidasker* dream offers a simple alternative: woman brings to man either organic ailments (syphilis, general paralysis) or functional difficulties (neuroses). Freud seems to have settled on the second choice, and like another Hercules he devotes his life to attempting to rid humanity of its "waste products"—that is, the neuroses, for which woman is considered primarily responsible. That these strange things revealed by Freud in *The Interpretation of Dreams* indeed concern woman's (the mother's?) sex is indicated by several features of the Brücke dream: the *parallel* established with the dream of the botanical monograph concerning the "genus *Cyclamen*," his wife's favorite flower, and the *occasion* that dictated the dream's formation: the book lent the previous evening to Louise N. was titled *She.* Freud calls it "'a *strange* book, but full of hidden meaning . . . the eternal feminine'"; moreover, in this novel a woman plays a major role. To publish *The Interpretation of Dreams* is to expose—along with his own criminal incestuous relations—woman's sex, the mother's sex; for such a book not to arouse horror, the reader would have to be familiar with the representation of incest and to have overcome castration anxiety. Freud's willingness to publish this book implies that he himself has overcome such anxiety and by the same token is no longer afraid to expose his *own femininity* as well, that most secret part of his most private being. The Brücke dream identifies Freud with the heroine of *She,* that woman guide who heads toward the unknown with the intention of winning immortality and who meets death in a subterranean fire. Another detail of the dream flaunts castration even while resisting it: Freud sees part of his own body (his pelvis) before him (detached from him, as it were), but at the same time he does not have the sensation that that part is missing from his body. To expose a "supplementary" pelvis is tantamount to a duplication of the genital organs; it has apotropaic value. Publishing *The Interpretation of Dreams* is a way for Freud simultaneously to display his castration and to defend himself against it. *The Interpretation of Dreams* is an apotropaic defense that is to protect Freud against castration and death, against his detractors, against anti-Semitism. We know, indeed, that circumcision for Freud is equivalent to castration, and that he attributes the same unconscious origin to misogyny and anti-Semitism: the horror provoked by female genital organs, the fear of castration. And we may perhaps relate the *Grauen* of the Brücke dream to the *Grauen* that we find

in the famous dream about Uncle Josef (who bears the name of that biblical figure with whom Freud often identifies). Uncle Josef, that "simpleton," as Freud's father Jakob used to call him, that criminal, that Jew who had made Freud's father's hair turn grey (*grauen*) in just a few days because of grief over his criminal conduct. The Uncle Josef for whom Freud, at the level of dreams, feels a great affection revealing in fact a deep hatred, a strange repulsion—in another dream Freud identifies that same Uncle Josef with colleagues who have been denied the post of professor by the ministry, yet he does not hesitate to identify himself with the minister, and thus to mistreat those learned and eminent colleagues simply because they are Jews. His uncle Josef's greatest crime, in the last analysis, was the fact that he was Jewish. This, even more than his misdeeds, is what made him an object of horror and revulsion to his own society—just like women, and for the same reasons.

By playing in his dream the role of persecutor, the role of the minister, Freud shows that *he* will not submit to the fate of his uncle or of his Jewish colleagues, that he will become a professor precisely because of his "Jewish tenacity" and the love of his Jewish mother. "In mishandling my two learned and eminent colleagues because they were Jews, and in treating the one as a simpleton and the other as a criminal, I was behaving as though I were the Minister, I had put myself in the Minister's place. Turning the tables on his Excellency with a vengeance! He had refused to appoint me *professor extraordinarius* and I had retaliated in the dream by stepping into his shoes."

The intimate, shameful secrets that Freud fears to expose to the public, because of the horror they are very likely to arouse, are thus inseparably linked with his Jewishness and with femininity, with castration anxiety. In this sense, *The Interpretation of Dreams* is another Medusa's head.

This long detour by way of Freud's dreams will prove not to have been useless, for these dreams are the royal road that may lead us to a better understanding of the status of female sexuality in Freud's theoretical texts. The detour has in any case allowed us to explain both Freud's delay in publishing on the subject of female sexuality and his ultimate haste, for fear of being overtaken by death. (pp. 20-32)

> *Sarah Kofman, in her* The Enigma of Woman: Woman in Freud's Writings, *translated by Catherine Porter, Cornell, 1985, 225 p.*

Toril Moi   (essay date 1981)

[*In the following essay, which was originally published in* Feminist Review *in 1981, Moi critiques Freud's famous case history of Dora formally known as "Fragment of an Analysis of a Case of Hysteria." She calls attention to the patriarchal, chauvinistic prejudices which she claims skewed Freud's analysis and which cast into doubt the veracity of his account.*]

Over the past few years Freud's account of his treatment of the eighteen-year-old Dora has provoked many feminists to take up their pen, in anger or fascination. Dora had for some time suffered from various hysterical symptoms (nervous cough, loss of voice, migraine, depression, and what Freud calls "hysterical unsociability" and *"taedium vitae"*), but it was not until the autumn of 1900, when her parents found a suicide note from her, that Dora's father sent her to Freud for treatment. Freud's case history reveals much about the situation of a young woman from the Viennese bourgeoisie at the turn of the century. Dora's psychological problems can easily be linked to her social background. She has very little, if any, scope for independent activity, is strictly guarded by her family, and feels under considerable pressure from her father. She believes (and Freud agrees) that she is being used as a pawn in a game between her father and Herr K., the husband of her father's mistress. The father wants to exchange Dora for Frau K. ("If I get your wife, you get my daughter"), so as to be able to carry on his affair with Frau K. undisturbed. Dora claims that her father only sent her to psychiatric treatment because he hoped that she would be "cured" into giving up her opposition to her father's affair with Frau K., accept her role as a victim of the male power game, and take Herr K. as her lover.

Freud, then, becomes the person who is to help Dora handle this difficult situation. But Freud himself is the first to admit that his treatment of Dora was a failure. Freud has his own explanations of this failure, but these are not wholly convincing. Feminists have been quick to point out that the reasons for Freud's failure are clearly sexist: Freud is authoritarian, a willing participant in the male power game conducted between Dora's father and Herr K., and at no time turns to consider Dora's own experience of the events. That Freud's analysis fails because of its inherent sexism is the common feminist conclusion.

But *Dora* is a complex text, and feminists have stressed quite different points in their reading of it. Hélène Cixous and Catherine Clément discuss the political potential of hysteria in their book *La jeune née* and agree that Dora's hysteria developed as a form of protest, a silent revolt against male power. They differ, however, as I shall show later, in their evaluation of the importance of hysteria as a political weapon. Cixous and Clément do not discuss in any detail the interaction between Freud and Dora, but Hélène Cixous returned to this theme in 1976, when she published her play *Portrait de Dora*. Here Dora's story is represented in dreamlike sequences from Dora's own viewpoint. Cixous plays skillfully with Freud's text: she quotes, distorts, and displaces the "father text" with great formal mastery. This technique enables her to create new interpretations of Dora's symptoms in a playful exposure of Freud's limitations.

Jacqueline Rose's article, "Dora: Fragment of an Analysis" differs considerably from these two French texts. Rose sees *Dora* as a text that focuses with particular acuteness on the problem of the representation of femininity and discusses several modern French psychoanalytical theories of femininity (particularly Michèle Montrelay and Luce Irigaray in relation to Lacan). She concludes by rejecting that simplistic reading of *Dora* which would see Dora the woman opposed to and oppressed by Freud the man. According to Rose, *Dora* reveals how Freud's concept of the feminine was incomplete and contradictory, thus delineating a major problem in psychoanalytical theory: its inability to account for the feminine. A valuable contribution to a feminist reading of psychoanalysis, Rose's essay is nevertheless silent on its political consequences.

The same is true of Suzanne Gearhart's "The Scene of Psychoanalysis: The Unanswered Questions of Dora." Gearhart reads *Dora* principally through Lacan's and Irigaray's discussions of Dora's case, arguing that the central problem in the text is "the symbolic status of the father." According to Gearhart, *Dora* must be seen as Freud's "interrogation of the principle of paternity"; it is in the correct understanding of the text's handling of this problem that we will find the key to the ultimate explanation of Dora's illness and also the basis of the identity of Freud and his work. Gearhart's highly sophisticated reading of *Dora* shows that the status of the father in *Dora* is problematical, and the father himself made marginal, because Freud wants to avoid the central insight that the (Lacanian) Imaginary and Symbolic realms are fundamentally complicit. Theoretically valuable though this essay is, it fails to indicate the consequences of its reading of *Dora* for a feminist approach to psychoanalysis.

Maria Ramas' long study of Dora, "Freud's Dora, Dora's Hysteria," is the most accessible article on Dora to date. Whereas Rose and Gearhart use a sophisticated theoretical vocabulary, Ramas writes in a lucid, low-key style. But her "theoretical" inquiry advances little beyond a scrupulous, somewhat tedious resumé of Freud's text. Ramas argues that "Ida's problem [Ramas uses Dora's real name, Ida Bauer, throughout her text] was her unconscious belief that "femininity, bondage, and debasement were synonymous." Since Freud unconsciously shared this belief, she claims, he could only reinforce Dora's problems rather than free her from them.

This, at least, is a traditional feminist reading: it implies that Dora could escape her hysteria only through feminist consciousness-raising—that if she could stop equating femininity with bondage she would be liberated. But it is also a sadly partial and superficial account, failing to encompass many controversial areas of Freud's text. Despite one brief reference to Jacqueline Rose's article, Ramas seems to find the status of the term *femininity* in the text quite unproblematical; she unquestioningly accepts Freud's automatic reduction of oral sex to fellatio (a point I shall return to later) and does not even notice many of Freud's more eccentric concerns in the case study. Qualifying her own essay as pure "feminist polemics," Ramas suggests that further study of *Dora* would lead beyond feminism: "If this were Freud's story, we would have to go beyond feminist polemics and search for the sources of the negative countertransference—the unanalyzed part of Freud—that brought the analysis to an abrupt end."

I believe that it is precisely through an exploration of the "unanalyzed part of Freud" that we may uncover the relations between sexual politics and psychoanalytical theory in *Dora,* and therefore also in Freud's works in general. In my reading of *Dora* I want to show that neither Rose's and Gearhart's depoliticized theorizing nor Ramas' rather simplistic "feminist polemics" will really do. Feminists must neither reject theoretical discussion as "beyond feminist polemics" nor forget the ideological context of theory.

The first version of *Dora* was written in 1901. Freud entitled it "Dreams and Hysteria" and had the greatest ambitions for the text: this was his first great case history, and it was to continue and develop the work presented in *The Interpretation of Dreams,* published in the previous year. But Freud recalled *Dora* from his publisher and curiously enough delayed publication until 1905, the year of the *Three Essays on Sexuality.* Why would Freud hesitate for more than four years before deciding to publish *Dora?* According to Jacqueline Rose, this hesitation may have been because *Dora* was written in the period between the theory of the unconscious, developed in *The Interpretation of Dreams,* and the theory of sexuality, first expressed in the *Three Essays. Dora* would then mark the transition between these two theories, and Freud's hesitation in publishing the text suggests the theoretical hesitation within it. Jacqueline Rose may well be right in this supposition. It is at any rate evident that among Freud's texts *Dora* marks an unusual degree of uncertainty, doubt, and ambiguity.

This uncertainty is already revealed in the title of the work: the true title is not "Dora," but **"Fragment of an Analysis of a Case of Hysteria."** Freud lists three reasons for calling his text a fragment. First, the analytic results are fragmentary both because Dora interrupted the treatment before it was completed and because Freud did not write up the case history until after the treatment was over. The only exceptions to this are Dora's two dreams, which Freud took down immediately. The text we are reading, in other words, is constructed from fragmentary notes and Freud's fragmentary memory. Second, Freud insists on the fact that he has given an account only of the (incomplete) analytic *results* and not at all of the *process* of interpretation—that is to say, Freud willfully withholds the *technique of the analytic work.* To describe the analytic technique, Freud argues, would have led to "nothing but hopeless confusion." Finally, Freud stresses that no *one* case history can provide the answer to *all* the problems presented by hysteria: all case histories are in this sense incomplete answers to the problem they set out to solve.

It is of course perfectly normal to state, as Freud does here, the limitations of one's project in the preface to the finished work, but Freud does more than that. In his Prefatory Remarks to *Dora,* Freud seems positively obsessed with the incomplete status of his text. He returns to the subject again and again, either to excuse the fact that he is presenting a fragment or to express his longings for a *complete* text after all. His Prefatory Remarks oscillate constantly between the theme of fragmentation and the notion of totality. These two themes, however, are not presented as straight opposites. Having expressed his regrets that the case history is incomplete, he writes: "But its shortcomings are connected with the very circumstances which have made its publication possible. . . . I should not have known how to deal with the material involved in the history of a treatment which had lasted, perhaps, for a whole year." Freud here totally undermines any notion of a fundamental opposition between fragment

and whole: it would have been impossible to write down a *complete* case history. The fragment can be presented as a complete book; the complete case history could not. Nevertheless, Freud insists on the fact that the fragment *lacks* something:

> In the face of the incompleteness of my analytic results, I had no choice but to follow the example of those discoverers whose good fortune it is to bring to the light of day after their long burial the priceless though mutilated relics of antiquity. I have restored what is missing, taking the best models known to me from other analyses; but like a conscientious archaeologist, I have not omitted to mention in each case where the authentic parts end and my construction begins.

Once again, Freud candidly admits that his results are incomplete—only to claim in the same breath that he has "restored what is missing": Freud's metaphors in this context are significant. Dora's story is compared to the "priceless though mutilated relics of antiquity," and Freud himself figures as an archeologist, digging relics out from the earth. His claim here is that when he adds something to the "mutilated relics," completeness is established *malgré tout.* But this new completeness is after all not quite complete. On the same page as the above quotation, Freud writes that the psychoanalytic technique (which he jealously retains for himself) does not by its nature lend itself to the creation of complete sequences: "Everything that has to do with the clearing-up of a particular symptom emerges piecemeal, woven into various contexts, and distributed over widely separated periods of time." The "completeness" achieved by Freud's supplementary conjectures is doubly incomplete: it consists of Dora's story (the "mutilated relics of antiquity"), to which Freud's own assumptions have been added. But Dora's story is not only a fragment: it is a fragment composed of information that has emerged "piecemeal, woven into various contexts, and distributed over widely separated periods of time." We must assume that it is Freud himself who has imposed a fictional coherence on Dora's story, in order to render the narrative readable. But Dora's story is in turn only one part of the finished work entitled **"Fragment of an Analysis of a Case of Hysteria."** The other part is supplemented by Freud. In itself Dora's story is too fragmentary; it is readable only when Freud supplies the necessary supplement. But that supplement is based on Freud's experience from other cases of hysteria, cases that must have been constructed in the same way as Dora's: by information provided "piecemeal, over widely separated periods of time." The fragment depends on the supplement, which depends on other fragments depending on other supplements, and so on ad infinitum.

We are, in other words, surprisingly close to Jacques Derrida's theories of the production of meaning as *"différance."* According to Derrida, meaning can never be seized as presence: it is always deferred, constantly displaced onto the next element in the series, in a chain of signification that has no end, no transcendental signified that might provide the final anchor point for the production of sense. This, need one say, is not Freud's own *conscious* theory: he clings to his dream of "complete elucidation," refusing to acknowledge that according to his own account of the status of the *Dora* text, completeness is an unattainable illusion. Even when he insists strongly on the fragmentary status of his text, he always implies that completeness is within reach. He can, for instance, write, "If the work had been continued, we should no doubt have obtained the fullest possible enlightenment upon every particular of the case." Freud's text oscillates endlessly between his desire for complete insight or knowledge and an unconscious realization (or fear) of the fragmentary, deferring status of knowledge itself.

We have seen that in his Prefatory Remarks Freud discloses that "Dora's story" *is* largely "Freud's story": he is the author, the one who has conjured a complete work from these analytic fragments. This in itself should alert the reader eager to discover Dora's own view of her case to the dangers of taking Freud's words too much at face value. His account of the analysis of Dora must instead be scanned with the utmost suspicion.

The better part of the Postcript is devoted to a discussion of the reasons why the analysis of Dora was at least in part a failure. Freud's main explanation is that he failed to discover the importance of the *transference* for the analysis; he did not discover in time that Dora was transferring the emotions she felt for Herr K. onto Freud himself. Psychoanalytic theory holds that transference is normal in the course of analysis, that it consists in the patient's transferring emotions for some other person onto the analyst, and that if the analyst, unaware of the transference, cannot counteract it, the analysis will in consequence go awry.

Freud adds this information in this Postscript. But if we are to grasp what is being acted out between Freud and Dora, it is important to keep in mind from the outset this transference on Dora's part from Herr K. to Freud. Transference, however, is something the patient does to the analyst. Freud does not mention at all the opposite phenomenon, *countertransference,* which consists in the analyst's transferring his or her own unconscious emotions onto the patient. Jacques Lacan has discussed precisely this problem in *Dora* in an article entitled "Intervention sur le transfert." According to Lacan, Freud unconsciously identifies with Herr K. in his relationship to Dora, which makes him (Freud) far too interested in Dora's alleged love for Herr K. and effectively blind to any other explanation of her problems. Thus the countertransference contributes decisively to the failure of Dora's analysis.

The fact of transference and countertransference between Freud and Dora considerably complicates the task of the *Dora* reader. Freud's attempts to posit himself as the neutral, scientific observer who is merely noting down his observations and reflections can no longer be accepted. The archeologist must be suspected of having mutilated the relics he finds. We must remember that Freud's version of the case is colored not only by his own unconscious countertransference but also by the fact that he signally fails to notice the transference in Dora, and therefore systematically misinterprets her transference symptoms throughout the text. This, oddly, is something the reader is not told until the "Postscript."

Freud's interpretation of Dora's case can be summarized as follows. Dora develops hysterical symptoms because she represses sexual desire. But her case has an added, oedipal dimension: one must suppose that Dora originally desired her father, but since her father disappointed her by starting an affair with Frau K., Dora now pretends to hate him. Herr K. represents the father for Dora, particularly because he is also Frau K.'s husband. Dora's repression of her sexual desire for Herr K. is therefore at once a hysterical reaction (repression of sexual desire) *and* an oedipal reaction (rejection of the father through rejection of Herr K.). Based on this interpretation, Freud's treatment of Dora consists in repeated attempts to get her to admit her repressed desire for Herr K., a "confession" Dora resists as best she can.

We have already seen that, according to Lacan, the analysis failed because of Freud's unconscious identification with Herr K. Since Dora is at the same time identifying Freud with Herr K., the result is inevitably that she must experience Freud's insistence on the necessity of acknowledging her desire for Herr K. as a repetition of Herr K.'s attempt to elicit sexual favors from her. In the end she rejects Freud in the same way she rejected Herr K.—by giving him two weeks' notice. Herr K. had earlier had an affair with the governess of his children, and Dora felt greatly insulted at being courted like a servant by the same man. Her revenge is to treat both Freud and Herr K. as servants in return.

But Freud's incessant identification with Herr K., the rejected lover, leads to other interesting aspects of the text. One of the most important episodes in the study is Freud's interpretation of Herr K.'s attempt to kiss Dora, then fourteen, after having tricked her into being alone with him in his office. Freud writes that Herr K.

> suddenly clasped the girl to him and pressed a kiss upon her lips. This was surely just the situation to call up a distinct feeling of sexual excitement in a girl of fourteen who had never before been approached. But Dora had at that moment a violent feeling of disgust, tore herself free from the man, and hurried past him to the staircase and from there to the street door.

At this moment in the text Freud is completely in the grip of his countertransference: he must at all costs emphasize that Dora's reaction was abnormal and writes that "the behaviour of this child of fourteen was already entirely and completely hysterical." Her reaction was hysterical because she was already repressing sexual desire: "Instead of the genital sensation which would certainly have been felt by a healthy girl in such circumstances, Dora was overcome by . . . disgust." It is, of course, resplendently clear to any scientific observer that any normal girl of fourteen would be overwhelmed by desire when a middle-aged man "suddenly clasps her to him" in a lonely spot.

Freud then links Dora's feeling of disgust to *oral* impulses and goes on to interpret as a "displacement" Dora's statement that she clearly felt the pressure from the upper part of Herr K.'s body against her own. What she really felt, according to Freud, and what aroused such strong oral disgust, was the pressure of Herr K.'s erect penis. The thought of this unmentionable organ was then repressed, and the feeling of pressure displaced from the lower to the upper part of the body. The oral disgust is then related to Dora's habit of thumb-sucking as a child, and Freud connects the oral satisfaction resulting from this habit to Dora's nervous cough. He interprets the cough (irritation of oral cavity and throat) as a revealing symptom of Dora's sexual fantasies: she must be fantasizing a scene where sexual satisfaction is obtained by using the mouth (*per os,* as Freud puts it), and this scene is one that takes place between Frau K. and Dora's father.

Having said as much, Freud spends the next few pages defending himself against accusations of using too foul a language with his patients. These passages could be read as betraying a certain degree of unconscious tension in Freud himself, but it is enough to point out here that he argues his way from exhortations to tolerance to the high social status of "the perversion which is the most repellent to us, the sensual love of a man for a man" in ancient Greece, before returning to Dora's oral fantasy and making it plain that what he had in mind was fellatio, or "sucking at the male organ." It would not be difficult to detect in Freud a defensive reaction-formation in this context, since on the next page he feels compelled to allude to "this excessively repulsive and perverted phantasy of sucking at a penis." It is little wonder that he feels the need to defend himself against the idea of fellatio, since it is more than probable that the fantasy exists, not in Dora's mind, but in his alone. Freud has informed us that Dora's father was impotent, and assumes this to be the basis of Dora's "repulsive and perverted phantasy." According to Freud, the father cannot manage penetration, so Frau K. must perform fellatio instead. But as Lacan has pointed out, this argument reveals an astonishing lack of logic on Freud's part. In the case of male impotence, the man is obviously much more likely, *faute de mieux,* to perform cunnilingus. As Lacan writes: "Everyone knows that cunnilingus is the artifice most commonly adopted by 'men of means' whose powers begin to abandon them." It is in this logical flaw that Freud's countertransference is seen at its strongest. The illogicality reveals his own unconscious wish for gratification, a gratification Freud's unconscious alter ego, Herr K., might obtain if only Dora would admit her desire for him.

Freud's countertransference blinds him to the possibility that Dora's hysteria may be due to the repression of desire, not for Herr K., but for his wife, Frau K. A fatal lack of insight into the transferential process prevents Freud from discovering Dora's homosexuality early enough. Dora's condition as a victim of male dominance here becomes starkly visible. She is not only a pawn in the game between Herr K. and her father; her doctor joins the male team and untiringly tries to ascribe to her desires she does not have and to ignore the ones she does have.

Freud's oppressive influence on Dora does not, however, stem only from the countertransference. There are also more general ideological tendencies to sexism at work in his text. Freud, for instance, systematically refuses to consider female sexuality as an active, independent drive. Again and again he exhorts Dora to accept herself as an object for Herr K. Every time Dora reveals active sexual desires, Freud interprets them away, either by assuming that Dora is expressing masculine identification (when she fantasizes about female genitals, Freud instantly assumes that she wants to penetrate them) or by supposing that she desires to be penetrated by the male (Dora's desire for Frau K. is interpreted as her desire to be in Frau K.'s place in order to gain access to Herr K.). His position is self-contradictory: he is one of the first to acknowledge the existence of sexual desire in women, and at the same time he renders himself incapable of seeing it as more than the impulse to become passive recipients for male desire. Lacan assumes precisely the same attitude when he states that the problem for Dora (and all women) is that she "must accept herself as the object of male desire" (Lacan) and that this is the reason for Dora's adoration of Frau K.

Feminists cannot help feeling relieved when Dora finally dismisses Freud like another servant. It is tempting to read Dora's hysterical symptoms, as do Cixous and Clément, as a silent revolt against male power over women's bodies and women's language. But at the same time it is disconcerting to see how inefficient Dora's revolt turned out to be. Felix Deutsch describes Dora's tragic destiny in an article written in 1957. She continued to develop various hysterical symptoms, made life unbearable for her family, and grew to resemble her mother (whom Freud dismissed as a typical case of "housewife psychosis"). According to Deutsch, Dora tortured her husband throughout their marriage; he concluded that "her marriage had served only to cover up her distaste of men." Dora suffers continuously from psychosomatic constipation and dies from cancer of the colon. Deutsch concludes, "Her death . . . seemed a blessing to those who were close to her. She had been, as my informant phrased it, one of the most repulsive hysterics he had ever met."

It may be gratifying to see the young, proud Dora as a radiant example of feminine revolt (as does Cixous); but we should not forget the image of the old, nagging, whining, and complaining Dora she later becomes, achieving nothing. Hysteria is not, *pace* Hélène Cixous, the incarnation of the revolt of women forced to silence but rather a declaration of defeat, the realization that there is no other way out. Hysteria is, as Catherine Clément perceives, a cry for help when defeat becomes real, when the woman sees that she is efficiently gagged and chained to her feminine role.

Now if the hysterical woman is gagged and chained, Freud posits himself as her liberator. And if the emancipatory project of psychoanalysis fails in the case of Dora, it is because Freud the liberator happens also to be, objectively, on the side of oppression. He is a male in patriarchal society, and moreover not just any male but an educated bourgeois male, incarnating *malgré lui* patriarchal values. His own emancipatory project profoundly conflicts with his political and social role as an oppressor of women.

The most telling instance of this deeply unconscious patriarchal ideology in *Dora* is to be found in Freud's obsession with the sources of his patient's sexual information. After stressing the impossibility of tracing the sources of Dora's sexual information, Freud nevertheless continually returns to the subject, suggesting alternately that the source may have been books belonging to a former governess, Mantegazza's *Physiology of Love,* or an encyclopedia. He finally realizes that there must have been an *oral* source of information, in addition to the avid reading of forbidden books, then sees, extremely belatedly, that the oral source must have been none other than the beloved Frau K.

The one hypothesis that Freud does not entertain is that the source of oral information may have been Dora's mother—the mother who is traditionally charged with the sexual education of the daughters. This omission is wholly symptomatic of Freud's treatment of Dora's mother. Although he indicates Dora's identification with her mother, he nevertheless strongly insists that Dora had withdrawn completely from her mother's influence. Dora's apparent hatred of her mother is mobilized as evidence for this view.

But Freud ought to know better than to accept a daughter's hatred of her mother as an inevitable consequence of the mother's objective unlikableness ("housewife's psychosis"). Even his own oedipal explanation of Dora's rejection of Herr K. should contribute to a clearer understanding of the mother's importance for Dora. Oedipally speaking, Dora would be seen as the mother's rival in that competition for the father's love, but this rivalry also implies the necessity of identifying with the mother: the daughter must become like the mother in order to be loved by the father. Freud notes that Dora is behaving like a jealous wife and that this behavior shows that "she was clearly putting herself in her mother's place," but he draws no further conclusions from these observations. He also points out that Dora identifies with Frau K., her father's mistress, but is still quite content to situate her mainly in relation to her father and Herr K. He fails to see that Dora is caught up in an ambivalent relationship to her mother and an idealizing and identifying relationship to Frau K., the other mother-figure in this text. Freud's patriarchal prejudices force him to ignore relationships between women and instead center all his attention on relationships with men. This grievous underestimation of the importance of other women for Dora's psychic development contributes decisively to the failure of the analysis and the cure—not least in that it makes Freud unaware of the *pre-oedipal* causes for Dora's hysteria. Maria Ramas writes: "By Freud's own admission, the deepest level of meaning of hysterical symptoms is not a thwarted desire for the father, but a breakthrough of the prohibited desire for the mother."

Freud's particular interest in the sources of Dora's sexual information does not, however, merely reveal that for as long as possible he avoids considering oral relations between women as such a source; it also indicates that Freud overestimates the importance of this question. There is nothing in Dora's story to indicate that a successful analysis depends on the elucidation of this peripheral problem. Why then would Freud be so obsessed by these sources of knowledge?

First, because he himself desires total knowledge: his aim is nothing less than the *complete elucidation* of Dora, despite his insistence on the fragmentary nature of his material. The absence of information on this one subject is thus tormenting, since it so obviously ruins the dream of completeness. But such a desire for total, absolute knowledge exposes a fundamental assumption in Freud's epistemology. Knowledge for Freud is a finished, closed whole. Possession of knowledge means possession of power. Freud, the doctor, is curiously proud of his hermeneutical capacities. After having interpreted Dora's fingering of her little purse as an admission of infantile masturbation, he writes with evident satisfaction:

> When I set myself the task of bringing to light what human beings keep hidden within them, not by the compelling power of hypothesis, but by observing what they say and what they show, I thought the task was a harder one than it really is. He that has eyes to see and ears to hear may convince himself that no mortal can keep a secret. If his lips are silent, he chatters with his finger tips; betrayal oozes out of him at every pore. And thus the task of making conscious the most hidden recesses of the mind is one which it is quite possible to accomplish.

Freud in other words possesses powers more compelling than those of hypnosis. He is the one who discloses and unlocks secrets; he is Oedipus solving the Sphinx's riddle. But like Oedipus he is ravaged by a terrible anxiety: the fear of castration. If Freud cannot solve Dora's riddle, the unconscious punishment for this failure will be castration. In this struggle for the possession of knowledge, a knowledge that is power, Dora reveals herself both as Freud's alter ego and as his rival. She possesses the secret Freud is trying to discover. At this point we must suspect Freud of countertransference to Dora: he identifies with the hysterical Dora in the search for information about sexual matters. Freud has his own secret, as Dora has hers: the analytic technique, which, as we have seen, cannot be exposed without causing "total confusion." Freud jealously keeps his secret, as Dora keeps hers: her homosexual desire for Frau K.

But since Dora is a woman, and a rather formidable one at that, a young lady who hitherto has had only scorn for the incompetent (and, surely, impotent) doctors who have treated her so far, she becomes a threatening rival for Freud. If he does not win the fight for knowledge, he will also be revealed as incompetent/impotent, his compelling powers will be reduced to nothing, he will be castrated. If Dora wins the knowledge game, her model for knowledge will emerge victorious, and Freud's own model will be destroyed. Freud here finds himself between Scylla and Charybdis: if he identifies with Dora in the search for knowledge, he becomes a woman, that is to say, castrated; but if he chooses to cast her as his rival, he *must* win out, or the punishment will be castration.

The last point (that the punishment in case of defeat will be castration) requires further explanation. We have seen that Dora's sources of knowledge have been characterized as female, oral, and scattered. Freud, on the contrary, presents his knowledge as something that creates a unitary whole. In both cases we are discussing sexual knowledge. But Freud's own paradigmatic example of the desire for sexual knowledge is the sexual curiosity in children, and

Freud's most important text on this topic is *Little Hans.* Moving from *Dora* to *Little Hans,* the reader is struck by this remarkable difference in tone between the two texts. The five-year-old little Hans, straining to understand the mysteries of sexuality, is strongly encouraged in his epistemophilia (Freud's own word, from ***Three Essays on Sexuality***). Freud never ceases to express his admiration for the intelligence of the little boy, in such laudatory statements as, "Here the little boy was displaying a really unusual degree of clarity," or "Little Hans has by a bold stroke taken the conduct of the analysis into his own hands. By means of a brilliant symptomatic act|. . . ." This tone is far removed from Freud's stern admonitions of Dora, his continuous *et tu quoque* ripostes to her interpretation of her own situation.

Why this differential treatment? It is arguable that in *Little Hans* Freud equates the desire for knowledge and the construction of theories with the desire to discover the role of the penis in procreation. The penis, in other words, becomes the epistemological object par excellence for Freud. But if this is so, knowledge and theory must be conceptualized as whole, rounded, finished—just like the penis. Little Hans becomes in this sense a penis for Freud. He is both a pleasurable object to be studied, a source of excitation and enthusiasm, *and* Freud's double: a budding sexual theoretician emerging to confirm Freud's own epistemological activities. But where Little Hans confirms, Dora threatens. Her knowledge cannot be conceptualized as a whole; it is dispersed and has been assembled piecemeal from feminine sources. Dora's epistemological model becomes the female genitals, which in Freud's vision emerge as unfinished, diffuse, and fragmentary; they cannot add up to a complete whole and must therefore be perceived as castrated genitals. If Freud were to accept Dora's epistemological model, it would be tantamout to rejecting the penis as the principal symbol for human desire for knowledge, which again would mean accepting castration.

Freud's masculine psyche therefore perceives Dora as more fundamentally threatening than he can consciously express. Instead, his fear of epistemological castration manifests itself in various disguises: in his obsessive desire to discover the sources of Dora's knowledge, and in his oddly intense discussion of the fragmentary status of the *Dora* text. To admit that there are holes in one's knowledge is tantamount to transforming the penis to a hole, that is to say, to transforming the man into a woman. Holes, empty spaces, open areas are at all cost to be avoided; and with this in mind we can discern further layers of meaning in the passage quoted earlier:

> In the face of the incompleteness of my analytic results, I had no choice but to follow the example of those discoverers whose good fortune it is to bring to the light of day after their long burial the priceless though mutilated relics of antiquity. I have restored what is missing.

"The priceless though mutilated relics of antiquity" are not only Dora's story: they are Dora herself, her genitals and the feminine epistemological model. Freud makes sure that the message here is clear: "mutilated" is his usual

way of describing the effect of castration, and "priceless" also means just what it says: price-less, without value. For how can there be value when the valuable piece has been cut off? The relics are mutilated, the penis has been cut. Freud's task is therefore momentous: he must "restore what is missing"; his penis must fill the epistemological hole represented by Dora.

But such a task can only be performed by one who possesses what is missing. And this is precisely what Freud occasionally doubts in his text: the fear of castration is also the fear of discovering that one has already been castrated. Freud's hesitation in *Dora* between insisting on completeness and admitting fragmentary status indicates that in his text the penis is playing a kind of *fort-da* game with its author (now you have it, now you don't). Freud's book about Dora is the narrative of an intense power struggle between two protagonists—a struggle in which the male character's virility is at stake and in which he by no means always has the upper hand.

When Dora dismisses Freud like a servant, she paradoxically rescues him from further epistemological insecurity. He is left, then, the master of the *writing* of Dora. And even though his text bears the scars of the struggle between him and his victim, it is a victorious Freud who publishes it. Dora dismissed him, but Freud got his revenge: Dora was the name Freud's own sister, Rosa, had foisted on her maid in place of her real one, which also was Rosa. So Ida Bauer, in a bitter historical irony, was made famous under the name of a servant after all.

Freud's epistemology is clearly phallocentric. The male is the bearer of knowledge; he alone has the power to penetrate woman and text; woman's role is to let herself be pen-

Freud and Wilhelm Fliess. From 1895 to 1902, they maintained an intense and emotional correspondence which aided Freud in his self-analysis.

etrated by such truth. Such epistemological phallocentrism is by no means specifically Freudian; on the contrary, it has so far enjoyed universal sway in our patriarchal civilization, and one could hardly expect Freud to emerge untouched by it. It is politically important, however, to point out that this pathological division of knowledge into masculine totality and feminine fragment is completely mystifying and mythological. There is absolutely no evidence for the actual existence of two such gender-determined sorts of knowledge, to be conceptualized as parallel to the shapes of human genitals. Dora can be perceived as the bearer of feminine epistemology in the study only because Freud selected her as his opponent in a war over cognition, creating her as his symbolic antagonist. To champion Dora's "feminine values" means meekly accepting Freud's own definitions of masculine and feminine. Power always creates its own definitions, and this is particularly true of the distinctions between masculine and feminine constructed by patriarchal society. Nowhere is patriarchal ideology to be seen more clearly than in the definition of the feminine as the negative of the masculine—and this is precisely how Freud defines Dora and the "feminine" epistemology she is supposed to represent.

To undermine this phallocentric epistemology means to expose its lack of "natural" foundation. In the case of *Dora,* however, we have been able to do this only because of Freud's own theories of femininity and sexuality. The attack upon phallocentrism must come from within, since there can be no "outside," no space where true femininity, untainted by patriarchy, can be kept intact for us to discover. We can only destroy the mythical and mystifying constructions of patriarchy by using its own weapons. We have no others. (pp. 181-98)

> *Toril Moi, "Representation of Patriarchy: Sexuality and Epistemology in Freud's Dora," in* In Dora's Case: Freud—Hysteria—Feminism, *edited by Charles Bernheimer and Claire Kahane, Columbia University Press, 1985, pp. 181-99.*

Jeffrey B. Abramson   (essay date 1984)

[*In the following excerpt from his* Liberation and Its Limits: The Moral and Political Thought of Freud, *Abramson discusses Freud's critique and repudiation of religion.*]

Freud's most insistent attempt to work out the cultural implications of psychoanalysis was in the area of religion. He devoted three book-length manuscripts to the origins and history of religion, including his first foray into the interpretation of culture (*Totem and Taboo*) and his last, posthumously published work (*Moses and Monotheism*). In between, Freud delivered his famous broadside at the truth of religion (*The Future of an Illusion*) and returned to the worrisome question of man's religiosity at the start of *Civilization and Its Discontents.*

Why religion, again and again? For Freud, religion represented the central elaboration of public meaning for the human species to date, and yet the epitome of untruth as revealed by the advent of psychoanalysis. Freud's tone,

cool and impartial elsewhere, is fiery, even combative on the coming clash between science and religion and on the inevitable triumph psychoanalysis makes possible over the "neurotic" or "infantile" phase of civilization. This triumph will be psychoanalysis' greatest cultural achievement; it will accomplish science's "appointed task" of reconciling man to civilization, but it will also unleash new dangers of nihilism. For if the existence of God is the "sole reason" that keeps persons from murdering their neighbors, then his death will surely provoke an unbounded reign of terror. And if hitherto it has taken a God to make nature meaningful, then when the world is disenchanted of belief, the question of whether science in place of religion can make life intelligible will come to the fore.

Freud typically scoffed at "the idea of life having a purpose. . . ." "Nobody," he taunted, "talks about the purpose of the life of animals," and the presumption that humans are uniquely created with some *telos,* or goal, in mind, "stands and falls with the religious system." In humbling man's presumptive uniqueness, Freud saw himself as following in the footsteps of Copernicus and Darwin—psychoanalysis as the "third" great "blow" to "the self-love of humanity." The Copernican revolution dismantled the "cosmological illusion" by which man "naively" placed himself at the center of creation; Darwinism put an end to man's arrogant claim to a "divine descent" and reinstituted the "bond of community between [man] and the animal kingdom." And psychoanalysis inflicted the "most wounding" blow of all—the news that "the ego is not master in its own house." The prior two revolutions had already made it difficult for persons to understand themselves according to the testament of Genesis. But it was psychoanalysis alone which recovered the hidden unconscious origins of religion itself and, in so doing, concluded the battle against culture's most powerful fiction.

Freud on intellectual religiosity:

You are right: one is in danger of overestimating the frequency of an irreligious attitude among intellectuals. I get convinced of that just now on observing the reactions to my *The Future of an Illusion.* That comes from the most varied drinks being offered under the name of "religion," with a minimal percentage of alcohol—really nonalcoholic; but they still get drunk on it. The old drinkers were after all a respectable body, but to get tipsy on pomerit (apple-juice) is really ridiculous.

Sigmund Freud, in a letter to Marie Bonaparte, cited in Ernest Jones' Life and Work of Sigmund Freud, Vol. 3, 1957.

Freud himself understood there was an important duality in his approach to the psychology of religion. He is best known, through the title of *The Future of an Illusion,* for debunking religion as springing purely from the individual's infantile motives for wishing God the Benevolent Father into existence. This is an important aspect of Freud's case against religion, but he combined it, especially in *Moses and Monotheism,* with a historical argument foreshadowed by his earlier inquiries into totemism. On this argument, religion is an illusion which is at the same time an act of historical recollection, a way of recalling deeply buried truths about the fearful, criminal origins of civilization. And when this latent historical content of religion is recomprehended, then its full Oedipal structure is also revealed in the two faces God wears—benevolence and vengeance.

In *The Future of an Illusion,* Freud develops the nonhistorical side of his argument against religious fiction as follows:

God is our own creation, an illusion we believe in precisely because it illustrates the world according to our infantile liking. Religion is the adult's last and lasting attempt at flight from nasty reality back into infantile fantasy, at conjuring up a world of make-believe we have no right to believe in but want to believe in very badly. God, heaven, life after death—these are psychological creations whose existence can be understood only in terms of the motives we have for inventing them. The very power of faith to ignore reason (*Credo quia absurdum*) indicates we are dealing with a set of ideas humanity must have the deepest of motives for believing. But, as is typical of Freud, these deep motives are rooted in material, not spiritual, puzzlement and perplexity. As I have pointed out previously and need only summarize here, early childhood is mired in the anxiety implicit in being dependent on the help of others to satisfy basic needs. Within the family, the child learns that instinctual satisfaction depends on parental mediation. The parents, and especially the perceived stronger father, are figures of protection to be relied on. The father is the hero combatant of the child's fears. And the infant's fearsome helplessness lasts long enough for a dependent mentality to take hold: the expectancy that parental care will reappear to conquer fear whenever fear appears.

This desire to be fathered proves difficult to give up. To face the world on one's own; to admit to the impersonality and hostility of natural forces; to reconcile oneself to a world under no one's loving control—for all these admissions the sheltered child is ill prepared. Far easier, in later life and new situations of fear and perplexity, to respond according to the infantile prototype—to personalize nature into a world of father deities:

> When the growing individual finds that he is destined to remain a child for ever, that he can never do without protection against strange superior powers, he lends those powers the features belonging to the figure of his father; he creates for himself the gods whom he dreads, whom he seeks to propitiate, and whom he nevertheless entrusts with his own protection. Thus his longing for a father is a motive identical with his need for protection against the consequences of his human weakness. The defence against childish helplessness is what lends its characteristic features to the adult's reaction to the helplessness which *he* has to acknowledge—a reaction which is precisely the formation of religion.

In the personification of nature, wishing plays the largest part; we make nature over into what we would like it to be, into what it seemed to the child's eye. The origin of God, like the origin of our dreams, is in wish fulfillment; in fact, one might say God is a dream answering to humanity's "oldest, strongest and most urgent wishes. . . . "

Freud's account of the psychological motives for religious belief has been criticized for slipping back into the "unsociological" Enlightenment view of religion as wholly irrational, an isolable error without functional relation to any part of the social world. But, despite the title of his most famous book on the subject, Freud knew religion is, or at least was, a functional illusion. He recognized, though he stood against, the use of religion to sanctify obedience to social authority. And he was interested, from early in his career until his last written work, in the latent, or historical, content of religion. "God," Freud wrote, "must be recognized as a memory—a distorted one, it is true, but nevertheless a memory." But, like a neurotic symptom, God cannot withstand conscious knowledge of his origins. To know the psychology of religion is to know why it is false.

On the subject of religion's historical origin, Freud adopted from Darwin and from anthropologists of his time the description of rudimentary human groups—"hordes"—organized around worship of a sacred animal, or "totem." The horde expressed its unity in terms of the common descent of clan members from the totem animal, whose slaughter was ordinarily prohibited on pain of death. Nevertheless, once a year worship of the totem would be temporarily suspended in favor of its ritual slaughter and ingestion.

The horde's sense of common descent was accompanied by the first appearance of the incest taboo in history, all members refraining from sexual relations with one another. No one can overlook, Freud writes, that these two prohibitions—neither to kill the totem nor to have sexual relations with a woman of the same totem—"coincide in their content with the two crimes of Oedipus . . . , as well as with the two primal wishes of children, the insufficient repression or the re-awakening of which forms the nucleus of perhaps every psychoneurosis." This first worship of a "sacred" creature must be understood as a collective symptom, a screen expressing in disguised form the repressed memory of the murder and overthrow of the father by the brothers of the horde ("primal crime"). The purpose of the symptom is to allay, by disguising, the sense of guilt caused by that memory. In totemic thought, the clan absolves its guilt for the original father murder by exalting the substitute animal into a god and prohibiting any repetition of its murder. (Freud's analysis of dreams and neurosis had long since revealed to him the use of animals by the unconscious to symbolize the father.) Simultaneously, the totemic law of exogamy punishes the sexual motive behind the father murder.

Alongside his account of the early religion of totemism, Freud late in life added an account of the Oedipal grounding of monotheism among the Jews. Monotheism represents a quantum leap over totemism in the social history of guilt—and in the progress of both culture and neurosis. Nowhere does Freud write more sympathetically about religion than when dealing with the achievements monotheism made possible among the Jews. But nowhere does he make clearer the intimacy of those achievements with neurosis.

Monotheism is the highest form the religion of the father can assume. The animal gods have become humanized, the competing forces ousted, and God the Father stands alone, omnipotent and omniscient, the Almighty Being. With monotheism, it would seem that the repressed memory of the primal father has returned to a remarkable degree and wears its most transparent disguise. Only "thus was it that the supremacy of the father of the primal horde was re-established and that the emotions relating to him could be repeated."

What happened among the Jews to make them the first full bearers of humanity's repressed father complex? What happened, says Freud in his largest tribute to the historical force of a single individual, was Moses. In Freud's interpretation, Moses was a lieutenant of the Pharoah Ikhanaton, whose attempt to impose a monotheistic religion on the Egyptians themselves proved abortive; after Ikhanaton's overthrow and death, Moses carried on the experiment among the formerly enslaved Jews, escaping into exile with them when a new dynasty turned hostile to his and Ikhanaton's ideas.

For a time, Moses' campaign proved successful—until the more primitive Jews rose up against his enlightened despotism and murdered him. Freud takes the biblical story of Moses' not being allowed by God into the promised land as a vague indication of the more earthly punishment Moses suffered. After their rebellion, the Jews lapsed from monotheism for a time, adopting the worship of the local deities of the Sinai peninsula—in particular the Midianite god Jahve.

But over a generation or more—perhaps the forty years in the wilderness—the Mosaic ideals returned to convert Jahve into the one and only God. And the Jews have remained with the Mosaic God ever since, a record of religious survival unparalleled in the West.

The peculiar fate of the Jews, then, the fate that determined them as history's first monotheists, was the repetition of the primal crime in regard to Moses. The killing of the founder made their Oedipal guilt twice born, and decreed that the repressed phylogenetic memory of father murder should haunt them most closely:

> It would be worthwhile to understand how it was that the monotheist idea made such a deep impression precisely on the Jewish people and that they were able to maintain it so tenaciously. It is possible, I think, to find an answer. Fate had brought the great deed and misdeed of primaeval days, the killing of the father, closer to the Jewish people by causing them to repeat it on the person of Moses, an outstanding father-figure. It was a case of "acting out" instead of remembering, as happens so often with neurotics during the work of analysis.

Jewish monotheism, then, symbolically represents the return of the repressed in collective life; and the repressed returns just as it does in neurosis. After a period of forget-fulness—Freud calls it a latency period—the memory of Moses (and through him of the primal crime) brushes consciousness, only to be repressed again via the suitable disguises provided by monotheistic culture.

For the Jews, monotheism was a mixed blessing. On the one hand, their "progress in spirituality" was nonpareil for the times. The prohibition of idolatry, for example, helped to subordinate sense perception to abstract ideas as they built their culture on the unpictured concept of God. This enforced a stunning intellectual advancement on Jewish culture:

> The new realm of intellectuality was opened up, in which ideas, memories and inferences became decisive in contrast to the lower psychical activity which had direct perceptions by the sense-organs as its content. This was unquestionably one of the most important stages on the path to hominization.

But Freud's affirmation of the progressive role of religion is halting, qualified always by his insistence that the history of monotheism is also the history of neurosis. For monotheism was a stinging and symptomatic expression among the Jews of guilty conscience: since they had sinned against their God, their religion could be only a perpetual piece of atonement—an atonement which could never placate the sense of guilt because the source of the guilt remained unacknowledged. This religion of permanent expiation the Prophets especially were to enforce upon the people, driving the Jews toward what Freud calls insatiable "transports of moral asceticism" and "ethical heights" of instinctual renunciation unknown in antiquity. The exhortations of the Prophets "possess the characteristic—uncompleted and incapable of completion—of obsessional neurotic reaction-formations."

The obsessive character of religion, Freud notes, "is in the nature of an axiom." From the time he first studied totemism,

> I have never doubted that religious phenomena are only to be understood on the pattern of the individual neurotic symptoms familiar to us—as the return of long since forgotten, important events in the primaeval history of the human family—and that they have to thank precisely this origin for their compulsive character and that, accordingly, they are effective on human beings by force of the historical truth of their content.

The obsessive nature of religion is crucial to Freud's point of view, for this is where the power of religion lies. Suppose one were to consider religion merely a "tradition" passed on from generation to generation by oral or written communication. Such a tradition "would be listened to, judged, and perhaps dismissed, like any other piece of information from outside; it would never attain the privilege of being liberated from the constraint of logical thought." Communication from the outside simply cannot account for either the continuity of religious culture or the remarkable hold that concepts beyond empirical experience have had on the human mind.

Religion, like any deeply seated part of culture, must be

passed on internally; the concept of God must be an external manifestation, a symptom of an unconscious memory obsessively plaguing human beings. There must be some experience whose memory God obliquely expresses. That experience is the primal crime, the murder of the father. This memory "must have undergone the fate of being repressed, the condition of lingering in the unconscious, before it is able to display such powerful effects on its return, to bring the masses under its spell. . . ." Religion accomplishes on a wider social scale what obsessive neurosis does for individuals: it uses illusion and fantasies to mask the threatened return of the repressed.

In Freud's treatment, Christianity forms a validating sequel to his interpretation of monotheism and the social origins of guilt. In a most intriguing way, Christian doctrine comes close to healing our obsession, replacing guilt with salvation precisely because it implicitly acknowledges—and absolves us from—the original source of human remorse. Christ the Son delivers man from his sins by laying down his life in expiation. What, then, must the original sin have been that demanded the son's life in return, if not the murder of the father?

> Paul, a Roman Jew from Tarsus, seized upon this sense of guilt and traced it back correctly to its original source. He called this the "original sin"; it was a crime against God and could only be atoned for by death. With the original sin death came into the world. In fact this crime deserving death had been the murder of the primal father who was later deified. But the murder was not remembered: instead of it there was a phantasy of its atonement, and for that reason this phantasy could be hailed as a message of redemption (*evangelium*). A son of God had allowed himself to be killed without guilt and had thus taken on himself the guilt of all men. It had to be a son, since it had been the murder of a father.

The ambivalence of the father complex, however, permeates Christian doctrine also. Meant to propitiate the murdered father, the murdered son nevertheless dethrones the father once again and creates a new religion in his own image.

In what sense do actual historical events lie behind the origins of religion and the rise of monotheism? I have argued previously that the dubious empirical status of the phylogenetic hypothesis is wrapped up with Freud's attempt to account for the universality of infantile Oedipal experiences by postulating actual Oedipal crimes in the primal horde, memory of which is somehow inherited by children. Doubt about such a hypothesis rested both on the impossibility of explaining how memory of actual events could be inherited and also on the absence of independent evidence for the occurrence of the alleged primal crime.

In **Totem and Taboo,** Freud seems to recognize these difficulties. He comes down only tentatively on the side of the primal crime as a historical event, "without laying claim to any finality of judgment. . . ." An alternative account is equally plausible. The mere hostile *impulse* against the father, the mere existence of a wishful *fantasy* of killing

and devouring him, "would have been enough to produce the moral reaction that created totemism and taboo."

Freud's writings on religion and history here reach a moment in 1912 parallel to what he had experienced at the turn of the century with his analysis of hysterics. Although he first regarded his patients' tales of childhood seduction or abuse as literal recollections, Freud finally came to believe he was dealing with unconscious wishes creating fantasies with all the force of reality to the patient. After this moment, psychoanalysis as theory as well as therapy centered on an "explanation of the stability, efficacy and relatively coherent nature of the subject's phantasy life."

Freud's final response to whether he is dealing with fact or fantasy on the historical level is revealing and in accord with the argument put forward earlier against Freud's reliance on mythological prehistory. "[T]he distinction, which may seem fundamental to other people, does not in our judgment affect the heart of the matter." In the beginning could be either the deed or the dream. If the brothers actually killed their father repeatedly in history, that, coupled with their ambivalence about such acts, would serve to explain the remorse that drove them toward the prohibitions of totemism. On the other hand, if our primitive ancestors, like today's children, only fancied the Oedipal crimes, those fantasies would still have been historically real and powerful; they would still have served to conjure up guilt and the Oedipal contents of religion. To call something a fantasy in psychoanalysis is not at all to dismiss it as unreal, a mistake, a powerless illusion.

Religion, for Freud, always remained the clearest example of culture's own illness, an accepted way of being moral and social which psychoanalysis nevertheless finds objectionable. Religion qualifies as the deepest social obstacle to human liberation. Just as an individual hides from reality inside his neurotic symptoms, so a whole people hides through its rituals, personifications, and anthropomorphisms. The collective repression of the Oedipal complex is no better than its individual repression. Both lead to a guilty refusal to acknowledge, let alone transform, the aggressive and sexual attractions of humanity. Religious pacification of guilt is an endless, obsessive repetition of the infantile attitude toward the father.

And yet one positive aspect of a communal neurosis is that it saves individuals the trouble of manufacturing their own personal sickness. Religion can, and once did, stave off guilt as well as foment it. Religion can save as well as condemn. This dual nature of religion's relation to guilt can be seen in the split which opened between the theory and practice of Calvinism, as outlined by Max Weber in his classic *The Protestant Ethic and the Spirit of Capitalism.* As a doctrine, Calvin's notion of predestination could succeed only in aggravating man's anxiety on the question of salvation. What after all could represent more of a return of guilt in history than the notion of the inscrutable, unreachable God who wills our fate freely without regard to our actions? In parish practice, however, Calvinism came to offer more certain knowledge of one's salvation from sin—through the "election" signified by the ascetic but energetic pursuit of one's worldly tasks. To be a Calvinist in practice was to be a member of a group who reinforced each other's sense of mutual salvation. Calvinism may have created anxious minds, but anxious minds also adopted Calvinism to salve their own anxiety.

But in his own age and among his patients, Freud thought that religious illusion was no longer even a saving lie. Religious culture in a scientific age had little imperative value, provided none of the old psychological reassurances. To the contrary: Freud saw nothing as more responsible for aggravating his patients' private neuroses than the dogmas of the priests. Religion had now gone over entirely to the side of guilt, demanding instinctual renunciation while providing no compensatory feeling of grace. Freud's patients lived in the worst of all possible religious worlds, a hypocritical one where churches extracted guilt without belief, obedience but not faith. And the force of religion sans faith is the force of repression outright.

There was no question in Freud's mind that humanity's long experiment with religion was ending and was ending in failure. This prolonged infantile answer to the nature of the universe, this mass delusion, this "neurotic phase" of civilization, had been dealt a fatal blow by empirical science and by psychoanalysis itself. Phrases which make the project of human liberation depend on the abolition of religion abound in Freud. Religion and its techniques are "neurotic relics," "an historical residue." A "turning-away from religion is bound to occur with the fatal inevitability of a process of growth. . . ." Its "infantilism is destined to be surmounted."

What makes religion the "infantile phase" of culture is its refusal to accept nature as a realm of law and necessity, its escape instead into the omnipotence of a God. Freud's irreverent sense of freedom leads him to replace God the Almighty with another god, known by its ancient name:

> Our God [Logos] will fulfill whichever . . . wishes nature outside us allows, but he will do it very gradually, only in the unforeseeable future, and for a new generation of men. He promises no compensation for us, who suffer grievously from life.

Logos and *Ananke* (necessity): these become the only guardians of nature Freud himself would allow. Resignation to natural law replaces the consolation of faith as psychoanalysis replaces religion. Here, Freud takes as his model the great Leonardo da Vinci. Leonardo the master painter and scientist was also a spiritual man in the sense that he expressed awe at the wonder of creation. But his appeal to Freud lies in his refusal to explore this awe through a personal relation with God. "The reflections in which he has recorded the deep wisdom of his last years of life breathe the resignation of the human being who subjects himself to . . . the laws of nature, and who expects no alleviation from the goodness or grace of God."

For Freud, nothing essential attaches culture to conventional religion any longer; we have nothing to lose but our illusions. Those Cassandras who counsel caution, who tell us only religion keeps the masses in line, who predict the end of culture with the end of religion, have it backward. With the alleged truth out about God, Freud sees civiliza-

tion running a greater risk if it maintains the present attitude toward religion than if it gives it up altogether. The "great mass of the uneducated and oppressed," Freud writes, already "have every reason for being enemies of civilization." When they hear of God's death,

> [i]s there not a danger here that the hostility of these masses to civilization will throw itself against the weak spot that they have found in their task-mistress? If the sole reason why you must not kill your neighbour is because God has forbidden it and will severely punish you for it in this or the next life—then, when you learn that there is no God and that you need not fear His punishment, you will certainly kill your neighbour without hesitation, and you can only be prevented from doing so by mundane force. Thus either these dangerous masses must be held down most severely and kept most carefully away from any chance of intellectual awakening, or else the relationship between civilization and religion must undergo a fundamental revision.

The "fundamental revision" for which Freud speaks is the passage of humanity from religious morality to rational ethics. All those instinctual renunciations that religion has traditionally enforced—we must publish the reasons for them or let them perish:

> [W]e may now argue that the time has probably come, as it does in an analytic treatment, for replacing the effects of repression by the results of the rational operation of the intellect. We may foresee, but hardly regret, that such a process of remoulding will not stop at renouncing the solemn transfiguration of cultural precepts, but that a general revision of them will result in many of them being done away with. In this way our appointed task of reconciling men to civilization will to a great extent be achieved.

How, then, are we to bring about, on a large scale, a morality of reason rather than repression? This is the great task psychoanalysis can yet set itself. But before following Freud in his attempt to outline how the "rational operation of intellect" would work, we must note Freud's questionable assumption that religion and rationality are mutually exclusive categories.

Consider, by way of analogy, Freud's discussion of the psychology of love. Like the devout meeting God, lovers meet in a thicket of Oedipal motives. At times, Freud wields the category of motives to make love sound hopelessly pathological or "duplicitous," in Rieff's term—as when Freud writes that we are condemned to love only those who resemble ourselves or our mothers or fathers.

Suppose a person were to ask Freud, "What will happen to my love of my spouse if you convince me my motives for seeking out this relationship are deviously Oedipal?" Freud could not answer for certain. It might be that a lover could not embrace his or her former feelings once the motive for loving had become clarified. But it is also possible and even likely that the person's motives do not exhaust the love, that grounds of love exist capable of surviving conscious and rational reflection on how the love began. If this were not conceded by Freud, then he would have no psychology, only a psychopathology of love.

Freud's conclusions ought to be similar in regard to religion and its relation to human freedom. One form of religion—the neurotic form—cannot withstand psychoanalysis, any more than could the deathly form of conscience Freud traced out in individuals. Once revealed, the Oedipal obsession with God the Father becomes unstable, and the believer finds his faith, to this extent, groundless. In debunking these motives for religion, Freud thus classically aids our search for freedom as independence, for autonomous action and a break with the "authority of the past."

But all this does not mean there could not remain grounds for continued belief in religion even after our motives for belief became transparent. There could be, this is to assert, a form of religious commitment whose basis we could consciously affirm. Freud typically does not allow for this. He writes as if rationality demands a strict choice between itself and any form of religious attachment.

At the beginning of *Civilization and Its Discontents,* Freud takes up this question of rationally reconstructed religion. The subject matter of *The Future of an Illusion,* he acknowledges, was limited to

> what the common man understands by his religion— . . . the system of doctrines and promises which on the one hand explains to him the riddles of this world with enviable completeness, and, on the other, assures him that a careful Providence will watch over his life and will compensate him in a future existence for any frustrations he suffers here.

Philosophers and large numbers of others sense that *such* a religion is untenable but "nevertheless try to defend it piece by piece in a series of pitiful rearguard actions." They "think they can rescue the God of religion by replacing him with an impersonal, shadowy and abstract principle. . . . " But

> [t]he common man cannot imagine . . . Providence otherwise than in the figure of an enormously exalted father. Only such a being can understand the needs of the children of men and be softened by their prayers and placated by the signs of their remorse. The whole thing is so patently infantile, so foreign to reality, that to anyone with a friendly attitude to humanity it is painful to think that the great majority of mortals will never be able to rise above this view of life.

Thus Freud shunts aside the question of rational commitment to religion as simply not relevant to what gives religion its mass appeal. At the same time, in *Civilization and Its Discontents,* Freud returns to the question of whether he has gotten the origins of this mass appeal right in his prior works. He recounts the response of a friend to whom he had sent a copy of *The Future of an Illusion.* While "entirely agree[ing] with my judgment upon religion," Freud writes,

> he was sorry I had not properly appreciated the true source of religious sentiments. This . . . consists in a peculiar feeling, which he himself

is never without, which he finds confirmed by many others, and which he may suppose is present in millions of people. It is a feeling which he would like to call a sensation of "eternity," a feeling as of something limitless, unbounded—as it were, "oceanic." This feeling, he adds, is a purely subjective fact, not an article of faith; it brings with it no assurance of personal immortality, but it is the source of the religious energy which is seized upon by the various Churches and religious systems. . . . One may, he thinks, rightly call oneself religious on the ground of this oceanic feeling alone, even if one rejects every belief and every illusion.

Freud begins his public response to this friendly criticism cautiously. He "cannot discover this 'oceanic' feeling" in himself, and it "is not easy to deal scientifically with feelings." But "this gives me no right to deny that [this feeling] does in fact occur in other people." What, then, does the feeling referred to consist in?

> If I have understood my friend rightly, he means . . . a feeling of an indissoluble bond, of being one with the external world as a whole. . . . [He means] an intimation of [one's] connection with the world . . . through an immediate feeling. . . .

But even granted the reality of such oceanic sensation, the notion that it is primary and irreducible ("immediate") is an interpretation psychoanalysis disputes and dares to challenge with its preference for genetic explanations. In religion, just as in love, oceanic feelings of the above sort are traceable back to an early stage of "ego-feeling" that must have accompanied the infant's as yet blurry sense of its distinction from the external world. And if

> we may assume that there are many people in whose mental life this primary ego-feeling has persisted to a greater or less degree, it would exist in them side by side with the narrower and more sharply demarcated ego-feeling of maturity, like a kind of counterpart to it. In that case, the ideational contents appropriate to it would be precisely those of limitlessness and of a bond with the universe—the same ideas with which my friend elucidated the "oceanic" feeling.

So explained as but an infantile relic irretrievable within the bounds set by the reality principle, the use of oceanic feelings to console man with the conventionally religious notion of eternity once again stands exposed, as Freud's friend had already acknowledged. However, Freud was not content to leave his response to his friend at this. For the notion that religious need is at bottom a need to retrieve a state of intimate attachment with others carries with it a hidden affirmation of religion, stripped of its illusions and mythic elaborations. Thus Freud characteristically disputes the claim of oceanic feelings to be the source of religiosity; "the part played by the oceanic feeling . . . is ousted from a place in the foreground" by the even stronger need which Freud had isolated in *The Future of an Illusion* and which he now reiterates to his friend:

> [A] feeling can only be a source of energy if it is itself the expression of a strong need. The derivation of religious needs from the infant's helpless-

ness and the longing for the father aroused by it seems to me incontrovertible, especially since the feeling is not simply prolonged from childhood days, but is permanently sustained by fear of the superior power of Fate. I cannot think of any need in childhood as strong as the need for a father's protection. . . . Thus . . . [t]he origin of the religious attitude can be traced back in clear outlines as far as the feeling of infantile helplessness. . . . There may be something further behind that, but for the present it is wrapped in obscurity.

Comprehended as parasitic on the theme of infantile helplessness, religion lacks its affirmative moment; it stands revealed in Freud's mind as pejoratively perpetuated infantilism.

In and of itself, Freud's rejection of religion might not be of much import in our modern scientific age. What is of more concern is the ideal of human liberation behind the rejection. Freud stands in danger of reducing all our moral and political beliefs, all our allegiances and felt belongings, to the infantile-obsessive sort. Whether in his psychology of love or politics or religion, we have seen Freud always at least partly sour about the need for consolation or "oceanic feeling." Psychoanalysis enters upon the scene in the name of resignation to a reality that offers no final deliverance from our sufferings.

But as is typical in Freud, an affirmative teaching breaks through his own resigned pessimism. In the same year as **Civilization and Its Discontents'** publication, **Totem and Taboo** received its first Hebrew translation. Freud added a surprising and moving preface to this edition, which begins as follows:

> No reader [of the Hebrew version of] this book will find it easy to put himself in the emotional position of an author who is ignorant of the language of holy writ, who is completely estranged from the religion of his fathers—as well as from every other religion—and who cannot take a share in nationalist ideals, but who has yet never repudiated his people, who feels that he is in his essential nature a Jew and who has no desire to alter that nature. If the question were put to him: "Since you have abandoned all these common characteristics of your countrymen, what is there left to you that is Jewish?" he would reply: "A very great deal, and probably its very essence."

This passage makes clear that Freud's attitude toward the survival of his own religious identity after God's death is more complex than his theory allowed. About himself, Freud understood that his complete estrangement from "the religion of his fathers" did not likewise estrange him from the religious loyalties and identifications that had long since become implicated in his own identity. Even as atheist and nonnationalist, Freud affirmed the virtue of his earthly, political bond to his "people," his "countrymen." The very "essence" of Judaism as a common identity survived God, and Freud had no desire to "repudiate" but on the contrary affirmed the "common characteristics" among Jews he could not abandon without at the same time abandoning deep parts of himself.

For Freud to recognize autobiographically that religious conviction and communal loyalty play a positive role in giving content and depth to a human character is for him to draw back from his usual tone of mistrust about communal feelings, whether of the religious or political variety. As on all questions of "psychosynthesis," Freud thus finally gives no determinate answer on the earthly future of religion. The "religion of the fathers," the religion of mass appeal: these forms Freud thought he had analyzed in a way that rendered them bankrupt. But he leaves open the possibility that others will follow his own example in discovering a rational allegiance to their defining religious tradition, even after being psychoanalytically dispossessed of their infantile forms of faith. (pp. 67-82)

> *Jeffrey B. Abramson, in his* Liberation and Its Limits: The Moral and Political Thought of Freud, *The Free Press, 1984, 160 p.*

Elizabeth Wright   (essay date 1984)

[*In the following excerpt from her* Psychoanalytic Criticism: Theory in Practice, *Wright traces the origins of psychoanalytic criticism to Freud's theory of dreams and discusses Freud's speculations on art.*]

Dreams have a privileged place in Freud's metapsychology: 'the interpretation of dreams is the royal road to a knowledge of unconscious activities of the mind'. As a result of investigating them, in himself and his patients, he found himself more and more engaged with conflict and the overlapping of interpretations. Dreams, *par excellence,* reveal themselves to be boundary phenomena, in that they occur where intentions are in opposition, where bodily desires have to come to terms with society. (pp. 17-8)

In the condition of sleep the force of repression, according to Freud, is relaxed, because there is no immediate likelihood of unconscious impulse being carried through into dangerous action. Constraint is still operative in that the incursions of what is repressed are deflected from action, that is, from awakening the sleeper. This is why Freud calls dreams 'the GUARDIANS of sleep and not its disturbers'. This view has now been challenged as an empirical hypothesis by the fact that dreams have been shown to be regularly occurring events during a distinct state of sleep, with the implication that dreaming is something given which may be capitalized upon by unconscious impulses, not something which is *causally dependent* on being a dual creation of impulse and repressing force. However, the duality, and moreover the ambiguity, of dreams remains. It is Freud's vigorous exploration of the workings of these ambiguities that is of special relevance for the language of the arts, and for the activities of reading, writing and criticism. All the arts deal in illusion and Freud's exploration of the ruses and stratagems of the psyche is of immediate relevance to aesthetic experience, at the level of both the medium (the sounds and colours of the dream) and its interpretation. (p. 18)

According to Freud, the energizing force of dreams springs from an unconscious impulse seeking fulfilment, a desire not fulfilled in waking life. Unable to find expression in action, the impulse gathers to itself material both from recent experience, such as the effects of present bodily need plus the recollections of the previous day (the 'day's residues'), and from distant memories involving infantile sexual wishes. An unconscious wish meets up with a preconscious thought and strives for an illusory satisfaction. But the 'censorship', the force of repression, at the frontier between unconscious and preconscious will not allow these powerfully charged memories to reach representation in their original form. Instead, under the influence of this censorship, the material is transformed into a series of images, that is the dream. Hence Freud's dictum: 'A dream is a (disguised) fulfilment of a (suppressed or repressed) wish'. The disguise may be total as regards the judgement of the dreamer, or it may be insufficient. In either case, the repressed material has both reacted to and evaded censorship by this encoding into a not immediately recognizable form. Hence Freud calls the dream a 'compromise' between the demands of impulse and the intensity of the repressing force. The more intense the force of repression, the more obscure the encodings: the distortions of the material present in the dream are thus traceable to the power of the censorship.

The apparent irrationality of the dream is not only traceable to the resistance to censorship of the unconscious material. That material is already in a form to which the word 'rational' cannot be applied. It is subject to the flow of the primary process, that activity of unconscious desire, whereby an impulse seeks the repetition of achieved satisfaction by finding again the perception that accompanied it: more is included in the perception than the conscious mind can recognize. Hence this perceptual sorting is not some pre-given recognition but a perceptual 'identifying' of sensory patterns, complexes of colour, shape and sound across time, that do not necessarily correspond to what the repressing force, involved in the secondary process, takes as identical. Linkages made in the (unconscious) primary process are already absurd from the point of view of the conscious mind, and these have a profound effect upon the dream. It is therefore difficult to understand precisely the distinction, if it is indeed viable, between the irrational connections pre-existing in the primary process and the 'distortions' insisted on by the censorship. The mechanisms involved seem to serve at one and the same time a subversive purpose (primary process functioning) and a defensive purpose (the censorship of the dream-work). As Freud said, 'in any case the censorship profits from it'. When a patient reports a dream later, the rationality of daytime experiences gives the censoring force another opportunity, in that it can impose on the apparent absurdity of the dream-sequence a narrative sense and coherence, what Freud calls 'secondary revision'. This further distortion-towards-coherence represents another clue from the mode of the actual censoring as to what is being repressed. It would be a mistake, however, to view the question as being an exclusive distinction between the subversions of the primary process (its determination to have its wishes fulfilled) and the distortions of the secondary process (its determination to prevent those wishes from being realized). It is much more a matter of the two forces in some way interacting simultaneously, though Freud himself did not reach this theoretical position, in that he

kept primary process and secondary process separate. It is precisely this lacuna in Freud which led to the polarization between id-psychology and ego-psychology and the consequent opposing literary-critical positions.

Nevertheless, Freud's discussion of the individual mechanisms of the dream-work show him to be operating with a concept of ambiguity. It is significant, and has been remarked upon before, that in *The Interpretation of Dreams* Freud is nowhere engaged in tracking down the repressed infantile wish. What Freud is interested in is not the same old primal wish, but the forms taken by the language of desire, that which he calls the 'dream-work'. (pp. 19-20)

According to Freud, 'the first achievement of the dream-work is *condensation*. By that we understand the fact that the manifest dream has a smaller content than the latent one, and is thus an abbreviated translation of it'. But this is far from being a simple process of the mere omission of elements. Composite figures and structures are formed so that as little as possible is left out. Hence the concept of 'overdetermination', whereby several latent wishes converge on one manifest item, or the reverse, where one wish is represented a number of times in the same dream-sequence. The result in each case is a superimposition of elements. This ambiguity is most clearly demonstrable in the way condensation treats words or names. A thing with one name may be associated in a dream with an event with a similar name, even though neither *word* occurred in the dream. Freud relates a case, where someone dreamt that *'his uncle gave him a kiss in an automobile.'* He went on at once to give me the interpretation, which I myself would never have guessed: namely that it meant 'auto-erotism'. The co-presence of the car and the kiss matches the linking of the two parts of the term 'auto-erotism' (inducing sexual pleasure in one's own body). Condensation is also one of the essential features of the joke since, as the above example shows, it produces an ambiguous word in which two thoughts come together. In his book on jokes Freud quotes a saying that old people tend to fall into their 'anecdotage'. Here condensation creates a neologism: the phonetic sequence /dout/ is the element where two meanings coincide—anec*dote* and *dot*age. Instead of saying that old people bore us with their endless stories in their old age, the two ideas are condensed into one sound-unit.

Rational associations with words can be disrupted even more markedly. It is in the nature of the primary process that the distinction between word-as-symbol and word-as-actual-sound can sometimes be wholly ignored. Words, which as sounds have an auditory form, are things in their own right, and associations can be made between the word-as-thing and the thing for which it stands. This is what happens in the case of the schizophrenic, where something in his experience has attracted a chain of associations onto a noise, and the actual word/thing distinction disappears altogether; the world gets sorted out according to private symbols instead of public ones. It is because absurdities of this kind occur in the dreams of normal persons that Freud was able to demonstrate that the unconscious has its own mode of operation.

The second activity of the dream-work is *displacement*, which, according to Freud, 'might equally be described [in

Nietzsche's phrase] as "a transvaluation of psychical values" '. This transvaluation is achieved by the elements in the manifest dream replacing elements in the latent dream-thoughts via a chain of associations for the purpose of disguise; this results in the intensity of an idea becoming detached from it and passing to other ideas, which in themselves are of little value. There is also the consequence that the manifest dream has a different centre from the dream-thoughts and does not reflect their relative importance: indeed they need not appear in the dream at all. Freud regards displacement as 'the most powerful instrument of the dream-censorship'. Displacement too has an affinity with the mechanisms of the joke in that a switch of context affords a play on words whereby the dream work achieves its forced and often far-fetched linkages. One such example is cited by Freud and concerns a patient caught up in a series of dreams, in which her father, whom she recently lost, reappears. In this particular dream the father said: 'It's a quarter past eleven, it's half past eleven, it's quarter to twelve.' To this she made associations that her father set great store on punctuality, but this did not explain the source of the dream. Another chain of associations, apparently unconnected with the dream, led to a remark which occurred in a conversation she had heard the previous day: 'The *Urmensch* [primal man] survives in all of us.' This had provided her with the pretext to bring her dead father back to life, for she had turned him into an *Uhrmensch* [clockman] by making him proclaim the regular passing of the quarter hours. The displacement here consists of a shift of association between the authoritarian father who insisted on punctuality and the clock to which he repeatedly made reference. What was associated with the father is shifted onto the telling of the quarters, in itself a trivial event. This example also illustrates the occurrence of condensation and displacement together, for not only is there a displacement from father to the recurrence of the quarters, but there is a pun between *Ur-* (primal) and *Uhr-* (clock). A number of displacements onto one element of itself produces condensation and facilitates overdetermination. Displacement and condensation are thus not exclusive and there is no limit to the modes of their occurrence. (pp. 21-3)

Both condensation and displacement can produce visual and auditory images for abstract thoughts, thus contributing to the actual process of representation in dreams. *Considerations of representability,* the way the dream-thoughts achieve representation in the dream via images, is the third activity of the dream-work. Freud stresses the affinity of this process to what already obtains in language. Just as words are created by appeal to sensory items, so latent material becomes imaged by them. The German for 'adultery' is *Ehebruch,* literally 'breach of marriage': 'you will forgive the dream-work for replacing an element so hard to put into pictures . . . by another breach—a broken leg [*Beinbruch*]'. The representation is a strange language, however, in that it is divested of logical and syntactical relations. It is nearer to a rebus, a series of ideograms or pictographs, in which the syntactical connections are left to be made by the dreamer. The dream has its own order of relations, which can be deduced from the visual elements that actually appear. Contradictions can coexist in an image, for one image can stand for the opposite poles of

conflict. Freud cites the phenomenon found by philologists that there are a number of words which are used equally for opposite meanings (Latin *sacer* meaning both 'sacred' and 'profane'). One thing that is the cause of another might appear in a close temporal sequence but without the causal relation being demonstrated. A chronological succession of events might be turned into an image containing them all in spatial proximity. All these transformations of rational linkages are accompanied by regression to infantile modes of thought and feeling.

Representations also make use of symbols that are independent of the individual dreamer, deriving from a variety of cultural sources: they either already have a fixed conventional meaning or else they are 'typical symbols' that recur in the reports of a large number of patients. In the first case, some feature of a familiar legend may make its appearance; in the second, there is a common identification of the male sexual organ with upright objects, and of the mother's body with horizontal ones or with enclosures of all kinds. The interpretation of such 'typical symbols' has led to what has become known as 'vulgar Freudian symbolism': a given and rigid code in which all images have a specific bodily association. Freud, while under the influence of Wilhelm Stekel, did accord a greater place to the conventional symbol, but in the course of his clinical practice he rejected such a mechanical approach, asserting that the interpretation of any symbol, however public, has to be mediated by the context in which it is found: 'as with Chinese script, the correct interpretation should be arrived at on each occasion from the context'. Freud was thus no vulgar Freudian, even though as analyst he could not ignore the stock-in-trade of familiar symbols that are present in the culture.

The analyst is not the first interpreter of the dream: in narrating a dream the dreamer already acts as his own biased interpreter. *Secondary revision* is logically the last distorting activity of the dream-work. It can occur in the course of the dream, in that the censorship may already be singling out and emphasizing certain elements of the dream, operating 'simultaneously in a conducive and selective sense upon the mass of material present in the dream-thoughts'. But secondary revision or 'elaboration', as Freud also called it, is most obviously at work when the dream is presented in the form of a verbal account. The conscious mind prefers to put the irrational dream-sequence into recognizable and familiar logical order, involving a further distortion of the 'distortion' already achieved by the three mechanisms discussed above. This final revision is in the form of a gestalt-switch in that the dream-sequence is not altered, but the sorting of it is. The 'intelligible pattern' which the conscious mind wants to impose on the visual material can ignore or falsify what is patently there, in the manner of a reader who is so engaged in the text that he ignores the misprints. What was visible to the mind's eye in the dream remains unchanged, but the conscious perspective produces a re-vision of it. The material is ignored in the determination to arrive at an acceptable rational narrative: the ready-made formulations of the dream are abandoned, and new ones are made of the very same material. One might illustrate this with an example from Afferbeck Lauder's *Let Stalk Strine,* the comic guide to Australian pronunciation, taking the phrase 'Baked Necks'. The first clue, the actual letters as spelled out, suggest that a curious Australian cooked meat is being offered—perhaps an exotic 'prepared neck-end of lamb'. This clue is subverted in the context by the rival second clues that follow: 'A popular breakfast dish. Others include emma necks; scremblex; and fright shops'. This is a fair analogy for the process of secondary revision: a first interpretation of a visual experience (the letters) was 'revised' by its being placed in a new context. In the patient/dreamer's account the censorship in its conflict with the primary process overlooks in its secondary revision obvious contextual clues. Secondary revision shows that it is a danger for all systematic thinking to ignore elements that do not fit into a desired pattern. Reading shares this danger with the reporting of a dream. Boundaries shift with contextual placings of the visual material of the dream or of any symbolic medium, including what we call art: the rivalry of interpretations both within subjects (conscious versus unconscious) and between subjects (teller versus hearer) remains a common characteristic of dream and art, in whatever other respects they may differ.

Although Freud's essays on art and literature are admired for their elegant exposition, they have not, until fairly recently, received much serious critical attention. This is because in the past these writings have been invoked reductively, quoted selectively against his aesthetic argument as a whole. He relates art to the dream, along a path that leads 'from the investigation of dreams to the analysis of works of imagination and ultimately to the analysis of their creators—writers and artists themselves'. He relates the artist to the neurotic, this being his most notorious statement:

> An artist is once more in rudiments an introvert, not far removed from neurosis. He is oppressed by excessively powerful instinctual needs. He desires to win honour, power, love, wealth, fame and the love of women; but he lacks the means of achieving these satisfactions.

Finally, the object of the whole enterprise is the fulfilment of an infantile wish: 'In the exercising of an art it [psychoanalysis] sees once again an activity intended to allay ungratified wishes—in the first place in the creative artist himself and subsequently in his audience or spectators'. Id-psychological criticism is founded on these reductions: the content of the wish is paramount and as a consequence a direct relation between the artist and the work is presupposed and usually made the centre of the inquiry.

The key question around which these issues circle, 'from what sources that strange being, the creative writer, draws his material, and how he manages to make such an impression on us and arouse in us emotions of which, perhaps, we had not even thought ourselves capable' has not stirred many minds outside psychoanalytic circles. The question is confined to motivation: it asks about the nature of the subject and not about the value of the object. It would therefore seem to testify to the inferiority of the psychological approach to aesthetics as compared to the philosophical. In the past this kind of argument has been influential, but more recently Paul Ricoeur and Richard Wollheim have argued for the relevance and modesty of Freud's investigations into aesthetics. Freud does not profess to deal with the question of aesthetic criteria: 'Before the problem of the creative artist analysis must, alas, lay down its arms'. Throughout his work he never departs from this view.

In **'Creative writers and Day-dreaming'** (1908) Freud frankly admits that psychoanalysis cannot say how the artist achieves his 'innermost secret'. Ricoeur takes this essay as a prototype to argue that these writings on art are fragmentary in a highly systematic way. First, Freud proceeds by a series of analogies. Far from being reductive, these analogies make up the organizing principle of Freud's essays on art. By a series of displacements he works from the child at play, to the writer's fantasy-world, to the novelist's hero, bringing together dream and fiction in their joint function of fulfilling a wish. But Freud, as Ricoeur points out, also distinguishes daydream from artistic creation, by including the role of play, which goes beyond hallucinatory wish-fulfilment, and by stressing that the daydream makes use of the relation of fantasy to time, by taking 'an occasion in the present to construct, on the pattern of the past, a picture of the future'. Second, Freud has something to say about how the pleasure the artist gives us (from 'what we are inclined to take to be his personal daydreams' is connected with the dynamics of the work of art, and this Ricoeur sees as the systematic aim of the Freudian aesthetic. Variously interpreted, there is no doubt that this theory has been an all-pervasive influence within psychoanalytic applied criticism. Dreams and art are not merely linked because they fulfil wishes, but because both have to make use of strategies in order to overcome the resistance of consciousness: 'work' is done by the dreamer and the artist to transform their primitive desires into culturally acceptable meanings. In order to undermine our resistance, the artist masks his egoistic daydream and at the same time lures us with the

> purely formal—that is, aesthetic—yield of pleasure which he offers us in the presentation of his phantasies. We give the name of *incentive bonus,* or *fore-pleasure,* to a yield of pleasure such as this, which is offered to us so as to make possible the release of still greater pleasure arising from deeper psychical sources.

For this Freud has continued to come under fire, not only from aestheticians and literary critics, but also from the proponents of ego-psychology, who wish to argue that aesthetic form has to do with the ego's attempt to maintain and extend its boundaries over the id. Freud is damned out of his own mouth: 'In **"Creative Writers and Day-Dreaming"**, Freud reduced form and beauty to resistance and defence . . . Form sugar-coats an offensive content, bribing critical powers with aesthetic pleasure (analogous to sexual forepleasure)'. While this school must be given credit for its attempts to relate form and content, it makes art, as will be seen, into an altogether fervent and solemn affair. It ignores the connection between the technique of the work of art and the effect of pleasure it produces, which Freud here adumbrates, albeit in a reductive fashion. For a full elaboration of his theory one needs to look at Freud's work on the technique of jokes, where the connection between the fore-pleasure generated (by the word-play) and the deeper instinctual pleasure released is brought out. The saving of the repression, the needless expenditure which gives rise to laughter, can only occur by means of the linguistic devices the 'joke-work' employs in order to divert the attention of those involved in the joke.

Freud does not stop at asking where the artist gets his material and how he achieves his effects; he is also interested in the devices whereby the wish gets through. In an essay entitled 'Freud and the understanding of art', Richard Wollheim examines what part these devices play in Freud's view of art. He argues that Freud was fully aware of the difference between treating art as biographical evidence and treating it as an aesthetic object. The essay entitled **'Leonardo da Vinci and a memory of his childhood'** is first and foremost an attempt at psychobiography, whereby Freud wishes to trace the continuing effects of sexuality as experienced in childhood on the adult life of a great man. In the course of tracing his subject's complex history Freud purports to explain why Leonardo turned from art to science and why even his homosexuality was present merely in an idealized form. Freud's study is rooted somewhat tenuously in a supposed 'childhood memory' of Leonardo's, a 'vulture' that opens the infant's mouth with its tail (and which turns out to be a mistranslation of the word *nibio,* meaning kite). He relates these biographical findings (which do not depend on the species of bird in any significant way) to certain of Leonardo's paintings, the *Mona Lisa* and the *Madonna and Child with St Anne.* As Wollheim stresses, Freud does not derive his biographical evidence from the paintings: he finds contextual information embedded within them which he decodes with the help of the findings already established. As regards the *Mona Lisa,* Freud argues that the smile condenses two images of Leonardo's first mother, one signifying tenderness and reserve, the other sensuality and seduction. As regards the other picture, both natural mother and equally loved stepmother are present and linked in a pyramidal structure; here the enigmatic smile can be read on both faces, doubly condensed in dreamlike fusion. The focus is thus on processes whereby a conflict of meanings can be discerned within the work itself: in psychoanalytic terms a wish, to yield to the tenderness of the mother, is confronted by a defence, the danger of yielding to this wish. In artistic terms there is an ambiguous element the viewer cannot account for, what has been called 'the daemonic magic of this smile'.

Dreams and fantasies require a frame of reference, the associations the dreamer/patient is expected to bring to them, that make salient their ambiguity for the analyst. The work of art has already itself provided that ambiguity. In his study of Jensen's story *Gradiva* Freud feels justified in investigating 'the class of dreams that have never been dreamt at all—dreams created by imaginative writers and ascribed to invented characters in the course of a story'. He finds all the associative elements in the story itself; his interpretation in no way depends on the intention of the author, conscious or otherwise. This is not to deny that Freud was primarily interested in the several ways in which the story corroborated his theories: indeed he treats it as an allegory of psychoanalysis, with patient as hero,

analyst as heroine, and analytic setting as archaeological building-site. The clinical object of Freud's study may be summarized as four-fold; the fourth point brings together psychoanalytic and aesthetic ambiguity.

First, Freud plays on the obvious analogy between archaeology and psychoanalytical investigation, a favoured image to which he returns again and again. In *Gradiva,* the hero, Norbert Hanold, is an archaeologist who is investigating the buried remains of a city, Pompeii, and also, unknowingly, his ' "buried" childhood'.

Second, the story illustrates for Freud what he regards as one of the cornerstones of his theory, the return of the repressed: 'There is, in fact, no better analogy for repression, by which something in the mind is at once made inaccessible and preserved, than burial of the sort to which Pompeii fell a victim and from which it could emerge once more through the work of the spade'. In the story the hero is wholly absorbed in his studies and has turned away from life and its pleasures. As Freud puts it, the emotions he is unable to give to women of flesh and blood he gives to women of marble and bronze. His fantasies come to centre upon a Roman relief and grow into a full-scale delusion. The sculpture is of a girl stepping out in an idiosyncratic way, whom he therefore names Gradiva, 'the walking one'. After searching for her in vain in his native city, Vienna, he has an anxiety-dream in which he sees her in Pompeii, where he had assigned her in his fantasy, as she lies down and is buried by a fall of rubble. Like the hero of Thomas Mann's *Death in Venice,* Hanold is now driven by 'an inner restlessness and dissatisfaction' to seek an uncertain destination until he finally 'finds himself' in Pompeii. There he is disgusted by the presence of couples all about him and soon his thoughts and feelings drift from the moderate carnality of mating couples to the gross animality of copulating houseflies. When he sees his Gradiva in flesh and blood he knows at last what drove him to Pompeii. Subsequently it becomes clear that Hanold's fantasy is not a hallucination, but derives from the repressed memories of his childhood, 'a kind of forgetting which is distinguished by the difficulty with which the memory is awakened even by a powerful external summons, as though some internal resistance were struggling against its revival'. What Freud is interested in is not the mere fact of the return of the repressed, but in 'the highly remarkable manner of that return'. The instrument used to repress the unconscious, the name Gradiva, becomes the very means by which the repression is subverted. The unconscious fulfils the wish by means of a trick: 'Gradiva' turns out to be the translation into Latin of the repressed surname of Hanold's childhood love, Zoe Bertgang, meaning 'one who steps along brightly'.

Third, Freud wishes to show (and this is what first draws him to this story) that dreams have a meaning and can be interpreted. Though they cannot foretell the future, as antiquity would have it, they do have intentional significance; when the dream-text is finally revealed it represents the wishes of the dreamer as fulfilled. The creative writer, Freud says with one of his favourite gestures, knows better than the scientist. Dreams are not mere somatic stimuli, but have sense and purpose: they are 'the physiological delusions of normal people', giving access to the unconscious. But can literary dreams be analysed, when there is no dreamer to supply the associations for each piece of the manifest dream? Freud says this can be done by dint of 'borrowing' from his *Interpretation of Dreams.*

One of the principles he laid down is that some element in the dream is a piece of reality. Taking Hanold's first dream, in which Hanold is in Pompeii at the same time as Gradiva, Freud transcribes this circumstance as signifying 'the girl he was looking for was living in a town and contemporaneously with him'. This is true inasmuch as it applies to Zoe Bertgang, the real elements being 'in a town contemporaneously with him'. But it is a displacement by way of a double reversal, because in the dream Hanold is living at the same time and in the same place as the historical Gradiva, whereas in 'reality' (the story's empirical world), she is living in *his* time and place, the Vienna of his day. It is this displacement which enabled the repressed wish to get through. According to Freud's dream theory there is a current wish which attaches itself to a wish to do with the past. In this case, the admissible wish of the archaeologist, 'to have been present as an eyewitness at the catastrophe in the year 79 A.D.,' attached itself to the inadmissible wish of the would-be lover, 'to be there when the girl he loved lay down to sleep'.

Fourth, Freud notes the overlap of psychoanalytic and artistic ambiguity in the course of the story's unfolding. The author of the story leaves the reader in suspense as regards the level of its reality, whether the Gradiva Hanold finds in Pompeii is a revenant or a hallucination. Freud points out that the reader's knowledge of the situation is in advance of the hero's and that this is part of the author's conscious strategy: 'Anyone who reads *Gradiva* must be struck by the frequency with which the author puts ambiguous remarks into the mouths of his two principal characters'. The Gradiva in the streets of Pompeii is Hanold's old childhood friend Zoe and she understands what is going on. Both Zoe and Hanold share the symbolism which structures the story, the analogies between childhood and Pompeii, repression and burial. Zoe can therefore maintain her Gradiva role and yet at the same time try slowly to free Hanold from his delusion. Like a good analyst she works towards her goal indirectly, cultivating the ambiguities of the situation. What happens is that Gradiva/Zoe sees two meanings where Hanold sees only one. Freud gives a number of examples, one when she says to her patient: 'I feel as though we had shared a meal like this once before, two thousand years ago; can't you remember?' Freud calls this handling of a double language 'a triumph of ingenuity and wit', but carried away by the psychoanalytic parallel of heroine-cum-analyst he seems to wish to assign the credit to the character rather than the author. This is because in the first instance he wishes to press home the analogy to psychoanalytic procedures: 'This striking preference for ambiguous speeches . . . is nothing other than a counterpart to the twofold determination of symptoms, in so far as speeches are themselves symptoms and, like them, arise from the compromises between the conscious and the unconscious'. Freud sees a relationship between the symptomatic character of speech (all words as compromise-formations even when not obvi-

ous Freudian slips) and the writer's skill in the strategic use of language. The author achieves his effects by means of ambiguity: he speaks to the reader through Zoe, thus sharing his superior knowledge. Two meanings go to the reader, where only one goes to the hero. In his analysis of the story Freud shows that the strategies of desire are partly performed by the text. Here the author is not the one who is being analysed (although Freud did write to Jensen, and despite getting no lead, indulged in some lively speculation). However, he discusses the workings of the text only from the analyst's point of view, whether as himself, the author, or Zoe in her role as analyst; he does not here pursue any analogy between 'patient' and reader.

In the essay **'Psychopathic characters on the stage'** the spotlight is more on the audience. One question which occupies Freud in this highly condensed essay is how the audience's understanding of the repressed material will affect their response. If too much gets through, resistance will come into force and the spectator will not allow himself to be drawn in. The dramatist will fail to purge the spectator of his emotions and thus, according to Freud, not open up a possible source of pleasure. It is once again a question of strategy. In **'Creative writers and Daydreaming'**, the reader was to be 'lured' away from the writer's personal unconscious by the work's formal properties. In the present essay the spectator is to be drawn into the character's psychopathology by means of having his attention 'diverted'. The focus has thereby shifted from the author's need to that of the reader.

Freud's argument takes a somewhat roundabout route. The spectator wishes to identify with the hero, to have an illusion of greatness, but he does not want to undergo any real suffering. 'Accordingly', says Freud, 'his enjoyment is based on an illusion.' There speaks Freud the positivist, the same Freud who assumes that the child at play is like the creative writer in separating his world 'sharply' from reality. This seems only to stress the negative aspect of illusion, not the positive one developed by Freud's later followers. Freud does come round to the pertinent question as to how this illusion, that is 'only a game', is to be maintained, but he never answers it straightforwardly. He approaches the problem of audience response by making a distinction between the theatre of the Ancients and the Moderns.

Greek tragedy essentially involves conflict with an authority, be it a struggle against divinity (religious drama), against the state (social drama), or against another individual (psychological drama); in all these examples two conscious impulses are in opposition. But, Freud argues, when instead of psychological drama we have psychopathological drama, 'the source of the suffering in which we take part and from which we are meant to derive pleasure is no longer a conflict between two almost equally conscious impulses but between a conscious impulse and a repressed one'. The neurotic spectator will react to the lifting of repression with a mixture of enjoyment (on account of the energy saved in not having to hold down the repression) and resistance (on account of any anxiety that may be caused). The dramatist, says Freud, must proceed with care to attune the *non*-neurotic spectator, whose gain

Freud at Clark University, Worcester, Massachusetts, in September 1909. With him in the front row are Stanley Hall and Carl Jung. Back row, from left to right, A. A. Brill, Ernest Jones and Sandor Fereczi.

is not so obvious; he must draw him in 'with his attention averted', lower his resistance, so that he does not know exactly where his emotions are leading him: 'After all, the conflict in *Hamlet* is so effectively concealed that it was left to me to unearth it'.

At the beginning of the essay Freud argues that in drama in general the spectator can identify with the hero without suffering: he can have the glory without paying the price. He knows his enjoyment is based on illusion and hence he does not mind plunging in. With 'psychopathological drama' there is the problem of coming up against resistance. Rebellion against an inner authority is a painful process. Even so, there might be a yield of 'masochistic satisfaction' in identifying with the hero's defeat (Freud is here touching on his later economy of the drives as it appears in ***Beyond the Pleasure Principle***). Hence a different strategy is required to draw in the spectator who does not consciously wish to be the person on the stage, one which takes account of an unconscious satisfaction. The first case, illusion, and the second case, 'diversion of attention', together are a joint strategy, applicable to all drama. The opening of Freud's essay is in keeping with the wish-fulfilment theory of **'Creative writers and Day-dreaming'**, in that it stresses the play aspect, now in the light of the spectator's willingness to enter the illusion created by the playwright and the actor, who 'enable' him to play. At the

end of the essay, however, the 'dramatist's skill' is presented as creating a surrogate neurosis. There is aesthetic pleasure in both, in providing the unconscious with a release, but in the former, play partakes of a collusion that is publicly validated, while in the latter the collusion is private. A new kind of space is thus created, a neurotic space. In his essay 'Theatricum analyticum', Philippe Lacoue-Labarthe points out that this has wide implications for a theory of the theatre, in that it marks a break with Aristotle's poetics of the drama. What takes place can no longer be taken as a representation of reality, the mere imitation of an action, but is to be seen as the production of reality 'outside representation'. Theatre, in Jean-François Lyotard's words, is 'de-realized space'.

'Psychopathic characters' has something of the richness of Freud's essay 'The uncanny,' where he also stresses the power of the writer to control the return of the repressed and demonstrates, albeit unconsciously, how it is done: in foregrounding the uncanny effects in E. T. A. Hoffmann's 'Der Sandmann' via an argument for the Oedipus complex, he succeeds in 'diverting attention' from the uncanny effects of the repetition-compulsion as figured in the essay as a whole. In these writings Freud discusses theory and practice together: he is interested in the work's devices and the pleasurable effect thereby achieved. Unfortunately id-psychology dropped this two-fold concern and took for granted that the ultimate task of the psychoanalytic critic was the recovery of a latent and true meaning, and that his meaning would inevitably be directly connected with the way the author was caught up in his private fantasy. Since, however, the scrupulous critics were interested in the way this fantasy was *figured* in the text, their readings, however predictable in terms of themes, already, before Trilling, linked psychoanalytic processes with rhetoric.

It must be said, however, that Freud's notion of collusion between writer and reader assumes that there is always a challenge from a neurotic infantile wish, never a wish that could be corrective of the repressive system, against that system. The ambiguities always work one way only, allowing spurious satisfaction, returning the repressed whence it came. This is indeed, as will be seen, the burden of D. H. Lawrence's objection, and, from an anything but radical position, that of the ego-psychologists and archetypal critics. Freud's theory, though it recognizes the subversive force of the unconscious, here neglects the possibility that on some occasions it may overcome the censor and produce an aggressive correction. . . . His theory of the joke does something to make up for this omission. (pp. 24-36)

> *Elizabeth Wright, "Classical Psychoanalysis: Freud," in her* Psychoanalytic Criticism: Theory in Practice, *Methuen, 1984, pp. 9-36.*

Frank Kermode   (essay date 1989)

[*Kermode is an English critic whose career combines modern critical methods with expert traditional scholarship, particularly in his work on Shakespeare. In his critical discussions of modern literature, Kermode has embraced many of the conceptions of structuralism and phenomenology. Kermode characterizes all human knowledge as poetic, or fictive: constructed by humans and affected by the perceptual and emotional limitations of human consciousness. Because perceptions of life and the world change, so do human knowledge and the meaning attached to things and events. Thus, there is no single fixed reality over time. Similarly, for Kermode, a work of art has no single fixed meaning, but a multiplicity of possible interpretations; in fact, the best of modern writing is constructed so that it invites a variety of interpretations, all of which depend upon the sensibility of the reader. Kermode believes his critical writings exist to stimulate thought, to offer possible interpretations, but not to fix a single meaning to a work of art. True or "classic" literature, to Kermode, is thus a constantly reinterpreted living text, "complex and indeterminate enough to allow us our necessary pluralities." In the following excerpt from his* An Appetite for Poetry, *Kermode considers Freud's assumptions about the nature of historical interpretation, placing them within the context of nineteenth-century hermeneutics.*]

In its origins psychoanalysis depended upon certain assumptions, not inherent in it, about the past. Having the support of the powerful natural sciences, nineteenth-century geology and biology, these assumptions were not even recognized as such; and so they were, for a time, ines-

capable. They controlled many other kinds of inquiry, for example, linguistics, biblical criticism, history generally and art history in particular. But well within the lifetime of Freud these assumptions came into question. Others began to replace them. There were new notions as to what constituted valid interpretation. The criteria appropriate to natural science no longer seemed so obviously and unproblematically appropriate to the human sciences. In particular, the relations between past and present became vexatious. Once upon a time it seemed obvious that you could best understand how things are by asking how they got to be that way. Now attention was directed to how things are in all their immediate complexity. There was a switch, to use the linguist's expressions, from the diachronic to the synchronic view. Diachrony, roughly speaking, studies things in their coming to be as they are; synchrony concerns itself with things as they are and ignores the question how they got that way.

More about that later. Crudely, then, my subject is this switch of attention from explanations assuming a very long and rather simple past to explanations focused rather intensely on the here and now, with the past either ignored or given a new and difficult role as a sort of hinterland, in which fact and fiction are not readily distinguished, and perhaps do not need to be. This raises the further question, on which I shall, like Milton's Satan, gloze but superficially, of the relation between historical fact and fiction in historical constructions, a matter to which Freud gave some attention. Like him, we still have a troublesome remnant of a conscience in such matters, though it is a very long time since St. Augustine remarked that "not everything we make up is a lie"; a fiction may be *figura veritatis*, a figure of the truth. Perhaps, in the end, we shall find some comfort in that observation.

A lot has been written lately about "the archaeology of knowledge"—about period systems of discourse which put invisible constraints on the *kind* of thing that can be said at any particular time. Only later, in a new period, can we identify the constraints of a former one; we cannot do it for our own. But it seems extravagant to maintain, as some do, that these epochs are necessarily discontinuous. With psychoanalysis, anyway, one may surely speak of an origin in one epoch and a development in the next. Freud himself, though the most important herald of a new era of interpretation, was formed under the old regime, at a time when it seemed right to give most things a historical explanation, and to be suspicious of explanations that did not appeal to objective historical truth. Science, especially geology and botany, had enormously extended the past of the planet and its occupants; and this new past provided a space for previously unthinkable explanations of how things came to be as they are. In such a climate it would have been extremely difficult to prefer explanations of another kind; that would have been to show less than the proper respect of historians and scientists for fact.

The reader might here wish to remind me that Freud did, on occasion, give some thought to the relation between fact and fiction, truth and the figure of truth. "In my mind I always construct novels," he told Stekel. He called his Leonardo piece "partly fiction," and ***Moses and Monothe-***

ism had as its working title "The Man Moses: An Historical Novel." He seems always to have felt the attraction of the storyteller's ways of making sense of the world. The case histories, and especially that of the Wolf Man, have often been thought to show a regard for narrative values— for coherence, development, closure—not entirely consistent with simple factual record. Even *Beyond the Pleasure Principle* has been plausibly studied as a fiction, a masterplot for psychoanalytic narration.

Yet, so far as I know, Freud, when he considered these matters, always reaffirmed the criteria of truthfulness he inherited from science, and from an idea of history deriving from science—an idea that took no account of its fictive qualities. As we shall see, there were, during Freud's lifetime, new approaches to such problems; but he seems to have taken very little notice of them. His own amazingly original work was founded in an older tradition. For example, when he decided to abandon the simpler version of the seduction hypothesis, he got out of the resulting dilemma not by appealing to some theory of fiction but by making use of the extended past. When he says in his *General Theory of the Neuroses* that neurotics are "anchored somewhere in their past," and that their symptoms repeat the past as distorted by the censorship, he does add that the *Kinderscenen* thus recovered are not always *true*— they can be phantasies disguising childhood history, much as nations use legends to disguise their prehistory. But he goes on to claim that psychoanalysis is a technique that can be applied to transindividual subjects such as the history of civilization; and the next step is to explain the phantasies of the individual as inherited by means of genetic memory traces. So, talking of anxiety, he maintains that its "first state" has been "thoroughly incorporated into the organism through a countless series of generations."

By these means it was possible to extend the history of a neurosis beyond the bounds of an individual life, and so to confer upon phantasy the status of historical truth. That the case history of the Wolf Man depends equally upon this move is so obvious as to need no elaboration: the analysis had to proceed as though phantasies were true recollections, and could not otherwise succeed. Patients believe in the reality of the primal scene, and their conviction "is in no respect inferior to one based on recollection." And later Freud remarks that while it would be agreeable to know whether a patient was describing a phantasy or recollecting a real experience, the point is not of much importance, for in either case what is being described has objective historical reality. The phantasies "are unquestionably an inherited endowment, a phylogenetic heritage." Here he found himself in agreement with Jung, with the important qualification that correct method requires one to exhaust onto genetic explanations before going on to phylogenetic ones. One goes behind the individual history only when historical validation is not to be found there.

The formula *ontogeny repeats phylogeny* thus provides Freud with the means to extend indefinitely the past of the individual, and so create space for acceptably historical explanations. *Totem and Taboo* (1913) clearly depends on the formula. Even more enthusiastic applications of it are to be found in Ferenczi, who mapped the findings of psychoanalysis onto the biological and geological record with much boldness and assiduity. Haeckel's idea had been around for quite a while, and as it happens he was a Darwinian. But Freud and Ferenczi, though keen on the idea of recapitulation, associated the formula not with Darwin's evolutionary biology but rather with the earlier theory of Lamarck, who believed much less ambiguously than Darwin in the inheritance of acquired characteristics. Lamarck suited psychoanalysis much better; it seemed to need what Ferenczi called a "depth biology" that would explain how phylogenetic memory-traces accumulated in the germ plasma, imprinting there "all the catastrophes of phylogenetic development."

Freud's own adherence to an outmoded evolutionary theory, strongly expressed in his letter to Groddeck in 1917 and lengthily expounded by Sulloway, was a source of distress to Ernest Jones; but he never gave it up. From his remarks in *The Future of an Illusion,* twenty-five years after the event, one sees that he was quite unperturbed that the ethnology of *Totem and Taboo* was said to be out of date, and he obviously felt the same about condemnations of Lamarck. It was important to be able to map neurosis, genitality, and so forth on to an indefinitely protracted past, or, as he himself put it, to "fill a gap in individual truth with prehistoric truth." Actual historical occurrences are somehow genetically inscribed in the individual. Behind the idea of "prehistoric truth" we detect the immense authority of nineteenth-century science and its new explanations of the planet's history.

I shall come back to Freud on this point, but it is now time to ask how this idea of a hugely extended past affected other disciplines outside the natural sciences, and how it began to be given up. The most striking case is probably that of linguistics, because here the twentieth-century break with the historical approach was so decisive, and so clearly marked by the publication of Ferdinand de Saussure's *Course in General Linguistics,* posthumously assembled from students' lecture notes and first published in 1915. It is to Saussure that we owe the distinction between synchronic and diachronic. Hitherto the prevailing mode of linguistics had naturally been historical; languages were studied along a chronological axis. From their interrelations one could construct prehistoric states and parent languages from which they descended. This kind of linguistics was fully warranted as a science, and we know from the early essay on antithetical primal words, and from *Totem and Taboo,* that Freud respected it. He shows no signs of having read Saussure, and it is not difficult to guess that had he done so he would have felt little sympathy with the new approach. For Saussure argued that although there is nothing wrong in studying language historically, the investigation of language here and now has clear priority. The speaker of a language is confronted not with a history but with a *state*. "That is why the linguist who wishes to understand a state must discard all knowledge of everything that produced it, since what produced it is not a part of the state"; at this stage he must ignore diachrony. He must look at the systematic interrelations of a language *as it is;* other studies must be subsequent to that one. The questions how things are, and how things got to be this way, are therefore sharply separated.

I should perhaps add what everybody knows, that modern semiology and structuralism grow directly from Saussure's emphasis on state or system, and accept his critique of diachronic assumptions. Freud had an inveterate suspicion of system, which he associated with magic, and with the prescientific, so it is conceivable that he would have thought Saussure's methods regressive. But Saussure never came to his notice, and the direct impact of synchronic linguistics on psychoanalysis was delayed until the advent of Lacan.

The authority of a single person can, it is clear, affect the rate of change in this way; and there is also, more vaguely, a kind of inertia, say of stubbornness, which also tends to slow it. I myself was taught pre-Saussurian linguistics in the 1930s, and the reception of Saussure's ideas did not happen everywhere all at once. So one should not make these changes seem quite as sudden as the importance of the date 1915 suggests. Nor, of course, should it be thought that the move into the here and now was wholly the work of Saussure, or that it always took precisely the same form. And here the example of biblical criticism may be useful.

The historical criticism of the Bible was an eighteenth-century development, but its flowering in the nineteenth century is rightly thought of as among the greatest intellectual achievements of the period. The Bible came to be thought of less as a divinely instituted unity than as a collection of miscellaneous documents, each with a prehistory of change and redaction and conflation over very long periods of time. What had been treated synchronically, as a homogeneous canon, was now to be explained diachronically, as a set of independent documents brought together by editors who did not manage to conceal every trace of their activities.

The Old Testament was sorted into various strands that had been put together in a way that left visible joins. Behind the written versions were oral sources, the subject of prehistoric constructions. The magical view of the Torah as a book somehow coextensive with creation, uniformly inspired, faded away. Something of the sort happened also in New Testament scholarship. It was established, to the satisfaction of most, that Mark's was the earliest Gospel, and that Matthew and Luke used it as a source. But where did they find the material in their books which was not in Mark's? The question is typical, and so is the answer: there must have been a sayings-source, a document having historical existence though now lost, which was labeled Q. But Q, thus constructed, cannot account for the material in Matthew that is not in Luke, and vice versa. So each had to have a private source, called M in one case and L in the other. And this was by no means the end of it.

Now it so happens that this practice of constructing historical precedents came in at about the same time as the discovery of an extended geological past. Now there was *time* for such things to happen; time became a space for interpretation to work in. What validated interpretation was history. The parallel with psychoanalysis seems obvi-

ous. The new biblical criticism was of course strongly contested, but it prevailed, and has still not lost its potency. In recent times, however, the grip of history has been somewhat loosened. The historical events of the New Testament themselves command a much less simple kind of assent, as we know from the existentialist theologians. The biblical canon, split, as I have said, into separate books, is once again studied synchronically, as a *state,* in Saussure's word, of which the internal relations may be considered without regard to actual or conjectural chronologies. In a different though related tradition, structuralist anthropology treats the Bible as it would any other corpus of myth, that is, synchronically rather than diachronically, as something that developed through time.

An obvious question now is how this shift of interest affected the writing of history in the ordinary sense. It is a large question, and I shall begin to answer it by giving an example from a subdepartment of the subject, namely art history. German art historians were attracted by theories of transindividual memory, with archaic traces in art that could by research be found to originate in prehistoric events; ancient terrors, according to Aby Warburg, were transmitted by the cultural memory to reappear as sources of energy and delight, as when a girl in a fresco by Ghirlandajo recapitulates, in a beneficently distorted form, the image of a primitive Maenad. The cultural transmission of such "mnemic traces" or engrams is parallel to the genetic survival of prehistory in Freud's individual patient. We may remind ourselves that similar notions were still extant in practitioners of the more exact sciences. The American neo-Lamarckian E. D. Cope, for instance, proposed a doctrine of mnemo-genesis, which said that the recapitulation by the embryo of phylogenetic history is made possible by the existence of unconscious memory-structures in the organism.

Warburg continued to think along these lines until his death in 1926; some of the methods he devised for the study of recurrence are still in use, though detached from his theories. He found support wherever he could for his mnemic traces, for instance in the work of Semon, which had much to say about memory traces. It is worth noting that only a few years later, in 1932, there appeared F. C. Bartlett's *Remembering,* a work remembered when other books on memory are forgotten, yet which has no ancient traces or reactivated engrams. Bartlett prefers to speak of personal interest in the here and now—adaptation and response to an immediate stimulus. Once again it seems that the older historical assumptions are set aside.

Indeed they were under question as early as the 1870s, when Nietzsche called history "the gravedigger of the present"; and among other inquirers it would seem that a characteristically modern philosophy of history began to develop. Where does history happen? One answer was, in the historian's head, now. The related question, what does it mean to do history? required of the historian a new effort of self-reflection. He could no longer claim to be merely arranging objective and verifiable facts. And the problem was to find new ways of talking about what now appeared to be the obscure relation of past to present. It fell within the domain of the revived discipline of hermeneutics.

Hermeneutics, as understood in our time, owes much to Wilhelm Dilthey (1831-1911). Dilthey distinguished between the natural and the human sciences (*Geisteswissenschaften*), and this distinction was later to be important for psychoanalysis and indeed to all the other interpretive sciences. Freud seems to have ignored Dilthey; he would probably not have liked the philosopher's insistence on taking into account the historical situation of the observer as well as that of the observed; which is to complicate something Freud insisted was simple. According to Dilthey, understanding is subject to time and change; no past is fixed, and no present is to be thought of as somehow outside time. We survey the past from within our own horizon, and that horizon is always changing. That is why, as a matter of course, we lose faith in world views formerly taken to be beyond controversy—in "any philosophy which attempts to express world order cogently through a series of concepts."

Dilthey's line of thought, much transformed, has persisted into our own time, and hermeneutics has spread itself over the whole body of philosophy. But it continues to hold that meaning changes, including past meaning; and that the past is inextricable from the present of the interpreter. *There and then* cannot be detached from *here and now,* and objectively inspected. The past becomes, at least in part, a construction of the present. Thus Lévi-Strauss can say quite flatly that historical narratives are "fraudulent outlines" imposed on the data, which are of course synchronic. Most hermeneutic claims are less nihilistic, but still fatal to the old idea of the past.

And with that I conclude this extremely superficial account of altered attitudes to the past in some of the human sciences with which psychoanalysis must acknowledge kinship. Before I return to psychoanalysis with the object of seeing how it looks in this changed context, I should summarize the summary. The new long view of the past provided by natural science was imposed upon and in various ways exploited by the interpretive disciplines. In psychoanalysis individual histories were projected onto a longer phylogenetic scale, so that a present neurosis could be interpreted by reference to a remote "prehistoric" catastrophe; thus phantasy acquired the status of historical (scientific) fact. Linguistics, biblical criticism, and historiography also made use of these new time scales, accepting that historical factuality was the ultimate source of authentic interpretation. However, we thought we could see in these studies a shift into a new set of assumptions—rather dramatic in the case of linguistics, where Saussure explicitly affirmed the primacy of the synchronic, but no less certain, though more gradual, in the other disciplines. The interpretive emphasis, in short, was shifting away from that long past, so receptive of narrative explanations, and into the actual moment, the here and now. It would be easy enough to provide more evidence of this shift, say from the various kinds of formalism practiced in literary and other sorts of criticism, as they developed in different ways in Russia, America, and England; all were more or less dismissive of the historical dimension, all were concerned with synchronicity, the words on the page, the verbal icon.

To some who experienced this shift a particular problem must have grown more vexatious, namely the exact demarcation between historical truth and fiction, and, as I have remarked, it sometimes occurred to Freud to give the matter thought. How he dealt with it we may perhaps see from a single example. In 1911 Hans Vaihinger published his *Philosophy of "As if,"* though in fact he had written it twenty-five years earlier. It is, roughly, a Nietzschean philosophy of fictions. It was often reprinted, and came to Freud's attention. Vaihinger's explanation of the heuristic value of "as-if" thinking seems at first to have impressed him; but he soon dismissed it with the Johnsonian observation that this was an argument "only a philosopher could put forward." For it was not philosophy but hard science that was in touch with the truth. When, in *The Future of an Illusion,* Freud defines illusion as the conformity of a belief with a wish, he obviously implies that psychoanalysis is saved from illusion by its observational basis. He allows the carping critic set up as a kind of Aunt Sally in that book to complain that Freud has set up his own system of illusions in place of another; science is neither system nor illusion, and psychoanalysis is a science.

At the same time, and with some inconsistency, he commends *Totem and Taboo,* despite its outdated ethnology, for the way in which it brought a number of disconnected facts into a coherent whole. Of course he knew very well that a capacity to be represented as whole and self-consistent does not guarantee theories against illusion. When he condemned Adler's theories as "radically false" he said that their very consistency constituted a distortion comparable with those introduced by secondary revision in dream theory. In short, Freud would have agreed with the poet Stevens that "to impose is not / To discover." Whatever theory imposes on observation is likely to induce distortion and illusion. The doctrine which holds that the innocent eye sees nothing would not have been acceptable to Freud. He affirmed, indeed, that the foundation of science was "observation alone"; and he held this to be as true of psychoanalysis as of physics.

Everybody is now much more skeptical about the possibility of context-free observation, and most are much more ready to allow that the criteria for valid interpretation in the human sciences are different from those obtaining in natural science. In particular, the notion that historical facts exist in simple and accessible objectivity has become hard to hold. And in the present climate few could be as calm and certain about the nature of historical constructions as Freud was. In the late essay entitled **"Constructions in Analysis"** he is still saying there is nothing delusive about the contact of such constructions with historical reality. And he denied that the issue was of much practical importance because all the relevant material, whether fact or phantasy, had *some* historical reality, however archaic and however distorted in transmission. He would have thought rather ill of the argument that everything relevant belongs to the here and now—that what occurred in the transference was not, in some perfectly real and genuine way, a recapitulation of actual events. To think in that way he would have had first to abandon the foreunderstanding he had inherited from the dominant science of his formative years.

Possessing a degree of hindsight, we may think it inevitable that psychoanalysis should one day break its bond with natural science and move into the more congenial context of the *Geisteswissenschaften.* I don't know if he was a pioneer in this, but I learned that in 1939 Kroeber suggested that it was a mistake to treat the Oedipus complex as historical in origin. More recently Jerome Neu (from whom I gained this information) has asked "Must actual remorse for an actual crime be an essential step in superego formation?" replying that it need not be. Freud's account of the matter would be unobjectionable, says Neu, only if Lamarckianism were true, which it isn't. For this as well as other reasons psychoanalysis might want to reconsider its position among the disciplines.

A rapprochement between psychoanalysis and hermeneutics was proposed in Ricoeur's monumental *Freud and Philosophy.* Ricoeur maintains that the proper questions to put to Freud are those one would put to Dilthey, Weber, or Bultmann rather than those one would put to a physicist or a biologist. "It is completely misleading," he says, *contra* Freud, "to raise the question [of theory in psychoanalysis] in the context of a factual or observational science." And he stresses the uniqueness of the transference, its unpredictability and its here-and-nowness, as the distinctive characteristic of psychoanalysis considered as a hermeneutic.

To treat it thus is to avoid the Popperian charge of pseudo-science by taking psychoanalysis out of the arena in which Popper's criteria apply. The move once made, it is possible to think of psychoanalysis not merely as a hermeneutic science, but as the paradigm of all such sciences, and this is what Jürgen Habermas has argued. The interpretive disciplines differ from natural science in that they cannot yield demonstrative certainty, and depend on different procedures. In outlining them Habermas follows Dilthey. He adds that Freud took no account of all this, but stuck to the view that psychoanalysis was fundamentally a positive science, though with certain peculiarities. For Habermas the distinctive characteristic of psychoanalysis as hermeneutic is that it deals with discourses the authors of which are deceiving themselves; that is, it is concerned more with distortion of meaning than with meaning, or, as he says, with the intrusion of an at first incomprehensible private language into everyday language games. Analysis seeks to cure these linguistic deformations. Its explanations are not, as is supposed of those proper to the natural sciences, determined by context-free laws, for here interpretation is a formative part of the discourse; its aim is "the reintroduction into public communication of a symbolic content that has been split off." Psychoanalysis, unlike the sciences which pretend to context-free observation, is necessarily self-reflexive, always making its concern as to what it is doing a part of what it is doing.

And here we may recall that it was during Freud's most active years that poets and novelists discovered, or rediscovered and exploited, the possibilities of reflexivity, the values of systematic distortion, and the benefits of what is sometimes called "spatial form"—a detemporalizing of narrative which, accompanied by all manner of dislocation, overlaps, gaps, condensations, displacements, called for a quasi-synchronic reading and heightened interpretive awareness on the part of the reader. Works so composed can be seen only as wholes, and can be made sense of only by a collaborative act on the part of the reader; all reading is of course collaborative, but now the reader's share of the work is quite deliberately increased. The analogy between psychological and fictional interpretation was there *in posse* from the earliest days of psychoanalysis, but the forces which bound Freud to objective history, and many novelists to the conventions of "secretarial" realism, prevented, and in some degree continue to prevent, its exploitation.

However that may be, it is now quite usual to speak of Freud's historical constructions as delusive. One commentator will lament Freud's "limited epistemology," which prevented him from understanding that historical truth, or the appearance of it, is entirely the product of the analytical session. "The reality tested and the reality created . . . claim no authority outside the analytic process. What authorizes the process is immanent in the process." Let us leave aside the question whether Dr. Schwartz has considered the possibility that he too has a limited epistemology, and remark that self-authorization of this sort is also commonly credited to poems and novels—to works of fiction. Skura, indeed, says that the analyst can now teach critics how to attend to details apparently too trivial to bear the weight of interpretation; but he can only do so because he has given up the "referential fallacy" and come to see "the psychoanalytical process as a self-conscious end in itself."

Such commentators take the death of the psychoanalytical past as a *fait accompli.* According to Merton Gill the analysis of transference ought to be "content-free," and the analysand's references to the past are to be interpreted as indirect, resistant allusions to the here and now. And Donald P. Spence attacks many aspects of psychoanalytical practice which seem to him to derive from mistaken assumptions governing the aims and techniques of traditional analysis: the partnership between free association and evenly hovering attention, thought to create the conditions for an interpretive recovery of the past, is nonexistent. Pasts, indeed, are not reconstructed; they are constructed here and now. Moreover, since the analyst inserts fictions into the discourse, he might be more usefully thought of as a kind of poet rather than as a kind of archaeologist. What psychoanalysis does is construct "truth in the service of self-coherence . . . It offers no veridical picture of the past." Like the poet, the novelist, and the historian, the analyst creates under his specific conditions a past that is really here and now, a fiction appropriate to the present. Any interpretation is true "only in its own analytic space." Moreover, it is pointless to call an interpretation erroneous; it works by contributing to narrative intelligibility, and is neither true nor false but only a means to an end.

Spence and Viderman (who seems to have originated the analogy with the poet) have been accused of seriously misrepresenting the analyst's role, which, says one critic, is less like that of a poet than like that of a detective breaking an alibi. This analogy might have a certain appeal to all who would rather deal even with a policeman than with a poet, but it simply assumes the old historical dimension Spence and the others reject. As so often, old assumptions linger on, wearing the guise of common sense.

It is of course part of the premise that what is new will become old, perhaps lingering for a while as common sense before sinking into disuse or being revived and given a new dress. The most appealing thing about the hermeneutic approach is that it forbids itself to suppose that it can stop all movement at exactly the right place, namely one's own moment, or that it has achieved an interpretive apparatus that is permanently valid. And of course the sort of paradigm change I have been discussing can only be represented as a matter of history, which at least to that extent is not dead at all, as linguists, theologians, and historians of the most modern sort perfectly well understand. But this is second-order history—the narrative not of events or linguistic change or whatever, but rather the narrative of such narratives. Anyway, the shift seems to have happened, and it is hardly a surprise that psychoanalysis, with its roots in one epoch and its branches in another, should demonstrably have been caught up in it.

There is, I think, one more thing to be said. The most radical theologians, some of them atheist to all intents and purposes, are still Christians. Philosophers eloquent in their distrust of history and system—as nowadays some influential thinkers are—remain for all that philosophers. The art-historical methods of a Warburg have become the possession of scholars who may think his theories of small concern. And all the critics of the Freudian concept of the past to whom I have referred in this essay are either psychoanalysts or friends of psychoanalysis. Nietzsche remarked in *The Use and Abuse of History* that every past is worth condemning; and it is possible to believe in psychoanalysis without thinking that any of its past pasts are exempt from this general rule. Nevertheless, certain values seem to survive the conceptual forms in which from time to time they have been—*have* to have been—embodied. The certainty that present structures of belief will also change is therefore not a reason for supposing that psychoanalysis will cease to figure among the arts or sciences of interpretation, or even that it will not dominate them, in times when they will probably be defined in ways quite unforeseeable by us.

For my own part I am happy to think that psychoanalytic interpretation may hold commerce with the theory of fiction. The theologians are interested in a similar concordat, having lost confidence in objective history. I promised comfort at the end: it is this, that we may all, under the special conditions of our trades, claim to be dealing with *figurae veritatis,* figures of the truth. (pp. 136-51)

> *Frank Kermode, "Freud and Interpretation," in his* An Appetite for Poetry, *Cambridge, Mass.: Harvard University Press, 1989, pp. 136-51.*

FURTHER READING

Bibliography

Grinstein, Alexander. *Sigmund Freud's Writings: A Comprehensive Bibliography.* New York: International Universities Press, 1977, 181 p.
  Standard bibliography.

Biography

Jones, Ernest. *The Life and Work of Sigmund Freud.* 3 vols. New York: Basic Books, 1957.
  Comprehensive and authoritative account of Freud's life and career by a close friend and colleague.

Criticism

Ades, Dawn. "Freud and Surrealist Painting." In *Freud: The Man, His World, His Influence,* pp. 138-49. Edited by Jonathan Miller. Boston: Little, Brown and Co., 1972.

Considers Freud's influence on such painters as Max Ernst, Salvador Dali, Joan Miró and Yves Tanguy, emphasizing their affinities with the founder of psychoanalysis as well as their formal divergences.

Berman, Jeffrey. *The Talking Cure: Literary Representations of Psychoanalysis.* New York: New York University Press, 1985, 362 p.
     Explores the psychoanalytic dimensions of literary language in the work of such authors as F. Scott Fitzgerald, T. S. Eliot, and Sylvia Plath. Simultaneously, considers the therapeutic function of literature for its authors, and the intense ambivalence of twentieth-century writers towards Freud and psychoanalysis.

Bloom, Harold. "Freud and the Sublime: A Catastrophe Theory of Creativity." In his *Agon: Towards a Theory of Revisionism*, pp. 91-118. Oxford: Oxford University Press, 1982.
     Applies Freud's concepts of primary process, the "uncanny" and anxiety to Bloom's own theories about the Romantic category of the sublime.

————. "Freud's Concepts of Defense and the Poetic Will." In his *Agon: Towards a Theory of Revisionism*, pp. 119-44. Oxford: Oxford University Press, 1982.
     Fuses Bloom's theories about poetry as agonistic revisionism with Freudian concepts of repression and creative sublimation.

————. "Wrestling Sigmund: Three Paradigms for Poetic Originality." In his *The Breaking of the Vessels*, pp. 43-70. Chicago: The University of Chicago Press, 1982.
     Juxtaposes Bloom's analysis of a parable in Genesis with Freud's theories on the "primal scene" in *Three Essays on the Theory of Sexuality.* Bloom discerns a thematics of agonistic struggle which finds expression both in the paradigm of the Oedipal conflict and in Freud's own development as a prose-poet of the sublime.

Bronfen, Elisabeth. "The Lady Vanishes: Sophie Freud and *Beyond the Pleasure Principle.*" *South Atlantic Quarterly* 88, No. 4 (Fall 1989): 961-91.
     Examines parallels between Freud's reaction to the death of his daughter, Sophie, and the themes of thanatos (death-drive) and narcissism in *Beyond the Pleasure Principle,* which he wrote shortly after her death.

Brooks, Peter. "Freud's Masterplot." *Yale French Studies,* Nos. 55-56 (1977): 280-300.
     Cites parallels between structuralist theories of narrative construction and Freud's ideas about death-instinct and the closure of desire in *Beyond the Pleasure Principle.*

Carroll, David. "Freud and the Myth of the Origin." *New Literary History* VI, No. 1 (Autumn 1974): 513-28.
     Illustrates the pitfalls and limitations of critical methodologies that assume a point of origin for meaning within a literary text, and demonstrates how Freud's techniques for diagnosing neuroses suggest a more sophisticated approach.

Derrida, Jacques. "Freud and the Scene of Writing." In his *Writing and Difference,* translated by Alan Bass, pp. 196-231. Chicago: University of Chicago Press, 1978.
     Analyzes Freud's "Note on the Mystic Writing-Pad" (1925) as a precursor to Derrida's own theories on writing and primary process functioning.

Dunn, Allen. "A Child Asleep in Its Own Life: Primary Narcissism as the Dream of Identity." *Literature and Psychology* XXXVI, No. 3 (1990): 16-31.
     Critques Freud's notion of "primary narcissism," demonstrating how it is subverted and contradicted by Freud's conception of repression and the divided psyche. Dunn suggests that primary narcissism is still a useful concept, provided that one interprets it as a fantasy which is internalized by the narcissitic ego.

Eagleton, Terry. "The Name of the Father: Sigmund Freud." In his *The Ideology of the Aesthetic.* Oxford: Basil Blackwell, 1990, 400 p.
     Situates Freud in a lineage of philosophers who view art as a sublimated expression of the body. Eagleton also cites Friedrich Nietzsche's writings as an important precursor to psychoanalysis.

Eastman, Max. "Differing with Sigmund Freud." In his *Great Companions: Critical Memoirs of Some Famous Friends,* pp. 171-90. New York: Farrar, Straus and Cudahy, 1942.
     Lively, colloquial account of Eastman's meeting and correspondence with Freud during the 1920s.

Ellis, Havelock. "Psycho-Analysis in Relation to Sex." In his *The Philosophy of Conflict, and Other Essays in War-Time,* pp. 195-223. New York: Houghton Mifflin Company, 1919.
     Popular exposition of Freud's ideas, with particular emphasis on his theory of infantile sexuality.

Gray, Paul. "The Assault on Freud." *Time* 142, No. 23 (29 November 1993): 47-51.
     Discusses recent controversies among Freudian scholars and psychologists, such as the dispute over the scientific and therapeutic value of psychoanalysis.

Hoffman, Frederick J. *Freudianism and the Literary Mind.* Baton Rouge: Louisiana State University Press, 1957, 350 p.
     Assesses the influence of Freud's theories on twentieth-century literature and literary criticism, with individual chapters on Franz Kafka and Thomas Mann, and D. H. Lawrence.

Jofen, Jean. "A Freudian Interpretation of Freud's *Moses and Monotheism.*" *The Michigan Academician* XII, No. 1 (Summer 1979): 231-40.
     Attempts to psychoanalyze Freud and discover the motives which prompted him to write *Moses and Monotheism.* Jofen bases his analysis on the contention that Moses symbolizes Carl Jung.

Koestenbaum, Wayne. "Privileging the Anus: Anna O. and the Collaborative Origin of Psychoanalysis." *Genders,* No. 3 (Fall 1988): 57-81.
     Speculates on the metaphor of childbirth in *Studies in Hysteria* and the homoerotic overtones of Freud's collaboration and correspondence with Josef Breuer and Wilhelm Fliess, relating this to the more general question of gender politics in psychoanalysis.

Lewis, Helen Block. *Freud and Modern Psychology.* 2 vols. New York: Plenum Press, 1983, 235 p.
     Extensive exegesis of psychoanalysis which censures Freud's misogyny and his ignorance of the social dimensions of human behavior.

Mazlish, Bruce. "Freud." In his *The Riddle of History: The Great Speculators from Vico to Freud,* pp. 381-427. New York: Harper & Row, Publishers, Inc., 1966.

Assesses Freud's stature as a philosopher of history, placing him in the tradition of Giambattista Vico, Georg Wilhelm Hegel, and Karl Marx. Mazlish's exposition emphasizes the latter stages of Freud's writing career, in which he attempted to diagnose the neurotic ills of civilization as a whole.

Miller, Henry. "Psychoanalysis: A Clinical Perspective." In *Freud: The Man, His World, His Influence,* pp. 112-23. Edited by Jonathan Miller. Boston: Little, Brown and Co., 1972.

Offers severe criticism of the clinical value of psychoanalysis, contending that Freud's theories are impossible to verify empirically, and that the majority of mental disturbances do not respond to psychoanalytic treatment.

Rogers, Robert. *Self and Other: Object Relations in Psychoanalysis and Literature.* New York: New York University Press, 1991, 195 p.

Repudiates Freud's sexual drive-oriented theory of object relations in favor of a model which emphasizes interpersonal conflict and attachment deficits. Remainder of the book applies this revised theory to selected works of Herman Melville, Albert Camus, Emily Dickinson, and William Shakespeare.

Santayana, George. "A Long Way Round to Nirvana: Development of a Suggestion Found in Freud's *Beyond the Pleasure Principle.*" In his *Some Turns of Thought in Modern Philosophy: Five Essays,* pp. 87-101. New York: Charles Scribner's Sons, 1934.

Speculates on the philosophical aspects of Freud's formulation of the death-instinct in *Beyond the Pleasure Principle.*

Schneider, Marius G. "Sigmund Freud and the Development of Psychoanalysis." In *Twentieth-Century Thinkers: Studies in the Work of Seventeen Modern Philosophers,* edited by John K. Ryan, pp. 239-65. Staten Island, NY: Alba House, 1965.

Describes the development of psychoanalysis, underscoring Freud's mechanistic, biologistic assumptions about the structure of the mind and his pessimistic and misanthropic view of human nature. Schneider goes on to deliver a harsh verdict on the value of psychoanalysis, which he labels "Freud's mythology, and scientific fantasy."

Soule, George. "Freud and *The Interpretation of Dreams.*" In *Books That Changed Our Minds,* edited by Malcolm Cowley and Bernard Smith, pp. 27-41. New York: Kelmscott Editions, 1938.

Summarizes Freud's influence on twentieth-century culture, balancing an account of the widespread opposition to psychoanalysis with a reminder of Freud's steadfast adherence to scientific methods and aims.

Sperber, Manès. "Freud and his Psycho-analysis." In his *The Achilles Heel,* translated by Constantine FitzGibbon, pp. 146-71. Garden City, NY: Doubleday and Co., 1960.

Offers a dismissive critique of psychoanalysis, citing Freud's professional hubris and his tendency to mythologize psychological phenomena as obstacles in his search for scientific truth.

Timms, Edward, and Segal, Naomi. *Freud in Exile: Psychoanalysis and Its Vicissitudes.* New Haven, CT: Yale University Press, 1988, 310 p.

Collection of essays which examines the question of Freud's influence subsequent to his exile from Vienna in 1938. Comprises four sections which focus on, respectively, the origins of psychoanalysis in Viennese culture, Freud's reception in the English-speaking world, the difficulties of translating Freud's works, and contemporary disputes in psychoanalysis.

Wollheim, Richard, and Hopkins, James, eds. *Philosophical Essays on Freud.* Cambridge: Cambridge University Press, 1982, 310 p.

Essay collection that focuses on the philosophical issues arising from the work of Freud. Includes essays by Ludwig Wittgenstein, Thomas Nagel, and Jean-Paul Sartre.

Additional coverage of Freud's life and career is contained in the following sources published by Gale Research: *Contemporary Authors,* **Vols. 115, 133; and** *Major 20th-Century Writers.*

An Enemy of the People

Henrik Ibsen

The following entry presents criticism of Ibsen's drama *En folkefiende* (*An Enemy of the People*), first published and performed in 1883. For discussion of Ibsen's complete career, see *TCLC*, Volumes 2, 8; for discussion of the drama *Vildanden* (1884; *The Wild Duck*), see *TCLC*, Volume 16; for discussion of the drama *Et dukkehjem* (1879; *A Doll's House),* see *TCLC*, Volume 37.

INTRODUCTION

An Enemy of the People is among the most popular of Ibsen's plays and is representative of those works by Ibsen, including *A Doll's House* and *Gengangere* (*Ghosts*), which introduced realism to a European theater previously dominated by romanticism. These plays were instrumental in bringing the theatergoing public of the late nineteenth century to an acceptance of drama not only as entertainment but also as social commentary. An indictment of the flaws in modern society, *An Enemy of the People* focuses on a moral conflict between one individual, Dr. Stockmann, and the community in which he lives.

Ibsen wrote *An Enemy of the People* during the second phase of his career, a period during which he turned from writing verse dramas with mythical and historical themes to addressing controversial subjects in such social problem plays as *A Doll's House* and *Samfundets støtter* (*The Pillars of Society*). In a third phase Ibsen's works became increasingly symbolic and introspective. Many critics have suggested that *An Enemy of the People* may have been Ibsen's response to the pervasive critical and popular outrage against his previous play, *Ghosts,* which presented a dark perspective on family relationships.

An Enemy of the People is set in a small Norwegian resort community that has recently become prosperous as a result of its successful mineral baths. When Dr. Stockmann, the public health officer, discovers evidence that the waters are polluted and have already caused several illnesses, he reports his findings, confident that the town will follow his directions to remedy the situation and that he will be rewarded for his discovery. Although Stockmann's announcement is initially supported by the press and the majority of taxpayers, opposing forces gather strength when his brother, the mayor, points out the financial loss that would result from temporarily closing the baths to detoxify the system. Nevertheless, Stockmann remains steadfastly determined to cleanse the town of not only water pollution, but also of what he perceives as the pervasive corruption of the town's citizens. However, he is soon abandoned by his followers and declared an "enemy of the people"; his house is stoned, his daughter dismissed from her teaching position, and his friends persecuted. Stockmann resolves to found a school through which he will attempt to

save young people from the town's conformity and hypocrisy. At the play's conclusion, Stockmann has lost his political battle but still believes in the truth and virtue of his position. The play concludes with his ambiguous statement that "the strongest man in the world is the one who stands most alone."

Commentary on *An Enemy of the People* is divided between two major interpretations. In what is often considered the standard approach, the play is viewed as a strongly polemical work addressing the tendency of a social majority, represented by the townspeople, to suppress the visionary ideas of an individual or minority, represented by Dr. Stockmann. Proponents of this assessment have frequently viewed Dr. Stockmann as a mouthpiece for Ibsen's social criticism. As Robert Brustein has stated: "Ibsen has invested this play with the quality of a revolutionary pamphlet; and Stockmann, despite some perfunctory gestures towards giving him a life of his own, is very much like an author's sounding board, echoing Ibsen's private conversations about the filth and disease of modern municipal life, the tyranny of the compact majority, the mediocrity of parliamentary democracy, the cupidity of the Conservatives, and the hypocrisy of the Liberal

Press." The other major perspective on *An Enemy of the People* regards the play as a satirical depiction of all aspects of a political controversy rather than a clearly-defined opposition between a righteous individual and a corrupted society. Advocates of this interpretation argue that Dr. Stockmann may be motivated by self-interest rather than a genuine concern for the truth and point to the negative aspects of his character, including egotism, stubbornness, and contempt for the people of his community.

Although a popular success, *An Enemy of the People* has received significantly less critical attention than such Ibsen plays as *A Doll's House* and *The Wild Duck.* This disparity has been attributed to the widespread perception of the work as the most simplistic, polemic, and unpoetic of Ibsen's plays. John Northam, for example, stated in 1953 that *An Enemy of the People* "is the least imaginative of all Ibsen's realistic prose dramas." However, such later critics as Thomas Van Laan have argued that the play is in fact a significant departure from Ibsen's previous works and anticipates his highly complex later plays. Richard Hornby has stated, "*An Enemy of the People* is a pivotal play for Ibsen. Dr. Stockmann prepares the way for the complex characters in the later plays, such as Gregers Werle, Rebekka West, Hedda Gabler, or Halvard Solness. Such characters are the sort that both audiences and actors have since come to prefer—intricate, realistic, well-rounded, 'modern.'"

CRITICISM

The New York Times   (essay date 1895)

[*In the following review of an English theater company's production of* An Enemy of the People, *the critic praises the play's structure and dialogue but asserts that it lacks originality.*]

[*An Enemy of the People* is] that single one of [Ibsen's] socal dramas which is absolutely pure, so far as its exposition of the relations of the sexes is concerned. Of course, the fanatical Ibsenites will laugh or sneer, according to their individual moods, about this qualification, but it is impossible to please them and be rational at the same time.

An Enemy of the People is a drama in five acts, and its protagonist is Dr. Thomas Stockmann, a Norwegian physician, a man whose experiences of the world have been narrowly restricted, and whose nature is unusually simple and unsuspicious. His tendencies are all toward goodness, but he is not free from vagaries. After many years of toil and privation, he has almost reached the summit of his ambition. He is medical director of the baths in his native town, and earns almost as much as he spends. He has a large family, and his house is liberty hall.

The town owes all its prosperity to the baths. Such is Stockmann's simplicity that he really believes, when he has discovered that the water contains fever germs, and proposes to make his discovery public, his fellow-townsmen will rejoice. He even fears that they will give him a banquet or erect a statue of him, and he feels nervous on that account. The play's interest depends upon the development of Stockmann's character from this starting point step by step, his new understanding of himself, his neighbors, and the world. He becomes a hero in the fight. He develops from a somewhat irrational and flighty individual into a strong, purposeful man, with a clear vision. It is his idea, in the end, that that man is strongest who stands most alone. He is, at that moment, deserted, despised, and rejected; his position is taken away from him, his motives are impugned, and his family is insulted. Yet it is a "happy ending."

The play is an excellent example of Ibsen's superior constructive skill and facility as a writer of stage dialogue. The dramatist resorts to no old tricks of the craft. Every incident is natural and effective. There is not a superfluous word. On the other hand, the interest aroused is never very deep or absorbing. The attention does not waver, and one is mildly entertained from first to last, but there is no emotional effect. One does not laugh—unless he is simple enough to think Mr. Lionel Brough's property wheeze is funny—nor do tears of sympathy ever come to his eyes. If he is very susceptible and has a poor memory, or lacks education, he may imagine, with the advanced Ibsenites, that *An Enemy of the People* sets forth a new view of life; that the will of the majority has never before been satirized on the stage. It is not worth while now to argue about this, but it is worth while to say distinctly that there is not a single good idea in *An Enemy of the People* that is new, and that the play is acceptable merely as a clever modern drama, free from the hoary devices of convention, and grateful to the actors.

> *"Mr. Beerbohm Tree in an Ibsen Play at Abbey's," in* The New York Times, *April 9, 1895, p. 5.*

William Archer   (essay date 1911)

[*A Scottish dramatist and critic, Archer is best known as one of the earliest and most important translators of Ibsen's plays and as a drama critic of the London stage during the late nineteenth and early twentieth centuries. Archer valued drama as an intellectual product and not as simple entertainment. For that reason he did a great deal to promote the "new drama" of the 1890s, including the work of Ibsen and Bernard Shaw. Throughout his career he protested critical overvaluation of Elizabethan and Restoration drama, claiming that modern works were in many respects equal to or better than their predecessors. In the following essay, Archer discusses the background and early productions of* An Enemy of the People *and considers the character of Dr. Stockmann as a mouthpiece for Ibsen's ideas.*]

From *Pillars of Society* to *John Gabriel Borkman,* all Ibsen's plays, with one exception, succeeded each other at intervals of two years. The single exception was *An Enemy of the People.* The storm of obloquy which greeted *Ghosts* stirred him to unwonted rapidity of production. *Ghosts* had appeared in December, 1881; already, in the spring of 1882, Ibsen, then living in Rome, was at work upon its successor; and he finished it at Gossensass, in the Tyrol, in the early autumn. It appeared in Copenhagen at the end of November. Perhaps the rapidity of its composition may account for the fact that we find no sketch or draft of it in the poet's *Literary Remains.*

John Paulsen relates an anecdote of Ibsen's extreme secretiveness during the process of composition, which may find a place here: "One summer he was travelling by rail with his wife and son. He was engaged upon a new play at the time; but neither Fru Ibsen nor Sigurd had any idea as to what it was about. Of course they were both very curious. It happened that, at a station, Ibsen left the carriage for a few moments. As he did so he dropped a scrap of paper. His wife picked it up, and read on it only the words, 'The doctor says. . . .' Nothing more. Fru Ibsen showed it laughingly to Sigurd, and said, 'Now we will tease your father a little when he comes back. He will be horrified to find that we know anything of his play.' When Ibsen entered the carriage his wife looked at him roguishly, and said, 'What doctor is it that figures in your new piece? I am sure he must have many interesting things to say.' But if she could have foreseen the effect of her innocent jest, Fru Ibsen would certainly have held her tongue. For Ibsen was speechless with surprise and rage. When at last he recovered his speech, it was to utter a torrent of reproaches. What did this mean? Was he not safe in his own house? Was he surrounded with spies? Had his locks been tampered with, his desk rifled? And so forth, and so forth. His wife, who had listened with a quiet smile to the rising tempest of his wrath, at last handed him the scrap of paper. 'We know nothing more than what is written upon this slip which you let fall. Allow me to return it to you.' There stood Ibsen crestfallen. All his suspicions had vanished into thin air. The play on which he was occupied proved to be *An Enemy of the People,* and the doctor was none other than our old friend Stockmann, the good-hearted and muddleheaded reformer, for whom Jonas Lie partly served as a model."

The indignation which glows in *An Enemy of the People* was kindled, in the main, by the attitude adopted towards *Ghosts* by the Norwegian Liberal press and the "compact majority" it represented. But the image on which the play rings the changes was present to the poet's mind before *Ghosts* was written. On December 19, 1879—a fortnight after the publication of *A Doll's House*—Ibsen wrote to Professor Dietrichson: "It appears to me doubtful whether better artistic conditions can be attained in Norway before the intellectual soil has been thoroughly turned up and cleansed, and all the swamps drained off." Here we have clearly the germ of *An Enemy of the People.* The image so took hold of Ibsen that after applying it to social life in this play, he recurred to it in *The Wild Duck,* in relation to the individual life.

The mood to which we definitely owe *An Enemy of the People* appears very clearly in a letter to George Brandes, dated January 3, 1882, in which Ibsen thanks him for his criticism of *Ghosts.* "What are we to say," he proceeds, "of the attitude taken up by the so-called Liberal press—by those leaders who speak and write about freedom of action and thought, and at the same time make themselves the slaves of the supposed opinions of their subscribers? I am more and more confirmed in my belief that there is something demoralising in engaging in politics and joining parties. I, at any rate, shall never be able to join a party which has the majority on its side. Björnson says, 'The majority is always right'; and as a practical politician he is bound, I suppose, to say so. I, on the contrary, of necessity say, 'The minority is always right.' Naturally I am not thinking of that minority of stagnationists who are left behind by the great middle party, which with us is called Liberal; I mean that minority which leads the van, and pushes on to points which the majority has not yet reached. I hold that that man is in the right who is most closely in league with the future."

The same letter closes with a passage which foreshadows not only *An Enemy of the People,* but *Rosmersholm*: "When I think how slow and heavy and dull the general intelligence is at home, when I notice the low standard by which everything is judged, a deep despondency comes over me, and it often seems to me that I might just as well end my literary activity at once. They really do not need poetry at home; they get along so well with the *Parliamentary News* and the *Lutheran Weekly.* And then they have their party papers. I have not the gifts that go to make a good citizen, nor yet the gift of orthodoxy; and what I possess no gift for I keep out of. Liberty is the first and highest condition for me. At home they do not trouble much about liberty, but only about liberties, a few more or a few less, according to the standpoint of their party. I feel, too, most painfully affected by the crudity, the plebeian element, in all our public discussion. The very praiseworthy attempt to make of our people a democratic community has inadvertently gone a good way towards making us a plebeian community. Distinction of soul seems to be on the decline at home."

So early as March 16, 1882, Ibsen announces to his publisher that he is "fully occupied with preparations for a new play." "This time," he says, "it will be a peaceable production which can be read by Ministers of State and wholesale merchants and their ladies, and from which the theatres will not be obliged to recoil. Its execution will come very easy to me, and I shall do my best to have it ready pretty early in the autumn." In this he was successful. From Gossensass on September 9, he wrote to Hegel: "I have the pleasure of sending you herewith the remainder of the manuscript of my new play. I have enjoyed writing this piece, and I feel quite lost and lonely now that it is out of hand. Dr. Stockmann and I got on excellently together; we agree on so many subjects. But the Doctor is a more muddleheaded person than I am, and he has, moreover, several other characteristics because of which people will stand hearing a good many things from him which they might perhaps not have taken in such very good part had they been said by me."

A letter to Brandes, written six months after the appearance of the play (June 12, 1883), answers some objection which the critic seems to have made—of what nature we can only guess: "As to *An Enemy of the People,* if we had a chance to discuss it I think we should come to a tolerable agreement. You are, of course, right in urging that we *must* all work for the spread of our opinions. But I maintain that a fighter at the intellectual outposts can never gather a majority around him. In ten years, perhaps, the majority may occupy the standpoint which Dr. Stockmann held at the public meeting. But during these ten years the Doctor will not have been standing still; he will still be at least ten years ahead of the majority. The majority, the mass, the multitude, can never overtake him; he can never have the majority with him. As for myself, at all events, I am conscious of this incessant progression. At the point where I stood when I wrote each of my books, there now stands a fairly compact multitude; but I myself am there no longer; I am elsewhere, and, I hope, further ahead." This is a fine saying, and as just as it is fine, with respect to the series of social plays, down to, and including, **Rosmersholm.**

To the psychological series, which begins with **The Lady from the Sea,** this law of progression scarcely applies. The standpoint in each is different; but the movement is not so much one of intellectual advance as of deepening spiritual insight.

I hold that that man is in the right who is most closely in league with the future.

—Henrik Ibsen

As Ibsen predicted, the Scandinavian theatres seized with avidity upon **An Enemy of the People.** Between January and March, 1883, it was produced in Christiania, Bergen, Stockholm, and Copenhagen. It has always been very popular on the stage, and was the play chosen to represent Ibsen in the series of festival performances which inaugurated the National Theatre at Christiania. The first evening, September 1, 1899, was devoted to Holberg, the great founder of Norwegian-Danish drama; **An Enemy of the People** followed on September 2; and on September 3 Björnson held the stage, with *Sigurd Jorsalfar.* Oddly enough, *Ein Volksfeind* was four years old before it found its way to the German stage. It was first produced in Berlin, March 5, 1887, and has since then been very popular throughout Germany. It has even been presented at the Court Theatres of Berlin and Vienna—a fact which seems remarkable when we note that in France and Spain it has been pressed into the service of anarchism as a revolutionary manifesto. When first produced in Paris in 1895, and again in 1899, it was made the occasion of anarchist demonstrations. It was the play chosen for representation in Paris on Ibsen's seventieth birthday, March 29, 1898. In England it was first produced by Mr. Beerbohm Tree at the Haymarket Theatre on the afternoon of June 14, 1893. Mr. (now Sir Herbert) Tree has repeated his performance of Stockmann a good many times in London, the provinces, and America. He revived the play at His Majesty's Theatre in 1905. Mr. Louis Calvert played Stockmann at

the Gentleman's Concert Hall in Manchester, January 27, 1894. I can find no record of the play in America, save German performances and those given by Mr. Tree; but it seems incredible that no American actor should have been attracted by the part of Stockmann. *Een Vijand des Volks* was produced in Holland in 1884, before it had even been seen in Germany; and in Italy *Un Nemico del Popolo* holds a place in the repertory of the distinguished actor Ermete Novelli.

Of all Ibsen's plays, **An Enemy of the People** is the least poetical, the least imaginative, the one which makes least appeal to our sensibilities. Even in **The League of Youth** there is a touch of poetic fancy in the character of Selma; while **Pillars of Society** is sentimentally conceived throughout, and possesses in Martha a figure of great, though somewhat conventional, pathos. In this play, on the other hand, there is no appeal either to the imagination or to the tender emotions. It is a straightforward satiric comedy, dealing exclusively with the everyday prose of life. We have only to compare it with its immediate predecessor, **Ghosts,** and its immediate successor, **The Wild Duck,** to feel how absolutely different is the imaginative effort involved in it. Realising this, we no longer wonder that the poet should have thrown it off in half the time he usually required to mature and execute one of his creations.

Yet **An Enemy of the People** takes a high place in the second rank of the Ibsen works, in virtue of its buoyant vitality, its great technical excellence, and the geniality of its humour. It seems odd, at first sight, that a distinctly polemical play, which took its rise in a mood of exasperation, should be perhaps the most amiable of all the poet's productions. But the reason is fairly obvious. Ibsen's nature was far too complex, and far too specifically dramatic, to permit of his giving anything like direct expression to a personal mood. The very fact that Dr. Stockmann was to utter much of his own indignation and many of his own ideas forced him to make the worthy Doctor in temperament and manner as unlike himself as possible. Now boisterous geniality, loquacity, irrepressible rashness of utterance, and a total absence of self-criticism and self-irony were the very contradiction of the poet's own characteristics—at any rate, after he had entered upon middle life. He doubtless looked round for models who should be his own antipodes in these respects. John Paulsen, as we have seen, thinks that he took many traits from Jonas Lie; others say that one of his chief models was an old friend named Harald Thaulow, the father of the great painter. Be this as it may, the very effort to disguise himself naturally led him to attribute to his protagonist and mouthpiece a great superficial amiability. I am far from implying that Ibsen's own character was essentially unamiable; it would ill become one whom he always treated with the utmost kindness to say or think anything of the kind. But his amiability was not superficial, effusive, exuberant; it seldom reached that boiling-point which we call geniality; and for that very reason Thomas Stockmann became the most genial of his characters. He may be called Ibsen's Colonel Newcome. We have seen from the letter to Hegel that the poet regarded him with much the same ironic affection which Thackeray must have felt for that other Thomas who, amid many differences, had the same simple-minded, large-hearted, child-like nature.

In technical quality, *An Enemy of the People* is wholly admirable. We have only to compare it with *Pillars of Society,* the last play in which Ibsen had painted a broad satiric picture of the life of a Norwegian town, to feel how great an advance he had made in the intervening five years. In naturalness of exposition, suppleness of development, and what may be called general untheatricality of treatment, the later play has every possible advantage over the earlier. In one point only can it be said that Ibsen has allowed a touch of artificiality to creep in. In order to render the peripetia of the third act more striking, he has made Hovstad, Billing, and Aslaksen, in the earlier scenes, unnaturally inapprehensive of the sacrifices implied in Stockmann's scheme of reform. It is scarcely credible that they should be so free and emphatic in their offers of support to the Doctor's agitation, before they have made the smallest inquiry as to what it is likely to cost the town. They think, it may be said, that the shareholders of the Baths will have to bear the whole expense; but surely some misgivings could not but cross their minds as to whether the shareholders would be prepared to do so. (pp. 3-11)

> William Archer, in an introduction to An Enemy of the People and The Wild Duck *by Henrik Ibsen, Charles Scribner's Sons, 1911, pp. 3-11.*

Bernard Shaw (essay date 1922)

[*Shaw is generally considered the greatest dramatist to write in the English language since Shakespeare. He succeeded in revolutionizing the English stage, disposing of the romantic conventions and devices of the "well-made play" and instituting a theater of ideas. During the late nineteenth century, Shaw was also a prominent literary, art, and music critic. In 1895 he became the drama critic for the* Saturday Review, *and his reviews therein became known for their biting wit and brilliance. During his three years at the* Saturday Review, *Shaw determined that the theater was meant to be a "moral institution" and "elucidator of social conduct." In the following excerpt from his* The Quintessence of Ibsenism, *he discusses Ibsen's negative opinion of democracy as revealed in* An Enemy of the People.]

[*An Enemy of the People*] deals with a local majority of middle-class people who are pecuniarily interested in concealing the fact that the famous baths which attract visitors to their town and customers to their shops and hotels are contaminated by sewage. When an honest doctor insists on exposing this danger, the townspeople immediately disguise themselves ideally. Feeling the disadvantage of appearing in their true character as a conspiracy of interested rogues against an honest man, they pose as Society, as The People, as Democracy, as the solid Liberal Majority, and other imposing abstractions, the doctor, in attacking them, of course being thereby made an enemy of The People, a danger to Society, a traitor to Democracy, an apostate from the great Liberal party, and so on. Only those who take an active part in politics can appreciate the grim fun of the situation, which, though it has an intensely

local Norwegian air, will be at once recognized as typical in England, not, perhaps, by the professional literary critics, who are for the most part *fainéants* as far as political life is concerned, but certainly by everyone who has got as far as a seat on the committee of the most obscure Ratepayers' Association.

As *An Enemy of the People* contains one or two references to Democracy which are anything but respectful, it is necessary to examine Ibsen's criticism of it with precision. Democracy is really only an arrangement by which the governed are allowed to choose (as far as any choice is possible, which in capitalistic society is not saying much) the members of the representative bodies which control the executive. It has never been proved that this is the best arrangement; and it has been made effective only to the very limited extent short of which the dissatisfaction which it appeases might take the form of actual violence. Now when men had to submit to kings, they consoled themselves by making it an article of faith that the king was always right, idealizing him as a Pope, in fact. In the same way we who have to submit to majorities set up Voltaire's pope, *Monsieur Tout-le-monde,* and make it blasphemy against Democracy to deny that the majority is always right, although that, as Ibsen says, is a lie. It is a scientific fact that the majority, however eager it may be for the reform of old abuses, is always wrong in its opinion of new developments, or rather is always unfit for them (for it can hardly be said to be wrong in opposing developments for which it is not yet fit). The pioneer is a tiny minority of the force he heads; and so, though it is easy to be in a minority and yet be wrong, it is absolutely impossible to be in the majority and yet be right as to the newest social prospects. We should never progress at all if it were possible for each of us to stand still on democratic principles until we saw whither all the rest were moving, as our statesmen declare themselves bound to do when they are called upon to lead. Whatever clatter we may make for a time with our filing through feudal serf collars and kicking off old mercantilist fetters, we shall never march a step forward except at the heels of "the strongest man, he who is able to stand alone" and to turn his back on "the damned compact Liberal majority." All of which is no disparagement of parliaments and adult suffrage, but simply a wholesome reduction of them to their real place in the social economy as pure machinery: machinery which has absolutely no principles except the principles of mechanics, and no motive power in itself whatsoever. The idealization of public organizations is as dangerous as that of kings or priests. We need to be reminded that though there is in the world a vast number of buildings in which a certain ritual is conducted before crowds called congregations by a functionary called a priest, who is subject to a central council controlling all such functionaries on a few points, there is not therefore any such thing in the concrete as the ideal Catholic Church, nor ever was, nor ever will be. There may, too, be a highly elaborate organization of public affairs; but there is no such thing as the ideal State. There may be a combination of persons living by the practice of medicine, surgery, or physical or biological research; or by drawing up wills and leases, and preparing, pleading, or judging cases at law; or by painting pictures, writing books, and acting plays; or by serving in regiments and battle ships; or by manual labor or industrial service. But when any of these combinations, through its organizers or leaders, claims to deliver the Verdict of Science, or to act with the Authority of the Law, or to be as sacred as the Mission of Art, or to revenge criticisms of themselves as outrages on the Honor of His Majesty's Services, or to utter the Voice of Labor, there is urgent need for the guillotine, or whatever may be the mode in vogue of putting presumptuous persons in their proper place. All abstractions invested with collective consciousness or collective authority, set above the individual, and exacting duty from him on pretence of acting or thinking with greater validity than he, are man-eating idols red with human sacrifices.

This position must not be confounded with Anarchism, or the idealization of the repudiation of Governments. Ibsen did not refuse to pay the tax collector, but may be supposed to have regarded him, not as the vicar of an abstraction called THE STATE, but simply as the man sent round by a committee of citizens (mostly fools as far as Maximus the Mystic's Third Empire is concerned) to collect the money for the police or the paving and lighting of the streets. (pp. 91-4)

> Bernard Shaw, in his The Quintessence of Ibsenism, *third edition, Constable and Company Ltd., 1922, 210 p.*

Hermann J. Weigand (essay date 1925)

[*Weigand was an American educator and critic specializing in German and medieval literature. In the following excerpt from his critical study* The Modern Ibsen: A Reconsideration, *he asserts that in* An Enemy of the People *Ibsen voices his views in a paradoxical, comic manner through the character of Dr. Stockmann.*]

The publication of *Ghosts* was followed by a storm of abusive criticism, the like of which Ibsen had never experienced before. So general was the tone of violent condemnation—no less in the Liberal than in the Conservative political camp—that even Frederic Hegel, whose generous policy as publisher of Ibsen's works had made for very cordial relations between them, felt called upon to utter a word of warning to the poet not to overstep the bounds of moderation. Ibsen's reply gave him to understand politely, but none the less firmly, that these were matters which exclusively concerned his own judgment. Numerous references to the reception of *Ghosts* in Ibsen's letters of this period show how deeply it affected him, despite his attempts to take the matter in a calm and unruffled way, as something entirely to be expected. These references show how much he had grown in the matter of self-control since the days of *Peer Gynt,* when he had felt ready to "club the life out of" an influential reviewer who had disparaged its poetic value. He could afford now to be calm, at least outwardly, for he was confident that the future was on his side.

Yet he would not have been Ibsen, had he not boiled inwardly with rage over the stupidity and the hypocritical cant of his detractors. But fortunately rage subsided into derisive humor; and in that frame of mind he conceived

and wrote his ringing dramatic defense, *An Enemy of the People.* For once, as is significant to note, he did not require the long period of incubation, characteristic of all the other productions of his maturity; the new play appeared in the fall of 1882, only a year after the publication of *Ghosts.* He could afford to forego it this time, since his breezy conception of the new subject from the comic angle allowed him to dispense on this occasion with the slow "laboratory work" of intimate psychological analysis.

Much has been written about whom Ibsen may have used as the model for Doctor Thomas Stockmann. The honor has been claimed for Björnson, Jonas Lie, Georg Brandes and more lately for a rather boisterous Christiania reformer, Harald Thaulow, who, among other things, wrote a pamphlet for which he borrowed from Ibsen the title of "Pillars of Society." Except so far as the sanguine Doctor's temperament is concerned, the discussion is idle; for the Doctor's ideas about society, as well as the vehement and paradoxical form of their utterance, are Ibsen's own; some of Doctor Stockmann's programmatic ideas are stoutly championed by Ibsen in his letters as far back as a decade before the play was written. It is clear, moreover, that in this case the ideas supplied the prime motive for writing the play. Ibsen was fairly aching to tell the world, and his Norwegian countrymen more specifically, what he thought of their governing classes, their political party life, their press, the catch words of the multitude and the march of progress in general. In Act IV, the brilliant climax of the play, he has his say out, shouting his convictions with the Doctor's voice above the din and the catcalls of the mob; and in Act V he gets his vicarious revenge on the press by having the irate hero brandish his umbrella aloft and put the rascals to flight.

From the point of view of stage mechanics, *An Enemy of the People* has no counterpart in Ibsen's works for lucid structure and drastic, swiftly moving action. By the first meeting of the two radically dissimilar and temperamentally antipathetic Stockmann brothers, the contrast that forms the basis of the dramatic conflict is sketched in bold relief, and our sympathies are manipulated with a deft hand that steers them in a predetermined path without friction or jostling. We witness the first preliminary tiff which is bound to be followed by a more serious clash. There is nothing for us to unlearn in the succeeding acts: no revelations are sprung in Ibsen's wonted fashion; the focus of our sympathies requires no readjusting. Thus the technique of retrospective analysis, by means of which Ibsen achieved both a complexity and an objectivity of character portrayal heretofore unknown in dramatic literature, is abandoned for once in favor of a directness and simplicity calculated to enlist our sympathies immediately and whole-heartedly on the side of the burly, obstreperous, artless and genial Doctor. A check is put on objective critical analysis; when we do not laugh *with* the Doctor because of the consternation he causes in the camp of his enemies, we laugh *at* his comic impetuousness and lack of sophistication; he endears himself irresistibly to us by the gratification he affords our sense of the comic; the essential attitude of comedy is sustained; the Doctor's sanguine temperament keeps us on the run, as it were, affording us no opportunity for critical detachment.

With a series of deft, sure strokes the first act outlines the situation and prepares for the conflict. In the course of the act all the characters, except Aslaksen and the "Badger," are introduced and tersely characterized. The economic and political situation of the little seaside resort is lucidly sketched,—the new era of prosperity, due to the Baths; the political truce between the Conservative and the Liberal faction, on economic grounds; the impending local elections, promising this time to be a tame affair; and withal the clearly discernible undercurrent of political and personal friction. The action is launched by the arrival of the letter confirming the Doctor's suspicion about the pollution of the Baths, and by the two consequential steps with which he follows up his discovery: the report, prepared in advance, is dispatched by a special messenger to the Burgomaster, and the news of the discovery is gleefully proclaimed to the convivial gathering in the Doctor's home. More sophisticated than the happy Doctor, we look forward to the breaking of the tempest.

Act II precipitates the conflict in earnest. The Doctor finds his cause espoused by the representatives of the Liberal press and of the compact majority of tax-payers. Tingling with elation because of this unsolicited support and still without guile, he receives his brother in the expectation of a grudgingly bestowed tribute of gratitude, only to be rudely jolted out of his bliss by the manner in which the latter has reacted to his discovery. Instead of being hailed as a public benefactor, he must hear himself scolded, abused, threatened and called an impossible person. His discovery is to be suppressed, and he is called upon to make good the mischief already wrought, by a public retraction of his statements. The Doctor comes to, out of his rosy dreams, under this rude attack. One illusion is definitely gone. If there is going to be a struggle, he is ready for a fight that will make the town ring.

Two more developments of importance occur in Act II besides the precipitating of the conflict. The attitude of Stockmann's father-in-law, Morten Kiil, gives us an idea of what a malicious interpretation will be put upon the Doctor's fight against his brother by one element of the population. The Morten Kiils—and there are many of them in every community—will not regard him as a disinterested benefactor. More important, however, is Hovstad's announced intention to make political capital out of the Doctor's find. With the publicist's eye for catchwords, he sees that the foulness bred by the stagnant waters of the swamp, symbolically interpreted, can be used with telling effect against the political stagnationists—the Conservative party; and with the local elections at hand, the time is most opportune for calling the political truce. Stockmann is taken aback at first by this unexpected turn; but it is sufficient for the canny journalist to play upon his artless zeal for enlightenment, by presenting the campaign as a crusade against "superstition," to win his conditional consent. And when he finds himself checked by his brother, a little later, this catchword of Hovstad's provides the spark that sets off the train of his own political and social fireworks.

Act III brings the turning-point. Intoxicated with a sense of power by the consciousness of having the Liberal press before him and the compact majority at his back, the Doctor sees red. He now has his mind set on nothing less than a thorough-going political revolution at home. He already sees the Burgomaster dethroned and himself in his place. But the collapse of his dreams comes with amazing swiftness. At the moment when the Doctor feels himself borne aloft on the crest of his enthusiasm, when he struts about in the office of the *Messenger,* parading the insignia of local authority before his brother's livid face, his allies desert him: A word of flattery on the part of the Burgomaster has clinched the defection of the wobbly Aslaksen; and Hovstad, bound to follow suit because he is financially at Aslaksen's mercy, moreover has a personal score to settle with the father of Petra. The suddenness of this change of fortune dazes the Doctor like a thunderclap, but only for a moment; then he realizes that this thunderclap has cleared the air to his advantage; it has swept away the cobwebs of illusion which distorted his vision and his thoughts. Far from his being defeated, the fight has just begun. Now for the first time he feels invincible in the face of the decisive contest impending.

In Act IV the Doctor stages his spirited come-back. Undaunted by the conspiracy of the press and the town to muzzle him, he has passed around the word that he would deliver a lecture; and curiosity has brought a representative crowd to the spacious dining-room of the old mansion which Captain Horster has put at his disposal. So far he has won; but he has failed to reckon with the concerted shrewdness of his opponents; for besides having prepared the ground by a campaign of whispers, they have had the boldness to appear in person. As the Doctor steps out upon the lecture platform, they play their trump card by insisting upon the election of a chairman, and this is followed by a resolution to deny him permission to read his lecture. He is out-maneuvered and beaten again, more decisively than the first time; so it seems. Then it is that a sort of Berserker wrath descends upon him, not unlike in effect to a divine inspiration,—a contingency with which his opponents had been unable to reckon beforehand. Having once gotten under way, nothing can check him before he has delivered himself of his indignation and of all the new ideas which have accumulated in his brain in the course of the last two days. Hissed, and finally mishandled by the mob, he none the less emerges as victor. He has achieved his purpose. He has had his say.

The last act presents a final series of concerted countermoves on the part of society to dislodge the Doctor from his position of victory in isolation. The broken glass and the rocks on the floor are simply the prelude to a thorough-going boycott of the Doctor, his family and their single friend. In addition, threats of moral blackmail and temptations to sell himself for a price drive in upon him from three different quarters. The Burgomaster threatens him with complete ostracism, but holds out the hope of eventual reinstatement—at a price. As the Doctor refuses to budge, his brother is overjoyed to find a lever against him in the admission that old Morten Kiil is taking delight in the rumpus. It will now be easy to represent his conduct in such a light as to indicate an existing deal between the Doctor and his rich old father-in-law, who has old scores to settle with the Baths Committee; hence further conciliatory moves are no longer dictated by prudence. The second attack upon his honesty is staged by old Morten Kiil himself. This time he is less shocked by the insinuations involved in the proposed deal—it was the sort of thing to expect from the canny old "Badger"—but he feels the turn of the screws in his flesh most painfully; for it is now no longer a question primarily of himself: By persisting in his course he will be robbing his wife of her paternal inheritance. The third attack on his integrity is delivered by his former allies, Hovstad and Aslaksen. Crediting him with a shrewdness and hypocrisy which staggers his imagination, they open his eyes to the opportunity of amassing wealth at a single stroke by artificially depressing the value of the stock of the Baths. To clinch the speculation safely, the spokesman of the press and the leader of the compact majority offer to put their forces at his disposal, in return for their getting a share in the deal. Thus the three attacks involve, objectively considered, a dynamic increase in the magnitude of the temptation: The Burgomaster offered eventual reinstatement; Morten Kiil held out financial security; Hovstad and Aslaksen put him within reach of wealth and power. The third temptation, by the utter depravity of its proponents and by their imputation of an equal depravity on the Doctor's part, neutralizes the earlier temptation, which he had felt as painfully real, and brings about the utter moral and physical rout of the whole rotten gang. This victory is decisive. The authorities, the press, the respectable middle class and the rabble have spent the shafts of their attacks. They have not succeeded in making the Doctor budge one inch from his position. He stands there, erect, a living proof of the final truth he has discovered: "The strongest man in the world is he who stands most alone."

In its lucid grouping of the forces, its brisk movement, the head-on clash of opposites, the rapid marshaling of moves and countermoves, the graphic presentation of the turning-point, the vigor of the dynamic climax and the drastic conclusion, the play resembles the staging of a spirited sham battle. *An Enemy of the People* is without question a brilliant feat of stage mechanics. Over against this fact, the looseness in this play of Ibsen's usually puncture-proof motivation scarcely cuts any figure. Stockmann's artless expectation to find the Burgomaster peeved over his discovery, because it will dim his own reputation of being the most deserving citizen of the town; his wife's concurring in this sentiment; her comic dread of that fearsome thing, the compact majority—these would strain plausibility to the breaking point, if we did not react to them in the spirit of a game. Similarly, we have not the critical patience to ponder over Hovstad's alarming shortsightedness in espousing a cause that is bound to be unpopular. And as for Aslaksen coming to offer the Doctor his unsolicited support—supposing we already knew this man for the cautious political pussy-footer that he is; supposing we remembered the Doctor's reputation for "fads and crack-brained notions"—how could we possibly reconcile the constitutional wariness of this apostle of moderation with the blundering rashness of such a step? The fact is, the absence of scrupulous care in the realistic treatment of detail does not impinge upon our consciousness, because there are no eddies in the impetuous rush of the current of action, to give us pause.

We lay the play aside, tingling with elation over the Doctor's victory. Ibsen has made certain of that, by marshaling nothing but crooks and fools on the side of the opposition. There is the anæmic Burgomaster, a stickler for form, a sour-faced kill-joy, petty in his transparent egotism, petrified in his sense of authority, craftily hypocritical in his guardianship of the public weal; the two shabby journalists, opportunists and rascals of the coarsest texture, loud-mouthed and dirtily treacherous; the respectable, whining, sanctimonious preacher of moderate discretion; the filthy old tanner, bestially ignorant like the peasant of Holberg's day, stingy, and cruel, and shrewd withal; and behind these, the mass of burghers, colorless and timid, cowardly like a herd of sheep, coarse in their brutality, and yet restrained by the cowing discipline of many generations. Not a one among them whom we do not heartily despise for his meanness. Against this background of sordidness the figure of the Doctor is bound to stand out in boldest relief. His brusque, unsophisticated geniality takes our hearts by storm. His temperamental enthusiasm is catching. His very simplicity is so lovable that from our superior vantage-point we applaud him and egg him on, like an impish child exposing the make-believes of convention. After witnessing his naïve delight in the juicy roast of beef and in his other newly acquired luxuries—the tablecloth, and the lamp-shade which really diffuses the light quite artistically—we could never be angry at him,—or take him quite seriously. No matter what unpleasant things he may say, we will never construe them as aimed at ourselves, since we feel so superior to him, intrenched as we are in the refinements of our civilization. We are grateful to him for making us laugh. We would forgive anything he did for the sake of such a choice remark as: "A man should never put on his best trousers when he goes out to battle for truth and freedom." But what stampedes the play-goer's sympathy even more than the Doctor's geniality, enthusiasm, and naïveté, is his indomitable fighting spirit. His conviction of righteousness is backed by the most tenacious pugnacity. He is blindly courageous. His fighting spirit once aroused, he is ready to charge a whole army single-handed. Now the average red-blooded man likes to see nothing so much as a good fight. He will always cheer the fighter who, though outnumbered, refuses to budge. And the greater the odds against the staunch, single-handed champion, the greater the number of cowardly toughs and bullies who fall upon him, the more wildly the spectator will cheer when the whole mob of them is eventually routed by the courage of the lone individual who cannot be beaten, because—as we say—he never knows when he is licked. Stockmann scores two such brilliant victories: the first, when he upsets the crafty plans of his opponents by his impromptu broadside, when he fills their ranks with consternation by having his say out; the second, when he puts Hovstad and Aslaksen to flight by the flourish of his umbrella. Without any doubt, it is the fighting qualities of the doughty Doctor, above all, which have made him a stage idol.

So much for the personal aspects of the Doctor's victory. At the same time, however, we see the struggle between the Doctor and the town from a larger perspective. A public-spirited citizen has made a discovery of vital importance to the whole town. The authorities enter into a conspiracy with the press and the leaders of the opposition to suppress the inconvenient discovery by all the tricks and stratagems at their disposal. By his fight to make himself heard, the Doctor automatically becomes the champion of truth versus lie, of right against might. That is the only issue we see or care about, once we are under the spell of the play's suggestion; and at the conclusion we tingle with satisfaction over the vindication of truth and the exposure of falsehood. We feel we have been assisting at a contest between God and the Devil, and that God won. We are intuitively aware, in fact, that the whole play is focussed upon this issue.

Is this issue justified by the situation? The very question may be startling to the reader,—so securely have we been enmeshed by the net of suggestion spread to capture our sympathies for the genial Doctor; so willingly have we yielded to the author's adroit manipulation of our feelings. However, once the above analysis of the basis of our sympathies has made it apparent that our critical reason was shunted off to a siding from the very outset, in order to clear the track for the fast express of our emotions,—then our exultation in the triumph of truth over lie, in the victory of God and the disgraceful rout of the Devil will appear premature. Our reason will clamor for a review of the situation, before our zealous moral approval becomes final.

In all fairness we must put the Doctor's righteous cause on the defensive and examine its claims reasonably, critically. We must stop our ears against the persuasive eloquence of the advocate. We must even spice our objectivity with a pinch of skepticism.

Let our critical gaze dwell for a moment on the Doctor, as he flourishes the fateful letter. After creating an atmosphere of breathless tension by his rhetorical questions punctuated by effective pauses, he announces his discovery with a burst of emphasis that carries a shock like the sudden release of a high-voltage current. His body can scarcely stand up under the exuberance of pride and joy with which his discovery fills him. His outward personal modesty merely accentuates the importance of his find. "He has only been doing his duty. He has been a lucky treasure-digger." Now, what is it, precisely, that he is overjoyed about? The fact, he would say, that a very significant truth has been brought to light. Of course, we find this unspeakably amusing. He is gratified, in reality, at this new proof of his cleverness, of his superior insight and at the opportunity it affords him to bring this fact home in a most humiliating manner to the Board of Directors. Why had he carried on his investigations in absolute secrecy? Not from any sense of discretion—subsequent acts of his show that there is no trace of this in his make-up—but plainly, in order to spring a dramatic surprise upon his hectoring brother. A very human way to feel, surely, and justified in part by the snobbery and stupidity of the authorities. This much should be clear, however, from the outset: The Doctor is animated by temperamental pugnacity, a fairly active feeling of personal jealousy and an extremely good opinion of himself. He fools himself right along by persuading himself that his conduct is dictated by an abstract love of truth. Now, to begin with, we are perfectly aware of the human-all-too-human animus of his

conduct. However, as the play progresses and the issue becomes defined, the Doctor imperceptibly glides into the position of a champion of righteousness against lying hypocrisy. . . . Glides into this position, I said. Is jockeyed into this position—formulates the fact more precisely.

Having dispatched his report to the Burgomaster and broadcast the news among his friends, the Doctor struts about in a state of bliss, ready to see things take their course. By his lack of discretion he has already prejudiced the success of his reform immeasurably. His report is couched in such language that his brother, who was primarily responsible for the initial blunder in laying the pipes, is bound to see in it the ax that threatens to cut off his political career. To be sure, we do not see the report, but we hear Billing's comment: "Strong! Why, strike me dead if it isn't crushing! Every word falls like a—well, like a sledge-hammer." So, if our sympathies had not been set against the Burgomaster from the outset, and if he did not continue to parade the stupidity of the ossified bureaucrat, we could not blame him overmuch for refusing to accept his brother's verdict without a struggle. Or is the Burgomaster not right in remarking during his interview with the Doctor the next day that the matter in question is not a purely scientific one; that it has both a technical and an economic side? And is he not right in insisting that the matter be taken under calm deliberation with a view to finding less costly remedies than the one dictated by the Doctor to the Board? But even more serious than the dispatching of his provocatively phrased report is the ill-timed publicity which the Doctor has given the matter. This action of his, by the way, is rooted in one of his fundamental maxims, linked up, significantly, with the concept of duty: "It is a citizen's duty, when he has conceived a new idea, to communicate it to the public!" Now it is only a question of days before the whole town, and then the surrounding communities, will get wind of the affair, and it requires very little imagination to picture how they will exploit the rumor to their own advantage and to the ruin of the discredited rival resort.

The Doctor does not look at his actions from this angle; in fact, he is prevented from following out their probable consequences and from feeling any regret at the threatening economic calamity by the soothing consciousness of having done his duty. Duty is the lodestar to which he hitches his wagon, and at which he gazes both before and after his fight. . . . A lodestar? In reality a will-o'-the-wisp that keeps dancing in front of the reckless driver instead of guiding his course; a word fetish that harbors a double danger; serving by its absoluteness both as a blinder against any possible enlargement of his vision and as a feed-supply, turning the whole volume of his energy into a single channel. This consciousness of having done nothing but his duty is precisely the most dangerous feature to society of the Doctor's mental make-up, for it allows him to wash his hands completely of the consequences of his discovery. It dispenses him from any responsibility to see facts in their social relations. Accordingly, the Doctor feels it as no concern of his to see what his discovery may lead to. Any person who had the welfare of the community really at heart would have been aghast at the perspectives opened up by such a discovery. Not so the Doctor.

He rides the hobby-horse of principle, and to the man who rigorously bases his conduct on principle it is, in fact, a matter of conscience not to shy any sidelong utilitarian glances in the direction of possible consequences, inasmuch as such glances would be apt to vitiate the precise moral aim of his conduct.

Thus Stockmann turns out to be an extremely dangerous individual to any community. For a man who is pugnacious by temperament, who is always ready to start a fight to prove that he is right, and who at the same time is conscious of merely doing his duty, of following the voice of his conscience and of "setting aside his personal interests for the sake of his deepest, holiest convictions"—this sort of man will always have occasion to take up arms for the sake of truth and justice. He will always see things as either black or white; his reformer's ardor will never be dampened by any disquieting realization of there being perhaps two sides, or even more than two sides to a question. His conscience will always unerringly tell him what path to pursue; for, since he sees things from only one angle, he can apply his crude moral yardstick to the most delicate question without the least sense of inadequacy. Matthew Arnold's formulation of the "Hebraistic" attitude of mind, pushed to its extreme, expresses his outlook upon life. The "Hebraist," we remember, is primarily, if not exclusively, concerned with acting according to the best light that he has; whereas the "Hellenist," less concerned with acting, is more intent on increasing his lights. By which I would not be understood to imply that the Burgomaster and his ilk are "Hellenists" in any sense of the word.

Of course, our criticism of the Doctor is based on the assumption that the social welfare is a vital matter,—the so-cial welfare, bound up in this specific case, with the actual carrying out of the necessary reforms. But on this very point the Doctor, if consistent, would most sharply take issue with us. The social welfare, he would say, is of only accidental import as compared with the vindication of truth for its own sake. It is man's supreme duty to tell the truth; and if society withers under its hot flame, so much the worse for society; let it perish! This is the position of the ethical absolutist, who looks upon life as but an agency for the realization of abstract morality, instead of viewing morality from the biological angle as the regulation of conduct in the interest of life. As in the Doctor's case, life itself invariably refutes the position of the ethical absolutist by demonstrating to him, as it did to Brand, that the earth has no use for such as he.

Now let us see how the Doctor continues in the course on which he has embarked so recklessly.

At noon, on the day after the Doctor had made his discovery, the Burgomaster visits his brother and gives him to understand that for personal "and other" reasons he is very loth to take official cognizance of the Doctor's report. He would be politically discredited, if the responsibility for bungling the construction of the waterworks were to be laid squarely at his door. The Doctor now has his choice between several courses of action. Supposing that he really cherished kindly feelings toward his brother, he could offer to revise his report in such a way as to eliminate its exultingly offensive tone and leave it to the initiative of the Board to investigate the means for remedying the trouble. On the other hand, if he is anxious to have his brother get his deserts, he has the perfect right to insist that his brother, in his capacity of chairman, submit the report to the Baths' Committee; and if his brother refuses, it would be perfectly in order for him to hand his report to the officer next in rank. Now supposing that the Board refused to consider his communication or to take energetic action, it would be up to the Doctor to resign his position. Then he would be free to give the matter the fullest publicity through the press, at home and abroad. It is reasonable to suppose that the fear of such action on his part would be sufficient to force the hand of the Board, from mere motives of prudence; for any board of directors can be credited with enough business sense to know that damaging publicity would ruin the whole enterprise. But the Doctor considers neither of these legitimate alternatives. Yielding to his personal animus against his hectoring and hypocritical brother, he rushes to the offices of the press and gives Hovstad full authority to bring the report out in print.

So much is clear by now: Whoever wins, whether it be the Doctor or the Burgomaster, the Baths are certain to be the loser. Their reputation abroad will be damaged beyond repair by the noisy airing of the dispute among the public of the borough. Supposing the Doctor wins, the closing of the Baths for a couple of years will be the signal for brisk competition among the neighboring towns for diverting the stream of invalids to their own shores. By the time the Baths are reconditioned, the confidence of the outside public will have been so thoroughly undermined that there will be no patients forthcoming. Facts are never the sole factor in maintaining or building a reputation. As a matter

Ibsen at the age of thirty.

of fact we know that the Doctor loses out, so far as the press and the sentiment of the town is concerned. Yet the result is the same. The day after the Doctor's speech the stocks of the Baths sell for a song. The undertaking is discredited. Doctor Stockmann has succeeded in ruining the town.

We never looked at the situation from that angle when we cheered the Doctor in his spectacular fight. The fact is, once the conflict had become acute, we didn't give a tinker's dam about the Baths or the Town. We had forgotten all about technical and economic considerations. All we saw was a moral issue, in which from moment to moment the contrast between white righteousness and black crookedness became more intense. It served them right, we felt, those grotesque mummies, those sanctimonious blackguards and the whole cowardly mass of their followers—it served them right to reap the fruits of their lying hypocrisy, to be shown up in their despicable rottenness by the stalwart hero, the champion of truth, who grows, in fact, to the stature of a martyr. For has he not sacrificed his future and made paupers of his family, all because he would not descend to the low level of hypocrisy where he would have had to feel like spitting in his own face?

The play began by sounding the keynote of temperamental antipathy and personal jealousy. Imperceptibly the focus of the conflict was warped and twisted, until we saw it—were forced to see it—as a struggle of right against might. This turn guaranteed the play the whole-hearted applause of the compact majority of right-minded citizens and æsthetic philistines (begging the reader's pardon and our own!). The moral issue is always popular. We have but to remember that when a government finds itself drifting into war, its first task is to find a moral issue around which to rally the idealism of the country. Call the war a crusade against the foe of morality and civilization, and you are certain of the support of the compact majority.

An Enemy of the People is undeniably a successful play. My quarrel with Ibsen is about the means by which he has achieved its success. He has tricked our judgment like a dexterous lawyer. By manipulating the conflict until it comes to look like a clean-cut moral issue, by dinning the terms truth and lie into our ears, he makes us succumb to the Doctor's own moral word-fetishism. We see the Doctor as uprightness personified, as the defender of truth for truth's sake; we are tricked into forgetting that it is personal jealousy, an extremely good opinion of himself, a thirst for power and the love of stirring up a tempest, which are at the bottom of his conduct. We are tricked into taking his word for it that he loves his native town very dearly, whereas in reality he shows the most callous indifference to its material welfare. The Doctor's glee over his discovery, his mania of rushing into print, are represented as harmless temperamental idiosyncrasies, serving to endear him to us all the more, by contributing to our comic gratification,—when in reality they are evidences of an alarmingly anti-social point of view. With an adroitness that would do credit to an accomplished demagogue, Ibsen has fooled us into believing that the unsocial anti-social Doctor Stockmann is a genuine friend of the people.

Let it be said at once: To make my point clear, I have been forced to overstate the case. That Ibsen should have sacrificed his objectivity through a deliberate desire to cater to the taste of the public is, of course, out of the question. The discrepancy between the premises and the conclusion of the play is due to a clash of forces in Ibsen's own self. We have only to reverse our approach to the problem to see this at once.

At the beginning of this chapter I stated that this play was fathered not by a problem but by a definite purpose. Ibsen felt the urge to find an outlet for his pent-up indignation, to lash his countrymen with his scorn for their political and social muddling, to drive home his conviction that the time for a radical house-cleaning was at hand. It was this urge that begot the situation and the characters of the play. The figure of Doctor Stockmann was conceived to fill Ibsen's need for a mouthpiece through which he could hurl at the world, in a single bombardment, all the unpleasant "truths" that had been accumulating in his mind for more than a decade. Now it happened that the psychologist in Ibsen was not dozing all the time while the irate reformer was on a rampage; at intervals he double-crossed his partner by sawing through the props on which the fine ethical facade of the Doctor's indignation was built. Of course, he had to do this furtively, as it was a piece of sabotage, directed against his own creation. It was a case of taking care not to let the right hand know what the left hand was doing; and to make this possible, the whole play had to be steeped in the changing, unreal, iridescent lights of comedy, where make-believe, somehow or other, contrives to take liberties which we do not tolerate in serious realistic drama.

An Enemy of the People marks in many respects a short-lived but all the more vigorous renewal of the turbulent ferment of Ibsen's earlier storm and stress. The political and social message of Ibsen-Stockmann's dramatic sermon, which it remains for us to study, is anything but the mellow fruit of mature wisdom. The indignant reformer chafes at the bit; time and again he jumps the traces to bolt away from the thinker, at a breakneck gallop, over cliffs and precipices.

The fiction, brilliantly sustained, that the ideas contained in the Doctor's impromptu broadside had crystallized in two days—hence their provocative paradoxical form—must not let us lose sight of the fact that ideas just as revolutionary in substance and not a whit less extreme in form had been churning in Ibsen's brain for more than a decade. Ibsen frankly admits the substantial identity of viewpoint uniting him with the Doctor, in the letter with which he posted his manuscript to his publisher. "Doctor Stockmann and I got on excellently together," he writes on September 9, 1882; "we agree on so many subjects. But the Doctor is a more muddle-headed person than I am, and he has, moreover, several other characteristics for the sake of which people will stand hearing a good many things from him which they might perhaps not have taken in such very good part had they been said by me." As we see, Ibsen, with his native caution, indorses the Doctor with reservations; moreover he admits that there was method in hiding his own caustic self under the winning geniality of the Doctor's temperament.

In two letters of the year 1872, written at an interval of less than two weeks, Ibsen formulates the tenets which stand out ten years later as the Doctor's most important discoveries. On March 21, in a letter to Frederick Gjertsen, he tersely refers to the statement that the minority is always in the right as "my fundamental principle in every field and domain." In a letter to Georg Brandes, dated April 4, we find the Doctor's final discovery stated as follows: "To me it appears that the man who stands alone is the strongest." It is at bottom the same view of things which finds expression in an earlier letter to Brandes. A man with a mission, he writes on March 6, 1870, can not afford the luxury of keeping friends. They are too costly, not because of anything one has to do in their behalf, but because of what one has to refrain from doing in order to keep their friendship. Friendship, Ibsen has found, involves the unavoidable compromise of rigid principle; and compromise, we know from "Brand," is the very devil.

Even in the revolutionary fervor of his radicalism Ibsen yields not an inch to the Doctor's excited outbursts. We must content ourselves here with touching on only a few of the high lights of his pertinent utterances. Among the most characteristic of these is a poem of 1869, addressed to a revolutionary agitator. In defending himself against the charge of political indifference, Ibsen here calls for a more radical revolution than any contemplated by the politicians. Only one thoroughgoing revolution in the world's history he admits: the deluge. But even that, according to him, was bungled, since Noah was left to float securely in his ark. Let the thing be done over again, he exclaims. The next time I'll put a torpedo under the ark! The trouble with the politicians—Ibsen says in the period of his most stimulating interchange of ideas by letter with George Brandes—is that they want only their own special revolutions—revolutions in externals, in politics. From special revolutions Ibsen expects no good. The whole race is on the wrong track; that is the trouble. In anticipating the dawn of the Third Empire, he embraces the creed of philosophic anarchism: "The state must be abolished! In that revolution I will take part. Undermine the idea of the state, make willingness and spiritual kinship the only essentials in the case of a union—and you have the beginning of a liberty that is of some value." He had startled Brandes by the paradox, a little earlier, in commenting on the termination of the Italian troubles: "And then the glorious aspiration after liberty—that is at an end now. Yes—I must confess that the only thing I love about liberty is the struggle for it; I care nothing for the possession of it." Brandes' skeptical rejoinder to the whimsically humorous tone of this confession provoked a serious explanation on Ibsen's part: "What I call the struggle for liberty is nothing but the constant, living assimilation of the idea of freedom. He who possesses liberty otherwise than as a thing to be striven for, possesses it dead and soulless; for the idea of liberty has undoubtedly the characteristic, that it develops steadily during its assimilation. So that a man who stops in the midst of the struggle and says: 'Now I have it'—thereby shows that he has lost it. It is, however, exactly this dead maintenance of a certain given standpoint of liberty that is characteristic of the communities which go by the name of states—and this it is that I have

called worthless." All very well as a philosophic attitude, Brandes doubtless said to himself; but what bearing has it on the concrete Italian situation?

Somewhat later, again, we find Ibsen dwelling on struggle as such, as the embodiment of real values. With reference to Brandes' own revolution in the world of letters, he writes: "What will be the outcome of this mortal combat between two epochs, I do not know; but, anything rather than the existing state of affairs—so say I. I do not promise myself that any permanent improvement will result from the victory; all development hitherto has been nothing more than a stumbling from one error into another. But struggle is good, wholesome, and invigorating." The same letter contains a concrete application of his ideas to Scandinavian politics: "Dear friend, the Liberals are freedom's worst enemies. Freedom of thought and spirit thrive best under absolutism; this was shown in France, afterwards in Germany, and now we see it in Russia."

Of particular interest as regards our play is a passage from a letter to Lorentz Dietrichson: "It appears to me doubtful whether better artistic conditions can be attained in Norway before the intellectual soil has been thoroughly turned up and cleansed, and all the swamps drained off." This bears the date of December 18, 1879. So the symbolism of poison-exuding stagnation had fastened on Ibsen's mind several years before *An Enemy of the People* was written, which makes it clear, by the way, that the metaphor antedates the plot, instead of the reverse.

Two more passages from Ibsen's letters to Brandes must be quoted because, contrary to the pessimistic keynote of his earlier utterances, they presuppose a belief in progressive evolution. On January 3, 1882, at the time when *An Enemy of the People* was germinating in his mind, he writes: "It will never, in any case, be possible for me to join a party that has the majority on its side. Björnson says: 'The majority is always in the right.' And as a practical politician he is bound, I suppose, to say so. I, on the contrary, must of necessity say: 'The minority is always right.' Naturally I am not thinking of that minority of stagnationists who are left behind by the great middle party which with us is called Liberal; but I mean that minority which leads the van, and pushes on to points which the majority has not yet reached. I mean: that man is right who has allied himself most closely with the future." And on June 12th of the following year he attempts to elucidate the Doctor's position in the following terms: "As to the *Enemy of the People,* if we had a chance to discuss it, I think we should manage to come to an agreement. You are, of course, right when you say that we must all work for the spread of our opinions. But I maintain that a fighter in the intellectual vanguard can never collect a majority around him. In ten years the majority will, possibly, occupy the standpoint which Doctor Stockmann held at the public meeting. But during these ten years the Doctor will not have been standing still; he will still be at least ten years ahead of the majority. He can never have a majority with him. As regards myself, at least, I am conscious of incessant progression. At the point where I stood when I wrote each of my books, there now stands a tolerably compact crowd; but I myself am no longer there; I am else-where; farther ahead, I hope."

All these quotations, besides establishing the solidarity of Ibsen with Doctor Stockmann in all essentials, bring home to us the complexity of Ibsen's own intellectual position. No single formula will avail to express Ibsen's outlook on life; it harbors too many contradictory elements. Indignation is the mother of his philosophy. The pathos of disillusioned idealism sounds the keynote of his thinking. Ibsen's favorite attitude is to take up his position in the impregnable fortress of absolute idealism. He does that in **Brand,** where he sounds the clarion call of All or Nothing, where he brands compromise—the law of life—as the radical evil. He does that again, in demanding that human society totally reorganize itself on lines of purely voluntary coöperation, unappalled by the fact that this demand flies in the face of the most deeply rooted instincts of human nature. Unappalled by this fact . . . , rather led on by it; for the impossibility of life's ever meeting his demands provides the surest guarantee against his ever having to relinquish his basic attitude of protest against life as existing and real. And protest, we know from **Love's Comedy, Brand** and **Peer Gynt,** had been the most stimulating factor in his creative production. Yet this fact should make us wary of taking his absolute idealism too seriously. In his reflective moments, at least, Ibsen resorted to it more as a fiction providing the best working basis for ethical progress. Only by willing the impossible, he thought, can the utmost possible be wrung from slothful human nature.

If we look sharply, we find, in fact, that Ibsen does concede a certain value to life as it is. At any rate he finds value in struggle. "Struggle is good, wholesome and invigorating." The permanent results may be negligible; it may be a mere see-saw from error to error; but his indorsement of struggle is essentially an affirmation of life. Life is good, he is compelled to say; for it harbors the possibility of fine tragedies.

And presently he goes farther: Life is not only struggle and movement, but the movement has a definite forward swing. He sees leaders in the van, and stragglers in the rear. The whole, seemingly inert mass is moving forward. Forward, that means it is good, if it means anything.

What then becomes of his indignation? By seeing life as a rhythmical process and pronouncing it good, he has deprived himself of any philosophical basis to fume in indignation against the whole universal process. But Ibsen's temperament comes to the rescue. Seen as a whole, the process of life is an invigorating struggle, with even a forward swing; but—its tempo is intolerably sluggish, measured against the tempo of Ibsen's own feverish blood. He would leap on and on, to ever greater heights, opening up wider and wider panoramas; but this onward rush is retarded by the snail's crawl of human nature—human nature around him and human nature within his own vitals, from which escape is impossible. Ever and again the feel of these fetters throws him into new paroxysms of rage. Then he forgets all that he has learned. He brandishes the absolute before the face of life, and finding it a misshapen caricature of the ideal, he flies at the throat of life in a frenzy of destructive ire.

Does this not also describe the position of the Doctor? Of course, it does one's heart good to hear his blunt and fearless exposure of the legends of democracy: the democratic myth of equality; the infallibility of the majority; the sham liberalism of our majority parties, whether they style themselves Liberal or Republican or Democratic as good Norwegians or one hundred per cent Americans. It is refreshing to hear party organization shown up in its character of a ruthless steam-roller that crushes and maims the spires of intellectual independence. The Doctor is perfectly right when he says that the masses, far from being the flower of a nation, as vote-catching demagogues and muddle-headed romanticists would have us believe, are but the raw material that must be fashioned into a people. But—all this perfectly sound criticism is vitiated by the indignation of the firebrand against the universal process of life as such. Hovstad has put the Doctor's mind on the track of using the poison-breeding stagnation of the Baths as a political catchword. Doctor Stockmann is too naïve to exploit a catchword deliberately: What happens is that the catchword takes possession of him; it becomes an obsession. From the moment he uses the word, it ceases to be a metaphor; it looms in his mind as a living reality. The absolute ideal has him in its grip, as he shouts: "All our sources of spiritual life are poisoned; our whole society rests upon a pestilential basis of falsehood." He has grasped the relativity of all political and social values; but he succumbs to the obsession of the metaphor in formulating this insight as follows: Truths are constantly turning into lies. A normal truth lives at most a space of twenty years; then, like a ham turned rancid, it spoils, becomes a lie and infects society with its moral scurvy. Now, in the nature of things, as the Doctor admits, the lethargic masses of the population, the majority, never come to adopt a truth until it has become stale and rotten; hence they are perpetually feeding on poison and will feed on it as long as the rhythm of life continues. So, from the standpoint of his metaphor he is perfectly logical in shouting: "The masses, the majority, this devil's own compact majority—it's that, I say, that's poisoning the sources of our spiritual life, and making a plague-spot of the ground beneath our feet." And the corollary is obvious: "All men who live upon a lie should be exterminated like vermin." Now, connecting up these statements, which all have their source in his indignant absolute idealism, we find that they range themselves into the following syllogism: Truths are forever turning into lies. All men who live upon a lie ought to be exterminated. The great mass of humanity is forever feeding on truths that have turned into lies. Hence, the whole human race, barring the small band of outposts who are fighting the poison, ought to be wiped off the face of the earth.

A fine conclusion for a physician to arrive at! Can't we see him cutting out his patients' diseased vitals, overjoyed at the confirmation of his diagnosis, despite the minor circumstance that he kills them the more quickly in the process? We remember that Brand, the physician of the soul, was just as radical. To him life was a little thing, compared to the vindication of the ideal. The soul of just one woman he managed to save, and her he killed in the process.

What is wrong with the Doctor's absolute idealism? Why does Life laugh at his impotent railing?

The Doctor's own insight into the relativity of values is his own logical undoing. Only, he manages to deceive himself by formulating his insight in terms that don't fit the case. He lays about himself with the double pair of terms "right and wrong"; "truth and lie"; and, besides failing to fit the case, these terms contradict each other.

It is senseless to say that the majority is always right, ipso facto, unless one means to utter a tautology expressing the basic conventional working rule of the political and social "game" as practiced in democratic communities. Nothing is thereby predicated about the wisdom of the majority's decision. But it is equally senseless to make a maxim of its opposite and say: The minority is always right. Of course, it goes without saying that the people who think independently are hopelessly outnumbered by the unthinking mob in any community at any time. But the statement, that the minority is always in the right, means something very different. It implies, in effect, that every issue resolves itself automatically into a clear-cut progressive and an equally clear-cut reactionary point of view. It schematizes and falsifies life by implying that all thinking dissenters point in the same direction. As if the present did not open as many vistas to the future as there are points to the compass!

In formulating the paradox about the minority always being in the right, the natural scientist got in the way of the social thinker. Strictly speaking, the terms right and wrong pertain only to relations of fact. When Galileo contended that the earth moved, in opposition to the compact majority of theologians, he was right and they were wrong. But what the Doctor has in mind is not matters of fact at all; "truths" of the sort which Galileo established do not become rancid and turn into lies in a space of twenty years. It is obvious that the Doctor is talking about matters very indirectly related to facts in the scientific sense, . . . matters like socialism, the open shop, prohibition, vivisection, birth control,—to mention only a few of the issues that at present agitate the popular consciousness.

In a developing society new issues are constantly coming to the fore, and issues which hotly agitated our forefathers are dead to us;—think of the religious wars! Principles which were felt as adequate to life, when formulated,—unrestricted economic competition, for instance—have to be modified as a result of the growing complexity of modern life. Life in all its phases is engaged in a constant process of adaptation to new conditions.

The Doctor is aware of this, after a fashion; but sees a hopeless tangle in which he involves himself by forcing the phases of this process into his ethical strait-jacket. . . . The exclusiveness of the Doctor's ethical outlook on life amounts to monomania. He reduces every issue to a struggle between staunch uprightness and wilful malice, to a fight between gods and devils; and the worst of it is: his gods turn into devils almost overnight and have to be fought by new gods, with tooth and claw.

How absurd when reduced to fundamentals; yet how refreshing as a comedy! We can show the Doctor's absurdity up piecemeal, only to find at the end of our labors that our comic delight in his racy personality is as vivid as it was at the outset!

In *An Enemy of the People,* Ibsen formulated his social philosophy in aphoristic and paradoxical fashion—or at least attempted to; this much is clear to every Ibsen student.

Hence we were bound to consider the Doctor's point of view in all seriousness and analyze it, with due reference to Ibsen's personal utterances, as to the kernel of its content.

Simple enough it seemed, no doubt, to the reader, as he saw us mount our charger and put our critical lance in rest.

But maybe, by the time we got through, he may have begun vaguely to suspect that we have been charging windmills.

Perhaps not; yet we have the feeling of having been caught up in the vortex of a whirlwind. The ground under our feet seemed solid enough when we began our critical analysis. But by and by everything began to reel most disconcertingly.

At first we felt tolerably sure that Ibsen stood squarely behind his doughty Doctor. When we showed up the contradictions in his views, we thought we had scored a victory over Ibsen.

But our confidence received a jar, when on several occasions we noticed what seemed like Ibsen furtively delivering an impish slap, behind our backs, at his temperamental hero. Worse still, the time came when we were no longer able to tell with any assurance whether Ibsen was serious or whether he was laughing at himself.

We begin to suspect that Ibsen felt it in his blood that he was about to react with his accustomed choleric vigor against the very ideas which he himself had so stoutly championed and of which he makes the Doctor the spokesman; that in order to accelerate this reaction he rushes with headlong violence to the aid of his Doctor; that he intentionally develops his one-sided ideas to the limit, in order to see them topple all the more swiftly by their inherent lack of poise.

Intentionally, I say, and yet not with full consciousness.

Perhaps this statement of the case approaches the truth: Ibsen wanted to drive it home to us, pound it in to us with sledge-hammers, that the Doctor was right. But, radical individualist that he was, he couldn't brook the idea of our agreeing with him; so, with the sure instinct that he would grow out of and above the Doctor's viewpoint, he subtly prepared the ground for reservations which he would some day utter as a surprising come-back.

Ibsen's very next play is such a come-back. In the *Wild Duck* the truth fanatic is mercilessly exposed as a sorry mischief-maker.

An Enemy of the People marks the last bright flare-up of the preacher in Ibsen. Not that the white-hot flame of his indignation could ever have turned into a warm mellow glow; but he never gave it full rein again in his subsequent plays. (pp. 101-32)

Hermann J. Weigand, in his The Modern Ibsen: A Reconsideration, *Henry Holt and Company, 1925, 416 p.*

Halvdan Koht   (essay date 1931)

[*Koht was a Norwegian historian, biographer, and critic. In the following excerpt from his* Life of Ibsen, *he discusses* An Enemy of the People *in the context of various philosophical ideas and personal relationships that may have influenced Ibsen.*]

[Ibsen had had the subject for **An Enemy of the People**] in mind even before he wrote **Ghosts.** It began to engage his thoughts already during the controversy about **A Doll's House,** but at that time it had not strained so hard for expression, and therefore **Ghosts** had been able to push it aside. Now it pressed powerfully forward, and already in the middle of March, 1882, only three months after **Ghosts** had come out, he was actively at work upon his new play.

The thoughts which thus took form were not new to him. On the contrary, they had lived in him from the time of his youth. They had come to him from that Danish fighter, Sören Kierkegaard—he who had turned his weapons sharply against all intellectual troop-drilling, and who had thrown out the apothegm: "The mob is falsehood." The idea was a part of the individualism which arose in the nineteenth century. A man like Tocqueville invented the catchword "the tyranny of the majority," and Stuart Mill explained philosophically the personal demand for freedom against the majority. From the opposite side came Bismarck, with his wish for at least some people in the State who would not submit to the majority; it was in a speech in November, 1881, that he poured his venom upon "die Höflinge der Majorität, die Registratoren der Majorität."

Ibsen had himself as early as . . . 1851 been in conflict with both the reactionary minority and the "liberal" majority. He had no reverence for inherited dogmas; he rejoiced in revolt, and in new ideas that sprang up. We hear the very ring of **An Enemy of the People** in the speech which Theodor Abildgaard, one of the first friends Ibsen won in Oslo, made at the labor meeting in 1850. He spoke of how the King with his veto could delay a law through three sessions of the Storthing, and then he asked: "But who can guarantee that a law which is made after the passage of so many years any longer answers to the need of the times?" He would not grant the old truths even so long a life as twenty years.

In **Brand** the cry had been: " 'Tis horrible to stand alone" and, "He hopeless fights who fights alone." But the meaning at bottom was that it was not honest or worthy of a human being to do anything else than to stand alone, to be one's self—for one's self. Both the Mayor and the Dean in the play are roundly satirized for their worship of the majority, and Peer Gynt, the antithesis to Brand, always goes with the majority; that is a foregone conclusion.

When Ibsen fled from Norway, it was in alarm at all that could bind a man in his association with other people, even if they were friends and kindred spirits; in 1872 he wrote and warned Georg Brandes against building any hopes for his campaign upon an association: "To me, at any rate, it appears that the lonely man is the strongest."

He developed hatred and contempt, especially for politics and political parties, most of all for everything called democracy. We know this mood well from **The League of Youth,** and through the seventies he constantly aired it in paradoxes and epigrams which became almost regular pet phrases in his conversations and letters. Especially in the letters to Georg Brandes in the early part of the seventies, while he was working to formulate his view of life, we find much of this—words and thoughts which later returned in **An Enemy of the People.** The continuity of his mental life was shown when, in 1875, in the foreword to the new edition of **Catiline,** he mentioned with scorn "Cicero, the assiduous advocate of the majority." We know that the same thoughts were particularly alive in him just before he wrote **Ghosts** in the winter of 1880-81.

On New Year's Eve, 1880, Ibsen had a conversation with Kristofer Janson about French politics, in which he found fault with the French for driving the monks out of their monasteries: "Is not that what I have always said, that you republicans are the most tyrannical of all? You do not respect individual freedom. A republic is that form of government in which individual freedom is given least opportunity." He only became more angry when Janson defended the campaign against the monks by saying that the majority of the people were on that side. "The majority?" said Ibsen: "What is the majority? The ignorant mass. Intelligence is always in the minority. How many of those who are in the majority do you think are entitled to have any opinion? Most of them are blockheads." The thought was personal enough, though it was almost like a quotation from Schiller, in the lines spoken by the only man who voiced opposition to the majority in the Polish Reichstag:

Was ist die Mehrheit? Mehrheit ist der Unsinn;

Verstand ist stets bes Wenigen nur gewesen.

Ibsen thought likewise of his own people. One time he said in all seriousness to Janson: "Norway has at least been given one good law since 1814, and that is the law to protect quack doctors. For now one can at least cherish the hope that a few more thousand idiots may be killed each year than would otherwise be the case." Another time he said: "Would that there might soon be a revolution at home! For then it should be one of my greatest delights to station myself on the barricade and shoot down Norwegian 'peasant aristocrats.' " He complained that there was no one at home who dared to think or put into action a great thought—there was nothing but petty trifles. "The only ones," he said, "who really have my sympathy, are the nihilists and socialists. They want something definite and are consistent." Immediately after the controversy over **Ghosts** he wrote in a letter: "Then, as at other times, the Norwegians proved to be the most cowardly of all; and the most cowardly among the cowards were, of course, the so-called liberals." In another letter he said about them: "They are poor stuff to man barricades with."

He himself wanted to stand on the barricade—in battle. After he had moved to Rome in 1880, he was assiduous in his attendance at the Scandinavian Club, and always he had something to complain of and blame the management for; even if his complaints were mere trifles, he always turned them into matters of "principle" and made an issue of them. There were some who wanted to make him president, but he was unwilling, and begged to be excused. Finally he said: "I tell you that I have to belong to the opposition."

It was indeed his own life and blood he infused into that Enemy of the People whom he created—the man whom life taught that "the strongest man in the world is he who stands most alone"—the obstinate fighter, Doctor Stockmann.

With all the bold aggressiveness of Ibsen's preceding plays, there was nevertheless something cool, something firmly restrained about the revolt in them. The dramatist had fathomed deeply enough the inner life which he described; but there was no rushing storm about the characters. Everything was subjected to the rules of a formal art.

This time the author gave free rein to his love of mockery, and created a comedy which truly gushed with life—in which the characters, and particularly the hero, were permitted to develop and play freely according to their own impulses, not always guided by the reins of dramatic laws. This was because Ibsen was here writing directly from life.

The name of the main character was taken from the house in Skien in which he himself was born. The name Stockmann took on a symbolic sound to him; he recognized himself in it, and he felt that he was on home ground again. "The badger" Morten Kiil likewise got his name from Skien. During the winter of 1880–81 Ibsen had amused himself with writing down some memories from his childhood in Skien; it was intended as an introduction to a complete autobiography, and Ibsen looked back upon himself with a little smile. The autobiography was never finished, but there was something of a portrait in *An Enemy of the People.* When he had completed the play, in September, 1882, he wrote to his publisher: "Doctor Stockmann and I get on splendidly together; we agree so well in many respects; but the Doctor has a more muddled head than I, and he has besides various other characteristics which make it possible that one may tolerate things from his mouth which might perhaps not be so well received if they had been spoken by me."

"Stockmann," he said many years later to a German friend, after having seen the play presented in Berlin, "ist zum Teil ein grotesker Bursche und ein Strudelkopf." To be sure, Doctor Stockmann had received much of Ibsen's own spirit; but for all that he became a living, independent personality, made up of traits and characteristics that were derived from many different sources.

In Munich, Ibsen had known a young German poet, Alfred Meissner, who had often told of something that had happened to his father. The father was a doctor in the well-known bathing resort of Teplitz in Bohemia in the 1830s, and when the cholera broke out there, he found it his duty to make this known to the public. By so doing he frightened all the guests away for that year, and the citizens of the town were enraged against him. They stoned his house, and he was forced to move away hurriedly. It is possible that this story may have given Ibsen the subject for the incident in *An Enemy of the People.* But the character of Stockmann he found much nearer home—in Norway.

In February, 1881, Harald Thaulow, an apothecary, had a terrific quarrel with the management of the Christiania Steam Kitchen. It was the last act of a struggle in which he had been engaged since 1872. In this struggle one of the incidents which made most noise was a meeting in October, 1874, three weeks after Ibsen had been back in Norway for his last visit. It was at this meeting that Thaulow read the protest which came to be known as his "truth-telling speech." He tried to assert against the management a whole series of unpleasant "truths"; and, as he said, he "must be unfaithful to his own nature if he did not, as he had done before, continue to speak the truth for its own sake."

This all sounded Ibsenesque enough, and in 1880 he sent out a pamphlet attacking the Steam Kitchen management under the Ibsenesque title "The Pillars of Society in Prose." At the February meeting in 1881 he read a supplement to this in which he attempted to prove that the Christiania Steam Kitchen was the greatest humbug in the city. There was a wild uproar at this meeting, and Thaulow could finally not be heard at all. "No one can stand against the mob," he cried, and he left the meeting with these words: "I will now have nothing more to do with you. I will not strew pearls in the sand. It is an infernal misuse of a free people in a free community. Now I will go. Kindly go to the dunce's corner and be ashamed of yourselves, all of you!" He went, and a fortnight later he suddenly died.

The account of this disturbed meeting, which was given yet stronger relief by the death of the main actor so soon after, may well have inspired Ibsen and helped him put life and color into the meeting where his own Doctor Stockmann tried to tell the truth to his people. And he may well have taken some traits from the apothecary Thaulow himself for his doctor. Thaulow was a bold and self-reliant man, and was besides a man of many impulses which often crossed each other in a somewhat unexpected manner. In 1881 Jonas Lie wrote about Henrik Wergeland, who was a cousin of Thaulow: "I have always seen the apothecary in him when he suffers from so many vagaries in his poetry."

But Ibsen himself has said that he had especially two men in mind when he created Stockmann. They were Jonas Lie and Björnstjerne Björnson.

The author Jonas Lie was one of his friends from the old days. It was Lie who had published *Love's Comedy* for him in 1862. Now they had lived as neighbors in Berchtesgaden in the summer of 1880; it was Ibsen who had directed Lie to this location, and there Ibsen had thoroughly en-

> The thing that gave *An Enemy of the People* vital power was not its opinions; it was the sap of life that rose lustily in it, the delightful boldly-carved persons that moved in it—all fostered and born of genuine poetic wrath.
>
> —*Halvdan Koht*

joyed studying his friend. Many an evening he stood out on the road and peered into Lie's living room. Jonas Lie was a great and remarkable person, with a big heart and an open mind. . . . But when he wrote, and even more when he spoke, it was sometimes difficult to follow his thoughts. Flash upon flash of lightning shot through his mind, and every single flash was clear and powerful in itself, but the inner current which drew the line between them, often lay hidden deep underneath. Much of the abruptness in Doctor Stockmann, as well as the goodness and joyousness, came from Jonas Lie.

But Björnson gave to Stockmann his indomitable strength and will. . . . Ibsen had thought much about Björnson in the winter of 1880–81, while Björnson was in America; and it must be remembered that it was precisely at this time that the subject for *An Enemy of the People* began to grow in his consciousness. Ibsen thought it a deed of great daring to set out on so long a journey, and every time he heard of storm or sickness, he became anxious. "Then it broke in upon my consciousness, how infinitely much you are to me, and to all of us," he wrote to Björnson on March 8, 1882, a week before the first letter in which he mentions that he is working on *An Enemy of the People.* "I felt that if anything should happen to you, if so great a disaster should strike our lands, then all joy of work would have departed from me." Some months later, when Björnson celebrated the twenty-fifth anniversary of his authorship, Ibsen wrote to him the highest praise he could give anyone: "His life was his best poem." He thought that Björnson had achieved the greatest thing a man can attain—"in his life to realize himself."

That which now impressed him with especial vividness, was how Björnson had never been afraid to risk his hide. He recalled the flag controversy in the spring of 1879—the stormy meeting over which Björnson had on that occasion presided in Oslo, with the entire city mob against him—a meeting which had led to the rabble's stoning the house of one of his brothers-in-arms. Ibsen had not the slightest sympathy with the movement for a pure flag—quite the contrary, and for that very reason Björnson would not call on him when passing through Munich the next fall. But Ibsen had been especially stirred by the persecution which Björnson was subjected to during the flag campaign. We learn that he inquired diligently for news about it. "It interests me," he said, "for it is outrageous." Then in the spring of 1881 came the boycott against Björnson by the Christiania élite when he was to speak for the Wergeland statue. There was indeed material enough here for an enemy of the people. The keen, reckless love of battle shown by Björnson through all of this was something which awakened both wonder and respect in Ibsen, and almost involuntarily Björnson must leave his mark on the fighter who took form in Ibsen's imagination.

Some of the joy of battle went into himself. . . . He wanted to ply the whip on people whom he held in contempt as a crowd of miserable slavish souls, and therefore his new controversial play became a merry comedy.

He himself suggested the connection between this and the earlier comedy, *The League of Youth,* by letting the printer Aslaksen appear anew, no longer now as the somewhat down-at-heels and unsettled fellow, but as a house-owner and respectable citizen. The old opposition had now become defenders of the old order; Lawyer Stensgård had become governor. How could one expect a true spirit of liberty among such people?

Ibsen took vast pleasure in writing the new play. And he did it rapidly, too; within nine months after *Ghosts* had come out, it was completed. He was soothed into good humor by the work, and again—as in the case of *The League of Youth*—he said that it was to be a "peaceable play," one "that may be read by cabinet ministers and big business men and by their ladies, and that the theaters need not be afraid of."

The new comedy had indeed much more of common humanity in its nature than *The League of Youth,* and it became a theater piece which could make a success anywhere in the world. In plot, in character-drawing, in language, it was fresher and more flexible than anything Ibsen had written before.

He could not escape the fact that people took sides for and against the opinions which were expressed in the play. Conservatives rejoiced over the ridicule of the democratic majority politics; anarchists welcomed it as a contribution to their social philosophy. But the thing that gave the play vital power was not its opinions; it was the sap of life that rose lustily in it, the delightful boldly-carved persons that moved in it—all fostered and born of genuine poetic wrath. (pp. 180-90)

> *Halvdan Koht, in his* The Life of Ibsen, Vol. 2, *translated by Ruth Lima McMahon and Hanna Astrup Larsen, The American-Scandinavian Foundation—W. W. Norton & Company, Inc., Publishers, 1931, 341 p.*

John Northam   (essay date 1953)

[*In the following excerpt from his critical study* Ibsen's Dramatic Method, *Northam analyzes Ibsen's stage directions for* An Enemy of the People *and finds the work to be the least visually imaginative of Ibsen's plays.*]

When William Archer wrote of this play that it was, of all Ibsen's works, 'the least imaginative, the one which makes least appeal to our sensibilities . . . ' he voiced what has become a general judgement—which this analysis will not attempt to reverse. At most a plea may be entered on the grounds that it contains some use of visual suggestion, and therefore demands the exercise of the imagination to some degree, even if that degree be slight.

In the study of visual suggestion we shall, however, be for the first time deprived of the corroboration of the drafts.

The play opens with a significant set:

> *Dr. Stockmann's sitting-room, simply but neatly decorated and furnished. In the wall to the right are two doors, the further one leading to the hall, the nearer one to the Doctor's study. In the opposite wall, facing the hall door, a door leading to the other rooms of the house. Against the middle of this wall stands the stove; further forward a sofa with a mirror above it, and in front of it an oval table with a cover. On the table a lighted lamp, with a shade. In the back wall an open door leading to the dining-room, in which is seen a supper-table, with a lamp on it.*
>
> *Billing is seated at the supper-table, with a napkin under his chin. Mrs. Stockmann is standing by the table and placing before him a dish with a large joint of roast beef. The other seats round the table are empty; the table is in disorder, as after a meal.*

Here it should be noted that the inner room has no rival for our attention: it is framed by a doorway, it occupies a central position on the stage, and it has its own localized illumination; it also contains the only actors within sight. When we look at the scene, three main impressions take shape: the first is untidiness—the meal-table and the solitary diner; the second, lavishness—it is, after all, a large joint which is so prominently displayed; the third concerns Billing—we note his preference for solitude.

Almost immediately the untidy extravagance of the scene is connected with the Doctor in Ibsen's usual manner, that is, by means of an oral reference which makes a character formally responsible for a set, as Torvald was for the room in *A Doll's House.*

> MRS. STOCKMANN. You know how Stockmann insists on regular meal-hours—
>
> BILLING. Oh, I don't mind at all. I almost think I enjoy my supper more when I can sit down to it like this, alone and undisturbed.
>
> MRS. STOCKMANN. Oh, well, if you enjoy it . . . !

No sooner have these impressions been received than the picture is broken up by the arrival of Peter Stockmann, Burgomaster and brother to the Doctor; but the dining-room remains open in the background to reveal its broad hints.

> *Burgomaster Stockmann enters, wearing an overcoat and an official gold-laced cap, and carrying a stick.*

Peter is first of all placed by his costume which, with its suggestion of a uniform, creates an impression of constraint and perhaps subterfuge, in conflict with the atmosphere of the inner room. The opposition is made clearer when the Burgomaster reacts to the first symbol:

. . . Good gracious! Hot meat in the evening! That wouldn't suit my digestion. . . . I stick to tea and bread and butter. It's more wholesome in the long run—and rather more economical, too.

He is, of course, in the minority: the dining-room is soon crowded with Hovstad, the local editor and Billing's chief, Captain Horster, the Doctor and his two sons; only the Burgomaster never enters the room. Now that there are more men on the stage, we notice that only the Burgomaster remains buttoned up in his overcoat. The others leave theirs in the hall. If this may be interpreted as a further sign of constraint, then an opposite significance can be derived from a remark of the Doctor's which otherwise seems pointless. As he enters, he says to Captain Horster, his naval friend:

. . . What, you don't wear an overcoat?

—a remark which seems to set the seal of youthful indifference on the Captain.

The Doctor strengthens the connection between himself and the inner room by displaying great pride in his roast joint. However, since he is the chief character, he must spend most of his time on the main stage, whither he will attract the others. The inner room thereupon loses its claim to our interest; but as soon as this happens, Ibsen produces a second symbol of extravagance:

> *The men sit round the table; Mrs. Stockmann brings in a tray with kettle, glasses, decanters, etc.*

The extravagance is being accentuated. If, as this analysis suggests, the material lavishness is indication of the Doctor's character, then an interesting light is thrown on his wife: since she does not oppose these extravagances, and yet never shares in them (she does not drink), she may be classified tentatively as a fence-sitter.

Petra, on the other hand, the Doctor's daughter, quickly proclaims her sympathies by joining the men:

> . . . (*mixes her toddy*) Ah, this will taste good.
>
> HOVSTAD. . . . Have you been teaching in the night-school as well to-day?
>
> PETRA. (*sipping from her glass*) Two hours. . . .

The first act contains no further visual suggestion except the pantomime at the curtain, which shows the Doctor revealing his extravagance in another way:

> *He puts both his arms round her neck, and whirls her round with him. Mrs. Stockmann screams and struggles. A burst of laughter, applause, and cheers for the Doctor. The boys thrust their heads in at the door.*

The impression of disordered exuberance, which was created by means of visual suggestion, has already coloured our attitude towards the Doctor in the preliminary stages of his struggle with his brother over the purification of the medicinal Baths on which the town's prosperity depends. This impression is not strengthened visually in Act II, which opens with an uncommunicative set:

The Doctor's sitting-room. The dining-room door is closed. Morning.

The inner room tells us nothing; the outer room is without associations. No connection has been established between interior and exterior, so that the change from 'Evening' to 'Morning' does not help us. In fact Act II is devoted almost entirely to the verbal identification of the Baths with Society, an identity so simple and so impersonal as to produce none of the emotional overtones which, in the other plays, demand to be emphasized by visual suggestion.

There is, however, a new character to introduce: Aslaksen, the leader of moderate opinion and printer of the *Messenger:*

> *Aslaksen, the printer . . . is humbly but respectably dressed in black, wears a white neck-tie, slightly crumpled, and has a silk hat and gloves in his hand.*

He is clearly a seedy conventionalist; the general appearance of his costume links him with the canons of respectability which were held to govern the 'upper classes'; his necktie warns us that he finds it impossible to live up to those conventions. Consequently, when he offers to support the Doctor's exposure of the unhealthy state of the Baths in opposition to the Burgomaster, we feel that the Doctor might have looked rather more closely at the proffered help; but of course the extravagance of his nature makes him ready to embrace any profession as truth.

Meanwhile the Burgomaster's regalia take on a sharper significance. As he deploys his implacable opposition to the Doctor's plan for re-laying the water system, he hides behind fictions which conveniently conceal selfish aims; he talks in the collective first person plural, in the name of the town, as Burgomaster, as Chairman of the Baths committee; but behind it all is the eager determination of Peter Stockmann to preserve his personal pre-eminence. The uniform-cap on the stage constantly reminds us of the discipline which has made him prominent and powerful—the discipline of hiding oneself in order to realize oneself in power.

At first it seems that Dr. Stockmann will be so strongly supported that his brother and those whom he represents will be forced to capitulate. Hovstad, Billing and Aslaksen offer to support the Doctor with their 'compact majority' under the flag of their newspaper, although 'compact' is a misnomer for a nondescript assemblage of self-seekers.

In Act III they are about to print the Doctor's report on the water supply; the set, the offices of the *Messenger,* is not significant, except in so far as it reflects the scrubbiness of the characters.

> *The room is dingy and cheerless, the furniture shabby, the arm-chairs dirty and torn. . . .*

It is noteworthy that, when the Burgomaster calls at the offices to prevent the printing of his brother's article, he enters by the back way. The Norwegian text runs:

> ASLAKSEN. . . . han kom ind bagvejen.

where 'bagvejen' carries connotations of crooked dealing,

'backdoor methods'. The idea is worked out more fully (and visually) in **Hedda Gabler.**

Thus we know at once that the Burgomaster's approach will not be straightforward. We also see very quickly that Hovstad is not the man to withstand authority; the significance of Billing's solitary meal in Act I, has been picked up in Act III where we learn that, unknown to his chief, he has been trying to worm his way into office with his professed enemies; he is an adventurer. His chief is no better; his willing self-abasement before the Burgomaster is given us in a significant action:

> HOVSTAD. You are very welcome, Burgomaster; I am at your service. Let me take your cap and stick. (*He does so, and puts them on a chair.*)

The Doctor arrives, but not before his brother has seduced his backers by an appeal to their pockets. At first unaware of this, the Doctor revels full-bloodedly in his prospective triumph; he sees himself public benefactor and new ruler of the town. The scene which follows demonstrates in pantomime his rise and fall:

> DR. STOCKMANN. Nonsense, Katrina—you go home and look after your house, and let me take care of society. How can you be in such a fright when you see me so confident and happy? (*rubbing his hands and walking up and down*) Truth and the People must win the day; you may be perfectly sure of that. Oh! I can see all our free-souled citizens standing shoulder to shoulder like a conquering army—! (*stopping by a chair*) Why, what the devil is that? . . . Why, here's the topknot of authority! (*He takes the Burgomaster's official cap carefully between the tips of his fingers and holds it up. . . . Dr. Stockmann has put on the Burgomaster's cap and grasped his stick; he now goes up to the door, throws it open, and makes a military salute. . . .*) Respect, my good Peter! Now it's I that am in power in this town. (*He struts up and down.*) . . . (*calmly*) And all these powers I have against me?
>
> ASLAKSEN. Yes, you have. It would be absolute ruin for the town if your article were inserted.
>
> DR. STOCKMANN. So that is the way of it!
>
> BURGOMASTER. My hat and stick! (*Dr. Stockmann takes off the cap and lays it on the table along with the stick.*)
>
> BURGOMASTER. (*taking them both*) Your term of office has come to an untimely end.

From which we gather that the Doctor is not suited by temperament for the exercise of conventional power. Refusing to be silenced, however, he proposes to deliver his article as a public lecture, in the belief that reason will overcome prejudice. The set of Act IV, the meeting-room, is not significant in itself. Ibsen naturally does not miss the opportunity of symbolizing the hostility of society towards the Doctor by making him and his family enter by one door, and the townsfolk, with their Burgomaster and other leaders of opinion, by another.

The Doctor, we notice, is conventionally dressed:

*Dr. Stockmann enters by the door on the right.
He wears a black frockcoat and white necktie.*

This tells us that he still hopes to carry his point by conventional means. In his struggle with the uniformed Burgomaster, he adopts a social uniform.

He fails, of course. The meeting turns against him in a manner which fully justifies Ibsen's oblique comment on ochlocracy contained in the figure of the Drunken Man. We have been shown the Doctor's extravagance and his attempt to harness it to conventional methods; now we see his courage and rectitude:

> MRS. STOCKMANN. (*in a low voice*) Thomas, dear, let us go out by the back way.
>
> DR. STOCKMANN. No back ways, Katrina! . . . (*The Doctor, with his family, goes towards the door.*)

—the door by which his enemies entered and are now leaving. Visual suggestion does also find a place in the setting of Act V:

> *Dr. Stockmann's study. Bookshelves and glass cases with various collections along the walls. In the back, a door leading to the hall; in front, on the left, a door to the sitting-room. In the wall to the right are two windows, all the panes of which are smashed. In the middle of the room is the Doctor's writing-table, covered with books and papers. The room is in disorder. It is forenoon.*
>
> *Dr. Stockmann, in a dressing-gown, slippers and skull cap, is bending down and raking with an umbrella under one of the cabinets: at last he rakes out a stone.*

In the first place, it is a room with personal associations; it is the Doctor's own room; its disorder thus attaches itself to the occupant, so reviving the impressions of the first scene of the play. Secondly, we note that Dr. Stockmann's costume no longer makes any attempt at the conventional; we are therefore prepared to find that he has abandoned all hope of changing society by conventional means. The connection between costume and character is made clearer by what is said early in the act:

> DR. STOCKMANN. And look here, Katrina, they've torn a hole in my black trousers, too.
>
> MRS. STOCKMANN. Oh dear, and these were the best you have!
>
> DR. STOCKMANN. A man should never put on his best trousers when he goes out to battle for freedom and truth.

The Doctor, that is, cannot see any way of combining his eagerness for reform with conventional processes. We are not, therefore, surprised to be shown, again in action, that the Doctor's attitude towards his brother's regalia has changed; he does not covet them even in fun:

> DR. STOCKMANN. I daresay you find it rather draughty in here today. Put on your cap.
>
> BURGOMASTER. Thanks, if I may. (*does so*)

One more example exhausts the supply of visual suggestion in the play. Hovstad and Aslaksen, having heard that the Doctor's father-in-law is busy buying up depreciated Baths stock, come to insist, as the price of their silence, on a share in the financial swindle, as they conceive it:

> DR. STOCKMANN. (*flaring up*) But I—I am an enemy of the people! (*striding about the room*) Where's my stick? Where the devil is my stick? . . . (*finds his umbrella and brandishes it*)

—and with it he chases the rogues out of the room. This inevitably recalls the only other scene in which a stick played an important part: the scene in which the Doctor briefly wields the insignia of office. The comparison between the Burgomaster's stick and the Doctor's umbrella is amusing, and serves to illustrate the difference in temperament between the two men. Whatever power the Doctor may wield, it is never directed along the channels of convention. He decides to fight with the weapons most suited to him, and, collecting his family around him, makes a statement as extravagant as any he has uttered during the play; the strongest man in the world is he who stands most alone.

With this amusing tableau we come to the end of the reckless, unmethodical yet courageous battle of Doctor Stockmann against the evil in society. Of him Ibsen wrote: 'Dr. Stockmann and I got on so very well together; we agree on so many subjects. But the Doctor is a more muddle-headed person than I am. . . . ' There has been little characterization by visual suggestion, but such as it is, it has kept before us the muddle-headedness of the admirable Doctor when our sympathy might have led us, at times, to overlook his amiable weaknesses.

On the whole, however, we return to Archer's estimate of the play in order to endorse it; it is the least imaginative of all Ibsen's realistic prose dramas; it was written in the shortest time; it contains the fewest examples of visual suggestion. (pp. 77-85)

> *John Northam, in his* Ibsen's Dramatic Method: A Study of the Prose Dramas, *Faber & Faber Limited, 1953, 230 p.*

Arno K. Lepke (essay date 1960)

[*In the following discussion of* An Enemy of the People, *Lepke analyzes Dr. Stockmann's character in the context of principles that have consistently influenced Ibsen's writings.*]

Of all great dramatic characters of the nineteenth century, Ibsen's have undoubtedly remained most controversial. Equally impressive arguments have been brought forth either to demonstrate that they truly reveal or to suggest that they are but puppets fabricated by a gloomy master.

Among his early admirers were those who did not hesitate to subscribe to the playwright's notion of a divine call he must obey, such as he defined it in a letter to the king in 1866: "I am not fighting for a sinecure but for the life task which, so I believe, God has imposed upon me; a mission which, it seems to me, is the most important and the most needed one for Norway: to arouse our people and to teach them a generous, heroic, and noble concept of life." In this camp, idolatry could produce a book entitled *Christ or Ibsen* in which the dramatist is hailed and haloed as the founder of a new religion. In a similar spirit, Heilborn, e.g., offered tribute to the master's genius when comparing his dramatic figures with the heroes of Dostoyevsky's novels " . . . whose mystery increases as you slowly seem to come closer to them, but when you leave an Ibsen character, you have entered into his most secret thoughts and motivations so that he has become all clear [sic]" [Ernst Heilborn, "Der hundertjährige Ibsen," *Die Neue Rundschau* (1928)]. More soberly but persuasively James Joyce voiced the feelings of many Ibsen followers at the turn of the century: "Through the perplexities of diverse criticism the great genius of the man is day by day coming out as a hero comes out amidst the earthly trials. The dissonant cries are fainter and more distant, the random praises are rising in steadier and more choral chant . . . it may be questioned whether any man has held so firm an empire over the thinking in modern times. Not Rousseau; not Emerson; not Carlyle; not any of those giants of whom almost all have passed out of human ken" [James Joyce, "Ibsen's New Drama," *Fortnightly Review* (1900)].

In the opposing camp, strong vocabulary is employed to argue that many of the characters are "brain spun concoctions," often basically warped or even morbid. Protests of contemporary British critics decried "ghastly caricature," "malign and perverse obscurity," or even "beatific anarchy" in the plays immediately preceding *An Enemy of the People.* The whole gamut of defamatory epithets heaped on the "nookshotten Norwegian" by an outraged British press can be found in the Ibsen essays of G. B. Shaw, who took great delight in juxtaposing the most vitriolic flareups. While the vehemence of such outbursts reflects more the true nature of Victorian conscience than that of Ibsen's plays, their basic contention that Ibsen wilfully and deliberately construed his characters is maintained in much present day adverse criticism. Mary McCarthy may, I think, be safely considered a spokesman of this negative approach: " . . . there is a great deal of bathetic 'studio' art in all great nineteenth century writers except for Tolstoy. . . . certainly they paid for being titans and for the power to move a mass audience by a kind of autointoxication or self-hypnosis that allowed them to manipulate their emotions like a stage hand cranking out a snowstorm from a machine containing bits of paper. This effect of false snow falling on a dramatic scene is more noticeable in Ibsen than in any of his great coevals, and he left it as his legacy to the American school of playwrights, to O'Neill, and now Tennessee Williams, Arthur Miller, and William Inge" ["The Will and Testament of Ibsen," *Partisan Review* (1956)]. While admirers and opponents would agree on the phenomenal influence Ibsen has exerted in the past as well as in our own time, the so-called "quintessence of Ibsenism" will indubitably remain a bone of contention.

No other figure in his mature plays has, in my estimation, caused as many discussions and conflicting evaluations, especially in our colleges and universities, as his Doctor Stockmann, "the man with the stick," in *An Enemy of the People.* Beginning with contemporary outcries calling him a "raving maniac" and Archer's early condemnation

"the least imaginative of all of Ibsen's works, the one which makes least appeal to our sensibilities" to Stockmann praises and glorifications in modern anthologies which cannot hope to sell without him, one could compile an impressive collection of mutually exclusive views.

The few comments Ibsen himself made on this play do not really provide reliable clues to the doctor's puzzling personality since they sound vague and inconsistent. The following appear relevant to illustrate this point: " . . . when you so praiseworthily endeavor to mold a population into a democratic society, you find yourself making quite some progress in turning them into a bunch of plebeians." "I am not sure whether I should call this play a comedy or a drama; it partakes of the nature of both or lies halfway between." " . . . it will be a very peaceable [!] play this time, one which may safely be read by the state councillors, the rich merchants, and their ladies and from which the theaters will not feel obliged to recoil. It will be easy to write. . . . " "Dr. Stockmann and I come along capitally with each other, in many aspects we agree, but the doctor is more muddleheaded and confused than I am." " . . . in a way, he is a strange person and a foolhardy fellow." When questioned whether he did not consider the strongest man him who stands most alone, Ibsen retorted: "I am not responsible for all the nonsense which he [Dr. Stockmann] produces." But was he not obviously in sympathy with his pioneer? Ibsen snapped back: "Do you really think you know that? Perhaps you are completely wrong." One can well imagine the impenetrable smile accompanying these laconic statements. Were they primarily intended to baffle the listener or reader and to enhance his curiosity? At best they betray irreconcilable feelings Ibsen had for his protagonist of minority truths. At worst they illustrate the "sphinx of the north" relishing her aloofness while remaining ensconced behind unassailable pronouncements.

This play however, more than any other one, should provide a major key to the so-called "Ibsen secret" since its first draft was written by an irate man rising spontaneously to defend his authentic self. There was certainly no cryptic smile on his face when he penned the doctor's indictments. Yet, after two revisions of the original draft, the final version of the play presents Doctor Stockmann as a highly questionable, blundering, paradoxical, and almost foolish rebel.

In order to find clues to this strange portraiture, one should, I think, completely disregard Ibsen's own elusive comments on the play and rather consider those basic principles of writing to which he adheres and which he reiterates throughout his notebooks and correspondence. They may be summarized in the form of the following three imperatives which the playwright has adopted for his creative hours: (1) Rebel against outworn creeds and conventions; (2) Conceal yourself from your persecutors; (3) Judge your true self and human nature unsparingly. Before showing how these three principles are reflected in the play, I shall analyze them separately and discuss why he adopted them. Especially do I want to contend in this article that imperatives two and three were given predominant importance over imperative one when Ibsen twice revised the original draft before allowing it to be printed in its present form.

1. *Rebel against outworn creeds and conventions:* This motto is usually considered to be the major message of the play. Unquestionably, the original motivation of the drama was, more than ever before, one of rebellion against his inquisitors, representatives of "that man made, authority ruled, and law stricken society." After **A Doll's House** and **Ghosts,** Ibsen heard himself branded on all sides a fiendish man indulging in revolting appetites and sickening details. Voices at home were clamoring to have him burned at the stake for his seduction of both Nora and Mrs. Alving to climax a tradition too long interrupted. Had he not dared to suggest that "the most wonderful thing to happen" in a marriage might never? Had he not thereby caused shock hazards in prospective and retrospective wedlocks everywhere? In England, **A Doll's House** had to be bowdlerized, embellished, and recast by contemporary censors until it could be re-released under the innocuous title *Breaking a Butterfly.* Pondering on the elasticity of Victorian conscience, Archer conceded: " . . . Ibsen is impossible on the English stage, he must be trivialized" [*Theatre* (1880)]. The German conscience had reacted in a similar, if more sentimental, way: sobbing at the sight of the youngsters and finally collapsing, Nora lets herself be realigned to the family fold which made an enraged Ibsen cry out over "such barbaric enslavement." (Nora was recently fully rehabilitated in Berlin when she was allowed to slam the final door three times.) While the small community of his worshippers was trying to light torches for him, Ibsen saw himself burned everywhere, if not at the stake, at least in effigy.

Arthur Miller on his American adaptation of *An Enemy of the People:*

Most of the time an adaptation is a playwright's excuse for not writing his own plays, and since I am not yet with my back against that particular wall, I think it wise to set down what I have tried to do with **An Enemy of the People,** and why I did it.

There is one quality in Ibsen that no serious writer can afford to overlook. It lies at the very center of his force, and I found in it—as I hope others will—a profound source of strength. It is his insistence, his utter conviction, that he is going to say what he has to say, and that the audience, by God, is going to listen. It is the very same quality that makes a star actor, a great public speaker, and a lunatic. Every Ibsen play begins with the unwritten words: "Now listen here!" And these words have shown me a path through the wall of "entertainment," a path that leads beyond the formulas and dried-up precepts, the pretense and fraud, of the business of the stage. Whatever else Ibsen has to teach, this is his first and greatest contribution.

Arthur Miller, in his Preface to his adaptation of An Enemy of the People, *1951.*

For this reason, the playwright is certainly venting his wrath at his persecutors in many of the doctor's self-defending tirades. The fierceness of Ibsen's temper in such moments can be measured by the violence of the language used throughout the play. When brought to the quick, Ibsen would not hesitate to shake threatening fists at his countrymen and to unleash abusive, even vulgar, vocabulary to characterize them: " . . . a dull herd trotting in line, victims of pastoral stupefaction." " . . . I had to get out of the dirty business up there in order to become cleaned up as much as possible. What we need first of all is a relentless destruction and thorough extermination of this whole sinister medieval monkery spirit we inherited because it narrows our world view and stupefies our heads." " . . . my contemporaries up there I shall attack individually, one after the other. I shall not spare the child unborn, nor shall I spare the thoughts and feelings concealed behind the words of anybody up there." In such moments of boiling indignation and contempt for mankind, Ibsen will don the same sacerdotal black frock coat and the same white tie of self-righteousness with which he attires his Stockmann when appearing before a hostile citizenry. He will then truly become "the man with the club," impatient with human frailties, and ready to assume the stature of an archangel dispensing justice on a benumbed people. "Hammerblow after hammerblow until my very last day, I must penetrate into the depths until I find the precious ores . . . ;" in such and similar rhymed mottoes will he persuade himself in these hours of his great and burdensome mission.

But this Ibsen-Stockmann relishing the "sledgehammer language" of his indictments in the play is not really Henrik but Knud the father's temper breaking through. Knud had ruled the family in a spirit of despotism borne of frustration and had terrorized the children with his tyrannical outbursts. When returning to his normally sober and brooding self, Henrik Ibsen fully realized that his "all or nothing" formula was sterile and inapplicable to human nature as he had well demonstrated in the devastating swath cut by Stockmann's predecessor Brand. A naive and infuriated rebel who defies the absolutes of a compact majority and subsequently finds himself branded public enemy No. 1 would be too cheap an issue and too superficial a key to account for the lasting and, as it appears, increasing challenge of **An Enemy of the People.** The tempestuous parts in Ibsen are counterbalanced and held in check by opposing voices, especially by the warning

2. *Conceal yourself from your persecutors:* The comments by Ibsen on Doctor Stockmann which I gave above have already illustrated this propensity, just as the generally elusive and enigmatic elements in practically all of his mature plays indicate how much he shunned an open and unequivocal commitment. The playwright was hypersensitive to the stings of adverse criticism to the degree that he abandoned plans for an autobiography from fear that its details might be misconstrued and slanderously abused. Because of this complex, sometimes bordering on the phobic, some of his contemporaries nicknamed him "the marmot." Escaping to Italy from an oppressive home environment, he bitterly reminisces on the dichotomy this world created in him: " . . . back home I could never lead an integrated life. I was one self in my production, another self in the external world. But this way my production was

nothing wholesome either." " . . . whatever I had to say from the very core of my being, it was always voiced with the wrong expression; and since I felt this so very deeply, I put a fence around myself." "I can never quite persuade myself to lay myself bare completely . . . I prefer it to seclude myself." Vacillating thus between voices challenging him to expose stagnation and others, equally strong, urging him to be on his guard so that he may remain invulnerable, Ibsen encounters himself now a rebel, now another "shy guest at the feast of the world's culture." The dramatic use of conflicting and incompatible voices in *Brand* and *Peer Gynt,* e.g., illustrates this point. Caught in this frustrating dilemma, Ibsen attempted to cope with it and to solve it by assigning himself the major task

3. *Judge your true self and human nature unsparingly:* This third imperative resulting almost with necessity from the conflicting postulates of the previous two offers, in my opinion, the most important and the safest key to an understanding not only of the controversial doctor but likewise of many major figures in Ibsen's mature plays. It was most succinctly and felicitously worded by the playwright in one of his well-known maxims: "To live is to war with fiends that beset the brain and the heart, to write is to summon the self and to play the judge's part." This motto often invoked as inspiring lodestar by the ambitious young writer or perhaps serving as purple patch to embellish a literary disquisition cannot be taken seriously and literally enough in the case of Ibsen. My conjecture is that it was the force of this predominant principle which made Ibsen rewrite the play twice. The full implication of this imperative is intimated in a letter to his friend Bjørnson: " . . . you may believe me that in my quiet hours I certainly wallow quite thoroughly in my own entrails and separate and anatomize, especially in those areas where it does hurt the most." In following the action of the play closely, one can discern how the lovable and persuasive pioneer of truth and of a better world to live in is allowed almost imperceptibly to develop into a selfish and conceited rebel without a cause. While playing the judge's part when reconsidering the Stockmann of the first draft and while separating and anatomizing "where it does hurt the most," Ibsen discovers that his protagonist should be distinguished by the following three painful characteristics which I shall presently discuss separately: (1) a quarrelsome and pugnacious bent; (2) naive and blindfolded idealism; (3) ill-concealed selfishness parading as virtue. The phenomenal aspect of the play is that these disqualifying features of the crusader will enter into view only after an almost microscopic examination of the details of the "Ibsen palimpsest" as, I think, many final versions of his mature plays might fittingly be called.

1. *Stockmann's quarrelsome and pugnacious bent:* This feature is underscored by the choice of the name Stockmann which, as mentioned before, means "the man with the stick," an appellation befitting either brother. Early in the play we hear of "this disastrous propensity of yours" which had shown itself in the past in "cascades of letters, pamphlets, and newspaper articles on every possible and impossible thing" which the doctor had apparently poured into the town. To check this ingrained aggressiveness, Peter had him appointed medical officer of the baths,

hoping thereby to stop the "cantankerous man" and to prevent him from further attacking the government, "pulling things to pieces, and picking quarrels, an old habit of yours," as he puts it. Although the doctor rejects this accusation when levelled against him, he does confirm its validity later on when he loses self-control before a hostile crowd of citizens: " . . . I can't stand leading men at any price, I have had enough of such people in my time. . . . they are like billy goats in a young plantation; they do mischief everywhere. They stand in a free man's way, whichever direction he may turn, and what I should like best would be to see them exterminated like any other vermin." This native love of violence is further emphasized at the beginning of the play where one learns that the doctor gleefully composed his report on water contamination in "hammerblow language" before his suspicions had even been scientifically confirmed. Billing, the journalist, comments on this report: " . . . crushing, indeed, every word falls, how shall I put it, like the blow of a sledgehammer." How much the doctor relishes his explosive parts is seen later when his voice is heard by the people. Instead of using the opportunity to try to turn the tide in his favor, he prefers to show his teeth and to launch volleys of abusive language at his hated brother, the epitome of stagnation: " . . . my brother Peter, slow-witted and hidebound in prejudice . . . is every bit as plebeian as anything that walks in two shoes."

This tempestuous Stockmann resembling a high-school bully shows again how enraged Ibsen can feel over "burgomaster ethics" which enslave the masses and paralyze the individual's initiative. The shouting Stockmann actually does not much more than rehash the impatient battlecry of *Pillars of Society:* "How we suffer here under the curse of our traditions, conventions, and customs. Rebel against it, all of you . . . create an event which will strike in the very face of all these 'proprieties and good conventional manners' . . . I don't want to become something which simply has been accepted." Ibsen was never sure what the better traditions, conventions, and customs would or even should be like. He certainly kept hammering away to come closer to "the precious ores," but did he ever find them or anything precious for that matter? A favorite dream of his, as fervent as it was vague, was the vision of "the third empire" of the future in which all nations and religions would be merged in unity. While unable to proclaim how this Eldorado should be brought about, he did frequently proclaim his contempt and undying hatred of most contemporary politicians for preventing the realization of whatever "it" might be like. In exposing thus the immature and bumptious trait of his Stockmann self, Ibsen also points out clearly in the play that a deeply rooted naiveté about life and people is the major cause of such conduct:

2. *Stockmann's naive and blindfolded idealism:* This feature is underscored by the choice of the name Tomas to illustrate the doctor's native inability to see things in a realistic perspective. He is easily *tartuffed* by the grandiloquent oratory on the ethics of revolution as delivered by Hovstad and his associate who are primarily bent on exploiting him. One notices how gladly he accepts their custom-tailored verbiage when they hail him a savior about

to descend on a stricken town whose cause reflects true morality: " . . . a journalist incurs a heavy responsibility, doctor, if he neglects a favorable opportunity of emancipating the masses, the humble and the oppressed," protests Hovstad; " . . . in exalted circles I shall be called an agitator and all that sort of thing. But they may call me what they like, if only my conscience does not reproach me." Stockmann has the most generous vocabulary for his would-be followers, calling them "the liberal and active minds," "the fermenting forces of the future," and frequently advises them not to worry about the approaching revolution, that "everything will run off smoothly, quite smoothly . . . " These assurances are avidly absorbed by his listener, Mr. "capital fellow" (Hovstad), who counts on gaining Stockmann's charming but reserved daughter as a free extra in the bargain. Sensing the apprehensions of his clear-sighted wife, the doctor attempts to persuade her that there will be "triumphant social forces" backing him up and ready to fight for his cause: " . . . do you imagine that in a free country it is no use having right on your side? You are absurd, Catherine; besides, haven't I got the liberal minded, independent press to lead the way and the compact majority behind me? That is might enough, I should think." What revolution will really do to the old order is enthusiastically enunciated by him before his awed appendage: " . . . all the incapables must be turned out, you understand, and that in every walk of life . . . endless vistas have opened themselves to my mind's eyes today . . . I cannot see it all quite clearly yet, but I shall in time . . . young and vigorous standard bearers,—those are what we need and must seek, my friends; we must have new men in command at all our outposts." The sudden and painful awakening from these glorious dreams occurs when Peter's wiles and financial threats have convinced the conspirators that their investment in the doctor was too risky. Finding himself deserted by both, "the newly awakened lion hearted people" and his profit-minded "standard bearers," Tomas stands helplessly before his wife who bitterly comments on her husband's thwarted ambitions: "I know quite well that you have more brains than any one else in town, but you are extremely easily duped, Tomas."

To show how the Icarus reach for the sun originates in utter ignorance of earthly conditions is, of course, one of Ibsen's favorite themes. Similar to other idealists of his plays who have "bitten themselves fast," Stockmann is sailing blindfolded and steering either into a vortex or straight on the cliffs. His fate follows the pattern set by Brand, "the scourge of mankind," who gains nothing and loses everything by preaching that "nothing is eternally gained but what is sacrificially lost." Shaw remarks correctly that "He dies a saint, having caused more intense suffering by his saintliness than the most talented sinner could possibly have done with twice his opportunities." In like manner, Pastor Manders in *Ghosts* keeps hiding in the folds of his dogmatic coat until he can no longer see the light of true life around him. Destructive ignorance passing under the name of the ideal would again be highlighted in Gregers Werle, the fanatic busy-body of *The Wild Duck*. This direct offspring of Dr. Stockmann who parades his barren "nothing but the truth" formula decides to pour his "clear water" into a happy domestic fireplace,

a fitting image to climax Ibsen's dramatization of deceptive idealism. The emphasis on the doctor's quixotic ignorance reflects that basically pessimistic orientation in Ibsen which will predominate more and more in his later years: " . . . when man demands to live and to develop humanity at the same time, it is all megalomania, all humanity and all the Christians suffer from megalomania." " . . . there are actually moments when the whole history of the world appears to me like a great shipwreck, and then the only important thing seems to save oneself." " . . . all mankind has miscarried." These are just a few typical utterances.

3. *Stockmann's ill concealed selfishness parading as virtue:* Far more disillusioning than the pugnacious and naive traits illustrated above appears the thinly disguised and even self-complacent egotism which Ibsen decided to project as a major feature of his pioneer. Early in the play when having his suspicions of water contamination confirmed, Stockmann immediately and almost triumphantly divulges to press reporters the news that "the whole place is a pesthouse," although he had just been specifically warned that he must go through channels in all matters concerning the welfare of the town. By yielding to his impulse and by spreading the unsavory news right away, he has placed a lasting stigma on his town even though the damage might be curable, a possibility which he later on concedes when he speaks of chemicals and antidotes which could provide a reliable safety margin. He is thus doing irreparable damage to his fellow citizens who have invested most of their earnings in the future "gold mine," the baths. Desiring to precipitate a moment of victorious elation irrespective of consequences, Stockmann even exults in "the nice upset" his discovery will cause in town and in his brother's office especially. During the whole play, one hears not a single word of his expressing compassion for seeing the town's investments undermined and welfare tottering. On the contrary: Shortly after his momentous discovery, he pointedly suggests that he would not accept a salary increase if the committee should vote for it, a hint strong enough to expedite appropriate action. He later resumes the game of declining "undeserved honors" in order to encourage such official recognition as he feels himself entitled to: " . . . you don't see how on earth it was any more than my duty,—my obvious duty as a citizen. Of course, it wasn't. I know that as well as you do. But, my fellow citizens, you know! Good Lord, think of all the good souls who think so highly of me!. . . . whatever it is, whether it is a demonstration in my honor, or a banquet, or a subscription list for some presentation to me,—whatever it is, you must solemnly and faithfully promise me to put a stop to it." Addressed as these words are to his "fellow rebels" who have just reverted their allegiance from the risky Tomas to the foxy Peter, the whole scene assumes grotesque proportions.

The egotism of the doctor becomes crass and depressing in the climactic scene of the play when his own financial security becomes unexpectedly involved in the town's fiasco: his father-in-law comes to tell him that he has bought most of the shares of the baths whose value had tumbled to practically zero over night. Pointing out to Tomas that he paid for them with the money his daughter will be inheriting from him, he leaves the doctor to decide whether "you are stark, staring mad, Tomas. . . . it will be exactly as if you were to flay broad strips of skin from Catherine's body, and Petra's, and the boys'; no decent man would do that,—unless he were mad. . . . " Under the impact of this alternative, the doctor for the first time reconsiders his sweeping condemnations of the baths in which he had adamantly maintained that the town's water contamination was of an irremediable nature. The same Stockmann who had previously decried as "pieces of trickery and downright crime" any attempts at "patching and tinkering at the poisonous whitened sepulchre" when the town's weal was at stake now reverses his position in view of his own personal potential predicament: " . . . but hang it all! It must be possible for science to discover some prophylactic, I should think, or some antidote of some kind. . . . to think that you could do such a preposterous thing! Risking Catherine's money in this way and putting me in such a horribly painful dilemma! When I look at you, I think I see the very devil himself !" It is the first time that the existence of a painful dilemma occurs to him.

In thus letting the social reformer and preacher of righteousness stagger at a most crucial moment in the play, Ibsen returns to his favorite theme of the "life lie" behind which man entrenches himself, no matter how idealistic his approach may seem to himself and others. To leave no cause unstained with the acid of hidden falseness often appears to assume the nature of an obsession to which Ibsen will almost greedily yield. His biographer Collin sees in it a predominantly morbid penchant: " . . . he almost enjoyed, and this was a devilish feature in his personality, to discover everywhere the imperfect in earthly man and then to show it up triumphantly, especially where it had managed to conceal itself dexterously behind the mask of the apparently good and noble. He knew how to discern selfishness, the most deadly enemy of the soul, even in those relationships where it was covered with a thick coat of altruism. His judgment was like Mephisto's in Goethe's 'Prologue in Heaven.' He spoke of the 'never-have-been' of true moral absolutes. . . . " [*Henrik Ibsen, Sein Werk, seine Weltanschauung, sein Leben*]. The frustrated missionary in Ibsen can easily turn around, stamp his foot on the ground, and cry: "If I am incapable of building, I shall still be the man to tear down everything around me."

I have deliberately emphasized these disqualifying features of Dr. Stockmann since they do not fit into the picture of the "martyr for truth" so often painted for reasons of expedience. By no means do I want to minimize those lovable and admirable parts of the doctor which remain in the final version and which have made thousands of his readers identify themselves enthusiastically with "the strongest man." His straightforward and singlehanded tackling of the problem at hand against a devilish encirclement is certainly inspiring, just as his ebullient zest to eradicate the forces of evil in human and social relations is most engaging. But the thoughtful reader feels more and more saddened as he realizes the doctor's unfitness for the pioneering task he has undertaken. In this respect, he undoubtedly reflects that self-despairing Ibsen who will con-

clude in his later works that he pursued a chimera when dreaming of his life's mission.

Most readers will take the doctor's side when Peter demands from him on pain of dismissal that (1) he will reach the conclusion upon further investigation that the matter of the town's water was by no means as dangerous or as critical as he had imagined at first, and that (2) he will make a public confession of his full confidence in the bath committee and in their readiness to consider fully and conscientiously whatever steps may be necessary to remedy any possible defects.

But even in this obvious case of pressure and duress exerted against him, a close look at Stockmann's reaction reveals his basic immaturity and selfishness: although the first demand of Peter is criminal in nature, it was already noted before that the doctor will concede the possibility of remedial steps later in the play when his private fortune unexpectedly becomes dependent on the hygienic sanity of the baths. At this point in the middle of the play where the interest of his "oppressed fellow citizens" is at stake, he should have conceded at least as much. However, a smashing defeat of his hated brother outweighs all other considerations at this stage. He should further have accepted without any reservations Peter's second demand since he had no evidence whatever to indicate that he was dealing with a rubberstamping body or that there was a lack of civic responsibility in the committee.

Stockmann in the last phase of the drama can no longer harness his extravagance when proclaiming the nature of the better world he envisages. In his defensive speech before the common people he must hold them high to show them how low they really are. To deliver his indictments on "that rancid and tainted ham of the past," he appears before the citizenry in a sacerdotal black frock coat decorated with the white tie of self-righteousness. Clinging to the idea of leadership remaining in martyrdom, he declares with pontifical finality that "all sources of our moral life are poisoned and the whole fabric of our civic community is founded on the pestiferous soil of falsehood." Then his barrages roll on like the charges of his demagogical successors in history, often assuming the nature of volcanic eruptions: " . . . Can you imagine it is right that the stupid folk of the compact majority should govern the clever ones? . . . There is the foul lie that the common folk, the ignorant and incomplete men of the community, should have the same right to pronounce judgment . . . and to govern as the isolated and intellectually superior personalities. . . . there is a tremendous difference between poodle men and cur men. . . . I am in the right, I and a few other scattered individuals; the minority is always right. . . . a normally constituted truth lives, let us say, as a rule seventeen or eighteen years, seldom longer. But truths as aged as that are always worn frightfully thin. . . . these majority truths are like last year's cured meat. . . . and they are the origin of the moral scurvy that is rampant in our communities. . . . what does the destruction of a community matter if it lives on lies! It ought to be razed to the ground, I tell you. All who live by lies ought to be exterminated like vermin. . . . I am not so forgiving as a certain Person: I do not say, I forgive ye, for ye know not what ye do!''

The crusader ever athirst for militant action leaves the stage like the drunkard who had cast the only vote for him. The proud poodle man has thus severed the bonds connecting him with "the ordinary, common, low-bred cur men" and has thereby shown himself, indeed, an enemy of the people in most of his speeches and actions. In his passionate but vague propositions, he has offered no acceptable formula for the improvement of mankind, except for a few shrewd comments on conventional insincerities which will always exist in human relations. To cope successfully with the irrationality of the human animal, a reformer would need sympathy, diplomacy, understanding, persuasion, and a willingness to take rebuff, none of which Stockmann has.

He does regain the reader's sympathy toward the end of the play when he faces the insinuation that he engineered the condemnation of the baths in collusion with his father-in-law in order to gain control of them, a suspicion staggering his imagination. It is quite understandable that he wants to punish his accusers by an immediate defenestration.

The depressing keynote throughout the final act, however, remains the doctor's conceit and strutting: ". . . that the common herd should dare to make this attack on me as if they were my equals, that is what I cannot for the life of me swallow." Recoiling from the stigma "folkefiende," he has muddled ideas of escaping either to America, or to some South Sea island, or even to a virgin forest because "that hateful name is sticking here in the pit of my stomach, eating into me like a corrosive acid, and no magnesia will remove it." But when circumstances thwart these runaway plans, the doctor plunges back into his suicidal armor: ". . . but now I am going to sharpen my pen until they can feel its point; I shall dig it in venom and gall; I shall hurl my inkwell at their heads,. . . . We are going to stay where we are, Catherine, this is the field of battle, this is where I shall triumph." To give immediate evidence of his imminent victory, he announces to the boys that they will never set foot in school again because he will educate them himself: "that is to say, you shan't learn a blessed thing, but I shall make liberal-minded and high-spirited men of you . . . " It is thus a beclouded and blindfolded Dr. Stockmann who pronounces his memorable final axiom "the strongest man in the world is he who stands most alone."

The subject matter of this drama has gained new significance at a time when the validity of traditional democratic principles and prerequisites is again challenged by "strong men" bent on casting into limbo "those rotten majority truths." Ibsen's projection of the problem leaves a bewildering portrait of man, either in restless and unscrupulous pursuit of his personal gains or thinly disguising his egotism with high flowing oratory about the ideal.

This interpretation does not intend to belittle the doctor's courage and zest for his cause, nor do I want to disparage the intrigues against him by the leader of "the puny, narrow-chested, shortwinded crew." Viciously though the burgomaster brother is acting to ward off his own fall from power, the government if led by Dr. Stockmann would probably be in less responsible hands: he would certainly institute Calvinistic decrees resembling those of his kinsman Brand; and unknowingly, but obediently, he would become the tool of his "standard bearers, those fermenting forces of the future," who would show him whom to eliminate where. For his attempts to exterminate all liars he would ultimately again be stoned, but then more effectively.

Stockmann had his forerunners in Parsifal, Don Quixote, and Candide, but they were Tomas without Stockmann. They bear that basic stamp of innocence in which we recognize our own guileless parts and never-ending aspirations. The "guileless fool," "the knight of the woeful figure," and the believer in "the best of all possible worlds" make us search with them for the Holy Grail, Dulcinea del Toboso, and Cunegonde. We suffer with them because we know better what we wish we never knew.

The Stockmann naiveté is of a different caliber: Alcestes has returned from his desert up north to show them again what is what and who is who. The reader finds it increasingly difficult to smile when following his onslaughts. He found imitators in history to rule and ruin.

The reader laying the play aside and asking himself whose philosophy could have and, perhaps, should have been followed in the imbroglio of all the intrigues cannot help but remember the words of timid Mr. Aslaksen who is always afraid of sudden changes: ". . . Nobody can take exception to a reasonable and frank expression of a citizen's views . . . but not violently, doctor, . . . proceed with moderation, or you will do nothing with them . . . you may take my advice, I have gathered my experience in the school of life . . . " It is thus the weakling, the epitome of "the dull herd trotting in line" rather than the idealist who knows best how to cope effectively with a "wounded humanity." Shaw seeking to coin a conclusive maxim suggests that "the idealist is a more dangerous animal than the Philistine, just as man is a more dangerous animal than a sheep."

At the end of the play, it is the voice of Aslaksen again which expresses the typical and ever-recurring message of Ibsen: ". . . he [the doctor] talks about the baths . . . but it is revolution he is aiming at; he wants to get the administration of the town put in new hands. . . . Dr. Stockmann has shown himself in a light I should never have dreamed of . . . "

It is this latter discovery of Aslaksen which strikes the playwright again and again in his "hour of the great disgust" with all potential values and ideals once he has focused his merciless searchlight on them. When Mrs. Alving in *Ghosts* finally dares to review the life she spent Procrusteanized in the teachings of her haloed adjunct, Pastor Manders, she breaks forth: ". . . I wanted only to unravel one point in your teachings, but as soon as I had that unravelled, the whole fabric came to pieces, and then I realized that it was only machine made." It is this dramatic encounter with nothingness rather than a few

Scene from a 1937 production of An Enemy of the People *in New York.*

shocking details which produced the violent Ibsen controversy which still re-echoes today.

Ibsen stated in 1873 that he passed through three phases when composing a drama: in the first one he would write as if he had met his characters but briefly on a train ride; in the second phase, he would describe the same people imagining that he had just spent four weeks with them in a resort place; in the third and final phase he would analyze them thoroughly feeling that nothing in them was any longer hidden from him and that he had come to know them deeply with all their weaknesses.

It is my conjecture that the Doctor Stockmann of the train ride was close to the inspiring idealist and pioneer of truth whom many of the present-day interpreters so dearly prefer to the complex man he really is. But, as stated before, the first draft of the play was destroyed by Ibsen and so was the second. The playwright was known to weigh and reconsider practically every word of the final version of a play before releasing it for print. The third and final revision of *An Enemy of the People* incorporates and emphasizes, I feel, those negative features in the doctor "no longer hidden" which I have attempted to trace in this essay: the quarrelsome, the naive, and the oppressingly selfish parts. Considering the pronouncements of Ibsen given

above, I surmise that these features of the doctor slowly emerged as irrefutable findings of the probing judge while meditating on himself and human nature in general in his quiet hours.

In scrutinizing the inner battlefield of conflicting selves warring with each other for supremacy, Ibsen will, of course, often resolutely espouse the Stockmann cause which tells him that he was chosen to rebuild. He will then contemptuously turn away from the Zola-type writer "who is going down in the human sewer to take a swim" and he will announce that he is going down there too, but in order "to clean it up." Joining sides with his iconoclastic Brand whom he once called fittingly "my true self in my best moments," he will escape stone throwing from the persecuting "gray hawk of compromise" and again envisage his goal "to become the healer of the sickness and disharmony of this world."

But as ambition drives him onward to scale the icy mountains, conscience slowly applies the brakes and makes him retrace his steps until he finds himself paralyzed and sicklied o'er with the pale cast of thought: " . . . good devils and evil devils; light-haired devils and black-haired devils. If only one could be sure all the time whether it is the forces of light or the power of darkness which hold you in their grip . . . hahaha, then the thing would be quite simple . . . " The sarcastic treatment so often given Dr. Stockmann in this play shows how bitter and how thought-riddled Ibsen must have felt seeing himself thus caught in the middle of mutually stultifying voices. The final version with its undercurrent of despair bears the imprint of that self-searching pessimism which made Ibsen disclaim responsibility for "all the nonsense produced by the doctor."

André Gide once commented: " . . . as soon as I make any statement about myself, the very opposite immediately appears so much more true . . . whatever I say or do, there is always one part of myself which stays behind and watches the other part compromise itself; when one is divided that way, how is it possible to be sincere?" Ibsen would have recognized himself in this question, but he would have recoiled from the Frenchman's ability to enjoy his Nobel-prized multiplicity. Similarly, but fearfully, aware of this inner dichotomy, Ibsen can but see a tragic implication in a hopeless struggle for authenticity. When man is separated from his true self by layers of insincerity and from other selves by a gulf that can never be bridged, what else can the playwright do but to probe on into the elusive recesses of the human psyche and to continue compiling his encyclopedia of shams and self-deceptions?

In leaving practically nothing that may stand erect under his scrutiny, Ibsen's Dr. Stockmann anticipates Kafka's country doctor who finds his patient stricken with an incurable wound. The question thus can be no longer how to heal but how to live with an irremediable ailment. The revised life task must be clothed in a face saving and self-consoling formula: "My office is to question, not to answer." The best the soul-searching playwright can hope to achieve will be to make the universal sphinx of life a more intelligible riddle. But the retrospective Ibsen ponders with Rubek in his last play: "I was experiencing the painful joy of wrestling with the impossible."

Dr. Stockmann, the fighter for truth in Sunday trousers, is neither hero nor atrocious madhead but Ibsen's attempt to distinguish between the two. Created impulsively in the middle of his career and directed most personally at his environment, the play offers, in my estimation, one of the finest clues to the ever-exciting "Ibsen secret." (pp. 57-75)

> *Arno K. Lepke, "Who Is Doctor Stockmann?"*
> in Scandinavian Studies, *Vol. 32, No. 2, May,*
> *1960, pp. 57-75.*

Zygmunt Adamczewski   (essay date 1963)

[*Adamczewski is a Polish-born American philosopher and critic. In the following excerpt, he contends that Dr. Stockmann's obsession with the notion of absolute truth renders him incompetent as a leader and alienated from his community.*]

The town; the native town of his birth, in which he wants to live and serve, to which he would belong completely, if anywhere he can belong: this is the world in which Doctor Thomas Stockmann lives. Only a town? Yes, a town, a polis which is respected as the natural habitat of civilized man, beginning in Hellas. A town which contains on a small scale an assembly of all human horizons, of powers, aspirations, fields of action, loves, discoveries, rights and wrongs. A miniature world, or better, a miniature of a whole world.

In such a world billions of humans have found themselves completely at home and at rest. How is it that Stockmann does not? Does he need a wider horizon for activity, a country, an empire? Is it the small size of his world that stifles him? Not as one hears him speak; he wants to belong just within those circumscribed boundaries of his native town—if he can. On the other hand, larger boundaries of national or supernational scope also could not contain him, would have to be burst, impatiently exploded if needs be, for the sake of—what? How can this paradox be accounted for that a small scope might satisfy a man like Stockmann, yet much larger scopes might not suffice at all? The answer is that the grave difficulty in finding himself at home has for Stockmann nothing to do with that home's size. What prevents him from fitting snugly into a factual area of life, no matter of what dimensions, is his being possessed in a way entirely non-dimensional and non-quantitative: by ideas.

The cutting diagnosis of his predicament is put forward early by that prosaic realist, Peter Stockmann, the mayor:

"Oh, ideas—yes! My brother has had plenty of them in his time—unfortunately. But when it is a question of putting an idea into practical shape, you have to apply to a man of different mettle."

How are ideas put into practical shape? This is the basic question confronting Dr. Stockmann as well as the people around him. No doubt they can be. But to know how, is to resolve the dilemma of a man of ideas who wants to belong to the world he lives in. Otherwise he can be torn apart by his two loyalties, in agony such as mediaeval men suffered whose bodies used to be massacred by horses pulling in opposite directions. Is this not an exaggeration? How can an idea draw such agonizing power, when it otherwise serves as a fount of glory, of boons and advancements for humanity? Where is its danger? Why should an idea-proud man not feel at home in the world of his people? Some answers to such questions should become available from a close study of the history of Dr. Stockmann.

It is not each and every idea that signals danger to human existence. To assert that would be to fall prey to a frustrating misology. It is not even the quality of the idea that decides the danger, but the mode of grasping it, or being grasped by it, in a man's character. One man's poison is another man's discovery. There is a way, proper to some, maybe to many men, of holding to an idea so that in its blinding radiance the temporal world is suspended, neither illuminated nor hidden from view, showing not enough yet too much. The men are then neither willing to live a life of thought, nor capable of giving precedence to the real demands of everyday merely because they are real, no matter how ill suited to their idea. The light of the idea is here too diffuse to point up its practical fitness in the world, yet much too brilliant to be forgotten. Existence in the shine of such an idea becomes a Hegelian contradiction within itself. A thesis and an antithesis are posed, only no synthesis will come forth. It is in such existence that IDEA becomes tragic. (pp. 143-44)

Thomas Stockmann is likely to appear as a little man, of no great depth or reach. This is the more likely, since greatness often dwells but in a haze of perspective. And here perspective is shortened with the entry into this familiar modern age which has not yet quite passed. Dr. Stockmann's time is in this secular history almost contemporary. It is a time of rationally flattened surfaces and streamlined whirls; a labyrinth, but scientific. It is the time of modern man who . . . turns to "this earth" uniquely, supremely confident of his indifference for a Below or an Above. As for this present twentieth century, so for the preceding one, the strongest power felt immediately by any human individual is not an obsolete God whose damnation is just a cliché, but the living and breeding society whose sanction is public opinion, as effective as hell. Immortality becomes a question of newspaper publicity, and the place of final repose is one of social register. If there is a problem about saving, it is expressed not in terms of devils and souls but of dollars and cents. Greatness in this world has surely a more precise synonym in "prestige." Here begins a twilight of those great and serious ideas which seemed so essential for the conception of the tragic. One of them is certainly alive, the idea of freedom, of man's lonely self-dependence, although that, too, is threatened with being talked out of mind by a congregation of physicists, sociologists and psychiatrists. For a modern spirit, this idea is not worth bothering about, except for a rhetorical invocation. The others are all dead, never to return; and with them has been buried tragedy. Or has it, indeed?

The figure of Dr. Stockmann on this horizon still fits the Aristotelian criteria of a tragic hero: one who completes an action, therein sustaining bad fortune, also one socially elevated, and certainly neither too good nor too evil. How his character and story correspond to further aspects of tragic being, will have to be shown, depending on how serious his existence will be for you. Transposed out of historical perspective, Stockmann appears much like Oedipus, though an Oedipus unmindful of God and immortality, as befits modern style. Like Oedipus, he is involved in the disquiets and conflicts of a community's leadership; like Oedipus, he is ruined by his service to that community; like Oedipus, the seeds of his fall he sows by own hand in his actions. Some of that ancient ethos thus persists here. But beyond these points, the similarity ceases; and anyway, for a more intimate insight into Stockmann's existence, such an atemporal transposition cannot be more than a passing note aside. Because Stockmann acts in the modern time. If he is tragic, he is so in such ways only as modern man may be. His actions concern municipal meetings rather than crown conspiracies; his bad fortune can be expressed in terms of ostracism by society, not of oracular secret. Thus you must view him, and try to assimilate the serious aspects of what is proper to him in his temporal limits. Then perhaps you can see whether this tragic existence may also be yours.

The protest which Stockmann expresses does not obvious-

ly exhibit any roots in what endures through history of man; rather, it seems addressed to transitory, even disposable, features of group living arranged by the political animal. Such features, introduced in his own times or shortly before, can clearly be amended or abolished, again in his times or shortly after. If they are, nothing is left of proper concern for those who come decades or centuries later. No straight reference points to some eternal deficiency in man's existence, but only to specific, datable blows of inhumanity between man and man. Hell or heaven is no future destiny, it is only a picturesque description of faulty interpersonal relations which can, with some good intentions, so easily turn the corner into a terrestrial and social paradise. Such is the outward import of what Stockmann has to protest against. In such a frame of protesting mind he certainly stays within the ranks of modern scientific humanity for which there are not things which could not be manipulable, adaptable, reformable, within some time, and a relatively brief time. Thus the apparent higher speed of modern living makes problems and predicaments obsolete; what could be serious one hundred years ago can hardly be a serious concern now. Is not this another way of saying that what might have been persistently, universally tragic for man as man has been abolished in the wake of progress?

Because of this difficulty, to pursue the search of the tragic also on these modern grounds, it is necessary to dig to some depth under their surface, not merely to attend to the literal content and goal of Stockmann's protest. That deals with the septic condition of the town baths, if you please: surely no one contemporary with all the deodorized, detergent, disinfected know-how of today can seriously treat that backward problem. It is not a question of fleeting appearance and particular form of Stockmann's dramatic experiences, but of how these are tied in his proper character and vision of the world. For this reason his words and external gestures must be interrelated with what he strives for and does and is. In such an examination I expect to display some contradictions of his own being, of such a character as need not be confined to the nineteenth, the twentieth, or any other century of human history. This can be serious.

When first encountered, in some youthful, enthusiastic experience, the character of Dr. Stockmann is easily impressed in admiration as that of a martyr, and the label of "an enemy of the people" appears as a gross perversion of justice. When time admits a more thorough consideration, this epithet may perhaps be seen as not entirely inappropriate to his character. To make a beginning, let it be observed that on the whole Stockmann's protest is raised against idols enslaving the life of man. Each of such idols is transient, no doubt, and of danger only to such or such group, for a longer or shorter epoch. But whether idolatry criticized by him is as such equally transient, that is another question. A negative possibility is suggested by the irony contained within his protest: the fact that Stockmann does not declare war on idols in the name of human existence but under the banner of what may very well be another idol. His own actions and insights are not exempt from what he finds himself in dissent with. And that can provide a deeper but darker impression of him, as dark as to be conceivably tragic. But this observation must be clarified and developed. Here are some illustrations of it.

Stockmann protests against a narrow-minded, short-sighted, self-enclosed attitude toward life. It should imply that what he offers instead proceeds from an entirely open mind, a broad and far-reaching vision. Is this exactly the disposition indicated in such words as: "I will show that I am right and that you are wrong," "I have right on my side," "I take my stand on right and truth"? His dedication to what is right need not be questioned. But what about his assurance that he is in possession of, or in intuitive touch with, what is right? Is it not the case that such a unidirectional self-insistence tends to see only straight forward, not at all to the sides, that it can be hampered by congenital blinkers? If there is that danger, then there is reason to suspect that Stockmann's mind is also perhaps too narrow, that there lies in it the seed of all narrow-mindedness: fanaticism. This crucial aspect of his character will have to be examined further, to disclose better this apparent kinship between what he is and what he is against.

Stockmann protests against party organization: "Party programmes strangle every young and vigorous truth," "Party leaders must be exterminated." "A party leader like a wolf requires victims to prey upon." But what are his steps in regard to the affair of the baths? Claiming the backing of the "compact majority," assuring himself of a public outlet through the press, planning a series of manifestoes, "one article every single day like bombshells." This kind of activity looks to an outside eye remarkably like the organization of a political party, even if to the eye of Dr. Stockmann himself it may deserve some other denomination.

Stockmann demands that leaders who prey upon and oppress others, shackling their freedom, should be removed altogether. Yet what else can he be considered as but a leader manqué? He certainly exhibits signs of leadership aspirations, accepts this and that to be put "at his disposal," plays around with his brother's insignia of office and taunts him—not in earnest? "I am the mayor, the master of the whole town"—are there no notions of leadership there? Anyone who would claim that those are jokes without subconscious currents should also affirm that Stockmann, if successful in his crusade and carried on by his spirit of mission to his town, would definitely refuse any political responsibility for himself; such a speculation is not too well supported by evidence.

Stockmann desires independence, fresh, free air and initiative in living, deploring official shackles of organization and dependence. All this, very clearly and explicitly, on his own behalf. At the same time he is unwilling to extend his cry for independence to others without limitation. He cannot believe that human "common curs" are also capable of independent living, that even if less clever in making use of free movements, they might in their own dim way appreciate freedom no less than his own "poodle's brain." "I don't intend to waste a word on the puny, narrow-chested, short-winded—life no longer concerns itself with them." Values, advancements, privileges, these are to be justified for the poodle race; because it is stronger, more

developed? No interest is shown in the narrow-chested curs, no hope for them. Only at the very end of his activities, when isolated from his town, Stockmann is reduced to this brilliant idea: "I am going to experiment with curs, just for once; there may be some exceptional heads amongst them." Restricted to curs, he is still interested in and looking for poodles amongst them.

Stockmann in his "poodle" creed finds objectionable the rule of the majority because of its implications of equality of human voices and of its foundation in overwhelming numbers. This equality and those numbers have turned against him and held him powerless. But before that happened, Stockmann felt no qualms in exclaiming: what a good thing it is "to have behind me the compact majority, to feel this bond of brotherhood between oneself and one's fellow citizens!" He finds definite attraction in the idea of citizenship, yet that idea precisely implies being one surrounded by many who are akin, alike, equal. It is hard to think of citizenship under Nero or Ivan the Terrible, yet perhaps they were poodles whom majority rule of curs would have overwhelmingly frustrated?

Stockmann protests against trickery and mishandling of truth, as though he believed in its lasting dignity and power. It comes then as a great shock to discover him in the act of introducing a view of truth in which it appears as relative to use, to possession and to time: "A normally constituted truth lives at most twenty years . . . Don't talk nonsense about well-ascertained truths! The truths of which the masses now approve are the very truths that the fighters at the outposts held to in the days of our grandfathers. We fighters at the outposts nowadays no longer approve of them; and I do not believe there is any other well-ascertained truth except this, that no community can live a healthy life if it is nourished only on such old marrowless truths." This is amazing. If truth belongs among such perishable commodities for quick consumption, if it is something too many people can not and should not share, then what is Stockmann talking about, when he declares, before his catastrophe: "Truth and the people will win! Do you imagine that you can silence me and stifle the truth?"; or after the disastrous meeting, when he claims he has been fighting "for freedom and truth?" Can it be the same truth, worth fighting for, which cannot be stifled? Is the winning power of truth contingent upon individuals' approval? Is it possible that some linguistic coincidence is interfering here and that a distinction must be made between "truths" and "Truth?" But a worse suspicion lingers: could it be that the qualification for capitalizing "truth" is that it should be yours, that it is truth which you hold to, fight for and consider as invincible? It is conceivable and natural among mortals among whom Stockmann belongs, to hypostatize truth which they consider as their own, appropriated in their existence. But such a tendency may overlook that whatever makes truth your own need not be the same as what makes it true; and further, that when it leads, as in Stockmann's case, to a double standard, to aggrandizement of "Truth with me" and destructive contempt for "truths of others"—despite their being true though not approved by him—then such a relation to truth is divided against itself and dangerous.

Stockmann in his devotion to ideas protests against over-estimation of what is material. He would wish to disregard the gross and degrading necessities of earthly living, those merely incidental and secondary realities of food and domicile and income. Early in his story he boasts: "I earn almost as much as we spend." In his final resolution he has for his wife those scarcely practical or even humane words: "Oh, you will have to pinch and save a bit—then we shall get along. That gives me very little concern." Little concern for what she is to pinch and save from! Yet he is not at all an ascetic, indifferent to material comforts. In his first appearance he sounds quite complacent: "Ah, it is good to be sitting snug and warm here," with cigars and a drink, after a roast-beef supper. And in his last conversation with his brother he responds: "What a blessed feeling it is to know one is provided for!" To be provided with what the body needs is good to him, but to provide it, that gives him little concern. Is he dishonest, is he ready to sponge and abuse others? No, such a moral criticism of him would be hard to justify. Still, it remains uncontroverted that the material realities of life Dr. Stockmann values and devalues at the same time. This, as much as the other introduced conflicts and inconsistencies, is all in his way to be.

What do these illustrations show? For one thing they point to this definite conclusion: that Stockmann's character is outstanding and uncommon, harboring such contradictions within itself. But on the other hand, if the contradictory aspect is left aside for the moment, it can also be said that Stockmann very plainly shows himself as all too human. He moves through ordinary aspirations, he has to rely on brotherhood with his neighbors, he sees only a limited horizon and a partial view of truth, he enjoys the creature comforts of material realities. In no way does he stand above the level of social sorrows and personal perplexities of man: he is no Prometheus. And this in turn points to a more universally significant, if darker, conclusion. If such as Stockmann who see the shocks and shortages of human existence, still cannot tear themselves above them, where is the dream of eradicating them? If protest undermines itself when he who protests is human, where is the remedy? If salt itself is not salty enough, wherewith can it be salted? The limitation of visions, and its potential fanaticism and hostility; social organization, and its choking hold on spontaneity and initiative; leadership, and its enslavement of the led; demand for freedom, and incapacity to make use of it; the strength, security, and possible tyranny of majority rule; the elusiveness of impersonal and lasting truth to shortsighted and partial subjects; the indispensable material needs of the body growing into irreparable materialistic service to the body. All these "natural shocks" may thus be viewed as incurable, as wholly ingrained in the life of man, indeed as creating the stuff of which it is composed. This, admittedly not the complete nor the only picture, is nevertheless a true and universal picture of mankind, so inadequate, so disintegrating within that its cries must resound vainly in the wilderness. If there is truth in such a vision, then it must be admitted that Stockmann, before being a modern man, is a man; that his protest, far from being restricted to transitory and disposable features of nineteenth century's society, goes against all living of men with themselves; that to appreci-

ate it more intimately, one must look not at the secular times of the present age but at the time of human existence.

In fact, one aspect of Stockmann's protest can only be inferred indirectly, and never studied in his words and actions. That is the very possibility of his putting forward an open protest. However correct his objections against the limitations and liabilities of "liberalism" may be, reflection can lead to those conditions and constitutions of human living where liberalism is either not yet or no longer actual, where the illusions of presuming men equal and being guided by the desires of the greatest number have been dispensed with. In such times, in such societies, the very opportunity for voicing a protest by one man, on his behalf or also on behalf of others, could never be given. This passing thought may suffice to recall again the human significance of protest, even if that protest be practically pointless, as with Prometheus, even if he who protests be not free of what he protests against, as with Stockmann. Sapienti satis.

In this sombre picture of mankind, transpiring through the protesting character of Thomas Stockmann, is there any positive trait? There is, but it is not accessible among the features of this world where Stockmann has been observed thus far: in his town, surrounded by his fellow-citizens, submerged in human society. It is revealed at the conclusion of Stockmann's tragic story, when he leaves behind this former world of his. The one integral, uncontradicted characteristic of man—indeed, his only property—is his persisting power to "be" none other than himself, his ability to dare remain faithful to his freedom, tied by nothing above his own conscience. Unfortunately, this property begins to shine for Stockmann as the source of strength in his existence only when he is already out of bounds of society. What kind of strength can be there involved, against what forces? Not any more against those social forces of his world which he is now dissociated from. An outcast claims: "I am the strongest man in the town," and corrects himself: "Strongest in the whole world." Because his town used to be his world; yet he has passed beyond it. His strength can avail him now only against what is in himself, his own temptations, ideas, choices, the germs from which another world may perhaps arise in his future. But there is none now in his present, no field for his unworldly strength. Does Stockmann glimpse now this truth that his character and destiny have been unwordly all along? He seems to, when his last words are: "The strongest man is he who stands most alone." His strength obtains from his standing: standing for himself, standing out, standing free. On this strength a man can build a world around him. But the strength itself is shadowed by another property: to stand for himself is to stand at the foundations of a world, to stand there—alone.

Must this be so? The question is incomplete. There is no particular thing that must be there for everybody. Whatever is, depends on choice, and choice determines man to be this rather than that, thereby determining what will be there for him because he is this rather than that—himself. Events are such for Dr. Stockmann, since he is such as he is. Any man's tragic perspectives are neither requirements nor compulsions but openings of his existence in the world, the range of which is to be explored. For the understanding of the tragic story of Dr. Stockmann, a closer look must be taken at the roots of his character, in distinction to people around him in his world. But before that another interhuman phenomenon in that world calls for attention: it uncovers the ground of Stockmann's ultimate position, where he stands alone.

The light which has been so far thrown upon Stockmann is hardly flattering. Such a harsh scrutiny of his words and actions may appear to be moved by dissent rather than consent. This impression should be redressed. Because however human, wanting, self-divided, he emerges from this examination with his own character outstanding from a background, with issues, inclinations, ideas, proper to himself. What now about this background on which he stands out? It is human but not characterized, it is the town-world to which Stockmann appears to belong, it is the matrix in which his clashes and struggles are laid. The background to Stockmann's existence is the relation between the personal character and the crowd. Man against society; how many words have been spoken and written about this phenomenon, allegedly peculiar or at least peculiarly striking in the modern epoch? While Stockmann's life and vision, as already argued, is properly modern, its ground covers what is not exclusive nor even specifically different in modern times. As such, it presents an opportunity to enquire, on an incomparably vivid example, into this relation of man and the crowd, not merely transitory but enduring, old as much as new.

The crowd is here taken generically, as an envelopment to which each existing man can be related so or otherwise, but to which he cannot remain entirely unrelated. So understood, the crowd is of course not restricted to its definite examples such as the crowd at a meeting or at a parade, the crowd in peace or in wartime, the crowd of proletarians, civil servants, or taxpayers. However unlike, these are specific manifestations from what can be viewed as the same source. Nor is the crowd essentially constituted by the occasion of its gathering, the duration of its presence, the spatial contiguity of its members. To be in a crowd, men need not loiter touching elbows in the street; they can be in their homes or in a forest, separated not by inches but by miles, silent rather than shouting. What makes the relation of a man to the crowd is his way to be.

This must be elucidated. In order to do that, I shall describe in turn three of the factors present: the crowd as such, the men in the crowd, and the men outside it. These observations will be illustrated from the story, actions, and misfortunes of Dr. Stockmann, and the events he lived through, but not only in his literal encounter with the crowd at the town meeting, which, for this way of thinking, was no more than a specimen.

The crowd is in the background of individual actions such as Dr. Stockmann's. More precisely it should be said that the crowd is the background, the social setting of a man's world, the undifferentiated milieu of all the "others" taken together—which always remains other, the invisible elastic wall from which personal drives rebound, in which they often sink. As such, the crowd is a static entity, mere-

ly continuing to be there yet never here where you are: the crowd is always elsewhere, around, behind or ahead. You can move toward or away from or even amongst the crowd, but in moving you carry with you your own "here," and the crowd just stays. Its principal feature is inertia, since a move, a push, an action, is ever yours or his; "theirs" is the always uncertain re-action. When the crowd "does" anything, it is more strictly the men in it who do it, although they may not recognize themselves as the doers. So a drifting boat moves but aimlessly floating, its direction due to the haphazard but genuine steps of people on board, or else to the pounding of waves. Inertly the crowd resists novelty and burdens with its deadweight the fulmination of progress. Listen to the mayor who can well know what he is talking about: "The public does not require any new ideas. The public is best served by the good, old-established ideas it already has." That is, if it has any. The possession of ideas is contingent upon aspiration and interest, and such modes of individual movement and heat need not occur within that which is just there, impersonally. Incipient interests and diffused aspirations are all that can be looked for in the crowd as a whole. They barely suffice for the crowd to be aware of some events, weakly orienting itself and waiting for a push. Unidentified voices among those who come to hear Stockmann's public address: "I go to every public meeting, I do . . . Tell me what is going on here tonight . . . Who are we to back up in this? . . . Watch Aslaksen and do as he does." Does this indicate trust in a certain leader who serves them in their love? No, the crowd is there only to support, not to trust, to follow, not to love. A possible change in its support can happen like the dislocation of a boat's balance by a barrel rolling across. It is a matter of push and pull, of whipping on the crowd so that it should not lose its momentum when rolling along. What is the lever to set the crowd in motion? Enlightenment, devotion, sacrifice? Hardly. The simplest lever is that of suspicion, in defense of its status quo, in resentment against any flash of novelty or brilliance, in assimilation to the lowest common denominator. "I say, what has come to the doctor? What are we to think of it? . . . Have you ever noticed if the fellow drinks? . . . I rather think he goes off his head sometimes . . . Any madness in his family? . . . No, it is nothing more than sheer malice, he wants to get even with somebody." Ignorance, lack of comprehension responding blindly, but to what? Drunkenness, lunacy, selfishness, those are the avenues of re-action to the puzzling, suspicious superiority of Stockmann. Can the crowd appreciate devotion? It would have to recognize where its interests lie; and that already lies beyond the receptivity of its dispersed power. Strongly pushed, demagogically warned against such curiosity, it obeys, since that agrees so well with its unwillingness to encounter anything novel and unknown to be coped with. Suspicious, it refuses information: "Don't talk about the baths! We won't hear you! None of that!" Yet although Stockmann is not the man to achieve it, there are some chances of a change of support in the meeting: there is some initial applause for him, some confusion later, some amused laughter especially at his words critical of authority and prominent citizens; that sort of speech could turn the motion of the crowd, ever suspicious of those who claim to stand in front of it as its leaders. Because the balance of weight in the crowd is as precarious as in a boat on stormy waters. Without a pilot, the crowd is shaky, insecure. Its only safety lies in sheer size, in anonymous numbers. And that kind of strength is illusory since every chain is as resistant as the most fragile link in it, every boat stays afloat as long as its whole water-exposed surface has no break anywhere. Hence the inert servility to anyone who appears the strongest; because the concern of the crowd is only to remain unbroken, to float as an anonymous whole, to be there in "safe" bulk. Hence the inert timidity, as in the crowd of Theban elders, suspicious of all daring, so in the crowd pursuing Stockmann, which despite all its momentary hostility can only gather enough impetus to throw small stones at his house. This is not to say that a crowd cannot be really dangerous and homicidal: but that only happens when a decided destructive intent is imparted to it by some leading individuals, or else when the collective insecurity of the crowd is so greatly disturbed and threatened that it thrashes out to break, often no matter whom.

What makes the crowd be as it is? Speaking generally, Stockmann provides a certain answer when he denies that "the crowd has the monopoly of broad-mindedness and morality and that vice and corruption and every kind of intellectual depravity are the result of culture." What he denies is the naive Rousseau-type of illusion that somehow the generality of mankind could be, or have been, more moral, deserving, not to say noble, in their "natural" vegetation, and that it is the more complex cultural transformations of social living which are at fault in degrading the crowd. No, such a pseudo-historical apology for the crowd's mode of being misconceives just that which it tries to account for in a short temporal perspective. The crowd and what it signifies is not a phenomenon of modern culture; it is as old as mankind. It is the unsafe, unresolved human being as such that is responsible for the crowd. To be sure, specific conditions can make for quality variations. This is what Stockmann visualizes when he continues: "That culture demoralizes is only an old falsehood that our forefathers believed in and we have inherited. No, it is ignorance, poverty, ugly conditions of life, that do the devil's work!" It is not the achievements of culture, of temporal changes in humanity, but its persistent lacks and perversions that can make specific examples of crowds particularly worthy of contempt. In other words, there can be qualitative differences, due to the menace of ignorance, poverty, ugliness, between a crowd of shivering, starving aborigines and a crowd of Athenian citizens, or between that and a crowd of automated laborers in the slums of a contemporary city. The arrow of history need not point toward improvement or deterioration of crowds through the ages. At any rate, for the initial grasp of the whole background of human activities the main target is not what the crowd is like but that it is a crowd. What makes the crowd be, as the undifferentiated others, as "they?" Whatever makes anything be, is a choice. But what choice is involved, and whose choice? The best light can be thrown onto this problem from enquiring into the constituence of the crowd. And that is—individual men, after all.

The men in the crowd. What is their way to be, their com-

mon ethos? . . . At this stage men of the crowd can only be spoken of in the plural, and that always means an uncertainly crowded description. If there is a word which can provide a clue to the conception of being of men in the crowd, it is: loss. Loss of himself by each member of it produces the selfless, driveless inertia of the crowd as a whole. How can such a losing choice or rather choice of loss occur in any man? To envisage that, one must remember that choice is not here treated as a conscious act of man, at least it need not be such and can still remain choice. Thus it would be vain and insufficient to try and find out for one man, then another and another, whether, when and how he has been aware of choosing to lose himself. The answers could be unmanageable or none at all. Not every individual retains, like Hamlet, his conscientious response to choice. Also one must not weight the scales in hastily assuming that the choice was his: perhaps he was chosen, determined not from within, to lose himself. But in that case, is it warranted at all to speak of choice of loss? Of choice man does not have full or safe knowledge; this was confessed at the outset of the whole exploration. Still, choice can be presumed as responsible for what is in existence, on the basis of what in it can be observed and known. What symptoms are there in the existence of individual men in the crowd, which would point to such a choice of loss?

The man in the crowd loses his self by giving it over to others, surrendering it to become common. Common property, one would say, if what is proper, own, his, could ever be common; rather it is the case that property of self becomes annihilated there. This is how men become common. Each one yields himself to all the others in toto, not just sharing with this or that other one. He remains subject: subject to their influence, an obedient subject, a receptive, manageable, loyal subject. Does this happen only in the slums of stupidity and superstition? Not according to Dr. Stockmann: "The kind of common people I mean are not only to be found low down in the social scale; they crawl and swarm all around us—even in the highest social positions. You have only to look at your own mayor . . . He thinks what his superiors think and holds the same opinions as they. People who do that are common." The mayor himself does not get the chance to reply to these words; would he deny them? Immediately before, another crowd specimen, Hovstad, is in his speech very far from disclaiming such an attitude: he boasts of being common: "I lay no claim to any sort of distinction. I am the son of humble countryfolk, and I am proud that I come from common people." This is what a man has to say in the crowd, and this is what the crowd applauds. What a bankruptcy of existence: no claim to any distinction, to anything proper, uniquely his own, and pride in being just common! Someone may perhaps suggest that such words are only spoken to an anticipating audience, as here in the meeting; but this would be underestimating that loss which makes men think and act on this common pattern also when they are alone by themselves. Sometimes even more so then: without the comfort of surrounding others, dismayed by isolation, what would they do or think? Just "obviously" what anyone else would do in their place; there only is safety. And the predicament might not be so acute if, as Stockmann has it, they suited themselves to their superiors only. But this is how he could put it, he who is not a man of the crowd and therefore can discriminate for himself between superior and inferior. Discrimination demands a judging, aiming, longing self, not a self which is being lost, surrendered, and which is a constituent of inertia. The man in the crowd, yielding his selective powers, is open to all influence, inferior as much as superior. To him the danger lies precisely in being left to himself, isolated on his own, just himself as an individual—that is what he abandons, that is what he endeavors to shut out of his mind altogether. His vision becomes common, his thinking plural: not "I" and "he," but "we" and "they." To be "all-one" is disastrously unthinkable, always to be replaced by being "one of many." Hence his failure to discriminate between the influence, ideas, actions of this one superior individual and that one, inferior. Influences, forces, achievements are plural, everything that matters in the world is plural, finally he himself is—common, reducible to many, plural. Oneness of character must be lost. Therewith goes the capacity of moving and standing on one's own feet, leaving only the shaky balance of people who are in the same boat.

Is it conceivable that such phenomena in men "just happen," that they are not due to choice which determines them? To say that, one would not only admit casting about in hardly penetrated substrata of existence, but also would leave them in darkness. It may be a help to point out an alternative in this choice, other than common loss. Such an alternative was seen in Hamlet's conscientious indwelling into himself; more of it will be seen in Orestes. But the alternative situation of man can also be approached through what properly happens to Thomas Stockmann. This perspective must be gradually approached now.

If, for the man in the crowd, being one for himself is to be escaped, yielded, lost from mind, and plurality of the multitude is the imagined haven of power and security, then it is easy to see how to his imagination that power is endowed with a voice. The expression of that plural power is what is known as public opinion. It has no individual shape and must remain strictly anonymous, hence its voice can sound rather hazy and cryptic. But this does not put it in doubt for the man in the crowd; on the contrary, that disembodied voice, shrouded in the mystery of might, inspires him with insuperable awe. How could a mere finite one stand up against it? And thus takes place the formal ritual of prostration before the anonymous power of plurality. The day after the meeting, the news from his town-world which reaches Stockmann has no other form but this irritating, repetitious formula which passing from mouth to mouth could almost be used as a chant: one dares not oppose public opinion. Who does not invoke its protective charm, one after another? The glazier, the landlord, the school principal, the members of the baths' committee, the householders' association, the press, the leader of the majority, in short: the whole crowd. It is this phenomenon of consecutive—and thus individual—prostration before the voice of public opinion that points up a task in Stockmann's words that "the common people are nothing more than the raw material of which a people is made." A people, for him, would have a thousand

voices, and not one mumbling distortion of a voice; because a people is composed of individual persons; that is the distinction he must have in mind, between a people and common people. The latter, the common lost men, are the raw material which should then be worked over with the aim toward a more finished, fine, or finite "product": a people. What working over can apply to this raw, undifferentiated conglomeration of material which is the crowd? Precisely the recovery from loss of finite limits, of finer awareness, of discriminating finish in place of common haze. To work over the men in the crowd is to pick them out of the crowd, to sharpen their vision so that they should appreciate distinctions of individuality, to raise them from prostration and to confront them with the bogus power of the multitude whose monstrous proportions are entirely due to obliterating additions of many single, finite, personal selves. A people can speak and dare only if it is composed, put together by existing individuals who dare to speak with their own voices. This task of working over the crowd's raw material, of proposing to each of its members the alternative of being himself just within his limits, is anything but easy. Its perspectives can frighten, stretching into an infinite future: because this task is nothing else but the reach of temporal progress.

To contrast the "safe" stability of being in the crowd against the dismaying alternative of being just oneself, it is now time to look at the mode of existence of men without the crowd, such as Stockmann himself. The individual who chooses himself as just one and stands on his own, must realize not only his unsafe position of all-oneness and hence aloneness, but also the natural negation of his background. He has to count with the suspicions and superstitions of those who are in the crowd and aim at his degradation into their common plural denominator, or else at his removal from their horizon. In such hostile surroundings he has to strive for a guiding vision of his own, for ideas which could assure his independence. Now the reason may dawn for the pull exercised on men who posit themselves against others by ideas. Ideas are logs for the building of an independent home in the wilderness, they can be tools for damming the spread of the crowd, and weapons for defending what is one's own. A man outside of the crowd can only rely on character in his own acts and vision in his ideas; in the un-owned sphere of events it can be quite proper for him to be ready for starvation, for stoning, for still worse outcomes. And yet he must be turned continually toward the future; it is out of the future that ideas may arrive to sweep over his present isolation, it is toward the future that every novelty, disturbing to the crowd, is addressed, expecting to be proved by time, to gain and work over those men lost in the present. Thus it is that individuals standing on their own bring about progress, they are its emissaries, "the fighters at the outposts" watching for tomorrow. Progress through time, properly grasped, can have no individual opponents. No one, thinking and striving for himself can be averse to novelty and transformation as such, since for himself he will always find lacks to be filled, disproportions to be emended, the drastic burden of his finitude to be alleviated. This is not to say that no serious disputes could arise among independent men about the details, the methods, the priorities in such striving; not, however, about progress as such. That is the reason why Stockmann dismisses as secondary in importance the adversity of older, slower, more prejudiced leaders. If they are capable of leading others, a fortiori of moving on their own, they are not genuine adversaries. Otherwise, if they are just chips off the structure of the crowd, which happened to be thrown on top, then their realm is entirely that of the past. "All these venerable relics of a dying school of thought are most admirably paving the way for their own extinction; they need no doctor's help to hasten their end . . . It is not they who are most instrumental in poisoning our life . . . not they who are the most dangerous enemies." The enemy of progress is no one, but only the plurality, "the compact majority," the crowd as such. Why? Because progress of mankind is nothing but the striving toward new independent existence for every one, the working over of the "raw material" into finished individuals ready for the future, the disintegration of the crowd's inertia of the present. Thus the crowd and those who bring progress are in antithesis; but while progress lasts, the crowd is immortal. Utopians dreaming of an inestimably future future, when all progress will have been accomplished, should decide whether that accomplishment can really be victorious, and that means whether the opposition to progress, the background of interhuman existence, the crowd, will ever be annihilated. Only then each man could find and be himself, all-one within and alone without.

Whatever the case may be with regard to what lies beyond a millennial horizon, life of the individual as one thus presents the alternative to losing oneself in plurality: to stay himself, alone within the temporal gravity of his ideas tending toward the future, faced with the tacit suspicious resistance of the social world around him in his present. Dr. Stockmann does not find himself alone, an outsider, only after the violent clash with his fellow-citizens at the meeting. He has been outside of their common life all along, and his inward strength of standing up for himself has been his outward weakness in the town. Perhaps it is now a little clearer why he could never be completely at home in this world of his native town, and how in the conflict tearing him, between belonging to the people around him and belonging to his own ideas, so many contradictions have accumulated in his character. His position is so precarious, because in the very same tendencies, thoughts, actions, he would sincerely wish to participate in the real life of the town-world, and also to preserve his idea-inspired independence. And also, because the world around him has precisely the nature of a town; and a town is just such a horizon on which the background of a crowd is most favorably raised. The town, the natural habitat of man, naturally furthers his loss in the crowd. Neither Prometheus raised above humanity, nor homeless Oedipus, neither Hamlet in his princely isolation, nor Faust storming through the universe, can be adequately characterized as town-dwellers. Stockmann, however, longs to belong to the town which is his native home; and yet, no less than they, he remains an outsider. The predicament of Hamlet afflicts him in another dimension, provided by the town crowd. While alone, standing for himself, he may appear strong and safe in his private sphere, completely devoted to ideas. But as soon as he decides to transform his ideas into deeds, he is immediately thrown into the whirl of conflicts due to the background wall presented by all the others around him, he is being sucked down into the crowd, and has seemingly insuperable disadvantage in his struggle for independence and progress. Then he may no longer be alone, but neither is he safe and strong. Only when the struggle in the public sphere appears conclusively lost, he recovers himself, and is again just one man, on his own.

It may be asked whether the phenomena described on the preceding pages are responsible for the tragic character of Stockmann. An affirmative answer would definitely take too much for granted. The relations indicated pertain to man's independence as oneself and to its possible loss. It would be presumptuous, however, to look for a clear demarkation line between where a man's self is his own and where it is no more than common—as will be still pointed out with regard to such men of the crowd as the mayor, Aslaksen, Hovstad. Also unjustified would be a positive assertion that all independent existence is tragic or that its loss must be, Even in the initial sense of "tragic," which amounts to a passage from good to bad fortune, it can hardly be maintained that every independent individual must suffer such. The reasons for the possibility, even perhaps the likelihood, of a crash have been outlined: what may await the man who stands alone against a crowd, who should not "wear his best trousers when going out to fight for freedom and truth." He must be ready for resentment, self-doubt, accusations of insanity or criminality, ostracism, punishment, death and forgottenness or damnation by all others. So wide are the vistas of social hell, where there is no longer an Evil One, but plenty of evil ones have stayed: in the crowd, inertly accepting the task of negation. But there is, as ever, no general inevitability of such infernal courses of events, since what must properly happen to one person need not happen to another in similar surroundings. And no events, not even those in hell, are tragic by themselves.

In order then to enquire into the tragic being of Thomas Stockmann, his character must be further brought into relief. Some observations of his own character have already been introduced, emphasizing the conflicts within himself, which relate to his staggering position, gravitating both toward his town without and toward his idea within. A "two-souled" character, Stockmann is in proper linear descendance from Faust; yet such hereditary resemblance is not sufficient to determine the proper disposition of his own existence. What is now required is a closer look at the color and mass of the idea dominating his relation to the world.

And that means finally coping with that shocking, injurious, seemingly alien label of "an enemy of the people." The vote at the meeting is for Stockmann much more than a passing incident easily dismissed as due to stupidity. "That hateful name—I can't get quit of it. It is sticking here in the pit of my stomach, eating into me like a corrosive acid. And no magnesia will remove it." Perhaps he could get rid of the corrosive effects of that name, if he were entirely clear in his innocence of which he is ostensibly so sure. But the poisonous staying power of the label is due to the fact that the devotion to his idea has driven him to qualify for it. And this, however much he may want to, Stockmann is too honest to forget beyond recall. Doctor Thomas Stockmann is an enemy of the people. Not simply because he has stood against the crowd. No, many may do that and be treated inimically by the common people, without innerly finding themselves to be such enemies. But Stockmann has gone further. He has spoken these words:

"My native town is so dear to me that I would rather ruin it than see it flourishing upon a lie . . . What does the destruction of a community matter! All who live by lies ought to be exterminated like vermin! . . . You will bring about such a state of things that the whole country will deserve to be ruined. And if things come to that pass, I shall say from the bottom of my heart: Let the whole country perish, let all these people be exterminated!"

On that follows the accusation. Is it improper? These words of Thomas Stockmann, shaking his whole world to its foundations, echo an ancient cry; Pereat mundus, fiat justitia. Desert, justice, truth, are here weighed in the balance of Stockmann's mind against nothing less and nothing more than the existence of men. And it is the abstract idea that prevails. In contraposition to that dis-ordering human benefactor, Prometheus, Stockmann finds people of less weight than principles. Of what tragic significance the very posing of this contrast has been to Prometheus, has been considered. It will not be surprising if the contrast is no less tragic for Stockmann. While for the Titan the threat in defying order could be pregnant with anarchy, for this man serving the ideal order at all costs, the threat arising is fanaticism. It is the first trait of the fanatic mind that the order of his ideas can suffer no imposition, no compromise, no rivalry. Stockmann is a fanatic, if for him the living human reality must yield precedence to abstraction. He is an enemy of the people not because he hates people, but because caring for them he sacrifices their existence to his idea. Men may not tolerate that their being there, for themselves, should ever be taken as second to anything that emerges within that being, even an idea. In Stockmann's vision, however, this is exactly what must take place: men are less important than principles and values of order, they ought to exist only if they are good, just, truthful, otherwise they deserve to perish. Order, value, idea is above human life: eternal essence precedes temporal existence.

What is the idea that has taken such complete possession of Thomas Stockmann? In his crucial words quoted above the main stress seems to be upon the destructive import of lies, and thus by implication upon the supreme merit of truth. But the dubious, inconsistent attitude of Stockmann toward truth has already been pointed out. The same man who here so despises absence of truth spoke earlier of truth's being perishable, marrowless, subject to individuals' approval. If truth were his central idea, could he ever express himself about it in such terms? Further, it may be noticed in those condemning words, what he finds to deserve annihilation is not the deficiency of lies for knowledge, but "living by lies" or "flourishing upon a lie." It is the relation of lies to activities of character, their part in men's ethos, that is being condemned. There is then reason for regarding as the central dominating force in Stock-

mann's life the ethical idea of duty. His first statement to follow the irrevocable outcry: "Let all people be exterminated!" and the subsequent frenzy of the crowd declaring him an enemy of the people, is this: "I have done my duty." This can mean: he has not failed to serve his duty—his deity or his idol. Because if it were to mean, more humanely, that he has rendered what was due, paid what he owed, then the question could not be repressed: to whom? And to that question there is no answer. Duty which can be served by a demand for the annihilation of all, is certainly no duty to man. It claims to be super-human and reaches beyond the world of human existence. It cannot be said that Stockmann always wants it to be of such a transcendent nature, nor that he claims his devotion to it in a possessive, world-excluding fashion. As soon as he makes his critical discovery about the baths, he immediately discards any pretensions to personal recognition or reward for himself: "I have done nothing more than my duty." He treats his service as higher than his self. Even more explicitly, when he optimistically begins his town campaign despite the warning of his brother, he declares: "I shall have done my duty towards the public, towards the community." There is no conflict yet between the service of idea and the service of humanity. But one may well wonder whether it is still the same duty "towards the community" he has "done" at the conclusion of the meeting, where he has spoken not about the communal cause of the town but about the inferiority of common people. Clearly it cannot be the same. At this stage the idea of duty has become dissociated from human realities. The choice has been imposed on Dr. Stockmann, between what he sees as duty and what surrounds him in his world. It is the idea which is victorious. It is his existence which sustains a tragic defeat in that choice.

The choice between the world and the idea determines the future of Stockmann. That such a choice confronts him is the root of his tragedy. Then, on the altar of his idea he immolates his past, he is willing to sacrifice both his own and his family's material welfare with his "three big No's" to Morten Kiil, which are none too easy for him, in view of his respect for comforts and of his genuine affection for his dependents. In accordance with his manifesto of the night before, he must be ready to sacrifice much more—everything and everybody. Now that the problem is seen in black and white, in terms of wrong and right, of filth and purity, of stagnation and reform, the frame is set and rigid, no compromise or return admissible. The second, visionary Faustian soul has got rid of its more worldly counterpart and has spread wings to soar in quest of the ideal. Has it, really?

His devotion to duty is noble, admirable, infrangibly moral. For such an attitude reverence is due and often loudly expressed. But what is the role of such grand idealist thrust in the wavering situations of existence, what effect does it have in temporal striving, what guidance does it provide in men's everyday world, where enthusiasm is but a start of moving power? In order to place Thomas Stockmann in some comparable relation to other individuals in his world, and before passing to the final conclusions about his tragic ethos, a brief glance may be cast at the people amongst whom he lives. No other character is so much in the foreground of attention, no other ethical attitude is so clearly delineated, but a glimpse of the others can supply a sensible reference for comparison. Some of these others must be seen as men of the crowd, as individuals in the process of losing their proper selves. It must therefore be emphasized that such loss, earlier referred to, is but a phase of a man's way to be, in the course of life not something final, terminated, irrecoverable. About a man who reached a total condition of loss, nothing whatever could be said in singular terms—if he were no longer one.

There is, first, at the side of Dr. Stockmann, his wife Katherine, a not unusual model of female realism. She believes in an appropriate spread of human concerns, with greatest concentration in the circle immediately around. For her, duty begins at home. To her husband's declaration about duty towards the public, Katherine can straight away counterpose: "But towards your family, your own home? Do you think that is doing your duty towards those you have to provide for?" Stockmann gives her no answer. The limits of her moral realism also show in her wondering: "What is the use of having right on your side if you have not got might?" That which is right and due must for her be supported by adequate power of agency, must not be divorced from effectiveness. But when it comes to executing that which she sees as duty, she does not fail. Realizing that her husband's position becomes hopeless with the desertion of his supposed supporters, she nevertheless provides her willing and unwavering support: "I am going to stand by you, Thomas." This she does, it may be supposed, less because her husband is right than because it is her husband; but what is due to him from her, she renders fully.

Then there is Petra, his daughter. In her untried youth worshipping her father's image, she is perhaps formed most closely to resemble him. After him, she sees life contrasts in black and white, she is devoted to unadulterated truth, offended by its lack in educational practices and the duplicity of those responsible for adult media of communication. She condemns Hovstad for mixing with the service of a noble "cause" a personal sentiment. Her sentiment for duty makes her negate sentiment as such. But—one may wonder, what does Petra's future hold in store? Will she, past the dependent stage of inexperience, keep faith with her paternal heredity or will she, more likely, enveloped in the role of her sex, find it proper to follow her mother?

Of men in Stockmann's milieu, first to be mentioned, and quickly passed over, is Hovstad, the editor. He is at the lowest rung of the scale, by his own confession: "We are not worth much." The plural may be well noted, it is for him perfectly proper; so is his earlier cited statement, claiming no distinction but boasting of being common. The loss of a personal self is well advanced here. Lying face down into the wind of opportunity, trembling with cowardice, ever unwilling to stand up alone, resentfully dreaming of a common revolution but servile to any one who dares to speak up in a show of strength, Hovstad, along with millions of his fairly anonymous brethren, is useful to others. But only in the way all utensils are useful.

There is, next, Aslaksen who happens to be a printer and also serves as chairman of the householders' association. Again clearly a man of the multitude, yet of a different brand. He rather prides himself on never doing things, at any rate not ever undertaking any decisive acts or deep commitments. Despite this, he enjoys influence and leadership of a kind among the "compact majority." For the inert crowd, his timidity is a fitting symbol; he succeeds in being more average than the average individuals. This is what unites common people around him: their trust that he is incapable of uncommon moves. Afraid of the dark of the future, recoiling before crisis and violence, Aslaksen neither gropes nor thrusts himself forward. But thus hampered, he exploits his turtle character. He is aware that "a politician should never be too certain of anything," and the less impressive his activities, the safer he can feel. Therefore, in the local affairs of his town he is timid, but in "higher politics" of central government he feels he need not be, safe to snap at adversaries at sufficient distance, who will not even notice him. And so his way of living is harmonized faithfully around his idea of moderation, his commitment not to be committed. This shapes a character, not inspiring, not greatly efficacious, but still a character of his own. Except where it gravely matters, Aslaksen can be relied on.

By way of contrast, Captain Horster gives a suggestion of a man who is really free, but only because he has chosen to be a wanderer on the seas. With much of his time spent sailing, outside of his home town—which is in no way his world—Horster finds and accepts himself as an outsider. He knows his task, the art of running his ship; despite this, or precisely because of this, he is not interested in the art of political navigation, and leaves that task to the men able or at least willing to take the wheel. In his withdrawn role, he is no factor in the struggle of impersonal ideas and forces, which occupies the town world. And still his peripheral presence can be active on behalf of individuals suffering within; he can occasionally be helpful to them, as he is to Stockmann, his cause and his family. Thus in choosing independence and even homelessness, he retains his integrity and his power of being an agent.

A different specimen of this power of an isolated agent is presented in Morten Kiil. His is entirely the strength of a selfish badger fending off common curs. He knows he is alone on account of common envy of his wealth. But he claims to be "jealous of my name and reputation." His morals, of an extremely primitive nature, make him say to Stockmann: "I mean to live and die a clean man. You shall cleanse me, Thomas." How is that cleansing to be accomplished? By Stockmann's dementi of what he is convinced to be the truth concerning the effects of Kiil's business activities. This, like everything the badger needs and gets, is to be paid for, in Stockmann's family's being "provided for." Clean name for purchase, highest moral reputation for the highest cash bidder. Despite such primitive character, despite his social isolation, it cannot be denied that Morten Kiil wields power in the world of Stockmann's life, and is capable not only of affecting Stockmann's standing there, which is shown in his last encounter with representatives of the press and of the majority, but also of effecting far-going changes in the horizons and balances of the whole community.

Lastly, the individual closest to being the counter-partner of Thomas Stockmann in the world, who by a poignant throw of origins, happens to be not only his enemy but also his brother. The mayor and "master of the whole town" is in the eyes of the doctor a plebeian and common man, but judging by his words and acts he is certainly not the clearest example of a self lost into anonymity. More definitely than Aslaksen, he retains features of a character of his own: ambition, striving, activities proper for him, a view of what can and should happen to whom in the inter-personal flow of events. Peter Stockmann happens to be the brother of Thomas; but one cannot say that he just "happens" to be his adversary. The two make themselves opposed to each other in all ways they see and shape their lives. To the transcendent reach of the doctor's ethos of duty the mayor opposes a morality which is utilitarian but limited to the greatest benefit only in the shorter temporal perspectives. Thus in the affair of the baths, when Thomas maintains that silence would be not only wrong absolutely but also disadvantageous to the town's welfare in the further future, Peter can always retort: but what about the values of the coming present? If there were an objective method for the human mind to draw a balance between a certain though limited evil in the present and a greater though uncertain good in the future, then one could definitely say that one of the two brothers is wrong in his judgment. But such a balance must always be drawn by the mind of a particular person on whose existence it is incumbent to judge and to choose his way of living in time. One way is that of Thomas, but quite different is the way of Peter. As to the pure right or wrong involved, a man of Peter's brand may understand that as completely dependent on the concrete advantage or disadvantage in question. Because for Peter Stockmann abstraction of ideas is an alien perversion. He is no less ambitious, no less capable of wholehearted involvement than his brother; but these traits of character are fulfilled for him not in creation of thoughts but in their application to what is at hand. If Thomas sins in theory, the vice and virtue of Peter lie only in practice. And while Thomas gets to the point of divorcing his idea from life, Peter who may be idea-blind will never be unfaithful to his life. Hence his qualification for putting forward the diagnosis of his brother which has been cited at the outset. In that field, of "putting ideas into practical shape," the mayor is at home, there he is jealous, possessive, authoritarian. There he may lie, trick, malevolently pretend some "good will"—so in his interpretation of his brother's report as "merely imagination"—but he will have his way. He is not crude in his reaching for goals, either. Like Aslaksen, he is always for compromise and caution but also for persistence. With all in the crowd he wants to represent, he bows low to public opinion, but in the moment: he has won the insight that "public opinion is an extremely mutable thing." Without courageous independence to stand against it, he can crawl around it in the bushes between today, tomorrow and the day after, and surreptitiously inject transforming doses of his own intentions. If great objectives can be cumulatively attained by creeping up on them, then mayor Stockmann is capable of them. It is dubious whether he should ever be entitled to claim credit for any deed as "mine" and not rather "ours," since alone he would neither stand up nor move on. Still, greatness is sometimes ascribed to the common power of not rocking the boat.

What follows from these observations of the people around Dr. Stockmann? Only this. None of the observed characters, attitudes, views of the world is sublime, none need evoke deep admiration. But—it is not too much to say, equally, that none of them is inferior to Stockmann's in "putting ideas into practical shape," none less effective in the welding of vision with act, none less mindful of risk to fulfillment through time, and—none is more apt to induce tragic disaster. What then must be said about the differing, the tragic character of Stockmann in such a world? What is it that he sees and chooses that prevents him from concretely enjoying his presence in the same world with all these others?

Duty, truthfulness, nobility—it does not primarily matter how one denominates what Dr. Stockmann is dedicated to. It is, whatever its name, an idea. That it is abstract, drawn off the world of everyday experience, is true but not extraordinary: intellectual abstraction is a normal process in the human being. But to call it abstract is not yet to characterize it sufficiently for the role it plays in Stockmann's life. The idea is here not only drawn off the world but actually drawn up against the world, in counter-position to it. The light of the idea in its brilliance shows up the shadows in all that lies around. The call of the idea contra-dicts the noise of merely human voices. Thus the idea enters into contradiction with what is there in life and a choice is imposed in disjunctive terms: either—or. Either what is or what ought to be, either temporal existence or eternal order, either people or principles. Specifically, in Stockmann's situation it means: either to effect some change in the life of the town or to "have done my duty," either to involve himself hopefully in the affairs of the crowd or to preserve the independent purity of an outsider, either to "soil himself with filth" of political actions or to stay "free" without touching or being touched. And on the future horizon: either to have his family "provided for" at the cost of "bowing his neck to the yoke" or to "have the right to look my sons in the face when they are grown men," though they be clad in rags, starving, or dead. One course is destructive for character through self-hatred and contempt, the other deprives it of a point d'appui in the world without which man cannot exist. Such is the extreme situation into which the human being can be pressed by ideas.

Is there no exit? There always is when choice is possible, the knot cut through, one course embraced decisively. For one thing, the choice outlined above need not appear as pressing, or one of the paths may only glimmer as a vague contingency. There can be people whose devotion to ideas is equal to Stockmann's but who can spend their life building and dwelling in abstractions, regarding everyday's sensory surroundings as mere show, and never waking up to disappointment as the "scientist" Faust does. And there certainly can be plenty of people who cast themselves toward what is for them ordinary, ascertained reality, without suspicion of its inadequacy to possible ideas, successfully producing and handling certain things with certain other people, even, inmidst, losing themselves without missing any thing. Then there may be individuals for whom there is a conceivable contradiction between the world and the idea, but whose disposition is easily preconceived so that they pass each choice with hardly a jolt. But Thomas Stockmann is not like any of those. His way of holding to his ideas is such that the imposition of an either-or becomes inescapable; but while he reaches his choice, he does not resolve it. He comes to see that for him to stand up for his independence is to stand against all the others in the crowd, and that to witness and protest is to accuse and protest against. Yet much of what he protests against he carries right along within himself: the faults of leadership and organization, the appreciation of material comforts and family affection, the limited outlook on super-personal truth and personal independence. And he is not resolved to give up the community with others entirely, to cease from touching and interfering with their lives, to abandon the conviction that his town world is real and important. In the crucial, culminating phase of his action, at the meeting, the choice befalls him in silence when he is waiting for the opportunity to speak. In his speech he gives evidence of what he has chosen as primary, and to that he remains loyal: to his idea. Because speaking as he does, insulting, provoking, challenging, he reveals himself in such an aspect as cannot possibly be accepted or tolerated by the others. He shakes and undermines his whole world, his home to which he has wanted to belong. But his time goes on; and then? Has he cut his ties irreparably, does he accept a static stand outside and alone? By no means. He wavers already, facing his father-in-law's proposal; this he discards eventually. Then he rejects the possibility of leaving this town and country for the "solitude" of an American wilderness. He decides to strive for a further fight on the same "field of battle" and even to lower himself to an "experiment with curs"; an experiment which to his idea-possessed view cannot but be disappointing, a fight which in this world he cannot help losing. He has not torn himself away, he still longs for more time in the same world he has tried to shatter, he is impaled upon the horns of his choice. This is his misfortune, his inward break, this is what makes him TRAGIC. And this is due to the tragic power of his idea.

What idea should be conceived as tragic? More precisely, what status of an idea in a man's existence makes such existence tragic? Surely, it would be a gross distortion to predict a tragic destiny for all men devoted to ideas, although perhaps it is true that no man of no ideas can be properly tragic. Yet the outcome of these reflections on Dr. Stockmann is this. An idea is tragic, if it is no more than an idea torn off from its foundations in being and presumed to subsist as such. Then in a man's fixed contemplation of it, it shines with a purely reflected light yet of unchanging radiance, it is forever set in terms borrowed but invested imaginatively with splendor unseen in the fleeting flow; and it can effectively contra-dict whatever human time has to offer. The contradiction enters the man's existence and tears him apart, making it impossible for him to find himself whole in the world and yet impossible to be without the world. His protest draws him against and into a battling within, in which there is no enemy but himself and hence no victor ever. This windmill fight is tragic.

Thomas Stockmann is determined to serve duty, if it costs him his life. But he will never attain his duty in his existence, since there is no such fixed star within it; although many deeds, intentions, thoughts are "due" to his world, his partners in living, and to himself. He wages a campaign in the name of truth, as if truth were a goddess or an idol and he the select defender, as if it were above and not within his own being there; and so he despises the "false" altars of truth erected by other men. He complains that men make a "hodge-podge of right and wrong," without realizing that if right and wrong were not for men commingled in their task and pressing through their time, if they were laid out in clear patterns of super-temporal order, then life would be a fatal play of puppets pulled on strings, then risk, commitment, choice, would be out of the human question, then men could not stand out and exist. Such is the limited outline of Stockmann's vision, a vision alluring for him and yielding the temptation of superhuman purity and static perfection, but a vision which dazzlingly envelops his character and appropriates for him the label of the people's enemy. That he becomes the enemy of the people without whom he cannot exist, this is the tragedy of Thomas Stockmann. (pp. 144-71)

> *Zygmunt Adamczewski, "The Tragic Idea—Stockmann, The People's Enemy/'Ibsen: An Enemy of the People'," in his* The Tragic Protest, *Martinus Nijhoff, 1963, pp. 143-71.*

Morris Freedman (essay date 1967)

[*In the following excerpt, Freedman discusses Ibsen's treatment of the relationship between character and morality in* An Enemy of the People.]

Paradox . . . is at the heart of *An Enemy of the People.* To oversimplify, we have a good honest man involved in a good honest project which he destroys because of his very goodness and honesty. It seems to me a serious limitation, however, to read the play only as a tract. Dr. Stockmann is not just a hero standing for justice, self-sacrifice, courage in the face of tyranny. He is certainly this, but he is also a very human, very confused man, who turns heroism into farce, who, more than any villain in the play, destroys his own cause. His character is highly particularized; he is no stock idealist. His motivation, for example, is a complicated mechanism, involving his relation to authority and, specifically, to his older and more important brother, his need for adulation, his extravagant generosity. Consider the embarrassing scene in which the doctor toys like a child with the symbols of the mayor's authority.

Opposed to Dr. Stockmann we have a bad dishonest man, who, we recognize, could bring the good, necessary project into being because of his very badness. Peter Stockmann's sense of political exigency, his Machiavellian instinct for reality, his ability to manipulate people to his ends, his hypocrisy, his shiftiness, his close management of everyday small and large affairs, make him ideal to be, if he wishes, the true friend of the people.

An Enemy of the People goes a step beyond *Ghosts.* Ideas by themselves, however noble and essential, cannot be expected to make their way by their own force. If ideas can destroy, as in *Ghosts,* they can also be destroyed. The whole town may become sick from the organisms in the water supply, lose its attraction as a tourist center, harm itself irrevocably, because Dr. Stockmann's revelations were not presented in terms of the realities of the moment. It requires a conscious misreading of the text, almost as flagrant as the townspeople's willful refusal to see the consequences of the polluted water, to be taken in entirely by Dr. Stockmann. His megalomanic anticipation of praise, his refusal to consider any alternatives to his solution of the problem, the very privacy of his research render suspect the altruism of his motives and even of his findings. (The doctor may well be right in his conclusions, but how can we trust him altogether once we know him? What "controls" were there for his "research"? What other hypotheses might account for the organisms? What other way than his might the pollution be handled?) Any crackpot may come up at some time with a genuine marvel of one sort or another, but it is asking too much of society not to be skeptical. Dr. Stockmann may well be right in his gloomy predictions of doom for the town, but the town may be right also in not promptly acclaiming him its savior.

We are not given any attractive alternative to Dr. Stockmann. If the doctor is a frivolous, sophomoric fool, his brother, the mayor, is a pompous, stuffy one. The several groups of townsfolk are cynically depicted as opportunistic, unstable, shallow. But it is not the mayor who is disappointed in the character of his constituents; it is the doctor who overestimates and idealizes his supporters, attributing enlightenment, courage, and intelligence to them. Perhaps all public servants should be like the brave, dedicated physician, and we are sure that citizens should be everything the doctor originally thinks of them as being. But it is wrong to condemn the citizens for turning out to be no more than what the mayor knew them to be all along, or to condemn the mayor for working within the narrow limits of political sophistication rather than within the broader ones of political naïveté.

We are close to having a misanthropic work on our hands if we must conclude that nobility and courage can be corrupted by innocence, if we conclude that everyone in the town is a villain or a fool. (The episode in which Morten Kiil, Dr. Stockmann's father-in-law, accuses Dr. Stockmann himself of venality is Swiftian in its sudden opening up of the pit of human ugliness.) If we develop any doubts about the doctor's findings and recommendations, we must also have them about the hypocrisy of the mayor. Our affection for the doctor is no reason for accepting without hesitation everything he says; our disaffection from the mayor is no reason for rejecting everything *he* says. We are at an impasse.

Only detachment, coolness, absence of commitment can now help us, and only one man, an outsider, displays these qualities, Captain Horster. The sea captain, of course, comes off no better than the doctor at the hands of the townspeople. But his willingness to judge fairly, to give the doctor a chance to be heard, are in and of themselves moral qualities. The town may indeed be doomed, for at the point where the captain appears to support Dr. Stock-

mann it is beyond being helped effectively by either the doctor or the mayor. Both have been carried beyond the operation of reason to gestures of faith and of mindless affirmation. The two brothers, both self-professed public servants, have worked themselves into passions which can no longer serve anyone, not even themselves; the captain, aloof and dispassionate, not even a rooted member of the community, alone holds for a moment the possibility of redemption for the town.

We are dizzied by the concentric circles of ironies: the doctor may or may not be right, but he cannot be listened to; the mayor may be corrupt, but he may not be altogether wrong in his opposition to his brother; the townspeople (much like the citizens in Shakespeare's Roman plays) scarcely deserve, in any event, all the concern lavished on them. Truth and need, the public good and the private lust, all get stirred together. Nobility becomes the victim of personality. Even if the town never suffers from any microorganisms, it has already been sickened and debilitated by its treatment of the doctor. Morally it is already diseased. In *Ghosts,* the inadequacy of a vessel to the ideas it contains causes individual tragedy; in *An Enemy of the People,* the incapacity of ideas to accommodate to the unyielding demands of person, time, and place causes social disaster. (pp. 9-12)

> *Morris Freedman, "The Morality of Paradox: Ibsen's Social Plays," in his* The Moral Impulse: Modern Drama from Ibsen to the Present, *Southern Illinois University Press, 1967, pp. 3-18.*

Hans Georg Meyer   (essay date 1972)

[*In the following excerpt from his critical study* Henrik Ibsen, *Meyer analyzes Dr. Stockmann's character and his ambiguous relationship to society in* An Enemy of the People.]

Why was Ibsen so drawn to a man like [Dr. Stockmann]? Because no one could be more effective than Stockmann, whose ideas stem from the irrational, for launching an assault on the rationalizations of a society that camouflages vested interests as common weal. Precisely by pursuing his projects wholeheartedly, "with ardent enthusiasm," without regard for property or family, Stockmann brings to the surface the material interests underlying the pretended concern with health and progress. He demonstrates the insincerity of bourgeois society; yet we must not forget that he is used by Ibsen throughout the play to serve himself as an illustration.

Stockmann is a progressivist by nature, so to speak; he has a creative enthusiasm for new realities. He brings this almost sensual delight in productive activity to bear on the task of getting the water pipes relaid. But his productivity fails in its purposes. It stems from bodily states, is rooted in private assumptions, and is given impulsive and heedless expression. Briefly, it is too spontaneous to be linked with society, which, as Marx says, always presents a historically developed relationship between nature and individual. Stockmann's tendency to regard reality as a raw fact that feeds his élan gives him a fresh, nonideological appeal, but his vanguardism is as strong as his awareness of any given situation is weak. His undeniable tinge of provincialism makes him informal and frankly unconventional, but it also gives him a plebeian awkwardness and tactical clumsiness. He is temperamentally incapable of understanding the social reality in which power and property are acquired and defended and conflicts of interest fought out. He recognizes no class structures, harbors no ideological suspicions; therefore, he mistakes opportunism for conviction, and unity of interest for "brotherly community." This man, whose conduct toward himself and others is guileless, is effectively made to recognize the force operative in a society. This happens in the second and third acts.

Stockmann's first and toughest opponent is his brother, mayor and chairman of the town council. The dialectic the play develops derives from the brothers' contrasting temperaments, which inevitably lead them into conflict—proof that Ibsen thinks in terms of characters even when this reduces the conflicts to a private, accidental level. So far as naturalness is concerned, the mayor is the very opposite of the doctor. A sufferer from dyspepsia, he fusses over himself with the untrusting watchfulness so characteristic of those with that ailment. Since he belongs to the established powers, his appetites have long been satisfied. He is therefore bent on stigmatizing his brother's unruly urge for self-realization and thoughtless desire for worldly goods as a threat to established order, while he canonizes vested interests as the common good, and the social hierarchy as "the well-ordered community."

This opposition of temperaments thus points to fundamental issues: the conflict between ideological rigidity and blind action and the interplay between "head" and "heart." These last two terms point to the mayor's reactionary mentality, which is focused on privilege and status, and to Stockmann's willful progressiveness, which improvises its goals and is without rational procedure because he conceives moral decision as a spontaneous outpouring of universal brotherhood. Thus, the two forces that might produce a community capable of mediating between the individual and society are struggling against each other.

Stockmann is the only one of the central characters who lives in a non- or preideological community—the family. Ibsen chose a family setting for the exposition of Stockmann's character, and the fifth act will take him back to the family setting. For a long time Stockmann fails to see the absurdity of his tendency to interpret social situations on the model of family relations, and to see that other characters are thinking and acting in accordance with their social functions or the ideological groups they represent. Nevertheless, Stockmann at first finds allies to support his project, though they do so out of common interests rather than common motives. These are Hovstad and Billing on the one hand, and Aslaksen, owner of the press, on the other.

These men are the spokesmen for two social forces, and they reflect the dispositions and tendencies of the two brothers. Hovstad and Billing, like the doctor, are progressive, "thirsty for action," and hungry for the future;

they are passionately involved in public affairs. Aslaksen is the chairman of the home owners' association and an active member of the temperance society. Like the mayor, he enjoys a "position of some authority" through his various official positions. He is dedicated to the "cause of moderation," not because he is interested in bringing, fresh, vigorous forces into action but simply because he wants to acquire power and manipulate the intellectual and economic means at his disposal to his own advantage.

The parallels, which extend from clothing, diction, and gesture to similarities of temperament, are so striking that it seems obvious which characters will rally around which brother. But Ibsen arouses this expectation only to disappoint it; he intends to make us aware of man as "the sum of all social factors" (to quote Brecht). Hovstad, Billing, and Aslaksen do not act in response to their individual endowment or to libidinously centered initiative. They act with an eye to economic conditions and power politics. The reactionary Aslaksen prints the liberal *People's Messenger;* the progressive newspapermen have to come to terms with him because they cannot print the paper on credit anywhere else. To attract readers, Hovstad, dedicated to "the fight for freedom and justice" and "the education of man through self-government," wants to publish a story implying that human destinies rest with a "supernatural power." Billing, an avowed revolutionary, is secretly trying to get himself appointed secretary of the town council. Aslaksen's heart puts him "on the side of the people," but his head draws him toward the local power bloc. They are all compromisers. Behind the back of the individual, as Marx put it, they all contribute to the survival of the dominant forms of social thought and life.

At first, however, the progressives and the law-abiding citizens support Stockmann's project of installing a new water system. The journalists support him because his discovery will be a trump card in their campaign to expose the infallibility of the established powers as superstition and to emancipate the oppressed. Aslaksen supports him because the home owners, whose livelihood depends on the baths, are bound to set great store by impeccable sanitary standards and because he hopes to remind the authorities—"with the utmost moderation, of course"—of the influence of the "compact majority" of the middle class, which stands behind him.

But the mayor has no trouble in getting them to reverse themselves. He only needs to present the cost of the proposed new installation. The taxpayers would have to raise hundreds of thousands of crowns, and the baths would have to be closed for two years. The property owners are not prepared to support a program that would restrict their profits; the progressive newspapermen cannot risk sponsoring a project that will cost their readers money. It is curious that a matter that calls for a moral stance should from the first be seen exclusively from the economic and political points of view.

The conversion of Stockmann's allies takes place in the third act—in the editorial room of the newspaper. Stockmann comes bursting in, impatient to see the proofs of his article, which vociferously attacked the obstructive authorities and called for action. The mayor has hurriedly taken cover in the next room, leaving behind his cap and staff of office in his hasty retreat. Stockmann, still living in a "happy daze," has no idea that the "dear, faithful friends," who had so misread the economic picture as to think that his plans promoted their interests, have had a change of heart. As he indulges in visions of the tremendous demonstrations of support awaiting him, his eye falls on his brother's cap and official staff. Carried away by a triumphant illusion, he dons the insignia of power, pompously summons his brother into the editorial office, and parades about as "authority" and "master of the town" until the true situation dawns on him and cuts short his hour of official glory.

This scene undoubtedly presents all the formal characteristics traditionally used to define peripeteia. As Aristotelian dramatic doctrine prescribes, Ibsen has timed it for the middle act, having followed just as closely the classical pattern of the rising action through exposition and climax. But the Aristotelian model does not lend itself sufficiently to the social situation of his time. As we shall see in this play, the peripeteia does not, strictly speaking, introduce a catabasis; it does not even lead up to a solution, tragic or comic. And the peripeteia itself is removed from its true function.

Instead of producing a sudden change in the hero's destiny, it forces him into the belated realization that his fate has changed under the impact of economic factors. Since his consciousness lags behind reality, his defiance (with which the audience morally identifies) becomes at least partly comic. It is disturbing that Stockmann's very nonconformity, pathetic as it may be, and the spontaneity that has held out against circumstances, should become ridiculous. Ibsen shows this very ironically. Stockmann's wife, who has hitherto advocated moderation and kept his extravagance in check for the sake of their own material interests, now relinquishes her caution to stand by her husband without any reservation. The audience cannot take one side or the other. The illusory nature of Stockmann's self-understanding has been exposed; so has the falseness of the other side's allegedly moral position. Thus the reversal does not precipitate a resolution of the drama; rather, Ibsen uses the reversal to establish distance from both hero and society. If the play is to proceed in the traditional five-act pattern, it must confine itself to proving the impossibility of deriving drama from this antagonism between hero and society.

In fact, in the last two acts Ibsen shows how the characters become more and more inextricably entangled in the positions they assumed in Act III. (This is why the critics so often dismiss the fifth act as a coda, without looking into the reasons why this should be so.) The polarities are intensified to an almost unbearable degree. As the dramatic action diminishes, didactic elements come to the fore. Ibsen demonstrates the psychology of the outsider and the fanatical majority. Stockmann steps up his diatribes intended to expose the corrupt social order to a pitch of pointless frenzy. Society defends itself through ostracism and boycott against the uncompromising moral challenge that is bound to jeopardize it. Stockmann is able to make his explosive diatribe to the public only because Captain

Horster allows him to use a room in his house. Even before he begins to speak, the meeting is cleverly manipulated by the mayor and his accomplices, who declare themselves "the voice of the majority." Aslaksen is elected moderator of the discussion by acclamation. They pay tribute to one another as guardians of the public welfare, even of the personal welfare of Stockmann. They brand the doctor as a revolutionary and, before the assembly can make up its mind, persuade it that he "has public opinion against him."

Then Stockmann bursts out in a violent indictment of society. Ibsen never wrote a more ruthless denunciation of the lying morality of the bourgeoisie, the anachronism of its dogmatically rigid norms, the enslaved conformity of its adherents than in this diatribe of Stockmann's. At last the problem seems to have been posed in decisive and purely moral terms. But it is not so. This unmasking is so hopelessly mixed up with the urgings of Stockmann's natural spontaneity and stems so obviously from his latent violence that its moral integrity is broken and distorted. His speech is wildly extravagant, full of intellectual wilfulness, overloaded with images, trailing off into banality and then rising again to moving heights.

The climax of the speech is a denunciation of "the compact majority," which he himself once identified with. Its only purpose is to scoff; it has no partner in dialogue and seeks none. Its aim is not consensus or the establishment of moral norms; it is merely preparing the way for the canonization of its own standpoint. Its language has a prophetic ring: "They must be exterminated like vermin—all men who live on lies! You will poison the whole country!" It also does not shrink from blasphemous allusions: "I do not say 'I forgive you, for you know not what you do.'" The assembly, bent on retaliation, pays Stockmann back in his own coin. It brands as a heretic the renegade who has indicted its mode of life, gets rid of him by unanimously declaring him "an enemy of the people." Only a drunk man who keeps making a disturbance in the back of the room, repeatedly thrown out and arguing his way back in, remains immune. He accepts Stockmann's aspersions with morose indignation, but he is the only man to vote against the censure.

With malicious irony, Ibsen has brought it home to us that except for this drunk, who is unsusceptible to the excesses of absolutism, no one shows any spirit of mediation. Society, rigidified in ideologies or concerned with inventing moral window dressing for profit- and power-seeking motives, falls into line against the outsider and reveals its own totalitarian, antihumane nature. Stockmann and his daughter lose their positions; his lease is canceled; his two sons are expelled from school. Demonstrators throw rocks at his house (the setting of Act V), doing serious damage. Totalitarianism betrays itself most clearly in society's effort to wage the battle by means of tactics of moral ostracism against the nonconformist who opposes the opportunism of the majority.

Stockmann has, of course, invited his ostracism, because his character has an antisocial trait, long concealed but called forth again by the heat of battle. He is not at ease with complex organization, which requires giving both sides their due. Anyone he encounters is either his friend or his enemy. So Stockmann's natural social sphere is the family. His acts and thoughts stem from his innate excessiveness and from his uncontrolled vitality. His desire for brotherly solidarity, as well as the impulsive initiative that realizes itself in his projects, prevents him from adjusting to a social role that would make him a part of the complicated structure of society as a whole.

Stockmann's desire to buy a primeval forest or a South Sea island and his wholesale scoffing at all majorities indicate his contempt for the phenomenon of society. The revolution he wants would end in rule by aristocracy. All this makes it doubtful whether his actions, the object of which is seemingly the realization of morality, can be called moral. If, that is, one defines the moral as being able to see one's own actions rationally at a distance, with an awareness of the alternative to one's own preferred direction. This approach is incompatible with Stockmann's absolutism.

Yet since the closed society must, after all, regard the outsider as a troublemaker who questions its sanctimonious image of itself, and since its pseudomoral ideology does not proscribe the promotion of vested interests but only cloaks it, that society perseveres in its attempt to bring Stockmann to heel or even make use of him. Or, it tries, as the mayor does, to find a way to cast suspicion on Stockmann's protest against the politics of vested interests posing as public welfare by implying that the protest itself is dictated by his own material advantage.

With the capital he had promised to leave to Stockmann's wife and children, his father-in-law, Morten Kiil, buys up stock in the baths for practically nothing, hoping in this way to blackmail Stockmann into retracting his story. When the newspapermen and Aslaksen hear of this transaction, they assume that Stockmann has spread the rumor that the medicinal springs are contaminated in order to acquire the stock cheaply through his father-in-law. Hoping to cash in on Stockmann's apparent financial coup, they offer him their newspaper and influence for propagating his views—for a price. But this attempt to bring Stockmann to his senses through self-interest rather than self-knowledge and self-control is bound to fail. Stockmann accepts the ruin of his family. He sends his father-in-law a calling card on which he has written "three large no's." He chases the journalists and the printer out of the house with a stick.

It is no accident that the visiting card should suggest a sleight of hand or that the expulsion of the journalists should recall another expulsion—the one from the Temple. In a brief interval the hosannas hailing the friend of the people have given way to the reviling cry of "Crucify him!" Threatened by pogrom, Stockmann is inclined, in the darkness of his unconscious, to see his fate as martyrdom. (This tendency is already obvious in his diatribe at the public meeting.) He sees Kiil, Hovstad, and Aslaksen as devils incarnate or as "emissaries of the devil." He rejects blackmail and friendly advances as temptations and undertakes to create society anew with "twelve youngsters." And indeed he is not entirely wrong, however much this interpretation may conflict with his self-

understanding. Society's persecution of him, extending even to stoning, is totalitarian inasmuch as it uses the tactics of religious ostracism.

Stockmann, a man with no talent for dialectics or for considered action, a man who never achieves freedom of action, is not cut out to be a tragic hero. On the other hand, he does not belong to a society that might make this comic hero aware of his insufficiencies, thus maneuvering him toward maturity. Ibsen leaves him hanging in the balance between saint and fool. What makes him look so harebrained is indeed his assumption that he is a saint. Since he can be neither destroyed nor bought off, the play is open-ended. He has made another "great discovery," one of those discoveries that give him a chance to develop his strained, unreflective nature to the full: "The strongest man in the world is the man who stands alone." The ending of the play fixes him in the tragicomic ambivalence to which Ibsen has exposed him:

> MRS. STOCKMANN. (*smiling and shaking her head*) Oh, Thomas!
>
> PETRA. (*grasping his hands trustingly*) Father!
>
> (pp. 78-92)

Hans Georg Meyer, in his Henrik Ibsen, *translated by Helen Sebba, Frederick Ungar Publishing Co., 1972, 201 p.*

Ronald Gray (essay date 1977)

[*In the following excerpt from his critical study* Ibsen—A Dissenting View: A Study of the Last Twelve Plays, *Gray presents an analysis of Dr. Stockmann and considers* An Enemy of the People *in relation to Ibsen's personality and his often turbulent relationship with critics and the public.*]

The hostile reception of *Ghosts* was not necessarily a sign of its having hit the mark. For many years, it is true, none of the bigger Scandinavian theatres would touch it. In Germany the police refused to allow public performances. In England, when at last it was performed in 1891, the Press reacted with violent abuse. Ibsen had good cause to feel that his diagnosis was correct, and so had his supporters. Yet the fact was that he had simply had the audacity to imply that a dutiful married woman might drive her husband to drink, that a husband who went to prostitutes might transmit disease to his son (though Ibsen was far from giving accurate information about this), and—more controversially—that the incurably diseased might have to be put to death. The almost fanatical efforts at suppressing the play, or condemning it for even dealing with syphilis, showed that the smothering of truth, which Ibsen had exposed, was all too prevalent. Yet this success was not achieved by the subtle analysis of society, but by simply telling people they were rotten within, and that tells us nothing about the play as a play. Preachers had been telling people as much for centuries, without being abused for it. The reaction of theatre-goers may have come partly from the fact that they had come to expect only entertainment from the theatre, partly from the all-embracing yet not specifically grounded accusations which Ibsen levelled at them, in which case it was a hysterical reaction. So far as dramatic criticism is concerned, Ibsen had again created a play with a good deal of crude characterisation and motivation, although with effective theatrical moments, and again, through the flat contradiction to established values which he represented, sent the pigeons flying. He had succeeded in 'bringing about the condition of the world' once again, by virtue of being so closely involved with its own crudities of response.

Something of his feelings at the time can be gauged from the tenor of his next play, *An Enemy of the People,* which appeared after only one year, in 1882, and bears many marks of an impatient reaction. Though begun before *Ghosts,* it was now splendidly appropriate to the new situation: the *Zeitgeist* was going Ibsen's way again. But by comparison with the plays which were to follow, this was a 'Sturm und Drang' work. No other of the later plays has so much pace, so much violence of speech and action, or so much outright conflict.

It is easy, by over-simplification, to see in the plot a straightforward allegory of the reception of *Ghosts.* It is also clear, though neither of these interpretations exhausts the new play, that *An Enemy of the People* reverses the situation of *Ghosts.* There, the attempt at concealing truth seemed to lead to unmitigated disaster. Now, the attempt at revealing truth leads to disaster, of a kind, but to a triumphant reaffirmation. Like Nora in the previous play but one [*A Doll's House*], the persistent seeker after truth is left at the end alone, but secure in his self-esteem.

For speed of development, the play has no rival in Ibsen's work. In Act One, Dr Stockmann, the medical officer at a Norwegian spa, receives confirmation that the water supplied to visitors at the pump-room is badly infected. In Act Two he enlists the help of the Liberal editor Hovstad, and the proprietor of his newspaper, Aslaksen. In the next Act the full implications of the medical findings for the prosperity of the town are realised by the Mayor, as well as by the 'compact majority', and Stockmann begins to see his prospects of effecting an improvement disappear. The fourth Act, far from supplying the *ritardando* which it often does in a five-act play, shows Stockmann addressing a public meeting, which turns into a riot against him. Finally, not only the Mayor and the businessmen, but the Liberals, including both Hovstad and Aslaksen, and most of the town, in short the 'compact majority', turn against Stockmann. He loses his money and all but one of his supporters, apart from his wife and children, but finishes up determined to continue the fight.

From the brief résumé, it sounds like a play in defence of a real liberty, a denunciation of so-called Liberals who are in fact only concerned with their personal profits. It is not, and in some places it sounds like the reverse of such a play. The ambivalence found in the other plays is found here too.

For two Acts, only the radical reformer in Stockmann is in evidence, though presented with a jollity that might have been meant to demonstrate a point about the supposedly pessimistic author of *Ghosts.* The atmosphere is unusually hearty as Stockmann's wife hands round plates of roast beef, and Stockmann keeps open house in a genial

way, also seldom found in an Ibsen play. This hospitality also serves the purpose of neatly bringing Hovstad and Aslaksen into Stockmann's house as guests, and, since the Mayor, who is of the conservative faction, is Stockmann's elder brother, there is nothing complicated about bringing him in either. A little suspense enters in Act One, as Stockmann drops a hint that the analyst's report on the spa-water is expected and, by the end of the Act, the news of the poisoned source has broken, just before the curtain comes down. In Act Two Ibsen introduces briefly Stockmann's father-in-law, Morten Kiil, who is to play a large part in the catastrophe at the end, then goes on to a demonstration of how the opposition to Stockmann develops.

At first sight, the opposition seems at least a little unlikely. Even though the replacing of the pipes is expected to last two years, a man working solely on business principles would see that if there is a risk of a serious outbreak of typhoid fever—only a few cases having been reported so far—the reputation of the spa might disappear for a generation. It would be worth losing money for two years to avoid the worse consequence. (It is true, however, that Ibsen was basing his play on an actual event of a similar kind, businessmen being as irrational as anyone else.) The Mayor's rooted objection to believing Stockmann's report is, therefore, difficult though not impossible to credit so long as only business seems to be at stake.

Ibsen wins the sceptic over when he lets Stockmann accuse the Mayor of having originally insisted, against opposition, that the spa-water be tapped at a place where it was likely to be infiltrated with foul water from a nearby tannery. That vanity can override business interests is clear enough, and, when this vanity swells by the end of the Act, to the point where the Mayor is ordering Stockmann to keep his information secret, all pretence of adequate measures to be undertaken without too much public clamour is demonstrably hypocritical. The Mayor, for reasons of his own, intends to do nothing at all about the report, and Stockmann has good reason to be preparing to make a stand.

By Act Three, however, Stockmann is doing more than making a stand. When he comes into Hovstad's office with instructions to the editor to print his report for publication in the paper, he announces that he has four or five similar articles in mind, not about the same thing, but 'all connected with the question of the water-supply and the sewers'. It soon appears that he has more than four or five, and that they have nothing directly to do with the sewers. He is, in fact, in a barely controllable rage, as Ibsen is careful to indicate when Stockmann speaks of 'slamming down' his report in front of the public, only to change the phrase, after he has heard somebody echo it, to 'submit it to the scrutiny of every intelligent citizen'. But such assumed humility lasts for only an instant. Stockmann sees himself as the descendant of an old Pomeranian pirate bombarding the people from off-shore with one explosive article after another and, as he soon goes on to say, 'it's no longer just the water-supply and the sewers now. No, the whole community needs cleaning up, disinfecting.'

In the following speech, Stockmann goes further: 'All these dodderers have got to be got rid of! Wherever they are! My eyes have been opened to a lot of things today.' A moment later he is talking of revolution and, though he does not yet develop the point, by the time he leaves Hovstad's office he has said enough to show that he is looking forward to all-out war.

The reasons for this are obscure, though partly due to Stockmann's aggressive personality. Ibsen has been at pains to show, in Act One, that Stockmann has only recently come to the town after a long stay in the North and that he is full of enthusiasm for what he now sees. Though he does say that he looks forward to young people 'stirring things up a bit' in the years to come, there is no indication of what he thinks needs to be stirred up, and what he says to his brother—which may be played as a quick covering-up of the slip about the young people—is that he now feels immensely happy, 'surrounded by all this vigorous, growing life':

> What a glorious age this is to live in! It's as if a whole new world were springing up all around

and

> . . . there's life here . . . and promise . . . and innumerable things to work and strive for.

If Stockmann were a shrewd plotter, the covering-up might be made more convincing. But he is not. On the contrary, he is a man of completely straightforward emotions and ideas. All the more unfortunately for the play, his outburst in Act Three is enough to alienate from him the sympathy that a more realistic liberal might attract, and this is damaging to the balance of the contending forces. Stockmann's overjoyed response to the town in Act One looks euphoric. His total disillusionment in Act Three might be dyspeptic.

He has learned nothing more about the town in the meanwhile. All that has happened is that his brother, largely from injured vanity, has refused to take his report seriously and has threatened him with dismissal. Hovstad and Aslaksen are still on his side. No one else as yet knows anything about the adverse report on the pump-room water, except the analyst. Stockmann has suffered—as yet—only a personal snub and a threat from an elder brother. Yet he launches into an attack that takes in the whole of the town, and goes on to include not only the whole of Norwegian society but the whole civilised world: by Act Five, Stockmann is longing for a piece of primeval forest or a South Sea Island to be alone in. Where, one might wonder, did he gain the experience on which to base his several other papers, or his attacks on the world at large? He has been living in remote parts: his attacks could well be derived from fantasies. The rapid swing from one extreme to the other is . . . equally baseless.

An essential point here concerns the timing. When Stockmann leaves Hovstad's office after his first visit in Act Three, he has only his brother's egotism to resent, and if he were capable of tact he could keep Hovstad and Aslaksen on his side. As things are, his outburst has already begun to incline Aslaksen to turn back to sympathy with the authorities, who have never been far from his thoughts.

It is true that Ibsen now includes a scene in which Hovstad's hypocritical attitude is shown up by Stockmann's daughter, Petra. But this does not show Stockmann to have any better grounds for his outburst. Hovstad temporises because he has to sell his newspaper: Petra cannot see this, and denounces him rather smugly. But Hovstad is clearly shown to be a man of conscience:

> HOVSTAD. You shouldn't say that too boldly, Miss Petra. Least of all now.
>
> PETRA. Why isn't it just as good now?
>
> HOVSTAD. Because your father can't do without my help.
>
> PETRA. (*looking down at him*) So you're one of those too, are you? Puh!
>
> HOVSTAD. No, no, I'm not. It came over me so unexpectedly. You mustn't believe that.
>
> PETRA. I know what to believe. Goodbye!

The degree to which Hovstad is affected for the worse by the necessity to compromise, and the degree to which he still remains able to maintain a freely critical stance, are both shown in that nicely balanced passage.

The point remains that Stockmann's exaggerated outburst has already alienated Aslaksen, and has at least annoyed Hovstad. The issue thus begins to arise, for the play as a play, whether the level of argument is going to be interesting enough to keep the spectator's attention to the end. A dramatic confrontation is in the offing, but any clash is dramatic to some degree, so far as that goes. Will this one be worth more than the kind of notice that one might give to a crank orator at Hyde Park Corner?

The first doubt occurs when Hovstad, as soon as he realises that the Mayor is opposing him, begins to crumble. Aslaksen, Hovstad's proprietor, has not yet decided against publishing Stockmann's report—he may be wavering, but he has not yet come down either way. Hovstad, however, begins to toady to the Mayor as soon as he is asked whether he is expecting to print the report, and this is too servile a capitulation to supply a continuing interest: the opposition to Stockmann is being too obviously put in the wrong. Nothing has happened yet to change Hovstad's situation, and his volte-face is craven. The Mayor then insists to Hovstad and Aslaksen that Stockmann has been impetuous, which they are too ready to believe, although Stockmann's behaviour in the office may have conduced to their believing it.

The two are still wavering when Stockmann returns, full of bonhomie ('Back again!' are his first words), to see how the printing of his report is getting on, and shortly begins to talk in paranoid terms. He is surely meant by Ibsen to be seen as a naïve egotist, when he speaks of a mass movement, with only a half-hearted and momentary attempt at disclaiming any interest in leading it:

> My fellow citizens, you know—good heavens, these good people, they're really so fond of me . . . Yes, and that's just why I'm afraid . . . What I mean is . . . a thing like this comes along, and they—especially the underprivileged

classes—take it as a rousing call to take the affairs of the town into their own hands in future.

The egotism is put in its place, to some extent, when Stockmann, sensing that he has said too much, pretends—it can be played or understood as a pretence—to have meant he wanted no public parade or banquet as his reward. It would take an un-self-centred man to see Hovstad's reaction so quickly, and to deflect the remark into something more harmless. But the correction of the balance is only temporary, and naivety again reasserts itself before long.

Stockmann now announces grander visions: 'Oh, I see the whole liberal middle-class (*borgerstund*) flocking to join a victorious army.' In high spirits, he puts on the Mayor's official hat and pretends to be 'head of the whole town', replying to the Mayor's indignant objection:

> Pooh! when a people rises from its slumber like a lion, do you think anybody's going to be scared by official hats? Because we are having a revolution in town tomorrow, let me tell you.

An actor may go on presenting this as a bit of a lark, if a ponderous one, even when, still wearing the hat, Stockmann dismisses his brother from office and assumes it himself. His self-conscious but strong egotism may be expending itself by such tomfoolery, just as Ibsen expends his own bitter feelings about the reception of **Ghosts** by projecting them into this semi-ridiculous figure. There is a certain raillery about it all, aimed partly at Ibsen's own reactions to the mud slung at him. But the play is now on a knife-edge. Hovstad and Aslaksen have just heard Stockmann speak, in terms they never suspected him of using, of a full-scale people's revolution, the likelihood of which is extremely remote. Though he has not mentioned any specific grievance apart from the sewage, he seems in earnest. The boisterous game with the hat must be a self-deflating joke, and the reference to a 'revolution *tomorrow*' sounds like a deliberate toning down, rather than a serious political prophecy. Yet there is a touch of egomania about it: one suspects something like Skule's 'kingly thought' in **The Pretenders** to be in the background. Why, otherwise, should thoughts of massed ranks and a people rising from its slumber enter his head at all, when it is only a matter of an item on the Council agenda which could prove troublesome, and why should he use such rhetorical language? Hovstad and Aslaksen are not in the wrong, in retreating instinctively from him.

This is interpreting the play in the expectation that it will be an interesting study in the relationships between the compromisers and the complete radical. Ibsen clearly sees the danger of presenting Stockmann without a suggestion that he is at least half in jest, yet the play is constantly running the risk of spilling over into solemn earnest. As it goes on, doubt increases because of the way in which Ibsen seems more intent on carrying a flag for Stockmann himself than with drama. The question of the artist's degree of control over his projected *alter ego* is close under the surface.

Stockmann's outburst in Act Three was based on ignorance, and completely reversed his euphoric vision of the society in the town in Act One, based on equal ignorance. He ended the argument between himself and the Mayor, Hovstad, and Aslaksen with an even more sweeping generalisation: finding that he would get no support from them, he declared that everybody was against him 'because all the men in this town are nothing but a lot of old women—like you [his wife]'. This in its turn completely reversed his expectation, if it really was one, that there could be the very large degree of dissatisfaction that would be needed to provide support for a revolution in the town. In Act Four, however, his last diagnosis seems to be proved correct. There is next to nobody—only his family and Captain Horster, in fact—who will stand by him.

The public meeting, summoned at Captain Horster's house since all public halls are denied to Stockmann, is addressed first by Aslaksen and Hovstad, who rightly point out that Stockmann is not now so much concerned about the Baths as about revolution. Their withdrawal of support is understandable, though in Aslaksen it looks more convenient than principled. Stockmann goes on, not improving the situation, to insult his audience:

> I have said I am going to speak about the tremendous discovery I have made in these last few days . . . the discovery that all the spiritual sources of our life are poisoned, and that our whole civic community is built on a foundation teeming with pestilential lies.

'These last few days' is worth noting. The euphoria of Act One was not play-acting, and it is in fact only since then that Stockmann has changed his mind. But he has in reality discovered so recently nothing more shattering than that three men are unwilling to support him, and certainly he has not learned enough to justify him in what he goes on to say:

> If there's anything I can't stand at any price— it's leading men. I've just about had enough of that kind of people in my time. They are just like a lot of goats in a young plantation—there's mischief everywhere they go. They'll get in the way of any free man at every move he makes. If I had my way I'd like to see them exterminated like any other pest.

This language of exasperation is not a momentary outburst, it is part of a coherent philosophy, partly anti-democratic, as Ibsen's own philosophy generally was, partly aristocratic, partly violent and massively intolerant. Stockmann is not the man to mean seriously his talk of exterminating the opposition, yet this leap from critical objection to total and ruthless contempt makes Stockmann one of Ibsen's more childish egoists—no ordinary distinction—and reduces the political interest considerably.

It is not only the leaders whom he attacks:

> The worst enemy of truth and freedom in our society is the compact majority. Yes, the damned compact, liberal majority.

This soon extends to what, as Hovstad rightly points out, amounts to a declaration that the whole community must be destroyed. 'Who cares if it's destroyed? I say it should simply be razed to the ground. And all the people living by these lies should be wiped out, like vermin', is Stockmann's answer to that, and he goes on to say he would not mind if the population of the whole country were wiped out, if it ever came to be similarly infected. He regards the majority as mongrels and asks how they could be trusted to rule at all.

People inquire if Stockmann is drunk; someone wonders if there is insanity in his family, others oddly suppose he wants a rise in salary. So Ibsen plants the suggestion of a different view of Stockmann than the one taken by the Doctor himself; yet his sympathy with him remained strong, as we know from his own words. The result is chaos and uproar,—the people become a mob, half-mad themselves—while Stockmann seems unaware that he has said anything outrageous and declares he has simply done his duty. His reversion to the calm of a just man resting in the conscience of a good job done is another volte-face after this burst of bad temper.

Ibsen's concern with symbols needs to be kept in mind here. Stockmann's reactions to the sewage report are incredibly far-reaching and cannot arise reasonably from the negative response of the three men who have actually seen it. It is rather because the sewage symbolised corruption in Ibsen's mind—not Stockmann's, since he knew nothing of corruption until a few days before his outburst—that he let the play develop as it does. Ibsen's knowledge of the world, particularly of the way in which *Ghosts,* his own 'report', had been received, entitled him to say things about its corruption which needed greater foundations in the play itself than he troubled to provide, if Stockmann was to appear more than an opinionated ranter. He did in fact share some of Stockmann's views. He told Georg Brandes that he would join a revolution that promoted the abolition of the State (though Stockmann is not so precise about what his revolution will lead to). He opposed the dramatist Bjørnson for saying that the majority was always right and retorted, as Stockmann does, that it is on the contrary the minority which is always right: which minority, he did not say. Ibsen even confessed, in a genial mood, that he and Stockmann got on excellently with one another:

> We agree about so many things, but the Doctor is more muddle-headed than I am, and apart from this he has a considerable number of other traits that make people more willing to hear certain things from him which, if I myself had said them, they would not perhaps have taken quite so well.

What Ibsen privately thought is only relevant to the play if there is any doubt about its interpretation, and even then is not authoritative. Only the play can ultimately answer for itself. Still, it is clear from these remarks that Ibsen did suppose there was some value in Stockmann's vague ideas, and that his audience would not be put off, as the stage audience is, by Stockmann's wild exaggerating, his lack of self-awareness, his paranoid tendencies, and his fondness for exterminating as well as leading vast numbers of people. 'In ten years,' Ibsen wrote in another letter, 'the majority might possibly have reached the point where Dr Stockmann stood at the meeting. But during these ten years the Doctor has not been standing still; he continues

to be at least ten years further on than the majority . . . As far as I personally am concerned, I am always conscious of continually advancing.' From this, it must appear that, despite his muddle-headedness, Stockmann really has Ibsen's admiration, that Ibsen really supposed him to be saying something valuable, ahead of his time, and that occasionally Ibsen could come close to identifying himself with him.

Stockmann is seen in the last Act back at home on the morning after the riot, with all his windows smashed in, and of course indignant at such treatment from the mob, which confirms his opinion of them all, and leads him to say that things would be exactly the same 'out West', that is, in America, where he has never been. He still cannot conceive that there could be any allies in his struggle, and the next events all bear him out in this. Ibsen, who as author directs these events, now shows how Stockmann's daughter is dismissed from her job, how Captain Horster loses the command of his ship, and how the Ratepayers' Association urges all respectable citizens to sign a list declaring they will boycott Stockmann's medical practice. Sympathy for Stockmann among the audience is actively enlisted by these means.

The fundamental innocence of the doctor is then suggested by the device of having the Mayor express the obviously unfounded suspicion that Stockmann has made this fuss about the sewage only because he hoped to ingratiate himself with his eccentric father-in-law by vilifying the leading members of the community, and thereby gaining a personal share in the bequests of the old man's will.

It appears that, though Stockmann knew nothing of it, the father-in-law, Morten Kiil, is a wealthy man. (Stockmann must have known at least that he owned one of the tanneries whose effluent caused the pollution.) Stockmann also denies having known that a large part of Kiil's fortune was to be left to his children, while he and his wife were to have the interest on the capital during Stockmann's lifetime. This strange ignorance on both counts does, it is true, enable Stockmann to play the injured innocent to perfection when the Mayor makes his fantastic suggestion, that the attack on himself and the others could have been 'part of a bargain', by means of which Kiil was induced to make over such large sums to the Stockmann family. Ibsen's exaggerated self-identification with Stockmann seems the more probable here, as he digs into his imagination for means of arousing even stronger sympathy for his *alter ego.*

At this point, in fact, his invention breaks down. A moment later, Kiil himself enters to give yet one more diabolical twist to the lion's tail. He has in his wallet a large number of shares in the Baths, which he has bought up while they are extremely cheap, using for the purpose the money he had intended for the Stockmanns. The Baths thus in effect belong to Stockmann himself (the shares belong to Kiil, while he still lives), and if Stockmann goes on saying that the water is polluted he will ruin himself and his children financially. Will he, Kiil demands, now withdraw his accusations? Stockmann is neatly placed on the horns of a dilemma at a climactic point in the play.

How Kiil has come by the shares so cheaply is a mystery. The whole point of the rejection of Stockmann is that nobody is willing to believe in the pollution for fear of losing money. It now appears as though the shareholders already believe the report and are ridding themselves of their useless holdings as cheaply as possible, without waiting to see what remedy could be applied. Ibsen, for the advantage of his plot, is having it both ways, and shortly turns the new revelation to still more account. Hovstad and Aslaksen have heard the rumour that Kiil and Stockmann are buying up the shares cheaply, and have put two and two together even more preposterously than the Mayor did. They seem to know nothing about Kiil's will, but are convinced, and insinuate the point with the slyness of regular villains, that Stockmann is a party to the purchase because he wanted to get control of the Baths himself. When Stockmann pretends, ironically, to agree, and suggests he intends to make merely a brief, inexpensive show of putting things right, without costing the town a penny, Hovstad is heartily with him, and promises the support of the newspaper, as Aslaksen promises that of the Ratepayers' Association.

This is an eye-opener. In the earlier scenes Hovstad was represented as a genuine Liberal, who gave in perhaps too readily under pressure, but all the same a man really concerned to see the pollution made public. Now he takes the most cynical view of Stockmann's motives, an extremely improbable one to anyone who has seen the naivety of Stockmann in action, and for no better reason than that the newspaper is 'a bit shaky at the moment; it just can't quite make ends meet.' In other words, Hovstad is replying to Stockmann's pointed question, 'What do *you* get out of all this?', that he would be glad of some money from Stockmann in exchange for his help with spreading any better news about the Baths that seems expedient.

The argument has thus developed to a confrontation between an innocent, righteous, truth-loving champion and a despicable, insinuating, bribe-taking hypocrite. The full chord of Victorian melodrama has been struck, and there remains only the determination of the hero to go on undaunted against overwhelming odds. It might almost be a preposterous joke at Stockmann's expense. Perhaps from time to time, in Ibsen's thoughts, it was.

The overwhelming odds come next. Stockmann's sons return early from school—the final blow—because the other boys harassed them and the master has sent them home. Stockmann himself is nearly penniless, having been dismissed from his job, and having refused to accept Kiil's shares in the Baths, but he decides to make independent and decent-minded men at least of his own children. He proposes now to run a school in Horster's house in which he can teach them along with a few others: 'at least a dozen boys to start with.' Who will patronise the school, who will pay fees, is not discussed. He will fetch in 'some of the street-corner lads . . . the real guttersnipes', or rather he blithely tells his son to 'get hold of one or two for me': the authoritarian voice is in that, as the would-be aristocrat is in this: 'Just for once, I'm going to try an experiment on these mongrels. You never know what you might find amongst them.' Stockmann has had a low re-

gard for humanity so far, and 'mongrels' is more or less his name for the town in general, though he has on the whole had a better opinion of youth. The attitude he now takes is not promising, but the words, said with a smile (if Stockmann were capable of saying, by means of that smile, that he was never too serious about the depravity he found), could sound bold and cheerful.

Still, the prospects are dim: no job, no money, and as yet no school and no pupils. These are the circumstances in which Stockmann chooses to make his final dramatic stand, and declare himself 'one of the strongest men in the whole world, *now*':

> MORTEN. (*his son*) Honestly?
>
> DR STOCKMANN. (*dropping his voice*) Sh! You mustn't say anything about it yet. But I've made a great discovery.
>
> MRS STOCKMANN. What, again?
>
> DR STOCKMANN. Yes I have. (*He gathers them about him and says confidentially.*) The thing is, you see, that the strongest man in the world is the man who stands most alone.
>
> MRS STOCKMANN. (*smiles and shakes her head*) Oh, Thomas, Thomas . . . !
>
> PETRA. (*bravely grasping his hands*) Father!

There is a note of irony in these final words—Mrs Stockmann is unconvinced, though condoling—but Petra, the daughter, ends with the right tone of heroic admiration, the 'My Master Builder!' touch. There may be a certain paradoxical truth, too, in what Stockmann says, though not a new one, for it was said by Schiller a hundred years earlier. The trouble is, it clearly does not apply to him. With his amiable ignorance and naive arrogance he may be strong in that he is unassailable, but he is not strong in the sense that he can expect to gain anything. He has made himself an enemy of the people, but the consequences Ibsen hoped for from the play are improbable: no public is likely to reach Stockmann's position within ten years or a hundred. Only a play on a different level, the level at which it seemed for a time, up to Act Three, that this one could become, could achieve that result, and that was a play Ibsen never wrote. As Edmund Gosse, one of his foremost champions, observed as early as 1889, he had taken his revenge (on the critics of *Ghosts*) in an 'interesting novelette in dialogue form.' The allegory was, Gosse concluded, rather transparent, and 'the play is really a piece of rather violent personal polemic'. It cannot be valued on any other grounds. The really surprising thing about it is that Ibsen was capable, as an artist, of reproducing so starily, and on the whole naively, the tantrums which he sometimes displayed as a man. If, on the other hand, Stockmann is taken as representing rather Ibsen's view of Bjørnson, the naivety still remains in the construction of the play, in the way that it turns into melodrama and heroics (or somewhat sour farce, if the play is produced that way) what might have been both tragic and real. (pp. 84-98)

Ronald Gray, in his Ibsen—A Dissenting

View: A Study of the Last Twelve Plays, *Cambridge University Press, 1977, 231 p.*

Thomas F. Van Laan   (essay date 1986)

[*In the following essay, Van Laan provides a reading of* An Enemy of the People *that contrasts with standard interpretations of this work as a "realistic social problem" play.*]

An Enemy of the People has always been one of Ibsen's most popular plays with producers and audiences and would probably be produced even more frequently were it not for its large cast and multiple settings. Arthur Miller was moved to create an adaptation of it in 1950, and Steve McQueen, in one of his last ventures, chose it as an appropriate vehicle when he decided to try his hand at a serious drama without a chase scene. In remarkable contrast, the play has been far less popular with Ibsen critics and commentators. Few individual studies have been devoted to it, and it tends to receive anything approaching full-scope treatment only in editions that accord every included play a uniform introduction or in studies dedicated to thorough coverage of the entire Ibsen canon or to significant portions of it. Many such studies, moreover, pay it little attention, dismissing it with a few hasty general observations in order to hurry on to work that apparently engages the commentators' interest more deeply.

This relative paucity of attention is striking, especially given the vast amount of commentary the other prose dramas of modern middle-class life have prompted in recent years, but the reasons can be readily discerned. According to McFarlane, "*An Enemy of the People* generally ranks as one of the thinnest of Ibsen's maturer works" [James Walter McFarlane, in his introduction to *Ibsen,* VI (1960)]. It also generally ranks as one of his most straightforward plays ever, lacking almost entirely the hallmarks of complexity and ambiguity that help make Ibsen one of the world's foremost dramatists. From its appearance, commentators have been inclined to adhere to a single uncomplicated reading of the play which is perhaps best summed up by Robert Brustein, who called *An Enemy of the People* "the most straight-forwardly polemical work Ibsen ever wrote." "Ibsen has invested this play with the quality of a revolutionary pamphlet; and Stockmann, despite some perfunctory gestures towards giving him a life of his own, is very much like an author's sounding board, echoing Ibsen's private conversations about the filth and disease of modern municipal life, the tyranny of the compact majority, the mediocrity of parliamentary democracy, the cupidity of the Conservatives, and the hypocrisy of the Liberal Press" [*The Theatre of Revolt: An Approach to Modern Drama*]. In this reading, *An Enemy of the People* dramatizes its protagonist's struggles against a mob of "crooks and fools" [Hermann J. Weigand, *The Modern Ibsen: A Reconsideration*] and his ultimate spiritual triumph in the midst of practical and material defeat. Without a doubt, there would seem to be ample warrant for this reading, for Dr. Stockmann's adversaries are mercilessly exposed, he himself is in many respects a very appealing figure, and his views generally coincide, often verbatim, with those Ibsen had been expressing in letters and conversations as early as 1872 and with particular vehemence during the time he wrote the play. In any event, whether warranted or not, this standard view continues to gain adherents; as recently as 1980, Bernard F. Dukore concluded his analysis of the play by coming down four-square as a staunch advocate of the prevailing view: "Clearly, Dr. Stockmann's interpretation of events is Ibsen's" [*Money and Politics in Ibsen, Shaw, and Brecht*].

This is not to say that those who adhere to the standard view have not been aware of certain qualities of the play's protagonist that might seem to call this view into question. From the beginning, they have noticed Dr. Stockmann's rashness, his lack of self-criticism and self-irony, his childish egotism, his naive ignorance of the complexity of human motivation, his inability to see more than one side of a question, the "illiberal note" he strikes "in modern ears" [Michael Meyer, *Ibsen: A Biography*], and his apparent animus against his far more successful brother. For Brian Downs, he is "a figure of fun" [*A Study of Six Plays by Ibsen*]; for Ronald Gray, he often "sounds like an opinionated ranter" [*Ibsen—A Dissenting View*]; and for William Archer, who saw the play as "a straightforward satiric comedy" directed against Stockmann's adversaries, he possesses a "simple-minded, large-hearted, childlike" nature [Introduction to *An Enemy of the People* (1911)]. Awareness of these potentially problematic qualities in the protagonist has not prompted most commentators to modify their adherence to the standard reading; instead, they have developed various strategies for accommodating them. [Arthur] Miller omitted most of them from his adaptation. Dukore dutifully records them in his analysis, but he constantly mitigates their importance, in effect denying that they carry any ultimate weight in our response to the action. Meyer saves Stockmann from responsibility for his disturbing "illiberal" ideas by showing that they were current in the social and political thinking of Ibsen's day. Others, such as Archer and McFarlane, come up with what is probably the most sophisticated strategy by concluding that "these temperamental and very human weaknesses in the main character . . . prevent the drama from degenerating into a theatrical tract"; Ibsen is able to put forth his ideas "and to enlist the sympathies of the audience unambiguously on the side of the lone champion without at the same time making him too offensively virtuous."

Recognition of Dr. Stockmann's "temperamental and very human weaknesses" has increased over the years, and recently it has prompted some commentators to take these weaknesses not as details to be accommodated but as sources of departure for new readings that break sharply with the standard view. Long ago Croce, after pointing out Ibsen's seeming failure to dramatize a clear-cut attitude toward Brand, went on to note that "Ibsen rarely fell into this error again, perhaps only in the character of Doctor Stockmann, the 'enemy of the people,' where, as in Brand, we remain in some doubt as to whether the poet wishes to portray a hero or a fanatic, a profound or an obtuse mind, a character who tends toward the sublime or the grotesque" [in *European Literature in the Nineteenth-Century*]. Croce thus opened up the possibility of an alternative to the standard reading, and this possibility was greatly enhanced in the early 1960's in discussions of the play by Arno K. Lepke and Maurice Valency, both of whom focus almost exclusively on some of Stockmann's major negative qualities. Lepke [in his "Who is Doctor Stockmann," *Scandinavian Studies* (1960)], concludes by surmising that Ibsen originally conceived the play along the lines of the standard view but then, after meditating upon the type of the inflexible social critic and relentlessly probing this tendency in his own nature, came to see the type as a danger rather than a blessing and consequently altered the characterization of his protagonist. For Valency, the negative qualities are the means by which Ibsen "took care to caricature Dr. Stockmann so broadly that this character's notions could not possibly be attributed to the author" [*The Flower and the Castle: An Introduction to Modern Drama*]. Both Lepke and Valency thus try to place Stockmann in Ibsen's intellectual biography, but unfortunately neither of them made an attempt to provide a coherent reading of the play, one in which the protagonist's negative qualities might have a meaningful dramatic function. This task has been left for later commentators, most importantly Richard Hornby and Helge Rønning.

Proceeding from a careful and thorough analysis of Dr. Stockmann's negative qualities, Hornby concludes that the protagonist is "neither good nor bad," but rather "multifaceted, mixing noble and base qualities, and developing out of a complex of formative pressures." Stockmann is more fully developed and more interesting than any of his adversaries, but all in all he is not essentially unlike them. *An Enemy of the People,* in this reading, is not a presentation of a truth, with a protagonist who serves as the dramatist's spokesman, but rather a study of how people—including the protagonist—respond to a truth in the light of their own human limitations and needs and bend it, consciously or otherwise, to their own purposes. Rønning, who approaches the play in a sociological perspective, notes many of Dr. Stockmann's problematic qualities but stresses his political naiveté, his "incomplete understanding of his own position in society and the rules of the game in which he is involved" as well as his failure to see "the connection between economic and moral power." Dr. Stockmann is important to the play, therefore, not as a voice of truth but as a powerful example of Ibsen's insight into the history of his own time. For Rønning [*Contemporary Approaches to Ibsen: Reports from the Third International Ibsen Seminar*], *An Enemy of the People* dramatizes some of the "problems of the development of a fullfledged capitalist society," particularly "the conflict of individuality versus common interests" which this development gave rise to.

These two recent readings of the play, both of which virtually ignore or implicitly deny two key concepts of the standard view—the protagonist's undaunting passion for truth and the melodramatic shape of the action—are not modifications of the standard view but outright rejections of it. They are typical of the current situation with regard to the interpretation of *An Enemy of the People;* although Dr. Stockmann continues to receive whole-hearted endorsement from some commentators, for the first time in the history of Ibsen criticism a substantial number of others views him far more skeptically. The question that natural-

ly arises is: What is the relationship between these two conflicting responses to the protagonist and thus to the meaning of the play? It is not, I would argue, that one is correct and the other wrong; nor would I endorse the suggestion of Hermann J. Weigand, one of the first to suggest the alternative reading, who saw the play as a schizophrenic piece that works one way in the theater—prompting the standard view—and another way once we have freed ourselves from theatrical manipulation and can study the details of characterization and action with greater leisure and detachment; this alternative version of the play never achieves full coherence, according to Weigand, because Ibsen suppressed it: in his eagerness to lash his audience Ibsen forced the psychologist in him to work only "furtively." The real source of the conflict is that the commentators are responding to different dimensions of the play. *An Enemy of the People* constitutes an unusual experiment in form in which one familiar pattern of dramatic action, that of the realistic social problem comedy—the pattern perceived by adherents of the standard view—is overlaid by two additional patterns, one traditional to comedy, the other more characteristic of tragedy.

Setting aside for the moment the problematic qualities of the protagonist which have briefly troubled some adherents of the standard view and prompted other commentators to devise alternative readings, formal analysis of *An Enemy of the People* readily isolates a number of major characteristics.

1. In contrast to almost all the rest of Ibsen's last twelve plays, his major prose dramas of modern middle-class life, *An Enemy of the People* focuses our attention primarily upon a single character, scarcely asking us to feel any concern for the fate of anyone else; other characters are defined in relation to Dr. Stockmann, either as subordinate allies or, more often, as adversaries and foils.

2. These other characters are sketched in rapidly and possess only a few decisive traits that keep recurring to our attention; the recurring traits are often linked to repeated verbal formulas (like Aslaksen's "compact majority" and "moderation"), and as a result the characters sometimes veer toward caricature.

3. The action concerns itself with a problem, or issue, which is carefully articulated and presented, and which represents the sort of social issue Georg Brandes had in mind when in 1872 he urged writers to "put problems under debate" [*Main Currents in Nineteenth-Century Literature*]. The problem in *An Enemy of the People* is twice defined as Right versus Might and involves such related issues as the relationship between the individual and society; the conflict between telling truth pure, whatever the cost, and tailoring it to serve some supposedly higher priority; the right of the individual to free expression of his ideas, especially to their expression without fear of reprisal (some call it tenure); the question of who most deserves to hold power in the community and guide its destiny, etc., etc. The problem in *An Enemy of the People,* moreover, is not only clearly dramatized but also to a considerable extent "solved," in that the protagonist constitutes our primary connection with the action, he is in most respects highly sympathetic, his adversaries possess obvious short-

comings, and his strong denunciations of them explicitly put forth a number of clear-cut assertions about the issues of the play.

4. In the exposure of the adversaries' shortcomings, the play contains a good deal of satire. These adversaries profess ideal motives, but in their behavior they constantly betray their power lust, their greed, their anxieties about social position and financial situation, their personal resentments, and other forms of self-interest; most of them, however, remain able to conceal these betrayals from themselves, at least, through repeating high-sounding slogans and other verbal formulas or abruptly adopting new ones.

5. The satire produces a good deal of comedy, and the play also contains comedy beyond that directly stemming from the satire.

6. The structure is simple and straightforward. The fundamental issue is quickly established, along with noticeable indications of probable difficulty (the mayor warns his brother not to overstep his bounds even before Dr. Stockmann learns definitely that the baths are poisoned and need radically to be rebuilt), and from there on the play unswervingly traces the consequences of Dr. Stockmann's efforts to do what he sees as right. In Act II, the probable difficulty from the mayor manifests itself as unequivocal opposition, but Dr. Stockmann seemingly gains strength through acquiring numerous allies. In Act III, it is the mayor's turn to triumph, as he begins to win over Dr. Stockmann's most important allies, and subsequently Dr. Stockmann's position grows weaker and weaker as he is driven further and further into isolation from his community, until he even considers abandoning it forever. Ultimately, however, he resolves to stay, finding strength in his very isolation.

7. The play contains a good deal of local color, not only in its use of familiar types such as Aslaksen, Morten Kiil, and others, but also in the care with which a setting like the newspaper office is reproduced and in the obvious interest in how things work in a town like Stockmann's.

The characteristics I have listed for *An Enemy of the People* are also the identifying characteristics of the most familiar type of realistic drama known in Europe up to the date of Ibsen's play, the social problem comedy produced by such writers as Dumas *fils* and Augier in France (as early as the 1850's) and in Norway by Bjørnson (*The Newly Weds,* 1865; *The Editor,* 1874; *A Bankruptcy,* 1875; *The New System,* 1879; and *Leonarda,* 1879) and by Ibsen himself (to a considerable extent in *The League of Youth, The Pillars of Society,* and *A Doll's House;* and to a lesser extent in *Ghosts*). Typical of Augier's plays is *Les Effrontés* (1861), which features an unscrupulous newspaper editor who uses the press to further his own ends, including achieving an advantageous marriage; *Les Effrontés* was produced in Christiania, Norway, in 1863—while Ibsen was there—under the title *Den offentlige mening* ("public opinion"), a phrase often recurring in *An Enemy of the People.*

Ibsen's familiarity with this dramatic type, his extensive use of it in preceding plays, and the prominence of its chief characteristics in *An Enemy of the People* would seem amply to justify perceiving this play as one more version of the then fashionable realistic social problem comedy. Ibsen had already, especially with *Ghosts,* moved realistic drama far beyond the limitations of the social problem comedy, but with *An Enemy of the People* he tended to revert to it and in the process created probably the best example of the type that we possess. Certainly, there is little in the drama of Dumas *fils,* Augier, and Bjørnson—rich though much of it is—that can measure up to the high standard of the last two acts of *An Enemy of the People,* in which the sheer abundance of unfailingly brilliant inventions almost makes up for the lack of typical Ibsen density.

The ultimate inadequacy of the preceding formal analysis has already been anticipated, for Stockmann's problematic qualities have no place in it, and yet they unequivocally exist. The first to allude to them was Ibsen himself, who, on completing the play, wrote to his publisher that "Dr. Stockmann and I get along so splendidly with one another; we are so much in agreement on many things; but the Doctor is more muddle-headed than I am, and he has besides several other peculiarities which have the effect that people will tolerate hearing from his mouth various things that they perhaps would not have accepted nearly as well if they had been said by me." Years later Ibsen is said to have told a German friend, after seeing a production of *An Enemy of the People* in Berlin, that Dr. Stockmann "*ist zum Teil ein grotesker Bursche und ein Strudelkopf*" ("is to some extent a grotesque kid and a hothead").

Dr. Stockmann's problematic qualities—his rashness, his naiveté about people, society, and politics, his lack of self-awareness, his egotism, his aristocratic sense of superiority, his eagerness to lock horns with the brother he so obviously resents—necessarily undermine his authority as the spokesman for the values of the play and should prompt us to view him with a certain amount of troubled detachment. Although most commentators have not acknowledged it, the play calls for two distinct and quite different responses to these problematic qualities, one of which is implied by the first of the above quotations from Ibsen. The adherents to the standard view are fond of this passage because it quite obviously indicates that Ibsen to some extent thought of Stockmann as a vehicle for making statements that he could not get away with in his own person. But in describing Dr. Stockmann as being "more muddleheaded than I am," he also paved the way for seeing his protagonist in something of a comic light.

Dr. Stockmann is far from being the "figure of fun" that Downs called him, but he definitely has his comic side. To some extent, this is a positive element in our response to him. The characteristics that initially distinguish him from his brother—his heartiness and conviviality, his love of food and drink, his enjoyment of companionship, his extravagance of speech, his propensity for violence—evoke the carnival atmosphere traditionally associated with the comic *hero*—as opposed to the comic protagonist who is subjected to ridicule. Moreover, Dr. Stockmann is the deliberate source of many of the jokes in the play: for example, his mocking (mild in Act II and ferocious in Act V) of his fellow citizens' tendency to speak in slogans and other formulaic language, and his successful efforts to demonstrate his serenity under fire, including his superb observation that "One should never wear his best trousers when he's out fighting for freedom and truth." During the first three acts, however, the majority of the jokes occur at Dr. Stockmann's expense, prompting us to laugh at him rather than with him.

This process begins mildly enough. In Act I, when Dr. Stockmann is informing his family and friends of his discovery about the baths, Ibsen has him speak as if he is making an announcement to an audience on a public occasion; a few minutes later occurs the first exploitation of his inability to remember the maid's name, and as the act concludes he insists he is only doing his duty, adding—although no one has suggested it—that if the management of the baths wants to grant him a salary increase, he will not accept it. These comic touches prompt us to smile, thereby *potentially* creating detachment from Dr. Stockmann and a feeling of superiority over him, but it is more likely that they serve instead, as McFarlane argues, to endear him to us. Early in Act II, Dr. Stockmann indulges in his own deliberate comedy by parodying the slogans of Hovstad and Aslaksen when he boasts to his wife that he has "the liberal, independent press" on his side and "the compact majority" behind him. But even as he mildly mocks, he is also pleased, and later in the act Ibsen turns Dr. Stockmann's mockery back on himself when, having become enraged by his brother's efforts to silence him, he repeats the slogans without irony, claiming that these supports surely give him as much "might" as the mayor.

This comic twist helps set up the comic effects of Act III, which underscore Dr. Stockmann's egotism, his political naiveté, and his essential ignorance of the immediate circumstances into which he charges forth so rashly. Most of these effects occur in the second half of the act, after the mayor has persuaded Hovstad and Aslaksen to withdraw their support from Stockmann and to side with him. Without knowing this, Dr. Stockmann returns to the newspaper office and, in an elaboration of a theme from Act I, modestly insists that if, as he expects, his fellow citizens start preparations for a parade or banquet in his honor or a collection toward a testimonial gift, Hovstad and Aslaksen must prevent them. Then Dr. Stockmann notices the hat and stick his brother has left in the outer office. In a deliberate challenge to the mayor, he seizes these insignia of office, puts on the hat, takes up the stick, and calls his brother forth. Demanding respect, he declares that now he is the authority in the town and then launches into a hubristic speech about the revolution he is going to achieve with the aid of Hovstad and Aslaksen, adding to the irony with his own adoption of sloganistic language as he refers to himself as an "awakening lion of the people." The episode concludes with Dr. Stockmann's deflation, as he learns that he has lost the support of Hovstad and Aslaksen and must quietly and defeatedly return the mayor his insignia. The act dramatizes the hollowness of Hovstad and Aslaksen and the ease with which the mayor subverts them; it thus helps expose Dr. Stockmann's adversaries. Nonetheless, rather than exploiting this in Dr. Stockmann's favor, Ibsen has chosen to use the occasion to undercut him by having him make a fool of himself. To add

to the effect, this episode evokes one in Adam Oehlenschläger's *Hakon Jarl* (1807), in which an unequivocally comic figure, Hakon's proud and ambitious but ultimately ineffectual thrall, unexpectedly finds himself alone with the crown being prepared for Hakon's enthronement as King of Norway, tries it on, wields a file in lieu of a sceptre, and proclaims himself king—only to tremble and grovel a moment later when Hakon catches him in the act. Ibsen undoubtedly knew this play well, for it is one of the major works of one of the few dramatists Ibsen admitted to having read; and since Oehlenschläger was a mainstay of Scandinavian literature and theater, Ibsen had reason to assume that his audience might respond to this echo.

The comic treatment of Stockmann as a whole recalls another dramatist, Ludwig Holberg, who was Ibsen's favorite and the first Dano-Norwegian dramatist of note. Holberg's better comedies embody the pattern on which Ibsen drew in subjecting Stockmann to comedy and thus giving his realistic social problem comedy an overlay of more traditional comedy. *Erasmus Montanus* (1723), one of Holberg's masterpieces, provides an excellent example. It concerns the protagonist's return to his home community after having been away at the university. Once home, he is beset by a collection of ignorant boors and fools, including the deacon and the bailiff—i.e., representatives of the religious and the secular authorities—all of whom are unwilling to listen to new ideas and show hostility to those bringing them into the community. The protagonist's adversaries try to force him to renounce his new ideas, especially the unequivocally ridiculous one that the world is round rather than flat as everyone knows. The father of his sweetheart even refuses to let him marry her unless he recants, but the protagonist stands his ground because, as he says, he is compelled to speak the truth. Only when his adversaries completely gain the upper hand does the protagonist give in and recant. What makes this play a comedy is that the protagonist is himself a pompous and pretentious fool for whom learning has served only as a means of self-glorification: it has provided him with the Latin that he spouts at his family and fellow citizens and the techniques of disputation with which he tries to gain power over them, and it has made him sufficiently knowledgeable to be able to alter his name from the plebeian Rasmus Berg to the more elegant and noble-sounding Erasmus Montanus. The protagonist is so insufferable, in fact, that when his adversaries force him to recant—even to deny that the world is round—we are tempted to cheer. *Erasmus Montanus* employs the same structure as *An Enemy of the People*—a central figure pitted against a number of adversaries—and it achieves a remarkable balance in which the dramatist ultimately endorses neither but holds both the adversaries *and* the protagonist up to ridicule. In the end the protagonist is made to rid himself of his excesses, the typical fate of a protagonist in Holberg. His adversaries do not change, but this is no sign that they have won Holberg's approval, for their folly is still very much in evidence as the play concludes.

Ibsen's familiarity with the pattern exemplified by *Erasmus Montanus* is well documented by the fact that he had already used it in *Love's Comedy* (1862). Like Montanus and Stockmann, Falk, the protagonist of *Love's Comedy*, insists on his devotion to "truth." Falk is a poet who worships the ideal and seeks absolute freedom to fulfill himself as an autonomous individual. He relentlessly attacks society because its conventions, particularly those concerning love and marriage, crush the spirit and destroy individuality in order to mold each person into a good citizen. He is, moreover, so merciless in his exposure of those who have abandoned their youthful ideals and sold out—e.g., Pastor Straaman with his fat wife and twelve daughters—that his adversaries threaten to expel him from the community. Falk's positive ideals remain vague and undefined, but Ibsen, as his contemporaries angrily realized, clearly endorses his protagonist's criticisms. In the great final act, however, the tables are turned. Here Ibsen gives the adversaries an opportunity to speak out eloquently in defense of their choices, and then Guldstad, the older wealthy merchant who is Falk's rival for the hand of Svanhild, makes a strong case for conventional marriage—so strong, in fact, that both Svanhild and Falk realize that she must choose Guldstad rather than Falk. To some extent, this is a triumph for Falk, for it saves him from the fate of his adversaries and allows him to go off in freedom, following his call toward complete self-fulfillment, heading "upward" toward his goal as poet. At the same time, however, Falk stands exposed as an impractical dreamer unable to function in the real world, and he must acknowledge that, whatever his status, every man "who glimpses the ideal behind his work" is a poet. In this way, *Love's Comedy* achieves a balance typical of Holberg, and, significantly, when his adversaries crowd around Falk, rejoicing that Svanhild's choice vindicates them, he somewhat ironically capitulates with an allusion to *Erasmus Montanus:* "I cry out like Montanus: / The World is flat, Messieurs;—I was deceived; / flat as a flatbread—are you now relieved?"

Certain details of *Erasmus Montanus* suggest that Ibsen may also have been thinking specifically of this play when he wrote *An Enemy of the People.* In addition to the basic situation in which a truth-telling protagonist utterly lacking the ability to compromise is confronted with the necessity of gainsaying truth in order to be accepted by society and enjoy its privileges, I would particularly cite Act IV, scene 2 of Holberg's play. This scene is a public confrontation pitting Montanus against the deacon and the bailiff, who maintain that he should recant because everyone in the community thinks that the world is flat, and "one must obviously sooner believe what so many say than one alone"; Montanus, however, replies that since his fellow citizens lack learning, "they must believe what I and other people say." Montanus then tries to prove, through disputation, that the deacon and the bailiff are animals, but he is threatened with violence and finally prevented from speaking. This scene has unmistakable parallels with Act IV of *An Enemy of the People,* and further parallels between the two plays could easily be identified. Nonetheless, my argument does not depend on proving any direct influence of this or any other Holberg play on *An Enemy of the People.* I cite *Erasmus Montanus* merely as an excellent example of the familiar pattern of traditional comedy that Ibsen, to the extent that he makes Dr. Stockmann a comic figure, has added as an overlay to the basic pattern of realistic social problem comedy.

The other dramatic pattern that Ibsen adds to *An Enemy of the People,* further complicating its tone and structure, is more in keeping with his later hostile dismissal of Dr. Stockmann as "a grotesque kid and a hothead." Despite the parallels between the fourth act of *Erasmus Montanus* and the public meeting in *An Enemy of the People,* during this meeting—in Ibsen's fourth act—the play veers toward the tragic. Some comedy continues in this act, primarily in the treatment of Aslaksen and the behavior of the drunk, but the main business of this act—the frustrating of Dr. Stockmann, his retaliation, and the further retaliation of his adversaries—pushes beyond comedy and even serious social analysis to a new dimension. Central to this are what Meyer calls Dr. Stockmann's "illiberal" ideas, the ideas that Miller found it expedient to leave out of his adaptation. Prevented from reading his article about pollution in the baths, Dr. Stockmann decides to speak on a different topic, his more recent discovery, inspired by the community's treatment of him, that the spiritual sources of society are poisoned. He denounces the authority figures of the town and then the even more dangerous enemies of truth and freedom, the compact majority. Implicitly defining himself as an aristocrat—as Hovstad notices—Stockmann declares that in contrast to the usual opinion it is the minority, the small handful who are in tune with the newest truths, that is always in the right and must be listened to. The others are no better than animals, as Stockmann insists by image after image in his denunciations of his extremely hostile audience, and they differ from the spiritually and intellectually aristocratic as mongrels differ from the purebred. He threatens to take his case about the baths to other communities because, he claims, he is so fond of his birthplace that he would rather destroy it than see it flourish on a lie. Then comes the climax of his denunciations:

> It makes no difference if a community built on lies gets destroyed! It ought to be leveled to the earth, I say! They ought to be exterminated like vermin, all those who live by lies! You'll infect the whole country in the end; you'll bring it to the point where the whole country will deserve to be laid waste. And if it does come that far, then I'll say, from my heart of hearts, *let* the whole country be laid waste; let all of its people be exterminated!

At this point the community brands Dr. Stockmann an "enemy of the people," and it is hard to see that they are wrong.

The "social commentary" of this realistic social problem comedy is, to say the least, far more radical than the sort of thing Dumas *fils,* Augier, and Bjørnson engaged in. Ibsen expressed ideas similar to these extreme ones of Dr. Stockmann's but privately rather than publicly, and it is unlikely, especially after the reception of *Ghosts,* that he could expect his audience—which in the theater necessarily becomes an extension of Dr. Stockmann's audience—to take them in stride. Even before this act, he had made most of the spectators somewhat uncomfortable with Stockmann by giving him such a foul mouth, and here he nears the point of alienating them from his protagonist altogether. The result of these provocations is an action that takes Stockmann from his initial charming but somewhat comically ridiculous naiveté, through a blustering, disproportionate indignation that we are bound to admire (even when it amuses us) because it is so clearly righteous, to his *self*-righteous display of superiority. Dr. Stockmann gains our sympathy, as those more clever than he victimize him and drive him into isolation, but he almost loses it when in retaliation he threatens to destroy the community that has driven him out. By the end of Act IV, Stockmann initiates the self-comparison to Christ that he will develop throughout Act V; it is a significant measure of how far this *quondam* friend of the people has gone in his separation from them and in his elevation of himself over them—indeed, of how far he has distanced himself from his own humanity (not to mention the ideas for which Christ stands). Dr. Stockmann thus begins by entering upon a course of action that he is entitled to pursue and ought to pursue, but then he goes too far, making it impossible for us to continue to endorse him or even to understand him. This, by the way, is what most links him with earlier Ibsen protagonists, most notably Lady Inger, Earl Skule, Brand, Mrs. Alving, and, to some extent, Nora.

Despite these other Ibsen plays, the best example of the tragic pattern that Ibsen adds as an overlay to *An Enemy of the People* is, of course, Shakespeare's *Coriolanus.* There can be no question that Ibsen knew this play. In 1852, when the Norwegian Theater in Bergen sent him on a study-tour to Copenhagen, Hamburg, and Dresden, he came across a new book by Herman Hettner that was then all the rage and was to have a major influence on Ibsen. This book is *Das moderne Drama,* and in it Hettner discusses, and lays down precepts for achieving excellence in, three dramatic genres: historical drama, drama of middle-class life, and *Märchenlustspiel,* or (as Meyer translates the term) "romantic fairy-tale comedy." For my purposes, the important discussion concerns historical drama, which to be a true work of art, Hettner insisted, must be a psychological character-tragedy in which the action and its outcome stem entirely from the character of the hero. To illustrate what he has in mind, Hettner provides a fairly lengthy analysis of *Coriolanus,* calling it an unrivalled model of the type and particularly admiring the third act, which corresponds to the fourth act of *An Enemy of the People,* as perhaps the best act Shakespeare wrote. It is unthinkable that Ibsen, the author of *Cataline* and a young dramatist eager to develop and perfect his craft, would not have obtained a copy of *Coriolanus* at his first opportunity after reading Hettner's account of it. That he did so is attested to by the almost certain fact that, as A. E. Zucker first pointed out, *Coriolanus* is the source for the title of *An Enemy of the People.*

Neither of the dramatic patterns which Ibsen introduces as overlays in *An Enemy of the People* ultimately replaces the basic pattern in pre-eminence. At the risk of oversimplifying the generic complexity of the play, one can say that, in effect, the three patterns operate in sequence. Acts I and II primarily dramatize the basic pattern, that of the realistic social problem comedy. During Act III, the basic pattern remains in force, but the pattern of traditional comedy, strongly anticipated in Act II, comes to dominate, especially toward the end of the act. Act IV contains

the most explicit social commentary, but its nature and the vehemence with which it is delivered and received tip the play almost irrevocably toward tragedy. Act V is more difficult to describe. The emphatic return to the basic pattern is obvious. Dr. Stockmann has all the best jokes, not only those attesting to his serenity under fire but also those with which he mocks his opponents, especially by ridiculing the formulaic language they use when trying to evade responsbility for their acts against him, his family, and his one supporter (note the repetitions of and variations on "I dared not do otherwise" throughout the act). We also rejoice at Dr. Stockmann's summary treatment of his tempters, even when he employs violence. On the other hand, the presentation of Dr. Stockmann in this act is not unmixed. The frightening dimension of Act IV must remain somewhere in our minds, and Stockmann keeps it fresh by his further denunciations of his fellow citizens as animals and by his developing self-comparison to Christ—for example, his decision to educate or "experiment with" twelve "street-louts" or "bums" or "mongrels." Twice—when he starts treating his family and Horster as a lecture audience, and when he announces having made another "great discovery"—he is undercut by remarks that call attention to his comic excesses, although here again the comic touches are of the sort that are likely to make their target endearing. The final moment of the act, in which Dr. Stockmann declares his latest discovery ("the strongest man in the world is the one who stands most alone") is particularly complicated. It embodies Stockmann's genuine triumph even in his current difficult circumstances. On the other hand, as many commentators have pointed out, the moment is ironic, for Dr. Stockmann, surrounded by his family and Horster, is by no means standing alone either onstage or within the world of the play. Moreover, the statement is one more of the many slogans in the play. Stockmann's penchant for picking up—and giving in to—the slogans of others has been carefully explored by Ibsen, particularly as it leads his protagonist into comedy or tragedy, and throughout the play, not least in this fifth act, sloganistic language has borne the brunt of Ibsen's ridicule. The complexity of this final moment is caught by the two last speeches of the play, the only reaction to Dr. Stockmann's new slogan. In the first, Mrs. Stockmann, smiling and shaking her head, says, "Oh, Thomas, Thomas—!" In the second, his daughter Petra, who has always been his most enthusiastic supporter, grasps his hands and approvingly exclaims, "Father!"

As E. D. Hirsch, Jr., has argued, we learn to interpret a literary work by discovering its "intrinsic genre," the "broad type idea" to which, according to its initial particulars, it seems to belong and which provides us a "way of grounding and unifying [our] transient encounter with details." Normally, our reading as a whole is a process whereby we gradually narrow and make more explicit the initial vague and broad type idea, but sometimes, as we encounter new details out of keeping with our discovered intrinsic genre, the "original type idea must be discarded or drastically revised." The standard view of *An Enemy of the People* foregrounds the details of its opening act, while the counter view extractable from the interpretations of Hornby, Rønning, and others foregrounds those that put Stockmann in a questionable light. But both views constitute examples of a failure to respond to details not in keeping with the intrinsic genre upon which the interpreter has fixed. *An Enemy of the People* differs from most realistic social problem comedies in that it is not a monolithic work. It is instead a complex generic experiment in which, at key points and to some extent throughout, the basic genre must share the stage with two other genres, which, although they are of ultimately lesser importance for the play, are not for that reason to be ignored. Any interpretation of *An Enemy of the People* that does not proceed from a recognition of its generic complexity is bound to reduce it to the "thin" and straightforward piece it has generally been taken to be. (pp. 95-111)

> *Thomas F. Van Laan, "Generic Complexity in Ibsen's 'An Enemy of the People'," in* Comparative Drama, *Vol. 20, No. 2, Summer, 1986, pp. 95-114.*

FURTHER READING

Biography

Jaeger, Henrik. *Henrik Ibsen: A Critical Biography.* Translated by William Morton Payne. Rev. ed. 1901. Reprint. New York: Hasken House, 1972, 320 p.

Early biography recounting critical reaction to Ibsen plays.

Koht, Halvdan. *The Life of Ibsen.* Translated by Ruth Lima McMahon and Hanna Astrup Larsen. 2 vols. New York: W. W. Norton & Co., 1931.

Important early biography.

Meyer, Michael. *Ibsen: A Biography.* New York: Doubleday & Co., 1971, 865 p.

Presents information about Ibsen's experience as a theater director and about his later years, periods Meyer believes were neglected in Halvdan Koht's earlier biography.

Criticism

Brustein, Robert. "Henrik Ibsen." In his *The Theatre of Revolt: An Approach to Modern Drama,* pp. 37-83. Boston: Little, Brown & Co., 1964.

Examines *An Enemy of the People* in the context of Ibsen's entire oeuvre and highlights the recurring theme of individual rebellion in Ibsen's plays.

Esslin, Martin. "Ibsen: *An Enemy of the People.*" In his *Reflections: Essays on Modern Theatre,* pp. 29-34. Garden City, N.Y.: Doubleday & Co., 1969.

Considers *An Enemy of the People* to be a strongly political play and praises the work's technical perfection.

Franc, Miriam Alice. *Ibsen in England.* Boston: The Four Seas Co., 1919, 195 p.

Discusses Ibsen's place in English drama.

Hornby, Richard. "The Validity of the Ironic Life: *An Enemy of the People.*" In his *Patterns in Ibsen's Middle Plays,* pp. 147-79. Lewisburg: Bucknell University Press, 1981.

Presents a detailed discussion of characters and settings in *An Enemy of the People,* arguing that the play is a pivotal work in Ibsen's career.

Review of *An Enemy of the People,* by Henrik Ibsen. *The New York Times* XLI, No. 12, 675 (9 April 1892): 5.

Positive assessment of the first American performance.

Tennant, P. F. D. *Ibsen's Dramatic Technique.* New York: Humanities Press, 1965, 135 p.

Examines Ibsen's creative process, biographical influences on his writings, and structural aspects of his works.

Thompson, Alan. Review of *An Enemy of the People,* by Henrik Ibsen. *Theatre Arts* 35, No. 3 (March 1951): 24-7.

Evaluates Arthur Miller's adaptation.

Additional coverage of Ibsen's life and career is contained in the following sources published by Gale Research: *Contemporary Authors,* Vol. 104; *Drama Criticism,* Vol. 2; *Twentieth-Century Literary Criticism,* Vols. 2, 8, 16, 37; and *World Literature Criticism.*

Finnegans Wake

James Joyce

The following entry presents criticism of Joyce's novel *Finnegans Wake,* published in 1939. For discussion of Joyce's complete career see *TCLC,* Volumes 3 and 8; an entry devoted to *A Portrait of the Artist as a Young Man* is included in *TCLC,* Volume 16; an entry devoted to "*Ulysses* and the Process of Textual Reconstruction" is included in *TCLC,* Volume 26; and an entry devoted to *Dubliners* is included in *TCLC,* Volume 35.

INTRODUCTION

Joyce was the most prominent writer of English prose in the first half of the twentieth century. Many critics maintain that his verbal facility equaled that of William Shakespeare or John Milton, and his virtuoso experiments in prose redefined both the limits of language and the form of the modern novel. *Finnegans Wake,* Joyce's last work, is regarded as his most complex and innovative novel.

Joyce was born in a suburb of Dublin to middle-class parents. Due to adverse financial circumstances, the family relocated several times into progressively poorer neighborhoods around Dublin, a situation that afforded Joyce a great familiarity with the city during his childhood and youth. After graduating from University College in Dublin in 1902, Joyce left Ireland and established himself in Paris in order to abandon the milieu that his short story collection *Dubliners* depicts in harsh detail. In 1903 he returned to Ireland when his mother developed a serious illness. Following her death in 1904 Joyce moved permanently to the Continent with his future wife, Nora Barnacle. In France and Italy, Joyce struggled to support himself and his family by working as a language instructor. For a time, they lived in Zurich, Switzerland, where Joyce wrote most of the novel *Ulysses.* In 1920 Joyce and his family moved to Paris, and, following the international renown accorded him upon the publication of *Ulysses,* he gained the financial patronship of Harriet Shaw Weaver, enabling him to devote himself exclusively to writing. Joyce began composing *Finnegans Wake* in 1922 shortly after *Ulysses* appeared. He published sections of the novel under the title "Work in Progress" in a number of avant-garde periodicals, most notably Eugene Jolas's *transition,* and produced five fragments in pamphlet form as well. The novel appeared in its final form in 1939.

Finnegans Wake compresses major aspects of Western culture into what Joyce termed a "nightmare of history" that occurs in a dreaming mind during a single night. To express his subject matter, Joyce developed through numerous drafts and revisions a dense "night language," prose that layers puns, Irish and English dialects, and numerous foreign languages to convey the complex workings of the subconscious. No single narrative line dominates in

the novel. Rather, many tales and episodes, some consisting of only one or two phrases, are related, interrupted, alluded to, or developed slowly throughout the novel. The tales related in the novel center around five characters who appear in many different guises and configurations throughout: Humphrey Chimpden Earwicker (often referred to as HCE), his wife Anna Livia Plurabelle (ALP), twin sons Shem and Shaun, and daughter Issy. A Dubliner who is the keeper of a pub in Chapelizod, Earwicker is the major figure of the work, in whose subconscious many critics believe the episodes in *Finnegans Wake* take place. Earwicker's workday at the pub and his relationships with Anna Livia Plurabelle and their children frame Joyce's retelling of history. Using material drawn from Irish culture and Dublin life, as well as legend, myth, literature, history, and tradition, Joyce constructed a microcosmic view of Western civilization. His principal characters Earwicker and Anna Livia Plurabelle take on mythic stature to symbolize Everyman and Everywoman, and the harmony that exists between such opposing forces as death and life.

Joyce structured his work according to the theories of eighteenth-century Italian historian Giambattista Vico, who argued in his *Principi di una Scienza Nuova d'intorno alla comune natura delle nazioni* (1725) that history is a series of cycles that can be divided into four phases or ages, the last of which is a *recorso,* meaning a return to the first phase. Thus, *Finnegans Wake* is divided into four sections, the final section being a *recorso* whose ending phrase "A way a lone a last a loved a long the" flows smoothly into the first phrase of the novel: "riverrun, past Eve and Adam's, from swerve of shore to bend of bay brings us by a commodius vicus of recirculation back to Howth Castle and Environs." The similarities between the characters and plots of the layered tales in each section reflect the repetition of events in all human history as well as the history of the Earwicker family.

Much critical attention has been devoted to explicating the language and the structure of the novel and to sorting out the bewildering array of characters and stories the work encompasses. Early critics either dismissed the work as utter nonsense or expressed regret that Joyce had written a work that was so rich in content and complex in technique that it was impossible to understand. On reading a draft of the opening of the work, Harriet Shaw Weaver wrote Joyce, "the poor hapless reader loses a very great deal of your intention; flounders, helplessly. . . ." Ezra Pound commented, ". . . up to present I make nothing of it whatever. Nothing so far as I make out, nothing short of divine vision or a new cure for the clap can possibly be worth all the circumambient peripherization." While most later critics believe *Finnegans Wake* is a work of genius with a relatively commonplace theme, they concede that the text is virtually unreadable in the usual sense due to its extensive use of puns, allusions, and portmanteau words. Numerous guides and dictionaries to the characters and language of *Finnegans Wake* have been created in an effort to develop an understanding of its complexities, but serious critical debate still centers on whether the work is more than nonsense. Many commentators maintain that the novel is a successful attempt to create a work of art that is almost limitless in its possibilities for interpretation, and thus accurately mirrors its subject, the history of the human race.

CRITICISM

Stuart Gilbert   (essay date 1929)

[*In the following essay, Gilbert provides an overview of the themes and techniques of* Finnegans Wake.]

"Great poets are obscure for two opposite reasons; now, because they are talking about something too large for anyone to understand and now, again, because they are talking about something too small for anyone to see". With this preamble Chesterton introduces his study of that profoundest of nineteenth-century English poets, Francis Thompson. "In one of his poems", Chesterton continues, "he says that the abyss between the known and the unknown is bridged by 'pontifical death'. There are

about ten historical and theological puns in that one word. That a priest means a pontiff, that a pontiff means a bridge-maker, that death certainly is a bridge, that death may turn out to be a reconciling priest, that at least priest and bridges both attest to the fact that one thing can get separated from another thing—these ideas, and twenty more, are all tacitly concentrated in the word 'pontifical' ". It is not an accident that in casting about for some anticipation in English literature of the uncompromising brilliance of James Joyce's latest work (for, after all, poets are born not made, and—unless another miracle be presumed—the conception of a poet cannot be wholly immaculate), the first name that suggests itself should be that of Francis Thompson, that Crashaw "born again, but born greater". For Thompson, too, wrote of "something too large for anyone to understand", and since infinite greatness is—but for certain flashes when our sight is focussed to a god's-eye view of the universe—intellectually and linguistically out of our reach, not only is the poet's vision, in itself, difficult of apprehension, but the language of common speech must often prove inadequate to express concepts perceived *sub specie æternitatis.*

There are, in fact, two difficulties (or, rather, two aspects of the same difficulty) to disconcert a reader of **Work in Progress.** Perplexed, he poses first the essential question "What is it all about?" adding, *sotto voce,* a plaintive afterthought "Why, anyhow, does the author make it so difficult?"

The subject of **Work in Progress** may easiest be grasped by a reference to Vico's *Scienza nuova,* a treatise on the philosophy of history which appeared about two hundred years ago. The reception of Vico's work was that which too often awaits the philosopher attempting a new synthesis of the disparate phenomena which make up world-history. The story goes that a contemporary *savant,* Capasso, after an unsuccessful attempt to digest Vico's work, ran ostentatiously to his doctor to have his pulse taken, and a certain Neapolitan noble, asked for news of the writer, tersely replied "Off his head!" Vico proposed the making of "an ideal and timeless history in which all the actual histories of all nations should be embodied". Human societies begin, he contended, develop and have their end according to certain fixed laws of rotation; there is a recurrent cycle in human "progress", as in the astronomical domain. (Observe the subtle implications of the title **Work in Progress**). But this natural history of man is not, as might be expected, to be discovered by a mere series of inductions from past events. The essential facts are embodied in the lives, true or legendary, of national heroes; they are revealed through human personalities, rather than by acts or events. In his preface to Vico's works Michelet has succinctly set out this relation between the heroic personality and the so-called "facts" of history.

> The principle of the *New Science* is this: humanity is its own creation. The heroes of myth, Hercules whose arms rend the mountains, Lycurgus or Romulus, law-givers who in a man's lifetime accomplished the long work of centuries—all these are creations of the peoples' thoughts. God alone is great. When man craved for men-like-gods he had his way by combining generations

in an individual, by incarnating in a single hero the ideas of a whole cycle of creation. Thus he fashioned his historical idols, a Romulus or a Numa. Before these shadowy heroes the peoples made obeisance. But the philosopher bids them rise: "That which you adore", he says, "is but yourselves, your own conception". Hitherto mankind believed that all progress was due to chance appearances of individual genius. Political, religious, poetic advance was ascribed to the unexplained talent of certain individuals, splendid but incomprehensible. History was a sterile show, at best a diverting shadow-play.

The aim of the new science was to illustrate the fundamental unity of history, God's work in progress, which is not based (as, at first sight, it would seem) on sporadic advances due to the accidental genius of individuals, but on a general and inevitable movement of mankind as a whole, a trend recurrent and predictable like that of the tides, embodied, crystallized in great personalities. Thus, speaking of the 'sages', Vico remarks that "Solon was neither more nor less than the people of Athens, awakened to consciousness of its rights, the true founder of democracy. Dracon was simply the emblem of an aristocratic tyranny which preceded the change". "The diversity of views as to Homer's birthplace forces us to the conclusion that, when the various races of Greece disputed among themselves the honour of claiming him as one of theirs, it was because *they themselves were Homer*".

Vico places the beginnings of human history one or two centuries after the Deluge. The earth had grown dry and a storm brooded dark above the hills, on whose summits lonely giants roamed. Suddenly sounded a crash of thunder and, "terrified by this happening whose reason they ignored, they raised their eyes and gazed for the first time heavenwards". That was the beginning of what we call civilisation. Their fear of the sky (the heavens personify the first of the gods to all primitive peoples) was the beginning of wisdom. It drove them to refuge in dark caverns of the earth and thus arose the idea of the family and man's first attempt at 'virtue'. Hitherto, these giants, like beasts of the field, had fornicated openly with the female of the moment. Now, after the sky-god had spoken by his thunder, they were ashamed of open coition; each took to his cave a single woman and with her, in darkness, founded a family. Thus, for Vico, the etymology of 'Jupiter' is *jus + pater:* the sky is not merely the allfather but also the source of law and justice, of the family tie and social consciousness. But not only did the voice of the thunder inspire the brutish giants with ideas of shame and justice; the strong emotion of their fear loosened their tongues and they ejaculated the first monosyllable of the language, the name of father, that word which in all tongues has the same root. It is significant that *Work in Progress* opens with a crash of thunder.

James Joyce's new work, in fact, (as far as can be judged from the portion of it which *Transition* has so far published) is, in one of its aspects, a realization of the Italian philosopher's conception of an "ideal history"; those "eternal laws which all nations observe in their beginnings and developments, in their decay and death, laws which, if world upon world were born in infinite eternity, would

still hold good for those new worlds". Under the variety of external forms there is an essential identity between all peoples, all histories, which is embodied in the legends and lives of their national heroes. *Work in Progress* is, indeed, a book of heroes, many of whom are merged in the pan-heroic figure of H. C. E. (Here Comes Everybody). Vico's work, moreover, is much preoccupied with the root-meanings of words (their associative rather than strictly etymological implications) and he "contemplated the formation of a 'mental vocabulary' ", whose object would be to explain all languages that exist by an ideal synthesis of their varied expressions. And now, after two centuries, such a synthesis of history and of language, a task which seemed almost beyond human achievement, is being realised by James Joyce in his latest work.

To a certain extent, therefore, the verbal difficulties of *Work in Progress* are accounted for by the nature of the subject. It is obvious that in this composite picture of the life of mankind, where mythical heroes of the past, characters of biblical legend and notabilities of recent times are treated as one and the same protagonist, the style was bound to reflect the kaleidoscopic permutations of the temporal, physical and spatial attributes of the "hero". But in the verbal structure of Mr Joyce's new work there is a personal element which had already manifested itself in *Ulysses* and was, strangely enough, overlooked even by appreciative critics. Thus, in a recent study of *Ulysses* a commentator quotes at length the following passage from the opening of the *Oxen of the Sun* (Lying-in Hospital) episode and condemns it as "unconditionally inept and unpardonable". "Merely to arrange words in the form of a Chinese puzzle is pointless. It is unfortunate that Mr Joyce has chosen to commit this folly so many times in a work of such significance." The passage is as follows.

> Universally that person's acumen is esteemed very little perceptive concerning whatsoever matters are being held as most profitably by mortals with sapience endowed to be studied who is ignorant of that which the most in doctrine erudite and certainly by reason of that in them high mind's ornament deserving of veneration constantly maintain when by general consent they affirm that other circumstances being equal by no exterior splendour is the prosperity of a nation more efficaciously asserted than by the measure of how far forward may have progressed the tribute of its solicitude for that proliferant continuance which of evils the original if it be absent when fortunately present constitutes the certain sign of omnipollent nature's incorrupted benefaction.

The obscurity of that passage, its prolixity and redundancy—all are deliberate, and artistically logical. For this whole episode of the *Oxen of the Sun* is constructed so as to follow the growth of the embryo from its dark and formless origin to the hour of its emergence into the light of day, a fully developed and perfected child. The style of this section of *Ulysses* is at first dark and shapeless. Gradually the diction takes form and clarifies itself till it culminates in a futurist cacophony of syncopated slang, the jargon of our latest and loudest *jeunesse nickelée*. But, before this outburst, the language ascends in orderly march the gamut of English styles—of Mallory, Mandeville, Bunyan, Addison, Sterne, Landor, Macaulay, Ruskin, Carlyle and others. (It may be noted, however, that, as in the unborn embryo there is often premature development of a certain part, so there are occasional patches in the first section of the *Oxen of the Sun* where the terseness and clarity of later styles are anticipated.)

In the *Sirens* episode, again, the structure of the chapter strictly follows the form of a *fuga per canonem*. Not only this, but the terminology is chosen so as to include musical metaphors and terms. "Fall flat", "sound as a bell", "all for his own gut", "stave it off"—these and many other such idioms were deliberately selected for their musical associations.

The literary device employed by Mr Joyce in these episodes is not, as might appear at first sight, a mere caprice or *tour de force,* but has its justification in the origins of human speech. The earliest language was (as Vico points out) that of signs; the human animal was, in fact, dumb. He indicated the subject of his thought by pointing a finger at the object. The next stage was the naming of objects by ejaculated monosyllables. Then the name of the thing itself was used by extension to signify a wider, even an abstract, concept. From this view of the origin of language it follows that the use of simile and trope was not, as is generally believed, a poetic artifice, but was imposed on primitive man by the very conditions of his development and limits of his vocabulary. If we talk of the mouth of a river, for instance, we do not use the word 'mouth' because it seems a felicitous metaphor but because the makers of the language could conceive of no possible alternative; indeed, unless we have recourse to scientific jargon, no better term has yet been invented. In carefully adapting his words to his subject-matter, Mr Joyce is not performing a mere conjuring-trick with the immense vocabulary he has at his command but is going back to the original and natural methods of human speech. By extension, in such passages as that quoted above, the adaptation of words to subject was carried into the domain of style; but the principle remained the same—the fixing of the reader's mind on the subject-matter by every possible means, the exploitation of every potentiality of the language to create a complete harmony between form and content.

A common error on the part of both professional and amateur critics is that of applying to new literary forms the quasi-ethical test: "Would I wish *all* modern literature to be composed after this model?" That test of the universal (of doubtful value even in the domain of conduct) is quite inapplicable to original works of art. It is, rather, the criterion of a masterpiece of literature that it stands alone, and this holds good as well for diction as for form and content. The unusual word-formation of *Work in Progress,* a constructive metabolism of the primal matter of language, was called for by its subject and is thereby justified, but it will in all probability remain a unique creation—once and only once and by one only. For it is inconceivable that such a method of writing could prevail in general or narrative literature and it would be wrong to see in *Work in Progress* the promise of a systematic disintegration of language, or any sort of propaganda for an international

tongue, a new Volapük or Esperanto. Indeed, disciples of the New Word would defeat their own ends. The word-building of *Work in Progress* is founded on the rock of petrified language, of sounds with solid associations; were this groundwork to be undermined by a general decomposition of words, the edifice would in time be submerged in the shifting sand of incoherence, there would be a dissolution of logical speech and thought and in the last end man would revert to his brutish state, as it was in the beginning before the Lawfather thundered.

A dangerous game, in truth, the *jeu de mots,* this vivisection of the Word made Flesh! But so, perhaps, was creation itself—the rash invention of a progressive Olympian with a penchant for practical jokes.

A consciousness of this "joky" side of creation pervades *Work in Progress.* The world is indeed a Wonderland of perpetual surprises for every Alice of us. In the *reductio ad absurdum* of the processes of human thought—for absurdity is latent there behind the looking-glass of logic—Lewis Carroll, that elfin dialectician, excelled; it is noteworthy that he, too, experimented in the composition of picturesque and amusing neologisms, "portmanteau words" as his Humpty Dumpty called them. But Carroll's inventions were exclusively English and went no further than the telescoping of English words together, whereas the Irish writer's vocabulary is world-wide—*Work in Progress* may well be easier reading for a polyglot foreigner than for an Englishman with but his mother tongue—and he compresses allusions rather than single words. The difference can best be shown by quotation. Here are two familiar lines from Carroll's "Jabberwocky".

> 'Twas brillig, and the slithy toves
> Did gyre and gimble in the wabe.

They are explained as follows.

> "That's enough to begin with", Humpty Dumpty interrupted: "there are plenty of hard words there. '*Brillig*' means four o'clock in the afternoon—the time when you begin *broiling* things for dinner . . . '*Slithy*' means 'lithe and slimy'. You see it's like a portmanteau—there are two meanings packed up into one word . . . '*Toves*' are something like badgers—they're something like lizards—and they're something like corkscrews . . . To '*gyre*' is to go round and round like a gyroscope. To '*gimble*' is to make holes like a gimlet".

Humpty Dumpty might have added that "*brillig*" also suggests the sunshiny hours and "*gimble*" implies "gambol"; but no doubt he guessed that Alice, a clever little girl, could see these allusions for herself.

With these a few lines from *Work in Progress* may now be compared.

> Not all the green gold that the Indus contains would over hinduce them (o. p.) [The critic adds in a footnote " 'our people': indicated by the preceding passage."] to steeplechange back to their ancient flash and crash habits of old Pales time [The critic notes "Pales, the oldest of woodland gods: 'Palestine' is also implied."] ere beam slewed cable or Derzherr, live wire, fired Benjer-

mine Funkling outa th'Empyre, sin right hand
son . . .

The last words of this passage are built on an old music-hall refrain, popular in those 'good old days' when the "Empire" in Leicester Square was the happy-hunting-ground of the pretty ladies of London town: "There's hair, like wire, coming out of the Empire". An electrical under-current traverses the whole of this passage, which alludes to the dawn of pre-history when Vico's thunderclap came to rescue man from his wild estate; the "flash and crash days". "Beam slewed cable" hints at the legend of Cain and Abel, which is frequently referred to in *Work in Progress.* "There's hair" has crystallized into "Derzherr"—*Der Erzherr* (arch-lord) –with a sidethrust at the hairy God of illustrated bibles. He is a "live wire"—a bustling director. "Benjamin" means literally "son-of-the-right-hand"; here the allusion is to Lucifer (the favourite arch-angel till his rebellion) as well as to Benjamin Franklin, inventor of the lightning-conductor. The end of his name is written "—jermine", in tune with the German word *Erzherr,* which precedes, and "Funkling" (a diminutive of the German *Funke*—a spark), which follows. Also we can see in this word a clear, if colloquial, allusion to the angel's panic flight before the fires of God. In the background of the passage a reference to the doom of Prometheus, the fire-bringer, is certainly latent. "Outa"—the Americanism recalls "live wire", as well as such associations as "outer darkness"—Lucifer's exile in the void. "Empyre" suggests *Empyrean,* highest heaven, the sphere of fire (from *"pyr"*, the Latinized form of the Greek root *"pur"*—fire). Finally, "sin" implies at once the German possessive *sein* (his), and the archangel's fall from grace.

This passage illustrates the manner in which a *motif* foliates outwards through the surrounding text, beginning from a single word—here the "flash" in "flash and crash" has "electrified" the words which follow, and a German formation has similarly ramified into the context. All through *Work in Progress* similar foliations may be traced, outspreading, overlapping, enmeshed together; at last deciduous, as new and stronger *motifs* thrust upwards into the light. The difference in texture between such complexity and Carroll's occasional use of "portmanteau words" is evident. A similar contrast can be established between the neologies of *Work in Progress* and the new-coined words of Edward Lear, which, though they have not the same currency as Carroll's, are no less rich in verbal humour. Lear, too, had a gift for depicting droll or fantastic personages.

> His Waistcoat and Trowsers were made of Pork Chops;
> His Buttons were Jujubes and Chocolate Drops;
> His Coat was all Pancakes with Jam for a border,
> And a girdle of Biscuits to keep it in order;
> And he wore over all, as a screen from bad weather,
> A Cloak of green Cabbage-leaves stitched all together.

In this "nonsense rhyme" of Lear, *The New Vestments,* there is a curious anticipation of the idea of comestible dress developed by Mr Joyce in a description of Shaun's apparel (*Transition,* no. 12); his "star-spangled zephyr . . . with his motto through dear life embrothered over it in peas, rice and yeggyolk," and his "gigotturn-ups".

Lear's method of dovetailing words together ("scroob-ious", "slobaciously") may be compared to an English-man's way of carving a leg of mutton; he cuts vertically through the meat of sound and the fat of common sense, with an eye only to the funny effect of the chunk removed; whereas the Irish writer (like Tristan at the *découpage* of the deer and to the wonderment of Mark's knights) carves his *gigot* in the continental manner, that is to say, parallel to the etymological bone, following the way the muscles are naturally and anatomically set. Again, like Gibbon's "solemn sneer", Lear's humour often depends on pairs of words, usually adjectives, unequally yoked together.

> All the bluebottle flies began to buzz at once in a sumptuous and sonorous manner, the melodious and mucilaginous sounds echoing all over the waters and resounding across the tumultuous tops of the transitory Titmice upon the intervening and verdant mountains with a serene and sickly suavity.

A travesty of Gibbon's use of paired words is found in *Ulysses.* "Silent in unanimous exhaustion and approbation the delegates, chafing under the length and solemnity of their vigil and hoping that the joyful occurrence would palliate a licence which the simultaneous absence of abigail and officer rendered the easier broke out at once into a strife of tongues." In *Work in Progress* the treatment of pairs of ideas is *symbolical,* in the exact meaning of that word; ideas are *fused together.* Thus in "gigot turnups" we have the ideas of leg-of-mutton sleeves and their inferior counterpart, pegtop trousers, turned up in the modern manner, fused into one. Both Lear and Joyce exploit the incongruous, basis of all humour, but, while Lear's incongruities are laid side by side in comic pairs, Joyce's are *symbolised,* merged in one—the exact opposite of the Lear-Gibbon hendiadys. This fusion of ideas is illustrated in the description of the tree of life, "our sovereign beings-talk," and the "origin of spices" (*Transition,* no. 15). Lear's *extravaganze* are airy nothings, soaring on dual wings of candid nonsense, whereas Mr Joyce's for all their subtle buoyancy, are gravid with the seeds of red magic.

There is also a radical contrast between the humour of Carroll and Lear and the almost demoniac ribaldry of parts of *Work in Progress.* In the lines quoted above it is significant that the nearly meaningless catch of a London music-hall song should serve Joyce as the warp whereon to weave the story of divine reprisal on a revolting archangel. Of all the aspects of *Work in Progress* this, perhaps, will prove the most disconcerting to the general reader. The boisterous joviality of certain passages, the verbal horseplay, for instance, of that past-master of conceit, Jaunty Jaun, will certainly offend those who hold that gravity should exclude buoyancy in treating of first and last things. But, after all, the terms "heavy" and "light" are relative; birth and death, the story of the Fall, God's mysterious ways to man—all these are tragic or absurd according to the observer's standpoint; exclusive seriousness, indeed, is a colour-blindness of the intellect.

Given the subject of **Work in Progress,** the form and language employed followed as a matter of course. The personality of H. C. E., polymorphous yet strangely self-consistent, heroic yet human all-too-human, dominates the book from its broken beginning, the point arbitrarily chosen (since for time-bound man a beginning there must be) for us to set foot upon the circular track of the New History. The difficulties of the text are conditioned by the subject, for the language is world-wide as the theme. Words are built up out of sounds whose associations range over many frontiers, whose echoes ricochet from the ends of the earth. In this spectral realm of gigantic shadows, of river and mountain seen nearly or dimly as the night-clouds now lift now close in again, lies revealed the ageless panorama of the race, our own world and yet another. To comprehend this new vision of a timeless world something is needed of the clairvoyant audacity of Francis Thompson's last poem:

> O World invisible, we view thee,
> O World intangible, we touch thee,
> O World unknowable, we know thee,
> Inapprehensible, we clutch thee!

(pp. 49-63)

> *Stuart Gilbert, "Prolegomena to 'Work in Progress'," in* Our Exagmination Round His Factification for Incamination of Work in Progress, *by Samuel Beckett and others, 1929. Reprint by A New Directions Book, 1962, pp. 47-75.*

Alex Glendinning   (essay date 1939)

[*In the following excerpt, Glendinning discusses Joyce's use of puns in* Finnegans Wake.]

Mr. James Joyce's new work, **Finnegans Wake,** has had a bad reception in the English Press, judging by the reviews I have seen. It has been attacked as meaningless, drivelling, the work of a madman, 'a colossal leg-pull,' and so on; even his most sympathetic critic has described Mr. Joyce as 'a writer without a theme.' This is the more curious since, during the past sixteen years, most of the work has already appeared in serial form, and has been accompanied by a great deal of comment and explanation. In the circumstances, perhaps no apology is needed for drawing attention to what is already known about this extraordinary book.

Finnegans Wake is based largely on the philosophy of the seventeenth-century Neapolitan, Vico, who elaborated the theory that history repeats itself, that the history of one nation is the history of all nations, that organised society sprang from primitive man's fear of the supernatural, literally from the terror produced by a thunderclap, and that from this terror proceeded the social institutions of church, marriage and burial. Vico was among the first to recognise mythology as a true and important kind of history. He had in mind the project of writing 'a timeless, ideal history' which would be all histories rolled into one, and of creating a universal language which would express the 'common nature of nations' and of human ideas.

In a sense **Finnegans Wake** is a realisation of this project.

Based on the history of Dublin, as Vico's work was based on the history of Rome, it is an attempt to display simultaneously past and present, gods, heroes and men, all the ages and attributes of mankind in a vast, composite mythology. Finnegan was the hero of a ballad, who died and came to life again at his own wake. That he should represent the progress of history, through life, death and renewal, is an indication of Mr. Joyce's approach to his theme. **Finnegans Wake** is an uproarious book, like the celebration which gives it a title.

This is far too simple an account of it, but may serve to correct the impression that Mr. Joyce is a writer without a theme. His prose technique derives naturally enough from what he is attempting. It is an extremely involved and novel technique; but I think that what is traditional in it has caused as much perplexity as what is new. Joyce uses language to impersonate, to perform, to involve the reader almost physically in what is being said. It is essentially a poetic use of language; it is the kind of speech which Vico assigns to his 'heroic' age, when all men were poets; but we need go no farther back than Rabelais to find words used in this compulsive, mimetic way. When Rabelais wishes to convey the exertions of Diogenes with his tub, he gives us a list of a hundred verbs to read, and when we have worked our way through the list we are in a position to appreciate Diogenes' performance, for we have had our share in it. This is the simplest kind of device, but if a modern writer were to make use of it I think he would find himself accused of revolutionary procedures.

As Mr. Eliot has put it: 'language in a healthy state presents the object, is so close to the object that the two are identified,' and he has described Mr. Joyce's language as 'that which is struggling to digest and express new objects, new groups of objects, new feelings, new aspects.' We are not nowadays accustomed to language in a healthy state; we prefer objects at a distance—whether in politics or literature—and this fact has, I think, tended to magnify the very real difficulties of Mr. Joyce's prose.

Already, in **Ulysses,** Mr. Joyce had carried manipulation of language to remarkable lengths. The structure of **Ulysses** is largely to be explained as verbal impersonation. When Sirens are the theme, words and sentences assume musical forms. When the theme is giants, casual phrases are elaborated and distended by circumlocution till they become gigantic. When the protagonists of **Ulysses** are worn out, the language becomes worn out too, and their actions are described in the exhausted clichés of journalism. The method pervades the book in its smallest details: when somebody yawns, we are not merely told so, but are given the yawn itself: 'Iiiiiiiiiaaaaaaach!' And when the Viceregal procession passes through Dublin and we see the 'outriders leaping, leaping in their, in their saddles,' the prose takes a leap too, just to show exactly what happened.

In purpose and technique **Finnegans Wake** is a natural sequel to **Ulysses.** In the earlier book Mr. Joyce's task was to imply the Homeric age in the events of an Edwardian day. The words which describe what Mr. Bloom is doing suggest at the same time the Homeric parallel, in a sort of pantomime. The effect is elaborately ambiguous, but it is nothing to the ambiguity of *Finnegans Wake.* Here the task is not to imply one age in terms of another, but to imply all ages, all cities, all peoples simultaneously in a narrative of Dublin. In order that his words shall carry as many implications and ambiguities as possible, shall have the widest possible range, Mr. Joyce has evolved a complicated technique of punning, and has produced a language unlike anything ever written before. His technique is not entirely without precedent, however, for there is a very good account of its principles in the prose miscellanies of Swift and Sheridan. 'The Art of Punning,' as set out by Sheridan, includes a rule which describes very well the device on which *Finnegans Wake* is constructed:

> The Rule of Transition; which will serve to introduce anything that has the most remote relation to the subject you are upon; *e.g.* If a man puns upon a *stable,* you may pun upon a *corn-field,* a *meadow,* a *horse-park,* a *smith's* or *saddler's* shop; *e.g.* One says, 'his horses are gone to *rack.*' Then you answer, 'I would turn *oat* the rascal that looks after them. *Hay,* sir! don't you think I am right?'

Here is the whole method of *Finnegans Wake*: a device 'which will serve to introduce anything that has the most remote relation to the subject you are upon,' and the whole purpose of the book is to establish relations of this kind.

The first sentence implies the general theme, not only by what it says, but by the fact that it is a completion of the last sentence in the book:

> riverrun, past Eve and Adam's, from swerve of shore to bend of bay, brings us by a commodius vicus of recirculation back to Howth Castle and Environs.

A few lines further down we have the Viconian thunder-clap:

> bababadalgharaghtakamminarronnkonnbronn-tonnerronntuonnthunntrovarrhounawnskawnt-oohoohoordenenthurnuk!

This word has caused reviewers some dismay, and has convinced one or two that Mr. Joyce is out of his mind, but it is a natural enough extension of a common device. When a pistol goes off in a detective novel, we allow the author to write 'Bang!' though a pistol-shot does not really sound like that. Mr. Joyce is availing himself of this liberty, with a more complicated noise to imitate. By the 'Rule of Transition' the thunderclap is associated with the fall of the angels, the fall of man, the fall of a wall and the fall of Humpty Dumpty; it is a theme which constantly recurs. Finnegan, who now appears, is a composite figure with implications of Balbus, and apparently met his end while wall-building. His wake is described a few pages later, and is conducted, we are told, with 'the shoutmost shoviality.' A parody of a line from Phil the Fluter's Ball occurs here. 'With a toot on the flute and a twiddle on the fiddle, O!' appears in an alcoholic context as 'Tee the tootal of the fluid hang the twoddle of the fuddled, O!' and this line recurs throughout the book in different guises. In an appropriate setting it reappears as: 'To the tumble of the toss tot the trouble of the swaddled, O!' and it is typical of the many recurring phrases or motifs which serve to relate one context to another.

Presently we meet the 'hero' of the book, Humphrey Chimpden Earwicker, the Viking founder of Dublin, whose symbols are mountain and city. He is described as 'a big cleanminded giant,' 'a veritable Napoleon the Nth,' and when he takes charge of the prose it assumes the dignity of a state procession. It is a precarious dignity, for Earwicker has a stutter, and is embarrassed by his efforts to explain away some offence which he is alleged to have committed in Phœnix Park, and which is a source of much rumour and gossip. Towards the end of the book he has a section to himself, in which he boasts of his achievements as a husband and founder of cities; but he is seldom absent from the text in some form or other, for Earwicker is all men; he shares with Adam a misdemeanour in a garden (in 'Fiendish Park' as Mr. Joyce puts it, to leave us in no doubt), and by Earwicker we are also to understand Wellington, Duke Humphrey, Noah, Napoleon, Finnegan, Swift—anyone you care to mention, including Dunlop, the inventor of the pneumatic tyre. His name has hundreds of variations, through which the initials H.C.E. persist; he appears variously as Haroun Childeric Eggeberth, Howth Castle and Environs, even as Hosty's and Co., Exports, but his most popular nickname is natural enough: Here Comes Everybody.

The 'heroine' of the book is his wife, Anna Livia Plurabelle, whose symbol is the river. She is at once Dublin's river Liffey and all rivers and all women. Her name and initials pervade the text like Earwicker's, and she brings with her a flowing, streamlike prose rhythm. Anna, too, has a section to herself, and it is one of the clearest and loveliest in the book.

There are also Shaun the postman and Shem the penman, children of Earwicker and Anna. Shem is amusingly identified with Mr. Joyce himself in a long, illuminating passage in which he gives an account of his book and its method. He appreciates the reader's difficulty in locating the word 'as cunningly hidden in its maze of confused drapery as a fieldmouse in a nest of coloured ribbons,' but reminds him that 'patience is the great thing, and above all things else we must avoid anything like being or becoming out of patience.' Among the legendary ramifications of Shem the penman, traces of autobiography appear: 'He even ran away with hunself and became a farsoonerite, saying he would far sooner muddle through the hash of lentils in Europe than meddle with Irrland's split little pea.' 'Irrland' is a typical and unflattering construction, in which the alteration of a letter implies the German for 'crazy.' Among other salient personages is Jaun (don Juan), whose lengthy sermon to an audience of girls, in the middle of the book, is a triumph of innuendo and tough moralising.

Earwicker and Anna, Shaun, Shem and Jaun stand out as entities of a sort, since the narrative method, as Mr. Joyce puts it, causes 'some features palpably nearer your pecker to be swollen up most grossly while the farther back we manage to wiggle the more we need the loan of a lens'; but they are liable at any point to be dispersed into the surrounding text, and to coalesce again in the guise of Napoleon or Finnegan, Tristan or Iseult, any man or any woman.

The method of *Finnegans Wake* precludes sharp edges and outlines, anything which tends to isolate one object from another. Mr. Joyce describes it in his own way:

> Well, almost any photoist worth his chemicots will tip anyone asking him the teaser that if a negative of a horse happens to melt enough while drying, well, what you do get is, well, a positively grotesquely distorted macromass of all sorts of horsehappy values and masses of meltwhile horse.

'Horsehappy values' rather than horse are what we must expect in *Finnegans Wake*; and in this respect the book resembles a musical composition: its 'characters' are themes rather than persons, and are managed like the themes in a symphony, with the same recurrences and ramifications. If ever Pater's well-worn pronouncement about the aspiration of art towards the condition of music had an application it is in *Finnegans Wake,* and the best approach to the book is probably the condition of mind in which one listens to music, as Mr. Robert McAlmon suggested in an essay published some years ago: 'Joyce,' he wrote, 'wishes to believe that anybody reading his work gets a sensation of understanding, which is the understanding which music is allowed without too much explanation.'

The obscurities of *Finnegans Wake* are partly due to its enormous range. No single reader could possibly recognise all the implications which have been worked into it. To grasp even the greater part of them his knowledge would have to include mythology in general, Irish history, papal history, the religious significance of numbers and colours, Dublin street-names, the Book of the Dead, the philosophies of Bruno and Vico, the careers of Swift, Duke Humphrey, Finn MacCoole and Mr. Joyce, the names of most of the rivers and cities of the world, some fifty languages, and a great deal more.

That much of *Finnegans Wake* survives these difficulties is a tribute to Mr. Joyce's incomparable mastery of speech, of the evocative powers of words. In the first section there is a dialogue between two primitive men, Mutt and Jute, whose names relate them, characteristically, to the simple humours of the comic strip. Jute greets Mutt:

> Jute.—Yutah!
> Mutt.—Mukk's pleasurad.
> Jute.—Are you jeff?
> Mutt.—Somehards.
> Jute.—But you are not jeffmute?
> Mutt.—Noho. Only an utterer.
> Jute.—Whoa? Whoat is the mutter with you?
> Mutt.—I became a stun a stummer.
> Jute.—What a hauhauhauhaudibble thing, to be cause! How, Mutt?
> Mutt.—Aput the buttle, surd.
> Jute.—Whose poddle? Wherein?
> Mutt.—The Inns of Dungtarf where Used awe to be he.
> Jute.—You that side your voise are almost inedible to me. Become a bitskin more wiseable, as if I were you.

The dialogue proceeds through a series of explanations and misunderstandings to the final question and answer:

> Mutt.—Ore you astoneaged, jute you?
> Jute.—Oye am thonthorstrok, thing mud.

'Astoneaged' for 'astonished' combines vocal difficulty with a suggestion of the period; 'thonthorstrok' has the same laborious effect while suggesting the thunderclap and the birth of the gods. There are implications in this dialogue which are beyond me, but though bits of foreign words and parodies of modern advertisements are worked into it, its whole texture never fails to suggest the primitive awkwardness of a social encounter in the Stone Age, the struggling, thick speech of two simple-minded giants to whom speech is a difficulty. The elements of the situation are physically present in the language, apart from its remoter implications.

The book is to be judged by the success with which this communication of essential qualities is maintained, and it must be said that in many places the communication breaks down. There is necessarily a point reached in writing of this kind where words have been loaded with all the implications they can carry if they are to keep their communicative vigour, and not degenerate into mere puzzles; and I think that Mr. Joyce, with his passion for ramification, has often allowed himself to be tempted beyond this point. Here and there, too, his cleverness is alarming. Consider this passage:

> All the vitalmines is beginning to sozzle in chewn and the hormonies to clingleclangle, fudgem, kates and eaps and naboc and erics and oinnos on kingclud and xoxxoxo and xooxox xxoxoxxoxxx till I'm fustfed like fungstif . . .

This seems to me a fair example of Mr. Joyce's verbal mimicry. Eating is the subject, and the effect is of somebody talking with his mouth full; the language is involved in a general munching; but when one has it explained that the letters of 'steak' have been rearranged as 'kates,' peas and bacon as 'eaps' and 'naboc,' duckling as 'kingclud,' and so on, to suggest the transformation of food as it is munched, and that the o's and x's represent not only the final anonymous condition, the lost identity of masticated food, but stand for 'cabbage' and 'boiled protestants,' *i.e.,* potatoes, because the x's and o's correspond to the consonants and vowels in those words—when one realises that Mr. Joyce has been at pains to work all this into his text, one feels a little uneasy. It is a moderately good joke here, but it is very nearly a private joke, and it is proof of an ingenuity not far removed from pedantry. The suspicion that many of the obscurities of *Finnegans Wake* may be due to ingenuity of this sort is disturbing.

Such criticisms must qualify one's appreciation of the book, but I think the emphasis should not lie there, but rather on its extraordinary achievements. Mr. Joyce is entitled to the benefit of a good many doubts till we have had time to become familiar with his completed work. Meanwhile, though there is much in it that is difficult, there is also a great deal that can be enjoyed. One has not to consult a reference book to appreciate the simpler humours of its constructions, such as its own account of itself in terms of food: 'once current puns, quashed quotatoes, messes of mottage,' or its reference to psychoanalysis in the phrase 'jung and easily freudened.' Jaun's sermon is no more difficult than anything in Rabelais, and invites the comparison on any level. The fairy-tale imagery and streaming melodies of the Anna Livia section are accessible to anyone who can enjoy Hans Andersen and has an ear for music. Consider Anna in this passage, as she prepares to visit 'her furzeborn sons and dribblederry daughters':

> And after that she wove a garland for her hair. She pleated it. She plaited it. Of meadowgrass and riverflags, the bulrush and waterweed, and of fallen griefs of weeping willow. Then she made her bracelets and her anklets and her armlets and a jetty amulet for necklace of clicking cobbles and pattering pebbles and rumble-down rubble, richmond and rehr, of Irish rhunerhinerstones and shellmarble bangles. That done, a dawk of smut to her airy ey, Annushka Lutetiavitch Pufflovah, and the lellipos cream to her lippeleens and the pick of the paintbox for her pommettes. . . . She wore a ploughboy's nail-studded clogs, a pair of ploughfields in themselves: a sugarloaf hat with a gaudyquiviry peak and a band of gorse for an arnoment and a hundred streamers dancing off it and a guildered pin to pierce it: owlglassy bicycles boggled her eyes: and a fishnetzeveil for the sun not to spoil the wrinklings of her hydeaspects: her nude cuba stockings were salmospotspeckled: she sported a galligo shimmy of hazevaipar tinto that never was fast till it ran in the washing: stout stays, the rivals, lined her length: her bloodorange bockknickers, a two in one garment, showed natural nigger boggers, fancyfastened, free to undo: her black-stripe tan joseph was sequansewn and teddybearlined with wavy rushgreen epaulettes and a leadown here and there of royal swansruff: a brace of gaspers stuck in her hayrope garters . . .

. . . . .

It is too soon to attempt a comprehensive judgment of *Finnegans Wake*; but it is clear that Mr. Joyce has created in it a medium which, in Mr. Eliot's words, is able 'to digest and express new objects, new groups of objects, new feelings, new aspects.' He has succeeded in restoring to language much of the vitality it has lost in this age of potboilers and newspapers; he has brought within its range states of feeling which have hitherto been inaccessible. Some years ago M. Auguste Bailly wrote a critique of *Ulysses,* in which he criticised the device of the 'inner monologue.' He said:

> The necessity of recording the flow of consciousness by means of words and phrases compels the writer to depict it as a continuous horizontal line, like a line of melody. But . . . it is wrong to suppose that we follow only one train of thought at a time; there are several trains of thought, one above another. . . . We attend or own to one series of reflexions or images; but we are all the time aware of other series which are unrolling themselves on obscurer planes of consciousness. Sometimes there are interferences,

irruptions, unforeseen contacts between these series. A stream of thought from a lower level suddenly usurps the bed of the stream which flowed on the highest plane of consciousness. . . . At every instant we are aware of such simultaneity and multiplicity of thought-streams.

Finnegans Wake might have been written in answer to that criticism; simultaneity and multiplicity are just what it achieves, and M. Bailly's account of thought-processes reads like a description of its methods.

One can allow many of the criticisms that have been made of this book: that it is pedantic, showy, unnecessarily obscure, and so on; and one can still say that it has extended the tradition of literature. In England it has been received with mingled rage and sorrow; but it would have had a sympathetic reception in the eighteenth century, if one may judge from the verses addressed to Sheridan by Dr. Delaney in *The Art of Punning.* They might very well be addressed to Mr. Joyce:

> Hail to the sage, who, from his native store,
> Produced a science never known before,
> Science of words, once jargon of the schools,
> The plague of wise men, and the boast of
>   fools . . .
> Till now not half the worth of sounds we knew,
> Their virtual value was reserved for you.
> To trace their various mazes, and set forth
> Their hidden force, and multiply their worth;
> For if t'express one sense our words we choose,
> A double meaning is of double use.

                                                      (pp. 73-82)

Alex Glendinning, "Commentary," in The Nineteenth Century and After, *Vol. CXXVI, No. 749, July, 1939, pp. 73-82.*

John Crowe Ransom   (essay date 1939)

[*An American critic, poet, and editor, Ransom is considered among the most influential literary theorists of the twentieth century. As a member of the Fugitive movement, he promoted the creation of literature that incorporates the best qualities of modern and traditional art. He subsequently became identified with the Agrarian writers, a group dedicated to preserving through literature the Southern way of life and Southern values. However, Ransom is best known as a pioneer in the New Criticism movement, which dominated the American academic scene for nearly three decades beginning in the 1940s. In* The New Criticism *(1941), his most important work, he proposed a close reading of poetic texts and insisted that criticism should be based on a study of the structure of a given poem, not its content. In the following essay, Ransom views the structure and language of* Finnegans Wake *as reactions against science and logic.*]

Critics who have found nothing to say for [*Finnegans Wake*], and critics who have found nothing to say against it, are both uncritical. The first understand only that Joyce disdains the positive achievements of the race, and these they are prepared to defend for the sake of innumerable biological, political, moral, and material advantages; they are pensioners, not critics, of our opulent society. The others are persons of incorruptible innocence, unless they are actually in the green time of youth itself, and they believe that Joyce is really a writer with a positive attitude, and "different" only in being too difficult for ordinary readers to grasp.

A few years ago I read a poem of Mr. Archibald Mac-Leish's which represented Einstein in the act of discovering relativity. It seemed that the act as Einstein himself reported it was intolerably abstract, though its effect might be of universal moment, and that the poet must redeem it by a representation which would put back into it the diffused and somewhat disorderly sensibility which makes any experience realistic. So Einstein was exhibited, as best I remember, walking in a formal garden, taking twelve paces forward and six to the left, waving an arm and placing a hand upon his brow, kicking up some gravel as he stopped and wheeled. The poet was discreet in evoking this sort of image of Einstein's act, for it was merely external or dramatic, and behavioristic; it was harmless, but it was almost without bearing, for Einstein's act was so strictly internal that it could not be gathered by the observer of his behavior. Drama could not handle this experience. But imaginative narrative might have done it; and especially the technique of "stream of consciousness," which would popularize Einstein's mind, and probably libel it, by finding marginal thoughts that formed and swelled in defiance of the calculus and the metaphysics at the center. For instance, the outer gardens, or the basement levels, of the Einstein consciousness might carry on in a bawdy manner regardless of the solemn exercises at the center; and bawdry is a universal human bond. Bawdry is the stock resource of the literary convention when it comes to deflating idealists whose intellectual or moral purity cannot be endured.

To experienced persons it will seem that too much attention to the bawdry will make the record of the mathematical feat incredible. It will outrage our sense of history. Einstein actually arrived at relativity, and we know that the stages, which would be the serial cross-sections of his mind, must have been just as pure and technical as the completed arrival.

A tender regard for that segment of experience, or even that segment of potential experience, which fails to engage in the effective action is not revolutionary but counter-revolutionary; for it is reactionary. It reacts, precisely, against the aesthetic poverty of the effective action; and the latter thing we could not know as an antarctic pole of human experience but for our modern attainments in science, specialized studies, and maximum economy of action. I do not know to what lengths the race will react, keeping company with its artists; nor whether for a total action such as is implied in our "age of science" there must be an equal and opposite reaction. But I believe that *Finnegans Wake* is the most comprehensive individual reaction we have yet seen to all that we have accomplished with our perverted ideal of perfect action.

Operating constantly through this book is the rule which punctually alters the terms of discourse as soon as discourse has started, and brings its effectiveness to an end.

We hear a good deal about the "fluidity" of Joyce's language, but it is fluid on principle, and on a principle consistently opposed to the straight logic of science. In Euclid, or for that matter in non-Euclidean geometry, it is said: Let a be this, and let b be that; the terms remain fixed in their meanings throughout the problem. But a has a homophone somewhere, or at least b has, and puns are possible since there are terms of like sound to these terms, and by these tricks Joyce is equal to providing enough distraction to drown the original operation. Joyce exploits at least two prime devices for obfuscating discourse. One is stream of consciousness, which is prepared to excrete irrelevances in any situation. The other is the verbal device of going from the relevant meaning of the word to the irrelevant meaning, or from the word to the like-sounding words, and then to the words like the like-words; a device that must be open to a literature from the moment when its language possesses a hundred words. Doubtless no other man ever lived with Joyce's sensibility for the poetic values or the joke-values that depend on pure phonetic associations of a given word.

Joyce plays with the history of civilization at any stage, and in terms of any great name or great deed that you please to ask for. I am prepared to think, as I am told to, that Vico furnished him with the cue for what slight structural frame the book possesses. Vico distinguished in the intellectual history of the race the hieroglyphic, the poetic, and the abstract or civilized stages. Modern positive philosophers have distinguished the same stages under the terms: the theological, the metaphysical, the scientific. But positive philosophers bask in perfect satisfaction with the third stage, whereas Vico thought it was merely a last stage, not particularly creditable, and preceding the return of another hieroglyphic stage, and the commencement of a new cycle. With this start Joyce can go anywhere. His book is the most allusive in literature, except for the dictionaries and encyclopedias, and the allusions are rarely used as structural elements, and never kept to their logical and historical identities, except by the loyal scholars who like to explain them for us. Greater love has never been had for the master artist than that of the Joyceans who argue that there is close logic in Joyce's book, and in its parts. Mr. Eliot has had similar attentions from his disciples, but with more reason in the greater degree in which his stiff allusions are really symbolic, and functional for his prophetic discourse. I should judge that Joyce's book is not a unit of design, because the sections do not obey it, but have their own disorderly energies; nor are the sections because they have pages; nor the pages because of the sentences; and as for the sentences, the little fragments of discourse dissipate themselves as readily as the great ones, and apparently for the same reason, in order to obtain a "maximum connotation." The sentences have the words.

Joyce's reaction is not Dada-ism, for that cancels the technical complex of civilization and resorts to meaningless sounds. It is not primitivism, for that undertakes to "return," and has its own powerful drives to embark on. To the literary critic Joyce suggests some extreme exponent of surrealist or "abstractionist" painting. The painting seems to intend to render genuine fragments of finished objects, but assembles them in confusion as if to say that these pieces of life will never add up into a whole. In Joyce's book, as in the paintings, there are some small solid parts. For instance, the little concealed jingles of verse, only half nonsense, sometimes rhymed, existing in profusion, enough of them altogether to furnish an Auden richly. There is ubiquitous sexual interest, and that is a very solid and history-making interest; though sex in Joyce has every possible curious manifestation, and brings up in impotence as readily as in power. And there are large solid blocks of Irish talk and Irish life, the biggest creative achievement in a work that is largely satirical, nonsensical, and negative; for the prose rhythms are beautiful, and the effect whether intended or not is to indicate a folk-culture that is both real and aesthetic.

Joyce is a literary giant, an object of universal attention, and I think a critic is not censorious in remarking with concern the rôle he has assumed on so prodigious a scale. One observes among poets those who should be ready to capitalize quickly on his example. And among critics, some. I should like to see how Richards and Empson might comment on this book. Long ago Mr. Richards laid down a canon of revelance: Anything is relevant to the total meaning which belongs to the psychological situation; it does not have to belong to the logical situation. The canon might as well read: Anything is relevant. For no meaning can be denied to the stream of an aimless consciousness, and none is too remote to be prompted by phonetic association. Mr. Empson has shown how much meaning the ingenious reader can import by these devices, especially the latter device, into poetry that looks transparently logical. He makes use of puns and word-likenesses as if he had seen the strange words written out by the poet, as if he were reading Joyce instead of Shakespeare, Milton, and Marvell.

Yet Joyce's book is on the side of the angels, and I do not like to abuse it. For the poets it is sure to become an inexhaustible source of courage. It shows at most places how to escape from conceptual prose, and into the contingent world; a difficulty that most poets seem unable to surmount.

It is a lesson book for aestheticians. If Joyce's art is almost completely irresponsible, any poem is, and by definition should be, bent on introducing into discourse something of what prose defines as irrelevance. And the fact certainly is that his kind of procedure may be read back in some degree into the most classical poem, and it will indicate that the intention of art is in reaction against the processes of science, and that it wants to set up an object which is different in metaphysical kind from the objects scrutinized by science. The poets do not quite propose to eat their cake and have it too, but they are willing to eat less cake, and to eat it more delicately, and not without a stubborn regard for the local qualities of the occasion. (pp. 424-28)

> *John Crowe Ransom, "The Aesthetic of 'Finnegans Wake',"* in The Kenyon Review, Vol. I, No. 4, Autumn, 1939, pp. 424-28.

Leon Edel   (essay date 1939)

[*An American critic and biographer, Edel is a highly ac-claimed authority on the life and work of Henry James. His five-volume biography* Henry James (1953-73), *considered the definitive account of the American novelist's life, brought Edel critical praise for his research and interpretive skill. John K. Hutchens has summarized Edel's views on the ideal literary biographer as follows: "He is . . . a sensitive critic as well as a scrupulous collector of facts, searches a writer's work not only for its own esthetic sake but for what it says about the writer's inner life, uses the psychoanalyst's techniques but is not confined by them, and by-passes the orthodox biographer's subservience to chronology in favor of grouping for dramatic emphasis outside a fixed-time schedule." Edel himself has noted, "My aim in biography is to achieve tightness of synthesis and a clear narrative 'line'. In criticism I like directness and lucidity." In the following excerpt, he evaluates Joyce's achievement with the language and scope of* Finnegans Wake, *particularly commenting on the aural quality of the novel.*]

It seemed a little sad to many who read James Joyce's **Work in Progress** when it was appearing in *transition* that this great Irish genius should spend years fashioning an apparently exaggerated, if energetic, *jeu d'esprit.* They asked themselves why he refused to turn his pen to the world about him and concerned himself exclusively with the past. Democracies tumbled; ideals were shattered; new generations sought to efface history. But James Joyce remained securely locked in the Dublin of the turn of the century.

The answer is important. We are dealing, in Joyce, not with a reporter of immediate things, but with a devoted craftsman whose interest is the versatility and the universality of his *métier*. While Europe was in flames, he was able to set down, in Trieste, Zurich, and finally Paris, his **Ulysses,** which dealt with man in a pre-war world. In the aftermath of the War—it has taken him seventeen years—he has set down **Finnegans Wake** which deals with the whole range of the human consciousness. For Joyce, the writer whose Jesuit strain serves his own ends exclusively, deals not only with the immediate world, which he has observed intensely, but with that world in relation to all time. The heroics of one age are to him but a repetition of the heroics of another. The dictators of today are but the Caesars of yesterday. "Birth and death are sufficiently violent for me," he once told Padraic Colum.

Of course he might have gone on writing other novels like **A Portrait of the Artist as a Young Man.** He might have done fifty or a hundred novels (like Mr Wells or Mr Bennett) or an endless series of plays (like Mr Shaw) in which there is constant reiteration of idea and constant revelation of the same personality. But Joyce does not seem to want to leave many pictures of his time. The process of turning out novel after novel does not excite him. He is a virtuoso who wishes to enlarge the writer's method and technique. He is a scientist in letters who likes nothing better than to rig out a new experiment. For him one book is but a sketch from which a larger canvas will grow, and each canvas is more ambitious than the last. In every sense Joyce is like a composer who essays many forms. He must write chamber music, overtures, piano compositions, and songs, but he must try his hand also at the symphony.

James Joyce has so far written only one book in each form, and after more than thirty years he has published only seven books, two of them slender volumes of poetry.

He started with verse, little songs such as come to the lips of a creative writer, much like the *villanelle* that is fashioned in the *Portrait.* From the song Joyce progressed to the prose-picture, the short story; and **Dubliners** gives us these "slices of life," stories of haunted and lonely people, of children first awakening to life, of patriots who weep for Parnell, of the delicate quivering threads that bind a husband to his wife and a wife to her husband.

The next step was the drama-picture, and Joyce wrote **Exiles,** a play, dealing again with the relations between husband and wife, a tightly-written play, filled with rhythmic speech and acutely probed psychological situations. It is conventional drama touched by the hand of a great poet.

And the next step? A fusion of the prose-picture and the drama-picture—the novel. **A Portrait of the Artist as a Young Man** marked Joyce's first real experiment, an attempt to dramatize the thoughts and impressions that flow through the mind mingling with the images and sounds that impinge upon one's consciousness through ear and eye. Writers had told their readers of thoughts going on in the minds of their characters. But now the writer stood back and allowed the reader to look directly into the mind and observe thought, image, sound, as if he were looking at a film projected on a screen.

Joyce did not stop there. Beyond the novel lay the epic, fusing all the forms he had previously essayed—poetry, the prose-picture, the drama-picture, the narrative—and in *Ulysses* he sang a mighty theme, the story of a day in Dublin, June 16, 1904, mighty because, as Mr S. Foster Damon points out, it is also a day lifted from all time, a day in the history of the world. Here for more than eight hundred pages he ranges through the complex detail of a day, from morning to night, resorting to elaborate literary devices to tell his story so that the reader may at all times move with the characters, hear with their ears, see with their eyes, and consistently be inside their minds, thinking with them. In *Ulysses* Joyce attempts the most complete literary picture we have yet had of the stream of consciousness.

In the striking image of William James, all effort to explore the stream of consciousness is like turning up the lights to see what the darkness looks like. Consciousness is mobile, evanescent, combining word, sound, image, following many simultaneous tracks. To put this on paper is to attempt to put into words the meaning of a piece of music. Where we touch this realm, words, magnificent, imperfect instruments that they are, become virtually useless.

For who is to nail down on paper a moving, ever-elusive thought-stream, and how is it to be done? Henry James (did they not say he wrote fiction like a psychologist?) looked into the consciousness and selected from it, and put on paper in logical, reasoned form the thoughts of highly civilized beings. Proust too, in his long sweeping sentences gave an impression of broad deep channels of thought. But it was left to Joyce to give us a moving picture of thought—its jumbled incoherence, its automatic combination of image with half-formed and deformed words, and above all its fluidity. He has not always succeeded, but in *Ulysses* he came closer to it than any other writer: in effect he was able to dramatize the mind.

Ulysses was the story of a day in Dublin, a day in the lives of Leopold Bloom and Stephen Dedalus, a day, as we have noted, in the history of the world, and a day in that bottomless eternity that Joyce's priest so vividly describes in the **Portrait.** *Finnegans Wake* is again an advance: it is the epic of a night plucked from that selfsame eternity, and yet because it is a night, merging with all the nights that have gone before in our individual and collective consciousness, it carries, floating in its mighty stream fragments of the epics that have gone before, the flotsam and jetsam of the ages. In it past and present come together in one dimension. Sleep and nightmare, unconsciousness and half-consciousness; history and literature; the stories of wars and deeds accomplished; fables; football field and theatre and tavern; the great and the near-great—the backwash of Time sweeps into the present, and sweeping out again carries the present with it. And words, words that came with the infancy of the race and grew with time, words are here in all their confusion, words as they have been heard mingling with words they resemble, words deformed and altered and mixed with words from other languages, often inter-marrying with them, in order to reproduce not only this vast panorama, but all the sounds and smells and sensations associated with it, to render phantasmagoria articulate while keeping it phantasmagorial.

My first glimpse of James Joyce was at the Paris opera ten years ago. Sullivan, the Franco-Irish tenor, was singing *Les Huguenots* that night. From my *loge* I saw Joyce, upright, graying hair combed back, immaculately dressed, assisted to his seat, peering through two pair of thick glasses, one superimposed on the other. There was no mistaking our contemporary Homer, the author of a modern Odyssey.

He was not blind, but he was going through a bad phase then in the struggle to overcome failing sight. I doubt whether he could see the "traffic" of the stage distinctly that night, but he must have heard more than comes to the ordinary ear. From time to time his fine voice—he wanted once to be an opera singer—would rise above others with a shout of "Bravo!" when Sullivan would finish some grand aria, and his applause continued after others ceased applauding.

During an intermission I saw him again, leaning on his stick (was it Stephen Dedalus' ashplant?) cocking his head to catch voices all about him and looking into blurred space. He gave me the feeling then that all life flowed into him through his ears, that it has always come to him in this way. Voices, bells, the sound of hammering, distant movement of traffic, music, the patter of rain, the whole world of sound that moves about and in our visible world must be recorded in his mind, much as most people record what they see. And part of these sound patterns are words, their relation to each other, their place in the sentence and in the rise and fall of the human voice. He has learned to render sound with the distinctness a pianist gives to his every note:

> The fellows were practising long shies and bowling lobs and slow twisters. In the soft grey silence he could hear the bump of the balls; and from here and from there through the quiet air the sound of the cricket bats: pick, pack, pock, puck: like drops of water in a fountain falling softly in the brimming bowl.

Finnegans Wake is rich in such direct rendering of sound from the "bababadalgharaghtakamminarronnkonnbronntonnerronntuonnthunntrovarrhounawnskawntoohoohoordenenthurnuk!" of thunder to the "Flip! Flep!" of wet clothes on wet stones:

> Will we spread them here now? Ay, we will. Flip! Spread on your bank and I'll spread on mine. Flep! It's what I'm doing. Spread!

Beyond and above this direct imprisonment of sound in the English alphabet is his rendition of emotion and sensation through the sound and pace and rhythm of the language used. From the infinitely varied associations of the ideas he has chosen to verbalize, Joyce has taken those whose *sounds* best suit his purpose. This play with the sound of words has naturally resulted in an enormous number of intricate puns. It has also created a work as near to music as prose can come.

Finnegans Wake must be read with the ear. It may not be a coincidence that Humphrey Chimpden Earwicker, the hero—if such a book can be said to have a hero—has been given that name and that Joyce substitutes forms of "earwig" for it. The earwig, we find in the *Oxford Dictionary,* is "an insect which is supposed to creep into the ear." But it is the Old English form of the word that is interesting— *éarwicga* (note the resemblance to Earwicker), which meant, literally, an "ear-punner." When we realize how important the pun is in this work we can believe that there is a definite reason for the choice of the name.

This extravagant bit of play can be pursued still further. Earwicker, the *ear* of whose name recalls Eire, figures in the book also as Persse O'Reilly, and we find that *perce-oreille* is French for "earwig." H. C. Earwicker is also known by his initials as H.C.E., and this becomes in the book Here Comes Everybody. It is he who lies asleep as the book opens, this "imposing everybody . . . constantly the same as and equal to himself and magnificently well worthy of any and all such universalisation." He is a Dublin pub-keeper, father of two children, and first as he sleeps lightly, the evening's events in jumbled form pass through his semi-conscious mind, mingling with the stream of history. Then comes deeper sleep; nightmare; restlessness and discomfort, until the prose grows heavy and dense and almost as meaningless as sleep. Gradually smoother slumber comes, "the night's unconsciousness abates," day breaks and the world (and the book) begins to stir with life again. (*Ulysses,* too, was written in this way. The morning scenes in Dublin are sharper and more clearly-defined than those of afternoon and evening which become increasingly blurred.)

That is the barest outline of the six-hundred-and-twenty-

eight-page book. It contains recurrent motifs and themes and characters which take on multiple forms. And it is built, we are told, on the philosophic system of the Neapolitan, Giambattista Vico. Mr Samuel Beckett explains the philosophical basis of the book as follows:

> In the beginning was the thunder: the thunder set free Religion, in its most objective and unphilosophical form—idolatrous animism: Religion produced Society, and the first social men were the cave-dwellers, taking refuge from a passionate Nature: this primitive family life receives its first impulse towards development from the arrival of terrified vagabonds: admitted, they are the first slaves: growing stronger, they exact agrarian concessions, and a despotism has evolved into a primitive feudalism: the cave becomes a city, and the feudal system a democracy: then an anarchy: this is corrected by a return to monarchy: the last stage is a tendency towards interdestruction: the nations are dispersed, and the Phoenix of Society arises out of their ashes.

Vico, then, is apparently as important in *Finnegans Wake* as Homer is in *Ulysses.* Joyce builds this book on his philosophy as he built *Ulysses* around the Odyssey. In the earlier work the hero was the wanderer and the incidents of his day's wanderings (a fragment of his life's wanderings) were patterned on the incidents that befell the Homeric hero in his years of travels. So in *Finnegans Wake* the hero, lying asleep and occasionally dreaming, is the product of Vico's conception of society. The ages and events have fashioned him. Dublin figures in the story, it is the city around which history has unfolded (like any other city) and the Liffey River flows through the dream, a river like any other river, but also the river of life; a river which is a woman, Anna Livia Plurabelle, or Iseult la Belle, but also woman, the source of life. And Earwicker is Tristram, and Adam and Humpty Dumpty—did not both of them fall?—and the man in the ballad of *Finnegan's Wake,* who also fell, but revived at his wake when the word whiskey was mentioned. . . . The first words of the book set the Liffey running past Earwicker's pub, apparently situated near Phoenix Park . . .

> riverrun, past Eve and Adam's, from swerve of shore to bend of bay, brings us by a commodious vicus of recirculation back to Howth Castle and Environs.

Joyce begins to pile up the complex problems which make this book a terror and a delight from the outset. The river is to run back through history, by way of (vicus) Vico and come back again to Howth Castle and Environs, in a word to H.C.E.—Humphrey Chimpden Earwicker, Here Comes Everybody.

In the third paragraph there is a clap of thunder. The evening has been stormy. Is it the thunder that set free Religion and started society on its long travail? It starts Earwicker certainly on his long night of uncomfortable sleep. The river is running past Earwicker's pub. He lies asleep by his wife, Maggie, and nearby are their children Kevin and Jerry, and they are Eve and Adam and all the daughters and sons through the ages of Eve and Adam.

As we venture further into the book we find ourselves in a labyrinth of words and images, constructed with the same technical virtuosity that we saw in *Ulysses.* We discover the familiar fragments published as *Work in Progress,* but now in their proper setting—the fable of the "Mookse and the Gripes," the magnificent chapter of Anna Livia Plurabelle and the washerwomen, the story of the "Ondt and the Gracehopper," and the section published as "Haveth Childers Everywhere" which contains the names of many cities, turned into words by elaborate punning even as the names of rivers are used to narrate the river chapter of Anna Livia.

The book cannot be described adequately and it is too complex an organism for anyone to claim that he has penetrated to its depth and uncovered every meaning and every allusion. To understand the work sentence by sentence one would have to be able to go through the same series of mental associations in reading, as Joyce went through in composing. "It is unlikely that Joyce himself understands from re-reading of his . . . writing all that he thought it had in the way of implication," Mr Robert McAlmon said once. And this is probably true. It will forever be a work into which one will dip time and again for the delightful play of fancy and the pleasure to be found in its inventive language. Mr Edmund Wilson's two illuminating articles published recently in the *New Republic* are probably the clearest interpretation of some of the problems in the book while being an excellent aid to reading it. The series of essays published by Sylvia Beach in 1929 and recently republished, *Our Exagmination Round His Factification for Incamination of Work in Progress* contains many clues, probably furnished by Joyce himself. They were published in *transition* when *Finnegans Wake* was but a series of fragments, but the writers knew Joyce and must have questioned him. The curious will find that these essays, and a few other articles, open pathways to further exploration.

Our best clue to Joyce's method is in the text itself. I have selected for closer examination the passage in the Anna Livia chapter, Joyce's reading of which was recorded some years ago. Night is falling on the Liffey; two washerwomen are talking about the people whose clothes they wash. As the shadows darken, the waters rush swiftly by into the night, the river widens, the women become an eternal elm and stone on the river bank. Hearing Joyce read this passage one realizes there is method to his madness; and one becomes acutely aware of the extent to which *Finnegans Wake* is addressed to the ear.

The section has been republished several times, and in almost every instance Joyce revised it. By comparing the different versions we can study the way in which the work grew. In its first form it is fairly easy to follow. In the attempt to find richer sounds and associations, Joyce made further changes and the final form differs considerably from the original. An interesting sidelight is thrown on the text by a French adaptation, published in the *Nouvelle Revue Française* in May, 1931, made by seven persons, with Joyce presiding. It took them about fifteen sessions of three hours each to translate this fragment.

I know of the existence of five versions. These are:

(1) The first draft, called **Work in Progress,** published in *Le Navire d'Argent,* Paris, Oct. 1, 1925.

(2) Expanded and revised, published in *transition,* no. 8, Nov., 1927, Paris, under the title **Work in Progress.**

(3) Again revised and published under the title of *Anna Livia Plurabelle* in New York by Crosby Gaige in a *de luxe* limited edition.

(4) *Anna Livia Plurabelle,* Criterion Miscellany no. 15, London, Faber and Faber, 1930. (This version may be the same as (3).)

(5) The final version in **Finnegans Wake,** pp. 196-216.

I have not had the opportunity of comparing all the versions, but a study of (1), (4), and (5) serves our purpose. With one or two exceptions, (4) and (5) are identical. But the differences between (1) and (4) are sufficiently great to afford us an interesting study in conscious complication.

The first draft, as we have remarked, is written for the most part in straightforward English. One is almost tempted to say that Mr Joyce wrote the whole book out first in traditional form and then proceeded to translate it into the special idiom he devised for the work.

> Well, you know or don't you know or haven't I told you every story has an end and that's the he and the she of it.

This direct statement becomes in (4):

> Well, you know or don't you kennet or haven't I told you every telling has a taling and that's the he and the she of it.

We observe at once the whole tendency of the work: substitution of related and associative words for the actual word . . . ; "every story has an end" has given Mr Joyce the opportunity to play with "tailing," "telling," and "taling" even as he has substituted "kennet," presumably "ken it," for "know." But read the two sentences aloud and compare their rhythm and style. The changes, in addition to the new associations introduced into the sentence, woo the ear cunningly.

A little further "What time is it?" becomes "What age is at?" and "It must be late" is changed to "it saon is late." The word "soon" and the river Saône combine to form the word "saon," because Joyce in this chapter uses all possible names of rivers and water associations, to evoke the flow of water, its freshness and clearness on the one hand, its capacity for stagnation and muddiness on the other.

"It's ages now since I or anyone last saw Waterhouse's clock." This was modified to " 'Tis endless now since eye or ereone last saw Waterhouse's clogh," and in the final version the "since" is further modified to "senne" which may refer to the river Seine. The "ereone" is apparently an allusion to Samuel Butler's *Erewhon.* The change from "clock" to "clogh" is not entirely clear, except that the softer "clogh" is closer to the washerwoman's Irish speech. In the name Waterhouse Joyce obtains another water allusion.

"They took it asunder, I heard them say," Joyce altered to "I hurd them sigh," and in the recording it is interesting to hear the author sigh as he reads "they took it asunder" and the following words "when will they reassemble it." There again is a notable example of the music of *Finnegans Wake.* Read aloud, the words "asunder," "sigh," "reassemble," in succession constitute a series of carefully-scaled sounds which the word "say" instead of "sigh" would disturb. Incidentally "sigh" again is closer to the way the Irishwoman would say it.

There are puns on all sides. The washerwoman complains that her back hurts and says she'd "want to go to Aches-les-Pains." Then they hear the bell:

> Pingpong! There's the Belle for Sexaloitez! And
> Concepta de Send-us-pray! Pang!

"Wring out the clothes! Wring in the dew!" says the washerwoman.

In all versions the phrase "It's churning chill" occurs and it is illustrative of the effects Joyce seeks to produce. Ingenious is Joyce's introduction of two rivers of this world and one of the next, the Aar of Switzerland, India's Irrawaddy, and Hades' Lethe. The river is widening. The washerwomen are shouting at each other above the rush of waters. And one of them complains:

> It's that irrawaddyng I've stoke in my aars. It all
> but husheth the lethest sound.

Joyce reads that sentence brilliantly. There is, first, annoyance in his voice because the washerwoman cannot hear, and then it sinks to a whisper as he slowly, deliberately, hauntingly enunciates "it all but husheth the lethest sound." In the final version "sound" becomes "zsound."

We come to a striking example of alteration. "Wait till the rising of the moon, love," Joyce wrote originally; "Wait till the honeying of the lune love," he wrote in later versions, introducing a play on honeymoon, the honey colour of the moon, and changing moon to the French *lune* to achieve alliterative and musical effect in the words "lune love." The French translation successfully carries out this idea with "Attends moun amour que la lune s'y mielle," but the effect of "lune love" is not there.

"Twinkletoes" is changed to "trinkettoes" and "queer" to "quair," "same" to "seim." In the French version a neat pun is obtained, throwing light on "howmulty plurators made eachone in person?" "Combien bien d'incestres pour faire chaque seul nous."

And then we come to the final lines, practically unchanged in all the versions, where Joyce seems from the outset to have achieved expression of his mood. The lines have been much quoted. To hear Joyce read them is to feel the night descend, with its water sounds, the moisture in the air, the washerwomen transformed into elm and stone . . .

> Can't hear with the waters of. The chittering waters of. Flittering bats, fieldmice bawk talk. Ho! Are you not gone ahome? What Thom Malone? Can't hear with bawk of bats, all thim liffeying waters of. Ho, talk save us! My foos won't moos. I feel as old as yonder elm. A tale told of Shaun or Shem? All Livia's daughtersons. Dark hawks hear us. Night! Night! My ho head halls. I feel as heavy as yonder stone. Tell me of John or

Shaun? Who were Shem and Shaun the living sons or daughters of? Night now! Tell me, tell me, tell me, elm! Night night! Telmetale of stem or stone. Beside the rivering waters of, hitherandthithering waters of. Night!

In the "What Thom Malone" Joyce changed "tom" to "Thom" in the final version and similarly "the" to "thim" in "all thim liffeying waters of," adding to the music with the related sounds of "thom" and "thim" and perhaps thinking of bringing the name Tim in juxtaposition with Tom.

But one cannot explain all the reasons for Joyce's changes. The principal reasons are clear enough.

Curious and revealing as the alterations in the different texts are, they are perhaps no more interesting than the different forms the same phrases take on in the book itself. "Dear dirty Dublin" becomes "Dear dirty dumpling," "hear Hubty Hublin," "deep dorfy doubtlings." And there are infinite variations on "The Rocky Road to Dublin"—"the quaggy way for stumbling," "the way to wumblin," and "the lucky load to Lublin."

So we find, too, queer echoes of phrases and passages from *Anna Livia Plurabelle* in other chapters:

> . . . every crowd has its several tones and every trade has its clever mechanics and each harmonical has a point of its own, Olaf's on the rise and Ivor's on the lift and Sitric's place's between them.
>
> . . . every dam had her seven crutches. And every crutch had its seven hues. And each hue had a differing cry. Sudds for me and supper for you and the doctor's bill for Joe John.

The rhythm in each passage is the same. Or,

> . . . like any Etrurian Catholic Heathen, in their pinky limony creamy birnies and their turkiss indienne mauves;
>
> . . . like any enthewsyass cuckling a hoyden in her rougey gipsylike chinka-minx pulshandjupeyjade and her petsybluse indecked o' voylets;

in which the second is an elaborate embroidery on the first. This passage in *Anna Livia*—

> Then all that was was fair. Tys Elvenland! Teems of times and happy returns. The seim anew—

becomes:

> When who was wist was ware. En elv, et fjaell. And the whirr of the whins humming us howe. His hume. Hencetaking tides we haply return. . . .

And about four hundred pages further on it develops into:

> For nought that is has bane. In mournenslaund. Themes have thimes and habit reburns. To flame in you.

This is all part of the pattern, much as a fragmentary idea in the opening pages of *Ulysses* develops as it recurs in Bloom's or Dedalus' consciousness until it springs into a

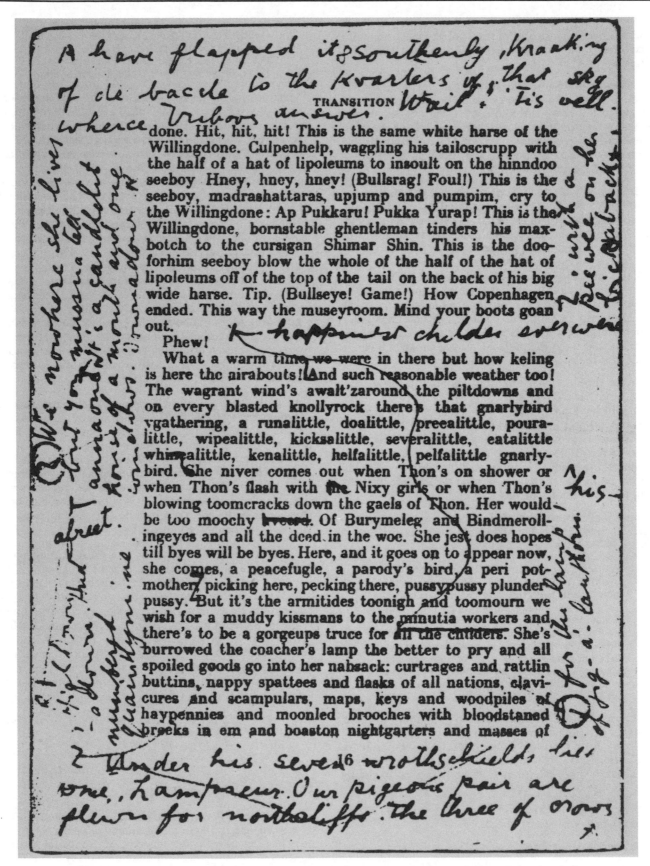

A have flapped itssoutherly, kraaking of de baccle to the Kvarters of, that sky wherce Trobow answers. Wail! 'Tis well.

TRANSITION

done. Hit, hit, hit! This is the same white harse of the Willingdone. Culpenhelp, waggling his tailoscrupp with the half of a hat of lipoleums to insoult on the hinndoo seeboy Hney, hncy, hney! (Bullsrag! Foul!) This is the seeboy, madrashattaras, upjump and pumpim, cry to the Willingdone: Ap Pukkaru! Pukka Yurap! This is the Willingdone, bornstable ghentleman tinders his max- botch to the cursigan Shimar Shin. This is the doo- forhim seeboy blow the whole of the half of the hat of lipoleums off of the top of the tail on the back of his big wide harse. Tip. (Bullseye! Game!) How Copenhagen ended. This way the museyroom. Mind your boots goan out.

Phew!

What a warm time we were in there but how keling is here the airabouts! And such reasonable weather too! The wagrant wind's awalt'zaround the piltdowns and on every blasted knollyrock there's that gnarlybird vgathering, a runalittle, doalittle, preealittle, poura- little, wipealittle, kicksalittle, severalittle, eatalittle whimealittle, kenalittle, helfalittle, pelfalittle gnarly- bird. She niver comes out when Thon's on shower or when Thon's flash with the Nixy girls or when Thon's blowing toomcracks down the gaels of Thon. Her would- be too moochy tweed. Of Burymeleg and Bindmeroll- ingeyes and all the deed in the woe. She jest does hopes till byes will be byes. Here, and it goes on to appear now, she comes, a peacefugle, a parody's bird, a peri pot- mother picking here, pecking there, pussypussy plunder pussy. But it's the armitides toonigh and toomourn we wish for a muddy kissmans to the minutia workers and there's to be a gorgeups truce for all the childers. She's burrowed the coacher's lamp the better to pry and all spoiled goods go into her nabsack: curtrages and rattlin buttins, nappy spattees and flasks of all nations, clavi- cures and scampulars, maps, keys and woodpiles of haypennies and moonled brooches with bloodstaned breeks in em and boaston nightgarters and masses of

Under his seven worthschields lies one, Lampseur. Our pigeons pair are flewn for northcliffs the three of crows full-blown image or sequence of ideas near the end of the book. So here themes and phrases intertwine, as complicated as an orchestral score, as subtle and often as difficult to follow.

An understanding of *Finnegans Wake* lies in an understanding of the roles of the eye and the ear in this work. For centuries now, since minstrels and ballad-singers yielded to the printed page and man gave his eye the work his ear had done, our auditory sense has to a considerable extent played second fiddle to the visual in literature—with the exception of the drama.

In *Finnegans Wake* Mr Joyce asks the eye to look at unfamiliar words and shapes on the printed page and expects it to communicate them to the ear. He asks the impossible. Only Mr Joyce's ear can catch all the sounds, all the beauties of his verbal fancies. The unprepared eye will invariably refuse to co-operate. Mr Joyce has put on paper a work that in reality should be heard, not read. That is why readers accustomed to having their eyes move comfortably and easily along the printed page find the book difficult. They trip and stumble. Their eye reads "soon" and suddenly discovers it is "saon." And even rougher obstacles than that lie in the path. Mr Joyce's road to Dublin is indeed a rocky one.

Mr Joyce should have committed his book to print only in the way that a composer prints the score of his work. He should have provided us with the facility for hearing it read aloud and the only way to do that is to record it. A tremendous task, for two pages of this long book fill a large-size record. But this record teaches more than hours of painstaking reading of the text. When Mr Joyce reads it aloud he indicates to us how little we are equipped to bring to life the notes he has written.

I should like to hear him read, for instance, the passage in which, apparently, Earwicker consoles his frightened child:

> You were dreamend, dear. The pawdrag? The fawthrig? Shoe! Hear are no phanthares in the room at all, avikkeen. No bad bold faathern, dear one. Opop opop capallo, muy malinchily malchik! Gothgorod father godown followay to-mollow the lucky load to Lublin for make his thoroughbass grossman's bigness. Take that two piece big slap slap bold honty bottomsside pap pap pappa . . . Sonly all in your imagination, dim. Poor little brittle magic nation, dim of mind!

Joyce puns all through here. There is even a pun in three languages, changing the Russian "muy malinchy malchik" (my little boy) to "malinchily" thus relating it to "melancholy" so that it might mean "my melancholy bad little chick," "mal" the French for bad prefixed to chick; "muy" is also Spanish for "very."

Or again, one would want to hear Joyce's rendition of the opening words of the last chapter:

> Sandhyas! Sandhyas! Sandhyas!

> Calling all downs. Calling all downs to dayne. Array! Surrection. Eireweeker to the wohld blu-

dyn world. O rally, O rally, O rally! Phlenxty, O rally! To what lifelike thyne of the bird can be. Seek you somany matters. Haze sea east to Osseania. Here! Here! Tass, Patt, Staff, Woff, Havv, Bluvv and Rutter. The smog is lofting.

A characteristic passage, evocative of morning. What would Joyce's voice make of them. "Array"—"arise, array thyself," and also a ray of sunshine, and equally "Hurray!" "Surrection"—Resurrection, perhaps also Insurrection. "Eireweeker"—Eire now becomes part of Earwicker's name. "The wohld bludyn world," with its play on "wold" and "world." And then more punning on O'Reilly, with the series of "O rally." The reference to Phoenix Park, the Phoenix, day rising from the dead ashes of the night. "Haze sea" and "haste ye." And then the allusions to the news agencies, spreaders of news to the "wohld bludyn world"—Tass of Russia, Pat of Poland, Stefani of Italy, Wolff of Germany (pre-Nazi; now the D.N.B.), Havas of France, and Great Britain's Reuters. "Calling all downs to dayne"—the "dayne" a reference to Earwicker's Scandinavian ancestors. There are probably many more allusions buried in these few words in which Joyce announces that the night is over, man is resurrected from sleep, the nightmare is gone, "the smog is lofting." "Smog," of course, like Lewis Carroll's "slithy" is a portmanteau word—for "smoke" and "fog."

Somewhere in the *Portrait* Stephen Dedalus asks himself: "Did he then love the rhythmic rise and fall of words better than their association of legend and colour?" Joyce loves words as probably no one in the whole reach of English literature loved them, their rise and fall, their associations of legend and of colour, the depth of history buried in each word. He sees with his ears as well as hears with them. He has all the sensitivity of a blind man but, being able to see, is the more richly endowed. And he must forgive us if we cannot go all the way with him.

Finnegans Wake, like *Ulysses,* is a great, a magnificent success—and failure. Both will remain books which will haunt us and to which we shall return, baffled, sometimes puzzled, and yet finding there great power and suggestiveness and inventiveness—an impression as of the complexity of the whole of life poured into a book's mould, which neither music, nor language, nor any artifice of man has yet captured. But where writers before him opened only small apertures on this world for all to see through, Joyce has flung open wide windows on vistas completely clear only to himself. (pp. 68-81)

Leon Edel, "James Joyce and His New Work," in University of Toronto Quarterly, *Vol. IX, No. 1, October, 1939, pp. 68-81.*

Louise Bogan   (essay date 1939)

[*Bogan was a distinguished American poet whose work is noted for its subtlety and restraint, evidencing her debt to the English metaphysical poets. She served for many years as the poetry critic at the* New Yorker *and is the author of* Achievement in American Poetry: 1900-1950, *a respected volume of criticism. In the following essay, which was originally published in 1939, she notes faults and virtues of* Finnegans Wake.]

Joyce has been writing **Finnegans Wake** for seventeen years. In 1922 **Ulysses** was published in Paris; this book was begun the same year. *Transition* has brought out about half of it, intermittently, under the title **Work in Progress**; and a number of fragments have appeared now and again in pamphlet form. A whole school of imitators has clustered around its linguistic and philosophical example, and its influence has been so strong that critics have been led to write of it in, as it were, its own terms. Something unheard-of and extraordinary was happening to language, history, time, space, and causality in Joyce's new novel, and the jaw-dropping and hat-waving of the front-line appreciators were remarkable in themselves. Because this subjective, or rolling-along-in-great-delight-with-a-great-work-of-art, school of criticism has had its innings with Joyce's books, the plain reviewer might do well to approach the work at first with a certain amount of leaden-footed objectivity, remaining outside the structure and examining it from as many sides as possible.

Joyce himself, as we shall see, has given a good many clues to what the book is about. The first thing that strikes the reader, however, is the further proof of Joyce's miraculous virtuosity with language. **Finnegans Wake** takes up this technical skill as it existed at the end of **Ulysses** and further elaborates it. Then Joyce's mastery of structure and his musician's feeling for form and rhythmic subtlety are here in a more advanced—as well as a more deliquescent—state of development. The chief reason for the book's opacity is the fact that it is written in a special language. But this language is not gibberish—unless it wants to be. It has rules and conventions. Before one starts hating or loving or floating off upon it, the attention might be bent toward discovering what it is, and how it works.

This private tongue is related to what Panurge called the "puzlatory," and it is cousin to the language of E. Lear, L. Carroll, and the writers of nonsense verse in general. It is based on the pun and is defined, by Fowler, as: "Paronomasia (Rhet.) 'word-shunting.' Puns, plays on words, making jocular or suggestive use of similarity between different words or of a word's different senses." Upon this rhetorical device **Finnegans Wake** is borne, no matter what limits of intelligibility or impenetrability it touches. Two examples may illustrate it:

> For a burning would is come to dance inane.
> Glamours hath moidered's lieb and therefore
> Coldours must leap no more.

> But listen to the mocking birde to micking
> bards making bared!

Now let us examine the texture of the writing. This, as one would expect, is firm. Moving for the most part in a private idiom, Joyce keeps unerringly to style's economy, precision, and weight. Through a thousand variations, through a confusion of tongues, the fundamental sinew of the writing persists; the book can be opened anywhere, and a page read at random, in proof of this. The remark of Richard Strauss to a young musician comes to mind: "Why do you write atonally? You have talent." Joyce is not writing as he is writing to cover up inexpertness. Prosodically, he is a master, as can readily be seen if he is compared with his apprentices.

He is a master-musician and a master-parodist. Here, even more clearly than in **Ulysses,** Joyce brings over into literature not only music's structural forms—as exemplified by the fugue, the sonata, the theme with variations—but the harmonic modulations, the suspensions and solutions, of music: effects in words which parallel a composer's effects obtained by working with relative or non-relative keys. Phrases and whole passages are transposed from a given style, mood, tempo, signature into a more contrasting one. Certain proper names—Finnegan, Earwicker, Anna Livia, Dublin, Phoenix, Howth, James and John, Lucan and Chapelizod—reappear in truncated, anagrammatically distorted, or portmanteau forms. The night-river leitmotif reads, at its most normal: "Beside the rivering waters of, hitherandthithering waters of. Night!" Its variants are numerous and remarkable. Joyce, the parodist, in **Ulysses** always effectively colored matter with manner. The number of styles parodied in **Finnegans Wake** is prodigious. But these present parodies differ somewhat from their predecessors; they are actually more limited. The punning language in which they are framed gives them all a mocking or burlesque edge (the prose poems, only, excepted). This limitation and defeat of purpose—for an immense book written in two main modes only is sure to grow monotonous—is the first symptom to strike the reader of the malady, to be later defined, which cripples **Finnegans Wake.**

Thus equipped, then, with his private vernacular, Joyce proceeds to attack what certainly seems to be every written or oral style known to man. A list of these styles would fill pages. The range and variety can only be indicated here. All forms of religious liturgy (Bible, prayer book, sermon, mass, catechism, litany); conversation; letters informal, formal, and illiterate; the fable, the examination paper, the chronicle; fashion notes and soap-box speeches; the hair-splitting argument and the sentimental narrative. And here are dialects and jargons—"every known *patois* of the English language." Slang, journalese, and specialized vocabularies: of heraldry, the race track, the courtroom, the nursery. Also uncounted foreign tongues, from Sanskrit through Anglo-Saxon to modern European, back to pidgin English, baby talk, and the sounds children make before speech. There are also just plain noises, onomatopoetically expressed, from bangs and howls to twitters and whimpers.

The "auditive faculty" of Stephen Dedalus has been expanded so that the functions of the other senses become subsidiary to it, Joyce has put down everything he has heard for the last seventeen years. We now can examine some evidence from Eugene Jolas, the editor of *Transition,* as to Joyce's method of work. Jolas says: "It was necessary [in compiling a complete MS for publication] to go through a number of notebooks, each of which had esoteric symbols indicating the reference to a given character, locality, event, or mood. Then the words accumulated over the years had to be placed in the segment for which they were intended." And what Joyce was up to in general—the underlying theme and philosophical purpose of the book—has been partially elucidated by Joyce to Jolas and others. Jolas says:

> We know that Mr. Joyce's ambition has been to write a book dealing with the night-mind of man. . . . We have tried to keep in mind that the dramatic dynamic is based on the Bruno theory of knowledge through opposites, and on the Vico theory of cyclic recurrence. . . . History being, in his earlier words "a nightmare," Mr. Joyce presents his phantasmagoric figures as passing back and forth from a mentality saturated with archetypal memories to a vision of future construction.

Another of Joyce's favorite exegetes sheds a little more light (and it can be definitely stated that light is needed, since the one actual fact which is clear to the reader, without exegesis, is that the action takes place in one night or one aeon of time, and is concerned with a man—a giant, an earth-force—asleep). Stuart Gilbert says:

> Joyce's new work is partly based on the historical speculations of Vico. . . . Vico held that there is a recurrent cycle in human "progress," as in the movement of the stars. Societies begin, continue, and have an end, according to universal laws. . . . Every nation passes through three stages, the divine, the heroic, the human. The prelude and aftermath of each cycle is complete disintegration. . . . Vico contemplated the writing of an "ideal and timeless history" in which all the actual histories of all nations should be embodied. . . . "Work in Progress" is, in many aspects, a realization of Vico's project. . . . It is interesting to note that an exceptionally intricate passage in Mr. Joyce's book is, in effect, a fantasia on the quinary scale. . . . Even the difficult passages of the "Anna Livia Plurabelle" fragment become lucid when read aloud in the appropriate rhythm and intonation by the author. In fact, rhythm is one of the clues to the meaning . . . for each of the polymorphous personages of the work has his appropriate rhythm, and many "references" can be located by reference to the rhythm of the prose.

With these few "clues" well in mind, the reader can only open the book, without further explanation, and battle his way into it. Life is too short to read all the glosses which have already multiplied around it and will continue to multiply. Some of its themes are perfectly clear. The pedestrian reviewer can add a few scattered notes, put down during her own two weeks' life with the literary monument.

There is every reason to believe that a *complete explanation* of the whole thing will come, after a longish lapse of time, from Joyce himself. This happened, it will be remembered, in the case of *Ulysses* after about nine years. . . . There is nothing whatever to indicate that Joyce has any real knowledge of the workings of the subconscious, in sleep or otherwise. Carroll has far more intuition than Joyce into the real structure of the dream. There are no sustained passages which give, for example, the feeling of nightmare. The punning style, as a matter of fact, precludes this. It is as though Joyce wished to be superior to

the unconscious. . . . At one point he brings in a long apologia for his own method and language. The effect of this interpolation is very queer. . . . Some sections start off with indicated time, but these indications seem to be afterthoughts. . . . The later versions of the fragments already published seem to be changed out of sheer perversity: a clause is omitted leaving nothing but a vestigial preposition; a singular noun is shifted to the plural, and the meaning is thereby successfully clouded. . . . The most frightening thing about the book is the feeling, which steadily grows in the reader, that Joyce himself does not know what he is doing; and how, in spite of all his efforts, he is giving himself away. Full control is being exercised over the minor details and the main structure, but the compulsion toward a private universe is very strong. . . . Joyce's delight in reducing man's learning, passion, and religion to a hash is also disturbing. . . . After the first week what one longs for is the sound of speech, or the sight of a sentence in its natural human context. . . . The book cannot rise into the region of true evocation—the region where Molly Bloom's soliloquy exists immortally—because it has no human base. Emotion is deleted, or burlesqued, throughout. The vicious atmosphere of a closed world, whose creator can manage and distort all that is humanly valuable and profound (cunningly, with Godlike slyness), becomes stifling. . . . *Ulysses* was based on a verifiable theme: the search for the father. The theme, or themes, of *Finnegans Wake* are retrogressive, as the language is retrogressive. The style retrogresses back to the conundrum. To read the book over a long period of time gives one the impression of watching intemperance become addiction, become debauch.

The book's great beauties, its wonderful passages of wit, its variety, its marks of genius and immense learning, are undeniable. It has another virtue: in the future "writers will not need to search for a compromise." But whatever it says of man's past, it has nothing to do with man's future, which, we can only hope, will lie in the direction of more humanity rather than less. And there are better gods than Proteus. (pp. 262-67)

Louise Bogan, "James Joyce," in her A Poet's Alphabet: Reflections on the Literary Art and Vocation, *edited by Robert Phelps and Ruth Limmer, McGraw-Hill Book Company, 1970, pp. 262-70.*

A. Walton Litz   (essay date 1961)

[*Litz is an American educator and critic who has written two book-length studies on Joyce's works. In the following excerpt, he traces the evolution and publication history of the* Finnegans Wake *manuscript.*]

When *Finnegans Wake* first appeared in 1939 most readers familiar with *Ulysses* were confounded by what seemed to be a radical change in Joyce's style and technique. Superficially, the dense language of the *Wake* bore little resemblance to even the most complex sections of *Ulysses.* Only those who had studied the fragments of Joyce's *Work in Progress* published during the 1920's and 1930's were prepared for the new language, realizing that it had developed gradually and inevitably out of the method of *Ulysses.* Today we are in a much better position to understand the affinities between *Ulysses* and *Finnegans Wake,* since the manuscript drafts and galley proofs of Joyce's last work provide complete and detailed evidence for every stage in the process of composition. Using this material as a foundation, we shall attempt—in Henry James's words—'to remount the stream of composition' and trace the growth of *Finnegans Wake.*

Over a year passed after the publication of *Ulysses* before Joyce could muster the strength and determination to begin a new work. When the *Wake* was finally begun, in the spring of 1923, neither the structure nor the ultimate style of the book had been determined. Of course, Joyce had been preoccupied for years with many of the *Wake*'s major themes and motifs. The philosophies of Giordano Bruno and Giambattista Vico, which support the *Wake*'s structure, were familiar to Joyce from his early reading in Dublin and Trieste, while some of the book's fundamental motifs (HCE's encounter with the Cad, the story of Buckley and the Russian General) belonged to the lore of the Joyce family. Many of the *Wake*'s important themes are foreshadowed in *Ulysses,* most notably Vico's cyclic view of history. But although the materials of the *Wake* had been accumulating in his imagination since childhood, the manner in which this ripening vision would be presented was still not clear when Joyce began work in 1923. The early years of *Work in Progress* were exploratory, and Joyce's first efforts reveal a search for some dominant structure and a gradual clarification of stylistic aims.

It seems likely that Joyce spent most of 1922 reviewing his previous achievements and waiting for his principal interests to 'fuse' into a new form. Certainly the collection and ordering of material was never completely abandoned. But if we have to choose an official date for the beginning of *Work in Progress* it must be 10 March 1923. On March 11th Joyce sent a letter to Harriet Weaver informing her that 'Yesterday I wrote two pages—the first I have written since the final *Yes* of *Ulysses*'. These two pages were the earliest version of the 'King Roderick O'Conor' piece, now pages 380-82 [of the 1939 Faber and Faber edition] of *Finnegans Wake.* On July 19th Joyce sent them to Harriet Weaver for typing, and then began sorting out his notes in preparation for future work. During the summer of 1923 he wrote three more sketches which were eventually incorporated into widely separated sections of the *Wake*: 'Tristan and Isolde' (now part of *Finnegans Wake* II. iv), 'St. Kevin' (*Finnegans Wake* 604-06), and 'pidgin fella Berkeley' (*Finnegans Wake* 611-12). In August Harriet Weaver typed these three pieces for Joyce, along with the 'King Roderick O'Conor' sketch.

These four early fragments, which were revised and incorporated into the *Wake* late in the process of composition, indicate the nature of Joyce's mature method. Instead of following a narrative sequence and beginning with a draft of the *Wake*'s first episode (which actually was not written until 1926), he first explored four of his major interests: the artistic possibilities of Irish history (King Roderick O'Conor), the seduction motif (Tristan and Isolde), the figure of Shaun (St. Kevin), and the argument between St.

Patrick and the archdruid. The last of these sketches is extremely significant. When Frank Budgen failed to take the 'pidgin fella Berkeley' passage seriously Joyce wrote to him:

> Much more is intended in the colloquy between Berkely the archdruid and his pidgin speech and Patrick in answer and his Nippon English. It is also the defence and indictment of the book itself, B's theory of colour and Patrick's practical solution of the problem.

The druid defends in obscure terms the language and design of *Finnegans Wake,* borrowing his arguments from Berkeley's subjective theory of vision, but common-sense Patrick dismisses the druid's reasoning and with it the night-world of the *Wake.* It was almost inevitable that this passage, which ultimately found its place near the end of the *Wake,* should have been one of the first written. Joyce in writing it seems to have been debating with himself the advantages and disadvantages of the task he was about to undertake.

On 2 August 1923 Joyce, who was then vacationing in Sussex, sent Harriet Weaver three early drafts of the 'pidgin fella Berkeley' episode. By comparing these versions we can gain some measure of his stylistic aims at the outset of *Work in Progress.* In the first version the archdruid explains his theory of colour in an abstract style less complex than that found in many parts of *Ulysses.* Here is the opening sentence:

> The archdruid then explained the illusion of the colourful world, its furniture, animal, vegetable and mineral, appearing to fallen men under but one reflection of the several iridal gradations of solar light, that one which it had been unable to absorb while for the seer beholding reality, the thing as in itself it is, all objects showed themselves in their true colours, resplendent with the sextuple glory of the light actually retained within them.

This first draft was cast into 'pidgin English' during a series of revisions. The 'final' 1923 draft opens as follows:

> Bymby topside joss pidgin fella Berkeley, archdruid of Irish chinchinjoss, in the his heptachromatic sevenhued septicoloured roranyellgreeblindigan mantle finish he show along the his mister guest Patrick with alb belonga him the whose throat he fast all time what tune all him monkafellas with Patrick he drink up words all too much illusiones of hueful panepiphanal world of lord Joss the of which zoantholithic furniture from mineral through vegetal to animal not appear to full up together fallen man than under but one photoreflection of the several iridals gradationes of solar light that one which that part of it (furnit of huepanepi world) had shown itself (part of fur of huepamvor) unable to absorbere whereas for numpa one seer in seventh degree of wisdom of Entis-Onton he savvy inside true inwardness of reality, tha Ding hvad in idself id ist, all objects (of panepiwor) alloside showed themselves in trues coloribus resplendent with sextuple gloria of light actually retained inside them (obs of epiwo).

Comparison of the two versions of the passage reveals several important characteristics of Joyce's method. As in *Ulysses* the revisions are expansive, an elaboration of the basic text. The names 'Berkeley' and 'Patrick' have been introduced in the final draft, but more important the language has been turned into Pidgin English so as to 'express' Joyce's conviction that early Irish religion was Eastern in nature. This process was continued in 1938, when Joyce re-worked the final 1923 version of this sentence for inclusion in Part IV of the *Wake*. He added allusions to several themes developed after 1923: the passage in *Finnegans Wake* opens with 'Tunc.', a reference to the 'TUNC' page of *The Book of Kells*, whose design Joyce felt was analogous to his own method. 'Berkeley' was also changed to 'Dalkelly' in 1938, to remind the reader of 'Buckley' (who shot the Russian General). But these changes were not extensive, and the general level of allusiveness and compression achieved in 1923 met Joyce's exacting standards of fifteen years later. In the revisions of 'pidgin fella Berkeley' made during July 1923 one can see Joyce moving toward an extension of certain technical goals already evident in the writing of *Ulysses*.

In August and September of 1923 Joyce turned from the four brief sketches already discussed to the composition of 'Mamalujo' (*Matthew-Mark-Luke-John*), an episode in which the Four Old Men witness the honeymoon of Tristram and Isolde (now *Finnegans Wake* II. iv). On October 17th Joyce wrote to Harriet Weaver that 'Mamalujo' was 'finished but I am filing the edges off it'. This 'filing process', as usual, took more time than Joyce had anticipated, and he was still revising 'Mamalujo' in the weeks before it was published in Ford Madox Ford's *Transatlantic Review* (April 1924). 'Mamalujo' was the first section of *Work in Progress* to be published; in 1938 it was amalgamated with the 'Tristan and Isolde' sketch to form the final version of II. iv.

During the early months of work on his new book Joyce felt compelled to justify in his letters the obscurity and fragmentary nature of his first sketches, which contrasted sharply with his early work on *Ulysses* 'where at least the ports of call were known beforehand.' In 1923 the ultimate structure of *Work in Progress* was still unclear, and Joyce had no narrative framework such as the *Odyssey* to follow. Therefore he adopted the technique of getting the book's major figures and motifs on paper as quickly as possible, feeling that these were 'not fragments but active elements' which would 'begin to fuse of themselves' in time. His favourite analogy for this mode of composition was that of an engineer boring into a mountain from different sides. 'I want to get as many sketches done or get as many boring parties at work as possible', he told Harriet Weaver. Later he used the same analogy in speaking to August Suter: 'I am boring through a mountain from two sides. The question is, how to meet in the middle'.

But although Joyce ranged widely in making his preliminary sketches for the *Wake*, he never lost sight of the family situation which lies at the centre of the work. By the middle of October 1923 he had drafted the first pages of I. ii., which review the origins of Humphrey Chimpden Earwicker's name and reputation. This fragment eventu-

ally reached print in the *Contact Collection of Contemporary Writers*, published in Paris in the spring of 1925. By the beginning of 1924 Joyce had filled a red-backed notebook with rough drafts of all the episodes of Part I except i and vi; this notebook was used as the basis for several fair copies of these episodes made in the first three months of 1924. The drafts contained in the notebook reveal how far advanced Joyce's conception of Part I was, and show him in full possession of his major types—Earwicker, Anna Livia, the antithetical twins, and the young daughter. The fundamental themes of guilt and resurrection, as well as the technique of metamorphosing a number of personages into a single type, are prominent in these early drafts.

The opening months of 1924 found Joyce rapidly filling-out the chapters of Part I already drafted. A fair copy of the 'Hen' piece (I. v) was finished in January; more material was added to Shem (I. vii) in February; and on March 7th Joyce completed a fair copy of *Anna Livia* (I. viii). Yet in spite of the firm grasp of themes and types displayed in the fair copy of *Anna Livia*, these early episodes for Part I were to undergo extensive revision before they found their place in *Finnegans Wake*. Every fragment of *Work in Progress* was subjected to a series of revisions which surpassed in scope and intensity the last-minute expansions of *Ulysses*.

There is no indication that Joyce had visualized as early as 1924 the basic four-part structure of the *Wake*, or that he thought of the early drafts in the red-backed notebook as belonging to a single unit. In March 1924 he began work on 'Shaun the Post' (now *Finnegans Wake* Part III), which was originally conceived as one piece but later expanded into four sections or 'watches', and work on Shaun occupied much of his time during 1924-25. There is some indication in an unpublished letter to Harriet Weaver that Joyce thought of Shaun as belonging with the pieces already drafted concerning HCE, Anna Livia and Shem, and that these were intended to form a second section of the *Wake* to follow a first section as yet unwritten. But as work on Shaun progressed through 1924 the problems of structure became more rather than less complex. On November 9th Joyce announced the solution to one problem:

> I think that at last I have solved one—the first—
> of the problems presented by my book. In other
> words one of the partitions between two of the
> tunnelling parties seems to have given way.

The nature of this first problem, and its solution, are obscure; the union of the two tunnelling parties led only to more confusion.

> [I am] pulling down more earthwork. The gangs
> are now hammering on all sides. It is a bewilder-
> ing business.

The composition of 'Shaun the Post', expanded by this time into four 'watches', continued through 1925, interrupted from time to time by the need for revising earlier episodes before their magazine publication. In April Joyce was rewriting 'The Hen' (I. v) for inclusion in the July *Criterion*, and encountering great difficulties. A month later, in spite of serious trouble with his eyes, he was correcting proofs of the first pages of I. ii for the *Contact Collection of Contemporary Writers,* edited by Robert McAlmon: 'I have some proofs to correct for Mr McAlmon', Joyce wrote to Harriet Weaver on April 25th, 'and I had better do it before the other eye gets disabled'. Later in the year he had to prepare an early version of *Anna Livia Plurabelle* for publication in the October issue of *Le Navire d' Argent,* and the Shem episode (I. vii) for the combined Autumn-Winter issue of *This Quarter.*

By the end of August 1925 Joyce had begun the fourth 'watch' of Shaun, and on October 10th he wrote:

> I began [Shaun] d (otherwise the last watch of Shaun) a few days ago and have produced about three foolscapes of hammer and tongs stratification lit up by a fervent prayer to the divinity which shapes our roads in favour of my ponderous protagonist and his minuscule consort.

The 'stratification' of Shaun d continued through the last months of 1925, and a first draft was finished sometime in November.

In the winter of 1925-26 Joyce's work was delayed by an eye operation, but the spring of 1926 found him revising the four 'watches' of Shaun as a unit. In April they were 'finished' and sent to the typist. The completion of 'Shaun the Post' seems to have acted as a catalyst on Joyce's imagination, for his letters of the succeeding two months reveal the final plan of the work crystallizing in his mind. On 21 May 1926 he wrote to Harriet Weaver:

> I have the book now fairly well planned out in my head. I am as yet uncertain whether I shall start on the twilight games of [Shem, Shaun and Issy] which will follow immediately after [Anna Livia] or on K[evin]'s orisons, to follow [the last watch of Shaun].

Early in the next month Joyce elaborated further on the episodes to follow *Anna Livia* (I. viii):

> Between the close of [Anna Livia] at nightfall and [the first watch of Shaun, III. i] there are three or four other episodes, the children's games, night studies, a scene in the 'public', and a 'lights out in the village'.

These two quotations show that by mid-1926, with a draft of Part III and a good deal of Part I already in hand, Joyce had solved most of his major structural problems and determined the final sequence of episodes. He had clearly visualized the four sections of Part II (the children's games, night studies, a scene in the 'public', and a 'lights out in the village') that were to be inserted between *Anna Livia* (I. viii) and the four 'watches' of Shaun (Part III). These episodes are a necessary 'bridge' between the heroic dimensions of Part I and the disintegration of the hero in the Shaun of Part III; they connect the past with the future, for in Part II the present-day companions of Earwicker and his wife—their children, the Twelve Citizens and the Four Old Men—rehearse the themes of the book. With the planning of this transitional section Joyce had conquered his major problem of composition. At approximately the same time he foresaw a concluding section which would include Kevin's orisons and follow as a Coda after the four 'watches' of Shaun.

With the plan for Part II now clearly before him, Joyce wrote in the summer of 1926 a piece called 'The Triangle', which later became 'The Muddest Thick That Was Ever Heard Dump' in *Tales Told of Shem and Shaun* (1929) and the middle of the classroom episode (II. ii) in **Finnegans Wake.** After finishing this fragment he paused to assess his position:

> I have done a piece of the studies, [Shem] coaching [Shaun] how to do Euclid Bk I, I. I will do a few more pieces, perhaps [Issy's] picture-history from the family album and parts of [the twelve] discussing A Pai (I would like to invent a satisfactory fountain pen!) *A Painful Case* and the [Earwicker-Anna Livia] household etc.

This letter shows Joyce well into the planning of Part II. The 'piece of the studies' mentioned is found in the same notebook with the fourth part of Shaun (III. iv), and at the end of this 1926 notebook we find the first draft of **Finnegans Wake** I. i. Joyce composed this initial chapter with special care, aware of its crucial position in the **Wake**'s structure; therefore we are justified in using it as a measure of his technical development during the years of exploratory writing (1923-26).

In 1926 Joyce asked Harriet Weaver to 'order' an episode by sending him some material which she would like to see incorporated in the **Wake.** Knowing his preoccupation with the prehistoric aspects of HCE, Miss Weaver responded by mailing Joyce a pamphlet on St. Andrew's Church, Penrith, which mentioned a fabulous 'giant' supposedly buried in the churchyard. After receiving the pamphlet Joyce began to adapt it and could soon reply:

> I set to work at once on your esteemed order and so hard indeed that I almost stupefied myself and stopped, reclining on a sofa and reading *Gentlemen Prefer Blondes* for three whole days. But this morning I started off afresh. I am putting the piece in the place of honour, namely the first pages of the book. Will try to deliver same punctual by Xmas. . . . The book really has no beginning or end. (Trade secret, registered at Stationers Hall.) It ends in the middle of a sentence and begins in the middle of the same sentence.

Seven days later, on November 15th, Joyce sent Miss Weaver an early version of the first paragraph accompanied by an extended commentary.

Between the inception of the **Wake**'s first paragraph in later 1926 and its publication in *transition* for April 1927 Joyce lavished many hours of correction and revision upon it. The earliest version is covered with marginal and interlinear additions; I shall quote it first as it was originally written, and then as it appears after the corrections and additions are included.

> Howth Castle & Environs! Sir Tristram had not encore arrived from North Armorica nor stones exaggerated themselves in Laurens county, Ga, doubling all the time, nor a voice answered mishe chishe to tuff-tuff thouartpatrick. Not yet had a kidscalf buttended an isaac not yet had twin sesthers played siege to twone jonathan. Not a peck of malt had Shem and Son brewed

> & bad luck to the regginbrew was to be seen on the waterface
>
> brings us to Howth Castle & Environs! Sir Tristram violer d'amores, had passencore rearrived on a merry isthmus from North Armorica to wielderfight his peninsular war, nor sham rocks by the Oconee exaggerated themselse to Laurens county, Ga, doubling all the time, nor a voice from afire bellowsed mishe chishe to tufftuff thouartpeatrick. Not yet though venisoon after had a kidscad buttended a bland old isaac not yet [though] all's fair in vanessy were sosie sesthers wroth with twone jonathan. Rot a peck of pa's malt had Jhem or Sen brewed by arclight & rory end to the regginbrew was to be seen ringsome on the waterface

After undergoing several further revisions the opening paragraph appeared in *transition* as follows:

> riverrun brings us back to Howth Castle & Environs. Sir Tristram, violer d'amores, fr' over the short sea, had passencore rearrived from North Armorica on this side the scraggy isthmus of Europe Minor to wielderfight his penisolate war: nor had topsawyer's rocks by the stream Oconee exaggerated themselse to Laurens County's gorgios, while they went doublin their mumper all the time; nor avoice from afire bellowsed mishe mishe to tauftauf thuartpeatrick: not yet, though venissoon after, had a kidscad buttended a bland old isaac; not yet, though all's fair in vanessy, were sosie sesthers wroth with twone nathandjoe. Rot a peck of pa's malt had Jhem or Shen brewed by arclight and rory end to the regginbrew was to be seen ringsome on the waterface

With the exception of 'waterface' being replaced by 'aquaface', the only changes between this version and that which opens *Finnegans Wake* occurred in the first sentence, which reads in the *Wake*:

> riverrun, past Eve and Adam's, from swerve of shore to bend of bay, brings us by a commodius vicus of recirculation back to Howth Castle and Environs.

Every important theme sounded in the final version of the opening paragraph is present in the earliest draft of the passage, and some are expressed in forms close to the final text. As usual, revision was primarily an elaboration of the basic form. In the earliest draft the geographical presence of HCE dominates the Dublin scene in 'Howth Castle & Environs!' The circular structure of 'the book of Doublends Jined' is evident in the immediate revision of the first sentence, where 'brings us to' is obviously a continuation of a concluding sentence already planned. By the *transition* version this has been expanded into 'riverrun brings us back to', thus introducing the Liffey's place in the cyclic plan of the book and emphasizing the fluid nature of Joyce's work. The words 'brings us back to', along with the change of 'arrived' to 'rearrived' in the revision of the first draft, imply that the cycles of the book are repetitions of archetypal cycles.

During the early development of the opening passage additional phrases were inserted to 'thicken' the fundamen-

tal motifs. 'By arclight', inserted into the first draft, prepares the way for succeeding references to Noah's rainbow, while 'topsawyer's' in the *transition* text suggests Tom Sawyer as the American counterpart of Shaun, the dominant brother. Even the smallest changes are significant: 'doubling' appears in *transition* as 'doublin' to remind the reader that the process being described is a universal one, as true of Dublin as of Georgia; and 'thouartpatrick' is altered to 'thouartpeatrick' so as to introduce an Irish 'peat rick'.

A more extended example of this 'stratification' is found in the development of the Swift-Stella-Vanessa motif through the early versions.

> . . . not yet had twin sesthers played siege to twone jonathan.

> . . . not yet [though] all's fair in vanessy were sosie sesthers wroth with twone jonathan.

> . . . not yet, though all's fair in vanessy, were sosie sesthers wroth with twone nathandjoe.

Here the additions amplify the original theme. 'Vanessy' suggests Vanessa. 'Sosie' replaces 'twin' as a combination of 'saucy' and 'Susannah'; 'wroth' hints at Ruth; Esther was already present in 'sesthers'; and the authors of the *Skeleton Key to 'Finnegans Wake'* [Joseph Campbell and H. M. Robinson] remind us that the Biblical stories of Susannah, Ruth and Esther, like that of Swift and his two lovers, involve 'the loves of old men for young girls'. 'Nathandjoe', which replaces 'jonathan' in the *transition* version, 'is an anagram for Jonathan (Dean Jonathan Swift) split in two and turned head over heels by his two young-girl loves, Stella and Vanessa'.

Joyce's skilful shaping of this passage indicates that by late 1926 the density which characterizes the final text of *Finnegans Wake* was already his ideal, and that he could achieve it with complete confidence. The years 1926-27 marked a turning point in the evolution of the *Wake.* From this point on Joyce was working to a clearly visualized structural pattern, and aiming for linguistic effects that he had already fully mastered in scattered passages. The remaining twelve years of laborious composition were given over to completing the design and recasting the entire work in his achieved 'final' style. This period could best be described, in the words of the young Stephen Dedalus [in *Stephen Hero*] as years of 'slow elaborative patience'.

Between 1927 and 1930 Joyce published advanced versions of the first and third Parts of *Finnegans Wake* in the *avant-garde* magazine *transition*. Although he did not share many of the radical theories held by *transition*'s editors and contributors, and remained aloof from most of the 'movements' and 'manifestoes' supported by the magazine, he welcomed the opportunity to revise the major portion of his early work for publication. Without the stimulus provided by the *transition* deadlines it is doubtful if Joyce would have ever finished the *Wake* in its present form. During 1927 the earliest complete version of Part I was published serially in the first eight issues of the new journal. The first chapter, which appeared in the April issue, was so well liked by the editors that Joyce agreed to fill in the gaps that still existed in Part I. He joined the section already published in the *Contact Collection of Contemporary Writers* (*Finnegans Wake* 30-34) with the episode that had appeared in the *Criterion* (*Finnegans Wake* 104-25) by 'finishing off' the intervening two episodes, which had been drafted in 1923-24. He then found it necessary to connect 'The Hen' (I. v) with 'Shem the Penman' (I. vii) by a new episode which was composed at high speed and under great pressure. Meanwhile all the previously published episodes were revised and expanded for their appearance in *transition*. Finally in November 1927 the eighth chapter appeared and the first Part of *Work in Progress* was in print, running without a break from 'riverrun' to the close of *Anna Livia Plurabelle*. Future revisions of this Part may be classified as 'secondary', consisting in the extension of major themes and the inclusion of dependent motifs.

An interesting view of the manner in which Joyce collected material during the *transition* years (1927-38) is provided by Eugene Jolas:

> We saw a good deal of him during those years. . . . All his friends collaborated then in the preparations of the fragments destined for *transition:* Stuart Gilbert, Padraic Colum, Elliot Paul, Robert Sage, Helen and Giorgio Joyce, and others. He worked with painstaking care, almost with pedantry. He had invented an intricate system of symbols permitting him to pick out the new words and paragraphs he had been writing down for years, and which referred to the multiple characters in his creation. He would work for weeks, often late at night, with the help of one or the other of his friends. It seemed almost a collective composition in the end, for he let his friends participate in his inventive zeal, as they searched through numberless notebooks with mysterious reference points to be inserted in the text. When finished, the proof looked as if a coal-heaver's sooty hands had touched it. ['My Friend James Joyce', in *James Joyce: Two Decades of Criticism,* edited by Seon Givens]

The method described by Jolas is reminiscent of the late revisions to *Ulysses.* Continual embroidery upon a fixed pattern characterized Joyce's work on both *Ulysses* and the *Wake*; the only difference is that the process was carried on for a much longer period of time in the later work, and that Joyce abandoned the conventional structure of language to permit this further elaboration.

The year 1928 opened with the publication of 'The Triangle' (later 'The Muddest Thick That Was Ever Heard Dump', now *Finnegans Wake* 282-304) in the February issue of *transition*. Then Joyce turned to the four 'watches' of Shaun and began to revise them; they appeared in *transition* between March 1928 and November 1929. At the same time he was re-working *Anna Livia* for separate publication by Crosby Gaige in October. Joyce had a great deal of trouble with his eyes during this period, and between June and October of 1928 he was able to write only one piece, 'a short description of madness and blindness descending upon Swift' which was never included in the *Wake.*

> Unslow, malswift, pro mean, proh noblesse, Atrahora, Melancolores, nears; whose glauque eyes glitt bedimmd to imm! whose fingrings creep o'er skull: till, qwench! asterr mist calls estarr and grauw! honath John raves homes glowcoma.

This passage mirrors Joyce's fear of blindness and madness which was accentuated by his ill health at the time, a fear that was to hamper the progress of his work more and more in the coming years. His letters contain frequent allusions to exhaustion and nervous strain, caused to some degree by his insistence on repeated and intensive revisions of each episode before publication. These last-minute changes often produced the added anxiety of delayed publication.

As soon as the proofs of the Crosby Gaige *Anna Livia* had been corrected in May 1928, Joyce began to concern himself with the revision of his three 'fables' which had already appeared in *transition* and were to comprise his next publication in book form: 'The Mookse and the Gripes', 'The Muddest Thick That Was Ever Heard Dump', and 'The Ondt and the Gracehoper'. The recasting of the fables extended well into the spring of 1929, and in August they appeared under the title *Tales Told of Shem and Shaun.*

In February 1929 the third 'watch' of Shaun was published in *transition* No. 15, and the fourth followed in November (*transition* No. 18), thus completing the initial publication of Part III. Part of the third watch was then revised for book publication, and came out in June 1930 under the title *Haveth Childers Everywhere.* In re-working this section Joyce utilized to full advantage his techniques of 'orchestration', creating more and more complex portmanteau words in his search for simultaneity of effect. This aim is exemplified in the 'stratification' of the following passage:

> That was Communicator a former colonel. A disincarnated spirit called Sebastiam may phone shortly. Let us cheer him up a little and make an appointment for a future date. Hello, Communicate! how's the butts? Everseptic! . . . So enjoying of old thick whiles, in tall white hat of four reflections he would puffout a smokefull bock. [1929]

> That was Communicator, a former Colonel. A disincarnated spirit, called Sebastion, from the Rivera in Januero, (he is not all hear) may fernspreak shortly with messuages from my deadported. Let us cheer him up a little and make an appunkment for a future date. Hello, Commudicate! How's the buttes? Everscepistic! . . . So enjoying of old thick whiles, in haute white toff's hoyt of our formcd reflections, with stock of eisen all his prop, so buckely hosiered from the Royal Leg, and his puertos mugnum. He would puffout a dhymful bock. [1930]

The revised text has been enriched with several geographical names: the Riviera and Rio de Janeiro ('Rivera in Januero'), Everest ('Everscepistic'), and Eisenstadt ('stock of eisen'). In the latter part of the passage HCE is a white-capped volcano; his snow-white head and smoking cigar are the mountain peak, while ports ('puertos mugnum') lie at his feet. This image has been foreshadowed in the second version by two revisions: the substitution of 'buttes' for 'butt', and the addition of 'deadported' (departed). 'Messuages', with its overtones of 'messages' and 'assuages', as well as its root meaning of 'house and lands', is a typical Joycean addition. 'Buckely hosiered' combines the image of buckled hose with a reference to Buckley (who shot HCE as the Russian General). The alteration of 'Everseptic' to 'Everscepistic' reflects a characteristic compression, for here three attributes of HCE have been merged into the original word. His identification with all mountains is in 'Everest'; he is a 'sceptic'; he is tainted—'septic'—and at the same time 'pistic', pure as the oil with which Mary anointed the feet of Jesus.

There can be no doubt that in revising this passage Joyce multiplied its references and enriched his text, but only at the expense of obscuring some of the original (and important) meanings: 'Everseptic' is overshadowed by the more complex 'Everscepistic'. Too often the process of deformation diffuses the basic effect instead of intensifying it; in many cases the earlier versions of a passage contain essential elements which are blurred in the final text. This is an inherent defect of Joyce's method.

In the late months of 1929, with Parts I and III of his work already in print, Joyce 'felt a sudden kind of drop' in the impetus behind his writing. The constant strain of working to a schedule, coupled with his ill health, had left him completely exhausted. It was not until September 1930 that he could bring himself to begin work on the virtually untouched Part II. With no deadlines to be met, the composition of II. i proceeded slowly. By November 22nd he had finished a 'first draft of about two thirds of the first section of Part II (2,200 words) which came out like drops of blood'.

The nervous illness of Joyce's daughter, Lucia, which reached a crisis during 1931-32, caused a drastic reduction in the pace of his work. The composition of Part II advanced slowly and under great difficulties, interrupted by occasional revisions of Part I. The draft of II. i was finally completed in 1932, but somehow the MS. disappeared and Joyce spent the best part of November reconstructing it from notes and his memory. The chapter finally appeared in February 1933 (*transition* No. 22).

Joyce's work of the 1930's may be distinguished from his earlier efforts by the complete control of his material that it exhibits. No longer was composition a process of exploration, a search for structural solutions or the perfection of linguistic devices. Instead the ultimate form of the book was fixed in his mind, and—as in the last stages of writing *Ulysses*—he elaborated like a mosaic worker upon a predetermined pattern. His friends of the time who were familiar with his methods, especially Louis Gillet and Eugene Jolas, have recorded their impressions of Joyce at work, and they attest that he held the incredibly complex form of the *Wake* in his mind as a single image, and could move from one section to another with complete freedom. The first drafts made during the 1930's were much more comprehensive than those of the 1920's, since Joyce had a precise notion of each episode's final shape and its rela-

tionship to surrounding episodes. The number of cross-references added in revision became fewer, and were of less importance, for each successive episode was written against a background of greater accumulated material and with more 'finished' sections in mind.

If we compare the version of II. i which appeared in *transition* (February 1933) with the corresponding episode in *Finnegans Wake,* these alterations in Joyce's method will become clear. The 1933 text of II. i was enlarged to one-third again its original length before final publication, but the changes were almost entirely minor additions which enrich the narrative with secondary references but leave the original intent untouched. The initial phrasing usually remains the same and the additions are inserted between phrases which they expand or qualify.

For example, on page 232 of *Finnegans Wake* the outcast Glugg (Shem), having thrown a fit and danced a jig, is about to recover control of himself when a message arrives from Izod renewing his hopes. In the 1933 version this paragraph is already associated with Swift and his girl-lover Esther Johnson through the use of the 'little language' (Ppt, MD) in the last two sentences.

> Stop up, mavrone, and sit in my lap. Pepette,
> though I'd much rather not. Like things are m.
> ds. is all in vincibles. Decoded.

In the 1939 version the correspondence between Izod and Stella is further strengthened by additions to a sentence earlier in the paragraph describing the 'message' from Izod.

> When a message interfering intermitting inter-
> skips from them on herzian waves, a butterfly
> from her zipclasped handbag, awounded dove
> astarted from, escaping out her forecotes.
> *transition* (February 1933)

> When (pip!) a message interfering intermitting
> interskips from them (pet!) on herzian waves,
> (call her venicey names! call her a stell!) a butter-
> fly from her zipclasped handbag, a wounded
> dove astarted from, escaping out her forecotes.
> **(Finnegans Wake)**

Through these additions Izod becomes a star ('a stell') containing both Stella and Vanessa ('venicey'): the rival lovers are one in her. 'Venice' in 'venicey' also suggests *Othello,* another story of tragic love between a young girl and an older man. The children in their games are re-enacting the Swiftian archetype of frustrated love, reminding one of Earwicker's incestuous desire for Issy. The message from Izod is a *Journal to Stella* in reverse, framed in the same 'little language'. However, Izod is not only Stella-Vanessa but Swift as well, and the twins are masculine versions of the rival lovers: a similar reversal occurs later in the chapter when she becomes 'la pau' Leonie' (Napoleon) who 'has the choice of her lives between Josephinus and Mario-Louis', obviously Joséphine and Marie Louise. But the important thing to notice about these revisions is that they do not add a new dimension to the passage but expand and refine allusions which are quite obvious in the 1933 version.

To obtain a clearer idea of Joyce's late revisions we must

examine the expansion of a longer passage, such as the following from near the end of II. i. The children are returning home from their games, and at the conclusion of the quotation the door is slammed behind them with an echo of the hundred-letter thunderclap first heard in the third paragraph of the *Wake.* I have italicized those words added in the course of revision; the entire 1933 text was retained without alteration.

> While, *running about their ways, going and coming, now at rhimba rhomba, now in trippiza trappaza, pleating a pattern Gran Geamatron showed them of gracehoppers, auntskippers and coneyfarm leppers,* they jeerilied along, *durian gay and marian maidcap, lou Dariou beside la Matieto, all boy more all girl singoutfeller longa house blong store Huddy,* whilest nin nin nin nin that Boorman's clock, a winny on the tinny side, ninned nin nin nin nin, about old Father Barley how he got up of a morning arley and he met with a plattonem blondes named Hips and Haws and fell in with a fellows of Trinity some header Skowood Shaws like (*You'll catch it, don't fret, Mrs Tummy Lupton! Come indoor, Scoffynosey, and shed your swank!*) auld Daddy Deacon who could stow well his place of beacon but he never could hold his kerosene's candle to (*The nurse'll give it you, stickypots! And you wait, my lasso, fecking the twine!*) bold Farmer Burleigh who wuck up in a hurlywurly where he huddly could wuddle to wallow his weg tillbag of the baker's booth to beg of (*You're well held now, Missy Cheekspeer, and your panto's off! Fie, for shame, Ruth Wheatacre, after all the booz said!*) illed Diddiddy Achin for the prize of a pease of bakin *with a pinch of the panch of the ponch in jurys* for (*Ah, crabeyes, I have you, showing off to the world with that gape in your stocking!*) Wold Forrester Farley who, *in deesperation of deispiration at the diasporation of his diesparation,* was found of the round of the sound of the lound of the. Lukkedoerendunandurraskewdylooshoofermoyportertooryzooysphalnabortan*sporthaokan*sakroidverjkapakkapuk.

The middle section of the thunder-word, 'fermoyporter', combines HCE's specific Dublin name (Porter) with *fermez la porte* and a cry for more drink ('moyporter'). The additions to the paragraph, which appear at first to be merely in the cause of onomatopœia, actually embody a number of significant expansions. 'Trippiza trappaza' and 'rhimba rhomba' point forward to 'triv and quad' and the lessons of the twins in the next episode, where Dolph helps Kev with a geometrical analysis of the 'Gran Geamatron' mentioned in this passage. 'Gracehoppers, auntskippers and coneyfarm leppers'—the followers of Glugg, Chuff and Izod—also foreshadow a later section, the fable of 'The Ondt and the Gracehoper'.

'Durian gay' relates the Glugg-Chuff antithesis to Oscar Wilde's tale of dual personality, *The Picture of Dorian Gray,* while simultaneously combining 'dour an' gay', the opposed temperaments of the two brothers who are each one-half of HCE's dual personality. The connection with Wilde himself is also significant, since he figures elsewhere in the *Wake* as part of the homosexual motif. 'Marian maidcap' is, of course, the giddy Izod, who plays Maid Marian in the children's adventures.

Among the other allusions added by Joyce, the recurring groups of four elements ('nin nin nin nin', 'with a pinch of the panch of the ponch in jurys') culminating in the series 'in deesperation of deispiration at the diasporation of his diesparation' reinforce the four-part rhythm which precedes the thunder-word in both versions: 'was found of the round of the sound of the lound of the'. The last of these four-part insertions can be identified by its '-ation' endings as a comment of the Twelve, the customers at Earwicker's pub. 'Deesperation' probably stems from the French *déesse* meaning 'goddess'. 'Deis' is an obsolete form of 'dais'; it introduces connotations of height and distinction, and suggests an elevated stage for acting. 'Diasporation' means 'fragmentation', specifically the Dispersion of the disobedient prophesied in the Old Testament (Deuteronomy xxviii. 25). And 'diesparation' reminds one of the *Dies irae* and the Last Judgment.

In the alphabetical sequence of these four words lies the plot of the episode: spurred on by the 'goddess' Izod, Glugg and Chuff strive to 'elevate' themselves in her eyes. Also, the machinery of the episode is that of a stage pro-

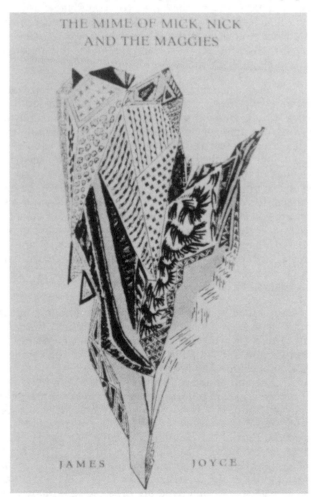

Dust jacket designed by Lucia Joyce for a section of Finnegans Wake *published in 1934.*

duction. When the games break up, the children are 'dispersed' to their various homes, and the thunderclap which will accompany the Last Judgment is heard when the father of the twins slams the door behind them.

But the progress of the episode has also been along 'Vico's road', down which the children march. The Divine age (*déesse*) is followed by the Heroic ('deis', the giants), which is in turn succeeded by the Dispersion of democracy and individualism, until the divine thunderclap ends the cycle and provides energy for 'recirculation': Omega becomes Alpha, New Zealand is replaced by Newer Aland, and the pattern is repeated. This presentation of Vico's scheme for the race is accompanied and paralleled by the individual cycle of Birth, Marriage, Death, and Resurrection. Thus Joyce's last insertion before the thunder-noise recapitulates the action of the chapter, relates it to the book's major philosophic theme, and explains the significance of the hundred-letter word that follows. Such was the multi-levelled condensation he aimed at in his later revisions. However, these late changes rarely add a new and significant dimension to the text; instead, they repeat and amplify elements of the basic narrative. Joyce's method was that of accretion, and such a method has no inherent boundaries. Often the final revisions enrich the text, but there are times when they lead to redundancy. Joyce's method, in its lack of discrimination and selection, reflects his ultimate purpose in the *Wake,* which was to make all his knowledge and experience implicit in the microcosmic life of a single family.

It is no coincidence that those who observed Joyce at work on *Finnegans Wake* often employ the same analogy that struck Frank Budgen while he watched the making of *Ulysses,* the analogy with mosaic-work. In a mosaic the basic outline is clear and simple, the individual pieces have fixed colours and dimensions. But within the intermediate divisions of the form the pieces are grouped according to less exact principles of design, and one piece can be exchanged for another similar unit without affecting the composition as a whole. In a like fashion, the intermediate divisions of the *Wake* are loosely-organized groups of associated items, and within their general context similar word-groups can be exchanged or moved about without greatly affecting the total impact of the passage. There is no inevitability to their placing.

The comparison with mosaic-work is illuminating, but it cannot be used as a justification for Joyce's final aesthetic aims. There is a crucial distinction between a composition in colour and line which can be viewed as a single image, and a composition in words which must be read over a period of time and united in retrospect. It is a commonplace of Joycean criticism to justify the techniques of *Finnegans Wake* by comparing them with early Celtic design, such as that found in the *Book of Kells.* Joyce encouraged this approach. Part of the chapter on ALP's 'Mamafesta' is a parody of Sir Edward Sullivan's description of the *Book of Kells,* as the authors of the *Skeleton Key to 'Finnegans Wake'* point out. Joyce seems to have regarded the 'TUNC' page of that work, the incredibly involved illumination of Matthew xxvii. 38 (TUNC CRU—CIFIXERANT—XPI CUM EO DU—OS LATRONES), as having a special affinity with his own art: the word 'Tunc' introduces 'pidgin fella Balkelly's' (and Joyce's) defence of the *Wake* in Part IV. The similarities between the two works are indeed striking. As Herbert Read has said, 'the closest analogy to the literary method of *Work in Progress* is perhaps to be found in the early graphic art of Joyce's own country, the abstract involved ornament of the Celts'. Here is a very good description of such art by a German writer:

> There are certain simple motives whose interweaving and commingling determines the character of this ornament. At first there is only the dot, the line, the ribbon; later the curve, the circle, the spiral, the zigzag, and an S-shaped decoration are employed. Truly, no great wealth of motives! But what variety is attained by the manner of their employment! Here they run parallel, then entwined, now latticed, now knotted, now plaited, then again brought through one another in a symmetrical checker of knotting and plaiting. Fantastically confused patterns are thus evolved, whose puzzle asks to be unravelled, whose convolutions seem alternatively to seek and avoid each other, whose component parts, endowed as it were with sensibility, captivate sight and sense in passionately vital movement. [From the prefatory letter to Charles Duff 's *James Joyce and the Plain Reader,* 1932]

But no matter how close the parallels, the undoubted success of Celtic illumination cannot stand as authority for Joyce's interminable elaborations upon the basic themes of the *Wake.* Few readers would deny that the effects Joyce achieved by subjecting his early drafts to 'a series of gross exaggerations' are partially negated by the loss of that sense of inevitability which Harry Levin sees as 'the touchstone of a more reserved style' [Levin, *James Joyce,* 1944].

Between 1932 and 1938 Part II of the *Wake* gradually took form. The first chapter was published separately in 1934 under the title *The Mime of Mick Nick and the Maggies.* The next year those portions of the schoolroom episode which surround 'The Muddest Thick That Was Ever Heard Dump' were published in *transition,* thus completing a version of II. ii. By February 1937 the first pages of II. iii were ready for publication, and the next year another large segment of II. iii was printed in *transition* (No. 27, April-May 1938).

The episode of the Twelve at the Tavern (II. iii), the longest and most complex in *Finnegans Wake,* was one of the last sections written. It stands at the physical centre of the *Wake* and serves a function similar to that of the *Circe* episode in *Ulysses:* most of the major motifs are recapitulated in it. It is interesting to note that the Tavern scene appears at approximately the same stage in the composition of the *Wake* as does *Circe* in the making of *Ulysses.* After *Circe* was completed only parts of the *Nostos* remained to be written, along with a general revision of the entire novel. After the Tavern scene had been constructed it only remained to combine the early 'Tristan and Isolde' fragment with 'Mamalujo', thus forming II. iv; to complete the concluding Part IV; and to tighten up the work as a whole. In *Work in Progress,* as in the making of *Ulysses,* Joyce composed from both ends at once, finally drawing the two halves together in a scene of transformation and recapitulation. We might compare those early (1923) fragments which ultimately found their place in Part IV of the *Wake* ('St. Kevin' and 'pidgin fella Berkeley') with the 'preliminary sketches for the final sections' of *Ulysses* that Joyce is said to have made early in 1914.

Joyce began to prepare *Finnegans Wake* for book publication in 1936, when he revised the latest printed text of Part I for submission to Faber and Faber. The next year the galleys for Part I were ready: the sheet for the first page of the *Wake* bears the printer's date '12 March 1937'. The fact that the book was being printed in England increased the difficulty of correcting proof, as did Joyce's habit of making extensive revisions on successive sets of galleys. During 1938 the proof sheets poured in while he was still composing Part IV. It was not until mid-November that the last words of the book were written, and final revisions were made after this. Louis Gillet remembers that corrections were being sent by telegram up to the very last moment. Although the trade edition of *Finnegans Wake* did not appear until 4 May 1939, Joyce received the first bound copy in time for his fifty-seventh birthday celebration on February 2nd, when he revealed the title that he had jealously guarded for so long. Sixteen years of exploration and elaboration had ended. (pp. 76-100)

A. Walton Litz, in his The Art of James Joyce: Method and Design in "Ulysses" and "Finnegans Wake," *Oxford University Press, London, 1961, 152 p.*

Frederick J. Hoffman   (essay date 1966)

[*In the following essay, Hoffman considers Joyce's attitude expressed in* Finnegans Wake *toward change and diversity, especially as manifested in the figure of the father, or creator.*]

It is scarcely an original thought, but surely one worth repeating: Joyce began his career hating and fearful of flux, chaos, and disorder; he ended it, in *Finnegans Wake,* by making a virtue of the reality of flux. The sensual world is ever-present in his work. Colors symbolically and imagistically dominate within it; tastes, sounds, tactile sensations provide the vibrancy of the Dublin scene and of the world abroad, always in the act of 'doublin their mumper'. Beyond these matters, there is the autobiographical reference, which is more difficult to measure. There are several significant facts it will be useful to remember. Joyce's father is the 'pivot' of his reflections upon family; in the beginning, he is shocked by the disorder (and its attendant filth and stinks) that his father can cause simply by not being a responsible family man. Later, his father's aberrant ways, while still recalled, are less important than his charm, his good voice, and his love of the 'good time'. In the end, in *Finnegans Wake* the father principle, and the father who exemplifies it, undergoes a curious change; Joyce, the son of his father, becomes through his role as creator, the father of the father image who suffers and himself creates. As he puts it in *Finnegans Wake*: 'Creator he has created for his creatured ones a creation'.

The story is perhaps a familiar one, and yet there are new insights into the family pattern. One of the major crises in modern literature (and, by implication, in modern society) concerns the stability of family. The great Jewish thinkers insist upon family cohesiveness; Catholics all but make a law of the inseparableness of man, wife and children. In the Protestant world, the individual responsibility overcomes family demands, and there occurs a breakdown of the idea of family as moral center. Max Weber and Carl Gustav Jung provide the economic and psychological versions of the decline.

The obvious truth is that the family is a microcosm of orders beyond it, geographical, cultural and universal. And, of course, the father becomes a 'major man', a creator and a primary cause at one and the same time. His acts, and the will behind them, are defined immediately and extensively in terms of their consequences. The disorder following upon the Joyce family's moves from one place to another, and upon the behavior of Joyce's father, is responsible for a crucial puzzle in Joyce's work. In the beginning, the creature tries to define himself simply by separating from the family and its religious supports. Joyce's attention is fixed upon the young creature who will rebel against his creator (both father and God, who are often interestingly merged in *Finnegans Wake*) by changing his status from that of creature to that of creator. Except in *Stephen Hero*, which we should really not consider as

---

Joyce's "Shorthand" for composing *Finnegans Wake:*

In compiling notes in his workbooks prior to the composition of the various sections of his book, Joyce made use of a number of signs, the so-called sigla, to designate characters. There are only a few of these signs. The principal ones and the name affixed to each are:

  ⋔ H.C.E., Humphrey Chimpden Earwicker, Finnegan
  △ Anna Livia Plurabelle
  [Shem
  ∧ Shaun
  ⊏ Shem-Shaun
  ⊥ Isolde (undifferentiated)
  ⊣ ⊢Isolde (the two Isoldes, Brittany and Ireland)
  ◠ Isolde (the Rainbow Girls)
  X The Four Historians (Mamalujo)
  O The Twelve
  S Sigurdsen
  K Kate
  P S. Patrick
  T Tristan
  ⚡ The Snake
  ☐ The Container (coffin, house or book)

Joyce used these symbols not only in the workbooks (for example, "⋔ smokes?" or "⋔ HcE chemical"), and in drafts but also in correspondence and even sporadically in the published text.

Danis Rose and John O'Hanlon, in their Understanding Finnegans Wake: A Guide to the Narrative of James Joyce's Masterpiece, *1982.*

being in the 'Joyce canon' because he himself did not so consider it, Joyce consistently poses father against son or sons, measures the spatial and psychological distances between them, and muses over the puzzle and (at times) the farce of creation itself.

I believe that one of the great contributions made by *Finnegans Wake* to modern literary thought is its suggestion concerning a solution of the problems of father-family and creator-creature relationship. This is a solution worked out without benefit of either clergy or psychiatrist. Joyce's sources are characteristically 'modern', in the fact that they are varied, even esoteric, and the result of intellectual improvisation in the establishment of a 'tradition'. The fact of most interest to us at this moment is not the cyclical theory of history, but the Viconian idea that God the creator, in the act of creation, commits 'original sin'. To say the least, Vico's God is bemused in consequence of the act of creation; it is preceded by thunder (which is God's way of stammering and hence His admission of guilt). Earwicker plays the God role as the father-creator, but (as the creature of God) in the sense of Joyce's remark 'Teems of times and happy returns. The seim anew', he is also a part of a recurring process, which God had set going by His initial creative act.

It ought surely to be illuminating to consider some of the characteristic images according to which Joyce has tried to define the father and his relationship to family. To begin with, there is the characteristic to-do of 'building'. The 'seim anew' involves creation and re-creation and rebuilding from ruins. Fathers topple, but they also create in the sense of fashioning, building, designing. So the Finnegan of folklore is a hod-carrier who, having tippled, loses his balance and topples from his ladder, which in itself rests against a structure in the act of being 'built'. But before this happens, he has been 'Bygmester Finnegan, of the Stuttering Hand', this man 'of hod, cement and edifices' who 'piled buildung supra buildung pon the banks for the livers by the Soangso'. Of course there is no doubt of the sexual implications; the physical image of the god Finnegan-Earwicker-*et al.* is that of the body beginning with the rock at Howth and extending to Phoenix Park, with the monolith 'erection' of the Wellington (Wellingdone, Willingdone, etc.) monument 'standing' in the phallic role. A *structure* honors a great builder (and destroyer), but it is also the phallic instrument of the business of building. 'Buildung' has several other meanings: *bildung,* as in the *bildungsroman* which recounts human development; and *dung,* which here signifies the state of decay to which the body and the substance which supports its life returns. After all, it is from a dungheap that the letter defending HCE is accidentally recovered.

We need to appreciate the 'grand mixture' here: building (creating, fathering) is closely identified with the counter-activity of destroying and dying. The basic source of the Viconian cycle is the steady move of man and society from beginnings to endings to renewals. Earwicker 'dies a little' with each addition to his family; but he also literally *co-habits,* lies next to and on Anna Livia. The Liffey *flows* at his side and provides a continuing source of amniotic anticipation of life. It, and she, also flows into the seas, and

thus is also dying; but in the course of moving out of life, she also moves back into it, the amniosis serving her as well as her children. The image of Earwicker's creativity is monolithic (his image is of rock and monumental structures); the key quality of Anna's is 'plurability'. Her resource is that of starting life, protecting it, and releasing it. Nothing so brilliantly defines this fusion of death and life as the closing-opening sentence of the *Wake*: 'A way a lone a last a loved a long the riverrun, past Eve and Adam's, from swerve of shore to bend of bay, brings us by a commodius vicus of recirculation back to Howth Castle and Environs'. Moving out into the sea of death, Anna Livia, 'a lone', becomes daughterwife to his sonhusband; the life process goes on, and she is 'allaniuvia pulchrabelled' because 'Now a younger's there'.

These acts of building, 'erecting', destroying, decaying, and renewing are more important in the perspective of Joyce's early creations. In a sense *Stephen Hero* was Joyce annotating his daily existence, and enhancing it; it is a diary of things happening and to come. Next, over a period of some eight years, Joyce replaced this manuscript with a 'portrait' [that became *A Portrait of the Artist as a Young Man*]. The word is itself important: Stephen is no longer 'heroic', but the subject of a work done by a man who looks at him from a distance. The distance is not great, but it is fairly important: not only years, but the act of exile have determined it. Joyce, in leaving Dublin, separated himself from the self who lived there. The consequences are partly viewed in the irony and skeptical reserve with which he views his creature. He has not yet reached the stage of the Viconian God's puzzlement over the results of his creative act; but the Stephen of *Portrait* is a model exercise in the drama of youthful separation from authority; more, it is a way of defining the arrogation of authority, removing it from the world of teachers, priests, fathers, and investing it in the rebellious self.

The squalor of Stephen's home life is a consequence of the father's decline. The breaking of the home forces Stephen into the streets, away from the family center, and he observes there poverty, filth, chaos. 'He wanted to meet in the real world the unsubstantial image which his soul so constantly beheld'. His mind and senses entertain the prospects of sensual bliss, but he is wary of actual contact. On a trip to Cork with his father, he visits Queen's College; there, in the anatomy theatre, Stephen reads the word *Foetus* 'cut several times in the dark stained wood'. The word startles him into thinking about past students, who have ironically left, as a 'symbol of permanence', this sign of their interest for others to see.

Stephen associates the biological implications of the word with the chaotic world his father's indulgences have created. Biology abases the intellect, as Stephen believes, inferring from the 'den of monstrous images' he has himself tolerated and encouraged. Disappointment in the father causes him to seek other sources of authority. The Church is revived in his mind as a father substitute: the priest will be father, and he may himself be priest, which is to say, 'father', without the implications the word has in his own family. The Church acts temporarily in the role of providing order and protecting him from the chaos of the outside world. But ultimately it will have an opposite effect: infinite extensions of both bodily pain and the pain of absence haunt Stephen in the days of the retreat sermons. To become a priest, after having made full confession, occurs to him as a way through.

The important point in Stephen's education is not his temporary sense of vocation, but his eventual act of secular conversion. This conversion is partway a recovery of his appreciation of sensual beauty: 'Heavenly God! cried Stephen's soul, in an outburst of profane joy'. It is also an attempt to set 'beauty' against chaos: Stephen walks through the disorder of Dublin, shaking from his ears the sound of 'a mad nun screeching', trying to replace it with the songs of Ben Jonson or the 'dainty songs of the Elizabethans'.

All of this is informed with an irony cultivated by Stephen's creator over a period of eight years of separation of creator from creature. The tone is sympathetic; he will 'hear him out'; and the discourses on beauty and creation are marvels in themselves. Like the library 'lecture' on Shakespeare's *Hamlet,* Stephen's discussion of *integritas, consonantia,* and *claritas* have the marks of genius but are nevertheless also locally and temporally caused. As before, he is trying to shut out the disorder caused by his father's defection. The 'many', the 'schwärmerei' of unordered life, is simply ugly and hateful, and needs to be kept within aesthetic bounds. Hence Stephen's mind works in terms of 'bounding lines', of precise forms and central illuminations. The great attractiveness of the 'epiphany' to him is not its divinity but its having marvellously worked in terms of a point of essence. In this way commonplace and even ugly moments may be invested with aesthetic power, in the sense that the 'ostensoir' of Baudelaire's 'Harmonie du soir' gives an aesthetic more than a religious illumination.

In all cases there is some one who assumes the role of the 'monothoid', the man who wishes to conquer the many by assuming it under the rubric of the one. Joyce's own conscience will not permit this easy way out of disorder; so the advocate of the one is not infrequently mocked, even—in the figure of a Lucifer, who arrogates God's power unto himself—treated as blasphemer. Stephen's career in *Ulysses* shows a further distance of created from creature. Here the riot of conundrum and paradox becomes even more outrageously amusing: two creators, who are two fathers (the one of the other, the other of himself); a father-god image who, having lost a son, seeks another and becomes not only father but God-companion to Stephen. Stephen's assertion of mind's power over thing is here even less convincing, because he is himself a victim of sensations which cannot be expelled as they were in the *Portrait.*

Ulysses is above all a testimony of the triumph of gestation over death. The 'Hades' episode reminds us clearly of the naturalistic odors and images of corruption; the 'conqueror worm' is treated as a comic inversion of its original function of horror. But the oncoming recurrences of life, as they do in *Finnegans Wake,* take the sting from the haunts of death (Bloom in the cemetery, Stephen staring in fright at the image of his dead mother who has risen to

haunt him). As in *Finnegans Wake,* the father becomes the 'maker', the builder, whose 'erections' are solid achievements:

> . . . By heaven, Theodore Purefoy, thou hast done a doughty deed and no botch! Thou art, I vow, the remarkablest progenitor barring none in this chaffering allincluding most farraginous chronicle. Astounding! In her lay a Godframed Godgiven preformed possibility which thou hast fructified with thy modicum of man's work. . . .
>
> (*Ulysses*)

In other words, the multiplicity of Dublin (the 'doublin their mumper' of *Finnegans Wake*) is no longer a frightful thing. The promise of Mrs Purefoy's ninth child, celebrated as it is in the 'farraginous chronicle' of 'Oxen of the Sun', has a significance beyond its adding to 'their mumper'.

Finnegans Wake is the culminating act in Joyce's conquest of his fear of the many. Not only are Shem's 'heroic acts' mocked (exile, the writings, the search for an aesthetic surrogate for life); all attempts to secure him against the flux are ignominiously defeated. Momentarily a Lucifer in *Ulysses* (in a scene which has at least a 'drunken glory'), Shem becomes a comic devil in *Finnegans Wake*; and his rebellion against not only father and family but life itself is treated with rich irony. Shem is no longer a lonely and arrogant spirit, proudly announcing his *non serviam;* he is actually (in being Shaun's twin, hence his 'identical opposite') the reverse of himself. I think one may say that *Finnegans Wake* is an immense 'accommodation' of the many, and that the multiplicity of life is given order as an intrinsic quality of renewal and recurrence.

The 'seim anew', the father is no longer a disrespected, irresponsible creator; like Lawrence, Joyce atoned for early unflattering portraits by establishing and defending a 'father principle' in his late work. The designs of explanation in *Finnegans Wake* are no longer confined to the neat indulgences of mind's-play; they have been based upon principles of organic growth and decay, recurrence, opposites which combine to make identities, a universal set of fluctuant geometries, with the minds of the participants playfully enacting the role of comically erudite annotator upon the facts of existence.

I do not mean that the father is glorified; and he is certainly not elevated to the level to which Lawrence brings his memory of the father image. Joyce's HCE is not so much a god figure as he is the representative 'maker' of vital abundance and disorder, the 'folks forefather' (*Finnegans Wake*). There is a constant stir and susurrus, which rises to loud clamor and subsides to 'confidential' gossip, but continues to surround his character. In other words, the 'truth' is as difficult to discover in *words* (each man uses words differently) as it is in things. Throughout, HCE is successor to Simon Dedalus, whose identity is public, associated with the children he has fathered, the friends he has made, the tavern, street, and out-of-doors comment and gossip he has stimulated and abetted. At the same time, HCE, like Bloom, is the alternate father figure as well: the foreigner, suspected of vague and shadowy sins, an intruder and invader. Joyce, the exile, makes his major figures exiles-in-Dublin, by way of compensation for his being Dubliner-in-Paris. The father of the *Wake* is therefore at the center of rumor, gossip, debate, and abuse; but he is solidly *there,* 'the pftjschute of Finnegan, erse solid man . . .'.

One way of interpreting the prevailing confusion in the *Wake* is to suggest that it is an indispensable part of being itself; the Joycean conception of life is, as we know from *Ulysses,* that it is a turmoil, a riot of opposites defying and at the same time seeking identities. In Joyce's notebooks, the data of life are patches and fragments of language, phrase, color, and sound. Each portmanteau word or phrase can be counted upon to multiply several-fold the suggestion and sound of meaning. That this brouhaha is dramatized in terms of family disputes is understandable; it is in the family that humanity 'settles', as water slows and moves toward the calm center of a pool. This is, at least, the view of it in *Finnegans Wake*; the family quarrels in *Dubliners* and *Portrait* testify to the fact that Joyce's acceptance of the family as center comes late in his life, and is defined in an entirely different intellectual atmosphere from the Catholic Dublin father-priest authority suggested to him at the beginning.

It is not so much that Joyce has simply 'got over' his rebellion, but rather that the distance from his creatures which maturity put at his disposal helped him immeasurably in assessing the actual depth and value of the noise and vibration of human *ambiance.* Identity is no longer what it was in the *Portrait*: there it meant what one *separately was.* In the *Wake* it emerges from a 'welter' that is caused partly by contemporary circumstances, partly by the everpresence, immanence, *or* imminence, of recurrent identities. Or, as Joyce says in the *Wake,* 'by the coincidance of their contraries reamalgamerge in that identity of undiscernibles'. The mixture is not only of gossip, rumor, and truth; it is also of good and evil. 'First we feel. Then we fall', Anna Livia says. The 'fall' is indispensable to being; guilt is indicated in HCE's stammering, which is matched in the recurrence, ten times, of the thunder, or God's stammering. But the awareness of guilt is not in itself a fact of paralysing effect or of stunning importance. HCE 'emerges' or rises from his fall; each time, he creates as he sins, or sins as he creates. Human fertility does eventually impress identity upon the world of relations; the identity which 'reamalgamerges' transcends the confusion of human strife over names, libels, lies, and similar calumnies. The ultimate aim is to provoke recognition of (1) the 'I' (the 'mishe mishe' of the *Wake*'s beginning), and (2) the family, which is a cluster of polarities and identities.

The family polarities rest chiefly with the twin sons. Shem is the great abstracter, the man who wants to push outward, in cyclical speculation, to put reality into the garments of semblance, in 'the weirdest of all pensible ways'. Further, he is the Dubliner in exile on the Continent, as his father is the 'invader exile' in Dublin. There is no doubt that section seven of part one is 'editorial', an echo of Joyce's critics, but at the same time an expression of Joyce's ultimate separation from the Stephen of *Portrait* and *Ulysses.* The passages are now familiar enough to the readers of the *Wake*: ' . . . Tumult, son of Thunder, self exiled in upon his ego, a nightlong a shaking betwixtween white or reddr hawrors, noonday-terrorised to skin and bone by an ineluctable phantom (may the Shaper have mercery on him!) writing the mystery of himsel in furniture'. The *doubles entendres* are sufficiently obvious: himself, but also him plus cell (which goes with 'self exiled in upon his ego'); furniture means things, patches and fragments fitted together in a design which is a mystery to all but himself. But he is also a 'premature gravedigger, seeker of the nest of evil in the bosom of a good word', a scavenger among ashes and dung, a connoisseur of obscenity and obscurity, 'shemming amid everyone's repressed laughter to conceal your scatchophily by mating, like a thoroughpaste prosodite, masculine monosyllables of the same numerical mus'.

That this characterization of Shem elides skillfully into the section devoted to Anna Livia Plurabelle is important enough. In the role of Mercius (the polar opposite of Justius), Shem appeals to his mother (' . . . I who oathily forswore the womb that bore you and the paps I sometimes sucked . . .'); and the sound of contentiousness becomes a punning mixture of the 'quoi?' for 'what', and a quacking sound, identical with the sound that Lucky makes in Beckett's *Waiting for Godot.* For Anna Livia, the sounds are resumed once again as gossip, but (in the tone of rivers, forever renewing themselves in their 'riverrun') also as a 'bildung' story, the move from the 'young thin pale soft shy slim slip of a thing' to the mother and the progenitress of the 'seim anew': 'Anna was, Livia is, Plurabelle's to be'.

In the end, the noise has abated, the lessons and lesions have been given, and we come back to the facts of gestation, of biological renewal, of the great erection and the smooth amniotic flow. As the great Theodore Purefoy is praised for his 'doughty deed' in *Ulysses,* so HCE merits the distinction of 'Haveth Childers Everywhere'. In the Mime of Mick, Nick and the Maggies, the game is to find ' . . . what is that which is one going to prehend?' Or, 'The howtosayto itiswhatis hemustwhomust worden schall'. Shem (in the role of Glugg) finds the teeming world 'Truly deplurabell!' But the 'coincidance' continues around poor Glugg, defying his effort to make one stand where once were many: the dance of cycles and generations, through 'Endles of Eons efter Dies of Eirae doeslike'; in other words, the 'seim anew' and many 'happy returns'. The 'essies' are 'impures', as they are in the world of Beckett's creatures. The ascent of man becomes the 'assent of man', and ultimately human reality is accepted as an ever-changing, always certain merging of 'essies' and 'possies'.

In *Finnegans Wake,* Joyce put the crown upon his celebration of the 'acceptance world', which in *Ulysses* had been featured in the mind of his street-roaming, musing exile, Bloom. Stephen saw the disorder and filth of life too, and even sought a fusion of space and time (the *nacheinander* and the *nebeneinander* of 'Proteus'); but his struggle against corruption and death becomes less and less an heroic and lonely stand against his 'duvlin sulph', and yields to the very teeming profusion of life that is graphically given in *Ulysses,* more complexly offered in the *Wake.* For not only is the Stephen figure of the *Wake* given with less respect; he moves into and out of his twin self, so that their polarities become identities. Evidences of resemblance, 'The seim anew' triumph over disparities. The father who earlier had merited the scorn of his rebellious son is now respected *and* opposed, fought *and* joined, because the principles of diffusion and twinness must eventually prove out as variations within a dominating and recurring identity. (pp. 16-25)

> *Frederick J. Hoffman, " 'The Seim Anew':
> Flux and Family in 'Finnegans Wake', " in*
> Twelve and a Tilly: Essays on the Occasion of
> the 25th Anniversary of Finnegans Wake, *ed-
> ited by Jack P. Dalton and Clive Hart, Faber
> & Faber, 1966, pp. 16-25.*

Roland McHugh   (essay date 1981)

[*McHugh is an English biologist who has studied and written extensively on* Finnegans Wake. *In the following excerpt, McHugh notes some of the difficulties the work poses for textual scholars.*]

Joyce's composition of *Finnegan Wake* occupied seventeen years, during which time he had few other occupations. He also, of course, spent a good deal of time lying down in darkened rooms, recovering from eye operations, and his poor vision helped to obscure his calligraphy. Thus one of the qualifications required of the manuscript scholar is the ability to decipher a jumble of cramped and distorted lettering.

For every chapter of the *Wake* there are a succession of *witnesses,* as they are called: drafts, typescripts, proofs and printed versions. Most of them are embellished with numerous additions and corrections in the author's hand. Joyce gave nearly all of this material to his patron, Miss Weaver, who later donated it to the British Museum. It is bound there in a collection of large volumes numbered B.M. Additional MSS 47471-47488.

The manuscripts spread their shadow slowly over the pathways of *Finnegans Wake* exegesis. Matthew Hodgart had a look at them in the 1950s and noticed, for example, that the rather similar III.1 and III.2 were originally constructed as a single chapter. In 1960 Clive Hart published a paper ["Notes on the Text of *Finnegans Wake,*" *Journal of English and Germanic Philology* LIX (1960)] noting certain disparities between the printed *Finnegans Wake* and the earlier versions, but this was ahead of its time and made little impact on pre-*Newslitter* society. The next phase was a controversy concerning Kiswahili. One Philipp Wolff, who had lived in Africa, recognized a number of words in *Finnegans Wake* as belonging to that language. He sent a list to Campbell, the *Skeleton Key* co-author, but received no acknowledgement. Then, hearing of the *Newslitter,* he passed the list to Fritz Senn and it appeared in the December 1962 issue ["Kiswahili Words in *Finnegans Wake,*" *A Wake Newslitter* (old series) 8, 1962].

Some of the words were undeniably correct. For instance at 199.19-20 Anna Livia offers ᴍ a ham sandwich (German, *Schinkenbrot,* made with French *jambon,* ham): 'a

shinkobread (hamjambo, bana?) for to plaise that man'. Wolff noticed the Kiswahili greeting *Hajambo, bwana?* At 200.33 'And what was the wyerye rima she made!' means 'And what was the weary rhyme (Italian, *rima*) she made?', plus the rivers Wye and Rima (the fluidity of I.8 is enhanced by the inclusion of over a thousand river-names). Here Wolff saw Kiswahili *rima,* 'pit for catching large animals'. Obviously a less useful gloss, but how can you presume to say that Kiswahili *rima* is 'wrong'? A paper by Jack P. Dalton in the April 1963 *Litter* provided the answer. You do it with the manuscripts:

> I am not so much interested in Kisuahili, or in Herr Wolff 's performance, or the Litter's performance, as I am concerned with the foundation of logical principles and practices on which *Finnegans Wake* scholarship must come to rest, if it is ever to amount to anything more than a stumbling block to the serious student, and a butt of derision for scoffers . . . Now the list I have presented [a modification of Wolff 's] . . . stands quite perfectly on its own two feet, as it were. However, there is a most interesting aspect of it not yet noted—*all the words in the list . . . were added to* Finnegans Wake *at the same time.* I refer to the second galleys for the *Finnegans Wake* ALP, B.M. Add. MS 47476A. 261-275 . . . There remain to note, then, the seven citations which I have completely dropped from Herr Wolff 's list . . . The items . . . were added . . . all 10 years or so prior . . . These items haven't a leg to stand on anyway, but the loss of context cuts the ground from under them as well.

In other words, if a number of items were all added to a particular witness of a *Finnegans Wake* chapter, they bolster one another in their chances of deriving from a specified source. Material like this tends to be clustered in small areas of text, so proximity to the main nucleus further increases the likelihood of relevance.

Of course the exigencies of reading *Finnegans Wake* leave few readers with the energy to check their findings against the MSS. There is also the problem of access. Until recently, if one did not live in London, it was necessary to purchase microfilm of the B.M. collection (and also, naturally, to have a microfilm reader at hand). But in 1977 publication began of a set of facsimiles, as part of a general edition of Joyce's manuscripts, *The James Joyce Archive.* The witnesses we are discussing take up twenty of the sixty-three *Archive* volumes, and are accompanied by a chronological analysis of the growth of each chapter, by Danis Rose, who also arranged the pages into a more coherent sequence than Miss Weaver's. The availability of the *Archive* will add considerable momentum to *Wake* studies: even Dublin now has a couple of sets, in the National Library and Trinity College.

We live in privileged times. When Dalton's paper on the Kiswahili appeared it must have seemed that the right of the layman to present his guesswork in the genial forum of the *Litter* was threatened. The next issue carried a rebuff from Clive Hart:

> It is certainly possible, by means of a reversal of Joyce's process of composition, to extract and

isolate the deposits of discrete pieces of denotation from which the book was originally compounded. I am not suggesting that this pursuit will lead to a denial of the interrelationships of constituent parts, nor that it claims the whole to be no more than the sum of its parts. What I am suggesting, however, is that it is a major example of a most restrictive fallacious intentionalism.

["The Elephant in the Belly: Exegesis of *Finnegans Wake*," *A Wake Newslitter* (old series) 13 (1963)]

Looming behind all the practicalities of *Finnegans Wake* research in the 1960s was the great schism between Dalton's Intentionalism and Hart's Anti-intentionalism. To the reader daunted by the volume of the MSS, the Anti-intentionalist approach has an obvious appeal, and as Hart says, it 'seems, paradoxically, to have Joyce's sanction—to have been, as it were, part of his intention'. For instance in [a letter of November 1926 from Joyce to his patron Harriet Weaver, the word 'violer' on the first page of *Finnegans Wake*] is glossed 'viola in all moods and senses'. Hart wrote to me in 1968: 'Most modern critics will say, rightly or wrongly, that it doesn't matter a damn what any author intended, except in so far as that intention is borne out by the work itself. "For all we know, JJ may have intended *Finnegans Wake* to be a cookery book. Who cares what he thought? What are the *book's* intentions?" '.

Now, this argument is theoretically unanswerable. But for most readers, a satisfied conviction that a particular interpretation is apt will rarely occur without at least a suspicion of authorial intent. And Anti-intentionalism is a fearful stimulus to what is known as the 'lunatic fringe' of *Finnegans Wake* studies. As Hart himself observes of the *Wake,* 'Too often its convolutions have been treated as a kind of endless verbal equivalent of the Rorschach Inkblot Test' [*Structure and Motif in Finnegans Wake*]. Against this backdrop, the restrictive quality of the manuscript approach seems a welcome curb. Instead of the uncommitted impartiality of the maximizer we see the jesuitical precision of the dealer in probabilities. The typical manuscript scholar is obsessed by the need for precision. A good example can be seen in Dalton's 'I Say It's Spinach—"Watch!" ', which took up the whole of the November 1963 *Litter.* This is a review of David Hayman's *A First Draft Version of Finnegans Wake.* Hayman had attempted to transcribe the earliest drafts of each *Finnegans Wake* chapter, but Dalton showed so many transcription errors in his work that its utility as a whole became questionable. The tone of his review—slow, nit-picking evisceration interspersed with clouds of vitriolic indignation and cheap sarcasm—has helped to create an image of the *Finnegans Wake* exegete as a man for whom worldly issues retreat before the conflicts of commas and semicolons. 'Damn it, Hayman, you make me ill with rage. The creation of such monstrous vile filth as this, and all the rest of it, should be a criminal offense, necessarily capital. That it is not is a grave defect of our society.'

This is all harmless comedy, but as Dalton edged forwards his pronouncements became more disconcerting. I think everyone interested in textual problems ought to read his 'Advertisement for the Restoration', which appeared in

1966 in a collection edited by Hart and himself, *Twelve and a Tilly.*

The article considers one of the most transparent portions of *Finnegans Wake,* the meditation of St Kevin (605.04-606.12). Various ecclesiastical and celestial hierarchies are dotted across it. Here is a dissected version, displaying one of them, the nine orders of angels. I have italicized the orders to facilitate recognition:

> Procreated . . . come their feast of precreated holy whiteclad *angels*. . . Kevin. . . came. . . to our own midmost Glendalough-le-vert by *archangel*ical guidance . . . whereof its lake is the ventrifugal *principulity,* whereon by prime, *power*ful in knowledge, Kevin . . . acolyte of cardinal *virtues* . . . carrying that privileged altar . . . ninthly en*throned* . . . his *cherub*ical loins . . . he meditated continuously with *seraph*ic ardour the primal sacrament of baptism or the regeneration of all man by affusion of water.

Pious readers will immediately remark the absence of one order, dominations, which ought to come between virtues and thrones. Dalton isn't pious, but he noticed it too, and went to the manuscripts. Looking at an early draft he found in place of 'carrying that privileged altar' an additional line of writing, making it 'carrying the lustral domination contained within his most portable privileged altar'. He concluded that 'mindful of the cardinal fact that *exactly one line* was excised, even the most sober attempts at justification seem to me sophistical in the extreme. In fact, it must be considered that the primary effect of omitting the line was not to leave out an order of angels, but to wreck the syntax of the sentence.'

Having demonstrated the existence of what might be described as an *error* in *Finnegans Wake,* Dalton went on to demonstrate more, and stated that he knew of over six hundred, adding however that 'not every one, of course, is as choice as these'. The solution he proposed was an emendation of the text. It is at this station that I cease to concur with his viewpoint.

Textual emendation is an issue relevant to other texts besides *Finnegans Wake,* for example *Ulysses.* At Munich, Hans Walter Gabler is currently directing the production of a critical edition, consisting of two parts. The 'synoptic text', on the left-hand pages, uses numbered half-brackets to label the stages of accretion and full brackets to label deleted items. Removal of the brackets and deletions gives the 'critical plain text', to be carried by the right-hand pages. Publication is expected around 1983, according to Hugh Kenner ["The Computerized *Ulysses,*" *Harper's* (April 1980)].

I will certainly buy Gabler's book and use it in place of the currently available *Ulysses.* There are bound to be a few erroneous changes, but by and large we understand the meaning of the novel. *Finnegans Wake,* however, is different. It can sometimes appear to be unreasonable nonsense whilst remaining utterly coherent for the reader who holds the key. And we never know what additional level of meaning might be lying dormant, waiting to shed illumination over some tract which looks fully explicated but isn't. In such cases what looks like a misprint might be a vital link in the new reading. Certainly, the line with 'domination' seems to have been omitted by Joyce's oversight, and its omission appears to be entirely reductive in impact, but it is in fact the thin end of the wedge. Admit it an error and a forest of new errors begin to clamour for attention.

Dalton believes, according to his article, that 'Siker of calmy days' (237.31) should be changed to read 'Siku of calmy days'. The word *siku* is Kiswahili for 'day', and we can certainly demonstrate that Joyce appreciated this when he inserted the item into the text. But what exactly did he insert? Dalton says 'Siku': 'The "u" Joyce wrote was sloppy, with suggestions of loops in the minims; the first was read as "e", the second followed as "r" '. I would maintain that the mark cannot be definitively judged a 'u' or an 'er': it is something between the two. But if we retain 'Siker' in the text I can still accept Kiswahili *siku* as an overtone in it. Change it to 'Siku' and you destroy the English overtone 'seeker', producing a less beautiful sentence which means solely 'day of calm/balmy days'. Being part of a speech addressed to a person, is it not more reasonable that he should be called a seeker than a day?

To appreciate the situation in relation to the progression of witnesses, we might look at the erosion which has affected 124.09-12. In his early paper on the text, Hart says 'This typographical carnival has suffered more corruption than any other single passage in *Finnegans Wake*' ["Notes on the Text of *Finnegans Wake*"]. Before we look at it, a word about its rationale might be in order.

I.5, as explained earlier, is an account of the letter (□), working towards the determination of its authorship. As one of the ingredients in □ is *The Book of Kells,* which was dated by an analysis of its punctuation, the punctuation marks of □ become significant at the end of I.5, and are said to have been 'provoked' by the fork of a professor, to introduce a notion of time [James S. Atherton, *The Books at the Wake*]. Because, as Samuel Beckett said, *Finnegans Wake* 'is not *about* something; *it is that something itself*', it is appropriate that a mass of distinctive punctuation should appear at just this point in the text [Beckett, "Dante . . . Bruno. Vico . . . Joyce," in Beckett et al., *Our Exagmination Round his Factification for Incamination of Work in Progress*]. This explains one piece of insanity, the double semicolon (;;), but to augment the effect Joyce sprinkled diacritics over the region indicated. As these differ in the different witnesses one might claim that dating by punctuation, as with *The Book of Kells,* can actually apply to the *Finnegans Wake* text itself.

We will examine only a fragment of the sentence. Part of the first draft, probably written around 26 February 1925, says of the marks that

> thĕy ăd bîn "provòked" by ʌ fork,
> ŏf ă grave Professor

Joyce's typist copied this fairly well, including the stroke through the second 's' in 'Professor', but making the marks above both 'of' and 'a' resemble slightly curved grave accents. Later the passage was retyped, and they were straightened in the process, becoming identical with the grave accent in 'Professor'. At the same time the sec-

ond 's' was removed, the stroke being presumably taken as a deletion mark, although Joyce does not normally delete in this fashion.

Next, the chapter was printed in the July 1925 number of T. S. Eliot's magazine *The Criterion,* and two new changes appeared: the second word was now 'ăd', and 'by' had become 'ay'. On *Criterion* pages prepared for the printer of another magazine, *transition,* Joyce changed the 'P' of 'Professor' to a 'B', but in the proofs they returned him they had not only complied with this request, but also removed the accent from its remaining 's', and those from 'ad', 'of' and 'provoked'. These alterations being retained in the August 1926 *transition,* it was left to the Faber and Faber printer to remove the mark over 'they' in 1937, and the words arrived at their present state.

Is it safe to assume that all those changes were accidents? Joyce did, after all, restore on all three sets of Faber galleys the grave accent five words further on, in 'professionally', presumably by reference to a copy of *transition.* Hart's paper notes 'the change to "ay" was probably intentional', but if so, why not also the change in 'ad' in *The Criterion,* which restores a type of accent used in the first draft, although on a different word? Ask somebody else and you'll get a third opinion. No two manuscript specialists can ever be expected to agree on what ought, and what ought not, to be altered. The conception of a 100% accurate text of *Finnegans Wake* strikes me as a dangerously idealistic abstraction.

Let's go back to 'Siker of calmy days'. Emendation of this phrase would be reductive: clarification of one level whilst another is obliterated. Nearly everything in *Finnegans Wake* means several different things at once, and the danger of the manuscript approach is that its proponents often fall prey to single-narrative readings, the narrative that the MS happens to account for. I suspect that Joyce would frequently observe some secondary interpretation or enrichment resulting from the ambiguity of a misprint. Although the effect might be to damage the syntax or coherence of the primary level, he might well opt for leaving it, such was his greed for multiplicity of meanings. Who are we to challenge such decisions?

In 1967, Peter du Sautoy, the vice-chairman of Faber and Faber, concluded in the *Newslitter* that a variorum edition might be 'the only way out, but I do not see it at the moment as something either feasible or economic for *Finnegans Wake*' ["The Published Text," *A Wake Newslitter* IV, No. 5 (1967)]. I'm inclined to agree that it's the only way out. But the first requirement is that the text be fully investigated, and Dalton's attention seems now to have swerved away to *Ulysses.* (He long ago submitted a '90% correct' version to Random House, which I hope they won't just sit on.) Most of the recent textual commentary has come from Danis Rose and Ian MacArthur.

At present Rose is apparently constructing a synoptic version of *Finnegans Wake* on the same lines as Gabler's *Ulysses.* This ought to provoke some disagreement when it appears, and the final aim, of course, is to replace the edition commonly found on bookshelves with a critical plain text extracted in the same manner as with *Ulysses.*

I think it unfortunate that one set of decisions should simply be adopted in bulk as the right answer, but of course a study of Rose's text ought to show up most of the apparent misprints (he claims there are about four thousand), and if these are then properly documented by checking against the MSS it should not be too difficult to convert the list into footnotes for a variorum edition.

In spite of his earlier committment to pure Daltonism in the *Litter,* Ian MacArthur tells me he now agrees that a variorum edition is the best solution [MacArthur, *A Wake Newslitter* XIII, No. 5 (1976)]. MacArthur is a chemist in Norwich, and has published various 'textual studies' of parts of the *Wake.* I particularly liked his piece on the 'F sigla', laterally inverted pairs of capital Fs which occur at a few points in *Finnegans Wake.* In some cases the printed letters are not precisely inverted. MacArthur observes 'From the various emendations that Joyce made, it appears that an essential feature of the motif is that the letters should be mirror images. Note, for example, 18.36, where the original pair was altered to enantiomorphs in draft [6]. The Fs at 121.03,07 underwent a rotation as Joyce altered the surviving original to mirror the corruption. The passage at 468.03 confirms this, where the Fs are directly linked to the pq motif' [MacArthur, "The F Sigla," *A Wake Newslitter* XV, No. 4 (1978)].

When we are dealing with issues as complex as this it is not enough for the manuscript expert merely to point out the stages at which a word or letter changed: he has to argue, to explain why the changes occurred. What I should like to see is not a synoptic version of *Finnegans Wake* but rather a thorough analytical discussion of possible textual abberations, preferably with photographs of particularly uncertain items in the handwriting. The footnotes in a variorum edition would be keyed to this volume for rapid reference, and would therefore be fairly compact in themselves, and not get in the reader's way. We just need somebody to do it. (pp. 70-81)

> *Roland McHugh, "The British Museum Manuscripts," in his* The "Finnegans Wake" Experience, *University of California Press, 1981, pp. 70-81.*

Clive Hart   (essay date 1982)

[*In the following essay, Hart describes a strategy for understanding* Finnegans Wake *as a whole, arguing that readings which place emphasis on minutiae and abstraction fail to promote a comprehensive understanding of the work.*]

For forty years and more most of us have been frightened of *Finnegans Wake.* Unsure how to respond to it, but hoping to establish some firm ground beneath our feet, we have concentrated overwhelmingly on detailed *explication de texte,* to the exclusion of critical commentary which would say something about the impact of the whole. Although large and usually deferential statements about the universality of its themes have appeared from time to time, not many critics have managed to guide us towards a satisfying aesthetic perspective. It is not even clear that most of us try to read it as we read other books. Do we believe

that *Finnegans Wake* offers us that *frisson,* that sense of delighted participation in creative imaginative achievements with which we are familiar from reading 'The longe love, that in my thought doeth harbar', or *Twelfth Night,* or *Ulysses*?

Perhaps it can do so, and it seems important to try to find an answer. So far, however, we appear to be in some doubt. The difficulties are many, including not only the book's notorious density of reference and multiplicity of linguistic signs, but also its confusingly, disturbingly mixed tone. We hear many voices without knowing which, if any, to believe. Are we invited to participate directly in 'And low stole o'cr the stillness the heartbeats of sleep'? Are we being addressed with ironic impatience in 'Shake it up, do, do! That's a good old son of a ditch! I promise I'll make it worth your while. And I don't mean maybe'? It does not help that the latter tone tends to predominate: a semi-exclamatory, slightly dismissive prickliness which both invites participation and simultaneously holds us a little apart.

The mixed tone may also be at least partly responsible for a disparity, which I know I am not alone in registering, between image and reality, between my sense of the book in tranquil recollection and my immediate impression whenever I have it open before me. Trying to maintain an uneasy grip on the whole, I inadvertently simplify it when remembering it. *Finnegans Wake* is richer, denser, than anything I can carry in my head. The same was true to a limited degree even of Joyce who, as the manuscript evidence shows, frequently forgot about some of the embellishments he had intended to include. (By contrast I tend to remember some other books, e.g. *Howards End,* as richer than they prove to be on rereading.)

It is perhaps inevitable that the gap appears to grow with increasing knowledge: the more one understands of the detail, thanks to the continuing flow of explication, the more difficult it becomes to sustain a satisfying sense of the whole. With some qualifications I nevertheless think it is worth our while to undertake the three centuries of meticulous work to which Joyce said he had condemned the professors. Some decades ago the task of explication was often undertaken in the expectation that patient research would lead to the elucidation of a mystery, on the analogy of the deciphering of Linear B. Despite the increasing production of specialist lexicons and annotations, much less is heard these days of comprehensive 'dictionaries' of *Finnegans Wake.* Not only our longer experience of the book, but also the growing familiarity of ideas of uncertainty, probability, approximation and open systems of thought, has led us to understand and to accept that in so far as there is a 'mystery' in *Finnegans Wake* it is fundamental, and fundamentally insoluble. Acceptance of 'mystery' at local level is, however, less easy. Ordinary human curiosity and frustration at bafflement combine to motivate the pursuit of meaning. When confronted by a strange word we naturally want to know what it means and why it takes this form rather than another. Virtually everything in *Finnegans Wake* was shaped with teasing forethought; almost nothing was left to chance. Distortions of ordinary English are not introduced because they are vaguely suggestive. Biographical and manuscript evidence, and the text itself, establish beyond doubt the dominance of semantic units, rationally controlled.

Many local delights arise from the pursuit of information elucidating the strange forms. At a microcosmic level it enriches one's sense of harmony and proportion to know that 'osghirs', which in the first place refers to Oscar Wilde, also contains the Armenian word for 'gold'. Placed in a context of scorn at worthless, destructive betrayers, the passage reads:

> They whiteliveried ragsups, two Whales of the Sea of Deceit, they bloodiblabstard shooters, three Dromedaries of the Sands of Calumdonia. As is note worthies to shock his hind! Ur greef to them! Such askors and their ruperts they are putting in for more osghirs is alse false liarnels. The frockenhalted victims!

There is much here that I do not understand. Among other things, however, an antithesis is established between the golden worth of betrayed, calumniated Oscar, and the accursed, blabbing accusers who are not worth a red cent ('liard'). A taste for such perceptions of detail is easy to develop. After a good deal of preparatory research, *Finnegans Wake* is an excellent *livre de chevet.* The interrelationships of image and idea within a short paragraph, re-read and pondered with a general if imperfect sense of the whole book in the background, frequently afford the same kind of aesthetic delight which one experiences in reading a short and highly wrought lyric such as Yeats's 'Leda and the Swan' (whose essential materials and double vision are of a kind that Joyce found congenial). A minor example is offered by Question 10 of I.vi: 'What bitter's love but yurning, what sour lovemutch but a bref burning till shee that drawes dothe smoake retourne?' Here Joyce rewrites Philip Rosseter's song: 'What then is love but mourning, / What desire, but a self-burning, / Till she that hates doth love return?' It grows both more bitter and more ironic: 'What makes love (more) bitter than the experience of yearning, what sours our lovematch as much as the brevity of our burning which lasts only until the (sophisticated) fairy-like, cigarette-smoking beloved herself returns to smoke?' An additional, and very Joycean, element is introduced with the spelling 'bref': the burning in the spirit and in the loins is ironically and antithetically reflected in the burning of a (Scandinavian) letter. The plaintive letter which echoes throughout *Finnegans Wake* is here transformed into a lover's *billet doux,* only to be cynically destroyed.

Local delights, even when they poignantly express recurrent themes of central human significance, are hardly a sufficient justification for struggling with a book of over 600 pages. Although reading *Finnegans Wake* in breaths of more than a paragraph or two can be unusually arduous, we are still in need of a satisfactory perspective which will allow us to respond more fully to the whole. While the outlines must inevitably remain less sharply defined than those of *Ulysses,* which Joyce thought he might have 'over-systematised', we need a better, a more satisfying sense of the movement, the rhythm, the shape of *Finnegans Wake.* Unless we are to wait another two and a half centuries, that sense will inevitably be based on incom-

plete evidence about the nature of the constituent parts. For various reasons I believe that this may matter a good deal less than in the case of books conceived in more conventional modes. In perhaps exaggerated form, Joyce suggested as much in a comment to Heinrich Straumann, Professor of English in Zürich: 'One should not pay any particular attention to the allusions to place-names, historical events, literary happenings and personalities, but let the linguistic phenomenon affect one as such.' We should be guarded in the weight we give to this. Joyce notoriously tempered his remarks to the tastes and background of his listeners; a Dubliner would almost certainly have been given different advice. It none the less seems clear that Joyce did not necessarily expect all the constituent details to be elucidated before the book could be read. It is an approach which I think worth cultivating at the present time.

I do not yet know how to read *Finnegans Wake,* but the more I can learn to read it simply, the happier I believe I shall be. Now that we have learned to understand a good proportion of the detail—and above all now that we have a reasonable grasp of the kind of materials from which it is built—I am inclined to advocate quite rapid reading. Unless one is willing to ignore local difficulties and to make the best of rather cursory attention to complexities, a grasp of the whole is, in my experience, very nearly impossible. For such a reading I suggest adopting the working hypothesis that, with the exception of three main kinds of phrase and a few other unclassifiable words, most of the text has a basic English sense, or sometimes two parallel

James, Nora, Lucia, and Giorgio Joyce in Paris, 1924.

senses, as in everyday punning. This basic thread of English sense we should always try to hear as clearly as possible, since it usually supplies the primary meaning of the book. The three main exceptions are (1) phrases specifically written in a foreign language and often signalled by italics (e.g. *'Hircus Civis Eblanensis!'*; (2) proper names and initials; (3) some exclamatory words and phrases which lie, so to speak, outside the controlling syntax of the text (e.g. 'Hou! Hou!'). Allowing 'the linguistic phenomenon [to] affect one as such', one absorbs additional meanings *en passant,* but with the emphasis always on a consecutive reading. Two examples may help to make the point, one simple, the second more difficult to accommodate to my proposed method:

> Liverpoor? Sot a bit of it! His braynes coolt parritch, his pelt nassy, his heart's adrone, his bluidstreams acrawl, his puff but a piff, his extremeties extremely so: Fengless, Pawmbroke, Chilblaimend and Baldowl. Humph is in his doge. Words weigh no no more to him than raindrips to Rethfernhim. Which we all like. Rain. When we sleep. Drops. But wait until our sleeping. Drain. Sdops.

In offering the following simplified version I do not wish to reduce this marvellously evocative passage to a flat paraphrase, but to propose that we attend to an underlying English utterance which holds the paragraph together:

> Is his liver poor? Not a bit of it! His brains are like cold porridge, his pelt is nasty, his heart's droning, his bloodstream is crawling, his puff is but a 'piff', his extremities are *in extremis:* he is fangless, broken, has chilblains and is as bald as an owl. Humphrey is in his dotage. Words weigh now no more to him than do raindrops to Rathfarnham. Which we all like: rain when we sleep. Drops. But wait until our sleeping train stops.

Much of what is omitted from such a version is obvious: the animals in 'His braynes coolt parritch' (the donkey's bray, the pigeon's coo, the young salmon in parr-), not to mention Humphrey's itches; the role-call of Dublin place-names; the drain in which all ends; above all, of course, the play of vowel and consonant. Most significant for my present purposes is the priority I give to 'nasty', in 'his pelt's nassy', over the more directly relevant 'damp' (German *nass*): his skin is clammy. For a moderately practised reader of *Finnegans Wake* 'damp' is the primary sense here. I nevertheless advocate trying to hear 'nasty' first.

For my more difficult example I return to the passage involving Oscar Wilde, quoted above. I cannot 'hear' it all in English, but suggest the following as a beginning:

> Those white-livered ragsups (?): two whales from the sea of deceit; those bloody, blasted shooters, three dromedaries from the sands of Calumdonia. As are not worthy to shake his hand. Our (?) grief to them. Such askers and their Ruperts (?), they are putting in for more 'oscar', and are all false Lionels (?). The faint-hearted victims!

('Oscar' is a slang word for money.) Apart from the lexicon, a difficulty, encountered quite frequently in *Finnegans Wake,* is presented by the syntax of the sentence beginning 'Such askors'. It is broken-backed, and one must do the best one can.

I do not suggest that the whole book will respond satisfactorily to this technique. Some passages mix so much non-English material into the English syntax as to make a simple paraphrase unworkable, as for example in the first sentence of the following:

> Dayagreening gains in schlimninging. A summerwint springfalls, abated. Hail, regn of durknass, snowly receassing, thund lightening thund.

'Day-greening' may perhaps make some sense. Joyce, writing about the dawn, produces a semi-calque on Swedish *daggryning* (dawn) which, however, literally means 'day-greying' rather than 'day-greening'. But 'gains in schlimninging'? The phrase, evidently including German *schlimm* (evil), yields no English echo to my ear.

Joyce composed *Finnegans Wake* using a technique akin to that of the creator of a mosaic. He selected appropriate particles of material to build up a large picture, sometimes finding the bits and pieces ready made, sometimes making them himself and storing them in notebooks ready for eventual use. Not only have we concentrated too often on the exact shape and structure of the bits, but we have hesitated to accept Joyce's assurance to Straumann that the whole is sufficiently visible even if our focus on the detail is often blurred. In proposing the pursuit of a thread of English meaning I believe that some points of obscure detail will be unexpectedly clarified and that we shall develop a better sense of the proportions of microcosm to macrocosm. It is all too easy to be 'lost in the bush' and cry in desperation: 'It is a puling sample jungle of woods'.

I plead for a simple reading for two further, related reasons. First, it is clear that a vast amount of redundancy is fundamental to the structure of *Finnegans Wake.* Not only does Joyce tell the same archetypal stories over and over again, but a given phrase will often say the same thing in two, three, or even more ways. That 'bludgeony . . . Sunday' is a Bloody Sunday, because of the bludgeons; the erector of myths is also master of them, Mister Rector ('myther rector'). Even when the meanings contradict rather than complement each other, as here, missing much of the sense often leaves us less badly off than we might suppose. At first it is frustrating to find that clarification of a local difficulty, after much hard work, merely leads to a statement parallel to one on a neighbouring line. Later, however, one takes comfort from the knowledge that remaining difficulties are unlikely to be obscuring a solution to the mystery of the universe.

I also seek a simple reading because I should like to pay as much attention as possible to the surface. We need, I believe, to see *Finnegans Wake* more clearly, rather than to read through it. Its exploration of structures and relationships, its colour, wit and pathos, achieved through immediacy of image and pattern, offer an inexhaustible commentary on how to look at the world. If we read it for abstract ideas it serves us ill. *Finnegans Wake* does not seem to me to be a book of profound philosophical significance. The playing with time and space in 'The Mookse and the

Gripes', the confrontation of unity and diversity in the Buckley–St-Kevin pages, are inventive, amusing and emotionally charged, but say nothing of consequence about philosophy. Again, much has been made of Joyce's interest in scholasticism and the Middle Ages, of which I believe he knew and understood very little. Nor does *Finnegans Wake* seem to me to have anything illuminating to say about linguistic theory or literary history: the famous quarrel with Wyndham Lewis strikes me as in itself an argument of low intellectual calibre which rapidly grows boring. We are misguided, I believe, if we read *Finnegans Wake* in search of Joyce's views on his literary contemporaries, on Irish politics, or on the controversies involving the Catholic Church.

I hope *Finnegans Wake* is more than the compendium of remarks about modern life, the super-commonplace book which many explicatory articles make it appear. I hope, too, that it is more than some recent nervous and self-protective modernist critics would have us believe. It is possible that Joyce wrote more than 600 pages over a period of more than sixteen years merely to explore the 'question of putting expressly and systematically the problem of the status of a discourse which borrows from a heritage the resources necessary for the deconstruction of that heritage itself' [Jacques Derrida, in his "Structure, Sign, and Play in the Discourses of the Human Sciences"], but, if so, *Finnegans Wake* is reduced to a massively redundant and tedious exercise in denying the powers of the creative imagination, a 'literary exemplar', as Margot Norris puts it [in her *The Decentered Universe of "Finnegans Wake": A Structuralist Analysis,* 1977], of 'destructive discourses of the twentieth century'. I hope, in fact, that *Finnegans Wake* is more than a pathological expression of the fear of authority, and that clear-sighted scrutiny of its surfaces through repeated rapid readings such as I have been advocating will show more of its freely imaginative constructive power.

In so far as post-Joycean writing may be invoked to place *Finnegans Wake* in context, I find it more profitable to appeal to the practitioners than to the theoreticians. And it is more useful, I believe, to try to read it in the light of *Marienbud,* of Pinget's *L'Inquisitoire* and *Quelqu'un,* than by comparison with more radically deconstructive work such as one often finds in the pages of *Minuit.* In *Quelqu'un,* as in *Finnegans Wake,* the sword of certainty never falls. Strenuous attempts are made in both to reconstruct simple narrative truths, but the pieces won't fit. In neither case do we lack information—indeed, we have a superfluity of it. I should like to be able to read *Finnegans Wake* as I read *Quelqu'un:* responding to a bustling and varied surface filled with evocative, lively and amusing detail, and listening to the wide-ranging registers of human speech. The banalities which make up the detailed utterances of *Quelqu'un* never tempt us to believe that anything profound is being said: it is a delightful interplay of images and minor events, the constructive juxtapositions being much more interesting than the self-evident point that the book also pulls to pieces the traditional structure of narrative reminiscence. And at the end one is aware that, against the odds, a shapely whole has emerged, expressing

something which approximates to the total content of a small world.

I should also like to appeal to *Marienbad* and *L'Inquisitoire,* the scope and aspirations of which more nearly approach those of *Finnegans Wake.* Although neither Robbe-Grillet nor Pinget would thank me for saying so, their châteaux suggest, if not the universe, at least whole complex worlds of experience. In exploring both we learn to accept that ultimate truths about those worlds are not merely difficult of access but non-existent. In experiencing both we need to exercise our eyes and ears as much as possible, and our abstracting faculties as little as possible. Again, like *Finnegans Wake* both use as a basic dynamism an interplay of fixed points and fluidity. In all three works the contradictions, the shifting perspectives, the changing emphases are made a great deal more disconcerting by the presence of some elements which are either wholly or almost wholly stable. Aggressors and victims are sometimes confused, the same event occurs in summer or in winter, the shape and furnishing of a room change inexplicably. But as these surrounding circumstances modulate, the personalities of central, plaintive consciousnesses remain identifiable, while the structural relationships, sometimes painful, remain as inescapable determinants of the universe.

Finnegans Wake is itself an afterword. After the Word of the beginning we are left to explore a fallen, post-created world in which things do not always hang together. Although fallen it is not quite wholly chaotic. Nor does it lack beauty, harmony and local wholeness. Less transcendental than some would have him, Joyce savoured the 'audible-visible-gnosible-edible world'. Like *L'Inquisitoire,* *Finnegans Wake* explores the multifarious nature of existence by reflecting it, by offering itself as a simulacrum. If they were to give the reader the sense of participating in something on that scale, both books had to be long, quasi-inexhaustible, and beyond the reach of total recall. No rejector of physical reality, Joyce celebrated it, reproduced it, represented it for our delighted apprehension. As in *Ulysses,* as in the novels of Pinget's middle period, the world of *Finnegans Wake* is essentially one of urban human interaction. The best things in it are the most immediately human: the Shem chapter, the portrait of Issy, Shaun's self-revelation and HCE's monologue in Book III seem to me to show *Finnegans Wake* at its most successful. I believe we may have heard too much about Joyce the revolutionary, the ironist making rude gestures towards the fiction of the past. While he wanted to 'make it new', the emphasis was on the making, on the creation of something to enhance our sense of life. Freed, like his successors the *nouveaux romanciers,* from the old constraints of 'character', Joyce nevertheless created highly individual human consciousnesses. The more directly we can perceive their relations with each other and with the curious environments in which Joyce placed them, the less tempted we shall be to treat *Finnegans Wake* in dreary terms of socio-literary history and the more we shall be able to profit from its acute perceptions of the everyday world around us. (pp. 155-64)

Clive Hart, "Afterword: Reading 'Finnegans Wake'," in A Starchamber Quiry: A James

Joyce Centennial Volume, 1882-1982, by Hugh Kenner and others, edited by E. L. Epstein, Methuen, 1982, pp. 155-64.

Northrop Frye (essay date 1985)

[*A Canadian critic and editor, Frye is the author of the highly influential and controversial* Anatomy of Criticism *(1957), in which he argued that literary criticism can be scientific in its method and results and that judgments are not inherent in the critical process. Believing that literature is wholly structured by myth and symbol, Frye viewed the critic's task as the explication of a work's archetypal characteristics. In the following essay, originally presented as a lecture in 1985, he traces the influence of Italian writers Giambattista Vico and Giordano Bruno on* Finnegans Wake *and discusses major themes of the novel.*]

Since the fourteenth century, there has never been a time when English literature has not been influenced, often to the point of domination, by either French or Italian literary traditions, usually both at once. For Chaucer, the major foreign influence was Boccaccio, whose *Teseide* and *Filostrato* form the basis for *The Knight's Tale* and *Troilus and Criseyde* respectively. In Tudor times the Petrarchan sonnet was the central model, both in technique and theme, for lyric poetry, and Ariosto at least contributed very heavily to the major epic of the period, Spenser's *Faerie Queene*. After the Restoration, French influence, of the neoclassical type, rose to dominance, headed by the critical theories of Boileau, whose slighting reference to "leclinquant de Tasse" marked the ascendancy of French satire over Italian romance. Romanticism, however, found Britain at war with France, when it was a patriotic duty to prove that French literature was second-rate, as we can see in Coleridge. The second generation of Romantics brought back Italian as the dominant foreign influence: Byron translated a canto of Pulci; Boiardo is a presence in Peacock's last story, *Gryll Grange;* Shelley (and Keats in translation) owed much to Dante, who had previously had, for religious reasons, relatively little influence. Romantic Italianism reached its climax in Browning, although Browning reflects the pictorial and visual culture of Italy more than its literature.

In the generation of Joyce, Eliot, and Pound, which came to maturity around the First World War, Eliot's main debts are to the French: the Italian influences are, again, confined largely to Dante, whom he imitates with great skill in an episode in *Little Gidding*. Ezra Pound's contacts with Italian literature, history, and art are of vast range and erudition, though they also include a good many red herrings. Joyce's Italianism is more centrally in the Romantic tradition. Stephen Dedalus in *Ulysses* complains, using the title of an Italian play, that he is the servant of two masters, one English and one Italian, but there he is talking about the political ascendancy of Great Britain and the Roman Catholic domination in religion. As literary masters, the Italians predominate in Joyce over all other non-English influences. Joyce's great debt to Dante, at every stage of his career, has been fully documented in a book-length study, and he owed much to other Italian

writers, including Gabriele D'Annunzio, who cannot be considered here. But *Finnegans Wake* is dominated by two Italians not previously represented to any extent in English literature before. One is Giambattista Vico, whom Joyce did much to make a major influence in our intellectual traditions ever since. The other is Giordano Bruno of Nola, in whom no previous writer in English except Coleridge seems to have been much interested, although he lived in England for a time and dedicated his two best-known books to Sir Philip Sidney.

During the years when Joyce was working on *Finnegans Wake,* publishing fragments of it from time to time under the heading of *Work in Progress,* a group of his disciples brought out a volume of essays with the eminently off-putting title of *Our Exagmination Round his Factification for Incamination of Work in Progress.* The first of these essays, by the disciple whose name is by far the best known today, Samuel Beckett, was on Joyce's debt to Italian writers, more especially Vico. Despite Beckett's expertise in Italian—all his major work reflects a masterly command of Dante—the essay is very inconclusive, mainly, I imagine, because the entire structure of *Finnegans Wake* was not yet visible, and the essays were designed to point to something about to emerge and not to expound on something already there. However, since then every commentary has been largely based on Joyce's use of Vico's cyclical conception of history.

Vico thinks of history as the repetition of a cycle that passes through four main phases, a mythical or poetic period, an age of the gods; then an aristocratic period dominated by heroes and heraldic crests; then a demotic period; and finally a *ricorso,* or return to chaos followed by the beginning of another cycle. Vico traces these four periods through the classical age to the fall of the Roman Empire, and speaks of a new cycle beginning in the medieval period. In the twentieth century Spengler worked out a similar vision of history, although he uses the metaphor of organisms rather than cycles. Spengler influenced Yeats to some degree, but not Joyce. The first section of *Finnegans Wake,* covering the first eight chapters, deals with the mythical or poetic period of legend and myths of gods; the second section, in four chapters, with the aristocratic phase; the third, also in four chapters, with the demotic phase, and the final or seventeenth chapter with the *ricorso.* The book ends in the middle of a sentence which is completed by the opening words of the first page, thus dramatizing the cycle as vividly as words can well do.

In contrast, there seems relatively little concrete documentation for the influence of Bruno of Nola, and one of the most useful commentaries, which has Vico all over the place, does not even list Bruno in the index. Yet Bruno was an early influence, coming to Joyce's attention before his growing trouble with his eyesight forced him to become increasingly dependent on the help of others for his reading. In his early pamphlet **"The Day of the Rabblement,"** he alludes to Bruno as "the Nolan," clearly with some pleasure in concealing the name of a dangerous heretic under a common Irish one. What the Nolan said, according to Joyce, was that no one can be a lover of the true and good without abhorring the multitude, which suggests that the immature Joyce, looking for security in a world where his genius was not yet recognized, found some reassurance in Bruno's habitual arrogance of tone. Bruno's "heresy," evidently, seemed to Joyce less an attack on or repudiation of Catholic doctrines than the isolating of himself from the Church through a justified spiritual pride—the same heresy he ascribes to Stephen in the *Portrait*. As far as Bruno's ideas were concerned, Joyce was less interested in the plurality of worlds, which so horrified Bruno's contemporaries, and concentrates on a principle largely derived by Bruno from Nicholas of Cusa, who was not only orthodox but a cardinal, the principle of polarity. Joyce tells Harriet Shaw Weaver in a letter that Bruno's philosophy "is a kind of dualism—every power in nature must evolve an opposite in order to realize itself and opposition brings reunion." Most writers would be more likely to speak of Hegel in such a connection, but that is not the kind of source one looks for in Joyce. In the compulsory period of his education Joyce acquired some knowledge of the Aristotelian philosophical tradition, and learned very early the numbing effect of an allusion to St. Thomas Aquinas. But there is little evidence that the mature Joyce read technical philosophy with any patience or persistence—not even Heraclitus, who could have given him most of what he needed of the philosophy of polarity in a couple of aphorisms.

In a later letter to Harriet Weaver, Joyce says, referring to both Vico and Bruno: "I would not pay overmuch attention to these theories, beyond using them for all they are worth." That is, cyclical theories of history and philosophies of polarity were not doctrines he wished to expound, the language of *Finnegans Wake* being clearly useless for expounding anything, but structural principles for the book. It is this question of structural principles that I should like to look into at the moment, rather than simple allusion. Many of Joyce's allusions, especially to run-of-the-mill fiction and poetry written in nineteenth-century Ireland, are there primarily because the setting is Irish; many of his structural principles derive from sources he seldom refers to. He owed a great deal more to Blake, for example, than one would realize from the number of references to him—more than he himself realized, probably. Again, if *Finnegans Wake* is a dream, the researches of Freud and Jung on dreams must be relevant to it, as both of these were prominent names in Joyce's milieu. Joyce's references to Freud and Jung are rare and usually in somewhat hostile contexts, but the hostility may be partly protective. When some of Freud was read to him he remarked that Vico had anticipated Freud, but in view of his use of Freud's Oedipal and censorship conceptions, his theory of wit, and his analysis of the condensation and displacement of the dreamwork, the remark seems to be something of a boutade. Again, Joyce had personal reasons for not wanting to come too close to Jung, but Jung's "collective unconscious" may also be a structural principle in the book.

Finnegans Wake was published in the year that I began continuous teaching, and within a few months I bought the copy that I still have, for ninety-eight cents on a remainder counter in Toronto. I was fascinated by the book, but was preoccupied at the time with the Blake prophe-

cies, and was in no position to go into orbit around it. When the Blake book was off my hands and I started working on the *Anatomy of Criticism,* I had to account, so to speak, for the existence of *Finnegans Wake.* True, there was a popular fallacy at the time, which I kept hearing for the next twenty years, that all works of literature were "unique," and that the critic should not try to detract from that uniqueness. The notion rested on a confusion between criticism as a body of knowledge about literature and the experience of reading, which is central to criticism but not part of it. Every experience is in some sense unique, but the unique as such cannot be an object of knowledge. So the task remained, as did, of course, the confusion. It seemed to me that there was an epic form that tended to expand into a kind of imaginative encyclopedia, and that the limit of this encyclopedic form was the sacred book, the kind of scriptural myth that we find in the Bible, the Prose Edda and in Hindu literature. The affinities of *Finnegans Wake,* for all its pervasive irony, appeared to be closest to that form, and I could see that the Bible (along with missals and prayer books, both Catholic and Anglican), the Koran, and the Egyptian Book of the Dead were much in Joyce's mind. Otherwise there seemed to be no critical theory that really illuminated what Joyce was doing. Joyce himself certainly did not provide one: his critical abilities were limited, and he seems to have been content to go along with the generally accepted statement that the language of *Finnegans Wake* is "dream language." But while it is true that the dream condenses and displaces and superimposes and puns and plays every kind of verbal trick, it hardly produces the linguistic Niagara that Joyce's seventeen years of work on *Finnegans Wake* accumulated. One cannot blame his contemporaries for insisting that he was wasting his genius on something that fell outside literature: one can only marvel at his persistence and inner confidence. But at his death, however extraordinary his achievement, it still seemed to be completely sui generis, and Eliot's remark that one *Finnegans Wake* was probably enough sounded like the most unassailable common sense. It was perhaps not until Jacques Derrida and his "deconstruction" techniques that the theory implied by *Finnegans Wake* really came into focus. The deconstructing critic tends to approach every text in the spirit in which Joyce approached the first drafts of his *Work in Progress* fragments. *Finnegans Wake* is a book in which practically every word provides, in addition to a surface meaning that may or may not be there, a great variety of "supplements" providing a number of further aspects to the meaning. Deconstruction implies a concept not far removed from Freud's concept of the censor, the process of achieving meaning by excluding unacceptable meanings; and Joyce's dream language, while the activity of censorship is certainly recorded in it, escapes, to a very unusual degree, from the kind of psychological gaps that mental censorship leaves in narrative-directed writing.

Then again, *Finnegans Wake* is a book of "traces." The central character, Finnegan himself, is effaced by his "death," or falling asleep—the two things seem to be much the same thing at the opening of the book—and what follows is a "differential" pursuit of echoes and reverberations into a world of words rather than a "logocentric" invoking of a presence. It is natural that commentators influenced by Derridean theories should be doubtful about the presence in the book of any continuous "story line" and regard the identity of the dreamer as an irrelevant question in a book where nothing has any consistent identity at all. I think, however, that Joyce, belonging to an older generation, was old-fashioned enough to prefer a set of narrative canons, however distinctively handled.

We begin with the figure of Finnegan, who is both Finn, the great legendary hero of Ireland, and the subject of a ballad about a hod carrier who fell off a ladder, broke his neck, had a funeral wake in his honor, and woke up in the middle of it demanding a share of the whiskey. In Joyce the twelve mourners at the wake persuade Finn to go back to sleep, and tell him that he is about to be superseded by another character, whose full name, we eventually learn, is Humphrey Chimpden Earwicker, but who is most commonly to be recognized by his initials HCE. Finn and HCE are frequently identified in the book, and both are married to the central female figure, whose full name is Anna Livia Plurabelle, with the initials ALP. Nevertheless we are told, as explicitly as we are told anything in the book, that Finn and HCE are distinguishable aspects of the same identity, like persons of the Trinity.

Finn seems to be Joyce's equivalent of the giant man out of whose body the world is made that we find in so many creation myths, although in *Finnegans Wake* his body seems to extend only from the Head of Howth on the northeast to Phoenix Park on the southwest. But this Dublin area is a world that mirrors and epitomizes the world, and in this sense Finn belongs to the family of the Indian Purusha, the Norse Ymir, the Cabalistic Adam Kadmon or Qodmon, and Blake's Albion. HCE, then, is Finn-again, Finn asleep and dreaming, whose dream is the recurring cycle of history. A dream ends by waking up, but although there are various intimations of an awakening throughout the book, especially in the final chapter, the dream of human history is an unending dream in which all attempts to wake up continue to be baffled as Finn was at the beginning. Stephen Dedalus in *Ulysses* speaks of history as a nightmare from which he is trying to awake, but it is clear that he never does wake up in that sense anywhere in the book. Similarly, the narrative of *Finnegans Wake* goes around in a circle to form the book of "Doublends Jined" (Dublin's Giant and double-ends joined), and the *ricorso* at the end is not a resurrection but only a return. All the dreamers in *Finnegans Wake,* so far as they are individual people, may wake up and go about their business in the morning, but even so they are still contained within the larger dream of time.

HCE has two sons, Shem and Shaun, who represent the conflict that is the pervading characteristic of history, although they are both essentially aspects of HCE, according to the principle of polarity. Near the beginning of the book we enter a "museyroom" with mementos of Napoleon and Wellington: this episode was evidently suggested by an illustration in Freud's treatise on wit and the unconscious. Wellington is or could be considered an Irish hero: one thinks of Bernard Shaw's remark that the only match for a French army led by an Italian would be a British army led by an Irishman. Apart from that, however, the result of the battle of Waterloo was not of great importance to Ireland, and in fact there are suggestions that Napoleon actually won the battle, as no doubt he did in his dreams on St. Helena. The essential point is that Napoleon and Wellington are both products of the same historical force of European imperialism, and in that context their opposition is illusory.

This is the simplest form of a conflict of polarities: in a slightly more complex one a defender of something in Ireland is fighting an invader who threatens it. Early in the book there is an encounter of two giants, Mutt and Jute: Jute seems to be connected with Danish invaders and Mutt with the Irish under Brian Boru, who stopped them at the Battle of Clontarf. A century later there was the twelfth-century English conquest under Henry II, along with which came the absorption of the native Irish church by the Roman Catholic organization. The link between the two is afforded by the fact that the pope at the time of Henry II's invasion was Adrian IV, Nicholas Brakespear, the only pope of English origin. But even here the polarities merge. In the colloquy between Mutt and Jute, Mutt says of the tide coming in and going out of Dublin Bay: "Hither, craching eastuards, they are in surgence; hence, cool at ebb, they requiesce." We note the prominence of the initial letters HCE at the beginning of each clause, indicating that invasion, resistance, withdrawal, and absorption, like the flow and ebb of the tide, are all aspects of the same force appearing as opposites.

In later historical periods the opposition can take a form like that of the "Devils" and "Angels" of Blake's *Marriage of Heaven and Hell,* where creative radicals struggle against established conservatives. As a rule the "Micks," the partisans of the "Angels" represented by St. Michael, are much more popular and highly regarded, especially by women, than the "Nicks," partisans of the opposite side, identified as that of "Old Nick" or the Devil by their opponents. In this aspect of the conflict "Shem," the writer and social misfit, becomes an exile and "Shaun" his brother assumes a great variety of social roles, including that of a highly indecorous priest. Joyce identifies himself to a great extent with Shem, and there is a good deal—many readers, including the present one, would say far too much—about Joyce's poverty and the neglect of his genius. Still, there is a good deal about Dante in Dante and even more about Bruno in Bruno. Vico also wrote an *Autobiography,* and, as Hugh Kenner reminds us, tells us that he fell off a ladder in the library and was for a time thought to be dead. There are other writer-heroes, notably Swift, and even a political one, Parnell.

The rivalry of brothers comes mainly from the Book of Genesis, where the chief archetypes are, first, Cain and Abel, and then Esau and Jacob. Often the two brothers expand into three. The line of succession runs through neither Cain nor Abel but through a third brother, Seth, and Noah also had three sons, of whom one was called Shem and another Ham, Ham being cursed and made subordinate to the others. Similarly the two "sons of thunder" (the significance of this word will meet us in a moment) among Jesus' disciples, James and John, whose names remind us of Shem and Shaun, are usually joined by a third,

Peter. The theme of three brothers comes into such popular phrases as "Tom, Dick, and Harry," often echoed in the book, and into Swift's *Tale of a Tub,* where three brothers, Peter, Jack, and Martin, each think up their own way of perverting the teachings of the New Testament.

In any case the sons, or more generally the younger generation, whether two or three, may direct their rivalries not only against one another but against their father. This may take the regular Oedipus form of trying to replace him in the affections of the mother (ALP), or simply of cuckolding an older man, as notably in the Irish story of Tristram and King Mark. This situation expands into the usual conflict of generations: the antagonism of Parnell to his predecessor Isaac Butt, of Joyce himself to Yeats, and above all of an interminable shaggy dog story (said to be originally a story in the repertoire of Joyce's father) of how a certain "Buckley" shot (or didn't shoot) a "Russian General."

The female characters in *Finnegans Wake* reflect the ambiguity between the elusive, tantalizing siren whose indifference is deplored in so much poetry and the cherishing wife and mother whose constant care is the fostering of life. This is the usual relation of the daughter-figure Issy or Isabel, who is linked to Isolde, and who is eloquently described by the Joyce scholar Adeline Glasheen as "a perfect triumph of female imbecility," to her mother ALP. Issy is usually portrayed as a narcissistic figure gazing into her own mirror reflection, recalling Alice before her adventures or the two women, Stella and her shadowy companion Rebecca Dingley, who were the recipients of Swift's Journal with its disguising "little language." Here, naturally, the second or shadow girl readily turns into the younger woman in Swift's life, Vanessa. Like HCE and his sons, ALP and her daughter often merge into the same identity, but again they are polar opposites: we may call them, borrowing from both Robert Graves and the Song of Songs, the white goddess and the black bride. The former is what Blake would call the "Female Will," the retreating figure who fascinates, beckons, or betrays, but always eludes. The latter, who is consistently associated with the Liffey river flowing through Dublin, is the power of renewal that flows out into the sea on the last page of the book, just before returning to the headwaters of the "riverrun" on the first page.

Most commentators believe that there is an individual dreamer at the core of the book, a tavernkeeper in Chapelizod, just up the Liffey river from Dublin. His name is generally assumed to be the filled-out form of HCE, but it is also possible that his name is Porter (there are other candidates), though his wife's name seems to be, in all of her contexts, consistently Anna Livia. This Earwicker, or Porter, seems to be of English, Protestant, and ultimately Scandinavian origin, his dream expressing some alienation about finding himself in Ireland (as he sinks into sleep we hear a voice saying "So This Is Dyoublong?"). Thus there is a latent conflict with the other aspect of himself, Finn, though the reality masked by that opposition appears to lie outside the book. The individual dreamer, if he is there, has two sons, usually called Jerry and Kevin, a daughter Isabel, at least two servants, a potboy and a cleaning woman; twelve customers in his pub (the mourners at Finn's wake), and a number of shadowy neighbors, including a mysterious "Magrath" and the "Maggies," who are evidently schoolmates of Issy or Isabel.

We seem to have, then, three major concentric circles of dream. The innermost is the individual dream of the tavernkeeper, the outermost the dream of mankind which is history, while in between there is the constant metamorphosis of the relations of Shem to Shaun, the universalized forms of Jerry and Kevin. The individual story assimilates the intensely studied scenes of Dublin life in *Dubliners* into the book; the Shem-Shaun rivalries incorporate *Portrait of the Artist as a Young Man* and *Stephen Hero,* with their focus on the social and cultural situation of Joyce himself; the dream of the many-sided Everyman whose *periplus* voyage covers the whole of the known world incorporates *Ulysses.* In *Ulysses* Stephen is an ex-Catholic intellectual and the figure who eventually becomes a symbolic father is Jewish; in *Finnegans Wake,* which was completed during the rise of Nazism in Europe, these affinities are reversed, Shem being "Semitic" and Shaun mainly parody Catholic. The activities of the tavernkeeper and his family during the previous day form the "manifest content" of the dream, the things on which the mind has not yet slept, as Freud says; the archetypal expansion of those activities to cover all human history forms the latent content. One would also expect the universal, autobiographical, and local imagery to predominate in turn through the three phases of Vico's cycle, and to some degree they do.

However expanded, the Dublin setting, or the Irish setting generally, remains constant throughout the book. One reason, not impossibly the decisive reason, why Vico and Bruno of Nola are so important in the dream is that there is a Vico Road just outside Dublin and a Dublin bookshop called Nowlan and Browne. It is clear that the *coincidentia oppositorum,* the real unity of apparent opposites, is only one small aspect of an epic quest in which the dragon to be slain, the enemy of the quest, is coincidence itself. A coincidence is a piece of design that one cannot find a use for, and in that sense there is no such thing as a coincidence in *Finnegans Wake.* If we ask who the hero is that is to achieve such a quest, the answer is, clearly, the reader of the book, "the ideal reader suffering from an ideal insomnia," as Joyce says. The reader is not only the hero of *Finnegans Wake*; he is also the only character involved with it who is never allowed to sleep or dream.

The merging of the individual dream with the total dream of mankind appears to be the central postulate on which Joyce's book is based. In one extraordinary interview, Joyce spoke of himself as a kind of psychopomp summoning the spirits of the dead. Naturally he would be most attracted to highly speculative thinkers who try to break out of the rigid Cartesian dualism in which so much of our intellectual attitude is still confined. One such thinker is Samuel Butler: Butler is not a major influence on *Finnegans Wake,* but there are several references to *Erewhon* and *The Way of All Flesh.* The latter is a bildungsroman in which the author examines a younger version of himself in order to objectify the younger self and break something of its hold on him, as Joyce's *Portrait* does with Stephen Dedalus.

In his biological writings, Butler deals with the conception of personality in such a way as to show that the personality has no clear circumference or center. All life interpenetrates with all other life, and all life constitutes a single being. In *The Way of All Flesh* he draws the inference that eventually we shall have to abolish the distinction of subject and object, internal and external, and live and work within a purely metaphorical universe. A few pages further on Butler quotes his hero as saying that no incontrovertible first premise for a philosophical system can ever be found, because "no one could get behind Bishop Berkeley." Joyce's references to the story of Buckley and the Russian General, already mentioned, often refer to Buckley as "Berkeley," which would associate the "Russian General" with, perhaps, Lenin, who made Berkeley the cockshy for the bourgeois idealism he was out to destroy. In itself this is probably overzealous commentary, but it is not inherently impossible that Berkeley should be for Joyce, as for Yeats, the Irish philosopher who had effectively removed the barriers between waking and dreaming life.

Butler and Berkeley lead us to an idealistic tradition from which Bruno also derived. In his book *God the Known and Unknown,* Butler equates his conception of the unity of all life with a "known" aspect of God. Such a foray into natural theology may seem unusual for a post-Darwinian writer, but it brings us close to Bruno's doctrine *natura est deus in rebus,* that nature is an incarnation of God in whom "all is in all." We referred earlier to Joyce's remark that Vico had anticipated Freud: perhaps, similarly, Bruno for him had anticipated something of Jung's "collective unconscious."

Like other scriptures, *Finnegans Wake* begins with the standard mythical themes of beginning: creation, fall (or some other myth about how man became mortal), and a universal deluge. In *Finnegans Wake* these are all essentially the same event: when man fell, the world he fell into was this one, and this world is symbolically submarine as well as subterranean. The assimilation of the three events is identical with Blake's myth of the fall when, as he says in *Europe:* "the five senses whelm'd / In deluge o'er the earth-born man." In Blake's *Jerusalem* Albion lies asleep in Atlantis at the bottom of the "Sea of Time and Space" for most of the poem, the archetypal leviathan or sea monster of the indefinite. Joyce's Finn is a land monster or "behemoth" whose "brontoichthyian form" can be dimly discerned in the landscape.

Freud's analysis of dreams gives us little sense of the real nature and importance of the anxiety dream, the deep uneasy guilt feelings that can hardly be explained as a mere blocking of desire. There is, however, an extraordinary flash of insight in De Quincey's mail-coach essay, where De Quincey speaks of a sudden crisis in his own experience passing into his dreams and merging there with a sense of original sin, of the kind which no doubt prompted the fall myth itself, and which, he suggests, perhaps everybody dreams over again every night. Nobody in *Finnegans Wake* seems to have heard of De Quincey except the least

likely character, Isabel, but the individual dream of the tavernkeeper at least is constantly losing or finding its identity in some myth of the fall of man.

Mysterious things are hinted at about the dreamer's sons, who have expanded into three soldiers and remind us of the sons of Noah, of whom one saw his drunken father as he should not have been seen. The daughter has become two girls, whose bladders begin the running of water that flows through the book, where the voyeurism goes in the opposite direction. There is also an encounter in Phoenix Park, a place associated with death (the Phoenix Park murders) and treachery (the attempt to involve Parnell in them which was frustrated by one conspirator's misspelling of "hesitancy"). HCE is accosted by a "cad" (cadet or younger son) with a "pipe" (French slang for penis) and asked for the time. He gives a stuttering answer and his "hesitancy" starts rumors spreading around the world. In a larger context the stutter marks the mechanical repetition of moments that is our experience of time, which according to St. Augustine began with the fall. The time when the question is asked appears to be 11:32, which is also twenty-eight to twelve, those being numbers prominent in human efforts to work out a calendar with the solar and lunar cycles. Both have associations in the book. Isabel's schoolmates, called the "Maggies," number twenty-eight, and the twelve mourners who persuade Finnegan to go back to sleep suggest a zodiacal cycle, just as, according to Blake, the twelve tribes of Israel in the desert were hypnotized by the zodiac ("sons of Albion") into giving up their revolution for a deified robot's legal code.

We are accustomed nowadays to hear that the unconscious, however defined, is linguistically structured as well as the consciousness. Here again is something that Joyce might have absorbed from earlier writers: Butler, for example, tells us that all genuine and achieved knowledge is unconscious knowledge, the consciousness being concerned only with exploring the new and as yet unassimilated. In the conscious world verbal exchange, though the chief means of communication, is also used quite as much to conceal or disguise communication. We build up ironic, self-enclosed verbal structures that others can penetrate only obliquely, or else we stylize what we say in dramatic attitudes conditioned by the characters of those we talk to. Meanwhile, the verbal currents boiling and swirling around in our unconscious keep up a constant jockeying for power, each trying to get to a place where it can dominate the ego. This gives a particular importance to the message from the outside that bypasses the conscious mind and strikes directly into the unconscious. According to Vico, the cycle of history begins with the thunderclap, interpreted by men (then giants) as the voice of God. Later, we have oracles purporting to carry the voice of divine authority, and eventually (to move outside Vico), the sacred scripture develops a codified body of such messages.

In *Finnegans Wake* the inner babble of the individual mind expands into a vision of mankind as dreaming a communal dream of conflicting voices, with occasionally a voice of command or exceptional authority penetrating and for an instant silencing the tumult. The series of thunderclaps, of a hundred letters each, that mark the beginning of a new phase of history begins on the opening page, and HCE is associated with the "earwig" or *perceoreille* ("Persse O'Reilly"), the insect that traditionally penetrates the ear of a sleeper. We may compare a line from the close of Blake's *Jerusalem,* just as the final apocalypse begins: "Her voice pierc'd Albions clay-cold ear." It is only the voice of the poet, the successor in society of the oracle and scripture, that carries this authority now, though the voice is constantly neglected. "Hear the voice of the Bard," Blake pleaded, and went on to say that the Bard's message is outside time and descends directly from the voice of God in Eden. It was also Blake who applied to himself the motto of John the Baptist, "The voice of one crying in the wilderness."

For a century after Blake's death poets were fascinated by the figure of John the Baptist, the herald and announcer of a new age, whose passion, unlike that of Jesus, involved their cherished theme of the femme fatale. Yeats, we remember, devoted much of his energy to proclaiming a new age and seeing signs of it in contemporary Ireland, even though, according to the most reliable of his clocks, the Christian era still has another thousand years to go. At the end of *Portrait of the Artist as a Young Man,* Stephen identifies his friend Cranly with John the Baptist, clearly reserving a greater role for himself, which in *Ulysses* it seems obvious he is not going to attain. *Finnegans Wake* seems to me largely based on the theme of annunciation, with Vico and Bruno standing guard over it partly because their first names, Giambattista and Giordano, suggest John the Baptist at the Jordan.

The struggles of Shem and Shaun, with their metamorphoses, form the main action of the book. Shem is the "penman" or "punman" who carries on the poetic and oracular tradition, and two elements in his technique are important for understanding his oracular role. One is the incessant use of the thematic phrase. Such phrases as "the same anew," "up guards, and at them," "Honi soit qui mal y pense," and dozens of others appear in astonishing variations throughout. This device is often linked to Wagner's leitmotif technique, although Joyce was not really a Wagnerian. In a preliterary age such thematic phrases would be magical formulas. The other technical element, which also harks back to preliterary magic, shows the poet as preeminently the knower of names, and, in the unconscious, calling a name can command an appearance. For all the distortion, there is a continuous orgy of naming in *Finnegans Wake*: books of the Bible, suras of the Koran, lyrics of Tom Moore, catalogues of rivers and cities, just for a start.

I have elsewhere spoken of two aspects of poetry deeply involved with the unconscious as charm and riddle. Charm in particular is linked to the oracular, to the sense of magical compulsion in its tradition, to an appeal to the past that takes the form "as that was, so may this be." Riddle is rather a perplexing of the conscious intelligence that prompts one to "guess" or identify the object it presents without naming. The riddle is the home of the pun, the metaphor, the verbal clusters formed in the unconscious and rising to the conscious surface. The charm is the home

of incantation, of the mystery hidden in sound. Charm and riddle are a psychological contrast, and if we stayed entirely within either area we should get a bad case of what Eliot calls dissociated sensibility. If we stayed with the oracular world of charm, everything would seem solemn, awful, portentous, and the least breath of humor or irreverence would destroy the mood. If we stayed with the world of riddle, we should be subjected to an endless stream of irresponsible wisecracks. To walk the razor's edge between the two, to achieve an oracular charm that is witty and a wit that evokes profound and haunting depths of linguistic experience, is a considerable tour de force, not to speak of keeping it up for over six hundred pages.

In the first chapter we are told a strange tale of a certain Jarl van Hoother, the earl of Howth in a Dutch or Scandinavian disguise, who is another context of HCE and who has two sons, named, in this tale, Tristopher and Hilary. A female figure known as a "prankquean" kidnaps first one son and then the other, keeping each in the wilderness for forty years and converting them to something else. Trisopher is converted to being a "luderman," presumably some form of playboy; Hilary is converted to a "tristian," a sorrowful Christian or Tristram. As we read this we are reminded of Bruno's personal motto, used at the beginning of his play *Il Candelaio* and elsewhere: *In tristitia hilaris, in hilaritate tristis.* The solemn and the gay are interchangeable aspects of the same thing, and this may well be the essence, for Joyce, of Bruno's theory of polarity.

Shem is the writer; Shaun is ultimately the product of what is written. Shaun is, first, the public that receives the poet's message, ridicules and belittles it when it cannot ignore it, and yet unconsciously keeps transforming and often perverting it into social institutions and codes of behavior. Shem works directly in the stream of time that supplies the energy of history; Shaun spatializes what Shem does, though he himself does not really know this, and regards himself as the intermediary between authority, whatever its source, and the public. Shem fails to guess the most important riddle with which he is confronted, the "heliotrope" riddle in the mime chapter, but Shaun answers a great many riddles, his confidence undiminished by the number of answers that are either wrong or irrelevant. Finally, in the fifteenth chapter near the end, Shaun is subjected to a close and sustained inquiry which brings out the fact that he is really the sum total of the book itself, as one of its characters after another emerges from him. The last one to emerge is HCE, who speaks as the builder of cities and civilizations throughout history.

Yet even HCE is not the fundamental force of history, for the great cities of the past are ruins now, and the most impressive erections disappear in a world where "Gricks may rise and Troysirs fall." Below him is the river of time, the ALP who continually renews herself, and HCE along with herself. All through the book we keep hearing about a "letter" written by ALP, lost in a dungheap but representing a creative energy of communication that Shem is in much closer touch with than either Shaun or HCE. Shaun supplies us with a greatly distorted version of this letter, but a more authentic one emerges at the very end, just before the final farewell speech by ALP as she flows out and merges with the sea. ALP herself can only die and renew: as she sinks into her father the sea we catch a glimpse of the conjunction of a bird and woman that marks the starting point of a new cycle of time, like those of Leda and the swan and the dove and the Virgin in Yeats: "If I seen him bearing down on me now under whitespread wings like he'd come from Arkangels, I sink I'd die down over his feet, humbly dumbly, only to wash-up." But unlike the Magdalen whom she echoes, she is not present at a resurrection, only at a renewal. The book goes around in the circle of the *ricorso*. But there is another kind of vision hinted at in the very end of her letter: "Hence we've lived in two worlds. He is another he what stays under the himp of holth."

Of the two worlds, the higher one is the world of the turning cycle of life, death, and renewal; below it is the still sleeping Finn who is all mankind. When we are told at the beginning of the book that Finn is about to be superseded by HCE, we can see an analogy with the relation of Ireland to the constant stream of Irish invaders, Danish, Roman, British, and the rest. At the end we get a glimpse of an apocalypse opening up from below that will swallow the cycle: this does not happen, but the last line of *Finnegans Wake* contains the little noticed phrase "till thou sends thee." What looks like the primary meaning of this is "till thou sends thee" or thyself, a second coming or reunion of HCE and ALP with a permanently awakened Finn. We are left with the sense that the imagery of the cycle, with its death followed by renewal and return, is the only imagery that human language, conscious or unconscious, can draw on to express whatever is beyond the cycle. Also that there is one polarity in which the opposed forces can never unite: the apocalyptic separation of the states of life and death.

We are left, finally, with the ultimate categories of time and space. Time is the inner energy of life, flowing in a relatively undisturbed form during sleep; our waking consciousness constructs a spatialized world, HCE's world of buildings and mountains. Joyce, who identifies with Shem, was told during his lifetime by various Shaun figures, such as Wyndham Lewis, that he ought to pay more attention to the spatial and objective world. Of Joyce's two mentors, Vico was particularly the theorist of time and history; Bruno, with his doctrine of an infinite universe, explored a new conception of space, pointing out that Aristotle, for example, who was so constantly quoted against him, had no word for space. Such words as *chora* and *topos* mean not space but place, space *there*. And yet Vico's cyclical conception of historical process is really a vision of time within a spatial metaphor, and Bruno's conception of the identity of polarized opposites a vision of the spatial subject-object confrontation dissolving back into a temporal flux. All our experience collapses in on a deadlock of categories, and there is nothing in human language, the expanded language of *Finnegans Wake* to get us out. Nothing, that is, except its confrontation with an insomniac reader who is still outside the book, struggling to make a sense of it that cannot ultimately be limited even to Joyce's sense. Such a reader is the closest we can come to Lewis Carroll's Humpty Dumpty, HCE before he fell off his

wall, who could explain all the poems that had ever been written, along with a number that hadn't been written yet.

When *Finnegans Wake* was published and the responses confused and disappointing, Joyce stressed the wit of the book as its more obvious appeal, and asked why nobody could see that it was funny. But we should not overlook its seriousness as well, or the fact that he apparently read, for instance, Blavatsky's *Isis Unveiled* with close attention, was genuinely interested in Yeats's *Vision,* except that he regretted, as do other readers of Yeats, its being imprisoned in a system disconnected from the poetry, and even spoke of minor and less seminal books on comparative mythology, such as Allen Upward's *Divine Mystery,* as coming close to doing what he was trying to do in his way. The merits of these books are not significant: what they indicate is the existence of a motive in Joyce's compulsively careful organization very different from what the puns and so-called obscenities indicate by themselves. One can match the charm-and-riddle language of the book with much of the Old Testament and the Vedic Hymns, but one can also find a good deal of it in both Vico and Bruno. Vico's "new science" opened up a whole new field of scholarly endeavor, yet his central myth, which begins with giants terrified of a thunderclap, running into caves dragging their wives behind them, and so instituting private property, reads almost like parody. Bruno is a writer whose satire and scatology almost matches Joyce's own, who wrote a great deal of self-obsessed braggadocio, abuse of contemporaries, long meaningless catalogues, and heavy-handed humor, but who nonetheless died a martyr to his vision. Both writers are full of the contradictions of creative power itself, and both find their tradition continued in the epic of a drunken Irishman's mock funeral wake that expands into the sleep of Eve and Adam under the circling stars. (pp. 356-74)

> *Northrop Frye, "Cycle and Apocalypse in 'Finnegans Wake'," in his* Myth and Metaphor: Selected Essays, 1974-1988, *edited by Robert D. Denham, University Press of Virginia, 1990, pp. 356-74.*

John Gordon   (essay date 1986)

[*In the following excerpt, Gordon asserts that Joyce's method of representing reality through the consciousness of his characters culminates in* Finnegans Wake.]

From beginning to end, Joyce remained a mimic in the root sense of the word. What changed, and deepened, between 1905 and the years that produced *Finnegans Wake* was not his mimetic intention but his understanding of the world he wished to render and the resourcefulness which he brought to the task. In particular he became, over these years, increasingly conscious of the paradox at the heart of the mimetic enterprise—that since the objective world must be represented, as it is experienced, through the prism of some individual consciousness, the artist seeking fidelity to fact must represent both simultaneously, must turn inward as well as outward. The quest for objectivity becomes the study of subjectivity, or rather the study of how the two interact. The author listening to the Seine must also attend to himself, listening, and indeed 'Anna Livia Plurabelle' is a *tour de force* not only for its rivering cadences but also for the voices of the women hearing it, making of it a symbol for their old lives, mingling their memories with its reality—and we can hear, if *we* listen, the purblind, ageing author doing the same thing, listening to a river in exile and remembering the river of his homeland: "Tis endless now senne eye or erewone last saw Waterhouse's clogh. They took it asunder, I hurd them sigh. When will they reassemble it?' The acutely sensitive presence of [Joyce's realistic] earlier work becomes 're-miniscensitive'. (pp. 1-2)

Now, there are many who feel that the last thing the world needs is another book about Joyce's symbols, and I understand their feeling. It is hard not to sympathise with the irritation of Clive Hart when he says, 'Our lives are full of fucking symbols: we don't need them in our reading matter as well' [quoted in Roland McHugh's *The 'Finnegans Wake' Experience*]. The natural reaction—exemplified in Joyce studies by Robert M. Adams and, before him, by Joyce's brother Stanislaus—is to echo Freud and insist that sometimes a cigar is just a cigar.

Well, yes and no. That a cigar is not necessarily a phallic symbol I agree. But which cigar are we talking about? I don't smoke, so if I had one on my desk here it would represent something unusual—probably the person who gave it to me, let us say to commemorate a recent birth. Behind that gesture would lie a slightly archaic custom towards which any American male of my generation is liable to feel ambivalent, and which I for one associate with movies of the 1930s and comic strips popular in the same period, movies and comic strips in which beaming males wearing vests and spats, released from the waiting room in which their pacing has worn a circular rut, present one another with blimp-shaped 'stogies' while slapping one another on the back and announcing 'It's A Boy!' (Joyce saw the same cartoons. . . .) Or it could be a cigar being smoked by a friend, either male (symbolising various things about him), or female, (symbolising various things about her plus, I suppose, liberation), or even child (symbolising stunted growth, etc). The cigar in the best-known picture of Freud symbolises, for me, cancer, needless suffering, and a pathetic infirmity in a great man who knew better.

That is the world of which *Finnegans Wake* is made, a world not of 'cigars' but of this cigar or that cigar. The objects surrounding its characters turn into symbols because that is what the objects we live with do. Man, said Aristotle, is the symbol-making animal, and *Finnegans Wake* is in that sense man-like: it is a vast symbol-making conjurer, replicating more faithfully than anything else ever written the process by which each individual generates, as opposed to receives, the meanings around him. Generates, not receives: that, it seems to me, is the distinction behind Joyce's objection to Freud—that he was not so much wrong as simplistic, fixedly translating certain things into certain other 'symbolic' things: house into womb, fire into phallus.

Being creatures of characters imagined by a man who was exceptionally sensitive to verbal and especially etymological nuance, a man who once made a point of hanging a pic-

ture of Cork in a cork frame, the symbols formed may have more to do with word-associations than we would normally expect: it matters, for instance, that the 'Argentine' in the sleeper's room is phonically close to both a kind of silvery fish and a South American country. In general, words are taken more literally than we're used to: it helps to be the kind of person who instinctively cringes on hearing an expression like 'pay through the nose' or 'peel your eyes'. But the essential process is identical to that discoverable by anyone who will look around and look within. All places we inhabit become middens of symbols. That is the reason that a book whose events virtually all occur in one room can be an autobiography and, because the life recounted has been lived in the world outside, over many days each 'dense as a decade', a (highly eccentric) universal history. In fact the history evoked can be dauntingly far-ranging and esoteric, because Joycean characters since *Ulysses* are permitted at times to plug into the intellectual resources of their erudite author. Leopold Bloom conjures up the hallucination of a figure, Virag, who gives utterance to his preoccupation with morbid sexual arcana through allusions unfamiliar to Bloom himself; the male principal of *Finnegans Wake,* reminded of Waterloo, refers readily to military *minutiae* beyond his ken.

That modification understood, the essential dramatic

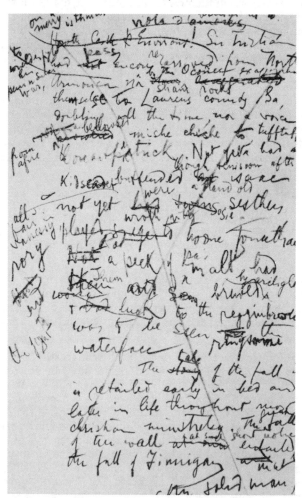

The first draft of the opening of Finnegans Wake.

premise of the *Wake* is a familiar one in the annals of dream literature and its analogues in other arts. It is the premise of, for instance, Ravel's *'L'enfant et les sortilèges'*, of the various 'Transformation Scene' effects in Buñuel and Dali's *'L'âge d'or* or Fritz Lang's *Metropolis,* of similar effects in children's classics such as Disney's *Dumbo* or Maurice Sendak's *Where the Wild Things Are:* under the influence of night or intoxication or imagination, familiar figures change into symbols generated from the interaction of their physical selves, the memories and conventions connected with them, and the state of the observer. The process is always to a certain extent one of projection, as in these two *Rashomon*-like set-pieces recording different characters' perceptions of, first, a stick with some sort of protuberance at one end, second the plink-plunking of water drops:

> Batty believes a baton while Hogan hears a hod yet Heer prefers a punsil shapner and Cope and Bull go cup and ball.

> The rushes by the grey nuns' pond: ah eh oh let me sigh too. Coalmansbell: behoves you handmake of the load. Jenny Wren: pick, peck. Johnny Post: pack, puck.

Most Wakean mutations are more elaborate than these examples because of their capacity for coming to life, for taking command of the text and making its story their story. The phenomenon itself begins as a familiar one in literature, essentially identical in origin with the common practice—variously called *'erlebte Rede', 'le style indirect libre',* or 'narrated monologue'—of letting a given character's idiom either take over or influence the narrator's style for as long as that character is the centre of attention. In Joyce's work this practice is often compounded by characters who are themselves, as it were, readers, their idioms infected by something recently read or heard. Here is a double-barrelled, and quite Joycean, example from Max Beerbohm's *Zuleika Dobson:*

> But, just as he set pen to paper, his hand faltered, and he sprang up, victim of another and yet more violent fit of sneezing.
> Dibuskined, dangerous. The spirit of Juvenal woke in him. He would flay. He would make Woman (as he called Zuleika) writhe. . . .

Like Beerbohm's character here, a Wakean figure who contemplates another symbol—a book of Juvenal, a calendar picture—will simultaneously revive, bring to life, its appropriate voice, and the narrative will record the process.

In the later Joyce particularly, both will go still further. They will, to a great extent, adopt the story or other set of conventions associated with that symbol—as if the young man of Beerbohm's book were for a page or ten to become Juvenal, and the events of the book thereafter were to be to some extent determined by the known pattern of Juvenal's life as well as by the requirements of the original Oxford fable. The practice is implicit in Joyce's work almost from the beginning. Florence L. Walzl has pointed out [in Bernard Benstock's *The Seventh of Joyce*] that the Eveline of *Dubliners* winds up acting out the story of a picture on her wall, that in effect 'Eveline' turns out

to be the story of that picture, transmuted through Eveline's consciousness. A more complicated version of the same thing occurs in the last story of *Dubliners,* 'The Dead'. Early on, Gabriel Conroy takes in two pictures:

> A picture of the balcony scene in *Romeo and Juliet* hung there and beside it was a picture of the two murdered princes in the Tower which Aunt Julia had worked in red, blue and brown wools when she was a girl.

It seems an idle enough observation, and yet consider: Gabriel is a professor of literature, attuned to the literary, and especially Shakespearian, ramifications of those pictures. The story of that balcony scene will return to him at the end of this night, when his wife tells him of her farewell to the young star-crossed lover who stood calling to her window from the back garden, under her window. Mingled with it will be the story of those two princes, murdered by Richard III in the play Gabriel knows well, whose ghosts return in the last act of that play to tell their assassin what the imagined ghost of the young Michael Furey tells Gabriel, at the end of *his* story: 'Despair and die!' (' . . . some impalpable and vindictive being was coming against him, gathering forces against him in its vague world'. Those two Shakespearian stories have entered into Gabriel through his eyes and memory, and after a spell of subterranean ferment their working-out comes to control his own story—comes in a way to write it, in fact, to determine its events as well as its style: the picture of the 'vindictive' haunter may be laid solely to Gabriel's literary imagination, but who or what has determined that his wife shall tell him her Romeo-and-Juliet story on this night? Who if not a narrator whose account of what is done and said is, in some strange way, conditioned by what occurs to the mind of his central character?

In fact the further along we get in Joyce's work the more it can seem as if the books are being improvised by the characters, the events related the product of fancies generated in the characters' minds by earlier events. There is an early, rudimentary version of the phenomenon in the first chapter of *A Portrait of the Artist as a Young Man,* where Stephen Dedalus reads about heroic Horatio-types in his book of Roman history and is immediately called on to stand fast against Father Dolan, the barbarian from without with his washerwoman's name. By the middle of *Ulysses* it is possible to find entire chapters being generated out of previous chapters by way of the central character's mediating sensibility: Leopold Bloom, for instance, leaves a bunch of men boozily singing an inflammatory patriotic song, 'The Croppy Boy', about a martyr being betrayed and hanged, and walks into a personification of such sentiments in a chapter, 'Cyclops', which is all about hanging and martyrdom, especially his.

By *Finnegans Wake* the improvisation is near-absolute. The character sees or hears things, or remembers or imagines seeing or hearing them, and the patterns and stories evoked in that act come to life and take command, become the patterns and stories of the text. He goes, or imagines going, to a privy containing a picture of a Waterloo battle scene, and the text is given over to rendering a notably faecal account of that battle. He hears, or imagines hearing, his daughter whisper to him from another room, and immediately the forbidden temptress of his desires appears, front and centre, casting everything else into background. To be sure in these as in other cases we cannot easily distinguish what is being imagined from what is being experienced, just as we may have trouble at times distinguishing what Stephen Dedalus is doing and what he is thinking of doing. All the events of *Finnegans Wake* occur in double focus at least: emanations depart from their dreaming original to go about their business, responding to stimuli in the way he would envision himself doing were he awake, and beget other emanations in turn, and so on; . . . it is the commonest thing in the Wakean world for a figure to be in two or more places at once. But the very difficulty in separating these multiple projections from one another, in distinguishing what is happening from what is imagined as happening, testifies to the extent to which they behave according to the same rules. All respond to the cues of their environment with improvisations compounded of public and private associations which immediately become the matter of the text. Imagination and experience are difficult to tell apart because the ways of the former follow the laws of the latter. (pp. 2-7)

John Gordon, in his Finnegans Wake: A Plot Summary, *Gill and Macmillan, 1986, 302 p.*

John Bishop   (essay date 1986)

[*In the following excerpt, Bishop defends the obscurity of* Finnegans Wake *as instrumental to Joyce's literary exploration of dreams and the unconscious.*]

Sooner rather than later, a reader of *Finnegans Wake* would do well to justify to himself its stupefying obscurity; for as even its most seasoned readers know, "*Finnegans Wake* is wilfully obscure. It was conceived as obscurity, it was executed as obscurity, it is about obscurity" [Adaline Glasheen, in her *A Second Census of "Finnegans Wake"*]. And to this one might add that nothing will ever make *Finnegans Wake* not obscure. Stories of the pains Joyce took to deepen the opacity of *Work in Progress* during its composition only intensify the impression thrown off by the finished text. Jacques Mercanton recalls finding Joyce and Stuart Gilbert "going over a passage that was 'still not obscure enough'" and gleefully "inserting Samoyed words into it" [Mercanton, "The Hours of James Joyce," in *Portraits of the Artist in Exile*, edited by Willard Potts]; Padraic Colum recalls [in *Our Friend James Joyce*] "from time to time [being] asked to suggest a word that would be more obscure than the word already there," only to have Joyce reply "five times out of six," in what amounts to an admission that his designs were darkly principled, "I can't use it." The essential question one wants answered in hearing these stories and in probing the murkinesses of the text itself is whether this relentless obscuration was really arbitrary and wilful—"sheer perversity," in Louise Bogan's phrase [in "Finnegans Wake," *Nation*, 6 May 1939]—or whether it was leading somewhere that would repay the study, time, and labor which *Finnegans Wake* demands of its reader. Joyce himself was unevenly helpful; as he put it to Frank Budgen on the less baffling matter of *Ulysses*, "If I can throw any obscurity

on the subject let me know" [*The Letters of James Joyce*, Vol. 3, edited by Richard Ellmann].

Not very expansively, he replied to the growing news that his readers simply were not following him by wondering out loud, with lamblike innocence, to William Bird: "About my new work—do you know, Bird, I confess I can't understand some of my critics, like Pound or Miss Weaver, for instance. They say it's *obscure*. They compare it, of course, with *Ulysses*. But the action of *Ulysses* was chiefly in the daytime, and the action of my new work takes place chiefly at night. It's natural things should not be so clear at night, isn't it now?" [quoted in *James Joyce* by Richard Ellmann, rev. ed., 1982]. Typically, he defended his methods by displacing attention from his style to his subject, as he did again when replying to objections raised by Jacques Mercanton over the obscurity of a passage in *Work in Progress*: "It is night. It is dark. You can hardly see. You sense rather" [quoted by Mercanton]. In Joyce's view, all obscurity came with the terrain he surveyed, and not with his treatment of it: "If there is any difficulty in reading what I write it is because of the material I use. In my case the thought is always simple" [quoted in *James Joyce and the Making of "Ulysses,"* by Frank Budgen]. He was only pointing out in all these remarks that "obscurity" is "darkness" rendered verbal (L. *obscuritas,* "darkness"), and that the night, his subject, was intractably obscure. Only a little reflection, I think, will demonstrate that the systematic darkening of every term in *Finnegans Wake* was an absolute necessity, dictated by Joyce's subject; and that *Finnegans Wake* has exactly what so cranky a critic as F. R. Leavis wished it had and of course judged it did not: "the complete subjection—subjugation—of the medium to the uncompromising, complex and delicate need that uses it" ["Joyce and 'Revolution of the Word,'" in *For Continuity*].

Suppose only that Joyce accomplished the least part of what he claimed when, over and over again throughout the 1920s and 1930s, he said that he "wanted to write this book about the night" [quoted in *James Joyce*]: "I reconstruct the nocturnal life" [quoted by Mercanton]. What would this sort of "reconstruction" have entailed? We might begin to appreciate the difficulties he would have faced by resorting to a simple experiment, an "appeal to experience" of the sort on which all modern forms of knowing—and the novel—are based. Suppose, that is, that we charged ourselves with the task of providing in chronological order a detailed account of everything that occurred to us *not* last night (such an account would be far too sketchy to be useful) but in the first half hour of last night's sleep; or better yet, suppose that we fall asleep tonight intent on preserving for liberal study in the morning a detailed memory of the first half hour of sleep. "The charges are, you will remember, the chances are, you won't." What we are likely to recall of this little slice of "Real life"—"you were there"—is a gap of obscurity far more stupefying than anything Joyce ever wrote. The "hole affair" (and a "hole," unlike a "whole," has no content) will likely summon up a sustained "blank memory"—"What a wonderful memory you have too!"—which in turn should generate vast "Questions" and "puzzling, startling, shocking, nay, perturbing" doubts about the possibility of literately filling in this blank "m'm'ry" ("m'm'ry," obviously, is "memory" with severe holes in it). "Now just wash and brush up your memoirias a little bit": even were we to simplify this exercise for the benefit of members of "the Juke and Kellikek families"—these were a clan of morons, prominent both in *Finnegans Wake* and in the press of Joyce's day, whom generations of inbreeding had reduced to a state of breathtaking feeble-mindedness—even were we to simplify this exercise by stipulating that we recall *anything* that passed through our minds in the half hour of "real life" under scrutiny, it isn't clear that there would be a great deal to say. Indeed, many of us will have only total "recoil" of "the deleteful hour" in question (not "recall"). A delightful Irish saying captures perfectly this kind of "recoil": "when a person singing a song has to stop because he forgets the next verse," according to the *Annotations,* "he says 'There's a hole in the ballad.' " Some such perturbing "hole in [the] tale" (of our "real life") seems also to entrench itself in the head when we begin to "recoil" the "hole affair" we endured last night. It is not simple obscurity that rises to meet us; "quite as patently there is a hole in the ballet trough which the rest fell out" (that "trough," not "through," deepens the emptiness of the "hole affair").

Was one dreaming throughout this half hour? And how does one know? Anyone's "m'm'ry" will attest that the average morning's catch of dreams runs exceedingly thin when compared to the length of time one lay asleep "during [the] blackout." Indeed, some people claim never to dream at all; people who do remember dreams are not likely to remember having them every night; and only the insane will claim to remember having undergone eight hours of nonstop dreaming on any night. Authorities on the subject will help us as little as our own "maimeries" ("maimed" "memories"): they have conducted for centuries an "embittered and apparently irreconcilable dispute as to whether the mind sleeps at night" [Sigmund Freud, *The Interpretation of Dreams*], arguing whether we dream continuously throughout the length of sleep and simply fail to remember most of what we dream, or whether dreaming interrupts sleep only erratically. Even the most respected of these authorities will not diminish our perplexities: in Freud's view, for instance, "a dreamless sleep is best, the only proper one. There ought to be no mental activity in sleep" [Freud, *Introductory Lectures on Psycho-analysis*]. If we simply assume, however, that "no mental activity" occupied the half-hour of "real life" we wished, in detail, to reconstruct, questions of an unsuspected order of obscurity would rise up to meet us. For dreams in their own ways may be obscure, and *Finnegans Wake* may also seem obscure, but both dreams and *Finnegans Wake* will only seem radiantly translucid when compared to those lengthy intervals of "real life" that occupy us in the space of sleep outside of dreams. Much of *Finnegans Wake,* of necessity, is about just this. What happens here? And how does one know? "Remember and recall, Kullykeg!" (Kallikak).

One of many reasons why Joyce's repeated claims about *Finnegans Wake* have seemed so improbable for so long is that people have customarily treated the book, at Joyce's invitation, as the "representation of a dream"—

doing so, however, as if dreams took place only in theory, and without concretely engaging the very strange and obscure question of what a dream is. Recollectible dreams are the rare, odd landmarks of sleep, and certainly not its norm; they rise out of the murk with a stunning clarity when compared to the darker, lengthier extents of the night that everywhere fall between. As a "nonday diary" seeking to "reconstruct the night," *Finnegans Wake* is not about a dream in any pedestrian sense of that word; treating it as a book about a "dream" is like treating *Ulysses* as a book about "human experience": both terms are far too broad to be useful. Joyce's comments on the relationship of *Finnegans Wake* to dreams and dreaming—comments that have bothered many readers—were therefore often appropriately cagey: to Edmond Jaloux he said that the book "would be written 'to suit the esthetic of the dream'," as indeed it must if it were to portray the average night in which dreams, "erigenating from next to nothing" [*Finnegans Wake*], punctuated the dark; and to Ole Vinding, comparably, he said "it's like a dream." But as many as his comments as not orient us less clearly in a "dream" per se than in "one great part of every human existence" [*The Letters of James Joyce,* Vol. 3] "about which we know almost nothing" [Mercanton]—in the night as an obscure totality. In the critical year 1927, when it became clear to Joyce that readers who had championed *Ulysses* were withdrawing their support, and when he began cultivating their encouragement by talking about abandoning *Work in Progress* to James Stephens, he replied to Harriet Shaw Weaver's objection that parts of his new work were "incorrigibly absurd" by remarking, "There is no such absurd person as could replace me except the incorrigible god of sleep and no waster quite so wasteful." He was implying what he said often and elsewhere more directly: "I want to describe the night itself" [quoted by Ole Vinding in "James Joyce in Copenhagen," in *Portraits of the Artist in Exile,* edited by Willard Potts]. And of the night: "Here is the unknown" [quoted by Mercanton].

"Recoil" again that "blank memory" of the "hole affair" we all went "trough," "even in our own nighttime." If we momentarily brush aside all the evident obscurities and arbitrarily assume that a continuous stream of "thought" purled through our minds in the half hour of "real life" we wished, in detail, to reconstruct, we would face the new problem not simply of replacing a "blank memory" with a presumed content, but of finding a means by which to do so. Particularly if we think of sleep (as opposed to "dreams") as that part of the night which cannot be remembered, this would mean finding a way of "reveiling" (note the occluding "veil") an interval of life inherently barred from "mummery" ("memory"). Since "in the night the mummery" is masked (or "mummed"), all such attempts to "recoil" will seem "unaveiling." Indeed, it is as if the persons we become in the "veiled world" (of the night) say "goodbye" to any potentially retrievable "mummeries" as soon as they "go by": "Dear gone mummeries, goby!" As if under hypnosis (Gr. *hypnos,* "sleep"), "[we] will remain ignorant of all . . . and draw a veil."

Can we nonetheless, by some determined exertion or inferential indirection, "reconstruct" a half hour of "real life" of which we have no "mummery" and which no amount of volition ("would") or obligation ("should") allows us to know? "You wouldnt should as youd remesmer. I hypnot" because sleep (*hypnos*) puts us in a trance ("mesmer") that moves us into "Metamnisia" (Gr. "metamnêsia," "beyond forgetfulness"); and from there, we find everything "leading slip by slipper to a general amnesia." What becomes obscure now is not simply the presumed content of the "blank memory" we all "recoil," but the operation of memory itself, and of "mummery's" darker underside, in forgetting. Any reconstruction of the night would of necessity have to open up bottomless inquiries into the complementary relations of memory and amnesia, and into our relations with the past. Since memory is the network of operations that gives us a sense of indivisible "sameness"—of "identity"—in time, what would become equally obscure, even questionable, is the stability of "identity." For "as I now with platoonic leave recoil," thinking about sleep is like being badly in "Platonic love": I have no real contact with the person in question, who seems to have taken "leave," at least of my senses. Worse, since presumably "I have something inside of me talking to myself," but I cannot "recoil" it, it must be that "I'm not meself at all." "You," therefore, "may identify yourself with the him in you"—where that "him" would refer to a "person suppressed for the moment."

Again, however, we might bypass all these obscure problems by supposing—improbably—that something awakened us after a half-hour of sleep last night, and enabled us to rise out of the murk of our own lives with dim memories and fleeting impressions that "something happened that time I was asleep": a dream. Although this would put us "mehrer the murk" ("nearer the mark"), a Beckettian cry of relief—"At last, a brain with content!"—would be far too hastily vented; for the retrieval of this dream "from the wastes a' sleep" would actually stir up more (Ger. *mehr*) rather than less "murk" (hence "mehrer the murk"). How do we know that the dream shakily falling together in "mummery" really happened during sleep and is not, for instance, a spontaneous after-effect of wakening? Since "we only know dreams from our memory of them after we are awake" [Freud, *The Interpretation of Dreams*], *not* from direct experience, everything we "know" is circumstantial, reaching us after the fact. What we have rashly labeled a dream, then, might more accurately be called the "murmury" of a dream. And since all such dreams occur to us—literally—when we wake up and assume the conscious capacity to "remumble" them ("mumble"), to articulate them to ourselves in "murmury" ("murmurs"), traducing them in the process, they will help only some in allowing us to know what really happened in the clearer few minutes of the dark half-hour that we wished, in detail, to reconstruct. This distinction is one that Freud made by partitioning the dream into a "manifest content" (of which the dreamer is conscious) and a "latent content" (of which the dreamer is not): "dreams only show us the sleeper in so far as he is not sleeping" [Freud, "A Metapsychological Supplement to the Theory of Dreams"]; the examination of "dreams is the royal road to the unconscious" [Freud, *The Interpretation of Dreams*], not the unconscious itself. Dreams in this customary sense, as Joyce pointed out to Jacques Mercan-

ton, are not what *Finnegans Wake* is about: " **'Work in Progress'**? A nocturnal state, lunar. That is what I want to convey: what goes on in a dream, during a dream. Not what is left over afterward, in the memory. Afterward, nothing is left."

Even were we to disregard as sophistic the evident epistemological problems surrounding dreams, new problems would make difficult our attempts to chronicle a half-hour fragment of the dark. For the question would arise of how we might arrange the dream chronologically, in history's clock-time and in linear script. Uncertainty would contaminate our knowledge of how long the dream lasted, surely, and of when exactly in the half-hour under our consideration it occurred. But even murkier questions would occlude our sense of its evolution in time: on what image did this dream begin? and what was going on immediately preceding its formation? On what last image did the dream end? and what followed that? Merely to ask these questions is to begin noting how bottomless any dream is in its obscurity, disappearing into a point that Freud called its "navel," "where it reaches down into the unknown" [*The Interpretation of Dreams*]. Trying to ascertain what happened before the first sketchy event that one recalls of any dream—"how the deepings did it all begin"—seems an exercise undertaken in vain, in vanity: "Fantasy! funtasy on fantasy, amnaes fintasies!" Thinking about these nocturnal "fantasies," one finds "everything" (L. *omnes*) "leading slip by slipper to a general amnesia" (hence "amnaes"), where thinking itself blurs out into "emptiness" (L. *vanitas*) and a contentless "void" (L. *vanus*). Any book purporting to reconstruct the night—and particularly an average night stirred by dreams—would have to show us how and why and when these "mummeries" ("masked performances") bled up out of the dark "from next to nothing," and there forced themselves into articulate "murmury."

Then, too, uncertainty would infect our knowledge not simply of the extension of the dream in linear time, but also of its own internal order in time. No one remembers the experience of sleep, if at all, as a sequence of events linked chronologically in time by cause and effect from the moment his head hit the pillow to the time the alarm clock startled him into rational accountability in the morning. Instead, memory of the night, often triggered by a random gesture or thought, seems to arise by association, dim particles of the dark standing out in "m'm'ry" and evoking others, and still others, until, by a process of mnemonic linking, one has filled in the gaps and reconstructed a spotty "m[e]m[o]ry." How does one know that this randomly drifting form of recollection does not replicate exactly the order in which dreams sequentially unfolded in the night—apparent last part first, apparent first part in the middle, "blackholes" everywhere else—and that what occurs to one as a jumble of disarranged impressions is not just that: a jumble of disarranged impressions, perhaps concealing a secret structure of its own, but perhaps not, upon which one imposes a coherent narrative structure after the fact in order to make logical sense of it?

Even supposing that we could dredge up a content for a half hour of "our own nighttime" and could order it sequentially, there would remain the vexing questions of what, if anything, the dream meant, and whether it was worth figuring out: not everyone agrees that dreams are meaningful; and not everyone who thinks that dreams are meaningful agrees on what dreams mean. "It is night. It is dark." And it is all very obscure. Indeed, "we are circumveiloped by obscuritads" (note again the "circumveloping" "veil").

Some such exercise in "nightwatch service" as the one we have just undertaken is crucial to any reading of Joyce's "nonday diary" because it will begin—merely begin—to "reveil" the essential obscurity of the material with which *Finnegans Wake* is literately dealing: "reading [the] Evening World" as we experience it "even in our own nighttime" is not easy. Such "night duty" will also begin to "reveil" why darkness and obscurity are integral aspects of Joyce's "book of the dark," and not mere mannerisms. Had Joyce made *Finnegans Wake* less obscure than it is, he would have annihilated everything about his material that is most essential, most engaging, funniest, and most profound—rather in the same way that an intrusive sweep of "floodlights" would destroy any nightscape. The obscurity of *Finnegans Wake* is its essence and its glory. In its own artful form of "chiaroscuro," the book renders the dark matters we have considered eminently "clearobscure" (the Eng. "chiaroscuro" derives from the It. *chiaroscuro,* "clear-dark"). (pp. 3-10)

As its spelling implies, the Joycean "UNGUMPTIOUS" has a lot of "gumption" and humor in it, and is both distinct from and yet related to the "Unconscious" in more orthodox forms. As its appearance in the text also suggests, and as many Joyceans have compellingly demonstrated, there can be no question that psychoanalysis had an impact, a deep one, on *Finnegans Wake*: the term appears in a phrase directing our attention to "LIPPUDENIES OF THE UNGUMPTIOUS" (a "libidinous unconscious"), in a book that has the "intrepidity" to call itself "an intrepidation of our dreams." Like all the many psychoanalytical tags drifting through *Finnegans Wake,* these terms suggest similarities and yet differences, both of which are important to weigh.

Mere mention of Freud will raise hackles on one side of the room and banners on the other; but sleep alone will elicit a version of the same bizarre politics. Merely having proposed as an exercise the reconstruction of a half-hour fragment of dark will already have raised in most minds unresolved questions on which there will be sides to take, and about which seasonably "fashionable" and unfashionable "factions" will form. A reader of Joyce would do well to try cultivating an indifference to these partisanships, by paying attention to the *Wake* itself: there we read that one must, "for a surview over all the factionables see Iris in the Evenine's World." The line invites its reader to sort these matters out not by resorting to programmatic responses, but by studying what is seen, "in fact, under the closed eyes" (hence the "iris"), in the "Evening World" (the night). ⊕ also suggests that in exploring the "Evening World," the *Wake* will, among all things else, "survey the factions" that have politicized the same dark domain.

It seems to me impossible for any reader seriously interested in coming to terms with *Finnegans Wake* to ignore [Sigmund Freud's] *The Interpretation of Dreams,* which broke the ground that Joyce would reconstruct in his own "intrepidation of dreams" and, arguably, made *Finnegans Wake* possible: it was in the cultural air that any early twentieth-century European would have breathed, and it is everywhere implicit in Joyce's "nonday diary." Its first chapter, not least, provides an excellent summary of the nineteenth-century literature on sleep and dreams, and those that follow have not been surpassed in exploring what dreams mean and how they work. No subsequent treatment of the subject fails to show its influence. The book is important to *Finnegans Wake,* however, not simply because it treats so elaborately *of Dreams,* but because it is equally about *Interpretation,* which is any reader's only business; and it is about interpretation of a kind that unyieldingly brings the simple and central question "What does it mean?" to a species of peculiarly nonsensical, obscure, and garbled literary text—"the text of the dream" [*The Interpretation of Dreams*], the puzzling and troubling "murmurrandoms" that any dreamer "remumble[s] from the night before" (note the "random" element in such "murmured memoranda" [Paul Ricoeur, *Freud and Philosophy*]). Particularly because the only real evidence of "dreaming" comes in the dark language of these "murmurable" "murmoirs" ("memorable" because "murmured" "memoirs"), some interpretive technique *distinct* from those brought to bear on consciously constructed narratives will be essential to a reading of what Joyce called his "imitation of the dream-state" [quoted by Mercanton]; and *The Interpretation of Dreams* offers not simply the most intricately developed and detailed example of such a technique, but also an account—no matter whether critical or not—of alternative interpretive techniques as well. It is, in short, an indispensable text to bring to *Finnegans Wake.*

On the other hand, it would be foolish to disregard Joyce's well-known derogations of Freud and "the new Viennese school" [*Ulysses*]: all of his recorded comments on psychoanalysis were dismissive. They suggest, perhaps, what should be obvious: that both as a "competent" thinker and man—a "competitor" and not a follower—and especially as an artist whose work consistently explored "the inner life," Joyce was of necessity in competition with psychoanalysis, and all the more particularly because of its claims to authority. This much, at least, is implied in remarks like the chastising aside he directed to Mary Colum when he heard that she was attending a series of lectures by Pierre Janet: "You could learn as much psychology from yourself as from those fellows" [*Our Friend James Joyce*]. And why not? A great deal has been said about the heroism of Freud's self-analysis, but relatively little about Joyce's, in the writing of *Ulysses,* which he regarded as "essentially the product of [his] whole life" [quoted by Jan Parandowski in "Meeting with Joyce," *Portraits of the Artist in Exile,* edited by Willard Potts]; it would be difficult to conceive of anyone spending seven years on a text that heavily autobiographical, reworking on a daily basis the personal and literary past, without emerging from the experience radically changed. One way of reading *Ulysses,* a work thematically absorbed with the issues of fathering and self-fathering, is to see it as the process whereby an arrogant little man, a young Joyce who in fact had published under the name "Stephen Dedalus," rewrote himself so entirely as to emerge from the experience not simply with the humane capabilities of a Leopold Bloom, and not simply even with the expansive good humor and affability that every reader of the biography will know, but as one of the twentieth century's great men of letters. The book, through its microscopic examination of the inner life, altered the past in every way possible.

It would do Joyce insufficient credit, then, to read *Finnegans Wake* as a "creative" reworking of understandings that might be had much more straightforwardly through a reading of Freud, and not simply because Joyce clearly went about reconstructing the night in his own idiosyncratic way, but also because if most of the night is void of recollectible dreams, a work aspiring to their interpretation would be only of partial relevance. Joyce thought about psychic interiors throughout his literary career and about "nightlife" daily for almost twenty years. It was his work. As an author who distrusted authority in all its forms, he preferred to all theory nagging, living, concrete immersion in the material under his scrutiny itself ("I hate generalities" [quoted in *James Joyce*]). If, as he said, "*Ulysses* is related to this book as the day is to the night" [quoted by Vinding], we should expect *Finnegans Wake* to behave with all the uncapturable richness of a *Ulysses,* exploring its dark subject thoroughly, systematically, but not systematically. Finally, too, as Joyce's comparative remarks on Freud and Vico suggest, his real authority in the study of the unconscious was Vico, and even here he distanced himself carefully ("I would not pay overmuch attention to these theories, beyond using them for all they are worth" [*The Letter of James Joyce,* Vol. 1]. (pp. 15-18)

[The healthily skeptical reader will wonder] how anyone could possibly know what goes on in a part of the night unyielding to "m'm'ry" and resistant in every way to any form of direct knowing. Particularly for a writer of Joyce's realist allegiances, the question would have raised larger questions about how one knows—anything. Capable as one may be in wakefulness of explicating allusions, for instance, or speaking cannily about the collapse of representational epistemologies, it would seem a genuine deficiency in any claim to knowledge not to know the content of one's own head in an wholly representative slice of "Real life." "Writing about the night," then, would have deepened in its purport for Joyce, and also in its obscurity, because it would have meant not simply generating a "nonday diary," but concurrently undertaking a sustained "epistlemadethemology for deep dorfy doubtlings"—a phrase that yields "two thinks at a time." *Finnegans Wake* launches on a dark "epistemology," to be sure, bending the questions "How do I know?" and "Where did thots come from?" ("thoughts") into "one great part of [our] existence" about which we must willingly entertain "deep doubts"—and "dorfy" ones, at that. But it is also, as an "epistle-made" artifact, an "epistlemadethemology" in which the status of language and letters ("epistles") will unrelentingly be "made [a] theme."

Although it is currently one trend to see *Finnegans Wake*

as a work "about language"—and it surely is—Joyce himself, whenever he was asked to clarify the book, problematically said that it was "about the night." This minor discrepancy as to what the book is "about" is extremely important . . . ; for while a book "about language" need say nothing at all "about the night," and in fact usually will not, a book "about the night" would of necessity have to undertake an intricate and wondrously obscure inquiry into the nature of language. "My heeders will recoil with a great leisure" (not "recall," not necessarily "pleasure") that big "blank memory" left suspended in their heads after last night's orgy of "leisure." Why do no words leap into the gap and fill this roomy space? *"If that [one] hids foregodden has nate of glozery"* ("has forgotten his night of glory"), is it because one has also "forgotten his native glossary"? If the experience of sleep entails the wholesale rubbling of language, out of what dark place in the mind do those "murmurable" "murmurrandoms" that we "recoil" in the morning come from?

The fullest possible response to the question of what happens to (literate) consciousness in the night—"Something happened that time I was asleep, torn letters or was there snow?"—would oblige us to wonder, at least if we think it improbable that language ever suddenly vacates the head, whether letters and literacy fell into a strange new order in the dark, like "torn letters"; or if sleep merely blanketed everything over, as if under a bleaching fall of "snow" ("We feel unspeechably thoughtless over it all here . . . "). In this latter case, the question would arise of how language could possibly capture the nothing that language, constantly about something, is not. For not the least obscure matter pertaining to our experimental reconstruction, in detail, of a half-hour of the night—presuming we could replace a profoundly "blank memory" with "somethink"—would be the question of what kind of language could adequately fill the spaciously "hole affair." English?—with words like "memory" and "recall," which are always of something? "Languish" too, then, is what *Finnegans Wake* is necessarily about ("language"), but primarily because it is "about the night." And in an already doubt-riddled "epistlemadethemology," letters—"epistles" and words—will be an ongoing "thematic" concern.

As to the question of how Joyce in particular could possibly know the interior of the night, we have the difficult evidence of *Finnegans Wake* itself to examine, but also oblique indications from the biography and the letters. All the evidence shows Joyce entering this area with extreme caution. He began to write *Work in Progress* in March 1923, in English, tentatively, unclear as to where it would lead him; and it took him the better part of a year, by the end of which he had sketched out half the book, to show the newly evolving work to anyone but his immediate friends, and then too, only tentatively ("May I ask you, by the way, to be rather reticent about my new book?" he wrote to Valery Larbaud. Nothing indicates that Joyce knew his "experiment in interpreting 'the dark night of the soul' " [*The Letters of James Joyce,* Vol. 1] would exhaust two decades of his life, half of his literary career, and the odd resources of some sixty languages. Only as he warmed to his material did he begin to realize the depth and extent of its obscurities, and these obviously challenged and allured him, but also frustrated him immensely: "The task I have set myself is dreadfully difficult," he wrote to Robert MacAlmon in early 1924, "but I believe it can be done." And to Harriet Shaw Weaver in the same year: "There are so many problems to be solved that I can face only one at a time"; "I have been thinking and thinking how and how and how can I and can't it"; "It is a bewildering business. . . . Complications to right of me, complications to left of me, complex on the page before me, perplex in the pen beside me, duplex in the meandering eyes of me, stuplex on the face that reads me. And from time to time I lie back and listen to the sound of my hair growing white" [*The Letters of James Joyce,* Vol. 1]. Nobody took these laments seriously; everybody thought he was dramatizing himself while really only doodling around with puns, indulgently parading the emptiest of eruditions, or inventing some kind of private mythology. Joyce: "I am rather discouraged about this as in such a vast and difficult enterprise I need encouragement. . . . but I cannot go back" [*The Letters of James Joyce,* Vol. 1].

Frank Budgen recalls being told by August Suter that "in the early days of the composition of *Finnegans Wake,*" Joyce said, "I am boring into a mountain from two sides. The question is how to meet in the middle." Suter recalls the formulation differently: when he asked Joyce about his new work, Joyce replied, "imagine a mountain which I am boring into from all sides without knowing what I am going to find." The comparison was to become a well-worked favorite, varying in form with the state of the work, and in these guises show Joyce thinking about the night much as anyone only can; for what happens "down there" can be inferred most clearly by working out of the two well-lit shafts through which one enters and leaves it, while falling asleep and waking up—although dreams pock the dark with innumerable random obscure points of entry. As the *Wake* puts it, of a hero obscurely called *"The Bearded Mountain,"* "there are two signs to turn to, the yest and the ist, . . . feeling aslip and wauking up": "the yest" here is where night fell and where "yest"erday disintegrated ("the west"), while "ist" (or "east") is where the day will break, and where the present always reappears ("is").

One of these two openings had already been amply cleared away, for two of Joyce's earlier three works of fiction had come to deadends at the threshhold beyond which *Finnegans Wake* was darkly to move. At the end of **"The Dead,"** "faintly falling" asleep in the Gresham Hotel, Gabriel Conroy feels "his own identity . . . fading out" as a reverie of snow drifts in his mind, to change his mind and the texture of the story as well; and at the end of *Ulysses,* Joyce sought comparably "to convey the mumbling of a woman falling asleep" [according to Louis Gillet in *Claybook for James Joyce*]. To note that Joyce's fiction pressed repeatedly against the dark borderland separating wakefulness from sleep is only to note one necessity that compelled him into the writing of the *Wake*—which, after all, is only an inflected synonym for "The Dead." A second necessity was the fact of *Ulysses* itself, through which, according to T. S. Eliot, Joyce "killed the nine-

teenth century, exposed the futility of all styles, and destroyed his own future." What could Joyce have done after writing *Ulysses*? A chronicle of June 17, 1904? Or a sweeping saga of three generations of family life whose culminating item would be a writer dense with sensitivity? The logical place for him to go was down, into the night. "Having written *Ulysses* about the day, I wanted to write this book about the night" [quoted in *James Joyce*].

The intensity with which Joyce studied dreams, read about dreams, and discussed dreams with family members and friends has been broadly documented. Jacques Mercanton, who is supposed to have become the official expositor of *Finnegans Wake* had Joyce lived, makes it seem in his recollection of Joyce that the going over of dreams may have been the first order of business of every day. But it clearly went further even than this: stray remarks in his letters show Joyce waking up at night, scribbling on paper in the dark, and falling back asleep: "I composed some wondrous devices for ∧d during the night," he informed Harriet Shaw Weaver, "and wrote them out in the dark very carefully only to discover that I had made a mosaic on top of other notes so I am now going to have to bring my astronomical telescope into play." Already he was teaching her, everywhere in the letters, how to read *Finnegans Wake*: "astronomical telescopes," unlike regular ones, work only at night, and they train on matters invisible to the light of day; they do what Joyce does in "his book of the dark." No amount of generalizing or mere assertion, however, will ultimately persuade anyone of anything. The only evidence that will show just how much Joyce thought and learned about the night is *Finnegans Wake* itself, "the Strangest Dream that was ever Half-dreamt."

Somewhere very early in a meditation of this sort, the busily put-upon reader will doubtlessly have paused to wonder why all of this should be important enough to merit his attention and time. Since the "hole affair" "amounts to nada in pounds or pence"—since it defies "sound sense" and is not very profitable either (hence the "pounds" and "pence"), he will likely want to ask of "Sleep, where in the waste is the wisdom?" Though the only fully satisfactory answer to this question can be a reading of *Finnegans Wake,* we might for now entertain a few orienting considerations.

Writers who deal with the subject are fond of pointing out that we spend one-third of our lives in sleep. The unyielding fraction, as anyone who has tried unsuccessfully to conform to a regulated eight-hour sleep schedule knows, is finally arbitrary, deriving from an Aristotelean partitioning of the day into three equal thirds of which one seems "reasonably" appropriate to the night. But the fraction is not simply arbitrary; it's conservative. For the forces that tow us into sleep, arguably, are always there under the surface of things, exerting an obliviating drag on our capacities to engage resourcefully and energetically in the world, blacking us out not just in those lengthy amnesias endured every night, but—an eyelid drooping here, attention lapsing there, best intentions crumbling everywhere—in the less noticeable amnesias, lapses of attentiveness, surrenders to passivity, and withdrawals from life that undermine the living of any day. Something of this nature surely overcomes Mr. Bloom, for instance, at 10 o'clock on a hot summer morning, when, theoretically well rested, he can barely bring himself to regard the world from "beneath his veiled eyelids" because the news of an unmanageable problem has left him sluggishly stupefied and stunned, in lotus-land [*Ulysses*]. "Nowtime" is just a variant of "nighttime," according to one of the *Wake*'s careful spellings as "night" is just "nowt." That big "blank memory" that we have all "recoil[ed]" from "our own nighttime," after all, did not simply vanish when night did; the roomily "hole affair" lingers on vexingly, now, very much a part of our present minds. If one-third of our lives is spent in sleep, then, so too one-third of us is never fully in the here-and-now. Inviting us to be conscious of the unconscious, or, in its own idiom, wakening the dead, *Finnegans Wake* wakes us up to the dark third of us that never comes to light.

At a complementary extreme, there are the forces that work against sleep. Toward the waking end of *Finnegans Wake*, its reader meets a figure who is given to venting, usually with great moral urgency, alarming statements on the order of "I'm the gogetter that'd make it pay like cash registers" and *"I've a terrible errible lot todue todie todue tootorribleday."* He represents, among much else, that part of the *Wake*'s sleeping mind whose anxiety about quotidian survival—making rational sound sense and tons of pounds and pence—is alarming him up into agony. The huffy-puffy rhythm tells it all: everyone is under pressure, "to do" "today" what's "due today," in "terror" and "error" and "horror," without perhaps stopping to wonder why all that pressure need be there, or where in one's life it originates. Sleep is what someone in this frame of mind doesn't want to think about, hasn't the time to think about, and can't afford to indulge in because of competing demands on his time and attention ("cash registers," "the cash system," and the whole "cash-dime problem," for example): "Dollarmighty!" Sleep is a sheer, unprofitable "waste of time." Still, since "today" is only "todie" in the terms given—since one's management of the limited amount of time in a day is only representative of one's management of the limited amount of time in a life—it may well be important to think about the night and one's dreams, before "today" slips into "to die," and to determine too where those pressurizing, sleep-annihilating demands come from and whether they need be met.

Sleep unfolds in "the darkness which is the afterthought of thy nomatter": to all quotidian appearances, it is absolutely trivial, a little "after-thought" "of no great matter" to much of anyone—particularly with all those "cash registers" in the background sonorously indicating what values are to be assigned to what things. Living as we do in a world where there are all kinds of pounds and pence and sounds and sense to make, we all mean business, if not literally. Who has time to think about the night in the morning when something else is always judged to be more centrally pressing? Wondering who makes these decisions as to what has value and what does not would in itself have fascinated Joyce, and also would have let him exercise a modernist inclination to detect precisely in the trivial—a single day, for example—the richest of revelations. Sleep

is the underside of the stone on whose sunlit upper surface is engraved the letter and the law of the land: no one wants to look at it. It is so trivial, so marginal, so unthinkable an "afterthought of thy nomatter," in fact, that even people writing about dreams and the centrality of the marginal and *Finnegans Wake* seem quite happy to overlook it, as if there were nothing there. So Joyce, "having done the longest day in literature"—in wording he co-opted from his brother—began "conjuring up the darkest night" [*The Letters of James Joyce,* Vol. 3], and for many good reasons: as we follow him into "our own nighttime," we find there, as intricately writ as anywhere else, "as human a little story as paper could well carry."

Within *Finnegans Wake*, Joyce refers to his sleepy subject as "the mountainy molehill": the phrase advises us that he knew quite well how big a "mountain" he was making out of a "molehill" by writing six hundred pages, over two decades, "about the night"; but it also serves notice that he found in the visionless and subterranean experience of sleep (a "molehill" of sorts) a vast "mountain" of material. By tunneling into this "mountain," Joyce not simply mined open the twentieth-century's analytical fascination with sleep, dreams, and the Unconscious, but developed as well a modernist eschatology (Gr. *eschatos,* "furthest, uttermost"): "modernist" because his efforts located in a trivial "afterthought of thy nomatter," in the absolutely unthinkable, precisely what is most apocalyptic and revealing about the precariously instituted order of things; an "eschatology" because it sends knowledge and thought to their limits and uttermost ends.

Even if one wanted to and had the time, sleep is what one cannot think about because it unfolds in a bottomless fissure within which thinking and all our quotidian ways of knowing disappear. At its interior, every epistemological category on which the novel, science, and empiricism are traditionally predicated—indeed, the totality of "the real"—crumbles into rich indefinition, and vanishes; and so too does "common sense." "Common sense," then, tells us that everything about *Finnegans Wake* must necessarily lie outside the pale of "common sense": no two people can ever empirically "sense" a dream in "common," and it isn't even clear that one can. Still, if we heed with Joyce "The Value of Circumstantial Evidence" ("dreams," for example), boring into the core of the dark from its two familiar well-lit wakened edges, much might be inferred about the heart of the night.

The best guide to *Finnegans Wake* is concentrated reflection on "our own nighttime." Joyce told Jacques Mercanton that he countered criticism of the book by saying that "it ha[d] to do with an ideal suffering caused by an ideal insomnia. A sentence in the book describes it in those terms." Since "ideal insomnia" differs from real insomnia by virtue of its ideality, the sentence is inviting us to be thoughtfully vigilant "in our own nighttime" and complementarily thoughtful in wakefulness about "how we sleep." Anyone wanting seriously to read *Finnegans Wake* must at some point go to "nightschool," take a few "Night Lessons," do a little "nightwatch service," exercise some "night duty," serve on "the vigilance committee," and, above all, "sleep on it." All of the characters inside the book do these things, and so did Joyce himself: "I am at present attending night school," he wrote jokingly to his son and daughter-in-law in 1934, and then went on to close the letter with a characteristic tag: "Good night, dear children. Nightynight everybody." Only daily reference to the "hole affair" you went "trough" last night will clarify this most "clearobscure" of books.

It was Joyce's lifelong rival, Doctor Oliver St. John Gogarty, who first reacted in exasperated disbelief [in a review in *Observer,* 7 May 1939] to *Finnegans Wake* by calling it "the most colossal leg-pull in literature since McPherson's Ossian." But even its most serious readers seem tacitly to have assumed that Joyce was only kidding when he said it was "about the night." The real obstacle to our comprehension of *Finnegans Wake* since its publication, in my view, has been a reluctance on the part of readers to think seriously about the very strange, literally unthinkable, and only apparently trivial material that it richly explores. As a consequence, Joyce's own many assertions about the book—his "reconstruct[ion of] the nocturnal life" and "imitation of the dream-state"—have been dismissed out-of-hand as improbable, or else explained away either as "conceits" that Joyce found useful for his own eccentric purposes, or as impressionistic "devices" that in practice have licensed interpretive mayhem on the one extreme hand and pedantic irrelevance on the other. As one consequence, the text perhaps most widely regarded as the great monolithic obstacle to our understanding of modernism has remained inaccessibly obscure since its publication in 1939—and not simply to the interested lay reader, but to many Joyceans as well. It is time that the putative bluff was called, and shown to be no bluff at all. *Finnegans Wake* is about "the night we will remember."

"But we'll wake and see." (pp. 18-25)

> *John Bishop, in his* Joyce's Book of the Dark: Finnegans Wake, *The University of Wisconsin Press, 1986, 479 p.*

Vincent J. Cheng   (essay date 1991)

[*In the following essay, Cheng argues that Joyce envisioned* Finnegans Wake *as a drama, creating characters who serve as versatile role players enacting what Joyce perceived as the recurring yet varied events of world history.*]

In James Joyce's vision, an artist is the god and creator of his own worlds—"After God, Shakespeare has created most," as John Eglinton asserts (quoting Dumas *père*)—while God is but a very major artist, "the playwright who wrote the folio of this world" ("and wrote it badly," Stephen Dedalus adds). In *Finnegans Wake,* Joyce confirms and restates this notion, referring to Shakespeare as "Great Shapesphere." To Joyce, artist and god were equivalent—the quintessential artist was the greatest bard of all, the lord of language at his Globe.

Since artists-creators-gods are the playwrights who write the folios of their worlds, Joyce similarly conceived of the world in the *Wake* as staged drama. Like Shakespeare before him, Joyce viewed all the world as a stage, the "world-

stage" of the *Wake.* This is the notion I will refer to as the dramatic metaphor.

HCE, the archetypal father who "Haveth Childers Everywhere" and who thus also creates and populates a world, is but another version of both poet and god—of "Great Shapesphere." Joyce himself, of course, is all of these things: like Stephen Dedalus' Shakespeare, he is "all in all." As a god and an artist, a poet triumphs over confining reality by creating worlds through the imagination—and each of his works is an exploration into the possible "history" of such worlds.

. . . . .

Myths are cyclical in nature, and Joyce centered *Ulysses* on an ancient myth. Bloomsday is a modern reenactment of the Odyssey: Homer's *Odyssey,* however, is not reenacted precisely, nor linearly, but in more modern variations; in the typical terms of everyman Leopold Bloom, it is "history repeating itself with a difference."

Bloom's comment could easily serve as a subtitle for *Finnegans Wake,* for Joyce carried the exploration of this general notion of cyclical history furthest—in *Finnegans Wake*—with the construct of a dream, the perfect vehicle for repeated motifs and variations, for everything happening at once, for all possibilities and all history in the course of a night's dream. He made *Finnegans Wake* into a Viconian river, "a commodius vicus of recirculation."

In contrast, for Stephen Dedalus, linear history ("a nightmare from which I am trying to awake") is a destroyer, an ouster of possibilities. "Kingstown pier, Stephen said. Yes, a disappointed bridge." "How, sir?" a student asks. A disappointed bridge, perhaps, simply because it *is* a pier—therefore severely limited in scope, the possibility of its being a bridge having been ousted by its clearly being a pier. Actual, factual history makes it so. Stephen Dedalus is himself remorseful because of the memory of his dead mother and the hurt he gave her. Her death is fact, and history makes it so; thus, his "agenbite of inwit" cannot be absolved—for she is dead, and nothing can change that absolute fact of history. This is why, to the aspiring artist, history is such a nightmare—because of its destructive qualities:

> Had Pyrrhus not fallen by a beldam's hand in Argos or Julius Caesar not been knifed to death? They are not to be thought away. Time has branded them and fettered they are lodged in the room of the infinite possibilities they have ousted. But can those have been possible seeing that they never were? Or was that only possible which came to pass?

In these crucial lines, Stephen is referring to Aristotle's theory in the *Poetics* ("Aristotle's phrase" in *Ulysses*) that there is a room of infinite possibilities—if Caesar had not been knifed to death, he might have lived to a ripe old age, might have developed cancer, might even have come to America—but history limits, and chooses from that room one possibility, thus destroying all others. Linear history, then, is seen by Stephen as a usurper and a destroyer of creative potential, a restrictive force which limits other, perhaps more interesting, possibilities. Stephen goes on to quote Milton:

> Weep no more, woful shepherd, weep no more
> For Lycidas, your sorrow, is not dead,
> Sunk   though   he   be   beneath   the   watery
>   floor. . . .

> It must be a movement then, an actuality of the possible as possible.

To Stephen, the conflict lies between history and poetry: Lycida's death is a historical fact; other possibilities are ousted by that certainty. The poet Milton, however, asserts that Lycidas is *not* dead; whereas factual history eliminates possibilities, poetry forges and creates new and other possibilities. Thus the poet, his poetry, and his imagination are placed in the role of revivifiers, recreators, constructive counters to history's destructiveness: "It must be a movement then, an actuality of the possible as possible."

Through artistic creation, the artist can counter the death-dealing destructiveness of history and fact by bringing to life all the dead chances ousted and destroyed by linear history. It is a great and moving moment in *Finnegans Wake,* when Shem-Joyce, reviled and ridiculed by his brother Shaun, gets up to defend himself, lifting his only weapon—the life wand, the godlike phallic pen/knife of the artistic imagination: "He lifts the lifewand and the dumb speak." The dead and the dumb can speak through the power of the creative, regenerative act; through the imagination are history and the past conquered. History, no longer just a nightmare, can be a dream vision, a resurrection of dead possibilities, a wake. Its destructive elements are exorcised through an exploration of myriad possibilities in the room of infinite ones.

Joyce's notions about the "room of the infinite possibilities" are carried out in the *Wake,* in which all history and literature are seen as uncertainty and gossip, the exploration of practically every possibility, and in which the study of the past is as uncertain as our knowledge of actual, factual truth. In a sense all of *Finnegans Wake* could be considered an attempt to answer the question, "What happened to HCE?" Finding the "truth"—if there is one—is a matter of digging (like Biddy the hen) through the countless possibilities, variations, and interpretations accumulated by the middenpile of time and cyclical history. Art and creation are, for the Joyce of the *Wake* as well as for Stephen Dedalus and Aristotle, a "movement, an actuality of the possible as possible," an exploration of potential actualities from the room of infinite possibilities. The problem is the same with the story of HCE: we try to choose one version. But which one? Unfortunately, "Zot is the Quiztune," and Joyce, like Hamlet (also seeking the truth) and Aristotle before him, knew it:

> . . . me ken or no me ken Zot is the Quiztune. . . . we are in for a sequentiality of improbable possibles though possibly nobody after having grubbed up a lock of cwold cworn aboove his subject probably in Harrystotalies [Aristotle] or the vivle [the Bible] will go out of his way to applaud him on the onboiassed back of his remark for utterly impossible as are all these events they are probably as like those which may

have taken place as any others which never took person at all are ever likely to be.

In describing the *Wake*'s explorations as "a sequentiality of improbable possibles," Joyce appeals to the dean of the Department of possibilities and probabilities, Aristotle. Joyce explains in this passage that the book explores a history of resonant uncertainty and indeterminate sequentiality, a sequentiality of improbable possibles that are as possible as anything, or as much so as the sequentiality put out by linear "history": "for utterly impossible as are all these events they are probably as like those which may have taken place as any others which never took person at all are ever likely to be." What actually "happened" is ultimately determined by the beholder (in the forms of gossip, criticism, history books, and so on), and nothing is ever conclusive: every generation reinterprets history, just as each generation reinterprets Shakespeare. *Finnegans Wake* studies this effect by exploring all possibilities and all viewpoints which "are probably as like those which may have taken place."

Finnegans Wake's world history is thus one about gossip and uncertainty, about incommunicability and the impossibility of learning the truth, about the attempts of literature, scholarship, and history to state truth by fabricating varying accounts and interpretations of every incident. Repeatedly the *Wake* collects opinions and evidence from a host of characters. Each one espouses his or her own versions of the HCE tale; nothing can be proved, and they are all probably "meer marchant taylor's fablings"—mere lies and fables about a sailor and a tailor. All this Irish gossip is erroneous misunderstanding, and, Joyce tells us, HCE, "the Man . . . [was] subjected to the horrors of the premier terror of Errorland, (perorhaps!)"—perhaps, for even that is uncertain. We can only listen to (or read) the *Wake*'s compilation of all the gossipy possibilities and speculative misunderstandings of history and the Ballad of Persse O'Reilly. Thus, we are called to "List! List!" (*Ulysses* and *Hamlet* I.v.22) to a review of human history: "*Hirp! Hirp! for their Missed Understandings! chirps the Ballat of Perce-Oreille.*" As such a compilation, the *Wake* is thus an exploration of the "Notpossible!"

"Learned scholarch[s]" also engage in such explorations. Scholarship and artistic creation, connected by the role of language (*litterae,* letters), are both concerned with finding, if possible, the right interpretation from the litterheap of infinite possibilities. Clearly aware of the similarity between reading the *Wake* and researching purple patches and problem passages of literature, Joyce, a twentieth-century followright, describes his own "problem passion play" as "the purchypatch of hamlock," the "patchpurple of the massacre," "[t]heirs porpor patches!," "paupers patch," and so on. Joyce further emphasizes this similarity by his repeated references to holographs, folios, librettos, original manuscripts, and Shakespearean scholars and ghosters.

Finnegans Wake is Joyce's attempt to compile these error-possibilities of HCE's comedy of errors—in other words, all history. A problem play has purple passages which engender much critical speculation and scholarly research; in this sense, *Finnegans Wake* is, like the letter unearthed by Biddy the hen, an attempt to dig into the middenheap and find the "gossiple" truth. Resonant with the pun of *litterae,* the "letter from litter" is broadly symbolic, representing both history and literature, especially *Finnegans Wake.* The letter contains all the contributions, from all generations, to the dirtmound of books, history and literature: "For that . . . is what papyr is meed of, made of, hides and hints and misses in prints"—all the errors and missed understandings (and misprints) of the Ballad of Persse O'Reilly. Therefore, you hardly need to ask if every story in the bound book of history has a score of versions and possible interpretations: "So you need hardly spell me how every word will be bound over to carry three score and ten toptypsical readings throughout the book of Doublends Jincd." Here Joyce is commenting on the interminable fecundity of the past and of literature, both subject to endless interpretation, by using the *Wake* as a symbol of both world and word.

The problem play of *Finnegans Wake* is, like the letter unearthed by Biddy the hen, an attempt to dig the truth out of the middenheap of possibilities. As with history or literature, there are an infinite number of possible meanings for the letter's sequentiality of improbables, and scholarly study results in numerous schools of interpretation. Equated with Joyce's works, the letter is thus similar to great literature, and specifically to Shakespeare's *Hamlet.* In *Finnegans Wake,* Joyce concludes about this "dummpshow" (the dumb show on the middendump)—that it is a "prepronominal *funferal* [the *Wake* as a funeral and a fun-for-all], engraved and retouched and edgewiped and pudden-padded, very like a whale's egg farced with pemmican, as were it sentenced to be nuzzled over a full trillion times for ever and a night till his noddle sink or swim by that ideal reader suffering from an ideal insomnia." In other words: this work, like Shakespeare's, has been retouched and worked over; and, like the plays or the *Wake,* it is meant to be puzzled over for a trillion nights by that ideal dreambook and insomniac reader. Finally, the passage describes the *Wake*'s Protean qualities as an exploration of infinite possibilities, which, like the cloud observed by Hamlet and Polonius, takes on many shapes, "very like a whale" (*Hamlet,* III.ii.367)—this line has been quoted before, by Stephen, in, appropriately, the "Proteus" episode, *Ulysses*'s exploration of infinite possibilities.

Like Shakespearean folios, then, or like littermounds, works of literature and of historical interpretation are comedies of errors, compilations of misunderstandings. The "purchypatch of hamlock" (*Hamlet*) is like the purple-patched *Wake.* In *Ulysses* and *Finnegans Wake,* Joyce's lifewand makes the dumb speak, exploring the infinite possibilities neglected by factual/linear history, those imaginative alternatives that allow a cloud to become a whale.

. . . . .

As we have seen, *Finnegans Wake* explores "a sequentiality of improbable possibles"—a history of resonant uncertainty, indeterminate sequentiality, and infinite possibilities: "for utterly impossible as are all these events they are probably as like those which may have taken place as any others which never took person at all are ever likely to be."

As early as 1962 Clive Hart had noted [in his *Structure and Motif in Finnegans Wake*] that "In *Finnegans Wake* [Joyce] was particularly concerned to reproduce relativity and the uncertainty principle. . . . There is in fact no absolute position whatever in *Finnegans Wake*. . . . [F]rom whichever standpoint we may examine the Joycean phenomena, all other possible frames of reference, no matter how irreconcilable or unpalatable, must be taken into account as valid alternatives." In his recent study of *Joyce's Uncertainty Principle,* Phillip F. Herring has argued that "Incertitude may be the dominant theme of the *Wake*. . . ."

After all, what the dream of all-history requires is a dream-like structure that allows for both specificity of detail and the endless flexibility of variable free-play—that is, both the concrete particulars of a specific possibility, and the simultaneous interchangeability of the particular for infinite possibilities. Characters and events must be infinitely flexible and variable. As Barbara DiBernard writes: "Correspondences juxtapose the individual and the universal, show the unity of life, and undercut any traditional notions of identity or reality. There are no characters or events in *Finnegans Wake* in the usual meanings of those terms"; Patrick McCarthy notes simply that "no character exists in his own right as a stable personality in the book [*Finnegans Wake*]" [Barbara DiBernard, "Technique in *Finnegans Wake,*" and Patrick McCarthy, "The Structures and Meanings in *Finnegans Wake,*" in eds. Zack Bowen and James F. Carens, *A Companion to Joyce Studies*].

The infinite possibilities and cycles of Joyce's "Viconian" history, then, require infinitely flexible structures and forms in *Finnegans Wake.* Narrative form/structure in *Finnegans Wake* has been a primary focus of *Wake* scholarship in recent years, and there have been a number of major contributions to our understandings of the different structures by which the *Wake*'s narrative is held together: Clive Hart's motifs, Michael Begnal's narrative and dream voices, Roland McHugh's sigla, Patrick McCarthy's riddles, John Bishop's sleeper—among others—have helped to elucidate the structural mysteries of Joyce's final work. I would propose still another structuring principle—the dramatic form of *Finnegans Wake,* the world as stage. This is a particularly illuminating structural principle given the nature of the *Wake*'s basis on history as infinite possibilities, history repeating itself with a difference. After all, the *Wake*'s fiction can hardly be considered a conventional narrative—and the usefulness of such necessary schemes and scaffolds as Adaline Glasheen's multitudinous charts titled "Who's Who When Everybody Is Somebody Else" suggests a shifting, kaleidoscopic set of references—like casts of characters in different plays.

Margot Norris's important deconstructionist formulation argues that in the *Wake* "[t]he substitutability of parts for one another, the variability and uncertainty of the work's structural and thematic elements, represent a decentered universe, one that lacks the center that defines, gives meaning, designates, and holds the structure together—by holding it in immobility." It is the mobility/variability of setting and character that allows for the *Wake*'s infinite possibilities; as Norris goes on to argue, "It is freeplay that makes characters, times, places, and actions interchangeable in *Finnegans Wake,* that breaks down the all-important distinction between the self and the other, and that makes uncertainty a governing principle of the work" [Norris, *The Decentered Universe of Finnegans Wake*]. In this sense, the dramatic stage provides both an appropriate analogy/metaphor and a precise form/vehicle for representing such infinitely varied reality: life/history are, in the *Wake,* presented as the infinitely varied repertory of plays produced nightly by a theater company, playing out the decentered variations of an archetypal all-play.

For, as Herring and many other commentators have long noted, in *Finnegans Wake* "Character is based on types that are identified in the *Wake* manuscripts and at *Finnegans Wake* 299 as sigla." "In one sense," McCarthy writes, *"Finnegans Wake* has a cast of thousands: the latest edition of Adaline Glasheen's invaluable *Census of Finnegans Wake* requires more than three hundred, double-column pages to list and identify the characters, real and fictitious, who appear or are mentioned in the *Wake.*" But Glasheen's charts ("Who's Who When Everybody Is Somebody Else") are also based on only a handful of sigla, suggesting archetypal character types playing out an infinite variety of story-possibilities, like casts of stock characters playing different parts ("changing every part of the time") in a multitude of different plays. This is the nature of the both predictably repetitious and infinitely shifting nature of *Finnegans Wake*: "every person, place and thing in the chaosmos of Alle anyway connected with the gobblydumped turkery was moving and changing every part of the time."

Thus, Joyce conceived of *Finnegans Wake* as essentially dramatic, a world-play acted out on the "worldstage" by the archetypal family members of a dramatic company. This "dramatic metaphor"—that is, that all the world is a stage and all the figures of history merely players—underlies all the "action" in *Finnegans Wake,* Joyce's chronicle of Viconian history: an exploration into Aristotle's "room of the infinite possibilities," different variations of basic archetypal structures within the patterns of Viconian cycles. Joyce sets his dream of all-history in the context of the dramatic milieu: the dream as drama.

In *Finnegans Wake* these possibilities take on the forms of various plays, each re-creating a different view of the possibilities of history. There are consequently thousands of allusions to drama and to the stage in *Finnegans Wake*—from the works of Ibsen to W. G. Wills's Napoleonic drama *A Royal Divorce* to Dion Boucicault's *Arrah-na-Pogue,* from Synge to Gilbert and Sullivan. Cheryl Herr has convincingly argued the importance and familiarity of such plays in the life of Dublin, in which "the theater provided an experience available in some form to almost all of Dublin's citizens" [Herr, *Joyce's Anatomy of Culture*]. [In *Shakespeare and Joyce*] I have shown how Shakespearean plays are particularly central matrixes, especially *Hamlet* (in defining the family relations between father and son, and between mother and son) and *Macbeth* and *Julius Caesar* (in defining the relations between rival brothers and the sister they fight over). Most importantly,

though, Joyce had come to think of an artist as a playwright and a creator-god, and of the artist's works as a stage peopled by his creations, "All the charictures in the drame."

The metaphor of playwright as god is most insistent in the *Wake,* Joyce's chronicle of world history. The prime mover behind the force of destiny is a playwright, "the compositor of the farce of dustiny"; this production of the play about Viconian history is presented by "the producer (Mr John Baptister Vickar)"—Joyce as the author of the *Wake* and God as the author of history, alias Giambattista Vico and John the Baptist. God-Shakespeare-Joyce-HCE is a "worldwright" and a "puppetry producer"; like Prospero, he is a "pageantmaster" and the "god of all machineries." In the *Wake,* the most recurrent symbol for the creator-father-god-figure is, however, Michael Gunn, manager of Dublin's Gaiety Theatre, and father of Joyce's friend Selskar Gunn; repeatedly HCE is referred to as, or compared with, Michael Gunn, in the role of manager of his worldstage. In II.i, that most "dramatic" of *Wake* chapters, HCE is introduced as "HUMP (Mr Makeall Gone)"; as stage managers, Michael Gunn and God can both make all things come or go. At the end of the same chapter, after loud applause, the exiting HCE is described as "Gonn the gawds, Gunnar's gustspells"; Gunn as god is gone; the play, Gunn's and God's gospels, is over. In 481.19 [of the 1939 Viking edition of *Finnegans Wake*] Joyce describes HCE as a builder of cities, a populator and a patriarch: "We speak of Gun, the farther"—HCE as Gunn and God the Father. So also he is described in 434.8-10 as "the big gun," waiting "for Bessy Sudlow" (Michael Gunn's wife, and an actress in his troupe) to serve him his dinner. In keeping with the theme of Viconian *ricorso,* HCE will also become, in a felicitous coinage, "the cropse of our seedfather"—the corpse will become the earth-laden seed and father of future crops and generations. Thus, finally, in the "worldwright" metaphor, HCE is a "gunnfodder": at once cannonfodder; a phallic gun; Michael Gunn, a father and a creator, a grandfather, and the fodder for future

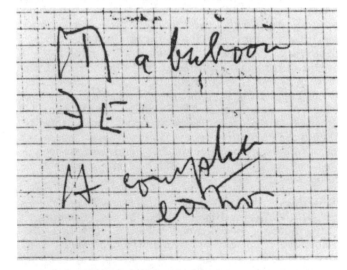

A fragment of a page from the Finnegans Wake *workbooks, showing Joyce's shorthand symbol for the character Humphrey Chimpden Earwicker.*

Gunns, guns, and generations. Even after death, after Makeall Gone has made all gone, himself being but cannon-fodder, even then will there be the "Hereweareagain Gaieties of the Afterpiece"—a joyous play (*pièce*) at the Gaiety in our afterlife. This will be supervised by this new Gaiety's manager, Michael Gunn, "the Royal Revolver of these real globoes," the god and gun who makes this world turn, the stage manager of "these real globoes"—the Globe Theater and the global world. As "Makeall Gone," "Gun, the farther," "gunnfodder," and "the big gun," Joyce is a playwright-god whose real-life phallic gun is the creative pen of Shem the Penman.

Joyce, conceiving of the artist-creator as a playwright, necessarily came to think of his own creations as plays. In the "Shem" episode, for example, Joyce describes *Ulysses*—"his usylessly unreadable Blue Book of Eccles"—as an S.R.O. hit and a Christmas pantomime at the Gaiety Theatre: "an entire operahouse (there was to be stamping room only in the prompter's box and everthemore his queque kept swelling) . . . in their gaiety pantheomime." More importantly, Joyce thought of the *Wake* itself as a drama. If Stephen Dedalus saw history as a nightmare, in the *Wake* Joyce presents history as a dream, the universal story of "Allmen"—at once the dream and drama of the world, dreamed and played nightly in countless versions and variations of the basic archetypal family drama about HCE, ALP, Shem, Shaun, and Issy. This dream unrolls the drama of universal history, a "dromo of todos"—a dream and drama of everything (Spanish *todos*), of today and of everyday. In the book itself, the word "dream" rarely appears unaccompanied by a pun on the word "drama"; this equation between dream and drama is enforced throughout. "In the drema" of the *Wake*, "We drames our dreams" of universal history, peopled with the characters and caricatures of the past, "All the charictures in the drame"; in the *Wake*, dreams are history, and one might say, "Me drames . . . has come through!"—my dreams have come true! In our own world of modern psychoanalysis, the drama of our dreams reveals our (and the world's) traumas; and so the *Wake* is (in the words of Shaun as "Professor Jones," alias Freudian/Shakespearean critic Ernest Jones) "a prepossessing drauma" (also *Traum*, German for dream). It may at times be depicted as *Hamlet*, "the drame of Drainophilias"—a dream and drama of Ophelia's; or as Bottom's eerie dream in a midsummer night's drama, "This eeridreme . . . From Topphole to Bottom"; or as Stephen's nightmare of history, "a lane picture for us, in a dreariodreama," a dreary Shakespearean drama at Drury Lane. However, behind the dream there is always the drama of cause and effect, of history-becoming-fact: "His dream monologue was over, of cause, but his drama parapolylogic had yet to be, affact."

"[I]n this drury world of ours," the Drury Lane counterpart to this dream-drama of the *Wake* is Shakespeare's "Miss Somer's nice dream." Whatever it is that Miss Somer or HCE or Yawn or mankind (or whoever) dreams, it is equated in the *Wake* with Bottom's dream in *A Midsummer Night's Dream*. (There are many references to "bully Bottom" throughout the *Wake*.) This is the central reason—as Father Boyle, Adaline Glasheen, and I have

all discussed in variant ways—that Bottom's dream in "Miss Somer's nice dream," along with the language of medieval and Elizabethan dream visions (methinks, meseems, etc.) is ubiquitous in *Finnegans Wake*: the Ass in *Finnegans Wake* remembers his dream of all-history on a "lukesummer night"; and since the *Wake* is both dream and drama, the Ass's dream vision thus finds a parallel in Bottom's dream from *A Midsummer Night's Dream*. The dream is at once a midsummer night's dream and all dreams, both "Miss Somer's nice dream" and "Mad Winthrop's delugium stramens." As such, it can be female ("Miss Somer") or male ("Mad Winthrop"), dream ("nice dream") or nightmare (delirium tremens), midsummer or midwinter ("Mad Winthrop"). It is all history.

The "prepossessing drauma," then, is both a traumatic dream sequence, the nightmare of history, and the archetypal family drama, *The Mime of Mick, Nick and the Maggies*. A poet-playwright—by analogy, HCE and all men—dreams the nightmare—"Me drames"—of all time, the "drema" of the world. The metaphor of the world as stage, the dramatic metaphor, is suggested recurrently in *Finnegans Wake* and most insistently on pages 30 to 33 and 219 to 221, the two passages in which Dublin's Gaiety Theatre is aptly transformed into the Globe.

James S. Atherton has observed [in his *Books at the Wake*] that "one of Joyce's favourite images for the world, or the *Wake*, is as a stage—although the famous quotation is never made." Of course, few direct quotations are made in *Finnegans Wake* without being refracted through puns and double meanings. Pages 30 to 33, however, contain a cluster of allusions to Shakespeare and to the stage, most conspicuous of which is the description of HCE as "our worldstage's practical jokepiece." Clearly, this is a direct reference to Jaques' (the "jokepiece"?) famous lines, "All the world's a stage, / And all the men and women merely players" (*As You Like It* II.vii.139-140). As a drama on the worldstage, HCE's story is a nightly reenactment, to which the public is invited, of an archetypal story, a "druriodrama" in this Drury Lane world of ours.

Here we first see HCE, like the "old gardener" Adam in his "prefall paradise," sitting about in his garden, "saving daylight under his redwoodtree" as the king approaches. These lines again echo *As You Like It* and "Under the greenwood tree," in a context which informs that the world has been a stage from the beginning of time, and that the Green World of the Forest of Arden, the world of dramatic romance, is none other than Eden and all gardens. The story which follows, the drama about human history, is a production to be "staged by Madame Sudlow" (Bessy Sudlow, actress and the wife of Michael Gunn) at the "king's treat house" (the Gaiety Theatre, a.k.a. King Street Theatre, was on King Street, Dublin) in a "command performance . . . of the problem passion play of the millentury." Admission to this "pantalime" (Christmas pantomimes were a tradition at the Gaiety) is "two pitts paythronosed" (two bits for patrons paying through the nose) to sit in the "pit stalls and early amphitheatre," or in the "Pit, prommer and parterre, standing room only." The habitual theatergoers are all out tonight to see "our worldstage's practical jokepiece," HCE: "Habituels conspiciously emergent." Like *Hamlet,* this piece is a "problem passion play"—and there are references in these pages to Ophelia ("Offaly"), Hamlet, Polonius with his "metheg in your midness," and the purple-patch of *Hamlet*—"the purchypatch of hamlock."

In any event, the drama of history here is a play or pantomime presented on a worldstage, in its "homedroned and enliventh performance . . . of the millentury, running strong since creation." As with *Hamlet* or with the plays of the "house of Atreox," the pantomime is an archetypal family drama: it is the tragedy of HCE's fall and his falling-out with his wife (*"A Royal Divorce"* and "Napoleon the Nth") and his daughters (*"The Bo Girl"* and *"The Lily"*). Brothers ("our red brother") and sisters ("his inseparable sisters, uncontrollable nighttalkers, Skertsiraizde with Donyahzade"—Scheherazade and Dunyazade, skirt-raised sisters from the *Arabian Nights*) are also here, as is the Holy Family, the "triptychal religious family symbolising puritas of doctrina, business per usuals and the purchypatch of hamlock."

The drama is a family affair. Joyce pursues this analogy in the *Wake* by frequently referring to the characters in the drama of the *Wake* as both family members and actors in a stage company. The drama on this worldstage is "real life"—or history—and the roles are played by a theatre company (whether the Gunns, Porters, Bonapartes, Hamlets, or Holy Family) whose cast members are the archetypal family itself: "Real life behind the floodlights as shown by the best exponents of a royal divorce." The cast members are, as we know by now, the members of HCE-Porter-Gunn's household, and their Gaiety Theatre globestage is none other than the publican's inn and residence in Chapelizod; thus, the word "house" is used throughout the *Wake* in three senses: domestic, tavernal, and theatrical (e.g., "the whole stock company of the old house of the Leaking Barrel"). The cast is first introduced on page 13 of the *Wake*:

> And here now they are. . . . A bulbenboss surmounted upon an alderman. . . . A shoe on a puir old wobban. . . . An auburn mayde, o'brine a'bride, to be desarted. . . . A penn no weightier nor a polepost. And so. And all.

The family members are an "older man" with a hump ("bulbenboss") and a stutter (Balbus), or Humphrey-HCE; his wife, ALP, a poor old woman; his daughter, Issy, an auburn maiden; and his twin sons, the Pen and the Post, Shem and Shaun. There are five so far in the cast, and yet that is not all. At other times this household troupe inflates to a "howthold of nummer seven," having two additional, nonfamily members in the household: a male servant (Sickerson, Sanderson, etc.) and a female servant (Kate). At the start of chapter 1 of Book II, the performance of *The Mime of Mick, Nick and the Maggies* is prefaced by the proper theatrical introductions of the cast; this reads: "featuring: GLUGG (Mr Seumas McQuillad). . . . IZOD (Miss Butys Pott). . . . CHUFF (Mr Sean O'Mailey). . . . ANN (Miss Corrie Corriendo). . . . HUMP (Mr Makeall Gone). . . . SAUNDERSON. . . . KATE"—that is, Shem the Penquill, Issy the Beauty Spot, Shaun the Post, Anna Livia (the running—

corriendo—waters of the Liffey), HCE-Michael Gunn, Saunderson, and Kate. These are the elements of our domestic drama, of "The family umbroglia."

In an acting troupe of only seven members, each actor or actress must be able flexibly to assume a number of roles on call, depending on the particular family imbroglio being performed that evening; thus, each member is symbolic of a family "type," able to be recast into almost any old play or version of a royal divorce. "Like the newscasters in their old plyable of *A Royenne Devours,*" they must be ready pliably to take over history's old plays, each actor performing the role assigned to him or her by the "worldwright" and puppetry producer. This concept is important and fundamental. The notion of an archetypal cast performing different plays, or interpretations of an archetypal play, corresponds marvelously with Joyce's concept of history as a resonant exploration of different possibilities. As the *Wake* is about history, the different variations (and possibilities) of reality and history become the different plays in the repertoire performed by the acting troupe and family, "the whole stock company of the old house," where each member is able to act the part for his or her particular "type" in each new play. The *Wake* is full of references to stock companies and acting troupes, with the same basic "types" playing different roles under each character "type." What better model could there be for Wakean history and Viconian *ricorso?* HCE can be the same basic actor under the various historical guises of Adam, Tim Finnegan, Finn MacCool, Shakespeare, and so forth; or the filial usurper (Cad, Hosty, Paul Horan, etc.), "Under the name of Orani . . . may have been the utility man of the troupe capable of sustaining long parts at short notice." The family is a house troupe, which performs "with nightly redistribution of parts and players by the puppetry producer and daily dubbing of ghosters, an archetypal cast and stock company acting out the different plays and infinitely various cycles of Viconian history.

Pages 323 and 324 provide an excellent illustration of how *Finnegans Wake* is presented as a stage drama played by "the whole stock company of the house":

> tummelumpsk . . . that bunch of palers. . . . Toni Lampi. . . . ghustorily spoeking, gen and gang, dane and dare, like the dud spuk of his first foetotype. . . . And ere he could catch or hook or line to suit their saussyskins, the lumpenpack. . . . Sot! . . . change all that whole set. Shut down and shet up. Our set, our set's allohn.

Fritz Senn has pointed out [in his "Notes on Dublin Theatres," in *A Wake Newslitter* Old Series 2, 6] that this passage (quoted here in part) refers to a particular stage performance of *Hamlet* in Dublin at the Crow Street Theatre. Referring to "the versatility of the Dublin stock companies" (and quoting from Samuel Fitzpatrick's *Dublin: A Historical and Topographical Account of the City* [1907], one of Joyce's source books for the *Wake*), Senn writes:

> "At Crow Street Digges ('Digges' in 313.26) was playing 'Hamlet' and ruptured a blood vessel. The play was immediately stopped and *She Stoops to Conquer* substituted for it. The manager's apologies having been accepted, the per-

formers, who were all in the house, hastily dressed and went on. A gentleman in the pit had left the building immediately before the accident to Digges, for the purposes of buying oranges. He was delayed for some little time, and having left 'Hamlet' in conversation with the 'Ghost,' found on his return the stage occupied by 'Tony Lumpkin' and his companions at the Three Jolly Pigeons. He at first thought he had mistaken the theatre, but an explanation showed him the real state of affairs" (Fitzpatrick, *Dublin*). In *Finnegans Wake*, all actors play multiple parts, often simultaneously, and we [readers] all think, again and again, that we have mistaken the theatre. In particular, Joyce used the incident in the paragraph beginning 323.25, where *She Stoops* and *Hamlet* are among the things that go on at the same time.

With much going on at once, the passage on pages 323 and 324 is a murky one at best; in context, it seems that HCE, in the role of the Norwegian Captain, has momentarily left the tavern for the outhouse (much as the spectator at Crow Street goes out to buy oranges), and returns to find the set (tavern = theater, of course) completely changed, as happened with *She Stoops to Conquer* and *Hamlet*. This historic worldstage seems to be constantly changing sets, exploring new and different variations and possibilities. The drinkers at the tavern have suddenly become "that bunch of palers" (a bunch of players); Tony Lumpkin appears as "tummelumpsk" and "Toni Lampi." The first play concerned Danish ghosts: both the ghost of King Hamlet, King of Denmark, ("ghustorily spoeking. . . . dane and dare") daring his son on (a father spooking and speaking, "like the dud spuk," to his firstborn, "his first foetotype"); and Ibsen's *Ghosts* (*Gengangere* in Dano-Norwegian; here, "gen and gang"). However, "ere he could catch or hook or line," the set has changed back to Tony Lumpkin and the Three Jolly Pigeons—back to the "lumpenpack" accompanied by the shout: "Sot! . . . change all that whole set. Shut down and shet up. Our set, our set's allohn"—our set's all one in the versatile drama of all-history. (The prop men, crying to shut down and set up, seem to be Sinn Feinners: ourselves, ourselves alone.) Change the set, but the show (and history) must go on, "like the newcasters in the old plyable." The archetypal family drama is a tale renewed and reenacted nightly on the worldstage, a daily dubbing of *Hamlet* (and all family dramas) at the Globe.

If all the world's a stage, then all stages are the world. As a result of this "dramatic metaphor," we find the pages of *Finnegans Wake* repeatedly and ubiquitously peppered and textured with references to theaters and stage history (the Globe, Bankside, Blackfriars, Drury Lane, Phoenix Playhouse, Dublin's Crow Street and Smock Alley Theaters, and so on), with stage directions ("On. Sennet"; "Exeunc throw a darras"; "Lights, pageboy, lights!"; "Act drop. Stand by! Blinders! Curtain up. Juice, please! Foots!" and so on). With such parameters, the players in our world-history then are naturally the great stage-actors, and there are repeated references in the *Wake* to Richard Burbage, David Garrick, Spranger Barry, Henry Mossop, Thomas Sheridan, Peg Woffington, Ellen Terry, and many others. There is much more to say (than I can suggest here) about the ways dramas and stage history structure *Finnegans Wake*. The more persistent references, of course, are to those actors most familiar to Joyce—the family troupe and stock company of Dublin's Gaiety Theatre on King Street, managed by Michael Gunn and Bessy Sudlow—who become the HCE and the ALP in the *Wake*'s "gaiety pantheomime" performed nightly by the house troupe. And so *Finnegans Wake* abounds with references to Gunn, Sudlow, the Gaiety, and other members of their troupe, such as Valentine Vousden and E. W. Royce.

Finnegans Wake is most explicitly a play in II.i, on page 219 and following, where *The Mime of Mick, Nick and the Maggies* is presented. This mime, put on by Michael Gunn's troupe, is a model of the *Wake* dream-drama. It is a play given by the children before their parents—a family drama of temptation and frustration (in which Izod-Issy is frustrated in her sexual temptations of Glugg-Shem). The story reenacts some of the old themes of the story of the parents, and is thus a "daily dubbing." Like the *Wake* and like Joyce's Viconian history, this play comes in four acts, and is a microcosm of *Finnegans Wake* itself.

To Joyce, always punning, a "play" is also a game—and the plot of the children's mime is literally a game, the children at play. The game that the girls ("the Maggies," led by Izod) are playing, Joyce said [in a letter], is one called "Angels and Devils or colours." Shaun-Chuff is Mick, or Michael the Archangel; Shem-Glugg is Nick, common nickname for the Devil; and the Maggies—rainbow girls or flower girls—are the "colours." Their sport is a guessing game in which Shem-Glugg is the victim: Izod poses a riddle to him three separate times, and thrice he is baffled and disgraced; the Maggies meanwhile dance rings around Shaun-Chuff, for the answer to their riddle is "heliotrope," and the heliotropic Floras find their sunshine in Shaun. HCE then returns to commence the fourth act, in which he ends the children's hour of game and sends them upstairs to bed. At this point the play is over, the curtain falls, and the chapter ends.

The introduction/playbill to *The Mime* is particularly important, for it forms a key statement of the *Wake*'s dramatic metaphor, equating the action of Joyce's novel (here, *The Mime*) with a stage performance. II.i. opens with a playbill announcing the performance of *The Mime*:

> Every evening at lightning up o'clock sharp and until further notice in Feenichts Playhouse. (Bar and conveniences always open, Diddlem Club douncestears.) Entrancings: gads, a scrab; the quality, one large shilling, Newly billed for each wickeday perfumance. Somndoze massinees. By arraignment, childream's hours, expercatered. Jampots, rinsed porters, taken in token. With nightly redistribution of parts and players by the puppetry producer and daily dubbing of ghosters, with the benediction of the Holy Genesius Archimimus and under the distinguished patronage of their Elderships. . . . while the Caesar-in-Chief looks. On. Sennet. As played to the Adelphi by the Brothers Bratislavoff (Hyrcan and Haristobulus), after humpteen dumpt-

een revivals. Before all the King's Hoarsers with all the Queen's Mum. And wordloosed over seven seas crowdblast in cellelleneteutoslavzendlatinsoundscript. In four tubbloids. . . . *The Mime of Mick, Nick and the Maggies,* adopted from the Ballymooney Bloodriddon Murther by Bluechin Blackdillain (authorways 'Big Storey'), featuring:

GLUGG (Mr Seumas McQuillad. . . .)

THE FLORAS. . . .

IZOD (Miss Butys Pott. . . .)

CHUFF (Mr Sean O'Mailey. . . .)

ANN (Miss Corrie Corriendo. . . .)

HUMP (Mr Makeall Gone. . . .)

THE CUSTOMERS. . . .

SAUNDERSON. . . .

KATE. . . .

. . . the show must go on.

Time: the pressant.

A partial explication for the playbill announcement reads thus: Performed every evening at lighting up time and until further notice in the Phoenix Playhouse. (Bar and conveniences always open, a club downstairs for "diddling," or passing the time.) Entrance fee: for vagabonds, a crab-apple; for the quality, one large shilling. Newly billed for each weekday performance. And Sunday matinees (for somnolent ones who doze through Sunday mass). By arrangement, there can be special children's hours, expurgated, and expertly catered, with jampots and rinsed porters taken in token. The play will be performed by the whole stock company, with nightly redistribution of parts and players by the puppetry producer (Michael Gunn, stage manager) and daily dubbing of ghosters with the blessing of the Holy Genesius Arch-Mime himself (St. Genesius, patron saint of actors; Greek *archimimos,* chief actor) and under the patronage of their Elderships . . . while the Caesar-in-Chief (God) looks on. Trumpets, please; begin the play. As previously performed at the Adelphi Theatre by the Brothers Bratislavoff (*brat* is slavic for brother; Greek *adelphoi,* brothers) after humpteen revivals (and revivals-ricorsos of HCE = Humpty-Dumpty). Played before all the King's Horses (Chamberlain's Men) and the Queen's Men. Wirelessed and broadcast over the seven seas in Celtic-Hellenic-Teutonic-Slavic-Zend-Latin-Sanskrit soundscript. In four tableaux. . . . Called *The Mime of Mick, Nick and the Maggies,* adopted from a Senecan tragedy of blood (like *Hamlet*) by Bluechin Blackdillain (otherwise known as the author of "Big Story") featuring: Glugg (Shem the Penman); The Flower (heliotrope) Girls; Izod (Miss Beauty Spot); Chuff (Sean the Postman); Anna Livia (the running waters of the Liffey); Hump (Michael Gunn); The Customers; Saunderson, the manservant; Kate, the maid. . . . The show must go on. Time: the present, urgent (French, *pressant*) and pressing ever onwards.

The playbill continues with a list of props used in "the

Pageant of Past History"—masks, lighting pipes, hats, bags, trees, rocks, venetian blinds, doorposts, gladstone bags, and so on. Credits are given for a musical score ("Accidental music providentially arranged by L'Archet and Laccorde"—John F. Larchet was the Abbey Theatre's orchestra leader), and singers are mentioned (including "Joan MockComic"—John McCormack). Next, "the whole thugogmagog . . . to be wound up for an after-enactment by a Magnificent Transformation Scene showing the Radium Wedding of Neid and Moorning and the Dawn of Peace, Pure, Perfect and Perpetual, Waking the Weary of the World"—the whole thingamajig is then to be wound up for an after-enactment in a Magnificent Transformation Scene showing the Radiant Wedding of Night and Morning, the Dawn of Peace, the Wake, and Ricorso. (Here, too, is found yet another play, Congreve's *Way of the World;* and, as in the Gaiety pantomimes, there is a "transformation scene.") These lines provide an apt description of Book IV of the *Wake,* and, thus, the four acts of *The Mime* appear to be a microscosm of the *Wake* itself.

Once again we have learned that the *Wake* family drama is being staged at the Gaiety, with "Makeall Gone" taking the lead role of Hump (HCE). "Every evening at lighting up o'clock sharp and until further notice in Feenichts Playhouse. . . . Newly billed for each wickeday perfumance": the nightly performance reminds us that HCE's story is an archetypal "drema," dreamt, performed, and reenacted during all times; and, like a reborn phoenix ("Feenichts"), Gunn-Hump rises each morning in order to replay a tragic fall in the evening's performance. The stage thus becomes a precise, concrete, and practical application of Joycean-Viconian *ricorso.* The various dramas in the *Wake* become the parameters of the dream-stories of cyclical history played out in its infinite possibilities. *The Mime* is thus a "nightly redistribution of parts and players by the puppetry producer and daily dubbing of ghosters." Our lives are, in this way, literally "played out" every night—in dream and drama. (pp. 69-82)

Vincent J. Cheng, " 'Finnegans Wake': All the World's a Stage," in James Joyce's "Finnegans Wake": A Casebook, *edited by John Harty III, Garland Publishing, Inc., 1991, pp. 69-84.*

FURTHER READING

Bibliography

Rice, Thomas Jackson. *James Joyce: A Guide to Research.* New York: Garland, 1982, 390 p.

   Selective, annotated bibliography with sections listing criticism on *Finnegans Wake* in English and major foreign-language studies of the novel. Rice's work includes materials published up to 1 January 1982.

Biography

Ellmann, Richard. *James Joyce.* Rev. ed. New York: Oxford

University Press, 1982, 887 p.

The authoritative biography. Upon its initial publication, Ellmann's widely praised work set a new standard for thoroughness in the examination of writers' lives.

Gorman, Herbert. *James Joyce*. New York: Farrar and Rinehart, 1939, 358 p.

The authorized biography. In spite of Joyce's participation in the preparation of Gorman's book, critics agree that this is not the best Joyce biography available, due largely to Joyce's failure to cooperate fully with his chosen biographer.

Criticism

Altieri, Charles. "*Finnegans Wake* as a Modernist Historiography." *Novel* 21, Nos. 2-3 (Winter-Spring 1988): 238-50.

Contends that in *Finnegans Wake* Joyce attempted to create a mode of expression suited to documenting human experience yet free of pitfalls associated with historiography.

Atherton, James S. *The Books at the Wake: A Study of Literary Allusions in James Joyce's "Finnegans Wake."* New York: Viking, 1960, 308 p.

Traces allusions in *Finnegans Wake* to literary works, classifying the references according to the degree that they influence the novel.

Attridge, Derek. "Finnegans Awake: The Dream of Interpretation." *James Joyce Quarterly* 27, No. 1 (Fall 1989): 11-29.

Suggests that "the notion of the dream as an interpretive context for *Finnegans Wake* is one among a number of such contexts which, though incompatible with one another, all have some potential value."

Bates, Ronald. "The Feast Is a Flyday." *James Joyce Quarterly* 2, No. 3 (Spring 1965): 174-87.

Attempts to show that Joyce conceived of the events described in *Finnegans Wake* as occurring on Easter, 3 April 1904.

Begnal, Michael H., and Senn, Fritz, eds. *A Conceptual Guide to "Finnegans Wake."* University Park: Pennsylvania State University Press, 1974, 236 p.

Comprises essays on *Finnegans Wake* by critics who "were each assigned an individual chapter or section of the novel and asked to deal with it from a specific angle or point of view."

Benstock, Bernard. *Joyce-again's Wake: An Analysis of "Finnegans Wake."* Seattle: University of Washington Press, 1965, 312 p.

Overview of *Finnegans Wake* intended, according to Benstock, for general readers rather than Joycean scholars.

———, ed. *Critical Essays on James Joyce*. Boston: G. K. Hall & Co., 1985, 236 p.

Employs "a chronological format to survey the varieties and dominant tendencies through the history of Joyce criticism."

Benstock, Shari. "Sexuality and Survival in *Finnegans Wake*." In *The Seventh of Joyce*, edited by Bernard Benstock, pp. 247-54. Bloomington: Indiana University Press, 1982.

Asserts that in *Finnegans Wake* "marital relationships survive by bonds of loyalty rather than sexual fulfill-ment" because "sexual experience that in and of itself is purely joyful exists only in youth."

Boldereff, Frances Motz. *Reading "Finnegans Wake."* Woodward, Pa.: Classic Nonfiction Library, 1959, 284 p.

Analyzes *Finnegans Wake* as the representation of a symbolic world, a history of Ireland, and an account of a day in the life of a man and his family. Boldereff supplements his study with a glossary of Irish words and phrases that appear in the novel.

Bowen, Zack, and Carens, James F. *A Companion to Joyce Studies*. Westport, Conn.: Greenwood Press, 1984, 818 p.

Includes "The Language of *Finnegans Wake*," by Michael H. Begnal; "Technique in *Finnegans Wake*," by Barbara DiBernard; and "The Structures and Meanings of *Finnegans Wake*," by Patrick A. McCarthy.

Campbell, Joseph, and Robinson, Henry Morton. *A Skeleton Key to Finnegans Wake*. New York: Harcourt, Brace and Co., 1944, 365 p.

Sketches the narrative outline of *Finnegans Wake* "page by page."

Chase, Richard V. "*Finnegans Wake*: An Anthropological Study." *The American Scholar* 13, No. 4 (Autumn 1944): 418-26.

Proposes that *Finnegans Wake* is an orthodox work of literature that addresses universal themes through "a religious pan-primitivism."

Cheng, Vincent John. *Shakespeare and Joyce: A Study of "Finnegans Wake."* University Park: Pennsylvania State University Press, 1984, 271 p.

Demonstrates Shakespeare's influence on *Finnegans Wake* through study of the novel's design, themes, and allusions. Cheng provides an annotated list of the allusions and the location of the corresponding lines in Shakespeare's works.

Christiani, Dounia Bunis. *Scandinavian Elements of "Finnegans Wake."* Evanston, Ill.: Northwestern University Press, 1965, 259 p.

Finds that *Finnegans Wake* evinces a significant Scandinavian influence. Some examples cited include: extensive use of Danish language in the novel; protagonist Humphrey Chimpden Earwicker's Norse lineage; and the founding of Dublin—Earwicker's native city—by Danes.

———. "The Polyglot Poetry of *Finnegans Wake*." In *Proceedings of the Comparative Literature Symposium, Vol. II: James Joyce—His Place in World Literature*, edited by Wolodymyr T. Zyla, pp. 23-38. Lubbock: Texas Technological College, 1969.

Contends that the language of *Finnegans Wake* enables Joyce to "express all-but-ineffable shades of awareness and feeling and compress more meaning and music, mimicry and wit into a few words than would be possible in any standard language."

Deming, Robert H., ed. *James Joyce: The Critical Heritage. Volume 2: 1928-1941*. London: Routledge & Kegan Paul, 1970, 821 p.

Reprints contemporary critical responses to both *Finnegans Wake* and passages from the novel that were published prior to its completion.

Devlin, Kimberly. "Self and Other in *Finnegans Wake*: A

Framework for Analyzing Versions of Shem and Shaun." *James Joyce Quarterly* 21, No. 1 (Fall 1983): 31-50.

Interprets *Finnegans Wake* as dramatizing the conflict between an individual's id and superego.

Dunleavy, Janet E.; Friedman, Melvin J.; and Gillespie, Michael Patrick, eds. *Joycean Occasions: Essays from the Milwaukee James Joyce Conference.* Newark: University of Delaware Press, 1991, 246 p.

Collects papers delivered at the James Joyce Conference in 1987. Among those discussing *Finnegans Wake* are "Murphy, Shem, Morpheus, and Murphies: Eumaeus Meets the *Wake*," by Susan Brienza and "Apostrophes: Framing *Finnegans Wake*," by Shari Benstock.

Finney, Michael. "Eugene Jolas, *transition,* and the Revolution of the Word." In *In the Wake of the "Wake,"* edited by David Hayman and Elliott Anderson, pp. 39-53. Madison: The University of Wisconsin Press, 1978.

Examines the theory underlying the Revolution of the Word—"a naive philosophy of linguistic nihilism" loosely associated with *Finnegans Wake*—in order to provide a context in which to understand Joyce's novel.

Fleming, William S. "Formulaic Rhythms in *Finnegans Wake.*" *Style* 6, No. 1 (1972): 19-37.

Determines that *Finnegans Wake* has patterns "at the phonetic and rhythmic levels" that attest to the "methodical coherence" of the novel.

Gillespie, Michael Patrick. "When Is a Man Not a Man?: Deconstructive and Reconstructive Impulses in *Finnegans Wake.*" *The International Fiction Review* 18, No. 1 (1991): 1-14.

States that *Finnegans Wake* requires suggestive and provisional interpretation rather than proscriptive analysis directed by "traditional cause-and-effect thinking."

Glasheen, Adaline. "Part of What the Thunder Said in *Finnegans Wake.*" *The Analyst,* No. XXIII (November 1964): 1-29.

Claims that notable words and names are incorporated in the thunder sounds phonetically spelled in *Finnegans Wake.* Glasheen places the thunder-words together on a graph from which she extracts phrases and terms.

Hart, Clive, and Senn, Fritz, eds. *A Wake Digest.* Sydney, Australia: Sydney University Press, 1968, 86 p.

Collects twenty-four essays that comment on various aspects of *Finnegans Wake.* Many of the essays were previously published in 1962 and 1963 in *A Wake Newslitter.*

Hayman, David, ed. Introduction to *A First-Draft Version of "Finnegans Wake,"* pp. 3-43. London: Faber and Faber, 1963.

Discusses Joyce's methods of composing and revising *Finnegans Wake* and comments on the manuscript history of each section of the novel.

——. "Pound at the Wake or the Uses of a Contemporary." *James Joyce Quarterly* 2, No. 3 (Spring 1965): 204-16.

Noting that Joyce and Ezra Pound were friends for several years, Hayman contends that Joyce incorporated "Pound's eccentricities, his foibles and follies, his passions, wit and rage" in *Finnegans Wake.*

Levin, Harry. "The Fabulous Artificer." In his *James Joyce: A Critical Introduction,* pp. 139-206. Norfolk, Conn.: New Directions Books, 1941.

Comments on ideas and themes central to *Finnegans Wake* and finds that Joyce's authorial intent and his use of language are congruous.

McCarthy, Patrick A. "Reading the Letter: Interpreting the *Wake.*" In *New Alliances in Joyce Studies,* edited by Bonnie Kime Scott, pp. 238-42. Newark: University of Delaware Press, 1988.

Discusses the significance of a correspondence that appears in *Finnegans Wake,* concluding that the letter—like the novel—resists selective and reductive interpretations.

Norris, Margot. *The Decentered Universe of "Finnegans Wake": A Structuralist Analysis.* Baltimore: Johns Hopkins University Press, 1976, 151 p.

Employs a structuralist approach based on Giordano Bruno's concept of binary opposition to examine the narrative, themes, perspective, and language of *Finnegans Wake.*

Phul, Ruth von. "Shaun in Brooklyn." *The Analyst,* No. XVI (February 1959): 1-22.

Maintains that Joyce based the character Shaun in *Finnegans Wake* on both his brother Stanislaus Joyce and his acquaintance J. F. Byrne.

Rose, Danis, and O'Hanlon, John. *Understanding "Finnegans Wake": A Guide to the Narrative of James Joyce's Masterpiece.* New York: Garland Publishing, 1982, 341 p.

Studies *Finnegans Wake* as a work that can be "apprehended by the conscious mind but which was written in the language of the unconscious." Rose and O'Hanlon attempt to uncover rules of vocabulary and grammar embedded in the novel, as well as demonstrate the significance of *Finnegans Wake* among intellectual achievements of the twentieth century.

Solomon, Margaret C. *Eternal Geomater: The Sexual Universe of "Finnegans Wake."* Carbondale and Edwardsville: Southern Illinois University Press, 1969, 164 p.

Explores the sexual symbolism of *Finnegans Wake.*

Staples, Hugh B. "Joyce and Cryptology: Some Speculations." *James Joyce Quarterly* 2, No. 3 (Spring 1965): 167-73.

Discusses Joyce's interest in cryptology, especially as evidenced in *Finnegans Wake* and *Ulysses.*

Tindall, William York. *A Reader's Guide to "Finnegans Wake."* New York: Farrar, Straus and Giroux, 1969, 399 p.

Chapter-by-chapter analysis of *Finnegans Wake.*

Wilson, Edmund. "The Dream of H. C. Earwicker." In his *The Wound and the Bow: Seven Studies in Literature,* pp. 243-71. Cambridge: Riverside Press, 1941.

Provides an overview and criticisms of *Finnegans Wake.*

Additional coverage of Joyce's life and career is contained in the following sources published by Gale Research: *Contemporary Authors,* Vols. 104, 126; *Concise Dictionary of British Literary Biography, 1914-1945; DISCovering Authors; Dictionary of Literary Biography,* Vols. 10, 19, 36; *Major 20th-Century Writers; Short Story Criticism,* Vol. 3; *Twentieth-Century Literary Criticism,* Vols. 3, 8, 16, 26, 35; and *World Literature Criticism.*

Curzio Malaparte

1898-1957

(Pseudonym of Kurt Erich Suckert) Italian journalist, essayist, novelist, poet, dramatist.

INTRODUCTION

Malaparte is best known for two memoirs, *Kaputt* and *La Pelle* (*The Skin*), in which he chronicled the political and social turmoil pandemic in Europe during World War II. These works also recount Malaparte's political and philosophical doctrines, principally his association with the fascist movement in Italy. Critical opinion suggests that the success of these books, which were both international bestsellers, was due to Malaparte's combination of journalistic talent and ability to anticipate and conform to trends in literature and politics.

Malaparte was born in Prato, in the province of Tuscany. His father was a German Jew, and his mother was an Italian from the northern province of Lombardy. Malaparte served in the Italian army in World War I and afterward, as a journalist and political activist, wholeheartedly promoted the rise of Benito Mussolini and his fascist regime in the 1920s. Malaparte's support for Mussolini continued into the next decade, but his propensity to be critical of fascist policies eventually resulted in censorship of his work and a period of exile on the island of Lipari. When Italy entered World War II in 1940, Malaparte's relationship with Italian fascist leaders had been restored sufficiently for him to return to his role as an Italian war correspondent. However, his frequent criticism of fascist leaders and a series of accurate but unfavorable articles detailing fascist progress on the Russo-German front finally resulted in his expulsion, in 1941, from German-held territory. By 1942, in one of several ideological conversions, Malaparte renounced fascism and became a war correspondent and liaison officer for the Allied forces. After World War II, Malaparte wrote a screenplay and two full-length dramas, none of which engendered significant critical acclaim or commercial success. He continued to publish political commentary, and, developing a political affinity for Maoist Communism, he traveled to China. During this journey he became seriously ill and returned to Rome. In one final ideological transformation, Malaparte converted to Roman Catholicism shortly before his death in 1957.

Critical commentary in English on Malaparte has focused almost exclusively on *Kaputt,* which is based on his experiences on the Russian front from 1941 to 1943, and on *The Skin,* which reflects the conditions in Naples following the Allied occupation of Italy. Common to both works are stark and often shocking imagery and a flamboyant prose style. In a typical passage from *Kaputt,* Malaparte writes: "The victim, tied to a pole, was stripped with a penknife piece by piece of all of his flesh, except for his nerves and his arteries and his veins. The man became a kind of trellis made of bones, the nerves and blood vessels through which the sun could shine and the flies could buzz." Fred R. Mabbutt has written that Malaparte's "grisly tales and grim humor are a nightmare not easily forgotten. The Croat Pavelich and his 'oyster' dinner of forty pounds of partisans' eyes; Russian prisoners being tested for literacy and those able to read shot . . . Jewish girls in Rumania coerced into brothels for twenty days and then shot . . . are episodes which Malaparte regards as 'horribly gay and gruesome.' " Some critics discern an undercurrent of fascist attitudes and ideals in both *Kaputt* and *The Skin* which belies Malaparte's public renunciation of the movement. Others question the historical accuracy of Malaparte's memoirs, while acknowledging their value as a reflection of the harsh and bizarre circumstances of the war. As Richard Watts, Jr., has observed: "I doubt that a single incident in [*Kaputt*] can be taken as possessing literal truth. What is important is that the whole leering, grimacing, corrupt and degenerate picture he paints of Fascist Europe . . . has, whatever the inventions and the arrogant fancies he may have added to it, an inescapable inner truth. The details may be lies, but the total effect is but too hideously and decadently true."

PRINCIPAL WORKS

La rivolta dei santi maledetti (nonfiction) 1921
Europa vivente (nonfiction) 1923
Italia barbara (nonfiction) 1925
L'arcitaliano (poetry) 1928
*Le technique du coup d'état (nonfiction) 1931
  [*Coup d'État: The Technique of Revolution,* 1932]
Il Volga nasce in Europa (journalism) 1943
  [*The Volga Rises in Europe,* 1957]
Don Camalèo (novel) 1946
Kaputt (memoirs) 1948
†*La peau* (memoirs) 1948
  [*The Skin,* 1952]
Das Kapital (drama) 1949
Cristo proibito (screenplay) 1951
Anche la donne hanno perso la guerra (drama) 1952
Maledetti toscani (nonfiction) 1956
  [*Those Cursed Tuscans,* 1964]
Opere complete di Curzio Malaparte. 9 vols. (novels, memoirs, essays, journalism, nonfiction, dramas, poetry, and correspondence) 1957-1971
Io in Russia e in Cina (journal) 1958

Il ballo al Cremlino   (short stories and unfinished novels) 1972

*This work was written in French and published in Italian as *Tecnica del colpo di stato* in 1948.

†This work, first published in French, appeared in Italian translation as *La pelle* in 1949.

CRITICISM

Joseph Shaplen   (essay date 1932)

[*In the following review of Coup d'Etat, Shaplen questions the validity of Malaparte's theory of political revolution.*]

Signor Malaparte is no parlor-Fascist. He is the real article. He took an active part in the seizure of Florence in 1922 and accompanied Mussolini on the march to Rome. He has been advertised as a poet, diplomat and close associate of Il Duce, and the present book, we are told, "has won the widest attention" in Europe as an exposition of the scientific theory of revolution in the machine age, as a warning to those countries which have not yet succumbed to dictatorship but which, according to Signor Malaparte, are all open to either a Communist or Fascist coup d'état.

Signor Malaparte asserts that this danger arises from the new technique of revolution conceived by Trotsky in November, 1917, and later developed with signal success by Mussolini. Signor Malaparte frankly admits, like Mussolini, "our masters are in Moscow." Because bourgeois-liberal-socialist Europe is not aware of this danger, because it clings to the old, simple, outworn "police methods" of protecting the State against insurrection, it may find itself drawn into the orbit of Italy or Russia.

This, in substance, is the main thesis of [*Coup d'Etat*], a book which opens large vistas only to run off on the narrow tangent of a pseudo-Machiavellian counter-revolutionary dilettantism, devoid of any understanding of the more profound springs of the social and political problems which form the background of his thesis.

Karl Kautsky has pointed out, and experience has certainly confirmed it, that only those who do not understand the nature of the modern State could have expected, as did the Russian Bolsheviki, that because a certain type of revolution, the objectively historical consequence of specific political, social and psychologic conditions peculiar to that country, occurred in Russia, other countries would indiscriminately follow suit. This, as is well known, is part of the original theory of "integral" Leninism.

Signor Malaparte makes the same mistake, but in even more vulgar fashion: he reduces the whole problem to a matter of technique.

What is this new technique of which Signor Malaparte speaks? Disregarding or minimizing the political elements, the complex of social and economic forces involved, it consists in the abandonment of frontal attack on the State and its representatives and the execution of a flank movement against its nerve centres: the seizure, as the first and essential step, of railway stations, post and telegraph offices and electric light plants. Only after thus cutting off the State from the social and economic body that feeds it is the assault on the State itself begun. Signor Malaparte would have us believe that had Trotsky been content to wait for the maturing of certain political events to which Lenin attached great importance, the Bolshevist coup d'état would not have been successful. In the author's opinion, Kerensky made his great mistake in failing to protect the nerve centres, the key positions on which Trotsky concentrated his fire. Having captured these centres, Trotsky proceeded to complete the task of insurrection by seizing the seat of government itself and arresting or dispersing its Ministers. To Trotsky, not to Lenin, whom Signor Malaparte depicts as, after all, only a Bolshevist Fabian, belongs the credit for the success of the Bolshevist coup d'état.

This is what has been termed history standing on its head. Signor Malaparte misrepresents the situation in Petrograd in November, 1917. Lenin was the brain, the will and the driving power of the Bolshevist coup d'état. Trotsky was his big stick. The power in Russia lay in the street amid increasing chaos, and Lenin and Trotsky had the courage to pick it up. That and nothing more constituted their "technique." Kerensky fought to the best of his ability and of the opportunities at his command. But these opportunities were limited. In the end he was betrayed—and this is the real immediate secret of the Bolshevist victory—by regiments commanded by Czarist officers who preferred to see the Bolsheviki rather than the revolutionary democracy in power, with the calculation that the Bolsheviki would not last long and permit the reactionaries to resume control.

So enamored is Signor Malaparte of his theory, which has neither historical nor political justification—with delightful nonchalance he does not hesitate to make his facts fit the theory—that he attributes Stalin's subsequent defeat of Trotsky to his mastery of Trotskist tactics and development of a counter-technique based upon the lesson of the November coup d'état.

The historical fact is that Stalin's victory over Trotsky was purely political. The story told by Signor Malaparte of a last-minute effort by Trotsky to seize power by means of his "technique" is fiction. Trotsky is a revolutionist in the grand style, but Stalin proved the better politician. The brilliant, sensitive, cultured Trotsky lost to the "epigones" because he thought too much of "style" and of striking attitudes and not enough of simple, concrete facts of the situation. When the climax came, the machine rode roughshod over Trotsky. His downfall simply served to emphasize that the romantic period of bolshevism was over and that it was time to talk prose. Mediocrity triumphed over brilliance, because the time for brilliance had passed.

Kapp in Germany, Primo de Rivera in Spain and Pilsudski in Poland are cited by Signor Malaparte as examples of dictators or would-be dictators who have failed because of their clinging to the obsolete methods of Bonapartism and pseudo-legality as means of accomplishing and maintaining a coup d'état. In what is perhaps the best and most brilliant chapter in the book, Signor Malaparte paints Hitler as a "would-be dictator" who does not have the courage of his dictatorial instincts and has permitted his revolutionary élan to degenerate to bourgeois-parliamentary legality. Unlike Mussolini he hesitates to strike, undermining the morale of his own forces. He has no understanding of the social forces at work in Germany and "shrinks from an encounter with the formidable power of the proletarian labor organizations which might bar the road of insurrection for him," as they once barred the road to success for Kapp. Hitler, in Malaparte's opinion, is only a tool of other reactionary elements, Prussian junkerdom and German heavy industry, a clown, a scarecrow. He has a certain immediate function to perform and having performed it he will disappear into the bourgeois obscurity whence he came.

Signor Malaparte's observations at this point are often shrewd, frequently brilliant, permeated with the cynical sophistication of one who has tasted violence and likes it. "It is revolutionary violence which legitimatizes a dictatorship, the coup d'état itself is its soundest foundation." With sadistic glee he describes the pogrom activities of the Fascist bands before and after the march on Rome. The ruthless destruction of trade unions and other working-class organizations, of cooperatives and organs of self-government, of the Republican and Catholic trade unions and of all democratic centres of resistance, possible and real, fill our Fascist poet with boundless admiration. This, too, is an essential part of his new "technique." In Italy, Signor Malaparte is frank enough to say the destruction of independent working-class organizations was carried out by Mussolini before the march on Rome as an essential pre-requisite to power.

Were not Signor Malaparte so obsessed with his purely militaristic approach to the problem and so eager to prove a wholly false thesis, he would understand that right at this point lies the crux of the whole question. No dictatorship, Bolshevist or Fascist, is possible in any modern State with a well-organized, trained and disciplined working class and a creative, virile bourgeoisie. It is precisely because these two elements were absent in Russia and Italy that bolshevism and fascism were victorious. Signor Malaparte himself shows clearly how helpless Kapp was despite his seizure of Berlin before the onslaught of the general strike in Germany. In Italy the working class, although more numerous and better organized than in Russia, had permitted itself to be weakened by internecine strife promoted by Communist propaganda and thus opened the road to Mussolini.

Signor Malaparte's advice to Europe is entirely gratuitous. It would be futile to deny the dangers of social disintegration lurking in certain spots in Europe. These dangers, particularly the danger of fascism, will remain as long as the economic crisis persists. But neither fascism nor communism has as yet demonstrated its ability to solve the social and economic problem. The victories they have won are not evidences of their strength or of the superiority of Signor Malaparte's "technique," but of the weakness of the democratic forces in Russia and Italy. No régime has ever justified itself merely by the fact of its being. Even Signor Malaparte admits that Western Europe will fight to the death for its liberty, but having admitted this he should be more concerned as a good Fascist with the task upon which his own camp lays most stress, the task of remaining in power, than with teaching Europe how to save itself from a coup d'état. Europe will take care of itself. Signor Malaparte should remember that the civil war in Europe, if it comes, like the great war, will be won on the Western front. The war was not won on the Roman Campagna or at Brest-Litovsk. The civil war would be won in those countries where freedom has always fought its greatest battles and gained its permanent victories.

The handbook on revolutionary tactics written by Signor Malaparte should contribute considerably to fanning the feverish imaginations of both Communists and Fascists. It is a clinical specimen of the social psychopathology of our time.

Joseph Shaplen, "Modern Revolutionary Technique as a Fascist Sees It," in The New York Times Book Review, *July 3, 1932, p. 3.*

Max Nomad   (essay date 1932)

[*Nomad was an Austrian-born political writer. In the following review of* Coup d'Etat, *he asserts that Malaparte fails to illuminate his subject—the reasons for and methods of political revolution.*]

Revolutions, coups d'etat, general strikes, terrorism, sabotage, barricades, skirmishes, massacres, executions—these are among the most fascinating episodes of the great human tragi-comedy. Torn from the intimate connection with the main propelling force of class and group interests, however, their descriptions are no more helpful to understanding social history than would be the mere photograph of a dynamo to an understanding of the nature of electromagnetism. ***Coup d'Etat: The Technique of Revolution*** fails primarily because it provides such descriptions without revealing those intimate connections which would give them genuine meaning.

Coup d'Etat is written vividly, with flashes of wit here and there, and this explains the *succès de scandale* the book has achieved in Europe. The author, the Italian Fascist Curzio Malaparte, candidly confesses:

> . . . the object of the book is not . . . to discuss the political, economic, and social programs of the conspirators, but to show that the problem of conquest and defense of the state is not a political one, that it is a technical problem . . . that the circumstances favorable to a coup d'etat are not necessarily of a political and social order and do not depend on the general condition of the country.

In another passage he points out that the technical problem consists in getting hold of the most vital arteries of the nation's economic life—the railway stations, postal and telegraph services, ports, power plants, gas works, and water mains.

History is thus made very easy. The disintegration of the Czarist army, the misery and destitution of the masses, the desire for peace, the land hunger of the peasantry, the growing disappointment of the industrial workers, as expressed by the growth of Bolshevist influence in the Soviets, the struggle for power between rival groups of the revolutionary intelligentsia—all these factors can be summarily dismissed. The coup d'etat of November, 1917, succeeded because Trotzky knew how to apply the right technique. The author stresses his argument with numerous "quotations" for which he gives no sources. During his struggle against the opposition, Stalin, according to Malaparte, referred to Trotzky as "a wretched Jew," and Trotzky, nothing daunted, called his rival "a miserable Christian." Just like that.

In the light of the fact that Trotzky's technique of the coup d'etat is so easy to understand, and, according to Malaparte, so easy to apply anywhere, one wonders why those tactics were not employed successfully by the Italian and Polish Communists in 1920, or by the German Communists between 1919 and 1923, and finally by Trotzky himself in 1926-27? Since Signore Malaparte dismisses political and economic circumstances as determining factors, he is forced to find other explanations. The Germans and Italians—well, they simply were "ignorant of the methods, the tactics, and the modern technique of the coup d'etat of which Trotzky had given a new and classic example." The Polish Communists understood Trotzky, but being mostly Jews, they did not have the guts. This applied also to Trotzky's followers during his struggle against Stalin.

Only Mussolini knew how to apply Trotzky's tactics. But there is a little hitch in Malaparte's epic picture of Benito's rise to power—that is, aside from his always too obvious embellishment of historical facts. The author says modestly that "it is not known" why the King refused to sign an order establishing a state of siege when the March on Rome was started. Malaparte knows that Madame Kollontai loved the sailor Dybenko "for his transparent eyes and for his cruelty"; but he does not know, that is, he affects not to know, what every historian knows, that the Italian Army Command, which hoped to establish a military dictatorship, was conspiring with, and giving all the necessary assistance to Mussolini, who, of course, later double-crossed his allies, as he double-crossed all his other associates. All of which was not exactly identical with Trotzky's "technique."

Despite his often grotesque distortions of the Russian events, the author is actually much less severe with the Bolsheviks than with the heroes of the counter-revolutionary coups d'etat outside of Italy. But he is much too cautious to give more than a faint hint of the actual class origin of his contempt for Kapp, Primo de Rivera, Pilsudski, and Hitler.

The fact of the matter is that the so-called "fascist" coups d'etat in the other countries can hardly be said to have revealed very much in common with the Italian brand. Mussolini and his original following of adventurous dissenters from the various radical and revolutionary groups, mostly déclassé intellectuals, ex-workers, and war veterans, had placed themselves at the disposal of the manufacturers, financiers, and land-holders for the double purpose of cowing the workers and destroying all the organizations headed by their former rivals in the radical camp. Having finished the job, they had no inclination to step aside as dismissed bullies who were no longer needed. They established a dictatorship of the fascist section of the intelligentsia over both workers and capitalists (and the rest of the population, for that matter)—ready to seize their former backers rudely by the throat whenever such a gesture was necessary for the maintenance of their own power. Neither the Kapp nor the Rivera dictatorships had anything in common with this essential feature of a fascist regime. Both the German and the Spanish coup meant simply the reestablishment or the strengthening of the old Junker and militarist rule—with the famished intellectual "outs" altogether removed from the picture. Pilsudski's coup of 1926 was likewise a purely military and quite "respectable" affair, while Hitler, in the opinion of Malaparte, is merely a hired agent in the service of the German manufacturers and Junkers—with no actual intention of reaching out for an exclusive fascist dictatorship, Italian style.

Malaparte's chapter on Hitler contains some very caustic and challenging remarks about dictators in general. It is a reasonable conjecture that the bitter sarcasm of some of these passages was aimed not exclusively at the eloquent Austrian yokel. The author no doubt was out to vent his spleen at the incomparable Master, Mussolini himself, who is apparently more feared than loved by his immediate entourage.

Malaparte has been known in Italy as an author of a volume of fascist lyrics. If in this line of his endeavor he has shown as much imagination as in his treatment of historical facts, he has done his country a great wrong by deserting the muses. (pp. 86-7)

Max Nomad, "Revolution as a Fine Art," in The Nation, New York, Vol. CXXXV, No. 3499, July 27, 1932, pp. 86-7.

Albert Hubbell   (essay date 1946)

[*In the following review of* Kaputt, *Hubbell expresses admiration for Malaparte's analysis of the "Fascist state of mind."*]

In the summer of 1943, while he was waiting at his home on Capri for the Allied soldiers to take him prisoner, Curzio Malaparte, an Italian diplomat and journalist of considerable reputation on the Continent, finished a book he had been working on secretly during the war. That book, **Kaputt**, has now been published by Dutton in an English translation. It is one of the most astonishing and forbidding documents of our time—a sort of Gothic nightmare, a masque of the Fascist death. In his introduction, or perhaps his apologia, Malaparte calls it a "horribly gay and gruesome book," and he is right.

What Malaparte has written is a clinical study of the Fascist state of mind in its purest, most hideous form. The gay gruesomeness of which he speaks is evident in his reports on the dinner parties given by high Axis functionaries, the gossip of titled German ladies at embassy receptions, the drinking bouts of Nazi officers, and the smart small talk around cocktail tables in Rome. It is also evident in the macabre vignette of the scene in a Finnish steam bath where Heinrich Himmler and his S.S. guards danced around naked—ten white, flabby bodies surmounted by grim, fishy-eyed German faces. The bodies were "wonderfully defenseless—bereft of secrecy . . . no longer frightening." The real skin of the German is his uniform, Malaparte remarks in recording this occasion; without his uniform, the German could not frighten a child. There is a grisly gaiety, too, in Malaparte's account of a dinner given by Governor-General Frank in Warsaw, an event of awesome vulgarity presided over by the piggish proconsul with the coarse neck and the fine, feminine hands (he played Chopin "like an angel"), who thought of himself as a Lorenzo de' Medici, a lover and patron of the arts, an architect of model ghettos who would wake the Polish people from their cultural apathy by introducing a German renaissance. Malaparte says Frank told his guests that he had just received a shipment of a new soap and that the nice ladies of Poland would now be able to keep themselves clean and pretty. The only trouble, he went on, was that this soap was made mostly of dung and unfortunately retained the color and smell of its main ingredient, at which the company shouted *"Wunderbar!"* and laughed until tears came.

Our country fought the Fascists and the Nazis in Europe, and our correspondents reported back to us on the fighting. The best of them did it well, but they could never quite explain the peculiar nature of our adversary. There has been writing by other men, of course, which indicates that the Fascist mind is different from anything else we have ever known, but there have been few men indeed who could tell us just how that mind worked. What was the *positive* side of Fascism? What did the Fascists hope for? How did they (as all human beings must) justify themselves to themselves? Malaparte experienced the war—or the most important part of it, ideologically—from the other side of the curtain, and the chief value of the testament he has written is in his revelation, conscious and unconscious, of a philosophy that is founded on self-hatred and a death wish. During the four years his part of the war lasted, Malaparte, because of his two professions, came to know intimately high-ranking Fascists—German, Italian, Spanish, Rumanian, Hungarian, and Finnish. He worked, ate, played, and suffered with those men who wanted to be the masters of the world—the sick people who could be stimulated only by death, who were in love with death, whose very fury was a sick fury.

Malaparte gives a thoughtful judgment of the master race. One of the things he found in them was a great strangeness. He shows you exactly how strange that strangeness is by setting down some conversations he had with his German acquaintances, most of whom were the élite of either the old or the new order. These men and women talked and thought on a plane not only different from ours but even different from that of an Italian in the good

graces of the Fascist government. As for the cruelty of the Germans, Malaparte believes that it is a result of fear. "They are ill with fear . . . they are afraid of everything and everybody; they kill and destroy out of fear. . . . They are afraid above all of the weak, of the defenseless, of the sick, of women, and of children. They are afraid of the aged. Their fear has always aroused a profound pity in me. If Europe were to feel sorry for them, perhaps the Germans would be healed of their horrible disease."

That last sentence is a clue to Malaparte's character, which is a significant element of his book. It is hardly the remark of a fighting man. Malaparte hated the slowly growing tyranny of the Nazis and the bondage in which his beloved, long-suffering Italy was held. But he was not a man to take overt action against any of this. He was tired, after twenty years of service to Fascist diplomacy and journalism, and he felt, he says, that he was no more than a whore. He understood the Nazis' disease because he was tainted with it himself, but he loathed the proconsuls and the proconsuls' ladies, the generals and the diplomats he had to associate with. He slyly ridiculed them to their faces, and he got away with it, because it did not occur to them that anyone would poke fun at them. He even made dangerous jokes at dinners with German generals.

Malaparte had, of course, already become acclimated to a tyranny, though it had been one that was, in comparison to the German, a rather old-fashioned autarchy—a tyranny that, like the one under which Voltaire lived and wrote, could conceivably be tempered by epigrams. He had disapproved of the homegrown tyranny, too, and criticized it, and on several occasions he had gone to jail for his remarks or for his impudent, defeatist dispatches. But he always returned to his old trade and his old friends in the ruling clique. It was only, one feels, when Mussolini's minor absolutism was merged with the larger one, the blackout of all human values that was to last for a thousand years, that Malaparte came to hate. Maybe "hate" is too strong a word for his emotion about the new despotism. He deplored it deeply, but he understood it and he understood the despair out of which it came. Though he might weep privately for the lost freedom of the spirit, or rage at the chicaneries about him, his final gesture was always a shrug. With his fashionable Roman friends—the brilliant ones, the beautiful, witty ones whose repartee was scented with the most delicious treason, who gathered every afternoon at the Acquasanta Golf Club and tried to engage the fitful favor of Count Ciano—Malaparte shared the misfortune of being *fin de siècle* in the middle of a very new century.

Malaparte saw a lot of the war we didn't hear about. He lived for a while in Finland with the young men of the German Army—the *Alpenjägers,* who had been sent north to patrol the forests and who, prematurely aged by the violent dissipations through which they had tried to escape boredom, were further aged by the unrelenting cold. Whatever the state of the German Army mind elsewhere, in Finland there was only a continual gloom. One of the soldiers told Malaparte that suicides among the troops had increased so alarmingly that Heinrich Himmler himself had had to come to the Finnish front to stop them. "He will place the dead under arrest," said this young man. "He will have them buried with tied hands. He had three *Alpenjägers* shot yesterday because they had tried to hang themselves." There are, in Malaparte's account of this campaign, other symbols of the night that would have settled over the planet if the Axis had won the war. There is a description of a wintry scene on the Finnish-Russian front in 1942 that, for grotesquerie and suggestion of world's end, outranks Hieronymus Bosch. There had been a terrible battle in the snowy forest beside Lake Ladoga, and in the afternoon the Finns had set fire to the forest. All the horses of the Soviet artillery, dragging their guns behind them, had plunged into the shallow waters in an effort to escape the awful heat. By morning, the lake was covered with a sheet of ice from which rose the heads of a thousand dead horses, upright and rigid, eyes bulging, and all despairingly facing the shore. Later that winter, Malaparte and a philosopher friend used to stroll out on the lake and sit on the heads while they talked about the war.

Malaparte writes a phrenetic prose. As he sweeps along through purple patches, through mystical threnodies, through stark and bloody paragraphs, you feel that he is barely keeping himself under control. It is an appropriate style for the content, but it occasionally betrays the writer into absurdities and obscurities. Whether or not every conversation he has recorded is verbatim is unimportant. What is important is that this book is, subjectively and objectively, a composite portrait of what is called Fascism—with all its senility, all its decay, its cynicism, its sad weariness exposed. Malaparte's word for it is perhaps as good as any. "Kaputt," the dictionary says, means "Done, broken, finished, gone to ruin." (pp. 131-32, 134-35)

> Albert Hubbell, *"The Great Strangeness,"* in The New Yorker, *Vol. XXII, No. 42, November 30, 1946, pp. 131-32, 134-35.*

Richard Watts, Jr.   (essay date 1946)

[*Watts was a journalist and drama critic whose career spanned forty years at the* New York Herald Tribune *and the* New York Post. *In the following review, he suggests that the ultimate value of Malaparte's* Kaputt *lies in its unintentional revelation of the author's fascist attitudes and principles.*]

In a moment of almost startled introspection, Curzio Malaparte, apparently still not quite believing it, said to a German princess: "I sometimes think that I, too, am partly responsible for what is now taking place in Europe." Since Malaparte, a playboy of Italian fascism, participated in Mussolini's march on Rome and fought for the Blackshirts in Florence, was a Fascist journalist of note and a specially favored Axis war correspondent, who numbered among his intimates such choice souls as Ciano and the butcher of Poland, Governor Hans Frank, this remark, which he says he made in Potsdam in 1942, would seem to be a triumph of understatement. It is, however, the sort of thing which gives *Kaputt* its unwholesome fascination and its undoubted importance.

Despite an occasional sojourn in Mussolini's jails and a disclaimer of sympathy for his Nazi friends, there is no denying that Malaparte is an extremely dubious and unhealthy character. It is even hard to dispute that *Kaputt* is an untrustworthy book which, despite his protestations, contains as much fiction as fact. Indeed, I doubt that a single incident in it can be taken as possessing literal truth. What is important is that the whole leering, grimacing, corrupt and degenerate picture he paints of Fascist Europe before the tide had turned against it has, whatever the inventions and the arrogant fancies he may have added to it, an inescapable inner truth. The details may be lies, but the total effect is but too hideously and decadently true.

Ironically, *Kaputt* is a more valuable and revealing book than its author realizes. In it, he is so busily engaged in showing what a remarkable fellow he is, with his charm, wit and courage, his contempt for those who are taken in by the illusions of fascism, his knowledge of the great and his intimacy with the powerful, and, above all, his great cultural sophistication, that he gives himself away. His joy in sadism is too great, his relish in the decadent too evident and his delight in evil too obvious. The more he protests that he suffered imprisonment under fascism and has risen above it, the clearer it is that he is a true child of its spirit. One of the makers and creatures of the Fascist era, he has persuaded himself that he is guiltless of its horrors.

The terrible thing is that he is not only sure of his innocence but has apparently convinced the gullible—or could it be culpable?—gentlemen of the Allied occupation forces of his rectitude, since it is reported that for two years he has been a liaison officer attached to the American high command in Italy. In short, he is just the type of unprincipled opportunist that is most cherished and given advancement by our policy makers abroad, in their blind conviction that they are propping up the respectable elements as a shield against communism. It is a chastening thought that from Spain eastward to Japan, men like Malaparte are regarded by American policy as representing the future of both Europe and Asia.

The literary world and the best journalists conceded that at best Malaparte was a brilliant juggler with words, a skilful craftsman who could write with ease in any of several fashionable styles, a maker of ephemeral verbal fireworks.

—Luigi Barzini, *"Remembering Curzio Malaparte,"* in Encounter, *April, 1982.*

It is the potential value of a book which revels in cruelty, lust, decadence, rottenness and general depravity that its author, in the firm conviction that he is proving his superiority to the diseased world in which he had happily participated, unconsciously gives the show away by his arrogant boastfulness. As much as he may have hoodwinked the

Allied Military Government authorities by his protestations of innocence, his frantic exhibitionism in *Kaputt* is so flagrant that the mask is torn from his face and his essential indecency stands exposed. He reveals the evil flowering of European fascism with vivid and memorable skill, but in the process he and his kind are also shown as characteristic examples of its noxious flora. The thought of turning Europe over to such men under the guise of democracy should be unthinkable.

No one who reads *Kaputt* is likely to forget for a long time its nightmare episodes. The Croat Pavelich and his basket of partisans' eyes; Russian prisoners being tested for literacy and those able to read executed; Jewish girls in Rumania forced into prostitution for twenty days and then shot; Himmler in a Finnish bathhouse; the Russian boy's guess concerning the German general's glass eye; the visit to the Warsaw ghetto with Max Schmeling and Frank when Frank gayly took a rifle-shot at a fleeing Jewish child; the pogrom in Jassy—such episodes do make up what Malaparte fancies as "a horribly gay and gruesome book." But the horror and the gruesomeness arise less from the evil of the things described than from the unspeakable quality of the author himself.

There is no denying that Curzio Malaparte is a skillful writer. He can not only provide macabre incidents that capture the obscenity of a diseased political system, but can catch the whole nauseating spirit of Franco's Spain in the character of the Spanish Ambassador to Finland or the magnitude of postwar Poland's problems in Frank's boast of the use he has made of the Polish clergy and aristocracy. *Kaputt,* both consciously and unconsciously, is less "horribly gay" than horribly illuminating. (pp. 737-38)

> *Richard Watts, Jr., "Life without Principle,"
> in* The New Republic, *Vol. 115, No. 22, December 2, 1946, pp. 737-38.*

Vincent Sheean (essay date 1952)

[*An American novelist, political journalist, and foreign correspondent, Sheean served the U.S. Army as an intelligence officer during World War II. In the following review, he focuses on the stylistic traits of* Kaputt *and* The Skin *and questions Malaparte's reliability in these works.*]

The peculiar talent of Malaparte grows no less distinct with the years. Its iridescence may come from putrefaction (indeed he never stops telling us so) but just the same it gleams and glows with a light that is not of every day. At the very outset of his career in the 1920s he became the darling of the Fascist régime for his *Technique of the Coup d'Etat,* which was also much admired by Communists; he flourished exceedingly in Axis high society until, like all spoiled children, he went too far in his witticisms and was exiled to the isle of Lipari; he operated with the Nazi armies as a war correspondent and observer. He seems to have been everywhere in Europe, and on pretty much all sides (except the Russian) during the many-sided war. He began his "collaboration" with the Americans as soon as

they landed in Italy, and would no doubt do the same for the Russians if they arrived there tomorrow.

[*The Skin*] describes his experiences with the American army from the time of the Salerno landings until the end of the war. His last book, *Kaputt,* described his experiences earlier in the war with Hitler's armies. The two books are similar in their tone of perverse and willful horror, cynicism and despair. It is self-humiliation of the most unrelieved kind. The title, *The Skin,* comes from a theme Malaparte introduces more than once in the text, which is that nowadays men struggle only for their skins, their putrid and evanescent skins, and not for any principle at all. He also says that the skin of a dead man horribly slain, so that there is nothing much left but skin, is the proper flag. "My country's only flag," he says.

Malaparte's self-abasement has nothing whatever to do with humility: it comes, on the contrary, from pride and contempt—pride in himself, contempt for others. He says that the Italian people have always kissed the feet of their conquerors, but in sovereign contempt. This theme recurs from beginning to end of a long book. Malaparte generalizes from his own very peculiar case and presents us with a view both of Italy and of Europe which many of us must reject. I have known Italy and the Italians for thirty years, and amongst my large acquaintance I can think of none who have kissed the feet of any conqueror at all. But Malaparte, with the artist's egoism (for he is an artist), extends the one to embrace the many, says that "all Europe is Naples now," and that he himself is "the soul of Europe." He never seems to understand that by making himself, with his extremely dubious past, a symbol for a whole continent, he is doing an ultimate disservice to the country he professes to love.

Furthermore, in this book (as in *Kaputt*) we are regaled with story after story of the most complex and perverse horror, and we are asked to believe them as facts. Many readers must remember from the previous book such things as the frozen horses in Finland, the trained mad dogs in the Ukraine. It is curious that nobody but Malaparte seems to have told these macabre stories. In *The Skin* we have many such. I was in Naples during the very time he writes about, and I never saw mothers selling their children to Moroccan soldiers in the public streets; I did not smell corpses wherever I went, and I entered Naples on the very first day (before Malaparte did). Malaparte sees corpses everywhere, smells them all the time, and writes of them with a sort of fiendish glee. It is almost impossible to make out whether he really expects us to believe all the stories he tells. They are narrated with such extravagance of detail, imagery and allusion that they make irresistible reading—that is, even when one is tempted to be sick one goes on reading. Such is his power as a writer that even his most disgusting passages command attention and refer the mind to larger realities which, for the time being, persuade the imagination of their validity even though they be rejected half an hour later.

One of the horror stories, late in the book, casts a doubt on all the others. He was lunching with General Guillaume and Pierre Lyautey near the Castel Gandolfo, with Rome and the valley spread out before them. (It was the day the 5th Army took Rome.) The Frenchmen were making fun of him, saying that all these horrors could not conceivably happen to any one man, and that much of what he told in *Kaputt* (then a great European success) must have been invented. Malaparte then and there, with a flow of language almost inimitable, invented a story of what had happened at lunch—a story involving cannibalism for the sake of politeness. They were shocked and sickened, and on his way down to Rome with his American friend Jack Hamilton, Malaparte indicates that it was all pure leg pull. If this could happen once it could happen more than once. Malaparte's perversity seems limitless, and his Grand Guignol talent must in itself be a temptation to pile on the spectral lights and ghastly coloration.

The book is extravagantly overwritten, like all that he does, and he cannot observe the simplest sunset without dragging into it allusions to everything from Homer to Jean-Paul Sartre. Much of this is what they used to call in Paris, at the end of the war, *"étalage factice"*—that is, false display. (A shop-window would show bottles of brandy or Burgundy, for instance, with a big sign saying *"éti-lage factice"* so that customers would know the bottles were empty.) But Malaparte's native gift is superior to his culture; it carries us along through totally unnecessary analogies and cross-references. There is at times a simple, breathless interest over what is going to happen next. The ending of the book is quite horrible, but even the nausea which he deliberately incites cannot keep us from reading it. He is staying in a friend's house in Rome. The friend is a gynecologist or obstetrician. The room in which Malaparte is quartered is surrounded by foetuses (he calls them foeti) in bottles of various sizes. In his final vision these monsters, relentlessly described, engage in dialogue, and the most monstrous of all is Mussolini, Malaparte's one-time patron. The disgust we feel is what the author intended us to feel. The last line of the book is as follows:

> "It is a shameful thing to win a war," I said in
> a low voice.

> *Vincent Sheean, "A Brilliant, Shocking Devil's Advocate," in* The New York Herald Tribune Book Review, *September 21, 1952, p. 6.*

Anthony West   (essay date 1952)

[*The son of Rebecca West and H. G. Wells, West is an English author who has written several novels concerned with the moral, social, psychological, and political disruptions of the twentieth century. In the following excerpt, West considers Malaparte's portrayal of postwar Europe to be profoundly pessimistic.*]

Curzio Malaparte's *The Skin,* a sour account of the passage of the Allied armies through Italy in the late war, is a fitting sequel to his *Kaputt,* published in this country in 1946. That memorable fantasia described his experiences as a war correspondent with the Fascist and Nazi armies in the East during the (for them) brighter opening years of the conflict. It was fascinating not so much for the material it contained (though that was striking enough, recalling Callot's Surrealist engravings of seventeenth-century warfare and its horrors) as for the dash and insou-

ciance with which its author treated his own delicate position. Malaparte wrote with such passionate distaste for Fascism, and with such hatred of the crass inhumanity of the German military machine, that it was painful to see him so closely tied to the German soldiery and forced to sit through dinner parties with Göring, Frank, and lesser Party bonzes. A cruel fate had wantonly forced Malaparte to snuggle up to the evil thing he detested, and one could not help wondering what catastrophic mistake, what misunderstood action, had earned the poor fellow such good standing in Fascist circles. But *Kaputt* passed over this question, rapidly and at great height, to exploit most successfully the prevailing anti-Fascist mood.

Time's chariot has moved on since then; there is no longer an anti-Fascist mood to exploit, because America bled, and the British bled themselves white, to break Fascism. The mood has changed, and if the sales of *The Skin* are any indication, Malaparte has spotted its new character with his usual acuity. . . . Malaparte is still suffering in *The Skin,* and still chained by the caprice of fate to a crass and brutal military machine—this time the United States Army, to which he gallantly offered his services when it was clear that the Fascist jig was up. The British barely come into the picture, and the only contribution on their part that Malaparte sees fit to mention was their provision of castoff uniforms for the reconstituted Italian Army. "Castoff" is perhaps the wrong term, since Malaparte says, and may believe, that they were stripped from the bodies of the British dead at El Alamein and Tobruk. When this necrophilic and indecent fancy has been toyed with to his satisfaction, Malaparte has done with the British, and it is the turn of the Americans to humiliate and distress him. He does not suffer alone; his pain is shared by one American officer. His partner is Staff Colonel Jack Hamilton, who is "pale and elegant, with gentlemanly, almost European manners." He is devoted to European culture, and especially to French literature, but his enthusiasm is not related to any profound knowledge, and Malaparte cannot resist poking sly fun at his slipshod quotations, his inaccurate references, and his naïve attempts to disguise his barbarism by speaking French. "His attitude to Europe, like that of nearly all true Americans, was conditioned by a subtle species of 'inferiority complex' which manifested itself not . . . in an inability to understand and forgive our misery and shame but in a fear of understanding, a reluctance to understand." Jack, an old U. P. man, blushes a good deal as he witnesses the indignities inflicted on the Italian people while the uncouth soldiers of the Fifth Army force their way through Naples, through Rome, and on to Florence. It is only after a time that one recognizes him as the twin brother to the decent German officer in Steinbeck's *The Moon Is Down,* or the Francophile German officer in Vercors's *Silence de la Mer,* figures who typify the sane recognition that the enemy was not wholly evil and that there was such a thing as a good German. To allow that a good American exists is a generous concession from Malaparte, considering what the American Army did to Italy and the rest of Europe. Nothing much was wrong when Mussolini's thugs castrated Matteotti and left him to die on the Via Appia, nothing much was wrong when Dachau and Buchenwald went into business; it was later that things went wrong.

The "plague" had broken out in Naples on October 1, 1943—the very day on which the Allied armies had entered that ill-starred city as liberators. . . . The extraordinary thing about this most modern of diseases was that it corrupted not the body but the soul. . . . Perhaps it was written that the freedom of Europe must be born not of liberation but of the plague. . . . The price of freedom is high—far higher than that of slavery. And it is not paid in gold, nor in blood, nor in the most noble sacrifices, but in cowardice, in prostitution, in treachery, and in everything that is rotten in the human soul.

After corrupting Naples, the American Army moved north to bring barbarism to Rome, an event Malaparte describes with relish. He parades a column of illiterate boobies past all the monuments that testify to the richness of the Roman past. They finally come to the Colosseum:

> Colonel Granger stood up in his jeep and for a long time surveyed the gigantic shell of the Colosseum in silence. He turned to me, and with a note of pride in his voice shouted, "Our bombers have done a good job!" Then, spreading out his arms, he added apologetically, "Don't worry, Malaparte, that's war!"

The column rolls on into the Via dell'Impero, and one of its Sherman tanks symbolically flattens a man. America has neither culture nor morality, nothing but machines that destroy people and culture. The tank reduces the man to a mere outline, a paper doll, the barest suggestion of a human being, with all its vital qualities ironed out. This is one of the things that led Malaparte to dedicate his book to the American soldiers "who died in vain in the cause of European freedom." They were incapable of anything but destruction. And, besides, freedom is an impossibility for Europeans:

> They will never know the meaning of riches, happiness, and freedom. They have always lived in slavery; they have always been victims of hunger and fear. They will always be slaves, they will always be victims of hunger and fear.

This level of pessimism, disheartening though it is, is nothing to what Malaparte can achieve. In a dialogue with the ghost of Mussolini, he remarks that

> Everything that man gives to man is a foul thing. Even love and hatred, good and evil—everything. The death which man gives to man. . . . Forgiveness is a foul thing, too.

It is impossible to dislike Malaparte after this, eager as he seems to be to win one's dislike. It is only possible to feel the tenderness for him that one feels for a person who unconsciously exhibits the symptoms of a fatal disease. Malaparte's anti-Americanism is a sick man's petulance, and one realizes that what inspires it is the invalid's hatred for those who offer him the burden of renewed hope, and the prospect of prolonging a struggle he is ready to give up, when all he wishes is to be left in his exhaustion to wait for the ease and comfort of darkness and silence. D. H. Lawrence diagnosed this disease, the real European plague, when he visited Germany immediately after the First World War. He detected in the exhausted and embittered German people a turning away from Mediterranean warmth and light and from the vital sources of European life. He felt that they were obsessed by a cold longing for the gloom of the primeval German forests and that they were turning toward the bleak, Icelandic cradle of the Saga culture in search of a Nihilist creed. He predicted that this longing would produce a mass movement of a purely destructive kind, and foresaw the eruption of the blackclad Fascist divisions all over Europe, carrying with them their tragic faith in violence, disorder, and destruction. Malaparte testifies to the virulence of the sickness, and to the Fascists' success in spreading it. They may have lost all their territories and all their power over men's bodies, but they have planted their cult of death and Nihilism deep in their real victims' minds, and hold them more securely in the cage of hopelessness than they were ever held in party organizations or behind wire. (pp. 123-26, 129)

> *Anthony West, "Turns for the Worse," in* The New Yorker, *Vol. XXVIII, No. 37, November 1, 1952, pp. 123-26, 129.*

Malaparte's penchant for attention:

Malaparte tried to squeeze publicity for himself out of the smallest event in his life. Everything—the books he wrote, his newspaper polemics, his political decisions, his love affairs, the scandals he provoked—was designed to shock the *bien pensants* and make people (and the press) talk about him. His darkest masterpiece was, perhaps, the exploitation of the suicide of an American girl he was bored with and had abandoned without money. She took barbiturates and swam naked far out to sea at Ostia; some fishermen rescued her and brought her to a hospital where she was in a coma for days. Malaparte played the role of the heartbroken lover to the hilt. He wept, tore his hair, declared life was not worth living without his one great love. He embraced Peter Ustinov (who had come consolingly to dine with him one night), cried on his shoulder, and sobbed: "I'm a wretched man, Peter . . . this girl is dying . . . she is *dying* . . . and there's nothing I can do to save her. . . ." Ustinov, who knew nothing of the matter, looked at him half-amused and half-amazed, and wondered, "Has Malaparte gone mad?" After the girl had died (and been buried at Malaparte's expense), Malaparte told Tamburi: "It didn't go at all badly. . . . Think of the publicity I got."

> *Luigi Barzini in* Encounter, *April, 1982.*

John van Eerde (essay date 1958)

[*In the essay below, van Eerde explores Malaparte's characteristic use of historical and literary names in his works.*]

Curzio Malaparte's works are noteworthy for the many names strewn through their pages. This article would suggest that the presence of these names is not a fortuitous circumstance, but rather a stylistic procedure of some importance. The article will address itself particularly to *La Pelle.*

Through reference to names, especially those associated with literary history, Malaparte consistently economizes in his descriptive passages, and forces the reader to form the picture evoked by a literary association rather than by the novelist himself. An example of this is his allusion to the encounter of the homosexuals residing in Italy during World War II:

> Si riconoscevano all'odore, a un accento, a uno sguardo: e con un alto grido di gioia si gettavano gli uni nelle braccia degli altri, come Virgilio e Sordello nell' *Inferno* di Dante, facendo risuonare le vie di Napoli delle loro morbide, e un po' rauche, voci femminili.

> They recognized each other by a scent, by an accent, by a look: and with a loud shout of joy would throw themselves into each other's arms, like Vergil and Sordello in Dante's *Inferno,* making the streets of Naples resound with their morbid and rather raucous feminine voices.

The mention of the meeting of Vergil and Sordello is obviously designated to enable the reader to enlarge Malaparte's image. There is a similar procedure in the description of Hamburg after a saturation bombing: "Per alcuni giorni Amburgo offrì l'aspetto di Ditte, la città infernale." ("For a few days Hamburg looked like Ditte, the city of Hell.")

Malaparte employs this method often enough to allow one to recognize in him a considerable unwillingness to create an autonomous imagery. What he seems consistently to do is to suggest pictures in the reader's mind through the evocative power of names. This is evident in his attempt to communicate the intellectual climate of a certain group in Italy during the war: ". . . i giovani recitano oggi la parte d'invertiti come, al tempo di Byron e di Musset, recitavan quella di eroi romantici, o, più tardi, quella di poeti maledetti, e più recentemente la parte di raffinati Des Esseintes." ("Youths today play the part of inverts as, in the time of Byron and Musset they played that of romantic heroes, or later, that of decadent poets, and more recently the part of refined Des Esseinteses.")

In the above passage, names are used to characterize periods of history. They are in fact Malaparte's chief characterizing agent. This is particularly true in the case of his description of language. By a list of names Malaparte will hope to enable his reader to hear the tongue spoken by certain people in his writings. The already mentioned homosexuals speak a language of which Malaparte has little to say directly, but which he likens to that of René, of Giraudoux, of Baudelaire, in what he calls a Stravinskian transcription of Proust:

> pieno di quelle cadenze affettuose e maligne che rievocano il tiepido clima di certi 'interni' proustiani, di certi paesaggi morbosi, tutto l' autunno di cui è ricca la stanca sensibilità degli omosessuali moderni. Essi stonavano, parlando in francese, non già come si stona nel canto, ma come si stona parlando in sogno: posavano l'accento fra una parola e l'altra, come fan Proust, Giraudoux, Valéry.

> full of those affettuoso and sly cadenzas which conjure up the warm climate of certain Proustian 'interiors,' of certain morbose landscapes, the whole autumn that enriches the tired sensibility of modern homosexuals. Speaking French, they were out of tune, not as one is in singing, but as one is when talking in a sleep: they would put the stress between one word and another, as Proust, Giraudoux, and Valéry do.

Thus Malaparte identifies a manner of speech with a name which evokes a literary style. Early in *La Pelle* Jack says he learned French from his concierge and from La Fontaine: "Tu ne trouve pas que je parle comme les animaux de La Fontaine? Ho imparato da lui 'qu un chien peut bien regarder un Evêque.' " ("Don't you think I speak like La Fontaine's animals? I learned from him 'that a dog can certainly look at a Bishop.' ") French is not the only language described in an indirect fashion by this writer. In the case of English he will again have recourse to names. He says that Walter de la Mare's English is like an ancient music, like Rupert Brooke's, the tongue of the last humanistic tradition of Edwardian England. And the Oxford accent of Fred, a character in *La Pelle,* is heard as a "frisson modulé" ("A modulated shudder"), the term used, Malaparte tells us, by Gerard de Nerval to describe Silvia's speech. Finally the previously mentioned homosexual group is said by the author to have spoken an English reminiscent of the Elizabethan sonnets and of passages uttered by certain of Shakespeare's characters in the comedies. Of course he names them: Theseus (opening *Midsummer Night's Dream* with "O, me thinks, how slow this old moon wanes!") or Hippolyta (saying "Four nights will quickly dream away the time") or Orsino (guessing Viola's sex in *Twelfth Night*).

As might be expected names figure prominently whenever Malaparte is describing people in an intellectual environment or as the product of a certain intellectual climate. He writes of a German woman in *La Pelle* thus:

> Gerda Von II . . . pareva muoversi e respirare in quel paesaggio convenzionale della poesia di Stephan George, dove le architteture neoclassiche di Winckelmann e gli scenari del secondo Faust fanno da sfondo alle spettrali Muse di Hölderlin e di Rainer Maria Rilke.

> Gerda Von H . . . seemed to move and breathe in that conventional landscape of Stephan George's poetry, in which the neoclassic architecture of Winckelmann and the scenarios of the second Faust act as a background for the spectral Muses of Hölderlin and Rainer Maria Rilke.

It is through reference to their readings that we are acquainted with the intellectual make-up of the homosexuals in *La Pelle.* Malaparte tells us that they looked for inspiration to Gide (who was their Goethe) and read André Breton, Paul Elouard, Sartre and Pierre-Jean Jouve.

This indirect method of characterization through names may involve more than one intermediary between the personage characterized and Malaparte's reader. For example, Jack in *La Pelle* is presented as being unlike the Americans in Paris in Hemingway's *The Sun Also Rises.* But the characterization does not stop there. Malaparte compounds the effect by adding that Hemingway's Americans were like those of Eleanor Green, of whom Sinclair Lewis once wrote that they were "Come i profughi intellettuali della Rive Gauche verso il 1925, o come T. S. Eliot, Ezra Pound, o Isadora Duncan, iridescent flies caught in the black web of an ancient and amoral european [sic] culture." ("Like the intellectual refugees of the Left Bank about 1925, or like T. S. Eliot, Ezra Pound, or Isadora Duncan. . . .") Even when Malaparte ventures a description of his own, he often invokes the name of a literary figure as a kind of ultimate confirmation. Thus he compares Italy's wartime homosexuals to Americans in Paris in the 1920's " . . . i cui visi appannati dall'alcool e dalle droghe appaiono incastrati l'uno nell'altro, come in un quadro bizantino, nella galleria dei personaggi dei primi romanzi di Hemingway. . . ." (" . . . whose faces dulled with alcohol and drugs seem wedged together, as in a byzantine painting, in the gallery of characters in Hemingway's first novels. . . .")

As can be seen, Malaparte has much to say about these inverts in *La Pelle.* He shows them meeting each other as Vergil and Sordello met, he describes their intellectual orientation in terms of several French writers whom he names. He pictures their physical appearance in the light of Hemingway. He also alludes to what he calls their bourgeois aestheticism, and his definition of this is again a series of names. Here, as elsewhere, Malaparte would seem to aim at a cumulative effect, as he finds their above mentioned aestheticism based on a group of writers including Novalis, the comte de Lautréamont, Wilde, Diaghilev, Rilke, D'Annunzio, Gide, Cocteau, Proust, Maritain, Apollinaire, Valéry and Barrès. He adds that later the homosexuals turned to Marx and the Soviet writer, Simonov.

The examples of Malaparte's use of names to characterize, given above, involve groups or members of a group forming a kind of collectivity. However, the same process is evident where the writer deals with an individual. Jack in *La Pelle* is described as inebriated, confusing Horace and Poe and putting Annabel Lee and Lydia in the same stanza. This is the Jack "Che conosceva tutto Rimbaud a memoria." ("Who knew all of Rimbaud by heart.") It is Jack whose kneeling on the sand at the Salerno landings prompts Malaparte to evoke Aeneas' arrival at the mouth of the Tiber.

We see the same dependence on literary reference in the comparison of Conseulo to the women "dai capelli trasparenti del color dell' ala delle cicale, che nelle commedie di Fernando de Rojas e di Gil Vicente parlano in piedi, con lunghi gesti e lenti." ("with transparent hair the color of the harvest-fly's wing, who in the plays of Fernando de Rojas and Gil Vicente stand talking with slow, sweeping gestures.")

Similarly Malaparte compares Consuelo to women " . . . dai capelli del colore del miele freddo, che nelle commedie di Lope de Vega, di Calderón de la Barca, di Ramon de la Cruz, parlano con voce stridula, camminando in punta di piedi . . . Anche Consuelo ha 'los ojos graciosos' della canzone di Melibea e di Lucrezia nella *Celestina,* che umiliano 'los dulces árboles sombrosos.' " (. . . "with hair the color of cold honey, who in the plays of Lope de Vega, of Calderón de la Barca, of Ramon de

la Cruz, speak in a shrieking voice, walking on tip-toe. Consuelo too has 'the attractive eyes' of the song of Melibea and Lucretia in the *Celestina,* which humble 'the sweet, shady trees.' ") The procedure is repeated in his comparison of Mrs. Fiat in *La Pelle* to Toutchevitch "quel personaggio di *Anna Karenina* di Tolstoi, che era dello stesso stile Luigi XV del salotto della Principessa Betsy Tverskaia." ("that character in Tolstoy's *Anna Karenina,* who was the same Louis XV style as Princess Betsy Tverskaia's drawing-room.") Jeanlouis in *La Pelle* is handsome in a way that elicits names: "Era, quella di Jeanlouis, la romantica bellezza virile che piaceva a Stendhal, la bellezza di Fabrizio del Dongo. Aveva la testa di Antinoo . . . . " ("Jeanlouis' beauty was the virile, romantic beauty that Stendhal liked, Fabrizio del Dongo's beauty. He had Antinoo's head.") The use of names in this instance is of particular interest in that the reader is placed two steps away from the quality of Jeanlouis' good looks. This quality is not merely that of the beauty of Fabrizio del Dongo, but specifically what pleased Stendhal in it. This relationship becomes important as Malaparte goes on to establish a parallel. "Quegli ufficiali francesi erano Stendhal di fronte a Fabrizio del Dongo. E anch' essi, come già Stendhal, non avertivano che la belleza di Jeanlouis era, come quella di Fabrizio, una belleza senza ironia, e senza inquietudini di natura morale." ("Those French officers were Stendhal facing Fabrizio Dongo. And they too, as Stendhal, paid no attention to the fact that Jeanlouis' beauty was, like that of Fabrizio, without irony and without any preoccupations of a moral nature.")

Malaparte applies his method of characterization not only to animate beings, but also to inaminates. Describing the sea as wine-colored, he remarks that this is the way it looks in Homer. And his Rome glistens in the Sun "Simile a quelle città di pietra chiara che appaiono in fonda all'orizzonte nei paesaggi dell' *Illiade.*" ("Like those cities of bright stone that appear deep on the horizon of the landscapes in the *Iliad.*") He thinks of a house once visited from time to time by Pierre Lyautey in terms of names: Napoleon (he had a room there) Stendhal (he and Angela Pietragrua shared and hence immortalized a bed there), and Parini (he wrote his poem "Il Giorno" on a desk in the house).

Malaparte's preoccupation with names is particularly striking in *La Pelle,* but it is not new with that work. An enumeration of names serves to describe Paris in *Kaputt:*

> . . . quella sua giovane Parigi, di Puvis de Chavannes, dei suoi amici pittori, Zorn, Wahlberg, Cederström, Arsenius, Wennerberg, di quei suoi anni felici. 'Paris était bien jeune, alors.' Era la Parigi di Madame de Morienval, di Madame de Saint-Euverte, della Duchessa di Luxembourg (e anche di Madame de Cambremer e del giovane Marchese di Beausergent), di quelle stesse déesses di Proust—

> . . . his young Paris, the Paris of Puvis de Chavannes, of his painter friends, Zorn, Wahlberg, Cederström, Arsenius, Wennerberg, of his happy years. 'Paris was very young then.' It was the Paris of Madame de Morienval, of Madame de Saint-Euverte, of the Duchess of Luxemburg

(and also of Madame de Cambremer and of the young Marquis de Beausergent), of those same goddesses of Proust. . . .

Paris furnishes a continued application of the method as Malaparte proceeds:

> Sulle immagini della remota Parigi di Madame de Guermantes e del Principio Eugenio, si sovrapponevano a poco a poco, davanti ai miei occhi, le dolorose e care immagini di una Parigi più giovane, più torbida, più inquieta, più triste, forse. Come i visi dei passanti che affiorano dalla nebbia di là dai vetri di un caffè, io vedevo affacciarsi alla memoria i volti di Albertine, di Odette, di Robert de Saint Loup, le ombre degli adolescenti che s'intravedono dietro le spalle di Swan e di M. de Charlus, le fronti segnate dall'alcool, dall'insonnia, e dalla sensualità, dei personaggi di Apollinaire, di Matisse, di Picasso, di Hemingway, gli spettri azzurri e grigi di Paul Elouard.

> On the images of the remote Paris of Madame de Guermantes and of Prince Eugene, there were gradually superimposed before my eyes, the sad and dear images of a younger, more troubled, a sadder Paris, perhaps. Like the faces of passersby that appear out of the mist from the other side of a café window, I could see looming in my memory the faces of Albertine, Odette, Robert de Saint Loup, the shades of the adolescents partially seen behind the backs of Swan and M. de Charlus, their foreheads marked with the alcohol, insomnia, and sensuality of the characters of Apollinaire, Matisse, Picasso, Hemingway, the blue and grey spectres of Paul Elouard.

A city, a whole country may be summed up in a name as Malaparte tells us, writing, "Parigi, per Victor Maurer, era il bar del Ritz, e la Francia era il suo amico Pierre Cot." ("Paris, for Victor Maurer, was the Ritz bar, and France was his friend Pierre Cot.")

It is not surprising that the Russian village of Alexandrowska should evoke a comment from Malaparte bearing on its name: "In Russia, i villaggi si assomigliano tutti, anche nel nome. Ci son molti villaggi che hanno il nome di Alexandrowska, nella regione di Balta." ("In Russia all villages resemble each other even as to name. There are many villages with the name Alexandrowska, in the region of Balta.")

The importance that Malaparte attaches to names as words used to designate persons or institutions is nowhere more clearly seen than in his fascinating comparison of Mussolini with Lord Perth. He notes their manner of speech as revealed, significantly enough, in their pronunciation of names. Mussolini sounded like a peasant of Romagna, saying "scopone," "Lambrusco," "Comizio," and "Forlì," when pronouncing such words as Mediterranean, Suez, Ethiopia, while Lord Perth pronounced the same words as he would the Serpentine, Whiskey, and Edinburgh.

As has been stated, Malaparte's dedication to names was a longstanding one. In **Don Camalèo** (1928) there are already examples of names in enumeration, resulting in a kind of cumulative effect. For example, he writes:

> Se l'Italia di questi anni fosse la Francia dell' ottantanove, e se i partigiani del governo di Ottobre avessero avuto a che fare con: *Les Actes des Apôtres,* con i due Rivarol, Suleau, Champcenetz, Mirabeau, 'Le Vicomte' Peltier, Bergasse, Monlosier, Lauragnais, Tilly, de Bonnay, Barruel-Bauvert, sareberro morti tutti quanti di paura.

> If the Italy of these years were the France of '89 and if the October Government partisans had had to deal with *The Acts of the Apostles,* with the two Rivarols, Suleau, Champenetz, Mirabeau, 'Le Vicomte' Peltier, Bergasse, Monlosier, Lauragnais, Tilly, De Bonnay, Barruel-Bauvert, the whole lot would have died of fright.

There is in the **Camalèo** the same use of a name to characterize as is seen in **La Pelle** and **Kaputt.** At one point Sebastiano remarks to his pupil Don Camalèo that Italy no longer has any courtiers left. There are only poultry in the courtyard of Rome. Don Camalèo asks whether these are animals such as one finds in Phaedrus: " 'Come quelli di La Fontaine, piuttosto' replicò Sebastiano cambiando discorso." (" 'Like those of La Fontaine rather' replied Sebastiano changing the conversation.") And on another page Don Camalèo complains that people treat him like a man who resembles an animal: " 'O come una specie di Scarron' interloquiva Sebastiano." (" 'Or like a kind of Scarron' interjected Sebastian.) It is natural in the same novel to find the author referring to Lamartine's characterization of Talleyrand as a muted Mirabeau in preface to his own characterization of the Italian people as " . . . tutti dei Machiavelli a mezza voce." (" . . . All muted Machiavellis.") And consistent with Malaparte's use of names to replace descriptive adjectives is his allusion to "Quello strano e magro personaggio alla Balzac." ("That odd, thin personage à la Balzac.") Indeed the whole book **Don Camalèo,** bitterly satirical of the prattling conqueror of defenseless Ethiopia, is an eloquent witness to Malaparte's emphasis on names. The name "Mussolini" seems to occur on almost every page of the novel. In the twelve pages of Chapter XXI "L'Uomo et la bestia," the name occurs thirty-four times.

The effect of Malaparte's use of names as a characterizing agent is to make his style a hurried one. It also injects a distinct superficiality to his descriptions. Quite aside from such inaccuracies as placing the meeting of Vergil and Sordello in the *Inferno* rather than in the *Purgatorio,* Malaparte sometimes calls on names for what they do not have to give. There is, for instance, no such instinctive recognition in the Vergil-Sordello meeting as in that of the homosexuals of **La Pelle.** Only when Sordello hears the word "Mantova" does he say "O Mantovano, io son Sordello de la tua terra." ("O Mantouan, I am Sordello from your land.")

Malaparte's avalanche of names tends to neglect the valid distinctions and nuances of literary criticism. Too many of them are used at the same time to qualify a person, a place, or an object. Only rarely does the author acknowledge chronology and the difference between generations, as for instance, when he writes: "Quel che appariva strano era il fatto che Barrès era altrettanto lontano da Jeanlouis e dai giovani della sua generazione quanto Gide: il Gide di 'moi, cela m'est égal, parce que j'écris *Paludes*.' " ("What appeared strange was the fact that Barrès was as far from the youth of his generation as Gide: the Gide of 'To me that makes no difference, because I wrote *Paludes*.' ")

This super-abundance is often self-defeating. One thinks of what Malaparte himself wrote in a novel: "Sebastiano aveva regione: lo scolaro pretendeva troppi maestri. Ora andava matto per l' autore del *Dizionario filosofico*, ora per Bossuet. Plutarco lo inamorò per una settimana, Amleto gli tolse sonno di due notti; finì per disgustarsi di Amleto leggendo Laforgue" (*Don Camalèo*). ("Sebastian was right: the pupil aspired to too many masters. Now he would go mad for the author of the *Philosophical Dictionary*, now for Bossuet. Plutarch enamoured him for a week, Hamlet cost him two nights sleep; he finally became disgusted with Hamlet reading Laforgue.") (pp. 88-96)

John van Eerde, "Names in Some Works of Malaparte," in Names, *Vol. VI, No. 2, June, 1958, pp. 88-96.*

Fred R. Mabbutt   (essay date 1975)

[*In the following essay, Mabbutt examines the relationship between Malaparte's literary works and his politics.*]

[It] is unnecessary to trace all of Malaparte's voluminous writings over his lengthy career. It will suffice to judge the Italian intellectual from his major works, for they reflect most of his variegated life: *Technique du coup d'état* from his Fascist past; *La Volga nasce in Europa* [*The Volga Rises in Europe*], *Kaputt,* and *La Pelle* from his period of disillusionment; and *Those Cursed Tuscans* from his post-World War II "reconstruction" when he hoped to employ his "writer's eye" to escape the imbroglio of politics and ideology.

When Malaparte wrote *Technique du coup d'état,* he was one of Mussolini's stalwart Black Shirts, and had helped to immobilize Florence during the March on Rome. His objective, as he explained it, was to "demonstrate how a modern State is captured and defended, which was, more or less, the subject treated by Machiavelli. . . ." Though affirming that his book "is in no sense an imitation of *The Prince*," Malaparte's argument is contradictory and unconvincing.

It is clear that Malaparte considered himself to be a modern Cataline of the Right, dedicated to the "necessity of a strongly organized State, with a severe control of political, social, economic life"; and his *Technique du coup d'état* is his latter-day version of *The Prince,* altered to suit modern dictatorships.

By the end of the First World War, people in almost every western European country had been fused into economic masses by the forces of economic production. Responding to a common stimulus or reacting against a common disorder, the psychology of people seemed to be fixed by their mass existence. In crowds, people could be moved by a

single voice or be swept into a mass movement led by a modern Cataline.

Coup d'état is reduced to a mere technique which will succeed, he alleges, whenever some courageous and "manly" individual applies it; and it will succeed irrespective of political or economic conditions. Echoing his tactical model of insurrection, Leon Trotsky, Malaparte (as always without documentation) confides to his readers that he shares with Trotsky his belief that "the tactics of insurrection are . . . independent of the general condition of the country or of a revolutionary state of affairs favorable to insurrection." Thus, history by Malaparte is rendered simple, torn from its intimate connection with class or group interests, and reduced to a distorted photograph of the surface of the dynamic process which undergirds it.

When he is not distorting history by reducing it to technique, Malaparte is standing it on its head with grotesque misrepresentations of past events. Since "the problem of conquest and defense of the state . . . is a technical problem" for Malaparte, history may be explained entirely in terms of men of violence who have the "courage" to apply the modern techniques of insurrection. Thus, the 1917 Communist coup d'état in Russia becomes a result of the tactics of Leon Trotsky through his seizure of the vital arteries of the nation's economic life—the railway stations, power plants, water mains, gas works, banks, post offices, and telegraph services. Summarily dismissed by Malaparte are factors which most scholars consider crucial: the disintegration of the Czarist army during the First World War, and land hunger of the peasantry, the misery of the masses, the desire among the populace and military rank-and-file for peace, the growing alienation (as expressed by the growth of Bolshevik influence in the soviets) of the industrial proletariat, and the estrangement of a large portion of the Russian intelligentsia from the Czarist regime.

In view of the fact that Trotsky's technique of coup d'état is so easy to understand, and, according to Malaparte so simply accomplished by virile, intelligent leadership, one wonders why those tactics were not successfully employed by Silone and the Italian Communists. Since determining factors have been dismissed by Malaparte, he is forced to use other "explanations." The Italian Communists, we are told, were simply "ignorant of the methods, the tactics, and the modern technique of coup d'état of which Trotsky had given a new and classic example." Only Mussolini, who we are reminded was brought up as a Marxist, knew how to apply Trotsky's tactics.

Even Malaparte, however, is hard pressed to explain his own epic picture of Mussolini's rise to power, for he modestly confesses that "it is not known" why the King refused to sign an order proclaiming a state of siege when the Fascist March on Rome began. He is at a loss to explain (or affects not to know) any reasons for the King's refusing to defend the parliamentary regimé, when it was a matter of common knowledge that Victor Emmanuel III doubted that his army would obey an order to suppress the Fascist march.

In what is perhaps Malaparte's most revealing chapter, "Mussolini," he paints with sadistic glee the pogrom activities of the Fascist Black Shirts as they maraud Italy before and after the march on Rome. As he described it:

> Mussolini's political battle in the last four years has not been fought with gentleness or cunning, but with violence, the hardest, the most inexorable scientific violence.

Fascist Black Shirts with silver death's heads embroidered on their shirts, wearing steel helmets painted red, and armed with bayonets and bombs, heap their destruction on trade unions and all centers of democratic resistance, all to the boundless admiration of the Fascist intellectual. After all, he argues, "It is revolutionary violence which legitimizes a dictatorship, the coup d'état itself is its soundest foundation."

It is Malaparte's passion for violence which leads him to reject Hitler as a "would-be dictator" who lacks the "courage" of his dictatorial instincts and heroic inclinations. As Malaparte puts it, "Hitler was a Julius Caesar who could not swim, and stood on the shores of a Rubicon that was too deep to ford." Hitler's fatal weakness, according to Malaparte, was that he was a "man-of-law." And in his pinnacle of "scientific analysis," Malaparte informs his readers that "the crisis which confronts National Socialism might well be called a process of 'social-democratisation.' It is a slow evolution toward legality. . . ." Malaparte's ideological perspectives have so skewed his objective judgment at this stage in his intellectual development that his ideas can only be described as warped and convoluted.

His exuberant Fascism began to sour, however, during the 1930s when his altercation with Balbo and Mussolini landed him in the *Regina Coeli* in Rome and a *confino* on the island of Lipari. In June, 1941, at the outset of the German invasion of the Soviet Union, his dispatches from the Ukraine as a correspondent for the *Corriere della Sera* were so far at variance from the Fascist line which predicted a short, "easy" war against the Soviet Union, that he was expelled from the war zone, and placed under house-arrest for a period of four months by Mussolini. When, in January, 1942, military events confirmed the soundness of Malaparte's judgment regarding the toughness of Soviet military resistance, he requested and was granted permission to be sent to Finland to resume his coverage of the war. His correspondence, as compiled in **La Volga nasce in Europa,** provides the reader with an opportunity to gauge the accuracy of the Italian intellectual's claim to have written "the only objective document, the only impartial testimony, to have come out of Soviet Russia since the beginning of the campaign."

Although Malaparte's history is far less distorted than in his earlier work, **Technique du coup d'état,** his old loves and hatreds remain as pronounced as ever. In much the same way that the earthquake of 1915 shaped the thoughts and actions of Silone, war continued to shape the ideas of Malaparte, though the type of war that he knew and loved existed only as a memory. As he put it:

> . . . the fact is that the [Second World] war is not present to me today as a living, cruel reality, it's present only as a memory—a kind of photo-

graphic image conjured up from the remotest depths of my consciousness.

"How different are the wounded of this war," he reports at another time, "from those of the war of twenty-five years ago! I have said it before: they look more like the workers who have been injured in an industrial accident than soldiers wounded in battle." The soldiers never speak of the war, and when they sing, it is to themselves, not in chorus. To Malaparte, the Second World War is a lonely, desperate struggle devoid of "humanness" because it is a mechanized, fluid warfare which denies the soldier and the camaraderie and heroic opportunities afforded by World War I.

It is this fact which helps to explain his hatred of technology as well as his continued idealization of the peasantry. To Malaparte, technology had produced a "race of mechanics," and flattened human values of the past. It had dehumanized human conflict into wars between machines. In a revealing passage, he explains the meaning of this new "industrial ethic." The Soviet Union, which for him represents a paradigm of the new "race of mechanics" illuminates the modern "industrial ethics." With its *udarniki* and mass-produced soldiers, it buries its dead (along with its past values) in a military cemetery outside of Leningrad. Viewing that cemetery, Malaparte reflects that, in this new industrial age, a man dies as if he were a machine—a steel-blue automobile whose engine has stopped—and that

> The inscriptions on the iron stelae of a Soviet cemetery should read, not "Here lies," etc., but "The appended figures show the maximum output achieved by the comrades buried beneath this mound. . . ."

For Malaparte, "the dead are like shipwrecked mariners" who have been marooned by an inhuman force. Only in the idealized conception he has of the peasantry can Malaparte find any spark of his "shipwrecked humanity" left. Only in the forests of Leningrad does Malaparte find that the "dead" come to life, and that the dynamos, cranes, and steel bridges of the present are engulfed or silenced by the crescendo of "strange noises," and the mysterious sounds of the trees and streams. Only there, in the form of the unpolished woodsman and peasant, are the ghosts of another age resurrected, and life, as Malaparte loves and understands it, renewed.

On July 27, 1943, after Mussolini's arrest, Malaparte claims that he returned to Italy "in order to assume my post of responsibility in the struggle against the Germans." Transferring his allegiance from Fascism to the Italian liberation forces and the Allies, Malaparte's role as liaison officer to the United States Fifth Army provided him with the experience which provides the setting for his two international bestsellers, **Kaputt** and **La Pelle.** Though Malaparte is a wily *poséur* in the *genre* of his understanding of Ulysses, and his political odyssey may be more fanciful than accurate, it is possible to curry out of his novels his ideological predisposition.

Kaputt is a clinical study of the Fascist state of mind in one of its most pure and hideous forms. Malaparte's hatred of the growing Nazi tyranny in Italy is nearly indelible. He was tired, after twenty years of Fascist diplomacy and journalism, and he felt, he said, that he was no more than a whore. He understood the disease of Nazism because he himself was tainted with it.

The basic plan of **Kaputt** has the simplicity of Boccaccio's *Decameron,* and the events take place in the midst of complete peace in the ancient and dreamy palace of old Prince Eugene of Sweden. His love of the cruelty of war, of action over ideas, and the brawling coarse peasantry is nowhere more clearly in evidence. When Count Galeazzo Ciano describes to Malaparte the Chinese tortures he witnessed in the streets of Peking, Malaparte confesses his love of "the sensual pleasure . . . in being cruel" and vicariously enjoys the experience of Ciano as he recalls the brutalities:

> The victim, tied to a pole, was stripped with a penknife piece by piece of all of his flesh, except for his nerves and his arteries and his veins. The man became a kind of trellis made of bones, the nerves and blood vessels through which the sun could shine and the flies could buzz.

Indeed, it is this kind of cruelty which Malaparte equates with human nature; and no doubt, it is this assumption which accounts for his idealization of the "manliness" of the peasantry. They alone remained human; they alone had not been reduced to yardsticks of industrial output by the new machine age.

Kaputt is an untrustworthy book which, despite his protestations, contains as much fiction as fact. Most often his memories of his wartime odyssey are recounted to interlocutors who credit him with a record of personal humanitarianism, and with daring *mots* and brilliant repartees which slyly ridicule the Nazi leaders who are in command in Finland and Poland.

His grisly tales and grim humor are a nightmare not easily forgotten. The Croat Pavelich and his "oyster" dinner of forty pounds of partisans' eyes; Russian prisoners being tested for literacy and those able to read shot; frozen Russian soldiers posted in the snow with their right arms outstretched to act as "silent police" for German *panzer* units; Jewish girls in Rumania coerced into brothels for twenty days and then shot; the visit to the Warsaw ghetto with Max Schmeling and Frank when "the Butcher of Poland" cheerfully fired a shot at a fleeing Jewish child; the pogrom in Jassy—are episodes which Malaparte regards as "horribly gay and gruesome." The details of these stories may be lies, but the portrait he paints of the Fascist mentality is revealing.

Malaparte also, rather unconsciously, reveals the tenuousness of the Fascist ideology as far as creating lasting personal relationships are concerned. As Professor Marquis once observed, "For the Fascist personal relations can only be cemented in combat. But when combat turned sour . . . there was nothing left." As the military tide turned against Fascist and Nazi alike in 1942-43, disillusionment set in to such an extent that suicides among Axis troops increased so alarmingly that Heinrich Himmler himself had to go to the Finnish front to stop them. "He will place the dead under arrest," said one young German

Alpenjäger. "He will have them buried with tied hands. He had three *Alpenjägers* shot yesterday because they tried to hang themselves."

Some Fascists, however, like Malaparte followed the time-honored tradition of *transformismo* and prostituted whatever beliefs they may have once held to save their skins. Certainly this is what Malaparte must have meant when, after admitting to being a whore, he confessed that the war will be won by the whores.

His second novel, **La Pelle**, emphasizes his point by observing that "human skin, which flapped and fluttered in the wind exactly as a flag does" is his true country. The locale of **La Pelle** is Naples during the period from 1943 to 1945 when the Allied forces were pushing their way north through the liberation of Rome. As always, his writing is a chamber of horrors and surrealistic terror which is tethered to unbridled egotism. His characteristic form of expression remains the symbolic anecdote which usually centers around one image like the soldier in **La Pelle** who is literally flattened by a Sherman tank.

> I laughed to myself as I thought how that flag of human skin was our flag, the true flag of us all, victors and vanquished, the only flag worthy to fly that evening from the tower of the Capitol.

The incident is revealing not only because it demonstrates how utterly uncommitted Malaparte is to an ethic of ultimate ends, but it also re-emphasizes Malaparte's obsessive hatred of technology. It matters little to him who runs the machines, Nazis or Americans. To him the results were the same: humanity, as he understood it, was crushed beneath the weight of dehumanizing machines.

The American military machine was responsible for much more than reducing man to a mere outline of his former self by ironing out all of his vital qualities. It was also a generator of a "plague" which crushed culture as it rolled on the Via dell' Impero. "The extraordinary thing about this most modern of diseases was that it corrupted not the body but the soul. . . ."

Italian girls selling themselves for a package of cigarettes; Italian mothers trading their boys to Moroccan soldiers in return for food to fill their larders; the blond wigs which Italian girls wear for the benefit of American Negroes; the discovery by Malaparte of his beloved dog, Febo, who had been his sole companion during his years of imprisonment and political exile on a vivisectionist rack with a probe stuck into his exposed liver—all of these events, and more, pointed to the new barbarism which Malaparte felt the American Army generated across Italy.

After corrupting Naples, the American Army extended its plague northward to Rome. Parading a column of illiterate ignoramuses past Roman monuments that testify to the richness of the past, Malaparte brings the American column to a halt in front of the Colosseum:

> Colonel Granger stood up in his jeep and for a long time surveyed the gigantic shell of the Colosseum in silence. He turned to me, and with a note of pride in his voice shouted, "Our bombers have done a good job!" Then spreading out his

arms, he added apologetically, "Don't worry, Malaparte, that's war!"

All of these themes—the prostitution of humanity, the despair of defeat, and the love of the histrionic act—combine and interact to provide the great tension of Malaparte's thought in the novel. On the one hand, there is the fierce moral nihilism whose essence provides the title, *La Pelle.* On the other hand, there is the promise of absolution and of rebirth which becomes explicit only near the end of the novel with his recounting an episode involving the eruption of Vesuvius. After the wrath of Vesuvius has waned, Malaparte dimly perceives life quivering anew as rivers of flame slowly cool and congeal. In that once molten inferno, he observes:

> Here and there the deposits of lava, after cooling off have taken on human shapes, the aspect of gigantic men, intertwined like wrestlers in a dark, silent affray.

What the phoenix-like rebirth will be like, Malaparte does not say. But he sees "for the first time . . . the ugliness of the human countenance, the loathsomeness of the substance of which we are made." Human nature, he believes, will remain constant. "A man is pride, cruelty, betrayal, degradation, violence." His hatred was not only of humanity, but of the technology which erased the past and compounded mankind's wretched condition by fusing him into a mass society devoid of individualism and a sense of belonging.

His war had been lost; his comrades were now gone. The machine age had erased his roots as they existed prior to and during the First World War. It had swamped man's individuality in the morass of mass society, and reduced even man's most sublime act of individualism—heroism—to an appendage of mechanized warfare.

Only in his romanticized peasantry in Tuscany could Malaparte recognize (or imagine) the traces of life in a pre-industrial age. To do this required him to romanticize his *peasantry* into a highly abstract group. In contradistinction to Silone who viewed rural people in the singular, as a concrete, boorish *cafone,* Malaparte viewed them in the abstract, plural form. In his last book, *Those Cursed Tuscans,* he observes that "above all, the people are the same." They are all lean and hungry; and in contrast to Silone, who judges them in terms of how they measure up to his ultimate ends, Malaparte judges them by their "mania" for realism, for their performance of things according to the measure of man rather than of God or saints. Sharing Silone's anti-urban bias. Malaparte notes that his "Pratese are Tuscans in a very special way. They have nothing in common with Rome or Romans." They are all members of the same clan who are the only real people left in the world. As he put it in *Those Cursed Tuscans:*

> What must be kept in mind when judging the people of Prato is this: at Prato what counts is the people, only the people, and that Prato is a workingman's town, entirely a workingman's town, the only one in Italy that is a workingman's town from top to bottom.

It is ironic that Malaparte should abstract the peasantry in such a way, for he notes that "They carry out their business in prose, not poetry." Though Malaparte claims to despise "playing the hero with the tongue," and rhetoric to clear language, he himself is the master of abstraction and theatrical language. Only in his claim that his peasantry has "reason with imagination," does he bear any significant resemblance to his romanticized people in the use of language.

Thus, Malaparte considers himself, like his peasants, to be part of an extinct breed of men who are at war with the new men of the machine age. He was born for battle, an intellectual whose ideas had been shaped by his time. To him life was an adventurous voyage, and "freedom is nothing more than an awareness of the relationship between life and death, between the world of the living and the world of the dead." In his Thrasymachan world, he believed "that a freeman should expect no justice, by the grace of God, except from himself." That is the origin of his harsh, often cruel, and implacable rebelliousness. In an industrial world of mass men, where individualism had succumbed to "industrial moral," Malaparte affected to be its last gladiator. Although the new industrial civilization limited or denied man his individual freedom in most areas, Malaparte believed that individual freedom existed only in the way one chooses to die. He hoped that his death would be glorious. Then, he would willingly go to Hell, like all proper Tuscans, but only to urinate. (pp. 13-16)

Fred R. Mabbutt, "Curzio Malaparte: An Intellectual and Fascism," in Forum, *Vol. 12, No. 3, 1975, pp. 9-17.*

FURTHER READING

Biography

Barzini, Luigi. "Remembering Curzio Malaparte." *Encounter* LVIII, No. 4 (April 1982): 85-7.
    Examination of Orfeo Tamburi's *Malaparte come me,* a collection of anecdotes and personal remembrances.

DeGrand, A. J. "Curzio Malaparte: The Illusion of the Fascist Revolution." *Journal of Contemporary History* 7, Nos. 1-2 (January-April 1972): 73-89.
    Focuses on Malaparte's career from 1917 to 1933, calling it "one response to the crisis which opened in 1914."

Talamonda, Marida. *Casa Malaparte.* New York: Princeton Architectural Press, 1992, 161 p.
    Examines Malaparte's role in the design and construction of his villa on the island of Capri from 1938 through 1945. Talamonda includes photos, architectural drawings, and translations of letters and legal documents.

Criticism

Evans, Arthur R., Jr. "Assignment to Armageddon: Ernst Jünger and Curzio Malaparte on the Russian Front, 1941-

43." *Central European History* XIV, No. 4 (December 1981): 295-321.

> Compares two accounts of events on the Russian Front during World War II: Jünger's *Kaukasische Aufzeich-nungen* and Malaparte's *Il Volga nasce in Europa,* characterizing Malaparte's book as "hyperbolic and exhibitionist," and Jünger's as "reticent and reclusive."

Goldstone, Herbert. "Malaparte and Moravia: Concerning Failure and Estimate." *Western Review* 17, No. 3 (Spring 1953): 229-34.

> Contrasts the stylistic differences in Malaparte's *The Skin* (1948) and Alberto Moravia's *The Fancy Dress Party* (1941).

Pick, Robert. "History as a Nude with Lesions." *The Saturday Review of Literature* (New York) XXIX, No. 46 (16 November 1946): 13-14.

> Proposes that Malaparte's *Kaputt* be considered well-written "fiction based on facts."

Slonim, Marc. "A People Set Apart." *The New York Times Book Review* (25 October 1964): 56.

> Review of *Those Cursed Tuscans.* Slonim suggests that Malaparte's analysis of the people of Tuscany, while well-written, is lacking in substance and convincing detail.

"A Saxon in the Ranks of Tuscany: The Changeable Career of Curzio Malaparte." *The Times Literary Supplement* (12 January 1973): 39-40.

> Features commentary on Malaparte's lesser-known writings and posthumously published works, including *Il ballo al Cremlino.*

Mary Roberts Rinehart

1876-1958

(Also wrote under the pseudonyms Roberts Rinehart and Elliott Roberts) American novelist, short story writer, playwright, essayist, autobiographer, and poet.

INTRODUCTION

Rinehart was a popular writer of mystery and romance novels during the first half of the twentieth century. Best known for her novel *The Circular Staircase,* she contributed significantly to the development of the mystery genre in the United States. Although her work has been criticized as unrealistic and improbable, she has also attracted praise for her exceptional abilities as a storyteller and for her distinctive combination of suspense, humor, and the macabre.

Rinehart was born and grew up in Pittsburgh. After completing high school, she enrolled in the Pittsburgh Training School for Nurses and, shortly following her graduation in 1896, married Dr. Stanley Rinehart. A stock market crash in 1903 left the Rineharts heavily in debt; in order to contribute to the family's finances, Rinehart began writing poems and short stories, selling them to such magazines as *All-Story* and *Munsey's.* Her first major success came in 1908 with the publication of *The Circular Staircase,* which received critical acclaim as well as becoming a best-seller. Over the next twenty-eight years, ten of her novels, both mysteries and romances, also appeared on best-seller lists, making her one of the most popular writers of the period. During World War I Rinehart served as a war correspondent, an experience she drew upon for her 1918 novel *The Amazing Interlude,* which tells the story of an American girl working in a canteen on the Western Front. Rinehart lived and worked in Washington, D.C., for ten years, from 1922 until her husband's death, before moving to New York, where she resided for the remainder of her life. When World War II began, she again made plans to serve as a correspondent, but ill-health prevented her from making the trip to Europe. Rinehart worked assiduously throughout her long career, publishing her final novel, *The Swimming Pool,* in 1952 and her last short story two years later. She died in 1958.

Rinehart's mysteries and romances are notable for introducing distinctive narrative formulas and character types. A typical Rinehart mystery focuses on an unmarried woman who, as narrator, reflects on a series of harrowing events surrounding a case of multiple murder. Unlike earlier detective narratives in which crimes were solved in the manner of a puzzle by one principal investigator, the "Rinehart formula" emphasized the suspense occasioned by an ongoing series of murders that increasingly threaten the narrator and people close to her, while simultaneously incorporating comic elements and developing romantic subplots. Rinehart's formula also features two detectives: a professional sleuth and the female narrator, who relies on intuition and leaps of insight rather than logic to assist the primary detective in discovering and assembling clues. In *The Circular Staircase,* for example, Rachel Innes, a wealthy middle-aged spinster, assists a detective in identifying the criminal responsible for a series of murders and disappearances in which she and her niece and nephew become personally involved: the boyfriend of Innes's niece disappears, her nephew's girlfriend is the stepdaughter of one of the victims, one of the murders occurs in the house in which Innes is spending the summer, and at one point she becomes trapped in a secret room with the murderer. Another important element is the personal growth which the narrator undergoes as a result of the experience. Innes, for instance, becomes more independent, learns to be a more astute judge of character, and concludes that her formerly complacent existence was rather boring and unfulfilling. Like her mystery novels, Rinehart's romances also adhere to a formula. These novels generally focus on love relationships complicated by previous engagements or marriages and share a common theme: the high price attached to personal freedom. Romances with male protagonists, such as *Dangerous Days* and *The Doctor,* conclude triumphantly when obstacles separating the lovers are overcome, while those centering on married women, such as *This Strange Adventure,* end in tranquil resignation, with the woman forsaking her lover and returning to her husband.

Critical commentary on Rinehart's work has focused on the style and structure of her novels and the value of her work as a reflection of cultural norms. Rinehart was the primary innovator of a highly melodramatic style of detective fiction that some critics refer to as the Had-I-But-Known school, named for the first-person narrator's frequent musings on what lives might have been saved or criminal deeds forestalled had she possessed a particular fact or clue earlier in her investigation. A number of critics find this stylistic trait fatal to an appreciation of Rinehart's works. Commentators critical of Rinehart's mysteries have also argued that her romantic subplots obstruct the flow of the narrative, that her characters have little if any relation to the real world, that she relies extensively on improbable coincidences, and that her main characters needlessly confuse and prolong the solution of the mystery by withholding information. Countering detractors of Rinehart's Had-I-But-Known style of narrative, some critics have asserted that it would be natural for someone reflecting on terrifying events from the past to consider what might have happened if another piece of information had been at their disposal. Others have suggested that Rinehart's melodramatic formula enabled strong reader identification with the narrator, whose personal involvement in the plot allowed Rinehart to create and sustain a high level of suspense and excitement. Critics concerned with analyzing Rinehart's mysteries and romances as reflections of American culture have noted that her characters and plots evolved over time as the dominant mores of society changed. As Arnold Hoffman has stated: "Rinehart avoided a hard didactic line on any of the social issues. . . . From the outset of her career Mrs. Rinehart manifested a feeling for both sides of the issue. Her detractors might say she simply knew what would sell to most people, but . . . I would say she observed and recorded the topical with an objective sensibility."

The Case of Jennie Brice   (novel)   1913
The After House   (novel)   1914
The Street of Seven Stars   (novel)   1914
"K"   (novel)   1915
Tish   (short stories)   1916
Bab: A Sub-Deb   (short stories)   1917
Long Live the King   (novel)   1917
The Amazing Interlude   (novel)   1918
Twenty Three and a Half Hours Leave   (novel)   1918
Dangerous Days   (novel)   1919
Love Stories   (short stories)   1919
Affinities   (short stories)   1920
The Bat [with Avery Hopwood]   (drama)   1920
A Poor Wise Man   (novel)   1920
The Breaking Point   (novel)   1921
More Tish   (short stories)   1921
Sight Unseen and the Confession   (novels)   1921
The Red Lamp   (novel)   1925
Tish Plays the Game   (short stories)   1926
Lost Ecstasy   (novel)   1927
This Strange Adventure   (novel)   1929
The Door   (novel)   1930
My Story   (autobiography)   1931; also published as *My Story: A New Edition and Seventeen New Years* [revised edition], 1948
Miss Pinkerton   (novel)   1932
The Album   (novel)   1933
The State vs. Elinor Norton   (novel)   1933
The Doctor   (novel)   1936
Tish Marches On   (short stories)   1937
The Wall   (novel)   1938
Writing Is Work   (essay)   1939
The Great Mistake   (novel)   1940
Haunted Lady   (novel)   1942
The Yellow Room   (novel)   1945
Episode of the Wandering Knife   (short stories)   1950
The Swimming Pool   (novel)   1952
The Frightened Wife and Other Murder Stories   (short stories)   1953

PRINCIPAL WORKS

A Double Life [as Roberts Rinehart]   (drama)   1906
The Circular Staircase   (novel)   1908
The Man in Lower Ten   (novel)   1909
Seven Days [with Avery Hopwood; adapted from the novel *When a Man Marries*]   (drama)   1909
When a Man Marries   (novel)   1909
The Window at the White Cat   (novel)   1910
The Amazing Adventures of Letitia Carberry   (short stories)   1911
Cheer Up   (drama)   1912
Where There's a Will   (novel)   1912

CRITICISM

The New York Times Review of Books   (essay date 1908)

[*In the following review, the critic focuses on the qualities that distinguish* The Circular Staircase *from previous works of detective fiction.*]

In **The Circular Staircase** Mary Roberts Rhinehart has given the jading reading public a tale of mystery with a new piquancy. It might be possible, though it would be difficult, to contrive a more involved network of circumstances and a create a more hopeless mystification. But it would not be possible to invent a more pleasantly diverting character than the lady (it would be a pleasure to call her young, but she confesses to gray hairs) who is at the centre of the mystery and who herself narrates it. Written in any old style, *The Circular Staircase* would be the sort of thing people sit up nights to finish; written in the delightfully humorous vein which makes it stand out so much above the ordinary detective story, it is bound to be, with more than usual deserts, a popular success.

It is all about an old house with an unsuspected secret chamber, a bank President who loots his own institution in order to hoard the spoil where he can feel it his own; a doctor who buries a pauper's corpse for the body of the bank President; an unruly son; two Nemesi in the forms of women; a matter of three or four murders; two unhappy love affairs and one tragic one; an automobile and a freight car, and a gentlemanly detective who ought to have married the lady who was no longer young—and who will do so yet if an entertaining author will be so good as to write another book.

> *"Entertaining Mystery," in* The New York Times Review of Books, *Vol. 13, August 22, 1908, p. 460.*

The Arena   (essay date 1908)

[*The following is a positive review of* The Circular Staircase.]

With the possible exception of *The House of a Thousand Candles,* [*The Circular Staircase*] is by far the best mystery or detective story of recent years. It is ingenious in plot and skilful in execution. From beginning to end we have a succession of dramatic, oftentimes exciting and frequently tragic happenings. While as in almost all mystery stories, the element of improbability is present, and while as literature it is not a romance to command attention, as a mystery tale in which the action is swift and interest kept keyed to a high pitch, and in which the human and love interest also is quite prominent, *The Circular Staircase* will appeal to the general present-day novel-reader intent on interest and amusement.

The story is concerned with the extraordinary series of events, embracing not a few tragedies, that follow the renting of a magnificent country estate by a woman of means who has yielded to the importunities of her two foster children: a young man named Halsey, and his sister Gertrude. The young people have completed their collegiate education. Both are in love with characters that are involved in the plots and counter-plots of the story. The suspicion that falls on the girl's lover and the equivocal position of Louise Armstrong, the one-time *fiancée* of Halsey, add materially to the interest of the romance, which is so cleverly told as to baffle the general reader who imagines from time to time that he has found the true clue, until the closing scenes, when the mystery is cleared up and with it the gloom and bitter anxiety that have filled the hearts of the lovers. (pp. 394-95)

> *A review of "The Circular Staircase," in* The Arena, *Vol. 40, No. 226, October, 1908, pp. 394-95.*

Blanche Colton Williams   (essay date 1920)

[*In the following excerpt, Williams discusses Rinehart's short stories, praising her ability to create intricate plots, suspense, and a realistic setting.*]

That story telling is the most popular of all kinds of discourse, spoken or written, has been exemplified from the time of Homer to the present. Whatever other elements may be conducive to longevity, it is narrative which draws numbers to the fireside, the printed page, or the screen. It is for her foremost ability to tell a tale that Mary Roberts Rinehart is successful. The fact that frequently there is small residuum after the "story" is subtracted is one proof of this ability. She knows this fact, knows that she is a narrator and modestly states that some day she may be a novelist. For she is aware that the novelist is biographer, analyst, philosopher—in many respects so much more than the story teller. But, as she must also know, the story teller's compensations are many in the direction of the dramatic, the picturesque and the vivid.

She is popular because she not only knows how to tell a story but how to tell the sort that most people seek to-day for entertainment. No other writer reflects more accurately the age of the motion picture. This is neither to assert nor to deny that she has been influenced by motion picture technique. It is to say that, being a child of the twentieth century, she recognizes the demand for rapid action and the eagerness for one unique visual impression after another. She supplies the demand by unreeling film after film from a mind fertile in invention and prodigal of picture-story stuff which, translated in terms of black and white, reel off before the reader. There is the same lack of depth, or "thickness," in her narrative which the motion-picture play illustrates. It is art of two dimensions. Bearing in mind that comparisons are odorous, but without invidious comparison, we find distinguishing characteristics in the narratives of three women writers who have been associated with the Steel City. Margaret Deland's stories have the depth of life, Willa Cather's have the finish of the sculptor, Mary Roberts Rinehart's have the finish of the screen play. Each method is well in its way; and if the first two contribute, in the main, to more enduring literature, the third contributes, on the whole, to the entertainment of the greater number. Moreover, each method shares with the others.

Take, for example, Mrs. Rinehart's "Tish" stories. After reading them, one knows that Tish is a daring eccentric spinster in the neighborhood of fifty; that to tell her a thing is dangerous means no power can restrain her; that she has mastered, in middle age, motoring, riding and skating; that she has run the hazards of camping out in Maine and the dangers of climbing the Rockies; that she has solved a mystery or two—that she is, in short, the representative of a contemporary type worthy to rank with the best creations of Mrs. Rinehart's contemporaries. For Tish, though typical, is an individual creation. She is promise of what the author of her being may do when she writes the novel as she will wish to write it. And yet, to revert to the point under discussion, when one reads about Tish it is the chronicle of her adventures that gives pleasure. One recalls from **"Mind Over Motor"** Tish triumphantly whizzing around the race course in Jasper's new car; from **"The Simple Lifers,"** Tish with a clamshell, "Indian nippers," advancing upon Percy's beard; from **"Tish's Spy,"** Tish, buoyed by a life-belt, headed for Island Number Eleven; from **"My Country Tish of Thee,"** Tish capturing a band of real bandits. All the pictures are screen studies, or pictures that cry out for screen presentation.

"Any one who has a sense of proportion can write a short story," Mrs. Rinehart has said to interviewers. "The main thing is to realize its essentials. The instinctive sense of what to tell and what to leave to the reader's imagination is what makes the born story teller." In addition to knowing that action is demanded by men readers, who go to baseball and polo, even if women, who are more introspective, are content to read analytical paragraphs, she believes that suspense is the vise that holds the reader. Therefore, she clamps it on early in the action, quite often hinting at just enough of the dénouement to cause curiosity as to what it was all about and how it all happened. She is a master of the art of suggestion. She believes that in a story the story's the thing: "You must have a good plot" (a particular in which the story is different from the novel). She recommends acquaintance with the market, since the writing of short stories is a game, and certain subjects are more or less in demand. Some subjects she regards as taboo—for instance, religion.

Mary Roberts was born in Pittsburgh, August 12, 1876. After being graduated from high school, she took the training school course for nurses offered by the Pittsburgh Homeopathic Hospital. That she draws largely from her hospital career is evident from her most successful fiction, from *The Amazing Adventures of Letitia Carberry* (1911) (albeit the title doth protest too much), through *"K"* (1915), the first long story of its kind, and *Love Stories* (1919). Though not a few authors have written hospital sketches, yet not one of them before Mrs. Rinehart wrote a body of narrative contributing definitely to local color and setting through hospital scenes and business. Even when she writes a story that has its action outside the hospital, she introduces bits of lore obviously gathered in her training career, odds and ends that rise spontaneously and become part of the whole. They form, incidentally, part of the realistic detail by which *à la Defoe*, the author, conveys the illusion of reality. For instance, you are rather sure Tish was in the Maine Woods; for you remember that a leech attached itself to her leg and was allowed to remain (by Aggie's advice): "One must leave it on until it was full and round and couldn't hold any more, and then it dropped off."

On April 21, 1896, according to *Who's Who,* Mary Roberts, not yet twenty, was married to Dr. Stanley Marshall Rinehart. In 1905, after the birth of her three sons, Mrs. Rinehart began to write. For the magazines she wrote poems and short stories—her first story went for $35—and in 1907 she produced her first play, *Double Life.* About this time Robert H. Davis, of *Munsey's,* suggested that she try a serial. The result was *The Circular Staircase* (1908), a mystery story, which she sold for $400. In 1914 she said she would not sell it for less than $20,000. This long story brought her popularity, popularity increased by

another mystery, *The Man in Lower Ten* (1909). *When a Man Marries* was also published in 1909, after which followed *The Window at the White Cat* (1910). Her deftness in plot construction, her skill in arousing suspense, her ability to hold off the climax relentlessly while apparently advancing relentlessly toward it, and her final seeming clever solution of the mystery—all are manifest in *The Window at the White Cat.* There is the lawyer narrator, Knox, whose employment as mouthpiece makes for reality; there is the disappearance of Allen Fleming, a piece of paper bearing the sign of Eleven Twenty Two, the only clue, there is his daughter Margery, who comes to the lawyer (the love story is drawn in, at once, with a tempestuous tug at the ears); there is the rival, young Wardrop, former secretary of Allen Fleming, about whom suspicion is thrown (with a rather strong odor of red herrings); there is the concomitant disappearance of Miss Jane, sister of Letitia (not the Letitia who is Tish, however); there are the stolen pearls, the lost traveling bag, the murder of Fleming and the final solution of the mystery at *The White Cat.* Clever "detective story" stuff it is, much like that of Anna Katherine Green and numerous followers of Poe, without particular distinguishing marks.

The Amazing Adventures followed, 1911. The volume includes three stories, in which the first, a mystery, introduces the heroine of all. **"Three Pirates of Penzance"** and **"That Awful Night,"** which fulfill the requisites of the short story, fill out the book; but the two hundred pages in which Letitia turns detective at the hospital are the most important. Mrs. Rinehart may have found the germinal idea in Poe's "The Murders in the Rue Morgue." So similar is the likeness at one point that, just as the reader begins to wonder whether she will solve the story similarly, she takes occasion to mention "The Murders" in such manner as to convey that her dénouement will be different. The solving, however, lacks the convincingness of Poe's story, as the manner lacks his clarity.

The author recognized the value of the material in her enterprising old maid and utilized it in stories published from 1912 on. In 1916 five of them were collected under the title, *Tish.* For the title of one, instanced above, we have not been able to forgive her: **"My Country Tish of Thee."** She likes punning as well, almost, as the Elizabethans and, admittedly, she ordinarily succeeds better than in this perpetration. When Aggie of **"The Amazing Adventures"** broke the thermometer in her mouth, Tommy Andrews remarked of her that having been quicksilvered she'd now probably be reflecting; when Lizzie, the other crony, who narrates **"My Country"** fell from her horse, which stepped on and over her, Tish said something about his having walked across a "bridge of size." On the whole, this volume is the best collection Mrs. Rinehart has published. To "Pendennis," of *The Forum,* she said in 1918: "Every man is a hundred types; he's a Puritan and a rake, a coward and a soldier, a shirker and a worker, a priest and a sinner. All the writer does is to take the dominant characteristic of that man and lay stress on it." Surely, she put much of herself into Tish, wide as seems the gap between the incorrigibly eccentric spinster and the lady of "erect force, of swift judgment, of irreproachable dignity; in manner gentle, feminine." They share a love of nature:

Tish's mountains and woods are to her a forest of Arden no less than to Mrs. Rinehart; doubtless the latter shares the sense of discomfort the three spinsters felt, but never would she have turned back with Aggie and Lizzie; she grimly enjoys the conquering of difficulties, one fancies, as Tish enjoyed struggling; and, in diverse ways, they share a sense of humor.

It is, again, the background of reality, of such settings as Mrs. Rinehart has seen summer after summer, which fixes the all but unbelievable adventures of the three maiden ladies. So much, then, for the three tales of *Tish* which show her going back to nature. That the author has insight into character of another sort is displayed in **"Like a Wolf on the Fold"** wherein the astute Syrian, Tufik, is as individual and as typical as toothless Aggie, fat Lizzie and enterprising Tish, all of whom finally flee from his outrageously calculated dependence upon his "mothers." The presentation of his character gains from the method best adapted to narrative—the objective. Tufik acts, and his acts are colored by the comments of the ladies; but the author keeps out of his mind and proves, again, her ability to succeed by steering clear of the psychological.

Meantime, beginning about 1909, Mrs. Rinehart was writing stories of another sort, which appeared that year, in 1913, 1914, and 1915 in various magazines and which were gathered up under the title of *Affinities,* and published in 1920. Apropos of her nomenclature, the author was asked in 1914 whether it was difficult to get names for her people. She smiled. "Once I was invited," she said, "to an affinity party. I did not go, but it suggested a story to me. Of course, I was very careful not to use the names of any one whom I knew. After the story came out I had a letter from a man in the West saying that his name was Ferdinand, and that his wife, his affinity, in fact the whole set, had names identical with the ones I had used in my story."

The title story may be cited, further, by way of indicating the all but unavoidable O. Henry influence. Fanny (the assumed narrator) and Ferd Jackson are affinities. The complication, at the basis of the surprise, lies in the fact that Day (Fanny's husband) and Ida Jackson (Ferd's wife) are also affinities, and unknown to the narrator and her picnic party are with another group on a neighboring island. After an exciting incident of a borrowed boat and a thrilling automobile race across country, Fanny and Ferd reach home. The shock emerges in the knowledge each acquires of the parts played by Day and Ida. Similar in construction are **"The Family Friend,"** and **"Clara's Little Escapade,"** testifying to Mrs. Rinehart's mastery of surprise. In all, the passing fad of a few years ago for affinities is treated in humorously satirical vein. **"The Borrowed House"** and **"Sauce for the Gander"** entrench upon the débutante ground which Mrs. Rinehart worked to best advantage in *Bab—A Sub-Deb.* The book was published in 1917, after appearing as a series of stories in periodicals.

Mrs. Rinehart has stated that her creed is service, and she has illustrated how her books bear it out by reference to these whimsical fabrications of Bab's sub-débutante days. Bab, she says, is typical of the service we give to that brilliantly adorned figure of our first dream ambitions—

romance. So again, as in the person of Letitia Carberry, Mrs. Rinehart draws upon her own personality for the psychology of Bab or draws upon what she might have been. In Bab Mrs. Rinehart has succeeded in approaching and describing, through narrative, the mental condition of ɪa young girl who, surrounded by wealth and culture, is eager to escape from the reality of life, who as indicated, is romantic. She is another of the gauges the author has flung down to her future novel. The fact that little Mary Roberts Rinehart, 2nd, who made a grandmother of Mary Roberts Rinehart, 1st, at 43, is familiarly known as Babs, may be an indication that the fictive heroine is popular in the family.

Tish and Bab are frequently spoken of as though characters in novels. But it is to be remembered that they figured, first, in a series of short stories. The quite unexplainable tradition among publishers that books of short stories do not sell so easily as novels is probably accountable for such works as Mr. Tarkington's *Penrod* and Mrs. Rinehart's *Bab* appearing in novel disguise.

From 1912 to 1917 Mrs. Rinehart published, from time to time, a number of hospital stories in which love is supreme. They are included in *Love Stories* (1919). There are critics who think the strongest element of her success lies in her appreciation of the joys and sorrows of the tender passion. **"Twenty-Two," "Jane," "In the Pavilion," "God's Fool,"** and **"The Miracle"** run the gamut of this emotion as it may be found, in varying aspects, in the private ward or Ward G, in the heart of the guiltless or the guilty. There is the young probationer, N. Jane Brown, who by a daring act loses her newly achieved position but saves a boy's life, and whose case is happily solved through the interest of the patient in Twenty-Two. There is another Jane, whom temper alone has brought to the hospital and who is conquered by the application of the principle that fire drives out fire. There is the nurse who marries, just to oblige him, a supposedly dying gentleman, and for whom he recovers. There is the Magdalen of **"The Miracle,"** which touches the misery of the degraded woman with an unusual sympathy and which shows the regenerating influence of the child. Of them all, **"God's Fool"** offers the one character worthy of being placed alongside Tish and Bab. The volume includes a war story, **"Are We Downhearted? No!"** which we should have liked to see published, rather, with *Twenty-Three and a Half Hours' Leave* (1919). The latter is one of the most humorous stories resulting from the Great Conflict and grows out of the author's intimate acquaintance, through her soldier son and her own war work, with actual conditions.

It is not to be forgotten that in these years Mrs. Rinehart's most impressive accomplishment has lain in her longer stories, her drama, and recently, in the motion picture dramatization of *Dangerous Days* and *It's a Great Life* [a film based on **"The Empire Builders"**]. It has been urged that some genius may do for the movies what Shakespeare did for the drama. This person might well be Mrs. Rinehart. She has the gift in that direction; she has evinced increasing interest in the medium. Only the other day she had a moving picture projector installed in her own home, finding it helpful to study picture production at close range. *The New York Tribune* of July 18, 1920, is responsible for the statement that the moving picture addition to her work necessitates her going to the California Coast about three times a year.

Her earlier long stories were continued in *Where There's a Will* (1912), *The Case of Jennie Brice* (1913), *The After House* (1914) and *The Street of Seven Stars* (1914). The psychic tale *"K"* was followed by a romance of lovable Otto IX, *Long Live the King!* (1917) and *The Amazing Interlude* (1917), a war theme of feminine courage. *A Poor Wise Man,* her latest long work, was first published serially in *The Ladies Home Journal* (1920). Among her dramas are *Seven Days* (1909), and *Cheer Up* (1913).

Through Glacier Park revealed this author a powerful writer of expository and descriptive prose. Her articles on the war, conceded to be among the most vivid and accurate written, were sent from the various army fronts she visited. On one occasion, according to her story, she reached France as a stowaway across the Channel. She interviewed the Queen of England, the Queen of Belgium, General Foch, and was decorated by the Belgian Queen.

Mrs. Rinehart lives at Sewickley, but has her office in Pittsburgh, where she works daily. After the manner of the modern professional, she waits not for inspiration, but picks up her pen and writes.

On her office wall hangs this motto: "Ideas and hard work are the keys to all success." (pp. 309-21)

> *Blanche Colton Williams, "Mary Roberts Rinehart," in her* Our Short Story Writers, *Moffat, Yard & Company, 1920, pp. 309-21.*

A. E. Murch on Rinehart and Anna Katharine Green:

The plot of *The Circular Staircase,* typical of Mrs. Rinehart's crime mysteries, is in many respects reminiscent of the pattern created by Anna Katharine Green almost thirty years earlier, with two lines of detective enquiry being followed, separately and often at cross purposes, by a police official and the strong-minded, inquisitive, kind-hearted elderly spinster who narrates the story. Miss Rachel Innes, in *The Circular Staircase,* is largely a re-incarnation of Miss Green's Amelia Butterworth in her personal qualities, social position and habits of thought, her relationship with her long-suffering maid, her sympathy with young lovers, as well as in her detective methods and her facility for 'happening' to discover important information by accident. Mrs. Rinehart, however, handles this plot technique with greater literary skill than her predecessor, and her first crime novels are particularly interesting because they owe nothing to French or English influences, and represent the emergence of a new vein of purely American detective fiction, with an authentic background of characteristically American social conditions.

> *A. E. Murch, in his* The Development of the Detective Novel, *1958.*

Mary Roberts Rinehart   (essay date 1939)

[*In the following excerpt from her essay* Writing Is Work, *Rinehart discusses the sources for some of her works, her writing habits, and the progress of her literary career.*]

There are two stock questions always asked any writer: How did he start to write, and where does he get his ideas for stories? Once again I can only speak from my own experience. For the first, I started because I liked to write and wanted to earn some money. For the second, my own work has divided itself into two parts.

One part comes very hard. Indeed, most of it comes very hard. Some ideas have taken two or three years before they ripened into any sort of shape, and even a short story, carefully thought out beforehand, may take a month to get on paper. But once in a blue moon something else occurs. Such an incident happened to me two years ago. I was in bed, resting before a serious operation, and I wakened in the morning with a short story in my mind, complete and ready to write. I sat up in the bed and wrote it that day, finishing at eleven o'clock that night. The next day I went to the hospital, carrying it with me for rewriting. Nurses came and went, but I hardly saw them. I sat up in my high bed, a board on a pillow in front of me and finished it at ten o'clock that night.

It is useless to ask any writer to explain that.

Other stories of course have had a definite origin. On the desk in front of me is the confession of a murder. It is written on a small slip of paper and was found under the telephone box on the floor of a cheap hotel. The woman who ran the hotel had been driven out of town, and when the telephone was being repaired the slip of paper had been found. It reads:

> To whom it may concern: On the 31st of May, 19—, I killed a woman in my house of sin at ———— St., ————. I hope you will not find this until I am dead.

She had signed her full name, and, so far as I know, she is living today. The police dug up the cellar of the house, but no body was ever found. But some time later I wrote a story called *The Confession* from it.

Not all origins are so specific, but all writers know them. It may take time for the idea to germinate. It was two years after I spent some time at a little sick-and-sorry house in Belgium during the war before I wrote from that experience a book called *The Amazing Interlude.* The Tish stories began many years ago from the purely accidental meeting with three spinster ladies living together who had been adopted by a strange dog. And a recent Tish story, in which she crosses the Atlantic in a blimp, owes its origin to a statement by some man whose name I have forgotten or never knew, that it was possible to fish for sharks from a small dirigible.

There are other origins equally easy to trace. At the Hofopera in Vienna I saw a little prince fidgeting in the royal box, and a book and a picture—with Jackie Coogan as the prince—was the result. One day in the same city I saw a street called the Siebensterngasse, and wrote a story called

The Street of Seven Stars from it. And a hideous murder at sea provided me with a book [*The After House*] which had the strange result of reopening the case and releasing, on parole, a man from Atlanta who had been imprisoned there for seventeen years.

So much for the origins. What about the work itself?

Writers who began before the war were trained in a hard school. We sent in our material, complete to the last semi-colon, got it back or had it accepted at any price an editor chose to pay, and that was that. But it made troupers of those who survived. The phrase that "the show must go on" does not refer only to the theatrical world. The professional writer carries on in spite of hell and high water. And the general idea that when I or any other writer wants something it is only necessary to toss off a story, drives me to fury. One day at my desk would disprove that, as well as discourage those amateurs who see in this profession an easy means to wealth and reputation. I have never been able to be a prima donna. Even had I shown such a tendency I had a happy humorous family which would simply have laughed at me. But the reliable trouper in this combination of art—if possible—business and profession does not throw temperament about the place. He is usually sober and industrious. If he writes humor his expression while doing it is generally that of an individual with a bad toothache. He does not expect to be nursed along by either editor or publisher. If he has a date line he tries to keep it. And always he works.

Not only is life always about, pressing on him with its problems and its incessant demands. It is frequently necessary to work against extremely adverse conditions. In fact, it is axiomatic with most writing people that there are no such things as perfect conditions for work. But even at the best the strain is very great.

For example, recently I finished a long story called *The Wall.* To write it I took notes of all sorts for some fourteen months before I began. In writing the story with pen and ink I did three and, in some parts, four and five complete versions, an estimated 375,000 words. The completed book ran 120,000 words. The work was done in five months, working from seven to nine hours a day. Then, the day after I finished the story I passed out, and had been two weeks in an oxygen tent before I returned to consciousness. And not too much of that!

This is the work which the writer is supposed to toss off in leisure moments between bridge and trips to Europe. Or when he wants a new car. Yet it has its amusing side. Some seven or eight years ago I was in a hospital, and was visited by a friend who was also a very eminent psychiatrist. He knew my long record of illness and operation; and he sat beside the bed and inspected me soberly.

> "Just what are you escaping from?" he inquired.
> "Me? Escaping?"
> "Certainly you are escaping. From what? Writing."
> "Would escape cause gall-stones?" I ask feebly.
> "Of course it would. You are escaping from work. You might as well know it."

Well, perhaps he was right. Some writers go fishing. Some

divorce their wives. Some take to drink. It is just possible that I escape into gall-stones or an oxygen tent! I do not know. But I do know that now and then I escape into writing, leaving a world I cannot face for a dream world of my own creating. Once, stricken with grief so profound that I felt I had reached the end of my road, I faced work half done, and had to go back to the desk again. I think it saved me.

I can write of that period now. I could not then. The first day, with my pen in my hand, and finally giving up and putting my head down on the desk. The second day, a few words; to be thrown away because they were undecipherable. And then at last after a long struggle the road opening up again, an escape for a few hours, and the blessed relief of work once more.

Perhaps that is why writers keep on writing. That and other things. They speak with loathing of their job, but few of the professionals really stop. For one thing, the early urge to write, in time, becomes the habit of writing. We are often miserable at our desks or typewriters, but not happy away from them. And most writers also must earn. It is an uncertain profession, at its best. It does not lend itself to the accumulation of wealth. True, prices are better today. I have already mentioned the small leather bank book, and here I quote the material I sold in those early days, and what I received for it.

Most of the entries mean nothing to me today. I cannot remember them at all. But in that Niagara Falls of work during the first year or two there are a dozen so-called poems which brought anywhere from two to twelve dollars. I remember vaguely only two of them, and they were pretty dreadful. There are also fifty-nine short stories, the earlier ones bringing me an average of twenty dollars, the later ones showing a slight rise. And, some time in that period, I wrote four serials and published them, and two novelettes. I do not remember anything about the novelettes, which is the way they are listed; but I see that one brought seventy-five dollars, which is certainly all it was worth. As to the four serials, two of them I have forgotten entirely, and have no idea what they were about. The other two, however, became my first two books. One of them, called *The Man In Lower Ten,* brought me four hundred dollars as a serial, and the second, *The Circular Staircase,* five hundred.

Certainly the dam had burst! But I came of a family where my father, its sole reading addict, had had rather fine literary tastes, and I was only a story teller, and barely that. Before my first book came out I warned all my friends that I was bringing out a penny shocker, and please not to read it. When the fatal day came I was hiding on a farm in the country, and its subsequent success, while gratifying, frightened me almost into a fit.

Every writer knows the terror of an unexpected success. How to carry on? How to repeat it?

But, willy-nilly, I had a business by that time, although it was not yet a profession. (pp. 5-11)

There was much in my favor, nevertheless. There was less competition. Fewer people were writing. And times were good. The magazines were prospering. I often think that I would not care to build a reputation of sorts under present conditions. In those early days I could get an idea while making a cake, write it in the afternoon, get it typed—I had a little Jewish girl who lived around the corner for that—and send the story off the next day. When, or if, it came back, I sent it off again to another magazine. It was as simple as that.

Or was it? I weighed ninety-six pounds. My health was bad. I had a big house with the nursery on the top floor, and the children had everything from measles and whooping cough to diphtheria. Part of that time there was only a general housework girl, and I had the house as well. Not an ordinary house, either. A doctor's house, with offices and telephone to watch and calls to follow up. Any doctor's wife knows what that means, to trace her husband and try to locate him for some emergency.

Nor has it been much easier since. The only difference is that the pressure has changed, not lessened. Small wonder that I have little or no patience with those writers who use temperament as an excuse for not working, and no belief at all in inspiration. I write now as I always have, when I can find the time for it.

I must have been writing for eight years or so before I dared to submit anything to *The Saturday Evening Post.* It was notably difficult to get into its pages, and its list of great and popular names among its authors, put it far beyond me. Then one day I took my courage in my hands and sent the first of the Tish stories to it. I had very little hope, but things began at once to happen with astonishing rapidity. The editors not only took the story; they sent an associate editor all the way to my home to see me. Such polishing of furniture as preceded his arrival, such anxiety over the lunch, and what I would wear! And then he could not stay for lunch, and I am sure he never saw the furniture or my new dress. What he wanted was more Tish stories, and the *Post* has had them—at intervals for twenty-five years.

I know that this is not the usual picture of the professional writer. He sits calmly and with dignity at his desk or his typewriter, indifferent to visiting editors or lunches or furniture polishing. When he writes he writes, and words become sacred as soon as he has put them down. There are some of us like that, of course; people with such utter self-confidence that every word they write is precious and must remain. But I have never known any. The average writer, especially if he is experienced, is a humble creature, ready to wag his tail at a kind word.

It is usually the dilettante who has the superiority complex. (pp. 12-3)

A question often asked of professional writers is as to their methods of work. Personally, I have always thought that Arnold Bennett had reduced that method to a science. He rose at six, with a tea outfit close at hand. He brewed and drank his tea and then went to work. At nine in the morning he had finished for the day. He never rewrote. I have seen some manuscripts of his, and there on his pages, done in a small beautiful hand, a word may be crossed out and another substituted. But that is all.

To me, he was a miracle. When I think of my own confused and often frenzied days, life pressing from all sides, people, clothes, food, letters, business and emergencies, I know that I manage badly. Yet, in case it is of interest, I do try to work systematically. I have no fixed hour for going to my desk, but it is always as soon in the morning as I can do it.

From then until one o'clock there is a theory that I shall not be disturbed. It is largely theory, but I go back, nevertheless, after each interruption. At one o'clock my lunch tray comes. I eat or not. If I am working hard I may take only a cup of coffee. After that I go on until one of two things happens. Either I am writing nonsense or my hand will no longer hold a pen. At the end of a nine-hour day, for instance, I may have to soak my right hand in hot water for some time, and my head feels as though it is filled with mush.

If the evening is free I go to bed, again to make notes for the next day's work; and this may go on for months. During that time I have an almost complete detachment from the world I live in, a sort of armor against distraction. I talk to people, move about, appear on the surface much as usual. But later on I have only a confused memory of what has happened during that period.

I am quite sure that this is true of all professional writers during any long piece of work.

Nevertheless, I have my own idiosyncrasies. I must have my own pen; a pen so important to me after eight years of use that it is kept carefully hidden lest some absent-minded visitor carry it off. I must use a certain kind of ink. I work badly if there is anything on my mind, from a dinner party to an unpaid bill. And—possibly due to my early experience—I do not work well in a large room.

It may be that this is temperament after all! The fact remains that, having built myself in more opulent times a large book-lined study, for years I was conscious of the room. It was too high, too spacious, perhaps too grand. Some memory of the first little black-walled office must have persisted, and today I am once more working in a small and unencumbered place.

Not long ago I found a writer in the depths of despair. He could not write. It was gone. It was over. I asked him where he was working, and discovered that he had a study the size and general proportions of a hay barn. I suggested a cubby-hole somewhere, and he agreed to try it. He is working again.

I have no explanation, unless it is that, in a small space, one feels more shut away from the active interesting world outside and alone with his characters. Or that the mental inversion essential to creation is somehow assisted by the closing in of walls. O. Henry writing in a prison cell.

This matter of characters is apparently a matter of general interest. People ask where the writer gets them, and if he is honest he will usually say he does not know. Certainly I never drew but one character direct from life, and that was in the very early days. I met a man, and later on I murdered him. He had been very kind to me, and I have been sorry ever since.

Actually I think that most writers invent their characters to fit the parts they are to play in the story. True, they change, these people. I have known a villain on my desk to become almost saintly before he left it. This is familiar to all writers, but it is generally the exigency of the story, and not the character walking away with the book, which causes it.

Style is also a subject of inquiry and interest. I know nothing about style, except to have an idea and to present it as lucidly and simply as I can. Writers have certain styles, of course. The staccato individual writes his jerky, staccato prose. The ponderous ones write the long involved sentences which represent their own mental ponderosity. The suave and sophisticated reflect what they are.

In plain truth these hurried days leave little time for style *per se*. People read more and more for subject matter and less and less for quality in writing. It is no time for a Macaulay rewriting one sentence thirty-two times. Which leads rather naturally to what leads to success in writing. Every writer wants that. In fact, he wants two things. He wants to be both the fair-haired child of the critics and to be a best-seller at the same time.

Sometimes, more often in recent years, this happens. It is no longer considered fatal to all literary craftsmanship to sell a lot of books, or to be a successful magazine writer. The result, however, of this dual objective is hard on the writer himself. He wants both to do the best possible work and also to reach the largest possible audience. The result is a fairly normal condition of discouragement.

There are, as I have already said, some few who are so cocksure of themselves that they never feel it. My own personal discouragement, however, is so keen that it reaches the point of neurosis, and I have never failed to have it. At some time during any given piece of work it overtakes me. The story seems pointless, the writing bad. I am overwhelmed by a sense of futility. I want desperately to quit, and I have a sense of actual nausea at the sight of my desk. But eventually I carry on; and here I think is the distinction, not only between success and failure, but between the temperamental aspirants and the professional group. The first gives up, the second goes back with grim determination and finishes the job. (pp. 16-9)

> *Mary Roberts Rinehart, in her* Writing Is Work, *The Writer, Inc. Publishers, 1939, 25 p.*

Howard Haycraft   (essay date 1941)

[*Haycraft is an American editor and critic who has written extensively on mystery fiction. In the following excerpt from his* Murder for Pleasure: The Life and Times of the Detective Story, *originally published in 1941, he denotes the strengths and weaknesses of the "Rinehart formula."*]

The dividing line between the *physical* type of detective story and the pure mystery story is often difficult to distinguish. The conclusive test might well be whether, in the final analysis, the solution is accomplished by incident (mystery story) or deduction (detective story). Even by

> **Mary Roberts Rinehart had what amounts to genius in the creation of atmosphere. By this is meant the ability to present a subtle background of suspense, almost of terror, and to repeat this process until the final climax has been reached.**
>
> —*Sutherland Scott, in his* Blood in Their Ink: The March of the Modern Mystery Novel, *1953.*

this test, it is not easy to decide in which of these categories the dramatic and highly popular murder stories of Mary Roberts Rinehart belong. They fall almost exactly on the border-line. (But it is possibly not without some significance that the average uncritical American reader, asked to list important writers of the "detective story," will almost invariably place Mrs. Rinehart's name first.) Examined in the light of careful scholarship, some of the Rinehart tales would likely be found to belong to the one type, some to the other. One day, perhaps, the academic world will forego its preoccupation with the dead bones of the past long enough to perform this practical service to literature! (p. 87)

Virtually all the Rinehart crime novels have detectives of a sort, which is one reason they are so difficult to classify. Most of them have two: an official detective of more of less astuteness; and the first-person narrator, usually a woman, most often a romantic spinster engaged in protecting young love from unjust suspicion, who alternately complicates the plot and aids detection in unpremeditated fashion—a combination of participating (usually interfering!) Watson, and detective-by-accident.

This is the readily recognizable "Rinehart formula," still delightful when practised by its originator, but becoming increasingly tedious in the hands of her far-too-numerous imitators among American women writers. It is, in fact, only Mrs. Rinehart's superlative talent as one of the great story-tellers of the age (and the intensely human quality of her writing) that induces us to overlook in her own tales breaches of detective etiquette we could excuse in nobody else: what Waldo Frank calls her "carpentry." Foremost in any catalogue of these flaws must be the manner in which romantic complications are allowed to obstruct the orderly process of puzzle-and-solution. Similarly, the plots are always being prolonged by accidents and "happenstances"—not honest mistakes of deductive judgment by the investigator, which would be a legitimate part of the game, but unmotivated interferences and lapses on the part of the characters, who are forever blundering into carefully laid traps and springing them prematurely, or "forgetting" to tell the official detective of important clues. ("Four lives might have been spared if I had only remembered. . . .") Only too frequently, it must be confessed, these clues turn out at the dénouement to have had no bearing on the puzzle anyway!

We can excuse, perhaps, the interminable "Had-I-But-Knowns" as a harmless but irritating species of auctorial mannerism. Much more serious is the writer's tendency to abuse the least-likely-person theme, to pin the crimes on psychologically (and sometimes physically) impossible characters. A final and vital flaw is the painful stretching of the long arm of coincidence which would have us believe, in utter defiance of the laws of probability, that Fate will obligingly and repeatedly bring together without other cause whole groups of persons who, usually unknown to themselves, are intimately related through some complex pattern of antecedent events. (Suggested mental exercise for bored readers: Try to chart—or even figure out—the relationships of the characters in the author's *The Great Mistake!*)

Unfortunately, it is too often these weaknesses that Mrs. Rinehart's imitators are prone to mimic, rather than her points of strength—of which there are many. For the "formula" she devised possesses immense technical advantages, quite apart from its inventor's personal narrative skill. Chief among them, as pointed out by the late Grant Overton, are the reader's participation in the adventure by self-identification with the narrator; and the "forward action" of the plot, the direct antithesis of the over-intellectualized puzzle story. In a Rinehart murder novel the initial crime is never the be-all and end-all but only the opening incident in a progressive conflict between the narrator and the criminal. As Overton further observed: "Here [is] no put-the-pieces-together formula; here [is] an out-guess-this-unknown-of-he'll-out-guess-you, life-and-death struggle." Sometimes this dramatic approach goes too far and carries the story past the border-line of detection and into the realm of mere mystery-adventure; but kept within bounds it is a technique that practitioners of the cut-and-dried Static School might profitably study. In Mrs. Rinehart's own skilled hands it results in a mood of sustained excitement and suspense that renders the reader virtually powerless to lay her books down, despite their logical shortcomings.

Whether mystery or detection, Mary Roberts Rinehart's works have played an incalculable rôle in introducing women, both readers and writers, to puzzle fiction. She represents the quintessence of the romantic mood in the literature. She is the unquestioned dean of crime writing by and for women. (pp. 89-91)

> Howard Haycraft, "America: 1890-1914 (The Romantic Era)," in his Murder for Pleasure: The Life and Times of the Detective Story, 1941. Reprint by Biblo and Tannen, 1972, pp. 83-102.

Arnold R. Hoffman (essay date 1972)

[*In the following excerpt, Hoffman examines Rinehart's crime fiction as a reflection of the changing social mores of American society.*]

In whatever way popular literature, as one segment of that popular culture (or mass culture, as Messrs. [Bernard] Rosenberg and [David Manning] White would have it), may in the end be defined by its many analysts—and in all like-

lihood the definitions will be nearly as diverse and divergent as the number of definers—if some account is taken of the author's term of production, the number of works published, and the number of sales tallied for those works, Mary Roberts Rinehart will be a major figure in American popular literature, and, thereby, in America's popular culture. The point of especial importance to this paper is that a major portion of her literary reputation rests on her mystery fiction.

Considering Mrs. Rinehart's "crime stories," as she preferred to call them, or indeed any aspect of her career in letters, with an intent and organization even approaching the conduct of historical or critical scholarship is really a new venture, one offering both the rewards and pitfalls of fresh research. It is surprising to this writer that, considering the general reputation of Mrs. Rinehart, very few commentators have noticed her and even fewer have given her more than cursory attention. One can be done very quickly with a recall of the commentary on her work, crime fiction or otherwise.

Apparently the earliest document is the slight monograph of 1924, from the company of George H. Doran, Mrs. Rinehart's publisher from 1915 to 1929. In addition to two articles by Mrs. Rinehart herself, *Mary Roberts Rinehart: A Sketch of the Woman and Her Work* contains an opening, sugary advertisement by Grant Overton and an insipid, embarrassing sketch by Robert H. Davis. A long stretch of time ensues, but in 1941 Howard Haycraft's *Murder for Pleasure* redeems the time by setting forth in five rather astute pages a simple outline of the virtues and vices of Mrs. Rinehart's mystery fiction. A much more representative treatment of Mary Roberts Rinehart is W. B. Mowery's *Professional Short-Story Writing*, in which Mrs. Rinehart is merely named in a sentence with three other authors as one who writes "detective fiction . . . as genuinely emotional as straight fiction." [Frank Luther Mott's] *Golden Multitudes* of 1947 . . . devotes two paragraphs of of text to Mrs. Rinehart, but largely to the publishing success of *The Circular Staircase.* John Tebbel's *George Horace Lorimer and The Saturday Evening Post* of 1948 is interesting, not as criticism but as a glimpse of Mary Roberts Rinehart as public and private personality. Being an interesting person outside of her books, Mrs. Rinehart—and I think Matthew Arnold would applaud my inability to call her merely "Rinehart"—was particularly appealing to interviewers. Two records of visits with her, the former more revelatory than the latter, are Robert van Gelder's ["An Interview With Mary Roberts Rinehart," *The New York Times Book Review* (1940)] and Harvey Breit's ["Talk With Mary Roberts Rinehart," *The New York Times Book Review* (1952)]. Sutherland Scott's *Blood in Their Ink* (1953) becomes at times a bit histrionic in its rhetoric, as much mystery "criticism" seems to, but through the several pages devoted to Mary Roberts Rinehart, one does perceive Scott's insight into atmosphere and motivation in her crime stories. Insight in a much briefer compass is the case with A. E. Murch's 1958 *The Development of the Detective Novel.* He gives Mrs. Rinehart two paragraphs. I have saved for the last what is perhaps the most prestigious of all the references to Mary Roberts Rinehart, slight as it is: that of Cleanth Brooks in *The Well Wrought Urn*. And, quite succinctly, Brooks speaks to the point dealt with by everyone interested in popular culture.

> For what is the sensibility of our age? Is there any one sensibility? Do we respond to T. S. Eliot, Dashiell Hammett, Mary Roberts Rinehart, or Tiffany Thayer? The objective answer must be that some of us respond to one and some to another.

From the foregoing it should be clear that, as I have said, this essay undertakes, even in its rather limited scope, to discuss what is virtually unresearched work.

Mary Roberts was born at Pittsburgh, Pennsylvania, in 1876 to a poor sewing machine maker and part-time inventor, whose veins flowed with, in his daughter's phrase, strict "Covenanter blood."

Her beginning in fiction was humble and honest enough. In 1896, while a student at the Pittsburgh Training School for Nurses, she married Dr. Stanley Marshall Rinehart. In a few years she was busily rearing three sons, who were later to distinguish themselves in the publishing industry. But as Haycraft records the fact,

> A stock-market slump in 1903 wiped out the Rinehart's small savings and left them $12,000 in debt. In a vague hope of contributing to the family support, Mrs. Rinehart began to write short stories in the intervals of bringing up her family of growing boys. Considerably to her surprise, her first story sold to *Munsey's Magazine* for thirty-four dollars. . . . While convalescing from an operation she wrote her first long story, and her first crime story, *The Man in Lower Ten,* which was published serially in 1907 but not in book form until 1909. Her first work to appear between covers was *The Circular Staircase* (1908). . . .

From that point—or, really, from the *Munsey's* story— Mrs. Rinehart's writing success closely imitated the proverbial snowball.

She wrote and published successfully for almost fifty years; as Haycraft notes, her first fiction was sold to *Munsey's Magazine* in 1903, and her last new novel was published in 1952. (The "new" is important, for three other books, collections of previous work, were to be published before her death in 1957.) Admittedly not to be compared with the prolific Erle Stanley Gardner, Mrs. Rinehart did produce an extraordinary amount of work, and in the final result, a very broad canon: crime fiction, humorous fiction, romances, travelogues, war reportage, commentary on writing (nothing that one could call literary criticism), an autobiography (updated once), plays, articles, and sketches. By 1933, forty-six books (including omnibuses) carried her name. In 1952, with the publication of her final novel, a mystery, Mrs. Rinehart's name stood below sixty-one book titles. The slackened pace in the years since 1938, necessitated by impaired health, hurt her average, but in 1952 it still stood at slightly over one book a year for forty-four years—an impressive output by almost any reckoning.

Indeed, in the quantitative terms of reception alone, she must be accounted a "popular" writer. In *60 Years of Best Sellers: 1895-1955,* Alice Payne Hackett asserts that Mrs. Rinehart is one of those writers with the most titles— eleven in her case—on the sixty annual lists by specific publishers. Too, she is among those enduring longest on the lists: from 1909 to 1936. *The Circular Staircase,* her first novel published as a book—by Bobbs-Merrill in 1908—sold in the regular edition 300,000 copies. Through the three Grosset & Dunlap reprint editions, sales reached nearly 250 thousand copies. Then, by way of a Triangle Books hardcover edition, a Pocket Books paper edition, and two Dell paperback issuings (the latter currently available in the paperbound racks), the novel's sales have gone substantially higher. In 1947 Mott cited the figure 750,000. By Mrs. Hackett's 1956 computation, the figure had climbed to 800,000, and the Dell publications follow that. The *Newsweek* review of her 1950 *Episode of the Wandering Knife* submitted that her books had sold "some 10,000,000" copies. Her crime story of 1909, *The Man in Lower Ten,* was the first American detective novel to make the annual best seller list.

Mrs. Rinehart's other books subsequently to make the list were: *The Window at the White Cat* (1910), *When a Man Marries* (1910), *"K"* (1915), *Amazing Interlude* (1918), *Dangerous Days* (1919), *Poor Wise Man* (1921), *The Breaking Point* (1922 and 1923), *Lost Ecstasy* (1927), *The Door* (1930), and *The Doctor* (1936). Of course, what such figures never reflect, and what it is impossible to know, is the number of *Saturday Evening Posts, Ladies Home Journals, Good Housekeepings,* and other periodicals that were brought just for the serializations of these and other Mary Roberts Rinehart books. At any rate, Mrs. Rinehart's best sellers alone are a qualitatively impressive production, even had she written no other books. And of those eleven best sellers, seven were crime stories.

Mary Roberts Rinehart's books were not only sold—they were read, by an immense and heterogeneous public. Among her high-placed or famous admirers, Mrs. Rinehart counted Herbert Hoover ("thirty years of continuous esteem") and Gertrude Stein. She endeared herself to masses of readers by a warm and personal response to all kinds of appeals, the answers to which made her address the public in print. After reaching an early fame substantial enough to occasion an influx of correspondence, Mrs. Rinehart chose Saturday as her weekly time for reading letters and dictating and signing answers to admiring fans, aspiring writers, and even distraught mothers and lonely wives, particularly during the two world wars.

An example of Mrs. Rinehart's public response—and not really as much of a footnote as it might seem—is her May Day, 1943 article for the *Saturday Review:* "To Mother, with Love. Some Thoughts About Books on Mother's Day." She wisely proposes different books for different mothers, depending upon the extent of their personal relation to the war; books on the war and foreign countries will not do for everyone, but she subtly suggests that crime fiction as escapism is suitable. She concludes:

> . . . I am a woman and a mother. Every book I have listed I have read and cared for. And a

book lasts, especially if on the fly-leaf it says, "To Mother, with love."

The obvious sentimentalism of the whole article has its reflections in her mysteries.

The remainder of this essay attempts to examine a major portion of the crime stories of Mary Roberts Rinehart as they reflect or comment upon the social mores of the United States. In *The Development of the Detective Novel,* A. E. Murch says,

> her first crime novels are particularly interesting because they owe nothing to French or English influences, and represent the emergence of a new vein of purely American detective fiction, *with an authentic background of characteristically American social conditions.* (my italics)

It must, of course, be remembered at all times that Mrs. Rinehart is the author, and, like other writers, even the most aesthetically polished, she selects and chooses from the background Murch observes.

From a survey of twenty-one of Mrs. Rinehart's books, the most coherent discussion of society in her crime fiction should begin according to categories. Therefore, I've chosen to isolate *swearing, drinking, smoking, attitudes toward race, violence, psychology, social classes,* and *sex.* For commentary upon both the validity of these categories and the representative quality of the mysteries, I have chosen also occasionally to glance at some of the immensely popular Tish stories, her humorous tales of three old maids' picaresque adventures. The stories about Miss Letitia Carberry and her cronies, first born in 1910 to a long run in the *Saturday Evening Post,* reflect all of the categories I have enumerated.

From the proposed list, the category that most clearly reflects an alteration in social attitude through the years is swearing, including both profanity and milder expletives. From *The Circular Staircase* of 1908 through *The Frightened Wife and Other Murder Stories* of 1953, one may observe an increasing use of profanity, qualified only in the

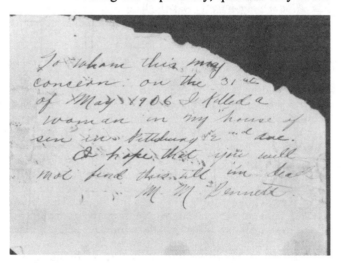

The scrap of paper that provided the inspiration for The Confession.

first and middle years if the narrator is female. In the last books, the sex of the story's teller seems irrelevant.

In that first novel, the narrator is Miss Rachel Innes, a middle-aged spinster given once only in a rare outburst of emotion to ejaculate "fiddlesticks." (This is Tish's best exclamation, too, in the early stories.) In speaking to Miss Innes, another character once has occasion for using "damned" and the phrase "I'll see him in hell," but in the manner of Chaucer's apology, the man emphasizes his wrestling with the morality of repeating these words that had been spoken by a third person. Once a strange man in a crowd, never to be identified or seen again, is heard to exclaim "What the hell!" but that suffices for the gratuitous profanity.

In *The Man in Lower Ten* (serial 1907, book 1909) the narrator is a young attorney, but not given to profanity. However, his somewhat wild-living law partner, McKnight, *is* given to colorful expressions like "Jove," "make an ass of oneself," "what in blazes," or "the blankety-blank thing." The narrator, apparently because he is our hero and must maintain an aura of gentility, utters only one "darned," all in all quite an example of self-restraint.

A particularly interesting development comes in 1910 with *The Window at the White Cat.* A variety of phrases entirely new to Mary Roberts Rinehart are introduced, e.g., "who in the devil's name," "Good God," "I'll be damned," "God only knows," and "for God's sake." The striking point is this: Mrs. Rinehart has the central crime and a great deal of the action take place in an urban men's club, devoted to heavy drinking, smoking, and much gambling. Yet in that atmosphere there is virtually no hard profanity; nor is there more in *The Case of Jennie Brice* (1913), *The After House* (1914), or two short novels published together in 1921, *The Confession* and *Sight Unseen.* The first, narrated by a young nurse, contains almost no profanity; only an unsavory character says "Hell." The second, important for its treatment of alcoholism, uses "damn" and "damned" frequently, but there is no swearing by the narrator-hero, an exemplary young medical school graduate.

The Breaking Point of 1922 really marks Mary Roberts Rinehart's emergence into the Twenties, if we think of that decade in the stereotype of freer language. The novel is only tangentially a mystery; there was a murder out West years before the novel opens, but the hero's amnesia and certain machinations by other principals have obscured the details of the homicide and the identity of the murderer. But for the first time in Mary Roberts Rinehart's crime fiction, the hero, a young man, regularly uses "damn" and "damned," for example, "I don't give a damn about it" and "I know damned well." Yet true to the established form, the strongest profanity is reserved for a "villain." The suspiciously foreign-looking character who wants to revenge himself upon the hero says at one point, for the expression's first time in Mrs. Rinehart's books, "I don't give a God-damn."

By 1930 and *The Door,* profanity and even the mild expressions, what Tish's maidenly, matronly friends would call "indecorous speech," are part and parcel of the narrative. No one is a foul mouth, but "damn" and "hell" are frequent; most importantly, when the men swear, they do so directly in front of women. In this pre-Depression world no one is struck by violated proprieties.

The State vs. Elinor Norton of 1934 is in many ways Mrs. Rinehart's most violent novel. Even more than *The Breaking Point,* this novel details the torture of a soul. Here a woman is psychologically racked through years of contest with a tyrannical mother embittered by poverty, an insensitive husband, and an immoral, belligerent lover. Of course, all comes right in the denouement, but until then her life is one torment. An objective correlative of that is the virtual ubiquity of "hell"—"the hell of a time," "the hell of a way," "giving it hell," "raise a merry little hell"—phrases all saying that circumstances have, in another of the book's phrases, "made her life actual hell." In 1938 with *The Wall,* Mrs. Rinehart achieves her most natural spectrum of swearing, traversing the range from the at once contemptible and pitiable Juliette's affectation of high-society in her "Thank God" and "God" every other word to the kindly old sheriff's "by the great horn spoon."

The Yellow Room of 1945 mirrors the general lessening of social restrictions that had followed with the exigencies of the war and the consequent general inattention to decorum. So, for the first time "bastard" appears in a book of Mrs. Rinehart's, although it is used in an innocuous phrase: "this house is an architectural bastard." For the first time someone, and not a ruffian says "God-dammitt," but at the same time, Mary Roberts Rinehart's third person narrator can write "here his language became unprintable. He used a few army words not common in polite society, and added some of his own invention." The observation to be made is that the words alluded to here are, on the evidence of what *is* printed in the novel, the four-letter Anglo-Saxon terms and some Freudian derivations. In surveying these and other novels, one sees Mary Roberts Rinehart moving through the years toward a more realistic, less forced use of profanity, no matter the sex of the narrator. There are dramatic shifts toward a wider usage at the opening of the Twenties and at the end of War War II. Her first heroes are generally restrained, especially before women, but by the time of *The Frightened Wife,* the hero is the roughest talking of all. In fifty years, Mary Roberts Rinehart shifts from the decorum of Wilkie Collins toward (but not too far) the colorful diction of Mickey Spillane.

Another aspect of Mary Roberts Rinehart's crime fiction that mirrors society's trends is drinking. It is, however, handled as a social amenity, not for its own sake, but because it reflects the behavioral attitudes of different generations in different periods. Observant to the fact that *anything* may have a point of interest or humor—compare, the myriad repetitions of "by the great horn spoon"—Mrs. Rinehart provides oddity in the imbibing of various characters. Miss Innes, narrator of *The Circular Staircase* and a middle-aged spinster, finds her refuge in the teapot, although she does accept a sociable glass of elderberry wine during one calling visit. Tish's blackberry cordial is ubiquitous, always held in readiness as a restorative, even

on a camping trip to the Rocky Mountains! An equally striking eccentric drinker is McKnight of *The Man in Lower Ten* who has already been observed as the narrator's sidekick, the scapegoat, the one upon whom a multitude of venial but lively sins can be cast. Accordingly, McKnight twice, in apparently typical actions, drinks a concoction of everything that's available to hand.

However, throughout the crime novels and the Tish stories, it is only those who are of the lower classes and of the theatre crowd who get drunk. Dramatic instances of the latter appear in *The Case of Jennie Brice* and *The Breaking Point.* (The single exception occurs in *The After House* (1914), a novel which deals with alcoholism as much as it can while its main business is being a mystery.) Yet Mrs. Rinehart was not unequivocally opposed to alcohol, for in the post-World War II novels, "cocktails" or "highballs" are an ordinary part of the characters' lives. On the other hand, Mrs. Rinehart can be ironic. In *The Swimming Pool* of 1952 there is an almost juvenile fascination with serving high-balls—constantly. But again, as with the swearing, the issue revolves upon the hero or heroine. From main characters who generally eschew liquor or take it only in extreme moderation, Mrs. Rinehart ends by developing principal figures who drink as a matter of course.

There is relatively little to say about smoking in Mary Roberts Rinehart's novels. Generally, the heroes smoke, but sometimes only cigars. And in *The Man in Lower Ten* the gentlemen make a point of asking the lady or ladies if they may smoke. In the Twenties—and dramatically in *The Door* of 1930—one suddenly finds young ladies of good family smoking, usually as acts of overt defiance. Throughout Mrs. Rinehart's mysteries, smoking, of whatever kind and even after it is quite acceptable, is used extensively as a narrative crutch: to show nervousness, in the shaky match; to show regained calm, in the steady match or smooth inhalation; to show deliberation, in the careful lighting; and to show poor taste or defiance, as in the case of the liberated young woman of *The Wall* (1938). Moreover, smoking plays its role in the detection of crimes: in *The Album* a cigar stub gives the lead to a certain person's presence, and in *The Wall,* a lipstick-stained cigarette butt is a major clue.

In the matter of reflected social attitudes toward race, there seems to be no pattern, no progression as one might from these other subjects expect to find, from a somewhat narrow prejudice to an enlightened liberalism or at least open-mindedness. In fact, the social critic inclined to accusation would probably find racism in the novels. *The Circular Staircase* has a real Uncle Tom, Thomas Johnson, a servant. (Blacks are seen in Mrs. Rinehart's fiction only as servants, and faithful ones at that.) Miss Innes "watched Thomas shuffle along" and later remarks that "Thomas shuffled out." Her servant Beulah is "coal-black." Believing the nature of Negroes to be distinct in all regards, one man observes "those darkies seldom have a penny;" similarly, *The Case of Jennie Brice* uses the archetypal loyal Negro retainer, given to shuffling and a softly muttered "praise Gawd." Again in *The Man in Lower Ten,* there is a "colored housemaid," this time named "Euphemia." Mrs. Rinehart attempts a Negro dialect for a porter on the train, but she fails so miserably and the porter is such a pitiful man that he is past all convincing and comes off merely ludicrous. *The Door* (1930) has an Amos, a superstitious and plainly devious servant whose presence and behavior prompt such statements as these: "There are some people to whom all Negroes look alike" (from the narrator); "Show a Negro a police badge and he'll come clean" (this from a stalwart, representative police officer); "his color was the peculiar gray of the terrified Negro" (this from a friend of the narrator).

However brief these stereotyped treatments of Blacks, other races are even more quickly dismissed and in clichés no less unkind. For a servant, McKnight has a "Jap," and McKnight's friend observes "it would take a Turk to feel at home in red and yellow pajamas." In *The Window at the White Cat,* "German cupidity" is assumed; and at a Chinese restaurant the diners get "a slanteyed welcome." Twenty-four years after McKnight's "Jap," the hero's maid in *The State vs. Elinor Norton* (1924) does not trust "Japs" or "them Orientals." From all of this in the pre-World War II decades, one might expect real enmity to develop after the war. But in the post-war novels "krauts" and "Japs" are mentioned, even in recollection of the war, without any vindictiveness beyond that in the slang. Only in *The State vs. Elinor Norton* is any kind of objectivity or sensitivity evident, and this after those references to "Japs." In Wyoming, one local character thinks of Indians as "lazy devils" and "shiftless cattle thieves"; but the narrator thinks to himself, "Our Indians are what we have made them."

In short, Mary Roberts Rinehart adheres to stereotyped, flat characterizations for non-Anglo-Saxon ethnic groups. The characterizations are so short, really, as to seem most of the time to be supercilious dismissals, nor does the picture become brighter as Mary Roberts Rinehart moves through her career. If one were to say that in the mysteries there simply is not time for full, sympathetic character development, one might turn to the Tish story **"Like a Wolf on the Fold"** (1913) for an illustrative comparison. This story is built entirely on the episode of Tish's good nature being imposed upon, and finally defrauded, by a "dratted Syrian." The attitude of the story's Anglo-Saxon principals, an attitude Mrs. Rinehart's tone never denies, can be summed up in two words: dirty foreigners.

However underplayed the racial element is in Mrs. Rinehart's crime fiction, the same cannot be said for violence. However, only a few generalizations on violence can be drawn with regard to Mrs. Rinehart's mysteries, and those are far more relevant to her brand of story than to her fiction as a social mirror. Usually, one murder precipitates, directly or obliquely, one to three others. Those killed subsequent to the principal murder know something about it, either the killer or his motivation. Again in general, Mrs. Rinehart is predisposed toward having the gore take place offstage. Often we learn of a person being struck on the head and then pushed downstairs in an always unsuccessful attempt to disguise the true mode of attack. Why that should be necessary is never clear. But with equal frequency neither the blow nor the fall kills the person. People are

shot at close range and from afar, stabbed to death while asleep, and killed with golf clubs and hypodermic injections of lethal drugs or air. But as these illustrations indicate, the means of death is never imaginative. The only deaths that stand apart are those in *The After House* (1914), in which the deceptively gentle old salt—patterned strongly in respect to his apparent wisdom on Melville's Old Dansker of *Billy Budd*—turns out to be a religious fanatic who "though himself a priest of heaven, appointed to make ghastly sacrifices at certain signals from on high." He dismembers three sleeping victims with an ax.

The problem of the old sailor is clearly a psychological one, and psychology as a broad area of interests and effects is a category of some importance in Mary Roberts Rinehart's mysteries. One might remember that Freud's first major works were published in translation in the first decade of this century and the ideas were immediately picked up, often at second and third hand, by a large American public. Mary Roberts Rinehart's *Window at the White Cat* (1910) is important for its incorporation of some instruments of experimental and diagnostic psychology. One chief suspect for the crime is put through a lengthy word association test. During the testing, the examining doctor asserts that "psychology is as exact a science as mathematics." (However, true to Mrs. Rinehart's code of reliance on detective intuition, the test does not reveal the true criminal.)

The Breaking Point of 1922 comes at the beginning of a decade and a half of intense interest in the possibilities of psychoanalysis and psychotherapy. *The Breaking Point* is a long novel for Mary Roberts Rinehart, and it hangs on the point that a traumatic experience can make a man forget a former existence, i.e., suffer amnesia. Suspicion arises that the young hero, Dr. Dick, was mixed up in some unlawful deed in a prior life that he cannot remember. To find out who he is, Dick Livingstone throws off his present existence and travels west to the place of his reputed trouble. By absolutely rejecting his life back East, he does regain his former identity and a partial knowledge of the murder in which he had been implicated. Then, to go back to those he has loved, he must throw off that regained life, which has become a slovenly existence; and through the sympathy of his foster-father, he succeeds in coming back. This is handled quite well, however vague its scientific aspects may seem, and at no time are the technicalities really more clear than when Dr. Dick's foster-father goes into the big city to see a "psycho-analyst," about his boy's troubles and is told "We've only commenced to dig into the mind."

After *The Breaking Point,* Mary Roberts Rinehart pays very little attention to psychology until the 1945 and post-war stories, when battle-fatigue and shell-shock—in short, war trauma—become frequent subjects. In *The Yellow Room* the hero is a veteran disabled by both physical and mental wounds. A principal figure of **"The Burned Chair"** (included in *The Frightened Wife and Other Murder Stories*) is a still-suffering victim of Korea. Another story of that volume, **"If It Were Only Yesterday,"** is a third person narrative, but the center of consciousness is the mind of the murderer, an insane young woman, obviously unbalanced by an automobile accident. A psychiatrist is briefly introduced, probing into her resentment toward the invalid sister whom she murders before committing suicide.

In addition to a concern with psychology and its intricacies, Mrs. Rinehart's crime fiction also manifests her and the public's interest in psychic phenomena. In her own life, she believed that she had twice received communication from Dr. Rinehart shortly after his death. Unsure of the outcome of such experiences if continued, she never again tried for contact. In the crime fiction, this first-hand communication with the spirit world is reflected a number of times in unexplained phenomena, such as the autonomous glowing of *The Red Lamp* (1925), and in incidental allusions to seances. Much of the action in *Sight Unseen* of 1921 takes place during seances when knowledge about certain crimes is cryptically transmitted through the medium. At the conclusion, there is no rational explanation offered for the supersensory knowledge which revealed the information. Interest in the unexplainable grew to a fad in the Twenties, but apparently was still relevant in 1938. *The Wall* of that year introduces sympathetically a secondary figure who is a regular seance participant and believer.

Being without effort very much an American, and having been born into and come to live in two strikingly different social classes, Mary Roberts Rinehart could be expected to be class conscious, and also conscious that class differences in America were at the best very shaky. Her early crime fiction, even through *The Wall* of 1938, is often told by a narrator whose position makes requisite the introduction of grand old homes (sometimes seemingly haunted), summer resorts, town cars, and servants of all types. Mrs. Rinehart never explicitly says that the good old days of dignified affluence are gone for America, but again and again her narrators or other major characters are now the genteel poor. Very clearly she caters to America's nostalgia for a time when large fortunes and *grande dames* ruled society. In the Twenties and Thirties there was a sharp awareness that the Gilded Age was only a memory, to be clung to by the few of that generation remaining. Finally, in Mrs. Rinehart's mysteries after 1945, there is no longer a concentration upon the details of managing inheritances, houses, and wild children.

Importantly, the wild children of Mrs. Rinehart's fiction in the first half of her career are not the sex-ridden creatures of today's hard-boiled fiction. Yet Mary Roberts Rinehart's crime fiction really is not of "another time"; it is of several times, through which decorous young ladies who might be kissed on the first anniversary of their "affairs" (*"K,"* 1915) have metamorphosed into witty females who can balance a cigarette, cocktail, and tennis racket all at once.

In the process of this radical change—and the men are a part of it, too—Mary Roberts Rinehart never plays for sensationalism. In only one of the mysteries is there anything other than a conventional marriage or romance (allowed its obstacles of money, position, and distance). And that is *The State vs. Elinor Norton* of 1934. A major portion of the story is involved first with Blair Leighton's attempts to get Elinor away from her husband and his rather offhand dalliance with a sluttish country girl while he maneuvers, and then with Elinor's agony after her husband has been killed and Blair begins sleeping with her, holding out the promise that he will marry her. There are no bedroom scenes, but at one point Elinor appears before the men in lounging pajamas, and it is clear later that adultery is taking place. However, it is the conclusion to the novel that is most important. The narrator, whom one hesitates to call the "hero," for his physical role in the story is severely limited, finally persuades Elinor to marry him, just before she is to enter an Episcopal convent. For the first time, a Mary Roberts Rinehart hero takes a sullied woman to wife.

In an essay on "The Simple Art of Murder," [in *Atlantic Monthly* (1944)] Raymond Chandler refers to Robert Graves' and Alan Hodge's *The Long Week End,* a study of English life and manners after World War I which gives some attention to detective stories. Their observation is that mysteries do not reflect what is going on in the world, because only writers without vision or ability write mysteries, a kind of unreal fiction. This essay differs with that point of view.

A reading of Mrs. Rinehart's "crime stories" and research into her life and the publication history of her books, indicates that there are two views under which her mysteries may be examined: as craft or art, and as a record of social thought and behavior across some fifty years. As a literary craftsman, Mary Roberts Rinehart worked imaginative variations on "mystery formulas" that are partly stock and partly germane to her own work. She was not the first to use notes behind baseboards or re-papered walls, but she often thought to use an old roll of the original paper for the job. And, although it is hardly to her credit, she is generally recognized as the founder of the "Had-I-But-Known" (or HIBK) school. Under the aspect of an artist, she was, in her own words, "primarily interested in people and their motivations" [Breit], and at times—very irregularly—she does achieve finely drawn, absorbing characterizations. That of Rachel Innes is one.

However, instead of looking at aesthetic issues, this essay has dealt with Mrs. Rinehart's sensitivity to and portrayal of cultural shifts during her long career. In the mysteries the narrators often survey the world of a waning—or better, moribund—Victorian upper class, sometimes from within, sometimes from the viewpoint of the genteel poor, and sometimes through the eyes of the middle class. In an aura of nostalgia that ebbs and flows, one sees old fortunes dwindling through too many heirs, no heirs at all, or mere waste. One sees social refinements, the proprieties, being stubbornly maintained by one generation and glaringly ignored by its successor. The generation gap is never more strikingly evident or more sensitively depicted than in *The Breaking Point* where the old man looks to God and trusts and the young man acknowledges a vague Providence but insists on searching. In a succession of images generally so deftly executed that they complement rather than obscure a good story—and Mrs. Rinehart always thought of herself as a storyteller, not as a literary figure—we watch the quickening pace of the workaday world and leisure life bring in cigarettes to replace pipes and cigars, fast driving to replace a walk on a picnic, and fifteen minutes alone for a young couple instead of five (*The Case of Jennie Brice*).

Significantly, Mrs. Rinehart avoided a hard didactic line on any of the social issues. In 1908 she was *not* a young rebel advocating social upheaval. In 1934 she was *not* a middle-aged law giver. And in 1952 she was *not* an entrenched old woman railing aginst the encroachments of the young and the new. Rather, from the outset of her career Mrs. Rinehart manifested a feeling for both sides of the issue. Her detractors might say she simply knew what would sell to most people, but at the end of this research I would say she observed and recorded the topical with an objective sensibility. (pp. 154-68)

> *Arnold R. Hoffman, "Social History and the Crime Fiction of Mary Roberts Rinehart," in* New Dimensions in Popular Culture, *edited by Russell B. Nye, Bowling Green University Popular Press, 1972, pp. 153-71.*

Rinehart on the crime story:

I've never written a detective story in my life. I'm not primarily interested in clues. I'm primarily interested in people and their motivations. When the crime story began to be interested in people it began to grow up. My contribution was *The Circular Staircase,* which came out in 1908; it was supposed to have helped the crime story grow up.

Mary Roberts Rinehart, as quoted by Harvey Breit, in his "Talk With Mary Roberts Rinehart," in The New York Times Book Review, *February 3, 1952.*

Julian Symons   (essay date 1972)

[*An English novelist, poet, biographer, and critic, Symons is best known for his highly praised crime novels in which he is less concerned with presenting a baffling mystery than with exploring the state of society from a skeptical and ironic perspective. In the following excerpt, he criticizes Rinehart's mysteries as implausible and unrealistic.*]

[The stories of Mary Roberts Rinehart] were stories written to a pattern. All of them deal with crime, and the crime is almost always murder. There is a detective, but his activities are often less important than those of the staunch middle-aged spinster, plucky young widow, or marriageable girl who finds herself hearing strange noises in the night, being shut up in cupboards, overhearing odd and apparently sinister conversations, and eventually stumbling upon some clue that solves the mystery. Much of what happens in these stories occurs by chance, and the mystery is prolonged only by the obstinate refusal of the characters to reveal essential facts. Mrs. Rinehart's books in particular became those of the Had I But Known school, the absurdities of which were wittily summed up by Ogden Nash:

Sometimes it is the Had I But Known what grim
      secret lurked
behind the smiling exterior, I would never have
      set foot
within the door;

Sometimes the Had I But Known then what I
      know now, I could
have saved at least three lives by revealing to the
Inspector the conversation I heard through that
      fortuitous
hole in the floor. . . .

And when the killer is finally trapped into a confession by
some elaborate device of the Had I But Knowners some
hundred pages later than if they hadn't held their
knowledge aloof,

Why, they say, Why, Inspector, I knew all along
      it was he,
but I couldn't tell you, you would have laughed
      at me
unless I had absolute proof.

These are the first crime stories which have the air of being written specifically for maiden aunts, and they exploited a market which, with the spread of library borrowing, proved very profitable. From Rinehart's second book and first success, *The Circular Staircase* (1908), at the climax of which spinster Rachel Innes finds herself shut up with the murderer in a small secret room behind the great old chimney piece ("I knew he was creeping on me, inch by inch"), the formula of needless confusion and mock terror did not change. The settings became more varied, yet also more enclosed. As one commentator has said, "It does not really matter much to the world view which emerges whether the backdrop is New York City or Connecticut, a town or a country house, the stability and balance most usually associated, sentimentally at least, with an agrarian order are assumed." People in the books die, but this is not important because in relation to the real world none of them was ever alive. Nobody is ever doing any work, although suspects may be labeled solicitor, doctor, chauffeur.

Sometimes the confinement of the society in which violence takes place is carried to fantastic lengths. Rinehart went on writing until a year or two before her death, and *The Album* (1933) is typical of her later novels. It deals with five families living in Crescent Place, "a collection of fine old semi-country houses, each set in its own grounds," insulated from the city outside by an entrance gate marked *Private,* "so that we resemble nothing so much as five green-embattled fortresses." The action literally never moves outside the Crescent. Reporters and photographers cause no trouble after an initial visit, and make no attempt to gain access to the houses, although four murders are committed, the first with an axe and the last involving a headless trunk. Within this totally closed circle, none of the characters works, although one apparently did, since we are told that "he had given up even the pretence of business since the depression, and spent a good bit of time tinkering with his car in the garage." Even such tinkering is unusual, for there are cooks, a gardener, a chauffeur, various helpers. These people really have nothing to do, apart from being suspected of murder. The murderer, naturally, is one of them. Her actions, when her identity is revealed, are outrageously unlikely. (pp. 96-8)

> *Julian Symons, "The Rise of the Novel," in his* Mortal Consequences: A History—From the Detective Story to the Crime Novel, *Harper & Row, Publishers, 1972, pp. 91-9.*

Jan Cohn (essay date 1977)

[*An American educator and critic, Cohn is the author of* Improbable Fiction: The Life of Mary Roberts Rinehart *(1980). In the following essay, she speculates on the elements of character and plot which contributed to the popularity of Rinehart's romance novels.*]

During her long lifetime, Mary Roberts Rinehart published nearly seventy volumes of fiction and essays. Her writing attracted and maintained a large and loyal audience for half a century. Her first novel, **The Circular Staircase,** was published in 1908 and has become an all-time best-seller. Between 1909 and 1936, eleven of her books made the best-seller list, more than those of any other American novelist. By 1967, a decade after her death, the paper-back sales of Rinehart's books had passed the fifteen million mark, and currently Dell continues to reissue her novels in paper.

Rinehart is probably best remembered as a writer of mystery novels; of her nearly three dozen full-length works of fiction, twenty are mysteries. However, in her own time, Rinehart was at least as well regarded for her romances as for her crime novels. Of her eleven best sellers, eight were romances. Like the mysteries, the romances were serialized before publication, and serialized for remarkably high prices. In 1919, for example, *The Pictorial Review* paid $25,000 for **Dangerous Days,** and in 1935, in the middle of the Depression, *Good Housekeeping* bought the rights to **The Doctor** for $75,000. Subsequent to serialization, both became best sellers.

An examination of Rinehart's romances ought to lead the student of popular literature toward some understanding of the dynamics of popularity itself, but unfortunately the romance, as a popular form, has not received the kind of attention devoted to other popular genres—the dime novel, the western, the detective story—and the methodology developed for those popular genres is not particularly well-adapted to the romance. In general, the most important work done with these forms has been done in the area of classification, in the discovery of common elements among a considerable number of specific works. Thus, attention has been paid to the larger elements: the overall shape of plot, the more notable and recurrent character types and stereotypes, the broadcast moral and ethical statements and implications.

Content analysis in the interest of classification has proven valuable, certainly, and the consequent identification of patterns and formulas in popular literature has prepared us to deal more intelligently with the important question of audience appeal. John Cawelti's theory of formula [in "The Concept of Formula in the Study of Popular Literature," *Journal of Popular Culture* (1969)], for example, focuses on the culture for which popular materials are produced. For Cawelti, formulas represent "the way in which culture has embodied both mythical archetypes and its own preoccupations in narrative form," and the function of formula is to provide a culture with a "way of simultaneously entertaining itself and of creating an acceptable pattern of temporary escape from the serious restrictions and limitations of human life."

As useful as this theory of formula has been for highly conventionalized forms like the classic detective novel, it is less valuable for the study of the romance, where conventions play a less determinative role in shaping a particular work. Moreover, if formula does not dominate the romance as it dominates other popular forms, then it is arguable whether or not formula provides the same significant source of popular appeal in the romance that it provides in other popular forms. It is worth asking whether it is indeed formula, in the romance, that serves as the mechanism to permit the "temporary escape" from the realities of life. The idea of literature as an escape from human frustrations is at least as old as Freud, but a good deal more evidence is needed to determine what particular elements of a literary work encourage the reader's escape into fantasy. In attempting to analyze Mary Roberts Rinehart's romances, then, there are two distinct but interrelated problems: can a methodology be devised that is appropriate to the romance? and, can that methodology lead toward a clearer understanding of the dynamics of audience response, of the escape into fantasy that undoubtedly lies at the heart of popular appeal?

The relationship established between a popular writer and his audience might be compared to an unwritten contract, a set of guarantees. In those genres where formulas are most stringently adhered to—for example, the classic detective story—those guarantees are fairly pervasive, involving specific fictional elements such as character, plot, setting, as well as the more general and abstract elements of theme and moral values. The reader, sharing the formula, anticipates the guarantee. When the contract is broken ("Chinatown" is an important example), the reader experiences a shock, sometimes distressing, sometimes pleasant, but his trust has been betrayed. As a result, both entertainment and escape are inhibited and different kinds of emotional and intellectual responses elicited.

A writer like Rinehart, on the other hand, worked within much less stringent formulas of plot and character in her romances, but she also provided guarantees for her audience. Those guarantees, however, had relatively little to do with specifics of plot and a great deal to do with moral values. The reader is somehow assured that conventional moral laws will not be overturned and that the status quo will be reaffirmed; he is, therefore, able to escape "from the serious restrictions and limitations of human life" by undertaking vicariously those kinds of normally unacceptable adventures the novelist describes. Moreover, the closer a particular adventure is to the temptations experienced in real life—the less exotic the plot and setting of the novel—the more tightly must the contract be drawn, the more sure must the reader be of the moral world the author is offering to share. As a result, quasi-realistic popular forms like the domestic novel and the love story demand greater securities from the writer than do spy novels and gothic thrillers, for the temptations they offer and the temporary escape they provide come much closer to answering the repressed needs of the audience. But paradoxically, the formulas for love stories are not so clear nor so rigidly drawn as they are for more exotic genres. Lovers must meet and they must be parted; beyond that, a writer of romances is fairly free, for both happy and unhappy endings are permissible and plots are much freer of conventional elements than are plots of classic detective fiction.

The problem is, then, to discover how the contract is drawn up between writer and reader for those popular forms which are not so rigidly controlled by the conventions of formula. To some extent, the contract probably exists as a function of an author's reputation; for a new author, reviews and advertising help readers know just how far they will be morally protected. Still, in any popular piece of fiction the overriding moral responsibility of the writer must be demonstrated at the same time that the novel examines dangerous territory.

Just such a contract must have existed between Rinehart and her audience, a contract promising escape but simultaneously affirming the moral status quo. In order to explore how these guarantees were established, a fairly complex analysis is called for; the general identification of patterns is not adequate to the task. That is not to deny the existence of patterns in these novels, for Rinehart always worked within the large formal plan of the love story: developing a love affair and then strewing obstacles in the paths of the lovers. Moreover, Rinehart frequently selected the same major obstacle; her lovers are customarily kept apart not by considerations of class or money, nor by difficult parents, but by the previous engagement or marriage of one or both of the lovers. While the pattern remains fairly constant throughout the half-century of Rinehart's career, the novels demonstrate movement in another way—by an increasingly realistic treatment of the conflict between love and marriage. In developing and emphasizing thematic material at odds with the popular morality of the early twentieth century, Rinehart provides moral compensations and moral compromises for her readers. Love may triumph but moral values remain absolutely intact.

Rinehart's earliest romances, however, are not so bold. *The Street of the Seven Stars,* 1914, is innocent of the problems of marriage. The obstacles for the lovers are minimal; that is, neither Peter, studying to be a doctor, nor Harmony, a promising violinist, is married or engaged. They meet in Vienna and they are both desperately poor. Poverty, pride, and social prejudices provide conventional difficulties for the lovers and keep the plot moving, but the only real obstacle, and the last to be resolved, is Harmony's professional future. Despite Rinehart's own double career as wife-mother and writer, her young heroine must surrender her violin. Peter tells her that he is "jealous of

every one about you. It would have to be the music or me." At the very end of the novel, as Peter is packing to leave Vienna, Harmony rushes to him, asserting that "I shall have a career. Yours!"

After *The Street of the Seven Stars,* Rinehart's romances begin to explore the tension created when her lovers are not free. At first, a previous engagement serves as the major obstacle. In *"K",* 1915, and *The Amazing Interlude,* 1917, the young female protagonists are engaged, and engaged to the wrong men. Although Sidney and Sara Lee are similar types in their relative poverty, their desire for work, and their armor-like innocence, the fiances are not type-cast. In *"K,"* he is Doctor Max, a pretentious surgeon who is carrying on an affair with another woman. In *The Amazing Interlude,* Harvey suffers from no moral blemishes, but he is dull and unimaginative, domineering and over-protective. Rinehart's heroines extricate themselves from their unsatisfactory commitments, but extrication is not accomplished without difficulty. Engagement may not be so final as marriage, but as a social contract it serves a useful representative purpose, suggesting the indissoluble bond of marriage while cautiously avoiding the dangerous subjects of divorce and adultery.

By 1921 Rinehart was prepared to deal with lovers who are already married. *Dangerous Days* represents a fairly bold departure for a popular woman novelist, and Rinehart signals her awareness of that departure, and her innate caution, by allowing to a man rather than a woman the central role in the book. Clay Spencer, a forty-five year old mill owner, is both older and richer than earlier lovers in Rinehart's novels, and he chafes under the restraints of marriage. He has justification for his dissatisfaction, for his wife, Natalie, belongs to the only character-type for whom Rinehart's tolerant imagination can find no sympathy: wealthy, lazy, society wives, "Women of futile lives." Although Clay is guarded all about with the author's rationalizations for his failed marriage, Rinehart's problems are not altogether solved. If it is less dangerous for male characters than for female to feel adulterous stirrings, there is still a dilemma about creating a female character for Clay to love, one who will not offend the moral sensibilities of her audience. A relationship between an unmarried girl and a married man would be out of the question. So married she must be, and Rinehart creates Audrey Valentine, a woman whose husband deserts her in the early pages of the novel and, for good measure, dies later on as a flyer in the war.

This particular configuration of the male protagonist, his indolent and futile wife, and the other woman—badly married and finally widowed—is repeated in Rinehart's one other novel in which lovers are finally freed from unsatisfactory marriages and united with one another. *The Doctor,* 1936, shares other elements with *Dangerous Days.* The union of the lovers is accomplished only after each has suffered loneliness and hopelessness for a good number of years and has gone beyond that suffering to the duty and the solace of work. Furthermore, the lovers must prove themselves capable "women of futile lives." Although Clay is guarded all about with the legal spouses. There is something of the medieval trial-by-ordeal in the sexual renunciation of the sympathetic characters in both novels. Conversely, the frivolous wives in both books indulge in their own perhaps more carnal and certainly more public affairs, eventually leaving and finally divorcing their husbands. Justifications are heaped up in both novels, absolving these errant husbands of any guilt.

The complex conditions established for extramarital romance in *Dangerous Days* and *The Doctor* reflect the caution and tact with which Rinehart handles the issue of failed marriage. Such marriages were tragedies, she believed; as she says in *Dangerous Days,* "Clayton Spencer faced the life tragedy of the man in his prime, still strong and lusty with life, with the deeper passions of the deepening years, who has outgrown and outloved the woman he married." But the system of morality that defended the home and militated against divorce and adultery was too powerful to offend. Rinehart solved the problem only through the development of a stringent set of conditions, and only for the male protagonist. Even then, the husband must be divorced by the willful wife; the woman he loves must be widowed.

How carefully Rinehart established these conditions can be seen best by comparison to those novels in which she dealt with the story of the unhappy wife. In 1929 Rinehart published *This Strange Adventure.* The protagonist is female and a good case could be made for seeing this novel as the obverse of *Dangerous Days,* as Audrey's story rather than Clay's. But a crucial difference in plotting occurs in this novel: we are given not only the dramatic years of a character's life, but her whole history from childhood. Missie is presented first as a child and we follow her through the loss of her parents, her life with her grandmother, and her years of enduring a more-or-less forced marriage. As *The Doctor* resembles *Dangerous Days* in structure, plot, and theme, so, a very late romance, *A Light in the Window,* 1948, echoes the patterning of *This Strange Adventure.* Decades are covered rather than years, and the central character, a woman, must learn the same lessons that Missie had learned twenty years earlier.

This Strange Adventure is Rinehart's boldest exploration of marriage and, it seems to me, her most convincing novel. At the same time, the very boldness in the depiction of a woman's experience in marriage calls for more measures of caution, even of repression, than had *Dangerous Days.* No conventional happy ending is awarded the unhappy married woman. The story of Missie's marriage falls into two parts that might be called Temptation and Repentance. Missie is tempted by Kirby, a young engineer with whom she falls in love. Meanwhile her marriage to Wesley—sensual, hard-drinking, unfaithful—grows more intolerable. It is not only the character of her husband, however, but marriage itself that chafes: "She had not enough money. She was his chattel, his creature." In a crucial scene, Wesley tries to embrace Missie, "A furious hatred began to shake her" and she strikes him with a poker, leaving him for dead. Eventually she takes the train to New York and Kirby, but one chaste night in a hotel is all she can manage. Repentance begins: she returns home humbled, prepared to spend the rest of her life under her husband's brutal domination. Her submission is encouraged by her motherhood, for she fears to lose her young son, but it is also the submission required as punishment for the crime she has been guilty of—not attempted murder, but the abortive flight to freedom.

Rinehart will not allow Missie the same resolution she permits Clay Spencer, but she does soften her judgement somewhat. Missie learns the woman's lesson: there is a kind of happiness to be found in marriage, a domestic devotion, a quiet affection, a shared life. These discoveries are made in the months when Wesley is dying, providing a kind of tranquil half-light to alleviate some of the misery of Missie's life. Once widowed, Missie has no more desire to find love; although Kirby has never married, they will remain only old friends who meet occasionally. The romances centered on the life of a married man end in eventual triumph; those concerned with the life of a married woman provide no more than the tranquility of resignation.

There is much that I have omitted in my brief analyses of these romances: minor characters, involved sub-plots, rich social and political detail; however, even so brief a consideration of the essential love story in each novel indicates how carefully Rinehart worked to provide her readers with vicarious sexual freedom and stern moral resolution. The reader is drawn to share experiences he or she has dimly desired, to participate in awful freedoms. But at the same time, the reader is shown the high price of that freedom, for even in *Dangerous Days* and *The Doctor,* where the lovers are finally united, the cost in suffering has been very high—has been, perhaps, exorbitant.

As Rinehart's carrot-and-stick approach to the issue of love and marriage suggests, the contract between the popular writer and the audience must depend on the writer's intuitive grasp of the desires and fears of the audience, perhaps because the writer shares these desires and fears. How important a part the hidden frustrations and wishes of the audience play in their response to popular fiction can only be guessed, and only theoretically can we explore the way in which the fantasy element of fiction satisfies the fantasy needs of individual readers. But a useful theory has been provided by the Freudian critic, Norman Holland, in *The Dynamics of Literary Response.* According to Holland, a reader's response to fiction involves a continuum of functions from conscious to unconscious. In the middle of the continuum is the response that Holland calls "affect," the reader's perception of the text itself. At the highest level, one of conscious intellection, the reader discovers the central meaning of the text and its thematic organization. At the deepest level, the reader absorbs—or "introjects"—the central fantasy of the text and, by analogy, creates his own personal, associated fantasies. It is at this level that what we more traditionally call "escape" or "vicarious experience" is allowed for. Theoretically, conscious and unconscious processes can operate with equal energy; however, in Holland's view, the amount of energy consumed by each process varies according to the kind of work we are reading. A "Masterpiece" demands considerable intellection, leaving little energy for unconscious processes. An "Entertainment," on the other hand, demands little intellection and provides a great deal of energy for fantasizing.

Elitist as this distinction may appear, it is worth considering in terms of formula and in terms of the configurations of Rinehart's romances. Heavily formulaic fiction—again let us take the classic detective novel—certainly frees the mental energies of the reader from a considerable number of tasks. The nearly ritualized elements of plot, including the ultimate success of the hero-detective and the final defeat of the criminal, as well as the guaranteed restoration of the status quo, demand little energy at the level of conscious intellection. Rinehart's fiction, on the other hand, does not provide so many assurances for the reader; the formulas are not so deep nor so pervasive.

Deep and pervasive are, however, the moral formulas, the sentimental laws of Rinehart's fiction. The romances, taken as a whole, provide a compendium of sentimental laws. Good women will be made to suffer and their reward will be hard-won, tranquil contentment. Good men *may* have to suffer, but that suffering will win them happiness. Although the laws of society may sometimes appear hard, they are, in fact, necessary and even benevolent. And while rewards may seem to be few and punishments heavy, in the final analysis they are distributed justly. The major lesson of life is that love is the greatest gift, but that work is the only good on which one may absolutely depend. Assured of Rinehart's support of these sentimental laws, the reader is free to fantasize. In other words, it is not the intellectual faculties that are excused from labor in reading a Rinehart novel, but the moral faculties. Or, in more acceptable psycho-analytic language, the censor relaxes its surveillance over the unconscious.

Holland's theory of literary response differentiates popular from elite fiction, "Entertainments" from "Masterpieces," in terms of the varying amount of energy demanded of the higher intellectual functions. It may be possible, however, to make this discrimination more explicit in terms of the reader-writer contract and the moral guarantees it carries. The sentimental laws shared by Rinehart and her audience are supported by her fiction. Unlike elite fiction, these novels work without irony; they do not unmask society in the interest of proving the simultaneous power and venality of society's laws. The absence of irony has two effects. In the first place, it enforces the contract; there are no radical, anti-social implications to undercut the reader's confidence. Secondly, the absence of irony is one element among several that accounts for the clarity, even the simplicity, of the text, and that clarity may itself play a part in eliciting or encouraging the reader's response.

Holland, in distinguishing the reader's response to elite literature from the response to popular literature, considers the question in terms of the expenditure of intellectual energy. While Holland is primarily concerned with the energy consumed at the highest level of intellection, it seems useful to consider as well the energy demanded at the middle level, what Holland calls "affect," the level of the perception of the text. Irony complicates a text, as do strained syntax, an arcane vocabulary, and complex metaphoric language. Rinehart's text, in the limited sense of the language itself, demands little energy from the reader. Her language never calls attention to itself; it is transparent, a medium to carry the story. The same point can be made for Rinehart's text in the larger sense, text as plot, character, setting, and structure. Rinehart's characters are not psychologically puzzling; they carry no moral ambiguity. The relation of plot to character, and of both to setting and theme, is without irony. The novels, to put it simply, say what they mean and mean what they say. To carry Holland's argument, then, to the level of affect, is to discover that Rinehart's texts are designed so as to make relatively few demands on the reader and, therefore, to leave unused a good deal of mental energy, energy which can be expended in the creation of fantasies analogous to the central fantasy of the novel.

A theory of the dynamics of reader-response to different kinds of fiction, from the most inventive to the most conventional, is an important step toward the discovery of useful and appropriate methods for the analysis of popular fiction. If, as I have argued, Rinehart's readers were free to create fantasies that provided them with a much-needed escape from the limitations and frustrations of their lives, and if that freedom to fantasize was indeed the result of the contract Rinehart offered, a contract guaranteeing the affirmation of popular morality, then our methods must be directed at discovering the configurations within Rinehart's novels that underwrote that guarantee.

I use the term configuration to discriminate what I have described in Rinehart's novels from larger patterns of more pervasive formulas. A configuration is made up of elements of plot and character as these elements appear, and reappear, in conjunction with one another. For example, the novel of the unhappy wife is a configuration of several character-types: the good wife, the weak and unfaithful husband, the hard-working and unmarried lover, and of a number of plot elements: the introduction of the protagonist as a child, a marriage entered into without enthusiasm, the slow realization of sexual distress, an awakening distrust of the marriage state itself, one abortive attempt at freedom, the death of the husband. The novel of the unhappy husband has different character types and different elements of plot. The indolent wife, the hard-working husband, the effete lover, the abandoned woman appear in a configuration that includes the denial of sexual fulfillment, long-term separation, financial hardship for one of the lovers, the final freeing of the male by divorce and the female by the death of her husband. Although each of these configurations is employed within the same general pattern of the love-story and for the same general theme of love and marriage, it is the configuration, not the pattern or the theme, that determines the moral solution in each novel.

The contract between writer and reader is expressed, I think, in these configurations, for they carry the moral code of the culture. And it is in the shared moral code that the reader finds not only the guarantees supporting the sentimental laws in which he believes but also the overriding sense of typicality, universal applicability that Rinehart's romances provide. For it is not, finally, the daring and unique act that Rinehart underlines for her reader, not Missie attacking her husband with the poker, but Missie assessing her life, finding it composed of "all the usual elements, the boyhood sweetheart, the unfaithful husband, the kind lover." That life story, as Rinehart tells us, was "a triumph of the ordinary." (pp. 581-89)

Jan Cohn, "The Romances of Mary Roberts Rinehart: Some Problems in the Study of Popular Culture," in Journal of Popular Culture, Vol. XI, No. 3, Winter, 1977, pp. 581-90.

Rinehart on writing:

I have a strong visual memory that is not unusual, but certainly is useful. I have no memory at all for names, remember only briefly what people say, but retain always a sharp image of how they looked, what they wore, what gestures they used, and what their surroundings were—to the last detail. At my desk writing a scene, the externals of action all are before me and I need simply to select what details to put down. Of course, finding the reason for putting them down, the point, is not simple at all.

Mary Roberts Rinehart, as quoted by Robert van Gelder, in his "An Interview with Mary Roberts Rinehart," in The New York Times Book Review, December 15, 1940.

Kathi L. Maio   (essay date 1983)

[*In the following excerpt, Maio discusses the characteristics of the Had-I-But-Known formula and identifies Rinehart as its principal innovator.*]

It was Ogden Nash who gave Had-I-But-Known its name. In a poem entitled "Don't Guess, Let Me Tell You," he proclaimed: "Personally, I don't care whether a detective-story writer was educated in night school or day school. / So long as he doesn't belong to the H.I.B.K. school" [*The Art of the Mystery Story*, edited by Howard Haycraft, 1946]. Nash's use of a male pronoun to describe the authors of such tales is nothing more than a case of semantic sexism, for HIBK has had, from its very beginnings, a distinctly female character. Needless to say, Nash was not alone in his disdain. Howard Haycraft once called HIBK "a school of mystery writing about which the less said the more chivalrous." Julian Symons dismissed HIBK [in his *Mortal Consequences*, 1972] as "the first crime stories which have the air of being written specifically for maiden aunts."

Now that chivalry is dead, now that one does not have to be apologetic for being a maiden aunt, it seems appropriate that we reexamine the "feminine" detective novel, HIBK, a detective fiction formula that celebrates its roots, Gothic romance.

The ties between Gothic and detective fiction are strong and undeniable. Even male critics will acknowledge that the official "father" of detective fiction, Edgar Allan Poe, was also a master of Gothic horror. Also, as Devendra Varma has pointed out [in his *The Gothic Flame*], "the ingenuity of plotting, characterization and background, the perennially fascinating situation of pursuit, coupled with the chief detective ware of 'suspense' are the gift of Gothic romance."

HIBK is quite obviously a Gothic-detective hybrid, and it has inherited characteristics of both parents. Like the Gothic, HIBK is an exercise in terror which is largely domestic terror and which focuses on a woman and her immediate ménage. An HIBK, like the Gothic, is unabashedly a thriller. While the detective story claims to be an intellectual exercise, the HIBK story openly appeals to our emotional sensibilities of sympathy, outrage, horror—and triumph. But HIBK, as a modern formula, employs a modern setting. Removing the Gothic from the crumbling castle and replanting it in a recognizable modern environment makes the HIBK-Gothic a less detached, more ominous, journey into fear. Mabel Seeley reported [in *Twentieth Century Authors: First Supplement*] that if she had a "premise, it was that terror would be more terrible, horror more horrible, when visited on people the reader would feel were real in places he [sic] would recognize as real."

HIBK is also a form of detective story. Like detective fiction, HIBK is, almost always, a "murder mystery" wherein the mystery is finally solved without recourse to the supernatural. A combined force of professional and amateur detectives solves the mystery, and captures or stops the murderer. But HIBK is unlike the "pure puzzle" detective story in many ways. The pure puzzle detective story generally features a single, nicely delineated murder for its primary mastermind sleuth to ponder—and eventually solve through the exercise of sparkling, detached logic. One feels secure that the hero-sleuth has everything firmly under control. The same is not true of HIBK. Here, there is no sense of security—no sense that a heroic male figure has things under control. In an HIBK novel, no one ever says "It's elementary, my dear Watson," because it never is. The situation is always complicated with sub-plots and emotional cross-currents. Events occur in a rapid and confounding chain reaction. Often there are multiple murders. Seldom is there a professional detective, and when there is, he is never a mastermind. Law and male authority figures are clearly not the heroes in HIBK.

Instead, the hero is a woman who tells her own story. Instead of starting from the murder and reconstructing to one, final, pat solution (as with most detective stories), she takes us back to the beginning—to *her* beginning with the story—and moves forward from there. When we begin an HIBK novel, the "solution" has already been found. In HIBK, the end is the beginning in one woman's voyage toward understanding that period in her life when "the world turn[ed] over, revealing its underside" [Mabel Seeley, *The Beckoning Door*].

HIBK has been attacked as unrealistic and "romanticized" in comparison with pure detective fiction. But is it really? When danger, violence, and death enter the lives of humans, does a dapper detective usually sweep in, solve the mystery, and resolve the situation so that all those involved (save the murderer and the victims) skip blithely into the sunset, never giving the matter another thought? Or, are we instead threatened to our very existence by violence and death until it comes back to us in nightmares and until we rethink during our waking hours all the many moments that lead to death and violence, saying to ourselves "If only I had:"

> For the seeds of the mystery lay either in happenings which seemed at the time to bear no relationship to each other . . . or else in very small things, in incidents which might easily have meant nothing at all; incidents which, at the time, I considered myself silly for noting and wondering over.

[Mabel Seeley, *The Listening House*]

Mary Roberts Rinehart is the "mother" of HIBK. Although there was a large body of first-person-female narrative mystery fiction before Rinehart (Anna Katharine Green's "Amelia Butterworth" novels are charming examples), it is Rinehart who clearly developed the narrative technique into a formula that went beyond pure detection. Rinehart's first nonserial novel, *The Circular Staircase* (1908), is the cornerstone work of HIBK. The narrator, spinster Rachel Innes, rents a summer country house called Sunnyside and is soon embroiled in a plot of multiple murder (five die) and general mayhem. She is clearly an innocent bystander to the original plot. But soon the reputations of her niece and nephew, and her own safety, are threatened. For a while she waits for the police to resolve things, but she soon finds their inaction "deadly," and the situation increasingly dangerous. In self-defense she becomes a detective, ferreting clues and suppressing those that implicate her household.

The official sleuth, Mr. Jamieson, his band of detectives, and the confused innocents involved all stumble at cross-purposes through a plot that becomes more deadly and dangerous with every moment. Miss Innes makes most of the key discoveries because she is not plagued by the need for "logical" (linear) thinking like the classic male sleuth. She does not expect human behavior to be a rational process. She does not expect physical evidence to tell the whole story. Curiosity and leaps of insight stand her in good stead. She tells us:

> Halsey always says: "Trust a woman to add two and two together and make six." To which I retort that if two and two plus *x* make six, then to discover the unknown quantity is the simplest thing in the world. That a household of detectives missed it entirely was because they were busy trying to prove that two and two makes four.

Rinehart would later freely admit [in *My Story: A New Edition and Seventeen New Years*] that *"The Circular Staircase* was intended to be a semi-satire on the usual pompous self-important crime stories."

The Circular Staircase was followed by many more Rinehart mysteries, and almost all are within the HIBK formula. Rinehart was masterful in the use of the older woman as spinster-heroine and narrator. While these women are sharp, fiercely independent, and skeptical about men, they often help foster the obligatory romance by playing fairy-godmother-as-vindicating-sleuth for one or more sets of young lovers. Other mysteries feature younger (but still

mature) women as central figures. In *The Wall* (1938) and *The Great Mistake* (1940), young women are actively brave in working to rid their households of danger. They are rewarded with romance and a happy ending. But theirs is a happy ending tempered by the need to look back, to reevaluate, and even to regret the past.

Rinehart, unlike most of her successors, made frequent small concessions to the supernatural demands of the Gothic. An example is her use of omens. In *The Case of Jennie Brice* (1913), the widow-narrator, Mrs. Pitman, finds that a dead kitten has floated into her flooded rooming house—a sure omen of misfortune. In *The Wall*, a servant observes a flock of crows overhead and predicts "bad luck"—which turns out to be the understatement of the year. In the same book, the mysterious ringing of certain bells by a "ghost" is never fully explained.

Rinehart was the innovator, and she was followed by many other HIBK practitioners. (pp. 82-5)

> Kathi L. Maio, "Had-I-But-Known: The Marriage of Gothic Terror and Detection," in The Female Gothic, *edited by Juliann E. Fleenor, Eden Press, 1983, pp. 82-90.*

James C. Dance   (essay date 1989)

[*In the following excerpt, Dance surveys Rinehart's mystery fiction and examines the characteristics of her female protagonists.*]

From about 1908, when *The Circular Staircase* was published in book form, until her death in 1958, Mary Roberts Rinehart reigned as the queen of American mystery writers (a title she professed to despise). Her 1909 book *The Man in Lower Ten* has the distinction of being the first American detective novel to appear on the annual bestseller list.

Critics have credited her, on the positive side, with the injection of humor and informality into the formal detective story, and, on the negative side, with the "Had I But Known" (HIBK) device in which the narrator, usually a heroine, teases the reader with intimations of events further along in the plot which could have been avoided except for her indiscreet behavior.

Both of these accomplishments can be seen, in retrospect, to rise out of her use, in most of her mystery novels and many of her short stories, of a fairly standard stock company of characters, chief among them the unmarried female whose domestic calm is shattered by the intrusion of murder.

An examination of MRR's spinster heroines produces the following discoveries:

1. MRR did not, with one possible exception, cast these women in the roles of major sleuths, thus observing Howard Haycraft's dictum that "women . . . do not make satisfactory principal detectives." They are, at the most, Watsons or assistants to various sheriffs or investigators; at the least, involved observers.

2. MRR's heroines, probably reflecting changes in Ameri-

can society and public taste, evolved from wealthy dowagers into less-well-to-do younger women.

3. MRR's technique of placing her heroines in dangerous situations to which they were not, by upbringing or experience, accustomed, provided more or less subtle learning stimuli in which their powers of intuition and observation were stretched and they tended to become, in the language of this decade, more liberated.

As early as 1907, when *The Circular Staircase* in its original serial form was being written, MRR created the character of an indomitable middle-aged spinster who is on the scene of the crime and assists in the detection. Of her first ten books, five were to feature such a heroine. After 1930, her novel-length mysteries continued to employ unmarried women in the major roles, but these were much younger—in their twenties and thirties—than the fifty-ish spinsters of her earlier works. MRR's autobiography *My Story* (1931, 1948) does not indicate why, just when she herself was reaching the age she had been attributing to her popular heroines, she should suddenly (in 1933's *The Album*) lop some 25 years off her narrator's age, and continue that pattern through the remainder of her full-length mystery fiction. One can surmise that, since most of those novels were first published serially in *The Saturday Evening Post,* she may have had editorial advice as to the kind of heroine to which her readers would most readily relate; but that is strictly conjecture.

It may be significant that MRR's early spinster heroines, self-described as "elderly" and "middle-aged," were actually, on closer reading, in their forties and fifties. The notion that people in this age span were "old," and that it was unusual, or eccentric, or humorous, for them to involve themselves in crimes and other adventures, quickly became a literary convention. But the speed with which the stereotype of "old" was changing is suggested by Agatha Christie's decision, in 1930, to make Miss Marple 74 years old in order to achieve the effect.

In addition to the reverse aging of her heroines, there was a progressive decline in their fortunes. From *The Circular Staircase* through *The Door* (1930), MRR's spinsters were, with one exception, depicted as women of wealth and social position. The modern reader gets an unintended chuckle when Elizabeth Bell, narrator of *The Door,* writes, "I live alone in the usual sense of the word," and then goes on to introduce her secretary, butler, cook, chauffeur, housemaid, laundress, and gardener.

The exception is the narrator of *The Case of Jennie Brice* (1931), who is not only a widow, breaking her out of the otherwise invariable spinster mold, but also an impoverished boarding-house keeper.

The families who inhabit The Crescent, locale of *The Album,* however, begin to show the inroads of the Depression. By the time of *The Wall* (1938), the young heroine is hard-pressed to maintain both the town house and her family's traditional summer home on "the island," as well as give employment to her elderly butler, cook, and maid. By 1940's *The Great Mistake,* she is so bad off as to have to seek work. The family in MRR's 1945 book *The Yellow Room* has to cope not only with a diminished fortune but

also with the deprivations of World War II—rationing, no gas, no telephone, no male servants. The heroine of *The Swimming Pool* (1952, MRR's last full-length mystery novel) has given up the town house and is living in the country house, managing by augmenting her brother's income as an attorney with her earnings as a writer.

Before we look in more detail at these ladies, however, let us try to clear up a quibble concerning MRR's best-known spinster character, Letitia Carberry—"Tish." This strong-minded maiden lady and her two companions, Lizzie and Aggie, apparently had drunk of the fountain of middle-age, remaining in their fifties from 1910 till 1955. Barzun and Taylor, in their monumental *A Catalogue of Crime* (1971), dismiss this trio with the statement, "The Tish stories are not detection and rely on feminine appeal." For the bulk of the stories, this may be true, but it overlooks the first Tish novelette, the title piece in *The Amazing Adventures of Letitia Carberry* (1911). Tish is convalescing in a hospital where a dead body is stolen from the morgue, a doctor is pushed through a skylight, and something ape-like and powerful menaces Aggie and kills a bunch of laboratory animals. If these circumstances are not mysterious, and if Tish's obstinate search for the explanation is not detection, then our definition is much less elastic than we have been led to believe.

Tish, Lizzie, and Aggie are comic exaggerations of the stock spinster character whom MRR used with such success in her early mysteries. All of them, each in her own way, battled the stereotype even as they perpetuated it.

Miss Rachel Innes is the narrator of *The Circular Staircase,* MRR's first and most consistently popular mystery novel, published in book form in 1908. (See *My Story* for the account of how her early magazine serials were converted into books.) Apparently in her late forties or early fifties, Miss Innes is a well-off single woman, aunt and surrogate parent to Gertrude and Halsey, a niece and nephew in their early twenties. Dreading a hot summer in the city, she snaps up a rental bargain in a palatial country estate, Sunnyside, so remote from civilization that all her servants except her talkative maid, Liddy, leave after one night. Over several suspenseful days, Sunnyside's real owner, a bank president whose institution is in trouble, suddenly dies out West; his ne'er-do-well son is found shot dead at the foot of the circular staircase; Gertrude's boyfriend, the bank cashier, disappears, and Halsey's girlfriend, the bank president's stepdaughter, appears; and certain clues suggest the presence in the house of a secret room where the embezzled bank funds may be cached.

Miss Innes finds herself assisting the detective, Mr. Jamieson, even to the extent of participating in an exhumation. After pursuing both red herrings and solid leads, she manages to get trapped in the secret room behind the mantel with the criminal.

Rachel Innes moves a long way toward liberation in the course of this story. She develops a closer relationship with her niece and nephew and countenances their love affairs. Her rapport with the detective is close and might, in a later book, have ripened into a middle-aged romance; but, for the spinster of this period, that was unacceptable.

She learns to look beneath the façades presented by the suspects, from society matrons to servants. Ultimately, she discovers that her former placid way of life bores her and, as the book ends, is planning to rent another summer home—"and I don't care if it has a Circular Staircase."

The Circular Staircase underwent a metamorphosis into *The Bat,* first a stage play co-authored with Avery Hopwood in 1920 and thence into a novel under MRR's name (but reputedly ghostwritten), published in 1926. Rachel Innes becomes Cornelia Van Gorder; the nephew is eliminated, the niece becomes Dale Ogden; Liddy becomes Lizzie, etc. The rented summer home is the same, but the circular staircase (except when some very ambitious stage designer opts otherwise) is reduced to the bottom steps of a plain back stair. Joining in the search for the embezzled money are a mysterious master criminal, the Bat, and a determined detective, Anderson. Miss Cornelia is portrayed as an older woman than was Rachel Innes, and she is not the narrator of the novelization, which is told in the third person. She is bored by domestic tranquility, takes up pistol shooting, follows newspaper stories of the Bat avidly and wishes she were a man so that she could take part in the sleuthing. At the climax, she effects the Bat's capture by bravely telling "The first lie of an otherwise blameless life."

To return to the chronology, MMR's next heroine-narrator was featured in *The Case of Jennie Brice* (1913). Mrs. Bess Pitman is in her early forties but looks older because of the hardships she has endured since running away from home as a teenager to marry Mr. Pitman. She has never been reconciled with her well-to-do family, but in the course of this mystery she meets and befriends her young niece. Mrs. Pitman runs a boarding house near the Pittsburgh theatre district. Located on the riverbank, it is annually flooded, and the disappearance of her roomer, actress Jennie Brice, occurs during such a flood. Suspicious clues—a bloodstained knife, a missing clock, an overheard conversation, a crumpled note—persuade Mrs. Pitman and her friend Mr. Holcombe that the story which the missing woman's husband tells is not true and that he has in fact murdered her. They confide in a reporter and eventually convince the police to investigate. There is never much doubt that Mrs. Pitman's suspicions are correct.

Bess Pitman is a strong, independent character, used to surviving in a rough world. She concludes her narrative by telling how she has continued to run her boarding house since the murder, but that Mr. Holcombe has asked her to marry him and she is seriously contemplating accepting his proposal and revealing her real identity to her sister and niece.

Mrs. Pitman seems less stereotyped than, and well differentiated from, MRR's other narrators of this period. Her often self-deprecating humor is a welcome touch, and her refusal to solicit sympathy for her failed marriage and her estrangement from her family marks her strength of character. While her story is not unsuspenseful, and the solution to the crime not uninventive, the weakness of the "whodunit" puzzle (compared with, say, *The Door*) keeps it from registering as strongly with the reader.

Sight Unseen and *The Confession,* two novelettes, were published together in book form in 1921 after magazine publication in, respectively, 1916 and 1917. MRR wrote that she based *The Confession,* the one with a spinster narrator, on a true story and that she possessed the handwritten slip of paper described by the title. Her middle-aged heroine, accompanied by her elderly, loquacious maid, rents a summer home and is repeatedly bothered by a feeling of unease in the vicinity of the hall telephone, heightened by a series of midnight phone calls from a caller who never speaks. In spite of locals who seek to prevent her finding out anything, she learns of an undiscovered murder but, considering the circumstances, joins the conspiracy to protect the murderer. MRR used her standard devices but failed to make anything memorable out of this situation.

Sight Unseen, the companion piece, may be considered a trial balloon for her longer, better novel of the occult, *The Red Lamp,* published in 1925.

In 1930, MRR's sons had formed the publishing company of Farrar & Rinehart, and for their first list she wrote what many consider her best mystery novel, *The Door.* Elizabeth Bell harks back to Rachel Innes: a middle-aged spinster with a niece and nephew often in residence. This wealthy family retains its own professional nurse, who circulates among the various households—chiefly those of Miss Bell, her sister Laura (mother and stepmother of the niece and nephew), and her cousin Jim. It is the nurse who is savagely murdered. Subsequently, Laura's husband is found dead, and cousin Jim is accused of both murders. Three more deaths are attributable to the killer, whose name MRR manages to conceal until the next to last sentence on the last page. This makes for excellent suspense, but it also makes it absolutely necessary to re-read the book with the killer's identity in mind, in order to see how everything is so carefully worked out.

Miss Bell does less detecting and more straight narrating, since she has to be kept in the dark until the very end, agonizing as the people she thinks the most of come under suspicion. She assists the toothpick-chewing detective in hunting for clues, but less daringly. The mood of danger and fear is well maintained, and the hints to the culprit's identity are fairly presented. Given the last-page gimmick, it is understandable that Miss Bell reacts rather than acts and that her character changes little except to be affected by shock, apprehension, and surprise.

In 1932, Farrar & Rinehart published *Miss Pinkerton,* featuring MRR's only series character and only professional detective: Nurse Hilda Adams, nicknamed "Miss Pinkerton" by Inspector Patton after he recruits her to do undercover work for the police in various cases involving invalids or others logically needing nursing care. This case takes her to the decaying mansion of Miss Juliet Mitchell, an elderly recluse whose nephew has apparently committed suicide. His death is, of course, actually murder, and Miss Juliet herself is soon to become the second victim; another character is left unconscious in a garage with the motor running; and the nurse herself is nearly strangled and locked in an airless closet. Although she does not pick the real criminal from among the suspects until the Inspector tells her whom he has arrested, she contributes information and collects clues that prove valuable to the police investigation. She participates not without considerable soul searching, feeling that the trust a patient places in a nurse assumes something of the confidentiality of the doctor-patient relationship. Fortunately for her conscience, in this instance she can innocently report her observations and leave the drawing of inferences to the Inspector.

Miss Pinkerton, fairly short as novels go, later was reprinted as the title story in a 1959 collection which also included two shorter stories, **"The Buckled Bag"** (1914), Nurse Adams's first case, nursing a wealthy woman whose socialite daughter vanishes and then turns up again with a questionable explanation of having been kidnapped; and **"Locked Doors"** (also 1914), caring for two small boys in a mysteriously barricaded house. The collection also contains the short novel *Haunted Lady* (1942), a locked-room murder case which, for once, "Miss Pinkerton" solves in advance of the Inspector.

In **"The Buckled Bag,"** Hilda gives her age as 29. In *Haunted Lady,* she is said to be 38, with "slightly graying" hair. She never reconciles herself to the contradictory demands made upon her by her dual professions and struggles with her conscience on every case, most notably *Haunted Lady.*

A fifth Miss Pinkerton story, **"The Secret,"** is one of three novelettes collected in 1950 in *The Episode of the Wandering Knife.*

In 1933, MRR produced *The Album,* with its gallery of eccentrics—one might say grotesques—unmatched in any other of her novels, and her youngest heroine-narrator to date. Louisa Hall is 28, the "baby" of the inhabitants of The Crescent, an elegant but declining block where five mansions front on a common lawn. One matriarch insists that all doors in her house be locked at all times, with herself the keeper of the keys. An elderly invalid keeps a fortune in a trunk under her bed. One husband and wife have not spoken to each other for years. Louisa's mother has worn deep mourning for her late husband for two decades. The newlywed Wellingtons, having recently moved into the house he inherited, with their wild parties and loud music, represent to the other inhabitants the worst of the Jazz Age. When the wealthy invalid is axed to death in her bed, and other murders follow, The Crescent is shaken to its foundations; but in the ensuing investigation Louisa loses many of her repressions and falls in love with Herbert Dean, a criminologist with sufficient eccentricities of his own.

The Album, besides being a thrilling if gory whodunit, is an excellent portrayal of a young woman suddenly forced to reassess all the values and priorities she has accepted unquestioningly all her life. Louisa blossoms visibly, and, although her behavior (including the cliché of walking alone into a dark, empty house where a trap has been set for the killer) tends to reinforce the criticisms of the HIBK name-callers, in context it seems logical (she is obeying her mother's command to retrieve her late father's portrait).

1938's *The Wall* was a high point in MRR's output. In the aftermath of the Depression, Marcia Lloyd must carefully husband her resources to be able to maintain two houses and keep a handful of elderly family retainers. The very day that she reopens Sunset House for the summer, her brother's amoral ex-wife and her maid show up and give every sign of entrenching themselves until Arthur makes a cash settlement, which will get Juliette out of some unspecified kind of trouble. Marcia co-operates with the bucolic local sheriff to solve Juliette's murder, but they are unable to prevent the deaths of her maid and the local doctor. A large roster of suspects (so large, in fact, that one begins to question how so many people with concealed connections to the dead woman should all turn up at the same time at the same place) is gradually whittled down. At the last, it is the sheriff's tenacity and not Marcia's intuition that identifies the murderer.

Orchidaceous Juliette dominates *The Wall* even after her death. She is MRR's best drawn "bitch" and served as a model for unsympathetic females that the author was to use in most of her subsequent mysteries. Marcia pales by comparison, and her reaction to the threatening events is chiefly anxiety. Her romance with the secretive artist Allen Pell seems perfunctory and immature; her interaction with the middle-aged countrified sheriff is much more interesting and well done.

In *The Great Mistake* (1940), orphaned Pat Abbott is thrust into the direct predicament of any MRR heroine: she is forced to take a secretarial course and get a job! But the job is as social secretary to Mrs. Maud Wainwright, the wealthy widow whose magnificent estate, The Cloisters, has always been an object of admiration to Pat. Generous and kindly, Mrs. Wainwright would seem to have no troubles; but then the unsuitable woman to whom her son has been married, and from whom he is separated, shows up—just as he and Pat have begun to respond to each other. In short order, both his mother and his wife are murdered, and he is the leading suspect. The "great mistake" is not, as the critical reader might suspect, Pat's habit of wandering around The Cloisters in the dark, but a secret from Mrs. Wainwright's past which someone is willing to kill to keep hidden.

The Great Mistake, though full of incident and detail, reads as if MRR's heart were not fully in it. She incorporates humor and suspense in adequate amounts, but echoes of earlier books ring in the reader's mind as the story unfolds, and the total effect is disappointing. (Could this be because MRR is forced to kill off an "elderly matron" character very much in the mold of her earlier heroines?)

Pat may be said to develop as a character in that she makes an effort to be independent, learns to type, learns to drive, learns to look beneath the façade that most of her friends and acquaintances are putting up; but she is rather faceless and forgettable.

Another less than wholehearted attempt is *The Episode of the Wandering Knife,* a 1948 novelette which MRR combined with two others for 1950 book publication. Some fairly inventive situations are pretty much wasted in the muddled story of the opportune murder of a wealthy scion's unfaithful wife on the night of the last big party before the family turn their estate over to be a wartime convalescent home. His discontented sister (who narrates) and his scatterbrained mother spend most of their time concealing evidence that points to his guilt. The gesture toward Judy Shepard's liberation is that she wants to give up the perks of a debutante to join the WACS.

One of the stories in this volume is **"The Secret,"** the fifth and final Miss Pinkerton mystery. Told in the third person, it is a wartime story with Hilda Adams forty-ish and unable to get into the Nursing Corps because of her age and a mild heart condition.

MRR returned to expected form in 1945's **The Yellow Room,** even though she made the awkward mistake of allowing an elevator to be operated in a house where the electricity was turned off (this in the serial version; for book publication, MRR hastily installed an independent power source for the elevator). Recycling some elements from **The Wall** and **The Wandering Knife,** MRR has her heroine, Carol Spencer, braving wartime shortages and hardships to open the family summer home in Bar Harbor. This is at her petulant mother's request, to welcome her brother, a decorated flyer, home on leave. The discovery of a woman's partly burned body in an upstairs linen closet adds a further discouraging element. The understaffed police chief enlists the help of Major Jerry Dane, who is recuperating from a war injury. The search for the identity of the dead woman brings Carol to painful discoveries about her idolized brother, her spoiled sister, and her Missing In Action fiancé.

Writing in the third person, MRR puts her cast of by now familiar characters through their paces with verve and ingenuity. Carol's romance with the major develops convincingly, and her relationship with the elderly father of her MIA fiancé, who refuses to believe his son is dead, is sensitively handled. Her mother is not as aggravating as the mother in **The Wandering Knife,** but then she is not given as much to do. The evocation of the wartime situation and its use to provide clues and motives are well done.

In 1952, six years before her death at the age of 82, MRR published her last full-length mystery novel, **The Swimming Pool.** It was also the only one of her mysteries not to be first serialized in a magazine. In this story, she again recycles plot elements she used in previous books. This time, the heroine, Lois Maynard, and her brother Phil have sold the city house and are living in the country house, The Birches, where, by combining his income as an attorney with hers as a mystery novelist, they can live economically and even keep on their elderly cook and hire an occasional maid. Suddenly—echoes of Juliette—their bitchy sister Judith shows up, bent on divorcing her wealthy, much older husband and seeking sanctuary. Two murders in the past and two in the present are eventually tied together and explained by the revelation of Judith's secret.

Lois does the narrating and shares the detection with a cop on leave whose reason for renting the gatekeeper's cottage and involving himself in the mystery is more than simple kindness. Lois is a strong enough character to prevent her glamorous sister from stealing all the scenes. The intro-

duction of a well-drawn teenaged nephew adds a fresh face to the MRR stock company.

Why were heroines not the narrators or point-of-view characters in MRR's other mysteries?

In **The Man in Lower Ten** (1909), her first book-length serial and second novel, the narrator is a young attorney. On a train trip, he inadvertently swaps berths with a stranger who is murdered during the night—in mistake from him?—and the train is involved in a catastrophic wreck. The hero, with a broken arm, is aided by a beautiful young woman who shows courage and resourcefulness in getting her injured companion and herself back to the city, during which time he falls in love with her. Alas, not only is she involved in the political scandal he is investigating but she is also engaged to the private detective with whom he works. Obviously, the heroine could not be the narrator of this mystery because it is her concealment of secrets from the hero which creates much of the suspense. The reader sees her through the hero's impassioned eyes, which credit her with being more brave and less pampered than she really is.

The Window at the White Cat (serialized in 1908 but not collected in book form until 1933) is also narrated by a love-smitten young attorney who finds his inamorata's father's just-murdered body in a roadhouse—the "White Cat" of the title. More interesting than the heroine are two of his other clients, "elderly" sisters who live together, one a martinet, one a doormat; they are also the aunts of the heroine. In a secondary plot, attorney Jack Knox puzzles over the meek sister's sudden, inexplicable disappearance from the Maitland mansion. Not only is the older sister called Miss Letitia but she has some of the headstrong, opinionated characteristics of MRR's Tish, without the latter's saving sense of humor.

MRR drew upon her investigation of a real crime, a series of murders on a yacht, for **The After House** (1914) and had the satisfaction of seeing the case reopened and the real murderer, whom she had correctly identified in her novel, caught. Her narrator is Ralph Leslie, a young medical student, working as a hand on a wealthy family's yacht, where he is attracted to the owner's sister-in-law. When three people are murdered, he is elected by the rest of the crew to take charge until they can get back to port, but once there he faces the accusation of having been the killer. Again, he is the logical viewpoint character, separated from the crew and the passengers, forced by his implication to seek the answer to the mystery. His heroine is not as conspicuous as the two previous ones, and it is clear that he is more highly motivated by his need to save his own skin than by his infatuation with her.

As MRR tells in her autobiography, she experienced numerous "supernatural" happenings during her life, happenings she could not explain but which failed to convince her of the presence of beings or forces from the afterlife. Some of these events are fictionalized incidentally in her books, but in **The Red Lamp** (1925) the occult occupies center stage. Somewhat anticipated by the novelette **Sight Unseen** in 1916, **The Red Lamp** tells of the experiences of a university professor (the narrator) and his family during the summer that they live in a cottage on the estate of his late uncle, with his niece's boyfriend occupying the boat-house and an elderly author and his male secretary renting the main house. The series of disappearances and murders that strikes the community seems somehow connected to a red-shaded lamp in the study of the mansion, which can be seen glowing through the windows when it has no business being turned on. While the niece and her boyfriend assist in the detecting, they are clones of similar characters in other MRR books; the unique heroine is the professor's wife, a quiet, self-contained lady who has ESP. Her attitude of refusal to admit her special abilities, and her reluctance to use them, are sensitively conveyed, as are the mixed emotions of her husband, who feels she could, if she would, contribute to the solution of the crimes. The mood of suspense created by facing "normal" people with both murder and the occult is powerfully maintained. It is possible that, if this story had been written ten years later, MRR might have considered using the niece as the narrator.

The Red Lamp was the last of MRR's long works with a male narrator until her late novelette *The Frightened Wife* was published as the title piece in a collection in 1953 after serialization. For this story, she disinterred the lawyer-protects-damsel-in-distress format of *The Man in Lower Ten* and *The Window at the White Cat.* The heroine, trapped in a loveless marriage by fear of reprisals to her infant son, can now afford to seek her freedom thanks to a small fortune she has earned as the secret author of a popular soap opera; then her husband is murdered and her child disappears.

In his well-known essay "The Rules of the Game," Howard Haycraft decreed: "In all fairness, women and boys do not make satisfactory principal detectives." One can picture Miss Marple, Miss Silver, Mrs. Pollifax, and their whole sorority simultaneously laying down their knitting and giving him a hard stare. MRR did not, with the possible exception of Nurse Adams, break this rule; her spinster heroines are relegated to secondary investigative functions. What she did was recognize the value of having an easily recognizable stereotype as the viewpoint character, and of facing that character with danger and mystery in order to force her or him to act out of type. It is the novelty of having an elderly maiden lady, or a complacent debutante, or a confirmed homebody mixed up with murder that attracts and keeps our interest in an MRR mystery.

And, although that novelty has worn thin with time and imitation, MRR's stories have not dated badly. One regrets the racial slurs, and younger readers may puzzle over details of early automotive and railroad transportation, but the crimes and the motives behind them are timeless.

Is it perhaps time to retire the character of the elderly spinster heroine? Have consciousness-raising arguments about "agism" given us a different picture of the physical appearance, health, and intellectual acuity of today's senior citizens? ZaSu Pitts and Edna Mae Oliver are not around to play these roles any more; instead, we have such admitted fifty-year-old actresses as Joan Collins and Barbara Eden. Even MRR at her peak would have been hard-pressed to intimidate those ladies with a house with a Circular Staircase! (pp. 29-37)

> *James C. Dance, "Spinsters in Jeopardy," in The Armchair Detective, Vol. 22, No. 1, Winter, 1989, pp. 28-37.*

FURTHER READING

Biography

Cohn, Jan. *Improbable Fiction: The Life of Mary Roberts Rinehart.* Pittsburgh: University of Pittsburgh Press, 1980, 293 p.
    Biography of Rinehart that also includes an extensive bibliography of her works.

Criticism

Davis, Robert H., ed. *Mary Roberts Rinehart: A Sketch of the Woman and Her Work.* New York: George H. Doran Co., 1924, 44 p.
    Contains two essays by Rinehart as well as essays by Robert H. Davis and Grant Overton.

Doran, George H. "Mary Roberts Rinehart." In his *Chronicles of Barabbas, 1884-1934: Further Chronicles and Comment, 1952,* pp. 187-94. New York: Rinehart & Co., 1952.
    Laudatory sketch of Rinehart and her family.

"Latest Fiction by Mrs. Rinehart, Mr. C. Morley, Sax Rohmer, and Others." *The New York Times Review of Books* 24 (6 July 1919): 357-58.
    Asserts that although the plot of *Dangerous Days* is unoriginal, Rinehart has created believable characters who command reader interest.

Overton, Grant. "The Vitality of Mary Roberts Rinehart." In his *When Winter Comes to Main Street,* pp. 102-17. New York: George H. Doran Co., 1922.
    Praises Rinehart's work for its variety and vitality which, he argues, "has its roots in a sympathetic feeling and a sanative humour."

———. "Mary Roberts Rinehart." In his *The Women Who Make Our Novels,* pp. 272-85. New York: Dodd, Mead & Co., 1928.

Examines Rinehart's development as a writer.

Additional coverage of Rinehart's life and career is contained in the following source published by Gale Research: *Contemporary Authors,* Vol. 108.

Edouard Rod

1857-1910

(Full name Louis-Edouard Rod) Swiss novelist, short story writer, critic, editor, and playwright.

INTRODUCTION

Rod is best known for his novels reflecting his theory of *Intuitivisme* (Intuitivism). In contrast with Naturalism, which emphasizes social forces and relationships, Intuitivism focuses on characters' psychology. Pessimistic in tone, Rod's works often depict sensitive characters who suffer as a result of moral conflicts.

Rod was born in 1857 in Nyon, Switzerland. The sense of fatalism evident in his work is often ascribed to his Calvinist upbringing and lonely childhood, during which he cared for his paralyzed mother. Rod attended universities in Lausanne, Bonn, and Berlin before moving to Paris in 1878. There Rod began working as a journalist, submitting articles and reviews to periodicals, and soon after founded and edited the critical journal *La revue contemporaine.* At this time he also began working on his first novel and frequented literary circles that included Emile Zola, the founder of the Naturalist school of literature, as well as such noted authors as J.-K. Huysmans, Maurice Barrès, and Anatole France. Between 1886 and 1893, Rod held a professorship of comparative literature at the University of Geneva. He also traveled to the United States and England, where he lectured on French literature. Rod remained a well-known figure in the French literary world until his death in 1910.

Among Rod's first published works was his pamphlet *A propos de "l'Assomoir,"* a defense of Zola's controversial novel *L'assommoir* (1877, *Gervaise*). Influenced by Zola, Rod established his initial reputation as a writer with several Naturalist novels in which he portrayed characters destroyed by circumstances imposed on them by their environments. In his first novel, *Les allemands à Paris,* Rod depicted the corruption and downfall of displaced working-class Germans who attempt to assimilate into the sophisticated city life of Paris. Despite his admiration for Zola and his doctrines, Rod never fully accepted Naturalism, which he felt did not adequately account for the characters' psychological states. Influenced by the psychological emphasis he discerned in works by such Russian authors as Fyodor Dostoevsky and Leo Tolstoy, Rod developed his philosophy of "Intuitivism," maintaining that an author need only look into his or her own mind to understand the human condition. Such Intuitivist works as *La course à la mort* and *Le sens de la vie,* which connect Rod with the development of the French psychological novel, reflect a pessimistic philosophy that views suffering and death as the dominant realities of life.

In later novels, which critics have termed *études passionelles* ("studies of passion"), Rod abandoned the introspection and pessimism central to his Intuitivism to create sympathetic portrayals of tragic characters struggling to resolve conflicts between passion and duty. Typical of these novels is *La ménage du Pasteur Naudié,* in which Rod depicted a widowed Protestant minister whose marriage to a young, capricious woman gradually leads him to neglect his children and his pastoral duties. In subsequent works, including *Mademoiselle Annette* and *L'eau courante,* Rod carefully detailed the life and manners of the peasants and burghers of his native canton of Vaud to show the destructive effects of modern economic and political developments on the region's traditional values of hard labor and self-sacrifice. While critics have faulted Rod's novels for their undistinguished prose style and generally pessimistic outlook, most agree that his works offer well-constructed examinations of moral predicaments. Since the close of World War I, Rod's works have fallen into obscurity, perhaps, as critic Michael G. Lerner speculates, because their examination of delicate questions of scruple has been viewed as outdated and out of touch with an increasingly permissive society.

PRINCIPAL WORKS

Le développement de la légende d'Œdipe dans la littérature Européene (criticism) 1879
A propos de l'Assommoir (criticism) 1879
Les allemands à Paris (novel) 1880
Palmyre Veulard (novel) 1881
La chute de Miss Topsy (novel) 1882
Côte à côte (novel) 1882
L'autopsie du Docteur Z. et autres nouvelles (short stories) 1884
La femme d'Henri Vanneau (novel) 1884
La course à la mort (novel) 1885
Études sur le XIXᵉ siècle (criticism) 1888
Le sens de la vie (novel) 1889
Scènes de la vie cosmopolite (short stories) 1890
Les trois cœurs (novel) 1890
Nouvelles romandes (short stories) 1891
Les idées morales du temps présent (criticism) 1892
La sacrifiée (novel) 1892
  [*The Sacrifice of Silence,* 1899]
La vie privée de Michel Teissier (novel) 1893
  [*The Private Life of an Eminent Politician,* 2 vols., 1893]
La seconde vie de Michel Teissier (novel) 1894
Le silence (novel) 1894
Les roches blanches (novel) 1895
  [*The White Rocks,* 1896]
Dernier refuge (novel) 1896
Scènes de la vie Suisse (short stories) 1896
Là-haut (novel) 1897
Le ménage du Pasteur Naudié (novel) 1898
  [*Pastor Naudier's Young Wife,* 1899]
Au milieu du chemin (novel) 1900
Mademoiselle Annette (novel) 1901
L'eau courante (novel) 1902
Nouvelles vaudoises (short stories) 1904
L'affaire J.-J. Rousseau (criticism) 1906
Le réformateur (drama) 1906
L'ombre s'étend sur la montagne (novel) 1907
Le glaive et le bandeau (novel) 1910
Les effeuilleuses (novel) 1911
Le pasteur pauvre (novel) 1911

CRITICISM

The Atlantic Monthly (essay date 1890)

[*In the following unsigned review of* Les trois coeurs, *the critic comments on the philosophy of Intuitivism set forth in Rod's preface to the novel.*]

We hear a good deal of talk nowadays about the impropriety of novelists taking upon themselves to explain their art instead of leaving it to be divined by their readers. But the phenomenon is not very surprising, after all, save in a country where the interest in literature is largely of an unliterary sort. True, we have not the authority of the older writers for such a proceeding, but with each generation customs arise which Moses omitted either to enjoin or prohibit. Literature is the natural medium for the expression of ideas upon literature, and the fullness with which writers nowadays take readers into their confidence results from the quickening on both sides of a conscious interest in the means by which literary works are produced, and in the relation which they bear to life. The critic, at least, cannot afford to censure; for a criticism which has for its primary object the perception and disclosure of an author's meaning will be ready to accept any aid in arriving at that object, even from so direct a source. In France, it is no new thing for an author to set forth his methods and convictions, or to presuppose an interest in them on the part of his readers. M. Edouard Rod's chapter of literary autobiography, given as a preface to **Les Trois Cœurs,** is by no means the least interesting part of the book. M. Rod set out, as he tells us, ten years ago, as an enthusiastic naturalist,—more enthusiastic than natural, we suspect; and now, at a considerable distance from the camp, he retraces the steps by which he left it. He characterizes his own naturalism as a matter of conviction rather than of temperament, and notes the existence throughout the school, and by his own confession in Zola himself, of a *levain romantique.* Our own acquaintance with the novels of M. Rod had not, we regret to say, begun, in the days when he was a naturalist; but, judging from the present book, and making full allowance for the rebound of a convert, it is difficult to imagine that his achievements in the realistic line can ever have been great. The first intellectual doubts came to him from the founder of the faith. Zola's theory of the experimental novel, substituting a potential for an indicative mood, and placing a larger executive responsibility in the hands of the novelist, was seized by his disciple as an escape from the novel of observation, of which the limitations—or the requirements—had proved irksome to some of the younger members of the school.

"It will not do to forget that there were developing within us cravings which naturalism could not satisfy; being in its essence limited, self-satisfied, materialistic; interesting itself in manners rather than in souls. We were—and we were destined to become in a still higher degree—restless minds, smitten with a longing for the infinite; idealists, careless of manners, and looking through appearances to man."

To disaffection within the ranks were joined beguiling voices from without. We will mention only two of the literary influences felt by M. Rod: that of the Russian novelists and that of Dante Rossetti. Having proceeded from naturalism to symbolism without, so far as we can perceive, experiencing any very radical change, M. Rod has set himself to discover a method of novel-writing by which he can embody some of his new convictions; and, while recognizing the fact that there have been too many attempts at schools in France, and that it requires "a unilateral faith" to believe implicitly in terms, he has erected for himself a sort of provisional government under the name "intuitivism."

What is an intuitive novel, and how does it differ from other novels whose writers may be supposed to have been blessed now and then with intuitions? Intuitivism M. Rod defines as inward observation; the study of self, not as an end, "but as a key to the mysteries of the human mind." With this key Shakespeare no doubt unlocked more hearts than his own, though he has left us no record of having done so. "Look into thine own heart and write" is no new maxim, and it is one which would have been pretty sure to be followed in some fashion or other, if it had never been formulated; for we comprehend the minds of others by our own, as we see through the eyes bestowed upon us. But the programme of intuitivism as set forth by M. Rod is a more special matter. It does away with most of the materials which are accumulated by other than intuitional methods. "I have sought, in this little book, to disengage the novel from some of the tares which prevent it from developing in the way that I have indicated: to free it, in the first place, from description, which appears to me affected and often illusory, since it takes up a great deal of space, says little, and explains nothing; secondly, from retrospective narrative, which, intended simply to introduce the characters, has become in time a stereotyped discussion on childhood, youth, and education, and which, when significant, has the drawback of making the outline too precise; and, finally,—though not to as great an extent as I could have wished,—from 'scenes,' which have always an artificial and theatrical air." Theoretically, these are steps in a right direction, though the old-fashioned novel-reader may be tempted to inquire what is left after this wholesale elimination. After an attentive reading of *Les Trois Cœurs,* we cannot say that we think there is much left. M. Rod might almost have included conversation among his omissions, for we get very little of it, except of a new order, which we might call solitary conversation, if we had not the better word "intuitive" supplied to us.

In his inward investigations, M. Rod has not failed to note the fact that, alongside of our active life, there takes place a sort of drama of idleness; that much of our existence is passed among imaginary scenes and conversations. The mind anticipates events, shapes them at its own will, and produces those castles in the air erroneously assumed to be the exclusive property of youth; those inward dialogues in which we ourselves shine so brilliantly, and the other party becomes a mere echo. One of the most striking points in the Russian novels, to one curious of methods in novel-writing, is the place given to this double action of the mind. Those men of the steppe know all the elves and demons by which solitude is peopled. Tolstoï and Turgenieff, with their rich storehouse of experience, gleaned from within and without, are observers, psychologists, realists, and idealists in one. But in France the differentiation of talent is carried, nowadays, to such excess that we meet with novelists apparently endowed, like M. Cherbuliez's duchess, with an incapacity for beholding two things at once. In *Les Trois Cœurs,* we are introduced to the hero, Richard Noral, and his wife, as they sit at their fireside, each carrying on a line of meditation, from which we get alternate passages, making a sort of unspoken dialogue. When a man dreams in a style too generally ascribed by novelists to members of the weaker sex,—"I have never loved enough! . . . Whenever a new feeling beat within my heart, I have driven it away by reason. I have never let myself go. I have analyzed all my desires.

I have known no intoxication;" when he is filled with *"un ardent soif d'inconnu,"* and aspires *"à des mystères d'âme et de chair,"* and his wife thinks, "He is unhappy, and my love for him is vain; I can do nothing for his happiness,"— there are rocks ahead, as any novel-reader can tell. This inward drama not only serves as the exclusive medium through which we watch M. Rod's characters; it also dominates and shapes their action. Richard Noral, egoist and dreamer, breaks three women's hearts in his attempts at an outward realization of his rather commonplace aspirations, and is rewarded by a momentary contact with the real aspect of things, and by the discovery that in pursuing the shadow he has let the substance flee. The scene of the book is an interior one. The inward, invisible symbol is substituted for the outward and visible fact. Were it not for the incident which disposes of the American adventuress, whose name M. Rod has sought across the Channel rather than on this side of the Atlantic, we should have been allowed to hope that M. Noral's misdemeanors and attractions had been taken a little too seriously by the author as well as by himself, and that the hearts of Hélène, Rose-Mary, and Madame d'Hays might be susceptible of recovery in a clearer atmosphere. But the breaking of hearts is a question which a prudent critic will forbear to meddle with. M. Rod's experiment in novel-writing has interested us more than his novel. No large result in fiction could ever be obtained by looking at life in sections, but we may reasonably expect interesting studies from such an undertaking. There are, no doubt, many lives wrecked upon unsubstantial reefs, and the life of an egoist, intuitively viewed, may bring to light a number of truths, of however unpleasant a variety. But M. Rod's intuitions play as persistently upon the surface as if his subject were contemporary manners. They give us no real insight, no new fact. His intuitive novel is neither realistic nor in any true sense ideal, but a slice of the conventional French fiction dipped in a solution of Rossetti. Even among his own countrymen, Rossetti has not always been happy as an influence, and an imitation House of Life is tolerably sure to meet with the fate of a house built upon sand. (pp. 277-80)

A review of "Les trois coeurs," in The Atlantic Monthly, *Vol. LXVI, No. CCCXCIV, August, 1890, pp. 277-80.*

Winifred Stephens   (essay date 1914)

[*In the following excerpt, Stephens provides an overview of Rod's life and major works.*]

The political, social, and religious controversies which have rent France in twain during the last ten years have profoundly affected the world of letters. Many of these disputes have been led by literary men; and even novelists have come down from the mount of pure contemplation into the arena of warfare. Emile Zola set the example. He was followed by Anatole France, Paul Bourget, Marcel Prévost, and many others. Thus the French public has come to expect its novelists to espouse definitely one side or the other in questions of the day.

M. Rod is one of the few French novelists who refuse to

be identified with any particular party, and his aloofness gives rise to a multitude of conjectures as to his future intellectual destiny. Some months ago, when he went to Rome and wrote thence to the *Figaro,* an eloquent letter on the historical greatness of the Roman Church, there was a loud outcry that at last he had shown his hand, that at length there was no longer any doubt as to his religious opinions, that he was about to follow the example of Huysmans and Bourget and to become a practising Catholic.

But M. Rod has not yet forsaken the world and entered a Benedictine monastery, nor has he openly espoused the cause of clericalism. The effect of these conjectures on the mind of M. Rod himself may be inferred from a paragraph in his last novel, *L'Ombre s'étend sur la Montagne,* where he writes of the philosophical author, M. Jaffé: "He was discussed with that violence always provoked by sincere writing in times of public agitation. Freethinkers considered him an apostate because he broke with their traditions and emancipated himself from their tyranny; conservatives hailed him as an unexpected recruit because he approved of certain items in their programme; one newspaper announced his imminent conversion; another maintained that he had gone to Rome to receive the papal benediction. He read all this without anger or astonishment, somewhat moved, however, to see what self-interest, discord, civil hatred, intolerance, and fanaticism will discover in the simple work of a detached investigator (*un chercheur désinteressé*)."

In this last expression, M. Rod describes himself exactly; for he is above all things *un chercheur désinteressé*, a detached patient investigator of human life,

> holding no form of creed,
> But contemplating all.

His inquiries have led him through many phases of experience, ranging from what he now holds to have been anarchic individualism to the serener air of collectivism. But throughout his spirit moves in a pessimistic cloud; he never escapes entirely from that moulding force of his early genius, the influence of Schopenhauer.

His novels are one long indictment of human life; and in his latest production, as well as in his first important work, he often appears to regard death as the one good thing in existence. But such an attitude is something of a pose. Occasionally he comes to himself and is sincere; then he confesses that life, terrible, cruel, iniquitous though it be, is better than annihilation.

Some of this pessimism may be the result of heredity and early environment. Though by choice and avocation he is a Parisian and an agnostic—"Paris is the city of my choice; I believe in her and love her"—*Paris demeure ma ville d'election, j'ai foi en Paris et je l'aime,* he writes—by birth he is a Swiss and a Calvinist. Both the manner and the matter of his novels betray his origin. They are full of the romantic poetry of the Swiss, while they lack the ethereal grace of style, the concise crispness of phrase which reveal the true Frenchman. The working out of their plots is too often in accord with that fatalism which, resulting from the Calvinistic creed of his boyhood, caused him to choose as the theme of his university thesis the *Development of the Legend of Œdipus.*

Hereditary influences were not alone in casting a gloom over the author's youthful spirit. What should have been the gladsome years of childhood, were passed by the sick couch of his paralysed mother. "A sad event completed my development," he writes in one of his novels [*Au Milieu du Chemin*]. "My mother was stricken with paralysis; I became her nurse; she was dying slowly while I was growing up."

The picture of human suffering thus engraved upon his memory has profoundly influenced his whole work. If there be one message more than another he considers it to be his duty to deliver it is that contained in his earliest great work [*La Course à la Mort*]: "*Prostrate yourselves before the suffering of humanity.*"

Edouard Rod was born in 1857 at Nyon, a picturesque town, figuring in more than one of his novels, on the Lake of Geneva. His grandfather had been a schoolmaster; and his father in early manhood had followed the same calling, and then relinquished it for that of a bookseller. Many months of the boy Edouard's childhood were passed with his invalid mother in peasants' cottages in villages whither she had gone in search of health. In these humble abodes her son learnt to love that simple life which he was later to reproduce with graphic touch in such novels as *L'Eau Courante* and *Là Haut.*

When he was at home he attended first that dame school described in one of the most delightful of his idyllic novels, *Mademoiselle Annette,* and later the college of Nyon. At fifteen he entered the Academy of Lausanne, and attended the lectures of the philosopher, Charles Secretan, whose originality and breadth of thought was one of the moulding influences of his boyhood. From Lausanne he passed to the University of Bonn, and from Bonn to Berlin, where he developed a passion for Wagner's music.

He was now studying his doctor's thesis, the completion of which took him to Paris, where he arrived in 1878, just after the appearance of Zola's *L'Assommoir,* when the controversy it excited was at its height. Into this controversy the young writer boldly plunged, and made his début in letters by a powerful pamphlet entitled *A Propos de l' Assommoir,* in which he defended the Realists, and gave an excellent exposition of Zola's literary system. Having identified himself with the realistic school, and come under the personal influence of Zola, he produced four novels of his own on realistic lines: *Palmyre Veulard, Côte à Côte, La Chute de Miss Topsy, L'Autopsie du Docteur Z.,* and *La Femme d' Henri Vanneau.*

These four volumes are greatly inferior to M. Rod's later work. Although the writer has long since ceased to call himself a realist, he is still regarded as tarred with Zola's brush by the peasants of his native canton. When you ask these good people about their illustrious fellow-countryman, they shake their heads mournfully and murmur the terrible name of Zola, which to them means all that is impious and impure in a decadent age. These simple Vaudois, alas! will never read the later works of their compatriot. There they would find him painting with a loving and a reverent hand the wholesome life of his native town, and the health-giving toil of the Swiss peasants on the shores of their beautiful lake, under the shadow of their majestic mountains.

M. Rod's realistic novels were merely a necessary phase through which his genius had to pass. It was obvious that they were the exercises of his 'prentice hand, and that he had not yet discovered his vocation. In 1885, he put realism on one side, and produced an entirely original work, *La Course à la Mort.*

Some years later, in his preface to *Trois Cœurs,* M. Rod described his literary evolution from naturalism into something its exact contrary, something he is pleased to term *Intuitivisme.*

"Ten years ago," he writes, "at the beginning of my literary career, I was a realist, like all the young men of the day; for Zola had intoxicated us. . . .

"We dreamed of forming a school, a school which should have battles and victories, a first night, like that of *Hernani,* a general and captains, a Victor Hugo, a Sainte Beuve. . . .

"Alas! that dream was never realised, and for more than one reason. . . . In conviction we might be realists, in temperament we never were. . . . We had aspirations that could never be satisfied by realism, which was essentially self-satisfied, narrow, materialist, more curious about manners than character, about things than souls: we were, and we were becoming more and more, restless, idealist, in love with the infinite, caring little for manners, in things seeking always man."

Among the influences carrying further and further from realism the youth of the early eighties, says Rod, were Wagner's music, Schopenhauer's and Leopardi's pessimism, pre-Raphaelite painting, English poetry, and Russian novels. These influences were driven home to the minds of the French youth by De Voguë's *Studies in Russian Novelists,* and Bourget's *Essays on Contemporary Psychology;* and they resulted in the case of Rod in a determination to write a novel devoid of all concrete incident, the action of which should take place entirely in the heart.

This resolve took shape in his first novel of mark, *La Course à la Mort,* his favourite among his books, he tells us, and the one which has cost him the greatest effort. Here he strikes the keynote of his genius. The whole of his later work has been evolved from the tendencies displayed in this little book of two hundred and ninety-eight pages.

The extreme pessimism of this volume, a kind of catechism based on the philosophy of Schopenhauer, aroused a great outcry. Monsieur Rod was accused of corrupting the youth of France. So, in a preface to a later edition, he found it necessary to defend his position. This he did somewhat feebly by maintaining the erroneous distinction between man's intellectual and his practical life. Still later in *Au Milieu du Chemin* he disproved this very statement.

Somewhat mistaken and unwholesome as may be the teaching of *La Course à la Mort,* it is, nevertheless, a work of power and insight; and it is indispensable reading for those who would understand the development of the writer's talent. Here we have the origin of the threefold cord of his subsequent work: his novels of pure passion, those of peasant life, and those dealing with social questions. In the two books which followed *La Course à la Mort, Le Sens de la Vie* and *Les Trois Cœurs,* Monsieur Rod continues in a series of more or less autobiographical studies the probing of his hero's heart, the analysis of a temperament which he himself has compared to that of René, Werther, and Lara. Of the most significant of these three novels, *Le Sens de la Vie,* Jules Lemaitre in *Les Contemporains* makes a striking analysis. For Rod the conclusion of the whole matter is that life has a meaning for those alone who believe and who love. He uses the word "believe" in the widest sense of the term.

These abstract studies in morals were followed by novels of pure passion. The first, *La Sacrifiée,* appeared in 1892; and then came *La Vie Privée de Michel Teissier* in 1893. Now the writer's fame crossed the Channel; and this novel, the plot of which, as the author hints, may have been suggested by Parnell's story, was translated into English. Its sequel, *La Seconde Vie de Michel Teissier,* in 1894, was followed in the next four years by *Le Silence, Les Roches Blanches, Le Dernier Refuge,* and *Le Ménage du Pasteur Naudié.* In this last we have a fine picture of life in a circle rarely depicted by French novelists, that of the Eglise Reformée of France, at La Rochelle and the University town of Montauban.

In all these books M. Rod, with a masterly hand, treats of love beating against the barriers of social law and other human relations, ending in the death of passion or in the shipwreck of the individual. In his later works, notably *Au Milieu du Chemin,* and *L'Ombre s'etend sur la Montagne,* the same problem finds a different solution, the storm of passion is stilled in a compromise between love and law.

M. Rod depicts passion with a power displayed by no other living writer. In such works as these we are reminded of the preponderant part love plays in French fiction, and love of the irregular sort. Why this is so was explained by M. Rod, when, in 1898, at the invitation of his English readers, he came to London and lectured on the contemporary French novel at Stafford House. Then with intense seriousness and admirable lucidity of thought and expression, addressing an audience largely composed of writers and critics, he justified the French novelist's method of concentrating his attention on love. "The moment of love," said the lecturer, "is the decisive moment, the only moment indeed when one of those obscure beings, who would otherwise leave no trace in history, may become a hero—at least in the poetical sense—may develop his innate energy and show his soul in all its truth. And because in irregular love the soul conflict is most violent, because regular love, unopposed as it is by the barriers of law, duty, or faith, has no history, it is in irregular love that the French novelist finds his most significant subject."

From these novels of passion, M. Rod to a great extent and of set purpose banishes descriptive passages in order to concentrate his attention on the movements of the soul. "Description," he writes, "appears to me tedious, and above all things illusionary: it holds an important place, and yet says little and explains nothing."

When he does describe the natural surroundings of his characters it is nearly always because they illustrate their state of mind. In 1897, however, he published the first of a series of novels in which, contrary to his previous method, description of natural scenery counts for much. *Là Haut* was the earliest of those novels, the first of those prose idylls of the Alps and the Jura, in which M. Rod appears as the Thomas Hardy of Switzerland. Even in *La Course à la Mort* his feverish soul had found relief in turning away from books *ces porte-voix où l'humanité a ciré tous ses désirs a chanté tous ses rêves, a pleuré toutes ses douleurs.* Treading in the footsteps of Rousseau, he had gone back to the country of his boyhood, to "the virgin mountain air, to the healing sights of nature." "Can I do better than passively to contemplate its useless blooming? (*ses inutiles floraisons*)," he had asked in the despairing mood of *La Course à la Mort.*

Thus he came to write a series of novels in which the atmosphere is healthier and the life simpler than in *La Vie de Michel Teissier* and similar works. The disappointed worldling, Sterny, in *Là Haut,* the hardened millionaire, Pierre Denys Nicollet, in *Mademoiselle Annette,* alike find peace and healing on the high mountain tops in the contemplation "of the ample spaces of the sky," sharing the simple life of the Vaudois peasants. These novels are full of idyllic pictures of peasant life and Alpine landscapes. So strong is the writer's love of the mountain country that he returns almost to pagan nature worship; he actually personifies the mountains and the valleys. In *Là Haut,* the fatal fall of the Alpinist, whose love of the mountains had been the passion of his existence, seems, like that of Empedocles from Etna, to be the perfecting of a life-long communion with nature. The chief personage of this novel is the Alpine village of Vallanches, endowed with a life really more intense than that of its human inhabitants. The towering peak, La Tour aux Fées, seemed to live with a life active, personal, almost human, as it looked down on the painful evolution of the primitive pastoral hamlet into a bustling fashionable village, with a railway line and big hotels. The tragedy of this book lies in the strife between "those eternal enemies: those who would have the world remain motionless, and those who would change everything." It is obvious that M. Rod is on the side of the former. Volland, the advocate of elementary simplicity, says to Monsieur Rarogne, the capitalist, "You say that money is a seed like any other. Yes, unfortunately. A sad seed, Monsieur de Rarogne, a seed which germinates in evil appetites, an accursed seed, which no ill wind had as yet wafted into this neighbourhood." M. Rod is no believer in the religion of the millionaire. In his opinion it is neither money nor worldly prosperity that is the cause of happiness. Those who can content themselves with little are richer than those who are always longing for more.

Such is the suggestive doctrine underlying the most delightful of these prose idylls: *Mademoiselle Annette.* "This is a true story, a catastrophe of real life," writes the author in his first chapter, "barely understood as it unrolled itself before my eyes in childhood, the details of which, however, have remained engraved on my memory."

Mademoiselle Annette, with large brown eyes, dimpled chin, heavy coils of dark brown hair, is the writer's favourite heroine. She attains as near as possible to perfection. Indeed, it is hard to find a single fault in the character of this Swiss schoolmistress. Some of the author's happiest years were passed at her school, he tells us. "There he was too happy to need even friends." "Mademoiselle Annette Nicollet's school was one of those true schools of Thelema, which existed before pedagogy became a science; at a time when there was no question of overwork, when the alphabet was still a pretty picture-book, when every year did not bring the invention of some new method of making straight strokes, when recreation was much and lessons little."

But ruin came upon Mademoiselle Annette's family. She had her own disappointment of the heart. And then she found her joy in ministering to others, not with a martyr's air, but as one simply following the bent of her own inclination. In the end she softens the heart of her millionaire uncle, and converts him from the worship of his banking account to the belief that "the spirit of sacrifice is the greatest of virtues, that it alone can bring true contentment, that it can cause greater happiness than any other disposition of the soul."

The background of this simple story is the little town of Bielle, in reality Nyon, the author's birthplace, on the Lake of Geneva. Already in *La Course à la Mort* he had introduced his readers to the tranquillity of its grass-grown streets, to the sad majesty of its huge Protestant temple, whither his mother took him every Sunday, and outside which there stood an ancient statue, thought by some to represent a goddess and by others a Roman empress. The old-world life of this little town and its inhabitants, *"gens figés dans la paix des habitudes,"* is admirably depicted. Mademoiselle Annette's uncle, the millionaire, Pierre Denys Nicollet, having heaped up wealth in America, returns to Bielle and attempts to transform it according to American ideas.

But Bielle, unlike Vallanches, clings to its primitive conditions, refuses to be Americanised, and in the end it is the millionaire who is converted. He is brought to reverence, as the two most important principles of life, the spirit of sacrifice which he discerns in his niece, and the spirit of primitive labour which he discovers in his brother, the gardener. He arrives at the conclusion that "simple and productive toil is infinitely superior to complicated, scientific, and lucrative work."

Both in *Là Haut* and *Mademoiselle Annette* it is obvious that economic problems have arrested the writer's attention. In *Un Vainqueur,* published in 1905, such a problem furnishes the chief interest of the story. The plot resolves itself into the duel between capital and labour, between employer and employed, between the middle class and the proletariat. The question is skilfully and impartially stated, but no solution is offered. "Perhaps we shall know some day" is the author's very vague conclusion. "The Conqueror," Alcide Délémont, who by the sweat of his brow has risen from the rank of employé to that of employer, is a fine figure, a very Hercules of industrialism willing to sacrifice himself, his family, and the human race, if needs be, to *Ce Moloch des affaires.* To him it is no matter whether the children employed in his workshops have or have not attained the legal age. His one concern is the prosperity of his factory, which needs children as well as coal, potassium, machinery, and men. This novel, in a *genre* quite different from the author's previous work, is as redolent of the atmosphere of the factory as those powerful scenes of *L'Assommoir* where the washerwoman meets her lover by his forge.

L'Indocile, M. Rod's next novel, appeared a few months after *Le Vainqueur,* to which it may be regarded as the sequel, in that we meet with many of the same characters in the two books. But the world of *L'Indocile* and the problems with which it deals are not those of the preceding work.

To find a clear presentment of the various currents of French intellectual life at the present day, one cannot do better than turn to *L'Indocile.* There we have a trio of friends, Paris University students: one, Urbain, is a pronounced Radical, a self-confident optimist, who cries "look without," who believes that the world is to be saved and saved rapidly by acts of parliament; another, Claude, is a fervent Catholic, who cries "look within," his only hope for mankind is in the changing of men's hearts; and, holding the balance between these two opposite poles of thought, stands the third friend, an anarchic individualist, Valentin, l'Indocile.

Agnostic as he is, M. Rod does not hesitate to expose the narrowness of the new secular religion which is growing up in France.

It has become a commonplace to say that in France, the country which has adopted the word *Liberté* as her motto, the true meaning of the term is unknown. "Liberty is to walk straight, to think rightly! No one has the liberty to fall into error or superstition," remarks one of the characters in this book; and such is the opinion of most intellectual Frenchmen to-day. Indeed, as M. Rod powerfully points out, this new secular religion is as intolerant as the old Church.

"Now it is our turn to excommunicate," cries the rich anti-clerical wine merchant in *L'Indocile.* "We will excommunicate the Pope! the Monks! the Priests!" Valentin, who holds himself aloof from all parties, hearing such language, remarks truly: "I see the dawn of a new religion, new idols, a new gospel, a new fanaticism."

Readers of Anatole France's *Sur la Pierre Blanche* will remember that in the last chapter of that book, where he anticipates the world in 2270, in a deeply significant passage he foretells the destruction of liberty. "Society cannot permit liberty, since there is none in nature," he writes. "There is no being in existence that is free. Formerly it was said that a man was free when he merely obeyed laws. That was puerile."

L'Indocile reveals the writer's wise comprehension of the significance of events and keen insight into the character of the young Frenchman of to-day. He sees clearly whither things are tending in France. He portrays admirably that temperament dominated by abstract logic which is much more common among Latin races than in our own country. In the phase of development his talent has reached, the interest of his novels is infinitely broader than in his earlier works.

In a novel with the title *L'Incendie,* published in 1906, he reverts to the earlier theme of Swiss peasant life. The plot recalls that of a previous tale, *L'Eau Courante.* In both novels the story is of those who vainly contend with rapidly approaching economic disaster. In *L'Incendie* the prevailing tone is a little less dark than in the earlier work. Our author recognises that good does exist side by side with evil; and we are grateful to him for painting as the closing scene a picture in which loving-kindness predominates.

M. Rod's last book, *L'Ombre qui s'etend sur la Montagne,* which appeared in the March of 1907, is a novel of passion. Here he deals with the problem treated seven years earlier in *Au Milieu du Chemin.* In both novels we have the waves of passion dashing against the barriers of conventional law, and ending not in the complete shipwreck of *Le Dernier Refuge,* the most pessimistic of all his writings, but in the sacrifice of the individual to society. Here, as elsewhere, it is the woman who makes the sacrifice.

Rather than break up her home and darken her daughter's life, Irène Jaffé parts from Lysel, whom for years she has loved with an ardent passion, strictly controlled within Platonic bounds. It is the old theme of the conflict between love and duty. Irène deciding in favour of duty, sacrifices her happiness. As the shadows fall upon the mountains, so does the sun fade from Irène's life. Death mercifully intervenes to end her joylessness. At the last her husband relents and summons the lover to Irène's death-bed. In the contemplation of the woman's unselfishness the two men are reconciled. "It was not to please herself that she stayed by my fireside," says the husband. "Neither was it through self-love that she gave her heart to me," says the lover.

Such a romantic conclusion is unsatisfactory from a realistic point of view; and the book would have done better to end with Irène's renunciation of her lover. Yet the volume as a whole, although less powerful than its prototype, *Au Milieu du Chemin,* is deeply interesting.

Increasing years and family ties transform the principles of husband and wife, while upon the lover they leave no imprint. Franz Lysel retains all the buoyancy and ardour of youth. A great musician, he is a typical artist, a Polish exile, without home or country. For him love is everything. His is an attractive child-like nature, ever young, impetuous, and irreflective, without guile and without malice. When Irène breaks with him, his love remains unchanged and reveals no bitterness. The husband, Monsieur Jaffé, in spite of a calm philosophical temperament, had in his youth held views so thoroughly individualist as to border on anarchy. He and his wife, when they married, had resolved that if ever weighty reasons should make them desire to separate, neither would raise any obstacle to the other's taking such a step; and they had gone so far as each to sign a paper to that effect. But, as the years drag on, and as their child grows up, although affinity between them has long since vanished, and although the husband is aware of his wife's attachment to Lysel, he allows things to remain as they are. Meanwhile, his philosophic studies are leading him from individualism to collectivism. He is arriving at the conclusion that "principles of the common moral code, arbitrary as they appear to us, repose nevertheless upon a minute knowledge of the sequence of causes and effects in the life of individuals and in that of the race." At the same time his daughter is growing obviously observant and critical of her parents' disunion and its chief cause. New influences bring Monsieur Jaffé to put that alternative before his wife, which results in her separation from her lover. For she has almost unconsciously been treading the same path of intellectual experience as her husband; and, although at first she repels his suggestion, she is afterwards bound to admit, "I too have sometimes had those ideas."

Irène Jaffé is the typical Rod heroine. Her yearning for self-sacrifice is the undercurrent of her being. As years advance she passes from the passion of youth to the serene reflectiveness of middle age; she controls the impulse of her early ardour, and it is only for Lysel's sake, not for her own, that she hesitates at first to sacrifice her love and serve "the universal order."

The minor characters in the story, like the protagonists, are well drawn, and have a strong grip on the memory. Madame Storm, Irène's mother, is a common butterfly type of person flitting from one fashionable resort to another, ever seeking pleasure and failing to find it. Anne Marie, the daughter, old for her years, is as grave and self-contained as her philosophic father. Hugo Meyer, the aged musician, and his companion Louise, stand out well, with strong individualities of their own.

Among the many beautiful descriptive passages of this work, the finest is the scene at the first night of Lysel's opera. M. Rod, himself a musician, has in reality here written a symphony in words. The succeeding waves of emotion passing over the audience, changing from approval to censure; the loud applause of sincere delight yielding to that of mere courtesy, merging again into murmurs of discontent and finally culminating in a storm of howls and hisses, are depicted with striking skill. In the early chapters of the book, where the action is laid in that Alpine country the writer loves, there is fine word painting in the romantic scenes of the sunset upon the Jungfrau and the bright freshness of a summer morning in the gardens of Interlaken.

As in earlier novels, the changing landscape is intended to indicate the future vicissitudes in the lives of those who gaze upon it; the dark shadows stretching over the Jungfrau are the symbols of the coming sorrow which is to overcast the lives of Irène Jaffé and Franz Lysel.

In psychological insight and high moral tone this last production of our author's pen takes equal rank with his previous work. It is not by the grace of his style, nor by the artistic construction of his plots, nor by the subtlety of his wit that M. Rod recommends himself to his readers. It is

above all things by the high seriousness of his work. He remains a powerful portrayer of passion, a patient seeker after moral truth devoid of prejudice, generally sincere and frank. His novels are the faithful record of the evolution of a thoughtful mind; and as such, rather than as great artistic creations, they cannot fail to interest the serious reader. (pp. 263-88)

> *Winifred Stephens, "Edouard Rod, 1857," in her* French Novelists of To-Day, *second edition, John Lane, The Bodley Head, 1914, pp. 263-88.*

George Saintsbury   (essay date 1917)

[*Saintsbury has been called the most influential English literary historian and critic of the late nineteenth and early twentieth centuries. His numerous literary histories as well as studies of European literature and individual authors have established him as a leading critical authority. Saintsbury maintained that "the novel has nothing to do with any beliefs, with any convictions, with any thoughts in the strict sense, except as mere garnishings. Its substance must always be life not thought, conduct, or belief, the passions of the intellect, manners, and morals not creeds and theories. . . . The novel is . . . mainly and firstly a criticism of life." In the following excerpt from an essay first published in 1917 and reissued in revised form in 1964, Saintsbury appraises Rod's novels.*]

I have quite a lively remembrance of the advent of M. Edouard Rod, of the crowning of *Le Sens de la Vie,* and so forth. That advent formed part of the just mentioned counter-attack on Naturalism, in which, as usual, some of the Naturalist methods and weapons themselves were used; but it had a distinct character of its own. Unless I mistake, it was not at first very warmly welcomed by "mortal" French criticism. There may have been something in this of that curious grudge against Swiss-French, on the part of purely French-French, men of letters which never seems to have entirely ceased. But there was something more than this, though this something more was in a way the reason, some might say the justification, of the grudge. M. Rod was exceedingly serious; the title of his laureated book is of itself almost sufficient to show it; and though the exclusive notion of "the gay and frivolous Frenchman" always was something of a vulgar error, and has been increasingly so since the Revolution, Swiss seriousness, with its strong Germanic leaven, is not French seriousness at all. But he became, if not exactly a popular novelist to the tune of hundreds or even scores of editions, a prolific and fairly accepted one. I think, though he died in middle age and produced other things besides novels, he wrote some twenty or thirty stories, and his production rather increased than slackened as he went on. With the later ones I am not so well acquainted as with the earlier, but there is a pervading character about these earlier ones which is not likely to have changed much, and they alone belong strictly to our subject.

Next to *Le Sens de la Vie* and perhaps in a way, as far as popularity goes, above it, may be ranked, I suppose, *La Vie Privée de Michel Teissier,* with its sequel, *La Seconde*

Vie de M. T. These books certainly made a bold and wide separation of aim and subject from the subject and the aim of most French novels in these recent years. Here you have, instead of a man who attempts somebody else's wife, one who wishes to get rid—on at least legally respectable terms—of his own, and to marry a girl for whom he has, and who has for him, a passion which is, until legal matrimony enfranchises it, able to restrain itself from any practical satisfaction of the as yet illicit kind. He avails himself of the then pretty new facilities for divorce (the famous "Loi Naquet," which used to "deave" all of us who minded such things many years ago), and the situation is (at least intentionally) made more piquant by the fact that Teissier, who is a prominent statesman and gives up not merely his wife but his political position for this new love of his, starts as an actual supporter of the repeal of the divorce laws. To an English reader, of course, the precise problem would not have the same charm of novelty, except in his capacity as a reader of French novels. But, putting that aside, the position is obviously capable of being treated with very considerable appeal. The struggles of the husband, who *has* loved his wife—M. Rod had not the audacity or the strength to make him love her still—between his duties and his desires; the indignant suffering of the wife; and most of all, the position of the girl who, by ill-fortune or the fault of others, finds herself expending, on an at first illicit and always ill-famed love, what she might have devoted to an honourable one, certainly has great capabilities. But I did not think when I read it first, and I do not think now when I have read it again, that these various opportunities are fully taken. It is not that M. Rod has no idea of passion. He is constantly handling it and, as will be seen presently, not without success occasionally. But he was too much what he calls his eidolon in one book, "Monsieur le psychologue," and the Psyche he deals with is too often a skinny and spectacled creature—not the love of Cupid and the mother of Voluptas.

If he has ever made his story hot enough to make this pale cast glow, it is in *La Sacrifiée.* This is all the more remarkable in that the beginning of the book itself is far from promising. There is a rather unnecessary usher-chapter—a thing which M. Rod was fond of, and which, unless very cleverly done, is more of an obstacle than of a "shoe-horn." The hero-narrator of the main story is one of the obligatorily atheistic doctors—nearly as great a nuisance as obligatorily adulterous heroines—whom M. Rod has mostly discarded; and what is more, he is one of the pseudo-scientific fanatics who believe in the irresponsibility of murderers, and do not see that, the more irresponsible a criminal is, the sooner he ought to be put out of the way. Moreover, he has the ill-manners to bore the company at dinner with this craze, and the indecency (for which in some countries he might have smarted) to condemn out loud, in a court of justice, the verdict of the jury and the sentence of the judge on his pet. Neither can one approve the haste with which he suggests to the wife of his oldest and most intimate friend that she is not happy with her husband. But this time M. Rod had got the forge working, and the bellows dead on the charcoal. The development of the situation has something of that twist or boomerang effect which we have noticed in *Michel Teissier.* Dr. Morgex begins by defending murderers; he does not end, but

starts the end, by becoming a murderer himself, though one with far more "extenuating circumstances" than those so often allowed in French courts. His friend—who is an advocate of no mean powers but loose life and dangerously full habit—has, when the doctor warns him against apoplexy, half scoffed, but also begged him, if a seizure should take place, to afford him a chance of euthanasia instead of lingering misery. The actual situation, though with stages and variations which are well handled, arises; the doctor, who has long since been frantically in love with the wife, succumbs to the temptation—which has been aggravated by the old request, by the sufferings of the victim, and by the urgent supplications of the family, that he *shall* give morphia to relieve these sufferings. He gives it—but in a dose which he knows to be lethal.

After a time, and having gone through no little mental agony, he marries the widow, who is in every sense perfectly innocent; and a brief period of happiness follows. But his own remorse continues; the well-meaning chatter of a lady, who has done much to bring about the marriage, and to whom Morgex had unwarily mentioned "obstacles," awakes the wife's suspicion, and, literally, "the murder is out." Morgex confesses, first to a lawyer friend, who, to his intense surprise, pronounces him legally guilty, of course, but morally excusable; then to a priest, who takes almost exactly the opposite point of view, and admitting that the legal crime may be excusable, declares the moral guilt not lessened; while he points out that while the wages of iniquity are retained, no pardon can be deserved or expected. And so the pair part. Morgex gives himself up to the hardest and least profitable practitioner-work. Of what the wife does we hear nothing. She has been perfectly guiltless throughout; she has loved her second husband without knowing his crime, and after knowing it; and so she is "La Sacrifiée." But this (as some would call it) sentimental appeal is not the real appeal of the book, though it is delicately led up to from an early point. The gist throughout is the tempering and purifying of the character and disposition of Morgex himself, through trial and love, through crime and sacrifice. It is not perfectly done. If it were, it would land the author at once in those upper regions of art which I cannot say I think he attains. But it is a very remarkable "try," and, with one other to be mentioned presently, it is nearest the goal of any of his books.

On the other hand, if he ever wrote a worse book than *Le Silence,* I have not read, and I do not wish to read, that. The title is singularly unhappy. Silence is so much greater a thing than speech that a speaker, unless he is Shakespeare or Dante or Lucretius, or at least the best kind of Wordsworth, had better avoid the subject, avoid even the word for it. And M. Rod's examples of silence, preluded in each case (for the book has two parts) by one of those curious harbingerings of his which are doubtfully satisfactory, are not what they call nowadays "convincing." The first and longest—it is, indeed, much too long and might have been more acceptable in twenty pages than in two hundred—deals with the usual triangle—brutal husband, suffering wife, interesting lover. But the last two never declare themselves, or are declared; and they both die and make no sign. In the second part there is another triangle, where the illegitimate side is established and results in a duel, the lover killing the husband and establishing himself with the wife. But a stove for tea-making explodes; she loses her beauty, and (apparently for that reason) poisons herself, though it does not appear that her lover's love has been affected by the change. In each case the situation comes under that famous and often-quoted ban of helpless and unmanageable misery.

Nor can I think highly of **Là-Haut,** which is quite literally an account of an Alpine village, and of its gradual vulgarisation by an enterprising man of business. Of the ordinary novel-interests there is little more than the introduction at the beginning of a gentleman who has triangled as usual, till, the husband has, in his, the lover's, presence, most inconsiderately shot his wife dead, has missed (which was a pity) M. Julien Sterny himself, and, more unconscionably still, has been acquitted by a court of justice, in which the officials, and the public in general, actually seemed to think that M. Sterny was to blame! He is much upset by this, and, coming to Vallanches to recuperate, is rewarded later for his good deeds and sufferings, by the hand of a very attractive young woman with a fortune. This poetic justice, however, is by no means the point of the book, which, indeed, has no particular point. It is filled up by details of Swiss hotel-life: of the wicked conduct of English tourists, who not merely sing hymns on Sunday, but dance on wet evenings in the week (nearly the oddest combination of crimes known to the present writer); of a death in climbing of one of the characters which is not in the least required by the story; of the scalding of her arm by a *paysanne* in a sort of "ragging" flirtation, and the operation on the mortifying member by a curé who knows something of chirurgy; and of the ruin of some greedy peasants who turn their châlet into a hotel with no capital to work it, and are bought out, with just enough to cover their outlay and leave them penniless, by the general *entrepreneur.* It is a curious book, but the very reverse of a successful one.

The centre, not by any means in the chronological sense (for they were among his earliest), but in the logical and psychological, of M. Rod's novel production, is undoubtedly to be found in the two contrastedly titled books *Le Sens de la Vie* and *La Course à la Mort.* The first, which, as has been said, received Academic distinction, I approached many years ago without any predisposition against it, and closed with a distinct feeling of disappointment. The other I read more recently with a distinct apprehension of disapproval, which was, if not entirely, to a very large extent removed as I went on. It was strongly attacked as morbid and mischievous at its first appearance in 1885; and the author, some years afterwards, prefixed a defence to his fifth edition, which is not much more effective than such defences usually are. It takes something like the line which . . . Mr. Traill took about Maupassant—that Pessimism was a fact like other facts, and one was entitled to take it as a subject or motive. But it also contained a slip into that obvious but, somehow or other, seldom avoided trap—the argument that a book is "dramatic," and does not necessarily express the author's own attitude. Perhaps not; but the rejoinder that almost all, if not all, M. Rod's books are "sicklied o'er" in this way is

rather fatal. One gets to expect, and seldom misses, a close and dreary air throughout, often aggravated by an actual final sentence or paragraph of lamentation and mourning and woe. But I do not resent the "nervous impression" left on me by *La Course à la Mort,* with its indefinitely stated but certain end of suicide, and its unbroken soliloquy of dreary dream. For it is in one key all through; it never falls out of tune or time; and it does actually represent a true, an existent, though a partial and morbid attitude of mind. It is also in parts very well written, and the blending of life and dream is sometimes almost Poesque. A novel, except by the extremest stretch of courtesy, it is not, being simply a panorama of the moods of its scarcely heroic hero. And he does not "set one's back up" like René, or, in my case at least, produce boredom like most of the other "World-pain"-ers. The still more shadowy appearances of the heroine Cécile, who dies before her lover, while the course of his love is more dream than action, are well brought in and attractive; and there is one passage descriptive of waltzing which would atone for anything. Many people have tried to write about waltzing, but few have done it well; this is almost adequate. I wonder if I dare translate it?

> We never thought that people might be turning an evil eye on us; we cared nothing for the indignation of the mammas sitting passive and motionless; we hardly felt the couples that we jostled. Thanks to the cradling of the rhythm, to the intoxication of our rapid and regular movement, there fell on us something like a great calm. Drunk with one another, hurried by the absorbing voluptuousness of the waltz, we went on and on vertiginously. People and things turned with us, surrounding us with a gyre of moving shadows, under a fantastic light formed of crossing reflections, in an atmosphere where one breathed inebriating perfumes, and where every atom vibrated to the ever more bewildering sound of music. Time passed, and we still went on; losing little by little all consciousness except that of our own movement. Then it even seemed that we came out of ourselves; we heard nothing but a single beat, marking the cadence with strokes more and more muffled. The lights, melting into one, bathed us in a dreamy glow; we felt not the floor under our feet; we felt nothing but an immense oblivion—the oblivion of a void which was swallowing us up.

And doubtless it was so, as has been seen of many in the Time of Roses.

To take one or two more of his books, *Le Ménage du Pasteur Naudié,* though less poignant than *La Sacrifiée* and with no approach to the extra-novelish merit of *La Course à la Mort,* starts not badly with an interesting scene, no less a place than La Rochelle, very rarely met, since its great days, in a French novel—a rather unfamiliar society, that of French Protestantism at Rochelle itself and Montauban—and a certainly unusual situation, the desire of a young, pretty, and wealthy girl, Jane Defos, to marry an elderly pastor who is poor, and, though a widower, has four children.

That nothing but mischief can come of this proceeding—

as of an abnormal leap-year—is clear enough: whether the way in which the mischief is brought about and recounted is good may be more doubtful. That a person like M. Naudié, simple, though by no means a fool, should be taken in by a very pretty girl falling apparently in love with him—even though, to the general dangers of the situation, are added frank warnings that she has been given to a series of freakish fancies—is not unnatural; that she should soon tire of him, and sooner still of the four step-children, is very natural indeed. But the immediate cause of the final disruption—her taking a new fancy to, and being atheistically converted by, a cousin who, after all, runs away from temptation—is not very natural, and is unconvincingly told. Indeed the whole character of Jane is insufficiently presented. She is meant to be a sort of Blanche Amory, with nothing real in her—only a succession of false and fleeting fancies. But M. Rod was not Thackeray.

With two or three more of his later-middle books (it does not seem necessary to deal with the very latest, which are actually beyond our limit, and could not alter the general estimate very favourably) the preparation of judgment may cease. *Mademoiselle Annette* is the history of a "house-angel" and her family, and the fortunes and misfortunes they go through, and the little town of Bielle on the Lake of Geneva. It is told, rather in M. Ferdinand Fabre's way, by a bystander, from the time when the heroine was his school-dame and, as such dames sometimes, if not often, are, adored by her pupils. Annette dies at last, and M. Rod strews the dust of many others on her way to death. An American brother of the typical kind plays a large part. He is tamed partly by Annette, partly by a charming wife, whom M. Rod must needs kill, without any particular reason. *L'Eau Courante* is an even gloomier story. It begins with a fair picture of a home-coming of bride and bridegroom, on a beautiful evening, to an ideal farm high up on the shore of Leman. In a very few pages M. Rod, as usual, kills the wife after subjecting her to exceptional tortures at the births of her children, and then settles down comfortably to tell us the ruin of the husband, who ends by arson of his own lost home and drowning in his own lost pond. The interval is all blunder, misfortune, and folly—the chief *causa malorum* being a senseless interference with the "servitude" rights of neighbours, whom he does not like, by stopping, for a week, a spring on his own land. Almost the only cheerful character in the book (except a delightful *juge de conciliation,* who carries out his benevolent duties in his cellar, dispensing its contents to soften litigants) is a black billy-goat named Samuel, who, though rather diabolical, is in a way the "Luck of the Bertignys," and after selling whom their state is doomed. But we see very little of him.

The summing up need probably not be long. That M. Rod was no mere stuffer of the shelves of circulating libraries must have been made clear; that he could write excellently has been (with all due modesty) confessed; that he could sometimes be poignant, often vivid, even occasionally humorous, is true. He has given us a fresh illustration of that tendency of the later novel, to "fill all numbers" of ordinary life, which has been insisted upon. But that he is too much of a "dismal Jemmy" of novel-writing is certainly

true also. The House of Mourning is one of the Houses of Life, and therefore open to the novelist. But it is not the *only* house. It would sometimes seem as if M. Rod were (as usual without his being able to help it) a sort of *jettatore,*—as if there were no times or places for him except that

> When all the world is old,
> And all the trees are brown,
> And all the sport is cold,
> And all the wheels run down.

But there is something to add, and even one book not yet noticed to comment on, which may serve as a real light on this remarkable novelist. The way in which I have already spoken of *La Course à la Mort,* which was a very early book, may be referred to. Even earlier, or at least as early, M. Rod wrote some short stories, which were published as *Scènes de la Vie Cosmopolite.* They include "Lilith" (the author, though far from an Anglophile, had a creditable liking for Rossetti), which is a story of the rejection of a French suitor by an English governess; the ending of a liaison between a coxcomb and a lady much older than himself ("Le Feu et l'Eau"); "L'Idéal de M. Gindre," with a doubtful marriage-close; a discovery of falseness ("Le Pardon"); "La Dernière Idylle" (which may be judged from some of its last words: "I have made a spectacle of myself long enough, and now the play is over"), and "Noces d'Or," the shortest and bitterest of all, in which the wife, who has felt herself tyrannised over for the fifty years, mildly retaliates by providing for dinner *nearly* all the things that she likes and her husband does not, though she effects a reconciliation with *pâté de canard d'Amiens.* I wonder if they ate duck-pies at Amiens in the spring of 1918?

The purpose of this postscript-account, and of the reference to *La Course,* should not be very obscure. It is clear that, at first and from the first, M. Rod's vocation was to be a prophet of discouragement and disappointment. You may be this and be quite a major prophet; but if you are not a major prophet your minority will become somewhat painfully apparent, and it will often, if not always, go near to failure. I think this was rather the case with M. Rod. (pp. 542-53)

> *George Saintsbury, "Other Novelists of 1870-1900," in his* A History of the French Novel (to the close of the 19th Century): From 1800-1900, Vol. II, *1917. Reprint by Russell & Russell, Inc., 1964, pp. 518-55.*

Stuart Henry (essay date 1921)

[*In the following excerpt, Henry characterizes Rod's works as sterile and pessimistic.*]

Edouard Rod lived in company with ideas. Life came to him second-handed. His existence was neutralized into his classroom, his study, his indoctrinations. His personality was not original, diversified nor piquant. It was sane, regular and praiseworthy even to commonplaceness. There were no pegs on which to hang one's human interest.

On the only occasion I ever met him he was afflicted with

a severe cold. He was bundled up, stuffed up, blinked up. Letters and life seemed through his eyes and feelings to be clogged up, barred off or at any rate dammed. As often as I have thought of him since, that impression has revived and I have always associated stuffiness and uncomfortableness with his literary legacy and outlook. This may illustrate the defect or danger of Sainte-Beuve's medium of personality in estimating the output of an author.

This trivial incident of Monsieur Rod's rheum, however, chances to fit in, in a way, with his innate and incurable pessimism. Yet his pessimism seemed rather a sort of indigestion of the very good things of earth. Success and prosperity were the *plats* from which he partook at the banquet of life, and still he could not but ask constantly, Why eat? Why enjoy? Why live?

Far lighter and pleasanter than his quasi masters Schopenhauer and Leopardi, he was of plainer, more substantial stuff than the typical Parisian skeptics of his day. One need not look to him for any disconsolate force, intensity, isolated grandeur nor, on the other hand, for any Pyrrhonic brilliancy and irony. He was never an ironist, though he belonged to the little circle of pungent jesters in the sanctum of the "Journal des Débats." In truth he was a genuine professor rather than a genuine literary man, and most truly belonged with Brunetière, Faguet and the others in the gray, somber, doctrinal portals of the "Revue des Deux Mondes."

Born and reared on the banks of the azure Leman with his face toward both Germany and France, Monsieur Rod finally decided to be French. In preferring not to develop the exotic within him, and thus not to add a distinctly new segment of horizon to the realm of French letters, he may have missed his greatest opportunity. If he had held himself aloof from and discussed Paris in his volumes as he held himself aloof from and discussed his theses, he might have originated a more valuable and entertaining work.

His hybrid nature partly explains that certain sterility which nearly always marks his ideas, impulses and productions. For instance, he neutralized the Calvinistic element within him by believing, like a royalist Frenchman, that the Holy See is on the whole sufficiently representative and reformative. If one had objected in the presence of Monsieur Rod to the effacement of the individual in the uniformity of Romanism, he would have responded by objecting to the personal wranglings rife in the individualistic Protestant parishes such as he was familiar with in his cherished canton of Vaud.

His stories are to be distinguished from the usual French novel by the fact that they are "clean"; yet, highly alive to the moral demands of the Protestant races, he was under the impression, as he told me, that the "immorality" of his fiction was the reason why it had not found a foothold in England and America. As for his own attitude toward religion, he would *believe,* but *could not*—like almost every psychologist of the Renan group. He was a "Calvinist free thinker."

His pronounced consciousness of *moi,* the source or sign of his as well as of all pessimism, was neither exaggerated, eccentric nor ailing. It was intellectual dilettantism. His

débuts in literature were extremely Naturalistic, but he soon revolted against Zola and willingly classified himself with Bourget and Barrès. He was legitimately the truest son of Goethe to be found in the family of contemporary French authors. He characterized Goethe as the father of modern dilettantism, and indicated himself when he defined a *goethéen* as one who is "above all intelligent or . . . comprehensive" because he embraces subjects rather than penetrates them, interests himself in everything for the purpose of enjoying all his faculties, yet gives himself wholly to nothing;—who is, in brief, largely tolerant and sympathetic because he is indifferent.

Thus Monsieur Rod's dilettantism—his rather plethoric, after-dinner indolence and indifference—assumed the guise of intellectual luxury. Now and then he exclaimed against such a fate: "Ah, thrice cursed is he who has touched the damned dilettantism!" But the die was cast and nothing was left to him except to make the most of it. And that he did with very good grace, for that matter. After all, like his own Michel Teissier, he loved his ailment.

Monsieur Rod was born in 1857, and studied at Berne and Berlin and at the Sorbonne. His belletristic career was divided between Paris and Geneva. He resided for quite a time on the slopes of the Seine at Auteuil where in his salon on Sunday afternoons one could meet many of the literary celebrities of France. He was a rather large man, fine looking, polished in manner, companionable. His voice was very soft and pleasant, and he had talents as a conférencier. He never liked teaching and apparently cared little for the title of erudite. He studied seriously many varied subjects such as Wagner's estheticism, contemporary Italian literature, Pre-Raphaelitism; yet he did not permit these exotic chiaroscuros and perspectives to enrich and beautify the grisaille pages of his fiction. (pp. 319-22)

Stuart Henry, "Edouard Rod," in his French Essays and Profiles, *E. P. Dutton & Company, 1921, pp. 317-22.*

Anatole France   (essay date 1922)

[*France was a French novelist and critic of the late nineteenth and early twentieth centuries. According to contemporary literary historians, France's best work is characterized by clarity, control, perceptive judgment of world affairs, tolerance and justice. A persistent tone of irony, varying in degrees of subtlety, is often considered the dominant trait of his writing. In his critical works, this device of ironic expression becomes an effective tool of literary analysis. In the following excerpt, France characterizes* Les trois coeurs *as a moralist's warning against the dangers of egoism.*]

[When] M. Edmond Scherer was analysing **Le sens de la vie** in *Le Temps,* he never foresaw the melancholy tale which has followed it to-day, and I fancy that **Les trois cœurs** would have caused him some surprise had he lived long enough to become acquainted with them. In **Le sens de la vie** M. Édouard Rod left his hero married and the father of a family. M. Scherer thought in all good faith that that was the end of the matter. It is true that the author had not finished, but the eminent critic concluded, on his behalf, that to get married and be a father is pretty well the whole art of Life: that if it is impossible for us to discover any meaning in what is called Life, it is expedient to wish what the gods wish, without knowing what they do wish, or even if they wish at all, and as it is a question of living, what matters is not why but how.

M. Edmond Scherer was a wise man, but not sufficiently mistrustful of the slyness of poets. He never penetrated M. Édouard Rod's secret design, which was to show us, in agreement with Ecclesiastes, that all is but vanity, and this is the design which appears in *Les trois cœurs.* For here is the hero Richard Noral, waking up in the arms of the gentle Helen, whom he has married, as disenchanted as King Solomon himself, who had had, truth to tell, an infinitely more extended experience of matrimony.

Helen has not brought Richard happiness, and yet she is a sweet, noble creature. But she is not the dream, the unknown, a thing out of reach. And this infirmity, common to all living beings, slowly lowers her in the sensitive, sterile mind of her dreamy husband. An artist without an art, Richard foolishly demands of life to bring him the form and soul of his dreams, as if there were any other chimeræ for us but those we ourselves invent. Having neither originality of mind nor a generous heart, he revels in a mystic sensuality while contemplating the works of the pre-Raphaelites. In company with Dante Gabriel Rossetti, he asks:

> By what magic word, the key of unexplored paths, can I descend to the bottom of love's abysses?

He nourishes himself on the *Vita nuova;* that is, he lives in the dream of a dream. M. Édouard Rod tells us that he was naturally "good and noble-hearted," but that in his bad moments he showed himself to be "egoistic, despotic, and cruel," and that there were two men in him. I can only see one, an egoist without a temperament, who regards love as a grace.

Tired of Helen, who has not given him the impossible, he takes his boredom and his curiosity to a vaguely American adventuress of uncertain age, perhaps a widow, Rose-Mary, who has passed through life in sleeping-cars, packet-boats, and hired carriages; she has very few memories, except of the eighteen trunks which she everlastingly drags with her from New York to Vienna, from Paris to San Francisco, to all the watering-places and seaside resorts. A glittering flower of the table d'hôte, a gaudy beauty, a vulgar nature under a singular exterior, she is fundamentally a very decent woman, fond of animals, sentimental, capable of love and of dying for it. She is a simple-hearted adventuress, who dreams of the fireside. She loves Richard devotedly. M. Édouard Rod tells us: "When Rose-Mary was his mistress, Richard felt unhappy." He was deeply distressed. He thought, "I have made a mistake. I am mistaken in her, in myself, and in everything! She is not at all like Cleopatra, and has none of the characteristics of the great lovers of history."

No, Rose-Mary does not resemble Cleopatra. That might have been foreseen. For lack of the necessary prevision, Richard is now in a painful situation. Helen has learnt all. She makes no complaints to her husband, but her modest grief, her silence and pallor are more eloquent than any complaints. Richard feels touched, for he has taste. His little daughter, Jeanne, suffers by sympathy. "The mother and daughter seem to live the same life, and languish of the same illness." The house has the look of an empty house; one breathes in it a miasmatic atmosphere. The work-room, the library, where formerly the family had assembled in smiling tranquillity, is now avoided, deserted, and full of memories that chill the heart, as though it were a death-chamber.

In passing from this lugubrious home to the little hotel sitting-room brightened by Rose-Mary with exotic bibelots, Richard only varied his boredom and depression. Rose-Mary, like Helen, loved and suffered. In grief, as in love, both of which are virtues, Rose-Mary towered above chaste and proud Helen, wife and mother. Before we pass on, there is one thing that I do not understand about the excellent Rose-Mary, who had such big hats and such a good heart. It is her resignation. She does not protect this love which is her life: she is always ready to yield. Neither jealous nor violent, she never inflicts the furies of an Ellénore on this new Adolphe. She is strangely inert and gentle, in the face of treachery and desertion. I do not say that such behaviour is untrue to life; I know nothing about it. Everything is possible. But I wish it were better indicated from what source this woman, deficient in taste and wit, derived so rare a virtue. She has no position in the world, neither husband nor son. I should like to know whence came her strength to suffer in silence and die secretly.

For she dies. One night she throws herself into the sea from the deck of one of the transatlantic steamers on which she had taken so many passages, and no one will ever know how or why she died. This is a great deal of discretion for a lady who wore startling dresses and had eighteen trunks.

The maid of Avalon—and the recollection would not have displeased Richard Noral—sung by Tennyson was less negligent in her suicide. Dying for Arthur, she wished that he should know it, and it was she herself who, lying dead in a boat, brought her confession to the knight in a letter.

> Living, they called me the Maid of Avalon.

While Rose-Mary was drowning herself very simply and sincerely for love of him, Richard was haunting the *salon* of Madame d'Hays. Widowed after a few months of marriage, she had, at little expense, acquired a freedom equally precious to herself and her adorers. Richard admired in Madame d'Hays "that marvellous harmony of features, colouring, looks, movements and tone of voice that made the young woman an exceptional being, a dream above and beyond the idea of beauty." And Madame d'Hays did not look unkindly on Richard. Coming back from the Bois in her landau she acknowledged his bow with a pretty smile; they went a great deal to the theatre together; they talked of Shelley and the pre-Raphaelites. So well, indeed, that Richard fell in love with her. He would, as usual, have applied himself painstakingly to the adventure, had not the death of his daughter recalled him sharply to the solitude of his home and Helen in tears. Little Jeanne has died of inflammation of the lungs, but it is her mother's misery and her father's indifference which have slowly exhausted this frail and ardent nature. Little Jeanne is dead; a few months pass by, and the garden in which she plucked flowers blossoms once more. Richard, thinking of the child, who was his own, murmurs:

What delicious recollections she has left us!

And he adds:

Are not these recollections worth the reality?

Horrible speech! He who forgives Nature for the death of a child is outside the human race. He must be partly a monster. No doubt it is terrible to think that children will grow into men, that is, into something pitiable and odious. But one does not think of it. For in loving them, educating them and wishing them to live we follow the reasons of the heart, which are the great, true, and only reasons.

Richard Noral is a miserable creature, who makes a mess of marriage and adultery, and seeks for Cleopatra. But what would you have done with Cleopatra, you fool, if you had met her? You are neither exquisite Cæsar, nor rough Antony, to intoxicate yourself with this living cup, and you are not the sort of man to lose a kingdom for a kiss. Look at your friend Baïlac. He is always happy. He does not search for Cleopatra, and he finds her in all women. He's always in love, and his wife never worries him. The clever fellow has foreseen everything; she is always enceinte. Your friend Baïlac is like Henry IV; he loves duchesses and servant-maids. What he asks of woman is woman, and not the infinite, the impossible, the unknown, God, everything, and literature. He behaves badly, I admit it; he behaves very badly; but not for nothing. He's a bad egg, but not a fool. He loves without wishing to, without thinking about it, with ingenuous ardour, quite naturally; and that clothes him with a sort of innocence.

You think him a brute because he does not understand Rossetti's sonnets; but be careful lest, when all is said and done, he has not more imagination than you have. He knows how to discover the native beauty of things. You, you want a ready-made ideal, a Pia, not as she really was in her poor mortal life, but such as the art of a courteous poet and an exquisite painter have made her. You want poetic shades, and harmonious phantoms. What else do you seek? And why did you trouble Rose-Mary?

In calling you an egoist, people flatter you. Had you been merely an egoist you would have been only half bad. Egoism adapts itself to a kind of love and passion; in refined natures it desires, for its satisfaction, pure forms animated by beautiful thoughts. It is sensual; its peaceful dreams softly caress the universe. But you, you are less than an egoist: you are incapable. And if women love you, I am rather surprised. They ought to guess that you rob them shamefully.

It is a novelty of these days to claim the right to passion, as it has been always to claim the right to happiness. I have at hand a little book of the last century called *De l'Amour,* which amuses me hugely, as it is written with extraordinary simplicity. The author, M. de Sevelinges, who was a cavalry officer, would have you understand that true love is only for officers. "A warrior," he says, "has great advantages in love. He is also more inclined thereto than other men. Beautiful law of Nature!"

M. de Sevelinges is amusing. But he rightly enough adds that it is well that love, passionate love, should be rare. He bases his argument on the fact that "its powerful effect is always to detach men from their surroundings, to isolate them, and make them independent of any connections which it has not itself formed," and he concludes that, "a civilized society which was composed of lovers would inevitably relapse into poverty and barbarism." I advise Richard Noral to study the maxims of M. de Sevelinges; they are not lacking in philosophy. Nevertheless one should resign oneself to forgo love, when one feels its impossibility.

Then what is to be done? you ask. Good Lord, cultivate your garden, till the soil, play the flute, hide yourself, and live all the same! Remember Sieyès' words, and remember that it is still something to have lived under that perpetual Terror which is human destiny. And again the incomparable M. de Sevelinges would say: "If I take away passion, I at least leave you peace and pleasure. Is that nothing?"

Without speaking of *Adolphe,* we have already met more than one hero of romance for vainly seeking passion. In a very fine book, *Crime d'amour,* M. Paul Bourget has shown us the Baron de Querne, who seduces an honest woman only in order to throw her into despair. M. de Querne has a suspicious mind and an arid heart; he is abominably hard. Without any profit to himself, he destroys the happiness of the woman who loves him. But it is his business; he is a professional seducer; moreover he does not fall into slushy sentiment, or give himself up to that absurd ravaging of lives which makes Richard Noral altogether odious, and rather ridiculous. I see there is still a moral in M. Édouard Rod's book, and it is that all is vanity to vain men, and a lie to those who lie to themselves.

"We shall have adultery and cigarettes," said Théophile Gautier in the age of red waistcoats. M. Édouard Rod leaves us only the cigarettes.

So his book, in its very despondency, warns us to fear egoism as the worst of evils. It teaches purity of heart and simplicity. It calls to mind this little verse of the *Imitation:* "When anyone seeks himself, love is stifled in him."

There is much talent in this bitter story. One cannot overpraise the sobriety of the telling, the alternately graceful and powerful rapidity of the scenes, and the elegant precision of the style. I must even praise the cold and affected touch which perfectly fits the subject.

M. Édouard Rod's methods of art and composition are very superior to those, now almost abandoned, of the naturalistic school. In a short preface to **Les trois cœurs** the young author describes himself as an Intuitivist. I have no objection. In any case, he is a thousand miles apart from the Naturalists. The new school, including the old pupils of the Master of Médan, appears to be entering upon a kind of idealism, of which M. Hennique has recently given us a pleasing and peculiar example. M. Édouard Rod believes that he can indicate the principal causes of this unexpected phenomenon. He finds them in the exoticism in which we are steeped, and notably in the powerful suggestions exercised over the younger generation by the music of Wagner, English poetry and Russian romances. These indeed are the causes whose action, already perceptible in the work of M. Paul Bourget, progresses to exaggeration in the *éthopées* of M. Joséphin Péladan. A clever critic, M. Gabriel Sarrazin, was in a position to say: "At the present moment our literature is flooded by exotic infiltration. Our thought becomes more and more composite. While the people and the middle class remain imperturbably faithful to our Gallic and classical traditions, and continue to appreciate wit, animation and rhetoric, many of our writers are making a collection of all human conceptions. With the keen, refined aroma of ideas, and the swift, penetrating, ironic, and, in a word, French imagination, they combine the heavy, morbid perfume of heady theories and imaginings transplanted from other lands" [*Poètes modernes de l'Angleterre*]. Let us not too greatly deplore these importations; literatures, like nations, live by exchange. (pp. 257-66)

> Anatole France, "Edouard Rod," in his On Life & Letters, third series, *translated by D. B. Steward, John Lane/The Bodley Head Ltd., 1922, pp. 257-66.*

James Raymond Wadsworth (essay date 1938)

[*In the following excerpt, Wadsworth discusses Rod's Intuitivist novels.*]

Notwithstanding the wide circulation of Zola's novels, time brought an inevitable reaction to naturalism. One of the most noteworthy manifestations of the growth of an anti-naturalistic spirit was the protest of the *Cinq purs* which followed the publication of *La Terre* in 1887. [The critic adds in a footnote, "Paul Bonnetain, Lucien Descaves, Paul Margueritte, Gustave Guiches, J. H. Rosny. For Bonnetain's account of this protest *vide* Huret, *Enquête.*"] In this connection, Brunetière, always one of Zola's most severe critics, proclaimed the bankruptcy of naturalism [*Le Roman naturaliste*]. An excessive study of the physiological man, as a logical consequence, directed attention to the observation of the psychological being, almost wholly neglected by the naturalists.

This movement found a leader in Paul Bourget, who had, as early as 1873, pointed out the necessity of developing a new type of novel [*Revue des deux mondes,* 15 juillet 1873]. His *Essais de psychologie contemporaine,* appearing in *La Nouvelle Revue* (1883-1885), bring to the field of literature the application of psychological analysis, a method which he follows in the novel, beginning with *L'Irréparable* (1884). Not only did Bourget do this, but he succeeded in stating so forcibly what he was accomplishing that he effected a revolution in the novel of his time. The novel of analysis assumed the predominant position held only a few years previously by naturalism.

Of the Médan group, Zola and Alexis alone remained naturalists. In *Pierre et Jean* (1888) Maupassant shows the influence of Bourget. With *Un caractère* (1889) Hennique had turned to spiritualism. Huysmans had left his earlier manner in *A rebours* (1884). Céard had written no novels since *Une Belle Journée.*

Edouard Rod had not awaited the publication of *La Terre* to break with the method of Zola. *La Course à la Mort,* which marks a definite departure from his previous style and connects him with the evolution of the novel of analysis, had already appeared in 1885. He himself recognizes the inevitability of such a rupture, declaring that the voice of authority influences youth, which later regains its independence [*Le Correspondant,* 25 août 1893]. This had been the nature of his attraction to Zola, whose vigorous campaign against his opponents had won for him as many followers as had his literary ability. Rod and his fellows had dreamed of a new literary crusade similar to that of 1830, with the *première* of *L'Assommoir* replacing the battle of *Hernani.* However, the young naturalists had failed to consider some essential facts. "Nous ne savions pas que la loi de la différenciation s'applique à la littérature qui a perdu ses traits collectifs, et ne produit que des œuvres de plus en plus individuelles" [*Les Trois Cœurs,* Préface]. Moreover, the narrow materialism of naturalism, more absorbed in things than in the study of souls, failed to satisfy their tendencies toward idealism.

Rod did not lose his personal admiration for Zola, nor did he underestimate the importance of his work ["The Place of Emile Zola in Literature," *Contemporary Review,* 1902, vol. 82]. Zola had defined a work of art as a corner of nature seen through a temperament. The first phase of an author's work, Rod declares, emphasizes the reproduction of the corner of nature. At the end of this period of realism he seeks rather to manifest his own temperament through the corner of nature. He wishes to pass beyond the mere representation of the object and to analyze the laws and the secret forces which determine the sentiments and the actions of his characters.

It was in Zola's own theory that Rod found the idea which led to the formation of his doctrine of intuitivism. The articles on *Le Roman expérimental* led him to make between experiment and observation comparisons wholly favorable to the former. The experimental method leaves the writer free to form conjectures and to deduce certain conclusions while observation restricts him in this respect. It has the additional advantage—and this constitutes a capital fact in the explanation of Rod's literary evolution,—"elle l'autorise, elle l'oblige même à tirer de son propre fonds les raccords qui existent entre les faits et échappent à l' observation" [*Les Trois Cœurs,* Préface]. This statement contains in germ the fundamental principle of the theory of intuitivism. Since the analysis of Rod's early works shows them to be of essentially experimental nature rather than based upon direct observation, he had already turned toward the intuitivist novel.

Among the foreign influences which contributed to his gradual emancipation from naturalism Rod places first the music of Wagner, which seems to him based on intuition. At the same time were introduced the pessimism of Leopardi and especially that of Schopenhauer. Then came the art of the Pre-Raphaelites, and modern English poetry which the studies of Rod's friend, Sarrazin, first revealed to France. Still more important than any of these importations was that of the Russian novel. Through their interpretation of the significance of these exotic elements Vogüé and Bourget exerted a profound influence upon the young men of their generation.

In addition to these foreign influences and the result of his own reflections on the subject of Zola's theories, Rod's relations with Hennequin, who became one of his most intimate friends, exercised an important direction upon his thought. In frequent discussions with him on the question of environment, Rod conceived a violent antipathy toward minute and useless descriptions and thought of replacing them by a study of the inner being. He proposes to apply still further in the novel the principle which Wagner had used in *Tristan und Isolde,* to divert the interest from externals to the play of passion going on in the hearts of the characters. Life as well as literature completing the process of his detachment from naturalism, Rod implies that we may seek in *Le Sens de la Vie* those influences which effected the final transformation. Marriage, paternity, altruistic aspirations, the serious consideration of religious problems, all produce a state of mind no longer suited to the materialism and brutality of naturalism.

It is not *La Course à la Mort* with which Rod publishes the explanation of his theory of intuitivism. Not until 1889, when he no longer believes in the possibility of forming a definite group with a single aim, does he expound his doctrine in the preface of *Les Trois Cœurs.* An *intuitif,* he explains, is a man who indulges in introspection, not for the purpose of seeing himself alone, but to discover the key to the mysteries of the soul of humanity. Intuitivism would apply intuition to literary psychology. Schopenhauer, in his solution of the problem of existence, proposes to conceive the world in analogy with his own *microcosmus.* Rod in like manner would have the author look within himself to know and love others, not himself.

The attainment of this end in the novel involves radical changes among which Rod mentions the suppression of descriptions of environment which, he declares, only occupy space and explain nothing, although here he contradicts Balzac. He suggests also the elimination of retrospective narratives which recount the childhood and adolescence of the characters and thus present too definite a picture. He attempts to avoid artificial and theatrical scenes. Even these alterations do not entirely satisfy him. He desires still more complete liberation from the tyranny of precise figures and concrete facts so that their general significance may stand out more clearly. "Il faudrait revenir, sous une forme à trouver, au *Symbole;* et je ne sais si le moule trop brutal du roman s'y prêtera jamais." Rod suggests for the novel the evolution which already characterized the idealistic movement in poetry. Never a naturalist in reality, Rod has now become an intuitivist. To exemplify his theory he writes three novels, *La Course à la Mort, Le Sens de la Vie,* and *Les Trois Cœurs.*

Rod's theory of intuitivism did not meet with complete success in its first application, *La Course à la Mort* (1885). *La Course à la Mort* analyzes the intimate sufferings of a soul afflicted by the pessimistic spirit of the time and finding escape from the miseries of life only in the aspiration toward death. His unhappiness does not result from the intellectual ambition of a Faust or a Manfred. He does not know the satiety of debauch of a Childe Harold, nor does he experience the proud revolt of Lara. He has little in common with Werther whose moral sufferings come from the struggle of a man against things, from a passion opposed in its development. While he more nearly resembles René and Obermann, he lacks the element of genius which enables René to establish the superiority of his soul over his environment; and although like Obermann, he personifies doubt with his impotent reveries, he seems less sure of his desires and does not render the same impression of moral elevation. He does not possess the profoundly religious spirit and the belief in duty, or the aspiration to mingle his personal life in the general existence which characterized Amiel. He exemplifies Schopenhauer's principle that a never resting, never satisfied want constitutes the kernel of existence. His pessimism has no real foundation as did that of Leopardi because nothing happens to him. [The critic adds in a footnote, "Leopardi declared, however, that his philosophy had no connection with his physical suffering. Cf. Rod, *Etudes sur le XIXe siècle,* 'Giacomo Leopardi'."] Those events which do occur change at once into sensations which an immediate but unconscious analysis decomposes.

He aspires to love, for "le jeune homme problème rencontre la jeune fille énigme" [Gaucher, *Revue Bleue,* 26 septembre 1885]. The attraction of Cécile remains unexplained but he believes she too shares his weariness with life. This romance with only an occasional meeting forms his constant preoccupation, forcing him to a continual introspection. Cécile, too, feels the same indefinable aspirations. In a passage of Wagnerian inspiration Rod describes the spiritual communion which occurs as they waltz together. With no necessity for words to express their common sentiments, their souls vibrate with conflicting emotions, their own unexpressed passions as well as the griefs of other lovers. [The critic adds in a footnote, "The prelude of *Tristan und Isolde* expresses this longing for the unattainable and this unquenchable desire. Cf. Wagner's interpretation cited in Krehbiel, *Studies in the Wagnerian Drama.*"] Gradually they rise above the notion of time to a higher sphere where all faculties melt into one— ceaseless, causeless suffering. Then comes the desire for deliverance through death. Their souls attain together a kind of Nirvana, in which time, space and the world have disappeared, while they hear only a murmur of voices glorifying this state of annihilation. After this ecstatic moment Cécile passes out of his existence so that the news of her death later leaves him untouched. Love seems to him only an instrument of torture which destroys our last illusion and reveals life as the immutable caricature of our dreams.

His literary ambitions appear futile, since universal uncertainty renders it impossible to prove anything. There remains nothing to discover in the field of thought, or at least an original idea would merely be lost in the mass of mediocrity. Art alone, because of its uselessness, merits our interest, but it tortures us by holding before our eyes an unattainable ideal. Schopenhauer praised art from a different point of view, advancing the conception of salvation through esthetic contemplation. He maintained that art alone can cause the sudden breaking forth of the faculty of intuition which results in the predominance of pure perception and the disappearance of the will which removes suffering with it.

The hero next explores literature, but only to find all books the living witnesses to the contradictions, errors, and defeats of human thought. From them all he deduces the Schopenhauerian doctrine that evil constitutes the positive principle of life and that good is merely a mood of thought like time and space.

Abandoning literature, he longs to find refuge in some remote spot, loving and loved by a naïve, ignorant creature. He aspires to the quiescence which Schopenhauer offers as a practical deliverance from suffering. Gradually he discovers the source of his complaint. He learns that the iron turning in his wound is Life. He hates life, and every living creature because it suffers and causes pain. Rod's hero does not, like Obermann, feel his own sufferings alone; he suffers for all. Yet in spite of his hatred of life he is not sure of desiring death. His dream of solitude brings doubts too when he discovers upon a mountain top two brothers, one contemplative, the other meditative as he himself would be. The latter, without having read Schopenhauer, preaches his same hopeless doctrine. The hero therefore begins to wonder whether solitude brings disillusionment or leads to paradise.

Rod on the decline of Naturalism among Emile Zola's disciples:

We had aspirations that could never be satisfied by realism, which was essentially self-satisfied, narrow and materialist, more curious about manners than about character, about things than about souls: we were, and we were becoming more and more restless, idealist, in love with the infinite, caring little for manners, in everything always seeking man.

Edouard Rod, in his preface to his Les trois coeurs, *1890.*

At Bayreuth he finds justification for Schopenhauer's belief in music as the highest art. In Wagner, as in Michel Angelo, the other master whom he profoundly admires, he learns that those who have seen and experienced all aspire only to quiescence. Although music has brought temporary cessation of suffering, he has not the energy to maintain the artistic attitude, and the will to live reasserts itself.

He seeks escape from the prison which life builds around him, and taking the five or six hundred books which for him epitomize the history of human thought, retires to an isolated spot. There his days pass in ineffable ennui; he loses interest in ideas, his poets disappoint him, inspiration fails to come and his will, already feeble, grows still weaker. In the midst of his boredom he discovers two desirable things, silence and immobility. More and more he absorbs himself in things, with no desire to leave the quiet valley.

Mon âme est prête à se perdre dans les plantes et dans l'air. Et la terre m'appelle . . . Je pourrais me coucher sur son sein pour m'endormir dans son mystère . . . Je pourrais lui demander enfin ma part de son inconscience . . . Ne ferais-je pas mieux que de contempler passivement ses inutiles floraisons!

In these final words he has attained the entire negation of the will to live and is passing into Nirvana.

An analysis of *La Course à la Mort* shows how much Rod owed to Schopenhauer and to Wagner and how far their influence predominated over that of Zola even during his naturalistic period, for he had begun the composition of the novel several years before its publication [Mlle. de Mestral Combremont, *La Pensée d'Ed. Rod*]. The extent to which the book reveals its author is not an easy question to determine. Critics offer conflicting opinions, Sabatier declaring that its evident sincerity forms the principal attraction of the work [*Journal de Genève,* 9 août 1885] and Sarcey likewise accepting it as the portrayal of a personal crisis. Fuster refuses to consider it more than an attempt to become the leader of a literary school [*Essais de Critique*], while Gaucher sees in the novel a sincere journal of the man combined with the exaggerated pose of the author [Gaucher, *Revue Bleue,* 26 septembre 1885]. Gabriel Sarrazin, probably Rod's most intimate friend at that time, should offer credible evidence. "Tout est vrai dans ce livre que j'ai vu vivre et écrire" [Mestral Combremont].

Rod himself insists that the philosophy which he developed to complete the intellectual mechanism of his hero must not be considered the expression of his own conception of life. Notwithstanding this public protest, one cannot deny Rod's fundamental pessimism, his belief in evil as the positive principle of life. Why he did not seek the Nirvana to which his hero aspired will become evident through the analysis of *Le Sens de la Vie.*

While Sarcey and Hennequin accept Rod's work as representative, Fuster maintains that Rod has analyzed an exceptional case. Upon the publication of *La Course à la Mort,* which Henry Bordeaux calls the poem of modern pessimism [*Pèlerinages litt.*], a Parisian journalist described Rod as a *"pessimiste pontifiant."* and devoted to *"la jeunesse où l'on s'ennuie"* a study in which he cites Rod as one of the most prominent examples of precocious old men, *"ânes bâtés qui se croient porteurs de reliques"* [Champsaur, *Le Cerveau de Paris*]. This group of morose pedants as he termed them, best represented by Edouard Rod, *"l'ennui fait homme,"* in reality possesses a deeper significance than Champsaur would have us believe, for by 1885, pessimism had profoundly affected French thought. Teodor de Wyzewa wrote in 1885: "Notre littérature française semble vouloir s'appeler aujourd'hui, décidément, le Pessimisme. Elle nous donne des romans pessimistes, des drames pessimistes, des poèmes pessimistes, des œuvres de critique pessimistes" [*Nos Maîtres*]. In an article on the pessimism of Bourget, Fuster himself makes a similar statement fully in accord with the opinion expressed by Georges Pellissier ["Le Pessimisme dans la littérature contemporaine" (written in 1890), *Essais de litt. cont.*]. No literary genre reveals this characteristic to a greater degree than the novel. In this literature of despair, *La Course à la Mort* holds an important place.

In *Le Sens de la Vie* (1889), the second volume of the intuitivist series, Rod attempts to answer the riddle of the meaning of life. Marriage and paternity have transformed his philosophy and he has learned that we live not merely to die but also to love. The hero, the anonymous protagonist of *La Course à la Mort,* has renounced his futile self-analysis. His marriage constitutes his first action in his emancipation from self, and to his surprise proves less disagreeable than he had imagined. However he can not banish entirely his habit of anticipating misfortunes. His ignorance of the knowledge of happiness menaces the future of their love. Marriage entails obligations, most important of all, that of living.

Tolstoy's *Confession* had appeared in French translation in 1887. The problem of the meaning of life, which had tormented the Russian author, now presents itself to Rod's hero and his reason rejects all solutions suggested to his mind. The collapse of the Greek and Roman civilization prevents him from accepting the ideal of the progress of humanity by which Renan in his youthful enthusiasm for science had replaced faith. He feels indifferent toward humanity, instead of sharing Schopenhauer's misanthropy. Pity, which in the complete application of the term means faith in the religion of human suffering, can no more be acquired than faith in Christianity. Agnosticism gives no answer. The problem still remains and his anxious curiosity persists. In spite of his uncertainty, he accepts life, he experiences joys, he loves.

Paternity brings with it a constant evolution of his sentiments. From his first stage of paternal jealousy, he passes to a feeling of pity for the helpless creature for whose presence in the evils of the world he is responsible. He has not forgotten Schopenhauer's declaration that the human race would cease to exist if children were brought into the world by an act of pure reason alone, for a man would in sympathy spare the coming generation the burden of existence. Pity develops into affection and finally love, which is revealed by the serious illness of the child. Disgust with life vanishes before the approach of death; he clings to life and finds it preferable to annihilation. A desire to sacrifice himself wholly to the child's happiness indicates that he is approaching the solution of his problem. Yet the question still presents itself as he considers the possibility of a higher ideal than family happiness.

The reading of *Humiliés et Offensés, Crime et Châtiment, La Guerre et la Paix,* and *Anna Karénine* reveals a new world. Wondering if dilettantism has merely found a new topic of discussion in this Russian religion of human suffering, he questions the sincerity of the enthusiasm of his fellows for the message "Love ye one another." As for himself, he hesitates and doubts, even though he admires the new gospel. A concrete example of its efficacy appears upon the death of an old friend, whose life of self-abnegation and suffering seems to have exemplified perfection in the art of living. This theme Rod will develop more completely in *Mademoiselle Annette.* The idea of the beauty of sacrifice appears likewise in figures like Maria Lidine, and Baron des Claies in the story **"Les Lilas sont en fleurs."**

The working of these various factors on the heart and mind of the hero results in a first step toward altruism, but pity must be accompanied by action and here a difficulty arises. As Tolstoy opposed the artificial philanthropy of the wealthy, so Rod rejects organized charity as a hypocritical compromise between actual sacrifice and the donation of our superfluous goods to our less fortunate neighbors. He determines to secure an intimate acquaintance with the people whom he hopes to help. One experience suffices to show him the folly of looking for good among so many hatreds. From this contact with the proletariat he gains an understanding of class hatred and becomes convinced that one can hope for nothing from the masses. Moreover he discovers that the Russian novels have deceived him in starting him upon a path which he can not follow. The religion of human suffering lies as far beyond our reach as any other creed. The failure of altruism to solve the problem teaches him that he must find happiness in the small circle of family affections and duties.

From altruism he turns to an analysis of his attitude toward religion. A friend who had once shared his opinions and who has since been reconverted to Protestantism points the way to escape from scepticism through the logical realization of the social and individual necessity for religion. He arrives at the conclusion reached a few years later by Paul Bourget [in the Préface to his *Essais de psychologie contemporaine*]. Confronted by this social need for faith, he found it through an act of the will.

The hero finds this difficult to comprehend and understands still less why his friend has returned to the Protestant faith, which he criticizes in words revealing that Rod still retained the aversion for Protestantism shown in *Côte à côte.* Rod proved elsewhere that he shared his hero's opinions by parallel statements declaring that the Christian religion at present does not entirely satisfy our conscience because the aridity of the abstract Protestant faith repels us and the concrete faith of Catholicism does not lie within the reach of all. Notwithstanding his condemnation of Protestantism, he admits that he may be nearer his friend's beliefs than appearances indicate.

He receives further light on the subject of religion through the apparition of his love who had died ten years before. The vision, who seems to have read Renan, characterizes religions as the error of limited brains attempting to imagine infinity. In spite of their illusory nature, we must not treat them as impostures. We must banish curiosity, and knowing not, seek not to know. "Savoir est la suprême duperie."

Experience has finally taught the hero that affection seems to hold the meaning of life. A desire comes to cease to question, and to take his wife and child to some tropical island where life would be as simple and pure as that depicted by Bernardin de Saint Pierre. The island vanishes when he thinks of the future of his child. For her he dreams of a typical *bourgeois* existence, happy in performing the ordinary duties of life.

The pessimist refuses to accept complete happiness. When

affection offers its keenest joy an anguishing obsession of approaching death for his loved ones steals over him. Love seems futile when annihilation awaits our affection. Seeing after the tortures of death itself an afterward of uncertainty, he envies the believers who have found an answer to the problem.

During a burst of exaltation produced by hearing a high mass at Saint Sulpice he enjoys with all his senses a moment of faith. He longs to participate in worship, but ignorant of the ritual, he is forced to read his hymn in his own heart and a chant inspired by Schopenhauer and Renan mingles with the words of the pious. He has only to banish his last doubts and find God in a humble prayer dictated by faith, but his lips alone murmur a *Pater noster.* His reason has refused to yield to his instinct and to his need for faith.

Amiel had said: "Savoir, aimer, et pouvoir, c'est là la vie complète." Rod learned from Renan the uncertainty of knowledge. "Pouvoir" in religion does not lie within his power. The book *Vouloir et pouvoir* which he undertook as the logical sequel to *Le Sense de la Vie,* he failed to finish, doubtless because he feared to have taken as autobiographical a work which did not sincerely represent his own beliefs. If Catholicism attracted him from the esthetic point of view, his Protestant training would forever keep him from a conversion like that of Huysmans. Rod's hero seems to have discovered one possible meaning of life in family affections and reaches a conclusion identical with that of Amiel. "Donner du bonheur et faire du bien, voilà notre loi, notre ancre de salut, notre phare, notre raison d'être." Yet since the earlier work, he has undergone the influence of Tolstoy, and if he still preaches despair it is no longer that of the individual in solitude but a nobler melancholy resulting from the spectacle of human suffering and our inability to relieve it. We feel too with Lemaître [in *Les Contemporains,* 5e série] that Rod concludes life has a meaning only for those who believe and love. His pessimism therefore depends partly upon his failure to achieve faith. This same longing for belief appears in **"La Transformation de l'idée de Dieu."** Rod elsewhere declared that tranquillity of mind requires illusions which we may take for certainties and that even though we may have liberated ourselves from religious beliefs, we cannot escape the need for religion. He might apply to himself his own description of Henri Warnéry as a religious soul and a free intelligence.

Le Sens de la Vie, perhaps to a greater extent than *La Course à la Mort,* presented an analysis of the state of mind of many of Rod's contemporaries. Lemaître characterized the book as too true, and confessed having experienced many of the same sentiments. Coinciding with the aspirations of the moment, it achieved a notable success and was crowned by the French Academy. Thus Rod vindicated his theory of intuitivism.

In *Les Trois Cœurs* (1890), the final novel of the intuitivist series, he endeavors to discredit self-analysis and to show man's duty to his family and to everyday life rather than to himself and the world of fancy represented by the poets of the past. Rod has here only partly succeeded in the application of his doctrine. If he created Richard Noral

through intuition, thinking him a general type, he deceived himself, for Noral is as exceptional as the nameless hero of *La Course à la Mort.* Having formed him thus, he does with this unusual character show the workings of the human heart under certain circumstances. He proves likewise the point in his theory which condemns wholly selfish introspection. The epigraph taken from the *Imitation* contains the whole substance of *Les Trois Cœurs.* "Dès que quelqu'un se cherche soi-même, l'amour s'étouffe en lui." Knowing men only through the mirror of himself, Noral instinctively avoids his fellow creatures. Fascinated by the dreams of vanished poets, he deplores his own ignorance of passion and the selfishness of his individuality. He curses the century which has banished the great emotions of the past. He feels his soul still capable of love, but like the hero of *La Course à la Mort,* he knows that pleasure can only bring final disillusionment.

At this opportune moment, an American, Rose-Marie, arriving in Paris, expresses her willingness to renew their former friendship. Selfish and hardhearted, Richard deserts the affections of his wife and his little daughter Jeanne in order to cultivate his ego, no longer in futile introspection, but in action, in love and pleasure. Noral soon discovers that his love for Rose-Marie too has passed, or rather, might have existed and did not. This intuitivist Adolphe succeeds only in weakening the affection he already possessed and degrading his soul through lies and hypocrisy. As Anatole France said, "Richard Noral est un misérable, qui gâche à la fois le mariage et l'adultère et qui cherche Cléopâtre." Noral's two victims have, however, something which he lacks,—the power to love. He finally extricates himself from a difficult situation by breaking both hearts for a third woman for whom he feels a strange affinity. Even so, he suspects that Madame d'Hays is only a pretext created by himself for the satisfaction of his ego. Rose-Marie discovers that she alone has loved, and heartbroken, she slips quietly into the ocean from her transatlantic liner. The love which Noral has just killed casts a shadow over his new passion. At this moment, his daughter Jeanne, whose resistance has been weakened by her mother's grief and her own unhappiness at her father's neglect, falls seriously ill. Richard abandons his egoism only too late and his daughter dies. This catastrophe brings him to his senses. Richard and his wife, united in suffering, feel that they have much to forgive each other, although one can scarcely understand how Hélène could have acted differently toward this egoist who has fed his soul on the compositions of the Pre-Raphaelites and on the *Vita Nuova.*

Richard at last perceives his mistake, but instead of blaming himself, reproaches the poets whose dreams have influenced him. This theme Rod will study from the author's point of view in *Au milieu du Chemin.* Having destroyed his possibility of happiness, he perceives that the man of to-day loves, but differently, and that the powers of affection and devotion which he once possessed in his own heart were worth quite as much as Dante's ecstasy or the passion of Musset. Anatole France points out the true significance of *Les Trois Cœurs* when he calls it a warning to fear egoism as the worst of evils and a lesson in simplicity and purity of heart. Thus the last of the intuitivist trio has its place in the idealistic movement of the time.

Intuitivism stands out in the work of Edouard Rod as his most original contribution to literature. He formulated a theory and applied it with sufficient success to be acclaimed the apostle of pessimism in *La Course à la Mort.* By the same method he expressed in *Le Sens de la Vie* the idealistic aspirations of the epoch and came into prominence as one of the leaders, along with Paul Desjardins, of a neo-Christian movement. While *Les Trois Cœurs,* with its study of the results of selfish introspection, fails to attain the same standard of excellence, it forms a valuable link in the proof of his theory. (pp. 9-21)

> *James Raymond Wadsworth, "Intuitivism,"* in University Studies, *Vol. XXXVIII, Nos. 3-4, 1938, pp. 9-21.*

Michael G. Lerner   (essay date 1975)

[*Lerner is an English critic and educator who often focuses on Rod's writing. In the following excerpt, he describes Rod's achievements as a novelist and speculates as to the decline of Rod's literary reputation.*]

As Charles Recolin stated already in 1898 [in his *L'Anarchie Littéraire*] Edouard Rod's life and work presented an individually interpreted yet highly representative picture of the pre-1914 literary world:

> Quand on voudra faire l'histoire de l'évolution des idées pendant le dernier quart de ce siècle, M. Rod sera certainement un des premiers témoins consultés. Nul mieux que lui ne s'est pénétré des pensées de son temps, et nul ne les a traduites avec plus de sincérité et de scrupule, tout en colorant ce qu'il réflétait, à la manière des lacs de son pays natal, de la teinte spéciale de son propre fond.

This was so particularly because Rod's personal circumstances largely coïncided with those on a much wider level of the French writer in general during this period of uncertainty and change, from which the present age of universal cataclysm, scientific invention, and sophisticated savagery was born.

Looking at these circumstances, it is observed that while the artist was becoming increasingly isolated in the French society to which he nevertheless belonged, Rod was by his family background as well as by intellect and sensibility exiled and at the same time rooted in his Swiss homeland; while French writers were mainly Catholic sceptics of varying degrees, Rod was a moralistic refugee of Protestantism; when the French sought spiritual succour in foreign reinterpretations of their threatened moral values, Rod as a Swiss in France, acquainted moreover with Sarrazin, Hennequin, Brewster and André Gladès, naturally and necessarily participated in the current cosmopolitanism; and when French minds turned in confusion to the social and moral issues of the Dreyfus case, of tradition and anarchy, and the European situation, Rod could similarly ponder on Rousseau's life, on his homeland and faith, and the tragedies of his last years. Indeed within Rod's very personality there was an anguish and

conflict found in French literary life as a whole. From the very beginning there was in his personality a dichotomy of his delicate sensibility of a sentimental Swiss and his intellect of the more sophisticated Parisian and that of his Protestant, realistic moral searching and an aesthetically spiritual desire for Catholic, stable self-completion. There was in Rod a conflict, mirrored in his literary themes, technique and style, between his real self and that into which he wished to escape from it, between the reality of himself and the destiny of his situation in life; a Pascalian moral consciousness of his relative *grandeur* and his infinite *petitesse,* epitomised in the role of the *Pasteur Pauvre* he liked to portray, that urged him to a Faustian striving to transcend fatal reality, to justify with faith his doubts in Fate and know himself; in fact, to escape the fate of Oedipus, whose spiritual human condition haunted Rod from his licentiate thesis to his last novels. As Lecigne points out in describing Rod's tentative flights from the *ombres* of life to the ideal *lumière* as those of an "aigle blessé," this inner craving for spiritual balance was essentially common to all his generation "et c'est pour cela que sa destinée est un des symboles qui caractérisent le mieux la génération d'hier avec ses souffrances, ses espoirs et son impuissance finale" [*Du Dilettantisme à l'Action*].

Rod's literary development, both encouraged by and encouraging those personal circumstances, gives a broad and clear reflection of the history of ideas before 1914 from the infatuation with Zola and Wagner and the vogues for the pre-Raphaelites, the Russians, the Scandinavians, the Italians, and Americanism to the social interest in tradition and nature and in the thought of Nietzsche, Stirner, Kropotkin, Ellen Key, Blum, Péguy, Sangier, and Sorel. It provides, too, insights into the literary evolution from physical realism to a neo-Symbolist concern for the inner man and a pseudo-political interest in the individual in society: the basic incompatibility of Zola's disciples and the fundamental fallacy of the Naturalist doctrine in its diverse application; the cumulative effect of the diagnostic studies of Bourget in his *Essais,* the curative *Roman Russe* of de Vogüé, and the *nouveau spiritualisme* of Bergson in moulding the cosmopolitan dilettantism that produced the idealistic trend away from Naturalism and towards Symbolism; the spiritual drift from psychological to sociological interest, from the individual to the individual's roots in society, from the mind in the present to the spirit of Man through the ages; the stresses and strains of the Dreyfus case and the subsequent dangers of exploitation and extremism in the social issues of change and reform it provoked; and finally, a pre-Proustian investigation into life's fatal course itself, which takes in the spiritual and moral problems latent in all Rod's literary production on a higher level of perspective. Rod like his age might then be termed in Tissot's words "un intellectuel s'intellectualisant d'expérience en expérience, de volume en volume" [*In Memoriam Edouard Rod*]; demonstrating the spiritual confusion in contemporary values from *Les Allemands à Paris* to *Le Glaive et le Bandeau* and their moral influences on the individual conscience and society in his *Etudes Passionnelles* and social studies; and thus participating in the modern search for the Graal, that in the second half of the last century could be exemplified in Flaubert's eclectic scepticism and Renan's metaphysical dilettantism and that in the present age has led to the *Bildungsroman* of Rolland and Mann, the Bergsonian works of Proust and Durrell, the 'stream of consciousness' novels of Joyce and Svevo, the theatre of Pirandello, and the existentialism of Malraux. But the fact that Rod's literary and critical preoccupation with the fatal course of "idées morales" in society was as representative of the period's thought and symptomatic of its problems as Flaubert's earlier sado-masochistic involvement with "idées reçues" has not, however, prevented the present virtual oblivion into which his pristine celebrity has regrettably fallen.

Various reasons can be suggested for the popular neglect of Rod despite the large volume of his work, its variety, and the diverse interest it stimulates and Bourget's assurance [in the 19 February 1910 *Revue Hebdomadaire*] that it has "sa place marquée pour toujours dans l'histoire de la haute littérature française." Chief among any such explanations must be placed the early death of Rod prior to the 1914-1918 cataclysm—unlike Bourget and Barrès who survived well after it—and his Swiss nationality. As Beuchat affirms [in *Edouard Rod et le Cosmopolitisme*], the War changed the face of the world and modified its features including the mark Rod had impressed on it; moreover, after the War there was no effort made in Switzerland to revive Rod's memory for some twenty years, in which time his reputation had faded in other countries and his works were out of print. Certainly too, the nature of his personality and work failed to appeal to the post-War world; the grave issues of his moral situations were not likely to be very popular at any time in the modern age of increasing licence and irresponsibility, particularly immediately after the soul-destroying First World War; and Rod's bourgeois conservative moral indecision in face of a changing society was hardly suited to the new world situation: events such as the rise of America, the Revolution in Russia, the growth of socialist democracy and of proletarian and feminist power, and even the War itself, had happened even sooner than Rod had rightly anticipated them, but they were nevertheless in the past and present and could no longer be looked to in debating the future. If, as Van Raalte asserts [in *L'Oeuvre d'Edouard Rod*], Rod's novels demand from the reader that sympathy for his ideas which he instilled into them by his sincerity, it is clear that such self-projection was now more difficult and artificial. Rod's works thus suffered partly due to their very contemporaneity and, in turn, because they had subordinated theme, technique, and style to the discussion of moral thought, much of which had now become, at least immediately after the War, redundant by its loss of actuality. Furthermore, Rod's stories are frequently too functionally calculated and his characters are too often types with a set outlook rather than full personalities to be memorable and achieve a more lasting significance. However, this loss of actuality and over-emphasis on ideas also affected the works of many of his contemporaries and does not fully explain why Rod's novels have not survived as well as those of Bourget, Barrès or France. An influential factor in this process was, however, the fact that Rod's novels were, as has been observed earlier, frequently misunderstood at the time of their publication and thus were neglected with his more doctrinaire works after the War.

All too often Rod's originality remained elusive and critics only recognised in his interpretations what he had already imitated from or what resembled other contemporary topics; certainly his Swiss works were never popular in France due to national taste and prejudice. Blame for this can perhaps be fixed on Rod to some extent for the complexity of his novels and for leaning so manifestly on occasions on Tolstoy, Wagner, or D'Annunzio; but it is to be set even more squarely on the shoulders of critics who have failed to reveal the precise yet sincere realism of Rod's delicately introspective comprehension of moral character, his gentle humour, his realistically shrewd and extremely far-sighted perspicacity in social issues, his religiously sentimental yet sympathetically detached simplicity of vision of village life, and the fluctuating classical beauty of his largely abstract style. It is these qualities that lend his work at times the charm of Puccini's music and Millais' portraits, the wit and irony of a Galsworthy or an E. M. Forster, the broad understanding of Verga and Deledda, and a language blended with the abstraction of Bourget, the oratory of Flaubert, and, occasionally the sensitivity of Proust. If Rod has been neglected, it is then, as his friend Hennequin would have diagnosed, a reflection of post-1914 society's lack of desire so far to re-examine and appreciate him. There is still hope, however, that with the awakening of interest in the culture of the period, that spans Rod's life and French literature from Zola to Proust and which so clearly but ominously resembles the fatal evolution of our own, his reputation will be revived and he might at last receive the homage of posterity he merits from the mysterious justice of Man's eternal destiny. (pp. 249-53)

> *Michael G. Lerner, in his* Edouard Rod (1857-1910): A Portrait of the Novelist and His Times, *Mouton, 1975, 272 p.*

FURTHER READING

Criticism

Review of *La seconde vie de Michel Teissier,* by Edouard Rod. *Blackwood's Edinburgh Magazine* CLVI, No. DCCCCXLIX (November 1894): 583-99.

    Characterizes *La seconde vie de Michel Teissier* as thoughtful and refined.

Lerner, Michael G. "Edouard Rod and Henry Brewster: An Unpublished Tribute." *Nottingham French Studies* VII, No. 2 (October 1968): 90-106.

    Examines Rod's friendship with and essay on American expatriate writer Henry Brewster.

———. "Edouard Rod and America." *Revue de littérature comparée* 44 (1970): 531-39.

    Describes Rod's tour of North America and its effect on his writings.

———. "A Literary Age in Evolution: 'Les idées morales du

temps présent' of Edouard Rod." *Nottingham French Studies* XI, No. 1 (May 1972): 27-38.
    Discusses the evolution of Rod's moral thought.

"M. Rod's New Novel." *The Saturday Review* (London) 86, No. 2235 (27 August 1898): 275.
    Characterizes *Le ménage du Pasteur Naudié* as a carefully executed, if overly austere, study of French Protestant morality.

"Les trois coeurs." *The Spectator* 64, No. 3223 (5 April 1890): 483-84.
    Characterizes Rod's novel as self-indulgent and unoriginal.

Review of *La vie privée de Michel Teissier,* by Edouard Rod. *The Westminster Review* 139, No. 3 (March 1893): 338-400.
    Includes a favorable appraisal of *La vie privée de Michel Teissier.*

Jules Verne

1828-1905

(Full name Jules Gabriel Verne) French novelist, short story writer, and playwright. For further information on Verne's career, see *TCLC,* Volume 6.

INTRODUCTION

Verne is regarded as one of the originators of modern science fiction. Remembered chiefly for the adventure novels in his series *Les voyages extraordinaires,* which includes *Vingt mille lieues sous les mers* (*Twenty Thousand Leagues under the Sea*), *Voyage au centre de la terre* (*Journey to the Center of the Earth*), and *Le tour du monde en quatre-vingt jours* (*Around the World in Eighty Days*), Verne was among the first writers to explore in his works the possibilities of technology. Intending to educate his readers, Verne infused general scientific knowledge into absorbing stories that typically explore nineteenth-century concerns about scientific innovation and its potential for human benefit or destruction.

Born in Nantes, Verne was educated in local schools before going to Paris in 1847 to study law, which was his father's profession. Verne had little interest in practicing law, and in Paris met numerous people in literary circles who encouraged him to write. After his marriage to Honorine du Fraysne de Viane in 1857, Verne worked as a stockbroker and wrote in his spare time. His early plays, short stories, and opera libretti met with little success. The publication in 1863 of *Cinq semaines en ballon* (*Five Weeks in a Balloon*), the first of the *voyages extraordinaires,* marked the beginning of Verne's long association with publisher Pierre-Jules Hetzel. Hetzel saw in Verne's work the opportunity to educate French readers about geography and modern science, while also providing them with an exciting story. This was to be the objective of all subsequent books in the *voyages* series, which proved to be commercially successful both in France and abroad. After the publication of *L'ile mystérieuse* (*The Mysterious Island*) in 1874, Verne's writing became darker and more pessimistic, reflecting the destructive potential that he had come to see in technology. Some commentators have seen this change in outlook as a result of several personal tragedies that befell Verne about this time. Other scholars have argued that even Verne's early work contains hints of pessimism, which were toned down at Hetzel's insistence and which later emerged more fully after Hetzel's death in 1886. None of Verne's later works has proved as popular or enduring as his earlier novels. By the time of Verne's death in 1905, he had been named a Chevalier of the French Legion of Honor and was internationally known as a highly imaginative adventure writer.

The early titles in Verne's *voyages extraordinaires,* such as *Twenty Thousand Leagues under the Sea, Journey to the*

Center of the Earth, and *De la terre à la lune, trajet direct en 97 heures* (*From the Earth to the Moon Direct in 97 Hours 20 Minutes: And a Trip around It*), express confidence in humankind's ability to know and control nature. In these works Verne's heroes journey to previously uncharted regions in order to gain knowledge for the betterment of humanity. Progress for Verne meant scientific achievement, exploration, and discovery; consequently, his most frequent hero is the scientist. Because his intention was to educate his readers, Verne included in his books an encyclopedic range of information relating to scientific discoveries and inventions. Many of his characters, such as Professor Lidenbrock of *Journey to the Center of the Earth,* frequently lecture their companions (and the reader) on scientific subjects in the midst of an adventure. Its educational properties notwithstanding, Verne's fiction is best remembered for its thrilling adventures and fantastic modes of transportation: the submarine *Nautilus* in *Twenty Thousand Leagues under the Sea,* the flying machine *Albatros* of *Robur-le-conquérant* (*Robur the Conqueror*), the powerful airship *Victoria* of *Five Weeks in a Balloon,* and a steam-powered mechanical elephant in *La maison à vapeur* (*The Steam House*).

Verne's later works, including *Maître du monde* (*Master of the World*), *Etonnante aventure de la mission Barsac* (*The Barsac Mission*), and the short story "L'éternel Adam" ("The Eternal Adam"), display less optimism about the future of humankind and technology and satirize humanity's attempts to control the universe. The scientists who appear in these works are unscrupulous, allowing others to use their inventions for evil, or menacing the world themselves with powerful futuristic weapons. Verne's last work, "The Eternal Adam," suggests that human progress is an illusion and scientific advancement futile.

While few critics have disputed Verne's importance in the evolution of science fiction, many have maintained that his ideas were of greater merit than his skills as a fiction writer. However, this charge has been countered by evidence that nineteenth-century English translators savaged Verne's work, making careless errors, and in many cases omitting or completely revising large portions of his original texts. Newer translations of some of the better known works have recently appeared. Some modern critics have faulted Verne's works because of their sometimes erroneous science, heavy-handed didacticism, wooden character portrayals, racial stereotypes, and a dearth of female characters. While Verne based much of the technology depicted in his books in fact, many critics have noted that he ignored science when it suited his purposes. Nevertheless, Verne is still praised for his ability to predict future uses of technology. He remains among the most-translated authors in world literature.

PRINCIPAL WORKS

Les pailles rompues (drama) 1850
*Cinq semaines en ballon: Voyages de découvertes en Afrique (novel) 1863
  [*Five Weeks in a Balloon*, 1869]
*Voyage au centre de la terre (novel) 1864
  [*A Journey to the Center of the Earth*, 1872]
*De la terre à la lune: Trajet direct en 97 heures. 2 vols. (novel) 1865
  [*From the Earth to the Moon: Passage Direct in 97 Hours and 20 Minutes*, 1869, also translated as *From the Earth to the Moon*, 1959]
*Les Aventures du capitaine Hatteras. 2 vols. (novel) 1865
  [*At the North Pole* (volume 1) and *The Desert of Ice* (volume 2), 1874, also translated as *The Adventures of Captain Hatteras*, 1876]
*Les enfants du Capitaine Grant. 3 vols. (novel) 1868
  [*In Search of the Castaways*, 1873, also translated as *Captain Grant's Children*, 1964]
*Autour de la lune (novel) 1870
  [*Round the Moon*, 1876]
*Vingt mille lieues sous les mers (novel) 1870
  [*Twenty Thousand Leagues under the Sea*, 1873]
*Une ville flottante, suivi de les Forceurs de blocus (novel and short story) 1871

[*A Floating City, and the Blockade Runners*, 1874]
*Le Pays des fourrures (novel) 1873
  [*The Fur Country*, 1874]
*Le Tour du monde en quatre-vingts jours (novel) 1873
  [*A Tour of the World in Eighty Days*, 1873; also translated as *Around the World in Eighty Days*, 1874]
*Le Docteur Ox; Maître Zacharias; Un Hivernage dans les glaces; Un Drame dans les airs (short stories) 1874
  [*Dr. Ox's Experiment, and Other Stories*, 1874]
*L'île mystérieuse. 3 vols. (novel) 1875
  [*The Mysterious Island*, 1875]
*Michel Strogoff, Moscou-Irkoutsk. 2 vols. (novel) 1876
  [*Michael Strogoff, the Courier of the Czar*, 1877]
*Hector Servadac: Voyages et aventures à travers le monde solaire. 2 vols. (novel) 1877
  [*Hector Servadac: Travels and Adventures Through the Solar System* 1877; also translated as *To the Sun?* and *Off on a Comet!*, 1878]
*Les Cinq Cents Millions de la Begúm, suivi de Les Revoltés de la "Bounty" (novel and short story) 1879
  [*The 500 Millions of the Begum*, 1879; also translated as *The Begum's Fortune*, 1880]
*Robur-le-conquérant (novel) 1886
  [*The Clipper of the Clouds*, 1887; also translated as *Robur the Conqueror*, 1887]
*Sans dessus dessous (novel) 1889
  [*Topsy Turvy*, 1890; also translated as *The Purchase of the North Pole*, 1891]
*L'ile à hélice. 2 vols. (novel) 1895
  [*The Floating Island*, 1896; also translated as *Propeller Island*, 1961]
*Face au drapeau (novel) 1896
  [*For the Flag*, 1897]
*Le Sphinx des glaces. 2 vols. (novel) 1897
  [*An Antarctic Mystery*, 1898; also translated as *The Mystery of Arthur Gordon Pym*, 1961]
*Maître du monde (novel) 1904
  [*The Master of the World*, 1914]
*Le Phare du bout du monde (novel) 1905
  [*The Lighthouse at the End of the World*, 1923]
*Les Naufragés du "Jonathan." 2 vols. (novel) 1909
  [*The Survivors of the Jonathan*, 1962]
*Hier et demain (short stories) 1910
  [*Yesterday and Tomorrow*, 1965]
*L'Etonnante aventure de la mission Barsac. 2 vols. (novel) 1919
  [*The Barsac Mission: Into the Niger Bend* (volume 1) and *The City in the Sahara* (volume 2), 1960]

*These volumes comprise the series *Les voyages extraordinaires.*

CRITICISM

The Nation (essay date 1905)

[*In the excerpt below, the critic praises Verne's works as imaginative adventure stories especially appropriate for the young.*]

The death of Jules Verne should strike with a sense of personal bereavement all boys who read and all men in whom the romantic imagination of boyhood has not yet perished. He was a prophet with honor in his own country, for he and the famous Cathedral of Amiens were the twin marvels of the provincial city. Their two pictures, in all sizes and styles, stare from hundreds of shop windows. But this tribute is only a faint echo of that which came to him from every corner of the globe. Wherever love of adventure, coupled with curiosity as to the mechanism of the universe, exists, there Jules Verne finds his disciples. *Around the World in Eighty Days, Twenty Thousand Leagues under the Sea, The Mysterious Island, A Voyage to the Centre of the Earth, From the Earth to the Moon*—here is a rollcall that should stir the pulses of graybeards, and almost summon back their irrevocable youth.

Verne's novels lack, we must admit, the great and enduring excellences of *Robinson Crusoe,* yet to fall short of that matchless tale is far from failure. Many have tried to shoot with the bow of Defoe, have come cheerfully near to the target, and have still missed the bull's-eye. Paltock's *Peter Wilkins* is, in spite of Lamb's generous praise, thin tissue in comparison with *Crusoe,* Stevenson's *Treasure Island* is the product of extraordinary intelligence and dexterity, but it wants bulk and depth. We lay down our *Crusoe,* notwithstanding all its prolixities, with the conviction that we know the man. Whether wearing his skin cap and attended by Friday, or dressed as a sailor or a merchant, that heroic embodiment of ingenuity, piety, and fortitude could not escape our instant recognition. Captain Nemo, on the other hand, would be unrecognizable off the *Nautilus* and with his clothes changed; Cyrus Harding is a mere walking handbook of *Facts Every Boy Should Know;* and even Phileas Fogg is not a convincing personality. In the art of characterization Verne is feeble. His creatures have certain tricks of dress or speech: they have specialties in knowledge, but no blood and vitality. They are hollow inside. Each, notwithstanding a fairly elaborate make-up, is, as Jean Passepartout described the redoubtable Phileas Fogg, "a genuine automaton."

Fortunately, boys are not contemplative philosophers. They will tolerate skilful character-drawing in a story that is crammed with incident; but, given the incident, they are entirely happy with characters which are differentiated in the most rudimentary fashion. "We read story-books in childhood," says Stevenson, "not for eloquence or character or thought, but for some quality of the brute incident." Nothing is better in its kind than the *Arabian Nights;* nothing was ever written in which the caliphs, beggars, and robbers are more palpably wood and pasteboard. The fascination of the tales lies in the enchantment and the astounding adventures which vivify every page. *Sindbad* thrusts upon us "brute incident," stripped of all the accessories which appeal to sophisticated taste, and captivates instantly the savage and the child.

The books of Jules Verne are the *Arabian Nights* elaborately fitted with all modern improvements. The genii and the sorcerers of a few centuries ago have their lineal descendants in the accomplished gentlemen who are sometimes described as "the wizards of science." A submarine boat, a fast express, an automobile, a dirigible balloon, or a hollow shell shot at the moon, is a comfortable and highly plausible substitute for a travelling carpet or a roc. Given the problem of annihilating space and time, the unknown authors of the *Arabian Nights* and Jules Verne both solve it according to formulas popular in their own day.

The charm of mystery is evident in the very title of Verne's works. No lad of twelve can resist the challenge of *Twenty Thousand Leagues under the Sea, Voyage to the Centre of the Earth,* and *The Mysterious Island.* Had the subject-matter belied the captions, many eager readers would still have pegged away, lured by the mere magic of the words stamped on the binding. But the stories are worthy of their delicious names. The island *is* mysterious. Once you learn that the dog Top has been snuffing about the well in the Granite House, you and Cyrus Harding will never rest satisfied till you have discovered what it is that the sagacious animal hears and smells, till you have penetrated to that secret cavern where the *Nautilus* lies with the dying Captain Nemo.

On the scientific side of Verne's writing one may easily lay undue stress. He is not the first to embed scientific knowledge in stories for boys, though he is uncommonly successful in sugar-coating the pill. The method of Abbott and his imitators is to let Rollo draw Uncle George into endless and often futile discussion of the wonders of earth and sky. There is too much talk and too little action. Verne, on the contrary—and he has had many followers, notably H. G. Wells—vitalizes the dead fact by employing it in some striking feat in mastery of man or nature. The discourse on air pressure, water pressure, and hydraulics in *Twenty Thousand Leagues under the Sea* is not knowledge for its own sake, but for the sake of managing the first and greatest of submarines in the delightful business of exploring the depths of the ocean. Nevertheless, as we have said, these contributions to science are not to be taken too seriously. The average boy can shed information as a duck sheds water. Who ever followed through those complicated calculations for constructing the great cannon and aiming it at the moon? If parents are severe-minded and doubtful about the propriety of the novel, the young reader can protest, "See, father, it tells us that, at 32,000 feet below the surface of the ocean, pressure on the human body would be 97,500,000 pounds"—an unanswerable argument. But the science, after all, is a mere husk. The kernel is of such stuff as dreams are made of. (pp. 242-43)

"*Jules Verne,*" in The Nation, *New York, Vol. 80, No. 2074, March 30, 1905, pp. 242-43.*

Kingsley Amis   (essay date 1960)

[*Amis is a distinguished English novelist, poet, essayist, and editor who is best known for his first novel,* Lucky Jim *(1954). Throughout his career Amis has sustained an interest in science fiction and was coeditor of the*

Spectrum *science fiction anthologies. In the following excerpt, Amis provides an overview of Verne's strengths and weaknesses as a writer and discusses how Verne influenced the development of science fiction as a genre.*]

With Verne we reach the first great progenitor of modern science fiction. In its literary aspect his work is, of course, of poor quality, a feature certainly reproduced with great fidelity by most of his successors. Although interspersed on occasion with fast and exciting narrative, for instance in the episode where Captain Nemo and his associates find their twenty-thousand-league voyage interrupted by the Antarctic ice pack, the story line is cluttered up again and again by long explanatory lectures and bald undramatised flashbacks. Even the more active passages are full of comically bad writing:

> What a scene! The unhappy man, seized by the tentacle and fastened to its blowholes, was balanced in the air according to the caprice of this enormous trunk. He was choking, and cried out, *"A moi! à moi!"* (Help! help!). Those French words caused me a profound stupor. Then I had a countryman aboard, perhaps several! I shall hear that heartrending cry all my life!
>
> The unfortunate man was lost. Who would rescue him from that powerful grasp? Captain Nemo threw himself on the poulp, and with his hatchet cut off another arm. His first officer was fighting with rage against other monsters that were climbing the sides of the *Nautilus.* The crew were fighting with hatchets.
>
> The Canadian, Conseil, and I dug our arms into the fleshy masses. A violent smell of musk pervaded the atmosphere. It was horrible.

One would have to blame Verne's translator for some of those ineptitudes, but such was the form in which the novels reached English-speaking readers, none of whom, to my knowledge, has bothered to complain. The story and the ideas were the thing. These ideas, the scientific ones at least, have naturally got a bit dated: the helicopter with seventy-four horizontal screws, the tunnel to the centre of the Earth, the moon-ship shot out of a gun at a speed that would have pulped the travellers before they were clear of the barrel. But these errors hardly matter, any more than Swift's Brobdingnagians cease to be impressive when we reason that they would have broken most of their bones whenever they tried to stand up. It matters hardly more that Verne did successfully foretell the guided missile, nor that this extract from *Five Weeks in a Balloon* (1862) has a bearing on events of eighty years later:

> "Besides," said Kennedy, "the time when industry gets a grip on everything and uses it to its own advantage may not be particularly amusing. If men go on inventing machinery they'll end by being swallowed up by their own inventions. I've often thought that the last day will be brought about by some colossal boiler heated to three thousand atmospheres blowing up the world."
>
> "And I bet the Yankees will have a hand in it," said Joe.

The general prophecy about invention overreaching itself is clearly far more interesting than the particular glimpse of something like the nuclear bomb, or rather of its possible outcome. Verne's importance is that, while usually wrong or implausible or simply boring in detail, his themes foreshadow a great deal of contemporary thinking, both inside and outside science fiction.

As regards the mode itself, Verne developed the tradition of the technological utopia, presenting in *The Begum's Fortune* a rival pair of these, the one enlightened and paternalistic, the other totalitarian and warlike. This was published in 1879, so it is no surprise to find that the nice utopia is French and the nasty one German. There are also several novels virtually initiating what has become a basic category of science fiction, the satire that is also a warning, and it is here that Verne is of some general interest. Thus in *Round the Moon,* after the projectile has fallen back into the sea—at a speed of 115,200 miles an hour, incidentally, and without hurting anyone inside—we find a company being founded to "develop" the moon after a fashion that anticipates *The Space Merchants.* The sequel to *Round the Moon, The Purchase of the North Pole,* involves not only the said purchase on the part of the Baltimore Gun Club, the people who set up the cannon to fire the moon-projectile, but a scheme whereby a monstrous explosion shall alter the inclination of the Earth's axis and so bring the polar region into the temperate zone. Since parts of the civilised world would correspondingly be shifted into new polar regions, the response of officialdom is unfavourable. However, the explosion takes place, and only an error in the calculations preserves the *status quo.* The notion of an advancing technology increasing the destructive power of unscrupulousness reappears on a smaller scale in *The Floating Island,* where the huge artifact breaks up in mid-ocean as a result of rivalry between two financial cliques. The book closes with a straightforward Vernean sermon on the dangers of scientific progress considered as an embodiment of human arrogance. The heavy moral tone of this and many passages in the other books is among the less fortunate of Verne's legacies to modern science fiction, and some of his other anticipations, if they are properly that, give no cause for congratulation. In particular, his sexual interest is very thin: Phileas Fogg, the hero of *Around the World in Eighty Days,* does pick up an Indian princess in the course of his travels, but we discover almost nothing about her, and Fogg treats her with an inflexible courtesy which goes beyond mere Victorianism and which any girl of spirit might find subtly unflattering. Even the villains rarely do so much as aspire to lechery. It is in his political tone, which, however vague and eccentric, is nearly always progressive, and even more in his attitude to technology, fascinated but sceptical and at times tinged with pessimism, that Verne's heritage is most interesting and valuable: his last book, **"The Eternal Adam,"** is a kind of proleptic elegy for the collapse of Western civilisation. These are the considerations which go some way to override his ineptitude and pomposity, his nineteenth-century boys'-story stuffiness, and make him, not only in a science-fiction sense, recognisably modern.

Whatever else he may or may not have been, Jules Verne is certainly to be regarded as one of the two creators of modern science fiction; the other, inevitably enough, is H. G. Wells. . . . The expected comparison with Verne, made often enough at the time (though repudiated by both), now shows not only a huge disparity in literary merit but certain differences in the direction of interest. A main preoccupation of Verne's, as I said, was technology itself, "actual possibilities," as Wells put it, "of invention and discovery," and this holds true equally when what were possibilities to Verne are impossibilities or grotesque improbabilities to us. The long scientific lectures interpolated in his stories—"If I created a temperature of 18°, the hydrogen in the balloon will increase by 18/480s, or 1,614 cubic feet" and so on—these lectures, however tedious, are highly germane to what Verne was doing. Wells, on the other hand, is nearly always concerned only to fire off a few phrases of pseudo-scientific patter and bundle his characters away to the moon or the 803rd century with despatch. Verne himself saw this point all right, and complained after reading (rather cursorily, it seems) *The First Men in the Moon:*

> I make use of physics. He fabricates. I go to the moon in a cannon-ball discharged from a gun. There is no fabrication here. He goes to Mars [*sic*] in an airship [*sic*], which he constructs of a metal that does away with the law of gravitation. That's all very fine, but show me this metal. Let him produce it.

(pp. 34-9)

Kingsley Amis, "Starting Points," in his New Maps of Hell: A Survey of Science Fiction, *Harcourt Brace Jovanovich, Inc., 1960, pp. 15-41.*

Verne and science fiction:

As in science, so in science fiction: new inventions, theories, stories, quickly become junk, archaisms, relics condemned to obsolescence and oblivion by an inexorable law of progress. As a progenitor of the genre of science fiction (the subject of conflicting paternity claims, the child of many putative fathers: Francis Bacon, Thomas More, Lucian of Samosata), Verne was bound to be of only minimal, marginal interest: founding-fathers, fathers of all sorts, are doomed to be surpassed in imaginative scope and technical latitude, overridden and despised by their progeny. . . .

Verne's fictions earn the epithet 'extraordinary' on more than one count. The *Voyages* were styled *extraordinaires* on the grounds that they exceeded the bounds of the ordinary. Now their imaginary itineraries—by virtue of their very success—are liable to seem only ordinary to an extraordinary degree. The term 'extraordinary' incorporates both these senses: on the one hand, beyond, surpassing the ordinary; on the other, exceedingly ordinary, ordinary in the extreme. Verne's fictions are extraordinary twice over: characteristically treating the possibilities and limitations of excess, the abnormal, the unlawful, they simultaneously constitute an exemplary instance of the genre, an almost perfect paradigm of fiction-making.

Andrew Martin, in his The Mask of the Prophet: The Extraordinary Fictions of Jules Verne, *Clarendon Press, 1990.*

Fernando Savater   (essay date 1979)

[*In the excerpt below, Savater explores the theme of initiation in* Journey to the Center of the Earth *and* 20,000 Leagues under the Sea.]

The initiatory nature of adventure novels whose plot consists of a journey is widely recognized even by critics who most obstinately resist the mythologization of storytelling. In fact, eighty percent of adventures either explicitly or implicitly take the form of a journey, always easily interpretable as a series of steps toward initiation. The pattern is obvious: the adolescent, still within the placental confines of the natural, receives the summons to adventure in the form of a map, a riddle, a fabulous tale, a magic object. Accompanied by an initiator, a figure of demoniacal energy whom he simultaneously fears and venerates, he undertakes a journey rich in sudden reversals, difficulties, and temptations. He must overcome successive trials and finally defeat a monster, or, more generally, confront death itself. In the end he is reborn into a new life which is no longer natural but artificial, a mature life and one of a delicately vulnerable kind.

This plot is so well known that I recall it to the reader's mind only as a clarification of the use I ordinarily make of the word *initiation*, employed in its least pretentious and most habitual sense. . . . [The] pattern of initiation itself can serve vastly different aims and that the result of the ritual can as well be the attainment of man's estate as resignation, the enrichment of possibilities, or acceptance of their finiteness. Both the journey of Gilgamesh and the quest for the Grail are initiatory tales: the denouement of the first is the inexorability of death, that of the second is immortality. Epic wisdom always sees the journey as something significant; for the storyteller, no one ever travels with impunity. But the initiate's experiences vary from the most unmistakable triumph of strength to the no less complete realization of weakness, solitude, or annihilation. Initiation does not offer a lesson with a single meaning; at its highest level, neither wisdom nor ignorance is alien to it. All these perspectives have already been minutely studied by modern critics. I would like to emphasize here some aspects of the actual experience of the journey in one of its possible variants—the descent.

To descend is to plunge into that which sustains us, to plumb the foundations that lie beneath us. It is a dangerous mission, perhaps one leading to madness, for everything seems to indicate that the earth sustains us precisely insofar as it preserves its opacity, its stubborn resistance to our investigative gaze. To open it in any way is to put it out of action as a support; the investigation which uncovers it to our eyes takes it out from under our feet by that very act. Not only our physical stability but also our mental equilibrium, our reason itself, can falter in the course of this attempt. When we descend radically—that is, not when we descend a staircase, which is something raised, but when we descend to what is really below—we lose our firmest coordinates and have to invert our points of reference very oddly. What formerly upheld us now becomes something that covers us; what is closed surrounds us and opens before us, while what was formerly open acquires a faraway, opaque indeterminateness; to leap upward takes us closer to the rocks while falling brings us closer to the air. Our head no less than our feet needs solid foundations, and this exercise in geographical perversion can make it spin. Nonetheless, throughout the ages what lies beneath us has always been particularly tempting. The kingdom of the dead is there but also hidden treasures. The secret places of all things are there, which will permit us to control them better when we return to the surface. Whatever is deepest and most profound is there, which verbal intuition tells us is the most desirable. Everything decayed lies there but also everything that is forgotten, feared, all that must be concealed, that is, *buried.* There the deepest darkness awaits us—dead or alive, we will go there in the end, and to descend while we are still alive predisposes and prepares us for the last descent of all—and everything denied to the light of day. And there, lastly, down there, must be the center, for we cannot forget that we crawl about upon a sphere—and that center is not so much a geometrical equidistance as a point of spiritual power, the terrible divine umbilicus that contains the whole meaning of the world. One day we emerge from the nether, the dark, the enclosed places, from the earth; and on any night we will return to it. We descend in order to rise again, that is, to be reborn. This second birth endows us with renewed strength, an impeccable desire to live tempered by contact with hell, and a familiarity with fundamental things which causes the unavoidable to lose its horrible prestige.

We shall take our examples of the essential pilgrimage from Jules Verne. Curiously, though some descry in Verne the very paradigm of the initiatory novelist, a critic as shrewd as Michel Foucault denies the initiatory nature of his tales, arguing that at the end of their heroes' journeys "nothing has changed, either on earth or in the depths of themselves." Perhaps here we would have to distinguish between the story of an initiation and an initiatory story: *Treasure Island* obviously belongs to the first category and Verne's novels to the second (with relative shades of difference which we will discuss). The story that narrates an initiation is the chronicle of the things that happen to a character in his progress toward initiatory enlightenment and maturity; in the initiatory story the reader is the initiate. Indeed, Verne's characters are usually purely external, eyes that see and hands that grasp, thermometers of temperature changes or bellows registering the absence of oxygen; their minimal inner selves are noted only in such primary phenomena as resistance to adventure (Axel in ***Journey to the Center of the Earth***) or mystery: Captain Nemo has a secret, not a psychology. Following the initiation that undeniably takes place in Verne's novels, the characters display about as much change as the odometer of an automobile after the twenty-four-hour race at Le Mans: they register the distance covered, but otherwise are exactly the same as when they started out. But they have done their job of being the reader's eyes and ears during the initiatory process. Hence the documentary nature of so many of Verne's novels, his obsession with giving the reader reliable data about the circumstances of an adventure which concerns him more closely than the characters who are supposedly experiencing it, and who are really no more than the *sensorium dei* of the reader-god.

Reading Verne is like going up in an unballasted balloon, like riding astride a kite, like being pulled down into the abyss on a bottomless waterfall: and all this within the strictest and even the most prosaic matter-of-factness. It means dreaming, of course, but without having to give up calculation, reflection, and even plans. It means joining hands with delirium and placing myth at our service, only to reach the fullest and most irrefutable realism, to install ourselves irrevocably in the soberest ordinariness which surrounds us, accepted as imagination brought to life.

Let us say, in order to make ourselves a little clearer, that there are "hard" fantasies and "soft" fantasies. These last are rambling, cumulative, and unstructured, like their prototype, Lucian's *True History;* things that are portentous, unlikely, or conceivable only in the last resort by a generous stretch of the imagination succeed each other with the suspicious arbitrariness of a world where everything is possible except order. It is the realm not so much of the chaotic, which at least postulates an absent cosmos with which it contrasts, but of the amorphous. Since it is the only kind of fantasy conceivable by persons who lack imagination, and since it permits a certain harmful proclivity toward the allegorical, it has produced unreadable and pretentious jumbles like certain subproducts of German romanticism or a few French "rêveries". Let us, rather, remember the masterworks it has given us: *Alice in Wonderland,* Lord Dunsany's *A Dreamer's Tales,* H. P. Lovecraft's *The Dream-Quest of Unknown Kadath.*

"Hard" fantasy, on the other hand, prefers what Borges calls "the secret adventures of order" and abhors the gratuitous reversal of fortune as much as the juggling of inverisimilitude or the absurd. In this kind of fantasy surprise arises from careful plotting, not from incongruousness, and its most prodigious element is precisely the familiar gradations by which we approach the improbable. Certain rules of the game are laid down and respected, certainly broader rules than the usual ones but profoundly indebted to them, of which they are both extrapolation and counterpoint. In hard fantasy the most strictly regulated realities, such as ethics or science, can become the nucleus of the novel's plot. Let us recall with a thrill of gratitude *The Strange Case of Dr. Jekyll and Mr. Hyde,* the works of H. G. Wells and Olaf Stapledon, Arthur C. Clarke's *Rendezvous with Rama,* and others. Need we say that the works of Jules Verne are paradigms of the hard fantasy, that they not only aspire to attain the ephemeral triumph of perplexity but also the deepest and most permanent spells of prophecy, the initiatory ritual, and utopian freedom?

Apparently, Verne is anything but an *écrivain maudit.* His work enjoyed tremendous popularity almost from the beginning of his career, and his fame has remained intact, or even increased, to the present day, when his books have been published dozens of times in all civilized languages. But it has not only been the common reader who has supported him in this spontaneous and permanent vote of confidence; some of his most illustrious contemporaries had no hesitation in proclaiming his genius, with unaccustomed agreement: Tolstoy as well as Alfred Jarry, Kipling and Gorki as well as Paul Claudel, Raymond Roussel, and the surrealists.

Present-day French critics like Butor, Michel Foucault, Roland Barthes, and Claude Roy have "rediscovered"— the fashionable phrase—Jules Verne, burying the simple flow of his writing under mountains of Freudian interpretations, structural diagrams, or sociological digressions. It is an effort in which one is astonished as much by the writers' ingenuity as by their repetitiveness and superfluity; but I will not belabor the point, for maybe I am making the same mistakes on this page—in this book—and maybe I lack the gift of simplicity more than other writers do.

Verne was an unknown writer, they tell us, and the prestige he gained arose from a misunderstanding: he was confused with a "minor" author of the same name, taken for a simple writer of adventure novels or scientific prophecy, and his symbolic value, the mythical and political levels made possible by more "adult" readings of his work, was ignored. Miguel Salabert, his translator into Spanish, sharply accuses Verne's own readers of concealing these levels: "Readers of 'adventure books' are bad readers. Carried away by interest in the sudden change of circumstance, the story line, they unabashedly skip everything that they do not think essential. Descriptions and digressions bore youngsters."

Well, well, so readers of adventure books are bad readers because they like good stories well told, without any false padding; good readers, on the other hand, enjoy putting up with the superfluous. So much for them, then, but where did Salabert get the idea that youngsters don't like descriptions and digressions? The youngster who is writing this read Salgari with other youngsters like himself, and it was not uncommon for us to rush off to verify in the pages of the encyclopedia one of the technical references to animals or trees that are scattered through his stories. No one is more meticulous than a child reader, my friend Salabert. In cases like Verne's, literary critics especially are made victims of their intrinsic limitations: *they* are the ones who have decided that writers of adventure or scientific prophecy are "minor," they are the ones who decree that adolescents enjoy only the picturesque or the unimportant, they are the ones who, in the nineteenth century, limited Verne's interest to his ability to foresee scientific advances and string together curious turns of plot. They are the ones who have always been mistaken about Verne; children, however, were right about him from the start. Now we must rescue Verne not only from his enthusiasts but from "serious" criticism's prejudices against "minor" literature. But even in the middle of this rescue operation, critics seize the opportunity to blame their own compulsions on those who have maintained a little freshness with respect to the stories' value, a freshness they have in large measure lost. Naturally mental retardation and childishness are not indispensable to make an adult interested in Verne: it is enough that he has not lost his capacity to enjoy reading. But this does not deny the fact that Jules Verne is indeed a writer of fantastic adventures and hence the possessor of a magnificent poetic and mythi-

cal spirit, like many other "minor" writers: Stevenson, Kipling, Wells, Salgari, Conan Doyle. Whether in the depths of the sea, in the clouds, in the impossible jungles of our nighttime terrors or on the moon, the voice of Jules Verne repeats his secret hymn, which sings persuasively of the many faces of courage, the miracles of reasoning power, and also—why not?—the paradoxical joys of resignation.

The first of the two Verne novels I have chosen to illustrate the downward journey is *A Journey to the Center of the Earth,* one of the most marvelous and unforgettable of the whole cycle. All of Verne is in it: the unusual scene, the tremendous enterprise, the timid and shrinking but resourceful adolescent, the energetic adult who performs the initiation, the untamable forces of the occult, the implicitly metaphysical meaning of risk and discovery. Professor Lidenbrock decides to give lessons in abysses to his nephew Axel: his plan is nothing less than to take him down to the very center of the earth. The adventure begins when they find an ancient manuscript written in unintelligible runic letters: it is the word of the Traveler, the Alchemist, which comes from far away, clothed in a ritual of concealment worthy of Poe. Axel does not want to answer this summons; his objections repeat those of a common sense that we might well call "superficial," since his chief argument is that everything that interests him in the world is on its surface and that he hasn't lost anything in that remote center. Lidenbrock, however, convinces him that to reach the center would best help him to possess the pleasures of the surface. What Paul Valéry said was true: "The deepest part of all is the skin"; the truth of this maxim lies in the fact that to regain the skin, one must first pass through the depths. Axel will take some time to learn this: he will take the whole novel, to be exact, for even when at the end of the journey he seems to be just as interested as Lidenbrock in reaching the center of the earth, this interest appears to be a sort of "rapture of the deep," more suicidal than regenerative. The center, after all, marks only half the journey: it is certain that the travelers have descended in order to come up, this time in a profound sense, to the surface.

We have spoken of *Treasure Island* as a reflection on audacity; we can undoubtedly think of *A Journey to the Center of the Earth* as an epic of effort. Few stories are so palpably toilsome, so humbly approving of effort and perseverance. It is made very clear that to descend is first of all a question of effort. Axel must undergo all the tests that effort has to face: hunger and thirst, exhaustion, vertigo, being alone in the dark, injuries, burns, disorientation, starting over, panic in the face of the unknown, monsters of the lower regions, storms, the power of lightning, rough waters, hurricane—and also obstructed paths and blind alleys. Only his persistence in what he has undertaken allows him to extract from weakness, in every case, the necessary strength to pass the test successfully. In the chronicle of other exploits, what shines brightest is the heroes' skill or courage; in this story the chief trait is obstinacy. Except for the proofs of his passage which the long-dead Arne Saknussemm tried to make in order to mark the downward path, and the positive indications in his manuscript, no special intelligent initiative guides the descent of the travelers, who are fundamentally carried along by stubborn inertia. Rather than descending they seem to fall. And their ascent through the volcano will be no less unplanned and will display the pneumatic automatism of the cork popping out of a champagne bottle. All that is left for the travelers to do is put up with the confusion of the different accidents of their journey, while they feel pressing above their heads those thousands of kilometers of rock which, miraculously, do not decide to crush them. Perseverance is second nature to Professor Lidenbrock, while the keenness of his scientific knowledge is considerably less obvious. But in this stressful descent wisdom is superfluous. All they need to do is want, not to know or even be able to act.

As he descends, Axel finds more and more open space where everything ought to be opaque, as we would think. Just as modern atomic physics has shattered the solidity of matter, making it identical to the near-emptiness of stellar space, so the ever larger caverns encountered by Verne's explorers reproduce the open expanse of the surface they had left behind. As Hermes Trismegistus said, "What is above is equal to that which is below." After descending many kilometers Axel reencounters breeze and ocean, clouds and vegetation. Everything is the same, but everything could not be more different. The lower world is the past of the surface world, its ocean is what our oceans have forgotten, its vegetation takes us back to the Jurassic period or even earlier, its formidable beasts no longer harass the earth's outer surface. A gigantic antediluvian shepherd drives a flock of mastodons among giant ferns; the dust that covers the ground comes from the calcareous remains of prehistoric mollusks. Just as memories of mute infancy pile up in our unconscious, which is our lower depths, so the earth's past is stratified and joined in its interior. The Herculean keeper of mastodons is Utnapishtim, the Eternal Ancestor, whom Gilgamesh approached in his search for immortality. What seemed hopelessly lost—the past—is only buried, has sunk, in order to offer a solid foundation for our present. To descend is to go backward. What sustains us is what precedes us. Axel will not succeed in carrying the flower of immortality to the surface, as Gilgamesh also was unable to do; the frozen, fundamental shadow of Utnapishtim awakens his horror and postulates an even more radical descent, of which he will no longer be capable. Really, only the young man has fulfilled the purpose of the journey, for Professor Lidenbrock belongs to the abstract scientific sphere of the dispute of forms, and the descent has chiefly affected him as a verification or rejection of existing theories. As for Hans, he fully belongs to the ferocious silence of the primitive, as is revealed in the raft crossing under the magical light of St. Elmo's fire. "Hans did not budge. His long hair, blown forward by the hurricane over his motionless features, gave him an odd appearance, for the end of every hair was tipped with little luminous plumes. This frightening mask reminded me of the face of antediluvian man, the contemporary of the ichthyosaurus and the megatherium."

Only Axel has truly descended, following the footsteps of the alchemist Arne Saknussemm, but he does not succeed in completing the journey of the perfect initiate. The cen-

Attack of the giant squid in 20,000 Leagues under the Sea. *Engraving by E. Riou, 1870.*

ter of the world, which is perhaps ultimately made of fire, is closed to him; the hasty violence of explosives he sets off will arouse the bowels of the earth against him and result in his expulsion. In fact this is the only initiative he takes during the whole trip, and it causes the end of his initiation before he has completed it. To descend is indeed a task for the tenacious man, not for the merely resourceful.

Verne himself offers us another version of the voyage of descent essentially different from the one we have just been discussing. In this second version what opens beneath us is not terrestrial solidity but the sea's unquiet skin. Here the descent is described as penetrating into another world that lies parallel to our own, not of diving into abysses that underlie and make possible the ground on which we move. **Twenty Thousand Leagues Under the Sea** promises by its very title a complete journey through this new territory. It is a parallel world, a qualitatively inverted reflection of the solid surface on which we live. This time the descent is not made simply to climb up again, as in the previous case, but to install oneself once and for all in the heart of everything that is different. The depths of the sea are literally for exiles. Those who choose it die to everything connected with their previous life. The crew of this wandering, ghostlike ship, the *Nautilus,* is made up exclusively of dead men. Its captain has lost his former name and rank and calls himself Nemo, Nobody, like Ulysses—but a Ulysses who does not perform this renunciation of his name as a subterfuge, the better to recover it later, but rather because this divesting himself of his name is meant to proclaim his permanent abandonment of the desire for Ithaca. To go down into the depths of the sea is a decisive step that does not admit compromise: it means turning toward absolute freedom. This is how Nemo puts it in his impassioned hymn to the sea:

> The sea does not belong to despots! Up there, on the *surface,* men can still administer unjust laws, fight, tear one another to pieces, be carried away with terrestrial horrors. But thirty feet below the surface, their influence is quenched, their power vanishes. Ah, professor, why not live—*live* in the bosom of the waters! Here only will you find true independence! Here I recognize no masters! Here I am free.

But this freedom is won after a previous death at the price of power, a price that none of the three unwilling guests whom Nemo has plucked from the surface of the sea is willing to pay. On the other hand, that cold blue paradise is full of terrors, and to survive in it one must become a no less formidable threat. First taken to be a giant narwhal or some other kind of dangerous marine beast, the *Nautilus* indeed displays a wild animal's free will: its independence mingles with the exercise of ferocity. In no other way can it share the watery jungle with the hundred-handed horror of the giant squid, the man-eating cachalot—which is "nothing but mouth and teeth"—or the shark's swift, gloomy shadow.

Captain Nemo uses his marvelous submarine to carry out real challenges to natural forces. No matter how much he abhors terrestrial powers and their abuses, there is in him a large measure of the Faustian impulse that motivates the conquerors of empires or the inventors of volcanic war machines. Although the flag he plants in the frozen solitude of the Pole is black, something in his action reminds us more of Alexander's pride than Livingstone's humanitarianism. Nemo too, like his enemies the despots, understands independence as greater strength and greater resistance. This explains his tigerish wanderings, his defiance of the heavy, oppressive ice pack which traps him in a gelid coffin, his stubborn approach to the unendurable oven of the underwater volcano, and his defiance of the terrible pressures of the Sargasso Trench, where the *Nautilus* too succumbs to the temptation to descend farther and farther in search of "those primordial rocks never visited by the light of heaven; the lowest granite, which forms the very base of the earth; those deep grottoes scooped out of the rocky mass. . . ."

De Neuville's drawings successfully capture the haughty stance of this imperious libertarian, who was not content with shared power and sought the limitless kingdom of the sea for himself alone. His prisoners never succeeded in really penetrating his personality, which, we must recognize, was by no means easy. Aronnax's interests were too quiet and contemplative for him to feel entirely congenial

with the pirate; Conseil's well-disciplined submissiveness might have pleased him even less. Ned Land, however, had a character that somewhat resembled Nemo's, but his perpetual rebellion did not awake in the captain the sympathy that might have been expected. After all, Land carried the earth in his soul, as indicated by his name itself; he was, moreover, extremely skeptical and dared to formulate objections against his very creator: "The common man believes in extraordinary comets crossing space, in the existence of antediluvian monsters in the heart of the earth, but astronomers and geologists don't believe in such fantasies."

Here is the voice of Verne himself, with his ***Hector Servadac*** and his ***Journey to the Center of the Earth.*** Axel at least undergoes a certain transformation, gradually becoming enthusiastic about the undertaking which his uncle and he have begun, but Nemo's three prisoners change nothing either in their relationship with him or in themselves in any fundamental way, though Aronnax duly marvels at the scientific aspects of the *Nautilus'* journey. In their best moments they behave like tourists and the rest of the time like prisoners avid to escape.

As we have said, however, the initiate that Verne's ritual of descent requires is neither young Axel nor the eminent Professor Aronnax but the reader himself. *Tua res agitur.*

Hetzel's influence on Verne:

While it was Jules Verne who had originally conceived of this new type of narrative which he called a "Roman de la Science"—a novel where the discoveries and innovations of modern science would act as the mainspring to the plot—it was Pierre-Jules Hetzel who insisted that Verne's narratives maintain a high level of didacticism: i.e., that they be oriented toward the *instruction* of science as well as its fictional applications. A fervent positivist, political activist, and firm believer in the Republican ideals of 1848, Hetzel viewed his knowledge—a lacuna he saw as the direct result of the outdated anti-science curricula of the Catholic-controlled French public schools.

As early as 1850, Hetzel began consistently to shift his publishing efforts toward literary works which would address this specific social need. In late 1862, he reviewed a newly completed manuscript entitled ***Cinq semaines en ballon*** by a certain Jules Verne and concluded that a series of such works could be a very effective fictional vehicle for supplementing the French public's scientific awareness. Verne agreed to Hetzel's close supervision and collaboration (some would say censorship) in this project, and a long-term contract was signed for two additional "utile y dulce" works of the same type each year—to be collectively called the ***Voyages extraordinaires.*** Appearing first in feuilleton format in Hetzel's bi-monthly family journal the *Magasin d'Education et de Récréation* and then published separately as individual novels, Verne's scientific-adventure "travel" narratives enjoyed an immediate and continuing success.

Arthur B. Evans in his "The Extraordinary Libraries of Jules Verne," L'Esprit Createur *XXVIII, No. 1 (Spring 1988).*

For you, bold reader, the hollow diamond, the echoing abyss down which the stone falls, bouncing from side to side, and the inner sea of our origins that awaits you in the center of the globe, if you dare to descend through the mouth of Sneffels which the shadow of Scartaris touches, before the calends of July. For you, reader who does not drown in a glass of water, the limitless turquoise sea teeming with creatures you have never seen or dreamed of, the shimmering ghost of Atlantis' sunken streets, the shining, blue-white torture of the ice—which Dante reserved for the lowest circle of Hell—contemplated from below, the spiral curse of the whirling maelstrom. Choose the way to the abyss that is best for you, the initials of the long-dead alchemist who preceded you in the descent, or the defiant sign of the great exile: the letters "A.S." scratched on the rock or the golden "N" that proudly marks the black flag. (pp. 41-52)

> *Fernando Savater, "The Journey Downward," in his* Childhood Regained: The Art of the Storyteller, *translated by Frances M. López-Morillas, Columbia University Press, 1982, pp. 39-52.*

Mark Rose (essay date 1983)

[*Rose is an American educator and the author of* Alien Encounters: Anatomy of Science Fiction *(1982). In the following excerpt, he explores the contradiction between Verne's materialistic themes and the romantic form of fiction he employs in* Journey to the Center of the Earth.]

Jules Verne's subject is nature. The **voyages extraordinaires** explore worlds known and unknown: the interior of Africa, the interior of the earth, the deeps of the sea, the deeps of space. Verne's imagination projects itself in terms of "inside" and "outside." Characteristically, Verne's voyagers travel in vehicles that are themselves closed worlds, snug interiors from which the immensity of nature can be appreciated in upholstered comfort. The *Nautilus* is the most familiar of these comfortable, mobile worlds; inside all is cozy elegance, the epitome of the civilized and human, while outside the oceans gleam or rage in inhuman beauty or mystery. Roland Barthes finds the principle at the heart of Verne's fictions to be the "ceaseless action of secluding oneself." The known and enclosed space, the comfortable cave, is safe while "outside the storm, that is, the infinite, rages in vain." The basic activity in Verne is the construction of closed and safe spaces, the enslavement and appropriation of nature to make a place for man to live in comfort. "The enjoyment of being enclosed reaches its paroxysm when, from the bosom of this unbroken inwardness, it is possible to watch, through a large window-pane, the outside vagueness of the waters, and thus define, in a single act, the inside by means of its opposite" [*Mythologies,* 1972].

Journey to the Center of the Earth (1864), is of course just such an exploration of "insideness," except that here rather than being the place of enclosed safety, the interior world, a realm of subterranean galleries, caverns, and seas, becomes an immensity, a fearful abyss. Abysses dominate the novel. Even before Professor Lidenbrock and his nephew, Axel, begin their journey into the interior, Axel, the story's narrator, has nightmares in which he finds himself "hurtling into bottomless abysses with the increasing velocity of bodies dropping through space." The idea of the abyss is continually kept before us, and always the danger is as much psychic as physical. Standing on the edge of the first real chasm, Axel speaks of the "fascination of the void" taking hold of him. "I felt my centre of gravity moving, and vertigo rising to my head like intoxication. There is nothing more overwhelming than this attraction of the abyss." The danger, evidently, is of losing one's sense of self and of disappearing, intoxicated, into the infinite void.

The abyss in ***Journey to the Center of the Earth*** is a version of the cosmic void, but the geometry of the earthly chasm differs from that of the astronomical infinity, for the earth is round and therefore has both poles and a center. Poles and center are magical loci, the three still places on the turning globe. When the earth is conceived as a bounded world located in unbounded space, the poles are extremities, the furthest points on the globe. Indeed, imagined in this way, the poles are magical precisely because they are the earth's boundaries and thus partake of the numinous power associated with any boundary zone. They

James Mason in the film version of Journey to the Center of the Earth *(1959).*

are the icy, uninhabitable regions in which human space—the habitable world—meets the nonhuman space of the infinite. To reach and explore the poles is to achieve the completion of the human sphere by defining the earth in its entirety. (This is the meaning that seems to generate the nineteenth- and early twentieth-century obsession with polar exploration.) To reach the center of the globe also means to achieve completion, except that now the earth itself has become the imagined immensity and the attainment of the center means the penetration of the essence, the achievement of the heart of the mystery. The liminal poles are frigid; the mystical center is generally imagined as hot, as the fluid, living core of the globe. The earthly chasm thus opens onto a different kind of imaginative space from the astronomical void; at the bottom of the bottomless abyss is the region not of transcendence but of immanence, the locus in which all knowledge, all being, all power are immediately present. To attain the center of the earth, then, means to penetrate the heart of nature, to possess nature absolutely. This is the object of Professor Lidenbrock and his nephew Axel's quest.

Extremes meet and magical opposites are always, in a sense, identical. At the time Verne was writing *Journey to the Center of the Earth* he was also writing *Captain Hatteras* in which an obsessed adventurer reaches the North Pole. The pole itself turns out to be an erupting volcano—magical heat in the center of the regions of cold—and standing on the lip of the polar crater, the margin of the space in which heat and cold, life and death, inside and outside, immanence and transcendence interpenetrate, Hatteras goes mad. Significantly, in *Journey to the Center of the Earth* Lidenbrock and Axel gain access to the interior by traveling north to the cold and barren arctic limits of the habitable world, Iceland, where they enter the subterranean regions through the cone of the extinct volcano Sneffels.

In traveling to Iceland Lidenbrock and Axel are following the directions given in a runic cryptogram that the professor has discovered in an ancient book. "Descend into the crater of Sneffels Yokul, over which the shadow of Scartaris falls before the kalends of July, bold traveller, and you will reach the centre of the earth. I have done this. Arne Saknussemm." Arne Saknussemm, Lidenbrock knows, was a sixteenth-century Icelandic alchemist. The deciphering of his coded message is the novel's first narrative concern and this initial action provides the paradigm for the fiction as a whole, for nature itself is conceived here as a kind of cryptogram to be decoded. The key to Saknussemm's message is that it must be read backward. Likewise, in their descent Lidenbrock and Axel must in effect read nature backward as they pass through the strata of successively earlier and earlier periods of natural history, eventually finding themselves in a marvelous underground world filled with plants from the era of the giant ferns. Here they discover long extinct animals and in one of the well-known Vernian set pieces witness a mortal battle between an ichthyosaur and a plesiosaur. Finally, and climactically, they have a brief glimpse of a giant prehistoric man guarding a herd of mastodons.

> *Immanis pecoris custos, immanior ipse. . . .*
> Yes, indeed, the shepherd was bigger than his

flock. . . . He was over twelve feet tall. His head, which was as big as a buffalo's, was half hidden in the tangled growth of his unkempt hair—a positive mane, like that of the primitive elephant. In his hand he was brandishing an enormous bough, a crook worthy of this antediluvian shepherd.

Lidenbrock and Axel's journey to the earth's center is thus also a journey into the abyss of evolutionary time, and this fusion of the spatial and temporal modes is one of the fiction's sources of power. Temporally projected, the quest for the center, the heart of the mystery, becomes the pursuit of origins, the quest for an ultimate moment of beginning. Understanding this fusion of modes helps to explain why the prehistoric giant is presented in the language of pastoral, a language which activates a literary code of origin that is simultaneously spatial and temporal in mode, both "there" and "then." Understanding this also helps to explain why Lidenbrock and Axel's journey is presented as a repetition of Arne Saknussemm's journey, as a recovery of an original knowledge once possessed by science in its primeval past. The professor and his nephew in following the mysterious alchemist's footsteps are in effect restoring science to its center and origin.

The process of decoding, of learning to read nature, is in this fiction essentially an action of naming. Like many of Verne's protagonists—think, for instance, of Aronnax and Conseil in *Twenty Thousand Leagues Under the Sea*—Lidenbrock and Axel are obsessive categorizers concerned to find the exact name for each geological stratum, the exact botanical and zoological classification for each underground species of plant or animal. As they descend they are concerned, too, with being able to name their precise position in relation to the surface, the exact number of vertical and lateral feet that they have traveled at each point. Moreover, since they are penetrating an unknown world, Lidenbrock and Axel are obliged not only to discover but at times to create names: the "Hansback" for the underground stream that guides them part of their way, "Port Gräuben," "Axel Island," "Cape Saknussemm." The imposition of human names on the nonhuman world is obviously an act of appropriation and conquest, for to be able to decipher and read nature is here to possess it, to drain it of its mysterious otherness and make it part of the human world.

In a characteristic moment Axel describes coming upon a dense subterranean forest composed of weird umbrella-like trees.

> I quickened my step, anxious to put a name to these strange objects. Were they outside the 200,000 species of vegetables already known, and had they to be accorded a special place among the lacustrian flora? No; when we arrived under their shade, my surprise turned to admiration. I found myself, in fact, confronted with products of the earth, but on a gigantic scale. My uncle promptly called them by their name.
>
> "It's just a forest of mushrooms," he said.
>
> And he was right. It may be imagined how big these plants which love heat and moisture had

grown. I knew that the *Lycopodon giganteum,* according to Bulliard, attains a circumference of eight or nine feet, but here there were white mushrooms thirty or forty feet high, with heads of an equal diameter. There were thousands of them; the light could not manage to penetrate between them, and complete darkness reigned between those domes, crowded together as closely as the rounded roofs of an African city.

Notice how this passage enacts a conquest, an annexation of alien territory. It begins in tension with Axel unable to name the "strange objects." As the passage develops the objects become "just" mushrooms. Next they are associated with the *"Lycopodon giganteum"*—that is, with a scientific or exact name. Finally they are transformed metaphorically into "the rounded roofs of an African city" so that we are now viewing a primitive but specifically human landscape.

Appropriately, it is Professor Lidenbrock rather than Axel who in this passage first names the "strange objects." From the beginning Lidenbrock is a figure of heroic will engaged in mortal combat with the nonhuman world. Arriving at the base of Sneffels, he is described as "gesticulating as if he were challenging" the volcano. "So that is the giant I am going to defeat!" he announces in a phrase that sustains this aspect of the fiction. Nothing daunts the professor. Obsessively, he presses forward through every difficulty that lies in the way of the total conquest of nature. "The elements are in league against me!" he cries at a moment when the battle is particularly furious. "Air, fire, and water combine to block my way! Well, they are going to find out just how strong-willed I am! I won't give in, I won't move back an inch, and we shall see whether man or Nature will get the upper hand!"

The narrative establishes the professor's significance in part by placing him in opposition to Hans, the phlegmatic Icelandic peasant who acts as guide. By trade an eiderdown hunter, an occupation that significantly involves no struggle with nature since the "hunter" merely collects the feathers from the elder's readily accessible nest, Hans is clever and resourceful but utterly without will. Indeed, Axel calls him "that man of the far West endowed with the fatalistic resignation of the East." The principal thing that Hans cares about is his salary; he insists upon having three rix-dollars doled out to him each Saturday evening no matter what the exploring party's situation or location. This mechanical action becomes a comic leitmotif in the novel, but it is also significant, suggesting the peasant's absolute unconcern about his surroundings, his obliviousness to nature's marvels. Curiously, Hans and Professor Lidenbrock, while in most respects opposed figures, are at one point seen as similar. Sailing across a magnificent underground sea, the professor expresses irritation that they are making no progress toward the center. Axel is delighted with the beautiful views, but Lidenbrock cuts his rapture short.

> "I don't give a damn for views. I set myself an object, and I mean to attain it. So don't talk to me about magnificent views. . . ."

> I took him at his word, and left the Professor to bite his lips with impatience. At six in the eve-

ning, Hans claimed his wages, and three rix-dollars were counted out to him.

Each imprisoned in his own form of obsession, Lidenbrock and Hans are equally blind to the magic of their surroundings. Paradoxically, the aggressive, passionately involved, Western attitude toward nature can isolate one from nature no less effectively than the passive unconcern of the East.

Both Hans's passivity and Lidenbrock's will to conquer nature are opposed to Axel's romanticism. In a characteristic exchange, the professor and his nephew discuss the fact that the subterranean sea has tides like those of the surface. Axel is amazed and delighted; his uncle, however, finds nothing marvelous in the discovery, pointing out that a subterranean sea will be as subject to the sun and moon's gravitation as any other.

> "You are right," I cried. "The tide is beginning to rise."

> "Yes, Axel, and judging by the ridges of foam I estimate that the sea will rise about ten feet."

> "That's wonderful!"

> "No, it's perfectly natural."

> "You may say what you like, Uncle, but it all seems extraordinary to me, and I can scarcely believe my eyes. Who would ever have imagined that inside the earth's crust there was a real ocean, with ebbing and flowing tides, winds and storms?"

Axel and his uncle live in different mental universes, Axel embodying the spiritualistic response to the nonhuman ("That's wonderful!"), Lidenbrock embodying bourgeois materialism ("No, it's perfectly natural."). Not surprisingly, each at various points in the story believes that the other has gone mad.

Near the end of the novel, however, Axel undergoes a conversion. Confronted with what appears to be an insurmountable obstacle to further descent—a huge boulder has sealed the gallery through which they must pass—the youth is suddenly seized by his uncle's demon of heroic conquest. Now it is Axel who is impatient with delay and who insists that they must immediately blow up the rock with explosive guncotton. "The Professor's soul had passed straight into me, and the spirit of discovery inspired me. I forgot the past and scorned the future." Nothing matters for him now except the imperative of penetration to the center. Demonically possessed, Axel has become, like his uncle, a "hero." His journey, then, has become an initiation into the bourgeois-heroic attitude toward nature, a "going in" in a social as well as a physical sense, and the story ultimately ratifies his new status as an adult male by granting him the hand of the professor's beautiful god-daughter, Gräuben. Nevertheless, as the comic ironies persistently directed against Professor Lidenbrock's limited vision suggest, in the youth's passage something has been lost as well as gained. Caring neither for past nor future, imprisoned in the narrow cage of his own will to dominate, Axel can no longer confront nature except as an antagonist, something utterly apart from himself. Demonically possessed, he is no longer a free agent.

Axel and his uncle never do reach the earth's mysterious center. The guncotton explosion triggers a volcanic eruption and, like an animal defending itself against an intrusion into its body, nature expels the explorers, vomits them out along a great volcanic shaft back into the air. Perhaps physical achievement of the center is impossible? Or perhaps reaching that magical locus would mean going mad like Captain Hatteras on the crater of the polar volcano? In any case, the point of furthest penetration, the journey's true climax, is reached, significantly, not by the professor but by his romantic nephew and not in literal reality but in a vision.

Before his conversion, Axel, reflecting upon "the wonderful hypotheses of paleontology," has an extended daydream in which, first, he supposes the subterranean world filling with long-extinct creatures: antediluvian tortoises, great early mammals, pterodactyls and other primeval birds. "The whole of this fossil world came to life again in my imagination." As his dream continues, however, the great animals disappear, the earth grows steadily warmer, and he finds himself in a still earlier age, the period of gigantic vegetation. Even here the dream does not end. Sweeping backward into the abyss of time in quest of the center, the point of origin, Axel finds the heat becoming more and more intense until the earth's granite liquifies and finally the planet itself dissolves into its original white-hot gaseous mass. "In the centre of this nebula, which was fourteen hundred thousand times as large as the globe it would one day form, I was carried through interplanetary space. My body was volatilized in its turn and mingled like an imponderable atom with these vast vapours tracing their flaming orbits through infinity." Climactically, Axel himself disappears, becoming part of the cosmic infinity. At the ecstatic center, the boundary between man and nature, the human and the nonhuman, melts and the explorer merges with the world being explored.

Axel's dream represents, of course, both a romantic alternative to the professor's treatment of nature as an antagonist to be conquered and a fusion of spiritualistic and materialistic world views. Moreover, in Axel's dream, the text calls attention to its own status as a fiction, an imaginary voyage. This kind of fictive self-consciousness was perhaps implicit in such earlier passages as Axel's rhetorical question, "Who would ever have imagined that inside the earth's crust there was a real ocean, with ebbing and flowing tides, winds and storms?" Now, however, in the description of the fossil world coming to life in Axel's imagination—these events are shortly to occur in the narrative proper as the explorers begin to encounter extinct animals and plants—the text's play with its own fictionality is particularly emphatic and we can hardly miss seeing Axel as momentarily a version of Verne.

Expelled from the interior, the explorers emerge in an eruption of Mount Stromboli in Sicily.

> We had gone in by one volcano and come out by another, and this other was more than three thousand miles from Sneffels, from that barren country of Iceland at the far limits of the inhab-

ited world! The chances of our expedition had carried us into the heart of the most beautiful part of the world! We had exchanged the region of perpetual snow for that of infinite verdure, and the gray fog of the icy north for the blue skies of Sicily!

Like the interior, the surface is a realm of infinities, but here the "infinity" is one of welcoming, protective vegetation. Since, in this novel, the interior space has become the void, the exterior world becomes the known and safe space. In reaching Sicily, Lidenbrock and Axel have, ironically, reached the earth's center, the primitive heart not of nature but of the human sphere. "We were in the middle of the Mediterranean," says Axel, "in the heart of the Aeolian archipelago of mythological memory, in that ancient Strongyle where Aeolus kept the winds and storms on a chain." Warm and nourishing in contrast with the icy polar verge, the Sicilian landscape is a paradise of olives, pomegranates, and vines hung with delicious fruit free for the taking, a landscape that recalls and fulfills the brief evocation of pastoral in the subterranean encounter with primeval man.

With the arrival in Sicily the narrative proper is over; in substituting one code of "centrality" for another, the text has achieved narrative closure. Nevertheless, a further detail remains to be treated in a coda. On the shore of the subterranean sea, after a fierce electrical storm, the explorers' compass seemed to indicate that they had been traveling for nearly 1,500 miles in the wrong direction. Had they really been going north when they thought they were going south? The mystery of the compass remains an unexplained phenomenon and a torment to Professor Lidenbrock since "for a scientist an unexplained phenomenon is a torture for the mind." One day, however, back in Hamburg, Axel notices that the compass needle points south instead of north and he realizes that the electrical storm in the earth's interior must have reversed the instrument's poles. The final mystery is explained, the puzzle is complete and, in a version of the lived-happily-ever-after formula, Axel tells us that "from that day onward, my uncle was the happiest of scientists."

This coda affirms the materialistic faith that the book of nature is readable to the last word, that nature is merely a cryptogram to be decoded, or, as Axel puts it, that "however great the wonders of Nature may be, they can always be explained by physical laws." And yet, despite this explicit positivistic affirmation, the narrative's romance structure suggests a more problematic view. Here "explaining nature" is represented by the idea of reaching the center, which, of course, the explorers never do attain. Did Arne Saknussemm ever in fact reach the center? Throughout the story, Axel and Lidenbrock debate the question of the earth's internal temperature. Is the earth's core molten or even gaseous with a temperature perhaps over two million degrees as Axel, the romantic, maintains? Or, as the positivistic Lidenbrock supposes, does the rise in temperature experienced as one descends into the earth reach a limit at a certain depth, leaving a core that can be explored by human beings? So far as the explorers descend the temperature remains comfortable, but the ultimate issue of whether the center itself is transcendently hot is never resolved, and in the narrative this debate becomes equivalent to the question of how nature can be known. Is the center literally reachable as Lidenbrock passionately believes? Or, as Axel's dream implies, is it in fact a magical place attainable only in dream or in vision or in fiction?

What I hope my analysis of Verne's novel has suggested is the way the narrative is built upon an unresolvable incompatibility between a fundamentally materialistic ideology and a literary form that projects the world as ultimately magical in nature. *Journey to the Center of the Earth* can be taken as representative of science fiction in general. Science fiction has typically asserted a materialistic point of view, and yet, at the same time, science fiction has typically expressed itself through the spiritualizing categories of romance. Most often, as in Verne, the contradiction at the heart of the narrative remains more or less disguised. This formula is characteristic of hard-core science fiction. Asimov's *Foundation* series, for example, asserts both a deterministic view of history and a spiritualistic belief in the efficacy of individual free will. Alternatively, instead of suppressing the incompatibility of spiritualism and materialism, a text may focus directly upon the contradiction, questioning its validity. Such narratives generally take the form of a progressive discovery of the interpenetration, or even of the identity, of matter and spirit. Olaf Stapledon's novels characteristically operate in this way, dissolving normally discrete categories of thought. At one point in *Last and First Men,* for example, the moon's orbit is found to be decaying faster than physical theory alone would predict, and the narrator explains that man had not yet discovered the "connexion between a planet's gravitation and its cultural development." C. S. Lewis's *Out of the Silent Planet,* Walter Miller's *A Canticle for Leibowitz,* and many recent fictions operate in a similar manner. What is the difference between matter and spirit in a world such as that of Brian Aldiss's *Cryptozoic* in which one can travel in time by taking a mind-altering drug?

Alfred North Whitehead, among others, points out [in *Science and the Modern,* 1967] that a tension between spiritualistic and materialistic world views is fundamental in modern—that is, post-Renaissance—culture. Oversimplifying, we might say that modern culture wishes to believe both in the priority of matter and of spirit, both in free will and in determinism. In the nineteenth century this tension generally took the form of fierce debates between the proponents of science, particularly evolution, and the proponents of religion and the dignity of man. At present we more often encounter the tension in displaced form, in, for example, the antipathy between humanistic and behavioristic psychology. (Curiously, Freudian psychology, which in the early part of the present century figured as another in the long series of deterministic threats to human dignity, now appears to have crossed a crucial semantic boundary and to figure as spiritualistic in opposition to properly "scientific" therapies. Psychoanalysis is regularly accused of being a religion rather than a science.) On the plane of popular culture, the tension is evident in recurrent waves of interest in such pseudo-sciences as astrology and parapsychology, and in oriental mysticism. In periods of social stress such as the 1960s in the United States, this tension is likely to become particularly evident as dissenters from the predominantly pragmatic and materialistic culture express their position by aligning themselves with various spiritualistic movements. Not surprisingly, dissent from the Vietnam War often manifested itself in such quasi-religious forms as "bearing witness."

What I am suggesting, then, is that science fiction characteristically operates within the space of a basic contradiction in modern culture. Indeed, as a genre, one of science fiction's functions appears to be to produce narratives that mediate between spiritualistic and materialistic world views. I realize of course that such a generalization requires a much fuller consideration of texts than I can possibly present here. I think, however, that it would be a relatively easy matter to illustrate the observation both from classic narratives such as those of Wells and from recent texts such as, say [Ursula K. LeGuin's] *The Left Hand of Darkness.* For the present let me be content with remarking that understanding science fiction's role as mediator helps to explain the genre's interest in such quasi-scientific topics as telepathy, teleportation, telekinesis, matter transmission (which may be understood as a mechanized version of teleportation), and time travel. We can note in passing that the paradox at the heart of the notorious time loop in such stories as Heinlein's "All You Zombies" is that both free will and determinism are asserted simultaneously, for here free agents are nevertheless caught in cycles of determined repetition. Understanding science fiction's role as mediator also helps to explain the genre's interest in mechanical spirits such as robots, androids, intelligent computers, and cyborgs. (Interestingly, computer psychiatrists have become a popular motif in current science fiction.) All of these topics can be understood as points at which the spiritual and the material intersect.

Do we believe in free will or in determinism, in the priority of spirit or priority of matter? According to Whitehead the "radical inconsistency at the basis of modern thought accounts for much that is half-hearted and wavering in our civilization." This may be true and yet in fiction contradiction is not necessarily a defect. Indeed, as Verne's *Journey to the Center of the Earth* perhaps suggests, the contradiction itself as embodied in narrative may be understood as a well of vitality, one of the sources from which science fiction as a genre draws its power. (pp. 31-41)

> Mark Rose, "Jules Verne: Journey to the Center of Science Fiction," in Coordinates: Placing Science Fiction and Fantasy, *George E. Slusser, Eric S. Rabkin, Robert Scholes, eds., Southern Illinois University Press, 1983, pp. 31-41.*

Jānis Svilpis (essay date 1983)

[*In the following excerpt, Svilpis examines the rite of passage theme in* Journey to the Center of the Earth.]

[*Journey to the Center of the Earth*], published in 1864, is an early and influential embodiment of many recurrent patterns, not least its blend of adventure and didacticism. The youthful protagonist, Axel, accompanies his uncle, Professor Lidenbrock, on a subterranean scientific expedition prompted by a sixteenth-century Icelandic manuscript that alludes to an earlier descent. Axel undergoes a rite of passage into manhood on the way. Lidenbrock's ward, Gräuben, his sweetheart, urges him to go, saying he will find a wife when he returns, and she welcomes him back with the promise, "Now that you are a hero, Axel . . . , you will never have to leave me again." He becomes a hero not only by braving dangers but also by absorbing a scientific perspective, and this process of absorption poses dangers of its own.

The book's slow opening detracts from the adventure by delaying the descent until Chapter 17, two fifths of the way through, but it serves a number of purposes, including the establishment of a pattern of testing associated with visionary experiences. Axel's perceptions of the world around him are modified and he becomes hardened to the resulting disorientation. He deciphers the manuscript "in the grip of a sort of hallucination," saving the household from a farcical threat of starvation caused by Lidenbrock's refusal to allow a meal until the problem is solved. Despite his fears, he finds himself maneuvered into going on the expedition. Lidenbrock browbeats him into climbing to the top of the Vor-Frelsers-Kirk in Copenhagen to give him "lessons in abysses," and five such lessons inure him to the vertiginous "optical illusion" that the world is spinning. From Sneffels Yokul, on Iceland, Axel sees the landscape "as if one of Helbesmer's relief-maps were spread out at my feet," and he becomes pleasantly intoxicated by this scientific mode of perception. To be sure, this *is* intoxicating, for it detaches him from his immediate surroundings and even from his personal identity, in an abstract and impersonal vision, a view from a height: "I forgot who I was and where I was, living the life of the elves and sylphs of Scandinavian mythology." This is vertigo in a more insidious form, and only a short while later, Axel must be restrained from throwing himself down the volcano's central chimney.

The testing pattern changes once the group moves underground. In two incidents, nearly miraculous rescues stress the importance of faith and courage. Lidenbrock takes a wrong turn, they run out of water, and Axel despairs, though his uncle counsels fortitude. Axel awakens from delirium to hear Hans, the Icelandic guide, announce in Danish his discovery of a subterranean river, and though he does not know Danish, he understands. A bit after this, like Moses in the wilderness, Hans smites the rock with his pickaxe and brings forth water. Subsequently, Axel strays from the others and becomes lost in the dark. By chance, he happens upon an acoustical phenomenon that enables him to speak with Lidenbrock, though they are almost four miles apart, and in this he sees God's providence, "for He had led me through those huge dark spaces to what was perhaps the only spot where my companions' voices could have reached me."

But his faith is not yet sufficient to let him stand his most severe visionary trial alone. When they enter the huge subterranean cavern and go rafting on the Lidenbrock Sea, he has a "prehistoric daydream," in which he looks back over the development of life on Earth, and farther back to the condensation of the planet out of a gaseous nebula. As before, he loses his sense of identity and his consciousness of his surroundings, overcome by a vision of the paleontological, geological, and cosmological past, and Hans has to stop him from throwing himself overboard. When this vision seems to come true, and especially when he glimpses the gigantic shepherd of mastodons, he flees in panic, as he did when lost, but this time Lidenbrock shares his fear. This sequence culminates in the discovery that Arne Saknussemm, Icelandic alchemist, heretic, explorer, and author of the manuscript that Axel has deciphered, had reached this place before them. Seeing this sign that faith and courage may be more successful than he has believed possible, Axel exchanges places with his uncle, temporarily becoming fearless and insisting that they press on: "the Professor's soul had passed straight into me, and the spirit of discovery inspired me." His enthusiasm leads to the blasting of a rock that bars the way, which plunges them into an abyss, and results ultimately in their return to the surface by being shot out of a volcano.

Axel still has fears, but he learns to control them, and he passes his final test of vision by emerging from this last abyss. That he has become a mature scientist is proven by his explanation of the puzzling malfunction of their compass, which baffles even Lidenbrock. Unlike his decipherment of the manuscript, this is an application of scientific reasoning, not a chance perception. From the first, he has been a knowledgeable commentator on geological matters—his identifications and classifications form much of the book's didactic content—but he becomes much more than a spouter of facts, and the progress of the story reflects this development. The opening is primarily travelogue, loaded with encyclopedic detail; after the subterranean descent the emphasis shifts to data-gathering, observation, and measurement, and then, as their instruments are lost or grow unreliable, it shifts again, this time to an imaginative grasp of the larger picture to which the isolated data belong. Axel proceeds from book-learning to active observation and finally to a vision of the order of the world which complements and helps create his new faith and courage.

Something akin to this vision, the presupposition that the world has an order, has been present from the beginning. Lidenbrock's reasons for undertaking the expedition include a desire to determine which of two competing hypotheses about the Earth's core is true. One, commonly accepted and supported by Axel, says that it is molten; the other, attributed to Humphry Davy and supported by Lidenbrock, holds that it is cold and that vulcanism is a surface phenomenon. Their disputes on this subject appear frequently, giving substance to Lidenbrock's otherwise unconvincing assertion that "I no longer regard you as my nephew, but as my colleague." In this debate, as in their other debates, Lidenbrock dominates until Axel supersedes him. The question about the Earth's core is answered inconclusively, but Axel's new intrepidity and force of personality show that he has emerged as his uncle's equal in authority.

Voyages of discovery are often voyages of self-discovery, and the archetype of Verne's story is very old. He applied it, however, to some specifically science-fictional themes, broadening the idea of discovery to include all past time, and the idea of self-discovery to include the individual's relationship to the cosmos. He explored the developing scientific mind's relationship to authority, both scientific and parental; he displayed that mind in the act of solving problems; and he analyzed the qualities required by both science and adulthood. Verne's primary concern in this book is with the intellectual, rather than the moral or social being, and in this he anticipates a major emphasis in twentieth-century science fiction. (pp. 22-3)

> Jānis Svilpis, "Authority, Autonomy, and Adventure in Juvenile Science Fiction," in Children's Literature Association Quarterly, Vol. 8, No. 3, Fall, 1983, pp. 22-6.

M. Hammerton (essay date 1987)

[Hammerton is an English psychologist and educator. In the excerpt that follows, he examines Verne's application of technical scientific matters in his writings.]

Jules Verne (1828-1905) has been variously estimated as a writer of poetic force, the father of Science Fiction and "a typical little bourgeois". ("Bourgeois" should really be spelled "B—", now that it has superceded "bugger" as "a vague term of abuse".) It is still the case that his purely literary reputation stands higher in France than in English-speaking countries; but the reasons for this are not his fault, and not far to seek. Briefly: Verne has been wickedly served by his translators.

His books were first translated, usually within a few years of their first appearance, by various hacks who seem to have known little English, less French, and no Science. Some of their renderings would make a schoolboy blush. I think my favourite howler is in Vingt Mille Lieues, where an irate captain calls for someone more skilled and is made to demand another, more to the right. (Ch. 6: " 'A un autre plus adroit!' cria la commandant . . . ") There are comparable gems, however, in almost every chapter of every book, besides blunders in elementary arithmetic. Subsequent hacks copied from the earlier ones, unless by some miracle they happened to make exactly the same arithmetical blunders; and his most recent editors, though properly respectful, have tended to cut out the very passages which, though they may give pause to the unenlightened, delight the connoisseur (such as the minute account in L'Ile Mystérieuse, of how to make nitroglycerine from the rawest of raw materials).

By this time, the reader may have surmised that I am something of an admirer of Verne. I do not deny it; and will attempt to offer some defence of this position.

Certainly he had failings, some of which are regarded more sternly now than in his own time: for example his racial prejudices read offensively today. But Victorians—Lincoln as well as Verne—could believe in the natural inferiority of some races whilst regarding their oppression with genuine horror. (There is no logical fallacy there—far less is there hypocrisy. Oppression is a moral act, which can be condemned irrespectively of any conclusions about abilities, which are an empirical matter.) His xenophobia, usually mild, could be unpleasant at times. This,

however, did not prevent him creating heroes and heroines—some of whom are surprisingly "modern" and "liberated"—who were English, Dutch, American, Russian, Indian or Chinese. And his humour was a saving grace.

A quality almost wholly lost by his translators is the ironic wit which pervades his work, especially the earliest books. Nevertheless, though his manner is light, his intentions were pervaded by a deep seriousness. His publishers produced his books in a series—collectively called Les Voyages Extraordinaires—explicitly dedicated to education as well as to entertainment; and Verne had no doubt that he intended to instruct as well as to amuse.

He was typically Victorian in this at least: he wished his instruction to be moral as well as factual; and his heroes are sometimes rather tryingly virtuous. They are brave, honest, determined, generous, kindly, and cheerful in the face of danger—and whilst twentieth-century men smile cynically at the string of adjectives, can they deny that they are indeed desirable qualities? Cynicism might equally be aroused by the prodigious learning of some of his heroes; but some astonishingly well-schooled persons do exist, and why not have one as the hero of an adventure tale?

The term "adventure tale" was used advisedly. Although Verne is mainly remembered for his science fiction—and it is with that that we are naturally most concerned—such works constituted less than a third of his enormous output. Out of over seventy volumes, altogether only a score or so are properly "sf": the remainder are adventures, packing a great deal of geographical and other information and favouring a "with-one-bound-Jacques-sprang-free" method of escaping from tight corners.

It was, perhaps, his high Victorian morality which led Verne to take the care he did over his future technology. It was not acceptable for him to deceive the aspiring young with vague phrases and graceful evasions. If he wanted to go to the moon, he checked on the Earth's velocity of escape (though, as we shall see, he made some mistakes in that area). If he wanted a balloon to remain airborne for weeks, he at least devised a theoretically workable method for doing it. If he wanted a submarine, he calculated its dimensions faithfully.

In various novels, Verne sent his heroes in navigable balloons, under the oceans, to the moon, in aircraft and in a flying-submarine-car. Another, though a villain rather than a hero, unintentionally launched an unmanned satellite, and yet other villainous wretches were armed with guided weapons, and a variety of assault VTOL machines. This makes a rather impressive list, the more so as many of these devices are described in enough detail to invite serious criticism.

Verne's first novel, and one which set the pattern for many to come, was Cinq semaines en ballon (1862). In this, three Britons cross then unknown Africa in a balloon, on the way establishing the source of the White Nile, discovering a gold mine, rescuing a missionary, eating an elephant, having an air-battle with some vultures, dispensing large dollops of geographical information for youthful readers, speculating on the future of the world, saving one-another's lives and generally behaving as true Verne heroes always would.

The problem with balloons, grasped within a very short time of their invention in 1783, was that they would only go where the wind happened to blow them. By Verne's day, it was known that winds often blow in different directions at different altitudes; so, in principle, the problem could be solved by probing at various altitudes until the right wind was found. However, in order to rise, ballast must be shed; and to sink gas must be valved away; and a very few vertical sweeps soon exhaust the reserves of both. Verne's way round this impasse was at once ingenious, odd, and terrifying.

Suppose a balloon, in shape a prolate ellipsoid, is completely closed, and contains exactly enough gas to be, with its payload, precisely in equilibrium with the surrounding air at ground level. Now warm the gas: it will expand, and the balloon will rise; let it cool again, and the balloon will sink. In order to achieve this happy result, Verne suggested what was, in effect, an electric central-heating system. A pipe was to lead from the lower part of the balloon to the heating system, another from thence to the upper segment. Thus, as heat was supplied, a circulation would be set up, and the whole body of gas eventually warmed.

Thus far his ingenuity: the oddity lay in the heating system itself. A battery was used to separate the constituent hydrogen and oxygen in a tank of water; the gasses were to recombine in an oxy-hydrogen flame heating the inside of a metal cone, the other side of which convected heat to the gas itself. Now why the complexity? You must, according to basic thermodynamics, recover *less* energy from the combustion of the gasses than you put into the water to separate them. Therefore, it were better and simpler to use the electricity directly in an element built into the inside of the cone.

It is, alas, decidedly possible—as we shall have cause to see again—that Verne quite simply never understood the ineluctable limitations of the laws of thermodynamics. More than one of his ideas depends on forbidden cheating of this kind; including precisely the above mistake again, in an aside in *L'Ile Mystérieuse.*

To justify the adjective "terrifying", I will merely observe that the reader is welcome to play with a flame near a balloon full of hydrogen—even a supposedly hermetically sealed one—but that I want to be a long way away when he does it.

A little arithmetic casts some further interesting light on Verne's ideas.

He carefully tabulates the mass of balloon and payload; and we readily compute (in close agreement with him, by the way) that the mass of the gas in the balloon was just under 130 kg. To attain an altitude of 300m—no great height—would roughly (necessarily roughly: the exact value would depend on the local temperature lapse-rate and other unknowns) require a 10°C increase in temperature. Since hydrogen has the rather high specific heat at constant pressure of 3.4 cal/gm/°C, this operation would require roughly 4 kw hr from the battery, making no allowance at all for inefficiency or loss. Making reasonable assumptions (many years ago, as a young heat-transfer engineer, I learnt to introduce that golden phrase every few lines) the batteries would have needed to supply at least 500 Kw hr during the journey. In 1862, that would have been a very remarkable battery indeed—and not a negligible one today. But Verne had a weakness for super-batteries.

It is worth noting this curious point. For Verne always seems to have shown the same two failings: he rarely solved the energy equations; and he never allowed for development—for the "ironing out of bugs" which is so invariable a part of making a new machine work. The power requirements of *Cinq Semaines* are typical as the assumption that the very first flight of the balloon is also its voyage: there is no test programme, no need for modification in the light of trials.

The second of these failings we might ascribe to an excess of Victorian confidence; but the first must be due to mere lack of knowledge. Let us not complain too much: at least four of his most enjoyable tales would never have been written if he had been too tender about power sources; and he always produced an ingenious and theoretically sound means of using the power he so blithely assumed.

Usually, the power he assumed was electric. Indeed, Verne may, with some justice, be called the Erasmus Darwin of Electricity, for the following lines can surely be compared with the famous ode to 'Unconquer'd Steam':

> "Listen", said Captain Nemo . . . "A powerful, controllable, and flexible form of energy is used for every purpose, and really runs my ship. It is used for everything: lighting, heating and power for the motors. I refer to electricity." (my translation).

The narrator expresses astonishment, reflecting how little anyone had achieved, at that time, in electrical engineering. And indeed, it was so: no electric motor was commercially available in 1870 with the power output of a good Watt beam engine, far less one which could compare with the best high pressure steam engines of the time.

The principle of the electric motor had been demonstrated by Faraday as early as 1821; but it remained a principle only. Gramme did not demonstrate his D.C. motor until 1873, nor Siemens his little (2 h.p.) traction engine until 1879. Also, the problem of supplying current was only being satisfactorily solved when Verne wrote: Gramme was building his generator whilst Verne was working on *Vingt Mille Lieues;* though some rather less satisfactory machines had been produced a few years before. Otherwise, if you wanted electricity, you had to use chemical means: in other words, batteries. A lot of effort was devoted, during the nineteenth century and since, to finding better and more powerful kinds of batteries; but with only modest success. The re-chargeable battery (accumulator) was being developed by 1870; but the best of these today cannot supply the kind of energies for the kind of weight that Verne demanded and confidently, if wrongly, expected.

He was not in the least inhibited by the "state of the art".

His submarine—the splendid *Nautilus*—incorporated many features that had already been tried by brave, if not very successful pioneers (e.g., in *La Plongeuse* of 1864), or which were obvious enough. Any thoughtful engineer of the time would have agreed that such a craft would need ballast tanks to submerge it, horizontal rudders to control it in a vertical plane, a pressure hull, and, above all, a form of motor which was not air-breathing. Verne realised that an electric motor would satisfy that requirement, and contributed to the whole a stupendous zest and confidence.

Nautilus is described as a 1500 ton boat, 70 m (230 ft) long and 8m (26 ft) in maximum diameter. It would therefore be comparable to a modern nuclear attack submarine, though rather smaller and slimmer. No nuclear submarine, however—indeed, no millionaire's yacht—boasts the luxurious splendours with which Verne endowed his creation: a library of 12,000 volumes (no less), a saloon 10m by 6, "truly a museum . . . (containing) all the treasures of Nature and of Art", and an organ, whereon the enigmatic Captain Nemo was wont to extemporise melodies in the Scottish style.

To descend from Verne's exuberance to numbers, it would require roughly 400 h.p. to drive such a craft at 10 kt; and to drive it at its full speed of 50(!) kt would require about 10,000 hp. During a journey of 80,000 km the batteries were only charged once; so assuming the lower speed for cruising, and only a small margin for high-speed bursts and contingencies, the batteries would have needed to hold a charge of the order of a million kilowatt hours.

Today, the motor would be no problem; but even if the hull were so full of batteries as to reduce the accommodation to a very spartan level, it would be impossible to run for more than, at most, a few days without re-charging. (Consider the performance of the best type of "conventional" submarines.)

Evidently, then, Verne was both reasonably confident and right about electric motors; but was his confidence in a new generation of super-batteries defensible, even though wrong as it turned out? Unfortunately, the answer is no, given that he could not have forseen nuclear energy. Fuels offering the most energetic chemical reactions known, even if that energy were converted into electrical energy with 100% efficiency would have required more mass than the *Nautilus* could have carried, even without engines and crew, to provide the charge he needed.

Nevertheless *Vingt Mille Lieues* is a great piece of technical prediction. Even though designers would have to content themselves with shorter voyages between re-charging, it summarised all the hints and suggestions of the pioneers, boldly provided them with a suitable motor (which was a bullseye) and transmuted the whole, with a soaring Victorian confidence, into a tale of assured wonder and great fun.

The element of Great Fun was present, if sometimes with a faintly gruesome tinge, when Verne temporarily deserted the sea for interplanetary space (*De la Terre à la Lune* and *Autour de la Lune*). The instigators of Verne's Moon-trip are a peace-weary (truly!) group of firearms fanatics, who have formed themselves into the Gun Club of Baltimore—a body comprising 1833 full members and more than 30,000 corresponding members, despite the criterion of entry being to have made some contribution to the design or development of weapons. As a result of practical experience on the battlefields of the American Civil War and sundry disasters in testing they are a somewhat battered lot, having "One arm between four members, and two legs between six".

To keep these bloodthirsty cripples out of mischief, and for the sheer glorious fun of the thing, their (intact) president suggests firing a projectile at the Moon. Later, a splendid and eccentric Frenchman, Michel Ardan (actually an affectionate portrait of Verne's old friend Felix Tournachon—who was among other things, the first man to take an aerial photograph from a balloon) insists on travelling in the projectile, taking with him the club president, and a rival engineer.

To achieve these noble ends, Verne's heroes fire an aluminium shell 9 ft in calibre (he gives all the dimensions in English measure) out of a gun 900 ft long, which has been cast *in situ,* in a specially prepared excavation on top of a hill in Florida: the muzzle is at ground level. A charge of 400,000 lbs of gun-cotton expels the projectile, which, for fine control in space, is equipped with steering rockets.

It is easy enough to laugh at this scheme. It was evident at the time that Verne made no allowance for air resistance: indeed, the shell would be vaporised before it even left the gun muzzle. Evidently also, the acceleration would have spread the heroic voyagers over the base of the inside at the initial shock. Nevertheless, it seems to me, the whole idea is worthy of the greatest praise.

Verne was not the first to write of travel to the Moon; but he was the first to talk about it as a great engineering problem, to be discussed in terms of quantity and material: he brought it from the merest fantasy to calculation. That he gave the escape velocity correctly is not, by itself, remarkable: the value had been estimated by Newton, and derived closely after Cavendish's work at the end of the previous century. Verne was the first to make any sort of serious suggestion of how such a velocity could be attained, and (for once!) his energetics were in the right bracket. A body travelling at escape velocity has an energy of rather less than 16,000 calories per gramme of its mass; gun-cotton yields around 1500 cals/gm; and, of course, not all the energy of the charge is conveyed to the projectile. In allowing 20 kg of propellant for each kg of projectile he was very reasonable. (Apollo did rather better a century later.) He realised that rockets would work in vacuum, and made the brilliant suggestion of using them for what is now called vernier control. (Why, one wonders, did he not take the next step of using rockets for the whole job?) Above all—it is worth repeating—he treated the project as a vast engineering enterprise, which indeed it was to be. Not for him the solitary genius and his one assistant fabricating a space-ship in a back yard—an improbable supposition which recurred again and again over the following decades. Reaching the Moon was a goal, he rightly saw, which would require the labour of thousands and the expenditure of millions.

Certainly, he made a lot of minor errors, some of them surprisingly silly ones. For example, his heroes encounter a tiny, hitherto-unknown close satellite of the earth; and the values Verne gives for its orbit and period do not match—although the computation is very easy. But these are trivial failings in the light of the major mental saltation he achieved: he made space-flight something to be rationally talked about.

Also, let this be noted: for him space-flight was a glorious and soul-stirring enterprise. He would have scorned our mean-minded contemporaries who merely sneered and carped about the expense. Nothing, indeed, could be further from such baseness than the fictional welcome he planned for his astronauts, who, owing to unforseen perturbations, had orbited the Moon, and returned to splash down in the Pacific. They toured the U.S.A. in a special train, whilst, at each station upon the way, local inhabitants dined on the platform, everything being so timed that they could toast the heroes as they came through; the dauntless three were thus enabled to drink with almost the entire population of the States. What a pity that N.A.S.A. did not take up this superlative idea!

Even today, space-flight remains worthy of remark; but flying has become such a commonplace that it needs some effort to remind ourselves that, within the life-time of persons still living, an aircraft was a sign and a wonder. Verne's story *Robur le Conquérant*—always known in English-speaking areas by the title *The Clipper of the Clouds*—when published in 1886 was considered almost as daring as his earlier Moon journeys.

It is, I hope, no denigration of a number of distinguished pioneers to say that the decades from the death of Cayley in 1853 to the work of Lilienthal in the '90s were unhappy ones in the story of powered flight. Cayley's own work might never have been done, for all the notice that was taken of it; and failure followed failure as one designer after another tried to start from scratch. One of the greatest physicists of the century, Lord Kelvin, went on record as believing that heavier-than-air flight was impossible; and such minor successes as there were came in the realms of lighter-than-air flight, i.e. with airships. Giffard, the Tissandiers and others, mostly in France, could justly claim that they had at least got off the deck; and if their craft were somewhat flattered in being called "dirigibles", at least they had some finite capacity for movement and control. In these circumstances, disputes between confident airship men and hopeful aircraft designers could become somewhat heated—though not, I imagine, quite as heated as Verne makes the row between his Philadelphia balloon enthusiasts and his hero Robur.

Verne came down firmly in favour of machines which were heavier than air. As he clearly stated, to be stronger than the air, it is necessary to be heavier; and he quoted with approval the indisputable observation of another pioneer that, after all, birds fly.

The Clipper of the Clouds is thin as a story. Two balloonists, arguing fiercely amongst themselves about the design of an airship they are planning, and more fiercely with a mysterious engineer named Robur, who interrupts one of the meetings of their club to tell them (rudely) that they are wasting their time, are kidnapped by their mysterious opponent, who takes them on board his helicopter, and demonstrates its paces in a world cruise. Subsequently they escape, obstinately finish building their airship, which bursts when challenged to a climbing-match by Robur in his machine, who concludes by reading everyone a lecture and flying off into the unknown.

Somehow the magic, which remains in *Vingt Mille Lieues* despite our familiarity with submarines, has disappeared. Perhaps also the character of Robur does not help: he is less credible than Nemo and much more offensive. However, *Albatros*, the helicopter (the word coined by Verne is "Aeronef", which never won acceptance: it was in fact a helicopter), is described in considerable detail.

The fuselage of the *Albatros* is exactly the shape of the hull of a small clipper ship complete with three deck-houses: it is 30m (98ft) long by 4m (13ft) in beam. Whereas modern helicopters generally have one large rotor, the *Albatros* boasts no less than 37 contra-rotating pairs of small ones, in three parallel rows: 15 on each side and 7 rather larger ones on the centre-line. These rotors are purely for lift; they are not tilted to provide translational movement. Instead, a 4-bladed tractor propellor in the prow, and a similar pusher in the stern suffice for a maximum speed of 200 km/hr (124 mph). The machine is built of a compressed, chemically bonded paper—apparently rather like Tufnol. The engines, one need hardly say, are electric; and power is drawn from batteries and accumulators. There is a crew of eight and the craft is armed with a 60mm gun, which comes in handy for rescuing sacrificial victims from anthropophagous celebrations in Dahomey. *Albatros* makes a complete circuit of the earth without re-charging.

Once again, the batteries are simply absurd. Electric motors would be worth considering for aircraft—their power-to-weight ratio can be quite reasonable—were it not for the problem of power sources. In effect, Verne was compelled to imagine it solved because no type of motor was then known which yielded enough power for sufficiently low weight: the internal combustion engine was in its infancy, hot air engines were manifestly too feeble, and steam required massive boilers, condensers and fuel supplies.

For the rest, the multiple small rotors would be less efficient than one very large one; though no one knew that at the time. Contra-rotation was a splendid idea, as it would obviate the need for the counter-torque rotor which is a feature of the modern helicopter, although it is not evident that Verne realised this; probably it should be put down to a fine stroke of intuition. The 60mm gun is quite acceptable: during the Second World War some marks of Mosquito aircraft carried a 57mm piece, and 75mm ones were mounted in some Mitchells.

Verne's main contribution, once again, is the utter confidence he manages to convey. The thing can be done, he says, given only a lighter prime mover than we have at the moment. And, of course, he was right and the sceptics were confounded.

The predictions of his later years tend to be less explicit,

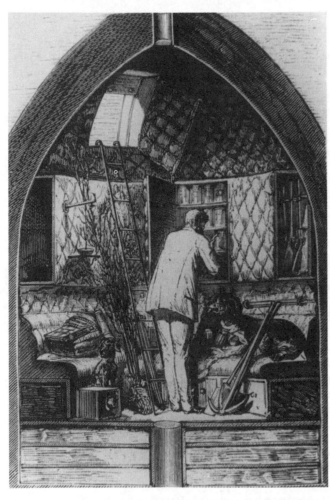

Interior of Verne's "space bullet," From the Earth to the Moon.
Engraving by H. de Montaut, 1865.

and, it must be admitted, less consistent and less carefully thought out. Probably the aging writer, maintaining a tremendous output, found it increasingly difficult to keep abreast of technical developments, and to work out the details of contrivances as he devised them. For example, I am unable to make sense of the description of the aircraft (called "planeurs", though they are not gliders) in the posthumously published *L'Etonnante Aventure du Mission Barsac.* It is, of course, the case that some parts of this book were only partially completed, and that it suffered from the editing of lesser hands. In any case, it contains the world's first radio-guided missile. The missile, apparently in the form of a model aircraft, is controlled—admittedly, over short distances only by means of Herz's electromagnetic waves, it being explained that an Italian named Marconi has recently discovered how to send them efficiently.

So evidently Verne had managed to keep track of one growing aspect of technology. However, the description of the flying-submarine-car with which the disagreeable Robur, now gone quite crackers, returns to attempt the conquest of the world in *Maître du Monde* includes some decided oddities.

The machine was spindle shaped, sharper for'ard than aft, the fuselage being aluminium, though I could not decide what material was used for the wings. It rested on four wheels . . . the spokes being broadened into paddles, which helped the *Epouvante* along when on or under the water. But . . . the principal drive comprised two Parsons turbines, one on either side of the keel. Driven with extreme rapidity by the machine, they acted as propellors in the water; and I wondered whether they were not also used in flying (my translation).

It really seems that Verne did not realise that Parsons turbines were *steam engines;* particularly as the narrator (predictably) goes on to say "The force which drove all these mechanisms could only be electricity"

I, at least, am baffled here. Had he read of Parsons turbines driving generators—a set often being called a "turbo-alternator"—and, when he read of their use in ships (*Turbinia* made her famous demonstration in 1897), assumed that the alternator was being used as a motor? It seems scarcely credible, yet I cannot think of another explanation.

Confusion likewise appears in *Les 500 millions de la Bégum;* though, in this case, the book as a whole is, perhaps, too lighthearted to warrant too nice a critical study. A Frenchman and a German each inherit half of a vast fortune left by an Indian Begum; and each decides to use his new wealth to found an "ideal city" in parts of the newly opened lands of the American West. Verne, no doubt getting something of his own back for the Franco-Prussian War, has his French hero found a Home of Culture and the Arts; whilst the German (surprise!) sets up an enormous armament works. Finding the close proximity of this model of French civilization offensive, the German (Herr Prof. Schultze) decides to eliminate it by firing a single enormous poison-gas shell from a monster cannon of his own design. What the Federal authorities were doing about this is nowhere made clear; but, although the gun is built, loaded and fired, all is well: the muzzle velocity is even greater than intended, and the deadly shell passes into orbit as an unintended artificial satellite!

Of course, this is nonsense—though such cheerful nonsense that one suspects that Verne knew it. It is not possible to fire a projectile straight into closed orbit from the surface of a planet: it would necessarily return to the surface. (Rocket-launched satellites receive their final urge whilst in flight, and roughly parallel to the surface.) Even forgetting this ineluctable conclusion of orbit mechanics, however, Verne—for once—gets the actual numbers wrong. He gives the final velocity of the shell 500 m/s; which is absurdly low. Concorde is about as fast; and whatever its fate may be, that beautiful aircraft stands no risk of going into orbit. This is very odd, since the man who wrote *De la Terre à la Lune* must have known that circular orbit velocity is escape velocity divided by 2, or a little less than 8000 m/sec.

Let us regard *Les 500 millions* then, as a farce. Overall, how does Verne stand in the sf pantheon?

Obviously, he must stand very high indeed as a predictor.

His major ideas—aircraft, submarines, and flight to the moon—have all been fulfilled. Certainly, he was almost always wrong in detail; and certainly, too, he wildly overestimated the future of electric storage. It must also be allowed that other men before him had thought of, and tried to construct, both submarines and aircraft; although, as has been remarked, he was the first to do serious sums on space-flight.

As a writer he had lightness of touch, sparkle and verve. If his characters often lack depth, his narrative, at its best, carries the reader along with an infectious gusto. Above all, he propagated a vibrant confidence and enthusiasm. It is impossible to guess how many readers he inspired into, or reinforced in, a decision to devote their lives to science and technology: it must, one feels, have been a lot. We could do with a new Jules Verne today. (pp. 30-8)

> *M. Hammerton, "Verne's Amazing Journeys,"*
> *in* Foundation, *No. 38, Winter, 1986-87, pp.*
> *30-8.*

Humanity's relationship to nature in Verne:

Verne had an obsession for plenitude: he never stopped putting a last touch to the world and furnishing it, making it full with an egg-like fullness. His tendency is exactly that of an eighteenth-century encyclopaedist or of a Dutch painter: the world is finite, the world is full of numerable and contiguous objects. The artist can have no other task than to make catalogues, inventories, and to watch out for small unfilled corners in order to conjure up there, in close ranks, the creations and the instruments of man. Verne belongs to the progressive lineage of the bourgeoisie: his work proclaims that nothing can escape man, that the world, even its most distant part, is like an object in his hand, and that, all told, property is but a dialectical moment in the general enslavement of Nature. Verne in no way sought to enlarge the world by romantic ways of escape or mystical plans to reach the infinite: he constantly sought to shrink it, to populate it, to reduce it to a known and enclosed space, where man could subsequently live in comfort: the world can draw everything from itself; it needs, in order to exist, no one else but man.

> *Roland Barthes, "The* Nautilus *and the Drunken Boat,"*
> *in his* Mythologies, *Hill and Wang, 1972.*

John J. Pierce   (essay date 1987)

[*In the excerpt below, Pierce explores Verne's impact on the development of science fiction as a genre.*]

Why call Jules Verne the father of science fiction? He wasn't the first ever to write it. His ideas were limited, and few would grant him the literary stature of Poe or Hawthorne, or even Mary Shelley. Yet he *was* the father of science fiction; for Verne was the one who made the world aware of science fiction and science fiction aware of itself. He was the first to be fully conscious of working in a new medium and, thus, the first to be conscious of its thematic significance.

Verne's name still *means* science fiction to millions. It brings to mind a particular genre as few names do. Suppose someone were to tell you Wladyslaw Uminski was the "Polish Cyrano de Bergerac" or the "Polish Mary Shelley" or the "Polish Edgar Allan Poe"? You might guess he wrote satire or gothic tales or detective fiction, but it would be a pretty nervous and uncertain guess. Let someone tell you Uminski was the Polish Jules Verne, however, and you'll know exactly what he means— without having read anything by him or knowing anything else about him.

Verne (1828-1905) could have been just another minor nineteenth century romantic. He was nurtured in the literary tradition of Victor Hugo and Alexandre Dumas, but his own career seemed to go nowhere for years. He would surely have been forgotten if we had nothing to remember him for but the light comedies, operetta libretti, and minor tragedies and melodramas he turned out between 1847 and 1861, often in collaboration with now-obscure writers like Charles Wallut. The patronage of Alexandre Dumas *fils* may have helped Verne get some of his works staged, but nothing promised a career breakthrough until *Five Weeks in a Balloon* (1863).

"I have just written a novel in a new form, one that is entirely my own," he reportedly wrote to a friend at the Paris Stock Exchange. "If it succeeds, I will have stumbled upon a gold mine. In that case, I shall go on writing and writing without pause." Verne proved to be as prophetic about his own career as about the coming of submarines and space travel. After more than a century, his *voyages extraordinaires* are still in print around the world in many languages, and they may have been filmed more than the works of any other writer.

Verne's formula seems a simple one today, but it was an imaginative revolution of the first order in 1863. For Verne was the first romancer of the future, the first to capture the spirit of scientific discovery and invention and romanticize it at a time when "romance" was almost always associated with the past. Romantic fiction meant the historical adventure novels of Dumas and Sir Walter Scott or, at most, an occasional contemporary work like Hugo's *Les Miserables.*

"Miniver Cheevy, born too late," ran Edwin Arlington Robinson's poem of cynical disillusionment with the romantic ideals of an imaginary and, in any case, lost past. But if Verne's readers felt any regret, it was in being born too soon. To them, romance was not something for nostalgia, but for anticipation.

Rather than just a mutation, the *voyage extraordinaire* was a true synthesis. The romantic movement in literature is usually characterized as having been a revolt against rationalism in favor of raw emotion and "natural" values— almost any encyclopedia will say as much. Most romantics have been suspicious of "science," and gothic sf is but one expression of that suspicion. Yet Verne's formula came to be called the scientific romance, a melding of values elsewhere regarded as antithetical.

What seems primitive today in the *voyage extraordinaires* can be compared with neoteny, the retention of juvenile characteristics by the adult organism, in biological evolution. Verne freed science fiction from the imperatives of the travel tale and embryonic forms of sf: the static perfection of the classical utopia, the narrow focus of satire, the gothic preoccupation with sin and retribution, and the cynicism of the hoax. All were "adult" characteristics, but they stood in the way of science fiction's emergence as a distinct genre. Only by stripping his fiction to the bare essentials of the adventure story motivated by scientific discovery or invention could Verne lay the groundwork for sf to evolve on its own terms. Science and technology, which had been peripheral to the traditional travel tale when they appeared at all, were now placed at the center and combined with the elementary appeal of romantic action and adventure. But once science was granted a literary reality of its own, the way was clear for the evolution of moral, psychological, social, and even philosophical themes arising out of scientific progress.

None of this was immediately apparent in *Five Weeks in a Balloon,* which seems conceptually but a small advance over Verne's earlier false starts in sf. **"A Winter amid the Ice"** (1855) involved polar exploration, while **"A Voyage by Balloon"** (1851) speaks for itself. Neither retains even the interest of **"Master Zacharias"** (1854), a medieval tale about a clockmaker who loses his soul to his obsession with his work, which shows that Verne was aware of gothic sf and tried his hand at it.

Samuel Ferguson's system for circulating heated hydrogen through the gas envelope of the *Victoria* to control its ascent and descent is the only real invention in *Five Weeks in a Balloon,* although that must have seemed impressive in 1863. More important is the pervasive spirit of scientific enterprise in the novel. For Ferguson and his comrades, science is not simply a scholarly pursuit, but a means of expanding human experience and achievement as they soar over the obstacles that have frustrated previous explorations of Africa.

It is significant that the heroes of Verne's first science fiction novel are Englishmen. While he has been accused of sharing many of the prejudices of his time, this is rarely apparent except in his least works. Nationality scarcely seems to matter in the *voyages extraordinaires*—science is an international enterprise, and the fraternity of scientific enterprise can know no boundaries. It may not be going too far to call the *voyages* the first truly international literature. Certainly there are few major languages in which they have not appeared and in which they have not changed literary consciousness.

Until Verne's works began to appear, neither critics nor readers seem to have had any concept of what we now call science fiction. In an "advertisement" (really a preface) to the 1859 William Gowans edition of *The Moon Hoax,* for example, the "publisher" compares Locke's work to the *Arabian Nights, Utopia, Gulliver's Travels,* and even to *Robinson Crusoe* and *Pilgrim's Progress.* It is the same perception of the travel tale Charles Garnier had used for his collection of *Voyages Imaginaires* in 1787-9; nothing really new is seen in *The Moon Hoax.*

Yet in 1874, shortly after the first translations of Verne appeared in America, George Cary Eggleston could observe that "the modern wonder story—a wonder story in which we practical, hard-headed, inquiring, fact-full people of today could in some sort believe—was not born until M. Jules Verne made a congenial marriage between science and fancy." Two years later, William H. L. Barnes could casually refer to Verne as the "master of scientific fiction"—a term which cannot have existed very long when he used it.

For all their technical background, the *voyages extraordinaires* are better remembered for the spirit of scientific enterprise than for the letter of science. In *Journey to the Center of the Earth* (1864), Verne exploits an inner world tradition that was hardly credible even then. Yet the journey itself is unforgettable: the descent into a volcanic crater in Iceland, the discovery of a new bed of coal from beneath, the rescue of a lost explorer because of a freak acoustical effect, and the voyage across the Central Sea in a vast cavern lit by phosphorescence and inhabited by prehistoric men and monsters.

Verne's astronauts in *From the Earth to the Moon* (1865) are fired off into space from a huge cannon. As has been pointed out seemingly countless times since, they would have been smashed to a pulp by the acceleration, and their spacecraft would have been vaporized by air resistance in any case. As it happens, the very year Verne's novel was published also saw publication of Achille Eyraud's *Journey to Venus,* in which rockets are first suggested as a means of launching spacecraft. To be sure, Eyraud had the odd notion that rockets could recycle their own exhaust thereby saving on fuel; even so, he was a better prophet than Verne. Only who reads *Journey to Venus* today? Who can even find it?

Whatever his limitations, Verne could communicate the excitement of an enterprise like the conquest of space. Impey Barbicane and his fellow enthusiasts of the Baltimore Gun Club are so dedicated to their dream of sending a man to the moon that their dedication is infectious. One hardly misses what is usually called "human interest"; or, to be more precise, Verne creates a new kind of human interest. And however wrong he was about how men would be sent into space, he was right on target about the human reaction:

> Since dawn, a vast crowd had covered the plain that stretched out around Stone Hill as far as the eye could see. Every quarter of an hour the railroad brought a new load of onlookers. This immigration took on fantastic proportions. According to the *Tampa Observer,* five million people trod the soil of Florida on that memorable day.

Here science is no longer the half-mystic process of secret rituals and incantations, carried on in shuttered rooms in back streets, which had characterized gothic sf. It is out in the open, part of the world; more than that, it is part of the *evolution* of the world. So are Verne's heroes part of the world. When Barbicane and his associates find themselves being offered unsolicited advice and assistance by the Frenchman Michel Ardan, they soon make common cause. Any resentments give way to a shared sense of mission which transcends traditional loyalties.

At his best, Verne could achieve almost mythic power. With *Twenty Thousand Leagues under the Sea* (1869-70), he added Captain Nemo to the pantheon of literary heroes that begins with Ulysses and embraces King Arthur, Robin Hood, Sherlock Holmes, and others. Originally intended to be a Polish nationalist whose family had been slain by the Russians, he was made a man of indeterminate origins and therefore a more universal figure—both as an idealist and as an outlaw.

Nemo shares Verne's own sense of wonder at the world of nature as revealed by science: "My flocks, like those of Neptune's shepherds, graze without fear on the immense prairies of the ocean," he tells Professor Aronnax. "I have vast properties, sown by the hand of the creator, and cultivated by me." But he also shares Verne's dream of harnessing the laws of nature: "There is a powerful agent, responsive, prompt and facile, that meets our every need on board," says Nemo of the electricity which powers the *Nautilus.* "It lights and warms our ship, it is the soul of our mechanical apparatus."

Nemo, with his romantic quest for vengeance, has reason to withhold his knowledge from the wider world. But Verne is eager to reveal all the secrets of the *Nautilus,* a submarine craft so sophisticated that some of its details (or at least its comforts) have yet to be realized. How drab and utilitarian our submarines seem next to one with a library, a museum, and picture windows opening on the Deep! And for all his obsession with vengeance, an obsession which dooms him as he is symbolically drawn into the maelstrom at the end of the novel, Nemo never loses sight of all the creative possibilities of the technology he has mastered: "There is the true Existence. And I can imagine the founding of nautical towns, clusters of submarine houses that like the *Nautilus* would rise every day to breathe at the surface—free towns, independent cities . . . " No wonder Jacques Cousteau's efforts to domesticate the undersea realm inspire a sense of déjà vu for readers of *Twenty Thousand Leagues under the Sea.*

Ironically, Verne doesn't seem to have understood the nature of his literary revolution as well as his readers; fewer than half the *voyages extraordinaires* were really science fiction. But those which weren't are all but forgotten today, save for *Around the World in Eighty Days* (1873), and even that exudes the spirit of science fiction. Phileas Fogg, for all his stiff-upper-lip British mannerisms, is very much a man of the new age of science, and his journey is an act of faith in technological progress. Yet, often in Verne's later sf, the only real heroes are the inventions, such as the steam-powered elephant in *The Steam House* (1880), or the heavier-than-air flying machine in *Robur the Conqueror* (1886).

Contemporary critics are finding more food for thought in Verne's works than previously suspected. Jean Chesneaux's *The Political and Social Ideas of Jules Verne* (1971), for example, explores the controversial thought lurking behind the romancer's "bourgeois façade." But while there seems to be something there, it isn't particular-ly relevant to Verne's role in the evolution of science fiction.

True, *The Begum's Fortune* (1879), based on a rough draft by exiled communard Paschal Grousset, introduces utopian and anti-utopian themes in contrasting the good and evil cities of Franceville and Stahlstadt, founded by rival heirs to an eccentric millionaire. The rival families whose quarrels bring destruction to a floating wonder city in *Propeller Island* (1895) may represent the self-destructive nature of capitalism. *Black Diamonds* (*Les Indes Noires,* 1877), in which part of a coal mine in Scotland is transformed into a brightly lit model city for workers, may indeed express Saint Simonian ideas of communal enterprise. These works, however, are little known or read and, except perhaps for the last, have had no discernible influence on science fiction.

In other cases, Verne was playing catch-up with novel modes of sf that had outdistanced him. A world war is threatened in *For the Flag* (1896), basis for Karel Zeman's delightful film, *The Fabulous World of Jules Verne* (1961). But world wars had actually been fought by 1896 in Victorian science fiction. **"In the Year 2889"** (1889) was Verne's only attempt to envision a society of the future, but Albert Robida's *The Twentieth Century* (1882) had already done it far better.

That Verne's youthful optimism about scientific progress failed him in later years is manifest. In *The Barsac Mission* (1914), edited by his son Michel Verne, deluded scientist Marcel Camaret puts his science at the service of a gangster empire in the Sahara. From an oasis of weather control and other wonders, Harry Killer and his Merry Fellows set out to plunder the world. Finally forced to face the truth, Camaret destroys his handiwork, proclaiming, "God has condemned Blackland!" Robur, heroic pioneer of aviation in *Robur the Conqueror,* returns as a madman in *Master of the World* (1904). After menacing the world with his combination automobile-submarine-airplane, he meets his doom when his hubris leads him to defy God by flying the *Terror* into a thunderstorm.

Perhaps Verne's last word is the stoicism of **"Eternal Adam"** (1910). A scientist of a far future time finds his faith in progress shaken by the discovery that his civilization was built on the ruins of another—our own—which was destroyed overnight in a worldwide cataclysm. All progress is illusion, the labor of Sisyphus repeated over and over as a blind and indifferent universe defeats human aspirations. All that is left is "an intimate conviction of the eternal recurrence of events."

Yet, whatever the significance of Verne's last works, it represents a footnote in the evolutionary history of sf. His impact remains that of the youthful works, on science fiction and even on the world. As in *Robur the Conqueror,* it is the vision of science that is Verne's legacy: "And now, who is this Robur? . . . Robur is the science of the future. Perhaps the science of to-morrow! Certainly the science that will come!" (pp. 33-8)

John J. Pierce, "Verne and the Verneans," in his Foundations of Science Fiction: A Study in Imagination and Evolution, *Greenwood Press, 1987, pp. 33-49.*

Verne and nature:

It is one of the chief characteristics of the Vernian planet that its population of objects and beings is endlessly proliferating; like the single grain of wheat (in *L'Ile mystérieuse*) that grows to reproduce itself several million-fold, they are self-multiplying. Even the polar North displays a tropical profusion of creatures. . . . This cornucopian abundance is beneficent since it promises the eternal satisfaction of appetite. But nature is potentially hazardous, and the image of the storm cloud, together with the emphasis on the monstrousness of the innumerable beings, and (later) their ambiguous *puissance*, suggest a sinister, maleficent aspect. The overflowing, immeasurable, dangerous world of monsters and sharks, if it is to be rendered anodyne and intelligible, fit for human consumption, must be contained. Containment, or enclosure, is the objective and rationale of Verne's scientific taxonomy.

Andrew Martin, in his The Knowledge of Ignorance: From Genesis to Jules Verne, *Cambridge University Press, 1985.*

Arthur B. Evans   (essay date 1988)

[*Evans is an American educator and critic whose works include* Jean Cocteau and His Films of Orphic Identity *(1975). In the following excerpt, Evans discusses the pessimism toward science and technology that imbues Verne's late fiction.*]

The second half of Verne's novelistic production is very different from the first in its general ideological focus. Such a change can most simply be described as a slow but steady metamorphosis away from the overall optimism of a Positivistic world view. And, correspondingly, one discerns a more frequent foregrounding of a generally pessimistic, cynical, and vehemently antiscience outlook. As might be expected, the scientific pedagogy within these particular texts grows less and less central to the plot structures—becoming progressively more abridged, watered down, or cut out altogether. Questions concerning environmental protection, human morality, and social responsibility are more often raised. Humor either disappears entirely or is recentered in irony and/or acidic satire. And the scientists themselves are increasingly portrayed as crazed megalomaniacs—using their technological know-how for purposes of world domination or fabulous wealth.

The underlying reasons for this palpable change of tone in Verne's works are very complex and the result of a variety of factors in the author's own life as well as in the social fabric of late nineteenth-century France. During a time in which he was experiencing serious problems with his rebellious son Michel, as well as growing financial worries, Verne also had to cope with the successive deaths of three individuals who were very close to him: his mis-

tress Madame Duchêne in 1885, his editor and *père spirituel* Hetzel in 1886, and his mother in 1887.

Further, an event still cloaked in mystery took place on March 9, 1886. Verne was attacked at gunpoint by his nephew Gaston and was shot in the lower leg. Lodged in the bone of his ankle, the bullet could not be removed. As a result, Verne remained partially crippled for the rest of his life. In December of the same year, he confessed to Hetzel fils: "As for the rest, I have entered into the darkest part of my life. But I am unwilling to let it conquer me. Believe me when I say that I take these things very philosophically. The future is rather threatening for me because of the business that you already know about, and I confess that if I couldn't take refuge in hard work, which pleases me, I would indeed be in a pitiful state." But a few years later, Verne seems to have grown less philosophical about such matters. In two letters to his brother Paul, he confides: "All that's left for me . . . are these intellectual distractions. . . . My character is profoundly changed, and I have received blows from which I will never recover . . . " and "my dear Paul, you are happy. Remain happy. As for me, I am rarely so any more . . . All told, I'm finishing up badly."

This growing pessimism in Verne's private life had its counterpart in the French social climate of the 1880s and 1890s. A severe long-term economic crisis lasted from 1882 to 1895, provoked in part by a series of agricultural disasters, a depressed manufacturing industry, skyrocketing unemployment, and a series of bank failures. Political strife worsened, precipitating the Boulangiste "uprising" and the fall from power of Jules Ferry. These and other occurrences created in the French public a general mood of disillusionment and frustration with the Positivist policies of the past. It was during this period that Verne began to serve as an elected official for the city of Amiens, putting him into constant confrontation with such matters as he and his fellow councilmen grappled with the local impact of these national issues.

It also seems far from coincidental that these same decades witnessed the rise of modern capitalistic imperialism and the frenetic rivalry among the various industrialized nations of the Western world to colonialize (and exploit) a greater and greater number of unexplored and/or undeveloped countries around the globe—particularly in Africa, the Far East, Indonesia, and the South Seas. And concurrently, on the domestic front finance capital came increasingly to replace industrial capital as the springboard for economic growth—intensifying the hegemonic power of banks, profit-conscious investors, and moneylenders in the politics of France's decision making.

Finally, this period also saw the birth of the modern military-industrial complex, where the advances of technology were unilaterally applied to the production of ever more lethal weapons systems. National military budgets soared, as France and the other industrialized powers of the world sought to consolidate their geo-strategic holdings through the practice of conscription . . . and the latest in advanced military hardware: iron-clad warships, land mines, machine-guns, poison gas canisters, long-range artillery, and more. Science and technology were increasingly becoming the handmaidens to international warfare—not only in the military confrontations with one's rivals, but also in the bloody repression of insurrections within one's own colonies.

Whether such developments directly affected the fundamental tone of his *Voyages Extraordinaires* is no doubt debatable. But Verne *was* undeniably a witness to, and very conscious of, these profound transformations in the overall tenor of his times. And the ideological texture of his novels *does* change during this period. Whether it be the product of the events in his own life or those in the world around him (or a combination of both), Verne's pessimism becomes much more palpable in these latter texts. His science turns increasingly misanthropic and his technology often verges on the satanic. And the idealistic Byronic Romanticism of his work becomes progressively tinged with overtones of Baudelarian *spleen,* of Huysmans-like introversion, or of Jarry-esque derision.

In illustrating how this change of ideological orientation manifested itself in the thematic makeup of Verne's fiction, the gradual shift in his portrayal of the scientist is especially suggestive. Viewed schematically, there are four types of scientists in the *Voyages Extraordinaires:* the heroic, the eccentric, the incompetent, and the dangerous.

Engraving of Jules Verne, age 50.

The first two types are positive (in both senses of the word); the latter two are negative. And their respective appearance in these works is usually mutually exclusive and successive in nature.

The first (and earliest) characterization of the Vernian scientist is unsparingly laudatory—albeit one-dimensional—where his courage and knowledge are exceeded only by his personal integrity and altruism. This sort . . . is typified by such individuals as Dr. Fergusson of *Five Weeks in a Balloon,* Cyrus Smith of *Mysterious Island,* or Dr. Clawbonny of *The Adventures of Captain Hatteras.* One might be tempted to say that Captain Nemo of *Twenty Thousand Leagues under the Sea* also belongs to this category of heroic scientist. But Nemo's solitary nature, his moments of brooding silence, and his thirst for vengeance make him much less one-dimensional as a fictional character and infinitely more intriguing—his mysterious and oxymoronic personality identifying him as a quite unique specimen in Verne's roster of protagonists.

The second type of scientist—still quite heroic (often inadvertently) but also very fallible—combines scientific expertise with comical personality quirks: for example, the excited stuttering of Professor Lidenbrock in *Journey to the Center of the Earth,* the "distracted" foibles of Paganel in *The Children of Captain Grant,* or the pedantic idiosyncrasies of Palmyrin Rosette in *Hector Servadac.* Each is what the author invariably calls "an original" and is depicted as a kind of *grand enfant:* adorably naïve and amusingly unconventional. And each, as mentioned, becomes so engrossed in his science that he fits the description of the proverbial absentminded professor—respected and competent in his field, devoted to his "students," but totally inept in the mundane matters of day-to-day living.

The third type is similar to the second but without the heroism, the scientific virtuosity, or the compassion. These scientists are treated with humor, but it is bitingly satirical and pejorative. They are shown to be narrow-minded, fastidious, egocentric, insensitive, verbose, and unproductive. Aristobulus Ursiclos of *The Green Ray* epitomizes this brand of quack-scientist (his name reflects his character), as well as William Falsten of *The Chancellor* whom Verne classifies as "the kind of scientist who thinks only of machines, who is so absorbed by mechanics and mathematics that he sees nothing beyond that." A number of statisticians throughout the *Voyages Extraordinaires* also belong to this group, such as Cokburn of *The Floating City* or Poncin of *The Amazing Adventure of the Barsac Mission*—professional mathematicians whom Verne considers not true scientists at all, but rather, in the words of Michel Ardan, individuals "who keep score while we play the game."

The fourth type of scientist grows more prevalent in Verne's later works: the mad scientist, the irresponsible scientist, the scientist who presents a serious danger to Nature, to society, and to humanity as a whole because he chooses to compromise his wisdom for power or money. There is no humor in these portrayals. There is neither heroism nor compassion. And "pure" scientific research (as exemplified by the naming and classifying topoi . . .) is no longer the driving force behind these scientists—just as the activities of exploration and discovery are no longer the ultimate goals of their "voyage." The majority of these wayward scientists are inventors, using their technological genius to create apocalypse-machines. They are shown to be uncommonly erudite and technologically brilliant, but also greedy, misanthropic, vainglorious, arrogant, and often insane.

The first novel in which this particular brand of scientific villain appears is *The Begum's Fortune* (1879), a text that is often cited as Verne's only technological utopia/dystopia. Two scientists, one French and one German, inherit a vast fortune from a distant and fabulously rich relative who was a sultan in India. Each decides to build the city of his dreams in the newly explored American territory of Oregon. The former constructs France-Ville, a harmonious prototype of perfect urban hygiene (reflecting the scientific specialty of its creator, Dr. Sarrasin). The latter constructs Stahlstadt—meaning the City of Steel—an immense and militaristic industrial complex devoted to the production of cannons and explosive shells that contain a variety of poison gases (the specialty of its Krupps-like creator, Herr Schultze). Schultze succeeds in revolutionizing modern warfare with his gigantic artillery and lethal missiles, and, needless to say, does a thriving business by providing the major powers of the world with potent new weapons. But his *idée fixe* is neither wealth nor political prestige; it is racial supremacy for the Germanic people. The narrator explains:

> The professor had heard of his rival's intention to build a French city where the physical and spiritual hygienic conditions would improve all the qualities of the race and create generations of young people who were strong and valiant. To him, this enterprise seemed both totally absurd and destined to fail because it was contrary to the laws of Progress—laws which dictated the fall of the Latin race, its subsequent servitude to the Saxon race, and, finally, its total disappearance from the face of the Earth . . . It was obvious that he was called upon by the creative and destructive force that is Nature to wipe out these pygmies who dared oppose her wishes. . . .
>
> Besides, this project [Stahlstadt] was of secondary importance to Herr Schultze. It was only a small part of a much greater plan to destroy all those who refused to merge with the German people and become united with the Vaterland.

Incarnating French attitudes toward Germany during the postwar years of the 1870s and foreshadowing certain events of the twentieth century, Herr Schultze is Verne's first truly evil scientist. As pointed out earlier, his vision of nature and humanity is focused uniquely on relationships of force, as dictated by cold analytical logic. Identifiably Nietzschean in his evolutionary beliefs and reflecting a kind of scientific social Darwinism, Schultze lectures the young Marcel Bruckmann in the manner of Zarathustra, saying:

> "My dear young man," answered Herr Schultze, "there appears to be in your otherwise very organized head a collection of Celtic ideas that would be of great harm to you, if you were to live very

long. Good and evil, right and wrong are purely relative things, simple human conventions. Nature's laws are the only absolute. The law of competition is like the law of gravitation. Fighting against it is senseless; accommodating oneself to it and then acting according to its dictates is both wise and reasonable. And that is why I will destroy Doctor Sarrasin's city."

Herr Schultze represents the dark underside of Verne's objective rationalism and the growing awareness on the author's part that, in Rabelais's words, "science without conscience leads to the ruin of the soul." It is significant in this respect that Schultze's scientific totalitarianism is ultimately foiled at the last moment by a kind of deus ex machina gas leak in his secret laboratory and he is instantly frozen solid—a form of justice that is doubly poetic given his lack of human warmth. But, quite characteristic of Verne's later works, it is this intervention of Providence that defeats him in the end, not the human forces of morality. This outcome aptly illustrates the twofold nature of Verne's growing pessimism: that science in the hands of evil people becomes evil, that it is all-powerful in its own right and, when misused, can be stopped only by suprahuman means.

But science can also corrupt good people. Even the most morally resilient of scientists can fall prey to the supreme omnipotence it offers. One excellent case in point is the metamorphosis of Robur from his initial appearance in *Robur the Conqueror* (1886) to his death in *Master of the World* (1904). In the final episode of the former novel, Robur is portrayed as a heroic *oberman* of the skies who, from the deck of his invincible *Albatros,* warns the general public of the potential dangers of science:

> "Citizens of the United States!" he said. "My experiment is completed. But my opinion is, as of now, that nothing should be rushed, not even Progress. Science must not get ahead of social customs. Evolution, not revolution, is what's needed. In a word, everything in its own time. My arrival today is much too early to overcome your contradictions and divisiveness. The nations of this world are not yet mature enough for unity.
>
> So I am leaving you, and I am taking my secret with me. But it will not be lost to humanity forever. It will belong to you the day that you become wise enough to use it constructively and never abuse it. Farewell, citizens of the United States! Farewell!"

Contrary to what occurs in Verne's earlier novels, the fruits of the scientist's discoveries are no longer bequeathed to humanity as a whole. The scientist himself judiciously decides that the human species is not yet fit to possess such technology and he disappears from sight, taking his secrets with him. But all is not lost—Robur promises to return someday—and there is still hope for the future. Thus, at this stage, Verne's pessimism is somewhat attenuated by the wisdom of Robur himself and by the assumption that Man will, at some point in time, be capable of using (but not abusing) the science that Robur symbolizes.

But the Robur of *Master of the World* breaks that promise and, with his new car-boat-plane vehicle called *Epouvante* (*Terror*), he begins openly to intimidate humanity for the pleasure of proving his superiority. Industrialized nations from around the world, seeing in this apparatus an incomparable military weapon (an increasingly frequent motif in Verne's later works), offer him millions for it, to which he defiantly responds:

> Proposals coming from the diverse nations of Europe as well as those lately received from the United States of America can expect no other answer than the following:
>
> I categorically refuse any offer for the purchase of my vehicle. This invention will be neither French, nor German, nor Austrian, nor Russian, nor English, nor American. The machine will remain my property, and I will do with it as I please.
>
> With it, I have control over the entire world. No human power exists, under any circumstances, that is strong enough to resist it.
>
> Do not try to take it from me. It is and will continue to be beyond your reach. Any harm that you attempt to do me will be repaid a hundredfold.
>
> As for the price I am offered, I have no interest whatsoever. I have no need of your millions. Besides, the day where I might wish to have millions or even billions, I would need only to reach out my hand for them.
>
> Let it be known on both the New and the Old Continents, they can do nothing against me—and I can do everything against them.
>
> This letter, I sign it: Master of the World.

As the narrative continues, a young, inexperienced, and somewhat hapless Inspector Strock attempts to track down Robur. Predictably, he succeeds only in finding himself a prisoner aboard the *Epouvante*. Upon face-to-face encounter, Strock realizes that the once-heroic Robur is now totally insane.

> We were face to face, two feet apart. With folded arms he looked at me, and I was shocked by his gaze. . . . It was not that of a sane man, a gaze that seemed to have nothing human left in it! . . .
>
> Obviously, Robur was obsessed. This gesture, that I had already observed when he was walking around the campsite, this gesture, he did it again . . . his arm raised and pointing to the sky . . . It was as if some irresistible force was drawing him toward the upper reaches, as if he no longer belonged on earth and was destined to live in space, a perpetual guest of the higher atmosphere. . . .

Robur's loss of reason is accompanied by a complete loss of communicativeness: an arrogant mutism in sharp contrast to his previous incarnation where he had proved to be surprisingly loquacious—explaining the details of *Albatros* to his (also) unwilling passengers, giving speeches before public assemblies, sounding his trumpet above all the major capitals of the world, and so on. In this text, however, it is Strock who communicates his observations to the reader. And such secondhand descriptions create an even greater "distance" between the identifying reader and the erstwhile hero, as well as severely undercutting the authoritativeness of the (very rare) passages of scientific pedagogy present in the novel.

The climax of *Master of the World* has Robur defiantly flying his *Epouvante* into the heart of a lightning storm, with dire consequences:

> With eyes blazing, the impassible Captain flew directly into the storm—*face to face* with it, as if to defy its power and to show that he had nothing to fear from it. To avoid the storm's fury, the *Epouvante* would need to immediately dive—a manoeuvre which Robur apparently had no intention of doing.
>
> No! He maintained his exalted bearing like a man who, in his intractable pride, believed himself above or outside all of humanity! To see him thus, I fearfully wondered if this man wasn't some fantastic being escaped from some supernatural world!
>
> Then he spoke, and amid the roaring of the storm and the crashing of the thunder I heard:
>
> "I . . . Robur . . . Robur . . . Master of the World! . . . "
>
> At that moment, all of my instincts and my sense of duty suddenly came to the fore. . . . Yes! it was totally crazy, but I had to try to arrest this criminal whom my country had outlawed, who was threatening the entire world with his terrible invention. I had to somehow handcuff him and bring him to justice! . . . Was I or was I not Strock, police inspector? . . . And, forgetting momentarily where I was, one against three above a seething ocean, I rushed toward Robur and, with a voice that could be heard above the storm's din, I shouted "In the name of the Law, I . . . "
>
> Suddenly, *Epouvante* shuddered as if jolted by a powerful electrical shock. Its members shook violently like those of a human when electrocuted. Its frame shattered, the machine broke into pieces and fell.
>
> The *Epouvante* had just been struck by lightning. With wings broken and turbines smashed, it plummeted from an altitude of more than a thousand feet into the depths of the ocean!

Once again it is the hand of Providence that succeeds in striking down the otherwise indomitable scientist and his technological marvel. Once again, the secrets of its construction disappear with its inventor—this time forever. And once again, the helplessness of humanity (and its reliance on supernatural intervention) is dramatically underscored: Strock's attempts at lawful arrest are upstaged by a higher law that takes matters into its own hands.

The Icarus-like moral to this story could be taken from any number of Verne's later texts. But it is important to realize that this particular lesson is not unique to these texts. It is present in the great majority of Verne's works, from the earliest of his *Voyages Extraordinaires* to the last. What is different, however, is that such an explicit challenge to the established order of things is now the central thematic element around which the entire plot unfolds. Earlier, it was always implicit—an unemphasized corollary to the many scientific explorations and discoveries portrayed, usually evoked in passing as the hero momentarily wondered: "Wasn't he walking on forbidden ground? Wasn't he, in this voyage, trying to overstep the limits of the impossible? Hadn't God reserved for some later century the knowledge of this continent . . . ?" But such fears, although serving to highlight the religious humility of the hero in question (and to heighten the suspense), were usually shown to be groundless and were quickly forgotten. If present at all, Providence was shown to be infinitely benevolent and a reliable source of "just-in-the-nick-of-time" assistance whenever the heroes found themselves in a tight spot: for example, saving Fergusson and companions from a ferocious lion attack, rescuing the survivors of the Hatteras expedition, providing the castaways of Lincoln Island with a grain of wheat to begin their crops, answering Dick Sand's call for help in fighting cannibals, and so on. Thus, the deus ex machina leitmotif is quite common throughout all of the *Voyages Extraordinaires.* But its use for the violent destruction of the hubris-filled scientist and his futuristic machine marks a new twist in the author's narrative practice, and one that would be utilized again and again throughout his later novels.

Among Verne's "dangerous" scientists, there exists yet another variant: the one who, although not crazed, is totally irresponsible and either refuses to understand the threat posed by his inventions or simply doesn't care. The final novel in the trilogy of *From the Earth to the Moon, Around the Moon,* and *Topsy Turvy* is a good case in point. Barbicane, Maston, and company (but not Michel Ardan for obvious reasons) are once again brought into the limelight. But this time it is to construct a giant cannon, which, when fired, will alter the earth's rotational axis. The rationale is that, once straightened, the earth's polar caps would partially melt, exposing hundreds of thousands of square miles of new land and access to fabulously rich coal and mineral deposits. Representing the commercial interests of the United States (a reflection of the author's changing attitudes toward America during the latter years of his life), they first "purchase" the Arctic at an international auction. Then Maston is charged with working out the mathematical formulate to accomplish the task. Finally, Barbicane and the remainder of the newly formed North Polar Practical Association begin construction of the cannon in central Africa near Mount Kilimanjaro (picked for its capacity to withstand the recoil of such a blast). During this time, however, the probable global effects of such an operation are calculated by civilian engineers and printed in newspapers around the world:

> In two of the sectors, situated opposite one another in the northern and southern hemispheres, the seas would withdraw and would flood the other two sectors of these hemispheres.
>
> In the first sector: the Atlantic Ocean would dry up almost totally . . . Consequently, between America and Europe vast new lands would emerge . . . But it must be noted that, with the drop in the water level, the breathable atmosphere would also drop proportionately. Thus, the coasts of Europe and America would be at such a great altitude that even cities located at twenty or thirty degrees would have at their disposition only the air normally found at an altitude of four kilometers. Hence, to take only the principal cities of New York, Philadelphia, Charleston, Panama, Lisbon, Madrid, Paris, London, Edinburg, Dublin, etc. . . . absolute impossibility of living there.
>
> Same effect in the opposing sector, which includes the Indian Ocean, Australia, and a quarter of the Pacific Ocean. . . .
>
> In the sector of the Northeast . . . Petersburg and Moscow on the one hand and Calcutta, Bangkok, Saigon, Peking, Hong Kong, and Yeddo on the other . . . these cities would disappear underwater. . . .
>
> In the sector of the Southwest . . . the disasters would be somewhat less severe . . . However, large territories would still be submerged by this artificial flood. . . .

Or, as the narrator blithely sums it up, with tongue undoubtedly in cheek and *humour noir* in full array (albeit with a certain amount of bitterness showing through the seams):

> Those threatened were divided into two categories: the asphyxiated and the drowned. . . .
>
> On the side of the asphyxiated, there were the Americans of the United States and the Europeans of France, England, Spain, etc. The prospect of annexing new territories on the ocean floor was not sufficient to make them accept the modifications involved. . . .
>
> On the side of the drowned, there were the inhabitants of South America, then the Australians, Canadians, Hindus, New Zealanders . . . Ah! If it had only been a question of burying under new seas the Samoyeds or the Lapons of Siberia the Fuegans, the Patagonians, the Tartars, the Chinese, the Japanese or a few Argentinians, perhaps the civilized States would've accepted this sacrifice. But too many Powers had too large a share of these catastrophes to not protest. . . .

But turning a deaf ear to the cries, the pleas, and the threats of their brethren from around the world, Barbicane and company complete their project. Their huge cannon is subsequently loaded and, with great ceremony, fired. As the peoples of all nations hold their collective breath and await the impending cataclysm, it quickly becomes evident that the attempt has failed. Why? Because of an unnoticed error in Maston's mathematics—an error that occurred at the outset of his complex algebraic formulations and that was caused (predictably?) by a deus ex machina intervention in the form of a lightning bolt:

> In fact, when the famous secretary of the Gun Club took as a base for his equations the circumference of the Earth, he marked it as forty thousand meters instead of forty thousand kilometers—which skewed the solution to the problem. . . .
>
> Yes! Three zeroes forgotten in the measurement of the Earth's circumference!
>
> Suddenly J. T. Maston remembered. It was at the beginning of his work, when he had just closed himself up in the study of Ballistic Cottage. He had correctly written the number 40,000,000 on the blackboard. . . .
>
> At that moment, the telephone rings! J. T. Maston heads towards it . . . He exchanges a few words with Mrs. Evangelina Scorbutt . . . And then a lightning bolt strikes the lines, knocking him off his feet and toppling his blackboard. . . . Then he gets up . . . He begins to rewrite the half-erased number on the blackboard . . . He had barely written 40,000 . . . when the phone rings a second time . . . And when he gets back to work once again, he forgets to add the last three zeroes to the measurement of Earth's circumference! (175-76, IA)

Once again humanity is saved from science by the intercession of Providence. And once again the text concludes on the following (somewhat awkward, given the scathingly satiric narrative voice used up to this point) moralizing note: "To change the conditions by which the Earth moves is an effort well beyond those permitted to humanity. Man cannot alter the order of the Universe as established by the Creator."

Many other examples of this brand of irresponsible scientist can be seen in Verne's later works: Orfanik of *The Carpathian Castle,* for instance, or Thomas Roch of *For the Flag,* or Wilhelm Storitz of *The Secret of Wilhelm Storitz,* among others. All are partly or totally deranged, all are a serious menace to society, all are seemingly invincible, all are ultimately foiled by Providence, and all are a testament to their creator's growing obsession with the dangers of advanced technology. But one "mad scientist" in particular merits special attention: Marcel Camaret of *The Amazing Adventure of the Barsac Mission.* This work is, quite appropriately, the very last novel of the *Voyages Extraordinaires* and was at least partially written by Verne's son Michel. But what is of importance is that, in his portrayal of Camaret, Verne directly addresses the question of the scientist's "responsibility" for the technical marvels that he brings into the world.

The scenario is as follows: the principal protagonists of the story have ventured deep into Africa in search of the lost brother of their organizer Jane Buxton. They are captured by men on strange flying machines and taken to the secret city of Blackland, located somewhere in the Sahara. Established by its tyrant "king" Harry Killer (another very appropriately named protagonist), Blackland is an inter-national criminal "utopia"—a highly advanced technological haven for escaped murderers, rapists, and thieves from all countries around the world:

> It was a very strange city. Built on perfectly flat land . . . it formed an exact semi-circle . . . Its area of approximately one hundred and thirty acres, was divided into three sectors of unequal size. . . .
>
> In the first lived the aristocracy of Blackland. . . .
>
> In the third lived the Civil Body, those White Men who could not enter the first sector. . . .
>
> Located between the first and the third, the second sector . . . took up the remainder of the city. It was the slaves' compound.
>
> On the north corner, adjacent to the public gardens, was a huge quadrangular building surrounded by parapeted walls . . . the Palace, as it was commonly called, where lived Harry Killer and nine of his early associates, now promoted to the rank of advisors . . . Located in front of the Palace was the Factory.
>
> The Factory was like an autonomous and independent city into which this dictator continually poured money . . . If it were he who had initially conceived of Blackland, it was the Factory that had created it for him and had furnished it not only with all the modern conveniences but also with a host of extraordinary inventions that Europe would not come to know until several years in the future.

A modern Sodom and Gomorrah, Blackland is portrayed as a city of consummate evil. And the rapacity of its inhabitants is exceeded only by the wonders of its futuristic technology—climate-control devices, electric flying machiens called *planeurs,* telephones, electric lighting, and automated agricultural machinery—all provided by the creative genius of the director of the Factory, the scientist Marcel Camaret.

In contrast to his surroundings, Camaret is portrayed as a quiet and timid man, soft-spoken and dreamy-eyed, but "endowed with unlimited energy" as well as a prodigious intellect. Typical of Verne's "eccentric" scientists, he is so absorbed in the abstractions of his craft that he has totally lost contact with the world around him:

> Marcel Camaret was the only inhabitant of the Factory who could leave it at will and wander the streets or the neighboring countryside of Blackland. Although he often took advantage of this liberty to stroll his daydreams around the city, it must not be concluded that he was any better informed than his workers about the unusual customs of Blackland—he was totally unaware of them, and even of the name of the city itself.
>
> One day, a worker asked him about the city's name. Camaret thought about it for a moment, and, to the astonishment of his subordinate, he replied hesitantly;
>
> "My word . . . I'm not sure. . . . "

Never, until that very instant, had he thought to inform himself about this detail. Nor did he think any more about it afterwards.

But where the rapt preoccupations of Verne's earlier "eccentric" scientists had led to burlesque situations of slapstick comedy, that of Camaret leads to human suffering and tragedy. He is completely unaware of the unscrupulous nature of his benefactor Harry Killer and the sinister use the latter has made of his inventions:

> Camaret . . . lived in a perpetual feverish state. All his dreams, he had managed to materialize them one after the other. After the rain-making machine, his brain produced a hundred other inventions which benefited Harry Killer, without their creator ever knowing how the latter made use of them.
>
> As for how his comrade might utilize such machines, the idea never entered Marcel Camaret's head. A being of pure abstraction, he had seen them only as problems to be solved. He never concerned himself with their practical application or with the origin of the materials put at his disposition for their construction. . . . He had asked, he was supplied. To him, nothing was simpler.

Driving this moral point home even further, the narrator continues:

> Of course, an inventor cannot be held responsible for the evil for which he was, indirectly, the cause. It would never occur to anyone, for example, to accuse the man who invented the revolver for all the crimes committed by this weapon—crimes which would have not taken place without it. But, nonetheless, the creator of such an instrument is aware that it can and must kill: it was with this goal in mind that he created it.
>
> Nothing of the sort in the case of Marcel Camaret. If he had ever had the idea of inventing a cannon that was larger and whose bullet was heavier than any in existence, he would have happily calculated the form of the piece, the weight and profile of the projectile and the necessary powder charge without ever considering this work as anything but an exercise in ballistics. He would have been greatly surprised to learn that his brain-child could, given the chance, be a brutal killer.

Quite obviously, the main ideological thrust of Verne's fiction has shifted. No longer a simple question of using science as a kind of narrative springboard to adventure and pedagogy, it is rather the social implications of science and the moral role of the scientist himself that now occupy center stage in the author's text, forming the thematic kernel around which his entire plot revolves. It is no longer a simple question of science in the hands of an evil or indifferent scientist who threatens the safety of the world, but rather of the responsibility of those who—innocently naïve though they may be in their own right—nevertheless create the means whereby such crimes can occur. The lesson is clear: scientists not only have a moral obligation to educate society (as pointed out earlier), but also to safeguard society from the fruits of their own labor.

It is significant in this regard that, unlike in his earlier pessimistic novels, it is not Providence that intervenes at the last moment to rescue the protagonists—it is Marcel Camaret himself. And it is not a bolt of lightning from the heavens that ultimately destroys Blackland and its corrupt inhabitants—it is, once again, Marcel Camaret. Upon finally learning the truth of how he had been manipulated and of the use to which his miraculous inventions had been put, Camaret's gentle madness turns into insane wrath and—likening himself to the vengeful God of the Apocalypse—he triggers a fiery holocaust that consumes the entire city, reducing it to lifeless rubble:

> "God has condemned Blackland! . . . "
>
> In his mind, God was obviously himself, judging by the gestures accompanying his shouted death-sentence. But before anyone could restrain him, Camaret had fled, screaming over and over again:
>
> "God has condemned Blackland! . . . "
>
> He closed himself up in the tower . . . Almost immediately, the first explosion was heard . . . The explosions continued without interruption, and even accelerated in number. . . .
>
> Blackland, blown to pieces by the one who had created her, was nothing more than ruins and debris. Of the admirable but dangerous handiwork of Marcel Camaret absolutely nothing remained.

Thus, Verne's treatment of the scientist seems to have traveled full circle. Initially, the scientist's status in his works was that of a "constructive" and salutary agent of human progress and knowledge (often aided by God). He then turned into a proud, unconquerable, and potentially destructive threat to humanity (and punished by God). And now, in his final incarnation, he appears as a well-intentioned but betrayed—and ultimately tragic—figure whose constructive genius is perverted by others, and who chooses to destroy (by his own hand) both them, himself, and his potentially humanitarian creations in a fit of remorseful rage. From saint to titan to angel of death, the metamorphosis of the scientist in the *Voyages Extraordinaires* says a great deal about Verne's evolving ideological stance concerning the fundamental relationship of science to human endeavor.

But the detrimental social effects of science are not limited to the corruption or megalomania of scientists or to the dangers that these misguided individuals represent to humanity. The industrial applications of science are also shown to pose grave threats to the human habitat and to the quality of life on this planet—a concern that increasingly haunts the pages of Verne's later novels. For example, one preferred image that the author begins to use in these texts when characterizing industry (and in sharp contrast to his portrayal of it in earlier works) is that of a "coal-eating monster." In *The Black Indies,* it is called "the monster of a million gullets that is industry," and in *Topsy Turvy* he states, "The stomach of industry thrives on coal; it will not eat anything else. Industry is a 'carbonivorous' animal. Industry's incessant hunger for more coal—provoking such rash attempts as that depicted in *Topsy Turvy* to procure new sources—is paralleled by its need for other natural resources to construct and maintain its machines or to manufacture its goods. And the resulting negative impact on the environment is shown to take a variety of forms. Among those cited by Verne is the near extinction of certain species of animals that have industrial uses, such as whales (for their oil) or elephants (for their ivory). Of the former he repeatedly warns: "for some years now . . . abusive destruction has reduced their number," and "it must be noted in passing that . . . whalers have all but abandoned the seas of the northern hemisphere. Due to excessive hunting, whales are becoming rare." Of the latter, he predicts:

> However plentiful they are, the species will eventually disappear. Since an elephant can bring in one hundred francs of ivory, they are hunted without mercy. Each year, according to the figures of M. Foa, no less than forty thousand of them are slaughtered on the African continent, which produces seven hundred and fifty thousand kilograms of ivory shipped to England. Before fifty years goes by, there will be no more of them, in spite of their long life expectancy.

Another such environmental concern is that of air pollution. Consider, for example, the following passage from *The Last Will of an Eccentric,* where the hero Max Réal is traveling through the state of Ohio and describes the impact of the many petroleum refineries located there:

> From Cleveland, I went to Warren, an important city in Ohio and very rich in petroleum. A blind man would recognize it by smell alone; its air is sickening. One could easily believe that it would ignite if a match were lit. And what a countryside! On the flatlands, as far as the eye can see, nothing but oil derricks and wells, and even on the hillsides and along the edges of creeks. All these, like so many oil lamps fifteen to twenty feet high . . . all that's lacking are the wicks!

But perhaps the most frequent criticism of modern industry in these texts is an esthetic one. That is to say, in ravaging Nature's resources and "making way" for progress, such industrialization destroys the beauty, the exoticism, and the natural poetry of the landscape. As Max Réal expressed it in a letter to his mother:

> You see, dear Mother, this region doesn't equal our poetic prairies of the Far West, nor the wild valleys of Wyoming, nor the distant views from the Rockies, nor the deep horizons of the Great Lakes and the Oceans! Industrial beauty is fine; artistic beauty is even better; natural beauty, nothing to match it! . . .
>
> So I continued heading southwest. Many stations paraded by on either side of the train: cities, burgs, villages, and, throughout this entire district, not a single corner of Nature that was left alone! Everywhere the hand of Man and his noisy machinery! . . . One day, the trees themselves will be made of metal, the prairies of felt, and the beaches of iron filings! . . . that's progress.

The considerable difference, for instance, in Verne's portrayal of locomotives and railroads between his earlier works and his later ones is especially revealing in this regard. Traditionally, Verne has been remembered as a Saint-Simonian apologist of progress who continually sang the praises of those "noble engines" and the gleaming "ribbons of steel" spreading gloriously across the land. And passages such as the following from *Around the World in 80 Days* served to validate these beliefs about him:

> The locomotive, glistening like a reliquary, with its large lantern throwing out tawny beams of light, its silver-plated bell, its "cow-catcher" that protrudes like a spur, blended its hisses and rumbles with those of the rivers' torrents and cascades and twisted its smoke into the black boughs of the fir trees.
>
> Few, if any, tunnels; nor any bridges along the route. The railroad hugged the flank of the mountainsides, not seeking by the straight line the shortest distance between one point and another, and not violating Nature.

But in his later works, the kinetic poetry of the locomotive and its harmonious integration into Nature are conspicuously absent. In a complete change of perspective (both

Verne's publisher, Pierre-Jules Hetzel, c. 1875.

narratologically and ideologically), the author now describes the many experiential disadvantages of train travel. Among others, it "alienates" the voyagers from personal contact with the countryside and the towns through which they travel. Also, railways tend to homogenize everything located along their routes, wiping out local color and the exotic "otherness" of foreign milieus:

> Yes! blinded by the smoke, the steam and the dust, and, even worse, by the rapidity of transport. . . . insulated within the compartment of a car, with no more field of vision than that offered by a tiny window . . . stopping only at train stations that all look alike, seeing of cities only their outside walls or the tips of their minarets, listening to the constant noise of the rumbling of the locomotive, the hissing of the boiler, the creaking of the rails and the screeching of the brakes, is *that* what you call traveling?

> So what can be done? During this end-of-the-century era, we always arrive too late, and the marvels of the Oriental countryside, their curious customs, the masterpieces of Asiatic art are now only memories or ruins. Railroads will eventually homogenize all the countries through which they pass, forcing them down to the same level, to the same likeness.

This loss of exoticism due to industrial progress (and to its political counterpart—colonialization) is most succinctly described in Verne's Polynesian "voyage" entitled *Propeller Island.* The sudden influx of European industriousness into these once pristine island cultures is shown to have brought with it the full panoply of Western customs, dress, and religious practices—all but replacing those more exotic conventions that were indigenous to these locales. This esthetic loss constitutes a major disappointment to the protagonists of this novel. But the worst effect of such industrial progress on these Shangri-Las, according to Verne, is neither its negative effect on their unspoiled environment nor its destruction of those esthetic pleasures enjoyed by tourists. Rather, it is its catastrophic impact on the heretofore happy and healthy natives of such cultures. As the artificial island of *Propeller Island* navigates from one South Seas archipelago to the next, its passengers begin to hear a sadly familiar refrain:

> Since they have begun to dress more "decently," the Nouka-Hivians and other natives have lost their original vitality as well as their natural gaiety. They are bored now, and their health has suffered. Before, afflictions such as bronchitis, pneumonia, and consumption were unknown to them. . . .

> At the time of Dumont d'Urville, the number of Nouka-Hivians had grown to eight thousand inhabitants . . . but since, their numbers have steadily declined. What is the cause of this decrease? Extermination by war, kidnapping of the males for plantations in Peru, abuse of hard liquor, and—why not admit it?—all the evils brought by . . . "civilized" races.

Thus, the lesson of these later *Voyages Extraordinaires* is quite clear: in much the same fashion as science corrupts the individual with its forbidden fruit of knowledge, indus-try corrupts the idyllic innocence of Nature. Neither is immune from what Verne now calls "this minotaur called Progress." And in both instances, the consequences of such corruption are necessarily and invariably the same—death.

Finally, the objective rationalism and analytical logic of Verne's earlier novels finds its opposite here as well. Human instinct is continually valorized as an effective problem-solving tool. But one must be careful to differentiate between two separate sorts of instinct in Verne's protagonists: the kind that has been learned (more often evoked in his earlier texts), versus the more atavistic kind that is a vestige of our animal ancestry (the benefits of which are portrayed more often in his later texts). The former is the product of experience, like the archetypal veteran sea captain who can foretell abrupt changes in the weather or, without the aid of his instruments, sense the ocean currents beneath his vessel. Or consider the young Dick Sand who, according to his captain, has already learned those nautical instincts necessary to becoming a truly fine sailor:

> "Look at him now, Mistress Weldon," continued Captain Hull. "He's at the helm, his eyes fixed on the top of the mainsail. No inattention on the part of this young sailor, and no lurching of the vessel! Dick Sand already has the sureness of a seasoned helmsman! A good start for a young seaman! Our trade, Mistress Weldon, is one that must be started as a young child. He who has not served as cabin-boy will never become a complete seaman, at least in the merchant marine. Everything must be a lesson, and thereby be both instinctive and well thought out in a good seaman—both the resolution made and the manoeuvre executed."

In these two instances, it is practical experience that provides these heroes with an "instinctual" feel of their respective ships. This brand of instinct is a physical (and somewhat mechanical) attribute: a product of hands-on learning over a long period of time, and of the continual repetition of certain cause-effect relationships. Such instincts are developed through trial and error, are subordinate to reasons' commands, and are measured by one's dexterity or deftness of movement in the execution of those commands.

In Verne's later works, in contrast, instinct is often portrayed as replacing reason in problem-solving situations, and superior to it. For example, take the case of the scientist Jeorling who is the narrator of *The Ice Sphinx.* At one point in the narrative, when all other means of analysis fail to account for the unusual magnetic phenomena that he and the crew of the *Halbrane* encounter in the Antarctic, he offers an hypothesis, saying: "It was in this way . . . that I came to explain the occurrence, by instinct." Or note the recurring premonitions among the heroes of *Little-Fellow, The Secret of Wilhelm Storitz,* and *The Thompson Travel Agency.* Or note the narrator's comments in *Mistress Branican* where he praises women's intuition: "Whereas a man relies on direct observation of fact and the consequences that derive from it, it is certain that a woman often has a clear vision of the future thanks to her intuitive qualities. It's a kind of inspiration that guides her and gives her a certain prescience about things." Or, finally, consider the following example, taken from *The Village in the Treetops,* where the lost protagonists must rely on the natural instincts of their African guide Khamis to lead them through the unexplored forest:

> In fact, a kind of instinct like that of animals—an inexplicable sixth sense that is found in some races of men—permits the Chinese, among others, and several tribes of Indians of the Far West to guide themselves by hearing and smell more than by sight, and to recognize direction by certain signs. Khamis possessed this faculty to a rare degree. He had many times proven it beyond a doubt. In a certain measure, the Frenchman and the American could put their entire trust in this ability . . . [that was] not prone to error.

Instinct is thus "not prone to error"—unlike the analyses of its rationalistic counterpart (see Maston's math error in *Topsy Turvy* or Lidenbrock's false compass headings in *Journey to the Center of the Earth,* among others). Thus, it is important to note that Verne's pessimism concerning the essential character of the human species is *not* unilateral in its applications. It is only humanity's acquired scientific nature that is in question in these texts and its blind faith in objective rationalism.

As a fitting conclusion to this chapter the following discussion concerns a text that is very emblematic of this ideological shift in Verne's portrayal of science. This particular short story is, appropriately, one of the author's final pieces of fictional writing. It was published posthumously in 1910 and was undoubtedly much revamped by his son Michel. It is entitled **"Eternal Adam"** and carries a footnote at the bottom of the title page informing the reader that it was "Written by Jules Verne in his final years and until now unpublished, this short story is somewhat unique in that it offers conclusions that are pessimistic—contrary to the proud optimism that animates the *Voyages Extraordinaires.* M.J.V." Aside from being an obvious attempt to validate the authenticity of this short story as being from the pen of his father, Michel's commentary also reflects (mistaken) public opinion in France during this period concerning the overall character of the *Voyages Extraordinaires*—a collection of which, in truth, only the earliest titles could be called "proudly optimistic." But the myth of Jules Verne as the "technological prophet" was already, in 1910, an established institution—so much so apparently that the publishers of this posthumous work felt the need for this explanatory note on the title page.

As for **"Eternal Adam"** itself, it is a story within a story. In the distant future, a scientist named Zartog Sofr-Ai-Sr (note the resemblance with Nietzsche's Zarathoustra, as first pointed out by Marcel Moré) is shown grappling with the theoretical details of human evolution. He is an inhabitant of the only land mass on Earth—an island continent called Hars-Iten-Schu, a kind of future Atlantis and occupying precisely the same geographic position as its prehistoric ancestor. Zartog Sofr-Ai-Sr is a true Positivist and the most highly respected archeologist of this advanced civilization. At one point during his rather Saint-Simonian musings, he states:

> Yes, comparing Man when he first appeared on the Earth naked and unarmed to what he has become today, one can only admire him. For centuries, despite his hatreds and his warring on his brothers, he has never retreated from his ongoing struggle with Nature and has ceaselessly increased his margin of victory over her. At first somewhat slow, his conquest has, during the past two hundred years, accelerated at a phenomenal pace. His achievement of political stability and universal peace has resulted in vigorous scientific growth. Humanity has learned to live by its brain and no longer by its limbs alone. Man has learned to think. That is why, during these past two hundred years, he has made so much progress in understanding and domesticating matter. . . .
>
> Yes, Man is great, greater even than the immense universe—a universe which, in the very near future, he will rule over. . . .
>
> So, in order to know the entire truth of his ascendancy, one last problem remains to be solved: "Exactly who is he? Where did he come from? Toward what mysterious end point is he evolving?"

But the hero of this tale encounters a fundamental problem in the evidence produced by his archeological excavations. Contrary to all logic, there seems to be no ascending continuity in human evolutionary development—at least according to the artifacts he unearths. In fact, hundreds of centuries of growth appear to alternate successively with rapid periods of de-evolution and degeneration in the human species. And what is even worse, at its highest point of development, ancient civilization seems further advanced than that of Sofr-Ai-Sr's own day!

> A conscientious examination of these sacred ruins was enough to remove all doubt: the men who lived during this ancient era had already acquired a cerebral development much superior to their successors, greater even than that of Zartog Sofr's contemporaries! There had obviously been, during some one hundred and sixty or one hundred and seventy centuries, a period of drastic regression followed by a long slow period of regrowth. . . .
>
> "What?" he murmured to himself. "Admit that, some forty thousand years ago, Man had attained a level of civilization comparable to—if not superior to—the one that we now enjoy? That his knowledge and his possessions suddenly disappeared without a trace, forcing his descendants to begin over from nothing as if they were pioneers on a world that was uninhabited before them? . . . But, to admit this would deny all hope for the future! It would brand all our efforts as useless, all progress as uncertain and precarious as a tiny soap bubble floating on an ocean's waves!

Predictably, the remainder of the narrative goes on to prove this very fact. During a fortuitous moment at the dig, Sofr uncovers a partially disintegrated aluminum canister containing ancient manuscripts written in an unknown language (French), which he spends the ensuing two years deciphering. Much to his surprise and chagrin, he finds himself face-to-face with the astonishing truth of the matter: it is a diary, written approximately 20 thousand years before by the sole survivor of a planetary cataclysm. This journal recounts the end of humankind, the abrupt disappearance of the known continents, and the subsequent social and intellectual retrogression of those few individuals remaining who had managed to find refuge on a large island that suddenly rose up in the mid-Atlantic.

This "discovered" narrative constitutes the story within the story of **"Eternal Adam"**—reiterating, in *mise-en-abŷme* fashion via the text's very format, the major lesson of the tale as a whole. Ironically, the author of this diary was likewise a successful and very "positive" mining executive during his own era (dated "2 . . . "). And just prior to the first earthquake tremors, he and his dinner guests were engaged in the following conversation—strangely reminiscent of Sofr's own panegyric to progress:

> Then, coming back to their topic of discussion, the two rivals agreed that, whatever his origin, Man was an admirable creature and had attained the highest level of civilization ever known. They proudly enumerated his conquests. All areas of endeavor were mentioned. Bathurst praised chemistry . . . Moreno delivered an encomium to modern medicine . . . They paid tribute to the machines of industry, each more ingenious than the next, each doing the work of a hundred men . . . They especially praised electricity, that incredible power-source which was so docile and whose properties and very essence were now so well understood. . . .
>
> In all, it was a real dithyramb—and one in which I contributed no small share myself. We all agreed that humanity had reached a pinnacle of intellectual development never achieved before our time, one which assured Man's imminent and total victory over Nature.

The biting irony of the lesson is not lost on the Zartog Sofr-Ai-Sr. **"Eternal Adam"** concludes with his (Verne's?) reactions to this irrefutable proof of the meaningless transience—and vanity—of all human effort:

> a kind of dread gripped his soul . . . Sofr's optimism was washed away forever. If the manuscript presented no specific technical details, its general indications were abundant. And it proved without a doubt that humanity had, much earlier, progressed to a higher state of knowledge than it had since. . . .
>
> Reading this narrative from beyond the grave, Sofr imagined the terrible drama that was perpetually unfolding in the universe, and his heart was full of pity. Feeling the pain of those who had suffered long before, crushed beneath the weight of so much effort, in vain, throughout the infinity of time, the Zartog Sofr-Ai-Sr slowly and

sorrowfully came to realize the eternal cycle of all things.

Thus concludes the final entry in Verne's epic to "homo rationalis," one of the final journeys of his *Voyages Extraordinaires.* Perhaps extraordinary in the mimetic sense of the term, it is nevertheless a succinct and fitting resumé to Verne's own ideological evolution since the 1880s—a recapitulation of his growing pessimism regarding the true status of science and of men and women living in a universe that exceeds their comprehension.

Seen in the context of his entire ouevre, this work marks the end of an ideological "voyage" that parallels the majority of Verne's fictional ones in its essential circularity. Prior to 1862 and his first contract with Hetzel to initiate the series to be known as the *Voyages Extraordinaires,* Verne (as mentioned) wrote a number of essays, plays, and short stories, among the latter **"Master Zacharias"** (1853). Like some of his earliest writings, this particular short story is Romantic in the extreme, but (in contrast to them) the variant used here is à la Hoffmann. It features a mad scientist/clockmaker who, in true Faustian fashion, barters his soul for the secrets of science. He achieves wealth and glory as the creator of the best timepieces in the world. But, as the years pass, his pride grows to insane proportions: "No! I cannot die! No more than the Creator of this universe—a universe that abides by His laws! I have become His equal! I have shared his power!" Suddenly, throughout the land, Zacharius's clocks begin to tick erratically and, one by one, grow silent. Zacharius comes down with a strange illness and, soon after, perishes miserably as the last of his marvelous timepieces stops ticking.

When viewed in this diachronic perspective, the overall ideological orientation of Verne's *Voyages Extraordinaires* seems to follow a distinctly cyclical pattern—similar to that of humanity in **"Eternal Adam"**. From the initial "generic" Romanticism of those texts dating from his early years (1850s-62), it then evolves into the proudly optimistic Positivism of what might be called his Hetzel-period (1862-86), to subsequently (re)become the sometimes trenchant anti-Positivist Romanticism of his later works (1886-1919).

The circle is thus closed. The journey is completed where it began. And the true unity of this oeuvre lies in its oscillating heterogeneity as it travels from one ideological pole to the other and back again. (pp. 79-101)

> *Arthur B. Evans, in his* Jules Verne Rediscovered, *Greenwood Press, 1988, 199 p.*

FURTHER READING

Criticism

Barthes, Roland. "The *Nautilus* and the Drunken Boat." In his *Mythologies,* translated by Annette Lavers, pp. 65-7. New York: Hill and Wang, 1972.

Provides a brief overview of Verne's major themes.

———. "Where to Begin." In his *New Critical Essays*, translated by Richard Howard, pp. 79-89. New York: Hill and Wang, 1980.
>   Analyzes the symbolism and structure of *The Mysterious Island.*

Bleiler, E. F. "Jules Verne and Cryptography." *Extrapolation* 27, No. 1 (Spring 1986): 5-18.
>   Examines Verne's use of codes, puzzles, and cryptograms in his fiction.

Bongie, Chris. "Into Darkest Asia: Colonialism and the Imperial Fiction of Jules Verne's *Michel Strogoff.*" *CLIO: A Journal of Literature, History, and the Philosophy of History* 19, No. 3 (Spring 1990): 237-49.
>   Examines Verne's representation of history in his epic set in Russia.

———. "The Hollow Men: Despotic Individuals and the Fiction of Imperialism." In his *Exotic Memories: Literature, Colonialism, and the Fin de Siècle,* pp. 33-70. Stanford, Calif.: Stanford University Press, 1991.
>   Examines the ideas of colonialism in Verne's work, particularly in *Michel Strogoff.*

Butor, Michel. "The Golden Age in Jules Verne." In his *Inventory,* pp. 114-45. New York: Simon and Schuster, 1968.
>   Discusses themes and use of symbolism in *Les voyages extraordinaires.*

Chambers, Ross. "Cultural and Ideological Determinations in Narrative: A Note on Jules Verne's *Les Cinq Cents Millions de la Begum.*" *L'Esprit Createur* XXI, No. 3 (Fall 1981): 69-78.
>   Examines the structure and themes of one of Verne's lesser known works.

Evans, Arthur B. "Science Fiction vs. Scientific Fiction in France: From Jules Verne to J.-H. Rosny Aîné." *Science-Fiction Studies* 15, No. 1 (March 1988): 1-11.
>   Contrasts Verne's "scientific" fiction with the *science* fiction of other prominent French science fiction writers.

———. "The Extraordinary Libraries of Jules Verne." *L'Esprit Createur* XXVIII, No. 1 (Spring 1988): 75-86.
>   Analyzes the motif of the library in Verne's works. Some of this material also appears in Evans's *Jules Verne Rediscovered: Didacticism and the Scientific Novel.*

Friedländer, Saul. "Themes of Decline and End in Nineteenth-Century Western Imagination," translated by Susan Rubin Suleiman. In *Visions of Apocalypse: End or Rebirth?* edited by Saul Friedländer, Gerald Holton, Leo Marx, and Eugene Skolnikoff, pp. 61-83. New York: Holmes and Meier, 1985.
>   Examines the theme of the end of humankind as treated by H. G. Wells and Jules Verne.

Ketterer, David. "Fathoming *Twenty Thousand Leagues under the Sea.*" In *The Scope of the Fantastic—Theory, Technique, Major Authors,* edited by Robert A. Collins and Howard D. Pearce, pp. 263-75. Westport, Conn.: Greenwood Press, 1985.
>   Explores the mythology and symbolism used in *Twenty Thousand Leagues under the Sea.*

Lynch, Lawrence. *Jules Verne.* New York: Twayne Publishers, 1992, 127 p.
>   Provides a concise biography of Verne, along with critical appraisals of his major works. Includes an annotated bibliography.

Additional coverage of Verne's life and career is contained in the following sources published by Gale Research: *Contemporary Authors,* **Vols. 110, 131;** *Dictionary of Literary Biography,* **Vol. 123;** *Major Authors and Illustrators for Children and Young Adults;* *Something about the Author,* **Vol. 21; and** *Twentieth-Century Literary Criticism,* **Vol. 6.**

Nikolai Zabolotsky

1903-1958

(Full name Nikolai Alekseyevich Zabolotsky; also transliterated as Zabolotskii and Zabolockij) Russian poet and translator.

INTRODUCTION

Misunderstood and persecuted during his lifetime, Zabolotsky is now recognized as one of the finest Russian modernist poets to emerge after the Communist revolution. Establishing him as a literary pioneer, his earliest verse collection, *Stolbtsy,* offers phantasmagoric explorations of Leningrad, blending realism with surrealistic images and striking linguistic constructions. His later work is more traditional, characterized by a reserved style and such conventional subjects as nature and the individual, while demonstrating virtuosic control of language.

Zabolotsky was born in 1903 in Kazan, the capital of the Soviet republic Tatar. The son of an agronomist, he lived in rural areas before leaving home in 1920 to study philology in Moscow. Zabolotsky continued his studies in Leningrad at the Herzen Pedagogical Institute and began to publish poems in literary journals. Upon graduating in 1925, he served in the army for two years and subsequently secured employment in Leningrad in the Division of Children's Literature of the State Publishing House. Zabolotsky's work as an author and translator of tales for children served as his primary source of income through the 1930s. He became a member of the avant-garde literary group OBERIU, an acronym formed from the Russian words for "Association for Real Creativity," and was largely responsible for formulating the group's manifesto, which was published in 1928. In this document, the OBERIU advocated an art that attempts to awaken a fresh appreciation and understanding of objects and surroundings through unconventional presentation. Because the OBERIU intended to supplant the proletarian writers sanctioned by the government as the creators of a new Soviet literature, the group suffered harsh verbal attacks from conservative critics, and several members were arrested. Published in 1929, Zabolotsky's collection *Stolbtsy* received recognition from the artistic community as a preeminent work of avant-garde poetry, but its deviation from the principles of Socialist Realism dismayed Soviet authorities. Zabolotsky's next work, the epic poem *Torzhestvo zemledeliya* (commonly known as *The Triumph of Agriculture*), was interpreted by government officials as a scathing satire of Soviet socialism. Arrested in 1938 on the fraudulent charge of participating in a terrorist organization, Zabolotsky was exiled to a work camp in a remote area. After his release in 1946, he resumed writing and eventually settled in Tarusa, a small town on the Oka River. He died in 1958.

Critics have tended to separate Zabolotsky's career into two distinct phases corresponding with the periods before and after his imprisonment. His earliest poetry more closely corresponds to the self-characterization offered in the OBERIU manifesto: "N. Zabolotsky, a poet of naked concrete figures brought close to the eyes of the spectator. One must hear and read him more with one's eyes and fingers than with one's ears. The object does not crumble; on the contrary, it becomes tighter and firmer, as though to meet the feeling hand of the spectator. The development of action and the setting play a secondary role to that main task." The early poems of *Stolbtsy* manifest an aesthetic vision which simultaneously attempts to give verbal expression to the essence of objects and employs language in a manner that embodies the tragicomic jumble which the urban environment of Leningrad represented to Zabolotsky. Scholars have praised Zabolotsky's vivid descriptions, fantastic metaphors, and startling juxtapositions of images. Also published during this period, *The Triumph of Agriculture* addresses humankind's place in nature, the active pursuit of utopia, and life as envisioned under the new political order. The story of a village undergoing collectivization, *The Triumph of Agriculture* was perceived by contemporary Soviet authorities as mocking the government's conception of social transformation through its overtly nationalistic tenor, sometimes hyperbolic descriptions, and ambiguous references to contemporary politics; in contrast, some subsequent critics have asserted that Zabolotsky actually supported collectivization as a means to human happiness. The post-exile poetry, while noted for its linguistic beauty and philosophical depth, is markedly less experimental than Zabolotsky's earlier work, evincing a closer affinity to the classical nineteenth-century Russian poetry of Alexander Pushkin, Fyodor Tyutchev, and others. In *Stikhotvoreniya*, Zabolotsky continued to address the theme of humanity's place in nature, offering contemplative observations of the natural world and portraits of human perseverance. Western critics initially criticized Zabolotsky's later poetry as dully conventional and speculated that he had succumbed to government pressure. While acknowledging significant superficial differences between the phases of his career, recent scholars have asserted that Zabolotsky's mastery of form and style and ongoing concern with humankind's place in the world indicate a more unified opus than had been previously presumed.

PRINCIPAL WORKS

*"OBERIU" (manifesto) 1928; published in journal *Afishi doma pechati*
 ["The Oberiu Manifesto," published in *Russia's Lost Literature of the Absurd,* 1971]
Stolbtsy (poetry) 1929 [*Scrolls: Selected Poems,* (partial translation), 1971]
Torzhestvo zemledeliya (poetry) 1933; published in journal *Zvezda*
Vitiaz' v tigrovoi shkure (translation) 1937
Vtoraya kniga (poetry) 1937
Slovo o polku Igoreve (translation) 1946
Stikhotvoreniya (poetry) 1948
Stikhotvoreniya i poemy (collected works) 1965

*Composed primarily by Zabolotsky, with assistance from other members of the OBERIU.

CRITICISM

Vera Sandomirsky (essay date 1960)

[*In the following excerpt, Sandomirsky investigates the relationship between Zabolotsky's poetry and his experience of life under communism.*]

Not long ago, Nikolai Zabolotsky asked those who "with notebooks full of poems" had journeyed ahead of him to "the country without ready-made shapes" whether it was easy and peaceful for them there. Now that he has joined them, the martyrdom that was his should earn him peace while his slender poetic output secures him a place among the major Russian poets of our time.

The ambivalence of officialdom toward this poet in Russia accompanied him to his grave with only the bare minimum of decorum and sour politeness. And what is more regrettable, the *émigré* literary world has so far failed to introduce Zabolotsky to the non-Russian public. His work is largely unknown, and to basic literary research he remains a challenge.

Fortunately, it is possible to bring to Russian readers the first effort to appraise Zabolotsky's work as a whole and to reveal its formative philosophical core. Because of his philosophy and because of his curiously anachronistic affinity with Tyutchev, the Stalinist regime attempted to destroy him. It was equally unforgiving of his other bizarre affinity with Zoshchenko. Georgii Petrov's long essay ["Kandidat bylykh stoletii, polkovodets novykh let," *Morty,* 1958], written with depth and love for the late poet shortly before he died is the first serious study, as far as I know, of Zabolotsky's unhappily scattered poetry. It is all the more valuable as Petrov examined first printings in the journals of the late 'twenties and 'thirties. By enforced revisions, censors frequently distorted Zabolotsky's poetry when it appeared in the few individual editions. It is to be hoped that original versions will someday be collected.

Zabolotsky was born in Kazan in 1903. His father was what may in English be called an agronomist. The family seems to have moved from place to place and Zabolotsky finished his secondary education in Urzhum in 1920. Thereupon, as a young man, he must have served in the Red Army after which by the mid-twenties, he moved to Leningrad. There, according to V. Zavalishin [in "Nikolai Zabolotsky," *Novy Zhurnal,* September, 1959], he transferred upon the advice of two evidently imaginative faculty members, from the department of biology to that of language and literature at the Herzen Institute. His first poems started to appear in newspapers in 1927.

If one is to look for a generic affiliation of the young provincial poet, his roots are in futurism and more precisely in that of Khlebnikov's recension. It is Zabolotsky of that early period whom Vladimir Orlov remembers in a cryptic and lopsided obituary notice:

> . . . still wearing out his Red Army overcoat and heavy soldier shoes, he used to come to our editorial office, young, red-cheeked, very modest, silent, somehow very much collected from within. ["Put Poeta," *Literaturnaya Gazeta,* December 20, 1958]

Inner control is the earmark of his work from the very beginning as well as a stringent, anti-lyrical sense of form. The word *classical* comes to mind, if paradoxically. In his best work, dating from the 'thirties, he has proven himself a narrative poet combining the afterglow of the Nekrasov tradition with a novel apocalyptic perception of the Bolshevik world.

As to that which is not known about his life, one might remember that the totalitarian condition fosters a dichotomy in the destiny of poets. Their lives are either mercilessly and to a great degree falsely exposed, as in the cases of Essenin and Mayakovsky, or, less vulgarly but not less tragically, their personal destiny is relegated to oblivion through either the rancor or indifference of those who implement the notorious *obshchestvennost.* Oblivion can descend in a poet's lifetime, with or without the purgatory of the concentration camp. If scarcely anything is known of the way Akhmatova manages to exist, Zabolotsky's last years are even more of a puzzle. We have only his poetry and through it alone access to his integrity as both poet and man.

One slender book of poems each decade, however, tells eloquently enough the story of his bitter lot. The first book, *Stolbtsy,* appeared in 1929. The very fact that the second, *Vtoraya Kniga,* only forty-five pages long, was published as late as 1937, hints at the difficulties he experienced with editors and censors. From the start, much like Pasternak, he was branded a bizarre and dangerous individualist. The third small book, *Stikhotvoreniya,* was published in 1948. Thus far, the fullest collection of his poetry, also under the last title, was published in 1957. Between 1937 and the end of the war, Zabolotsky was prevented from publishing at all.

Suffice it today to reread his transcript of the collectivization of peasants, **"Torzhestvo Zemledeliya"** and the fragments of the never finished **"Lodeinikov"** to see that the courage of detachment from the political system under which he lived and the depth of his questioning pessimism could not have remained unpunished. Sometime in 1937 he was arrested, accused of belonging to a subversive group, and sentenced to solitary confinement in a Far-Eastern concentration camp.

In *Pisatelskie Sudby,* a concise first-hand martyrology of the intelligentsia under Stalin, the late and well-informed R. V. Ivanov-Razumnik cites a letter which circulated among the *literati* of both capitals. Zabolotsky managed to send it from concentration camp. It was addressed to Nikolai Tikhonov with the request to forward it to Konstantin Fedin as well. It is a fantastic document. Not long after Zabolotsky disappeared, both Fedin and Tikhonov were decorated by the government for their achievements. The pertinent passage reads as follows:

> A year and a half ago, a group of writers and I were arrested and accused of belonging to a terrorist Trotskyist group. During interrogation and under the pressure of most convincing arguments, we were forced to admit that we were members of that group and that we were recruited by the two writers who headed it: Nikolai Tikhonov in Leningrad and Konstantin Fedin in Moscow. You will understand now my joy for you. You are alive and you are free. You will also understand my deepest consternation. How is it possible that both of you, the heads of a terrorist organization, having recruited me among its members, should have received a high governmental reward whereas I, a rank and file member of that very organization, have received for the same thing not a medal but ten years of solitary confinement. It is clear that something is very strange here and that ends do not meet.

> It behooves you—you who are free and decorated by the government—to attempt to untie this fantastic knot and either to admit your guilt and request to be sent into solitary confinement or to do all you can to liberate us who sit here entirely without guilt. . . .

It seems that thereupon, frightened and embarrassed, Tikhonov and Fedin, if not exactly requesting solitary confinement for themselves, had worked feverishly to get Zabolotsky's sentence reduced. But there seems to be no doubt that he did not return to freedom until eight years had elapsed, that is, at the end of the war.

> An overall view of Zabolotsky's work shows that his course as a poet started in the complexity of interlocked themes and images, in hyperbolic surrealistic tension, and ended in simplicity of form, taking one theme at a time.
>
> —*Vera Sandomirsky*

The early Zabolotsky belonged to that small group of difficult modern poets and was, like Pasternak, a poet for poets. He started out as an innovator. The "newness" in him was a nervous, fragmented, surrealistic, sharply dichotomized vision of the Soviet urban world. With objects, animals, and new philistines adrift in a flat and airless sky, the vision was suspended between satire and despair. The postwar Zabolotsky is a far less modern poet. His form has become more traditional, and, with this transformation, his agony over the ugliness of life, mutilated by the apocalyptic NEP man with all his progeny, has become blunted. In compensation, perhaps, his Platonic concern with personal reality, which he has always seen as very different from the reality of nature, and his concern with death have revealed themselves with majestic calm. He too, at last, was permitted to become lyrical, a modest reward Khrushchevism doles out to those who survive.

Against this background, Orlov's friendly words in the official *Literaturnaya Gazeta* sound less cynical than tragic. Today's fashionable half-truths are more corrosive, perhaps, of simple decency than the monstrous untruths of earlier Soviet periods. In comparing the satirical pathos of Zabolotsky's grotesque nightmares with the simplicity of his postwar style, Orlov evaluates this transformation as growth in the positive direction and establishes, as he must, a causality:

> . . . above all, of course, life itself had helped Zabolotsky . . . One can see clearly . . . how life, the real life of the people with its passions and struggle had re-taught the poet and had led him forward and upward from invented schemes to the poetry of clear and goal-directed thinking, to poetry glorifying labor and creativity.

Having omitted any mention of the years the poet spent

in solitary confinement in a Northern concentration camp, *Literaturnaya Gazeta,* for one, might have refrained, especially in a last farewell, from attributing Zabolotsky's growth to the beneficial conditions of Soviet life.

It struck me in this connection that the sardonically nostalgic *desideratum* expressed in the concluding paragraph of the now-famous critique, of socialist realism by the anonymous brilliant Soviet mind had long since been fulfilled by the young Zabolotsky among all too few others at the juncture of the 'twenties and 'thirties.

> At present, I place my hopes in a fantasmagorical art, which would have hypotheses instead of a goal, an art in which the grotesque would replace the realistic in the description of everyday life. This is what would best respond to the spirit of our epoch. May the unearthly imaginations of Hoffmann and Dostoevsky, of Goya and Chagall, of Mayakovsky . . . as well as those of many other realists and non-realists—may these teach us how to express truth with the aid of the absurd and fantastic! [**"A Voice from the Depths,"** *Soviet Survey,* July-September, 1959]

In this fantasmagorical school Zabolotsky could have been an excellent teacher.

> . . . The large saucer of water
> On high tipped over.
> A woodsprite plucks the bark
> out of his shaggy beard;
> from behind a cloud,
> a siren points down
> with her little foot;
> the cannibal nibbles
> a gentleman's unspeakables.
> Mixed up in a general dance,
> hamadryads and Britons,
> witches, fleas, and the dead
> wing about everywhere.
> My intellect, you candidate
> of bygone epochs,
> commander of new years,—
> these monsters are
> but fiction and fever
> but fiction and dreams,
> the rocking of sleepy thought,
> inconsolable agony—
> that which does not exit.
>   [**"Merknut znaki zodiaka"**]

But pupils under socialist realism were reluctant to learn. Even if they had been eager, the course would have been strenuous. Zabolotsky's craft did not lend itself to imitation, nor even to parody, primarily because of its acute timeliness. Pointing to the essential in its character, V. Zavalishin says:

> The peculiarity of Zabolotsky's grotesques consists in that the most common, the most simple things of the world of reality assume nightmarish outlines and shapes. Here the borders between everyday phenomena and the oppressive dream are swept away. And, therefore, the epoch of the "great change" is perceived as if through an attack of brain fever or while screaming at night.

A secret net of antennae seems to stretch from visions of one artist of fantasmagoria to those of another. It has been found that Zabolotsky's distorted world has something in common with that of, for instance, Hieronymous Bosch and Gogol. But, curiously, if Gogolesque elements were discovered in his poetry, so also were elements derived from classicism. It is not difficult to foresee a future Ph.D. thesis in which everyone the poet has been compared with will be catalogued: Derzhavin and Tyutshev; Khlebnikov and Mayakovsky; Hieronymous Bosch and Henri Rousseau. The topsy-turvy world of Marc Chagall seems to me at times to have illustrated best of all Zabolotsky's visions, although the painter has never been as dark as the poet. Affinities, however, have not made of Zabolotsky an eclectic, a mere receptacle of influences. Comparing Zabolotsky to such widely disparate figures actually reflects more on the critics than on the subject. On the one hand, the connections that some readers sense, point to the poet's roots in and response to a literary tradition as well as his groping for a new form. On the other hand, other readers, once exposed to any newness, themselves grope for an interpretation through analogies. Leaving comparisons aside, the central literary fact remains that the young Zabolotsky responded to the new social order with nightmarish, shattered, upside-down visions. The submerged pantheist in him, the poet who through eerie, static illuminations of distorted fragments of reality, groped in vain for a vanished whole, inevitably turned to the death motif. Stalinist censors, who saw to it that socialist realism produced a literature without the themes of death and tragedy, took a poor view of Zabolotsky's preoccupation with death. This was pessimism and pessimism was treason.

> Lodeinikov began to listen. Over the garden
> Hovered the vague rustle of thousands of deaths.
> Nature, having turned into hell,
> Performed her deeds without ado.
> The beetle ate the grass, the bird pecked at the
>   beetle,
> The ferret drank the brain from the bird's head,
> And the faces of night creatures,
> Contorted with fear, peered out of the grass.
> The eternal crushing machine of nature
> Brought death and being
> Into one tangle. But reason failed
> To unite both these mysteries . . .
>   [*Stikhotvoreniya,* 1957]

This all-too brief homage should be concluded with a word about Zabolotsky's postwar poetry. One is forced here to take a somewhat uneasy stand. Respect for a man's personal character should not, theoretically, interfere with the evaluation of his art. True, it has become fashionable among those who value the young poet highly to dismiss his recent work as lacking in real literary interest. I cannot share this position even at the risk of being accused of inconsistency. An overall view of Zabolotsky's work shows that his course as a poet started in the complexity of interlocked themes and images, in hyperbolic surrealistic tension, and ended in simplicity of form, taking one theme at a time. In this sense, his course parallels that of Pasternak. Zabolotsky, who began as a bizarre narrative poet became a lyricist of controlled and masculine sorrow; the angular, harsh, urban poet turned more and more to nature. But, although now a quasi botanist—

> I have become the nervous system of plants
> I have become the meditations of stony cliffs . . .
>
> ["Gomborskii les"]

—his concern for people did not decline. Nor did he cease to be a masterful teller of the inner story, even if on a reduced scale. **"Staraya Aktrisa," "Nekrasivaya Devochka,"** and the surprisingly sunlit and springlike **"Skvorez"** are among the best pages of poetry written in Russian in the last fifteen years. (pp. 267-74)

> *Vera Sandomirsky, "Nikolai Alekseevich Zabolotsky: 1903-1958," in* The Russian Review, *Vol. 19, No. 3, July, 1960, pp. 267-74.*

Margaret Dalton   (review date 1966)

[*In the following review, Dalton contrasts Zabolotsky's early and later poetry.*]

Zabolockij's wide poetic range—including modernistic, Futurist practices in the early period, and the adherence to "classical" traditions of Russian eighteenth- and nineteenth-century poetry in his later period—was less the result of a specific artistic development than of political pressures and persecutions which marked Zabolockij's whole life. Nevertheless, the fact that Zabolockij could express himself through such divergent poetic forms testifies to his creative powers and his acute sense for language.

Zabolockij's early manner is most clearly manifested in *Stolbcy,* a collection of poems deceptively simple and even primitive at first glance, but laden with complexity and density of imagery and meaning. *Stolbcy* earned Zabolockij his literary reputation among poets, and the permanent enmity of Party functionaries. Following the example of Xlebnikov, his acknowledged master, Zabolockij concentrated on verbal play rather than on metrical experimentation and startled the reader by the unexpectedness of his images, his grotesque comparisons, and incompatible combinations of diverse lexical and logical elements. One need think only of such images as the prostitutes who "raised their enamel hands toward heaven and ate sandwiches from boredom," of the "furious conclave of glasses" which "kindled like a church-chandelier" (**"Krasnaja bavarija"**), of the night "walking around inopportunely" while drunken laughter "flies in the shape of a parrot" (**"Belaja noč"**), etc. Zabolockij's vision of the large modern city in *Stolbcy* is grotesque and nightmarish: people appear in it as marionettes manipulated by an unseen hand, while inanimate objects become independent of their usual associations and acquire a life of their own— much as Gogol's "Nose" paraded around St. Petersburg in the uniform of a state councilor. Zabolockij's connection with Gogol in portraying a topsy-turvy world with strange mechanical prostitutes and puppet-like Ivanovs on the one hand, and animated cupboards, couches, and lamps on the other, was immediately recognized. It became equally obvious, however, that under the guise of the temporal Zabolockij, like Gogol, was presenting the "eter-

nal" themes of mediocrity, stupidity, and *pošlost,* which were as current in 1930 as they had been a hundred years earlier.

By 1934 Zabolockij had to abandon his early manner (cf. his poem **"Proščanie,"** on the death of Kirov). His poetry from then on became progressively more muted and conventional in imagery and form. The satiric barb was lost, while a more "positive" tenor appeared in its place. Whether Zabolockij was actually groping for a more organic conception of the world (in contrast to his early fragmented, chaotic vision) or whether this was an enforced development is difficult to ascertain. His themes became more diverse and quietly objective: a large number of poems are descriptions of landscapes and of various seasons of the year. The conquest of nature by man and by modern technology is a recurring theme, as are the poet's musings on life and death. The problem of immortality, however, never acquires any religious connotation, but reflects rather a pantheistic belief in continuous reincarnations. Although Zabolockij seems to have become more distant to the world of man in his late period, he at times presents human portraits with sensitivity and keen psychological insight. A very interesting place in Zabolockij's late poetry is occupied by a small cycle of love poems entitled "Poslednjaja ljubov," evoking the memory of Tjutčev. The poems are characterized by a simplicity of diction and a directness that is far removed from the early, exuberant Zabolockij. The poem **"Vstreča,"** with its tantalizing poetic groping to express a moment of love, belongs among Zabolockij's best poems.

Bent, but not broken, Zabolockij found even in his last years enough creative power to see the beauty of this

---

Helen Muchnic on Zabolotsky's poetic evolution:

[Zabolotsky] developed and emphasized certain tendencies in his work that had always been present in it and suppressed others that were a threat to his survival. And he could do this without mendacity, for what mattered to him above all was the process of setting things down in poetry, not the subject to be set down, nor any one way of doing so. Unlike Akhmatova and Mandelshtam who seem possessed by insights and emotions, Zabolotsky is moved by nothing other than the desire to write. But this desire is powerful; he is the nightingale-Antony of his lyric, irrevocably tied to his Cleopatra-song. This is why it was possible for him to change his style without being untrue to his poetic self. He suppressed the grotesque boisterousness of his early verse— his philosophizing animals, his battles of syntax, in which warring elephants are forces of the subconscious, his pastry cooks who look like "idols in tiaras," and the bald guests at a wedding feast, sitting "like shots fired from a gun"—all the amusing fantasies which gave a surrealist quality to his poetry, and cultivated instead the classical, traditional, eighteenth-century elements that had also been part of his work from the beginning.

Helen Muchnic, in her "Three Inner Emigrés: Anna Akhmatova, Osip Mandelshtam, Nikolai Zabolotsky," The Russian Review, *January 1967.*

---

world and to glorify it in poems of brilliant colors and acute freshness of vision. He also preserved a quiet dignity which few of his contemporaries managed to retain. As a poet he is, however, most memorable in **Stolbcy,** and a poem like **"Krasnaja bavarija"** in its strange intensity and muffled drama may remain as memorable as Blok's famous "Neznakomka," to which it is doubtlessly, though distantly, related. (pp. 215-16)

> *Margaret Dalton, in a review of "Stikhot-voreniia," in* Slavic and East-European Journal, *n.s. Vol. X, No. 2, Summer, 1966, pp. 215-16.*

Fiona Björling   (essay date 1973)

[*In the following excerpt, Björling characterizes the OB-ERIU aesthetic through study of the group's manifesto, which was written largely by Zabolotsky.*]

OBERIU stands for *Obedinenie Realnogo Iskusstva.* The key-word is of course *realnoe,* and its proper interpretation will take us a long way towards an understanding of the position of OBERIU art within the context of Soviet art in the twenties. In fact the term *realnoe iskusstvo* can be understood in two ways: either art itself is concrete, an artefact, as much a part of reality once it has been made as a table or chair; or, alternatively, the concern of art is with real existing things, the objectively perceptible world.

In the first place we have to do with the social position of art, with its function and place in Soviet society. In this case, the term *realnoe* puts OBERIU art in opposition to any sort of mimetic or didactic art. In his article, "K tipologii literaturnyx učenij dvadcatyx godov" [in *Slavica Pragensia XII,* 1970], Aleksandar Flaker differentiates three basic approaches towards art; these he calls 'teachings' or 'doctrines'.

Flaker calls the first teaching "avantgarde-constructivist", and it comprises the aftermath of futurism, the leftists and the constructivists. According to this teaching, the function of art was considered to be practical rather than aesthetic, hence the futurist cry, "iskusstvo v žizn, k polnomu rastvoreniiu v nej!" [S. Tretjakov, "Otkuda i kuda?", *Lef* 1923] The purpose of art was not merely to convert people to a new socio-political outlook, it was to equip them with the capacity to live life in a quite new way on every level, to arouse within them a new 'feel for life' (*mirooščuščenie*). Once this new 'feel for life' is established art, in theory, will be superfluous.

Flaker calls the second teaching, "učenie o mimeticeško-pozna-vatelnom obščestvennom naznačenii literatury".The cognitive approach to literature was associated with the development of realism in the twenties, and in particular with the name of Voronskij. According to this view, man in the street is too absorbed in his daily round to be able to appreciate the essence of life. In order to comprehend reality he resorts to art: art reflects reality as it is, the good along with the bad, but it has the advantage of standing outside reality. From its vantage point art can appreciate what is essential reality as opposed to what is irrelevant and circumstantial. Art is *poznanie žizni*

where the stress is on comprehension of reality, rather than on direct confrontation or involvement with it. Art does not dive down into reality, it hovers above taking aerial photographs.

Flaker defines the third teaching as "učenie o socialno-peda-gogičeskoj funkcii literatury a vmeste s nej i drugix iskusstv". This doctrine was held by those who maintained that literature had a direct function within the class struggle and demanded that it be used as a weapon in bringing social awareness to the proletarian class. Accordingly literature is primarily a political instrument, and its relation to reality is channelled through its conception of how that reality should be.

Against this background it is obvious that OBERIU art adheres to the first of Flaker's teachings, namely the "avantgarde-constructivist". . . . Concerning the artefact character of a work of art we note that the OBERIU members call themselves 'workers', *čestnye rabotniki svoego iskusstva.*

OBERIU art then is integrated with life and society, it plays its part within reality as a component part of that reality. As such it is distinct from the mimetic and didactic teachings of art in which is implicit the fundamental assumption that art is essentially different from reality; art is not of reality, it is about reality, not an equivalent to direct experience, but a way of comprehending direct experience.

If on the other hand we interpret *realnoe iskusstvo* as referring not to the position of art itself, but to its subject-matter, then we may conclude that OBERIU art is concerned with the simple, concrete things of a reality which every human being is able to perceive. The [OBERIU] Declaration itself supports this interpretation with its continual stress on *predmet,* the 'object': "OBERIU *ne skolzit po temam i verxuškam tvorčestva,—ono iščet organičeski novogo mirooščuščenija i podxoda k veščam.*" The object is to appear naked, freed from the 'slime' of emotions which has become attached to it: "*Posmotrite na predmet golymi glazami i vy uvidite ego upervye očiščennym ot vetxoj literaturnoj pozoloty.*"

The object, usually confronted in a specific context, appears isolated, a thing in its own right. Thus physical feel, sensual reality take the place of significance from the human or social point of view. The reader is encouraged to confront the object with exploring fingers and eyes rather than with his ears (i.e. as a word to be comprehended). Man must experience the object like a child, in innocence, that is without any preconceived idea of the object and its significance. OBERIU interest in the child's or the mentally disturbed's view of reality is frequently underlined. It should be pointed out however that the focal point of this interest is the light that such a displaced view casts on the object itself. The OBERIU is not interested in the child's mind *per se,* just as it is not interested in any subjective or emotional experience other than as a means by which to discover the object of the experience.

The significance of the word *predmet* ['object'] for the OB-ERIU is reminiscent of the futurist insistence on the 'thing' or *vešč.* (pp. 6-9)

[The] term *realnoe iskusstvo* undoubtedly alludes in part to the OBERIU preoccupation with the 'object'. And this in turn ties up with the first interpretation of the word *realnoe,* namely that art is a part of reality where it has a practical function to fulfil. For if the practical task of art is to arouse within the new Soviet man a new sensibility with which to face life on every level, then it must begin at the beginning, at the basic everyday level, and reawaken perception of the most ordinary things, those things which we most take for granted.

The Declaration is divided into four sections, the first of which is called "The Social Face of the OBERIU". In this section is considered the vital question of the function of art in Soviet society, and the problem as to which sort of art can best fulfil that function. The ideas put forward confirm what we have already deduced from the designation *real noe,* and as we might have expected the OBERIU makes a bid for left art as the only true art of the first proletarian state. . . . (pp. 9-10)

Either the references [Declaration] to proletarian art are clichés, part of the language of manifestoes, necessarily inserted because of the cultural-political situation of the time; or, and this is certainly worth considering, the OBERIU did genuinely believe in the establishment of a proletarian culture. But in this case they understood 'proletarian culture' to mean something quite different from the proletarian culture advocated by the proletarian writers, by the Proletkult, the Smithy and the RAPP organizations etc. For the OBERIU the word 'proletarian' was not used in its strictly class-relating sense, that is to say as relating to the working class. The OBERIU used the word in a much broader sense and seem to imply that it refers to something which might be defined as 'the new Soviet citizen', 'post-revolutionary man'. It was not a question of proletarian versus bourgeois, but of new versus old, and 'proletarian' was equivalent to 'new', 'revolutionized'. Like most left artists the OBERIU expected a revolution penetrating all levels of human activity, emotional and perceptual as well as political and intellectual. The establishment of a new proletarian culture was for them tantamount to the establishment within every man of a new way of experiencing life itself.

As for the timing of the Declaration and its views, this was indeed curious. While the identification of a political and a cultural revolution was possible in the years of turmoil surrounding the revolution, by 1928, ten years later, it must have become obvious that 'proletarian culture' meant officially 'a culture suitable for the working class', a culture which would give this class literacy and a schooling in correct political and social thinking. The political situation was far too precarious to encourage a radical, questioning approach to life; it needed on the contrary a consolidating, orthodox approach. With the adoption of the first five-year plan in 1928 avant-garde art was virtually extinguished. It would seem that the OBERIU Declaration is a lost cry, a final and fated blossoming of left art before its extinction.

A precise understanding of what is meant [in the Declaration] by 'left art' is essential if we are to appreciate what OBERIU art is about. The Declaration itself gives no definition of 'left art', but it quotes three names by way of example, namely Filonov, Malevič and Terentev. Filonov's School, Malevič's architectural work and Terentev's production of *Revizor*—this is the sort of art which the OBERIU is advocating.

Why does the OBERIU pick out these three artists in particular? What is the quality in common to these artists which, for the OBERIU, constitutes 'left art'? There are several possible answers to the first question. Firstly it is feasible that the choice of these particular artists reflects Zabolockij's personal taste. We do know that Zabolockij was extremely interested in the visual arts. But beyond this lies the simple explanation that it was in these fields—painting and the visual arts, the cinema, the theatre—that left art was most keenly felt; no poetry corresponding to the OBERIU ideas was published at this time. Consequently the fate of these three artists was indicative of the fate of left art as a whole. All three artists named had currently provoked strong negative criticism.

But apart from the political-cultural topicality of these artists, what was the quality which the OBERIU admired in them? It seems strange that Malevič with his extreme abstraction, or idealization, of reality into its basic elements of form should appeal to the OBERIU with its impassioned plea for the naked object, visible and tangible etc. Filonov, on the other hand, advocated the 'analytical method' and in the 1920's founded and ran his School of Analytical Art; he looked upon art as upon an equivalent to science: through art both the artist himself and his viewer developed their minds. Every detail should be meticulously analysed, it was not a question of 'creation', but of 'making' or 'constructing'; a work of art is a *sdelannaja vešč.*

Igor Terentev was a celebrated *zaumnik* who defended *zaum* as late as in 1928, i.e. after the publication of the OBERIU Declaration. From the few reports of the production of *Revizor* referred to, it would seem that the production exploited techniques which might meaningfully be termed 'absurd', rather than 'transrational'.

It would seem that the factor which these artists had in common was an analytical approach to reality. They sought to make direct contact with the raw material of reality and were prepared to break through all conventional ways of thought and perception to achieve this end. In order to know reality anew, they had first to break it down into its smallest part and examine it from every angle. In my opinion it is this radical, analytical approach to reality which the OBERIU admired in Malevič, Filonov and Terentev, and which they took to be the essence of 'left art'. (pp. 10-13)

Zabolockij's poetry professes to show the reverse process, construction as opposed to dissection, but it amounts to the same thing: the artist handles reality as a child handles a jigsaw puzzle or a box of building bricks: he takes it to pieces, examines each piece and builds it up again aware of the concrete feel of each of the units with which he is building.

In the light of this analytical approach, we may interpret the statement: "OBERIU vgryzaetsja v serdcevinu slova, dramatičeskogo dejstvija i kino-kadra" to mean that the artistic material itself must also be analysed, dissected, re-appraised. The word in poetry must be stripped of every-thing which is not essentially poetic; the dramatic action must be stripped of all that is not essentially dramatic. By 'heart of the word' is meant that part of the word which functions poetically. For while all forms of culture work side by side to create a new civilization, each works in its own way and according to its own logic. Thus poetry can-not be made to replace philosophy, drama cannot take the place of a history lesson; the functions of poetry and drama are just as 'real' and necessary as the functions of philosophy, history, etc., but they are different. A point which is repeatedly stressed in the Declaration, especially in the sections concerned with the cinema and the theatre, is that the logic of art is not identical to the logic of life; "Možet byt vy budete utverždat, čto naši sjužety ne-realny i ne-logičny? A kto skazal, čto žitejskaja logika objazatel-na dlja *iskusstva?*"

And not only that—within art, each branch works in its own particular way, depending on the nature of its materi-al: "Sjužet teatral nogo predstavlenija—teatralnyj, kak sjužet muzykalnogo proizvedenija—muzykalnyj. Vse oni izobražajut odno—mir javlenij, no v zavisimosti ot materi-ala,—peredajut ego po-raznomu, po-svoemu."

In the theatre the object is presented dramatically: the dra-matical presentation singles out an object—often irrele-vant from the point of view of the narrative theme or in-trigue—for special attention. It is the chain of such appar-ently absurd scenic moments which constitutes the theme proper of a dramatic production. In poetry we have to do with the object as it is expressed in language. The task of poetry is to exploit the power of words to associate with one another in new and stimulating ways. Underlying this conception of poetry is the belief that language, the verbal designation of an object, actually affects the way in which we perceive that object; in other words the object and its name are intimately bound together. Thus a sterile lan-guage which relies on automatic, stereotyped associations instead of experimenting with new ones can actually help to blunt the readers' perceptive senses. In OBERIU poetry it is the 'clash of verbal meanings' which is to express the object 'with the exactitude of mechanics' and hereby to awaken the readers' powers of perception.

What the OBERIU calls *stolknovenie slovesnyx smyslov* was termed *sdvig* by the futurists. The OBERIU do not actually use this term themselves but it seems the most appropriate term in the context and may be translated into English as 'displacement'. The purpose of the *sdvig* is to displace the object referred to from its accustomed context into a new and unexpected one, thereby revealing aspects of the ob-ject which had hitherto been overlooked or forgotten. The newly revealed aspects are in this case objective, they be-long to the object concerned and are not dependent on any subjective interpretation. The way poetry achieves this displacement is by combining words in such a way that they create unusual associations: for example, two or more words which do not appear to make sense together from the semantic point of view are made grammatically depen-dent on each other. Displacement can occur on any lin-guistic or poetic level: it can be semantic, syntactic or rhythmic etc. But the important thing is that it is the se-mantic associations of the words which are exploited: syn-tax, rhythm, euphony etc. are used not as ends in them-selves, but as a means of manipulating the associative power of the word, for it is this which is 'the heart of the word' from the poetic point of view.

The Declaration . . . comes to a sensitive and interesting point, namely the relationship of OBERIU to *zaum* or 'transrational language'. The OBERIU dissociates itself from *zaum* in defensive and indignant tones: "Net školy bolee vraždebnoj nam čem zaum. Ljudi real nye i konkret-nye do mozga kostej, my—pervye vragi tex, kto xolostit slovo i prevraščaet ego v bessilnogo i bessmyslennogo ubl-judka." What does the OBERIU understand by the term *zaum?* The phrase 'impotent and nonsensical mongrel' suggests that the term is used in its current (1928) mean-ing as a useful slander to be hurled at anything which does not appear to make sense.

Confusion arises out of a failure to distinguish between true *zaum* and the displacement techniques which have just been discussed. Describing the poetry of Vvedenskij and defending it against any accusation of indulgence in *zaum*, the Declaration gives a warning: "Nužno byt pobolše ljubopytnym i ne polenitsja rassmotret stolknove-nie slovesnyx smyslov. Poèzija ne mannaja kaša, kotoruju glotajut ne žuja i o kotoroj totčas zabyvajut." A poem based on the principle of displacement might be every bit as difficult to understand as a poem which is written in *zaum;* the distinction does not lie in the degree of obscuri-ty.

The distinction between *zaum* and poetry which is con-structed on the displacement principle is fundamental; in fact these two constructive principles are mutually exclu-sive. This becomes clear if we look back at prerevolution-ary futurism where the term *zaum* was used in its strict sense. Here we find a clear dichotomy in the use to which language was put. On the one side is *zaum*—the notion that poetical language is not made up of signs used to refer to something beyond themselves, but of self-contained words which possess an inherent power of expression above and beyond their denotative function. The meaning of language, as far as poetry is concerned, lies within the material itself and not in the use to which it is put. Op-posed to this and very much central to futurism is the no-tion that the value of language lies in the use to which it can be put, in the way in which it can be constructed: words are signs, their value is primarily semantic. But, and this is the important point, their semantic meanings are not fixed once and for all, but dynamic, designed to keep pace with and even forestall a dynamically evolving reali-ty. Hence the possibility and the function of displacement in poetry.

By far the greater part of futurism is concerned with the construction of language rather than with the material as an end in itself. So also the OBERIU makes quite clear that it is concerned with language in construction. (pp. 13-17)

The point is that we are dealing with a quite modern type of poetry, poetry which can be called metonymic as opposed to metaphoric. The terms and their definitions are taken from Roman Jakobson's article, "Two Aspects of Language and Two Types of Aphasic Disturbances" [in his *Fundamentals of Language,* 1956]. According to Jakobson, each speech utterance involves two processes: on the one hand the speaker must select the appropriate word from his code, or the lexical storehouse at his command, in other words he must name the object; on the other he must use the word he has chosen in a specific context, he must combine this word with others, in order to communicate in a meaningful way. It is a question of similarity or contiguity. In a normal speech utterance both processes are involved, but there may nevertheless be a swing towards either of the two poles:

> The development of a discourse may take place along two different semantic lines: one topic may lead to another either through their similarity or through their contiguity. The *metaphoric way* would be the most appropriate term for the first case and the *metonymic way* for the second, since they find their most condensed expression in metaphor and metonomy respectively.

Here we come to the relevance of these two poles of language for poetry and poetry analysis. According to this distinction, metaphoric poetry is poetry which explores similarities, poetry which represents one thing which exists within the given context by another which does not. A comparative conjunction such as *kak, slovno, kak budto* is always understood. By way of example, we may consider the following lines:

> i past otkryta slovno dver,
> i golova—kak bljudo,
>
> ["Na rynke"]

Within the context of these lines, *past* and *dver, golova* and *bljudo* are two pairs of equivalents or alternatives: the context describes an open jaw, but it could replace this image by the figurative 'door'. The reader is given the choice: either he can see the open jaw as it is, or he can 'translate' the image and imagine a door instead, but what he cannot do is to see both pictures simultaneously, in juxtaposition. Jakobson mentions "the primacy of the metaphoric process in the literary schools of romanticism and symbolism". We can say that the associations move 'vertically' out of the actual context to something beyond it.

Opposed to the "metaphoric way" is the "metonymic way": here it is a question not of similarity but of contiguity. We can say that the words associate 'horizontally', that is forwards, through the context itself. The poetic association is between two words in juxtaposition, between all the words within the same context. On the metonymic principle one image is not replaceable by another, it is rather that one image leads on to another. The "metonymic way" could be characterized by that game in which one member of a group begins a story and then passes it on to another, each member picking up the thread in turn. It is a question of stringing together various details to form a chain. Accordingly such poetry is dependent on its constructive means in a very special way. Syntax, rhythm, semantic and euphonic patterns assume a role of utmost importance: it is these elements which hold the poem together, it is they which transform a catalogue of isolated fragments into a meaningful chain of associations.

The following lines illustrate what is meant by metonymic representation:

> Uželi tam najti mne mesto,
> gde ždet menja moja nevesta,
> gde stulja vystroilis v rjad,
> gde gorka,—slovno Ararat,
> povityj kruževcem bumažnym,
> gde stol stoit i trexétažnyj
> v železnyx latax samovar
> šumit domašnim generalom?
>
> ["Ivanovy"]

The description contains metaphors (e.g., *slovno Ararat, samovar . . . šumit domašnim generalom*), but basically it is constructed on the metonymic principle: a series of details are described one after the other; each detail describes one fragment of the room which the poet is imagining. The reader deduces the nature of the whole room from the four concrete details which are described: the waiting girl, the arrangement of the chairs, the cabinet and the bubbling samovar. The details are united into a whole through their syntactic and rhythmic organization: each detail is introduced by the adverb *gde;* coming as it does each time at the beginning of the line, where it takes a slight emphatic, or hypermetric stress, it forms not only a verbal but also a rhythmic repetition. The details are further united by the rhythmic regularity of the verse, especially in its latter half, and again euphonically through the wealth of spirants (/ž/ and /š/) in lines 5-8.

Metonymic poetry—poetry of which the associations are according to contiguity as opposed to similarity—tends to be both fragmentary and concrete or objective. The reader is expected to deduce the whole from a few parts; at the same time the poet does not give direct expression to his subjective thoughts and feelings, instead he allows these to be deduced from a concrete, objective detail.

Jakobson quotes "the so-called 'realistic' trend" in literature as being predominantly metonymic. In the other arts he mentions "the manifestly metonymical orientation of cubism, where the object is transformed into a set of synecdoches". Further he names "the art of the cinema, with its highly developed capacity for changing the angle, perspective and focus of 'shots', (which) has broken with the tradition of the theater and ranged an unprecedented variety of synecdochic 'close-ups' and metonymic 'set-ups' in general".

In the following sections of the Declaration, entitled *Na putjax k novomu kino* and *Teatr obériu,* we understand just how essential is the metonymic approach to the OBERIU way of thinking. The OBERIU expresses it as follows: each form of art possesses a logic which is peculiar to itself; words placed side by side react with one another in one way, film-shots in another, scenic moments in another; the business of each branch of art is to exploit just those associative possibilities which are peculiar to its material. The emphasis is on construction and not on the development of a plot which exists beyond the work of art itself. (pp. 17-20)

This is not to say that art is devoid of content, that a theatrical producer has nothing to say; he has indeed something to say, but it is not a story with an exposition, a climax and a dénouement. The real subject of a theatrical production is the chain of tiny flashes of reality which become manifest when laid bare by an apparently 'absurd' scenic moment. An object isolated from the ostensible plot of a play is displaced, it catches the audience's attention and is appreciated anew, for itself, beyond its usual context.

In fact this metonymic approach is intimately bound up with the OBERIU preoccupation with the 'object', to be seen 'with naked eyes', by people who are 'real and concrete to the marrow of their bones'. Such a 'real' and concrete approach precludes excessive concern with similarity associations ('correspondances'), since these tend to become abstract, vague, esoteric, in a word—*ne-real nymi.*

From the foregoing argument it should be quite clear that verbal texture or poetical make-up is of the utmost importance in OBERIU poetry. It is not only the lexical or coded meaning of each word which is important, but also its contextual meaning which is the result of its manipulation by syntax and rhythm etc. (pp. 20-1)

> *Fiona Björling, in her* "Stolbcy" *by Nikolaj Zabolockij: Analyses, Almqvist and Wiksell, 1973, 112 p.*

Robin R. Milner-Gulland   (essay date 1974)

[*In the following essay, Milner-Gulland contends that Zabolotsky's poetry has been neglected and misinterpreted because critics fail to acknowledge his oeuvre as diverse yet unified.*]

If Nikolai Zabolotsky is still an "unread writer" in the West, it is not only for the predictable reasons: that poetry is hard to translate well (and makes no literary impact at all until this happens), that the usual "time-lag" in appreciation is still operating against him, that no spectacular extra-literary events made his life good journalistic copy, that it is almost impossible to make political capital out of his work (though this has been attempted). Beyond these causes there are others, more peculiar to Zabolotsky's special situation.

Like one or two others of the best Soviet writers (Platonov comes to mind) he was too individual a figure to fit easily into histories of literature; our pundits, both Eastern and Western, unable to place him in the "mainstream" of literary development as they conceived it, have tended to pass him over in silence or with hurried and inadequate comment. This individuality meant isolation in his lifetime; so did his life's very circumstances, since coming from the backwoods of Vyatka province he had no influential connections among the established metropolitan intelligentsia and literary groupings of 1920s Russia, who might have promoted his career—the small circle of Leningrad writers and artists who radically affected the outset of his mature work (in 1926) were mostly as young and unknown as himself. His first small book (*Stolbtsy,* 1929) was viciously attacked—above all by RAPP-ists, but equally (e.g.) by the leading emigré critic Khodasevich. Generally

regarded thereafter, in East and West as, at best, a curiosity, he joined the significant band of "underpublished" writers. He began to gain a small measure of serious esteem and popularity in Russia only from the mid 1950s, when he had not long to live. He remained "unread," both at home and abroad, not so much through mere lack of critical and public interest as through the inaccessibility of basic materials: only in 1965 were fairly comprehensive selections of his work published in the U.S.S.R. and U.S.A., while the first more-or-less complete edition appeared in 1972.

And the work itself? Even for those—and by now they must include almost all discriminating lovers of Russian poetry—who have come under its spell, it can itself contribute to misapprehensions and consequent undervaluation of the poet. The chief trouble is the chance fact that newcomers to Zabolotsky usually approach him simultaneously from the opposite extremes of his career: from the last works, which gained widest publication, and from the *Stolbtsy* poems, notorious for their modernistic *épatage.* Sensing (rightly) that a single poetic vision ought to lie behind both manners—the earlier nightmarishly grotesque, often obscure, fragmented, parodistic, the later classically-even, humane, rather didactic—they fail to find any connection between what are often termed the "two Zabolotskys." Until recently, a typical "mirror-image" situation used to obtain in Zabolotsky criticism: Soviet critics guardedly welcomed the "second," post-war Zabolotsky while remaining uneasy about the "formalistic" horrors lurking in the background; Western commentators draw easy morals about the plight of the Soviet artist from the contrast between the early "heterodoxy" they praised and the apparent late "conformism" they despised. Consider for example (a gem of literary-critical impertinence) the entire reference to Zabolotsky in R. Poggioli's still standard book on modern Russian poetry [*The Poets of Russia,* 1960]: (Before 1930) " . . . there resounded the mischievous and whimsical voice of Nikolai Zabolotsky, who was, however, first reprimanded into silence, and then tamed into that parrotry which seems to be the supreme law of Soviet art." Even a well disposed critic (Helen Muchnic), after rightly pointing out [in her essay, "Three Inner Emigrés," *Russian Review,* No. 1 (1967)] that in his second phase Zabolotsky develops themes latent in his early work, "explains away" the change in terms of pressure brought to bear on him, and speculates that" . . . What mattered to him above all was the process of setting things down in poetry, not the subject to be set down, nor any one way of doing so. Unlike Akhmatova or Mandelstam, who seem possessed by insights and emotions, Zabolotsky is moved by nothing other than the desire to write . . . That is why it was possible for him to change his style without being untrue to his poetic self. . . ." She consequently concludes that " . . . he is not equal to the greatest in poetic grandeur, emotional depth or philosophic insight. . . ."

Yet what emerges from the editions of the last few years is that there are not two Zabolotskys, but many; and then again there is only one, for the links become apparent that join, and make sense of his sharply diverse manners. His progress to "simplicity" no longer seems forced, but reveals its logic; this very simplicity, in the total context of his work, becomes a vehicle for far-from-simple reverberations and profundities. I believe that all Zabolotsky's work is best read as a series of cycles, formally and thematically differentiated from each other, yet passing by logical steps through different territories of a recognizably-unified poetic world. And Zabolotsky certainly saw his life's work as necessarily a whole. For all his changes of manner, he never conceived of a proper retrospective edition without his early work; he constantly revisited it, tinkering with it (to the annoyance of purists, perhaps, but to the considerable interest of anyone wishing to follow his development), reworking his canon, and ruthlessly rejecting much that he had written. There can seldom have been a poet so wholeheartedly and stubbornly dedicated, from first to last, to the realization over a lifetime of his inner vision and the hardworking service to his art than Zabolotsky; a poet, one should add, almost impervious to exterior pressures if they did not correspond with inwardly-felt necessity. The Soviet writer Vera Ketlinskaya recalls how (while still in his twenties) "Zabolotsky talked about the secret essence of literary creativity, of how such work demands the whole of a person, with nothing left over, how he must abandon all side issues—in particular the thirst for success and money—and of how a writer cannot have an easy life. This conversation was a turning point in my career "[*My znali Evgeniia Shvartsa: sbornik statei*, 1966].

I believe that all Zabolotsky's work is best read as a series of cycles, formally and thematically differentiated from each other, yet passing by logical steps through different territories of a recognizably-unified poetic world.

—*Robin R. Milner-Gulland*

If words like these conjure up an image of grim-faced dedication, for all its nobility perhaps rather offputting to the reader, he will soon discover as he explores Zabolotsky's work that there are many facets to his personality. Zabolotsky was, for instance, a born master of the witty (occasionally scabrous) epigram—he would trade them in impromptu sessions with his friend and colleague Yevgeny Shvarts, the playwright. Most of these have alas been destroyed; but there is a remarkable vein of wit, sometimes subterranean, which surfaces particularly in his early work. It may take blackly-humorous, grotesque, absurd, surreal, punning or parodistic forms; indeed the feeling that the reader is being "teased," the continual switches of the poet's tone of voice, heighten the bewildering effect which so disconcerted the first critics of *Stolbtsy* (needless to say, translation can scarcely follow such effects). He was to make of playful, parodistic or pastiche effects a tool that he was capable of using in basically serious contexts to the end of his life: his last important work, the cycle *Rubruk v Mongolii,* sparkles with the exuberance of his

youth, for all its real seriousness. Zabolotsky is continually able to surprise us when we think we have the measure of him; above all with wit, but also with such effects as unexpected pathos, self-mockery, childlike simplicity. This constant ability to do something new, the energy and variegation of his poetic quest, its continual implicit self-renewal gives his career intriguing parallels (they can be developed further) with that of Boris Pasternak, and, to me at least, these are a sign of a truly great, and not merely narrowly-talented, writer. But (born in 1903) Zabolotsky was much younger than Pasternak, and was intellectually formed after 1917; he could be claimed as the finest properly-Soviet poet—the only classic on a European level—to grow up after the Revolution. Nor does he retreat from his country and his age, despite eschewing political writing; his civic consciousness—like Pasternak's—was all the sharper for his standing outside the Soviet mainstream (a stance, in fact, that did not prevent his going to prison and exile from 1938 to 1946).

A poet who deserves reading, then, though not altogether an easy one: it is worth following up such clues as we have to see how best we may approach him.

In 1958, the last year of his life, Zabolotsky made a comment of considerable interest in a letter to his acquaintance A. K. Krutetsky:

> A poem is like a person: it has its own face, mind and heart. If a person is neither a savage nor an idiot, his face is always more or less impassive. Just as impassive should be the face of a poem. The intelligent reader can perfectly well see the whole great interplay (*igralishche*) of mind and heart beneath the veil of external impassivity. I count upon the intelligent reader. I don't want to be over-familiar with him, since I respect him.

Zabolotsky, by nature rather reticent, here for once throws out several hints about the nature of his work and his poetic method, and we shall come back to these shortly. But first it is worth lingering on the striking words with which Zabolotsky describes the relationship he wants to set up with the reader.

This desire for the "intelligent reader" may seem daunting to the ordinary poetry-lover, foreign or indeed Russian, who does not overvalue his own intellectual powers. But it should not be. Though it was Zabolotsky's fate to be little read in his lifetime, he certainly did not write for a highbrow coterie, least of all in the 1950s when the comment was made. Rather, he was laying down ground rules for civilized behavior in the dialectic conversation between the writer and reader, and asking not for a reader of any exceptional intellectual gifts, but one who was ready to use his mind as well as his feelings in the appreciation of poetry. Throughout his life Zabolotsky strove for balance: a balance in poetry between "thought, image and music" (to quote the title of a short article written in 1957), between emotion and intellect. But for a poet to claim even equal rights for intellect in our post-Romantic era is rather unusual. It marks Zabolotsky out as a poet of "cognitive," rather than primarily self-expressive or rhetorical intensions. I have dealt with this aspect of Zabolotsky's art in greater detail [in my "Zabolotsky: Philosopher-Poet," *So-*

viet Studies, April 1971], so shall not argue the point now; suffice it to say that to the "cognitive" poet ideas are of vital importance—ideas that can be expressed and communicated only through poetry. And the comment quoted above gives a clear indication that the reader should seek for meaning or meanings below the surface of his poem.

Such meanings can be, but seldom are, strictly allegorical. Plainly there would be no point in poetry if its *podtekst* were reducible to plain prose: Zabolotsky is in fact a committed master of *inoskazanie* (metaphorism). He sets up a narrative structure of verse—dislocated and complex in his early work, more lucid as time went on—beneath which the larger issues whose essence Zabolotsky sought to perceive and comprehend may be seen stirring. Time after time these turn out to be, in a literal sense, problems of life and death: of the metamorphoses of living and inanimate beings, of how mortality can be overcome, of how man can order his place in the vast chaos of Nature, help her to perfect herself and be perfected in turn. But sometimes Man as a social being (with all his defects in that respect) emerges as the prime object of attention: above all—a curious link—in some of the later poems and in the basic **Stolbtsy** cycle, set in a grotesquely-perceived Leningrad under NEP. For the poet's own personality there might seem to be little place in such a scheme, and Zabolotsky indeed tended to efface his own *persona* in any role more active than that of observer; yet passionate feeling is not far below the surface, particularly from the mid-1930s onwards, and the balance between "heart" and "mind" is maintained. Late in his life he actually produced a memorable, sad and strange cycle of love poems (**Poslednaya liubov',** 1956-57).

A writer to whom ideas are important invites us, if not requires us, to enter into his own "thought-world," and the reader wishing to approach him may like to know the chief landmarks on Zabolotsky's mental map. In 1932 he wrote in a letter to the self-taught *savant* Tsiolkovsky: "concerning people and books, I have always struck exceptionally lucky." What figures can we briefly list as important in the development of his individual outlook? Scientists and thinkers hold first place: Tsiolkovsky himself, the experimental botanists Burbank and Michurin, Engels of the *Dialectics of Nature,* the 18th century Ukrainian pantheist philosopher Skovoroda, perhaps at the end of his life Teilhard de Chardin (a born rationalist, he nevertheless worked out a "religionless religion"—which has been memorably described by Nikolai Chukovsky—in an attempt to "overcome" death). At least one visual artist had great importance for him: P. N. Filonov, whose principle of *sdelannost'* ("made-ness," involving the concept of unremitting hard work on the art-object) affected him deeply. Among other writers he exercised ruthless selectivity. Although there are many "pastiche" echoes of the Derzhavin-Pushkin period of Russian Classicism in his work, he reserved his chief respect for his "philosophical" predecessors, Baratynsky and Tyutchev. Few contemporary writers meant much to him, save Mandelstam and (*after* the basic **Stolbtsy** cycle had been written, despite what most commentators say) Khlebnikov. It is worth pointing out that he was never truly a Futurist, and had no time for Mayakovskian utilitarianism on the one hand

or for *zaumnyi iazyk* on the other; he must have come into contact with literary experimentalism through his young friends on the "left-wing" of the Leningrad Poet's Union. To end the list it is essential to remember Zabolotsky's most illustrious predecessor in the attempt to synthesize science and poetry: the later, classical Goethe, with whom this solitary figure had more in common than with almost any of his contemporaries.

Zabolotsky is not a "bookish" writer, fortunately; except in one or two early poems there are few "private references" that the uninitiated reader will miss. But some knowledge of, and sympathy with, the thinkers and writers listed above help the reader at least to understand Zabolotsky's concern with basic phenomena and their "architecture," with varied modes of perception and communication, with the ordering of man's place in the sinister jungle of the city, the vastness of the natural world, or the web of social life. Particularly in the "middle-period" work of the 1930s and 40s—ironically, the least-known part of the poet's output—the reader will find opening before him, in lucid form yet still with sudden moments of "strangeness" that take him by surprise, a poetic world which has all the "grandeur, emotional depth and philosophic insight" that give Zabolotsky a place among the great originals of the twentieth century. (pp. 385-91)

> *Robin Milner-Gulland, "Zabolotsky and the Reader: Problems of Approach," in* Russian Literature Triquarterly, *No. 8, 1974, pp. 385-92.*

A critic characterizes the evolution of Zabolotsky's literary status:

[Zabolotsky] was until recently dismissed or ignored outside Russia as well as within: after his extraordinary first volume **Stolbtsy** (*Scrolls*) and a few related poems had appeared in 1929-33, the leading emigré poet, Khodasevich, ridiculed him in terms that outdid the sharp attacks of the Soviet RAPP activists. Yet critical opinion is now moving towards a situation in which Zabolotsky will be accepted as *the* Soviet poet (*the* Soviet writer?) in a sense that Mayakovsky (who died in 1930), Pasternak (ambassador from another cultural age) or the greenhorns of the "Thaw" generation cannot be. He is perhaps the only major poet—on a European scale—to have grown up under Soviet rule. He was fourteen at the Revolution; his first work is a startling product of the experimental and libertarian 1920s; he muted and harmonized his style; he went into obscurity and eight years (1938-46) of exile; he enjoyed a late upsurge of creativity and finally a small measure of recognition, though his early poems have not been reprinted until now; before he died in 1958 he was a significant figure in the post-Stalin literary revival.

Times Literary Supplement, No. 3402, 11 May 1967.

I. Masing-Delic   (essay date 1974)

[*In the essay below, Masing-Delic studies themes in* Stolbtsy, *arguing that the work seeks to contrast reality with an ideal.*]

After a long period of neglect, the poetry of N. Zabolockij has in recent years become the object of a great deal of interest, in the Soviet Union, as well as in the West. While Soviet critics [such as A. Turkov in *Nikolaj Zabolockij*, 1966, and A. Makedonov in *Nikolaj Zablockij, Žizn, Tvorčestvo, Metamorfozy*, 1968] pay more attention to the later works of the poet, critical interest in the West favours *Stolbcy* (1929) and other early works. These are more complex and "modernistic" than the later "classical" production; while the later Zabolockij offers many difficulties for interpretation, the earlier bewilders and puzzles and often seems to defy understanding. Clearly, there exists a need for detailed critical analyses, particularly of the early poems. This need has recently been filled to a certain extent by [Fiona Björling's *"Stolbcy" by Nikolaj Zabolockij: Analyses*, 1973] which solves many riddles in three poems of *Stolbcy*, clarifies complex interweaving techniques of text and sub-text and discusses the influence of the OBERIU-declaration upon the style of *Stolbcy*. The present [essay] has as its aim to trace some recurring themes and motifs in *Stolbcy* and to suggest an overall interpretation of the cycle on this basis. It is intended rather to suggest than to prove.

It is generally accepted that *Stolbcy* offers a critique of NEP-times and its neo-*meščanstvo*. Poems like **"Novyj byt"** or **"Na rynke"** or **"Ivanovy"** clearly deal with the theme of the "sov-meščanin" and his way of life. It is possible to trace the *byt* and *mirovozzrenie* of the *sov-meščanin* in *Stolbcy* in great detail: he visits the bar *Krasnaja Bavarija* (title of the first poem of the cycle) where he listens to *žestokie romansy* and gets drunk. In what seems to be a parody on Blok's famous *Ja prigvožden k traktirnoj stojke*, the drunk NEP-man shouts: " . . . ja—iisusik, / molites mne—ja na kreste, / pod myškoj gvozdi i vezde . . ." (st. 3:24-27). For NEP-mentality revolutionary time leaps forward too quickly and the "babe" (*mladenec*) that was born in the "birth-pangs of revolution" to become the "new man", all of a sudden "lezet okarač" (**"Novyj byt"**, st. 1:12). As old times recede into the past and with them the older generation ("A vremja sochnet i želteet, / stareet papenka-otec", st. 2:1-2), the "babe" grows accumulating the attributes, necessary for his neo-bourgeois *byt*—a big flat, a *nevesta*, plenty of food and all that makes life *blagoprijatno* (5:5). The "NEP-*manki*" drift about town in search of sexual adventures without which they are forlorn creatures, unable to fill out their time: "Kuda idti, / komu nesti krovavyj rotik, komu skazat segodnja "kotik", / u č'ej posteli brosit' botik / i dernut knopki na grudi? / Neužto nekuda idti?!" (**"Ivanovy,"** st. 3:10-st. 4). Their NEP-mentality is—in addition to their excessive sexual interest—revealed in the vulgar choice of caressing word (*"kotik"*) and the repetition of the diminutive rhyme reveals the poet's ironic attitude towards them, as well as the "infantility" of their minds. The NEP-men and NEP-women in *Stolbcy* reveal a *"Per Skripkin—mentality"* with their love of *Fokstrot* (title of a poem), Hawaiian jazz-bands (mentioned in **"Fokstrot"**), cinemas called *Pikadilli* (**"Krasnaja Bavarija"**) and other foreign "realii nepovskogo byta". It has been pointed out [by Make-

donov] that Zabolockij's poem **"Svadba"**, as also his description of a wedding in the poem **"Novyj byt"**, "remind of " and "anticipate" the wedding-scene in Majakovskij's drama *Klop*, but it is noteworthy how, in general, writers dealing with the NEP-period single out the same targets of NEP-*byt* for attack. Thus the *žestokie romansy*, which play such an important part in *Stolbcy*, as evidence of spiritual poverty, as an indication of sham feelings and as cheap art-substitutes (**"Krasnaja Bavarija"**, **"Brodjačie muzykanty"**),—in K. Fedin's novel *Goroda i gody* (1924) increase Andrej Starcov's depression; he singles them out as an essential part of NEP-*byt* in his "speech" (in the first chapter of the book, entitled *Reč*) addressed to the windows of the court-yard where he lives (court-yards, by the way, also play an important part in *Stolbcy*): "Ja mog by rasskazat vam o každom iz ètich okon, no ja znaju—vy ne budete menja slušat. Poètomu prošu vas obratit svoi vzory tolko na okno von tam, vnizu, gde razvilas polosataja perina, . . . I ešče na okno von tam, pravee, otkuda s utra do noči sypletsja brenčanie dombry, i ešče na to, v samom verchu, pod čerdakom, gde neprestanno otcharkivaet romansy grammofon; . . . " The *dombra* and the guitar were also symbols of stifling *byt* and pseudo-emotions in Majakovskij's *Klop*, where the guitar is Prisypkin's—Per Skripkin's constant attribute. Lines from a *žestokij romans* are used to offer a grotesque parallel to Marusja's tragic fate in Majakovskij's poem *Marusja otravilas* (1927). Marusja poisoned herself because her lover, *èlektrotechnik Žan*—a precursor of the Prisypkin-Per Skripkin-type—criticized her for not being up-to-date enough. Marusja's departure from this world—caused by cheap and false values—is parodied in this line from a *žestokij romans*: "Smer-tel-nyj / ja-ad / ispit . . ." "Cats" were another common symbol of *byt*. Together with canaries they symbolize neo-petty-bourgeois life in e.g. Majakovskij's *O drjani* (1920), where a *kotenok*, sprawled out over *Izvestija* presumably represents the triumph of *byt* over revolutionary political ideals, while a *kanareica*, another symbol of petty bourgeois self-satisfaction, happily chirps away. "Cats" surround the unpleasant widow Anečka in Ju. Oleša's *Zavist* (1927), and it is in her soft bed, where, no doubt, soft and bulging *periny* abound (cf. Starcov's "speech") that the two "heroes" Kavalerov and Ivan Babičev find their proper place in life. *"Žir"* inevitably accompanies all persons caught in *byt*, whether of the pre- or postrevolutionary type in Majakovskij's works. In *Oblako v štanach* the symbol of *žir* recurs with insistent frequency to indicate a base, limited, "bourgeois" mentality. Thus the reader's *mysl* is likened to a *vyžirevšij lakej*, a mistress of Rotschildt's is *obžirevšaja* and the city is filled with "fat athletes" and fat people *proevšis naskvoz*, as a result of which *sočilos skvoz treščiny salo*. In *Stolbcy* similar unappetizing *žir*-images form the background of NEP-life, e.g. in the poem **"Leto"**: "ljudskie tela nalivalis kak gruši, / i zreli golovki, kačajas na nich. / Obmjakli derevja. Oni ožireli / kak sal'nye sveči . . ." (3-6). These examples could be endlessly multiplied, as guitars, dombras, violins, *žestokie romansy*, gypsy songs, feather-beds, samovars, cats and fat belong to the most common paraphernalia of the NEP-*byt*-image.—This image receives an interesting new variant in Zabolockij's poem **"Pekarnja"** in *Stolbcy*. **"Pekarnja"** describes yet another of the Leningrad microcosms that *Stolbcy* is full of—the setting is a bakery and its surrounding *malenkij kvartal* (st. 1:1). The *byt*-theme is struck when a *kot* appears. In the beginning he seems harmless enough with his charming *chvostik* (1:9), but this very *chvostik* in the last stanza of the poem proves to be *zlovonnyj* and before the *kot* leaves the scene where he has occupied a *početnoe mesto* (5:5), he leaves an unpleasant puddle on the floor. The scene that he has previously been witnessing is the birth of a *mladenec-chleb*—a birth which has caused its mother—the oven—no mean efforts (*chrapit beremennaja peč*, 2:10). No wonder that when the birth of the *mladenec-chleb* is finally accomplished the baker announces it *vo mrak nočnoj* (4:10). There is clearly something extraordinary about the birth of the *mladenec-chleb*: "I v étoj krasnoj ot natugi / peščere vsech metamorfoz / mladenec-chleb pripodnjal ruki / i slovo strojno proiznes" (4:5-9). Yet its birth leaves no permanent traces—even its mother all of a sudden assumes an air of maidenly and coquettish innocence the moment her delivery is accomplished, thus pretending that nothing ever happened (*A peč . . . stoit stydlivaja, kak deva . . .*, 5:1-4). If the oven—*peščera vsech metamorfoz*—represents the womb and birth-pangs of the revolution and her "baby-bread" the new "word" of a new life, then her pretense that nothing has happened in combination with the house-cat's mysterious and knowing smile (*Sidit—sidit i ulybnetsja*, 5:10) would indicate that *byt* has triumphed over all life-giving metamorphoses and that the revolution has betrayed "herself", denying what "she" "herself" has produced.

That "birth-babe" imagery in *Stolbcy* would apply to the ideology of NEP-existence seems confirmed by other poems in the cycle. Thus **"Nezrelost"** re-introduces a *mladenec* in a seemingly fitting combination with *kaška* (1). Yet the image is not idyllic but strange: "Mladenec kašku sostavljaet / iz mannych zeren golubych" (1-2). Perhaps some light is cast upon the "porridge-image" by a statement of Zabolockij's on poetry not being like "mannaja kaša, kotoruju glotajut ne žuja . . ." The immature babe, i.e. the "new man" turned NEP-man, makes his life (and presumably also art) into a predigested porridge, makes something impotent, feeble, weak and infantile out of it. Naturally a diet of "light-blue porridge" does not give strength enough for passion. Encountering a "naked girl", the "babe" declines her offer of love: "Krasot tvoich mne styden vid, / zakroj že nožki beloj tkanju, / smotri, kak moj koster gorit / i ne gotovsja k poruganju!" (25-29). Instead of passion, the "babe" chooses to return to his pot of porridge. His way of life is based upon "philistine wisdom" and a rat-like desire to collect material goods; this interpretation is suggested by the line: "Zerno k zernu—goršok napolnen" (5), indicating a rat or hamster mentality and the obviously ironic statement: "on mudro kašu pomešal—/ tak on urok živoj nauki / duše nesčastnoj prepodal" (30-32) reveals "philistine" wisdom. Naturally the *goršok* is a "base" symbol, and, perhaps, a symbol in the tradition of Puškinian imagery, namely the very opposite of poetry.—Sexual and other kinds of importence mark the "*mladenec*-man" also in the poem **"Figury sna,"** where "sick" imagery emphasizes the inability of the "babes" to lead a genuinely human life. Thus the *mladency* are said to have *bolšie belye tela* (2:7), a white-

ness which is matched by the whiteness of the moon, described as *dlinnoe bel'mo* (2:1). Other negative features are their *čašečki umov* (2:2); one *mladenec* is described as *suchoj* and *zolotušnyj* in appearance (2:13), while another in a Dostoevskian image is described as *žirnyj kak pauk* (2:14). This *mladenec* dreams of *prizračnye podrugi*, but all of them seem to pursue some unreal fancy, revealing their lack of strength. Thus one of them is said to be *v rubache goluboj* (2:10), where *goluboj* does not stand for naiveté and innocence, as the babe-image could lead one to believe, but for an insufficient grasp of life, for "infantility", as it did in the poem **"Nezrelost"** with its porridge *iz mannych zeren golubych*. Also here, as was the case in *Novyj byt*, a time-generation complex is indicated, as we also here find a *starik-otec*, asleep "za černoj zanaveskoj, / vo mrake dedovskich vremen", (3:1-2). Although the *starik* is engrossed in "dark times", he compares favourably with his off-spring, as he, at least, can show up one positive attribute—a *stameska*. Yet his *premudrost* seems doubtful, and the other attributes of his *byt*—a regally pompous cupboard, reminiscent of king David (*Tam škaf gljadit carem Davidom*—, 3:5), presumably when the latter was [according to the Old Testament] "old and stricken in years" and needed the warmth of a "young virgin", as well as a *kušetka,* exuding the temptations that Adam fell victim to (*kušetka Evoj obernulas*—, 3:7)—perhaps explain the mentality of his "babes".

The theme of unfulfilment, infantilism and sickliness, characterizing the "babe-man", is contrasted, or perhaps complemented, by the theme of lust. "Biology" is an important component in the thematic set-up of *Stolbcy,* as "V dvadcatye gody na prirodu dovol'no často smotreli kak na dvojnik kosnogo byta, podležaščij zaodno s nim revoljucionnoj pereplavke". In *Stolbcy* "nature" and "biology" do not undergo any significant amount of "revolutionary transformation", however, but—like *byt*—reign triumphantly. In the linking of *byt* and "naturalism", the critic Makedonov sees a positive aspect to *Stolbcy*: "Ibo temnoe, meščanskoe, zverinoe i "veščnoe", perežitki ego v čeloveke v konečnom ščete dejstvitelno imejut svjaz so stichiej biologičeskoj, zverinoj žiznju, iz kotoroj vyros čelovek i kotoruju on preodolevaet, . . . " If we agree that philistinism and biology are linked in *Stolbcy* and opposed to "spirit" and "mind", then Turkov's statement that "Meščanstvo kažetsja emu (Zabolockij, I.M-D.) kakim-to izvečnym zlom", should be added. The ugly and "evil" aspects of life, as expressed in *Stolbcy,* transcend mere NEP-*byt* and lead to more fundamental questions about human nature. *Pošlost',* as often before in Russian literature, arises as an "eternal category".

In the poem **"Belaja noč"** there is more "uninhibited biology" than "realnaja skazočnost bytija". The lyrical romanticism associated with the notion of "white nights" is here replaced by crude sexuality: "Ljubov stenaet pod listami,/ Ona menjaetsja mestami,/ to podojdet, to otojdet . . ./ A muzy ljubjat kruglyj god" (1:9-12). In the gliding from physical reality to a spiritual one, the poet may be suggesting an alternative to "mere biology", contrasting permanency in art with change in "biology"—in a self-ironic tone.—All these mass-orgies in public places sicken night "herself": "Noč legla,/ vdol po trave, kak mel bela", (4:1-2), but in spite of sickness "love" continues: "torčkom kusty nad neju vstali/ v nožnach iz raznocvetnoj stali, . . ." In the last stanza the sick "white night" is dying (*na ladan dyšit*)—to the inevitable accompaniment of a vulgar *romans* (in the previous stanza: "šel parochodik/ s muzykoj tomnoj po bortam, . . .") Her death evokes the image of a *nedonosok*: ". . . noč . . ./ kačaetsja kak na vesach./ Tak nedonosok ili angel,/ otkryv moločnye glaza,/ kačaetsja v spirtovoj banke/ i prositsja na nebesa" (6:3-8). This complex of images does justice to the sexual activities of the night, which will doubtlessly produce some *nedonoski*, as well as to its anaemic quality and strange spirituality, culminating in a longing to leave this world of vulgarity. The *nedonosok*-image may have been inspired by literature, as well as—as is suggested in Björling's book—by realia, the *Kunstkamera* in Leningrad. In Fedin's *Goroda i gody* a visit of Starcov's to a fair at the city of Erlangen is described, as also his previous visit to a medical museum in the same town. There he sees: ". . . v banočkach, . . . , plavali želtovatye komočki zarodyšej—celyj sonm neroždennych duš. Potom tjanulis somknutye rjady golovastych čelovečkov s prižatymi k životam tonkimi nožonkami i perepončatymi pal'cami ruk." (The unusual word *perepončatyj* occurs also in *Stolbcy* in the poem "Ofort"). Later in the chapter it is suggested that the results of sexual activities at the fair finally land in this museum.—The constellation of *angel* and *prositsja na nebesa* in **"Belaja noč"** may allude to Lermontov's *Angel*.

Sensuality and lust take on Boschian forms in the poem **"Svadba,"** where grotesque imagery reveals the beastliness of man (and woman, as in this case the description mainly applies to *mjasistych bab bol'šaja staja,* 3:5): "Oni edjat gustye slasti,/ chripjat v neutolennoj strasti,/ i, raspuskaja životy,/ v tarelki žmutsja i cvety" (3:10-14). The "philistine aspect" is given in a diatribe against the hypocritical morality of the wedding-guests and in the fate of the *ženich,* who was intended to become a "warrior" but forgot *grom kopyt* (4:4) to become *pridelannyj k neveste* (4:3). Yet this "philistine" aspect of NEP conquering a nobler ideal of life is swallowed up in an "eternal" perspective, as "ogromnyj dom, viljaja zadom,/ letit v prostranstvo bytija", (5:16-18), unhindered by *truda i tvorčestva zakon* (5:21).—Lust and impotence are strangely blended in the eternal category of *pošlost,* where "sound and fury" indeed "signify nothing". The poem **"Fokstrot"** introduces such a mixture of contradictory elements in the figure of a "hero" who: "V botinkach koži goluboj,/ v noskach blistatelnogo franta,/ parit na vozduche . . . / v dymu gavajskogo džaz-banda" (1:1-4). The extraordinary music, which makes the "hero" float in mid-air is produced by a *maéstro* who represents *"kartonnost"* in the sense it was presented in Blok's *Balagančik* (drama and poem). Thus the *maéstro* has a *grud kartonnaja* (in "reality" naturally a starched shirt-front) and he *mašet palkoj v pustotu* (1:10). His activities are partly grotesque (*bet rukoj po životu,* 1:9), partly pompously ridiculous (*kak žrec kačaetsja maéstro,* 1:8). Perhaps he is a black magician, like M. Bulgakov's later *Voland,* since what he produces is *gavajskij fokus nad Nevoju* (2:2), which leads to the effect mentioned above: *Geroj parit* (2:1). This *geroj* who spends a "lively" night under circumstances just described, is characterized as the "most splendid of cripples" (4:3)—as a weak and deformed creature in spite of outer elegance—as a betrayal of the human ideal: "I, tak igraja, čelovek, / rodil v poslednjuju minutu / prekrasnejšego iz kalek— / ženopodobnogo Iudu" (4:1-4). In this statement the "philosophy" of the poem comes out—the concern with *čelovek* and his existence, a concern extending beyond the ideology of NEP-man to a concern with mankind. The time expression *v poslednjuju minutu* may indicate that this "traitor of mankind" is the last product of a diseased time—a "bacillus", to use Majakovskian imagery,— from the past, by mistake let into the garden of (future) paradise, but it could also indicate that even this time paradise will not be perfect.—The "philosophy" of *Stolbcy* is not presented in the form of speculation and reasoning—it comes in an aside, often in the form of irony and travesty. Travesty follows the statement about the "Judas of our times" in the line: "Ego muzykoj ne budi—" (4:5), which alludes to Fet's "Na zare ty ee ne budi"; the mysterious image: "on spit segodnja pomertvelyj/ s cypljač'im znakom na grudi/ rostok boleznennogo tela", is to be deciphered as the hero's blond and sparse growth of hair, reminding of chicken down, and "chickeness" no doubt characterizes the whole image of this "hero of our times". A both horrified and amused fascination with the "crippledness" of man comes out in the poem **"Na rynke"**, where a series of defect human specimens is presented. Their bodily deficiencies evoke no pity as they are presented with "black humour" and horror is tampered by fairy-tale elements: "Na dolju étomu geroju/ ostalos brjucho s golovoju / da rot bol'šoj, kak rukojat,/ rulem veselym upravljat !" (5:9-12). The grotesque element prevails in the last stanza, describing the passion between an invalid who is *bezrukij, puchlyj* (7:16) and a *slepaja vedma* (7:17) whose intense flirt in a *tanec-kozerog* has the effect that "bryznut iskry iz-pod nog . . ./ I lampa vzvoet kak surok" (7:20-21). The last line deflates the wildness of the dance by indicating that the *tanec-kozerog* is about as lively as a marmot.

The most powerful manifestation of nature is death, and the theme of death occupies a most important place in *Stolbcy.* It appears both as a motif and as the sujet for an entire poem, and the frequency of the theme reveals an intense preoccupation with it.—Death is sung of in the bar *Krasnaja Bavarija,* where "sirens" sing of "kak, iz razbitogo viska,/izmučennuju grud obryzgav,/ on vdrug upal" (3:14-16). In the poem **"Čerkešenka"**, death is not sung of but interrupts the singing of the Circassian girl, who carries the river Terek in her breast, until the "stream" forces open her mouth "i trupom padaet ona" (2:11). Characteristically enough the colour "white" with its in *Stolbcy* negative symbolism, re-appears here in a new and original form in the expression *trupik izvestkovyj* (3:3). In both these examples death has been sudden, violent and melodramatic, with blood spurting over the victim. In the mysterious poem **"Ofort"**, a *pokojnik* is endowed with an unusual amount of energy and activity: "Pokojnik po ulicam gordo idet,/ . . ./ on golosom trubnym molitvu poet / i ruki lomaet naverch" (2:1, 3-4), but motion is inevitably put to rest and the *pokojnik* is already "perepolnen do gorla podzemnoj vodoj" (2:6) and forgetful of this world; the movement attributed to him, apparently "really" belongs to the funeral procession, and **"Ofort"** offers yet another example of the *smeščenie*-technique that is characteristic for *Stolbcy*.—Death befalls not only man, but, naturally, also other creatures, e.g. the poor chicken, doomed to die without ceremonies and to be devoured by *mjasistych bab bol'šaja staja* in the poem **"Svadba"**. The idea of infancy and death linked together—as in the *nedonosok*-image—re-appears here with the chicken "cursing his childhood" and the epithet *detskie*: " . . . proklinaet detstvo / cyplenok, sinij ot mytja— / on glazki detskie zakryl, / namorščil raznocvetnyj lobik / i telce sonnoe složil / v fajansovyj stolovyj grobik" (2:7-12). The diminutives also evoke the same idea of helplessness before death as, before, the Circassian girl's white *trupik*.—Sudden death strikes the silvery herrings with "meek eyes" (in **"Na rynke"**) who "razrezany nožom—/ . . . svivajutsja užom" (2:7-8). In addition to the death of individuals, such as the forward's in **"Futbol"** or the Circassian girl's in **"Čerkešenka"** and the death of animals, there is the death of nature, in imagery. "Night" dies in **"Belaja noč"** after sickness and debauchery; in **"Pekarnja"** the "meek evening" dies "kak lampočka v stekljannoj banke" (1:3), where through the word *banka* associations to scientific tests are evoked and to the image of the *nedonosok* in its *banka*. The dying evening is also stigmatized with *pričudlivye ranki* (1:4).—Mysterious is the poem **"Časovj"**, which appears to treat the theme of death in a "philosophical" vein. It begins with an allusion to Tjutčev's poem *Videnie,* as its first line "Na karaule noč' gusteet", evokes Tjutč's "Todga gusteet noč'". In **"Časovoj,"** night is, as in Tjutčev's poem, a *čas javlenij i čudes,* insofar as "unreal figures" appear, e.g. a *proletarij na kone* and a flying girl who *dudit v prozračnuju trubu* (9 and 16). The appearance of the latter is easier to explain than the existence of the former—at any rate in artistic terms, as she and those cows that gather around her *s ulybkoj blednoj na gubach* have a distinct Chagallian flavour. As for the *proletarij na kone,* it could be assumed that he is a dead and entombed "hero of the Soviet army", in honour of whom the *časovoj* stands on guard. The idea that the *časovoj* is guarding a tomb or coffin is suggested by *belyj domik* (13) *s kvadratnoj bašenkoj vverchu* (14), as such small towers, adorned by a red star, often can be found on the graves of Soviet soldiers. A *zvezdy požarik krasnyj* (21) is mentioned a few lines later. That somebody is dead in the poem **"Časovoj"** is also suggested by the appearance of mice *s glazami traurnymi* (26), where the epithet indicates more than merely the colour black. A sense of death is also conveyed by the absolute stillness and immobility of the guard who *stoit, kak kukla* and in whose *glazach odervenelych* (2 and 3) the bayonet, which he holds stiffly in front of him, is reflected. In fact, the presumably deceased *proletarij na kone* is alive in comparison with the immobile guard, as the *proletarijto—gremit, igraja pri lune* (9-10). In the end of the poem the roles of guard and guarded are reversed, as the *proletarij—ego chranit, raspraviv kopja* (33). It appears that a mysterious bond exists between the two soldiers—the dead one and the living—a bond of honour, perhaps, the awareness that they defend the same cause, perhaps the same "new world". Thus the same banners that hang down from the ceiling in front of the standing *časovoj,* form the *izgolove* of the

proletarij (34) and "day", peering in after the night has passed, is said to be "satisfied with them", i.e. both of them. The fact that the deceased is presented *na kone* and as a *proletarij* who *gremit, igraja pri lune* could be explained simply in terms of the essence of the deceased's warriorlike nature, but perhaps also by some representation of him there—a picture of him mounted on a horse, which comes "alive" in the moonlight. The girl, hovering *na stene* with her "transparent trumpet" could, if the interpretation is correct so far, represent the spiritual bond between the *časovoj* and the dead *proletarij,* in fact even the soul-spirit of the *časovoj* whose immobile body is left standing on the ground while his spirit hovers in different realms. There is a later poem in Zabolockij's production, which appears to treat the same theme as the one in **"Časovoj"**, namely the poem **"Prochožij"**, where a passerby, stopping at the grave of a dead young pilot, begins to "communicate" with him, and so real is their spiritual communication, transmitted *v medlennom šume vetvej* that the body of the passer-by begins walking along the road while his spirit remains somewhere else. It could be argued that the theme of death receives a philosophical resolution in **"Časovoj"**—the idea is indicated that a spiritual affinity can be established beyond the dividing line of death—at least between the spirit of a dead hero and a future one. Here death receives a treatment, typical of Soviet literature,—death can be overcome in heroism, as the memory of a hero remains a living reality.

If the problem of death can be solved philosophically in an ennobling and elevating vein, the problem of "life" with its crude biological manifestations presents more difficulties, as "small-dimensioned" life constantly undermines the noble hero-ideal, as presented in **"Časovoj"** e.g. To the inhabitants of *Narodnyj dom* (at any rate its female inhabitants) the "whole world" can be encompassed *obojami* (I:1:1) in a *peščerka malaja ljubvi* (I:1:2), where the word *peščerka* emphasizes both the brutish aspect of this world as well as its ridiculous pettiness. Naturally such *peščerki* exist only to small minds, yet their preponderance colours the whole world of *Stolbcy,* creating the impression that the poet of *Stolbcy* shared the opinion of the poet of *Černyj voron v sumrake snežnom* in finding: "Strašnyj mir! On dlja serdca tesen!" The final poem-triptych of the cycle **"Narodnyj dom"**, presents a microcosm of the "world", at the same time closing the world of *Stolbcy* by returning (in the third section) to the setting of the first poem of the cycle. Those drunkards that were presented in **"Krasnaja Bavarija"** re-appear in **"Narodnyj dom"** and their *butyločnyj raj*—(**"Krasnaja Bavarija"**, 2:1) is both locally and spiritually the same. But more is known about their "background" now and their "whisperings" with the bottle, as they bid farewell to "fiery youth" have to be seen in the perspective of what "youth" has been shown to mean. They substitute a "bottle paradise" for the *raj* where "každyj mal'čik ulybaetsja, / a devočka naoborot— / zakryv glaza, otkryla rot / i ručku vybrosila tepluju / na pripodnjavšijsja život" (III:2:6-10). **"Narodnyj dom"** shows life to be strongly reminiscent of a farce with certain recurring gags, "biology" being one of the more ridiculous. Thus the succession of generations and the repetition of the birth-decline-pattern fetters mankind in an eternal trap that allows for no surprises. The *devka* who just bought some oranges off an *apel'sinščik* wandering about the streets, turns into the eternal Eve *kušaja plody* (II:3:10) and, as is to be expected, the consequences of this action are not far away: "V kačeljach devočka-duša / visela, nožkoju šurša, / ona po vozduchu letela / i teploj nožkoju vertela / i teploj ručkoju zvala" (II:4). If the *devočkaduša* here is an infant ready to be born into this world, and if she will survive infancy without turning into a *nedonosok,* no doubt her devočka-aspect will not last long and she will turn into yet another *devka,* whose *pripodnjavšijsja život* will produce yet other *devki* and "*malčiki*". That "time" distorts and disfigures originally better forms also comes out in a small scene in "**Narodnyj dom II**" where a 40 year old man stands in front of a distorting mirror. Distortion and refraction here do not serve a purely aesthetic purpose, as so often in the work of Oleša, but a moral one. The "funny mirror" shows the man's face as it really is, shows what it has become like in the course of time and therefore the man cannot laugh at his funny face (*chotel smejatsja, no ne mog,* II:5:4) but seeks *pričinu iskrivlenija* (II:5:5). He therefore attempts to become a child again—the word *rebenok* being used here,

as it is less discredited than *mladenec* and *malčik*—in the sense that he retraces the past in order to find himself there: "on kak by delalsja rebenkom / i šel nazad na četverenkach- / pod sorok let—četveronog." (II:5:6- 8.) This then—an attempt to retrieve genuine values—is perhaps a solution to be preferred to the one that the drunkards in "**Krasnaja Bavarija**" recourse to when they have given up *ambar radosti* (III:1:3) and the joys of a *kurjatnik* happiness (II:1:1), namely the bottle which has become to them *slovno matuška* (III:1:11).

As critics have pointed out, the "tone" of **Stolbcy** is very difficult to establish, but whether one interprets the "tone" as mainly ironical and playful, dark and pessimistic, "concrete" or "literary", it would seem that the "tone" is also carried by a strong sense of morals and morality and the question, what should be considered as "true values". There is a strong dose of "philosophy" in **Stolbcy** in the sense that "ugly life" is opposed (both directly to "heroism" and "art" and indirectly through its very grotesqueness) to an ideal; also the question of death is posed and even "solved". A dream of a "pure world" and of reconciliation with death indicates the pattern of a *mirovozzrenie* that would find more explicit expression in Zabolockij's later works. (pp. 13-25)

> *I. Masing-Delic, "Some Themes and Motifs in N. Zabolockij's 'Stolbcy',"* in Scando-Slavica, *Vol. XX, 1974, pp. 13-25.*

Irene Masing-Delic (essay date 1983)

[*In the following essay, Masing-Delic explicates* The Triumph of Agriculture, *contending that the poem presents collectivization as an integral part of social transformation.*]

Nikolai Zabolotsky's long poem **The Triumph of Agriculture (Torzhestvo zemledeliia)** has been an object of controversy since its publication. As with Blok's *The Twelve,* critics have not been able to agree about the poem's stance towards contemporary events. For **The Triumph of Agriculture,** the basic question is whether the poem satirizes the collectivizers of Soviet agriculture or hails them as founders of a better world. A valid interpretation of the poem hangs upon the resolution of this question. The purpose of this essay is to establish whether the poem is a positive, even utopian, vision of collectivization or rather a satire upon it.

Initially, **The Triumph of Agriculture** was greeted with indignation. Soviet critics interpreted the poem as a vicious satire on the collectivization process then going on and as an attempt to "make socialist ideas into a laughing-stock" [cited in A. Makedonov, *Nikolai Zabolotskii. Zhizn, tvorchestvo, metamorfozy,* 1968]. Some critics in the West have also understood the poem as a satire. [In *Russian Literature under Lenin and Stalin,* 1972] Gleb Struve sees Zabolotsky as "mocking Soviet society or the modern world in general." [In "K voprosu o siurrealizme v russkoi literature," *American Contributors to the Seventh International Congress of Slavists,* 1973] Ludmilla Foster finds that the mixture of the absurd and comic in the poem serves "satir-

---

George Gibian on "The OBERIU Manifesto":

"**The Oberiu Manifesto,**" in some of its sections, carried on a polemic with the Proletarian groups—a polemic not likely to get the Oberiuty very far, since the press and all the instruments of power were against them. The Oberiu anti-Proletarian attack was two-pronged. On the one hand the "**Manifesto**" tried to occupy ground claimed by the Proletarians. The Oberiuty affirmed that they, not the Proletarian writers, truly filled the need of the new society and supplied, or would supply, art worthy of the new classless Soviet people. The Proletarian writers, they asserted, were not doing the job: their books were piling up in warehouses; the Soviet people would not read them.

The Oberiu went on to assert that "artistic methods of the old schools" could not satisfy the proletariat. Proletarian art was old-fashioned and a failure; the Oberiuty, on the other hand, "penetrate into the center" and "seek an organically new concept of life and a new approach to things."

The Oberiu, however, also defined itself carefully in relation to various non-Proletarian groups. It was easy for the Oberiuty to differentiate themselves from the Proletarians: that was a matter of two opposites. It is more difficult to separate the Oberiu from various kindred Futurist groups. A primary distinction is that the Oberiu rejected pure formalism, or art for art's sake. "**The Oberiu Manifesto**" did not oppose the view that art ought to concern itself with life and reality. It claimed that Oberiu art was realistic, that it did concern itself with life: "It finds a way to represent any subject." The "**Manifesto**" did not view art as separate from life or as an autonomous realm. Art was to be related to life; it ought to be a representation of life, but not a complete or slavish imitation or reproduction.

George Gibian, in the introduction to The Man with the Black Coat—Russia's Literature of the Absurd, *edited and translated by George Gibian, 1987.*

ical purposes," and quotes the following lines as an example: . . .

> A cow bedecked with formulas and ribbons
> Was baking a pie out of chemical elements,
> And before her, in a tin,
> Tall chemical rye was growing.

Here the thrust is directed against "pseudo-specialists on agronomy," she finds.

Was Zabolotsky really mocking pseudo-agronomists, or collectivization, or the Soviet state, or the modern world? Was he even mocking "vulgar materialism" or "vulgar sociology" while recognizing essential socialist values, as Pavlovsky argues [in "Nıkolai Zabolotskii," in *Poety— sovremenniki,* 1966], classifying *The Triumph of Agriculture* as a "mock-heroic poem?" Many critics, particularly in the Soviet Union and Eastern Europe, now discern a serious rather than mocking tonality in the poem. The East German critic Fritz Mierau sees *The Triumph of Agriculture* as one of the poet's "utopian visions of a nature free from suffering and completely assimilated by mankind" [*Revolution und Lyrik,* 1973]. A. Makedonov characterizes the mood of the poem as "genuine pathos without hidden mockery," defines the genre not as satire but as a "philosophical-symbolical fairy tale," and discerns in it a viewpoint that greets the transformation of nature through collective effort. Makedonov finds the initial Soviet reaction to *The Triumph of Agriculture,* a "strange misunderstanding, unheard of in the history of literature."

The utopian interpretation also has its adherents in the West. Boris Filipoff (like Makedonov, but ten years earlier) saw the basic theme of the poem as the transformation of nature. He also pointed to the source of this theme, stating [in *Stikhotvorenija,* edited by Gleb Struve and Boris Filipoff, 1965] that "Zabolotsky's remarkable epos" has a great affinity with "Fedorov's religious materialism." The Russian religious thinker Nikolai Fedorov (1828-1903), whose influence on Russian and Soviet literature is gaining recognition, maintained [in *Filosofiia obshchego dela. Stati, mysli, pisma Nikolaia Fedorovicha Fedorova*] that a mankind united in the "common task" of constant research and collective labor would unfailingly gain complete control over nature, including the natural phenomenon of death. Filipoff sees *The Triumph of Agriculture* as pervaded by the idea that mankind will transform the word "through the conquest of death," thus putting the poem into a utopian category. Indeed, Makedonov makes the same point when he writes that *The Triumph of Agriculture* deals with the striving of "man for a victory over time with the help of 'good sciences' and a new social organization." This wording puts the Fedorovian program in cautious terms: "victory over time" instead of "victory over death" or the "resurrection of the dead," as Fedorov would have put it. He also writes "new social organization" instead of "rediscovered universal kinship," but he implies what Fedorov states.

Filipoff correctly discerns Fedorovian ideas in *The Triumph of Agriculture,* but I disagree with him as regards the poem's presumed anti-Soviet stance. For Filipoff also finds in *The Triumph of Agriculture* a satire on "the ruling ideology," a satire that is intertwined with the enormous theme of "rebuilding the world through labor and love." There is no such "intertwining." Fedorovian ideas on overcoming death are indeed present in *The Triumph of Agriculture,* but the satirical elements are not aimed at any aspect of the ruling ideology but solely at the "remnants of the past." The ensuing analysis will demonstrate that a Fedorovian utopian transformation program underlies the system of ideas in the poem and that collectivization figures as an organic part of that transformation. *The Triumph of Agriculture* does not present a utopia in the strict sense of the world, but a Zabolotskian "legend in the making"—the world of today viewed from the perspective of tomorrow, just as the canons of socialist realism would require. Detailed analysis will show how collectivization advances "the common task" and how collectivizers such as the soldier realize the Fedorovian program. No critic has undertaken a detailed examination of the Fedorovian elements in *The Triumph of Agriculture,* because Soviet scholars hesitate to spell out utopian ideas linked to concrete events and Western critics cannot free themselves from the view that the poem is a satire on Soviet ideology and collectivization. It is time to examine *The Triumph of Agriculture* from a Fedorovian perspective.

In *The Triumph of Agriculture* the reader meets with a reality that is wondrous because of what it is and even more because of what it is bound to become, and therefore already "is." But this does not mean that there are no negative aspects in the village undergoing collectivization. The dark legacy of the past still exerts its influence. In the midst of the collectivizing village there is still the egotistic world of private property. This world is clearly negative in *The Triumph of Agriculture* and may be thought of as the "old world" to be overcome through collectivization. What is the most negative aspect of this "old world?" It is its irresponsible neglect of nature, which led to its decline and deterioration. According to the "old man" in chapter 1 ("Discussion on the Soul"), nature has reached a stage where it is only a "heap of ruins." The horse appearing in chapter 2 ("The Sufferings of Animals") agrees with him, stating that nature "is declining all around." The narrator agrees with both as he presents a nature in which the very springs of vitality are drying up. "Nature produces a pitiful juice," he states, and the plants "are filled with silence." They are also "short, feeble and blind." The animal kingdom, too, is degenerating.

Neglect of nature in the old world took the form of lack of planning. Nature was abandoned to its inherent self-destructiveness—a self-destructiveness that spells ruin to man and all other living organisms. In *The Triumph of Agriculture* nature is in a state of "wild disorder," and time rushes past "in a haphazard manner." This is so because nature "does not understand anything," as the soldier, the main personage of *The Triumph of Agriculture,* correctly remarks. Nature is not man's conscious enemy and does not knowingly threaten and often destroy him. It is, as Zabolotsky puts it in a later poem, [**"Ia ne ishchu garmonii v prirode"**], "a loving but demented mother." Therefore the soldier's antagonist in the first chapter, the shepherd, is also right when he states that he regards all of nature "as a home." He sees nature as a loving mother providing a home for mankind and forgets her outbursts of "insanity," manifest in elemental disasters, crop failures, and other forms of "wild disorder." Neither the soldier nor the shepherd is entirely right. The complete truth about nature is that she is both bountiful and cruel, both benevolent and destructive. Nature's "insanity" is schizophrenia.

What does a child owe its sick mother, or mankind the *magna mater* of nature that "bore" it and took as good care of it as its "insanity" allowed? Mankind owes its mother care, attention, and rational planning. In the old world mankind could not give nature the care it needed. A disunited society torn by class antagonism, lacking the solidarity that the Common Task demands, could not heal disintegrating nature; a sick mankind could not care for its "sick mother." The blame for nature's deterioration must therefore be put on the leaders of the old world, those who for egotistical reasons upheld class divisions, the dividers of the land and profiteers of human disunity—the kulaks.

In chapter 3 of *The Triumph of Agriculture,* "The Exile," the kulak is unmasked. This representative of his class is characterized as "blind, like a feudal lord," because he does not wish to see beyond the confines of his "egocentric world." He belongs to those who have fragmented nature by dividing it into artificial units such as "my hut" and "my new lovely granary." The kulak's clinging to his property hinders the rise of an integrated society that in collective labor could heal a "ruined nature," hence exile is his appropriate fate. But not only greed and "individualism" make the kulak an "anachronism" and obstacle to progress. So does his religiosity.

The Triumph of Agriculture offers a merciless critique of Russian Orthodoxy. In this respect it resembles Blok's *The Twelve.* Using Tolstoyan *ostranenie* devices, Zabolotsky lets his desperate kulak, who feels his end approaching, pray to "dishevelled, feeble and two-legged gods," i.e., icons. These "hairy gods" are shown to be as primitive as any heathen idols, and the epithet "two-legged" indicates their all too human status. Devoid of divine power these "feeble gods" cannot help the kulak or anybody else, however fervent the prayers addressed to them. "Kulak religion" fosters a fatal inertia and passivity in men. The kulak loves the status quo to the point where he is intent upon destroying "the signs of the future." To "leave everything to God" is the kulak's way of avoiding mental activity.

The Triumph of Agriculture's standard Marxist critique of religion as a passivity-inducing "opium" could in some respects also be called Fedorovian. Fedorov, it is true, regarded himself as an Orthodox Christian, but he did abhor a passive Christianity that relied on prayer instead of action. He regarded most Christians as "heathens" because they accepted nature as it "is," instead of transforming it through the Common Task. Fedorov might easily have put the label "heathen" on Zabolotsky's orthodox kulak, for he, neglecting the soil, replaced practical activity with prayers for personal well-being and wealth.

There is no doubt that in *The Triumph of Agriculture* the kulak is a negative figure. He and his religion are harmful to the new society being built; both must be eliminated. There is no hidden sympathy for the "exile" in *The Triumph of Agriculture,* as Filipoff implies. Nature itself finds the kulak guilty. Nature's spokesman, night, tells the kulak that the time has come to accept responsibility for his neglect of the soil. Then, without compunction, night pushes the kulak and his cart into the "abyss" of nonexistence. His elimination is part of the general retribution meted out to the old world. In the village, the church is closed or even "exorcised." The impression of exorcism is created by a wooden beam being used to close up the belltower. It is as if a vampire were being prevented from ever rising from the grave again. The impression is reinforced by the fact that another "enemy of mankind," the wooden plow, is being interred simultaneously. Also the presence of "witches" (bats) thickens the demonic aura of this passage. With the help of vampiric exorcism the "Third Rome" of Russian Orthodoxy does fall in the year of collectivization, clearing the path for the "triumph of agriculture."

Who is responsible for the fall of the old world, kulak empire, and kulak church? Who ushers in the new world and organizes the "triumph of agriculture?" The answer is the soldier, who, like the kulak, represents an entire class—the proletariat. The soldier is the kulak's antipode and replaces him as a leader of men. The qualities that make him a leader suited for realizing the "Common Task" are energy and courage. The soldier scorns death on the battlefield, is not overawed by Mother Nature, even when she is in her most "demented" moods (as during the terrible storm described in chapter 4), and he dares to challenge the authority of the forefathers who represent Russia's entire past. The soldier is not a crude materialist, petty *Besserwisser* and local dictator, as most Western and Soviet critics see him; he is rather the brave simple soldier of many a Russian fairytale as well as many literary works of the time. Although of their stock, the soldier is superior to the peasants around him. He is a rebel, and they, still enmeshed in kulak culture, are not. The soldier's rebellious character and "promethean" stance (the qualities that make him a true proletarian) come out most clearly in his confrontation with the Faustian *chorus infernalis* of deceased forefathers. He dares to challenge the authority of these "kulaks of the underworld," fanatically devoted to tradition, custom, and all forms of the status quo.

The forefathers want men to remain what they have been and still largely are, primitive creatures of nature. The very idea that men may transcend themselves angers them. Mediocrity is their ideal, as they plainly state: . . .

> We prefer average people—
> Those who give birth,
> Those who sing
> And don't threaten anyone
> And create nothing at all.

The forefathers so cling to the status quo of the "human condition" that they welcome death as a safeguard of mediocrity. Death, forcing every new generation to overcome infantile ignorance and juvenile inexperience, puts an effective check to collectivization, which the forefathers see, not as a grandiose plan to transform nature, but as "feverish fantasies." In their view the new mankind, realizing its dream of controlling nature and thus its own destiny, is possessed by *hubris.* They believe that mortality will shackle the pride of their living descendants.

The soldier, who represents a promethean mankind, rejects the forefathers' philosophy of acquiescence. The dead, he realizes, exert a fateful influence upon the living by their attempt to make the living look upon reality with their eyes. Retaining the values of the forefathers, their descendants uphold stagnation. Therefore the old world cannot become truly new until the "moles" have been revealed in all their "stupidity." Acknowledging that the forefathers' attitudes may have been right for their time, the soldier points out to them that now "their truth" is but "the overeagerness of inert ignoramuses!" He grants that the forefathers are right in presenting nature as a mighty mother, feeding mankind at her ample bosom, but he also insists that the infancy of mankind must end. The two babes that Mother Nature nourishes—man and woman relying on nature's bounty—ought to be weaned. Taking this attitude, the soldier proves to be a "Fedorovian." Fedorov saw in man's refusal to "come of age" and shoulder his responsibilities towards nature the main obstacle to his taking control over nature. Also Fedorovian is the soldier's statement that Mother Nature is fated to remain forever a "naked woman" if her children do not provide her with the fine garb of technology. The soldier sums up this complex of ideas by asking the forefathers, "Won't we regress/If all we do is give birth?" The forefathers become so irate at this question that they call the soldier the "aborted fetus of a redhaired old hag." Probably they feel stung by the soldier's just criticism of their outmoded position. They fear that the future might indeed belong to a promethean mankind and they be proved wrong. The soldier, in turn, is angered by their uncompromising position and retaliates with crude threats of execution, apparently not realizing that the dead cannot be killed. However ridiculous, the soldier's threats reveal his uncompromising stance towards "enemies of the revolution." The author of *The Triumph of Agriculture* blames the soldier as little for his "sacred anger" as the author of *The Twelve* blames his "apostles" for theirs.

Even though the soldier is the positive hero of the tale, he is shown to be flawed. He is uneducated; mingled with deep intuitive insights, such as his realization that men and women must "come of age" and renounce their infantile dependence on nature, there are some simplifications in his reasoning. Oversimplified (but not entirely wrong) is his approach to the question of immortality. He annoys the peasants with his offhand dismissal of their speculations on the afterlife and his reduction of the soul to mere "particles of phosphor." The narrator is aware of the ambiguity that surrounds the soldier in the eyes of the simple peasants. It is he who poses the question, who is the soldier and what does he stand for?

> There he goes—the soldier, bloodred
> From his boots to his head.
> In the midst of a great herd,
> Who is he—a demon or a god?
> And his winged star
> Glistens like a rhinoceros.

The answer to this question is that the soldier is not a "demon" bent upon the destruction of the peasant village, but a "god," liberating the village from the disasters to which a mismanaged and hence destructive nature exposes it. This "god" also shows the peasants how to overcome their all-too-human state and rise above the level of "herd creature." In this liberating activity, he is guided by the star of the new faith that realizes Fedorovian ideas in collective action—without relying on divine blessing; this faith replaces the passivity-inducing religion of kulaks and icons. It stipulates that man can change his fate, if only he is willing to put in the effort that the transformation of nature costs. It is this new message of salvation that the soldier disseminates in the village, becoming, like Blok's twelve, the "apostle" of a new faith. Involved in historical events that at first surpass his understanding, the soldier grows in stature and understanding, and becomes the true savior of the village.

One important factor that is usually overlooked in the evaluation of the soldier is his "conversion" induced by the "revelation" granted to him. Immediately after his debate with the obstinate forefathers, the soldier has a dream vision. In his vision he sees the "heavens suddenly open up" and, beyond, the world of the future. This revelation adds a dimension to the soldier's attitudes, which now also include love for mankind. If the soldier, before his "conversion," was overly severe to the villagers, he now realizes that he must lovingly guide them into a future more wondrous than he himself initially suspected. The soldier no longer makes his "winged star" into a "rhinoceros" of crude rebuttals. He has discovered his "kinship" with all men (except enemies of the Task). This sense of kinship extends even to man's "little brothers," the animals.

Part of the soldier's revelation is an "animal institute" (*zhivotnyi institut*). In this institute, the soldier tells eagerly listening cows, the consciousness of animals is being scientifically developed. In fact, they are to be brought to the level of human beings, given "full consciousness." This is entirely feasible, as man was but an animal not so long ago, and perhaps still is at the moment when collectivization comes to the village. The difference between human beings of today and animals is not unbridgeable. As the horse points out, his brain is not at all a "pitiful drone" but even now able to perceive "the pale window of consciousness." In the institue his brain capacity and consciousness will be further developed. This theme—the humanization of animals—is clearly stated in *The Triumph of Agriculture.* A wolf studying the stars through an "iron microscope" belongs to those who in *The Triumph of Agriculture*'s "animal institute" gain full consciousness. They are all profiting from evolutionary change induced scientifically by chemical and other means. Thus the horses who are "friends of chemistry" and the "chemical oats" growing in a tin are being improved to their full capacity in order to yield perfect specimens of their species and eventually transcend it in the process of becoming "highly organized beings."

The "animal institute" has tasks beyond giving animals (and plants) full consciousness. It deals with the question of consciousness *per se,* and therefore ultimately with the question of life itself, as consciousness and life are one. The "animal institute" where "life is always healthy" is also a "life institute" where the very springs of life are studied. The adjective *zhivotnyi* evokes the Church Slavonic *zhivot* (life) as well as its derivative *zhivotnoe* (animal). In the expression *dukh zhivotnyi* used by the old man during the peasants' discussion on the soul and afterlife, it seems to have the meaning of "life" rather than "animal." The chemical problems studied in the institute where "life is always healthy" may well center on the chemical causes of death and how these can be eliminated with the help of chemistry and other branches of science.

The problem that truly occupies all living creatures is the problem of mortality. All nature's creatures dream of immortality and fear death. Chapter 1 of *The Triumph of Agriculture* is devoted to a discussion of death and immortality by human beings, chapter 2 to a similar discussion among animals. Both men and animals experience sorrow and fear in the face of death, whose power seems so unshakable that it is taken for granted, and the living quickly forget the dead, who are unable to communicate with them. Fedorov strongly criticized this attitude towards the dead, and in *The Triumph of Agriculture* the dead do communicate with the living. They remind them that they do still exist, as they are part of the earth. Thus the "severe muzhik" in chapter 1 reports that when he is plowing his family plot, he sees a "throng" before him—the throng of forefathers buried in the ground he is tilling. One of the dead and buried souls of *The Triumph of Agriculture* suffers so intensely from her neglect by the living that this poor soul even voices her sentiments, telling the living that she is "the same" as they are and that she is bored to be all by herself.

The poor soul who laments her and all other souls' fate in an oblivious world is echoed by the old bull who laments the decay of the body in death. Fearing his own imminent death, the bull envisions how he will be "dumped" on the "cow cemetery" to dissolve in unmarked mass graves. Just like the old man in chapter 1, the bull fears becoming the object of nature's cruel mockery of the living form. Whereas the old man fears old age, the bull fears the putrefaction process, in which his identity will be dissolved and his form submerged into primeval matter.

It is this problem—the problem of mortality—that is the central task lying before the animal institute. During his revelation the soldier realized that immortality is the ultimate goal of the task begun by collectivization. He understood then that men who have gained knowledge of the laws of evolution and learned how to humanize animals also know how to make "gods" out of themselves, pushing their own evolution forward. It is true that the humanization of animals is dealt with in great detail in *The Triumph of Agriculture,* whereas the "divinization" of men is merely indicated. The soldier only briefly mentions that horses "hanging in the air" will be watching out for visitors from other planets and that these visitors will be "harmonious formations of people" who descend from the "pastures of ether." Future mankind is "interstellar" and in this respect clearly godlike, as Fedorov, who saw conquest of space as a corollary to achieving immortality, envisioned.

Are we to assume, then, that the peasants of the collectivizing village are making it possible for mankind to achieve an interstellar, immortal state of being?

Immortality (and freedom from all natural laws, such as the law of gravity) is the hallmark of a godlike state, and there is no doubt that some generation of post-collectivization mankind will achieve it. The realization of immortality is the main theme of *The Triumph of Agriculture.* The theme emerges from the description of the Common Task, the first phase of which is collectivization crowned by the "triumph of agriculture." What then exactly are the various phases of the Common Task and how is it realized concretely in the poem?

An important initial element of the Fedorovian task is the so-called "transfer" of technology from the city to the rural areas. This transfer should be carried out under the guidance of "military instructors." In general, the army is assigned an important role in Fedorov's transformation program. He saw in it a model institution of cooperation, discipline, and brotherly relations. But the army of the future must not be engaged in wars of the conventional type. The new army was to engage in battles with nature and its moral foundation was to be found in "sacred-scientific militarism." It was to become an army devoted to research on a gigantic scale, research conducted not in artificial laboratories in the city, but in the natural laboratory of nature itself. It was to be devoted to a research that had as its ultimate aim the conquest of the enemy of all mankind—death.

Zabolotsky's brave soldier, who in the Civil War did not hesitate to sacrifice his life for his brethren, and who helped to eliminate the non-fraternal class of kulaks, is now yearning to fight this ultimate enemy. In this aim he is a "Fedorovian" soldier. He also belongs to a new type of army, the army of collectivizers, which is determined to transform nature by purging it of all its dark and lethal aspects. Keen on battle with death itself, the soldier is the appropriate leader of the transfer of city technology to the village, which forms the first phase of collectivization. The soldier is therefore the one to lead the tractor and tractor-driver into the village to engage them in a "close battle with nature." Under his guidance, tools of war are transformed into tools of agriculture, as Fedorov (following Old Testament prophets) demanded. Furthermore, he also initiates the "burial of the plow" and the discarding of other outmoded tools of agriculture. These have been an obstacle to progress and the instruments of a labor that tied man to the soil, leaving him no time for resolving essential problems, such as the problem of mortality. Forcing man to "labor in the sweat of his brow" these tools became "instruments of torture" and one of them, the wooden plow, even a symbol of death (as the main instrument of torture). Hence the burial of the plow, which occupies an important place in *The Triumph of Agriculture,* is a symbolic burial of death itself, or at least a symbolic act marking the anticipation of the burial of death.

The wooden plow, which is buried in the village realizing collectivization, is a kind of female *Kashchei Bessmertnyi* (*sokha,* plow, is feminine, as is the word for death). She is a "wicked old monster"—as wicked, old, and monstrous as death itself—and she is dry and bony. A kind of "Kashchei vocabulary" surrounds her as "bones" and "skulls" are associated with her, as with the other outmoded tools. Like the bony Kashchei, this old "hag" of a plow is convinced of her immortality and eternal power. She thinks she rules the world because the "god of private property" whose power in the old world is undisputed, "hops" on her wooden "stomach" "like a flea." In other words, she trusts the power of capitalism (in *The Triumph of Agriculture* presented as a disuniting force) to preserve the principle of disintegration in the world, thus also ensuring the power of all-disintegrating death. Death exists as long as *any* form of disintegration exists, Fedorov stresses; it is bound to disappear when *all* forms of disintegration have been replaced by all-pervading unity and total integration. But the wooden plow, like Kashchei in many fairytales, learns the bitter lesson that her day of reckoning has come. The "half-open grave" teaches her that she is not immortal, but only a temporary phenomenon. Some day death too will learn that "time is up," as Velimir Khlebnikov prophesizes in *Ladomir.*

The tractor is thus much more than a fine piece of machinery—it is a "liberator" from death (the plow). Only this function can warrant the worship that is accorded the tractor by the villagers. They realize that the tractor's "snout" "cuts through the centuries," enabling a mankind, freed from inhuman labor, to establish links between generations by creating a planned transfer of knowledge, which will accelerate the growth of knowledge. No longer will death ensure mediocrity. On the contrary, it will itself be overcome by brilliant thought and the product of brilliant thought, technology. With the help of the tractor and other machinery, a deathless world will ultimately arise to replace the old one, where death rules. In the new world, ushered in by collectivization and the tractor, death will be buried like the plow; everything will be new, with a "new sun" and "new grass." In more biblical terms there will be a "new heaven" and a "new earth" and, consequently, "no more death," as nothing old (and death is old) can dwell in a world where "the former things are passed away." It can be argued that this reference, drawn from the religion of the old world that is rejected in *The Triumph of Agriculture,* cannot be relevant to the new world posited in the poem, but the allusion to the Book of Revelation is unmistakable in the phrases "new sun" and "new grass," and the fact that the soldier himself has a revelation also points to this source. There is nothing incompatible between the rejection of "kulak religion" and allusions to the Bible. The new religion introduced by the soldier superficially shares the aspiration of Christianity to give man immortality, but it envisions different means for realizing this aspiration. Immortality in *The Triumph of Agriculture* is seen in purely material terms. Although this is also the case in Fedorov's philosophy, he still relies on divine inspiration and intervention. *The Triumph of Agriculture* dispenses with that element—mankind saves itself. The soldier's revelation is a vision of the march of History but not a divine revelation.

One of the means of realizing what the vision promises has just been discussed. But technology, transferred from the city to the countryside, is not the whole answer to the problem posed by death. Another answer is to be found in a genuine soil science, which is not only concerned for the improvement of crops, but above all for earth's innermost contents—the dead. As Fedorov puts it, science must deal with the "mold on ancestral graves" and learn how to "extract the ashes of the forefathers" from earth's innermost depths. The agriculture that "triumphs" in *The Triumph of Agriculture* is undoubtedly of this kind; it can locate the "molecules and atoms into which the bodies of the (once) living disintegrate" [Fedorov's phrase]. When "science is applied to agriculture," [according to Fedorov] it is inevitably transformed "into resurrecting," at least when this science is in the hands of loving descendants, concerned for their forefathers. This type of science offers the answer to the bull's lament; there is no need for the bull to envision his imminent disintegration with such horror (although Fedorov does recommend that all graves be properly marked to facilitate the work of resurrectors). Nor does the poor soul have to feel that she will be forgotten forever when the last remnants of her "shrunken breasts" dissolve in earth. They and presumably even the retrograde forefathers, will eventually be redeemed when mankind will know the soil and other elements into which body particles disperse. At that stage of knowledge, the reconstruction of bodies will be a reality. The body is a kind of machine, in Fedorov's view. Once its parts have been reassembled, consciousness unfailingly returns. The "triumph of agriculture" in *The Triumph of Agriculture* is thus essentially the triumph of a necrological science that will master the art of locating body particles for the purpose of reassembling them. It can be argued that nowhere in *The Triumph of Agriculture* is it stated that disintegrated bodies can be reassembled. But scientific reintegration of scattered body tissue is the answer to the questions posed in chapter 1 with its discussion "on the soul" and chapter 2 describing the "sufferings of animals" (and man too is still an animal), including the suffering caused by knowledge of the disintegration death brings. The morbid interest in disintegration phenomena, which permeates *The Triumph of Agriculture,* points to the exponent of "scientific ressurection," Fedorov. There are also other indications of Fedorovian influence, such as the concept of procreation as a "non-progressive" force linked to death, but a discussion of that point would lead far afield. The vision of the "interstellar" people ought to be mentioned once more, however. These people do seem to possess bodies permeated by consciousness down to the last cell, or even atom; they are able to defy the laws of nature (as we know them), their bodies being indestructible. Fedorov believed that once human beings learned to govern all their body processes, making them fully conscious, they would be immortal. They would be "transfigured." It is possible that the interstellar people are collecting "particles" of the deceased in space. Fedorov points out that ancestral particles may scatter into the stratosphere and beyond. Possibly they are resurrected forefathers. These were destined by Fedorov to inhabit the universe. Whoever they are— the resurrected or the resurrectors—immortality is the ultimate goal of mankind; it is the triumph of a series of triumphs begun by the "triumph of agriculture." The animals who are listening to the soldier telling them about the future, understand the full scope of his utopian aspirations, which culminate in the vision of realized immortality. The horse tells the soldier that he has "fantasized enough for a hundred years." But the soldier rejects scepticism and tells the horse to be ashamed of himself. He is offering the animals and peasants of rural Russia a scientific transformation program of the world, which may be vast and time-consuming but is certain to become reality, once it has been begun. The certainty of success fully applies to the transformation of death into immortality. The triumph of agriculture is bound to end with the triumph of immortality over death.

When *The Triumph of Agriculture* ends, this ultimate triumph of life over death has not yet been accomplished. The parting scenes of the village are scenes of labor begun. The new world is still a "babe" when we leave it, but it is a "babe" that is learning not to suck nature dry, but to restore health to it. We see a peaceful community of men, animals, plants, and even minerals, learning to co-exist in an atmosphere of ever-increasing consciousness. Over this village the "sun of rebirth" rises in the morning, and the evenings do not bring darkness and despair, but are light-blue, like forget-me-nots. The last scene of the poem with its light-blue sky and "babes" making music, allows the reader to glimpse an earthly paradise, where man is innocent and will be immortal, as he once was before the Fall.

If *The Triumph of Agriculture* really deals with a scientific quest for immortality and the triumph of human reason over "insane" nature, why has it so persistently been regarded as a satire? Soviet criticism sees the reason for this misunderstanding in the technical deficiences of the poem. An overly naturalistic idiom gives the impression that the poet is parodying what he in fact holds dear, Turkov suggests [in his introductory essay to Zabolotsky's *Stikhotvoreniia i poemy*, 1965]. Grinberg sees in the clash between an optimistic finale and "the hopelessly pessimistic tonality" of the rest of the poem the cause of its apparent parodistic quality [as he stated in *Puti sovetskoi poezii*]. Western criticism tends to see *The Triumph of Agriculture* as a satire because of its "lunatic" quality, which is interpreted as parodistic exaggeration. Furthermore, the knowledge of the sharply negative reception of the poem at home, as well as the poet's subsequent harsh fate, enforced the impression that *The Triumph of Agriculture* is a parody. Why else should there have been such a sharp reaction? The irony is that part of the success of *The Triumph of Agriculture* in the West stems from its assumed satirical quality, whereas its initial failure in the Soviet Union was caused by the inability of the critics to decipher a text that went beyond the canons of socialist realism and therefore was believed to be satire. Although the poem has been "rehabilitated" at home and given full credit for good intentions, it is still not considered a success, as the critical remarks just quoted show.

Was Zabolotsky a convinced Stalinist, then, and a man in harmony with his times? According to Nataliya Roskina [in *Chetyre glavy*, 1980], the poet shunned all political discussions, declaring that he did not understand politics. This declaration was made by a man whose bitter experiences had taught him to be wary of politics. But undoubtedly also the author of *The Triumph of Agriculture* created a non-political poem. *The Triumph of Agriculture* offers a glorification of the Common Task and a collectivization that is seen to be part of it. It is an expression of faith in man's ultimate victory over death. It is not a tribute to Stalin or the Communist Party. Does this non-political quality and the poet's conviction that collectivization serves fraternal relations conducive to the Task "absolve" him from having supported a dubious cause? Does it absolve him from having condoned the elimination of the kulak class, even if he may have envisioned the elimination as being ultimately for "its own good" (resurrection presumably eventually benefiting all)? Similar questions could be asked about many Russian post-revolutionary writers. The answer to these questions depends, perhaps, on subjective moral evaluations. Our present task is to determine whether the author of *The Triumph of Agriculture* supported collectivization or not. The answer is that he did, as the inauguration of the Common Task. Some day, *The Triumph of Agriculture* promises, the dead will be located and reassembled, animals gain full consciousness and men become immortal gods, populating the sky. To Zabolotsky, when he wrote *The Triumph of Agriculture,* collectivization offered the concrete evidence that miracles could come true in a scientific and certain way. (pp. 360-76)

> *Irene Masing-Delic, "Zabolotsky's 'The Triumph of Agriculture': Satire or Utopia?" in* The Russian Review, *Vol. 42, No. 4, October, 1983, pp. 360-76.*

FURTHER READING

Biography

Slonim, Mark. "Posthumous Revivals." In his *Soviet Russian Literature,* rev. ed., pp. 352-62. London: Oxford University Press, 1977.

> Discusses Zabolotsky's literary career and his artistic repression by the Soviet government.

Zabolotsky, Nikolai. "The Story of My Imprisonment," translated by Robin Milner-Gulland. *Times Literary Supplement,* No. 4097 (October 1981): 1179-81.

> Recounts his arrest and experiences as a prisoner of the Soviet government.

Criticism

Björling, Fiona. " 'Ofort' by Nikolaj Zabolockij: The Poem and the Title." *Scando-Slavica* 23 (1977): 7-16.

> Argues that Zabolotsky's poem "Ofort" is a mock heroic challenge to the epic tradition in general and to Leo Tolstoy's poem "Vasilij Šibanov" in particular.

Goldstein, Darra. "Zabolotskii and Filonov: The Science of Composition." *Slavic Review* 48, No. 4 (Winter 1989): 578-91.

> Provides an overview of OBERIU poetics and compares the philosophical and aesthetic visions that inform Zabolotsky's poetry and Pavel Filonov's paintings.

————. " 'Moscow in Fences': Viktor Sosnora at the Gate." *The Russian Review* 51, No. 2 (April 1992): 230-37.

Demonstrates that through the verse "Moscow in Fences," Russian poet Viktor Sosnora is "transmitting to the reader Zabolotskii's experience, and in effect Zabolotskii himself." According to Goldstein, "Moscow in Fences" sharply renders Zabolotskii's "supreme sense of existential confinement."

Karlinsky, Simon. "Surrealism in Twentieth-Century Russian Poetry: Churilin, Zabolotskii, Poplavskii." *Slavic Review* XXVI (Winter 1989): 605-17.

Cites Zabolotsky's use of unpredictably juxtaposed images and burlesquely distorted quotations as examples of Russian appropriation of surrealist poetic techniques.

Masing-Delic, Irene. " 'The Chickens Also Want to Live': A Motif in Zabolockij's *Columns.*" *The Slavic and East European Journal* 31, No. 3 (Fall 1987): 356-69.

Claims that in *Columns* (*Stolbtsy*) Zabolotsky contrasted his own faith in collective human effort with the passive concept of human glory which Fyodor Dostoevsky presented in *Brothers Karamazov.*

Milner-Gulland, Robin R. "Zabolotsky: Philosopher-Poet." *Soviet Studies* XXII, No. 4 (April 1971): 595-608.

Studies influences on Zabolotsky's aesthetics.

————. "Grandsons of Kozma Prutkov: Reflections on Zabolotsky, Oleynikov, and Their Circle." In *Russian and Slavic Literature,* edited by Richard Freeborn, R. R. Milner-Gulland, and Charles A. Ward, pp. 313-27. Cambridge, Mass.: Slavica Publishers, 1976.

Focuses on one of Zabolotsky's contemporaries, the poet Nikolay Oleynikov, partially in an attempt "to explain, or set in context, some of the odder qualities of Zabolotsky's work."

————. "Zabolotsky's 'Vremya'." *Essays in Poetics* 6, No. 1 (April 1981): 86-95.

Finds the poem "Vremya" characteristic of Zabolotsky's middle-period poems because, according to Milner-Gulland, it exhibits tension between his early and later poetic styles.

Pratt, Sarah. " 'Antithesis and Completion': Zabolockij Responds to Tjutčev." *The Slavic and East European Journal* 27, No. 2 (Summer 1983): 211-27.

Contends that Zabolotsky's view of nature as presented in the poem "I Do Not Seek Harmony in Nature" "is at once antithetical to . . . yet seeks to complete the same basic notion" as that which Fyodor Tyutchev presents in "There Is Melodiousness in the Waves of the Sea."

Additional coverage of Zabolotsky's life and career is contained in the following source published by Gale Research: *Contemporary Authors,* **Vol. 116.**

Twentieth-Century Literary Criticism

Cumulative Indexes
Volumes 1-52

How to Use This Index

The main references

> **Calvino, Italo**
> 1923-1985.....CLC 5, 8, 11, 22, 33, 39,
> 73; SSC 3

list all author entries in the following Gale Literary Criticism series:

CLC = *Contemporary Literary Criticism*
CLR = *Children's Literature Review*
CMLC = *Classical and Medieval Literature Criticism*
DC = *Drama Criticism*
LC = *Literature Criticism from 1400 to 1800*
NCLC = *Nineteenth-Century Literature Criticism*
PC = *Poetry Criticism*
SSC = *Short Story Criticism*
TCLC = *Twentieth-Century Literary Criticism*

The cross-references

> See also CANR 23; CA 85-88;
> obituary CA 116

list all author entries in the following Gale biographical and literary sources:

AAYA = *Authors & Artists for Young Adults*
AITN = *Authors in the News*
BLC = *Black Literature Criticism*
BW = *Black Writers*
CA = *Contemporary Authors*
CAAS = *Contemporary Authors Autobiography Series*
CABS = *Contemporary Authors Bibliographical Series*
CANR = *Contemporary Authors New Revision Series*
CAP = *Contemporary Authors Permanent Series*
CDALB = *Concise Dictionary of American Literary Biography*
CDBLB = *Concise Dictionary of British Literary Biography*
DA = *DISCovering Authors*
DLB = *Dictionary of Literary Biography*
DLBD = *Dictionary of Literary Biography Documentary Series*
DLBY = *Dictionary of Literary Biography Yearbook*
HW = *Hispanic Writers*
JRDA = *Junior DISCovering Authors*
MAICYA = *Major Authors and Illustrators for Children and Young Adults*
MTCW = *Major 20th-Century Writers*
SAAS = *Something about the Author Autobiography Series*
SATA = *Something about the Author*
WLC = *World Literature Criticism, 1500 to the Present*
YABC = *Yesterday's Authors of Books for Children*

A.
See Arnold, Matthew

A. E. .... TCLC 3, 10
See also Russell, George William
See also DLB 19

A. M.
See Megged, Aharon

Abasiyanik, Sait Faik 1906-1954
See Sait Faik
See also CA 123

Abbey, Edward 1927-1989 ...... CLC 36, 59
See also CA 45-48; 128; CANR 2, 41

Abbott, Lee K(ittredge) 1947- ...... CLC 48
See also CA 124; DLB 130

Abe, Kobo 1924-1993 .... CLC 8, 22, 53
See also CA 65-68; 140; CANR 24; MTCW

Abelard, Peter c. 1079-c. 1142 ... CMLC 11
See also DLB 115

Abell, Kjeld 1901-1961............ CLC 15
See also CA 111

Abish, Walter 1931- .... CLC 22
See also CA 101; CANR 37; DLB 130

Abrahams, Peter (Henry) 1919- ..... CLC 4
See also BW; CA 57-60; CANR 26;
DLB 117; MTCW

Abrams, M(eyer) H(oward) 1912-... CLC 24
See also CA 57-60; CANR 13, 33; DLB 67

Abse, Dannie 1923-............. CLC 7, 29
See also CA 53-56; CAAS 1; CANR 4;
DLB 27

Achebe, (Albert) Chinua(lumogu)
1930- ..... CLC 1, 3, 5, 7, 11, 26, 51, 75
See also BLC 1; BW; CA 1-4R; CANR 6,
26; CLR 20; DA; DLB 117; MAICYA;
MTCW; SATA 38, 40; WLC

Acker, Kathy 1948- .... CLC 45
See also CA 117; 122

Ackroyd, Peter 1949-.......... CLC 34, 52
See also CA 123; 127

Acorn, Milton 1923-.............. CLC 15
See also CA 103; DLB 53

Adamov, Arthur 1908-1970 ...... CLC 4, 25
See also CA 17-18; 25-28R; CAP 2; MTCW

Adams, Alice (Boyd) 1926- ... CLC 6, 13, 46
See also CA 81-84; CANR 26; DLBY 86;
MTCW

Adams, Douglas (Noel) 1952- ... CLC 27, 60
See also AAYA 4; BEST 89:3; CA 106;
CANR 34; DLBY 83; JRDA

Adams, Francis 1862-1893....... NCLC 33

Adams, Henry (Brooks)
1838-1918 .... TCLC 4, 52
See also CA 104; 133; DA; DLB 12, 47

Adams, Richard (George)
1920- .... CLC 4, 5, 18
See also AITN 1, 2; CA 49-52; CANR 3,
35; CLR 20; JRDA; MAICYA; MTCW;
SATA 7, 69

Adamson, Joy(-Friederike Victoria)
1910-1980 .... CLC 17
See also CA 69-72; 93-96; CANR 22;
MTCW; SATA 11, 22

Adcock, Fleur 1934-............. CLC 41
See also CA 25-28R; CANR 11, 34;
DLB 40

Addams, Charles (Samuel)
1912-1988 .... CLC 30
See also CA 61-64; 126; CANR 12

Addison, Joseph 1672-1719 .... LC 18
See also CDBLB 1660-1789; DLB 101

Adler, C(arole) S(chwerdtfeger)
1932-...................... CLC 35
See also AAYA 4; CA 89-92; CANR 19,
40; JRDA; MAICYA; SAAS 15;
SATA 26, 63

Adler, Renata 1938-............ CLC 8, 31
See also CA 49-52; CANR 5, 22; MTCW

Ady, Endre 1877-1919 .... TCLC 11
See also CA 107

Aeschylus 525B.C.-456B.C....... CMLC 11
See also DA

Afton, Effie
See Harper, Frances Ellen Watkins

Agapida, Fray Antonio
See Irving, Washington

Agee, James (Rufus)
1909-1955 .... TCLC 1, 19
See also AITN 1; CA 108;
CDALB 1941-1968; DLB 2, 26

A Gentlewoman in New England
See Bradstreet, Anne

A Gentlewoman in Those Parts
See Bradstreet, Anne

Aghill, Gordon
See Silverberg, Robert

Agnon, S(hmuel) Y(osef Halevi)
1888-1970 .... CLC 4, 8, 14
See also CA 17-18; 25-28R; CAP 2; MTCW

Aherne, Owen
See Cassill, R(onald) V(erlin)

Ai 1947-.................. CLC 4, 14, 69
See also CA 85-88; CAAS 13; DLB 120

Aickman, Robert (Fordyce)
1914-1981 .... CLC 57
See also CA 5-8R; CANR 3

Aiken, Conrad (Potter)
1889-1973 ... CLC 1, 3, 5, 10, 52; SSC 9
See also CA 5-8R; 45-48; CANR 4;
CDALB 1929-1941; DLB 9, 45, 102;
MTCW; SATA 3, 30

Aiken, Joan (Delano) 1924-........ CLC 35
See also AAYA 1; CA 9-12R; CANR 4, 23,
34; CLR 1, 19; JRDA; MAICYA;
MTCW; SAAS 1; SATA 2, 30, 73

Ainsworth, William Harrison
1805-1882 .... NCLC 13
See also DLB 21; SATA 24

Aitmatov, Chingiz (Torekulovich)
1928- .... CLC 71
See also CA 103; CANR 38; MTCW;
SATA 56

Akers, Floyd
See Baum, L(yman) Frank

Akhmadulina, Bella Akhatovna
1937-...................... CLC 53
See also CA 65-68

Akhmatova, Anna
1888-1966 .... CLC 11, 25, 64; PC 2
See also CA 19-20; 25-28R; CANR 35;
CAP 1; MTCW

Aksakov, Sergei Timofeyvich
1791-1859 .... NCLC 2

Aksenov, Vassily .... CLC 22
See also Aksyonov, Vassily (Pavlovich)

Aksyonov, Vassily (Pavlovich)
1932-...................... CLC 37
See also Aksenov, Vassily
See also CA 53-56; CANR 12

Akutagawa Ryunosuke
1892-1927 .... TCLC 16
See also CA 117

Alain 1868-1951 .... TCLC 41

Alain-Fournier.................... TCLC 6
See also Fournier, Henri Alban
See also DLB 65

Alarcon, Pedro Antonio de
1833-1891 .... NCLC 1

Alas (y Urena), Leopoldo (Enrique Garcia)
1852-1901 .... TCLC 29
See also CA 113; 131; HW

Albee, Edward (Franklin III)
1928- ... CLC 1, 2, 3, 5, 9, 11, 13, 25, 53
See also AITN 1; CA 5-8R; CABS 3;
CANR 8; CDALB 1941-1968; DA;
DLB 7; MTCW; WLC

Alberti, Rafael 1902- .... CLC 7
See also CA 85-88; DLB 108

Alcala-Galiano, Juan Valera y
See Valera y Alcala-Galiano, Juan

Alcott, Amos Bronson 1799-1888 .. NCLC 1
See also DLB 1

Alcott, Louisa May 1832-1888 .... NCLC 6
See also CDALB 1865-1917; CLR 1; DA;
DLB 1, 42, 79; JRDA; MAICYA; WLC;
YABC 1

Aldanov, M. A.
See Aldanov, Mark (Alexandrovich)

Aldanov, Mark (Alexandrovich)
1886(?)-1957 . . . . TCLC 23
See also CA 118

Aldington, Richard 1892-1962 . . . . . . CLC 49
See also CA 85-88; DLB 20, 36, 100

Aldiss, Brian W(ilson)
1925- . . . . CLC 5, 14, 40
See also CA 5-8R; CAAS 2; CANR 5, 28;
DLB 14; MTCW; SATA 34

Alegria, Claribel 1924- . . . . CLC 75
See also CA 131; CAAS 15; HW

Alegria, Fernando 1918- . . . . CLC 57
See also CA 9-12R; CANR 5, 32; HW

Aleichem, Sholom . . . . TCLC 1, 35
See also Rabinovitch, Sholem

Aleixandre, Vicente 1898-1984 . . . CLC 9, 36
See also CA 85-88; 114; CANR 26;
DLB 108; HW; MTCW

Alepoudelis, Odysseus
See Elytis, Odysseus

Aleshkovsky, Joseph 1929-
See Aleshkovsky, Yuz
See also CA 121; 128

Aleshkovsky, Yuz . . . . CLC 44
See also Aleshkovsky, Joseph

Alexander, Lloyd (Chudley) 1924- . . CLC 35
See also AAYA 1; CA 1-4R; CANR 1, 24,
38; CLR 1, 5; DLB 52; JRDA; MAICYA;
MTCW; SATA 3, 49

Alfau, Felipe 1902- . . . . CLC 66
See also CA 137

Alger, Horatio, Jr. 1832-1899 . . . . . NCLC 8
See also DLB 42; SATA 16

Algren, Nelson 1909-1981 . . . . CLC 4, 10, 33
See also CA 13-16R; 103; CANR 20;
CDALB 1941-1968; DLB 9; DLBY 81,
82; MTCW

Ali, Ahmed 1910- . . . . CLC 69
See also CA 25-28R; CANR 15, 34

Alighieri, Dante 1265-1321 . . . . CMLC 3

Allan, John B.
See Westlake, Donald E(dwin)

Allen, Edward 1948- . . . . CLC 59

Allen, Roland
See Ayckbourn, Alan

Allen, Woody 1935- . . . . CLC 16, 52
See also AAYA 10; CA 33-36R; CANR 27,
38; DLB 44; MTCW

Allende, Isabel 1942- . . . . CLC 39, 57
See also CA 125; 130; HW; MTCW

Alleyn, Ellen
See Rossetti, Christina (Georgina)

Allingham, Margery (Louise)
1904-1966 . . . . CLC 19
See also CA 5-8R; 25-28R; CANR 4;
DLB 77; MTCW

Allingham, William 1824-1889 . . . NCLC 25
See also DLB 35

Allison, Dorothy 1948- . . . . CLC 78

Allston, Washington 1779-1843 . . . . NCLC 2
See also DLB 1

Almedingen, E. M. . . . . CLC 12
See also Almedingen, Martha Edith von
See also SATA 3

Almedingen, Martha Edith von 1898-1971
See Almedingen, E. M.
See also CA 1-4R; CANR 1

Almqvist, Carl Jonas Love
1793-1866 . . . . NCLC 42

Alonso, Damaso 1898-1990 . . . . CLC 14
See also CA 110; 131; 130; DLB 108; HW

Alov
See Gogol, Nikolai (Vasilyevich)

Alta 1942- . . . . CLC 19
See also CA 57-60

Alter, Robert B(ernard) 1935- . . . . . . CLC 34
See also CA 49-52; CANR 1

Alther, Lisa 1944- . . . . CLC 7, 41
See also CA 65-68; CANR 12, 30; MTCW

Altman, Robert 1925- . . . . CLC 16
See also CA 73-76

Alvarez, A(lfred) 1929- . . . . CLC 5, 13
See also CA 1-4R; CANR 3, 33; DLB 14,
40

Alvarez, Alejandro Rodriguez 1903-1965
See Casona, Alejandro
See also CA 131; 93-96; HW

Amado, Jorge 1912- . . . . CLC 13, 40
See also CA 77-80; CANR 35; DLB 113;
MTCW

Ambler, Eric 1909- . . . . CLC 4, 6, 9
See also CA 9-12R; CANR 7, 38; DLB 77;
MTCW

Amichai, Yehuda 1924- . . . . . . CLC 9, 22, 57
See also CA 85-88; MTCW

Amiel, Henri Frederic 1821-1881 . . NCLC 4

Amis, Kingsley (William)
1922- . . . . . . CLC 1, 2, 3, 5, 8, 13, 40, 44
See also AITN 2; CA 9-12R; CANR 8, 28;
CDBLB 1945-1960; DA; DLB 15, 27,
100; MTCW

Amis, Martin (Louis)
1949- . . . . CLC 4, 9, 38, 62
See also BEST 90:3; CA 65-68; CANR 8,
27; DLB 14

Ammons, A(rchie) R(andolph)
1926- . . . . CLC 2, 3, 5, 8, 9, 25, 57
See also AITN 1; CA 9-12R; CANR 6, 36;
DLB 5; MTCW

Amo, Tauraatua i
See Adams, Henry (Brooks)

Anand, Mulk Raj 1905- . . . . CLC 23
See also CA 65-68; CANR 32; MTCW

Anatol
See Schnitzler, Arthur

Anaya, Rudolfo A(lfonso) 1937- . . . . CLC 23
See also CA 45-48; CAAS 4; CANR 1, 32;
DLB 82; HW; MTCW

Andersen, Hans Christian
1805-1875 . . . . NCLC 7; SSC 6
See also CLR 6; DA; MAICYA; WLC;
YABC 1

Anderson, C. Farley
See Mencken, H(enry) L(ouis); Nathan,
George Jean

Anderson, Jessica (Margaret) Queale
. . . . CLC 37
See also CA 9-12R; CANR 4

Anderson, Jon (Victor) 1940- . . . . CLC 9
See also CA 25-28R; CANR 20

Anderson, Lindsay (Gordon)
1923- . . . . CLC 20
See also CA 125; 128

Anderson, Maxwell 1888-1959 . . . . . TCLC 2
See also CA 105; DLB 7

Anderson, Poul (William) 1926- . . . . CLC 15
See also AAYA 5; CA 1-4R; CAAS 2;
CANR 2, 15, 34; DLB 8; MTCW;
SATA 39

Anderson, Robert (Woodruff)
1917- . . . . CLC 23
See also AITN 1; CA 21-24R; CANR 32;
DLB 7

Anderson, Sherwood
1876-1941 . . . . . . TCLC 1, 10, 24; SSC 1
See also CA 104; 121; CDALB 1917-1929;
DA; DLB 4, 9, 86; DLBD 1; MTCW;
WLC

Andouard
See Giraudoux, (Hippolyte) Jean

Andrade, Carlos Drummond de . . . . . . CLC 18
See also Drummond de Andrade, Carlos

Andrade, Mario de 1893-1945 . . . . . TCLC 43

Andrewes, Lancelot 1555-1626 . . . . LC 5

Andrews, Cicily Fairfield
See West, Rebecca

Andrews, Elton V.
See Pohl, Frederik

Andreyev, Leonid (Nikolaevich)
1871-1919 . . . . TCLC 3
See also CA 104

Andric, Ivo 1892-1975 . . . . CLC 8
See also CA 81-84; 57-60; MTCW

Angelique, Pierre
See Bataille, Georges

Angell, Roger 1920- . . . . CLC 26
See also CA 57-60; CANR 13

Angelou, Maya 1928- . . . . CLC 12, 35, 64, 77
See also AAYA 7; BLC 1; BW; CA 65-68;
CANR 19, 42; DA; DLB 38; MTCW;
SATA 49

Annensky, Innokenty Fyodorovich
1856-1909 . . . . TCLC 14
See also CA 110

Anon, Charles Robert
See Pessoa, Fernando (Antonio Nogueira)

Anouilh, Jean (Marie Lucien Pierre)
1910-1987 . . . . . . CLC 1, 3, 8, 13, 40, 50
See also CA 17-20R; 123; CANR 32;
MTCW

Anthony, Florence
See Ai

Anthony, John
See Ciardi, John (Anthony)

Anthony, Peter
See Shaffer, Anthony (Joshua); Shaffer,
Peter (Levin)

Anthony, Piers 1934- . . . . CLC 35
See also CA 21-24R; CANR 28; DLB 8;
MTCW

Antoine, Marc
See Proust, (Valentin-Louis-George-Eugene-) Marcel

Antoninus, Brother
See Everson, William (Oliver)

Antonioni, Michelangelo 1912- ..... **CLC 20**
See also CA 73-76

Antschel, Paul 1920-1970. ...... **CLC 10, 19**
See also Celan, Paul
See also CA 85-88; CANR 33; MTCW

Anwar, Chairil 1922-1949 .... **TCLC 22**
See also CA 121

Apollinaire, Guillaume .. **TCLC 3, 8, 51; PC 7**
See also Kostrowitzki, Wilhelm Apollinaris de

Appelfeld, Aharon 1932- .... **CLC 23, 47**
See also CA 112; 133

Apple, Max (Isaac) 1941-........ **CLC 9, 33**
See also CA 81-84; CANR 19; DLB 130

Appleman, Philip (Dean) 1926- ..... **CLC 51**
See also CA 13-16R; CAAS 18; CANR 6, 29

Appleton, Lawrence
See Lovecraft, H(oward) P(hillips)

Apteryx
See Eliot, T(homas) S(tearns)

Apuleius, (Lucius Madaurensis)
125(?)-175(?) .... **CMLC 1**

Aquin, Hubert 1929-1977. .... **CLC 15**
See also CA 105; DLB 53

Aragon, Louis 1897-1982. .... **CLC 3, 22**
See also CA 69-72; 108; CANR 28; DLB 72; MTCW

Arany, Janos 1817-1882. .... **NCLC 34**

Arbuthnot, John 1667-1735 .... **LC 1**
See also DLB 101

Archer, Herbert Winslow
See Mencken, H(enry) L(ouis)

Archer, Jeffrey (Howard) 1940- .... **CLC 28**
See also BEST 89:3; CA 77-80; CANR 22

Archer, Jules 1915- .... **CLC 12**
See also CA 9-12R; CANR 6; SAAS 5; SATA 4

Archer, Lee
See Ellison, Harlan

Arden, John 1930- .... **CLC 6, 13, 15**
See also CA 13-16R; CAAS 4; CANR 31; DLB 13; MTCW

Arenas, Reinaldo 1943-1990 .... **CLC 41**
See also CA 124; 128; 133; HW

Arendt, Hannah 1906-1975 .... **CLC 66**
See also CA 17-20R; 61-64; CANR 26; MTCW

Aretino, Pietro 1492-1556 .... **LC 12**

Arguedas, Jose Maria
1911-1969 .... **CLC 10, 18**
See also CA 89-92; DLB 113; HW

Argueta, Manlio 1936-............ **CLC 31**
See also CA 131; HW

Ariosto, Ludovico 1474-1533. .... **LC 6**

Aristides
See Epstein, Joseph

Aristophanes
450B.C.-385B.C........ **CMLC 4; DC 2**
See also DA

Arlt, Roberto (Godofredo Christophersen)
1900-1942 .... **TCLC 29**
See also CA 123; 131; HW

Armah, Ayi Kwei 1939-......... **CLC 5, 33**
See also BLC 1; BW; CA 61-64; CANR 21; DLB 117; MTCW

Armatrading, Joan 1950-.......... **CLC 17**
See also CA 114

Arnette, Robert
See Silverberg, Robert

Arnim, Achim von (Ludwig Joachim von Arnim) 1781-1831 .... **NCLC 5**
See also DLB 90

Arnim, Bettina von 1785-1859.... **NCLC 38**
See also DLB 90

Arnold, Matthew
1822-1888 .... **NCLC 6, 29; PC 5**
See also CDBLB 1832-1890; DA; DLB 32, 57; WLC

Arnold, Thomas 1795-1842 ...... **NCLC 18**
See also DLB 55

Arnow, Harriette (Louisa) Simpson
1908-1986 .... **CLC 2, 7, 18**
See also CA 9-12R; 118; CANR 14; DLB 6; MTCW; SATA 42, 47

Arp, Hans
See Arp, Jean

Arp, Jean 1887-1966. .... **CLC 5**
See also CA 81-84; 25-28R; CANR 42

Arrabal
See Arrabal, Fernando

Arrabal, Fernando 1932- ... **CLC 2, 9, 18, 58**
See also CA 9-12R; CANR 15

Arrick, Fran..................... **CLC 30**

Artaud, Antonin 1896-1948 ..... **TCLC 3, 36**
See also CA 104

Arthur, Ruth M(abel) 1905-1979.... **CLC 12**
See also CA 9-12R; 85-88; CANR 4; SATA 7, 26

Artsybashev, Mikhail (Petrovich)
1878-1927 .... **TCLC 31**

Arundel, Honor (Morfydd)
1919-1973 .... **CLC 17**
See also CA 21-22; 41-44R; CAP 2; SATA 4, 24

Asch, Sholem 1880-1957 .... **TCLC 3**
See also CA 105

Ash, Shalom
See Asch, Sholem

Ashbery, John (Lawrence)
1927- ...... **CLC 2, 3, 4, 6, 9, 13, 15, 25, 41, 77**
See also CA 5-8R; CANR 9, 37; DLB 5; DLBY 81; MTCW

Ashdown, Clifford
See Freeman, R(ichard) Austin

Ashe, Gordon
See Creasey, John

Ashton-Warner, Sylvia (Constance)
1908-1984 .... **CLC 19**
See also CA 69-72; 112; CANR 29; MTCW

Asimov, Isaac
1920-1992 ...... **CLC 1, 3, 9, 19, 26, 76**
See also BEST 90:2; CA 1-4R; 137; CANR 2, 19, 36; CLR 12; DLB 8; DLBY 92; JRDA; MAICYA; MTCW; SATA 1, 26, 74

Astley, Thea (Beatrice May)
1925- .... **CLC 41**
See also CA 65-68; CANR 11

Aston, James
See White, T(erence) H(anbury)

Asturias, Miguel Angel
1899-1974 .... **CLC 3, 8, 13**
See also CA 25-28; 49-52; CANR 32; CAP 2; DLB 113; HW; MTCW

Atares, Carlos Saura
See Saura (Atares), Carlos

Atheling, William
See Pound, Ezra (Weston Loomis)

Atheling, William, Jr.
See Blish, James (Benjamin)

Atherton, Gertrude (Franklin Horn)
1857-1948 .... **TCLC 2**
See also CA 104; DLB 9, 78

Atherton, Lucius
See Masters, Edgar Lee

Atkins, Jack
See Harris, Mark

Atticus
See Fleming, Ian (Lancaster)

Atwood, Margaret (Eleanor)
1939- ..... **CLC 2, 3, 4, 8, 13, 15, 25, 44; SSC 2**
See also BEST 89:2; CA 49-52; CANR 3, 24, 33; DA; DLB 53; MTCW; SATA 50; WLC

Aubigny, Pierre d'
See Mencken, H(enry) L(ouis)

Aubin, Penelope 1685-1731(?)........ **LC 9**
See also DLB 39

Auchincloss, Louis (Stanton)
1917- .... **CLC 4, 6, 9, 18, 45**
See also CA 1-4R; CANR 6, 29; DLB 2; DLBY 80; MTCW

Auden, W(ystan) H(ugh)
1907-1973 ...... **CLC 1, 2, 3, 4, 6, 9, 11, 14, 43; PC 1**
See also CA 9-12R; 45-48; CANR 5; CDBLB 1914-1945; DA; DLB 10, 20; MTCW; WLC

Audiberti, Jacques 1900-1965 ...... **CLC 38**
See also CA 25-28R

Auel, Jean M(arie) 1936-.......... **CLC 31**
See also AAYA 7; BEST 90:4; CA 103; CANR 21

Auerbach, Erich 1892-1957 .... **TCLC 43**
See also CA 118

Augier, Emile 1820-1889 .... **NCLC 31**

August, John
See De Voto, Bernard (Augustine)

Augustine, St. 354-430. .... **CMLC 6**

Aurelius
See Bourne, Randolph S(illiman)

Austen, Jane
1775-1817 .... **NCLC 1, 13, 19, 33**
See also CDBLB 1789-1832; DA; DLB 116;
WLC

Auster, Paul 1947- .... **CLC 47**
See also CA 69-72; CANR 23

Austin, Frank
See Faust, Frederick (Schiller)

Austin, Mary (Hunter)
1868-1934 .... **TCLC 25**
See also CA 109; DLB 9, 78

Autran Dourado, Waldomiro
See Dourado, (Waldomiro Freitas) Autran

Averroes 1126-1198 .... **CMLC 7**
See also DLB 115

Avison, Margaret 1918- .... **CLC 2, 4**
See also CA 17-20R; DLB 53; MTCW

Axton, David
See Koontz, Dean R(ay)

Ayckbourn, Alan
1939- .... **CLC 5, 8, 18, 33, 74**
See also CA 21-24R; CANR 31; DLB 13;
MTCW

Aydy, Catherine
See Tennant, Emma (Christina)

Ayme, Marcel (Andre) 1902-1967... **CLC 11**
See also CA 89-92; CLR 25; DLB 72

Ayrton, Michael 1921-1975 .... **CLC 7**
See also CA 5-8R; 61-64; CANR 9, 21

Azorin........................... **CLC 11**
See also Martinez Ruiz, Jose

Azuela, Mariano 1873-1952........ **TCLC 3**
See also CA 104; 131; HW; MTCW

Baastad, Babbis Friis
See Friis-Baastad, Babbis Ellinor

Bab
See Gilbert, W(illiam) S(chwenck)

Babbis, Eleanor
See Friis-Baastad, Babbis Ellinor

Babel, Isaak (Emmanuilovich)
1894-1941(?) .... **CLC 73**
See also CA 104; TCLC 2, 13

Babits, Mihaly 1883-1941 .... **TCLC 14**
See also CA 114

Babur 1483-1530................. **LC 18**

Bacchelli, Riccardo 1891-1985 ..... **CLC 19**
See also CA 29-32R; 117

Bach, Richard (David) 1936-....... **CLC 14**
See also AITN 1; BEST 89:2; CA 9-12R;
CANR 18; MTCW; SATA 13

Bachman, Richard
See King, Stephen (Edwin)

Bachmann, Ingeborg 1926-1973..... **CLC 69**
See also CA 93-96; 45-48; DLB 85

Bacon, Francis 1561-1626 .... **LC 18**
See also CDBLB Before 1660

Bacovia, George................. **TCLC 24**
See also Vasiliu, Gheorghe

Badanes, Jerome 1937-............ **CLC 59**

Bagehot, Walter 1826-1877 ...... **NCLC 10**
See also DLB 55

Bagnold, Enid 1889-1981 .... **CLC 25**
See also CA 5-8R; 103; CANR 5, 40;
DLB 13; MAICYA; SATA 1, 25

Bagrjana, Elisaveta
See Belcheva, Elisaveta

Bagryana, Elisaveta
See Belcheva, Elisaveta

Bailey, Paul 1937- .... **CLC 45**
See also CA 21-24R; CANR 16; DLB 14

Baillie, Joanna 1762-1851 .... **NCLC 2**
See also DLB 93

Bainbridge, Beryl (Margaret)
1933- .... **CLC 4, 5, 8, 10, 14, 18, 22, 62**
See also CA 21-24R; CANR 24; DLB 14;
MTCW

Baker, Elliott 1922- .... **CLC 8**
See also CA 45-48; CANR 2

Baker, Nicholson 1957- .... **CLC 61**
See also CA 135

Baker, Ray Stannard 1870-1946... **TCLC 47**
See also CA 118

Baker, Russell (Wayne) 1925-...... **CLC 31**
See also BEST 89:4; CA 57-60; CANR 11,
41; MTCW

Bakshi, Ralph 1938(?)-............ **CLC 26**
See also CA 112; 138

Bakunin, Mikhail (Alexandrovich)
1814-1876 .... **NCLC 25**

Baldwin, James (Arthur)
1924-1987 ...... **CLC 1, 2, 3, 4, 5, 8, 13,
15, 17, 42, 50, 67; DC 1; SSC 10**
See also AAYA 4; BLC 1; BW; CA 1-4R;
124; CABS 1; CANR 3, 24;
CDALB 1941-1968; DA; DLB 2, 7, 33;
DLBY 87; MTCW; SATA 9, 54; WLC

Ballard, J(ames) G(raham)
1930- .... **CLC 3, 6, 14, 36; SSC 1**
See also AAYA 3; CA 5-8R; CANR 15, 39;
DLB 14; MTCW

Balmont, Konstantin (Dmitriyevich)
1867-1943 .... **TCLC 11**
See also CA 109

Balzac, Honore de
1799-1850 .... **NCLC 5, 35; SSC 5**
See also DA; DLB 119; WLC

Bambara, Toni Cade 1939- .... **CLC 19**
See also AAYA 5; BLC 1; BW; CA 29-32R;
CANR 24; DA; DLB 38; MTCW

Bamdad, A.
See Shamlu, Ahmad

Banat, D. R.
See Bradbury, Ray (Douglas)

Bancroft, Laura
See Baum, L(yman) Frank

Banim, John 1798-1842 .... **NCLC 13**
See also DLB 116

Banim, Michael 1796-1874 ...... **NCLC 13**

Banks, Iain
See Banks, Iain M(enzies)

Banks, Iain M(enzies) 1954- .... **CLC 34**
See also CA 123; 128

Banks, Lynne Reid .... **CLC 23**
See also Reid Banks, Lynne
See also AAYA 6

Banks, Russell 1940- .... **CLC 37, 72**
See also CA 65-68; CAAS 15; CANR 19;
DLB 130

Banville, John 1945-.............. **CLC 46**
See also CA 117; 128; DLB 14

Banville, Theodore (Faullain) de
1832-1891 .... **NCLC 9**

Baraka, Amiri
1934- ... **CLC 1, 2, 3, 5, 10, 14, 33; PC 4**
See also Jones, LeRoi
See also BLC 1; BW; CA 21-24R; CABS 3;
CANR 27, 38; CDALB 1941-1968; DA;
DLB 5, 7, 16, 38; DLBD 8; MTCW

Barbellion, W. N. P................ **TCLC 24**
See also Cummings, Bruce F(rederick)

Barbera, Jack 1945-.............. **CLC 44**
See also CA 110

Barbey d'Aurevilly, Jules Amedee
1808-1889 .... **NCLC 1**
See also DLB 119

Barbusse, Henri 1873-1935 .... **TCLC 5**
See also CA 105; DLB 65

Barclay, Bill
See Moorcock, Michael (John)

Barclay, William Ewert
See Moorcock, Michael (John)

Barea, Arturo 1897-1957 .... **TCLC 14**
See also CA 111

Barfoot, Joan 1946- .... **CLC 18**
See also CA 105

Baring, Maurice 1874-1945 .... **TCLC 8**
See also CA 105; DLB 34

Barker, Clive 1952- .... **CLC 52**
See also AAYA 10; BEST 90:3; CA 121;
129; MTCW

Barker, George Granville
1913-1991 .... **CLC 8, 48**
See also CA 9-12R; 135; CANR 7, 38;
DLB 20; MTCW

Barker, Harley Granville
See Granville-Barker, Harley
See also DLB 10

Barker, Howard 1946-............. **CLC 37**
See also CA 102; DLB 13

Barker, Pat 1943-................. **CLC 32**
See also CA 117; 122

Barlow, Joel 1754-1812 .... **NCLC 23**
See also DLB 37

Barnard, Mary (Ethel) 1909-....... **CLC 48**
See also CA 21-22; CAP 2

Barnes, Djuna
1892-1982 ... **CLC 3, 4, 8, 11, 29; SSC 3**
See also CA 9-12R; 107; CANR 16; DLB 4,
9, 45; MTCW

Barnes, Julian 1946-.............. **CLC 42**
See also CA 102; CANR 19

Barnes, Peter 1931- .... **CLC 5, 56**
See also CA 65-68; CAAS 12; CANR 33,
34; DLB 13; MTCW

Baroja (y Nessi), Pio 1872-1956 .... **TCLC 8**
See also CA 104

Baron, David
See Pinter, Harold

Baron Corvo
　See Rolfe, Frederick (William Serafino
　　Austin Lewis Mary)

Barondess, Sue K(aufman)
　1926-1977 . . . . CLC 8
　See also Kaufman, Sue
　See also CA 1-4R; 69-72; CANR 1

Baron de Teive
　See Pessoa, Fernando (Antonio Nogueira)

Barres, Maurice 1862-1923 . . . . TCLC 47
　See also DLB 123

Barreto, Afonso Henrique de Lima
　See Lima Barreto, Afonso Henrique de

Barrett, (Roger) Syd 1946- . . . . CLC 35
　See also Pink Floyd

Barrett, William (Christopher)
　1913-1992 . . . . CLC 27
　See also CA 13-16R; 139; CANR 11

Barrie, J(ames) M(atthew)
　1860-1937 . . . . TCLC 2
　See also CA 104; 136; CDBLB 1890-1914;
　　CLR 16; DLB 10; MAICYA; YABC 1

Barrington, Michael
　See Moorcock, Michael (John)

Barrol, Grady
　See Bograd, Larry

Barry, Mike
　See Malzberg, Barry N(athaniel)

Barry, Philip 1896-1949 . . . . TCLC 11
　See also CA 109; DLB 7

Bart, Andre Schwarz
　See Schwarz-Bart, Andre

Barth, John (Simmons)
　1930- . . . . . . CLC 1, 2, 3, 5, 7, 9, 10, 14,
　　　　　　　　　　　　　27, 51; SSC 10
　See also AITN 1, 2; CA 1-4R; CABS 1;
　　CANR 5, 23; DLB 2; MTCW

Barthelme, Donald
　1931-1989 . . . . . . CLC 1, 2, 3, 5, 6, 8, 13,
　　　　　　　　　　　　23, 46, 59; SSC 2
　See also CA 21-24R; 129; CANR 20;
　　DLB 2; DLBY 80, 89; MTCW; SATA 7,
　　62

Barthelme, Frederick 1943- . . . . CLC 36
　See also CA 114; 122; DLBY 85

Barthes, Roland (Gerard)
　1915-1980 . . . . CLC 24
　See also CA 130; 97-100; MTCW

Barzun, Jacques (Martin) 1907- . . . . CLC 51
　See also CA 61-64; CANR 22

Bashevis, Isaac
　See Singer, Isaac Bashevis

Bashkirtseff, Marie 1859-1884 . . . NCLC 27

Basho
　See Matsuo Basho

Bass, Kingsley B., Jr.
　See Bullins, Ed

Bass, Rick 1958- . . . . CLC 79
　See also CA 126

Bassani, Giorgio 1916- . . . . CLC 9
　See also CA 65-68; CANR 33; DLB 128;
　　MTCW

Bastos, Augusto (Antonio) Roa
　See Roa Bastos, Augusto (Antonio)

Bataille, Georges 1897-1962 . . . . . . CLC 29
　See also CA 101; 89-92

Bates, H(erbert) E(rnest)
　1905-1974 . . . . CLC 46; SSC 10
　See also CA 93-96; 45-48; CANR 34;
　　MTCW

Bauchart
　See Camus, Albert

Baudelaire, Charles
　1821-1867 . . . . NCLC 6, 29; PC 1
　See also DA; WLC

Baudrillard, Jean 1929- . . . . CLC 60

Baum, L(yman) Frank 1856-1919 . . . TCLC 7
　See also CA 108; 133; CLR 15; DLB 22;
　　JRDA; MAICYA; MTCW; SATA 18

Baum, Louis F.
　See Baum, L(yman) Frank

Baumbach, Jonathan 1933- . . . . . . CLC 6, 23
　See also CA 13-16R; CAAS 5; CANR 12;
　　DLBY 80; MTCW

Bausch, Richard (Carl) 1945- . . . . . . CLC 51
　See also CA 101; CAAS 14; DLB 130

Baxter, Charles 1947- . . . . CLC 45, 78
　See also CA 57-60; CANR 40; DLB 130

Baxter, George Owen
　See Faust, Frederick (Schiller)

Baxter, James K(eir) 1926-1972 . . . . CLC 14
　See also CA 77-80

Baxter, John
　See Hunt, E(verette) Howard, Jr.

Bayer, Sylvia
　See Glassco, John

Beagle, Peter S(oyer) 1939- . . . . CLC 7
　See also CA 9-12R; CANR 4; DLBY 80;
　　SATA 60

Bean, Normal
　See Burroughs, Edgar Rice

Beard, Charles A(ustin)
　1874-1948 . . . . TCLC 15
　See also CA 115; DLB 17; SATA 18

Beardsley, Aubrey 1872-1898 . . . . . NCLC 6

Beattie, Ann
　1947- . . . . CLC 8, 13, 18, 40, 63; SSC 11
　See also BEST 90:2; CA 81-84; DLBY 82;
　　MTCW

Beattie, James 1735-1803 . . . . NCLC 25
　See also DLB 109

Beauchamp, Kathleen Mansfield 1888-1923
　See Mansfield, Katherine
　See also CA 104; 134; DA

**Beauvoir, Simone (Lucie Ernestine Marie
　Bertrand) de**
　1908-1986 . . . . CLC 1, 2, 4, 8, 14, 31, 44,
　　　　　　　　　　　　　　50, 71
　See also CA 9-12R; 118; CANR 28; DA;
　　DLB 72; DLBY 86; MTCW; WLC

Becker, Jurek 1937- . . . . CLC 7, 19
　See also CA 85-88; DLB 75

Becker, Walter 1950- . . . . CLC 26

Beckett, Samuel (Barclay)
　1906-1989 . . . . . . CLC 1, 2, 3, 4, 6, 9, 10,
　　　　　　　　　11, 14, 18, 29, 57, 59
　See also CA 5-8R; 130; CANR 33;
　　CDBLB 1945-1960; DA; DLB 13, 15;
　　DLBY 90; MTCW; WLC

Beckford, William 1760-1844 . . . . NCLC 16
　See also DLB 39

Beckman, Gunnel 1910- . . . . CLC 26
　See also CA 33-36R; CANR 15; CLR 25;
　　MAICYA; SAAS 9; SATA 6

Becque, Henri 1837-1899 . . . . NCLC 3

Beddoes, Thomas Lovell
　1803-1849 . . . . NCLC 3
　See also DLB 96

Bedford, Donald F.
　See Fearing, Kenneth (Flexner)

Beecher, Catharine Esther
　1800-1878 . . . . NCLC 30
　See also DLB 1

Beecher, John 1904-1980 . . . . CLC 6
　See also AITN 1; CA 5-8R; 105; CANR 8

Beer, Johann 1655-1700 . . . . LC 5

Beer, Patricia 1924- . . . . CLC 58
　See also CA 61-64; CANR 13; DLB 40

Beerbohm, Henry Maximilian
　1872-1956 . . . . TCLC 1, 24
　See also CA 104; DLB 34, 100

Begiebing, Robert J(ohn) 1946- . . . . . CLC 70
　See also CA 122; CANR 40

Behan, Brendan
　1923-1964 . . . . CLC 1, 8, 11, 15, 79
　See also CA 73-76; CANR 33;
　　CDBLB 1945-1960; DLB 13; MTCW

Behn, Aphra 1640(?)-1689 . . . . LC 1
　See also DA; DLB 39, 80, 131; WLC

Behrman, S(amuel) N(athaniel)
　1893-1973 . . . . CLC 40
　See also CA 13-16; 45-48; CAP 1; DLB 7,
　　44

Belasco, David 1853-1931 . . . . TCLC 3
　See also CA 104; DLB 7

Belcheva, Elisaveta 1893- . . . . CLC 10

Beldone, Phil "Cheech"
　See Ellison, Harlan

Beleno
　See Azuela, Mariano

Belinski, Vissarion Grigoryevich
　1811-1848 . . . . NCLC 5

Belitt, Ben 1911- . . . . CLC 22
　See also CA 13-16R; CAAS 4; CANR 7;
　　DLB 5

Bell, James Madison 1826-1902 . . . TCLC 43
　See also BLC 1; BW; CA 122; 124; DLB 50

Bell, Madison (Smartt) 1957- . . . . . . CLC 41
　See also CA 111; CANR 28

Bell, Marvin (Hartley) 1937- . . . . . CLC 8, 31
　See also CA 21-24R; CAAS 14; DLB 5;
　　MTCW

Bell, W. L. D.
　See Mencken, H(enry) L(ouis)

Bellamy, Atwood C.
　See Mencken, H(enry) L(ouis)

Bidart, Frank 1939- .... **CLC 33**
See also CA 140

Bienek, Horst 1930- .... **CLC 7, 11**
See also CA 73-76; DLB 75

Bierce, Ambrose (Gwinett)
1842-1914(?) ..... **TCLC 1, 7, 44; SSC 9**
See also CA 104; 139; CDALB 1865-1917;
DA; DLB 11, 12, 23, 71, 74; WLC

Billings, Josh
See Shaw, Henry Wheeler

Billington, Rachel 1942- .... **CLC 43**
See also AITN 2; CA 33-36R

Binyon, T(imothy) J(ohn) 1936- .... **CLC 34**
See also CA 111; CANR 28

Bioy Casares, Adolfo 1914- .... **CLC 4, 8, 13**
See also CA 29-32R; CANR 19; DLB 113;
HW; MTCW

Bird, C.
See Ellison, Harlan

Bird, Cordwainer
See Ellison, Harlan

Bird, Robert Montgomery
1806-1854 .... **NCLC 1**

Birney, (Alfred) Earle
1904- .... **CLC 1, 4, 6, 11**
See also CA 1-4R; CANR 5, 20; DLB 88;
MTCW

Bishop, Elizabeth
1911-1979 ...... **CLC 1, 4, 9, 13, 15, 32;**
PC 3
See also CA 5-8R; 89-92; CABS 2;
CANR 26; CDALB 1968-1988; DA;
DLB 5; MTCW; SATA 24

Bishop, John 1935- .... **CLC 10**
See also CA 105

Bissett, Bill 1939- .... **CLC 18**
See also CA 69-72; CANR 15; DLB 53;
MTCW

Bitov, Andrei (Georgievich) 1937- ... **CLC 57**

Biyidi, Alexandre 1932-
See Beti, Mongo
See also BW; CA 114; 124; MTCW

Bjarme, Brynjolf
See Ibsen, Henrik (Johan)

Bjornson, Bjornstjerne (Martinius)
1832-1910 .... **TCLC 7, 37**
See also CA 104

Black, Robert
See Holdstock, Robert P.

Blackburn, Paul 1926-1971 ...... **CLC 9, 43**
See also CA 81-84; 33-36R; CANR 34;
DLB 16; DLBY 81

Black Elk 1863-1950 .... **TCLC 33**

Black Hobart
See Sanders, (James) Ed(ward)

Blacklin, Malcolm
See Chambers, Aidan

Blackmore, R(ichard) D(oddridge)
1825-1900 .... **TCLC 27**
See also CA 120; DLB 18

Blackmur, R(ichard) P(almer)
1904-1965 .... **CLC 2, 24**
See also CA 11-12; 25-28R; CAP 1; DLB 63

Black Tarantula, The
See Acker, Kathy

Blackwood, Algernon (Henry)
1869-1951 .... **TCLC 5**
See also CA 105

Blackwood, Caroline 1931- .... **CLC 6, 9**
See also CA 85-88; CANR 32; DLB 14;
MTCW

Blade, Alexander
See Hamilton, Edmond; Silverberg, Robert

Blaga, Lucian 1895-1961 .... **CLC 75**

Blair, Eric (Arthur) 1903-1950
See Orwell, George
See also CA 104; 132; DA; MTCW;
SATA 29

Blais, Marie-Claire
1939- .... **CLC 2, 4, 6, 13, 22**
See also CA 21-24R; CAAS 4; CANR 38;
DLB 53; MTCW

Blaise, Clark 1940- .... **CLC 29**
See also AITN 2; CA 53-56; CAAS 3;
CANR 5; DLB 53

Blake, Nicholas
See Day Lewis, C(ecil)
See also DLB 77

Blake, William 1757-1827 .... **NCLC 13**
See also CDBLB 1789-1832; DA; DLB 93;
MAICYA; SATA 30; WLC

Blasco Ibanez, Vicente
1867-1928 .... **TCLC 12**
See also CA 110; 131; HW; MTCW

Blatty, William Peter 1928- .... **CLC 2**
See also CA 5-8R; CANR 9

Bleeck, Oliver
See Thomas, Ross (Elmore)

Blessing, Lee 1949- .... **CLC 54**

Blish, James (Benjamin)
1921-1975 .... **CLC 14**
See also CA 1-4R; 57-60; CANR 3; DLB 8;
MTCW; SATA 66

Bliss, Reginald
See Wells, H(erbert) G(eorge)

Blixen, Karen (Christentze Dinesen)
1885-1962
See Dinesen, Isak
See also CA 25-28; CANR 22; CAP 2;
MTCW; SATA 44

Bloch, Robert (Albert) 1917- .... **CLC 33**
See also CA 5-8R; CANR 5; DLB 44;
SATA 12

Blok, Alexander (Alexandrovich)
1880-1921 .... **TCLC 5**
See also CA 104

Blom, Jan
See Breytenbach, Breyten

Bloom, Harold 1930- .... **CLC 24**
See also CA 13-16R; CANR 39; DLB 67

Bloomfield, Aurelius
See Bourne, Randolph S(illiman)

Blount, Roy (Alton), Jr. 1941- ..... **CLC 38**
See also CA 53-56; CANR 10, 28; MTCW

Bloy, Leon 1846-1917............. **TCLC 22**
See also CA 121; DLB 123

Blume, Judy (Sussman) 1938- .... **CLC 12, 30**
See also AAYA 3; CA 29-32R; CANR 13,
37; CLR 2, 15; DLB 52; JRDA;
MAICYA; MTCW; SATA 2, 31

Blunden, Edmund (Charles)
1896-1974 .... **CLC 2, 56**
See also CA 17-18; 45-48; CAP 2; DLB 20,
100; MTCW

Bly, Robert (Elwood)
1926- .... **CLC 1, 2, 5, 10, 15, 38**
See also CA 5-8R; CANR 41; DLB 5;
MTCW

Bobette
See Simenon, Georges (Jacques Christian)

Boccaccio, Giovanni 1313-1375
See also SSC 10

Bochco, Steven 1943- .... **CLC 35**
See also CA 124; 138

Bodenheim, Maxwell 1892-1954 ... **TCLC 44**
See also CA 110; DLB 9, 45

Bodker, Cecil 1927- .... **CLC 21**
See also CA 73-76; CANR 13; CLR 23;
MAICYA; SATA 14

Boell, Heinrich (Theodor) 1917-1985
See Boll, Heinrich (Theodor)
See also CA 21-24R; 116; CANR 24; DA;
DLB 69; DLBY 85; MTCW

Boerne, Alfred
See Doeblin, Alfred

Bogan, Louise 1897-1970..... **CLC 4, 39, 46**
See also CA 73-76; 25-28R; CANR 33;
DLB 45; MTCW

Bogarde, Dirk .... **CLC 19**
See also Van Den Bogarde, Derek Jules
Gaspard Ulric Niven
See also DLB 14

Bogosian, Eric 1953- .... **CLC 45**
See also CA 138

Bograd, Larry 1953- .... **CLC 35**
See also CA 93-96; SATA 33

Boiardo, Matteo Maria 1441-1494 .... **LC 6**

Boileau-Despreaux, Nicolas
1636-1711 .... **LC 3**

Boland, Eavan 1944- .... **CLC 40, 67**
See also DLB 40

Boll, Heinrich (Theodor)
1917-1985 .... **CLC 2, 3, 6, 9, 11, 15, 27,**
39, 72
See also Boell, Heinrich (Theodor)
See also DLB 69; DLBY 85; WLC

Bolt, Lee
See Faust, Frederick (Schiller)

Bolt, Robert (Oxton) 1924- .... **CLC 14**
See also CA 17-20R; CANR 35; DLB 13;
MTCW

Bomkauf
See Kaufman, Bob (Garnell)

Bonaventura.................... **NCLC 35**
See also DLB 90

Bond, Edward 1934- .... **CLC 4, 6, 13, 23**
See also CA 25-28R; CANR 38; DLB 13;
MTCW

Bonham, Frank 1914-1989 . . . . **CLC 12**
See also AAYA 1; CA 9-12R; CANR 4, 36;
JRDA; MAICYA; SAAS 3; SATA 1, 49,
62

Bonnefoy, Yves 1923- . . . . **CLC 9, 15, 58**
See also CA 85-88; CANR 33; MTCW

Bontemps, Arna(ud Wendell)
1902-1973 . . . . **CLC 1, 18**
See also BLC 1; BW; CA 1-4R; 41-44R;
CANR 4, 35; CLR 6; DLB 48, 51; JRDA;
MAICYA; MTCW; SATA 2, 24, 44

Booth, Martin 1944- . . . . **CLC 13**
See also CA 93-96; CAAS 2

Booth, Philip 1925- . . . . **CLC 23**
See also CA 5-8R; CANR 5; DLBY 82

Booth, Wayne C(layson) 1921- . . . . . **CLC 24**
See also CA 1-4R; CAAS 5; CANR 3;
DLB 67

Borchert, Wolfgang 1921-1947 . . . . . **TCLC 5**
See also CA 104; DLB 69, 124

Borel, Petrus 1809-1859 . . . . **NCLC 41**

Borges, Jorge Luis
1899-1986 . . . **CLC 1, 2, 3, 4, 6, 8, 9, 10,
13, 19, 44, 48; SSC 4**
See also CA 21-24R; CANR 19, 33; DA;
DLB 113; DLBY 86; HW; MTCW; WLC

Borowski, Tadeusz 1922-1951 . . . . . . **TCLC 9**
See also CA 106

Borrow, George (Henry)
1803-1881 . . . . **NCLC 9**
See also DLB 21, 55

Bosman, Herman Charles
1905-1951 . . . . **TCLC 49**

Bosschere, Jean de 1878(?)-1953 . . . **TCLC 19**
See also CA 115

Boswell, James 1740-1795 . . . . **LC 4**
See also CDBLB 1660-1789; DA; DLB 104;
WLC

Bottoms, David 1949- . . . . **CLC 53**
See also CA 105; CANR 22; DLB 120;
DLBY 83

Boucicault, Dion 1820-1890 . . . . . . **NCLC 41**

Boucolon, Maryse 1937-
See Conde, Maryse
See also CA 110; CANR 30

Bourget, Paul (Charles Joseph)
1852-1935 . . . . **TCLC 12**
See also CA 107; DLB 123

Bourjaily, Vance (Nye) 1922- . . . . **CLC 8, 62**
See also CA 1-4R; CAAS 1; CANR 2;
DLB 2

Bourne, Randolph S(illiman)
1886-1918 . . . . **TCLC 16**
See also CA 117; DLB 63

Bova, Ben(jamin William) 1932- . . . . **CLC 45**
See also CA 5-8R; CAAS 18; CANR 11;
CLR 3; DLBY 81; MAICYA; MTCW;
SATA 6, 68

Bowen, Elizabeth (Dorothea Cole)
1899-1973 . . . . . . **CLC 1, 3, 6, 11, 15, 22;
SSC 3**
See also CA 17-18; 41-44R; CANR 35;
CAP 2; CDBLB 1945-1960; DLB 15;
MTCW

Bowering, George 1935- . . . . **CLC 15, 47**
See also CA 21-24R; CAAS 16; CANR 10;
DLB 53

Bowering, Marilyn R(uthe) 1949- . . . **CLC 32**
See also CA 101

Bowers, Edgar 1924- . . . . **CLC 9**
See also CA 5-8R; CANR 24; DLB 5

Bowie, David . . . . **CLC 17**
See also Jones, David Robert

Bowles, Jane (Sydney)
1917-1973 . . . . **CLC 3, 68**
See also CA 19-20; 41-44R; CAP 2

Bowles, Paul (Frederick)
1910- . . . . **CLC 1, 2, 19, 53; SSC 3**
See also CA 1-4R; CAAS 1; CANR 1, 19;
DLB 5, 6; MTCW

Box, Edgar
See Vidal, Gore

Boyd, Nancy
See Millay, Edna St. Vincent

Boyd, William 1952- . . . . **CLC 28, 53, 70**
See also CA 114; 120

Boyle, Kay
1902-1992 . . . . . **CLC 1, 5, 19, 58; SSC 5**
See also CA 13-16R; 140; CAAS 1;
CANR 29; DLB 4, 9, 48, 86; MTCW

Boyle, Mark
See Kienzle, William X(avier)

Boyle, Patrick 1905-1982 . . . . **CLC 19**
See also CA 127

Boyle, T. Coraghessan 1948- . . . . **CLC 36, 55**
See also BEST 90:4; CA 120; DLBY 86

Boz
See Dickens, Charles (John Huffam)

Brackenridge, Hugh Henry
1748-1816 . . . . **NCLC 7**
See also DLB 11, 37

Bradbury, Edward P.
See Moorcock, Michael (John)

Bradbury, Malcolm (Stanley)
1932- . . . . **CLC 32, 61**
See also CA 1-4R; CANR 1, 33; DLB 14;
MTCW

Bradbury, Ray (Douglas)
1920- . . . . **CLC 1, 3, 10, 15, 42**
See also AITN 1, 2; CA 1-4R; CANR 2, 30;
CDALB 1968-1988; DA; DLB 2, 8;
MTCW; SATA 11, 64; WLC

Bradford, Gamaliel 1863-1932 . . . . . **TCLC 36**
See also DLB 17

Bradley, David (Henry, Jr.) 1950- . . **CLC 23**
See also BLC 1; BW; CA 104; CANR 26;
DLB 33

Bradley, John Ed 1959- . . . . **CLC 55**

Bradley, Marion Zimmer 1930- . . . . . **CLC 30**
See also AAYA 9; CA 57-60; CAAS 10;
CANR 7, 31; DLB 8; MTCW

Bradstreet, Anne 1612(?)-1672 . . . . **LC 4**
See also CDALB 1640-1865; DA; DLB 24

Bragg, Melvyn 1939- . . . . **CLC 10**
See also BEST 89:3; CA 57-60; CANR 10;
DLB 14

Braine, John (Gerard)
1922-1986 . . . . **CLC 1, 3, 41**
See also CA 1-4R; 120; CANR 1, 33;
CDBLB 1945-1960; DLB 15; DLBY 86;
MTCW

Brammer, William 1930(?)-1978 . . . . **CLC 31**
See also CA 77-80

Brancati, Vitaliano 1907-1954 . . . . . **TCLC 12**
See also CA 109

Brancato, Robin F(idler) 1936- . . . . . **CLC 35**
See also AAYA 9; CA 69-72; CANR 11;
CLR 32; JRDA; SAAS 9; SATA 23

Brand, Max
See Faust, Frederick (Schiller)

Brand, Millen 1906-1980 . . . . **CLC 7**
See also CA 21-24R; 97-100

Branden, Barbara . . . . **CLC 44**

Brandes, Georg (Morris Cohen)
1842-1927 . . . . **TCLC 10**
See also CA 105

Brandys, Kazimierz 1916- . . . . **CLC 62**

Branley, Franklyn M(ansfield)
1915- . . . . **CLC 21**
See also CA 33-36R; CANR 14, 39;
CLR 13; MAICYA; SAAS 16; SATA 4,
68

Brathwaite, Edward (Kamau)
1930- . . . . **CLC 11**
See also BW; CA 25-28R; CANR 11, 26;
DLB 125

Brautigan, Richard (Gary)
1935-1984 . . . . **CLC 1, 3, 5, 9, 12, 34, 42**
See also CA 53-56; 113; CANR 34; DLB 2,
5; DLBY 80, 84; MTCW; SATA 56

Braverman, Kate 1950- . . . . **CLC 67**
See also CA 89-92

Brecht, Bertolt
1898-1956 . . . . . **TCLC 1, 6, 13, 35; DC 3**
See also CA 104; 133; DA; DLB 56, 124;
MTCW; WLC

Brecht, Eugen Berthold Friedrich
See Brecht, Bertolt

Bremer, Fredrika 1801-1865 . . . . . **NCLC 11**

Brennan, Christopher John
1870-1932 . . . . **TCLC 17**
See also CA 117

Brennan, Maeve 1917- . . . . **CLC 5**
See also CA 81-84

Brentano, Clemens (Maria)
1778-1842 . . . . **NCLC 1**

Brent of Bin Bin
See Franklin, (Stella Maraia Sarah) Miles

Brenton, Howard 1942- . . . . **CLC 31**
See also CA 69-72; CANR 33; DLB 13;
MTCW

Breslin, James 1930-
See Breslin, Jimmy
See also CA 73-76; CANR 31; MTCW

Breslin, Jimmy . . . . **CLC 4, 43**
See also Breslin, James
See also AITN 1

Bresson, Robert 1907- . . . . **CLC 16**
See also CA 110

Breton, Andre   1896-1966... **CLC 2, 9, 15, 54**
  See also CA 19-20; 25-28R; CANR 40;
  CAP 2; DLB 65; MTCW

Breytenbach, Breyten   1939(?)- .. **CLC 23, 37**
  See also CA 113; 129

Bridgers, Sue Ellen   1942- .... **CLC 26**
  See also AAYA 8; CA 65-68; CANR 11,
  36; CLR 18; DLB 52; JRDA; MAICYA;
  SAAS 1; SATA 22

Bridges, Robert (Seymour)
  1844-1930 .... **TCLC 1**
  See also CA 104; CDBLB 1890-1914;
  DLB 19, 98

Bridie, James..................... **TCLC 3**
  See also Mavor, Osborne Henry
  See also DLB 10

Brin, David   1950-.............. **CLC 34**
  See also CA 102; CANR 24; SATA 65

Brink, Andre (Philippus)
  1935- .... **CLC 18, 36**
  See also CA 104; CANR 39; MTCW

Brinsmead, H(esba) F(ay)   1922- .... **CLC 21**
  See also CA 21-24R; CANR 10; MAICYA;
  SAAS 5; SATA 18

Brittain, Vera (Mary)
  1893(?)-1970 .... **CLC 23**
  See also CA 13-16; 25-28R; CAP 1; MTCW

Broch, Hermann   1886-1951...... **TCLC 20**
  See also CA 117; DLB 85, 124

Brock, Rose
  See Hansen, Joseph

Brodkey, Harold   1930-........... **CLC 56**
  See also CA 111; DLB 130

Brodsky, Iosif Alexandrovich   1940-
  See Brodsky, Joseph
  See also AITN 1; CA 41-44R; CANR 37;
  MTCW

Brodsky, Joseph .... **CLC 4, 6, 13, 36, 50**
  See also Brodsky, Iosif Alexandrovich

Brodsky, Michael Mark   1948- ..... **CLC 19**
  See also CA 102; CANR 18, 41

Bromell, Henry   1947-.............. **CLC 5**
  See also CA 53-56; CANR 9

Bromfield, Louis (Brucker)
  1896-1956 .... **TCLC 11**
  See also CA 107; DLB 4, 9, 86

Broner, E(sther) M(asserman)
  1930- .... **CLC 19**
  See also CA 17-20R; CANR 8, 25; DLB 28

Bronk, William   1918-............. **CLC 10**
  See also CA 89-92; CANR 23

Bronstein, Lev Davidovich
  See Trotsky, Leon

Bronte, Anne   1820-1849.......... **NCLC 4**
  See also DLB 21

Bronte, Charlotte
  1816-1855 .... **NCLC 3, 8, 33**
  See also CDBLB 1832-1890; DA; DLB 21;
  WLC

Bronte, (Jane) Emily
  1818-1848 .... **NCLC 16, 35**
  See also CDBLB 1832-1890; DA; DLB 21,
  32; WLC

Brooke, Frances   1724-1789 .... **LC 6**
  See also DLB 39, 99

Brooke, Henry   1703(?)-1783 .... **LC 1**
  See also DLB 39

Brooke, Rupert (Chawner)
  1887-1915 .... **TCLC 2, 7**
  See also CA 104; 132; CDBLB 1914-1945;
  DA; DLB 19; MTCW; WLC

Brooke-Haven, P.
  See Wodehouse, P(elham) G(renville)

Brooke-Rose, Christine   1926- ...... **CLC 40**
  See also CA 13-16R; DLB 14

Brookner, Anita   1928-...... **CLC 32, 34, 51**
  See also CA 114; 120; CANR 37; DLBY 87;
  MTCW

Brooks, Cleanth   1906-............. **CLC 24**
  See also CA 17-20R; CANR 33, 35;
  DLB 63; MTCW

Brooks, George
  See Baum, L(yman) Frank

Brooks, Gwendolyn
  1917- ...... **CLC 1, 2, 4, 5, 15, 49; PC 7**
  See also AITN 1; BLC 1; BW; CA 1-4R;
  CANR 1, 27; CDALB 1941-1968;
  CLR 27; DA; DLB 5, 76; MTCW;
  SATA 6; WLC

Brooks, Mel...................... **CLC 12**
  See also Kaminsky, Melvin
  See also DLB 26

Brooks, Peter   1938-.............. **CLC 34**
  See also CA 45-48; CANR 1

Brooks, Van Wyck   1886-1963...... **CLC 29**
  See also CA 1-4R; CANR 6; DLB 45, 63,
  103

Brophy, Brigid (Antonia)
  1929- .... **CLC 6, 11, 29**
  See also CA 5-8R; CAAS 4; CANR 25;
  DLB 14; MTCW

Brosman, Catharine Savage   1934-.... **CLC 9**
  See also CA 61-64; CANR 21

Brother Antoninus
  See Everson, William (Oliver)

Broughton, T(homas) Alan   1936- ... **CLC 19**
  See also CA 45-48; CANR 2, 23

Broumas, Olga   1949-.......... **CLC 10, 73**
  See also CA 85-88; CANR 20

Brown, Charles Brockden
  1771-1810 .... **NCLC 22**
  See also CDALB 1640-1865; DLB 37, 59,
  73

Brown, Christy   1932-1981........ **CLC 63**
  See also CA 105; 104; DLB 14

Brown, Claude   1937- .... **CLC 30**
  See also AAYA 7; BLC 1; BW; CA 73-76

Brown, Dee (Alexander)   1908- .. **CLC 18, 47**
  See also CA 13-16R; CAAS 6; CANR 11;
  DLBY 80; MTCW; SATA 5

Brown, George
  See Wertmueller, Lina

Brown, George Douglas
  1869-1902 .... **TCLC 28**

Brown, George Mackay   1921-.... **CLC 5, 48**
  See also CA 21-24R; CAAS 6; CANR 12,
  37; DLB 14, 27; MTCW; SATA 35

Brown, (William) Larry   1951-...... **CLC 73**
  See also CA 130; 134

Brown, Moses
  See Barrett, William (Christopher)

Brown, Rita Mae   1944- ..... **CLC 18, 43, 79**
  See also CA 45-48; CANR 2, 11, 35;
  MTCW

Brown, Roderick (Langmere) Haig-
  See Haig-Brown, Roderick (Langmere)

Brown, Rosellen   1939-............ **CLC 32**
  See also CA 77-80; CAAS 10; CANR 14

Brown, Sterling Allen
  1901-1989 .... **CLC 1, 23, 59**
  See also BLC 1; BW; CA 85-88; 127;
  CANR 26; DLB 48, 51, 63; MTCW

Brown, Will
  See Ainsworth, William Harrison

Brown, William Wells
  1813-1884 .... **NCLC 2; DC 1**
  See also BLC 1; DLB 3, 50

Browne, (Clyde) Jackson   1948(?)-... **CLC 21**
  See also CA 120

Browning, Elizabeth Barrett
  1806-1861 .... **NCLC 1, 16; PC 6**
  See also CDBLB 1832-1890; DA; DLB 32;
  WLC

Browning, Robert
  1812-1889 .... **NCLC 19; PC 2**
  See also CDBLB 1832-1890; DA; DLB 32;
  YABC 1

Browning, Tod   1882-1962 .... **CLC 16**
  See also CA 141; 117

Bruccoli, Matthew J(oseph)   1931- .. **CLC 34**
  See also CA 9-12R; CANR 7; DLB 103

Bruce, Lenny..................... **CLC 21**
  See also Schneider, Leonard Alfred

Bruin, John
  See Brutus, Dennis

Brulls, Christian
  See Simenon, Georges (Jacques Christian)

Brunner, John (Kilian Houston)
  1934- .... **CLC 8, 10**
  See also CA 1-4R; CAAS 8; CANR 2, 37;
  MTCW

Brutus, Dennis   1924-.............. **CLC 43**
  See also BLC 1; BW; CA 49-52; CAAS 14;
  CANR 2, 27, 42; DLB 117

Bryan, C(ourtlandt) D(ixon) B(arnes)
  1936- .... **CLC 29**
  See also CA 73-76; CANR 13

Bryan, Michael
  See Moore, Brian

Bryant, William Cullen
  1794-1878 .... **NCLC 6**
  See also CDALB 1640-1865; DA; DLB 3,
  43, 59

Bryusov, Valery Yakovlevich
  1873-1924 .... **TCLC 10**
  See also CA 107

Buchan, John   1875-1940 .... **TCLC 41**
  See also CA 108; DLB 34, 70; YABC 2

Buchanan, George   1506-1582 .... **LC 4**

Buchheim, Lothar-Guenther   1918- ... **CLC 6**
  See also CA 85-88

Buchner, (Karl) Georg
  1813-1837 .... **NCLC 26**

Cameron, Peter 1959-............ **CLC 44**
See also CA 125

Campana, Dino 1885-1932........ **TCLC 20**
See also CA 117; DLB 114

Campbell, John W(ood, Jr.)
1910-1971 .... **CLC 32**
See also CA 21-22; 29-32R; CANR 34;
CAP 2; DLB 8; MTCW

Campbell, Joseph 1904-1987....... **CLC 69**
See also AAYA 3; BEST 89:2; CA 1-4R;
124; CANR 3, 28; MTCW

Campbell, (John) Ramsey 1946- .... **CLC 42**
See also CA 57-60; CANR 7

Campbell, (Ignatius) Roy (Dunnachie)
1901-1957 .... **TCLC 5**
See also CA 104; DLB 20

Campbell, Thomas 1777-1844 .... **NCLC 19**
See also DLB 93

Campbell, Wilfred................. **TCLC 9**
See also Campbell, William

Campbell, William 1858(?)-1918
See Campbell, Wilfred
See also CA 106; DLB 92

Campos, Alvaro de
See Pessoa, Fernando (Antonio Nogueira)

Camus, Albert
1913-1960 .... **CLC 1, 2, 4, 9, 11, 14, 32,
63, 69; DC 2; SSC 9**
See also CA 89-92; DA; DLB 72; MTCW;
WLC

Canby, Vincent 1924-............. **CLC 13**
See also CA 81-84

Cancale
See Desnos, Robert

Canetti, Elias 1905- ...... **CLC 3, 14, 25, 75**
See also CA 21-24R; CANR 23; DLB 85,
124; MTCW

Canin, Ethan 1960-............... **CLC 55**
See also CA 131; 135

Cannon, Curt
See Hunter, Evan

Cape, Judith
See Page, P(atricia) K(athleen)

Capek, Karel
1890-1938 .... **TCLC 6, 37; DC 1**
See also CA 104; 140; DA; WLC

Capote, Truman
1924-1984 ...... **CLC 1, 3, 8, 13, 19, 34,
38, 58; SSC 2**
See also CA 5-8R; 113; CANR 18;
CDALB 1941-1968; DA; DLB 2;
DLBY 80, 84; MTCW; WLC

Capra, Frank 1897-1991.......... **CLC 16**
See also CA 61-64; 135

Caputo, Philip 1941-............. **CLC 32**
See also CA 73-76; CANR 40

Card, Orson Scott 1951- .... **CLC 44, 47, 50**
See also CA 102; CANR 27; MTCW

Cardenal (Martinez), Ernesto
1925- .... **CLC 31**
See also CA 49-52; CANR 2, 32; HW;
MTCW

Carducci, Giosue 1835-1907....... **TCLC 32**

Carew, Thomas 1595(?)-1640....... **LC 13**
See also DLB 126

Carey, Ernestine Gilbreth 1908-.... **CLC 17**
See also CA 5-8R; SATA 2

Carey, Peter 1943-............. **CLC 40, 55**
See also CA 123; 127; MTCW

Carleton, William 1794-1869..... **NCLC 3**

Carlisle, Henry (Coffin) 1926-...... **CLC 33**
See also CA 13-16R; CANR 15

Carlsen, Chris
See Holdstock, Robert P.

Carlson, Ron(ald F.) 1947-........ **CLC 54**
See also CA 105; CANR 27

Carlyle, Thomas 1795-1881...... **NCLC 22**
See also CDBLB 1789-1832; DA; DLB 55

Carman, (William) Bliss
1861-1929 .... **TCLC 7**
See also CA 104; DLB 92

Carossa, Hans 1878-1956........ **TCLC 48**
See also DLB 66

Carpenter, Don(ald Richard)
1931- .... **CLC 41**
See also CA 45-48; CANR 1

Carpentier (y Valmont), Alejo
1904-1980 .... **CLC 8, 11, 38**
See also CA 65-68; 97-100; CANR 11;
DLB 113; HW

Carr, Emily 1871-1945........... **TCLC 32**
See also DLB 68

Carr, John Dickson 1906-1977 ...... **CLC 3**
See also CA 49-52; 69-72; CANR 3, 33;
MTCW

Carr, Philippa
See Hibbert, Eleanor Alice Burford

Carr, Virginia Spencer 1929-....... **CLC 34**
See also CA 61-64; DLB 111

Carrier, Roch 1937-........... **CLC 13, 78**
See also CA 130; DLB 53

Carroll, James P. 1943(?)-........ **CLC 38**
See also CA 81-84

Carroll, Jim 1951- .... **CLC 35**
See also CA 45-48; CANR 42

Carroll, Lewis.................. **NCLC 2**
See also Dodgson, Charles Lutwidge
See also CDBLB 1832-1890; CLR 2, 18;
DLB 18; JRDA; WLC

Carroll, Paul Vincent 1900-1968.... **CLC 10**
See also CA 9-12R; 25-28R; DLB 10

Carruth, Hayden 1921- .... **CLC 4, 7, 10, 18**
See also CA 9-12R; CANR 4, 38; DLB 5;
MTCW; SATA 47

Carson, Rachel Louise 1907-1964... **CLC 71**
See also CA 77-80; CANR 35; MTCW;
SATA 23

Carter, Angela (Olive)
1940-1992 ...... **CLC 5, 41, 76; SSC 13**
See also CA 53-56; 136; CANR 12, 36;
DLB 14; MTCW; SATA 66;
SATA-Obit 70

Carter, Nick
See Smith, Martin Cruz

Carver, Raymond
1938-1988 ... **CLC 22, 36, 53, 55; SSC 8**
See also CA 33-36R; 126; CANR 17, 34;
DLB 130; DLBY 84, 88; MTCW

Cary, (Arthur) Joyce (Lunel)
1888-1957 .... **TCLC 1, 29**
See also CA 104; CDBLB 1914-1945;
DLB 15, 100

Casanova de Seingalt, Giovanni Jacopo
1725-1798 .... **LC 13**

Casares, Adolfo Bioy
See Bioy Casares, Adolfo

Casely-Hayford, J(oseph) E(phraim)
1866-1930 .... **TCLC 24**
See also BLC 1; CA 123

Casey, John (Dudley) 1939-........ **CLC 59**
See also BEST 90:2; CA 69-72; CANR 23

Casey, Michael 1947-............. **CLC 2**
See also CA 65-68; DLB 5

Casey, Patrick
See Thurman, Wallace (Henry)

Casey, Warren (Peter) 1935-1988... **CLC 12**
See also CA 101; 127

Casona, Alejandro................. **CLC 49**
See also Alvarez, Alejandro Rodriguez

Cassavetes, John 1929-1989........ **CLC 20**
See also CA 85-88; 127

Cassill, R(onald) V(erlin) 1919-... **CLC 4, 23**
See also CA 9-12R; CAAS 1; CANR 7;
DLB 6

Cassity, (Allen) Turner 1929- .... **CLC 6, 42**
See also CA 17-20R; CAAS 8; CANR 11;
DLB 105

Castaneda, Carlos 1931(?)-......... **CLC 12**
See also CA 25-28R; CANR 32; HW;
MTCW

Castedo, Elena 1937-............. **CLC 65**
See also CA 132

Castedo-Ellerman, Elena
See Castedo, Elena

Castellanos, Rosario 1925-1974..... **CLC 66**
See also CA 131; 53-56; DLB 113; HW

Castelvetro, Lodovico 1505-1571..... **LC 12**

Castiglione, Baldassare 1478-1529 ... **LC 12**

Castle, Robert
See Hamilton, Edmond

Castro, Guillen de 1569-1631........ **LC 19**

Castro, Rosalia de 1837-1885 ..... **NCLC 3**

Cather, Willa
See Cather, Willa Sibert

Cather, Willa Sibert
1873-1947 ...... **TCLC 1, 11, 31; SSC 2**
See also CA 104; 128; CDALB 1865-1917;
DA; DLB 9, 54, 78; DLBD 1; MTCW;
SATA 30; WLC

Catton, (Charles) Bruce
1899-1978 .... **CLC 35**
See also AITN 1; CA 5-8R; 81-84;
CANR 7; DLB 17; SATA 2, 24

Cauldwell, Frank
See King, Francis (Henry)

Caunitz, William J. 1933-......... **CLC 34**
See also BEST 89:3; CA 125; 130

Chomette, Rene Lucien 1898-1981 .. CLC 20
See also Clair, Rene
See also CA 103

Chopin, Kate .... TCLC 5, 14; SSC 8
See also Chopin, Katherine
See also CDALB 1865-1917; DA; DLB 12, 78

Chopin, Katherine 1851-1904
See Chopin, Kate
See also CA 104; 122

Chretien de Troyes
c. 12th cent. - .... CMLC 10

Christie
See Ichikawa, Kon

Christie, Agatha (Mary Clarissa)
1890-1976 ...... CLC 1, 6, 8, 12, 39, 48
See also AAYA 9; AITN 1, 2; CA 17-20R;
61-64; CANR 10, 37; CDBLB 1914-1945;
DLB 13, 77; MTCW; SATA 36

Christie, (Ann) Philippa
See Pearce, Philippa
See also CA 5-8R; CANR 4

Christine de Pizan 1365(?)-1431(?) .... LC 9

Chubb, Elmer
See Masters, Edgar Lee

Chulkov, Mikhail Dmitrievich
1743-1792 .... LC 2

Churchill, Caryl 1938- .... CLC 31, 55
See also CA 102; CANR 22; DLB 13;
MTCW

Churchill, Charles 1731-1764........ LC 3
See also DLB 109

Chute, Carolyn 1947-............. CLC 39
See also CA 123

Ciardi, John (Anthony)
1916-1986 .... CLC 10, 40, 44
See also CA 5-8R; 118; CAAS 2; CANR 5,
33; CLR 19; DLB 5; DLBY 86;
MAICYA; MTCW; SATA 1, 46, 65

Cicero, Marcus Tullius
106B.C.-43B.C............... CMLC 3

Cimino, Michael 1943-............ CLC 16
See also CA 105

Cioran, E(mil) M. 1911-........... CLC 64
See also CA 25-28R

Cisneros, Sandra 1954-............ CLC 69
See also AAYA 9; CA 131; DLB 122; HW

Clair, Rene...................... CLC 20
See also Chomette, Rene Lucien

Clampitt, Amy 1920- .... CLC 32
See also CA 110; CANR 29; DLB 105

Clancy, Thomas L., Jr. 1947-
See Clancy, Tom
See also CA 125; 131; MTCW

Clancy, Tom.:.................... CLC 45
See also Clancy, Thomas L., Jr.
See also AAYA 9; BEST 89:1, 90:1

Clare, John 1793-1864........... NCLC 9
See also DLB 55, 96

Clarin
See Alas (y Urena), Leopoldo (Enrique
Garcia)

Clark, (Robert) Brian 1932-........ CLC 29
See also CA 41-44R

Clark, Eleanor 1913- .... CLC 5, 19
See also CA 9-12R; CANR 41; DLB 6

Clark, J. P.
See Clark, John Pepper
See also DLB 117

Clark, John Pepper 1935- .... CLC 38
See also Clark, J. P.
See also BLC 1; BW; CA 65-68; CANR 16

Clark, M. R.
See Clark, Mavis Thorpe

Clark, Mavis Thorpe 1909-........ CLC 12
See also CA 57-60; CANR 8, 37; CLR 30;
MAICYA; SAAS 5; SATA 8, 74

Clark, Walter Van Tilburg
1909-1971 .... CLC 28
See also CA 9-12R; 33-36R; DLB 9;
SATA 8

Clarke, Arthur C(harles)
1917- ...... CLC 1, 4, 13, 18, 35; SSC 3
See also AAYA 4; CA 1-4R; CANR 2, 28;
JRDA; MAICYA; MTCW; SATA 13, 70

Clarke, Austin 1896-1974......... CLC 6, 9
See also CA 29-32; 49-52; CAP 2; DLB 10,
20

Clarke, Austin C(hesterfield)
1934- .... CLC 8, 53
See also BLC 1; BW; CA 25-28R;
CAAS 16; CANR 14, 32; DLB 53, 125

Clarke, Gillian 1937-............. CLC 61
See also CA 106; DLB 40

Clarke, Marcus (Andrew Hislop)
1846-1881 .... NCLC 19

Clarke, Shirley 1925-............. CLC 16

Clash, The .... CLC 30
See also Headon, (Nicky) Topper; Jones,
Mick; Simonon, Paul; Strummer, Joe

Claudel, Paul (Louis Charles Marie)
1868-1955 .... TCLC 2, 10
See also CA 104

Clavell, James (duMaresq)
1925-....................... CLC 6, 25
See also CA 25-28R; CANR 26; MTCW

Cleaver, (Leroy) Eldridge 1935- .... CLC 30
See also BLC 1; BW; CA 21-24R;
CANR 16

Cleese, John (Marwood) 1939- ..... CLC 21
See also Monty Python
See also CA 112; 116; CANR 35; MTCW

Cleishbotham, Jebediah
See Scott, Walter

Cleland, John 1710-1789 .... LC 2
See also DLB 39

Clemens, Samuel Langhorne 1835-1910
See Twain, Mark
See also CA 104; 135; CDALB 1865-1917;
DA; DLB 11, 12, 23, 64, 74; JRDA;
MAICYA; YABC 2

Cleophil
See Congreve, William

Clerihew, E.
See Bentley, E(dmund) C(lerihew)

Clerk, N. W.
See Lewis, C(live) S(taples)

Cliff, Jimmy...................... CLC 21
See also Chambers, James

Clifton, (Thelma) Lucille
1936-.................... CLC 19, 66
See also BLC 1; BW; CA 49-52; CANR 2,
24, 42; CLR 5; DLB 5, 41; MAICYA;
MTCW; SATA 20, 69

Clinton, Dirk
See Silverberg, Robert

Clough, Arthur Hugh 1819-1861.. NCLC 27
See also DLB 32

Clutha, Janet Paterson Frame 1924-
See Frame, Janet
See also CA 1-4R; CANR 2, 36; MTCW

Clyne, Terence
See Blatty, William Peter

Cobalt, Martin
See Mayne, William (James Carter)

Coburn, D(onald) L(ee) 1938- ...... CLC 10
See also CA 89-92

Cocteau, Jean (Maurice Eugene Clement)
1889-1963 .... CLC 1, 8, 15, 16, 43
See also CA 25-28; CANR 40; CAP 2; DA;
DLB 65; MTCW; WLC

Codrescu, Andrei 1946- .... CLC 46
See also CA 33-36R; CANR 13, 34

Coe, Max
See Bourne, Randolph S(illiman)

Coe, Tucker
See Westlake, Donald E(dwin)

Coetzee, J(ohn) M(ichael)
1940- .... CLC 23, 33, 66
See also CA 77-80; CANR 41; MTCW

Coffey, Brian
See Koontz, Dean R(ay)

Cohen, Arthur A(llen)
1928-1986 .... CLC 7, 31
See also CA 1-4R; 120; CANR 1, 17, 42;
DLB 28

Cohen, Leonard (Norman)
1934- .... CLC 3, 38
See also CA 21-24R; CANR 14; DLB 53;
MTCW

Cohen, Matt 1942-................ CLC 19
See also CA 61-64; CAAS 18; CANR 40;
DLB 53

Cohen-Solal, Annie 19(?)- .... CLC 50

Colegate, Isabel 1931- .... CLC 36
See also CA 17-20R; CANR 8, 22; DLB 14;
MTCW

Coleman, Emmett
See Reed, Ishmael

Coleridge, Samuel Taylor
1772-1834 .... NCLC 9
See also CDBLB 1789-1832; DA; DLB 93,
107; WLC

Coleridge, Sara 1802-1852....... NCLC 31

Coles, Don 1928- .... CLC 46
See also CA 115; CANR 38

Colette, (Sidonie-Gabrielle)
1873-1954 ...... TCLC 1, 5, 16; SSC 10
See also CA 104; 131; DLB 65; MTCW

Collett, (Jacobine) Camilla (Wergeland)
1813-1895 .... NCLC 22

Cowley, Malcolm 1898-1989 . . . . **CLC 39**
See also CA 5-8R; 128; CANR 3; DLB 4,
48; DLBY 81, 89; MTCW

Cowper, William 1731-1800 . . . . **NCLC 8**
See also DLB 104, 109

Cox, William Trevor 1928- . . . **CLC 9, 14, 71**
See also Trevor, William
See also CA 9-12R; CANR 4, 37; DLB 14;
MTCW

Cozzens, James Gould
1903-1978 . . . . **CLC 1, 4, 11**
See also CA 9-12R; 81-84; CANR 19;
CDALB 1941-1968; DLB 9; DLBD 2;
DLBY 84; MTCW

Crabbe, George 1754-1832 . . . . . . **NCLC 26**
See also DLB 93

Craig, A. A.
See Anderson, Poul (William)

Craik, Dinah Maria (Mulock)
1826-1887 . . . . **NCLC 38**
See also DLB 35; MAICYA; SATA 34

Cram, Ralph Adams 1863-1942 . . . . **TCLC 45**

Crane, (Harold) Hart
1899-1932 . . . . **TCLC 2, 5; PC 3**
See also CA 104; 127; CDALB 1917-1929;
DA; DLB 4, 48; MTCW; WLC

Crane, R(onald) S(almon)
1886-1967 . . . . **CLC 27**
See also CA 85-88; DLB 63

Crane, Stephen (Townley)
1871-1900 . . . . . **TCLC 11, 17, 32; SSC 7**
See also CA 109; 140; CDALB 1865-1917;
DA; DLB 12, 54, 78; WLC; YABC 2

Crase, Douglas 1944- . . . . **CLC 58**
See also CA 106

Craven, Margaret 1901-1980 . . . . . . **CLC 17**
See also CA 103

Crawford, F(rancis) Marion
1854-1909 . . . . **TCLC 10**
See also CA 107; DLB 71

Crawford, Isabella Valancy
1850-1887 . . . . **NCLC 12**
See also DLB 92

Crayon, Geoffrey
See Irving, Washington

Creasey, John 1908-1973 . . . . **CLC 11**
See also CA 5-8R; 41-44R; CANR 8;
DLB 77; MTCW

Crebillon, Claude Prosper Jolyot de (fils)
1707-1777 . . . . **LC 1**

Credo
See Creasey, John

Creeley, Robert (White)
1926- . . . . . **CLC 1, 2, 4, 8, 11, 15, 36, 78**
See also CA 1-4R; CAAS 10; CANR 23;
DLB 5, 16; MTCW

Crews, Harry (Eugene)
1935- . . . . **CLC 6, 23, 49**
See also AITN 1; CA 25-28R; CANR 20;
DLB 6; MTCW

Crichton, (John) Michael
1942- . . . . **CLC 2, 6, 54**
See also AAYA 10; AITN 2; CA 25-28R;
CANR 13, 40; DLBY 81; JRDA;
MTCW; SATA 9

Crispin, Edmund . . . . **CLC 22**
See also Montgomery, (Robert) Bruce
See also DLB 87

Cristofer, Michael 1945(?)- . . . . **CLC 28**
See also CA 110; DLB 7

Croce, Benedetto 1866-1952 . . . . . **TCLC 37**
See also CA 120

Crockett, David 1786-1836 . . . . **NCLC 8**
See also DLB 3, 11

Crockett, Davy
See Crockett, David

Croker, John Wilson 1780-1857 . . **NCLC 10**
See also DLB 110

Crommelynck, Fernand 1885-1970 . . **CLC 75**
See also CA 89-92

Cronin, A(rchibald) J(oseph)
1896-1981 . . . . **CLC 32**
See also CA 1-4R; 102; CANR 5; SATA 25,
47

Cross, Amanda
See Heilbrun, Carolyn G(old)

Crothers, Rachel 1878(?)-1958 . . . . . **TCLC 19**
See also CA 113; DLB 7

Croves, Hal
See Traven, B.

Crowfield, Christopher
See Stowe, Harriet (Elizabeth) Beecher

Crowley, Aleister . . . . **TCLC 7**
See also Crowley, Edward Alexander

Crowley, Edward Alexander 1875-1947
See Crowley, Aleister
See also CA 104

Crowley, John 1942- . . . . **CLC 57**
See also CA 61-64; DLBY 82; SATA 65

Crud
See Crumb, R(obert)

Crumarums
See Crumb, R(obert)

Crumb, R(obert) 1943- . . . . **CLC 17**
See also CA 106

Crumbum
See Crumb, R(obert)

Crumski
See Crumb, R(obert)

Crum the Bum
See Crumb, R(obert)

Crunk
See Crumb, R(obert)

Crustt
See Crumb, R(obert)

Cryer, Gretchen (Kiger) 1935- . . . . . . **CLC 21**
See also CA 114; 123

Csath, Geza 1887-1919 . . . . **TCLC 13**
See also CA 111

Cudlip, David 1933- . . . . **CLC 34**

Cullen, Countee 1903-1946 . . . . . **TCLC 4, 37**
See also BLC 1; BW; CA 108; 124;
CDALB 1917-1929; DA; DLB 4, 48, 51;
MTCW; SATA 18

Cum, R.
See Crumb, R(obert)

Cummings, Bruce F(rederick) 1889-1919
See Barbellion, W. N. P.
See also CA 123

Cummings, E(dward) E(stlin)
1894-1962 . . . . . . **CLC 1, 3, 8, 12, 15, 68;**
                                              PC 5
See also CA 73-76; CANR 31;
CDALB 1929-1941; DA; DLB 4, 48;
MTCW; WLC 2

Cunha, Euclides (Rodrigues Pimenta) da
1866-1909 . . . . **TCLC 24**
See also CA 123

Cunningham, E. V.
See Fast, Howard (Melvin)

Cunningham, J(ames) V(incent)
1911-1985 . . . . **CLC 3, 31**
See also CA 1-4R; 115; CANR 1; DLB 5

Cunningham, Julia (Woolfolk)
1916- . . . . **CLC 12**
See also CA 9-12R; CANR 4, 19, 36;
JRDA; MAICYA; SAAS 2; SATA 1, 26

Cunningham, Michael 1952- . . . . **CLC 34**
See also CA 136

Cunninghame Graham, R(obert) B(ontine)
1852-1936 . . . . **TCLC 19**
See also Graham, R(obert) B(ontine)
Cunninghame
See also CA 119; DLB 98

Currie, Ellen 19(?)- . . . . **CLC 44**

Curtin, Philip
See Lowndes, Marie Adelaide (Belloc)

Curtis, Price
See Ellison, Harlan

Cutrate, Joe
See Spiegelman, Art

Czaczkes, Shmuel Yosef
See Agnon, S(hmuel) Y(osef Halevi)

D. P.
See Wells, H(erbert) G(eorge)

Dabrowska, Maria (Szumska)
1889-1965 . . . . **CLC 15**
See also CA 106

Dabydeen, David 1955- . . . . **CLC 34**
See also BW; CA 125

Dacey, Philip 1939- . . . . **CLC 51**
See also CA 37-40R; CAAS 17; CANR 14,
32; DLB 105

Dagerman, Stig (Halvard)
1923-1954 . . . . **TCLC 17**
See also CA 117

Dahl, Roald 1916-1990 . . . . . **CLC 1, 6, 18, 79**
See also CA 1-4R; 133; CANR 6, 32, 37;
CLR 1, 7; JRDA; MAICYA; MTCW;
SATA 1, 26, 73; SATA-Obit 65

Dahlberg, Edward 1900-1977 . . . **CLC 1, 7, 14**
See also CA 9-12R; 69-72; CANR 31;
DLB 48; MTCW

Dale, Colin . . . . **TCLC 18**
See also Lawrence, T(homas) E(dward)

Dale, George E.
See Asimov, Isaac

Daly, Elizabeth 1878-1967 . . . . **CLC 52**
See also CA 23-24; 25-28R; CAP 2

Deloria, Vine (Victor), Jr. 1933-.... **CLC 21**
See also CA 53-56; CANR 5, 20; MTCW;
SATA 21

Del Vecchio, John M(ichael)
1947- .... **CLC 29**
See also CA 110; DLBD 9

de Man, Paul (Adolph Michel)
1919-1983 .... **CLC 55**
See also CA 128; 111; DLB 67; MTCW

De Marinis, Rick 1934-........... **CLC 54**
See also CA 57-60; CANR 9, 25

Demby, William 1922-............ **CLC 53**
See also BLC 1; BW; CA 81-84; DLB 33

Demijohn, Thom
See Disch, Thomas M(ichael)

de Montherlant, Henry (Milon)
See Montherlant, Henry (Milon) de

de Natale, Francine
See Malzberg, Barry N(athaniel)

Denby, Edwin (Orr) 1903-1983..... **CLC 48**
See also CA 138; 110

Denis, Julio
See Cortazar, Julio

Denmark, Harrison
See Zelazny, Roger (Joseph)

Dennis, John 1658-1734........... **LC 11**
See also DLB 101

Dennis, Nigel (Forbes) 1912-1989.... **CLC 8**
See also CA 25-28R; 129; DLB 13, 15;
MTCW

De Palma, Brian (Russell) 1940-.... **CLC 20**
See also CA 109

De Quincey, Thomas 1785-1859 ... **NCLC 4**
See also CDBLB 1789-1832; DLB 110

Deren, Eleanora 1908(?)-1961
See Deren, Maya
See also CA 111

Deren, Maya .... **CLC 16**
See also Deren, Eleanora

Derleth, August (William)
1909-1971 .... **CLC 31**
See also CA 1-4R; 29-32R; CANR 4;
DLB 9; SATA 5

de Routisie, Albert
See Aragon, Louis

Derrida, Jacques 1930-............ **CLC 24**
See also CA 124; 127

Derry Down Derry
See Lear, Edward

Dersonnes, Jacques
See Simenon, Georges (Jacques Christian)

Desai, Anita 1937-............ **CLC 19, 37**
See also CA 81-84; CANR 33; MTCW;
SATA 63

de Saint-Luc, Jean
See Glassco, John

de Saint Roman, Arnaud
See Aragon, Louis

Descartes, Rene 1596-1650 .... **LC 20**

De Sica, Vittorio 1901(?)-1974 ..... **CLC 20**
See also CA 117

Desnos, Robert 1900-1945........ **TCLC 22**
See also CA 121

Destouches, Louis-Ferdinand
1894-1961 .... **CLC 9, 15**
See also Celine, Louis-Ferdinand
See also CA 85-88; CANR 28; MTCW

Deutsch, Babette 1895-1982 .... **CLC 18**
See also CA 1-4R; 108; CANR 4; DLB 45;
SATA 1, 33

Devenant, William 1606-1649 .... **LC 13**

Devkota, Laxmiprasad
1909-1959 .... **TCLC 23**
See also CA 123

De Voto, Bernard (Augustine)
1897-1955 .... **TCLC 29**
See also CA 113; DLB 9

De Vries, Peter
1910- .... **CLC 1, 2, 3, 7, 10, 28, 46**
See also CA 17-20R; CANR 41; DLB 6;
DLBY 82; MTCW

Dexter, Martin
See Faust, Frederick (Schiller)

Dexter, Pete 1943-............ **CLC 34, 55**
See also BEST 89:2; CA 127; 131; MTCW

Diamano, Silmang
See Senghor, Leopold Sedar

Diamond, Neil 1941- .... **CLC 30**
See also CA 108

di Bassetto, Corno
See Shaw, George Bernard

Dick, Philip K(indred)
1928-1982 .... **CLC 10, 30, 72**
See also CA 49-52; 106; CANR 2, 16;
DLB 8; MTCW

Dickens, Charles (John Huffam)
1812-1870 .... **NCLC 3, 8, 18, 26**
See also CDBLB 1832-1890; DA; DLB 21,
55, 70; JRDA; MAICYA; SATA 15

Dickey, James (Lafayette)
1923- .... **CLC 1, 2, 4, 7, 10, 15, 47**
See also AITN 1, 2; CA 9-12R; CABS 2;
CANR 10; CDALB 1968-1988; DLB 5;
DLBD 7; DLBY 82; MTCW

Dickey, William 1928-.......... **CLC 3, 28**
See also CA 9-12R; CANR 24; DLB 5

Dickinson, Charles 1951-.......... **CLC 49**
See also CA 128

Dickinson, Emily (Elizabeth)
1830-1886 .... **NCLC 21; PC 1**
See also CDALB 1865-1917; DA; DLB 1;
SATA 29; WLC

Dickinson, Peter (Malcolm)
1927-.................... **CLC 12, 35**
See also AAYA 9; CA 41-44R; CANR 31;
CLR 29; DLB 87; JRDA; MAICYA;
SATA 5, 62

Dickson, Carr
See Carr, John Dickson

Dickson, Carter
See Carr, John Dickson

Didion, Joan 1934-..... **CLC 1, 3, 8, 14, 32**
See also AITN 1; CA 5-8R; CANR 14;
CDALB 1968-1988; DLB 2; DLBY 81,
86; MTCW

Dietrich, Robert
See Hunt, E(verette) Howard, Jr.

Dillard, Annie 1945-............ **CLC 9, 60**
See also AAYA 6; CA 49-52; CANR 3;
DLBY 80; MTCW; SATA 10

Dillard, R(ichard) H(enry) W(ilde)
1937- .... **CLC 5**
See also CA 21-24R; CAAS 7; CANR 10;
DLB 5

Dillon, Eilis 1920-................ **CLC 17**
See also CA 9-12R; CAAS 3; CANR 4, 38;
CLR 26; MAICYA; SATA 2, 74

Dimont, Penelope
See Mortimer, Penelope (Ruth)

Dinesen, Isak........... **CLC 10, 29; SSC 7**
See also Blixen, Karen (Christentze
Dinesen)

Ding Ling....................... **CLC 68**
See also Chiang Pin-chin

Disch, Thomas M(ichael) 1940-... **CLC 7, 36**
See also CA 21-24R; CAAS 4; CANR 17,
36; CLR 18; DLB 8; MAICYA; MTCW;
SAAS 15; SATA 54

Disch, Tom
See Disch, Thomas M(ichael)

d'Isly, Georges
See Simenon, Georges (Jacques Christian)

Disraeli, Benjamin 1804-1881 .. **NCLC 2, 39**
See also DLB 21, 55

Ditcum, Steve
See Crumb, R(obert)

Dixon, Paige
See Corcoran, Barbara

Dixon, Stephen 1936-............. **CLC 52**
See also CA 89-92; CANR 17, 40; DLB 130

Doblin, Alfred .... **TCLC 13**
See also Doeblin, Alfred

Dobrolyubov, Nikolai Alexandrovich
1836-1861 .... **NCLC 5**

Dobyns, Stephen 1941-............ **CLC 37**
See also CA 45-48; CANR 2, 18

Doctorow, E(dgar) L(aurence)
1931- ..... **CLC 6, 11, 15, 18, 37, 44, 65**
See also AITN 2; BEST 89:3; CA 45-48;
CANR 2, 33; CDALB 1968-1988; DLB 2,
28; DLBY 80; MTCW

Dodgson, Charles Lutwidge 1832-1898
See Carroll, Lewis
See also CLR 2; DA; MAICYA; YABC 2

Dodson, Owen (Vincent)
1914-1983 .... **CLC 79**
See also BLC 1; BW; CA 65-68; 110;
CANR 24; DLB 76

Doeblin, Alfred 1878-1957........ **TCLC 13**
See also Doblin, Alfred
See also CA 110; 141; DLB 66

Doerr, Harriet 1910- .... **CLC 34**
See also CA 117; 122

Domecq, H(onorio) Bustos
See Bioy Casares, Adolfo; Borges, Jorge
Luis

Domini, Rey
See Lorde, Audre (Geraldine)

Dominique
See Proust, (Valentin-Louis-George-Eugene-)
Marcel

Dunbar, William   1460(?)-1530(?) .... **LC 20**

Duncan, Lois   1934-.............. **CLC 26**
See also AAYA 4; CA 1-4R; CANR 2, 23, 36; CLR 29; JRDA; MAICYA; SAAS 2; SATA 1, 36, 75

Duncan, Robert (Edward)
1919-1988 .... **CLC 1, 2, 4, 7, 15, 41, 55; PC 2**
See also CA 9-12R; 124; CANR 28; DLB 5, 16; MTCW

Dunlap, William   1766-1839 .... **NCLC 2**
See also DLB 30, 37, 59

Dunn, Douglas (Eaglesham)
1942- .... **CLC 6, 40**
See also CA 45-48; CANR 2, 33; DLB 40; MTCW

Dunn, Katherine (Karen)   1945- ..... **CLC 71**
See also CA 33-36R

Dunn, Stephen   1939- .... **CLC 36**
See also CA 33-36R; CANR 12; DLB 105

Dunne, Finley Peter   1867-1936.... **TCLC 28**
See also CA 108; DLB 11, 23

Dunne, John Gregory   1932-........ **CLC 28**
See also CA 25-28R; CANR 14; DLBY 80

Dunsany, Edward John Moreton Drax
Plunkett   1878-1957
See Dunsany, Lord; Lord Dunsany
See also CA 104; DLB 10

Dunsany, Lord................... **TCLC 2**
See also Dunsany, Edward John Moreton Drax Plunkett
See also DLB 77

du Perry, Jean
See Simenon, Georges (Jacques Christian)

Durang, Christopher (Ferdinand)
1949- .... **CLC 27, 38**
See also CA 105

Duras, Marguerite
1914- ...... **CLC 3, 6, 11, 20, 34, 40, 68**
See also CA 25-28R; DLB 83; MTCW

Durban, (Rosa) Pam   1947-........ **CLC 39**
See also CA 123

Durcan, Paul   1944-............ **CLC 43, 70**
See also CA 134

Durrell, Lawrence (George)
1912-1990 .... **CLC 1, 4, 6, 8, 13, 27, 41**
See also CA 9-12R; 132; CANR 40; CDBLB 1945-1960; DLB 15, 27; DLBY 90; MTCW

Durrenmatt, Friedrich
.... **CLC 1, 4, 8, 11, 15, 43**
See also Duerrenmatt, Friedrich
See also DLB 69, 124

Dutt, Toru   1856-1877........... **NCLC 29**

Dwight, Timothy   1752-1817...... **NCLC 13**
See also DLB 37

Dworkin, Andrea   1946- .... **CLC 43**
See also CA 77-80; CANR 16, 39; MTCW

Dwyer, Deanna
See Koontz, Dean R(ay)

Dwyer, K. R.
See Koontz, Dean R(ay)

Dylan, Bob   1941- ...... **CLC 3, 4, 6, 12, 77**
See also CA 41-44R; DLB 16

Eagleton, Terence (Francis)   1943-
See Eagleton, Terry
See also CA 57-60; CANR 7, 23; MTCW

Eagleton, Terry .... **CLC 63**
See also Eagleton, Terence (Francis)

Early, Jack
See Scoppettone, Sandra

East, Michael
See West, Morris L(anglo)

Eastaway, Edward
See Thomas, (Philip) Edward

Eastlake, William (Derry)   1917-..... **CLC 8**
See also CA 5-8R; CAAS 1; CANR 5; DLB 6

Eberhart, Richard (Ghormley)
1904- .... **CLC 3, 11, 19, 56**
See also CA 1-4R; CANR 2; CDALB 1941-1968; DLB 48; MTCW

Eberstadt, Fernanda   1960-........ **CLC 39**
See also CA 136

Echegaray (y Eizaguirre), Jose (Maria Waldo)
1832-1916 .... **TCLC 4**
See also CA 104; CANR 32; HW; MTCW

Echeverria, (Jose) Esteban (Antonino)
1805-1851 .... **NCLC 18**

Echo
See Proust, (Valentin-Louis-George-Eugene-) Marcel

Eckert, Allan W.   1931- .... **CLC 17**
See also CA 13-16R; CANR 14; SATA 27, 29

Eckhart, Meister   1260(?)-1328(?) .. **CMLC 9**
See also DLB 115

Eckmar, F. R.
See de Hartog, Jan

Eco, Umberto   1932-........... **CLC 28, 60**
See also BEST 90:1; CA 77-80; CANR 12, 33; MTCW

Eddison, E(ric) R(ucker)
1882-1945 .... **TCLC 15**
See also CA 109

Edel, (Joseph) Leon   1907-...... **CLC 29, 34**
See also CA 1-4R; CANR 1, 22; DLB 103

Eden, Emily   1797-1869 .... **NCLC 10**

Edgar, David   1948-............... **CLC 42**
See also CA 57-60; CANR 12; DLB 13; MTCW

Edgerton, Clyde (Carlyle)   1944- .... **CLC 39**
See also CA 118; 134

Edgeworth, Maria   1767-1849...... **NCLC 1**
See also DLB 116; SATA 21

Edmonds, Paul
See Kuttner, Henry

Edmonds, Walter D(umaux)   1903- .. **CLC 35**
See also CA 5-8R; CANR 2; DLB 9; MAICYA; SAAS 4; SATA 1, 27

Edmondson, Wallace
See Ellison, Harlan

Edson, Russell .... **CLC 13**
See also CA 33-36R

Edwards, G(erald) B(asil)
1899-1976 .... **CLC 25**
See also CA 110

Edwards, Gus   1939-.............. **CLC 43**
See also CA 108

Edwards, Jonathan   1703-1758....... **LC 7**
See also DA; DLB 24

Efron, Marina Ivanovna Tsvetaeva
See Tsvetaeva (Efron), Marina (Ivanovna)

Ehle, John (Marsden, Jr.)   1925-.... **CLC 27**
See also CA 9-12R

Ehrenbourg, Ilya (Grigoryevich)
See Ehrenburg, Ilya (Grigoryevich)

Ehrenburg, Ilya (Grigoryevich)
1891-1967 .... **CLC 18, 34, 62**
See also CA 102; 25-28R

Ehrenburg, Ilyo (Grigoryevich)
See Ehrenburg, Ilya (Grigoryevich)

Eich, Guenter   1907-1972.......... **CLC 15**
See also CA 111; 93-96; DLB 69, 124

Eichendorff, Joseph Freiherr von
1788-1857 .... **NCLC 8**
See also DLB 90

Eigner, Larry..................... **CLC 9**
See also Eigner, Laurence (Joel)
See also DLB 5

Eigner, Laurence (Joel)   1927-
See Eigner, Larry
See also CA 9-12R; CANR 6

Eiseley, Loren Corey   1907-1977..... **CLC 7**
See also AAYA 5; CA 1-4R; 73-76; CANR 6

Eisenstadt, Jill   1963-............. **CLC 50**
See also CA 140

Eisner, Simon
See Kornbluth, C(yril) M.

Ekeloef, (Bengt) Gunnar
1907-1968 .... **CLC 27**
See also Ekelof, (Bengt) Gunnar
See also CA 123; 25-28R

Ekelof, (Bengt) Gunnar............. **CLC 27**
See also Ekeloef, (Bengt) Gunnar

Ekwensi, C. O. D.
See Ekwensi, Cyprian (Odiatu Duaka)

Ekwensi, Cyprian (Odiatu Duaka)
1921- .... **CLC 4**
See also BLC 1; BW; CA 29-32R; CANR 18, 42; DLB 117; MTCW; SATA 66

Elaine......................... **TCLC 18**
See also Leverson, Ada

El Crummo
See Crumb, R(obert)

Elia
See Lamb, Charles

Eliade, Mircea   1907-1986 .... **CLC 19**
See also CA 65-68; 119; CANR 30; MTCW

Eliot, A. D.
See Jewett, (Theodora) Sarah Orne

Eliot, Alice
See Jewett, (Theodora) Sarah Orne

Eliot, Dan
See Silverberg, Robert

Eliot, George
1819-1880 .... **NCLC 4, 13, 23, 41**
See also CDBLB 1832-1890; DA; DLB 21, 35, 55; WLC

Eliot, John 1604-1690 .... **LC 5**
See also DLB 24

Eliot, T(homas) S(tearns)
    1888-1965 ..... **CLC 1, 2, 3, 6, 9, 10, 13,**
                        15, 24, 34, 41, 55, 57; PC 5
See also CA 5-8R; 25-28R; CANR 41;
    CDALB 1929-1941; DA; DLB 7, 10, 45,
    63; DLBY 88; MTCW; WLC 2

Elizabeth 1866-1941 .... **TCLC 41**

Elkin, Stanley L(awrence)
    1930- ... **CLC 4, 6, 9, 14, 27, 51; SSC 12**
See also CA 9-12R; CANR 8; DLB 2, 28;
    DLBY 80; MTCW

Elledge, Scott .... **CLC 34**

Elliott, Don
See Silverberg, Robert

Elliott, George P(aul) 1918-1980 ..... **CLC 2**
See also CA 1-4R; 97-100; CANR 2

Elliott, Janice 1931- .... **CLC 47**
See also CA 13-16R; CANR 8, 29; DLB 14

Elliott, Sumner Locke 1917-1991 ... **CLC 38**
See also CA 5-8R; 134; CANR 2, 21

Elliott, William
See Bradbury, Ray (Douglas)

Ellis, A. E. .... **CLC 7**

Ellis, Alice Thomas .... **CLC 40**
See also Haycraft, Anna

Ellis, Bret Easton 1964- .... **CLC 39, 71**
See also AAYA 2; CA 118; 123

Ellis, (Henry) Havelock
    1859-1939 .... **TCLC 14**
See also CA 109

Ellis, Landon
See Ellison, Harlan

Ellis, Trey 1962- .... **CLC 55**

Ellison, Harlan 1934- .... **CLC 1, 13, 42**
See also CA 5-8R; CANR 5; DLB 8;
    MTCW

Ellison, Ralph (Waldo)
    1914- .... **CLC 1, 3, 11, 54**
See also BLC 1; BW; CA 9-12R; CANR 24;
    CDALB 1941-1968; DA; DLB 2, 76;
    MTCW; WLC

Ellmann, Lucy (Elizabeth) 1956- .... **CLC 61**
See also CA 128

Ellmann, Richard (David)
    1918-1987 .... **CLC 50**
See also BEST 89:2; CA 1-4R; 122;
    CANR 2, 28; DLB 103; DLBY 87;
    MTCW

Elman, Richard 1934- .... **CLC 19**
See also CA 17-20R; CAAS 3

Elron
See Hubbard, L(afayette) Ron(ald)

Eluard, Paul .... **TCLC 7, 41**
See also Grindel, Eugene

Elyot, Sir Thomas 1490(?)-1546 ..... **LC 11**

Elytis, Odysseus 1911- .... **CLC 15, 49**
See also CA 102; MTCW

Emecheta, (Florence Onye) Buchi
    1944- .... **CLC 14, 48**
See also BLC 2; BW; CA 81-84; CANR 27;
    DLB 117; MTCW; SATA 66

Emerson, Ralph Waldo
    1803-1882 .... **NCLC 1, 38**
See also CDALB 1640-1865; DA; DLB 1,
    59, 73; WLC

Eminescu, Mihail 1850-1889 ..... **NCLC 33**

Empson, William
    1906-1984 .... **CLC 3, 8, 19, 33, 34**
See also CA 17-20R; 112; CANR 31;
    DLB 20; MTCW

Enchi Fumiko (Ueda) 1905-1986.... **CLC 31**
See also CA 129; 121

Ende, Michael (Andreas Helmuth)
    1929- .... **CLC 31**
See also CA 118; 124; CANR 36; CLR 14;
    DLB 75; MAICYA; SATA 42, 61

Endo, Shusaku 1923- ..... **CLC 7, 14, 19, 54**
See also CA 29-32R; CANR 21; MTCW

Engel, Marian 1933-1985 .... **CLC 36**
See also CA 25-28R; CANR 12; DLB 53

Engelhardt, Frederick
See Hubbard, L(afayette) Ron(ald)

Enright, D(ennis) J(oseph)
    1920- .... **CLC 4, 8, 31**
See also CA 1-4R; CANR 1, 42; DLB 27;
    SATA 25

Enzensberger, Hans Magnus
    1929- .... **CLC 43**
See also CA 116; 119

Ephron, Nora 1941- .... **CLC 17, 31**
See also AITN 2; CA 65-68; CANR 12, 39

Epsilon
See Betjeman, John

Epstein, Daniel Mark 1948- .... **CLC 7**
See also CA 49-52; CANR 2

Epstein, Jacob 1956- .... **CLC 19**
See also CA 114

Epstein, Joseph 1937- .... **CLC 39**
See also CA 112; 119

Epstein, Leslie 1938- .... **CLC 27**
See also CA 73-76; CAAS 12; CANR 23

Equiano, Olaudah 1745(?)-1797...... **LC 16**
See also BLC 2; DLB 37, 50

Erasmus, Desiderius 1469(?)-1536.... **LC 16**

Erdman, Paul E(mil) 1932- .... **CLC 25**
See also AITN 1; CA 61-64; CANR 13

Erdrich, Louise 1954- .... **CLC 39, 54**
See also AAYA 10; BEST 89:1; CA 114;
    CANR 41; MTCW

Erenburg, Ilya (Grigoryevich)
See Ehrenburg, Ilya (Grigoryevich)

Erickson, Stephen Michael 1950-
See Erickson, Steve
See also CA 129

Erickson, Steve .... **CLC 64**
See also Erickson, Stephen Michael

Ericson, Walter
See Fast, Howard (Melvin)

Eriksson, Buntel
See Bergman, (Ernst) Ingmar

Eschenbach, Wolfram von
See Wolfram von Eschenbach

Eseki, Bruno
See Mphahlele, Ezekiel

Esenin, Sergei (Alexandrovich)
    1895-1925 .... **TCLC 4**
See also CA 104

Eshleman, Clayton 1935- .... **CLC 7**
See also CA 33-36R; CAAS 6; DLB 5

Espriella, Don Manuel Alvarez
See Southey, Robert

Espriu, Salvador 1913-1985........ **CLC 9**
See also CA 115

Espronceda, Jose de 1808-1842... **NCLC 39**

Esse, James
See Stephens, James

Esterbrook, Tom
See Hubbard, L(afayette) Ron(ald)

Estleman, Loren D. 1952- .... **CLC 48**
See also CA 85-88; CANR 27; MTCW

Evan, Evin
See Faust, Frederick (Schiller)

Evans, Evan
See Faust, Frederick (Schiller)

Evans, Marian
See Eliot, George

Evans, Mary Ann
See Eliot, George

Evarts, Esther
See Benson, Sally

Everett, Percival
See Everett, Percival L.

Everett, Percival L. 1956- .... **CLC 57**
See also CA 129

Everson, R(onald) G(ilmour)
    1903- .... **CLC 27**
See also CA 17-20R; DLB 88

Everson, William (Oliver)
    1912- .... **CLC 1, 5, 14**
See also CA 9-12R; CANR 20; DLB 5, 16;
    MTCW

Evtushenko, Evgenii Aleksandrovich
See Yevtushenko, Yevgeny (Alexandrovich)

Ewart, Gavin (Buchanan)
    1916- .... **CLC 13, 46**
See also CA 89-92; CANR 17; DLB 40;
    MTCW

Ewers, Hanns Heinz 1871-1943 ... **TCLC 12**
See also CA 109

Ewing, Frederick R.
See Sturgeon, Theodore (Hamilton)

Exley, Frederick (Earl)
    1929-1992 .... **CLC 6, 11**
See also AITN 2; CA 81-84; 138; DLBY 81

Eynhardt, Guillermo
See Quiroga, Horacio (Sylvestre)

Ezekiel, Nissim 1924- .... **CLC 61**
See also CA 61-64

Ezekiel, Tish O'Dowd 1943- .... **CLC 34**
See also CA 129

Fagen, Donald 1948- .... **CLC 26**

Fainzilberg, Ilya Arnoldovich 1897-1937
See Ilf, Ilya
See also CA 120

Fair, Ronald L. 1932- .... **CLC 18**
See also BW; CA 69-72; CANR 25; DLB 33

Fairbairns, Zoe (Ann) 1948- .... **CLC 32**
See also CA 103; CANR 21

Falco, Gian
See Papini, Giovanni

Falconer, James
See Kirkup, James

Falconer, Kenneth
See Kornbluth, C(yril) M.

Falkland, Samuel
See Heijermans, Herman

Fallaci, Oriana 1930- .... **CLC 11**
See also CA 77-80; CANR 15; MTCW

Faludy, George 1913-.............. **CLC 42**
See also CA 21-24R

Faludy, Gyoergy
See Faludy, George

Fanon, Frantz 1925-1961.......... **CLC 74**
See also BLC 2; BW; CA 116; 89-92

Fanshawe, Ann .... **LC 11**

Fante, John (Thomas) 1911-1983 ... **CLC 60**
See also CA 69-72; 109; CANR 23;
DLB 130; DLBY 83

Farah, Nuruddin 1945-............. **CLC 53**
See also BLC 2; CA 106; DLB 125

Fargue, Leon-Paul 1876(?)-1947 ... **TCLC 11**
See also CA 109

Farigoule, Louis
See Romains, Jules

Farina, Richard 1936(?)-1966 .... **CLC 9**
See also CA 81-84; 25-28R

Farley, Walter (Lorimer)
1915-1989 .... **CLC 17**
See also CA 17-20R; CANR 8, 29; DLB 22;
JRDA; MAICYA; SATA 2, 43

Farmer, Philip Jose 1918-....... **CLC 1, 19**
See also CA 1-4R; CANR 4, 35; DLB 8;
MTCW

Farquhar, George 1677-1707....... **LC 21**
See also DLB 84

Farrell, J(ames) G(ordon)
1935-1979 .... **CLC 6**
See also CA 73-76; 89-92; CANR 36;
DLB 14; MTCW

Farrell, James T(homas)
1904-1979 .... **CLC 1, 4, 8, 11, 66**
See also CA 5-8R; 89-92; CANR 9; DLB 4,
9, 86; DLBD 2; MTCW

Farren, Richard J.
See Betjeman, John

Farren, Richard M.
See Betjeman, John

Fassbinder, Rainer Werner
1946-1982 .... **CLC 20**
See also CA 93-96; 106; CANR 31

Fast, Howard (Melvin) 1914- ...... **CLC 23**
See also CA 1-4R; CAAS 18; CANR 1, 33;
DLB 9; SATA 7

Faulcon, Robert
See Holdstock, Robert P.

Faulkner, William (Cuthbert)
1897-1962 ..... **CLC 1, 3, 6, 8, 9, 11, 14,
18, 28, 52, 68; SSC 1**
See also AAYA 7; CA 81-84; CANR 33;
CDALB 1929-1941; DA; DLB 9, 11, 44,
102; DLBD 2; DLBY 86; MTCW; WLC

Fauset, Jessie Redmon
1884(?)-1961 .... **CLC 19, 54**
See also BLC 2; BW; CA 109; DLB 51

Faust, Frederick (Schiller)
1892-1944(?) .... **TCLC 49**
See also CA 108

Faust, Irvin 1924-.................. **CLC 8**
See also CA 33-36R; CANR 28; DLB 2, 28;
DLBY 80

Fawkes, Guy
See Benchley, Robert (Charles)

Fearing, Kenneth (Flexner)
1902-1961 .... **CLC 51**
See also CA 93-96; DLB 9

Fecamps, Elise
See Creasey, John

Federman, Raymond 1928- ...... **CLC 6, 47**
See also CA 17-20R; CAAS 8; CANR 10;
DLBY 80

Federspiel, J(uerg) F. 1931-........ **CLC 42**

Feiffer, Jules (Ralph) 1929-... **CLC 2, 8, 64**
See also AAYA 3; CA 17-20R; CANR 30;
DLB 7, 44; MTCW; SATA 8, 61

Feige, Hermann Albert Otto Maximilian
See Traven, B.

Fei-Kan, Li
See Li Fei-kan

Feinberg, David B. 1956-......... **CLC 59**
See also CA 135

Feinstein, Elaine 1930-............ **CLC 36**
See also CA 69-72; CAAS 1; CANR 31;
DLB 14, 40; MTCW

Feldman, Irving (Mordecai) 1928-.... **CLC 7**
See also CA 1-4R; CANR 1

Fellini, Federico 1920-............. **CLC 16**
See also CA 65-68; CANR 33

Felsen, Henry Gregor 1916- .... **CLC 17**
See also CA 1-4R; CANR 1; SAAS 2;
SATA 1

Fenton, James Martin 1949-....... **CLC 32**
See also CA 102; DLB 40

Ferber, Edna 1887-1968........... **CLC 18**
See also AITN 1; CA 5-8R; 25-28R; DLB 9,
28, 86; MTCW; SATA 7

Ferguson, Helen
See Kavan, Anna

Ferguson, Samuel 1810-1886..... **NCLC 33**
See also DLB 32

Ferling, Lawrence
See Ferlinghetti, Lawrence (Monsanto)

Ferlinghetti, Lawrence (Monsanto)
1919(?)-........ **CLC 2, 6, 10, 27; PC 1**
See also CA 5-8R; CANR 3, 41;
CDALB 1941-1968; DLB 5, 16; MTCW

Fernandez, Vicente Garcia Huidobro
See Huidobro Fernandez, Vicente Garcia

Ferrer, Gabriel (Francisco Victor) Miro
See Miro (Ferrer), Gabriel (Francisco
Victor)

Ferrier, Susan (Edmonstone)
1782-1854 .... **NCLC 8**
See also DLB 116

Ferrigno, Robert 1948(?)-.......... **CLC 65**
See also CA 140

Feuchtwanger, Lion 1884-1958 ..... **TCLC 3**
See also CA 104; DLB 66

Feydeau, Georges (Leon Jules Marie)
1862-1921 .... **TCLC 22**
See also CA 113

Ficino, Marsilio 1433-1499 .... **LC 12**

Fiedler, Leslie A(aron)
1917-................ **CLC 4, 13, 24**
See also CA 9-12R; CANR 7; DLB 28, 67;
MTCW

Field, Andrew 1938-.............. **CLC 44**
See also CA 97-100; CANR 25

Field, Eugene 1850-1895 .... **NCLC 3**
See also DLB 23, 42; MAICYA; SATA 16

Field, Gans T.
See Wellman, Manly Wade

Field, Michael .... **TCLC 43**

Field, Peter
See Hobson, Laura Z(ametkin)

Fielding, Henry 1707-1754 .... **LC 1**
See also CDBLB 1660-1789; DA; DLB 39,
84, 101; WLC

Fielding, Sarah 1710-1768 .... **LC 1**
See also DLB 39

Fierstein, Harvey (Forbes) 1954- ... **CLC 33**
See also CA 123; 129

Figes, Eva 1932-.................. **CLC 31**
See also CA 53-56; CANR 4; DLB 14

Finch, Robert (Duer Claydon)
1900-..................... **CLC 18**
See also CA 57-60; CANR 9, 24; DLB 88

Findley, Timothy 1930- .... **CLC 27**
See also CA 25-28R; CANR 12, 42;
DLB 53

Fink, William
See Mencken, H(enry) L(ouis)

Firbank, Louis 1942-
See Reed, Lou
See also CA 117

Firbank, (Arthur Annesley) Ronald
1886-1926 .... **TCLC 1**
See also CA 104; DLB 36

Fisher, M(ary) F(rances) K(ennedy)
1908-1992 .... **CLC 76**
See also CA 77-80; 138

Fisher, Roy 1930-................. **CLC 25**
See also CA 81-84; CAAS 10; CANR 16;
DLB 40

Fisher, Rudolph 1897-1934 .... **TCLC 11**
See also BLC 2; BW; CA 107; 124; DLB 51,
102

Fisher, Vardis (Alvero) 1895-1968.... **CLC 7**
See also CA 5-8R; 25-28R; DLB 9

Fiske, Tarleton
See Bloch, Robert (Albert)

Frederick the Great 1712-1786 ...... **LC 14**

Fredro, Aleksander 1793-1876 ..... **NCLC 8**

Freeling, Nicolas 1927- .... **CLC 38**
  See also CA 49-52; CAAS 12; CANR 1, 17;
  DLB 87

Freeman, Douglas Southall
  1886-1953 .... **TCLC 11**
  See also CA 109; DLB 17

Freeman, Judith 1946- .... **CLC 55**

Freeman, Mary Eleanor Wilkins
  1852-1930 .... **TCLC 9; SSC 1**
  See also CA 106; DLB 12, 78

Freeman, R(ichard) Austin
  1862-1943 .... **TCLC 21**
  See also CA 113; DLB 70

French, Marilyn 1929- ...... **CLC 10, 18, 60**
  See also CA 69-72; CANR 3, 31; MTCW

French, Paul
  See Asimov, Isaac

Freneau, Philip Morin 1752-1832 .. **NCLC 1**
  See also DLB 37, 43

Freud, Sigmund 1856-1939 .... **TCLC 52**
  See also CA 115; 133; MTCW

Friedan, Betty (Naomi) 1921- ...... **CLC 74**
  See also CA 65-68; CANR 18; MTCW

Friedman, B(ernard) H(arper)
  1926- .... **CLC 7**
  See also CA 1-4R; CANR 3

Friedman, Bruce Jay 1930- .... **CLC 3, 5, 56**
  See also CA 9-12R; CANR 25; DLB 2, 28

Friel, Brian 1929- .... **CLC 5, 42, 59**
  See also CA 21-24R; CANR 33; DLB 13;
  MTCW

Friis-Baastad, Babbis Ellinor
  1921-1970 .... **CLC 12**
  See also CA 17-20R; 134; SATA 7

Frisch, Max (Rudolf)
  1911-1991 ..... **CLC 3, 9, 14, 18, 32, 44**
  See also CA 85-88; 134; CANR 32;
  DLB 69, 124; MTCW

Fromentin, Eugene (Samuel Auguste)
  1820-1876 .... **NCLC 10**
  See also DLB 123

Frost, Frederick
  See Faust, Frederick (Schiller)

Frost, Robert (Lee)
  1874-1963 .... **CLC 1, 3, 4, 9, 10, 13, 15,
                        26, 34, 44; PC 1**
  See also CA 89-92; CANR 33;
  CDALB 1917-1929; DA; DLB 54;
  DLBD 7; MTCW; SATA 14; WLC

Froy, Herald
  See Waterhouse, Keith (Spencer)

Fry, Christopher 1907- .... **CLC 2, 10, 14**
  See also CA 17-20R; CANR 9, 30; DLB 13;
  MTCW; SATA 66

Frye, (Herman) Northrop
  1912-1991 .... **CLC 24, 70**
  See also CA 5-8R; 133; CANR 8, 37;
  DLB 67, 68; MTCW

Fuchs, Daniel 1909- .... **CLC 8, 22**
  See also CA 81-84; CAAS 5; CANR 40;
  DLB 9, 26, 28

Fuchs, Daniel 1934- .... **CLC 34**
  See also CA 37-40R; CANR 14

Fuentes, Carlos
  1928- ...... **CLC 3, 8, 10, 13, 22, 41, 60**
  See also AAYA 4; AITN 2; CA 69-72;
  CANR 10, 32; DA; DLB 113; HW;
  MTCW; WLC

Fuentes, Gregorio Lopez y
  See Lopez y Fuentes, Gregorio

Fugard, (Harold) Athol
  1932- .... **CLC 5, 9, 14, 25, 40; DC 3**
  See also CA 85-88; CANR 32; MTCW

Fugard, Sheila 1932- .... **CLC 48**
  See also CA 125

Fuller, Charles (H., Jr.)
  1939- .... **CLC 25; DC 1**
  See also BLC 2; BW; CA 108; 112; DLB 38;
  MTCW

Fuller, John (Leopold) 1937- .... **CLC 62**
  See also CA 21-24R; CANR 9; DLB 40

Fuller, Margaret .... **NCLC 5**
  See also Ossoli, Sarah Margaret (Fuller
  marchesa d')

Fuller, Roy (Broadbent)
  1912-1991 .... **CLC 4, 28**
  See also CA 5-8R; 135; CAAS 10; DLB 15,
  20

Fulton, Alice 1952- .... **CLC 52**
  See also CA 116

Furphy, Joseph 1843-1912 .... **TCLC 25**

Fussell, Paul 1924- .... **CLC 74**
  See also BEST 90:1; CA 17-20R; CANR 8,
  21, 35; MTCW

Futabatei, Shimei 1864-1909 ..... **TCLC 44**

Futrelle, Jacques 1875-1912 ...... **TCLC 19**
  See also CA 113

G. B. S.
  See Shaw, George Bernard

Gaboriau, Emile 1835-1873 ...... **NCLC 14**

Gadda, Carlo Emilio 1893-1973 .... **CLC 11**
  See also CA 89-92

Gaddis, William
  1922- .... **CLC 1, 3, 6, 8, 10, 19, 43**
  See also CA 17-20R; CANR 21; DLB 2;
  MTCW

Gaines, Ernest J(ames)
  1933- .... **CLC 3, 11, 18**
  See also AITN 1; BLC 2; BW; CA 9-12R;
  CANR 6, 24, 42; CDALB 1968-1988;
  DLB 2, 33; DLBY 80; MTCW

Gaitskill, Mary 1954- .... **CLC 69**
  See also CA 128

Galdos, Benito Perez
  See Perez Galdos, Benito

Gale, Zona 1874-1938 .... **TCLC 7**
  See also CA 105; DLB 9, 78

Galeano, Eduardo (Hughes) 1940- ... **CLC 72**
  See also CA 29-32R; CANR 13, 32; HW

Galiano, Juan Valera y Alcala
  See Valera y Alcala-Galiano, Juan

Gallagher, Tess 1943- .... **CLC 18, 63**
  See also CA 106; DLB 120

Gallant, Mavis
  1922- .... **CLC 7, 18, 38; SSC 5**
  See also CA 69-72; CANR 29; DLB 53;
  MTCW

Gallant, Roy A(rthur) 1924- .... **CLC 17**
  See also CA 5-8R; CANR 4, 29; CLR 30;
  MAICYA; SATA 4, 68

Gallico, Paul (William) 1897-1976 ... **CLC 2**
  See also AITN 1; CA 5-8R; 69-72;
  CANR 23; DLB 9; MAICYA; SATA 13

Gallup, Ralph
  See Whitemore, Hugh (John)

Galsworthy, John 1867-1933 .... **TCLC 1, 45**
  See also CA 104; 141; CDBLB 1890-1914;
  DA; DLB 10, 34, 98; WLC 2

Galt, John 1779-1839 .... **NCLC 1**
  See also DLB 99, 116

Galvin, James 1951- .... **CLC 38**
  See also CA 108; CANR 26

Gamboa, Federico 1864-1939 ...... **TCLC 36**

Gann, Ernest Kellogg 1910-1991 .... **CLC 23**
  See also AITN 1; CA 1-4R; 136; CANR 1

Garcia, Christina 1959- .... **CLC 76**

Garcia Lorca, Federico
  1898-1936 .. **TCLC 1, 7, 49; DC 2; PC 3**
  See also CA 104; 131; DA; DLB 108; HW;
  MTCW; WLC

Garcia Marquez, Gabriel (Jose)
  1928- .... **CLC 2, 3, 8, 10, 15, 27, 47, 55;
                                              SSC 8**
  See also Marquez, Gabriel (Jose) Garcia
  See also AAYA 3; BEST 89:1, 90:4;
  CA 33-36R; CANR 10, 28; DA;
  DLB 113; HW; MTCW; WLC

Gard, Janice
  See Latham, Jean Lee

Gard, Roger Martin du
  See Martin du Gard, Roger

Gardam, Jane 1928- .... **CLC 43**
  See also CA 49-52; CANR 2, 18, 33;
  CLR 12; DLB 14; MAICYA; MTCW;
  SAAS 9; SATA 28, 39

Gardner, Herb .... **CLC 44**

Gardner, John (Champlin), Jr.
  1933-1982 ..... **CLC 2, 3, 5, 7, 8, 10, 18,
                                          28, 34; SSC 7**
  See also AITN 1; CA 65-68; 107;
  CANR 33; DLB 2; DLBY 82; MTCW;
  SATA 31, 40

Gardner, John (Edmund) 1926- ..... **CLC 30**
  See also CA 103; CANR 15; MTCW

Gardner, Noel
  See Kuttner, Henry

Gardons, S. S.
  See Snodgrass, W(illiam) D(e Witt)

Garfield, Leon 1921- .... **CLC 12**
  See also AAYA 8; CA 17-20R; CANR 38,
  41; CLR 21; JRDA; MAICYA; SATA 1,
  32

Garland, (Hannibal) Hamlin
  1860-1940 .... **TCLC 3**
  See also CA 104; DLB 12, 71, 78

Garneau, (Hector de) Saint-Denys
  1912-1943 .... **TCLC 13**
  See also CA 111; DLB 88

Author Index

Gravel, Fern
See Hall, James Norman

Graver, Elizabeth 1964- . . . . CLC 70
See also CA 135

Graves, Richard Perceval 1945- . . . . CLC 44
See also CA 65-68; CANR 9, 26

Graves, Robert (von Ranke)
1895-1985 . . . . . . CLC 1, 2, 6, 11, 39, 44,
45; PC 6
See also CA 5-8R; 117; CANR 5, 36;
CDBLB 1914-1945; DLB 20, 100;
DLBY 85; MTCW; SATA 45

Gray, Alasdair 1934- . . . . CLC 41
See also CA 126; MTCW

Gray, Amlin 1946- . . . . CLC 29
See also CA 138

Gray, Francine du Plessix 1930- . . . . CLC 22
See also BEST 90:3; CA 61-64; CAAS 2;
CANR 11, 33; MTCW

Gray, John (Henry) 1866-1934 . . . . TCLC 19
See also CA 119

Gray, Simon (James Holliday)
1936- . . . . CLC 9, 14, 36
See also AITN 1; CA 21-24R; CAAS 3;
CANR 32; DLB 13; MTCW

Gray, Spalding 1941- . . . . CLC 49
See also CA 128

Gray, Thomas 1716-1771 . . . . . . LC 4; PC 2
See also CDBLB 1660-1789; DA; DLB 109;
WLC

Grayson, David
See Baker, Ray Stannard

Grayson, Richard (A.) 1951- . . . . CLC 38
See also CA 85-88; CANR 14, 31

Greeley, Andrew M(oran) 1928- . . . . CLC 28
See also CA 5-8R; CAAS 7; CANR 7;
MTCW

Green, Brian
See Card, Orson Scott

Green, Hannah . . . . CLC 3
See also CA 73-76

Green, Hannah
See Greenberg, Joanne (Goldenberg)

Green, Henry . . . . CLC 2, 13
See also Yorke, Henry Vincent
See also DLB 15

Green, Julian (Hartridge)
1900- . . . . CLC 3, 11
See also Green, Julien
See also CA 21-24R; CANR 33; DLB 4, 72;
MTCW

Green, Julien 1900- . . . . CLC 77
See also Green, Julian (Hartridge)

Green, Paul (Eliot) 1894-1981 . . . . . . CLC 25
See also AITN 1; CA 5-8R; 103; CANR 3;
DLB 7, 9; DLBY 81

Greenberg, Ivan 1908-1973
See Rahv, Philip
See also CA 85-88

Greenberg, Joanne (Goldenberg)
1932- . . . . CLC 7, 30
See also CA 5-8R; CANR 14, 32; SATA 25

Greenberg, Richard 1959(?)- . . . . CLC 57
See also CA 138

Greene, Bette 1934- . . . . CLC 30
See also AAYA 7; CA 53-56; CANR 4;
CLR 2; JRDA; MAICYA; SAAS 16;
SATA 8

Greene, Gael . . . . CLC 8
See also CA 13-16R; CANR 10

Greene, Graham
1904-1991 . . . . CLC 1, 3, 6, 9, 14, 18, 27,
37, 70, 72
See also AITN 2; CA 13-16R; 133;
CANR 35; CDBLB 1945-1960; DA;
DLB 13, 15, 77, 100; DLBY 91; MTCW;
SATA 20; WLC

Greer, Richard
See Silverberg, Robert

Greer, Richard
See Silverberg, Robert

Gregor, Arthur 1923- . . . . CLC 9
See also CA 25-28R; CAAS 10; CANR 11;
SATA 36

Gregor, Lee
See Pohl, Frederik

Gregory, Isabella Augusta (Persse)
1852-1932 . . . . TCLC 1
See also CA 104; DLB 10

Gregory, J. Dennis
See Williams, John A(lfred)

Grendon, Stephen
See Derleth, August (William)

Grenville, Kate 1950- . . . . CLC 61
See also CA 118

Grenville, Pelham
See Wodehouse, P(elham) G(renville)

Greve, Felix Paul (Berthold Friedrich)
1879-1948
See Grove, Frederick Philip
See also CA 104; 141

Grey, Zane 1872-1939 . . . . TCLC 6
See also CA 104; 132; DLB 9; MTCW

Grieg, (Johan) Nordahl (Brun)
1902-1943 . . . . TCLC 10
See also CA 107

Grieve, C(hristopher) M(urray)
1892-1978 . . . . CLC 11, 19
See also MacDiarmid, Hugh
See also CA 5-8R; 85-88; CANR 33;
MTCW

Griffin, Gerald 1803-1840 . . . . NCLC 7

Griffin, John Howard 1920-1980 . . . . CLC 68
See also AITN 1; CA 1-4R; 101; CANR 2

Griffin, Peter . . . . CLC 39

Griffiths, Trevor 1935- . . . . CLC 13, 52
See also CA 97-100; DLB 13

Grigson, Geoffrey (Edward Harvey)
1905-1985 . . . . CLC 7, 39
See also CA 25-28R; 118; CANR 20, 33;
DLB 27; MTCW

Grillparzer, Franz 1791-1872 . . . . . . NCLC 1
See also DLB 133

Grimble, Reverend Charles James
See Eliot, T(homas) S(tearns)

Grimke, Charlotte L(ottie) Forten
1837(?)-1914
See Forten, Charlotte L.
See also BW; CA 117; 124

Grimm, Jacob Ludwig Karl
1785-1863 . . . . NCLC 3
See also DLB 90; MAICYA; SATA 22

Grimm, Wilhelm Karl 1786-1859 . . NCLC 3
See also DLB 90; MAICYA; SATA 22

Grimmelshausen, Johann Jakob Christoffel
von 1621-1676 . . . . LC 6

Grindel, Eugene 1895-1952
See Eluard, Paul
See also CA 104

Grossman, David 1954- . . . . CLC 67
See also CA 138

Grossman, Vasily (Semenovich)
1905-1964 . . . . CLC 41
See also CA 124; 130; MTCW

Grove, Frederick Philip . . . . TCLC 4
See also Greve, Felix Paul (Berthold
Friedrich)
See also DLB 92

Grubb
See Crumb, R(obert)

Grumbach, Doris (Isaac)
1918- . . . . CLC 13, 22, 64
See also CA 5-8R; CAAS 2; CANR 9, 42

Grundtvig, Nicolai Frederik Severin
1783-1872 . . . . NCLC 1

Grunge
See Crumb, R(obert)

Grunwald, Lisa 1959- . . . . CLC 44
See also CA 120

Guare, John 1938- . . . . CLC 8, 14, 29, 67
See also CA 73-76; CANR 21; DLB 7;
MTCW

Gudjonsson, Halldor Kiljan 1902-
See Laxness, Halldor
See also CA 103

Guenter, Erich
See Eich, Guenter

Guest, Barbara 1920- . . . . CLC 34
See also CA 25-28R; CANR 11; DLB 5

Guest, Judith (Ann) 1936- . . . . CLC 8, 30
See also AAYA 7; CA 77-80; CANR 15;
MTCW

Guild, Nicholas M. 1944- . . . . CLC 33
See also CA 93-96

Guillemin, Jacques
See Sartre, Jean-Paul

Guillen, Jorge 1893-1984 . . . . CLC 11
See also CA 89-92; 112; DLB 108; HW

Guillen (y Batista), Nicolas (Cristobal)
1902-1989 . . . . CLC 48, 79
See also BLC 2; BW; CA 116; 125; 129;
HW

Guillevic, (Eugene) 1907- . . . . CLC 33
See also CA 93-96

Guillois
See Desnos, Robert

Guiney, Louise Imogen
1861-1920 . . . . TCLC 41
See also DLB 54

Guiraldes, Ricardo (Guillermo)
1886-1927 . . . . TCLC 39
See also CA 131; HW; MTCW

Gunn, Bill .... CLC 5
See also Gunn, William Harrison
See also DLB 38

Gunn, Thom(son William)
1929- .... CLC 3, 6, 18, 32
See also CA 17-20R; CANR 9, 33;
CDBLB 1960 to Present; DLB 27;
MTCW

Gunn, William Harrison 1934(?)-1989
See Gunn, Bill
See also AITN 1; BW; CA 13-16R; 128;
CANR 12, 25

Gunnars, Kristjana 1948- .... CLC 69
See also CA 113; DLB 60

Gurganus, Allan 1947- .... CLC 70
See also BEST 90:1; CA 135

Gurney, A(lbert) R(amsdell), Jr.
1930- .... CLC 32, 50, 54
See also CA 77-80; CANR 32

Gurney, Ivor (Bertie) 1890-1937 ... TCLC 33

Gurney, Peter
See Gurney, A(lbert) R(amsdell), Jr.

Gustafson, Ralph (Barker) 1909- .... CLC 36
See also CA 21-24R; CANR 8; DLB 88

Gut, Gom
See Simenon, Georges (Jacques Christian)

Guthrie, A(lfred) B(ertram), Jr.
1901-1991 .... CLC 23
See also CA 57-60; 134; CANR 24; DLB 6;
SATA 62; SATA-Obit 67

Guthrie, Isobel
See Grieve, C(hristopher) M(urray)

Guthrie, Woodrow Wilson 1912-1967
See Guthrie, Woody
See also CA 113; 93-96

Guthrie, Woody .... CLC 35
See also Guthrie, Woodrow Wilson

Guy, Rosa (Cuthbert) 1928- .... CLC 26
See also AAYA 4; BW; CA 17-20R;
CANR 14, 34; CLR 13; DLB 33; JRDA;
MAICYA; SATA 14, 62

Gwendolyn
See Bennett, (Enoch) Arnold

H. D. ...... CLC 3, 8, 14, 31, 34, 73; PC 5
See also Doolittle, Hilda

Haavikko, Paavo Juhani
1931- .... CLC 18, 34
See also CA 106

Habbema, Koos
See Heijermans, Herman

Hacker, Marilyn 1942- .... CLC 5, 9, 23, 72
See also CA 77-80; DLB 120

Haggard, H(enry) Rider
1856-1925 .... TCLC 11
See also CA 108; DLB 70; SATA 16

Haig, Fenil
See Ford, Ford Madox

Haig-Brown, Roderick (Langmere)
1908-1976 .... CLC 21
See also CA 5-8R; 69-72; CANR 4, 38;
CLR 31; DLB 88; MAICYA; SATA 12

Hailey, Arthur 1920- .... CLC 5
See also AITN 2; BEST 90:3; CA 1-4R;
CANR 2, 36; DLB 88; DLBY 82; MTCW

Hailey, Elizabeth Forsythe 1938-... CLC 40
See also CA 93-96; CAAS 1; CANR 15

Haines, John (Meade) 1924- .... CLC 58
See also CA 17-20R; CANR 13, 34; DLB 5

Haldeman, Joe (William) 1943-..... CLC 61
See also CA 53-56; CANR 6; DLB 8

Haley, Alex(ander Murray Palmer)
1921-1992 .... CLC 8, 12, 76
See also BLC 2; BW; CA 77-80; 136; DA;
DLB 38; MTCW

Haliburton, Thomas Chandler
1796-1865 .... NCLC 15
See also DLB 11, 99

Hall, Donald (Andrew, Jr.)
1928- .... CLC 1, 13, 37, 59
See also CA 5-8R; CAAS 7; CANR 2;
DLB 5; SATA 23

Hall, Frederic Sauser
See Sauser-Hall, Frederic

Hall, James
See Kuttner, Henry

Hall, James Norman 1887-1951 ... TCLC 23
See also CA 123; SATA 21

Hall, (Marguerite) Radclyffe
1886(?)-1943 .... TCLC 12
See also CA 110

Hall, Rodney 1935- .... CLC 51
See also CA 109

Halliday, Michael
See Creasey, John

Halpern, Daniel 1945- .... CLC 14
See also CA 33-36R

Hamburger, Michael (Peter Leopold)
1924- .... CLC 5, 14
See also CA 5-8R; CAAS 4; CANR 2;
DLB 27

Hamill, Pete 1935- .... CLC 10
See also CA 25-28R; CANR 18

Hamilton, Clive
See Lewis, C(live) S(taples)

Hamilton, Edmond 1904-1977 .... CLC 1
See also CA 1-4R; CANR 3; DLB 8

Hamilton, Eugene (Jacob) Lee
See Lee-Hamilton, Eugene (Jacob)

Hamilton, Franklin
See Silverberg, Robert

Hamilton, Gail
See Corcoran, Barbara

Hamilton, Mollie
See Kaye, M(ary) M(argaret)

Hamilton, (Anthony Walter) Patrick
1904-1962 .... CLC 51
See also CA 113; DLB 10

Hamilton, Virginia 1936-.......... CLC 26
See also AAYA 2; BW; CA 25-28R;
CANR 20, 37; CLR 1, 11; DLB 33, 52;
JRDA; MAICYA; MTCW; SATA 4, 56

Hammett, (Samuel) Dashiell
1894-1961 .... CLC 3, 5, 10, 19, 47
See also AITN 1; CA 81-84; CANR 42;
CDALB 1929-1941; DLBD 6; MTCW

Hammon, Jupiter 1711(?)-1800(?).. NCLC 5
See also BLC 2; DLB 31, 50

Hammond, Keith
See Kuttner, Henry

Hamner, Earl (Henry), Jr. 1923- ... CLC 12
See also AITN 2; CA 73-76; DLB 6

Hampton, Christopher (James)
1946- .... CLC 4
See also CA 25-28R; DLB 13; MTCW

Hamsun, Knut .... TCLC 2, 14, 49
See also Pedersen, Knut

Handke, Peter 1942- .. CLC 5, 8, 10, 15, 38
See also CA 77-80; CANR 33; DLB 85,
124; MTCW

Hanley, James 1901-1985 ...CLC 3, 5, 8, 13
See also CA 73-76; 117; CANR 36; MTCW

Hannah, Barry 1942- .... CLC 23, 38
See also CA 108; 110; DLB 6; MTCW

Hannon, Ezra
See Hunter, Evan

Hansberry, Lorraine (Vivian)
1930-1965 .... CLC 17, 62; DC 2
See also BLC 2; BW; CA 109; 25-28R;
CABS 3; CDALB 1941-1968; DA;
DLB 7, 38; MTCW

Hansen, Joseph 1923-............. CLC 38
See also CA 29-32R; CAAS 17; CANR 16

Hansen, Martin A. 1909-1955..... TCLC 32

Hanson, Kenneth O(stlin) 1922-.... CLC 13
See also CA 53-56; CANR 7

Hardwick, Elizabeth 1916- .... CLC 13
See also CA 5-8R; CANR 3, 32; DLB 6;
MTCW

Hardy, Thomas
1840-1928 ...... TCLC 4, 10, 18, 32, 48;
SSC 2
See also CA 104; 123; CDBLB 1890-1914;
DA; DLB 18, 19; MTCW; WLC

Hare, David 1947- .... CLC 29, 58
See also CA 97-100; CANR 39; DLB 13;
MTCW

Harford, Henry
See Hudson, W(illiam) H(enry)

Hargrave, Leonie
See Disch, Thomas M(ichael)

Harlan, Louis R(udolph) 1922-..... CLC 34
See also CA 21-24R; CANR 25

Harling, Robert 1951(?)- .... CLC 53

Harmon, William (Ruth) 1938-..... CLC 38
See also CA 33-36R; CANR 14, 32, 35;
SATA 65

Harper, F. E. W.
See Harper, Frances Ellen Watkins

Harper, Frances E. W.
See Harper, Frances Ellen Watkins

Harper, Frances E. Watkins
See Harper, Frances Ellen Watkins

Harper, Frances Ellen
See Harper, Frances Ellen Watkins

Harper, Frances Ellen Watkins
1825-1911 .... TCLC 14
See also BLC 2; BW; CA 111; 125; DLB 50

Harper, Michael S(teven) 1938- .. CLC 7, 22
See also BW; CA 33-36R; CANR 24;
DLB 41

Helyar, Jane Penelope Josephine 1933-
See Poole, Josephine
See also CA 21-24R; CANR 10, 26

Hemans, Felicia 1793-1835 ...... NCLC 29
See also DLB 96

Hemingway, Ernest (Miller)
1899-1961 .... CLC 1, 3, 6, 8, 10, 13, 19,
30, 34, 39, 41, 44, 50, 61; SSC 1
See also CA 77-80; CANR 34;
CDALB 1917-1929; DA; DLB 4, 9, 102;
DLBD 1; DLBY 81, 87; MTCW; WLC

Hempel, Amy 1951- .... CLC 39
See also CA 118; 137

Henderson, F. C.
See Mencken, H(enry) L(ouis)

Henderson, Sylvia
See Ashton-Warner, Sylvia (Constance)

Henley, Beth .... CLC 23
See also Henley, Elizabeth Becker
See also CABS 3; DLBY 86

Henley, Elizabeth Becker 1952-
See Henley, Beth
See also CA 107; CANR 32; MTCW

Henley, William Ernest
1849-1903 .... TCLC 8
See also CA 105; DLB 19

Hennissart, Martha
See Lathen, Emma
See also CA 85-88

Henry, O. .... TCLC 1, 19; SSC 5
See also Porter, William Sydney
See also WLC

Henryson, Robert 1430(?)-1506(?).... LC 20

Henry VIII 1491-1547 .... LC 10

Henschke, Alfred
See Klabund

Hentoff, Nat(han Irving) 1925- ..... CLC 26
See also AAYA 4; CA 1-4R; CAAS 6;
CANR 5, 25; CLR 1; JRDA; MAICYA;
SATA 27, 42, 69

Heppenstall, (John) Rayner
1911-1981 .... CLC 10
See also CA 1-4R; 103; CANR 29

Herbert, Frank (Patrick)
1920-1986 .... CLC 12, 23, 35, 44
See also CA 53-56; 118; CANR 5; DLB 8;
MTCW; SATA 9, 37, 47

Herbert, George 1593-1633 .... PC 4
See also CDBLB Before 1660; DLB 126

Herbert, Zbigniew 1924- .... CLC 9, 43
See also CA 89-92; CANR 36; MTCW

Herbst, Josephine (Frey)
1897-1969 .... CLC 34
See also CA 5-8R; 25-28R; DLB 9

Hergesheimer, Joseph
1880-1954 .... TCLC 11
See also CA 109; DLB 102, 9

Herlihy, James Leo 1927- .... CLC 6
See also CA 1-4R; CANR 2

Hermogenes fl. c. 175- .... CMLC 6

Hernandez, Jose 1834-1886 ...... NCLC 17

Herrick, Robert 1591-1674 .... LC 13
See also DA; DLB 126

Herring, Guilles
See Somerville, Edith

Herriot, James 1916- .... CLC 12
See also Wight, James Alfred
See also AAYA 1; CANR 40

Herrmann, Dorothy 1941- .... CLC 44
See also CA 107

Herrmann, Taffy
See Herrmann, Dorothy

Hersey, John (Richard)
1914-1993 .... CLC 1, 2, 7, 9, 40
See also CA 17-20R; 140; CANR 33;
DLB 6; MTCW; SATA 25

Herzen, Aleksandr Ivanovich
1812-1870 .... NCLC 10

Herzl, Theodor 1860-1904 .... TCLC 36

Herzog, Werner 1942- .... CLC 16
See also CA 89-92

Hesiod c. 8th cent. B.C.- .... CMLC 5

Hesse, Hermann
1877-1962 .... CLC 1, 2, 3, 6, 11, 17, 25,
69; SSC 9
See also CA 17-18; CAP 2; DA; DLB 66;
MTCW; SATA 50; WLC

Hewes, Cady
See De Voto, Bernard (Augustine)

Heyen, William 1940- .... CLC 13, 18
See also CA 33-36R; CAAS 9; DLB 5

Heyerdahl, Thor 1914- .... CLC 26
See also CA 5-8R; CANR 5, 22; MTCW;
SATA 2, 52

Heym, Georg (Theodor Franz Arthur)
1887-1912 .... TCLC 9
See also CA 106

Heym, Stefan 1913- .... CLC 41
See also CA 9-12R; CANR 4; DLB 69

Heyse, Paul (Johann Ludwig von)
1830-1914 .... TCLC 8
See also CA 104; DLB 129

Hibbert, Eleanor Alice Burford
1906-1993 .... CLC 7
See also BEST 90:4; CA 17-20R; 140;
CANR 9, 28; SATA 2; SATA-Obit 74

Higgins, George V(incent)
1939- .... CLC 4, 7, 10, 18
See also CA 77-80; CAAS 5; CANR 17;
DLB 2; DLBY 81; MTCW

Higginson, Thomas Wentworth
1823-1911 .... TCLC 36
See also DLB 1, 64

Highet, Helen
See MacInnes, Helen (Clark)

Highsmith, (Mary) Patricia
1921- .... CLC 2, 4, 14, 42
See also CA 1-4R; CANR 1, 20; MTCW

Highwater, Jamake (Mamake)
1942(?)- .... CLC 12
See also AAYA 7; CA 65-68; CAAS 7;
CANR 10, 34; CLR 17; DLB 52;
DLBY 85; JRDA; MAICYA; SATA 30,
32, 69

Hijuelos, Oscar 1951- .... CLC 65
See also BEST 90:1; CA 123; HW

Hikmet, Nazim 1902-1963 .... CLC 40
See also CA 141; 93-96

Hildesheimer, Wolfgang
1916-1991 .... CLC 49
See also CA 101; 135; DLB 69, 124

Hill, Geoffrey (William)
1932- .... CLC 5, 8, 18, 45
See also CA 81-84; CANR 21;
CDBLB 1960 to Present; DLB 40;
MTCW

Hill, George Roy 1921- .... CLC 26
See also CA 110; 122

Hill, John
See Koontz, Dean R(ay)

Hill, Susan (Elizabeth) 1942- .... CLC 4
See also CA 33-36R; CANR 29; DLB 14;
MTCW

Hillerman, Tony 1925-............. CLC 62
See also AAYA 6; BEST 89:1; CA 29-32R;
CANR 21, 42; SATA 6

Hillesum, Etty 1914-1943 .... TCLC 49
See also CA 137

Hilliard, Noel (Harvey) 1929-...... CLC 15
See also CA 9-12R; CANR 7

Hillis, Rick 1956-................. CLC 66
See also CA 134

Hilton, James 1900-1954 .... TCLC 21
See also CA 108; DLB 34, 77; SATA 34

Himes, Chester (Bomar)
1909-1984 .... CLC 2, 4, 7, 18, 58
See also BLC 2; BW; CA 25-28R; 114;
CANR 22; DLB 2, 76; MTCW

Hinde, Thomas .... CLC 6, 11
See also Chitty, Thomas Willes

Hindin, Nathan
See Bloch, Robert (Albert)

Hine, (William) Daryl 1936-....... CLC 15
See also CA 1-4R; CAAS 15; CANR 1, 20;
DLB 60

Hinkson, Katharine Tynan
See Tynan, Katharine

Hinton, S(usan) E(loise) 1950- ..... CLC 30
See also AAYA 2; CA 81-84; CANR 32;
CLR 3, 23; DA; JRDA; MAICYA;
MTCW; SATA 19, 58

Hippius, Zinaida .... TCLC 9
See also Gippius, Zinaida (Nikolayevna)

Hiraoka, Kimitake 1925-1970
See Mishima, Yukio
See also CA 97-100; 29-32R; MTCW

Hirsch, E(ric) D(onald), Jr. 1928-... CLC 79
See also CA 25-28R; CANR 27; DLB 67;
MTCW

Hirsch, Edward 1950- .... CLC 31, 50
See also CA 104; CANR 20, 42; DLB 120

Hitchcock, Alfred (Joseph)
1899-1980 .... CLC 16
See also CA 97-100; SATA 24, 27

Hoagland, Edward 1932-.......... CLC 28
See also CA 1-4R; CANR 2, 31; DLB 6;
SATA 51

Hoban, Russell (Conwell) 1925- .. CLC 7, 25
See also CA 5-8R; CANR 23, 37; CLR 3;
DLB 52; MAICYA; MTCW; SATA 1, 40

Hobbs, Perry
See Blackmur, R(ichard) P(almer)

Howells, William Dean
1837-1920 . . . . **TCLC 41, 7, 17**
See also CA 104; 134; CDALB 1865-1917;
DLB 12, 64, 74, 79

Howes, Barbara 1914- . . . . **CLC 15**
See also CA 9-12R; CAAS 3; SATA 5

Hrabal, Bohumil 1914- . . . . **CLC 13, 67**
See also CA 106; CAAS 12

Hsun, Lu . . . . **TCLC 3**
See also Shu-Jen, Chou

Hubbard, L(afayette) Ron(ald)
1911-1986 . . . . **CLC 43**
See also CA 77-80; 118; CANR 22

Huch, Ricarda (Octavia)
1864-1947 . . . . **TCLC 13**
See also CA 111; DLB 66

Huddle, David 1942- . . . . **CLC 49**
See also CA 57-60; DLB 130

Hudson, Jeffrey
See Crichton, (John) Michael

Hudson, W(illiam) H(enry)
1841-1922 . . . . **TCLC 29**
See also CA 115; DLB 98; SATA 35

Hueffer, Ford Madox
See Ford, Ford Madox

Hughart, Barry 1934- . . . . **CLC 39**
See also CA 137

Hughes, Colin
See Creasey, John

Hughes, David (John) 1930- . . . . **CLC 48**
See also CA 116; 129; DLB 14

Hughes, (James) Langston
1902-1967 . . . . . **CLC 1, 5, 10, 15, 35, 44;**
DC 3; PC 1; SSC 6
See also BLC 2; BW; CA 1-4R; 25-28R;
CANR 1, 34; CDALB 1929-1941;
CLR 17; DA; DLB 4, 7, 48, 51, 86;
JRDA; MAICYA; MTCW; SATA 4, 33;
WLC

Hughes, Richard (Arthur Warren)
1900-1976 . . . . **CLC 1, 11**
See also CA 5-8R; 65-68; CANR 4;
DLB 15; MTCW; SATA 8, 25

Hughes, Ted
1930- . . . . **CLC 2, 4, 9, 14, 37; PC 7**
See also CA 1-4R; CANR 1, 33; CLR 3;
DLB 40; MAICYA; MTCW; SATA 27,
49

Hugo, Richard F(ranklin)
1923-1982 . . . . **CLC 6, 18, 32**
See also CA 49-52; 108; CANR 3; DLB 5

Hugo, Victor (Marie)
1802-1885 . . . . **NCLC 3, 10, 21**
See also DA; DLB 119; SATA 47; WLC

Huidobro, Vicente
See Huidobro Fernandez, Vicente Garcia

Huidobro Fernandez, Vicente Garcia
1893-1948 . . . . **TCLC 31**
See also CA 131; HW

Hulme, Keri 1947- . . . . **CLC 39**
See also CA 125

Hulme, T(homas) E(rnest)
1883-1917 . . . . **TCLC 21**
See also CA 117; DLB 19

Hume, David 1711-1776 . . . . **LC 7**
See also DLB 104

Humphrey, William 1924- . . . . **CLC 45**
See also CA 77-80; DLB 6

Humphreys, Emyr Owen 1919- . . . . . **CLC 47**
See also CA 5-8R; CANR 3, 24; DLB 15

Humphreys, Josephine 1945- . . . . **CLC 34, 57**
See also CA 121; 127

Hungerford, Pixie
See Brinsmead, H(esba) F(ay)

Hunt, E(verette) Howard, Jr.
1918- . . . . **CLC 3**
See also AITN 1; CA 45-48; CANR 2

Hunt, Kyle
See Creasey, John

Hunt, (James Henry) Leigh
1784-1859 . . . . **NCLC 1**

Hunt, Marsha 1946- . . . . **CLC 70**

Hunter, E. Waldo
See Sturgeon, Theodore (Hamilton)

Hunter, Evan 1926- . . . . **CLC 11, 31**
See also CA 5-8R; CANR 5, 38; DLBY 82;
MTCW; SATA 25

Hunter, Kristin (Eggleston) 1931- . . . **CLC 35**
See also AITN 1; BW; CA 13-16R;
CANR 13; CLR 3; DLB 33; MAICYA;
SAAS 10; SATA 12

Hunter, Mollie 1922- . . . . **CLC 21**
See also McIlwraith, Maureen Mollie
Hunter
See also CANR 37; CLR 25; JRDA;
MAICYA; SAAS 7; SATA 54

Hunter, Robert (?)-1734 . . . . **LC 7**

Hurston, Zora Neale
1903-1960 . . . . **CLC 7, 30, 61; SSC 4**
See also BLC 2; BW; CA 85-88; DA;
DLB 51, 86; MTCW

Huston, John (Marcellus)
1906-1987 . . . . **CLC 20**
See also CA 73-76; 123; CANR 34; DLB 26

Hustvedt, Siri 1955- . . . . **CLC 76**
See also CA 137

Hutten, Ulrich von 1488-1523 . . . . **LC 16**

Huxley, Aldous (Leonard)
1894-1963 . . . . . **CLC 1, 3, 4, 5, 8, 11, 18,**
35, 79
See also CA 85-88; CDBLB 1914-1945; DA;
DLB 36, 100; MTCW; SATA 63; WLC

Huysmans, Charles Marie Georges
1848-1907
See Huysmans, Joris-Karl
See also CA 104

Huysmans, Joris-Karl . . . . **TCLC 7**
See also Huysmans, Charles Marie Georges
See also DLB 123

Hwang, David Henry 1957- . . . . **CLC 55**
See also CA 127; 132

Hyde, Anthony 1946- . . . . **CLC 42**
See also CA 136

Hyde, Margaret O(ldroyd) 1917- . . . **CLC 21**
See also CA 1-4R; CANR 1, 36; CLR 23;
JRDA; MAICYA; SAAS 8; SATA 1, 42

Hynes, James 1956(?)- . . . . **CLC 65**

Ian, Janis 1951- . . . . **CLC 21**
See also CA 105

Ibanez, Vicente Blasco
See Blasco Ibanez, Vicente

Ibarguengoitia, Jorge 1928-1983 . . . . **CLC 37**
See also CA 124; 113; HW

Ibsen, Henrik (Johan)
1828-1906 . . . . **TCLC 2, 8, 16, 37, 52;**
DC 2
See also CA 104; 141; DA; WLC

Ibuse Masuji 1898-1993 . . . . **CLC 22**
See also CA 127; 141

Ichikawa, Kon 1915- . . . . **CLC 20**
See also CA 121

Idle, Eric 1943- . . . . **CLC 21**
See also Monty Python
See also CA 116; CANR 35

Ignatow, David 1914- . . . . . . **CLC 4, 7, 14, 40**
See also CA 9-12R; CAAS 3; CANR 31;
DLB 5

Ihimaera, Witi 1944- . . . . **CLC 46**
See also CA 77-80

Ilf, Ilya . . . . **TCLC 21**
See also Fainzilberg, Ilya Arnoldovich

Immermann, Karl (Lebrecht)
1796-1840 . . . . **NCLC 4**
See also DLB 133

Inclan, Ramon (Maria) del Valle
See Valle-Inclan, Ramon (Maria) del

Infante, G(uillermo) Cabrera
See Cabrera Infante, G(uillermo)

Ingalls, Rachel (Holmes) 1940- . . . . . **CLC 42**
See also CA 123; 127

Ingamells, Rex 1913-1955 . . . . **TCLC 35**

Inge, William Motter
1913-1973 . . . . **CLC 1, 8, 19**
See also CA 9-12R; CDALB 1941-1968;
DLB 7; MTCW

Ingelow, Jean 1820-1897 . . . . **NCLC 39**
See also DLB 35; SATA 33

Ingram, Willis J.
See Harris, Mark

Innaurato, Albert (F.) 1948(?)- . . **CLC 21, 60**
See also CA 115; 122

Innes, Michael
See Stewart, J(ohn) I(nnes) M(ackintosh)

Ionesco, Eugene
1912- . . . . **CLC 1, 4, 6, 9, 11, 15, 41**
See also CA 9-12R; DA; MTCW; SATA 7;
WLC

Iqbal, Muhammad 1873-1938 . . . . . **TCLC 28**

Ireland, Patrick
See O'Doherty, Brian

Irland, David
See Green, Julian (Hartridge)

Iron, Ralph
See Schreiner, Olive (Emilie Albertina)

Irving, John (Winslow)
1942- . . . . **CLC 13, 23, 38**
See also AAYA 8; BEST 89:3; CA 25-28R;
CANR 28; DLB 6; DLBY 82; MTCW

Kaufman, George S. 1889-1961..... **CLC 38**
See also CA 108; 93-96; DLB 7

Kaufman, Sue .... **CLC 3, 8**
See also Barondess, Sue K(aufman)

Kavafis, Konstantinos Petrou 1863-1933
See Cavafy, C(onstantine) P(eter)
See also CA 104

Kavan, Anna 1901-1968........ **CLC 5, 13**
See also CA 5-8R; CANR 6; MTCW

Kavanagh, Dan
See Barnes, Julian

Kavanagh, Patrick (Joseph)
1904-1967 .... **CLC 22**
See also CA 123; 25-28R; DLB 15, 20;
MTCW

Kawabata, Yasunari
1899-1972 .... **CLC 2, 5, 9, 18**
See also CA 93-96; 33-36R

Kaye, M(ary) M(argaret) 1909-..... **CLC 28**
See also CA 89-92; CANR 24; MTCW;
SATA 62

Kaye, Mollie
See Kaye, M(ary) M(argaret)

Kaye-Smith, Sheila 1887-1956..... **TCLC 20**
See also CA 118; DLB 36

Kaymor, Patrice Maguilene
See Senghor, Leopold Sedar

Kazan, Elia 1909-.......... **CLC 6, 16, 63**
See also CA 21-24R; CANR 32

Kazantzakis, Nikos
1883(?)-1957 .... **TCLC 2, 5, 33**
See also CA 105; 132; MTCW

Kazin, Alfred 1915- .... **CLC 34, 38**
See also CA 1-4R; CAAS 7; CANR 1;
DLB 67

Keane, Mary Nesta (Skrine) 1904-
See Keane, Molly
See also CA 108; 114

Keane, Molly.................... **CLC 31**
See also Keane, Mary Nesta (Skrine)

Keates, Jonathan 19(?)-........... **CLC 34**

Keaton, Buster 1895-1966 .... **CLC 20**

Keats, John 1795-1821...... **NCLC 8; PC 1**
See also CDBLB 1789-1832; DA; DLB 96,
110; WLC

Keene, Donald 1922- .... **CLC 34**
See also CA 1-4R; CANR 5

Keillor, Garrison.................. **CLC 40**
See also Keillor, Gary (Edward)
See also AAYA 2; BEST 89:3; DLBY 87;
SATA 58

Keillor, Gary (Edward) 1942-
See Keillor, Garrison
See also CA 111; 117; CANR 36; MTCW

Keith, Michael
See Hubbard, L(afayette) Ron(ald)

Kell, Joseph
See Wilson, John (Anthony) Burgess

Keller, Gottfried 1819-1890....... **NCLC 2**
See also DLB 129

Kellerman, Jonathan 1949- .... **CLC 44**
See also BEST 90:1; CA 106; CANR 29

Kelley, William Melvin 1937-...... **CLC 22**
See also BW; CA 77-80; CANR 27; DLB 33

Kellogg, Marjorie 1922-............ **CLC 2**
See also CA 81-84

Kellow, Kathleen
See Hibbert, Eleanor Alice Burford

Kelly, M(ilton) T(erry) 1947-....... **CLC 55**
See also CA 97-100; CANR 19

Kelman, James 1946-............ **CLC 58**

Kemal, Yashar 1923- .... **CLC 14, 29**
See also CA 89-92

Kemble, Fanny 1809-1893 ...... **NCLC 18**
See also DLB 32

Kemelman, Harry 1908-............ **CLC 2**
See also AITN 1; CA 9-12R; CANR 6;
DLB 28

Kempe, Margery 1373(?)-1440(?) ..... **LC 6**

Kempis, Thomas a 1380-1471 .... **LC 11**

Kendall, Henry 1839-1882....... **NCLC 12**

Keneally, Thomas (Michael)
1935- ...... **CLC 5, 8, 10, 14, 19, 27, 43**
See also CA 85-88; CANR 10; MTCW

Kennedy, Adrienne (Lita) 1931- .... **CLC 66**
See also BLC 2; BW; CA 103; CABS 3;
CANR 26; DLB 38

Kennedy, John Pendleton
1795-1870 .... **NCLC 2**
See also DLB 3

Kennedy, Joseph Charles 1929-...... **CLC 8**
See also Kennedy, X. J.
See also CA 1-4R; CANR 4, 30, 40;
SATA 14

Kennedy, William 1928-... **CLC 6, 28, 34, 53**
See also AAYA 1; CA 85-88; CANR 14,
31; DLBY 85; MTCW; SATA 57

Kennedy, X. J..................... **CLC 42**
See also Kennedy, Joseph Charles
See also CAAS 9; CLR 27; DLB 5

Kent, Kelvin
See Kuttner, Henry

Kenton, Maxwell
See Southern, Terry

Kenyon, Robert O.
See Kuttner, Henry

Kerouac, Jack ..... **CLC 1, 2, 3, 5, 14, 29, 61**
See also Kerouac, Jean-Louis Lebris de
See also CDALB 1941-1968; DLB 2, 16;
DLBD 3

Kerouac, Jean-Louis Lebris de 1922-1969
See Kerouac, Jack
See also AITN 1; CA 5-8R; 25-28R;
CANR 26; DA; MTCW; WLC

Kerr, Jean 1923-.................. **CLC 22**
See also CA 5-8R; CANR 7

Kerr, M. E.................... **CLC 12, 35**
See also Meaker, Marijane (Agnes)
See also AAYA 2; CLR 29; SAAS 1

Kerr, Robert .... **CLC 55**

Kerrigan, (Thomas) Anthony
1918-...................... **CLC 4, 6**
See also CA 49-52; CAAS 11; CANR 4

Kerry, Lois
See Duncan, Lois

Kesey, Ken (Elton)
1935- .... **CLC 1, 3, 6, 11, 46, 64**
See also CA 1-4R; CANR 22, 38;
CDALB 1968-1988; DA; DLB 2, 16;
MTCW; SATA 66; WLC

Kesselring, Joseph (Otto)
1902-1967 .... **CLC 45**

Kessler, Jascha (Frederick) 1929-.... **CLC 4**
See also CA 17-20R; CANR 8

Kettelkamp, Larry (Dale) 1933- .... **CLC 12**
See also CA 29-32R; CANR 16; SAAS 3;
SATA 2

Keyber, Conny
See Fielding, Henry

Khayyam, Omar 1048-1131...... **CMLC 11**

Kherdian, David 1931-............ **CLC 6, 9**
See also CA 21-24R; CAAS 2; CANR 39;
CLR 24; JRDA; MAICYA; SATA 16, 74

Khlebnikov, Velimir .... **TCLC 20**
See also Khlebnikov, Viktor Vladimirovich

Khlebnikov, Viktor Vladimirovich 1885-1922
See Khlebnikov, Velimir
See also CA 117

Khodasevich, Vladislav (Felitsianovich)
1886-1939 .... **TCLC 15**
See also CA 115

Kielland, Alexander Lange
1849-1906 .... **TCLC 5**
See also CA 104

Kiely, Benedict 1919-.......... **CLC 23, 43**
See also CA 1-4R; CANR 2; DLB 15

Kienzle, William X(avier) 1928- .... **CLC 25**
See also CA 93-96; CAAS 1; CANR 9, 31;
MTCW

Kierkegaard, Soren 1813-1855.... **NCLC 34**

Killens, John Oliver 1916-1987..... **CLC 10**
See also BW; CA 77-80; 123; CAAS 2;
CANR 26; DLB 33

Killigrew, Anne 1660-1685.......... **LC 4**
See also DLB 131

Kim
See Simenon, Georges (Jacques Christian)

Kincaid, Jamaica 1949- .... **CLC 43, 68**
See also BLC 2; BW; CA 125

King, Francis (Henry) 1923- ..... **CLC 8, 53**
See also CA 1-4R; CANR 1, 33; DLB 15;
MTCW

King, Stephen (Edwin)
1947-.............. **CLC 12, 26, 37, 61**
See also AAYA 1; BEST 90:1; CA 61-64;
CANR 1, 30; DLBY 80; JRDA; MTCW;
SATA 9, 55

King, Steve
See King, Stephen (Edwin)

Kingman, Lee..................... **CLC 17**
See also Natti, (Mary) Lee
See also SAAS 3; SATA 1, 67

Kingsley, Charles 1819-1875..... **NCLC 35**
See also DLB 21, 32; YABC 2

Kingsley, Sidney 1906-............ **CLC 44**
See also CA 85-88; DLB 7

Kingsolver, Barbara 1955-......... **CLC 55**
See also CA 129; 134

Kingston, Maxine (Ting Ting) Hong
1940- .... CLC 12, 19, 58
See also AAYA 8; CA 69-72; CANR 13,
38; DLBY 80; MTCW; SATA 53

Kinnell, Galway
1927- .... CLC 1, 2, 3, 5, 13, 29
See also CA 9-12R; CANR 10, 34; DLB 5;
DLBY 87; MTCW

Kinsella, Thomas 1928- .... CLC 4, 19
See also CA 17-20R; CANR 15; DLB 27;
MTCW

Kinsella, W(illiam) P(atrick)
1935- .... CLC 27, 43
See also AAYA 7; CA 97-100; CAAS 7;
CANR 21, 35; MTCW

Kipling, (Joseph) Rudyard
1865-1936 .... TCLC 8, 17; PC 3; SSC 5
See also CA 105; 120; CANR 33;
CDBLB 1890-1914; DA; DLB 19, 34;
MAICYA; MTCW; WLC; YABC 2

Kirkup, James 1918- .... CLC 1
See also CA 1-4R; CAAS 4; CANR 2;
DLB 27; SATA 12

Kirkwood, James 1930(?)-1989 ...... CLC 9
See also AITN 2; CA 1-4R; 128; CANR 6,
40

Kis, Danilo 1935-1989 .... CLC 57
See also CA 109; 118; 129; MTCW

Kivi, Aleksis 1834-1872 .... NCLC 30

Kizer, Carolyn (Ashley) 1925-... CLC 15, 39
See also CA 65-68; CAAS 5; CANR 24;
DLB 5

Klabund 1890-1928 .... TCLC 44
See also DLB 66

Klappert, Peter 1942- .... CLC 57
See also CA 33-36R; DLB 5

Klein, A(braham) M(oses)
1909-1972 .... CLC 19
See also CA 101; 37-40R; DLB 68

Klein, Norma 1938-1989 .... CLC 30
See also AAYA 2; CA 41-44R; 128;
CANR 15, 37; CLR 2, 19; JRDA;
MAICYA; SAAS 1; SATA 7, 57

Klein, T(heodore) E(ibon) D(onald)
1947- .... CLC 34
See also CA 119

Kleist, Heinrich von 1777-1811.... NCLC 2
See also DLB 90

Klima, Ivan 1931- .... CLC 56
See also CA 25-28R; CANR 17

Klimentov, Andrei Platonovich 1899-1951
See Platonov, Andrei
See also CA 108

Klinger, Friedrich Maximilian von
1752-1831 .... NCLC 1
See also DLB 94

Klopstock, Friedrich Gottlieb
1724-1803 .... NCLC 11
See also DLB 97

Knebel, Fletcher 1911-1993 .... CLC 14
See also AITN 1; CA 1-4R; 140; CAAS 3;
CANR 1, 36; SATA 36; SATA-Obit 75

Knickerbocker, Diedrich
See Irving, Washington

Knight, Etheridge 1931-1991 ...... CLC 40
See also BLC 2; BW; CA 21-24R; 133;
CANR 23; DLB 41

Knight, Sarah Kemble 1666-1727 ..... LC 7
See also DLB 24

Knowles, John 1926- ...... CLC 1, 4, 10, 26
See also AAYA 10; CA 17-20R; CANR 40;
CDALB 1968-1988; DA; DLB 6; MTCW;
SATA 8

Knox, Calvin M.
See Silverberg, Robert

Knye, Cassandra
See Disch, Thomas M(ichael)

Koch, C(hristopher) J(ohn) 1932- ... CLC 42
See also CA 127

Koch, Christopher
See Koch, C(hristopher) J(ohn)

Koch, Kenneth 1925- .... CLC 5, 8, 44
See also CA 1-4R; CANR 6, 36; DLB 5;
SATA 65

Kochanowski, Jan 1530-1584........ LC 10

Kock, Charles Paul de
1794-1871 .... NCLC 16

Koda Shigeyuki 1867-1947
See Rohan, Koda
See also CA 121

Koestler, Arthur
1905-1983 .... CLC 1, 3, 6, 8, 15, 33
See also CA 1-4R; 109; CANR 1, 33;
CDBLB 1945-1960; DLBY 83; MTCW

Kogawa, Joy Nozomi 1935-........ CLC 78
See also CA 101; CANR 19

Kohout, Pavel 1928-.............. CLC 13
See also CA 45-48; CANR 3

Koizumi, Yakumo
See Hearn, (Patricio) Lafcadio (Tessima
Carlos)

Kolmar, Gertrud 1894-1943 ...... TCLC 40

Konrad, George
See Konrad, Gyoergy

Konrad, Gyoergy 1933- ...... CLC 4, 10, 73
See also CA 85-88

Konwicki, Tadeusz 1926-..... CLC 8, 28, 54
See also CA 101; CAAS 9; CANR 39;
MTCW

Koontz, Dean R(ay) 1945-......... CLC 78
See also AAYA 9; BEST 89:3, 90:2;
CA 108; CANR 19, 36; MTCW

Kopit, Arthur (Lee) 1937- .... CLC 1, 18, 33
See also AITN 1; CA 81-84; CABS 3;
DLB 7; MTCW

Kops, Bernard 1926-.............. CLC 4
See also CA 5-8R; DLB 13

Kornbluth, C(yril) M. 1923-1958.... TCLC 8
See also CA 105; DLB 8

Korolenko, V. G.
See Korolenko, Vladimir Galaktionovich

Korolenko, Vladimir
See Korolenko, Vladimir Galaktionovich

Korolenko, Vladimir G.
See Korolenko, Vladimir Galaktionovich

Korolenko, Vladimir Galaktionovich
1853-1921 .... TCLC 22
See also CA 121

Kosinski, Jerzy (Nikodem)
1933-1991 .... CLC 1, 2, 3, 6, 10, 15, 53,
70
See also CA 17-20R; 134; CANR 9; DLB 2;
DLBY 82; MTCW

Kostelanetz, Richard (Cory) 1940-.. CLC 28
See also CA 13-16R; CAAS 8; CANR 38

Kostrowitzki, Wilhelm Apollinaris de
1880-1918
See Apollinaire, Guillaume
See also CA 104

Kotlowitz, Robert 1924-............ CLC 4
See also CA 33-36R; CANR 36

Kotzebue, August (Friedrich Ferdinand) von
1761-1819 .... NCLC 25
See also DLB 94

Kotzwinkle, William 1938- ... CLC 5, 14, 35
See also CA 45-48; CANR 3; CLR 6;
MAICYA; SATA 24, 70

Kozol, Jonathan 1936-............ CLC 17
See also CA 61-64; CANR 16

Kozoll, Michael 1940(?)- .... CLC 35

Kramer, Kathryn 19(?)- .... CLC 34

Kramer, Larry 1935- .... CLC 42
See also CA 124; 126

Krasicki, Ignacy 1735-1801 .... NCLC 8

Krasinski, Zygmunt 1812-1859 .... NCLC 4

Kraus, Karl 1874-1936........... TCLC 5
See also CA 104; DLB 118

Kreve (Mickevicius), Vincas
1882-1954 .... TCLC 27

Kristeva, Julia 1941- .... CLC 77

Kristofferson, Kris 1936-.......... CLC 26
See also CA 104

Krizanc, John 1956-.............. CLC 57

Krleza, Miroslav 1893-1981......... CLC 8
See also CA 97-100; 105

Kroetsch, Robert 1927- ...... CLC 5, 23, 57
See also CA 17-20R; CANR 8, 38; DLB 53;
MTCW

Kroetz, Franz
See Kroetz, Franz Xaver

Kroetz, Franz Xaver 1946- .... CLC 41
See also CA 130

Kroker, Arthur 1945-............. CLC 77

Kropotkin, Peter (Aleksieevich)
1842-1921 .... TCLC 36
See also CA 119

Krotkov, Yuri 1917-.............. CLC 19
See also CA 102

Krumb
See Crumb, R(obert)

Krumgold, Joseph (Quincy)
1908-1980 .... CLC 12
See also CA 9-12R; 101; CANR 7;
MAICYA; SATA 1, 23, 48

Krumwitz
See Crumb, R(obert)

Krutch, Joseph Wood 1893-1970.... CLC 24
See also CA 1-4R; 25-28R; CANR 4;
DLB 63

Krutzch, Gus
See Eliot, T(homas) S(tearns)

Krylov, Ivan Andreevich
  1768(?)-1844 .... NCLC 1

Kubin, Alfred 1877-1959 .... TCLC 23
  See also CA 112; DLB 81

Kubrick, Stanley 1928-............ CLC 16
  See also CA 81-84; CANR 33; DLB 26

Kumin, Maxine (Winokur)
  1925- .... CLC 5,13, 28
  See also AITN 2; CA 1-4R; CAAS 8;
  CANR 1, 21; DLB 5; MTCW; SATA 12

Kundera, Milan
  1929- .... CLC 4, 9, 19, 32, 68
  See also AAYA 2; CA 85-88; CANR 19;
  MTCW

Kunitz, Stanley (Jasspon)
  1905- .... CLC 6, 11, 14
  See also CA 41-44R; CANR 26; DLB 48;
  MTCW

Kunze, Reiner 1933-.............. CLC 10
  See also CA 93-96; DLB 75

Kuprin, Aleksandr Ivanovich
  1870-1938 .... TCLC 5
  See also CA 104

Kureishi, Hanif 1954(?)-........... CLC 64
  See also CA 139

Kurosawa, Akira 1910-............ CLC 16
  See also CA 101

Kuttner, Henry 1915-1958........ TCLC 10
  See also CA 107; DLB 8

Kuzma, Greg 1944-................ CLC 7
  See also CA 33-36R

Kuzmin, Mikhail 1872(?)-1936 .... TCLC 40

Kyd, Thomas 1558-1594...... LC 22; DC 3
  See also DLB 62

Kyprianos, Iossif
  See Samarakis, Antonis

La Bruyere, Jean de 1645-1696...... LC 17

Lacan, Jacques (Marie Emile)
  1901-1981 .... CLC 75
  See also CA 121; 104

Laclos, Pierre Ambroise Francois Choderlos
  de 1741-1803 .... NCLC 4

La Colere, Francois
  See Aragon, Louis

Lacolere, Francois
  See Aragon, Louis

La Deshabilleuse
  See Simenon, Georges (Jacques Christian)

Lady Gregory
  See Gregory, Isabella Augusta (Persse)

Lady of Quality, A
  See Bagnold, Enid

**La Fayette, Marie (Madelaine Pioche de la
  Vergne Comtes** 1634-1693....... LC 2

Lafayette, Rene
  See Hubbard, L(afayette) Ron(ald)

Laforgue, Jules 1860-1887........ NCLC 5

Lagerkvist, Paer (Fabian)
  1891-1974 .... CLC 7, 10, 13, 54
  See also Lagerkvist, Par
  See also CA 85-88; 49-52; MTCW

Lagerkvist, Par
  See Lagerkvist, Paer (Fabian)
  See also SSC 12

Lagerloef, Selma (Ottiliana Lovisa)
  1858-1940 .... TCLC 4, 36
  See also Lagerlof, Selma (Ottiliana Lovisa)
  See also CA 108; CLR 7; SATA 15

Lagerlof, Selma (Ottiliana Lovisa)
  See Lagerloef, Selma (Ottiliana Lovisa)
  See also CLR 7; SATA 15

La Guma, (Justin) Alex(ander)
  1925-1985 .... CLC 19
  See also BW; CA 49-52; 118; CANR 25;
  DLB 117; MTCW

Laidlaw, A. K.
  See Grieve, C(hristopher) M(urray)

Lainez, Manuel Mujica
  See Mujica Lainez, Manuel
  See also HW

Lamartine, Alphonse (Marie Louis Prat) de
  1790-1869 .... NCLC 11

Lamb, Charles 1775-1834........ NCLC 10
  See also CDBLB 1789-1832; DA; DLB 93,
  107; SATA 17; WLC

Lamb, Lady Caroline 1785-1828.. NCLC 38
  See also DLB 116

Lamming, George (William)
  1927- .... CLC 2, 4, 66
  See also BLC 2; BW; CA 85-88; CANR 26;
  DLB 125; MTCW

L'Amour, Louis (Dearborn)
  1908-1988 .... CLC 25, 55
  See also AITN 2; BEST 89:2; CA 1-4R;
  125; CANR 3, 25, 40; DLBY 80; MTCW

Lampedusa, Giuseppe (Tomasi) di ... TCLC 13
  See also Tomasi di Lampedusa, Giuseppe

Lampman, Archibald 1861-1899 .. NCLC 25
  See also DLB 92

Lancaster, Bruce 1896-1963........ CLC 36
  See also CA 9-10; CAP 1; SATA 9

Landau, Mark Alexandrovich
  See Aldanov, Mark (Alexandrovich)

Landau-Aldanov, Mark Alexandrovich
  See Aldanov, Mark (Alexandrovich)

Landis, John 1950-.............. CLC 26
  See also CA 112; 122

Landolfi, Tommaso 1908-1979... CLC 11, 49
  See also CA 127; 117

Landon, Letitia Elizabeth
  1802-1838 .... NCLC 15
  See also DLB 96

Landor, Walter Savage
  1775-1864 .... NCLC 14
  See also DLB 93, 107

Landwirth, Heinz 1927-
  See Lind, Jakov
  See also CA 9-12R; CANR 7

Lane, Patrick 1939- .... CLC 25
  See also CA 97-100; DLB 53

Lang, Andrew 1844-1912........ TCLC 16
  See also CA 114; 137; DLB 98; MAICYA;
  SATA 16

Lang, Fritz 1890-1976 .... CLC 20
  See also CA 77-80; 69-72; CANR 30

Lange, John
  See Crichton, (John) Michael

Langer, Elinor 1939- .... CLC 34
  See also CA 121

Langland, William 1330(?)-1400(?) ... LC 19
  See also DA

Langstaff, Launcelot
  See Irving, Washington

Lanier, Sidney 1842-1881 .... NCLC 6
  See also DLB 64; MAICYA; SATA 18

Lanyer, Aemilia 1569-1645 .... LC 10

Lao Tzu .... CMLC 7

Lapine, James (Elliot) 1949-....... CLC 39
  See also CA 123; 130

Larbaud, Valery (Nicolas)
  1881-1957 .... TCLC 9
  See also CA 106

Lardner, Ring
  See Lardner, Ring(gold) W(ilmer)

Lardner, Ring W., Jr.
  See Lardner, Ring(gold) W(ilmer)

Lardner, Ring(gold) W(ilmer)
  1885-1933 .... TCLC 2, 14
  See also CA 104; 131; CDALB 1917-1929;
  DLB 11, 25, 86; MTCW

Laredo, Betty
  See Codrescu, Andrei

Larkin, Maia
  See Wojciechowska, Maia (Teresa)

Larkin, Philip (Arthur)
  1922-1985 .... CLC 3, 5, 8, 9, 13, 18, 33,
                                           39, 64
  See also CA 5-8R; 117; CANR 24;
  CDBLB 1960 to Present; DLB 27;
  MTCW

Larra (y Sanchez de Castro), Mariano Jose de
  1809-1837 .... NCLC 17

Larsen, Eric 1941- .... CLC 55
  See also CA 132

Larsen, Nella 1891-1964 .... CLC 37
  See also BLC 2; BW; CA 125; DLB 51

Larson, Charles R(aymond) 1938-... CLC 31
  See also CA 53-56; CANR 4

Latham, Jean Lee 1902-........... CLC 12
  See also AITN 1; CA 5-8R; CANR 7;
  MAICYA; SATA 2, 68

Latham, Mavis
  See Clark, Mavis Thorpe

Lathen, Emma .... CLC 2
  See also Hennissart, Martha; Latsis, Mary
  J(ane)

Lathrop, Francis
  See Leiber, Fritz (Reuter, Jr.)

Latsis, Mary J(ane)
  See Lathen, Emma
  See also CA 85-88

Lattimore, Richmond (Alexander)
  1906-1984 .... CLC 3
  See also CA 1-4R; 112; CANR 1

Laughlin, James 1914-........... CLC 49
  See also CA 21-24R; CANR 9; DLB 48

Laurence, (Jean) Margaret (Wemyss)
 1926-1987 . . **CLC 3, 6, 13, 50, 62; SSC 7**
 See also CA 5-8R; 121; CANR 33; DLB 53;
 MTCW; SATA 50

Laurent, Antoine 1952- . . . . **CLC 50**

Lauscher, Hermann
 See Hesse, Hermann

Lautreamont, Comte de
 1846-1870 . . . . **NCLC 12**

Laverty, Donald
 See Blish, James (Benjamin)

Lavin, Mary 1912- . . . . . . **CLC 4, 18; SSC 4**
 See also CA 9-12R; CANR 33; DLB 15;
 MTCW

Lavond, Paul Dennis
 See Kornbluth, C(yril) M.; Pohl, Frederik

Lawler, Raymond Evenor 1922- . . . . **CLC 58**
 See also CA 103

Lawrence, D(avid) H(erbert Richards)
 1885-1930 . . . . **TCLC 2, 9, 16, 33, 48;
                                     SSC 4**
 See also CA 104; 121; CDBLB 1914-1945;
 DA; DLB 10, 19, 36, 98; MTCW; WLC

Lawrence, T(homas) E(dward)
 1888-1935 . . . . **TCLC 18**
 See also Dale, Colin
 See also CA 115

Lawrence Of Arabia
 See Lawrence, T(homas) E(dward)

Lawson, Henry (Archibald Hertzberg)
 1867-1922 . . . . **TCLC 27**
 See also CA 120

Lawton, Dennis
 See Faust, Frederick (Schiller)

Laxness, Halldor . . . . **CLC 25**
 See also Gudjonsson, Halldor Kiljan

Layamon fl. c. 1200- . . . . **CMLC 10**

Laye, Camara 1928-1980 . . . . **CLC 4, 38**
 See also BLC 2; BW; CA 85-88; 97-100;
 CANR 25; MTCW

Layton, Irving (Peter) 1912- . . . . . **CLC 2, 15**
 See also CA 1-4R; CANR 2, 33; DLB 88;
 MTCW

Lazarus, Emma 1849-1887 . . . . **NCLC 8**

Lazarus, Felix
 See Cable, George Washington

Lazarus, Henry
 See Slavitt, David R(ytman)

Lea, Joan
 See Neufeld, John (Arthur)

Leacock, Stephen (Butler)
 1869-1944 . . . . **TCLC 2**
 See also CA 104; 141; DLB 92

Lear, Edward 1812-1888 . . . . **NCLC 3**
 See also CLR 1; DLB 32; MAICYA;
 SATA 18

Lear, Norman (Milton) 1922- . . . . . . **CLC 12**
 See also CA 73-76

Leavis, F(rank) R(aymond)
 1895-1978 . . . . **CLC 24**
 See also CA 21-24R; 77-80; MTCW

Leavitt, David 1961- . . . . **CLC 34**
 See also CA 116; 122; DLB 130

Leblanc, Maurice (Marie Emile)
 1864-1941 . . . . **TCLC 49**
 See also CA 110

Lebowitz, Fran(ces Ann)
 1951(?)- . . . . **CLC 11, 36**
 See also CA 81-84; CANR 14; MTCW

le Carre, John . . . . **CLC 3, 5, 9, 15, 28**
 See also Cornwell, David (John Moore)
 See also BEST 89:4; CDBLB 1960 to
 Present; DLB 87

Le Clezio, J(ean) M(arie) G(ustave)
 1940- . . . . **CLC 31**
 See also CA 116; 128; DLB 83

Leconte de Lisle, Charles-Marie-Rene
 1818-1894 . . . . **NCLC 29**

Le Coq, Monsieur
 See Simenon, Georges (Jacques Christian)

Leduc, Violette 1907-1972 . . . . **CLC 22**
 See also CA 13-14; 33-36R; CAP 1

Ledwidge, Francis 1887(?)-1917 . . . **TCLC 23**
 See also CA 123; DLB 20

Lee, Andrea 1953- . . . . **CLC 36**
 See also BLC 2; BW; CA 125

Lee, Andrew
 See Auchincloss, Louis (Stanton)

Lee, Don L. . . . . **CLC 2**
 See also Madhubuti, Haki R.

Lee, George W(ashington)
 1894-1976 . . . . **CLC 52**
 See also BLC 2; BW; CA 125; DLB 51

Lee, (Nelle) Harper 1926- . . . . . . **CLC 12, 60**
 See also CA 13-16R; CDALB 1941-1968;
 DA; DLB 6; MTCW; SATA 11; WLC

Lee, Julian
 See Latham, Jean Lee

Lee, Larry
 See Lee, Lawrence

Lee, Lawrence 1941-1990 . . . . **CLC 34**
 See also CA 131

Lee, Manfred B(ennington)
 1905-1971 . . . . **CLC 11**
 See also Queen, Ellery
 See also CA 1-4R; 29-32R; CANR 2

Lee, Stan 1922- . . . . **CLC 17**
 See also AAYA 5; CA 108; 111

Lee, Tanith 1947- . . . . **CLC 46**
 See also CA 37-40R; SATA 8

Lee, Vernon . . . . **TCLC 5**
 See also Paget, Violet
 See also DLB 57

Lee, William
 See Burroughs, William S(eward)

Lee, Willy
 See Burroughs, William S(eward)

Lee-Hamilton, Eugene (Jacob)
 1845-1907 . . . . **TCLC 22**
 See also CA 117

Leet, Judith 1935- . . . . **CLC 11**

Le Fanu, Joseph Sheridan
 1814-1873 . . . . **NCLC 9**
 See also DLB 21, 70

Leffland, Ella 1931- . . . . **CLC 19**
 See also CA 29-32R; CANR 35; DLBY 84;
 SATA 65

Leger, (Marie-Rene) Alexis Saint-Leger
 1887-1975 . . . . **CLC 11**
 See also Perse, St.-John
 See also CA 13-16R; 61-64; MTCW

Leger, Saintleger
 See Leger, (Marie-Rene) Alexis Saint-Leger

Le Guin, Ursula K(roeber)
 1929- . . . . **CLC 8, 13, 22, 45, 71; SSC 12**
 See also AAYA 9; AITN 1; CA 21-24R;
 CANR 9, 32; CDALB 1968-1988; CLR 3,
 28; DLB 8, 52; JRDA; MAICYA;
 MTCW; SATA 4, 52

Lehmann, Rosamond (Nina)
 1901-1990 . . . . **CLC 5**
 See also CA 77-80; 131; CANR 8; DLB 15

Leiber, Fritz (Reuter, Jr.)
 1910-1992 . . . . **CLC 25**
 See also CA 45-48; 139; CANR 2, 40;
 DLB 8; MTCW; SATA 45;
 SATA-Obit 73

Leimbach, Martha 1963-
 See Leimbach, Marti
 See also CA 130

Leimbach, Marti . . . . **CLC 65**
 See also Leimbach, Martha

Leino, Eino . . . . **TCLC 24**
 See also Loennbohm, Armas Eino Leopold

Leiris, Michel (Julien) 1901-1990 . . . **CLC 61**
 See also CA 119; 128; 132

Leithauser, Brad 1953- . . . . **CLC 27**
 See also CA 107; CANR 27; DLB 120

Lelchuk, Alan 1938- . . . . **CLC 5**
 See also CA 45-48; CANR 1

Lem, Stanislaw 1921- . . . . **CLC 8, 15, 40**
 See also CA 105; CAAS 1; CANR 32;
 MTCW

Lemann, Nancy 1956- . . . . **CLC 39**
 See also CA 118; 136

Lemonnier, (Antoine Louis) Camille
 1844-1913 . . . . **TCLC 22**
 See also CA 121

Lenau, Nikolaus 1802-1850 . . . . . . **NCLC 16**

L'Engle, Madeleine (Camp Franklin)
 1918- . . . . **CLC 12**
 See also AAYA 1; AITN 2; CA 1-4R;
 CANR 3, 21, 39; CLR 1, 14; DLB 52;
 JRDA; MAICYA; MTCW; SAAS 15;
 SATA 1, 27, 75

Lengyel, Jozsef 1896-1975 . . . . **CLC 7**
 See also CA 85-88; 57-60

Lennon, John (Ono)
 1940-1980 . . . . **CLC 12, 35**
 See also CA 102

Lennox, Charlotte Ramsay
 1729(?)-1804 . . . . **NCLC 23**
 See also DLB 39

Lentricchia, Frank (Jr.) 1940- . . . . . . **CLC 34**
 See also CA 25-28R; CANR 19

Lenz, Siegfried 1926- . . . . **CLC 27**
 See also CA 89-92; DLB 75

Leonard, Elmore (John, Jr.)
 1925- . . . . **CLC 28, 34, 71**
 See also AITN 1; BEST 89:1, 90:4;
 CA 81-84; CANR 12, 28; MTCW

Leonard, Hugh
See Byrne, John Keyes
See also DLB 13

Leopardi, (Conte) Giacomo (Talegardo
    Francesco di Sales Save
    1798-1837 .... NCLC 22

Le Reveler
See Artaud, Antonin

Lerman, Eleanor 1952-............ CLC 9
See also CA 85-88

Lerman, Rhoda 1936-............. CLC 56
See also CA 49-52

Lermontov, Mikhail Yuryevich
    1814-1841 .... NCLC 5

Leroux, Gaston 1868-1927........ TCLC 25
See also CA 108; 136; SATA 65

Lesage, Alain-Rene 1668-1747........ LC 2

Leskov, Nikolai (Semyonovich)
    1831-1895 .... NCLC 25

Lessing, Doris (May)
    1919- ..... CLC 1, 2, 3, 6, 10, 15, 22, 40;
                                        SSC 6
See also CA 9-12R; CAAS 14; CANR 33;
    CDBLB 1960 to Present; DA; DLB 15;
    DLBY 85; MTCW

Lessing, Gotthold Ephraim
    1729-1781 .... LC 8
See also DLB 97

Lester, Richard 1932-............. CLC 20

Lever, Charles (James)
    1806-1872 .... NCLC 23
See also DLB 21

Leverson, Ada 1865(?)-1936(?) .... TCLC 18
See also Elaine
See also CA 117

Levertov, Denise
    1923- ...... CLC 1, 2, 3, 5, 8, 15, 28, 66
See also CA 1-4R; CANR 3, 29; DLB 5;
    MTCW

Levi, Jonathan.................... CLC 76

Levi, Peter (Chad Tigar) 1931-..... CLC 41
See also CA 5-8R; CANR 34; DLB 40

Levi, Primo
    1919-1987 .... CLC 37, 50; SSC 12
See also CA 13-16R; 122; CANR 12, 33;
    MTCW

Levin, Ira 1929- .... CLC 3, 6
See also CA 21-24R; CANR 17; MTCW;
    SATA 66

Levin, Meyer 1905-1981 .... CLC 7
See also AITN 1; CA 9-12R; 104;
    CANR 15; DLB 9, 28; DLBY 81;
    SATA 21, 27

Levine, Norman 1924- .... CLC 54
See also CA 73-76; CANR 14; DLB 88

Levine, Philip 1928-.. CLC 2, 4, 5, 9, 14, 33
See also CA 9-12R; CANR 9, 37; DLB 5

Levinson, Deirdre 1931-........... CLC 49
See also CA 73-76

Levi-Strauss, Claude 1908- .... CLC 38
See also CA 1-4R; CANR 6, 32; MTCW

Levitin, Sonia (Wolff) 1934- .... CLC 17
See also CA 29-32R; CANR 14, 32; JRDA;
    MAICYA; SAAS 2; SATA 4, 68

Levon, O. U.
See Kesey, Ken (Elton)

Lewes, George Henry
    1817-1878 .... NCLC 25
See also DLB 55

Lewis, Alun 1915-1944............ TCLC 3
See also CA 104; DLB 20

Lewis, C. Day
See Day Lewis, C(ecil)

Lewis, C(live) S(taples)
    1898-1963 .... CLC 1, 3, 6, 14, 27
See also AAYA 3; CA 81-84; CANR 33;
    CDBLB 1945-1960; CLR 3, 27; DA;
    DLB 15, 100; JRDA; MAICYA; MTCW;
    SATA 13; WLC

Lewis, Janet 1899- .... CLC 41
See Winters, Janet Lewis
See also CA 9-12R; CANR 29; CAP 1;
    DLBY 87

Lewis, Matthew Gregory
    1775-1818 .... NCLC 11
See also DLB 39

Lewis, (Harry) Sinclair
    1885-1951 .... TCLC 4, 13, 23, 39
See also CA 104; 133; CDALB 1917-1929;
    DA; DLB 9, 102; DLBD 1; MTCW;
    WLC

Lewis, (Percy) Wyndham
    1884(?)-1957 .... TCLC 2, 9
See also CA 104; DLB 15

Lewisohn, Ludwig 1883-1955...... TCLC 19
See also CA 107; DLB 4, 9, 28, 102

Lezama Lima, Jose 1910-1976 ... CLC 4, 10
See also CA 77-80; DLB 113; HW

L'Heureux, John (Clarke) 1934-.... CLC 52
See also CA 13-16R; CANR 23

Liddell, C. H.
See Kuttner, Henry

Lie, Jonas (Lauritz Idemil)
    1833-1908(?) .... TCLC 5
See also CA 115

Lieber, Joel 1937-1971............. CLC 6
See also CA 73-76; 29-32R

Lieber, Stanley Martin
See Lee, Stan

Lieberman, Laurence (James)
    1935- .... CLC 4, 36
See also CA 17-20R; CANR 8, 36

Lieksman, Anders
See Haavikko, Paavo Juhani

Li Fei-kan 1904-................. CLC 18
See also CA 105

Lifton, Robert Jay 1926-......... CLC 67
See also CA 17-20R; CANR 27; SATA 66

Lightfoot, Gordon 1938-.......... CLC 26
See also CA 109

Ligotti, Thomas 1953- .... CLC 44
See also CA 123

Liliencron, (Friedrich Adolf Axel) Detlev von
    1844-1909 .... TCLC 18
See also CA 117

Lima, Jose Lezama
See Lezama Lima, Jose

Lima Barreto, Afonso Henrique de
    1881-1922 .... TCLC 23
See also CA 117

Limonov, Eduard.................. CLC 67

Lin, Frank
See Atherton, Gertrude (Franklin Horn)

Lincoln, Abraham 1809-1865..... NCLC 18

Lind, Jakov .... CLC 1, 2, 4, 27
See also Landwirth, Heinz
See also CAAS 4

Lindsay, David 1878-1945 .... TCLC 15
See also CA 113

Lindsay, (Nicholas) Vachel
    1879-1931 .... TCLC 17
See also CA 114; 135; CDALB 1865-1917;
    DA; DLB 54; SATA 40; WLC

Linney, Romulus 1930- .... CLC 51
See also CA 1-4R; CANR 40

Linton, Eliza Lynn 1822-1898.... NCLC 41
See also DLB 18

Li Po 701-763................. CMLC 2

Lipsius, Justus 1547-1606 .... LC 16

Lipsyte, Robert (Michael) 1938-.... CLC 21
See also AAYA 7; CA 17-20R; CANR 8;
    CLR 23; DA; JRDA; MAICYA;
    SATA 5, 68

Lish, Gordon (Jay) 1934-.......... CLC 45
See also CA 113; 117; DLB 130

Lispector, Clarice 1925-1977....... CLC 43
See also CA 139; 116; DLB 113

Littell, Robert 1935(?)- .... CLC 42
See also CA 109; 112

Littlewit, Humphrey Gent.
See Lovecraft, H(oward) P(hillips)

Litwos
See Sienkiewicz, Henryk (Adam Alexander
    Pius)

Liu E 1857-1909............... TCLC 15
See also CA 115

Lively, Penelope (Margaret)
    1933- .... CLC 32, 50
See also CA 41-44R; CANR 29; CLR 7;
    DLB 14; JRDA; MAICYA; MTCW;
    SATA 7, 60

Livesay, Dorothy (Kathleen)
    1909- .... CLC 4, 15, 79
See also AITN 2; CA 25-28R; CAAS 8;
    CANR 36; DLB 68; MTCW

Livy c. 59B.C.-c. 17............ CMLC 11

Lizardi, Jose Joaquin Fernandez de
    1776-1827 .... NCLC 30

Llewellyn, Richard .... CLC 7
See also Llewellyn Lloyd, Richard Dafydd
    Vivian
See also DLB 15

Llewellyn Lloyd, Richard Dafydd Vivian
    1906-1983
See Llewellyn, Richard
See also CA 53-56; 111; CANR 7;
    SATA 11, 37

Llosa, (Jorge) Mario (Pedro) Vargas
See Vargas Llosa, (Jorge) Mario (Pedro)

Lloyd Webber, Andrew   1948-
See Webber, Andrew Lloyd
See also AAYA 1; CA 116; SATA 56

Locke, Alain (Le Roy)
1886-1954 . . . . TCLC 43
See also BW; CA 106; 124; DLB 51

Locke, John   1632-1704 . . . . LC 7
See also DLB 101

Locke-Elliott, Sumner
See Elliott, Sumner Locke

Lockhart, John Gibson
1794-1854 . . . . NCLC 6
See also DLB 110, 116

Lodge, David (John)   1935- . . . . CLC 36
See also BEST 90:1; CA 17-20R; CANR 19;
DLB 14; MTCW

Loennbohm, Armas Eino Leopold   1878-1926
See Leino, Eino
See also CA 123

Loewinsohn, Ron(ald William)
1937- . . . . CLC 52
See also CA 25-28R

Logan, Jake
See Smith, Martin Cruz

Logan, John (Burton)   1923-1987 . . . . . CLC 5
See also CA 77-80; 124; DLB 5

Lo Kuan-chung   1330(?)-1400(?) . . . . . . LC 12

Lombard, Nap
See Johnson, Pamela Hansford

London, Jack . . . . TCLC 9, 15, 39; SSC 4
See also London, John Griffith
See also AITN 2; CDALB 1865-1917;
DLB 8, 12, 78; SATA 18; WLC

London, John Griffith   1876-1916
See London, Jack
See also CA 110; 119; DA; JRDA;
MAICYA; MTCW

Long, Emmett
See Leonard, Elmore (John, Jr.)

Longbaugh, Harry
See Goldman, William (W.)

Longfellow, Henry Wadsworth
1807-1882 . . . . NCLC 2
See also CDALB 1640-1865; DA; DLB 1,
59; SATA 19

Longley, Michael   1939- . . . . CLC 29
See also CA 102; DLB 40

Longus   fl. c. 2nd cent. - . . . . CMLC 7

Longway, A. Hugh
See Lang, Andrew

Lopate, Phillip   1943- . . . . CLC 29
See also CA 97-100; DLBY 80

Lopez Portillo (y Pacheco), Jose
1920- . . . . CLC 46
See also CA 129; HW

Lopez y Fuentes, Gregorio
1897(?)-1966 . . . . CLC 32
See also CA 131; HW

Lorca, Federico Garcia
See Garcia Lorca, Federico

Lord, Bette Bao   1938- . . . . CLC 23
See also BEST 90:3; CA 107; CANR 41;
SATA 58

Lord Auch
See Bataille, Georges

Lord Byron
See Byron, George Gordon (Noel)

Lord Dunsany . . . . TCLC 2
See also Dunsany, Edward John Moreton
Drax Plunkett

Lorde, Audre (Geraldine)
1934- . . . . CLC 18, 71
See also BLC 2; BW; CA 25-28R;
CANR 16, 26; DLB 41; MTCW

Lord Jeffrey
See Jeffrey, Francis

Lorenzo, Heberto Padilla
See Padilla (Lorenzo), Heberto

Loris
See Hofmannsthal, Hugo von

Loti, Pierre . . . . TCLC 11
See also Viaud, (Louis Marie) Julien
See also DLB 123

Louie, David Wong   1954- . . . . CLC 70
See also CA 139

Louis, Father M.
See Merton, Thomas

Lovecraft, H(oward) P(hillips)
1890-1937 . . . . TCLC 4, 22; SSC 3
See also CA 104; 133; MTCW

Lovelace, Earl   1935- . . . . CLC 51
See also CA 77-80; CANR 41; DLB 125;
MTCW

Lowell, Amy   1874-1925 . . . . TCLC 1, 8
See also CA 104; DLB 54

Lowell, James Russell   1819-1891 . . NCLC 2
See also CDALB 1640-1865; DLB 1, 11, 64,
79

Lowell, Robert (Traill Spence, Jr.)
1917-1977 . . . CLC 1, 2, 3, 4, 5, 8, 9, 11,
15, 37; PC 3
See also CA 9-12R; 73-76; CABS 2;
CANR 26; DA; DLB 5; MTCW; WLC

Lowndes, Marie Adelaide (Belloc)
1868-1947 . . . . TCLC 12
See also CA 107; DLB 70

Lowry, (Clarence) Malcolm
1909-1957 . . . . TCLC 6, 40
See also CA 105; 131; CDBLB 1945-1960;
DLB 15; MTCW

Lowry, Mina Gertrude   1882-1966
See Loy, Mina
See also CA 113

Loxsmith, John
See Brunner, John (Kilian Houston)

Loy, Mina . . . . CLC 28
See also Lowry, Mina Gertrude
See also DLB 4, 54

Loyson-Bridet
See Schwob, (Mayer Andre) Marcel

Lucas, Craig   1951- . . . . CLC 64
See also CA 137

Lucas, George   1944- . . . . CLC 16
See also AAYA 1; CA 77-80; CANR 30;
SATA 56

Lucas, Hans
See Godard, Jean-Luc

Lucas, Victoria
See Plath, Sylvia

Ludlam, Charles   1943-1987 . . . . . CLC 46, 50
See also CA 85-88; 122

Ludlum, Robert   1927- . . . . CLC 22, 43
See also AAYA 10; BEST 89:1, 90:3;
CA 33-36R; CANR 25, 41; DLBY 82;
MTCW

Ludwig, Ken . . . . CLC 60

Ludwig, Otto   1813-1865 . . . . NCLC 4
See also DLB 129

Lugones, Leopoldo   1874-1938 . . . . . TCLC 15
See also CA 116; 131; HW

Lu Hsun   1881-1936 . . . . TCLC 3

Lukacs, George . . . . CLC 24
See also Lukacs, Gyorgy (Szegeny von)

Lukacs, Gyorgy (Szegeny von)   1885-1971
See Lukacs, George
See also CA 101; 29-32R

Luke, Peter (Ambrose Cyprian)
1919- . . . . CLC 38
See also CA 81-84; DLB 13

Lunar, Dennis
See Mungo, Raymond

Lurie, Alison   1926- . . . . CLC 4, 5, 18, 39
See also CA 1-4R; CANR 2, 17; DLB 2;
MTCW; SATA 46

Lustig, Arnost   1926- . . . . CLC 56
See also AAYA 3; CA 69-72; SATA 56

Luther, Martin   1483-1546 . . . . LC 9

Luzi, Mario   1914- . . . . CLC 13
See also CA 61-64; CANR 9; DLB 128

Lynch, B. Suarez
See Bioy Casares, Adolfo; Borges, Jorge
Luis

Lynch, David (K.)   1946- . . . . CLC 66
See also CA 124; 129

Lynch, James
See Andreyev, Leonid (Nikolaevich)

Lynch Davis, B.
See Bioy Casares, Adolfo; Borges, Jorge
Luis

Lyndsay, Sir David   1490-1555 . . . . . . LC 20

Lynn, Kenneth S(chuyler)   1923- . . . . CLC 50
See also CA 1-4R; CANR 3, 27

Lynx
See West, Rebecca

Lyons, Marcus
See Blish, James (Benjamin)

Lyre, Pinchbeck
See Sassoon, Siegfried (Lorraine)

Lytle, Andrew (Nelson)   1902- . . . . . . CLC 22
See also CA 9-12R; DLB 6

Lyttelton, George   1709-1773 . . . . LC 10

Maas, Peter   1929- . . . . CLC 29
See also CA 93-96

Macaulay, Rose   1881-1958 . . . . . TCLC 7, 44
See also CA 104; DLB 36

Macaulay, Thomas Babington
1800-1859 . . . . NCLC 42
See also CDBLB 1832-1890; DLB 32, 55

Malraux, (Georges-)Andre
1901-1976 . . . . . . **CLC 1, 4, 9, 13, 15, 57**
See also CA 21-22; 69-72; CANR 34;
CAP 2; DLB 72; MTCW

Malzberg, Barry N(athaniel) 1939-. . . **CLC 7**
See also CA 61-64; CAAS 4; CANR 16;
DLB 8

Mamet, David (Alan)
1947- . . . . **CLC 9, 15, 34, 46**
See also AAYA 3; CA 81-84; CABS 3;
CANR 15, 41; DLB 7; MTCW

Mamoulian, Rouben (Zachary)
1897-1987 . . . . **CLC 16**
See also CA 25-28R; 124

Mandelstam, Osip (Emilievich)
1891(?)-1938(?) . . . . **TCLC 2, 6**
See also CA 104

Mander, (Mary) Jane 1877-1949. . . **TCLC 31**

Mandiargues, Andre Pieyre de. . . . . . . **CLC 41**
See also Pieyre de Mandiargues, Andre
See also DLB 83

Mandrake, Ethel Belle
See Thurman, Wallace (Henry)

Mangan, James Clarence
1803-1849 . . . . **NCLC 27**

Maniere, J.-E.
See Giraudoux, (Hippolyte) Jean

Manley, (Mary) Delariviere
1672(?)-1724 . . . . **LC 1**
See also DLB 39, 80

Mann, Abel
See Creasey, John

Mann, (Luiz) Heinrich 1871-1950. . . **TCLC 9**
See also CA 106; DLB 66

Mann, (Paul) Thomas
1875-1955 . . . . **TCLC 2, 8, 14, 21, 35, 44;**
SSC 5
See also CA 104; 128; DA; DLB 66;
MTCW; WLC

Manning, David
See Faust, Frederick (Schiller)

Manning, Frederic 1887(?)-1935 . . . **TCLC 25**
See also CA 124

Manning, Olivia 1915-1980 . . . . . . **CLC 5, 19**
See also CA 5-8R; 101; CANR 29; MTCW

Mano, D. Keith 1942- . . . . **CLC 2, 10**
See also CA 25-28R; CAAS 6; CANR 26;
DLB 6

Mansfield, Katherine. . . **TCLC 2, 8, 39; SSC 9**
See also Beauchamp, Kathleen Mansfield
See also WLC

Manso, Peter 1940- . . . . **CLC 39**
See also CA 29-32R

Mantecon, Juan Jimenez
See Jimenez (Mantecon), Juan Ramon

Manton, Peter
See Creasey, John

Man Without a Spleen, A
See Chekhov, Anton (Pavlovich)

Manzoni, Alessandro 1785-1873 . . **NCLC 29**

Mapu, Abraham (ben Jekutiel)
1808-1867 . . . . **NCLC 18**

Mara, Sally
See Queneau, Raymond

Marat, Jean Paul 1743-1793 . . . . **LC 10**

Marcel, Gabriel Honore
1889-1973 . . . . **CLC 15**
See also CA 102; 45-48; MTCW

Marchbanks, Samuel
See Davies, (William) Robertson

Marchi, Giacomo
See Bassani, Giorgio

Margulies, Donald. . . . . **CLC 76**

Marie de France c. 12th cent. -. . . . **CMLC 8**

Marie de l'Incarnation 1599-1672. . . . **LC 10**

Mariner, Scott
See Pohl, Frederik

Marinetti, Filippo Tommaso
1876-1944 . . . . **TCLC 10**
See also CA 107; DLB 114

Marivaux, Pierre Carlet de Chamblain de
1688-1763 . . . . **LC 4**

Markandaya, Kamala . . . . **CLC 8, 38**
See also Taylor, Kamala (Purnaiya)

Markfield, Wallace 1926-. . . . . **CLC 8**
See also CA 69-72; CAAS 3; DLB 2, 28

Markham, Edwin 1852-1940 . . . . . . **TCLC 47**
See also DLB 54

Markham, Robert
See Amis, Kingsley (William)

Marks, J
See Highwater, Jamake (Mamake)

Marks-Highwater, J
See Highwater, Jamake (Mamake)

Markson, David M(errill) 1927-. . . . **CLC 67**
See also CA 49-52; CANR 1

Marley, Bob. . . . . **CLC 17**
See also Marley, Robert Nesta

Marley, Robert Nesta 1945-1981
See Marley, Bob
See also CA 107; 103

Marlowe, Christopher
1564-1593 . . . . **LC 22; DC 1**
See also CDBLB Before 1660; DA; DLB 62;
WLC

Marmontel, Jean-Francois
1723-1799 . . . . **LC 2**

Marquand, John P(hillips)
1893-1960 . . . . **CLC 2, 10**
See also CA 85-88; DLB 9, 102

Marquez, Gabriel (Jose) Garcia. . . . . . **CLC 68**
See also Garcia Marquez, Gabriel (Jose)

Marquis, Don(ald Robert Perry)
1878-1937 . . . . **TCLC 7**
See also CA 104; DLB 11, 25

Marric, J. J.
See Creasey, John

Marrow, Bernard
See Moore, Brian

Marryat, Frederick 1792-1848 . . . . **NCLC 3**
See also DLB 21

Marsden, James
See Creasey, John

Marsh, (Edith) Ngaio
1899-1982 . . . . **CLC 7, 53**
See also CA 9-12R; CANR 6; DLB 77;
MTCW

Marshall, Garry 1934-. . . . . **CLC 17**
See also AAYA 3; CA 111; SATA 60

Marshall, Paule 1929- . . **CLC 27, 72; SSC 3**
See also BLC 3; BW; CA 77-80; CANR 25;
DLB 33; MTCW

Marsten, Richard
See Hunter, Evan

Martha, Henry
See Harris, Mark

Martin, Ken
See Hubbard, L(afayette) Ron(ald)

Martin, Richard
See Creasey, John

Martin, Steve 1945-. . . . . **CLC 30**
See also CA 97-100; CANR 30; MTCW

Martin, Violet Florence
1862-1915 . . . . **TCLC 51**

Martin, Webber
See Silverberg, Robert

Martin du Gard, Roger
1881-1958 . . . . **TCLC 24**
See also CA 118; DLB 65

Martineau, Harriet 1802-1876. . . . **NCLC 26**
See also DLB 21, 55; YABC 2

Martines, Julia
See O'Faolain, Julia

Martinez, Jacinto Benavente y
See Benavente (y Martinez), Jacinto

Martinez Ruiz, Jose 1873-1967
See Azorin; Ruiz, Jose Martinez
See also CA 93-96; HW

Martinez Sierra, Gregorio
1881-1947 . . . . **TCLC 6**
See also CA 115

Martinez Sierra, Maria (de la O'LeJarraga)
1874-1974 . . . . **TCLC 6**
See also CA 115

Martinsen, Martin
See Follett, Ken(neth Martin)

Martinson, Harry (Edmund)
1904-1978 . . . . **CLC 14**
See also CA 77-80; CANR 34

Marut, Ret
See Traven, B.

Marut, Robert
See Traven, B.

Marvell, Andrew 1621-1678. . . . . **LC 4**
See also CDBLB 1660-1789; DA; DLB 131;
WLC

Marx, Karl (Heinrich)
1818-1883 . . . . **NCLC 17**
See also DLB 129

Masaoka Shiki. . . . . **TCLC 18**
See also Masaoka Tsunenori

Masaoka Tsunenori 1867-1902
See Masaoka Shiki
See also CA 117

Masefield, John (Edward)
1878-1967 . . . . **CLC 11, 47**
See also CA 19-20; 25-28R; CANR 33;
CAP 2; CDBLB 1890-1914; DLB 10;
MTCW; SATA 19

Maso, Carole 19(?)- . . . . **CLC 44**

McInerney, Jay 1955- . . . . **CLC 34**
See also CA 116; 123

McIntyre, Vonda N(eel) 1948- . . . . . **CLC 18**
See also CA 81-84; CANR 17, 34; MTCW

McKay, Claude . . . . **TCLC 7, 41; PC 2**
See also McKay, Festus Claudius
See also BLC 3; DLB 4, 45, 51, 117

McKay, Festus Claudius 1889-1948
See McKay, Claude
See also BW; CA 104; 124; DA; MTCW;
WLC

McKuen, Rod 1933- . . . . **CLC 1, 3**
See also AITN 1; CA 41-44R; CANR 40

McLoughlin, R. B.
See Mencken, H(enry) L(ouis)

McLuhan, (Herbert) Marshall
1911-1980 . . . . **CLC 37**
See also CA 9-12R; 102; CANR 12, 34;
DLB 88; MTCW

McMillan, Terry (L.) 1951- . . . . . **CLC 50, 61**
See also CA 140

McMurtry, Larry (Jeff)
1936- . . . . **CLC 2, 3, 7, 11, 27, 44**
See also AITN 2; BEST 89:2; CA 5-8R;
CANR 19; CDALB 1968-1988; DLB 2;
DLBY 80, 87; MTCW

McNally, Terrence 1939- . . . . . . **CLC 4, 7, 41**
See also CA 45-48; CANR 2; DLB 7

McNamer, Deirdre 1950- . . . . **CLC 70**

McNeile, Herman Cyril 1888-1937
See Sapper
See also DLB 77

McPhee, John (Angus) 1931- . . . . . . **CLC 36**
See also BEST 90:1; CA 65-68; CANR 20;
MTCW

McPherson, James Alan
1943- . . . . **CLC 19, 77**
See also BW; CA 25-28R; CAAS 17;
CANR 24; DLB 38; MTCW

McPherson, William (Alexander)
1933- . . . . **CLC 34**
See also CA 69-72; CANR 28

McSweeney, Kerry . . . . **CLC 34**

Mead, Margaret 1901-1978 . . . . **CLC 37**
See also AITN 1; CA 1-4R; 81-84;
CANR 4; MTCW; SATA 20

Meaker, Marijane (Agnes) 1927-
See Kerr, M. E.
See also CA 107; CANR 37; JRDA;
MAICYA; MTCW; SATA 20, 61

Medoff, Mark (Howard) 1940- . . . **CLC 6, 23**
See also AITN 1; CA 53-56; CANR 5;
DLB 7

Meged, Aharon
See Megged, Aharon

Meged, Aron
See Megged, Aharon

Megged, Aharon 1920- . . . . **CLC 9**
See also CA 49-52; CAAS 13; CANR 1

Mehta, Ved (Parkash) 1934- . . . . **CLC 37**
See also CA 1-4R; CANR 2, 23; MTCW

Melanter
See Blackmore, R(ichard) D(oddridge)

Melikow, Loris
See Hofmannsthal, Hugo von

Melmoth, Sebastian
See Wilde, Oscar (Fingal O'Flahertie Wills)

Meltzer, Milton 1915- . . . . **CLC 26**
See also AAYA 8; CA 13-16R; CANR 38;
CLR 13; DLB 61; JRDA; MAICYA;
SAAS 1; SATA 1, 50

Melville, Herman
1819-1891 . . . . . . **NCLC 3, 12, 29; SSC 1**
See also CDALB 1640-1865; DA; DLB 3,
74; SATA 59; WLC

Menander
c. 342B.C.-c. 292B.C. . . . . **CMLC 9; DC 3**

Mencken, H(enry) L(ouis)
1880-1956 . . . . **TCLC 13**
See also CA 105; 125; CDALB 1917-1929;
DLB 11, 29, 63; MTCW

Mercer, David 1928-1980 . . . . **CLC 5**
See also CA 9-12R; 102; CANR 23;
DLB 13; MTCW

Merchant, Paul
See Ellison, Harlan

Meredith, George 1828-1909 . . . **TCLC 17, 43**
See also CA 117; CDBLB 1832-1890;
DLB 18, 35, 57

Meredith, William (Morris)
1919- . . . . **CLC 4, 13, 22, 55**
See also CA 9-12R; CAAS 14; CANR 6, 40;
DLB 5

Merezhkovsky, Dmitry Sergeyevich
1865-1941 . . . . **TCLC 29**

Merimee, Prosper
1803-1870 . . . . **NCLC 6; SSC 7**
See also DLB 119

Merkin, Daphne 1954- . . . . **CLC 44**
See also CA 123

Merlin, Arthur
See Blish, James (Benjamin)

Merrill, James (Ingram)
1926- . . . . **CLC 2, 3, 6, 8, 13, 18, 34**
See also CA 13-16R; CANR 10; DLB 5;
DLBY 85; MTCW

Merriman, Alex
See Silverberg, Robert

Merritt, E. B.
See Waddington, Miriam

Merton, Thomas
1915-1968 . . . . **CLC 1, 3, 11, 34**
See also CA 5-8R; 25-28R; CANR 22;
DLB 48; DLBY 81; MTCW

Merwin, W(illiam) S(tanley)
1927- . . . . . . **CLC 1, 2, 3, 5, 8, 13, 18, 45**
See also CA 13-16R; CANR 15; DLB 5;
MTCW

Metcalf, John 1938- . . . . **CLC 37**
See also CA 113; DLB 60

Metcalf, Suzanne
See Baum, L(yman) Frank

Mew, Charlotte (Mary)
1870-1928 . . . . **TCLC 8**
See also CA 105; DLB 19

Mewshaw, Michael 1943- . . . . **CLC 9**
See also CA 53-56; CANR 7; DLBY 80

Meyer, June
See Jordan, June

Meyer, Lynn
See Slavitt, David R(ytman)

Meyer-Meyrink, Gustav 1868-1932
See Meyrink, Gustav
See also CA 117

Meyers, Jeffrey 1939- . . . . **CLC 39**
See also CA 73-76; DLB 111

Meynell, Alice (Christina Gertrude Thompson)
1847-1922 . . . . **TCLC 6**
See also CA 104; DLB 19, 98

Meyrink, Gustav . . . . **TCLC 21**
See also Meyer-Meyrink, Gustav
See also DLB 81

Michaels, Leonard 1933- . . . . **CLC 6, 25**
See also CA 61-64; CANR 21; DLB 130;
MTCW

Michaux, Henri 1899-1984 . . . . . . **CLC 8, 19**
See also CA 85-88; 114

Michelangelo 1475-1564 . . . . **LC 12**

Michelet, Jules 1798-1874 . . . . . . **NCLC 31**

Michener, James A(lbert)
1907(?)- . . . . **CLC 1, 5, 11, 29, 60**
See also AITN 1; BEST 90:1; CA 5-8R;
CANR 21; DLB 6; MTCW

Mickiewicz, Adam 1798-1855 . . . . . **NCLC 3**

Middleton, Christopher 1926- . . . . . . **CLC 13**
See also CA 13-16R; CANR 29; DLB 40

Middleton, Stanley 1919- . . . . **CLC 7, 38**
See also CA 25-28R; CANR 21; DLB 14

Migueis, Jose Rodrigues 1901- . . . . . **CLC 10**

Mikszath, Kalman 1847-1910 . . . . . **TCLC 31**

Miles, Josephine
1911-1985 . . . . **CLC 1, 2, 14, 34, 39**
See also CA 1-4R; 116; CANR 2; DLB 48

Militant
See Sandburg, Carl (August)

Mill, John Stuart 1806-1873 . . . . . **NCLC 11**
See also CDBLB 1832-1890; DLB 55

Millar, Kenneth 1915-1983 . . . . **CLC 14**
See also Macdonald, Ross
See also CA 9-12R; 110; CANR 16; DLB 2;
DLBD 6; DLBY 83; MTCW

Millay, E. Vincent
See Millay, Edna St. Vincent

Millay, Edna St. Vincent
1892-1950 . . . . **TCLC 4, 49; PC 6**
See also CA 104; 130; CDALB 1917-1929;
DA; DLB 45; MTCW

Miller, Arthur
1915- . . . . **CLC 1, 2, 6, 10, 15, 26, 47, 78;
DC 1**
See also AITN 1; CA 1-4R; CABS 3;
CANR 2, 30; CDALB 1941-1968; DA;
DLB 7; MTCW; WLC

Miller, Henry (Valentine)
1891-1980 . . . . **CLC 1, 2, 4, 9, 14, 43**
See also CA 9-12R; 97-100; CANR 33;
CDALB 1929-1941; DA; DLB 4, 9;
DLBY 80; MTCW; WLC

Miller, Jason 1939(?)- . . . . **CLC 2**
See also AITN 1; CA 73-76; DLB 7

Morgan, Edwin (George) 1920- ..... **CLC 31**
See also CA 5-8R; CANR 3; DLB 27

Morgan, (George) Frederick
1922- .... **CLC 23**
See also CA 17-20R; CANR 21

Morgan, Harriet
See Mencken, H(enry) L(ouis)

Morgan, Jane
See Cooper, James Fenimore

Morgan, Janet 1945- .... **CLC 39**
See also CA 65-68

Morgan, Lady 1776(?)-1859 ...... **NCLC 29**
See also DLB 116

Morgan, Robin 1941- .... **CLC 2**
See also CA 69-72; CANR 29; MTCW

Morgan, Scott
See Kuttner, Henry

Morgan, Seth 1949(?)-1990 .... **CLC 65**
See also CA 132

Morgenstern, Christian
1871-1914 .... **TCLC 8**
See also CA 105

Morgenstern, S.
See Goldman, William (W.)

Moricz, Zsigmond 1879-1942 ..... **TCLC 33**

Morike, Eduard (Friedrich)
1804-1875 .... **NCLC 10**
See also DLB 133

Mori Ogai .... **TCLC 14**
See also Mori Rintaro

Mori Rintaro 1862-1922
See Mori Ogai
See also CA 110

Moritz, Karl Philipp 1756-1793 ...... **LC 2**
See also DLB 94

Morland, Peter Henry
See Faust, Frederick (Schiller)

Morren, Theophil
See Hofmannsthal, Hugo von

Morris, Bill 1952- .... **CLC 76**

Morris, Julian
See West, Morris L(anglo)

Morris, Steveland Judkins 1950(?)-
See Wonder, Stevie
See also CA 111

Morris, William 1834-1896 .... **NCLC 4**
See also CDBLB 1832-1890; DLB 18, 35, 57

Morris, Wright 1910- ... **CLC 1, 3, 7, 18, 37**
See also CA 9-12R; CANR 21; DLB 2;
DLBY 81; MTCW

Morrison, Chloe Anthony Wofford
See Morrison, Toni

Morrison, James Douglas 1943-1971
See Morrison, Jim
See also CA 73-76; CANR 40

Morrison, Jim .... **CLC 17**
See also Morrison, James Douglas

Morrison, Toni 1931- ..... **CLC 4, 10, 22, 55**
See also AAYA 1; BLC 3; BW; CA 29-32R;
CANR 27, 42; CDALB 1968-1988; DA;
DLB 6, 33; DLBY 81; MTCW; SATA 57

Morrison, Van 1945- .... **CLC 21**
See also CA 116

Mortimer, John (Clifford)
1923- .... **CLC 28, 43**
See also CA 13-16R; CANR 21;
CDBLB 1960 to Present; DLB 13;
MTCW

Mortimer, Penelope (Ruth) 1918- .... **CLC 5**
See also CA 57-60

Morton, Anthony
See Creasey, John

Mosher, Howard Frank 1943- ...... **CLC 62**
See also CA 139

Mosley, Nicholas 1923- .... **CLC 43, 70**
See also CA 69-72; CANR 41; DLB 14

Moss, Howard
1922-1987 .... **CLC 7, 14, 45, 50**
See also CA 1-4R; 123; CANR 1; DLB 5

Mossgiel, Rab
See Burns, Robert

Motion, Andrew 1952- .... **CLC 47**
See also DLB 40

Motley, Willard (Francis)
1912-1965 .... **CLC 18**
See also BW; CA 117; 106; DLB 76

Mott, Michael (Charles Alston)
1930- .... **CLC 15, 34**
See also CA 5-8R; CAAS 7; CANR 7, 29

Mowat, Farley (McGill) 1921- ..... **CLC 26**
See also AAYA 1; CA 1-4R; CANR 4, 24,
42; CLR 20; DLB 68; JRDA; MAICYA;
MTCW; SATA 3, 55

Moyers, Bill 1934- .... **CLC 74**
See also AITN 2; CA 61-64; CANR 31

Mphahlele, Es'kia
See Mphahlele, Ezekiel
See also DLB 125

Mphahlele, Ezekiel 1919- .... **CLC 25**
See also Mphahlele, Es'kia
See also BLC 3; BW; CA 81-84; CANR 26

Mqhayi, S(amuel) E(dward) K(rune Loliwe)
1875-1945 .... **TCLC 25**
See also BLC 3

Mr. Martin
See Burroughs, William S(eward)

Mrozek, Slawomir 1930- .... **CLC 3, 13**
See also CA 13-16R; CAAS 10; CANR 29;
MTCW

Mrs. Belloc-Lowndes
See Lowndes, Marie Adelaide (Belloc)

Mtwa, Percy (?)- .... **CLC 47**

Mueller, Lisel 1924- .... **CLC 13, 51**
See also CA 93-96; DLB 105

Muir, Edwin 1887-1959 .... **TCLC 2**
See also CA 104; DLB 20, 100

Muir, John 1838-1914 .... **TCLC 28**

Mujica Lainez, Manuel
1910-1984 .... **CLC 31**
See also Lainez, Manuel Mujica
See also CA 81-84; 112; CANR 32; HW

Mukherjee, Bharati 1940- .... **CLC 53**
See also BEST 89:2; CA 107; DLB 60;
MTCW

Muldoon, Paul 1951- .... **CLC 32, 72**
See also CA 113; 129; DLB 40

Mulisch, Harry 1927- .... **CLC 42**
See also CA 9-12R; CANR 6, 26

Mull, Martin 1943- .... **CLC 17**
See also CA 105

Mulock, Dinah Maria
See Craik, Dinah Maria (Mulock)

Munford, Robert 1737(?)-1783 .... **LC 5**
See also DLB 31

Mungo, Raymond 1946- .... **CLC 72**
See also CA 49-52; CANR 2

Munro, Alice
1931- .... **CLC 6, 10, 19, 50; SSC 3**
See also AITN 2; CA 33-36R; CANR 33;
DLB 53; MTCW; SATA 29

Munro, H(ector) H(ugh) 1870-1916
See Saki
See also CA 104; 130; CDBLB 1890-1914;
DA; DLB 34; MTCW; WLC

Murasaki, Lady .... **CMLC 1**

Murdoch, (Jean) Iris
1919- ...... **CLC 1, 2, 3, 4, 6, 8, 11, 15,
22, 31, 51**
See also CA 13-16R; CANR 8;
CDBLB 1960 to Present; DLB 14;
MTCW

Murphy, Richard 1927- .... **CLC 41**
See also CA 29-32R; DLB 40

Murphy, Sylvia 1937- .... **CLC 34**
See also CA 121

Murphy, Thomas (Bernard) 1935- ... **CLC 51**
See also CA 101

Murray, Albert L. 1916- .... **CLC 73**
See also BW; CA 49-52; CANR 26; DLB 38

Murray, Les(lie) A(llan) 1938- ..... **CLC 40**
See also CA 21-24R; CANR 11, 27

Murry, J. Middleton
See Murry, John Middleton

Murry, John Middleton
1889-1957 .... **TCLC 16**
See also CA 118

Musgrave, Susan 1951- .... **CLC 13, 54**
See also CA 69-72

Musil, Robert (Edler von)
1880-1942 .... **TCLC 12**
See also CA 109; DLB 81, 124

Musset, (Louis Charles) Alfred de
1810-1857 .... **NCLC 7**

My Brother's Brother
See Chekhov, Anton (Pavlovich)

Myers, Walter Dean 1937- .... **CLC 35**
See also AAYA 4; BLC 3; BW; CA 33-36R;
CANR 20, 42; CLR 4, 16; DLB 33;
JRDA; MAICYA; SAAS 2; SATA 27, 41,
70, 71

Myers, Walter M.
See Myers, Walter Dean

Myles, Symon
See Follett, Ken(neth Martin)

Nabokov, Vladimir (Vladimirovich)
1899-1977 ..... **CLC 1, 2, 3, 6, 8, 11, 15,
23, 44, 46, 64; SSC 11**
See also CA 5-8R; 69-72; CANR 20;
CDALB 1941-1968; DA; DLB 2;
DLBD 3; DLBY 80, 91; MTCW; WLC

Norton, Andre 1912- .... CLC 12
See also Norton, Alice Mary
See also CA 1-4R; CANR 2, 31; DLB 8, 52;
JRDA; MTCW

Norway, Nevil Shute 1899-1960
See Shute, Nevil
See also CA 102; 93-96

Norwid, Cyprian Kamil
1821-1883 .... NCLC 17

Nosille, Nabrah
See Ellison, Harlan

Nossack, Hans Erich 1901-1978 ..... CLC 6
See also CA 93-96; 85-88; DLB 69

Nosu, Chuji
See Ozu, Yasujiro

Nova, Craig 1945- .... CLC 7, 31
See also CA 45-48; CANR 2

Novak, Joseph
See Kosinski, Jerzy (Nikodem)

Novalis 1772-1801 .... NCLC 13
See also DLB 90

Nowlan, Alden (Albert) 1933-1983 .. CLC 15
See also CA 9-12R; CANR 5; DLB 53

Noyes, Alfred 1880-1958 .... TCLC 7
See also CA 104; DLB 20

Nunn, Kem 19(?)- .... CLC 34

Nye, Robert 1939- .... CLC 13, 42
See also CA 33-36R; CANR 29; DLB 14;
MTCW; SATA 6

Nyro, Laura 1947- .... CLC 17

Oates, Joyce Carol
1938- ...... CLC 1, 2, 3, 6, 9, 11, 15, 19,
33, 52; SSC 6
See also AITN 1; BEST 89:2; CA 5-8R;
CANR 25; CDALB 1968-1988; DA;
DLB 2, 5, 130; DLBY 81; MTCW; WLC

O'Brien, E. G.
See Clarke, Arthur C(harles)

O'Brien, Edna
1936- ... CLC 3, 5, 8, 13, 36, 65; SSC 10
See also CA 1-4R; CANR 6, 41;
CDBLB 1960 to Present; DLB 14;
MTCW

O'Brien, Fitz-James 1828-1862... NCLC 21
See also DLB 74

O'Brien, Flann .... CLC 1, 4, 5, 7, 10, 47
See also O Nuallain, Brian

O'Brien, Richard 1942- .... CLC 17
See also CA 124

O'Brien, Tim 1946-......... CLC 7, 19, 40
See also CA 85-88; CANR 40; DLBD 9;
DLBY 80

Obstfelder, Sigbjoern 1866-1900... TCLC 23
See also CA 123

O'Casey, Sean
1880-1964 .... CLC 1, 5, 9, 11, 15
See also CA 89-92; CDBLB 1914-1945;
DLB 10; MTCW

O'Cathasaigh, Sean
See O'Casey, Sean

Ochs, Phil 1940-1976............ CLC 17
See also CA 65-68

O'Connor, Edwin (Greene)
1918-1968 .... CLC 14
See also CA 93-96; 25-28R

O'Connor, (Mary) Flannery
1925-1964 .... CLC 1, 2, 3, 6, 10, 13, 15,
21, 66; SSC 1
See also AAYA 7; CA 1-4R; CANR 3, 41;
CDALB 1941-1968; DA; DLB 2;
DLBY 80; MTCW; WLC

O'Connor, Frank .... CLC 23; SSC 5
See also O'Donovan, Michael John

O'Dell, Scott 1898-1989........... CLC 30
See also AAYA 3; CA 61-64; 129;
CANR 12, 30; CLR 1, 16; DLB 52;
JRDA; MAICYA; SATA 12, 60

Odets, Clifford 1906-1963 .... CLC 2, 28
See also CA 85-88; DLB 7, 26; MTCW

O'Doherty, Brian 1934-........... CLC 76
See also CA 105

O'Donnell, K. M.
See Malzberg, Barry N(athaniel)

O'Donnell, Lawrence
See Kuttner, Henry

O'Donovan, Michael John
1903-1966 .... CLC 14
See also O'Connor, Frank
See also CA 93-96

Oe, Kenzaburo 1935- .... CLC 10, 36
See also CA 97-100; CANR 36; MTCW

O'Faolain, Julia 1932-....... CLC 6, 19, 47
See also CA 81-84; CAAS 2; CANR 12;
DLB 14; MTCW

O'Faolain, Sean
1900-1991 .... CLC 1, 7, 14, 32, 70;
SSC 13
See also CA 61-64; 134; CANR 12;
DLB 15; MTCW

O'Flaherty, Liam
1896-1984 .... CLC 5, 34; SSC 6
See also CA 101; 113; CANR 35; DLB 36;
DLBY 84; MTCW

Ogilvy, Gavin
See Barrie, J(ames) M(atthew)

O'Grady, Standish James
1846-1928 .... TCLC 5
See also CA 104

O'Grady, Timothy 1951- .... CLC 59
See also CA 138

O'Hara, Frank
1926-1966 .... CLC 2, 5, 13, 78
See also CA 9-12R; 25-28R; CANR 33;
DLB 5, 16; MTCW

O'Hara, John (Henry)
1905-1970 .... CLC 1, 2, 3, 6, 11, 42
See also CA 5-8R; 25-28R; CANR 31;
CDALB 1929-1941; DLB 9, 86; DLBD 2;
MTCW

O Hehir, Diana 1922- .... CLC 41
See also CA 93-96

Okigbo, Christopher (Ifenayichukwu)
1932-1967 .... CLC 25; PC 7
See also BLC 3; BW; CA 77-80; DLB 125;
MTCW

Olds, Sharon 1942-............ CLC 32, 39
See also CA 101; CANR 18, 41; DLB 120

Oldstyle, Jonathan
See Irving, Washington

Olesha, Yuri (Karlovich)
1899-1960 .... CLC 8
See also CA 85-88

Oliphant, Margaret (Oliphant Wilson)
1828-1897 .... NCLC 11
See also DLB 18

Oliver, Mary 1935-............ CLC 19, 34
See also CA 21-24R; CANR 9; DLB 5

Olivier, Laurence (Kerr)
1907-1989 .... CLC 20
See also CA 111; 129

Olsen, Tillie 1913- .... CLC 4, 13; SSC 11
See also CA 1-4R; CANR 1; DA; DLB 28;
DLBY 80; MTCW

Olson, Charles (John)
1910-1970 ..... CLC 1, 2, 5, 6, 9, 11, 29
See also CA 13-16; 25-28R; CABS 2;
CANR 35; CAP 1; DLB 5, 16; MTCW

Olson, Toby 1937- .... CLC 28
See also CA 65-68; CANR 9, 31

Olyesha, Yuri
See Olesha, Yuri (Karlovich)

Ondaatje, (Philip) Michael
1943-............... CLC 14, 29, 51, 76
See also CA 77-80; CANR 42; DLB 60

Oneal, Elizabeth 1934-
See Oneal, Zibby
See also CA 106; CANR 28; MAICYA;
SATA 30

Oneal, Zibby .... CLC 30
See also Oneal, Elizabeth
See also AAYA 5; CLR 13; JRDA

O'Neill, Eugene (Gladstone)
1888-1953 .... TCLC 1, 6, 27, 49
See also AITN 1; CA 110; 132;
CDALB 1929-1941; DA; DLB 7; MTCW;
WLC

Onetti, Juan Carlos 1909-....... CLC 7, 10
See also CA 85-88; CANR 32; DLB 113;
HW; MTCW

O Nuallain, Brian 1911-1966
See O'Brien, Flann
See also CA 21-22; 25-28R; CAP 2

Oppen, George 1908-1984 .... CLC 7, 13, 34
See also CA 13-16R; 113; CANR 8; DLB 5

Oppenheim, E(dward) Phillips
1866-1946 .... TCLC 45
See also CA 111; DLB 70

Orlovitz, Gil 1918-1973........... CLC 22
See also CA 77-80; 45-48; DLB 2, 5

Orris
See Ingelow, Jean

Ortega y Gasset, Jose 1883-1955 ... TCLC 9
See also CA 106; 130; HW; MTCW

Ortiz, Simon J(oseph) 1941-....... CLC 45
See also CA 134; DLB 120

Orton, Joe .... CLC 4, 13, 43; DC 3
See also Orton, John Kingsley
See also CDBLB 1960 to Present; DLB 13

Orton, John Kingsley 1933-1967
See Orton, Joe
See also CA 85-88; CANR 35; MTCW

Paustovsky, Konstantin (Georgievich)
  1892-1968 .... CLC **40**
  See also CA 93-96; 25-28R

Pavese, Cesare 1908-1950 .... TCLC **3**
  See also CA 104; DLB 128

Pavic, Milorad 1929- .... CLC **60**
  See also CA 136

Payne, Alan
  See Jakes, John (William)

Paz, Gil
  See Lugones, Leopoldo

Paz, Octavio
  1914- .... CLC **3, 4, 6, 10, 19, 51, 65;**
  PC 1
  See also CA 73-76; CANR 32; DA;
  DLBY 90; HW; MTCW; WLC

Peacock, Molly 1947-............ CLC **60**
  See also CA 103; DLB 120

Peacock, Thomas Love
  1785-1866 .... NCLC **22**
  See also DLB 96, 116

Peake, Mervyn 1911-1968 ...... CLC **7, 54**
  See also CA 5-8R; 25-28R; CANR 3;
  DLB 15; MTCW; SATA 23

Pearce, Philippa .... CLC **21**
  See also Christie, (Ann) Philippa
  See also CLR 9; MAICYA; SATA 1, 67

Pearl, Eric
  See Elman, Richard

Pearson, T(homas) R(eid) 1956- .... CLC **39**
  See also CA 120; 130

Peck, John 1941- .... CLC **3**
  See also CA 49-52; CANR 3

Peck, Richard (Wayne) 1934- ...... CLC **21**
  See also AAYA 1; CA 85-88; CANR 19,
  38; JRDA; MAICYA; SAAS 2; SATA 18,
  55

Peck, Robert Newton 1928-........ CLC **17**
  See also AAYA 3; CA 81-84; CANR 31;
  DA; JRDA; MAICYA; SAAS 1;
  SATA 21, 62

Peckinpah, (David) Sam(uel)
  1925-1984 .... CLC **20**
  See also CA 109; 114

Pedersen, Knut 1859-1952
  See Hamsun, Knut
  See also CA 104; 119; MTCW

Peeslake, Gaffer
  See Durrell, Lawrence (George)

Peguy, Charles Pierre
  1873-1914 .... TCLC **10**
  See also CA 107

Pena, Ramon del Valle y
  See Valle-Inclan, Ramon (Maria) del

Pendennis, Arthur Esquir
  See Thackeray, William Makepeace

Pepys, Samuel 1633-1703.......... LC **11**
  See also CDBLB 1660-1789; DA; DLB 101;
  WLC

Percy, Walker
  1916-1990 .... CLC **2, 3, 6, 8, 14, 18, 47,**
  65
  See also CA 1-4R; 131; CANR 1, 23;
  DLB 2; DLBY 80, 90; MTCW

Perec, Georges 1936-1982 .... CLC **56**
  See also CA 141; DLB 83

Pereda (y Sanchez de Porrua), Jose Maria de
  1833-1906 .... TCLC **16**
  See also CA 117

Pereda y Porrua, Jose Maria de
  See Pereda (y Sanchez de Porrua), Jose
  Maria de

Peregoy, George Weems
  See Mencken, H(enry) L(ouis)

Perelman, S(idney) J(oseph)
  1904-1979 ... CLC **3, 5, 9, 15, 23, 44, 49**
  See also AITN 1, 2; CA 73-76; 89-92;
  CANR 18; DLB 11, 44; MTCW

Peret, Benjamin 1899-1959 .... TCLC **20**
  See also CA 117

Peretz, Isaac Loeb 1851(?)-1915... TCLC **16**
  See also CA 109

Peretz, Yitzkhok Leibush
  See Peretz, Isaac Loeb

Perez Galdos, Benito 1843-1920 ... TCLC **27**
  See also CA 125; HW

Perrault, Charles 1628-1703 .... LC **2**
  See also MAICYA; SATA 25

Perry, Brighton
  See Sherwood, Robert E(mmet)

Perse, Saint-John
  See Leger, (Marie-Rene) Alexis Saint-Leger

Perse, St.-John .... CLC **4, 11, 46**
  See also Leger, (Marie-Rene) Alexis
  Saint-Leger

Peseenz, Tulio F.
  See Lopez y Fuentes, Gregorio

Pesetsky, Bette 1932-............ CLC **28**
  See also CA 133; DLB 130

Peshkov, Alexei Maximovich 1868-1936
  See Gorky, Maxim
  See also CA 105; 141; DA

Pessoa, Fernando (Antonio Nogueira)
  1888-1935 .... TCLC **27**
  See also CA 125

Peterkin, Julia Mood 1880-1961.... CLC **31**
  See also CA 102; DLB 9

Peters, Joan K. 1945-............ CLC **39**

Peters, Robert L(ouis) 1924-........ CLC **7**
  See also CA 13-16R; CAAS 8; DLB 105

Petofi, Sandor 1823-1849....... NCLC **21**

Petrakis, Harry Mark 1923-........ CLC **3**
  See also CA 9-12R; CANR 4, 30

Petrov, Evgeny .... TCLC **21**
  See also Kataev, Evgeny Petrovich

Petry, Ann (Lane) 1908- ...... CLC **1, 7, 18**
  See also BW; CA 5-8R; CAAS 6; CANR 4;
  CLR 12; DLB 76; JRDA; MAICYA;
  MTCW; SATA 5

Petursson, Halligrimur 1614-1674 .... LC **8**

Philipson, Morris H. 1926-........ CLC **53**
  See also CA 1-4R; CANR 4

Phillips, David Graham
  1867-1911 .... TCLC **44**
  See also CA 108; DLB 9, 12

Phillips, Jack
  See Sandburg, Carl (August)

Phillips, Jayne Anne 1952- ..... CLC **15, 33**
  See also CA 101; CANR 24; DLBY 80;
  MTCW

Phillips, Richard
  See Dick, Philip K(indred)

Phillips, Robert (Schaeffer) 1938-... CLC **28**
  See also CA 17-20R; CAAS 13; CANR 8;
  DLB 105

Phillips, Ward
  See Lovecraft, H(oward) P(hillips)

Piccolo, Lucio 1901-1969......... CLC **13**
  See also CA 97-100; DLB 114

Pickthall, Marjorie L(owry) C(hristie)
  1883-1922 .... TCLC **21**
  See also CA 107; DLB 92

Pico della Mirandola, Giovanni
  1463-1494 .... LC **15**

Piercy, Marge
  1936- .... CLC **3, 6, 14, 18, 27, 62**
  See also CA 21-24R; CAAS 1; CANR 13;
  DLB 120; MTCW

Piers, Robert
  See Anthony, Piers

Pieyre de Mandiargues, Andre 1909-1991
  See Mandiargues, Andre Pieyre de
  See also CA 103; 136; CANR 22

Pilnyak, Boris .... TCLC **23**
  See also Vogau, Boris Andreyevich

Pincherle, Alberto 1907-1990 ... CLC **11, 18**
  See also Moravia, Alberto
  See also CA 25-28R; 132; CANR 33;
  MTCW

Pinckney, Darryl 1953-........... CLC **76**

Pineda, Cecile 1942-............. CLC **39**
  See also CA 118

Pinero, Arthur Wing 1855-1934 ... TCLC **32**
  See also CA 110; DLB 10

Pinero, Miguel (Antonio Gomez)
  1946-1988 .... CLC **4, 55**
  See also CA 61-64; 125; CANR 29; HW

Pinget, Robert 1919- .... CLC **7, 13, 37**
  See also CA 85-88; DLB 83

Pink Floyd....................... CLC **35**
  See also Barrett, (Roger) Syd; Gilmour,
  David; Mason, Nick; Waters, Roger;
  Wright, Rick

Pinkney, Edward 1802-1828 ..... NCLC **31**

Pinkwater, Daniel Manus 1941-.... CLC **35**
  See also Pinkwater, Manus
  See also AAYA 1; CA 29-32R; CANR 12,
  38; CLR 4; JRDA; MAICYA; SAAS 3;
  SATA 46

Pinkwater, Manus
  See Pinkwater, Daniel Manus
  See also SATA 8

Pinsky, Robert 1940-........ CLC **9, 19, 38**
  See also CA 29-32R; CAAS 4; DLBY 82

Pinta, Harold
  See Pinter, Harold

Pinter, Harold
  1930- .. CLC **1, 3, 6, 9, 11, 15, 27, 58, 73**
  See also CA 5-8R; CANR 33; CDBLB 1960
  to Present; DA; DLB 13; MTCW; WLC

Pirandello, Luigi 1867-1936..... TCLC **4, 29**
See also CA 104; DA; WLC

Pirsig, Robert M(aynard)
1928- .... CLC **4, 6, 73**
See also CA 53-56; CANR 42; MTCW;
SATA 39

Pisarev, Dmitry Ivanovich
1840-1868 .... NCLC **25**

Pix, Mary (Griffith) 1666-1709 .... LC **8**
See also DLB 80

Pixerecourt, Guilbert de
1773-1844 .... NCLC **39**

Plaidy, Jean
See Hibbert, Eleanor Alice Burford

Planche, James Robinson
1796-1880 .... NCLC **42**

Plant, Robert 1948- .... CLC **12**

Plante, David (Robert)
1940- .... CLC **7, 23, 38**
See also CA 37-40R; CANR 12, 36;
DLBY 83; MTCW

Plath, Sylvia
1932-1963 ..... CLC **1, 2, 3, 5, 9, 11, 14, 17, 50, 51, 62; PC 1**
See also CA 19-20; CANR 34; CAP 2;
CDALB 1941-1968; DA; DLB 5, 6;
MTCW; WLC

Plato 428(?)B.C.-348(?)B.C........ CMLC **8**
See also DA

Platonov, Andrei .... TCLC **14**
See also Klimentov, Andrei Platonovich

Platt, Kin 1911- .... CLC **26**
See also CA 17-20R; CANR 11; JRDA;
SATA 21

Plick et Plock
See Simenon, Georges (Jacques Christian)

Plimpton, George (Ames) 1927-..... CLC **36**
See also AITN 1; CA 21-24R; CANR 32;
MTCW; SATA 10

Plomer, William Charles Franklin
1903-1973 .... CLC **4, 8**
See also CA 21-22; CANR 34; CAP 2;
DLB 20; MTCW; SATA 24

Plowman, Piers
See Kavanagh, Patrick (Joseph)

Plum, J.
See Wodehouse, P(elham) G(renville)

Plumly, Stanley (Ross) 1939- ...... CLC **33**
See also CA 108; 110; DLB 5

Poe, Edgar Allan
1809-1849 ... NCLC **1, 16; PC 1; SSC 1**
See also CDALB 1640-1865; DA; DLB 3,
59, 73, 74; SATA 23; WLC

Poet of Titchfield Street, The
See Pound, Ezra (Weston Loomis)

Pohl, Frederik 1919- .... CLC **18**
See also CA 61-64; CAAS 1; CANR 11, 37;
DLB 8; MTCW; SATA 24

Poirier, Louis 1910-
See Gracq, Julien
See also CA 122; 126

Poitier, Sidney 1927-.............. CLC **26**
See also BW; CA 117

Polanski, Roman 1933- .... CLC **16**
See also CA 77-80

Poliakoff, Stephen 1952- .... CLC **38**
See also CA 106; DLB 13

Police, The...................... CLC **26**
See also Copeland, Stewart (Armstrong);
Summers, Andrew James; Sumner,
Gordon Matthew

Pollitt, Katha 1949- .... CLC **28**
See also CA 120; 122; MTCW

Pollock, (Mary) Sharon 1936-...... CLC **50**
See also CA 141; DLB 60

Pomerance, Bernard 1940-........ CLC **13**
See also CA 101

Ponge, Francis (Jean Gaston Alfred)
1899-1988 .... CLC **6, 18**
See also CA 85-88; 126; CANR 40

Pontoppidan, Henrik 1857-1943 ... TCLC **29**

Poole, Josephine .... CLC **17**
See also Helyar, Jane Penelope Josephine
See also SAAS 2; SATA 5

Popa, Vasko 1922- .... CLC **19**
See also CA 112

Pope, Alexander 1688-1744.......... LC **3**
See also CDBLB 1660-1789; DA; DLB 95,
101; WLC

Porter, Connie 1960- .... CLC **70**

Porter, Gene(va Grace) Stratton
1863(?)-1924 .... TCLC **21**
See also CA 112

Porter, Katherine Anne
1890-1980 ...... CLC **1, 3, 7, 10, 13, 15, 27; SSC 4**
See also AITN 2; CA 1-4R; 101; CANR 1;
DA; DLB 4, 9, 102; DLBY 80; MTCW;
SATA 23, 39

Porter, Peter (Neville Frederick)
1929- .... CLC **5, 13, 33**
See also CA 85-88; DLB 40

Porter, William Sydney 1862-1910
See Henry, O.
See also CA 104; 131; CDALB 1865-1917;
DA; DLB 12, 78, 79; MTCW; YABC 2

Portillo (y Pacheco), Jose Lopez
See Lopez Portillo (y Pacheco), Jose

Post, Melville Davisson
1869-1930 .... TCLC **39**
See also CA 110

Potok, Chaim 1929- .... CLC **2, 7, 14, 26**
See also AITN 1, 2; CA 17-20R; CANR 19,
35; DLB 28; MTCW; SATA 33

Potter, Beatrice
See Webb, (Martha) Beatrice (Potter)
See also MAICYA

Potter, Dennis (Christopher George)
1935- .... CLC **58**
See also CA 107; CANR 33; MTCW

Pound, Ezra (Weston Loomis)
1885-1972 ...... CLC **1, 2, 3, 4, 5, 7, 10, 13, 18, 34, 48, 50; PC 4**
See also CA 5-8R; 37-40R; CANR 40;
CDALB 1917-1929; DA; DLB 4, 45, 63;
MTCW; WLC

Povod, Reinaldo 1959-............. CLC **44**
See also CA 136

Powell, Anthony (Dymoke)
1905- .... CLC **1, 3, 7, 9, 10, 31**
See also CA 1-4R; CANR 1, 32;
CDBLB 1945-1960; DLB 15; MTCW

Powell, Dawn 1897-1965 .... CLC **66**
See also CA 5-8R

Powell, Padgett 1952-............. CLC **34**
See also CA 126

Powers, J(ames) F(arl)
1917- .... CLC **1, 4, 8, 57; SSC 4**
See also CA 1-4R; CANR 2; DLB 130;
MTCW

Powers, John J(ames) 1945-
See Powers, John R.
See also CA 69-72

Powers, John R. .... CLC **66**
See also Powers, John J(ames)

Pownall, David 1938-............. CLC **10**
See also CA 89-92; CAAS 18; DLB 14

Powys, John Cowper
1872-1963 .... CLC **7, 9, 15, 46**
See also CA 85-88; DLB 15; MTCW

Powys, T(heodore) F(rancis)
1875-1953 .... TCLC **9**
See also CA 106; DLB 36

Prager, Emily 1952-............. CLC **56**

Pratt, E(dwin) J(ohn)
1883(?)-1964 .... CLC **19**
See also CA 141; 93-96; DLB 92

Premchand...................... TCLC **21**
See also Srivastava, Dhanpat Rai

Preussler, Otfried 1923-........... CLC **17**
See also CA 77-80; SATA 24

Prevert, Jacques (Henri Marie)
1900-1977 .... CLC **15**
See also CA 77-80; 69-72; CANR 29;
MTCW; SATA 30

Prevost, Abbe (Antoine Francois)
1697-1763 .... LC **1**

Price, (Edward) Reynolds
1933- .... CLC **3, 6, 13, 43, 50, 63**
See also CA 1-4R; CANR 1, 37; DLB 2

Price, Richard 1949- .... CLC **6, 12**
See also CA 49-52; CANR 3; DLBY 81

Prichard, Katharine Susannah
1883-1969 .... CLC **46**
See also CA 11-12; CANR 33; CAP 1;
MTCW; SATA 66

Priestley, J(ohn) B(oynton)
1894-1984 .... CLC **2, 5, 9, 34**
See also CA 9-12R; 113; CANR 33;
CDBLB 1914-1945; DLB 10, 34, 77, 100;
DLBY 84; MTCW

Prince 1958(?)-.................. CLC **35**

Prince, F(rank) T(empleton) 1912- .. CLC **22**
See also CA 101; DLB 20

Prince Kropotkin
See Kropotkin, Peter (Aleksieevich)

Prior, Matthew 1664-1721.......... LC **4**
See also DLB 95

Pritchard, William H(arrison)
1932- .... CLC **34**
See also CA 65-68; CANR 23; DLB 111

Pritchett, V(ictor) S(awdon)
1900- . . . . CLC 5, 13, 15, 41
See also CA 61-64; CANR 31; DLB 15;
MTCW

Private 19022
See Manning, Frederic

Probst, Mark 1925- . . . . CLC 59
See also CA 130

Prokosch, Frederic 1908-1989 . . . . CLC 4, 48
See also CA 73-76; 128; DLB 48

Prophet, The
See Dreiser, Theodore (Herman Albert)

Prose, Francine 1947- . . . . CLC 45
See also CA 109; 112

Proudhon
See Cunha, Euclides (Rodrigues Pimenta) da

Proust, (Valentin-Louis-George-Eugene-)
Marcel 1871-1922 . . . . TCLC 7, 13, 33
See also CA 104; 120; DA; DLB 65;
MTCW; WLC

Prowler, Harley
See Masters, Edgar Lee

Prus, Boleslaw . . . . TCLC 48
See also Glowacki, Aleksander

Pryor, Richard (Franklin Lenox Thomas)
1940- . . . . CLC 26
See also CA 122

Przybyszewski, Stanislaw
1868-1927 . . . . TCLC 36
See also DLB 66

Pteleon
See Grieve, C(hristopher) M(urray)

Puckett, Lute
See Masters, Edgar Lee

Puig, Manuel
1932-1990 . . . . CLC 3, 5, 10, 28, 65
See also CA 45-48; CANR 2, 32; DLB 113;
HW; MTCW

Purdy, Al
See Purdy, Al(fred Wellington)
See also CAAS 17; DLB 88

Purdy, Al(fred Wellington)
1918- . . . . CLC 3, 6, 14, 50
See also CA 81-84; CANR 42

Purdy, James (Amos)
1923- . . . . CLC 2, 4, 10, 28, 52
See also CA 33-36R; CAAS 1; CANR 19;
DLB 2; MTCW

Pure, Simon
See Swinnerton, Frank Arthur

Pushkin, Alexander (Sergeyevich)
1799-1837 . . . . NCLC 3, 27
See also DA; SATA 61; WLC

P'u Sung-ling 1640-1715 . . . . LC 3

Putnam, Arthur Lee
See Alger, Horatio, Jr.

Puzo, Mario 1920- . . . . CLC 1, 2, 6, 36
See also CA 65-68; CANR 4, 42; DLB 6;
MTCW

Pym, Barbara (Mary Crampton)
1913-1980 . . . . CLC 13, 19, 37
See also CA 13-14; 97-100; CANR 13, 34;
CAP 1; DLB 14; DLBY 87; MTCW

Pynchon, Thomas (Ruggles, Jr.)
1937- . . CLC 2, 3, 6, 9, 11, 18, 33, 62, 72
See also BEST 90:2; CA 17-20R; CANR 22;
DA; DLB 2; MTCW; WLC

Qian Zhongshu
See Ch'ien Chung-shu

Qroll
See Dagerman, Stig (Halvard)

Quarrington, Paul (Lewis) 1953- . . . . CLC 65
See also CA 129

Quasimodo, Salvatore 1901-1968 . . . CLC 10
See also CA 13-16; 25-28R; CAP 1;
DLB 114; MTCW

Queen, Ellery . . . . CLC 3, 11
See also Dannay, Frederic; Davidson,
Avram; Lee, Manfred B(ennington);
Sturgeon, Theodore (Hamilton); Vance,
John Holbrook

Queen, Ellery, Jr.
See Dannay, Frederic; Lee, Manfred
B(ennington)

Queneau, Raymond
1903-1976 . . . . CLC 2, 5, 10, 42
See also CA 77-80; 69-72; CANR 32;
DLB 72; MTCW

Quevedo, Francisco de 1580-1645 . . . . LC 23

Quin, Ann (Marie) 1936-1973 . . . . . . CLC 6
See also CA 9-12R; 45-48; DLB 14

Quinn, Martin
See Smith, Martin Cruz

Quinn, Simon
See Smith, Martin Cruz

Quiroga, Horacio (Sylvestre)
1878-1937 . . . . TCLC 20
See also CA 117; 131; HW; MTCW

Quoirez, Francoise 1935- . . . . CLC 9
See also Sagan, Francoise
See also CA 49-52; CANR 6, 39; MTCW

Raabe, Wilhelm 1831-1910 . . . . TCLC 45
See also DLB 129

Rabe, David (William) 1940- . . . CLC 4, 8, 33
See also CA 85-88; CABS 3; DLB 7

Rabelais, Francois 1483-1553 . . . . LC 5
See also DA; WLC

Rabinovitch, Sholem 1859-1916
See Aleichem, Sholom
See also CA 104

Radcliffe, Ann (Ward) 1764-1823 . . NCLC 6
See also DLB 39

Radiguet, Raymond 1903-1923 . . . . TCLC 29
See also DLB 65

Radnoti, Miklos 1909-1944 . . . . TCLC 16
See also CA 118

Rado, James 1939- . . . . CLC 17
See also CA 105

Radvanyi, Netty 1900-1983
See Seghers, Anna
See also CA 85-88; 110

Raeburn, John (Hay) 1941- . . . . CLC 34
See also CA 57-60

Ragni, Gerome 1942-1991 . . . . CLC 17
See also CA 105; 134

Rahv, Philip . . . . CLC 24
See also Greenberg, Ivan

Raine, Craig 1944- . . . . CLC 32
See also CA 108; CANR 29; DLB 40

Raine, Kathleen (Jessie) 1908- . . . CLC 7, 45
See also CA 85-88; DLB 20; MTCW

Rainis, Janis 1865-1929 . . . . TCLC 29

Rakosi, Carl . . . . CLC 47
See also Rawley, Callman
See also CAAS 5

Raleigh, Richard
See Lovecraft, H(oward) P(hillips)

Rallentando, H. P.
See Sayers, Dorothy L(eigh)

Ramal, Walter
See de la Mare, Walter (John)

Ramon, Juan
See Jimenez (Mantecon), Juan Ramon

Ramos, Graciliano 1892-1953 . . . . . TCLC 32

Rampersad, Arnold 1941- . . . . CLC 44
See also CA 127; 133; DLB 111

Rampling, Anne
See Rice, Anne

Ramuz, Charles-Ferdinand
1878-1947 . . . . TCLC 33

Rand, Ayn 1905-1982 . . . . . CLC 3, 30, 44, 79
See also AAYA 10; CA 13-16R; 105;
CANR 27; DA; MTCW; WLC

Randall, Dudley (Felker) 1914- . . . . . . CLC 1
See also BLC 3; BW; CA 25-28R;
CANR 23; DLB 41

Randall, Robert
See Silverberg, Robert

Ranger, Ken
See Creasey, John

Ransom, John Crowe
1888-1974 . . . . CLC 2, 4, 5, 11, 24
See also CA 5-8R; 49-52; CANR 6, 34;
DLB 45, 63; MTCW

Rao, Raja 1909- . . . . CLC 25, 56
See also CA 73-76; MTCW

Raphael, Frederic (Michael)
1931- . . . . CLC 2, 14
See also CA 1-4R; CANR 1; DLB 14

Ratcliffe, James P.
See Mencken, H(enry) L(ouis)

Rathbone, Julian 1935- . . . . CLC 41
See also CA 101; CANR 34

Rattigan, Terence (Mervyn)
1911-1977 . . . . CLC 7
See also CA 85-88; 73-76;
CDBLB 1945-1960; DLB 13; MTCW

Ratushinskaya, Irina 1954- . . . . CLC 54
See also CA 129

Raven, Simon (Arthur Noel)
1927- . . . . CLC 14
See also CA 81-84

Rawley, Callman 1903-
See Rakosi, Carl
See also CA 21-24R; CANR 12, 32

Rawlings, Marjorie Kinnan
1896-1953 . . . . TCLC 4
See also CA 104; 137; DLB 9, 22, 102;
JRDA; MAICYA; YABC 1

Ray, Satyajit 1921-1992 . . . . CLC 16, 76
See also CA 114; 137

Read, Herbert Edward 1893-1968.... **CLC 4**
See also CA 85-88; 25-28R; DLB 20

Read, Piers Paul 1941- ...... **CLC 4, 10, 25**
See also CA 21-24R; CANR 38; DLB 14;
SATA 21

Reade, Charles 1814-1884 .... **NCLC 2**
See also DLB 21

Reade, Hamish
See Gray, Simon (James Holliday)

Reading, Peter 1946- .... **CLC 47**
See also CA 103; DLB 40

Reaney, James 1926- .... **CLC 13**
See also CA 41-44R; CAAS 15; CANR 42;
DLB 68; SATA 43

Rebreanu, Liviu 1885-1944 .... **TCLC 28**

Rechy, John (Francisco)
1934- .... **CLC 1, 7, 14, 18**
See also CA 5-8R; CAAS 4; CANR 6, 32;
DLB 122; DLBY 82; HW

Redcam, Tom 1870-1933 .... **TCLC 25**

Reddin, Keith. .... **CLC 67**

Redgrove, Peter (William)
1932- .... **CLC 6, 41**
See also CA 1-4R; CANR 3, 39; DLB 40

Redmon, Anne .... **CLC 22**
See also Nightingale, Anne Redmon
See also DLBY 86

Reed, Eliot
See Ambler, Eric

Reed, Ishmael
1938- .... **CLC 2, 3, 5, 6, 13, 32, 60**
See also BLC 3; BW; CA 21-24R;
CANR 25; DLB 2, 5, 33; DLBD 8;
MTCW

Reed, John (Silas) 1887-1920 ...... **TCLC 9**
See also CA 106

Reed, Lou. .... **CLC 21**
See also Firbank, Louis

Reeve, Clara 1729-1807 .... **NCLC 19**
See also DLB 39

Reid, Christopher (John) 1949- ..... **CLC 33**
See also CA 140; DLB 40

Reid, Desmond
See Moorcock, Michael (John)

Reid Banks, Lynne 1929-
See Banks, Lynne Reid
See also CA 1-4R; CANR 6, 22, 38;
CLR 24; JRDA; MAICYA; SATA 22, 75

Reilly, William K.
See Creasey, John

Reiner, Max
See Caldwell, (Janet Miriam) Taylor
(Holland)

Reis, Ricardo
See Pessoa, Fernando (Antonio Nogueira)

Remarque, Erich Maria
1898-1970 .... **CLC 21**
See also CA 77-80; 29-32R; DA; DLB 56;
MTCW

Remizov, A.
See Remizov, Aleksei (Mikhailovich)

Remizov, A. M.
See Remizov, Aleksei (Mikhailovich)

Remizov, Aleksei (Mikhailovich)
1877-1957 .... **TCLC 27**
See also CA 125; 133

Renan, Joseph Ernest
1823-1892 .... **NCLC 26**

Renard, Jules 1864-1910 .... **TCLC 17**
See also CA 117

Renault, Mary .... **CLC 3, 11, 17**
See also Challans, Mary
See also DLBY 83

Rendell, Ruth (Barbara) 1930- .. **CLC 28, 48**
See also Vine, Barbara
See also CA 109; CANR 32; DLB 87;
MTCW

Renoir, Jean 1894-1979 .... **CLC 20**
See also CA 129; 85-88

Resnais, Alain 1922-............... **CLC 16**

Reverdy, Pierre 1889-1960 .... **CLC 53**
See also CA 97-100; 89-92

Rexroth, Kenneth
1905-1982 ...... **CLC 1, 2, 6, 11, 22, 49**
See also CA 5-8R; 107; CANR 14, 34;
CDALB 1941-1968; DLB 16, 48;
DLBY 82; MTCW

Reyes, Alfonso 1889-1959 .... **TCLC 33**
See also CA 131; HW

Reyes y Basoalto, Ricardo Eliecer Neftali
See Neruda, Pablo

Reymont, Wladyslaw (Stanislaw)
1868(?)-1925 .... **TCLC 5**
See also CA 104

Reynolds, Jonathan 1942-....... **CLC 6, 38**
See also CA 65-68; CANR 28

Reynolds, Joshua 1723-1792 .... **LC 15**
See also DLB 104

Reynolds, Michael Shane 1937- .... **CLC 44**
See also CA 65-68; CANR 9

Reznikoff, Charles 1894-1976 .... **CLC 9**
See also CA 33-36; 61-64; CAP 2; DLB 28,
45

Rezzori (d'Arezzo), Gregor von
1914- .... **CLC 25**
See also CA 122; 136

Rhine, Richard
See Silverstein, Alvin

R'hoone
See Balzac, Honore de

Rhys, Jean
1890(?)-1979 .... **CLC 2, 4, 6, 14, 19, 51**
See also CA 25-28R; 85-88; CANR 35;
CDBLB 1945-1960; DLB 36, 117; MTCW

Ribeiro, Darcy 1922-............. **CLC 34**
See also CA 33-36R

Ribeiro, Joao Ubaldo (Osorio Pimentel)
1941- .... **CLC 10, 67**
See also CA 81-84

Ribman, Ronald (Burt) 1932- .... **CLC 7**
See also CA 21-24R

Ricci, Nino 1959-............... **CLC 70**
See also CA 137

Rice, Anne 1941- .... **CLC 41**
See also AAYA 9; BEST 89:2; CA 65-68;
CANR 12, 36

Rice, Elmer (Leopold)
1892-1967 .... **CLC 7, 49**
See also CA 21-22; 25-28R; CAP 2; DLB 4,
7; MTCW

Rice, Tim 1944- .... **CLC 21**
See also CA 103

Rich, Adrienne (Cecile)
1929- .... **CLC 3, 6, 7, 11, 18, 36, 73, 76;
PC 5**
See also CA 9-12R; CANR 20; DLB 5, 67;
MTCW

Rich, Barbara
See Graves, Robert (von Ranke)

Rich, Robert
See Trumbo, Dalton

Richards, David Adams 1950-...... **CLC 59**
See also CA 93-96; DLB 53

Richards, I(vor) A(rmstrong)
1893-1979 .... **CLC 14, 24**
See also CA 41-44R; 89-92; CANR 34;
DLB 27

Richardson, Anne
See Roiphe, Anne Richardson

Richardson, Dorothy Miller
1873-1957 .... **TCLC 3**
See also CA 104; DLB 36

Richardson, Ethel Florence (Lindesay)
1870-1946
See Richardson, Henry Handel
See also CA 105

Richardson, Henry Handel. .... **TCLC 4**
See also Richardson, Ethel Florence
(Lindesay)

Richardson, Samuel 1689-1761 .... **LC 1**
See also CDBLB 1660-1789; DA; DLB 39;
WLC

Richler, Mordecai
1931- .... **CLC 3, 5, 9, 13, 18, 46, 70**
See also AITN 1; CA 65-68; CANR 31;
CLR 17; DLB 53; MAICYA; MTCW;
SATA 27, 44

Richter, Conrad (Michael)
1890-1968 .... **CLC 30**
See also CA 5-8R; 25-28R; CANR 23;
DLB 9; MTCW; SATA 3

Riddell, J. H. 1832-1906 .... **TCLC 40**

Riding, Laura. .... **CLC 3, 7**
See also Jackson, Laura (Riding)

Riefenstahl, Berta Helene Amalia 1902-
See Riefenstahl, Leni
See also CA 108

Riefenstahl, Leni. .... **CLC 16**
See also Riefenstahl, Berta Helene Amalia

Riffe, Ernest
See Bergman, (Ernst) Ingmar

Riley, James Whitcomb
1849-1916 .... **TCLC 51**
See also CA 118; 137; MAICYA; SATA 17

Riley, Tex
See Creasey, John

Rilke, Rainer Maria
1875-1926 .... **TCLC 1, 6, 19; PC 2**
See also CA 104; 132; DLB 81; MTCW

Rimbaud, (Jean Nicolas) Arthur
1854-1891 .... **NCLC 4, 35; PC 3**
See also DA; WLC

Rinehart, Mary Roberts
1876-1958 .... **TCLC 52**
See also CA 108

Ringmaster, The
See Mencken, H(enry) L(ouis)

Ringwood, Gwen(dolyn Margaret) Pharis
1910-1984 .... **CLC 48**
See also CA 112; DLB 88

Rio, Michel 19(?)- .... **CLC 43**

Ritsos, Giannes
See Ritsos, Yannis

Ritsos, Yannis 1909-1990 ..... **CLC 6, 13, 31**
See also CA 77-80; 133; CANR 39; MTCW

Ritter, Erika 1948(?)- .... **CLC 52**

Rivera, Jose Eustasio 1889-1928 ... **TCLC 35**
See also HW

Rivers, Conrad Kent 1933-1968 ...... **CLC 1**
See also BW; CA 85-88; DLB 41

Rivers, Elfrida
See Bradley, Marion Zimmer

Riverside, John
See Heinlein, Robert A(nson)

Rizal, Jose 1861-1896 .... **NCLC 27**

Roa Bastos, Augusto (Antonio)
1917- .... **CLC 45**
See also CA 131; DLB 113; HW

Robbe-Grillet, Alain
1922- ...... **CLC 1, 2, 4, 6, 8, 10, 14, 43**
See also CA 9-12R; CANR 33; DLB 83;
MTCW

Robbins, Harold 1916- .... **CLC 5**
See also CA 73-76; CANR 26; MTCW

Robbins, Thomas Eugene 1936-
See Robbins, Tom
See also CA 81-84; CANR 29; MTCW

Robbins, Tom .... **CLC 9, 32, 64**
See also Robbins, Thomas Eugene
See also BEST 90:3; DLBY 80

Robbins, Trina 1938- .... **CLC 21**
See also CA 128

Roberts, Charles G(eorge) D(ouglas)
1860-1943 .... **TCLC 8**
See also CA 105; DLB 92; SATA 29

Roberts, Kate 1891-1985 .... **CLC 15**
See also CA 107; 116

Roberts, Keith (John Kingston)
1935- .... **CLC 14**
See also CA 25-28R

Roberts, Kenneth (Lewis)
1885-1957 .... **TCLC 23**
See also CA 109; DLB 9

Roberts, Michele (B.) 1949- .... **CLC 48**
See also CA 115

Robertson, Ellis
See Ellison, Harlan; Silverberg, Robert

Robertson, Thomas William
1829-1871 .... **NCLC 35**

Robinson, Edwin Arlington
1869-1935 .... **TCLC 5; PC 1**
See also CA 104; 133; CDALB 1865-1917;
DA; DLB 54; MTCW

Robinson, Henry Crabb
1775-1867 .... **NCLC 15**
See also DLB 107

Robinson, Jill 1936- .... **CLC 10**
See also CA 102

Robinson, Kim Stanley 1952- ...... **CLC 34**
See also CA 126

Robinson, Lloyd
See Silverberg, Robert

Robinson, Marilynne 1944- .... **CLC 25**
See also CA 116

Robinson, Smokey .... **CLC 21**
See also Robinson, William, Jr.

Robinson, William, Jr. 1940-
See Robinson, Smokey
See also CA 116

Robison, Mary 1949- .... **CLC 42**
See also CA 113; 116; DLB 130

Rod, Edouard 1857-1910 .... **TCLC 52**

Roddenberry, Eugene Wesley 1921-1991
See Roddenberry, Gene
See also CA 110; 135; CANR 37; SATA 45

Roddenberry, Gene .... **CLC 17**
See also Roddenberry, Eugene Wesley
See also AAYA 5; SATA-Obit 69

Rodgers, Mary 1931- .... **CLC 12**
See also CA 49-52; CANR 8; CLR 20;
JRDA; MAICYA; SATA 8

Rodgers, W(illiam) R(obert)
1909-1969 .... **CLC 7**
See also CA 85-88; DLB 20

Rodman, Eric
See Silverberg, Robert

Rodman, Howard 1920(?)-1985 ..... **CLC 65**
See also CA 118

Rodman, Maia
See Wojciechowska, Maia (Teresa)

Rodriguez, Claudio 1934- .... **CLC 10**

Roelvaag, O(le) E(dvart)
1876-1931 .... **TCLC 17**
See also CA 117; DLB 9

Roethke, Theodore (Huebner)
1908-1963 ...... **CLC 1, 3, 8, 11, 19, 46**
See also CA 81-84; CABS 2;
CDALB 1941-1968; DLB 5; MTCW

Rogers, Thomas Hunton 1927- ..... **CLC 57**
See also CA 89-92

Rogers, Will(iam Penn Adair)
1879-1935 .... **TCLC 8**
See also CA 105; DLB 11

Rogin, Gilbert 1929- .... **CLC 18**
See also CA 65-68; CANR 15

Rohan, Koda .... **TCLC 22**
See also Koda Shigeyuki

Rohmer, Eric .... **CLC 16**
See also Scherer, Jean-Marie Maurice

Rohmer, Sax .... **TCLC 28**
See also Ward, Arthur Henry Sarsfield
See also DLB 70

Roiphe, Anne Richardson 1935- ... **CLC 3, 9**
See also CA 89-92; DLBY 80

Rojas, Fernando de 1465-1541 ...... **LC 23**

**Rolfe, Frederick (William Serafino Austin
Lewis Mary)** 1860-1913 ...... **TCLC 12**
See also CA 107; DLB 34

Rolland, Romain 1866-1944 .... **TCLC 23**
See also CA 118; DLB 65

Rolvaag, O(le) E(dvart)
See Roelvaag, O(le) E(dvart)

Romain Arnaud, Saint
See Aragon, Louis

Romains, Jules 1885-1972 .... **CLC 7**
See also CA 85-88; CANR 34; DLB 65;
MTCW

Romero, Jose Ruben 1890-1952 ... **TCLC 14**
See also CA 114; 131; HW

Ronsard, Pierre de 1524-1585 .... **LC 6**

Rooke, Leon 1934- .... **CLC 25, 34**
See also CA 25-28R; CANR 23

Roper, William 1498-1578 .... **LC 10**

Roquelaure, A. N.
See Rice, Anne

Rosa, Joao Guimaraes 1908-1967 ... **CLC 23**
See also CA 89-92; DLB 113

Rosen, Richard (Dean) 1949- .... **CLC 39**
See also CA 77-80

Rosenberg, Isaac 1890-1918 .... **TCLC 12**
See also CA 107; DLB 20

Rosenblatt, Joe .... **CLC 15**
See also Rosenblatt, Joseph

Rosenblatt, Joseph 1933-
See Rosenblatt, Joe
See also CA 89-92

Rosenfeld, Samuel 1896-1963
See Tzara, Tristan
See also CA 89-92

Rosenthal, M(acha) L(ouis) 1917- ... **CLC 28**
See also CA 1-4R; CAAS 6; CANR 4;
DLB 5; SATA 59

Ross, Barnaby
See Dannay, Frederic

Ross, Bernard L.
See Follett, Ken(neth Martin)

Ross, J. H.
See Lawrence, T(homas) E(dward)

Ross, Martin
See Martin, Violet Florence

Ross, (James) Sinclair 1908- .... **CLC 13**
See also CA 73-76; DLB 88

Rossetti, Christina (Georgina)
1830-1894 .... **NCLC 2; PC 7**
See also DA; DLB 35; MAICYA;
SATA 20; WLC

Rossetti, Dante Gabriel
1828-1882 .... **NCLC 4**
See also CDBLB 1832-1890; DA; DLB 35;
WLC

Rossner, Judith (Perelman)
1935- .... **CLC 6, 9, 29**
See also AITN 2; BEST 90:3; CA 17-20R;
CANR 18; DLB 6; MTCW

Rostand, Edmond (Eugene Alexis)
1868-1918 .... **TCLC 6, 37**
See also CA 104; 126; DA; MTCW

Roth, Henry 1906- . . . . CLC **2, 6, 11**
See also CA 11-12; CANR 38; CAP 1;
DLB 28; MTCW

Roth, Joseph 1894-1939 . . . . TCLC **33**
See also DLB 85

Roth, Philip (Milton)
1933- . . . . . . CLC **1, 2, 3, 4, 6, 9, 15, 22,**
31, 47, 66
See also BEST 90:3; CA 1-4R; CANR 1, 22,
36; CDALB 1968-1988; DA; DLB 2, 28;
DLBY 82; MTCW; WLC

Rothenberg, Jerome 1931- . . . . CLC **6, 57**
See also CA 45-48; CANR 1; DLB 5

Roumain, Jacques (Jean Baptiste)
1907-1944 . . . . TCLC **19**
See also BLC 3; BW; CA 117; 125

Rourke, Constance (Mayfield)
1885-1941 . . . . TCLC **12**
See also CA 107; YABC 1

Rousseau, Jean-Baptiste 1671-1741 . . . LC **9**

Rousseau, Jean-Jacques 1712-1778 . . . LC **14**
See also DA; WLC

Roussel, Raymond 1877-1933 . . . . . TCLC **20**
See also CA 117

Rovit, Earl (Herbert) 1927- . . . . CLC **7**
See also CA 5-8R; CANR 12

Rowe, Nicholas 1674-1718 . . . . LC **8**
See also DLB 84

Rowley, Ames Dorrance
See Lovecraft, H(oward) P(hillips)

Rowson, Susanna Haswell
1762(?)-1824 . . . . NCLC **5**
See also DLB 37

Roy, Gabrielle 1909-1983 . . . . CLC **10, 14**
See also CA 53-56; 110; CANR 5; DLB 68;
MTCW

Rozewicz, Tadeusz 1921- . . . . CLC **9, 23**
See also CA 108; CANR 36; MTCW

Ruark, Gibbons 1941- . . . . CLC **3**
See also CA 33-36R; CANR 14, 31;
DLB 120

Rubens, Bernice (Ruth) 1923- . . . CLC **19, 31**
See also CA 25-28R; CANR 33; DLB 14;
MTCW

Rudkin, (James) David 1936- . . . . . . CLC **14**
See also CA 89-92; DLB 13

Rudnik, Raphael 1933- . . . . CLC **7**
See also CA 29-32R

Ruffian, M.
See Hasek, Jaroslav (Matej Frantisek)

Ruiz, Jose Martinez . . . . CLC **11**
See also Martinez Ruiz, Jose

Rukeyser, Muriel
1913-1980 . . . . CLC **6, 10, 15, 27**
See also CA 5-8R; 93-96; CANR 26;
DLB 48; MTCW; SATA 22

Rule, Jane (Vance) 1931- . . . . CLC **27**
See also CA 25-28R; CAAS 18; CANR 12;
DLB 60

Rulfo, Juan 1918-1986 . . . . CLC **8**
See also CA 85-88; 118; CANR 26;
DLB 113; HW; MTCW

Runeberg, Johan 1804-1877 . . . . . . NCLC **41**

Runyon, (Alfred) Damon
1884(?)-1946 . . . . TCLC **10**
See also CA 107; DLB 11, 86

Rush, Norman 1933- . . . . CLC **44**
See also CA 121; 126

Rushdie, (Ahmed) Salman
1947- . . . . CLC **23, 31, 55**
See also BEST 89:3; CA 108; 111;
CANR 33; MTCW

Rushforth, Peter (Scott) 1945- . . . . . CLC **19**
See also CA 101

Ruskin, John 1819-1900 . . . . TCLC **20**
See also CA 114; 129; CDBLB 1832-1890;
DLB 55; SATA 24

Russ, Joanna 1937- . . . . CLC **15**
See also CA 25-28R; CANR 11, 31; DLB 8;
MTCW

Russell, George William 1867-1935
See A. E.
See also CA 104; CDBLB 1890-1914

Russell, (Henry) Ken(neth Alfred)
1927- . . . . CLC **16**
See also CA 105

Russell, Willy 1947- . . . . CLC **60**

Rutherford, Mark . . . . TCLC **25**
See also White, William Hale
See also DLB 18

Ruyslinck, Ward
See Belser, Reimond Karel Maria de

Ryan, Cornelius (John) 1920-1974 . . . CLC **7**
See also CA 69-72; 53-56; CANR 38

Ryan, Michael 1946- . . . . CLC **65**
See also CA 49-52; DLBY 82

Rybakov, Anatoli (Naumovich)
1911- . . . . CLC **23, 53**
See also CA 126; 135

Ryder, Jonathan
See Ludlum, Robert

Ryga, George 1932-1987 . . . . CLC **14**
See also CA 101; 124; DLB 60

S. S.
See Sassoon, Siegfried (Lorraine)

Saba, Umberto 1883-1957 . . . . TCLC **33**
See also DLB 114

Sabatini, Rafael 1875-1950 . . . . TCLC **47**

Sabato, Ernesto (R.) 1911- . . . . . . CLC **10, 23**
See also CA 97-100; CANR 32; HW;
MTCW

Sacastru, Martin
See Bioy Casares, Adolfo

Sacher-Masoch, Leopold von
1836(?)-1895 . . . . NCLC **31**

Sachs, Marilyn (Stickle) 1927- . . . . . CLC **35**
See also AAYA 2; CA 17-20R; CANR 13;
CLR 2; JRDA; MAICYA; SAAS 2;
SATA 3, 68

Sachs, Nelly 1891-1970 . . . . CLC **14**
See also CA 17-18; 25-28R; CAP 2

Sackler, Howard (Oliver)
1929-1982 . . . . CLC **14**
See also CA 61-64; 108; CANR 30; DLB 7

Sacks, Oliver (Wolf) 1933- . . . . CLC **67**
See also CA 53-56; CANR 28; MTCW

Sade, Donatien Alphonse Francois Comte
1740-1814 . . . . NCLC **3**

Sadoff, Ira 1945- . . . . CLC **9**
See also CA 53-56; CANR 5, 21; DLB 120

Saetone
See Camus, Albert

Safire, William 1929- . . . . CLC **10**
See also CA 17-20R; CANR 31

Sagan, Carl (Edward) 1934- . . . . CLC **30**
See also AAYA 2; CA 25-28R; CANR 11,
36; MTCW; SATA 58

Sagan, Francoise . . . . CLC **3, 6, 9, 17, 36**
See also Quoirez, Francoise
See also DLB 83

Sahgal, Nayantara (Pandit) 1927- . . . CLC **41**
See also CA 9-12R; CANR 11

Saint, H(arry) F. 1941- . . . . CLC **50**
See also CA 127

St. Aubin de Teran, Lisa 1953-
See Teran, Lisa St. Aubin de
See also CA 118; 126

Sainte-Beuve, Charles Augustin
1804-1869 . . . . NCLC **5**

Saint-Exupery, Antoine (Jean Baptiste Marie
Roger) de 1900-1944 . . . . TCLC **2**
See also CA 108; 132; CLR 10; DLB 72;
MAICYA; MTCW; SATA 20; WLC

St. John, David
See Hunt, E(verette) Howard, Jr.

Saint-John Perse
See Leger, (Marie-Rene) Alexis Saint-Leger

Saintsbury, George (Edward Bateman)
1845-1933 . . . . TCLC **31**
See also DLB 57

Sait Faik . . . . TCLC **23**
See also Abasiyanik, Sait Faik

Saki . . . . TCLC **3; SSC 12**
See also Munro, H(ector) H(ugh)

Salama, Hannu 1936- . . . . CLC **18**

Salamanca, J(ack) R(ichard)
1922- . . . . CLC **4, 15**
See also CA 25-28R

Sale, J. Kirkpatrick
See Sale, Kirkpatrick

Sale, Kirkpatrick 1937- . . . . CLC **68**
See also CA 13-16R; CANR 10

Salinas (y Serrano), Pedro
1891(?)-1951 . . . . TCLC **17**
See also CA 117

Salinger, J(erome) D(avid)
1919- . . . . CLC **1, 3, 8, 12, 55, 56; SSC 2**
See also AAYA 2; CA 5-8R; CANR 39;
CDALB 1941-1968; CLR 18; DA;
DLB 2, 102; MAICYA; MTCW;
SATA 67; WLC

Salisbury, John
See Caute, David

Salter, James 1925- . . . . CLC **7, 52, 59**
See also CA 73-76; DLB 130

Saltus, Edgar (Everton)
1855-1921 . . . . TCLC **8**
See also CA 105

Saltykov, Mikhail Evgrafovich
1826-1889 . . . . NCLC **16**

Schwartz, Muriel A.
See Eliot, T(homas) S(tearns)

Schwarz-Bart, Andre 1928- .... CLC 2, 4
See also CA 89-92

Schwarz-Bart, Simone 1938- .... CLC 7
See also CA 97-100

Schwob, (Mayer Andre) Marcel
1867-1905 .... TCLC 20
See also CA 117; DLB 123

Sciascia, Leonardo
1921-1989 .... CLC 8, 9, 41
See also CA 85-88; 130; CANR 35; MTCW

Scoppettone, Sandra 1936- .... CLC 26
See also CA 5-8R; CANR 41; SATA 9

Scorsese, Martin 1942- .... CLC 20
See also CA 110; 114

Scotland, Jay
See Jakes, John (William)

Scott, Duncan Campbell
1862-1947 .... TCLC 6
See also CA 104; DLB 92

Scott, Evelyn 1893-1963 .... CLC 43
See also CA 104; 112; DLB 9, 48

Scott, F(rancis) R(eginald)
1899-1985 .... CLC 22
See also Scott, Frank
See also CA 101; 114; DLB 88

Scott, Frank
See Scott, F(rancis) R(eginald)
See also CA 141

Scott, Joanna 1960- .... CLC 50
See also CA 126

Scott, Paul (Mark) 1920-1978 .... CLC 9, 60
See also CA 81-84; 77-80; CANR 33;
DLB 14; MTCW

Scott, Walter 1771-1832 .... NCLC 15
See also CDBLB 1789-1832; DA; DLB 93,
107, 116; WLC; YABC 2

Scribe, (Augustin) Eugene
1791-1861 .... NCLC 16

Scrum, R.
See Crumb, R(obert)

Scudery, Madeleine de 1607-1701 ..... LC 2

Scum
See Crumb, R(obert)

Scumbag, Little Bobby
See Crumb, R(obert)

Seabrook, John
See Hubbard, L(afayette) Ron(ald)

Sealy, I. Allan 1951- .... CLC 55

Search, Alexander
See Pessoa, Fernando (Antonio Nogueira)

Sebastian, Lee
See Silverberg, Robert

Sebastian Owl
See Thompson, Hunter S(tockton)

Sebestyen, Ouida 1924- .... CLC 30
See also AAYA 8; CA 107; CANR 40;
CLR 17; JRDA; MAICYA; SAAS 10;
SATA 39

Secundus, H. Scriblerus
See Fielding, Henry

Sedges, John
See Buck, Pearl S(ydenstricker)

Sedgwick, Catharine Maria
1789-1867 .... NCLC 19
See also DLB 1, 74

Seelye, John 1931- .... CLC 7

Seferiades, Giorgos Stylianou 1900-1971
See Seferis, George
See also CA 5-8R; 33-36R; CANR 5, 36;
MTCW

Seferis, George .... CLC 5, 11
See also Seferiades, Giorgos Stylianou

Segal, Erich (Wolf) 1937- .... CLC 3, 10
See also BEST 89:1; CA 25-28R; CANR 20,
36; DLBY 86; MTCW

Seger, Bob 1945- .... CLC 35

Seghers, Anna .... CLC 7
See also Radvanyi, Netty
See also DLB 69

Seidel, Frederick (Lewis) 1936- ..... CLC 18
See also CA 13-16R; CANR 8; DLBY 84

Seifert, Jaroslav 1901-1986 ..... CLC 34, 44
See also CA 127; MTCW

Sei Shonagon c. 966-1017(?) ...... CMLC 6

Selby, Hubert, Jr. 1928- ..... CLC 1, 2, 4, 8
See also CA 13-16R; CANR 33; DLB 2

Selzer, Richard 1928- .... CLC 74
See also CA 65-68; CANR 14

Sembene, Ousmane
See Ousmane, Sembene

Senancour, Etienne Pivert de
1770-1846 .... NCLC 16
See also DLB 119

Sender, Ramon (Jose) 1902-1982 .... CLC 8
See also CA 5-8R; 105; CANR 8; HW;
MTCW

Seneca, Lucius Annaeus
4B.C.-65 .... CMLC 6

Senghor, Leopold Sedar 1906- ...... CLC 54
See also BLC 3; BW; CA 116; 125; MTCW

Serling, (Edward) Rod(man)
1924-1975 .... CLC 30
See also AITN 1; CA 65-68; 57-60; DLB 26

Serna, Ramon Gomez de la
See Gomez de la Serna, Ramon

Serpieres
See Guillevic, (Eugene)

Service, Robert
See Service, Robert W(illiam)
See also DLB 92

Service, Robert W(illiam)
1874(?)-1958 .... TCLC 15
See also Service, Robert
See also CA 115; 140; DA; SATA 20; WLC

Seth, Vikram 1952- .... CLC 43
See also CA 121; 127; DLB 120

Seton, Cynthia Propper
1926-1982 .... CLC 27
See also CA 5-8R; 108; CANR 7

Seton, Ernest (Evan) Thompson
1860-1946 .... TCLC 31
See also CA 109; DLB 92; JRDA; SATA 18

Seton-Thompson, Ernest
See Seton, Ernest (Evan) Thompson

Settle, Mary Lee 1918- .... CLC 19, 61
See also CA 89-92; CAAS 1; DLB 6

Seuphor, Michel
See Arp, Jean

Sevigne, Marie (de Rabutin-Chantal) Marquise
de 1626-1696 .... LC 11

Sexton, Anne (Harvey)
1928-1974 .... CLC 2, 4, 6, 8, 10, 15, 53;
PC 2
See also CA 1-4R; 53-56; CABS 2;
CANR 3, 36; CDALB 1941-1968; DA;
DLB 5; MTCW; SATA 10; WLC

Shaara, Michael (Joseph Jr.)
1929-1988 .... CLC 15
See also AITN 1; CA 102; DLBY 83

Shackleton, C. C.
See Aldiss, Brian W(ilson)

Shacochis, Bob .... CLC 39
See also Shacochis, Robert G.

Shacochis, Robert G. 1951-
See Shacochis, Bob
See also CA 119; 124

Shaffer, Anthony (Joshua) 1926- .... CLC 19
See also CA 110; 116; DLB 13

Shaffer, Peter (Levin)
1926- .... CLC 5, 14, 18, 37, 60
See also CA 25-28R; CANR 25;
CDBLB 1960 to Present; DLB 13;
MTCW

Shakey, Bernard
See Young, Neil

Shalamov, Varlam (Tikhonovich)
1907(?)-1982 .... CLC 18
See also CA 129; 105

Shamlu, Ahmad 1925- .... CLC 10

Shammas, Anton 1951- .... CLC 55

Shange, Ntozake
1948- .... CLC 8, 25, 38, 74; DC 3
See also AAYA 9; BLC 3; BW; CA 85-88;
CABS 3; CANR 27; DLB 38; MTCW

Shanley, John Patrick 1950- .... CLC 75
See also CA 128; 133

Shapcott, Thomas William 1935- ... CLC 38
See also CA 69-72

Shapiro, Jane .... CLC 76

Shapiro, Karl (Jay) 1913- .. CLC 4, 8, 15, 53
See also CA 1-4R; CAAS 6; CANR 1, 36;
DLB 48; MTCW

Sharp, William 1855-1905 .... TCLC 39

Sharpe, Thomas Ridley 1928-
See Sharpe, Tom
See also CA 114; 122

Sharpe, Tom .... CLC 36
See also Sharpe, Thomas Ridley
See also DLB 14

Shaw, Bernard .... TCLC 45
See also Shaw, George Bernard

Shaw, G. Bernard
See Shaw, George Bernard

Shaw, George Bernard
1856-1950 .... TCLC 3, 9, 21
See also Shaw, Bernard
See also CA 104; 128; CDBLB 1914-1945;
DA; DLB 10, 57; MTCW; WLC

Shaw, Henry Wheeler
    1818-1885 . . . . NCLC 15
    See also DLB 11

Shaw, Irwin 1913-1984. . . . . . CLC 7, 23, 34
    See also AITN 1; CA 13-16R; 112;
    CANR 21; CDALB 1941-1968; DLB 6,
    102; DLBY 84; MTCW

Shaw, Robert 1927-1978 . . . . CLC 5
    See also AITN 1; CA 1-4R; 81-84;
    CANR 4; DLB 13, 14

Shaw, T. E.
    See Lawrence, T(homas) E(dward)

Shawn, Wallace 1943- . . . . CLC 41
    See also CA 112

Sheed, Wilfrid (John Joseph)
    1930- . . . . CLC 2, 4, 10, 53
    See also CA 65-68; CANR 30; DLB 6;
    MTCW

Sheldon, Alice Hastings Bradley
    1915(?)-1987
    See Tiptree, James, Jr.
    See also CA 108; 122; CANR 34; MTCW

Sheldon, John
    See Bloch, Robert (Albert)

Shelley, Mary Wollstonecraft (Godwin)
    1797-1851 . . . . NCLC 14
    See also CDBLB 1789-1832; DA; DLB 110,
    116; SATA 29; WLC

Shelley, Percy Bysshe
    1792-1822 . . . . NCLC 18
    See also CDBLB 1789-1832; DA; DLB 96,
    110; WLC

Shepard, Jim 1956- . . . . CLC 36
    See also CA 137

Shepard, Lucius 1947- . . . . CLC 34
    See also CA 128; 141

Shepard, Sam
    1943- . . . . CLC 4, 6, 17, 34, 41, 44
    See also AAYA 1; CA 69-72; CABS 3;
    CANR 22; DLB 7; MTCW

Shepherd, Michael
    See Ludlum, Robert

Sherburne, Zoa (Morin) 1912- . . . . . . CLC 30
    See also CA 1-4R; CANR 3, 37; MAICYA;
    SATA 3

Sheridan, Frances 1724-1766 . . . . LC 7
    See also DLB 39, 84

Sheridan, Richard Brinsley
    1751-1816 . . . . NCLC 5; DC 1
    See also CDBLB 1660-1789; DA; DLB 89;
    WLC

Sherman, Jonathan Marc . . . . CLC 55

Sherman, Martin 1941(?)- . . . . CLC 19
    See also CA 116; 123

Sherwin, Judith Johnson 1936- . . . CLC 7, 15
    See also CA 25-28R; CANR 34

Sherwood, Robert E(mmet)
    1896-1955 . . . . TCLC 3
    See also CA 104; DLB 7, 26

Shiel, M(atthew) P(hipps)
    1865-1947 . . . . TCLC 8
    See also CA 106

Shiga, Naoya 1883-1971. . . . . CLC 33
    See also CA 101; 33-36R

Shimazaki Haruki 1872-1943
    See Shimazaki Toson
    See also CA 105; 134

Shimazaki Toson . . . . TCLC 5
    See also Shimazaki Haruki

Sholokhov, Mikhail (Aleksandrovich)
    1905-1984 . . . . CLC 7, 15
    See also CA 101; 112; MTCW; SATA 36

Shone, Patric
    See Hanley, James

Shreve, Susan Richards 1939- . . . . . . CLC 23
    See also CA 49-52; CAAS 5; CANR 5, 38;
    MAICYA; SATA 41, 46

Shue, Larry 1946-1985. . . . . CLC 52
    See also CA 117

Shu-Jen, Chou 1881-1936
    See Hsun, Lu
    See also CA 104

Shulman, Alix Kates 1932- . . . . . . CLC 2, 10
    See also CA 29-32R; SATA 7

Shuster, Joe 1914- . . . . CLC 21

Shute, Nevil . . . . CLC 30
    See also Norway, Nevil Shute

Shuttle, Penelope (Diane) 1947- . . . . . CLC 7
    See also CA 93-96; CANR 39; DLB 14, 40

Sidney, Mary 1561-1621 . . . . LC 19

Sidney, Sir Philip 1554-1586. . . . . LC 19
    See also CDBLB Before 1660; DA

Siegel, Jerome 1914- . . . . CLC 21
    See also CA 116

Siegel, Jerry
    See Siegel, Jerome

Sienkiewicz, Henryk (Adam Alexander Pius)
    1846-1916 . . . . TCLC 3
    See also CA 104; 134

Sierra, Gregorio Martinez
    See Martinez Sierra, Gregorio

Sierra, Maria (de la O'LeJarraga) Martinez
    See Martinez Sierra, Maria (de la
    O'LeJarraga)

Sigal, Clancy 1926- . . . . CLC 7
    See also CA 1-4R

Sigourney, Lydia Howard (Huntley)
    1791-1865 . . . . NCLC 21
    See also DLB 1, 42, 73

Siguenza y Gongora, Carlos de
    1645-1700 . . . . LC 8

Sigurjonsson, Johann 1880-1919 . . . TCLC 27

Sikelianos, Angelos 1884-1951 . . . . TCLC 39

Silkin, Jon 1930- . . . . CLC 2, 6, 43
    See also CA 5-8R; CAAS 5; DLB 27

Silko, Leslie Marmon 1948- . . . . CLC 23, 74
    See also CA 115; 122; DA

Sillanpaa, Frans Eemil 1888-1964. . . CLC 19
    See also CA 129; 93-96; MTCW

Sillitoe, Alan
    1928- . . . . CLC 1, 3, 6, 10, 19, 57
    See also AITN 1; CA 9-12R; CAAS 2;
    CANR 8, 26; CDBLB 1960 to Present;
    DLB 14; MTCW; SATA 61

Silone, Ignazio 1900-1978 . . . . CLC 4
    See also CA 25-28; 81-84; CANR 34;
    CAP 2; MTCW

Silver, Joan Micklin 1935- . . . . CLC 20
    See also CA 114; 121

Silver, Nicholas
    See Faust, Frederick (Schiller)

Silverberg, Robert 1935- . . . . CLC 7
    See also CA 1-4R; CAAS 3; CANR 1, 20,
    36; DLB 8; MAICYA; MTCW; SATA 13

Silverstein, Alvin 1933- . . . . CLC 17
    See also CA 49-52; CANR 2; CLR 25;
    JRDA; MAICYA; SATA 8, 69

Silverstein, Virginia B(arbara Opshelor)
    1937- . . . . CLC 17
    See also CA 49-52; CANR 2; CLR 25;
    JRDA; MAICYA; SATA 8, 69

Sim, Georges
    See Simenon, Georges (Jacques Christian)

Simak, Clifford D(onald)
    1904-1988 . . . . CLC 1, 55
    See also CA 1-4R; 125; CANR 1, 35;
    DLB 8; MTCW; SATA 56

Simenon, Georges (Jacques Christian)
    1903-1989 . . . . CLC 1, 2, 3, 8, 18, 47
    See also CA 85-88; 129; CANR 35;
    DLB 72; DLBY 89; MTCW

Simic, Charles 1938-. . . CLC 6, 9, 22, 49, 68
    See also CA 29-32R; CAAS 4; CANR 12,
    33; DLB 105

Simmons, Charles (Paul) 1924- . . . . . CLC 57
    See also CA 89-92

Simmons, Dan 1948-. . . . . CLC 44
    See also CA 138

Simmons, James (Stewart Alexander)
    1933- . . . . CLC 43
    See also CA 105; DLB 40

Simms, William Gilmore
    1806-1870 . . . . NCLC 3
    See also DLB 3, 30, 59, 73

Simon, Carly 1945-. . . . . CLC 26
    See also CA 105

Simon, Claude 1913-. . . . . . . CLC 4, 9, 15, 39
    See also CA 89-92; CANR 33; DLB 83;
    MTCW

Simon, (Marvin) Neil
    1927- . . . . CLC 6, 11, 31, 39, 70
    See also AITN 1; CA 21-24R; CANR 26;
    DLB 7; MTCW

Simon, Paul 1942(?)- . . . . CLC 17
    See also CA 116

Simonon, Paul 1956(?)- . . . . CLC 30
    See also Clash, The

Simpson, Harriette
    See Arnow, Harriette (Louisa) Simpson

Simpson, Louis (Aston Marantz)
    1923- . . . . CLC 4, 7, 9, 32
    See also CA 1-4R; CAAS 4; CANR 1;
    DLB 5; MTCW

Simpson, Mona (Elizabeth) 1957-. . . CLC 44
    See also CA 122; 135

Simpson, N(orman) F(rederick)
    1919- . . . . CLC 29
    See also CA 13-16R; DLB 13

Sinclair, Andrew (Annandale)
    1935- . . . . CLC 2, 14
    See also CA 9-12R; CAAS 5; CANR 14, 38;
    DLB 14; MTCW

Somerville & Ross
See Martin, Violet Florence; Somerville,
Edith

Sommer, Scott 1951- . . . . **CLC 25**
See also CA 106

Sondheim, Stephen (Joshua)
1930- . . . . **CLC 30, 39**
See also CA 103

Sontag, Susan 1933- . . . **CLC 1, 2, 10, 13, 31**
See also CA 17-20R; CANR 25; DLB 2, 67;
MTCW

Sophocles
496(?)B.C.-406(?)B.C. . . . . **CMLC 2; DC 1**
See also DA

Sorel, Julia
See Drexler, Rosalyn

Sorrentino, Gilbert
1929- . . . . **CLC 3, 7, 14, 22, 40**
See also CA 77-80; CANR 14, 33; DLB 5;
DLBY 80

Soto, Gary 1952- . . . . **CLC 32**
See also AAYA 10; CA 119; 125; DLB 82;
HW; JRDA

Soupault, Philippe 1897-1990 . . . . . . **CLC 68**
See also CA 116; 131

Souster, (Holmes) Raymond
1921- . . . . **CLC 5, 14**
See also CA 13-16R; CAAS 14; CANR 13,
29; DLB 88; SATA 63

Southern, Terry 1926- . . . . **CLC 7**
See also CA 1-4R; CANR 1; DLB 2

Southey, Robert 1774-1843 . . . . **NCLC 8**
See also DLB 93, 107; SATA 54

Southworth, Emma Dorothy Eliza Nevitte
1819-1899 . . . . **NCLC 26**

Souza, Ernest
See Scott, Evelyn

Soyinka, Wole
1934- . . . . **CLC 3, 5, 14, 36, 44; DC 2**
See also BLC 3; BW; CA 13-16R;
CANR 27, 39; DA; DLB 125; MTCW;
WLC

Spackman, W(illiam) M(ode)
1905-1990 . . . . **CLC 46**
See also CA 81-84; 132

Spacks, Barry 1931- . . . . **CLC 14**
See also CA 29-32R; CANR 33; DLB 105

Spanidou, Irini 1946- . . . . **CLC 44**

Spark, Muriel (Sarah)
1918- . . . . **CLC 2, 3, 5, 8, 13, 18, 40;
SSC 10**
See also CA 5-8R; CANR 12, 36;
CDBLB 1945-1960; DLB 15; MTCW

Spaulding, Douglas
See Bradbury, Ray (Douglas)

Spaulding, Leonard
See Bradbury, Ray (Douglas)

Spence, J. A. D.
See Eliot, T(homas) S(tearns)

Spencer, Elizabeth 1921- . . . . **CLC 22**
See also CA 13-16R; CANR 32; DLB 6;
MTCW; SATA 14

Spencer, Leonard G.
See Silverberg, Robert

Spencer, Scott 1945- . . . . **CLC 30**
See also CA 113; DLBY 86

Spender, Stephen (Harold)
1909- . . . . **CLC 1, 2, 5, 10, 41**
See also CA 9-12R; CANR 31;
CDBLB 1945-1960; DLB 20; MTCW

Spengler, Oswald (Arnold Gottfried)
1880-1936 . . . . **TCLC 25**
See also CA 118

Spenser, Edmund 1552(?)-1599 . . . . . . **LC 5**
See also CDBLB Before 1660; DA; WLC

Spicer, Jack 1925-1965 . . . . . . **CLC 8, 18, 72**
See also CA 85-88; DLB 5, 16

Spiegelman, Art 1948- . . . . **CLC 76**
See also AAYA 10; CA 125; CANR 41

Spielberg, Peter 1929- . . . . **CLC 6**
See also CA 5-8R; CANR 4; DLBY 81

Spielberg, Steven 1947- . . . . **CLC 20**
See also AAYA 8; CA 77-80; CANR 32;
SATA 32

Spillane, Frank Morrison 1918-
See Spillane, Mickey
See also CA 25-28R; CANR 28; MTCW;
SATA 66

Spillane, Mickey . . . . **CLC 3, 13**
See also Spillane, Frank Morrison

Spinoza, Benedictus de 1632-1677 . . . . **LC 9**

Spinrad, Norman (Richard) 1940- . . . **CLC 46**
See also CA 37-40R; CANR 20; DLB 8

Spitteler, Carl (Friedrich Georg)
1845-1924 . . . . **TCLC 12**
See also CA 109; DLB 129

Spivack, Kathleen (Romola Drucker)
1938- . . . . **CLC 6**
See also CA 49-52

Spoto, Donald 1941- . . . . **CLC 39**
See also CA 65-68; CANR 11

Springsteen, Bruce (F.) 1949- . . . . . . **CLC 17**
See also CA 111

Spurling, Hilary 1940- . . . . **CLC 34**
See also CA 104; CANR 25

Squires, (James) Radcliffe
1917-1993 . . . . **CLC 51**
See also CA 1-4R; 140; CANR 6, 21

Srivastava, Dhanpat Rai 1880(?)-1936
See Premchand
See also CA 118

Stacy, Donald
See Pohl, Frederik

Stael, Germaine de
See Stael-Holstein, Anne Louise Germaine
Necker Baronn
See also DLB 119

**Stael-Holstein, Anne Louise Germaine Necker
Baronn** 1766-1817 . . . . **NCLC 3**
See also Stael, Germaine de

Stafford, Jean 1915-1979 . . . **CLC 4, 7, 19, 68**
See also CA 1-4R; 85-88; CANR 3; DLB 2;
MTCW; SATA 22

Stafford, William (Edgar)
1914- . . . . **CLC 4, 7, 29**
See also CA 5-8R; CAAS 3; CANR 5, 22;
DLB 5

Staines, Trevor
See Brunner, John (Kilian Houston)

Stairs, Gordon
See Austin, Mary (Hunter)

Stannard, Martin . . . . **CLC 44**

Stanton, Maura 1946- . . . . **CLC 9**
See also CA 89-92; CANR 15; DLB 120

Stanton, Schuyler
See Baum, L(yman) Frank

Stapledon, (William) Olaf
1886-1950 . . . . **TCLC 22**
See also CA 111; DLB 15

Starbuck, George (Edwin) 1931- . . . . **CLC 53**
See also CA 21-24R; CANR 23

Stark, Richard
See Westlake, Donald E(dwin)

Staunton, Schuyler
See Baum, L(yman) Frank

Stead, Christina (Ellen)
1902-1983 . . . . **CLC 2, 5, 8, 32**
See also CA 13-16R; 109; CANR 33, 40;
MTCW

Stead, William Thomas
1849-1912 . . . . **TCLC 48**

Steele, Richard 1672-1729 . . . . **LC 18**
See also CDBLB 1660-1789; DLB 84, 101

Steele, Timothy (Reid) 1948- . . . . **CLC 45**
See also CA 93-96; CANR 16; DLB 120

Steffens, (Joseph) Lincoln
1866-1936 . . . . **TCLC 20**
See also CA 117

Stegner, Wallace (Earle)
1909-1993 . . . . **CLC 9, 49**
See also AITN 1; BEST 90:3; CA 1-4R;
141; CAAS 9; CANR 1, 21; DLB 9;
MTCW

Stein, Gertrude
1874-1946 . . . . **TCLC 1, 6, 28, 48**
See also CA 104; 132; CDALB 1917-1929;
DA; DLB 4, 54, 86; MTCW; WLC

Steinbeck, John (Ernst)
1902-1968 . . . . . . **CLC 1, 5, 9, 13, 21, 34,
45, 75; SSC 11**
See also CA 1-4R; 25-28R; CANR 1, 35;
CDALB 1929-1941; DA; DLB 7, 9;
DLBD 2; MTCW; SATA 9; WLC

Steinem, Gloria 1934- . . . . **CLC 63**
See also CA 53-56; CANR 28; MTCW

Steiner, George 1929- . . . . **CLC 24**
See also CA 73-76; CANR 31; DLB 67;
MTCW; SATA 62

Steiner, Rudolf 1861-1925 . . . . **TCLC 13**
See also CA 107

Stendhal 1783-1842 . . . . **NCLC 23**
See also DA; DLB 119; WLC

Stephen, Leslie 1832-1904 . . . . **TCLC 23**
See also CA 123; DLB 57

Stephen, Sir Leslie
See Stephen, Leslie

Stephen, Virginia
See Woolf, (Adeline) Virginia

Stephens, James 1882(?)-1950 . . . . . . **TCLC 4**
See also CA 104; DLB 19

Summers, Andrew James 1942-..... **CLC 26**
See also Police, The

Summers, Andy
See Summers, Andrew James

Summers, Hollis (Spurgeon, Jr.)
　　1916- .... **CLC 10**
See also CA 5-8R; CANR 3; DLB 6

Summers, (Alphonsus Joseph-Mary Augustus)
　　Montague 1880-1948........ **TCLC 16**
See also CA 118

Sumner, Gordon Matthew 1951-.... **CLC 26**
See also Police, The

Surtees, Robert Smith
　　1803-1864 .... **NCLC 14**
See also DLB 21

Susann, Jacqueline 1921-1974....... **CLC 3**
See also AITN 1; CA 65-68; 53-56; MTCW

Suskind, Patrick
See Sueskind, Patrick

Sutcliff, Rosemary 1920-1992 ...... **CLC 26**
See also AAYA 10; CA 5-8R; 139;
　　CANR 37; CLR 1; JRDA; MAICYA;
　　SATA 6, 44; SATA-Obit 73

Sutro, Alfred 1863-1933.......... **TCLC 6**
See also CA 105; DLB 10

Sutton, Henry
See Slavitt, David R(ytman)

Svevo, Italo .... **TCLC 2, 35**
See also Schmitz, Aron Hector

Swados, Elizabeth 1951- .... **CLC 12**
See also CA 97-100

Swados, Harvey 1920-1972 .... **CLC 5**
See also CA 5-8R; 37-40R; CANR 6;
　　DLB 2

Swan, Gladys 1934- .... **CLC 69**
See also CA 101; CANR 17, 39

Swarthout, Glendon (Fred)
　　1918-1992 .... **CLC 35**
See also CA 1-4R; 139; CANR 1; SATA 26

Sweet, Sarah C.
See Jewett, (Theodora) Sarah Orne

Swenson, May 1919-1989..... **CLC 4, 14, 61**
See also CA 5-8R; 130; CANR 36; DA;
　　DLB 5; MTCW; SATA 15

Swift, Augustus
See Lovecraft, H(oward) P(hillips)

Swift, Graham 1949- .... **CLC 41**
See also CA 117; 122

Swift, Jonathan 1667-1745.......... **LC 1**
See also CDBLB 1660-1789; DA; DLB 39,
　　95, 101; SATA 19; WLC

Swinburne, Algernon Charles
　　1837-1909 .... **TCLC 8, 36**
See also CA 105; 140; CDBLB 1832-1890;
　　DA; DLB 35, 57; WLC

Swinfen, Ann..................... **CLC 34**

Swinnerton, Frank Arthur
　　1884-1982 .... **CLC 31**
See also CA 108; DLB 34

Swithen, John
See King, Stephen (Edwin)

Sylvia
See Ashton-Warner, Sylvia (Constance)

Symmes, Robert Edward
See Duncan, Robert (Edward)

Symonds, John Addington
　　1840-1893 .... **NCLC 34**
See also DLB 57

Symons, Arthur 1865-1945 .... **TCLC 11**
See also CA 107; DLB 19, 57

Symons, Julian (Gustave)
　　1912- .... **CLC 2, 14, 32**
See also CA 49-52; CAAS 3; CANR 3, 33;
　　DLB 87; DLBY 92; MTCW

Synge, (Edmund) J(ohn) M(illington)
　　1871-1909 .... **TCLC 6, 37; DC 2**
See also CA 104; 141; CDBLB 1890-1914;
　　DLB 10, 19

Syruc, J.
See Milosz, Czeslaw

Szirtes, George 1948-............. **CLC 46**
See also CA 109; CANR 27

Tabori, George 1914-.............. **CLC 19**
See also CA 49-52; CANR 4

Tagore, Rabindranath 1861-1941.... **TCLC 3**
See also CA 104; 120; MTCW

Taine, Hippolyte Adolphe
　　1828-1893 .... **NCLC 15**

Talese, Gay 1932-................. **CLC 37**
See also AITN 1; CA 1-4R; CANR 9;
　　MTCW

Tallent, Elizabeth (Ann) 1954- ..... **CLC 45**
See also CA 117; DLB 130

Tally, Ted 1952-.................. **CLC 42**
See also CA 120; 124

Tamayo y Baus, Manuel
　　1829-1898 .... **NCLC 1**

Tammsaare, A(nton) H(ansen)
　　1878-1940 .... **TCLC 27**

Tan, Amy 1952- .... **CLC 59**
See also AAYA 9; BEST 89:3; CA 136;
　　SATA 75

Tandem, Felix
See Spitteler, Carl (Friedrich Georg)

Tanizaki, Jun'ichiro
　　1886-1965 .... **CLC 8, 14, 28**
See also CA 93-96; 25-28R

Tanner, William
See Amis, Kingsley (William)

Tao Lao
See Storni, Alfonsina

Tarassoff, Lev
See Troyat, Henri

Tarbell, Ida M(inerva)
　　1857-1944 .... **TCLC 40**
See also CA 122; DLB 47

Tarkington, (Newton) Booth
　　1869-1946 .... **TCLC 9**
See also CA 110; DLB 9, 102; SATA 17

Tarkovsky, Andrei (Arsenyevich)
　　1932-1986 .... **CLC 75**
See also CA 127

Tartt, Donna 1964(?)-............. **CLC 76**

Tasso, Torquato 1544-1595 .... **LC 5**

Tate, (John Orley) Allen
　　1899-1979 .... **CLC 2, 4, 6, 9, 11, 14, 24**
See also CA 5-8R; 85-88; CANR 32;
　　DLB 4, 45, 63; MTCW

Tate, Ellalice
See Hibbert, Eleanor Alice Burford

Tate, James (Vincent) 1943- ... **CLC 2, 6, 25**
See also CA 21-24R; CANR 29; DLB 5

Tavel, Ronald 1940-............... **CLC 6**
See also CA 21-24R; CANR 33

Taylor, Cecil Philip 1929-1981 ..... **CLC 27**
See also CA 25-28R; 105

Taylor, Edward 1642(?)-1729........ **LC 11**
See also DA; DLB 24

Taylor, Eleanor Ross 1920-......... **CLC 5**
See also CA 81-84

Taylor, Elizabeth 1912-1975 ... **CLC 2, 4, 29**
See also CA 13-16R; CANR 9; MTCW;
　　SATA 13

Taylor, Henry (Splawn) 1942-...... **CLC 44**
See also CA 33-36R; CAAS 7; CANR 31;
　　DLB 5

Taylor, Kamala (Purnaiya) 1924-
See Markandaya, Kamala
See also CA 77-80

Taylor, Mildred D.................. **CLC 21**
See also AAYA 10; BW; CA 85-88;
　　CANR 25; CLR 9; DLB 52; JRDA;
　　MAICYA; SAAS 5; SATA 15, 70

Taylor, Peter (Hillsman)
　　1917- ...... **CLC 1, 4, 18, 37, 44, 50, 71;**
　　　　　　　　　　　　　　　SSC 10
See also CA 13-16R; CANR 9; DLBY 81;
　　MTCW

Taylor, Robert Lewis 1912-........ **CLC 14**
See also CA 1-4R; CANR 3; SATA 10

Tchekhov, Anton
See Chekhov, Anton (Pavlovich)

Teasdale, Sara 1884-1933.......... **TCLC 4**
See also CA 104; DLB 45; SATA 32

Tegner, Esaias 1782-1846......... **NCLC 2**

Teilhard de Chardin, (Marie Joseph) Pierre
　　1881-1955 .... **TCLC 9**
See also CA 105

Temple, Ann
See Mortimer, Penelope (Ruth)

Tennant, Emma (Christina)
　　1937- .... **CLC 13, 52**
See also CA 65-68; CAAS 9; CANR 10, 38;
　　DLB 14

Tenneshaw, S. M.
See Silverberg, Robert

Tennyson, Alfred
　　1809-1892 .... **NCLC 30; PC 6**
See also CDBLB 1832-1890; DA; DLB 32;
　　WLC

Teran, Lisa St. Aubin de .... **CLC 36**
See also St. Aubin de Teran, Lisa

Teresa de Jesus, St. 1515-1582 ...... **LC 18**

Terkel, Louis 1912-
See Terkel, Studs
See also CA 57-60; CANR 18; MTCW

Torrey, E(dwin) Fuller 1937-....... **CLC 34**
See also CA 119

Torsvan, Ben Traven
See Traven, B.

Torsvan, Benno Traven
See Traven, B.

Torsvan, Berick Traven
See Traven, B.

Torsvan, Berwick Traven
See Traven, B.

Torsvan, Bruno Traven
See Traven, B.

Torsvan, Traven
See Traven, B.

Tournier, Michel (Edouard)
1924-.................. **CLC 6, 23, 36**
See also CA 49-52; CANR 3, 36; DLB 83;
MTCW; SATA 23

Tournimparte, Alessandra
See Ginzburg, Natalia

Towers, Ivar
See Kornbluth, C(yril) M.

Townsend, Sue 1946-............. **CLC 61**
See also CA 119; 127; MTCW; SATA 48,
55

Townshend, Peter (Dennis Blandford)
1945-.................... **CLC 17, 42**
See also CA 107

Tozzi, Federigo 1883-1920........ **TCLC 31**

Traill, Catharine Parr
1802-1899 .... **NCLC 31**
See also DLB 99

Trakl, Georg 1887-1914........... **TCLC 5**
See also CA 104

Transtroemer, Tomas (Goesta)
1931-.................... **CLC 52, 65**
See also CA 117; 129; CAAS 17

Transtromer, Tomas Gosta
See Transtroemer, Tomas (Goesta)

Traven, B. (?)-1969............ **CLC 8, 11**
See also CA 19-20; 25-28R; CAP 2; DLB 9,
56; MTCW

Treitel, Jonathan 1959- .... **CLC 70**

Tremain, Rose 1943-............. **CLC 42**
See also CA 97-100; DLB 14

Tremblay, Michel 1942-........... **CLC 29**
See also CA 116; 128; DLB 60; MTCW

Trevanian (a pseudonym) 1930(?)-... **CLC 29**
See also CA 108

Trevor, Glen
See Hilton, James

Trevor, William
1928- .... **CLC 7, 9, 14, 25, 71**
See also Cox, William Trevor
See also DLB 14

Trifonov, Yuri (Valentinovich)
1925-1981 .... **CLC 45**
See also CA 126; 103; MTCW

Trilling, Lionel 1905-1975 .... **CLC 9, 11, 24**
See also CA 9-12R; 61-64; CANR 10;
DLB 28, 63; MTCW

Trimball, W. H.
See Mencken, H(enry) L(ouis)

Tristan
See Gomez de la Serna, Ramon

Tristram
See Housman, A(lfred) E(dward)

Trogdon, William (Lewis) 1939-
See Heat-Moon, William Least
See also CA 115; 119

Trollope, Anthony 1815-1882 .. **NCLC 6, 33**
See also CDBLB 1832-1890; DA; DLB 21,
57; SATA 22; WLC

Trollope, Frances 1779-1863 ..... **NCLC 30**
See also DLB 21

Trotsky, Leon 1879-1940........ **TCLC 22**
See also CA 118

Trotter (Cockburn), Catharine
1679-1749 .... **LC 8**
See also DLB 84

Trout, Kilgore
See Farmer, Philip Jose

Trow, George W. S. 1943-........ **CLC 52**
See also CA 126

Troyat, Henri 1911-............. **CLC 23**
See also CA 45-48; CANR 2, 33; MTCW

Trudeau, G(arretson) B(eekman) 1948-
See Trudeau, Garry B.
See also CA 81-84; CANR 31; SATA 35

Trudeau, Garry B................. **CLC 12**
See also Trudeau, G(arretson) B(eekman)
See also AAYA 10; AITN 2

Truffaut, Francois 1932-1984...... **CLC 20**
See also CA 81-84; 113; CANR 34

Trumbo, Dalton 1905-1976 .... **CLC 19**
See also CA 21-24R; 69-72; CANR 10;
DLB 26

Trumbull, John 1750-1831....... **NCLC 30**
See also DLB 31

Trundlett, Helen B.
See Eliot, T(homas) S(tearns)

Tryon, Thomas 1926-1991 .... **CLC 3, 11**
See also AITN 1; CA 29-32R; 135;
CANR 32; MTCW

Tryon, Tom
See Tryon, Thomas

Ts'ao Hsueh-ch'in 1715(?)-1763....... **LC 1**

Tsushima, Shuji 1909-1948
See Dazai, Osamu
See also CA 107

Tsvetaeva (Efron), Marina (Ivanovna)
1892-1941 .... **TCLC 7, 35**
See also CA 104; 128; MTCW

Tuck, Lily 1938-................. **CLC 70**
See also CA 139

Tunis, John R(oberts) 1889-1975 ... **CLC 12**
See also CA 61-64; DLB 22; JRDA;
MAICYA; SATA 30, 37

Tuohy, Frank..................... **CLC 37**
See also Tuohy, John Francis
See also DLB 14

Tuohy, John Francis 1925-
See Tuohy, Frank
See also CA 5-8R; CANR 3

Turco, Lewis (Putnam) 1934- ... **CLC 11, 63**
See also CA 13-16R; CANR 24; DLBY 84

Turgenev, Ivan
1818-1883 .... **NCLC 21; SSC 7**
See also DA; WLC

Turner, Frederick 1943-........... **CLC 48**
See also CA 73-76; CAAS 10; CANR 12,
30; DLB 40

Tusan, Stan 1936-................ **CLC 22**
See also CA 105

Tutuola, Amos 1920- .... **CLC 5, 14, 29**
See also BLC 3; BW; CA 9-12R; CANR 27;
DLB 125; MTCW

Twain, Mark
.... **TCLC 6, 12, 19, 36, 48; SSC 6**
See also Clemens, Samuel Langhorne
See also DLB 11, 12, 23, 64, 74; WLC

Tyler, Anne
1941-........ **CLC 7, 11, 18, 28, 44, 59**
See also BEST 89:1; CA 9-12R; CANR 11,
33; DLB 6; DLBY 82; MTCW; SATA 7

Tyler, Royall 1757-1826.......... **NCLC 3**
See also DLB 37

Tynan, Katharine 1861-1931....... **TCLC 3**
See also CA 104

Tytell, John 1939- .... **CLC 50**
See also CA 29-32R

Tyutchev, Fyodor 1803-1873..... **NCLC 34**

Tzara, Tristan .... **CLC 47**
See also Rosenfeld, Samuel

Uhry, Alfred 1936-............... **CLC 55**
See also CA 127; 133

Ulf, Haerved
See Strindberg, (Johan) August

Ulf, Harved
See Strindberg, (Johan) August

Unamuno (y Jugo), Miguel de
1864-1936 .... **TCLC 2, 9; SSC 11**
See also CA 104; 131; DLB 108; HW;
MTCW

Undercliffe, Errol
See Campbell, (John) Ramsey

Underwood, Miles
See Glassco, John

Undset, Sigrid 1882-1949.......... **TCLC 3**
See also CA 104; 129; DA; MTCW; WLC

Ungaretti, Giuseppe
1888-1970 .... **CLC 7, 11, 15**
See also CA 19-20; 25-28R; CAP 2;
DLB 114

Unger, Douglas 1952-............. **CLC 34**
See also CA 130

Unsworth, Barry (Forster) 1930-.... **CLC 76**
See also CA 25-28R; CANR 30

Updike, John (Hoyer)
1932- ...... **CLC 1, 2, 3, 5, 7, 9, 13, 15,**
23, 34, 43, 70; SSC 13
See also CA 1-4R; CABS 1; CANR 4, 33;
CDALB 1968-1988; DA; DLB 2, 5;
DLBD 3; DLBY 80, 82; MTCW; WLC

Upshaw, Margaret Mitchell
See Mitchell, Margaret (Munnerlyn)

Upton, Mark
See Sanders, Lawrence

Voigt, Cynthia 1942- . . . . CLC 30
See also AAYA 3; CA 106; CANR 18, 37,
40; CLR 13; JRDA; MAICYA;
SATA 33, 48

Voinovich, Vladimir (Nikolaevich)
1932- . . . . CLC 10, 49
See also CA 81-84; CAAS 12; CANR 33;
MTCW

Voltaire 1694-1778 . . . . LC 14; SSC 12
See also DA; WLC

von Daeniken, Erich 1935- . . . . CLC 30
See also von Daniken, Erich
See also AITN 1; CA 37-40R; CANR 17

von Daniken, Erich . . . . CLC 30
See also von Daeniken, Erich

von Heidenstam, (Carl Gustaf) Verner
See Heidenstam, (Carl Gustaf) Verner von

von Heyse, Paul (Johann Ludwig)
See Heyse, Paul (Johann Ludwig von)

von Hofmannsthal, Hugo
See Hofmannsthal, Hugo von

von Horvath, Odon
See Horvath, Oedoen von

von Horvath, Oedoen
See Horvath, Oedoen von

von Liliencron, (Friedrich Adolf Axel) Detlev
See Liliencron, (Friedrich Adolf Axel)
Detlev von

Vonnegut, Kurt, Jr.
1922- . . . . . . CLC 1, 2, 3, 4, 5, 8, 12, 22,
40, 60; SSC 8
See also AAYA 6; AITN 1; BEST 90:4;
CA 1-4R; CANR 1, 25;
CDALB 1968-1988; DA; DLB 2, 8;
DLBD 3; DLBY 80; MTCW; WLC

Von Rachen, Kurt
See Hubbard, L(afayette) Ron(ald)

von Rezzori (d'Arezzo), Gregor
See Rezzori (d'Arezzo), Gregor von

von Sternberg, Josef
See Sternberg, Josef von

Vorster, Gordon 1924- . . . . CLC 34
See also CA 133

Vosce, Trudie
See Ozick, Cynthia

Voznesensky, Andrei (Andreievich)
1933- . . . . CLC 1, 15, 57
See also CA 89-92; CANR 37; MTCW

Waddington, Miriam 1917- . . . . CLC 28
See also CA 21-24R; CANR 12, 30;
DLB 68

Wagman, Fredrica 1937- . . . . CLC 7
See also CA 97-100

Wagner, Richard 1813-1883 . . . . NCLC 9
See also DLB 129

Wagner-Martin, Linda 1936- . . . . CLC 50

Wagoner, David (Russell)
1926- . . . . CLC 3, 5, 15
See also CA 1-4R; CAAS 3; CANR 2;
DLB 5; SATA 14

Wah, Fred(erick James) 1939- . . . . . . CLC 44
See also CA 107; 141; DLB 60

Wahloo, Per 1926-1975 . . . . CLC 7
See also CA 61-64

Wahloo, Peter
See Wahloo, Per

Wain, John (Barrington)
1925- . . . . CLC 2, 11, 15, 46
See also CA 5-8R; CAAS 4; CANR 23;
CDBLB 1960 to Present; DLB 15, 27;
MTCW

Wajda, Andrzej 1926- . . . . CLC 16
See also CA 102

Wakefield, Dan 1932- . . . . CLC 7
See also CA 21-24R; CAAS 7

Wakoski, Diane
1937- . . . . CLC 2, 4, 7, 9, 11, 40
See also CA 13-16R; CAAS 1; CANR 9;
DLB 5

Wakoski-Sherbell, Diane
See Wakoski, Diane

Walcott, Derek (Alton)
1930- . . . . CLC 2, 4, 9, 14, 25, 42, 67, 76
See also BLC 3; BW; CA 89-92; CANR 26;
DLB 117; DLBY 81; MTCW

Waldman, Anne 1945- . . . . CLC 7
See also CA 37-40R; CAAS 17; CANR 34;
DLB 16

Waldo, E. Hunter
See Sturgeon, Theodore (Hamilton)

Waldo, Edward Hamilton
See Sturgeon, Theodore (Hamilton)

Walker, Alice (Malsenior)
1944- . . . . CLC 5, 6, 9, 19, 27, 46, 58;
SSC 5
See also AAYA 3; BEST 89:4; BLC 3; BW;
CA 37-40R; CANR 9, 27;
CDALB 1968-1988; DA; DLB 6, 33;
MTCW; SATA 31

Walker, David Harry 1911-1992 . . . . CLC 14
See also CA 1-4R; 137; CANR 1; SATA 8;
SATA-Obit 71

Walker, Edward Joseph 1934-
See Walker, Ted
See also CA 21-24R; CANR 12, 28

Walker, George F. 1947- . . . . CLC 44, 61
See also CA 103; CANR 21; DLB 60

Walker, Joseph A. 1935- . . . . CLC 19
See also BW; CA 89-92; CANR 26; DLB 38

Walker, Margaret (Abigail)
1915- . . . . CLC 1, 6
See also BLC 3; BW; CA 73-76; CANR 26;
DLB 76; MTCW

Walker, Ted . . . . CLC 13
See also Walker, Edward Joseph
See also DLB 40

Wallace, David Foster 1962- . . . . CLC 50
See also CA 132

Wallace, Dexter
See Masters, Edgar Lee

Wallace, Irving 1916-1990 . . . . . . CLC 7, 13
See also AITN 1; CA 1-4R; 132; CAAS 1;
CANR 1, 27; MTCW

Wallant, Edward Lewis
1926-1962 . . . . CLC 5, 10
See also CA 1-4R; CANR 22; DLB 2, 28;
MTCW

Walpole, Horace 1717-1797 . . . . LC 2
See also DLB 39, 104

Walpole, Hugh (Seymour)
1884-1941 . . . . TCLC 5
See also CA 104; DLB 34

Walser, Martin 1927- . . . . CLC 27
See also CA 57-60; CANR 8; DLB 75, 124

Walser, Robert 1878-1956 . . . . TCLC 18
See also CA 118; DLB 66

Walsh, Jill Paton . . . . CLC 35
See also Paton Walsh, Gillian
See also CLR 2; SAAS 3

Walter, Villiam Christian
See Andersen, Hans Christian

Wambaugh, Joseph (Aloysius, Jr.)
1937- . . . . CLC 3, 18
See also AITN 1; BEST 89:3; CA 33-36R;
CANR 42; DLB 6; DLBY 83; MTCW

Ward, Arthur Henry Sarsfield 1883-1959
See Rohmer, Sax
See also CA 108

Ward, Douglas Turner 1930- . . . . CLC 19
See also BW; CA 81-84; CANR 27; DLB 7,
38

Ward, Peter
See Faust, Frederick (Schiller)

Warhol, Andy 1928(?)-1987 . . . . CLC 20
See also BEST 89:4; CA 89-92; 121;
CANR 34

Warner, Francis (Robert le Plastrier)
1937- . . . . CLC 14
See also CA 53-56; CANR 11

Warner, Marina 1946- . . . . CLC 59
See also CA 65-68; CANR 21

Warner, Rex (Ernest) 1905-1986 . . . . CLC 45
See also CA 89-92; 119; DLB 15

Warner, Susan (Bogert)
1819-1885 . . . . NCLC 31
See also DLB 3, 42

Warner, Sylvia (Constance) Ashton
See Ashton-Warner, Sylvia (Constance)

Warner, Sylvia Townsend
1893-1978 . . . . CLC 7, 19
See also CA 61-64; 77-80; CANR 16;
DLB 34; MTCW

Warren, Mercy Otis 1728-1814 . . . NCLC 13
See also DLB 31

Warren, Robert Penn
1905-1989 . . . . CLC 1, 4, 6, 8, 10, 13, 18,
39, 53, 59; SSC 4
See also AITN 1; CA 13-16R; 129;
CANR 10; CDALB 1968-1988; DA;
DLB 2, 48; DLBY 80, 89; MTCW;
SATA 46, 63; WLC

Warshofsky, Isaac
See Singer, Isaac Bashevis

Warton, Thomas 1728-1790 . . . . LC 15
See also DLB 104, 109

Waruk, Kona
See Harris, (Theodore) Wilson

Warung, Price 1855-1911 . . . . TCLC 45

Warwick, Jarvis
See Garner, Hugh

Washington, Alex
See Harris, Mark

Washington, Booker T(aliaferro)
1856-1915 .... **TCLC 10**
See also BLC 3; BW; CA 114; 125;
SATA 28

Wassermann, (Karl) Jakob
1873-1934 .... **TCLC 6**
See also CA 104; DLB 66

Wasserstein, Wendy 1950- ...... **CLC 32, 59**
See also CA 121; 129; CABS 3

Waterhouse, Keith (Spencer)
1929- .... **CLC 47**
See also CA 5-8R; CANR 38; DLB 13, 15;
MTCW

Waters, Roger 1944- .... **CLC 35**
See also Pink Floyd

Watkins, Frances Ellen
See Harper, Frances Ellen Watkins

Watkins, Gerrold
See Malzberg, Barry N(athaniel)

Watkins, Paul 1964- .... **CLC 55**
See also CA 132

Watkins, Vernon Phillips
1906-1967 .... **CLC 43**
See also CA 9-10; 25-28R; CAP 1; DLB 20

Watson, Irving S.
See Mencken, H(enry) L(ouis)

Watson, John H.
See Farmer, Philip Jose

Watson, Richard F.
See Silverberg, Robert

Waugh, Auberon (Alexander) 1939- .. **CLC 7**
See also CA 45-48; CANR 6, 22; DLB 14

Waugh, Evelyn (Arthur St. John)
1903-1966 ... **CLC 1, 3, 8, 13, 19, 27, 44**
See also CA 85-88; 25-28R; CANR 22;
CDBLB 1914-1945; DA; DLB 15;
MTCW; WLC

Waugh, Harriet 1944- .... **CLC 6**
See also CA 85-88; CANR 22

Ways, C. R.
See Blount, Roy (Alton), Jr.

Waystaff, Simon
See Swift, Jonathan

Webb, (Martha) Beatrice (Potter)
1858-1943 .... **TCLC 22**
See also Potter, Beatrice
See also CA 117

Webb, Charles (Richard) 1939- ...... **CLC 7**
See also CA 25-28R

Webb, James H(enry), Jr. 1946- .... **CLC 22**
See also CA 81-84

Webb, Mary (Gladys Meredith)
1881-1927 .... **TCLC 24**
See also CA 123; DLB 34

Webb, Mrs. Sidney
See Webb, (Martha) Beatrice (Potter)

Webb, Phyllis 1927- .... **CLC 18**
See also CA 104; CANR 23; DLB 53

Webb, Sidney (James)
1859-1947 .... **TCLC 22**
See also CA 117

Webber, Andrew Lloyd .... **CLC 21**
See also Lloyd Webber, Andrew

Weber, Lenora Mattingly
1895-1971 .... **CLC 12**
See also CA 19-20; 29-32R; CAP 1;
SATA 2, 26

Webster, John 1579(?)-1634(?) .... **DC 2**
See also CDBLB Before 1660; DA; DLB 58;
WLC

Webster, Noah 1758-1843 .... **NCLC 30**

Wedekind, (Benjamin) Frank(lin)
1864-1918 .... **TCLC 7**
See also CA 104; DLB 118

Weidman, Jerome 1913- .... **CLC 7**
See also AITN 2; CA 1-4R; CANR 1;
DLB 28

Weil, Simone (Adolphine)
1909-1943 .... **TCLC 23**
See also CA 117

Weinstein, Nathan
See West, Nathanael

Weinstein, Nathan von Wallenstein
See West, Nathanael

Weir, Peter (Lindsay) 1944- .... **CLC 20**
See also CA 113; 123

Weiss, Peter (Ulrich)
1916-1982 .... **CLC 3, 15, 51**
See also CA 45-48; 106; CANR 3; DLB 69,
124

Weiss, Theodore (Russell)
1916- .... **CLC 3, 8, 14**
See also CA 9-12R; CAAS 2; DLB 5

Welch, (Maurice) Denton
1915-1948 .... **TCLC 22**
See also CA 121

Welch, James 1940- .... **CLC 6, 14, 52**
See also CA 85-88; CANR 42

Weldon, Fay
1933(?)- .... **CLC 6, 9, 11, 19, 36, 59**
See also CA 21-24R; CANR 16;
CDBLB 1960 to Present; DLB 14;
MTCW

Wellek, Rene 1903- .... **CLC 28**
See also CA 5-8R; CAAS 7; CANR 8;
DLB 63

Weller, Michael 1942- .... **CLC 10, 53**
See also CA 85-88

Weller, Paul 1958- .... **CLC 26**

Wellershoff, Dieter 1925- .... **CLC 46**
See also CA 89-92; CANR 16, 37

Welles, (George) Orson
1915-1985 .... **CLC 20**
See also CA 93-96; 117

Wellman, Mac 1945- .... **CLC 65**

Wellman, Manly Wade 1903-1986 .. **CLC 49**
See also CA 1-4R; 118; CANR 6, 16;
SATA 6, 47

Wells, Carolyn 1869(?)-1942 ...... **TCLC 35**
See also CA 113; DLB 11

Wells, H(erbert) G(eorge)
1866-1946 ...... **TCLC 6, 12, 19; SSC 6**
See also CA 110; 121; CDBLB 1914-1945;
DA; DLB 34, 70; MTCW; SATA 20;
WLC

Wells, Rosemary 1943- .... **CLC 12**
See also CA 85-88; CLR 16; MAICYA;
SAAS 1; SATA 18, 69

Welty, Eudora
1909- .... **CLC 1, 2, 5, 14, 22, 33; SSC 1**
See also CA 9-12R; CABS 1; CANR 32;
CDALB 1941-1968; DA; DLB 2, 102;
DLBY 87; MTCW; WLC

Wen I-to 1899-1946 .... **TCLC 28**

Wentworth, Robert
See Hamilton, Edmond

Werfel, Franz (V.) 1890-1945 ...... **TCLC 8**
See also CA 104; DLB 81, 124

Wergeland, Henrik Arnold
1808-1845 .... **NCLC 5**

Wersba, Barbara 1932- .... **CLC 30**
See also AAYA 2; CA 29-32R; CANR 16,
38; CLR 3; DLB 52; JRDA; MAICYA;
SAAS 2; SATA 1, 58

Wertmueller, Lina 1928- .... **CLC 16**
See also CA 97-100; CANR 39

Wescott, Glenway 1901-1987 .... **CLC 13**
See also CA 13-16R; 121; CANR 23;
DLB 4, 9, 102

Wesker, Arnold 1932- .... **CLC 3, 5, 42**
See also CA 1-4R; CAAS 7; CANR 1, 33;
CDBLB 1960 to Present; DLB 13;
MTCW

Wesley, Richard (Errol) 1945- .... **CLC 7**
See also BW; CA 57-60; CANR 27; DLB 38

Wessel, Johan Herman 1742-1785 .... **LC 7**

West, Anthony (Panther)
1914-1987 .... **CLC 50**
See also CA 45-48; 124; CANR 3, 19;
DLB 15

West, C. P.
See Wodehouse, P(elham) G(renville)

West, (Mary) Jessamyn
1902-1984 .... **CLC 7, 17**
See also CA 9-12R; 112; CANR 27; DLB 6;
DLBY 84; MTCW; SATA 37

West, Morris L(anglo) 1916- ..... **CLC 6, 33**
See also CA 5-8R; CANR 24; MTCW

West, Nathanael
1903-1940 .... **TCLC 1, 14, 44**
See also CA 104; 125; CDALB 1929-1941;
DLB 4, 9, 28; MTCW

West, Owen
See Koontz, Dean R(ay)

West, Paul 1930- .... **CLC 7, 14**
See also CA 13-16R; CAAS 7; CANR 22;
DLB 14

West, Rebecca 1892-1983 .. **CLC 7, 9, 31, 50**
See also CA 5-8R; 109; CANR 19; DLB 36;
DLBY 83; MTCW

Westall, Robert (Atkinson)
1929-1993 .... **CLC 17**
See also CA 69-72; 141; CANR 18;
CLR 13; JRDA; MAICYA; SAAS 2;
SATA 23, 69; SATA-Obit 75

Westlake, Donald E(dwin)
1933- .... **CLC 7, 33**
See also CA 17-20R; CAAS 13; CANR 16

Westmacott, Mary
See Christie, Agatha (Mary Clarissa)

Weston, Allen
See Norton, Andre

Wurlitzer, Rudolph 1938(?)- ... **CLC 2, 4, 15**
See also CA 85-88

Wycherley, William 1641-1715 .... **LC 8, 21**
See also CDBLB 1660-1789; DLB 80

Wylie, Elinor (Morton Hoyt)
1885-1928 .... **TCLC 8**
See also CA 105; DLB 9, 45

Wylie, Philip (Gordon) 1902-1971 ... **CLC 43**
See also CA 21-22; 33-36R; CAP 2; DLB 9

Wyndham, John
See Harris, John (Wyndham Parkes Lucas)
Beynon

Wyss, Johann David Von
1743-1818 .... **NCLC 10**
See also JRDA; MAICYA; SATA 27, 29

Yakumo Koizumi
See Hearn, (Patricio) Lafcadio (Tessima
Carlos)

Yanez, Jose Donoso
See Donoso (Yanez), Jose

Yanovsky, Basile S.
See Yanovsky, V(assily) S(emenovich)

Yanovsky, V(assily) S(emenovich)
1906-1989 .... **CLC 2, 18**
See also CA 97-100; 129

Yates, Richard 1926-1992 ..... **CLC 7, 8, 23**
See also CA 5-8R; 139; CANR 10; DLB 2;
DLBY 81, 92

Yeats, W. B.
See Yeats, William Butler

Yeats, William Butler
1865-1939 .... **TCLC 1, 11, 18, 31**
See also CA 104; 127; CDBLB 1890-1914;
DA; DLB 10, 19, 98; MTCW; WLC

Yehoshua, Abraham B. 1936- ... **CLC 13, 31**
See also CA 33-36R

Yep, Laurence Michael 1948- ...... **CLC 35**
See also AAYA 5; CA 49-52; CANR 1;
CLR 3, 17; DLB 52; JRDA; MAICYA;
SATA 7, 69

Yerby, Frank G(arvin)
1916-1991 .... **CLC 1, 7, 22**
See also BLC 3; BW; CA 9-12R; 136;
CANR 16; DLB 76; MTCW

Yesenin, Sergei Alexandrovich
See Esenin, Sergei (Alexandrovich)

Yevtushenko, Yevgeny (Alexandrovich)
1933- .... **CLC 1, 3, 13, 26, 51**
See also CA 81-84; CANR 33; MTCW

Yezierska, Anzia 1885(?)-1970 ..... **CLC 46**
See also CA 126; 89-92; DLB 28; MTCW

Yglesias, Helen 1915- .... **CLC 7, 22**
See also CA 37-40R; CANR 15; MTCW

Yokomitsu Riichi 1898-1947 ...... **TCLC 47**

Yonge, Charlotte (Mary)
1823-1901 .... **TCLC 48**
See also CA 109; DLB 18; SATA 17

York, Jeremy
See Creasey, John

York, Simon
See Heinlein, Robert A(nson)

Yorke, Henry Vincent 1905-1974 ... **CLC 13**
See also Green, Henry
See also CA 85-88; 49-52

Young, Al(bert James) 1939- .... **CLC 19**
See also BLC 3; BW; CA 29-32R;
CANR 26; DLB 33

Young, Andrew (John) 1885-1971 .... **CLC 5**
See also CA 5-8R; CANR 7, 29

Young, Collier
See Bloch, Robert (Albert)

Young, Edward 1683-1765 .... **LC 3**
See also DLB 95

Young, Neil 1945- .... **CLC 17**
See also CA 110

Yourcenar, Marguerite
1903-1987 .... **CLC 19, 38, 50**
See also CA 69-72; CANR 23; DLB 72;
DLBY 88; MTCW

Yurick, Sol 1925- .... **CLC 6**
See also CA 13-16R; CANR 25

Zabolotskii, Nikolai Alekseevich
1903-1958 .... **TCLC 52**
See also CA 116

Zamiatin, Yevgenii
See Zamyatin, Evgeny Ivanovich

Zamyatin, Evgeny Ivanovich
1884-1937 .... **TCLC 8, 37**
See also CA 105

Zangwill, Israel 1864-1926 .... **TCLC 16**
See also CA 109; DLB 10

Zappa, Francis Vincent, Jr. 1940-
See Zappa, Frank
See also CA 108

Zappa, Frank .... **CLC 17**
See also Zappa, Francis Vincent, Jr.

Zaturenska, Marya 1902-1982 .... **CLC 6, 11**
See also CA 13-16R; 105; CANR 22

Zelazny, Roger (Joseph) 1937- ..... **CLC 21**
See also AAYA 7; CA 21-24R; CANR 26;
DLB 8; MTCW; SATA 39, 57

Zhdanov, Andrei A(lexandrovich)
1896-1948 .... **TCLC 18**
See also CA 117

Zhukovsky, Vasily 1783-1852 .... **NCLC 35**

Ziegenhagen, Eric .... **CLC 55**

Zimmer, Jill Schary
See Robinson, Jill

Zimmerman, Robert
See Dylan, Bob

Zindel, Paul 1936- .... **CLC 6, 26**
See also AAYA 2; CA 73-76; CANR 31;
CLR 3; DA; DLB 7, 52; JRDA;
MAICYA; MTCW; SATA 16, 58

Zinov'Ev, A. A.
See Zinoviev, Alexander (Aleksandrovich)

Zinoviev, Alexander (Aleksandrovich)
1922- .... **CLC 19**
See also CA 116; 133; CAAS 10

Zoilus
See Lovecraft, H(oward) P(hillips)

Zola, Emile (Edouard Charles Antoine)
1840-1902 .... **TCLC 1, 6, 21, 41**
See also CA 104; 138; DA; DLB 123; WLC

Zoline, Pamela 1941- .... **CLC 62**

Zorrilla y Moral, Jose 1817-1893 .. **NCLC 6**

Zoshchenko, Mikhail (Mikhailovich)
1895-1958 .... **TCLC 15**
See also CA 115

Zuckmayer, Carl 1896-1977 .... **CLC 18**
See also CA 69-72; DLB 56, 124

Zuk, Georges
See Skelton, Robin

Zukofsky, Louis
1904-1978 .... **CLC 1, 2, 4, 7, 11, 18**
See also CA 9-12R; 77-80; CANR 39;
DLB 5; MTCW

Zweig, Paul 1935-1984 .... **CLC 34, 42**
See also CA 85-88; 113

Zweig, Stefan 1881-1942 .... **TCLC 17**
See also CA 112; DLB 81, 118

Literary Criticism Series
Cumulative Topic Index

Topic Index

Spasmodic School of Poetry NCLC 24: 307-52
  history and major figures, 307-21
  the Spasmodics on poetry, 321-27
  Firmilian and critical disfavor, 327-39
  theme and technique, 339-47
  influence, 347-51

Steinbeck, John, Fiftieth Anniversary of *The Grapes of Wrath* CLC 59: 311-54

Sturm und Drang NCLC 40: 196-276
  definitions, 197-238
  poetry and poetics, 238-58
  drama, 258-75

Supernatural Fiction in the Nineteenth Century NCLC 32: 207-87
  major figures and influences, 208-35
  the Victorian ghost story, 236-54
  the influence of science and occultism, 254-66
  supernatural fiction and society, 266-86

Supernatural Fiction, Modern TCLC 30: 59-116
  evolution and varieties, 60-74
  "decline" of the ghost story, 74-86
  as a literary genre, 86-92
  technique, 92-101
  nature and appeal, 101-15

Surrealism TCLC 30: 334-406
  history and formative influences, 335-43
  manifestos, 343-54
  philosophic, aesthetic, and political principles, 354-75
  poetry, 375-81
  novel, 381-86
  drama, 386-92
  film, 392-98
  painting and sculpture, 398-403
  achievement, 403-05

Symbolism, Russian TCLC 30: 266-333
  doctrines and major figures, 267-92
  theories, 293-98
  and French Symbolism, 298-310
  themes in poetry, 310-14
  theater, 314-20
  and the fine arts, 320-32

Symbolist Movement, French NCLC 20: 169-249
  background and characteristics, 170-86
  principles, 186-91
  attacked and defended, 191-97

  influences and predecessors, 197-211
  and Decadence, 211-16
  theater, 216-26
  prose, 226-33
  decline and influence, 233-47

Theater of the Absurd TCLC 38: 339-415
  "The Theater of the Absurd," 340-47
  major plays and playwrights, 347-58
  and the concept of the absurd, 358-86
  theatrical techniques, 386-94
  predecessors of, 394-402
  influence of, 402-13

Tin Pan Alley
  See **American Popular Song, Golden Age of**

Transcendentalism, American NCLC 24: 1-99
  overviews, 3-23
  contemporary documents, 23-41
  theological aspects of, 42-52
  and social issues, 52-74
  literature of, 74-96

Travel Writing in the Twentieth Century TCLC 30: 407-56
  conventions and traditions, 407-27
  and fiction writing, 427-43
  comparative essays on travel writers, 443-54

***Ulysses* and the Process of Textual Reconstruction** TCLC 26: 386-416
  evaluations of the new *Ulysses,* 386-94
  editorial principles and procedures, 394-401
  theoretical issues, 401-16

Utopian Literature, Nineteenth-Century NCLC 24: 353-473
  definitions, 354-74
  overviews, 374-88
  theory, 388-408
  communities, 409-26
  fiction, 426-53
  women and fiction, 454-71

Vampire in Literature TCLC 46: 391-454
  origins and evolution, 392-412
  social and psychological perspectives, 413-44
  vampire fiction and science fiction, 445-53

Victorian Autobiography NCLC 40: 277-363
  development and major characteristics 278-88
  themes and techniques 289-313
  the autobiographical tendency in Victorian prose and poetry 313-47
  Victorian women's autobiographies 347-62

Victorian Novel NCLC 32: 288-454
  development and major characteristics, 290-310
  themes and techniques, 310-58
  social criticism in the Victorian novel, 359-97
  urban and rural life in the Victorian novel, 397-406
  women in the Victorian novel, 406-25
  Mudie's Circulating Library, 425-34
  the late-Victorian novel, 434-51

World War I Literature TCLC 34: 392-486
  overview, 393-403
  English, 403-27
  German, 427-50
  American, 450-66
  French, 466-74
  and modern history, 474-82

Yellow Journalism NCLC 36: 383-456
  overviews, 384-96
  major figures, 396-413
  the role of reporters, 413-28
  the Spanish-American War, 428-48
  Yellow Journalism and society, 448-54

Young Playwrights Festival
  1988—CLC 55: 376-81
  1989—CLC 59: 398-403
  1990—CLC 65: 444-48

TCLC Cumulative Nationality Index

Nationality Index

ISBN 0-8103-2430-X